THE BEST 294
BUSINESS SCHOOLS

2017 EDITION

The Staff
of The Princeton Review

The Princeton Review
24 Prime Parkway, Suite 201
Natick, MA 01760
editorialsupport@review.com

Published in the United States by Penguin Random House LLC, New York, and in Canada, a division of Penguin Random House Ltd.,Toronto.

ISBN: 978-1-101-92041-1
ISSN: 2161-5772

Production: Best Content Solutions, LLC
Production Editor: Melissa Duclos

The Princeton Review is not affiliated with Princeton University.

9 8 7 6 5 4 3 2 1

2017 Edition

Editorial
Robert Franek, Senior VP, Publisher
David Soto, Director of Content
    Development
Kristen O'Toole, Editorial Director
Stephen Koch, Student Survey Manager
Pia Aliperti, Editor

Penguin Random House Publishing Team
Tom Russell, VP, Publisher
Alison Stoltzfus, Publishing Director
Jake Eldred, Associate Managing Editor
Ellen L. Reed, Production Manager
Suzanne Lee, Designer

CONTENTS

INTRODUCTION

A RETURN TO OUR ROOTS

Over the past 20 years, The Princeton Review has annually published a guide to business schools. For the early editions of the guide, we collected opinion surveys from thousands of students at a select group of graduate business schools as well as school statistics from school administrators that include enrollment and demographic figures, tuition, and the average GMAT scores of entering students. We used the students' opinions to craft descriptive narratives of the schools they attended and reported the statistics in the sidebars of those narrative profiles.

For the 2001–2004 editions of this guide, we discontinued collecting opinion surveys from students and writing narrative descriptions of the schools; instead, we focused solely on collecting and reporting school statistics. While we were able to report statistics for many more business schools in the new format, we learned over the next few years that readers are interested in more than just school-reported statistics. They want to read what the experts—current graduate business school students—have to say about the experiences of today's graduate business student. They want from-the-horse's-mouth accounts of what's great (*and* what's not) at each school.

So, in 2005, we decided to reintroduce the student survey-driven descriptive narrative, offering students a more intimate look at the inner workings of each school, and we've continued with this approach ever since.

We also brought back several top 10 lists that rank the profiled schools according to various metrics (more on the rankings later). You'll find these rankings in Part II of this book.

Taken together, we believe that these candid student opinions, school statistics, and rankings provide a unique and helpful resource to help you decide what business schools to apply to. But let us stress that we hope that this book will not be the *only* resource you turn to when making this expensive (both in terms of time and treasure) decision to enter a graduate business program. Do additional research on the Internet and in newspapers, magazines, and other periodicals. Talk to admissions officers and current students at the programs that interest you. If at all possible, visit the campuses you are seriously considering. But treat the advice of all these resources (including ours) as you would treat advice from anyone regarding any situation: as input that reflects the values and opinions of others as you *form your own opinion*.

TWO TYPES OF ENTRIES

For each of the 438 business programs in this book, you will find one of two possible types of entries: a two-page profile with lots of descriptive text and statistics, or a straight statistical listing. Our descriptive profiles are driven primarily by 1) comments business students provide in response to open-ended questions on our student survey, and 2) our own statistical analysis of student responses to the many multiple-choice questions on the survey. While many business students complete a survey unsolicited by us at http://survey.review.com, in the vast majority of cases we rely on business school administrators to get the word out about our survey to their students. In the ideal scenario, the business school administration sends a Princeton Review-authored e-mail to all business students with an embedded link to our survey website (again, http://survey.review.com). If for some reason there are restrictions that prevent the administration from contacting the entire graduate business school student body on behalf of an outside party, they often help us find other ways to notify students of the fact that we are seeking their opinions, such as advertising in business student publications or posting on business student community websites. In almost all cases, when the administration is cooperative, we are able to collect opinions from a sufficient number of students to produce an accurate descriptive profile and ratings of its business school.

There is a group of business school administrators, however, that doesn't agree with us that current business school student opinions presented in descriptive profile and rankings formats are useful to prospective business school students. Administrators at the many AACSB-accredited business schools not appearing with two-page descriptive profiles are a part of this group. They either ignored our multiple attempts to contact them in order to request their assistance in notifying their students about our survey, or they simply refused to work with us at all. While we would like to be able to write a descriptive profile about each of these many schools anyway, we won't do so with minimal business student opinion.

So if you are a prospective business school student and would like to read current business student opinion about schools that do not appear with a two-page descriptive profile, contact the schools and communicate this desire to them. (We include contact information in each of the business school data listings.) If you are a current business student at one of the many AACSB-accredited business schools without a two-page descriptive profile, please don't send us angry letters; instead, go to http://survey.review.com, complete a survey about your school, and tell all of your fellow students to do the same.

You will find statistics for business schools whose administrators were willing to report their school statistics to us but were unwilling to allow us to survey their students under the school's name in the section of the book entitled "Business School Data Listings."

One more thing to note about the different entries: The majority of our various rankings lists are based wholly or partly on student feedback to our survey. Only one top 10 ranking, The Toughest to Get Into, is based on school-reported statistics alone. So while *any* of the 438 programs listed in the book may appear on that list, *only those schools with two-page descriptive profiles will appear on all other rankings lists.*

BUT SOME THINGS NEVER CHANGE

Admission to the business school of your choice, especially if your choice is among the most selective programs, will require your absolute best shot. One way to improve your chances is to make sure you apply to schools that are a good fit—and the comments provided by students in our descriptive profiles will provide more insight into the personality of each school than does its glossy view book.

In addition, you'll find plenty of useful information in Part I of this book on how to get in to business school and what to expect once you arrive. You'll find out what criteria are used to evaluate applicants and who decides your fate. You will also hear directly from admissions officers on what dooms an application and how to ace the interview. We've even interviewed deans at several of the top schools to share with you their take on recent events, including trends in business, b-school applications, recruitment, and placement.

Again, it is our hope that you will consult our profiles as a resource when choosing a list of schools that suit your academic and social needs, and that our advice is helpful to you during the application process. Good luck!

HOW WE PRODUCE THIS BOOK

How do we choose which b-schools to survey and profile? And why do some competitive schools have only a data listing?

Any business school that is AACSB-accredited and offers an on-campus Master of Business Administration degree may have a data listing included in the book, as long as that school provides us with a sufficient amount of school-specific data. In addition, this year we offered each of those accredited schools in which the primary language of instruction is English an opportunity to assist us in collecting online business student surveys.

Some schools were unable to solicit surveys from their students via e-mail due to restrictive privacy policies; others simply chose not to participate. Schools that declined to work with us to survey their students remain in the book, although they do not have a descriptive profile. Listing only the data for a school does not suggest that the school is less competitive or compelling; we only separated these profile types into two sections for easier reference. If you're not sure where to find information on a school in which you're interested, you can refer to our alphabetical b-school listing in the back of the book.

There is no fee to be included in this book. If you're an administrator at an accredited business school and would like to have your school included, please send an e-mail to surveysupport@review.com.

What's the AACSB, and by what standards are schools accredited?

The AACSB stands for the Association to Advance Collegiate Schools of Business. In April 2003, the AACSB made some significant changes to its standards for accreditation. In fact, the actual number of standards went from 41 to 21. Some of the changes in accreditation included a shift from requiring a certain number of full-time faculty members with doctorates to a focus on teacher participation. Schools may employ more part-time faculty members if they are actively involved in the students' business education. The onus of both the development of a unique curriculum and the evaluation of the success of that curriculum will fall on each b-school, and schools will be reviewed by the association every five years instead of every ten. As a result of the changes in accreditation standards, a number of schools have been newly accredited or reaccredited.

How were the student surveys collected?

Back in fall 2015, we contacted Admissions Officers at all accredited graduate b-schools and requested that they help us survey their students by distributing our Princeton Review-authored survey message to the student body via e-mail. The survey message explained the purpose of the survey and contained a link to our online business student survey. We had a phenomenal response from students.

The surveys are made up of seventy-eight multiple-choice questions and seven free-response questions, covering five sections: About Yourself, Students, Academics, Careers, and Quality of Life. Students may complete the secure online survey at any time and may save their survey responses, returning later, until the survey is complete and ready for submission. Students sign in to the online survey using their school-issued .edu e-mail address to ensure that their response is attributed to the correct school, and the respondent certifies before submission that he or she is indeed a current student enrolled in said program. In addition, an automated message is sent to this address once the student has submitted the survey, and they must click on a link in the e-mail message in order to validate their survey.

We use the resulting responses to craft descriptive profiles that are representative of the respondents' feelings toward the b-school they attend. Although well-written and/or humorous comments are especially appreciated, they would never be used unless they best stated what numerous students had told us.

What about the ranking lists and ratings?

When we decided to bring the student opinion-driven resources back into the fold, we updated our online survey and reconsidered all ranking lists. You will find that only a few of the rankings in this year's book resemble our b-school rankings of yesteryear. We've done our best to include only those topics most vital to success in business school. Most recently we added a new ranking list to the book, "Best Green MBA."

We offer several ranking lists on a variety of considerations, from academic experience to career expectations, to the atmosphere for women and minority students. It must be noted, however, that none of these lists purport to rank the business schools by their overall quality. Nor should any combination of the categories we've chosen be construed as representing the raw ingredients for such a ranking. We have made no attempt to gauge the "prestige" of these schools, and we wonder whether we could accurately do so even if we tried. What we have done, however, is presented a number of lists using information from two very large databases—one of statistical information collected from business schools and another of subjective data gathered via our survey of 22,000 business students at 295 AACSB-accredited business schools. We do believe that there is a right business school for you, and that our rankings, when used in conjunction with our profile of each school, will help you select the best schools to apply to.

Since the 2009 edition of this book, we have included "Best Classroom Experience" list, based on students' answers to survey questions concerning their professors' teaching ability and recognition in the field, the integration of new business trends and practices into course offerings, and the level of student engagement in the classroom.

What do the schools have to say about all this?

Our contact at each school is kept abreast of the profile's status throughout the production process. After establishing a contact through whom we are able to reach online student respondents, we get to work writing our profiles and crunching the data. Once this information has been poured into profile pages, we send a copy of the school's profile to our contact via e-mail. We request that the administrator review the data and comments included in the profile, and we invite their corrections to any inaccurate data, or text that may be misrepresentative of overall student opinion. With their suggestions in hand, we revisit survey responses and investigate any such claims of inaccuracy.

We are aware that a general distaste for rankings permeates the business school community, and that top schools have recently backed down from providing the data necessary for such calculations. We agree that overall rankings that purport to decide the "best" overall school are not so helpful to students, and that they may be tainted by the agendas of school administrators hoping to advance their schools' reputations, without taking the necessary measures to actually improve the quality of the school. This is why the meat of our book is the schools' descriptive profiles, which are meant to showcase each school's unique personality. The ranking lists are simply used as reference tools for students looking for a particular attribute in a prospective b-school. We don't claim to be the final word on what school has the best MBA program in the country—that's nearly impossible to determine. We simply relay the messages that the students at each school are sending us, and we are clear about how our rankings are determined.

HOW THIS BOOK IS ORGANIZED

This book is packed with information about business schools, and we want to make sure you know how to find what you're looking for. So here's a breakdown of how this book is organized.

Part I is comprised of several chapters that give you an idea of what to expect at business school and tell you how to put together a winning application.

Part II has our b-school ranking lists. Of the ten lists, six are based entirely on student survey responses; one is based solely on institutionally reported data, while four others are based on a combination of survey responses and statistical information. Along with each list, you will find information about which survey questions or statistical factors were used to calculate the rankings.

Part III contains profiles of all AACSB-accredited graduate schools with MBA programs divided into two sections: those with descriptive profiles based on student surveys, and those with only a statistical listing.

PART III-A: BUSINESS SCHOOL DESCRIPTIVE PROFILES

Please see the sample descriptive profile below.

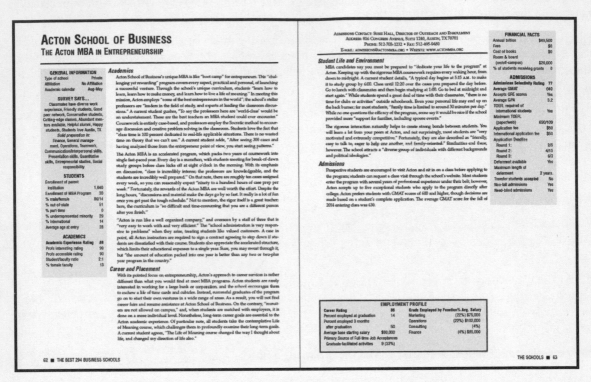

Each two-page spread is made up of eight major components. At the top of each page, you'll find the name of the business school, along with the name of an admissions contact and his or her address, phone number, fax number, if applicable, and e-mail address. This section also includes the b-school's website address. There are two sidebars (the narrow columns on the outer edge of each page) that contain information reported by the schools through the Business Data Set (BDS) and some student survey data as well. The Survey Says information reflects aspects of the school about which students feel the strongest; there are nine different possible results. We also offer an Employment Profile for each school, which is made up of statistical information from the BDS. The main body of the profile contains descriptive text discussing Academics, Placement and Recruiting, Student/Campus Life, and Admissions. Each description is based on student survey responses and may call upon statistical data where necessary.

The Sidebars

All information in the sidebars falls under the following categories: General Information, Academics, Financial Facts, and Admissions. Please note that not every category will appear for every school; in some cases the information is not reported or not applicable. These are the same data fields that are reported for those schools listed in Part III-B: Business School Data Listings, save for four of the five ratings, which appear only in the descriptive profiles.

Here is what each sidebar heading tells you.

General Information

Type of school

Public or private school.

Affiliation

Any religious order with which the school is affiliated.

Academic Calendar

Whether the school schedule runs according to trimesters, semesters, quarters, or another calendar type like a 4-1-4 (4-month semester, 1-month interim term, 4-month semester).

Survey Says

Survey Says gives you an at-a-glance look at what students are most in agreement about at their school. You'll find up to six results per school. Three will reflect the top three subject areas as indicated by responses to the following question:

How well has your school prepared you in the following areas:

Marketing	Presentation skills
Finance	Quantitative skills
Accounting	Computer skills
General management	Doing business in a global economy
Operations	Entrepreneurial studies
Teamwork	Environmental/Sustainability Issue Awareness
Communication/Interpersonal skills	Social Responsibility

In addition, Survey Says may include (up to) three things from the following list that students were most in agreement about:

- Students like Hometown, State. Based on level of agreement with the statement, "I like the town where my school is located."

- Friendly students. Based on level of agreement with the statement, "Your business school classmates are friendly."

- Good social scene. Based on level of agreement with the statement, "Your business school classmates have active social lives."

- Good peer network. Based on level of agreement with the statement, "Your business school classmates are the type of people you want to network with after graduation."

- Cutting-edge classes. Based on responses to the question, "How well has your school integrated new business trends and practices into course offerings?"

- Helpful alumni. Based on responses to the question, "How helpful have alumni been in assisting you in your job search?"

- Happy students. Based on level of agreement with the statement, "Overall, I am happy here."

Students

Enrollment of parent institution

Total number of undergraduate and graduate students enrolled in parent institution program.

Enrollment of MBA program

Total number of students enrolled in MBA programs at the business school, including both full- and part-time programs.

"% male/female" through "% international"

Items based on demographic information about full-time b-school students as reported by the schools.

Average age at entry

The average age of incoming first-year MBA students.

Average years work experience at entry

The average years of work experience for incoming first-year MBA students.

Academics

Academic Experience Rating

This rating measures the quality of the learning environment. Each school is given a score between 60 and 99. Factors taken into consideration include GMAT scores and undergraduate grades of enrolled students; percent accepted; percent enrolled; student/faculty ratio; and student survey questions pertaining to faculty, fellow students, and realization of academic expectations. This rating is intended to be used only to compare those schools within this edition of the book whose students completed our business student survey.

Please note that if a 60* Academic Experience Rating appears for any school, it means that the school didn't report all the rating's underlying data points by our deadline, so we were unable to calculate an accurate rating. In such cases, the reader is advised to follow up with the school about specific measures this rating takes into account.

Please also note that many foreign institutions use a grading system that is different from the standard U.S. GPA; as a result, we approximated their Admissions Selectivity and Academic Ratings, indicating this with a † following the rating.

Student/Faculty Ratio

The ratio of full-time graduate instructional faculty members to all enrolled MBA students.

Professors Interesting Rating

Based on the answers given by students to the survey question, "Overall, how good are your professors as teachers?" Ratings fall between 60 and 99. This rating is intended to be used to compare those schools within this edition of the book whose students completed our business student survey.

Professors Accessible Rating

Based on the answers given by students to the survey question, "How accessible are your professors outside of the classroom?" Ratings fall between 60 and 99. This rating is intended to be used to compare those schools within this edition of the book whose students completed our business student survey.

% female faculty

Percent of graduate business faculty in the 2015–2016 academic year who were women.

% minority faculty

Percent of graduate business faculty in the 2015–2016 academic year who were members of minority groups.

Joint Degrees

A list of joint degrees offered by the business school. See Decoding Degrees on page 723 for the full name of each degree.

Prominent Alumni

School administrators may submit the name, title, and company of up to five prominent alumni.

Financial Facts

Please note that we rely on foreign institutions to convert financial figures into U.S. dollars. Please check with any foreign schools you are considering for up-to-date figures and conversion rates.

"Tuition (in-state/out-of-state)" and "Fees (in-state/out-of-state)"

In-state and out-of-state tuition and fees per academic year. At state-supported public schools, in-state tuition and fees are likely to be significantly lower than out-of-state expenses.

Books and supplies

Estimated cost of books and supplies for one academic year.

Room and board

Cost of room and board on campus per academic year, and estimate of off-campus living expenses for this time period.

"% of students receiving aid" through "% of students receiving grants"

Percent of students receiving aid, then specifically those receiving grants and loans. These numbers reflect the percentage of all enrolled MBA students that receive financial aid, regardless of whether or not they applied for financial aid or for specific aid types. Likewise, the second figure, "% of first year students receiving aid" takes into account all first-year MBA students, regardless of whether they applied for financial aid or specific aid types.

Average award package

For students who received financial aid, this is the average award amount.

Average grant

For students who received grants, this is the average amount of grant money awarded.

Average student loan debt

The average dollar amount of outstanding educational MBA loans per graduate (class of 2014) at the time of graduation.

Admissions

Admissions Selectivity Rating

This rating measures the competitiveness of the school's admissions. Factors taken into consideration include the average GMAT score and undergraduate GPA of the first-year class, the percent of students accepted, and the percent of accepted applicants who ultimately enroll. No student survey data is used in this calculation. Ratings fall between 60 and 99. This rating is intended to be used to compare all schools within this edition of the book, regardless of whether their students completed our business student survey.

Please note that if a 60* Admissions Selectivity Rating appears for any school, it means that the school did not report all of the rating's underlying data points by our deadline, so we were unable to calculate an accurate rating. In such cases, the reader is advised to follow up with the school about specific measures this rating takes into account.

Please also note that many foreign institutions use a grading system that is different from the standard U.S. GPA; as a result, we approximated their Admissions Selectivity and Academic Ratings, indicating this with a † next to the rating.

of applications received

The total number of applications received for any and all MBA programs at the school.

% applicants accepted

The percentage of applicants to which the school offered admission.

% acceptees attending

Of those accepted students, the percentage who enrolled.

Average GMAT

The average GMAT score for the first-year class.

Average GPA

The average undergraduate GPA of the first year class, reported on a four-point scale.

TOEFL required of international applicants?

For those international students interested in applying, the b-school reports whether the Test of English as a Foreign Language (TOEFL) is required.

Minimum TOEFL (paper/computer/web)

The minimum TOEFL score necessary for consideration. We list acceptable scores for both the paper and computer versions of the test.

Application fee

The amount it costs to file an application with the school.

International Application Fee

The amount it costs an international student to file an application with the school if it is different from the cost of the regular application.

"Application deadline" and "Regular notification"

This regular application deadline reflects the date by which all materials must be postmarked; the notification date tells you when you can expect to hear back.

"Early decision program" and "ED deadline/notification"

If a school offers an early decision option, we'll tell you when early decision apps are due to be postmarked, and when you'll be notified of the school's decision.

"Deferment available?" and "Maximum length of deferment"

Some schools allow accepted students to defer enrollment for a year or more, while others require students who postpone attendance to reapply.

Transfer students accepted?

Whether or not students are accepted from other MBA programs.

Transfer Application Policy

Lets you know how transfer applications are reviewed and how many credits will be allowed to transfer from another program.

Non-fall admissions?

Some business schools may allow students to matriculate at the beginning of each semester, while for others, the invitation to attend stipulates that fall attendance is mandatory.

Need-blind admissions?

Whether or not the school considers applications without regard to the candidate's financial need.

Applicants also look at

The school reports that students applying to their school are also known to apply to a short list of other schools.

EMPLOYMENT PROFILE
Career Rating

Taking into account both student survey responses and statistical data, this rating measures the confidence students have in their school's ability to lead them to fruitful employment opportunities, as well as the school's own record of having done so. Factors taken into consideration include statistics on the average starting salary and percent of students employed within three months of graduation from the Business Data Set and comments from the student survey, assessing the efforts of the placement office, the quality of recruiting companies, level of preparation, and opportunities for off-campus projects, internships, and mentorships. Ratings fall between 60 and 99. This rating is intended to be used to compare only those schools within this edition of the book whose students completed our business student survey.

* Please note that if a 60* Career Rating appears for any school, it means that the school did not report all of the rating's underlying data points by our deadline, so we were unable to calculate an accurate rating. In such cases, the reader is advised to follow up with the school about the specific attributes this rating takes into account.

% grads employed within three months of graduation

This reflects the percentage of MBA grads who earned a job within three months of graduation.

Average starting salary

Average starting salary of all 2015 graduates.

Primary source of full-time job acceptances

This reflects the percentage of full-time job acceptances that are the result of school-facilitated, graduate-facilitated, or unknown activities.

Grads employed by field %: avg. salary

Reflects the distribution of 2015 graduates across many different industries and the average starting salary for each field.

Top five employers hiring grads

Reflects the top five employers who hired 2015 job seeking full-time MBA graduates, and the number of students they hired.

DESCRIPTIVE PROFILE

Each school's descriptive profile is made up of four sections which highlight those qualities that characterize the school as a unique institution. *Academics* covers students' opinions on the quality of professors, curriculum, special or noteworthy programs, the administration, and anything else academic in nature. *Career and Placement* deals with the school's efforts to secure internships and jobs for its current students and graduates; information about alumni assistance and popular recruiters of MBAs at the school may also be included. In *Student Life and Environment*, you'll find out how students balance work and play and whether they find it manageable to do so; often, you'll also find reviews of the school's facilities as well. Finally, the *Admissions* section describes what the Admissions Committee is looking for in potential students.

All quotes in these sections are taken from students' responses to our survey. We choose quotes that were consistent with the overall survey results.

PART III-B: BUSINESS SCHOOL DATA LISTINGS

This section contains all of the statistical information that is presented in the sidebars of the descriptive profile. Each school in this section will include an Admissions Selectivity rating but will not include the other three ratings, the Survey Says section, or a descriptive profile.

PART IV: SCHOOL SAYS

Part IV offers more detailed information about particular business schools authored by the schools themselves. The business schools included in this section pay a small fee for this space.

EVERYTHING ELSE

Next is a section entitled *Decoding Degrees* that will help you make sense of the myriad degree abbreviations you'll see listed in the book. You'll then find the indexes—alphabetical by school name, and then by location.

Enjoy and good luck!

PART I
ALL ABOUT BUSINESS SCHOOL

CHAPTER 1

THIS ISN'T YOUR FATHER'S (OR MOTHER'S) B-SCHOOL ANYMORE

THE NEW MBA CLASS: FEWER, YOUNGER, AND WORKING WHILE THEY LEARN

The MBA has always been seen as a golden passport; the trip ticket to romance and riches. The destination: career acceleration, power networks and recruiters, elite employers, and, of course, generous paychecks.

But not everyone wants to make the trip. Several factors will always impact on the popularity of the MBA: 1) the state of the economy—interest in getting the MBA has generally waxed and waned with economic times; 2) trends and favorable or unfavorable press—in the 1980s, a rash of insider trading scandals in which MBAs were ensnared made the degree look smarmy and other graduate programs, notably law and medicine, look more appealing; 3) the immediacy of good professional opportunities—the collapse of the dot-com boom, followed by the severe retrenchment of traditional MBA destinations (such as investment banks and consulting firms) in a depressed economy, has left many current MBAs stranded; and 4) recruiter demand for newly minted MBAs—do employers see the skill sets of today's MBAs bringing measurable value to their companies?

B-SCHOOL: INTEREST AND APPLICATIONS ON UPSWING

According to the 2014 GMAC Application Trends Survey, application volume to full-time two-year MBA programs has increased slightly over the past year (and for the second year in a row). After a spike in applications following the start of the recession in late 2007, most programs saw their application numbers decline slightly through 2011, but these numbers began to climb again in 2012. Part-time programs and executive MBA programs also saw small gains in applications.[1]

YOUNGER MINDS

Although lower application numbers can spell better fortunes for those currently applying to MBA programs, there are also some unrecognized opportunities for candidates with less than the traditional two to four years of work experience to make a strong case for admittance.

Admissions officers at large benchmark schools such as Stanford say that this trend pre-dates the economic downturn. Derek Bolton, Assistant Dean of MBA Admissions at Stanford notes, "The pendulum has gone too far in one direction in terms of the number of younger candidates applying to b-school. It has not kept pace with the overall pace of applicants. We want more young applicants applying. The goal is to bring the average age down in the next couple of years."

"What's driving this is the willingness on the part of the b-schools to not be rigidly fixed on what's right for someone. We may not always be the best judge of when the best time is for a candidate to go to b-school," continues Bolton.

Wharton's former Director of Admissions Rose Martinelli observed "a shift in that we became more tuned in to when students are ready in their leadership, professional, and personal development. We see so many nontraditional students that we don't want to have rules on when they can apply. We don't want to miss out on fabulous applicants because they don't think they can get in."

---

1. Graduate Management Admissions Council, 2014 Application Trends Survey Report, www.gmac.com/market-intelligence-and-research/research-library/admissions-and-application-trends/2014-app-trends-report.aspx (accessed April 29, 2015).

"When the applicant pool continues to get older and older, then we're closing out younger applicants who are on a fast track." Martinelli continues, "Why should we wait? Why should they wait? We want to catch the human element in the application process."

This perspective continues to hold true. As The University of Chicago's Stacey Kole sums up, "The pendulum had swung too far in terms of the type of student who should be admitted and when. Now schools are correcting that and experimenting, taking less experienced candidates. We believe that this experimentation is a good thing."

There may be more to the story, too. Because they may be less likely to be in committed relationships or have families, younger students are more active, generous alumni, and b-schools can't afford to ignore the market that these younger students represent. Despite the heightened competition, candidates with less experience are increasingly being deemed worthy of a coveted b-school acceptance.

THE DRAW OF THE PART-TIME PROGRAM

Because part-time education programs continue to attract applicants, pundits say that the future of b-school may lie in programs that offer more flexible part-time opportunities, allowing students to get the degree without making a full-time commitment. In fact, Stacey Kole, deputy dean for the full-time MBA Program and clinical professor of economics at The University of Chicago Graduate School of Business states, "There is this tendency to think of the MBA as a full-time-only product. But schools like Chicago offer MBA programs in the evening, on weekends, and in executive program formats. For us, whether the student matriculates in our part-time or full-time program, the process is exactly the same. Ours is the same degree, only delivered in full-time, part-time, and weekend formats with different scheduling options. Chicago GSB offers individuals interested in an MBA considerable flexibility in how they pursue their education."

Kole continues, "Part-time and executive programs are now providing more of the outside-the-classroom, extracurricular experience that did not exist 10 years ago. For example, they are offering student-led clubs, speakers, and recruiter events that historically were the exclusive domain of full-time programs. This is one explanation for why part-time programs are looking like better substitutes for a full-time program."

PAYBACK TIME

The MBA, particularly at the top schools, continues to pay out high dividends to grads. That's a hefty return on investment. But the degree doesn't come with any promises. The world of business requires some risk, as many MBA wannabes found out several years go: You can enter a business school program at the height of the economy only to graduate when things are dismal. But you can also enter b-school at low tide then watch as the job market swells and employers are fighting over the newest and brightest MBA grads, including you. Indeed, the current economic climate has many MBA students and grads concerned about their job prospects, however, it's important to realize that with these financial challenges come opportunities for innovative and dedicated individuals.

MBA CONCENTRATIONS

The MBA has changed a lot over the years. Once upon a time, it was enough to simply earn your degree and enter the working world a more knowledgeable and employable individual for it. Nowadays, business represents an increasingly multi-faceted and diverse world, meaning that MBA students can't be jacks-of-all-trades—they need areas of specialization. When looking at potential business schools, it's imperative to know if they offer the concentration you're keen on. To help you decide what your concentration might be, we've added these helpful indexes to the back of our book (see page 743) along with brief explanations of what each entails below.

ACCOUNTING

As an accounting specialist, you'll become an expert in the gathering and interpretation of financial data, and the ways in which that data can affect a company.

ENTREPRENEURSHIP

A concentration in entrepreneurship offers you the chance to develop real business savvy, network with potential collaborators and investors, and try out new ideas with fewer risks than you'll encounter in the real world.

FINANCE

The finance concentration is about money: how to make it, manage it, and make more of it. A specialization in finance will prepare you to make smart financial decisions for individuals, institutions, and companies.

HEALTHCARE ADMINISTRATION

This specialization will teach you how the nation's healthcare system works, as well as the challenges facing healthcare organizations—from government agencies to hospitals to biotech, pharmaceutical, and medical technology companies.

HUMAN RESOURCES MANAGEMENT

In this concentration, you'll learn how to maximize human output in a business environment, from understanding individual behavior to designing effective management structures, training programs, and compensation schemes.

INTERNATIONAL MANAGEMENT

A concentration in international management will prepare you to succeed in today's global business environment. Many programs actually require students to spend a semester overseas, working at a company or studying at a partner university.

LEADERSHIP

This concentration is designed to help students develop skills that are essential to success in any field: critical thinking, problem-solving, communicating, negotiating, and acting ethically in professional situations.

MARKETING

Marketing professionals anticipate consumer demands, help to create products and services that consumers want, attract consumers to that product or service, and retain consumers over the long haul. They also have their hand in pricing and distribution; figuring out what products should cost and how they'll get to customers.

Non-Profit Management

Running a non-profit requires many of the same skills needed to run a business: raising capital, managing organization for maximum cost efficiency, and effectively delivering a service to your "clients."

Supply Chain Management

A specialization in supply chain management will prepare you to create and manage the entire selling process for any company with a good or service to vend. In a world of global suppliers and tight profit margins, effective supply chain management can mean the difference between profitability and bankruptcy.

THE CONTINUING RELEVANCE OF BUSINESS SCHOOL

The MBA is such an attractive option because it *does* confer huge value on the recipient. Business schools know how to keep pace with the rapidly changing face of business. After all, that's *their* business, so you're never really out of the game. In fact, if you look at the nation's top business programs, you'll find exciting innovations in curriculum that reflect all that's new and relevant. This includes unique opportunities for teamwork, internships, and laboratory simulations that replicate real-world, real-time business scenarios.

The integration of these real-world experiences into the basics produces better-trained, more well-rounded managers, as graduates are more adept at discerning the correlation between principle and reality. Even so, programs and students in search of business knowledge that is more widely applicable and more relevant long-term has caused a strong return to fundamentals.

Backpedaling to the Basics

Many top schools are reviving the old classics: It's back to basics. Both schools and students now have enough of a perspective to look back at the frenzy of the last business cycle and understand that enduring values are rooted in a solid foundation. Gone is the frothy demand for trendy courses on e-commerce and other hype-driven topics. Just five years ago, a class at Stanford on the principles of Internet marketing was oversubscribed. Last year, only a few people signed up for it.

So here's a sampler of the back-to-basics you'll get at b-school: An in-depth immersion in all of the key functional areas of an organization: marketing, management, sales, finance, operations, logistics, and so on. You'll look at these areas across dozens of industries and organizational types, from start-ups to *Fortune* 500 companies.

The renewed focus on basics doesn't mean that you'll find yourself shorted on current trends and events. Expect plenty of case study debate on corporate governance and the Enron debacle, and expect the themes of global perspective and technological competence to permeate many programs. You'll also find classes and seminars on leadership gaining popularity. "We're seeing a resurgence of leadership courses as students seek out professions and business models that are other-oriented," notes Stanford's Bolton. "This may be a new generation. But these are students who look at business as a positive force in the world, a more noble calling."

Survivor Power

Once you have your MBA, you can expect to hit the ground running. You'll start off your post b-school career with a load of contacts that you will periodically leverage over your career. Many graduates use the degree to embark on entirely new career paths than those that brought them to the school; consultants become bankers, entrepreneurs become consultants, marketers become financiers, and so on. The MBA has and will continue to be a terrific opportunity to reinvent oneself.

"An MBA is unlike any other professional degree because the breadth of knowledge poises you for a multitude of career choices," says Julia Min Hwang, assistant dean of career management services at UC Berkeley's Haas School of Business. "You can be an investment banker, yet two years from that point, segue into nonprofit work. You can move from banking to corporate finance, to a venture-capital proposition, to ultimately having an entrepreneurial experience. So it's a credential that allows you the flexibility to explore different industries; it's a long-term investment that will give you the tools to transition if you want to."

"What's wonderful about the MBA is that it provides fundamental skills that you can use whenever and wherever you need them," champions Martinelli. "I'm a cheerleader for the nontraditional because I feel the MBA is such a fundamental tool. It offers an ability to enter the business world and link passion with functionality.

"For example, for folks who want to go into public service or nonprofit, even the arts industry, they're very narrow fields. You need the passion and vision to be successful in them. But often credibility is undermined when you don't understand the business world's perspective," states Martinelli.

"You've got to know that industry if you're going to make it viable for the future. But you have to be able to know how to talk to the business world in order to get those investments to make it happen. And that's one of the reasons why an MBA is so valuable. It bestows credibility in the marketplace and helps us maintain these organizations in a world that doesn't often respect passion over the bottom line," she continues.

Despite the nation's current financial woes, MBA grads still have plenty of prospects. Hundreds of companies continue to visit and recruit from business school campuses, with today's MBA candidates receiving two job offers on average. Recruiters exist in a symbiotic relationship with business schools. Employers like to maintain a strong presence on campus—even during an economic downturn—so that they'll have their top picks of MBA talent when the good times return. Thus, MBA programs remain one of the most effective means to get oneself in front of recruiters and senior managers from the most desirable companies. And while that may not grant you "immunity" from an economy characterized by up and downs, it will absolutely improve your survivor power.

COMPETITION HAS EASED UP

With an economic recovery seemingly underway, the chance to dive into any number of secure, well-paying jobs will lure a percentage of professionals away from the MBA. After years of struggling through economic hardship, a decent paycheck from the pocket of a much improved labor market may seem the best bet. There's no doubt that risk-averse individuals would prefer the stability of a secure job to what might-be, could-be, or should-be two years down the road—even with an MBA in hand. This may keep the applicant pool smaller.

Additionally, the continued decrease in the number of foreign applicants, who at many schools comprised more than 20 percent of students, will keep applications down, too. Other factors include the fact that there are currently smaller percentages of people in the country who are in the typical age bracket of business school applicants. Lastly, the increased interest in flexible and part-time MBA programs may continue to drive the decline in full-time business school applications.

What does all of this mean? Basically this: If you have a handsome application and you plan on applying to the most competitive programs this year, you may find yourself met with welcoming arms.

As the Song Goes...Money, Money, Money, Money...

But don't go buying the flashy car to go with that flashy degree quite yet. It needs to be said that, after several years of a slump, there could actually be a surge in this upcoming applicant pool that would correspond with improvements in the economy. Recruiters are once again canvassing the top business schools as hiring slowly returns to healthy levels. At programs like Chicago, Harvard, and Stanford, six-figure salaries and signing bonuses of $15,000-plus are still the norm. That's why it's important to remember that the MBA from the right school can deliver an immediate and hefty return on investment. According to the GMAC 2014 Global Management Education Graduate Survey, Job Search: Class of 2014 Report, members of the class of 2014 reported that they expected salary increases of at least 80 percent over their pre-MBA pay.[2]

Another trend worth noting: Although applications have come down over the past 5 years, that doesn't mean the quality of applicants has suffered. Notes Chicago's Kole, "Our applications are of high quality, and applicants appear to be quite focused with regard to why they seek an advanced degree. Whether they are career switchers or planning to resume their career path, those applicants who present a compelling story for why they want to be here leave a stronger impression with the admissions committee."

Top schools are always going to have people knocking at their doors. The possibility that business school applications in general could once again rise means you'll still want to be competitive. The long application process starts with developing a solid application strategy and applying to a diverse portfolio of schools.

Let Us Help You Decide

There are many factors to consider when deciding whether or not to pursue an MBA, and we'll help you make that decision in the following chapters. We'll also tell you a bit about each school in our profiles and prepare you to do further research on the schools on your list. We've worked hard to provide you with thorough information on every aspect of the MBA, but you don't have to take our word for it—see for yourself. Stanford's Bolton advises future applicants, "Start early. Visit as many schools as you can, because it's very hard to differentiate among programs from websites, books, and marketing materials. You need to get a feeling from walking down the halls."

After you decide to go, finding the right program can be extremely difficult. Bolton explains, "Applicants really have to dig beneath the programs they're looking at to determine what's going to make them happy. A lot of people wind up going to the wrong school. A lot of external factors contribute to that. People shouldn't worry about justifying the decision to others, but to themselves."

Making the Decision to Go

The next step for you may be b-school. Indeed, armed with an MBA you may journey far. But the success of your trip and the direction you take will depend on knowing exactly why you're going to b-school and just what you'll be getting out of it.

The most critical questions you need to ask yourself are the following: Do you really want a career in business? What do you want the MBA to do for you? Are you looking to gain credibility, accelerate your development, or move into a new job or industry? Perhaps you're looking to start your own business, in which case entrepreneurial study will be important.

---

2. Graduate Management Admissions Council, 2014 Global Management Education Graduate Survey Report, www.gmac.com/market-intelligence-and-research/research-library/curriculum-insight/2014-gmegs-survey-report.aspx (accessed April 29, 2014).

Knowing what you want doesn't just affect your decision to go, it also affects your candidacy; admissions committees favor applicants who have clear goals and objectives. Moreover, once at school, students who know what they want make the most of their two years. If you're uncertain about your goals, opportunities for career development—such as networking, mentoring, student clubs, and recruiter events—are squandered.

You also need to find a school that fits your individual needs. Consider the personal and financial costs. This may be the single biggest investment of your life. How much salary will you forego by leaving the workforce? What will the tuition be? How will you pay for it? If you have a family, spouse, or significant other, how will getting your MBA affect them?

If you do have a spouse, you may choose a program that involves partners in campus life. If status is your top priority, you should simply choose the most prestigious school you can get into.

The MBA presents many opportunities but no guarantees. As with any opportunity, you must make the most of it. Whether you go to a first-tier school or to a part-time program close to home, you'll acquire the skills that can jump-start your career. But your success will have more to do with you than with the piece of paper your MBA is printed on.

Chapter 2

Smart Phones and Power Lunches: What Does an MBA Offer?

NUTS-AND-BOLTS BUSINESS SKILLS

Graduate business schools teach the applied science of business. The best business schools combine the latest academic theories with pragmatic concepts, hands-on experience, and real-world solutions.

B-schools also teach the analytical skills used to make complicated business decisions. You learn how to define the critical issues, apply analytical techniques, develop the criteria for decisions, and make decisions after evaluating their impact on other variables.

After two years, you're ready to market a box of cereal. Or prepare a valuation of the cereal company's worth. You'll speak the language of business. You'll know the tools of the trade. Your expertise will extend to many areas and industries. In short, you will have acquired the skills that open doors.

ACCESS TO RECRUITERS, ENTRÉE TO NEW FIELDS

Applicants tend to place great emphasis on "incoming" and "outgoing" statistics. First they ask, "Will I get in?" Then they ask, "Will I get a job?"

Obviously, the first is largely dependent on how selective the school is and the quality of your credentials. The latter question can almost assuredly be answered in the positive, "Yes, you will."

But the real question is: How many—and what kind—of offers will you receive? Again, that is dependent on the appeal of the school to recruiters (what companies recruit on campus and how often is a readily available statistic you can get from each school) and the particular industry you elect to pursue. For example, investment banks and consulting firms are always going to come to the schools for formal recruiting periods, whereas more off-the-beaten-path choices will possibly require you to go off campus in search of opportunity.

It's Good to Be Wanted, It's Great to Be Paid

According to the Graduate Management Council, MBA alumni typically recouped one third of their financial investment in their graduate degree within the first year after graduation, and 100 percent of their tuition and education expenses after four years.[3] Presumably, starting salaries will continue to increase as the economy improves.

The majority of top grads receive a generous relocation package too. Indeed, if you were fortunate enough to have spent the summer between your first and second year at a consulting company, then you will, in all likelihood, also receive a "rebate" on your tuition. These companies often pick up a student's second-year tuition bill. The best package, however, goes to those MBA students who worked at the firm before b-school. These lucky capitalists often get their whole tuition paid for.

---

3. Graduate Management Admissions Council, 2015 Alumni Perspectives Survey General Data Report, http://www.gmac.com/market-intelligence-and-research/gmac-surveys/alumni-perspectives-survey/alumni-perspectives-survey.aspx (accessed April 29, 2015).

Getting the MBA for the Long Run

Despite its potential value, going to business school still requires you to take a bit of a gamble. Leaner years make business school a riskier proposition. The nation appears to be heading out of what has been a lingering recession, but economic factors are always unpredictable. Furthermore, the world has witnessed great political turmoil. All of these factors can quickly and negatively impact the job market for newly minted MBAs.

So as you make plans to go to b-school, you need to accept that there is some risk that the labor market won't greet you with open arms at graduation. Consider the plight of current MBAs: when they entered b-school, the economy was roaring ahead. The immediate future looked exceptionally bright. Most MBAs probably thought that once they got in, they had it made, and they looked forward to generous starting salaries and bonuses. Few probably anticipated that tough times could hit so dramatically.

But that's just the point. Good times and bad times cycle in and out. Many economic experts agree that the economy is starting to look up and the markets will continue to improve. This means traditional hirers of MBAs, such as the investment banks and consulting firms, may once again be wooing many a b-school grad. Still, it's hard to know when all of the recruiters who typically hire MBAs will feel comfortable again about bringing their hiring levels back up to what they were before the downturn.

The best way to consider the value of the degree is by focusing on its long-lasting benefits. "When people come here for their MBA, they talk about retooling for their life. They think about the long term and recognize that there are some short term hurdles," says Rose Martinelli, former director of admissions at the Wharton School. "Just out of business school, this is the very first job in a long career. This is really about building blocks and going for the long run. You may have to work harder to find a job now, but building your career is a lifelong process." The MBA gives you the tools, networking, and polish to meaningfully enhance your long-term prospects and earning potential.

"There is real opportunity here. The opportunity right now is to pursue your passion and perhaps not your wallet," continues Martinelli. "We're seeing more of an equalization in salary. Those high-paying jobs in finance, investment banking, and consulting are fewer and harder to find. So here you have an opportunity for a job with a true learning experience rather than one that just pays a lot. More people are going into nonprofit and government and making contributions back to the community."

Brand Power Counts

Of course, there is great variability with placement rates and starting salaries among schools. The MBA does not swap your tuition bill for a guarantee that you'll get rich quick. As we've noted, it is at the best schools—those that have the greatest prestige and global recognition—where the strongest recovery is taking place. It's brand power at work. Even in an uncertain economy, top schools will continue to produce in-demand MBAs for the marketplace.

Branded schools tend to have an extensive history with big recruiting companies because the schools are a steady source of exceptional talent. As the economy stabilizes and hiring creeps up again, recruiters are naturally going to orient themselves at the top-brand schools.

At the University of Chicago, Deputy Dean Stacey Kole notes: "Hiring activity has really skyrocketed. . . . We had thousands of interviews available for our grads."

At less prominent schools, the picture may not be quite as optimistic. It is important to consider placement rates and the list of companies that typically recruit on campus at any school you are considering.

GETTING A JOB

For most would-be MBAs, b-school represents a fresh beginning—either in their current profession or in an entirely different industry. Whatever promise the degree holds for you, it's wise to question what the return on your investment will be.

Several factors affect job placement and starting salary. School reputation and ties to industries and employers are important. At the top programs, the lists of recruiters read like a "Who's Who" of American companies. These schools not only attract the greatest volume of recruiters, but consistently get the attention of those companies considered to be "blue chip."

Not to be overlooked are lesser-known, regional schools that often have the strongest relationships with local employers and industries. Some b-schools (many of them state universities) are regarded by both academicians and employers as number one in their respective regions. In other words, as far as the local business community is concerned, these programs offer as much prestige and pull as a nationally ranked program.

Student clubs also play a big part in getting a job because they extend the recruiting efforts at many schools. They host a variety of events that allow you to meet leading business people, so that you can learn about their industries and their specific companies. Most important, these clubs are very effective at bringing in recruiters and other interested parties that do not recruit through traditional mainstream channels. For example, the high-tech, international, and entertainment student clubs provide career opportunities not available through the front door.

Your background and experiences also affect your success in securing a position. Important factors are academic specialization, academic standing, prior work experience, and intangibles such as your personal fit with the company. These days, what you did before b-school is particularly important; it helps establish credibility and gives you an edge in competing for a position in a specific field. For those using b-school to switch careers to a new industry, it's helpful if something on your resume ties your interest to the new profession. It's also smart to secure a summer job in the new area.

Finally, persistence and initiative are critical factors in the job search. Many fast tracks have been narrowed since the beginning of the decade. Increasingly, even at the best schools, finding a job requires off-campus recruiting efforts and ferreting out the hidden jobs.

A RETURN ON YOUR INVESTMENT

Not everyone measures their return on investment from business school with a dollar amount. We've heard many b-school grads explain that the fundamental skills, the network of people, and the proper environment in which to formulate their long-term career path were the most valuable things they wanted to get back from their MBA programs—in doing so, they considered the experience a success, regardless of their starting salary at graduation.

But for those who are anxious to start paying back those school loans, it's important to note that the industry in which you are hired can strongly affect your job prospects. Traditionally heavy hirers such as investment banking and consulting companies continue to lead the salary pack. Historically these sectors have offered the highest starting salaries and sign-on bonuses, with recruiters gravitating to the name-brand schools. At Chicago, Kole notes, "We saw tremendous activity in consulting, investment banking, investment management, and in leadership development programs. We are up in all of these areas, but most significantly in management consulting."

Also impacting your placement outlook is the geographic location of the school. Regional powerhouses such as Rutgers University in New Jersey may hold great sway at nearby, national employers such as Johnson & Johnson and Warner Lambert/Pfizer, providing graduates of those programs a unique competitive advantage. Although these companies reach out far and wide to recruit everywhere, a homegrown MBA may catch their attention and hold greater appeal.

As always, prioritize your criteria for school selection. Research who the top hirers are at any school you are considering. If you know what field you are interested in, look at how strong a particular business school's track record is in finding jobs for their graduates in that industry. To cement the relationships between school and recruiter, companies often foster a partnership with the school that includes sponsoring academic projects and internships, and hosting school club functions and informational cocktail hour events.

You may indeed be accepted at one of the nation's most prestigious schools, but if they lack real access to the type of industry you desire to work in, you are better off elsewhere.

FRIENDS WHO ARE GOING PLACES, ALUMNI WHO ARE ALREADY THERE

Most students say that the best part about b-school is meeting classmates with whom they share common goals and interests. Many students claim that the "single greatest resource is each other." Not surprisingly, with so many bright and ambitious people cocooned in one place, b-school can be the time of your life. It presents numerous professional and social opportunities. It can be where you find future customers, business partners, and mentors. It can also be where you establish lifelong friendships. After graduation, these classmates form an enduring network of contacts and professional resources.

Alumni are also an important part of the b-school experience. While professors teach business theory and practice, alumni provide insight into the real business world. When you're ready to interview, they can provide advice on how to get hired by the companies recruiting at your school. In some cases, they help you secure the interview and shepherd you through the hiring process.

B-schools love to boast about the influence of their alumni network. To be sure, some are very powerful, but this varies from institution to institution. At the very least, alumni will help you get your foot in the door. A resume sent to an alum at a given company, instead of to "Sir or Madam" in the personnel department, has a much better chance of being noticed and acted on.

After you graduate, the network continues to grow. Regional alumni clubs and alumni publications keep you plugged in to the network with class notes detailing who's doing what, where, and with whom.

Throughout your career, an active alumni relations department can give you continued support. Post-MBA executive education series, fund-raising events, and continued job placement efforts are all resources you can draw on for years to come.

CHAPTER 3

ADMISSIONS

PREPARING TO BE A SUCCESSFUL APPLICANT

GET GOOD GRADES

If you're still in school, concentrate on getting good grades. A high GPA says you've got not only brains but also discipline. It shows the Admissions Committee you have what you need to make it through the program. If you're applying directly from college or have limited job experience, your grades will matter even more. The Admissions Committee will have little else on which to evaluate you.

It's especially important that you do well in courses such as economics, statistics, and calculus. Success in these courses is more meaningful than success in classes like "Monday Night at the Movies" film appreciation. Of course, English is also important; b-schools want students who communicate well.

STRENGTHEN MATH SKILLS

Number-crunching is an inescapable part of b-school. If your work experience has failed to develop your quantitative skills, take an accounting or statistics course for credit at a local college or b-school. If you have a liberal arts background and did poorly in math, or got a low GMAT Math score, this is especially important. Getting a decent grade will go a long way toward convincing the Admissions Committee you can manage the quantitative challenges of the program.

WORK FOR A FEW YEARS—BUT NOT TOO MANY

Business schools have traditionally favored applicants who have worked full-time for several years. There are three primary reasons for this:

1. With experience comes maturity.

2. You're more likely to know what you want out of the program.

3. Your experience enables you to bring real-work perspectives to the classroom. Because business school is designed for you to learn from your classmates, each student's contribution is important.

Until recently, b-schools preferred to admit only those students with two to five years of work experience. The rationale was that at two years you have worked enough to be able to make a solid contribution, while beyond four or five, you might be too advanced in your career to appreciate the program fully. However, as we noted earlier in this book, there is a new trend among top schools toward admitting "younger" applicants—that is, candidates with limited work experience as well as those straight from college.

Depending on the schools to which you're applying and the strength of your resume of accomplishments, you may not need full-time, professional work experience. Of course, there's a catch: The younger you are, the harder you'll have to work to supply supporting evidence for your case as a qualified applicant. Be prepared to convince Admissions Committees that you've already done some incredible things, especially if you're hailing straight from college.

If you've targeted top-flight schools like Wharton, Columbia, or Stanford, applying fresh out of college is still a long shot. While your chances of gaining admission with little work experience have improved, your best shot is still to err on the conservative side and get a year or two of some professional experience under your belt.

If you're not interested in the big league or you plan on attending a local program, the number of years you should work before applying may vary. Research the admissions requirements at your target school. There's no doubt the MBA will jumpstart your career and have long-lasting effects on your business (and perhaps personal) outlook. If you're not ready to face the real world after college, plenty of solid b-schools will welcome you to another two years of academia.

There is one caveat to this advice, however. If your grades are weak, consider working at least three years before applying. The more professional success you have, the greater the likelihood that Admissions Committees will overlook your GPA.

Let Your Job Work for You

Many companies encourage employees to go to b-school. Some of these companies have close ties to a favored b-school and produce well-qualified applicants. If their employees are going to the kinds of schools you want to get into, these may be smart places to work.

Other companies, such as investment banks, feature training programs, at the end of which trainees go to b-school or leave the company. These programs hire undergraduates right out of school. They're known for producing solid, highly skilled applicants. Moreover, they're full of well-connected alumni who may write influential letters of recommendation.

Happily, the opposite tactic—working in an industry that generates few applicants—can be equally effective. Admissions Officers look for students from underrepresented professions. Applicants from biotechnology, health care, not-for-profit, and even the Peace Corps are viewed favorably.

One way to set yourself apart is to have had two entirely different professional experiences before business school. For example, if you worked in finance, your next job might be in a different field, like marketing. Supplementing quantitative work with qualitative experiences demonstrates versatility.

Finally, what you do in your job is important. Seek out opportunities to distinguish yourself. Even if your responsibilities are limited, exceed the expectations of the position. B-schools are looking for leaders.

March from the Military

A surprising number of b-school students hail from the military (although the armed forces probably had commanders in mind, not CEOs, when they designed their regimen). Military officers know how to be managers because they've held command positions. And they know how to lead a team under the most difficult of circumstances.

Because most have traveled all over the world, they also know how to work with people from different cultures. As a result, they're ideally suited to learn alongside students with diverse backgrounds and perspectives. B-schools with a global focus are particularly attracted to such experience.

The decision to enlist in the military is a very personal one. However, if you've thought of joining those few good men and women, this may be as effective a means of preparing for b-school as more traditional avenues.

Check Out Those Essay Questions Now

You're worried you don't have interesting stories to tell. Or you just don't know what to write. What do you do?

Ideally, several months before your application is due, you should read the essay questions and begin to think about your answers. Could you describe an ethical dilemma at work? Are you involved in anything outside the office (or classroom)? If not, now is the time to do something about it. While this may seem contrived, it's preferable to sitting down to write the application and finding you have to scrape for or, even worse, manufacture situations.

Use the essay questions as a framework for your personal and professional activities. Look back over your business calendar, and see if you can find some meaty experiences for the essays in your work life. Keep your eyes open for a situation that involves questionable ethics. If all you do is work, work, work, get involved in activities that round out your background. In other words, get a life.

Get involved in community-based activities. Some possibilities are being a big brother/big sister, tutoring in a literacy program, or initiating a green initiative on campus. Demonstrating a concern for others looks good to Admissions Committees, and hey, it's good for your soul, too.

It's also important to seek out leadership experiences. B-schools are looking for individuals who can manage groups. Volunteer to chair a professional committee or run for an office in a club. It's a wide-open world; you can pick from any number of activities. The bottom line is this: The extracurriculars you select can show that you are mature, multifaceted, and appealing.

We don't mean to sound cynical. Obviously, the best applications do nothing more than describe your true, heartfelt interests and show off your sparkling personality. We're not suggesting you try to guess which activity will win the hearts of admissions directors and then mold yourself accordingly. Instead, think of projects and activities you care about, that maybe you haven't gotten around to acting on, and act on them now!

Pick Your Recommenders Carefully

By the time you apply to business school, you shouldn't have to scramble for recommendations. Like the material for your essays, sources for recommendations should be considered long before the application is due.

How do you get great recommendations? Obviously, good work is a prerequisite. Whom you ask is equally important. Bosses who know you well will recommend you on both a personal and professional level. They can provide specific examples of your accomplishments, skills, and character. Additionally, they can convey a high level of interest in your candidacy.

There's also the issue of trust. B-school recommendations are made in confidence; you probably won't see exactly what's been written about you. Choose someone you can trust to deliver the kind of recommendation that will push you over the top. A casual acquaintance may fail you by writing an adequate, yet mostly humdrum letter.

Cultivate relationships that yield glowing recommendations. Former and current professors, employers, clients, and managers are all good choices. An equally impressive recommendation can come from someone who has observed you in a worthwhile extracurricular activity.

We said before you won't see *exactly* what's being written about you, but that doesn't mean you should just hand a blank piece of paper to your recommender. Left to their own devices, recommenders may create a portrait that leaves out your best features. You need to prep them on what to write. Remind them of those projects or activities in which you achieved some success. You might also discuss the total picture of yourself that you are trying to create. The recommendation should reinforce what you're saying about yourself in your essays.

About "big shot" recommendations: Don't bother. Getting some professional athlete who's a friend of your parent's to write you a recommendation will do you no good if he or she doesn't know you very well. Don't try to fudge your application; let people who really know you and your work tell the honest, believable, and impressive truth.

Prepare for the Graduate Management Admission Test (GMAT) or the Graduate Record Examinations (GRE)

Most b-schools require you to take the GMAT. The GMAT is now a three-and-a-half-hour computer adaptive test (CAT) with multiple-choice Math and Verbal sections as well as an essay section. Many schools will accept Graduate Record Examinations, or GRE, general test scores as a substitution for the GMAT. If you're interested in applying to both MBA and other master's programs, you may want to consider taking the GRE.

The GMAT begins with the Analytical Writing Assessment (AWA) containing one essay question. In the past, all questions that have appeared on the official GMAT have been drawn from a list of about 150 topics that appear in *The Official Guide to the GMAT* (published by the Educational Testing Service). Review that list and you'll have a pretty good idea of what to expect from the AWA. You will have 30 minutes to write your essay using a generic word processing program.

Next comes the multiple-choice section which has three parts: a 30-minute, 12-question Integrated Reasoning section (more on that below); a 75-minute Math section, and a 75-minute Verbal section. The Math section includes problem-solving questions (e.g., "Train A leaves Baltimore at 6:32 A.M.") and data-sufficiency questions. Data-sufficiency questions require you to determine whether you have been given enough information to solve a particular math problem. The good news about these types of questions is that you don't actually have to solve the problem; the bad news is that these questions can be very tricky. The Verbal section tests reading skills (reading comprehension), grammar (sentence correction), and logic (critical reasoning).

The Integrated Reasoning section was introduced in June 2012 and replaced a second essay question. It combines verbal and quantitative reasoning skills. There are only twelve questions in this section, but each will have multiple parts. For the entire section, you'll actually need to select approximately thirty different responses. Unlike the Quantitative and Verbal sections, the Integrated Reasoning section is not adaptive.

For those unfamiliar with CAT exams, here's a brief overview of how they work: On multiple-choice sections, the computer starts by asking a question of medium difficulty. If you answer it correctly, the computer asks you a question that is slightly more difficult than the previous question. If you answer incorrectly, the computer asks a slightly easier question next. The test continues this way until you have answered enough questions that it can make an accurate (or so they say) assessment of your performance and assign you a score.

Most people feel they have no control over a standardized test. They dread it as the potential bomb in their application. Relax; you have more control than you think. Whether you choose to take the GMAT or the GRE, you can take a test-preparation course to review the material, learn test-taking strategies, and build your confidence. Test-prep courses can be highly effective. The Princeton Review offers what we think are the best GMAT and GRE courses available. Even better, it offers two options for online preparation in addition to the traditional classroom course and one-on-one tutoring. Another option is to use our books *Cracking the GMAT* and *Cracking the GRE* to prepare for the tests. Updated annually, they include access to full-length practice tests plus reviews of all the subjects you'll find on the tests and many of our proven techniques for raising your scores on these tests that you would learn in one of our courses.

How many times should you take the test of your choice? More than once if you didn't get your desired score on the first try. But watch out: Multiple scores that fall in the same range make you look unprepared. Don't take the test more than once if you don't expect a decent increase, and don't even think of taking it the first time without serious preparation. Limiting your attempts to two is best. Three tries are okay if there were unusual circumstances. If you take it more than three times, the Admissions committee will think you have an unhealthy obsession. A final note: If you submit more than one score, most schools will take the highest.

If you don't have math courses on your college transcript or numbers-oriented work experience, it's especially important to get a solid score on the quantitative section. There's a lot of math between you and the MBA.

HOW THE ADMISSIONS CRITERIA ARE WEIGHTED

Although admissions requirements vary among business schools, most rely on the following criteria: GMAT (or GRE) score, college GPA, work experience, your essays, letters of recommendation (academic and/or professional), an interview with an admissions representative, and your extracurriculars. The first four are generally the most heavily weighted. The more competitive the school, the less room there is for weakness in any area. Any component out of sync, such as a weak test score, is potentially harmful.

Happily, the admissions process at business school is one where great emphasis is placed on getting to know you as a person. The essay component is the element that allows the schools to do just that. Your essays can refute weaknesses, fill in gaps, and in general, charmingly persuade an admissions board you've got the right stuff. They are the single most important criteria in business school admissions.

But as we've just said, they're not the only criteria. All pieces of your application must come together to form a cohesive whole. It is the *entire application* that determines whether you win admission.

ANTICIPATE AND COORDINATE

The application process is very time-consuming, so anticipating what you need to accomplish within the admissions time frame is critical. To make the best use of our advice, you should first contact each of the programs on your personal list of schools. Their standards and criteria for admission may vary, and you'll need to follow their specific guidelines. Please note that the less competitive a school is, the more easily you may be able to breeze through (or completely omit) the rigorous requirements we identify as crucial in the application process for the top programs.

In addition, business school applicants are often overwhelmed by how much they have to do to complete not only one, but several applications. Proper management of the process is essential, since there are so many factors to coordinate in each application.

You'll have to prep for the GMAT and/or GRE, then actually take the test, round up some writers for your recommendations, follow up with those chosen to write recommendations, make sure the recommendations are mailed in on time, have your college transcript sent, and finally, write the essays. Of course, some schools require an interview as well. What makes all of this particularly challenging is that many applicants have to do all of this while balancing the demands of a full-time job.

We know that it takes a supreme force of will to complete even one application. As grad school applications go, a top business school's is pretty daunting. So if you don't stay focused on the details and deadlines, you may drop the ball.

There are many common and incredibly embarrassing mistakes you can avoid with prudent early planning. These include allowing your recommenders to miss the deadline, submitting an application full of typos and grammatical errors, sending one school an essay intended for another, or forgetting to change the school name when using the same essay for several applications. Applicants who wind up cramming for the GMAT (or GRE) or squeezing their essay writing into several all-nighters end up seriously shortchanging themselves.

APPLY EARLY

The best advice is to plan early and apply early. The former diminishes the likelihood of an accidental omission or a missed deadline. The latter increases your chances of acceptance.

The filing period ranges anywhere from six to eight months. The earlier you apply, the better your chances. There are a number of reasons for this:

First, there's plenty of space available early on. Many b-schools have rolling admissions, and as the application deadline nears, spaces fill up. The majority of applicants don't apply until the later months because of procrastination or unavoidable delays. As the deadline draws close, the greatest number of applicants compete for the fewest number of spaces.

Second, in the beginning, Admissions Officers have little clue about how selective they can be. They haven't reviewed enough applications to determine the competitiveness of the pool. An early application may be judged more on its own merit than on how it stacks up against others. This is in your favor if the pool turns out to be unusually competitive. Above all, Admissions Officers like to lock their classes in early; they can't be certain they'll get their normal supply of applicants. Admissions decisions may be more generous at this time.

Third, by getting your application in early you're showing a strong interest. The Admissions Committee is likely to view you as someone keen on going to their school.

To be sure, some Admissions Officers report that the first batch of applications tend to be from candidates with strong qualifications, confident of acceptance. In this case, you might not be the very first one on line; but being closer to the front is still better than getting lost in the heap of last-minute hopefuls.

ROUNDS VERSUS ROLLING ADMISSIONS

Applications are processed in one of two ways: rounds or rolling admissions. Schools that use rounds divide the filing period into three or so timed cycles. Applications are batched into the round in which they are received and reviewed in competition with others in that round. A list of a b-school's round dates can be obtained by contacting its Admissions Office if it employs this method. Applications to schools with rolling admissions are reviewed on an ongoing basis as they are received.

GMAT OR GRE AND GPA

Test scores and GPA are used in two ways. First, they're "success indicators" for the academic work you'll have to slog through if admitted—will you have the brainpower to succeed in the program? Second, they're used as benchmarks to compare each applicant to other applicants within the pool. At the more selective schools, you'll need a higher score and average to stay in the game.

Research the schools to which you're planning to apply and identify which test makes the most sense for you. You'll need to register for the GMAT at mba.com or the GRE at ets.org/gre. Many applicants take the exam more than once to improve their scores. Test preparation is also an option for boosting your numbers—visit PrincetonReview.com for more information about The Princeton Review's GMAT and GRE courses.

Your college transcript is a major factor in the strength of your candidacy. Some schools focus more closely on the junior- and senior-year grades than the overall GPA, and most consider the reputation of your college and the difficulty of your course selections. A transcript loaded with offerings like "Environmental Appreciation" and "The Child in You" won't be valued as highly as one packed with calculus and history classes.

THE ESSAYS

Admissions committees consider the essays the clincher, the swing vote on the admit/deny issue. Essays offer the most substantive information about who you really are. Your admissions test scores and GPA reveal little about you, only that you won't crash and burn. Your work history provides a record of performance and justifies your stated desire to study business. But the essays tie all the pieces of the application together and create a summary of your experiences, skills, background, and beliefs.

The essays do more than give answers to questions. They create thumbnail psychological profiles. Depending on how you answer a question or what you present, you reveal yourself in any number of ways—creative, witty, open-minded, articulate, mature, to name a few. On the other hand, your essay can also reveal a negative side, such as arrogance, sloppiness, or an inability to think and write clearly.

> **CHECK IT OUT:** Most top schools require multiple essays, and our popular e-book *Business School Essays that Made a Difference* lets you know how to ace them all. Including sample essays from successful applicants with comments from admissions officers on what worked and what didn't, *Business School Essays that Made a Difference* lets you know how to write the essays that will get you admitted. Pick it up at PrincetonReview.com/bookstore.

LETTERS OF RECOMMENDATION

Letters of recommendation function as a reality check. Admissions committees expect them to support and reinforce what they're seeing in the rest of your application. When the information doesn't match up with the picture you've painted, it makes you look bad. Because you won't see the recommendation (it's sent in "blind"), you won't even know there's a problem. This can mean the end of your candidacy.

That's why you need to take extreme care in selecting your references.

Scan each application for guidelines on choosing your references—business schools typically request an academic and a professional reference. The academic reference should be someone who can evaluate your performance in an academic environment. It's better to ask an instructor, teacher's aide, or mentor who knew you well than a famous professor who barely knew your name.

The same holds true for your professional reference. Seek out individuals who can evaluate your performance on many levels. The reference will be far more credible. Finding the right person to write your professional reference, however, can be trickier. You may not wish to reveal to your boss early on that you plan on leaving, and if the dynamics of your relationship are not ideal (hey, it happens once in a while), he or she might not make an appropriate reference. If this is the case, seek out a boss at a former job or someone who was your supervisor at your current job but has since moved to another organization. Avoid friends, colleagues, and clients as references unless the school explicitly says it's okay.

Advise your writers on themes and qualities you highlighted in your application. Suggest that they include real-life examples of your performance to illustrate their points. In other words, script the recommendation as best you can. Your boss, even if he or she is your biggest fan, may not know what your recommendation should include.

A great recommendation is rarely enough to save a weak application from doom. But it might push a borderline case over to the "admit" pile. Mediocre recommendations can be damaging; an application that is strong in all other areas now has a weakness, an inconsistency.

A final warning on this topic: Procrastination is common here. Micromanage your references so that each recommendation arrives on time! If need be, provide packaging for an overnight letter, have your reference seal it up, and then ship it out yourself.

THE INTERVIEW

Not all business schools attach equal value to the interview. For some, it's an essential screening tool. For others, it's used to make a final decision on those caught somewhere between "admit" and "reject." Some schools may encourage, but not require, the interview. Others make it informative, with little connection to the admissions decision.

Like the letters of recommendation, an interview may serve as a reality check to reinforce the total picture. It may also be used to fill in the blanks, particularly in borderline cases.

If an interview is offered, take it. In person, you may be a more compelling candidate. You can use the interview to further address weaknesses or bring dull essays to life. Most importantly, you can display the kinds of qualities—enthusiasm, sense of humor, maturity—that can positively sway an admissions decision.

Act quickly to schedule your interview. Admissions Departments often lack the time and staff to interview every candidate who walks through their doors. You don't want your application decision delayed by several months (and placed in a more competitive round or pool) because your interview was scheduled late in the filing period.

A great interview can tip the scale in the "admit" direction. How do you know if it was great? You were calm and focused. You expressed yourself and your ideas clearly. Your interviewer invited you to go rock climbing with him or her the following weekend. (Okay, let's just say you developed a solid personal rapport with the interviewer.)

A mediocre interview may not have much impact, unless your application is hanging on by a thread. In such a case, the person you're talking to (harsh as it may seem) is probably looking for a reason not to admit you, rather than a reason to let you in. If you feel your application may be in that hazy, marginal area, try to be extra-inspired in your interview.

Approach this meeting as you would a job interview. Remember, you're being sized up as a person in all of your dimensions. Here are a few tips to use during the interview.

- Dress and act the part of a professional but avoid being stiff or acting like a stuffed shirt.

- Limit your use of business jargon. Interviewers often hear a lot of the same generic answers. They are more interested in you being your witty, charming, natural self.

- Be personable and talk about your passions, such as hobbies or a recent trip you've taken. The idea is to get the interviewer thinking of you as someone who will contribute greatly to the quality of campus life.

Highlight your achievements and excellence, even in something like gourmet cooking, but avoid stunts, such as pulling out a platter of peppercorn pâté sautéed in anchovy sauce.

Chapter 4
Quotas, Recruitment, and Diversity

B-schools don't have to operate under quotas—governmental or otherwise. However, they probably try harder than most corporations to recruit diverse groups of people. Just as the modern business world has become global and multicultural, so too have b-schools. They must not only teach diversity in the classroom but also make it a reality in their campus population and, if possible, faculty.

Schools that have a diverse student body tend to be proud of it. They tout their success in profiles that demographically slice and dice the previous year's class by gender, race, and geographic and international residency. Prospective students can review this data and compare the diversity of the schools they've applied to.

However, such diversity doesn't come naturally from the demographics of the applicant pool. Admissions Committees have to work hard at it. In some cases, enrollment is encouraged with generous financial aid packages and scholarships.

While they don't have quotas per se, they do target groups for admission, seeking a demographic balance in many areas. Have they admitted enough women, minorities, foreign students, marketing strategists, and liberal arts majors? Are different parts of the country represented?

As we've said before, the best b-schools tend to attract top talent, students, and recruiters to their campus. Women and minorities are the most sought-after groups targeted for admission. So it's no surprise that programs that report higher-than-average female and minority enrollments tend to be among the very best.

INITIATIVES FOR MINORITIES

Some schools report higher minority enrollments than others, so our advice is consistent: You need to thoroughly research the program you've set your sights on. Consider your goals. Do you simply want to attend the most prestigious program? How will social factors impact your goals and experiences on campus?

Most business schools aspire to diversify their programs. It's the number of minorities applying to business school that has remained consistently low. The Graduate Management Admissions Council offers schools resources to diversify their recruitment efforts to reverse this trend and increase the number of underrepresented minorities pursuing a business career. GMAC has an extremely useful list of resources for prospective students, too, at http://www.gmac.com/reach-and-recruit-students/recruit-students-for-your-program/diversify-your-candidate-pool/diversity-resources-2.aspx. These organizations provide information on current opportunities for mentorships, internships, and financial assistance, services, and educational opportunities.

As you make up your mind about where you want to go for b-school, know that the scenario is positive and that new infrastructures exist to support your business career.

FEMALE APPLICANTS AND STUDENTS

If you've toured the campus and classrooms of a business school, you may have noticed something: On average, roughly 65 percent of any given MBA program's students are male. While this may make a nice pool of dating prospects for the women who are enrolled, it's not something business schools are happy with—far from it! In fact, it's something they are working to change as quickly as they can.

Beyond showing significantly higher application volume, MBA programs of all types are seeing female applications increase. For example, for the incoming 2014–2015 class, women made up the majority of applicants in master's programs for marketing and communications and accounting. They also make up about 40 percent or more of the applicants to part-time programs.[4] While these numbers may not match the male-to-female ratio of other graduate programs, closing the b-school gender gap is only a matter of time.

School Initiatives

How can we be sure that female enrollment will continue to increase? One reason is that getting women enthused about a career in business is a sky-high priority at business schools across the country these days. To wit, many business schools have launched their own women-only outreach and recruiting events. Columbia University hosts an annual "Women in Business" conference that brings together more than 300 alumnae, business leaders, students and prospective students to network and share ideas on achieving success in the marketplace. Linda Meehan, former assistant dean and executive director or admissions at Columbia Business School, knows that this outreach is working because "applicants walk away wowed by the extraordinary experience of being surrounded by so many intelligent, passionate, and successful women." Events like these aim to dispel myths, discuss the perceived lack of role models, and help women make informed decisions.

Stanford's events, says Wendy Hansen, former associate director of admissions at the Stanford Business School, "focus on the educational experience, but also on the unique types of issues women have, such as: how does getting the MBA fit in with having a family or having a spouse? How do I make this experience fit in with my life?" Julia Min Hwang, assistant dean of career management services at UC Berkeley's Haas School of Business, says attendees often find comfort in numbers. "Seeing such a large presence of women is empowering. They realize they're not in this alone, that there are other women around like them."

If all this sounds like good public relations, it is. Schools want to get the word out: MBAs offer women viable opportunities. But if the business schools are talking the talk, they're also walking the walk. There's nothing superficial about this campaign. Bit by bit, the MBA landscape for women is changing.

Opportunities begin even before the first day of class. At Stanford, admitted women are treated to one-on-one admit-lunches with female alumni. Once an admit gets to campus, they find MBA life is chock-full of student-run women and management programs, support groups, retreats, executive conferences, mentoring programs, and other dedicated resources for women only.

For many years now, most business programs have had an on-campus Partners Club for spouses and significant others—a benefit to both female and male students. Newcomers to the business-school scene include groups like The Parents Club and Biz Kids where students can find family-oriented classmates and activities. Columbia University's Mother's Network is an initiative that provides a formal support network for new, current, and future b-school moms. Perhaps the most symbolic gesture of the increasing influence of women in business school is Stanford's provision of a private nursing room for MBA moms and their babies in its main classroom facility.

More Flexibility and Making it Work

Of course, there's still room for improvement. A continuing problem at business schools is a lack of course work and case study material featuring women leaders. Likewise, there is an absence of female professors on the academic front.

---

4.   Graduate Management Admission Council, 2014 Application Trends Survey Report, http://www.gmac.com/market-intelligence-and-research/gmac-surveys/app-survey/application-trends-survey.aspx (accessed May 22, 2015).

Apart from these lingering issues, business schools continue to tackle the particular challenges female students face. For many women, the late starting age can be a turn-off. But even here, there are new options and opportunities to consider.

If you're stressed out from trying to have it all and have written off getting an MBA, new early-initiative programs might make you pause and reconsider your decision. Harvard and Stanford have developed an early career track that aims to minimize the impact of the biological clock on a prospective applicant's decision to pursue an MBA. Other schools are likely to follow suit.

The early career track offers a solution that is as simple as it is practical: Admit women (and men) to the MBA program either straight out of college or with just a few years of work experience. Business schools hope that the option to attain their MBA early on in their careers will prompt more women to apply to their programs. With a bigger window to accomplish their professional goals, more women will turn to the MBA as a viable option that won't require them to sacrifice their personal lives.

Beginning a business career earlier eliminates the immediate problem of timing. But what happens down the road? While it helps to remove one timing issue, it can't indefinitely postpone the balancing act that shadows many women's careers. It's hard to rationalize the opportunity costs of the MBA knowing that the investment might be forsaken when tough choices have to be made.

Business schools blame misconceptions about the utility of the MBA for women's reticence on this front. They feel that many women underestimate the broad reach of the degree. The MBA is not just for hard-core careers like banking and finance, but is also useful in not-for-profit work, less high-stress industries such as consumer goods, and leadership positions in a wide range of fields.

Further, says Hansen, "There is a tremendous amount of flexibility in a general management degree. The MBA positions you much more effectively to make an impact wherever you fall at different points in your life. It gives you the tools and framework to apply those skills at different levels and in different intensities. For example, women can rise to a partner level or a senior leadership position and then scale back to a different role within the organization. They can also scale back to part-time work." In other words, the investment doesn't have to be forsaken; it might instead be redirected.

There's no doubt the return on investment (that's ROI in business speak) for the MBA is high. Six-figure salaries and sign-on bonuses that pay you back for the cost of your MBA tuition are hard to beat (and unlike medical, veterinary, and law school grads, you won't have malpractice premiums eating into your take-home pay). If you've thought business school might be right for you, keep investigating—you might be right.

WHERE ARE THE WOMEN IN MBA PROGRAMS?

Are you a professional woman in her mid-to-late twenties? Do you see graduate school in your future? During these tough times, you might envision yourself back on campus sooner rather than later. Downturns do tend to fuel grad school applications. After all, what better place to wait out the economy and avoid the gaping pit of joblessness?

Grad school can be a cure-all for many ills: It can jump-start or redirect a stubbornly off-track career; it can give you a place to hang out while you figure out what you want to be when you grow up (law school, a three-year degree, offers an even longer alternative); and it can transform your personal life as you vault into a new career. Even in uncertain times there is certainty in knowing that after two years in school you can emerge reborn as a professional with a spanking new identity, prescribed career track, and a solid alumni network.

Despite the huge appeal of graduate school, be it as an escape from bad times or as your true, chosen path, MBA programs have remained a problematic choice for many women. Female enrollment at law, medical, and veterinary schools now hovers at, or near, the 50 percent mark. So what's up with business schools? Why has female enrollment at business schools stagnated at about 30 percent?

Even during the best of times, business schools have struggled to attract women. Is this due to the unique challenges women face in building and sustaining their careers over a lifetime of choices, both professional and personal, or is there another reason? Clearly an MBA presents many opportunities, but, for women, will these opportunities upset their already delicate balancing acts?

THINKING OF FAMILY

Let's start with biology—as in biological clocks. Since a prerequisite for admission to many business programs is prior work experience, first-year business school students are typically a bit older than their law or med school counterparts. In fact, the average age for entering full-time MBA students is twenty-eight. This means that by the time graduation rolls around, MBA students are heading into their thirties—a prime time for marriage and children. For some women, that timing couldn't be worse.

Newly minted MBAs in their early thirties are just starting to reap the rewards of their business school investments by scoring brand new, mid-to-senior level jobs. With these jobs come ever-greater demands and time pressures. But, for many, the pressure to have a personal life is just as great. Those kinds of competing priorities are the very headaches women hope to avoid. Making matters worse, MBA jobs at the senior level can vault women into a culture that may still be dominated by old-school thinking (translation: men) and a culture that may be less tolerant of efforts to balance work commitments with family.

These dilemmas begin long before business school graduation. Again, because MBA students tend to be older, many women have to factor a partner or child into their graduate school decision, especially if it involves relinquishing a paycheck and/or relocation. Many of these women encounter a potential double standard: Husbands and boyfriends, especially those with careers, are often less willing to relocate on their female partner's behalf than vice versa.

NO URGENT MATTER

Another reason business school enrollment for women may be low is that an MBA is not a barrier to entry nor is it a requirement for success in business. In addition, it isn't a rite of passage in many fields that appeal to high numbers of women: marketing, publishing, fashion, and teaching. By contrast, notes Eileen Chang, former Associate Director of Admissions at the Harvard Business School, "If your objective is to be a lawyer or doctor, you simply can't practice without the requisite degree. Business school is fundamentally different because the career path is one where the MBA can put you on any number of tracks—be it banking, accounting, or management—but doesn't require a credential." Between the lack of a required degree for entering business and the late starting age to enter a program, some women perceive a high opportunity cost for the MBA.

FEAR OF MATH?

Why more women aren't pursuing an MBA is a question that business schools have been asking themselves for years. Some hard answers came in the form of a recent study by the University of Michigan's Business School Center for the Education of Women and the Catalyst Foundation. The following issues were identified as key deterrents to business school for women: the MBA is still seen as a male domain; there is a lack of support from employers; a lack of career opportunity and flexibility; a lack of access to powerful business networks and role models; and a perception that b-school is overloaded with math.

According to many schools, math fears are just that—fears. Chang observes, "Maybe historically, math was considered a hurdle. But we see so many women who have strong skills coming from fields that are quantitative, such as banking and engineering, that I think the math fears are almost a myth. But this is a myth we want to work against. We want applicants to know they can handle the math."

Julia Min Hwang, assistant dean of career management services at UC Berkeley's Haas School of Business, concurs, "The math phobia may be unfounded to a certain degree, and still it's a perception that has been long-lasting. Women [enter business school] and perform extremely well."

If you're frightened by math, you need to know that a business school education does require a basic command of the subject. "You do need to be comfortable with numbers," advises Wendy Hansen, former associate director of admissions at the Stanford Business School. "The strongest MBA programs are going to be rigorous in math. Knowing how to influence and lead an organization requires understanding the language of business, which includes accounting and finance."

Still, prospective MBAs with a math phobia need not panic; most programs will work with students who lack the necessary math background. "At Stanford, we have a pre-term program of courses before classes begin to get students up to speed," says Hansen, "We also encourage people to take quantitative courses before they come to our school to develop their skills."

If your math fears are not so easily assuaged, concerns about a persistent Old Boys Network might be. As Hansen notes, "Women may say, 'I don't see the masses of female role models doing what I want to do.' That is going to change slowly. But it is going to change. We have to reach a point where those in school reach a place where they are out in the world having an impact."

OUR ADVICE

Look at the number of female MBA students attending your targeted school and evaluate whether you would feel comfortable there. Research the number and range of student organizations for women and speak with female MBAs about school life.

Chapter 5
Money Matters

HOW MUCH WILL IT COST?

The Truth

To say that business school is an expensive endeavor is an understatement. In fact, to really gauge how expensive business school is, you need to look not only at your tuition costs and living expenses, but also at the opportunity cost of foregoing a salary for the length of your program. Think about it: You'll have a net outflow of money.

But keep in mind that, unlike law school or medical school, business school is just a two-year program. Once those two years are over, you can expect to reap the rewards of your increased market value. Unfortunately, business school differs from law school and medical school in a much less desirable way as well—there are serious limitations on the amount of money available through scholarships and grants. Most business school students seeking financial aid will be limited to loans, and lots of them.

Try not to get too upset about borrowing the money for business school; think of it as an investment in yourself. But, like all investments, it should be carefully thought out and discussed with everyone (spouse, partner, etc.) concerned. This is especially important for those of you considering business school. You need a law degree to practice law, and a medical degree to practice medicine, but a business degree is not required to work in business. That said, certain professional opportunities may be tougher to pursue without an MBA on your resume.

The Cost of B-School

So get out some paper, a pencil, and a calculator, and figure out how much it will cost you to attend school. What should you include? Your opportunity cost (lost income) and your cost of attending b-school (tuition and fees). One more thing: For a more accurate assessment of your investment, you should figure taxes into the equation by dividing tuition cost by 0.65 (this assumes taxes of about 35 percent). Why? Because in order to pay tuition of $35,000, you would have to make a pre-tax income of about $54,000. If you are lucky enough to have a source of aid that does not require repayment, such as a grant, scholarship, or wealthy benefactor, subtract that amount from the cost of attending b-school.

For example, if you currently make $60,000 and plan to attend a business school that costs $35,000 per year, your investment would be approximately $228,000.

$$(60,000 \times 2) + [(35,000 \times 2)/.65] = \$227,692.31$$

Now say you receive an annual grant of $5,000. Your investment would now be approximately $212,300.

$$(60,000 \times 2) + [(30,000 \times 2)/.65] = 212,307.69$$

HOW LONG WILL IT TAKE YOU TO RECOUP YOUR INVESTMENT?

To estimate this figure, you first need to estimate your expected salary increase post-MBA. Check out the average starting salaries for graduates of the programs you are looking at and adjust upward/downward based on the industry you plan to enter. Subtract your current salary from your expected salary and you'll get your expected salary increase.

Once you complete the step above, divide your investment (tuition and fees plus lost income) by your expected salary increase, and then add 2 (the length of a full-time MBA program). If you are contemplating a one-year MBA program, just add 1.

Going back to the example above, if your pre-MBA salary is $60,000 and you expect to make $80,000 when you graduate, your expected salary increase is $20,000 (a 33 percent increase). Let's assume you did not receive a grant and that your investment will be about $228,000.

$$(228,000/20,000) + 2 = 13.4$$

It will take you approximately 13 years to earn back your investment.

Keep in mind, these are approximations and don't take into account annual raises, inflation, and so on. But it is interesting, isn't it?

While business school is an expensive proposition, the financial rewards of having your MBA can be immensely lucrative as we discussed before. You won't be forced into bankruptcy if you finance it correctly. There are tried-and-true ways to reduce your initial costs, finance the costs on the horizon, and manage the debt you'll leave school with—all without selling your soul to the highest bidder.

COMPARISON SHOPPING

While cost shouldn't be the first thing on your mind when you are choosing a school, depending on your goals in getting an MBA, it might be fairly high on your list. Private schools aren't the only business schools. Many state schools have fantastic reputations. Regional schools may be more generous with financial aid. Tuition costs will vary widely between public and private schools, especially if you qualify as an in-state student. Keep in mind, however, that salary gains tend to be less dramatic at more regional schools.

HOW DO I FUND MY MBA?

The short answer: loans. Unless your company is underwriting your MBA, or you're able to pay your way in cash, you'll be financing your two years of business school through a portfolio of loans. Loans typically come in one of two forms: federal and private. Only a few of you will be lucky enough to qualify for, and get, grants and scholarships.

Anyone with reasonably good credit, regardless of financial need, can borrow money for business school. If you have financial need, you will probably be eligible for some type of financial aid if you meet the following basic qualifications:

- You are a United States citizen or a permanent U.S. resident.

- You are registered for Selective Service if you are a male, or you have documentation to prove that you are exempt.

- You are not in default on student loans already.

- You don't have a horrendous credit history.

International applicants to business school should take note: Most U.S. business schools will require all international students to pay in full or show proof that they will be able to pay the entire cost of the MBA prior to beginning the MBA program.

FEDERAL LOANS

The federal government funds federal loan programs. Federal loans are usually the "first resort" for borrowers because many are subsidized by the federal government and offer generous interest rates. Some do not begin charging you interest until after you complete your degree. Most federal loans are need-based, but some higher interest federal loans are available regardless of financial circumstances. Your business school's Financial Aid Office will determine what your need is, if any.

PRIVATE LOANS

Private loans are funded by banks, foundations, corporations, and other associations. A number of private loans are targeted to aid particular segments of the population. You may have to do some investigating to identify private loans for which you might qualify. As always, contact your law school's Financial Aid Office to learn more.

ALTERNATIVE SOURCES OF FUNDING

We've already mentioned these in one form or other, but they are worthy of a bit more attention.

The first alternative is sponsorship of your employer or educational reimbursement. Not all companies treat this the same way, but if you are able to get your employer to kick in a portion of the cost, you are better off than before. But beware, this benefit also comes with strings attached. Most companies that pay for your MBA will require a commitment of several years upon graduation. If you renege, you could be liable for the full cost of your education. Others will require that you attend business school part-time, which you may or may not want to do. Often, part-time students are unable to participate in on-campus recruiting and networking efforts to the same extent as full-time students.

Educational reimbursement can come in another form as well. Some companies will provide sign-on bonuses to new MBAs that will cover the cost of a year's tuition. This is a fantastic development from the years of a robust economy, but it is by no means a guarantee during tougher times. Don't assume that you will have this option open to you just because it has been a common occurrence in past years.

The other "alternative" source of funding is a financial gift from family or another source. Either you have a resource that is willing and able to fund all or part of your MBA, or you don't. If you do, be thankful.

APPLYING FOR FINANCIAL AID

In order to become eligible for financial aid of any kind, you will need to complete the Free Application for Federal Student Aid, also known as the FAFSA. You complete and submit this form after January 1 of the year in which you plan to enter business school. You should aim to complete and submit this form as soon as possible after the first of the year to avoid any potential delays. The FAFSA is available from a school's Financial Aid Office. You can also download the form directly from the website of the U.S. Department of Education at FAFSA.ed.gov. A third option is to use the FAFSA Express software (also downloadable from the website) and transmit the application electronically.

It is important to note that the form requires information from your federal income tax returns. Plan to file your taxes early that year.

In addition to the FAFSA form, most schools will have their own financial aid form that you will be required to complete and submit. These often have their own deadlines, so it is wise to keep careful track of all the forms you must complete and all their respective deadlines. Yes, it's a lot of paperwork, but get over it. You'll be much happier when the tuition bill arrives.

LOAN SPECIFICS

GUIDE TO FEDERAL LOANS

Direct Subsidized and Unsubsidized Loans

Subsidized and Unsubsidized federal loans require you to complete the FAFSA form in order to qualify. These are very desirable loans because they offer low-interest rates fixed for the life of the loan and are federally guaranteed. There is a limit to how much you can borrow in this program. The maximum amount per year you may borrow as a graduate student is $20,500. The maximum amount you may borrow in total is $138,500. The aggregate amount includes any Direct loans you may have from your undergraduate or other graduate studies.

You may have borrowed Direct Subsidized or Unsubsidized federal loans as an undergraduate. It's important to remember that all direct loans for graduate students are unsubsidized. Unsubsidized loans are not need-based and do charge interest from the time of disbursement to the time of full repayment. You can pay the interest while you are in school or opt for capitalization, in which case the interest is added to the principal. You will pay more in the long run if you choose capitalization. Interest payments may be tax deductible, so be sure to check. The standard repayment period for generally between ten and twenty-five years.

You will pay a small origination and guarantee fee for each loan, but this is not an out-of-pocket expense. It is simply deducted from the loan amount. Some schools will allow you to borrow the money under the Direct federal loan program directly from them, while others will require you to borrow from a bank. Direct federal loans are typically paid to the school to cover tuition, fees, and room and board (if you are living in campus housing). Any remaining balance will be paid to you by the school bursar. Repayment is handled by a loan servicer, which is a company that handles collection and administrative duties related to a loan. You will be contacted by your servicer upon receipt of your Direct loan. For more information on federal loans, call the Federal Student Aid Information Center at 800-433-3243 or visit studentaid.ed.gov.

Perkins Loans

Perkins loans are available to graduate students who demonstrate exceptional financial need. The financial aid office will determine your eligibility for a Perkins Loan. If you qualify for a Perkins Loan as part of your financial aid package, take it. The loans are made by the schools and are repaid to the schools, although the federal government provides a large portion of the funds. You can borrow up to $8,000 for each year of graduate study up to a total of $60,000 (this includes any money borrowed under this program during undergraduate study). The interest rates on this loan are low, currently 5 percent. There are no fees attached. The grace period is nine months upon graduation.

Direct PLUS Loans

Direct PLUS loans are made available through schools, though the U.S. Department of Education is actually the lender. You may borrow up to the full cost of attendance as determined by your school, less any other financial aid received. Like other federal loans, Direct PLUS loans have a small origination fee and a fixed interest rate, which is currently 7.21 percent. These funds are paid directly to your school to cover tuition, fees, and room and board. Any remaining balance will be refunded to you to cover other expenses associated with your education—when a school determines the cost of attendance, books, travel, and other expenses are typically included.

Private/Commercial Loans

This is expensive territory. Not only are interest rates high, but terms are also quite different from those found with federal loans. You may not be able to defer payment of interest or principal until after graduation. Origination and guarantee fees are also much higher since these loans are unsecured. After all, banks and other specialized lenders exist to loan money to folks like you, and unlike the federal government, want to make money doing it. If you go this route, shop around diligently. Think of it as good practice for your post-MBA executive career.

Scholarships and Grants

The usual sources for this type of funding are alumni groups and civic organizations. This funding is limited, and actual awards tend to be small. Even if you benefited from generous scholarship funding as an undergraduate, it would be unwise to assume you'll have the same experience as a graduate student. But do investigate. You never know what's out there. Schools will frequently list any scholarships and grants that are available at the back of their financial aid catalog.

For more information

Find out more about your financing options for business school education at PrincetonReview.com.

CHAPTER 6
WHAT B-SCHOOL IS REALLY LIKE

AN ACADEMIC PERSPECTIVE

The objective of all MBA programs is to prepare students for a professional career in business. One business school puts it this way:

Graduates should be all of the following:

1. Able to think and reason independently, creatively, and analytically.

2. Skilled in the use of quantitative techniques.

3. Literate in the use of software applications as management tools.

4. Knowledgeable about the world's management issues and problems.

5. Willing to work in and successfully cope with conditions of uncertainty, risk, and change.

6. Astute decision makers.

7. Ethically and socially responsible.

8. Able to manage in an increasingly global environment.

9. Proficient in utilizing technology as a mode of doing business.

Sound like a tall order? Possibly. But this level of expectation is what business school is all about.

Nearly all MBA programs feature a core curriculum that focuses on the major disciplines of business: finance, management, accounting, marketing, manufacturing, decision sciences, economics, and organizational behavior. Unless your school allows you to place out of them, these courses are mandatory. Core courses provide broad functional knowledge in one discipline. To illustrate, a core marketing course covers pricing, segmentation, communications, product-line planning, and implementation. Electives provide a narrow focus that deepen the area of study. For example, a marketing elective might be entirely devoted to pricing.

Students sometimes question the need for such a comprehensive core program, but the functional areas of a real business are not parallel lines. All departments of a business affect each other every day. For example, an MBA in a manufacturing job might be asked by a financial controller why the company's product has become unprofitable to produce. Without an understanding of how product costs are accounted for, this MBA wouldn't know how to respond to a critical and legitimate request.

At most schools, the first term or year is devoted to a rigid core curriculum. Some schools allow first-years to take core courses side by side with electives. Still others have come up with an entirely new way of covering the basics, integrating the core courses into one cross-functional learning experience, which may also include sessions on topics such as globalization, ethics, and managing diversity. Half-year to year-long courses are team-taught by professors who will see you through all disciplines.

TEACHING METHODOLOGY

Business schools employ two basic teaching methods: case study and lecture. Usually, they employ some combination of the two. The most popular is the case study approach. Students are presented with either real or hypothetical business scenarios and are asked to analyze them. This method provides concrete situations (rather than abstractions) that require mastery of a wide range of skills. Students often find case studies exciting because they can engage in spirited discussions about possible solutions to given business problems and because they get an opportunity to apply newly acquired business knowledge.

On the other hand, lecturing is a teaching method in which—you guessed it—the professor speaks to the class and the class listens. The efficacy of the lecture method depends entirely on the professor. If the professor is compelling, you'll probably get a lot out of the class. If the professor is boring, you probably won't listen, which isn't necessarily a big deal since many professors make their class notes available online.

THE CLASSROOM EXPERIENCE

Professors teaching case methodology often begin class with a "cold call." A randomly selected student opens the class with an analysis of the case and makes recommendations for solutions. The cold call forces you to be prepared and to think on your feet.

No doubt, a cold call can be intimidating. But unlike law school, b-school professors don't use the Socratic Method to torture you, testing your thinking with a pounding cross-examination. They're training managers, not trial lawyers. At worst, particularly if you're unprepared, a professor will abruptly dismiss your contribution.

Alternatively, professors ask for a volunteer to open a case, particularly someone who has had real industry experience with the issues. After the opening, the discussion is broadened to include the whole class. Everyone tries to get in a good comment, particularly if class participation counts heavily toward the grade. "Chip shots"—unenlightened, just-say-anything-to-get-credit comments—are common. So are "air hogs," students who go on and on because they like nothing more than to hear themselves pontificate.

Depending on the school, class discussions can degenerate into wars of ego rather than ideas. But for the most part, debates are kept constructive and civilized. Students are competitive, but not offensively so, and learn to make their points succinctly and persuasively.

A GLOSSARY OF INSIDER LINGO

B-school students, graduates, and professors—like most close-knit, somewhat solipsistic groups—seem to speak their own weird language. Here's a sampler of MBA jargon (with English translations):

Admissions Mistake: How each student perceives him or herself until getting first-year grades back from midterms.

Air Hogs: Students who monopolize classroom discussion and love to hear themselves speak.

B2B: "Business to Business"—a company that sells not to retail consumers, but to other enterprises. With the renewed focus on more traditional industries, this now stands for "Back to Basics."

B2C: "Business to Consumer"—a company that sells primarily to individual retail consumers. As with the above joke about B2B, business students occasionally say this really means "Back to Consulting."

Back of the Envelope: A quick analysis of numbers, as if scribbled on the back of an envelope.

Benchmarking: Comparing a company to others in the industry.

Burn Rate: Amount of cash a money-losing company consumes during a period of time.

Case Study Method: Popular teaching method that uses real-life business cases for analysis.

Cold Call: Unexpected, often dreaded request by the professor to open a case discussion.

Chip Shot: Vacant and often cheesy comments used not to truly benefit class discussion, but rather to get credit for participation.

Cycle Time: How fast you can turn something around.

Deliverable: Your end product.

Four P's: Elements of a marketing strategy: Price, Promotion, Place, Product.

Fume Date: Date the company will run out of cash reserves.

Functional Areas: The basic disciplines of business (e.g., finance, marketing, R&D).

HP12-C: A calculator that works nothing like a regular one, used by finance types when they don't have Excel handy.

Lingo Bingo: A furtive game of Bingo whereby he who "wins" must work a decided upon, often trite phrase (see "chip shot") into the class discussion. For example: "I didn't actually read the case last night, but the protagonist is *two beers short of a six-pack*." The winner also earns a prize and the admiration of classmates.

Low Hanging Fruit: Tasks or goals that are easiest to achieve (consultant jargon).

Monitize: To turn an idea into a moneymaking scheme.

Net Net: End result.

Power Nap: Quick, intense, in-class recharge for the continually sleep-deprived.

Power Tool: Someone who does all the work and sits in the front row of the class with his or her hand up.

Pre-enrollment Courses: Commonly known as MBA summer camp—quantitative courses to get the numerically challenged up to speed.

Pro Forma: Financial presentation of hypothetical events, such as projected earnings.

Quant Jock: A numerical athlete who is happiest crunching numbers.

Rule of Three: You should not talk more than three times in any given class, but you should participate at least once over the course of three classes.

Run the Numbers: Analyze quantitatively.

Shrimp Boy: A student who comes to a corporate event just to scarf down the food.

Skydeck: Refers to the back row of the classroom, usually when it's amphitheater style.

Slice and Dice: Running all kinds of quantitative analysis on a set of numbers.

Soft Skills: Conflict resolution, teamwork, negotiation, oral and written communication.

Take-aways: The key points of a lecture or meeting that participants should remember.

The Five Forces: Michael Porter's model for analyzing the strategic attractiveness of an industry.

Three C's: The primary forces considered in marketing: Customer, Competition, Company.

Value-Based Decision Making: Values and ethics as part of the practice of business.

YOUR FIRST YEAR

The first six months of b-school can be daunting. You're unfamiliar with the subjects. There's a tremendous amount of work to do. And when you least have the skills to do so, there's pressure to stay with the pack. All of this produces anxiety and a tendency to overprepare. Eventually, students learn shortcuts and settle into a routine, but until then, much of the first year is just plain tough. The programs usually pack more learning into the first term than they do into each of the remaining terms. For the schools to teach the core curriculum (which accounts for as much as 70 percent of learning) in a limited time, an intensive pace is considered necessary. Much of the second year will be spent on gaining proficiency in your area of expertise and on searching for a job.

The good news is that the schools recognize how tough the first year can be. During the early part of the program, they anchor students socially by placing them in small sections, sometimes called "cohorts." You take many or all of your classes with your section-mates. Sectioning encourages the formation of personal and working relationships and can help make a large program feel like a school within a school.

Because so much has to be accomplished in so little time, getting an MBA is like living in fast-forward. This is especially true of the job search. No sooner are you in the program than recruiters for summer jobs show up, which tends to divert students from their studies. First-years aggressively pursue summer positions, which are linked with the promise of a permanent job offer if the summer goes well. At some schools, the recruiting period begins as early as October, at others in January or February.

A DAY IN THE LIFE

Matt Camp, First Year
Tuck School of Business, Dartmouth College

7:00 A.M.: Get dressed. Out of the door by 7:45 A.M. to head to the campus dining hall for breakfast. If I have time, I'll scan both the *Financial Times* and *The Wall Street Journal*. Today, I have an informal get-to-know-you-better meeting with a marketing professor over breakfast.

8:30 A.M.: Core class in Corporate Finance. Grab any seat in a tiered classroom set-up. I'm usually in the middle toward the side. If possible, the front row stays empty.

10:00 A.M.: Check e-mail. Read the *Times*.

10:30 A.M.: Macroeconomics lecture/case study class. Again, no assigned seating. Expect cold calls on case. Cold calls are not terrifying. Professors are supportive, not out to embarrass you. Class discussion is lively, with a mix of people offering their views.

Noon: Back to the cafeteria. Tuck may be one of the few schools where everyone eats together at the same place. There isn't much in town, and you're tight on time, so it doesn't make sense to go back home or elsewhere. It's crowded, so I look for friends, but basically grab a seat anywhere at one of the large tables that seat six to seven. Professors, administrators, and students all eat at the same place. Food is above-average.

1:15 P.M.: Classes are over for the day. From this point, I begin to start homework; there's a lot of work to do. I can go to a study room on campus, but they get booked up pretty quickly for groups, so I head to the library. The majority of the people are doing work for tomorrow. It's rare to have someone working on a project that's due the following week. It's pretty much day-to-day.

4:00 P.M.: I head off to one of the scheduled sports I've signed up for. Today it's soccer, played about one mile from campus. I drive; friends hitch a ride with me. This is a big international scene, mostly men, but there's a small group of women too. It's definitely a game we play hard, but in a very congenial way.

6:00 P.M.: Head back to campus. I'm hungry. It's off to the dining hall again. Most first-years live in dorms, so home cooking is not an option. Almost all second-years live off-campus, so they head back for a home-cooked meal. Cafeteria is not crowded; I may eat alone.

7:00 P.M.: Head home for a quick shower and change. The night is just beginning.

7:30 P.M.: Meet with study group at school to flesh out rest of work that needs to be done in preparation for tomorrow's classes.

11:00 P.M.: Students and their wives/husbands or partners head out to play ice hockey at one of the two rinks here. Wives/husbands and partners play. There are different games going on for different skill levels. It's a lot of fun.

Midnight: Time to go and celebrate either a hard game or a sore butt, but everyone goes to get some wings and a beer. There are only two bars on campus, and they close at 1:00 A.M. so we head to one of them.

1:00 A.M.: After the bar closes, people head home.

1:15 A.M.: Exhausted, I go to bed. No TV. I've forgotten what that is.

YOUR SECOND YEAR

Relax, the second year is easier. By now, students know what's important and what's not. Second-years work more efficiently than first-years. Academic anxiety is no longer a factor. Having mastered the broad-based core curriculum, students now enjoy taking electives and developing an area of specialization.

Anxiety in the second year has more to do with the arduous task of finding a job. For some lucky students, a summer position has yielded a full-time offer. But even those students often go through the whole recruiting grind anyway because they don't want to cut off any opportunities prematurely.

Most MBAs leave school with a full-time offer. Sometimes it's their only offer. Sometimes it's not their dream job, which may be why most grads change jobs after just two years. One student summed up the whole two-year academic/recruiting process like this: "The first-year students collapse in the winter quarter because of on-campus recruiting. The second-years collapse academically in the first quarter of their second year because it's so competitive to get a good job. And when a second-year does get a job, he or she forgets about class entirely. That's why pass/fail was invented."

A DAY IN THE LIFE

KRISTIN HANSEN, SECOND-YEAR
Tuck School of Business, Dartmouth College

9:00 A.M.: Wake-up (my first class is at 10:30 A.M.) and finish work for Monday classes.

10:15 A.M.: Ride my bike to campus for 10:30 A.M. class.

10:30 A.M.: Head to International Economics class, an elective. I have only three classes this semester, my last. Prior to this I had four and a half classes each term. I front-loaded so I would have a light last semester. Grab a yogurt and juice on way in. Eat in class. We discuss a currency crisis case.

Noon: Head to study room and check e-mail. Finish work for next class.

1:00 P.M.: Grab a quick lunch in the dining hall. Will bring it to eat during class.

1:15 P.M.: Managerial Decision Making class, another elective. Today is the very last class that second-years will have at Tuck; we're off to graduation! Our professor brings in strawberries and champagne to celebrate. We all hang out and toast each other. This obviously doesn't happen everyday, but this is just the kind of thing a Tuck professor would do.

2:45 P.M.: I'm one of four Tuck social chairpersons, so I use this time to send e-mails to my co-chairs about the upcoming chili cook-off and farm party. Then I send a message to the school regarding other social events for the weekend. I get an e-mail from the New York office of CS First Boston, with whom I've accepted a job offer, with a calendar of the dates for my private client-services training.

3:00 P.M.: Go for a run, swim, or bike ride.

5:00 P.M.: Head home to shower and change. Usually I'd make dinner at home and eat, but tonight, I'm heading out to a social event. So I relax a bit and do an hour of preparation for the next day. On Monday, Tuesday, and Wednesday nights, the workload is heavier.

7:00 P.M.: Off to a Turkey Fry Dinner. This is a meal that will be prepared by my two economics professors. They donated this "dinner" for the charity student auction. Friends of mine bid on it and won. Each of eight bidders gets to bring a guest, and I'm one of the guests. The professors are hosting this at one of their homes. Basically, they're taking three large turkeys and fry-o-lating them.

8:30 P.M.: We all head out to an open mic night, led by the same two economics professors that hosted the Turkey Fry. It's held at a local bar. Anyone in the audience can get onstage and perform. I'm a member of the Tuck band, so I get up on stage with my acoustic guitar and play various folk and bluegrass songs. This is a great warm-up for the open mic night at Tuck.

10:45 P.M.: We head out for Pub Night in downtown Hanover.

1:00 A.M.: The bar closes, so we head to "The End Zone," one of the second-year houses close to campus. All the second-year houses are named; these are names that have been passed down from generation to generation. On a typical Thursday night at Tuck, a small number of students will stay out until 3:00 A.M. I'm usually one of them.

3:00 A.M.: I walk home. My house, called "Girls in the Hood," is just a ten-minute stroll away. I may grab a 3:00 A.M. snack. Then, I quickly fall asleep, exhausted.

Life Outside of Class

Business school is more than academics and a big-bucks job. A spirited community provides ample opportunity for social interaction, extracurricular activity, and career development.

Much of campus life revolves around student-run clubs. There are groups for just about every career interest and social need—from MBAs for a Greener America to the Small Business Club. There's even a group for significant others on most campuses. The clubs are a great way to meet classmates with similar interests and to get in on the social scene. They might have a reputation for throwing the best black-tie balls, pizza-and-keg events, and professional mixers. During orientation week, these clubs aggressively market themselves to first-years.

Various socially responsible projects are also popular on campus. An emphasis on volunteer work is part of the overall trend toward good citizenship. Perhaps to counter the greed of the 1980s, "giving back" is the b-school style of the moment. There is usually a wide range of options—from tutoring in an inner-city school to working in a soup kitchen to renovating public buildings.

Still another way to get involved is to work on a school committee. Here you might serve on a task force designed to improve student quality of life, or you might work in the admissions office and interview prospective students.

For those with more creative urges there are always the old standbys: extracurriculars such as the school paper, yearbook, or school play. At some schools, the latter is a dramatization of "b-school follies" and is a highlight of the year. Like the student clubs, these are a great way to get to know your fellow students.

Finally, you can play on intramural sports teams or attend the numerous informal get-togethers, dinner parties, and group trips. There are also plenty of regularly scheduled pub nights, just in case you thought your beer-guzzling days were over.

Most former MBA students say that going to b-school was the best decision they ever made. That's primarily because of nonacademic experiences. Make the most of your classes, but take the time to get involved and enjoy yourself.

PART II
SCHOOLS RANKED BY CATEGORY

On the following pages you will find eleven top 10 lists of business schools ranked according to various metrics. As we noted earlier, none of these lists purports to rank the business schools by their overall quality. Nor should any combination of the categories we've chosen be construed as representing the raw ingredients for such a ranking. We have made no attempt to gauge the "prestige" of these schools, and we wonder whether we could accurately do so even if we tried. What we have done, however, is presented a number of lists using information from two very large databases—one of statistical information collected from business schools, and another of subjective data gathered via our survey of 25,000 business students at 294 business schools.

Ten of the ranking lists are based partly or wholly on opinions collected through our business student survey. The only schools that may appear in these lists are the 294 business schools from which we were able to collect a sufficient number of student surveys to accurately represent the student experience in our various ratings and descriptive profiles.

One of the rankings, "Toughest to Get Into," incorporates *only* admissions statistics reported to us by the business schools. Therefore, any business school appearing in this edition of the guide, whether we collected student surveys from it or not, may appear on this list.

Under the title of each list is an explanation of what criteria the ranking is based on. For explanations of many of the individual rankings components, turn to the "How This Book is Organized" section, on page 5.

It's worth repeating: There is no one best business school in America. There is a best business school for you. By using these rankings in conjunction with the descriptive profiles and data listings in subsequent sections of this book, we hope that you will begin to identify the attributes of a business school that are important to you, as well as those schools that can best help you to achieve your personal and professional goals.

The top schools in each category appear in descending order.

TOUGHEST TO GET INTO

BASED ON THE ADMISSIONS SELECTIVITY RATING (SEE PAGE 10 FOR EXPLANATION)

1. Stanford University
2. Harvard University
3. University of California-Berkeley
4. Massachusetts Institute of Technology
5. Columbia University
6. University of Pennsylvania
7. Cornell University
8. The University of Chicago
9. Northwestern University
10. New York University

BEST CAREER PROSPECTS

BASED ON THE CAREER RATING (SEE PAGE 12 FOR EXPLANATION)

1. Columbia University
2. Stanford University
3. Harvard University
4. University of California-Berkeley
5. Dartmouth College
6. Duke University
7. University of Virginia
8. Massachusetts Institute of Technology
9. University of Pennsylvania
10. Northwestern University

BEST CLASSROOM EXPERIENCE

BASED ON STUDENT ASSESSMENT OF PROFESSORS' TEACHING ABILITIES AND RECOGNITION IN THEIR FIELDS, THE INTEGRATION OF NEW BUSINESS TRENDS AND PRACTICES IN THE CURRICULA, AND THE INTELLECTUAL LEVEL OF CLASSMATES' CONTRIBUTIONS IN COURSE DISCUSSIONS

1. University of California, Los Angeles
2. Harvard University
3. Georgia Institute of Technology
4. Stanford University
5. University of Florida
6. New York University
7. University of California, Davis
8. University of Virginia
9. Dartmouth College
10. The Ohio State University

BEST PROFESSORS

BASED ON THE PROFESSORS INTERESTING AND PROFESSORS ACCESSIBLE RATINGS (SEE PAGE 9 FOR EXPLANATION)

1. Indiana University-Bloomington
2. Vanderbilt University
3. University of Virginia
4. University of North Carolina at Chapel Hill
5. College of William and Mary
6. University of Notre Dame
7. Emory University
8. Brigham Young University
9. Washington University in St. Louis
10. Duke University

MOST COMPETITIVE STUDENTS

BASED ON STUDENT ASSESSMENT OF HOW COMPETITIVE CLASSMATES ARE, HOW HEAVY THE WORKLOAD IS, AND THE PERCEIVED ACADEMIC PRESSURE

1. Acton School of Business
2. IMD(International Institute for Management Development)
3. Southern Methodist University
4. Rice University
5. University of Virginia
6. Rollins College
7. Pepperdine University
8. Texas Christian University (TCU)
9. Howard University
10. University of Florida

MOST FAMILY FRIENDLY

BASED ON STUDENT ASSESSMENT OF: HOW HAPPY MARRIED STUDENTS ARE, HOW MANY STUDENTS HAVE CHILDREN, HOW HELPFUL THE BUSINESS SCHOOL IS TO STUDENTS WITH CHILDREN, AND HOW MUCH THE SCHOOL DOES FOR THE SPOUSES OF STUDENTS

1. Brigham Young University
2. IMD(International Institute for Management Development)
3. Dartmouth College
4. Pittsburgh State University
5. Harvard University
6. University of North Carolina at Chapel Hill
7. Duke University
8. Indiana University-Bloomington
9. Rice University
10. University of Notre Dame

BEST CAMPUS ENVIRONMENT

BASED ON STUDENT ASSESSMENT OF THE SAFETY, ATTRACTIVENESS, AND LOCATION OF THE SCHOOL

1. University of California-Los Angeles
2. Dartmouth College
3. University of North Carolina at Chapel Hill
4. University of Virginia
5. Vanderbilt University
6. Emory University
7. Duke University
8. University of Texas at Austin
9. Stanford University
10. University of Michigan-Ann Arbor

BEST GREEN MBA

BASED ON STUDENTS' ASSESSMENTS OF HOW WELL THEIR SCHOOL IS PREPARING THEM IN ENVIRONMENTAL/SUSTAINABILITY AND SOCIAL RESPONSIBILITY ISSUES, AND FOR A CAREER IN A GREEN JOB MARKET

1. University of Oregon
2. University of Vermont
3. Yale University
4. University of Denver
5. University of North Carolina at Chapel Hill
6. University of San Diego
7. University of Michigan-Ann Arbor
8. San Francisco State University
9. Portland State University
10. Stanford University

BEST ADMINISTERED

BASED ON STUDENT ASSESSMENT OF HOW SMOOTHLY THE SCHOOL IS RUN, AND THE EASE WITH WHICH STUDENTS CAN GET INTO REQUIRED AND POPULAR COURSES

1. Acton School of Business
2. University of Florida
3. University of Arkansas—Fayetteville
4. Elon University
5. Dartmouth College
6. Colorado State University
7. Georgia Institute of Technology
8. Texas Christian University (TCU)
9. University of Louisville
10. Rice University

GREATEST OPPORTUNITY FOR MINORITY STUDENTS

BASED ON THE PERCENT OF STUDENTS FROM MINORITIES, THE PERCENT OF FACULTY FROM MINORITIES, AND STUDENT ASSESSMENT OF RESOURCES FOR MINORITY STUDENTS, HOW SUPPORTIVE THE CULTURE IS OF MINORITY STUDENTS, AND WHETHER FELLOW STUDENTS ARE ETHNICALLY AND RACIALLY DIVERSE

1. Howard University
2. Texas Southern University
3. Florida International University
4. University of Massachusetts-Boston
5. Harvard University
6. University of North Carolina at Greensboro
7. Bowling Green State University
8. Drexel University
9. University of San Diego
10. University of North Carolina at Charlotte

GREATEST OPPORTUNITY FOR WOMEN

BASED ON THE PERCENT OF STUDENTS WHO ARE FEMALE, THE PERCENT OF FACULTY WHO ARE FEMALE, AND STUDENT ASSESSMENT OF: RESOURCES FOR FEMALE STUDENTS, HOW SUPPORTIVE THE CULTURE IS OF FEMALE STUDENTS, WHETHER THE BUSINESS SCHOOL OFFERS COURSEWORK FOR WOMEN ENTREPRENEURS, AND WHETHER CASE STUDY MATERIALS FOR CLASSES PROPORTIONATELY REFLECT WOMEN IN BUSINESS

1. Simmons College School of Management
2. University of San Diego
3. Harvard University
4. Tulane University
5. University of Virginia
6. Columbia University
7. Stanford University
8. Babson College
9. American University
10. University of Washington

PART III-A
BUSINESS SCHOOL
DESCRIPTIVE PROFILES

ACTON SCHOOL OF BUSINESS
THE ACTON MBA IN ENTREPRENEURSHIP

Academics

Acton School of Business's unique MBA is like "boot camp" for entrepreneurs. This "challenging yet rewarding" program covers every aspect, practical and personal, of launching a successful venture. Through the school's unique curriculum, students "learn how to learn, learn how to make money, and learn how to live a life of meaning." In meeting this mission, Acton employs "some of the best entrepreneurs in the world"; the school's stellar professors are "leaders in the field of study, and experts at leading the classroom discussions." A current student gushes, "To say the professors here are 'world-class' would be an understatement. These are the best teachers an MBA student could ever encounter." Coursework is entirely case-based, and professors employ the Socratic method to encourage discussion and creative problem solving in the classroom. Students love the fact that "class time is 100 percent dedicated to real-life applicable situations. There is no wasted time on theory that we can't use." A current student adds, "After seeing 300 cases and having analyzed those from the entrepreneur point of view, you start seeing patterns."

The Acton MBA is an accelerated program, which packs two years of coursework into single fast-paced year. Every day is a marathon, with students meeting for break-of-dawn study groups before class kicks off at eight o'clock in the morning. With its emphasis on discussion, "class is incredibly intense; the professors are knowledgeable, and the students are incredibly well prepared." On that note, there are roughly ten cases assigned every week, so you can reasonably expect "ninety to a hundred hours of case prep per week." Fortunately, the rewards of the Acton MBA are well worth the effort. Despite the long hours, "discussions and material make the days go by so fast. It really is a lot of fun once you get past the tough schedule." Not to mention, the rigor itself is a great teacher; here, the curriculum is "so difficult and time-consuming that you are a different person after you finish."

"Acton is run like a well organized company," and overseen by a staff of three that is "very easy to work with and very efficient." The "school administration is very responsive to problems" when they arise, treating students like valued customers. A case in point, all Acton instructors are required to sign a contract agreeing to step down if students are dissatisfied with their course. Students also appreciate the accelerated structure, which limits their educational expenses to a single year. Sure, you may sweat through it, but "the amount of education packed into one year is better than any two or two-plus year program in the country."

Career and Placement

With its pointed focus on entrepreneurship, Acton's approach to career services is rather different than what you would find at most MBA programs. Acton students are rarely interested in working for a large bank or corporation, and the school encourages them to eschew a life of time cards and cubicles. Instead, successful graduates of the program go on to start their own ventures in a wide range of areas. As a result, you will not find career fairs and resume assistance at Acton School of Business. On the contrary, "recruiters are not allowed on campus," and, when students are matched with employers, it is done on a more individual level. Nonetheless, long-term career goals are essential to the Acton academic experience. Of particular note, all students take the contemplative Life of Meaning course, which challenges them to profoundly examine their long-term goals. A current student agrees, "The Life of Meaning course changed the way I thought about life, and changed my direction of life also."

ADMISSIONS CONTACT: SUSIE HALL, DIRECTOR OF OUTREACH AND ENROLLMENT
ADDRESS: 816 CONGRESS AVENUE, SUITE 1240, AUSTIN, TX 78701
PHONE: 512-703-1232 • FAX: 512-495-9480
E-MAIL: ADMISSIONS@ACTONMBA.ORG • WEBSITE: WWW.ACTONMBA.ORG

Student Life and Environment

MBA candidates say you must be prepared to "dedicate your life to the program" at Acton. Keeping up with the rigorous MBA coursework requires every waking hour, from dawn to midnight. A current student details, "A typical day begins at 5:15 A.M. to make it to study group by 6:00. Class until 12:20 over the cases you prepared the day before. Go to lunch with classmates and then begin studying at 1:00. Go to bed at midnight and start again." While students spend a great deal of time with their classmates, "there is no time for clubs or activities" outside schoolwork. Even your personal life may end up on the back burner; for most students, "family time is limited to around 30 minutes per day." While no one questions the efficacy of the program, some say it would be nice if the school provided more "support for families, including spouse events."

The rigorous interaction naturally helps to create strong bonds between students. You will learn a lot from your peers at Acton, and not surprisingly, most students are "very motivated and extremely competitive." Fortunately, they are also described as "friendly, easy to talk to, eager to help one another, and family-oriented." Similarities end there, however. The school attracts a "diverse group of individuals with different backgrounds and political ideologies."

Admissions

Prospective students are encouraged to visit Acton and sit in on a class before applying to the program; students can request a class visit through the school's website. Most students enter the program with several years of professional experience under their belt; however, Acton accepts up to five exceptional students who apply to the program directly after college. Acton prefers students with GMAT scores of 600 and higher, though decisions are made based on a student's complete application. The average GMAT score for the fall of 2014 entering class was 630.

FINANCIAL FACTS

Annual tuition	$49,500
Fees	$0
Cost of books	$0
Room & board (on/off-campus)	$20,000
% of students receiving grants	0

ADMISSIONS

Admissions Selectivity Rating	77
Average GMAT	640
Accepts GRE scores	Yes
Average GPA	3.2
TOEFL required of international students	Yes
Minimum TOEFL (paper/web)	630/109
Application fee	$50
International application fee	$50
Application Deadline	
Round 1:	2/5
Round 2:	4/15
Round 3:	6/3
Deferment available	Yes
Maximum length of deferment	2 years.
Transfer students accepted	No
Non-fall admissions	Yes
Need-blind admissions	Yes

EMPLOYMENT PROFILE

Career Rating	86	Grads Employed by Function	% Avg. Salary
Percent employed at graduation	14	Marketing	(22%) $75,000
Percent employed 3 months after graduation	50	Operations	(22%) $102,000
Average base starting salary	$80,000	Consulting	(4%)
Primary Source of Full-time Job Acceptances		Finance	(4%) $85,000
Graduate-facilitated activities	9 (33%)		

ALFRED UNIVERSITY
SCHOOL OF BUSINESS

GENERAL INFORMATION
Type of school	Private
Affiliation	No Affiliation

SURVEY SAYS...
Good social scene, Cutting-edge classes
Solid preparation in:
Accounting

ACADEMICS
Academic Experience Rating	60*
Profs interesting rating	60*
Profs accessible rating	62
Student/faculty ratio	5:1
% female faculty	38
% underrepresented minority faculty	38
% part-time faculty	33

Academics

If you're looking for an "intimate environment" for your MBA experience, Alfred University is well worth a look. This program serves a population of just a few dozen graduate students. The result is a "solid business school that's convenient," where "students are not just another number." As one student told us, "The greatest strength of Alfred University is its size." The classes are around thirty people, and "the interaction is incredible." The school recently added an MBA accounting program that qualifies accounting students to be able to obtain their CPA license (the teachers "are some of the strongest teachers in the business school"), and there are also graduate assistantships available to any full-time MBA students who are willing to assist graduate faculty members in their area of interest in exchange for a portion of their tuition. The school is especially strong in entrepreneurial studies.

Professors at Alfred have the time to go the extra mile for students, and they "work hard to make sure you understand what they are teaching, but they also expect you to do your share of the work." Students also appreciate that "professors here are very diverse" and "have a lot of experience in the business world." With no crowd to fight, Alfred students have a better chance to shine. Although, keep in mind, this also means there's no anonymity. "Professors know everyone in the program well." Another student writes, "One professor liked a paper I wrote for his class. He offered to co-author another paper with me and pursue getting it published. These opportunities are so valuable to me and something I would never have expected." This sense of support and enterprise doesn't end in the classroom. As one student explains, "One-on-ones outside of the classroom are extremely helpful, and I'm able to gain additional insight on my career path."

Of course, a small school can only offer students so much. Some students find that there are "few academic options within the program" and "concepts and theories are left at the basics," but "the new acting dean is also looking to change things around and improve elective options." Regardless, students appreciate that "most MBA classes are scheduled in the late afternoon and early evening, which is convenient for people who work." Students approve of the school's active learning strategies, which emphasize teamwork, case studies, simulations, and field experience (usually gained through an internship).

Career and Placement

All Alfred students receive career services through the Robert R. McComsey Career Development Center. The office provides one-on-one counseling sessions; workshops in interviewing, resume writing, and networking; a career library with online and conventional print resources; and annual job fairs. The school also boasts a 100-percent placement rate for its MBAs. Students point out, however, that Alfred's remote location complicates their search for jobs and internships. Many agree that "Alfred is a small community" and that "outside internships and projects are more difficult to obtain due to the University's rural location." However, over the past few years the administration has worked "to expand local and international opportunities with a particular focus on MBA students," and there is "the clear sense that the school, administrators and professors want you to succeed."

Prominent employers of Alfred MBAs include Alstom, AOL Communications, Avantt Consulting, Met Life/New England Financial, General Electric Company, Eli Lilly and Company, Citynet, Corning, Dresser Rand, Nestlé, NYSEG, Toro Energy, and Wal-Mart.

ADMISSIONS CONTACT: SARA LOVE, GRADUATE ADMISSIONS
ADDRESS: OFFICE OF GRADUATE ADMISSIONS, ALUMNI HALL, SAXON DRIVE, ALFRED, NY 14802
PHONE: 800-541-9229 • FAX: 607-871-2198
E-MAIL: GRADINQUIRY@ALFRED.EDU • WEBSITE: BUSINESS.ALFRED.EDU/MBA.HTML

Student Life and Environment

Alfred, New York, is a normal small town "with only the essentials in the village"; however, the campus provides plenty of entertainment, resources, and opportunities to keep students "engaged and happy." The University is "a fun-loving community" of about 2,000 students, including 210 business undergrads and a few dozen "competitive, ambitious, friendly, [and] hard working" MBAs, who comprise a "mix of recent grads and experienced professionals." The "wide variety of clubs and organizations offer great opportunity for individual growth," and if you want a club "all you have to do is ask." One student explains, "Alfred's clubs and activities are astounding. Diverse clubs and organizations regularly attend student senate to discuss concerns that are circulating the student population."

Alfred's sixteen Division-III intercollegiate teams provide entertainment, as does the popular intramural sports program. The school's divisions of music, theater, and dance frequently hold performances. Alfred also has an active visual-arts community; it houses one of the best ceramic arts programs in the country. The "peaceful and safe" village of Alfred has a year-round population of 1,000 and surrounding towns are not much larger. These "secluded" surroundings lessen "the chances of distractions from studies," though when students need a break from the books, Rochester is only eighty miles away, and Buffalo is only a little farther down the road—provided you have four-wheel drive in the winter.

Admissions

Applicants must provide the school with official copies of undergraduate transcripts, TOEFL scores (for international students whose first language is not English), a statement of intent, professional resume, and two letters of recommendation (preferably from former employers or professors). Previous work experience is not required, and an interview, while always recommended, is optional.

FINANCIAL FACTS

Annual tuition (in-state/ out-of-state)	$38,020/$38,020
Fees	$970
Cost of books	$1,250
Room & board	$11,618
% of students receiving aid	100
% of first-year students receiving aid	100
% of students receiving grants	100
Average award package	$19,010
Average grant	$19,010

ADMISSIONS

Admissions Selectivity Rating **60***

EMPLOYMENT PROFILE

Career Rating	75	Grads Employed by Function	% Avg. Salary
Average base starting salary	$43,482	Marketing	(21%)
Primary Source of Full-time Job Acceptances		Operations	(5%)
School-facilitated activities	3 (16%)	Consulting	(5%)
Graduate-facilitated activities	4 (21%)	Management	(11%)
Unknown	12 (63%)	Finance	(32%)
		MIS	(5%)
		Other	(21%)

Top 5 Employers Hiring Grads
Alstom Power (1), Dresser-Rand (1), Excellus Blue Cross Blue Shield (1), Gunlocke Company (1), Buffamante Whipple & Buttafaro P.C. (1)

AMERICAN UNIVERSITY
KOGOD SCHOOL OF BUSINESS

GENERAL INFORMATION

Type of school	Private
Affiliation	Methodist
Academic calendar	Semester

SURVEY SAYS...

Classmates have diverse work experience, Friendly students, Liberal students, Happy students, Students love Washington, DC
Solid preparation in:
Teamwork, Communication/interpersonal skills, Presentation skills, Quantitative skills

STUDENTS

Enrollment of MBA Program	182
% male/female	54/46
% part-time	52
Average age at entry	27
Average years work experience at entry	4

ACADEMICS

Academic Experience Rating	**86**
Profs interesting rating	90
Profs accessible rating	96
% female faculty	32
% part-time faculty	46

Joint Degrees
MBA/JD LLM/MBA MBA/MA

Prominent Alumni
David Wajsgras, President of Intelligence, Information and Services, Raytheon; Victoria Harker, CFO, Gannett; Richard Clark, former chairman & CEO, Merck; Mark Murphy, CEO and President of the Green Bay Packers; Richard Hocker, founder, chief investment officer & CEO, Penn Capital Management

Academics

With an "emphasis on global learning" and fulfilling academics enriched by guest speakers from different industries, the Kogod School of Business at American University lets students enroll in an international program. Each of the first two semesters of the full-time program kicks off with a two-week intensive Signature Course that "prepares [students] for working in the global economy," and Full-Time, Professional, and Online MBA options ensure that any qualified and willing student can make a Kogod program work for their schedule; the professional program even benefits from the school providing concierge style service to its members, which includes dinner before class.

"A very organized, easy-to-interpret class framework" sets the tone for these seamless programs, where a focus on presentation skills and case analysis runs throughout. Full-time students can apply their knowledge to real-world client projects, choosing between a consulting focus, an elective schedule forged from Kogod's variety of offerings, or a managerial emphasis. All full-time students must also complete a global consulting project with an international client in their second year (professional students do a study abroad trip).

Professors at Kogod are "genuinely interested in seeing us succeed and extend themselves as much as possible." Their "willingness to help you with anything, whether its academics, external projects, or career advice" is a notable benefit of the small class sizes, and it means that "each student can ensure that they can get attention on a particular topic that they may be struggling with." "I have had some great professors who have taken out the time to really go deep into the material being taught to make sure that the class is understanding and grasping the subject," says a student. The administration is similarly "mindful of needs of working professional students and move quickly to increase the ease of our user experience" and is "active in addressing issues that we bring to them to ensure that we are getting the best possible education."

Career and Placement

All employment services are done through the Kogod Center for Career Development, which sets up site visits with employers and interested students, provides one-on-one counseling on résumés and job searches, and sponsors numerous industry-specific career fairs throughout the year. Students appreciate the "individual attention for career help and public speaking assistance" they receive through the KCCD, including the always popular Business Leadership in D.C. Luncheon Series that brings together top executives and students in an intimate, relaxed atmosphere. The "central location to large business centers" and "connection to politics and international affairs are a major plus" in terms of networking; graduates end up in a number of industries, with around a third going into consulting.

Recent employers of Kogod grads include CSC, Deloitte Consulting, LLP, TaylorMade Experience, PricewaterHouse Coopers, Capgemini, World Bank, and Raytheon, with an average starting salary of $74,183.

Student Life and Environment

There is a distinct "emphasis on cooperation rather than competition" across all three programs, and "even though we all want to do our best, we do not tear each other down to do so." There are "lots of good clubs" on this "very active" campus that is "small and easy to get around," and students form study groups to help each other understand the information being taught and meet regularly. The small cohorts of the professional program tend to grow especially close: "After every exam, almost the entire class meets up at a local watering hole afterwards to talk about our personal lives, not the test we just took," says one student. "It takes a certain type of character to work full-time and go to school, but these people do it flawlessly."

Admissions

The Kogod Admissions Office requires the following from all applicants: a completed online application form; a personal statement of purpose in pursuing the MBA; a current résumé; two letters of recommendation; an official transcript from all attended undergraduate and graduate institutions; and an official GMAT or GRE score report. International applicants whose first language is not English must also submit an official score report for other the TOEFL or the IELTS. An interview is required of all applicants.

FINANCIAL FACTS

Room & board	
(on/off-campus)	$20,000
% of students receiving grants	56
Average grant	$12,312

ADMISSIONS

Admissions Selectivity Rating	82
# of applications received	96
% applicants accepted	70
% acceptees attending	48
Average GMAT	580
Accepts GRE scores	Yes
Average Verbal GRE	154
Average Quantitative GRE	152
Average GPA	3.0
TOEFL required of international students	Yes
Minimum TOEFL (paper/web)	600/100
Application fee	$100
International application fee	$100
Application Deadline/Notification	
Round 1:	11/15 / 1/15
Round 2:	2/1 / 4/1
Round 3:	5/1 / 6/15
Deferment available	Yes
Maximum length of deferment	1 year
Transfer students accepted	Yes
Non-fall admissions	No
Need-blind admissions	Yes

EMPLOYMENT PROFILE

		Grads Employed by Function% Avg. Salary	
Career Rating	82		
Percent employed at graduation	46	Marketing	(11%)
Percent employed 3 months		Consulting	(32%) $83,167
after graduation	21	Management	(11%)
Average base starting salary	$74,183	Finance	(37%) $78,358
Primary Source of Full-time Job Acceptances		Other	(11%)
School-facilitated activities	8 (42%)	**Top 5 Employers Hiring Grads**	
Graduate-facilitated activities	11 (58%)	CSC, PwC, Raytheon	

APPALACHIAN STATE UNIVERSITY
WALKER COLLEGE OF BUSINESS

GENERAL INFORMATION
Type of school   Public
Affiliation   No Affiliation
Academic calendar   Semester

SURVEY SAYS...
Good social scene, Happy students
Solid preparation in:
Accounting, Presentation skills,
Doing business in a global economy

STUDENTS
Enrollment of parent
  institution   18,000
Enrollment of MBA Program   100
% male/female   65/35
% out-of-state   6
% part-time   32
% underrepresented minority   6
% international   6
Average age at entry   27
Average years work
  experience at entry   8

ACADEMICS
Academic Experience Rating   66
Profs interesting rating   69
Profs accessible rating   65
Student/faculty ratio   3:1

Academics

Nested in the Blue Ridge Mountains of North Carolina, the Walker College of Business at Appalachian State University offers an affordable MBA program. The Walker College of Business provides three options for students interested in pursuing the MBA—an accelerated one-year full-time program, a part-time night program on its main campus in Boone, and a part-time program at the university's satellite campus in Hickory, North Carolina. In the accelerated MBA, the entire degree, including a business practicuum, can be completed in only one year. Despite its speedy schedule, the MBA covers all functional areas of business, including accounting, economics, finance, management, marketing, supply chain management, business analytics, and statistics. In addition to the core curriculum, students have the option of tailoring their education through a concentration in one of seven fields: business analytics, economics, interdisciplinary business, international business, leading and managing human resources, supply chain management, or sustainable business. There is also a focus on international exposure throughout the curriculum, which helps students "gain the knowledge [they] will need to compete in today's global economy." Of particular note, all students are required to participate in an International Experience, which generally includes a trip overseas. Recent international experiences include China, Cuba, France, Costa Rica, Japan, and Poland. While the program is scarcely large enough to support more variety, students feel, "the MBA program needs to add a computer information systems option" to the current offerings.

For full-time students, the schedule is rigorous and "the days are pretty packed." Throughout the program, "students spend about two hours in class each day, Monday through Thursday," while their afternoons are "spent working on group projects, homework, and/or actually working at a job." Fortunately, classes in the full-time MBA program are small, with around twenty-four students per class. The result is a caring, student-oriented atmosphere, and plenty of personal attention. Offering guidance and support, "the school has a great administration that is willing to work with the students in order to help the students achieve their goals." In addition, "the professors, on the whole, are easy to get along with and are always willing to help the students." Academically, the program is strong, but the teachers can be hit or miss. A student admits, "There have been some professors who have challenged me and were at the caliber that I expected, but there were also some who I felt were inadequate to be teaching graduate-level classes." Overall, Walker "teachers are knowledgeable and excited for students to learn."

In addition to the campus-based MBA program, ASU offers a part-time off-site MBA at a satellite facility in Hickory, North Carolina. In content, this program is similar to the Boone MBA, yet students learn through various delivery formats, including interactive audio-video sessions and web-based instruction, as well as in-person lectures from ASU faculty. No matter where you choose to study, the icing on the cake is the program's "low cost." This public school maintains a "very reasonable" tuition price, while also offering "scholarship and assistantship" programs, which can lower the price tag even further.

Career and Placement

While the MBA program does not have its own career office, it does have a dedicated Career Services and Executive Coach. Each student receives individualized advising. Along with individual coaching, the MBA program offers a three-course Executive Skills program designed to build leadership skills, business acumen, and communication skills. The Career Development Center on the Appalachian State University campus serves the entire undergraduate and graduate student body, as well as ASU alumni. In addition, the Career Development Center organizes networking events and "career fairs

ADMISSIONS CONTACT: ANNA BASNIGHT
ADDRESS: ASU BOX 32068, BOONE, NC 28608-2068
PHONE: 828-262-2130 • FAX: 828-262-2709
E-MAIL: BASNIGHTAL@APPSTATE.EDU • WEBSITE: WWW.MBA.APPSTATE.EDU

that bring in companies that have positions all over the U.S. and around the world." With a strong local reputation, ASU "does well with helping the students find a job," but nothing's perfect and "there are still improvements that can be made."

Student Life and Environment

Located on a "beautiful campus" in Boone, North Carolina, "life is fabulous" at ASU. On this pleasant, hilltop campus, "students hang out as a collective most times and crime rates are relatively low." Not to mention, this Southern city boasts "terrific weather" and great outdoor activities, including hiking and fishing. MBA classes take place in Peacock Hall, which boasts wireless Internet, computer labs, and student lounges. On the Boone campus, students have access to study labs and a large library system. Students also have the opportunity to join the Executive Impact MBA Club, which provides studetns with networking and professional growth opportunities.

Bringing a positive attitude to the classroom, ASU students "are willing to learn, as well as willing to begin friendships that have lasted the length of the program." While the accelerated schedule keeps them busy, "students find time to attend sporting events, concerts, and many other extra curricular activities. All of the students also find time to hang out with one another and with their friends." While there are some local student hangouts, students say "nightlife could be a little better," in Boone. Most students, however, feel that "being in a small town has been wonderful for my school experience." A current student writes, "In general, I wouldn't have chosen anywhere else to go."

Admissions

Appalachian State University's small MBA program enrolls about sixty students each year. Prospective students are evaluated based on their GMAT score, three letters of recommendation, undergraduate academic performance, interview, and current resume. To be eligible for the program, students must have completed a series of prerequisite courses in accounting, finance, economics, management, marketing, and statistics, with a grade point average of B– or better. Professional work experience is not required.

FINANCIAL FACTS

Annual tuition (in-state/ out-of-state)	$12,177/$30,990
Fees	$4,338
Cost of books	$1,200
Average grant	$1,000
Average loan	$5,000

ADMISSIONS

Admissions Selectivity Rating	68
# of applications received	43
% applicants accepted	93
% acceptees attending	90
Accepts GRE scores	Yes
Average GPA	3.5
TOEFL required of international students	Yes
Application fee	$55
International application fee	$55
Regular application deadline	7/1
Application Deadline	
Round 1:	4/1
Round 2:	7/1
Round 3:	11/1
Deferment available	Yes
Maximum length of deferment	one year
Transfer students accepted	Yes
Transfer application policy	
Up to nine hours of graduate credit may be transferred for equivalent courses completed with at least grade of B.	
Non-fall admissions	Yes
Need-blind admissions	Yes

EMPLOYMENT PROFILE

Career Rating	86	Grads Employed by Function	% Avg. Salary
Percent employed at graduation	59	Marketing	(23%) $53,250
Percent employed 3 months after graduation	72	Operations	(13%) $49,100
		Consulting	(5%) $50,000
Average base starting salary	$53,200	Management	(10%) $45,000
Primary Source of Full-time Job Acceptances		Finance	(28%) $54,636
School-facilitated activities	0 (0%)	HR	(5%) $46,000
Graduate-facilitated activities	37 (95%)	MIS	(10%) $60,750
Unknown	2 (5%)	Other	(5%) $43,500

Top 5 Employers Hiring Grads
Wells Fargo (3), Lowe's Home Improvement (2), Grant Thornton (2), Georgia Pacific (1), MetLife (1)

ARIZONA STATE UNIVERSITY
W.P. CAREY SCHOOL OF BUSINESS

GENERAL INFORMATION
Type of school   Public
Affiliation   No Affiliation
Academic calendar   Quarter

SURVEY SAYS...
Classmates have diverse work experience, Friendly students, Happy students, Students love Tempe, AZ
Solid preparation in:
General management, Operations, Teamwork, Communication/interpersonal skills, Quantitative skills

STUDENTS
Enrollment of parent
  institution   51,984
Enrollment of MBA Program   150
% male/female   71/29
% out-of-state   47
% part-time   1
% underrepresented minority   17
% international   28
Average age at entry   28
Average years work
  experience at entry   5

ACADEMICS
Academic Experience Rating   **96**
Profs interesting rating   96
Profs accessible rating   TK
Student/faculty ratio   3:1
% female faculty   25
% underrepresented
  minority faculty   34
% part-time faculty   15

Joint Degrees
MBA/Master of Science in Information Management; MBA/ Master of Accountancy; MBA/ Master of Legal Studies; MBA/ Master of Taxation; MBA/MD with Mayo Medical School MBA/ Juris Doctorate; MBA/Master of Architecture

Academics

With the full weight of Arizona State University behind it, the W.P. Carey School of Business provides its students with small classes, a top name degree, and a "wealth of information and resources." Even with its stellar reputation, "professors and admin are hungry to improve" and the school "constantly evaluates the MBA programs to optimize/improve according to feedback, needs of the business community, and trends in business teaching." Academics are "demanding but rewarding, and extremely thorough," with multiple concentrations available for students to customize their education in areas such as Healthcare Management, International Business, and the lauded Supply Chain Management program. Students can expect "group projects galore" with the first year bringing "an enormous amount of information" and very little time to do much else; by the second year, "the coursework has decreased significantly."

The "outstanding" professors are "brilliant technically and readily make themselves available outside of class" and are always encouraging the students to attend office hours if the students feel if they are falling behind. "Our professors have held us to the highest level of professionalism and demand," says a student. The administration is similarly accessible, and "regularly hold town hall meetings to get a feel of the vibe of the student body and get feedback." "It has been a pleasure to work with school administration and faculty on adjusting class setups and extracurricular activities. They only want what the students want and proactively try to accommodate for those preferences," says a student.

Career and Placement

The career placement center has "a variety of effective resources" and plenty of job-finding events such as case competitions, business competitions, networking events, and corporate connections. There is a real focus on leadership at Arizona State, and students are directed towards career leadership courses from the start. Full-time MBAs must complete a required summer internship, and "outreach trips and case competitions are coordinated with various companies in different industries." The executive coaching program is a great way "to network with leadership within the local community and how they are able to operate in the real world." The Supply Chain Management concentration is definitely the crown jewel of the W. P. Carey crown and receives attention as such as far as resources go, and say that there are "[fewer] employers in non-SCM related fields" and wish the spectrum of recruiters could be broadened. Employers who frequently hire Arizona State MBAs include Amazon, Intel, CVS, Applied Materials, and Dell.

Student Life and Environment

The student body itself is composed of "interesting folks from around the country accompanied by a strong international component." Cohorts tend to be knit tightly, and the overall sense among the student body is "competitive but not cutthroat, [and] very collaborative," with diverse industry backgrounds encouraging new ideas and ways of approaching problems. Arizona State does an excellent job of providing social structure to what can feel like hectic times; regular happy hours are held for students every Thursday, and "there are many intramural teams that we are encouraged to participate in to get our mind off school for a couple hours out of the week." Every Monday, faculty will set up coffee and snacks before class starts and have everyone in the lobby congregate to socialize, and after class brings student-run club meetings for which the school provides lunch. The business school also has "a dedicated graduate-students only floor with team rooms, technology assistance, and food and beverages on elective days and Saturdays."

Admissions

When it comes to assessing applicants, the admissions committee at Arizona State takes a holistic approach. All application facets, from undergraduate GPA and GMAT score to résumé, work experience, letters of recommendations, essays and interviews are given thoughtful consideration. Fortunately, a bachelor's degree in business (or related discipline) is not required. Neither is previous coursework in math or statistics. Finally, applications to Arizona State are typically reviewed within two weeks of completion, interview or notification date (whichever is later).

Prominent Alumni

Robert Zollars, Executive Chairman/Mobile Technology; Charles Robel, Chairman/Software; Eddie LeVian, CEO/Jewelry; William Keitel, Former CFO/Communications Technologies; Craig Weatherup, Former CEO/Food and Beverage

FINANCIAL FACTS

Annual tuition (in-state/out-of-state)	$25,610/$42,086
Fees	$1,014
Cost of books	$1,054
Room & board (on/off-campus)	$11,080/$11,080
% of students receiving aid	99
% of first-year students receiving aid	100
% of students receiving grants	98
Average award package	$40,001
Average grant	$30,916
Average loan	$24,835
Average student loan debt	$45,662

ADMISSIONS

Admissions Selectivity Rating	94
# of applications received	443
% applicants accepted	31
% acceptees attending	62
Average GMAT	672
Range of GMAT	640–710
Accepts GRE scores	Yes
Average Verbal GRE	153
Range of Verbal GRE scores	147–157
Average Quantitative GRE	153
Range of Quantitative GRE scores	150–156
Average Writing GRE	3.9
Range of Writing GRE scores	3.5–4.0
Average GPA	3.4
TOEFL required of international students	Yes
Minimum TOEFL (paper/web)	550/80
Application fee	$70
International application fee	$90
Early application deadline	10/1
Early notification date	12/11
Regular application deadline	11/30
Regular application notification	2/5
Deferment available	No
Transfer students accepted	No
Non-fall admissions	No
Need-blind admissions	Yes

EMPLOYMENT PROFILE

Career Rating	95	Grads Employed by Function% Avg. Salary	
Percent employed at graduation	71	Marketing	(7%)
Percent employed 3 months after graduation	91	Operations	(57%) $100,220
Average base starting salary	$98,945	Consulting	(10%) $100,000
Primary Source of Full-time Job Acceptances		Management	(5%)
School-facilitated activities	45 (75%)	Finance	(13%) $98,000
Graduate-facilitated activities	15 (25%)	HR	(3%)
Unknown	0 (0%)	MIS	(2%)
		Other	(3%)

Top 5 Employers Hiring Grads

Intel Corporation (7), Amazon.com (6), Apple (4), Deloitte (2), Mattel (2)

AUBURN UNIVERSITY
RAYMOND J. HARBERT COLLEGE OF BUSINESS

Academics

Auburn University offers one of the South's premiere business programs. Those interested in earning their MBA are often attracted to the school's great location and "reasonable price." Students at Auburn are quick to highlight the "small class [size] and student faculty ratio," which virtually guarantees "close relationships with professors." The curriculum allows students to master the fundamentals of business theory and focus on a particular area of interest, such as finance, supply chain management, management of information technology, or business analytics.

While opinions on professors do vary, by and large students are very happy with their teachers. The vast majority are "very helpful and resourceful" and extremely "knowledgeable." And one pleased student adds that professors are "always willing to help with your classes or even other ventures." Indeed they "care about students' progress in and outside of the classroom."

MBA students are thankful for the program's administrators, who are "a big help to students." Time and again the "staff members [show that they] care about the students and handle their problems on a timely basis."

The MBA candidates at Auburn really believe that the University offers "great and numerous opportunities for students to get involved and to find jobs. There are so many tools available to them to achieve success." As one content student sums up, "Overall, I think [Auburn] is a hidden gem in terms of an MBA program in Alabama."

Career and Placement

The Office of Professional and Career Development serves the Business school's entire undergraduate and graduate student population and has a dedicated MBA career adviser. The career specialists understand that job hunting is an in-depth process and provide the tools and techniques for success. They help students develop and implement an effective job search strategy, showing them how to create a marketing plan and craft a target list of potential companies. Additionally, they host numerous seminars and events, offering students everything from resume writing workshops to mock interviews. The office also hosts several career fairs each academic year and city trips to visit corporations. The college attracts companies hiring students into consulting roles such as CapGemini, Deloitte, Ernst & Young, KPMG, and Quorum Business Solutions, as well as major companies focusing on supply chain management, including Delta, Exel Logistics, Home Depot, Lexmark, Target and Walmart. Financial services organizations including AFLAC, BB&T, BBVA, Regions Financial, and SunTrust, as well as the FDIC, Federal Reserve, OCC, the Alabama Securities Commission, and the Georgia Department of Banking and Finance also recruit Auburn's MBA students.

Student Life and Environment

MBA candidates at Auburn speak very highly of their peers. They are "very friendly" and are always "helpful when doing projects together." Students are also quick to report that their classmates are "easy going" and "highly intelligent." For the most part, they all seem to make a concerted effort "to contribute their opinions and share in class." This appears to be greatly appreciated as they often "provide [great] insight" and "bring great examples of real-time issues." Another student attempts to illuminate life at Auburn by stating, "There seem to be distinct groups: younger students, who participate in activities and clubs and hang out on campus vs. those like me, who come to school [just] for class."

Athletics play an important role in the social life on campus, particularly in the fall,

ADMISSIONS CONTACT: JULIE VAUGHT, MBA ADMISSIONS ADVISOR
ADDRESS: 415 W. MAGNOLIA AVENUE, SUITE 503 LOWDER BUSINESS BUILDING
AUBURN UNIVERSITY, AL 36849 • PHONE: 334-844-4060 • FAX: 334-844-2964
E-MAIL: MBADMIS@AUBURN.EDU • WEBSITE: WWW.MBA.AUBURN.EDU

where SEC football reigns supreme. Auburn's football team won the BCS National Championship in January 2011, and tailgating activities before each game provide an opportunity to network with alumni, prospective employers, and other students. Intramural sports are popular; outstanding golf courses are nearby, and the beaches of the Gulf of Mexico are three hours away by car. Since 2008, a ten-day International study trip has been built into the cost of the program; each spring groups of students and faculty travel worldwide to learn about doing business in various countries. Previous student groups have gone to Argentina, Brazil, China, France, Germany, Italy, South Africa, and other countries. Students say that this trip is a highlight of their Auburn experience.

Atlanta is a two-hour drive from Auburn, and provides a popular big-city weekend road trip destination, as well as permanent employment location for many students after graduation. Nearby Columbus, Georgia and Montgomery, Alabama, also offer plenty of entertainment options and distraction from schoolwork. Columbus is also the home of Fort Benning, one of the Army's largest bases.

Admissions

Full-time MBA students interested in attending Auburn University's Harbert College of Business should submit their application materials by a priority admission date of February 1 prior to the start of the fall semester they wish to enter. Each applicant's undergraduate transcripts, GMAT or GRE scores, letters of recommendation, essays, and resume are closely examined. Admissions officers note that GMAT or GRE scores must be from within the last five years. After a review of academic records and standardized test scores, selected candidates will be interviewed.

FINANCIAL FACTS

Annual tuition (in-state/ out-of-state)	$8,802/$26,406
Fees	$5,216
Cost of books	$1,200
Room & board (on/off-campus)	$12,178/$12,178
% of students receiving aid	97
% of first-year students receiving aid	98
% of students receiving grants	93
Average award package	$23,252
Average grant	$18,336
Average loan	$18,585

ADMISSIONS

Admissions Selectivity Rating	88
# of applications received	101
% applicants accepted	47
% acceptees attending	85
Average GMAT	578
Range of GMAT	528–623
Accepts GRE scores	Yes
Average Verbal GRE	156
Range of Verbal GRE scores	153–158
Average Quantitative GRE	154
Range of Quantitative GRE scores	150–160
Average Writing GRE	4.0
Range of Writing GRE scores	4.0–4.0
Average GPA	3.3
TOEFL required of international students	Yes
Minimum TOEFL (paper/web)	550/79
Application fee	$60
International application fee	$70
Regular application deadline	2/1
Deferment available	Yes
Maximum length of deferment	1 year
Transfer students accepted	Yes
Transfer application policy	AACSB schools only. Case-by-case basis and accepted in lieu of elective courses only. Limit of 12 credit hours.
Non-fall admissions	No
Need-blind admissions	Yes

EMPLOYMENT PROFILE

Career Rating	82	**Grads Employed by Function% Avg. Salary**	
Percent employed at graduation	32	Consulting	(67%) $58,667
Percent employed 3 months		Management	(11%) $40,000
after graduation	55	Finance	(11%) $40,000
Average base starting salary	$54,111	MIS	(11%) $55,000
Primary Source of Full-time Job Acceptances			
School-facilitated activities	7 (58%)		
Graduate-facilitated activities	3 (25%)		
Unknown	2 (17%)		

AUBURN UNIVERSITY—MONTGOMERY

SCHOOL OF BUSINESS

GENERAL INFORMATION

Type of school	Public
Affiliation	No Affiliation
Academic calendar	Rolling enrollment

SURVEY SAYS...

Friendly students, Happy students
Solid preparation in:
Marketing, Accounting, General management, Teamwork, Presentation skills, Quantitative skills

STUDENTS

Enrollment of parent institution	4,919
Enrollment of MBA Program	80
% male/female	59/41
% out-of-state	2
% part-time	30
% underrepresented minority	7
% international	30
Average age at entry	31

ACADEMICS

Academic Experience Rating	**85**
Profs interesting rating	91
Profs accessible rating	94
% female faculty	22
% underrepresented minority faculty	9
% part-time faculty	26

Academics

The AACSB-accredited MBA program at Auburn University Montgomery is "a great place to get your MBA at night," according to the program's locally-based student body. Students here also appreciate the "affordable" tuition as well as the school's "reputation for academic excellence" and "instructors who bring real-life business experiences to the classroom" and "have connections in the business world." The program is designed for part-time students; in fact, any student wishing to exceed a course load of nine hours per semester must first receive approval from the dean of the School of Business.

The MBA program at AUM is divided into three parts. The first is called the Basic Program, consisting of eleven half-term courses covering business concepts typically taught at the undergraduate level (accounting, management, marketing, business law, microeconomics, macroeconomics, operations management, statistics, MIS, and finance). Students who can demonstrate sufficient background in these areas may petition to be exempted from some or all of these requirements. The second part of the program is the Business Core, a seven-course set of classes covering such integrative concepts as managerial applications of accounting information and synergistic organizational strategy (the latter is a capstone course), as well as such essential functions as marketing, data analysis, and managing personnel. The program concludes with either three or four electives, depending on whether the student chooses a General MBA or a specialization. Specializations are offered in accounting, contract management, economics, finance, global business management, information systems, management of information technology, management, and marketing. Students earning a GPA below 3.25 must pass comprehensive exams at the end of the program in order to graduate. The program must be finished within five years of starting.

AUM MBAs brag that "professors are extremely knowledgeable, helpful, and outstanding in their areas," and that they also "understand that most of the evening students are fully employed and try to incorporate their day-to-day activities" into the curriculum. Most here "would like to see the use of more technology in the classroom" and complain that the school needs "all classrooms to be enabled with things like wireless internet access." Classrooms could also be improved by making them "resemble the real world, i.e. u-shaped seating"; at the very least, the school "needs to upgrade classroom furniture to make it feel less like a high school/junior high," students tell us.

Career and Placement

The Career Development Center (CDC) at AUM serves all university students and alumni. The office maintains a library of career-related material, including documents tracking salary and hiring trends around the region, state, country, and world. Career counseling services are available, as are job fairs, and seminars and workshops in interviewing, job hunting, and resume and cover letter writing. The office arranges internships and recruiting events for qualifying MBA students.

ADMISSIONS CONTACT: SHARON JONES, ADMISSION SPECIALIST
ADDRESS: P. O. BOX 244023, MONTGOMERY, AL 36124-4023
PHONE: 334-244-3623 • FAX: 334-244-3927
E-MAIL: VJONES1@AUM.EDU • WEBSITE: WWW.AUM.EDU

Student Life and Environment

AUM MBAs are "mostly working students between their mid-twenties and mid-thirties in age, with some being older." Most "work full time and go to school at night" and, despite their busy schedules, find a way to remain "extremely focused on their class work and understanding of the material" while also being "extremely helpful, kind, open for conversation, and willing to do whatever it takes to see that everyone in class is successful." They "don't seem to have any specific clubs or organizations available to them, especially in the evening hours," but most agree that their extracurricular schedule wouldn't allow them time to participate.

Montgomery is a midsize southern city well known for its integral part in the civil rights movement. The population of the city is about evenly split between whites and blacks, with small Hispanic, Native American, and Asian populations accounting for a small minority. The city is home to the Alabama Shakespeare Festival, a year-round enterprise that mounts a dozen or more productions and attracts over 300,000 visitors annually. Another major attraction is the minor-league baseball Montgomery Biscuits, the AA affiliate of the Tampa Bay Devil Rays. And no Montgomery summer is complete without Jubilee CityFest, a three-day outdoor festival that in recent years has attracted such headlining musical acts as Taylor Swift, Erykah Badu, the Goo Goo Dolls, Ludacris, and Vince Gill.

Admissions

Applicants to the AUM MBA program must submit official transcripts for all previous post-secondary academic work, official GMAT score reports, and a completed application form. The screening committee may request an interview, typically in the case of borderline candidates; otherwise, interviews are not required. International applicants must meet all of the above requirements and must also provide certified English translations of any academic transcripts in a foreign language and a course-by-course evaluation of undergraduate work "by a recognized, expert service in the field of foreign credential evaluations and international admissions." Applicants whose first language is not English must submit TOEFL scores. Candidates may be admitted conditionally pending completion of prerequisite undergraduate-level classes in business.

FINANCIAL FACTS

Fees	$817
Room & board (on/off-campus)	$4,320/
% of students receiving aid	51
% of first-year students receiving aid	53
% of students receiving grants	28
Average award package	$10,792
Average grant	$5,878
Average loan	$15,658

ADMISSIONS

Admissions Selectivity Rating	80
# of applications received	57
% applicants accepted	79
% acceptees attending	89
Average GMAT	467
Range of GMAT	420–520
Accepts GRE scores	No
Average GPA	3.1
TOEFL required of international students	Yes
Minimum TOEFL (paper/web)	500/
Application fee	$25
Deferment available	No
Transfer students accepted	No
Non-fall admissions	Yes
Need-blind admissions	Yes

EMPLOYMENT PROFILE

Career Rating	72	Top 5 Employers Hiring Grads
		Kelley Services, Connector Manufacturing Company, Arby's Restaurant Group, Fortis College, Coca Cola

AUGUSTA UNIVERSITY (FORMERLY GEORGIA REGENTS UNIVERSITY)
HULL COLLEGE OF BUSINESS

GENERAL INFORMATION

Type of school	public
Affiliation	No Affiliation
Academic calendar	Trimester

SURVEY SAYS...

Classmates have diverse work experience, Friendly students, Conservative students, Happy students
Solid preparation in:
Accounting, General management, Presentation skills, Quantitative skills

STUDENTS

Enrollment of parent	
Institution	8,333
Enrollment of MBA Program	79
% male/female	58/42
% out-of-state	19
% part-time	48
% underrepresented minority	34
% international	8
Average age at entry	31
Average years work	
experience at entry	8

ACADEMICS

Academic Experience Rating	85
Profs interesting rating	91
Profs accessible rating	95
Student/faculty ratio	25:1
% female faculty	17
% underrepresented	
minority faculty	25
% part-time faculty	17

Academics

Convenience and cost are the two main reasons students cite for choosing the MBA program at Augusta University (which formed in 2013 when Augusta State University merged with Georgia Health Sciences University). Many students here tell us that they attended the school as undergraduates and saw no reason to leave.

At Augusta's MBA program, "Personal attention and career development are a given. Students have to actively work at not being known by the administration and faculty of the business school." Service is key; despite its relatively small MBA enrollment, "[Augusta] has a dedicated educational professional to usher graduate students through the program." One student notes, "The school is the perfect size. It is small enough to allow for more personal relations between the student and the teacher but is big enough to enjoy all the aspects of attending a college." A "low teacher/student ratio" and "professors who are approachable and willing to help students" are among the other perks of attending. Augusta University works hard to accommodate its students' schedules by offering "almost every needed subject in the program" during the fall and spring semesters.

MBAs at Augusta must complete a fourteen-course sequence that includes two foundation courses, two electives and ten required courses in human resources management, marketing, finance, accounting, economics, operations management, leadership, management information systems, business analytics, and an integrating course in strategic management. Students tell us that the school has traditionally been recognized for strengths for economics, finance, and accounting, as well as in "certain quantitative-based courses like market research." In addition, Augusta has taken steps in order to better prepare the students for information-based knowledge. Those steps include "recently naming an information technology professor to chair the program."

Career and Placement

The Augusta University Career Center serves all undergraduates and graduate students at the university. Services are geared primarily toward undergraduates, in part because the school's graduate divisions are so small and in part because many graduate students—including many MBAs—attend while continuing in jobs they intend to keep post-graduation. The office sponsors an annual Career Fair and offers the standard battery of career services: job posting, counseling, mock interviews, on-campus recruiting, and more.

Student Life and Environment

Most Augusta University MBAs "work full-time during the day and attend classes at night," which means they have limited time to devote to extracurricular activities. Students tell us that "many professors acknowledge the average students' work/demand schedule and design their courses to allow students to catch up on the weekends." MBAs also appreciate how the small-school environment creates "the opportunity to get to know the students and faculty on a greater than superficial level," an opportunity students take advantage of by "congregating in a small centralized area of the building before classes." With so many chances to bond with peers and professors, it's no wonder students tell us that "the school feels like a family."

Full-time students—consisting primarily of international students and undergraduates proceeding directly from their BA program to the MBA—tell us that "there is an active campus life at [Augusta] even though few students actually live on campus. There are so many groups to be involved with and [there are] always activities going on. The school spirit at [Augusta] is so alive, and the students there really love their campus. Most of the MBA students are graduates of [Augusta University], so I believe they feel the same as well." Clubs "are very active on campus." Beta Gamma Sigma is one of the major ones for business students. MBAs tell us that the school has worked hard to beautify and improve this campus, which, they note, "was an arsenal during the Civil War. The school has done a great job of keeping that heritage intact" while simultaneously adding such assets as a "beautiful new student center" that "provides study areas, gym equipment, billiards, and a host of other activities for students that help to release school stress." Commuters warn that "parking is limited during morning hours, but afternoon and evening parking is very good."

The student body is "broadly diverse in age, occupation, race, and educational background, but [they are] uniformly goal oriented, serious, and competitive, [while also] capable or working in a team environment." Students seem to appreciate this diversity. One student says, "I have come in contact with people from many different cultures, and it gives me a different outlook on business." Even though there are "so many international students," most "seem to be regular people with careers who have felt a need to improve themselves."

Admissions

Applicants to the Hull College of Business MBA program must submit all of the following: official transcripts for all undergraduate and graduate work; an official score report for the GMAT (test score can be no more than five years old); an up-to-date resumé; three letters of recommendation; and a completed application form. In addition, international students whose first language is not English must submit an official score for the TOEFL and a financial responsibility statement. International transcripts must be submitted via Educational Credential Evaluators, Inc., Joseph Silney & Associates, Inc., or World Education Services, companies that match international course work to its American equivalent. The admissions committee looks for students with significant and diverse work experience, varied educational backgrounds, and sound academic achievement. Incoming students must be able to run word processing, spreadsheet, and database programs.

FINANCIAL FACTS

Annual tuition (in-state/ out-of-state)	$5,328/$17,712
Fees	$2,535
Cost of books	$3,200
Room & board (on/off-campus)	$10,250/$10,250

ADMISSIONS

Admissions Selectivity Rating	**81**
# of applications received	38
% applicants accepted	39
% acceptees attending	65
Average GMAT	510
Range of GMAT	340–630
Accepts GRE scores	Yes
Average Verbal GRE	149
Range of Verbal GRE scores	147–154
Average Quantitative GRE	150
Range of Quantitative GRE scores	144–162
Average Writing GRE	3.0
Range of Writing GRE scores	2.5–3.0
Average GPA	3.2
TOEFL required of international students	Yes
Minimum TOEFL (paper/web)	550/79
Application fee	$50
International application fee	$50
Deferment available	Yes
Maximum length of deferment	One year.
Transfer students accepted	Yes
Transfer application policy Must meet regular MBA admission standards. Up to nine semester credit hours from a regionally accredited institution may be accepted for transfer.	
Non-fall admissions	Yes
Need-blind admissions	Yes

BABSON COLLEGE
F. W. OLIN GRADUATE SCHOOL OF BUSINESS

GENERAL INFORMATION
Type of school — Private
Affiliation — No Affiliation
Academic calendar — Semester

SURVEY SAYS...
Classmates have diverse work experience, Friendly students, Good peer network, Good social scene, Cutting-edge classes, Happy students, Abundant clubs and activities
Solid preparation in:
Finance, General management, Teamwork, Communication/interpersonal skills, Presentation skills, Quantitative skills, Doing business in a global economy, Entreprenurial studies, Environmental sustainability

STUDENTS
Enrollment of parent institution	3,154
Enrollment of MBA Program	919
% male/female	69/31
% out-of-state	57
% part-time	62
% underrepresented minority	10
% international	62
Average age at entry	28
Average years work experience at entry	5

ACADEMICS
Academic Experience Rating	**90**
Profs interesting rating	93
Profs accessible rating	96
% female faculty	23
% underrepresented minority faculty	11
% part-time faculty	21

Prominent Alumni
Ruthie Davis, President & Designer, Ruthie Davis; Diane Sullivan, President, Chairman, and CEO, Caleres Inc; Akio Toyoda, President, Toyota Motor Corporation; James Poss, Founder & President, BigBelly Solar Inc.; Geoffrey Molson, Owner, Montreal Canadiens

Academics

Consistently known as one of the most entrepreneurially-focused business programs in the country, the F.W. Olin Graduate School of Business at Babson College in Wellesley, MA offers students the "knowledge, support, flexibility and mentorship to enable students to exercise entrepreneurial thought and action." The word "action" in the Entrepreneurial Thought and Action® pedagogy should be stressed as practical application is a major component of the MBA curriculum, which incorporates experiential learning throughout (such as the first year consulting project). Additionally, the giant Arthur M. Blank Center for Entrepreneurship offers numerous cocurricular resources and services dedicated to supporting students in their entrepreneurial endeavors, as well as the largest entrepreneurship faculty in the world. "Babson prepares its students to make things happen and to discover the way to maintain an entrepreneurship mindset in big corporate companies, which is something that I think is absolutely relevant for future executives in this world," says a student.

There are four options for the "innovative" Babson MBA, presenting a unified curriculum and the same options for electives: the One-Year, Two-Year, Evening, and Blended Learning Programs, the latter of which is delivered partly through distance learning and is typically chosen by working professionals. The One- and Two-Year Programs are both full-time, and are composed of more than half international students. "Teamwork is a key element" of all Babson courses, and results in students "leaving with strong management skills" to bring to their positions.

Most who come to Babson are drawn in by the reputation for the entrepreneurial specializations, and a visit to the school usually seals the deal. "Everyone associated with Babson that I talked to prior to enrolling (alumni, faculty, current students) seemed very, very happy and satisfied in life," says a current student. Teachers are "highly qualified" and "outstanding," and challenge students to support their answers. "If you make a statement be prepared to offer your logic behind it," says one. The intellectual capital of the faculty never stops growing, as members remain fully dedicated to continuing researching and developing the field of study "without disregarding the needed time to help students."

The administration "has always been on top of their game." They are "flexible and change classes and professors if needs be." Everyone ("including the Dean") has an open door policy and "always enjoy discussing ideas"; "the amount of support given to student initiatives is amazing."

Career and Placement

Babson's reputation within the Northeast is stellar, and the school often "teams up with BC, BU, Harvard, MIT, etc. to have events and network" (the national brand image is also "growing" at a nice clip, as helped by the San Francisco campus). There are plenty of meet and greets with different companies, info sessions, and CEO speeches that occur throughout the day for when one has time.

In terms of application upon graduation, Babson does an excellent job at relating the entrepreneurial spirit to more than just a new business. "From growing a small business, M&A or large business expanding in a new market, the general business acumen is excellent at all levels." Students without jobs are encouraged to "take advantage of the powerful alumni network in every aspect possible!"

Employers of Babson graduates include athenahealth, CVS Caremark, Bain Capital, EMC Corporation, Novartis Pharmaceuticals, iRobot.

ADMISSIONS CONTACT: PETIA WHITMORE, DEAN OF GRADUATE ADMISSIONS
ADDRESS: OLIN HALL, BABSON PARK (WELLESLEY), MA 02457-0310
PHONE: 781-239-4317 • FAX: 781-239-4194
E-MAIL: GRADADMISSION@BABSON.EDU • WEBSITE: WWW.BABSON.EDU/GRADUATE

Student Life and Environment

While there is a common thread of entrepreneurship, the common entrepreneurial denominator draws a varied crowd, and Babson students come from "very, very diverse backgrounds, work experiences, [and] ethnicities"; another universal thread is that "everybody has a unique and exciting story and goals." In this "extremely driven" group, people are "competitive but not at the expense of others." "We all are friends and are involved in each other's family life. It has been a great place to make lifelong business contacts, as well as lifelong friends," says a student.

There are a lot of different cultural activities sponsored by different clubs and different ethnic groups to create cultural awareness. Students who live on campus (or nearby) can take advantage of the "countless events going on" ("more social activities than any one person could possibly attend"), ranging from academic, to business-related, to just-for-fun events such as ski trips, Class Olympics, and Red Sox games. While public transportation is available via the MBTA Green line and free shuttle service, some students note that private transport is "essential" for commuting to Babson. Still, with MBA studies mostly concentrated in one building there is a lot of interaction with students, and "having on-campus offices for work teams makes the campus very lively at every time of day."

Admissions

Babson operates several rounds of admission for each graduate program—evening, Blended Learning, and full-time MBAs. There is no minimum GMAT score required for admission, though the score range for accepted applicants ranges between 580 and 690 each year (25th and 75th percentile). All programs require an admissions interview.

FINANCIAL FACTS

Annual tuition (in-state/ out-of-state)	$65,278/$65,278
Fees	$0
Cost of books	$2,112
Room & board (on/off-campus)	$17,728/$17,728
% of students receiving aid	76
% of first-year students receiving aid	80
% of students receiving grants	75
Average award package	$18,692
Average grant	$16,606
Average loan	$49,723
Average student loan debt	$77,063

ADMISSIONS

Admissions Selectivity Rating	87
# of applications received	636
% applicants accepted	54
% acceptees attending	45
Average GMAT	628
Range of GMAT	600–663
Accepts GRE scores	Yes
Average Verbal GRE	155
Range of Verbal GRE scores	153–156
Average Quantitative GRE	155
Range of Quantitative GRE scores	154–159
Average Writing GRE	4.1
Range of Writing GRE scores	3.0–4.5
Average GPA	3.2
TOEFL required of international students	Yes
Minimum TOEFL (web)	100
Application fee	$100
International application fee	$100
Application Deadline/Notification	
Round 1:	11/1 / 12/18
Round 2:	1/4 / 2/19
Round 3:	3/1 / 4/8
Round 4:	4/1 / 4/29
Deferment available	Yes
Maximum length of deferment	1 year
Transfer students accepted	No
Transfer application policy	
We do not accept transfer students to our Full-Time programs. However, we do accept transfer credit from AACSB accredited programs into our Evening program.	
Non-fall admissions	Yes
Need-blind admissions	Yes

EMPLOYMENT PROFILE

Career Rating	92	Grads Employed by Function% Avg. Salary	
Percent employed at graduation	50	Marketing	(19%) $78,207
Percent employed 3 months after graduation	86	Operations	(4%) $92,000
		Consulting	(11%) $84,369
Average base starting salary	$81,715	Management	(24%) $74,657
Primary Source of Full-time Job Acceptances		Finance	(13%) $89,027
School-facilitated activities	47 (34%)	MIS	(3%) $84,333
Graduate-facilitated activities	93 (66%)	Other	(27%) $83,831
Unknown	0 (0%)	**Top 5 Employers Hiring Grads**	
		Staples (4), Santander Bank (3), athenahealth (2), Fidelity Investments (2), Liberty Mutual (2)	

BALL STATE UNIVERSITY
MILLER COLLEGE OF BUSINESS

GENERAL INFORMATION
Type of school	Public
Affiliation	No Affiliation
Academic calendar	Semester

SURVEY SAYS...
Classmates have diverse work experience, Friendly students, Conservative students, Happy students
Solid preparation in:
Marketing, General management, Quantitative skills

STUDENTS
Enrollment of parent institution	21,196
Enrollment of MBA Program	232
% male/female	61/39
% out-of-state	19
% part-time	69
% underrepresented minority	8
% international	14
Average age at entry	28
Average years work experience at entry	3

ACADEMICS
Academic Experience Rating	**85**
Profs interesting rating	91
Profs accessible rating	91
Student/faculty ratio	30:1
% female faculty	6
% underrepresented minority faculty	42
% part-time faculty	0

Prominent Alumni
James Spencer, Exec VP of Operations Delphi Automotive; Chris Muhlenkamp, Sr. VP Allegion; Will Davis, Ontario Systems; E. Renae Conley, EVP-HR, Former Pres & CEO-Energy; Rick Lagore, EVP/COO Transportation Services LLC

Academics

Long a pioneer in distance learning, the Miller College of Business at Ball State University in Muncie, Indiana offers an MBA program that is "broad and extensive, providing several different paths to earning your degree." The extraordinarily flexible (not to mention "very affordable") school offers numerous delivery options that can accommodate almost any student's situation, including full-time, part-time, on-campus, and online courses. Classes are generally offered in the evenings, which "is very appealing to those who work full time or have to travel frequently." "I didn't know where I would be living before starting the program, and didn't want to start at a school only to have to not be able to attend anymore. Since most schools don't accept transfer MBA credit, I would have lost that time," reasons a student.

The greatest strengths of the school include "the professors and facilities"; professors have "extensive real world expertise" and "you can tell they LOVE what they do, which translates into excitement for the class, program and university." These "very engaging" teachers even communicate this to distance learning students through Skype, email and whiteboard, using "their professional experience to help us learn." "Everything is immersive," and the course work is certainly challenging. "I have to work really hard to achieve good grades," says one student. "Ball State provides immersive learning experiences to its students, [which] are difficult but necessary to understand the dynamic nature of the business world."

Uniquely, "there is a desire to get to know other distance learning students and collaborate in order to get more out of the taught materials." "I feel as though I am a traditional student even though I am connecting via the internet," says a student. The "cutting edge" technology and "access to the latest and greatest...software" truly makes for a "fantastic learning environment" that is "educating people of the future." The ease with which students can sign up for classes and complete their degree "is amazing." "Away with the old, go to Ball State, the way of the future universities!" says a student.

Career and Placement

The wide swath of backgrounds and experiences covered by each class is a blessing for all. "Everyone is interested in so many areas and has experience in a variety of jobs/ internships to share with each class." The school does an excellent job of putting together job/internship fairs and attracting a variety of recruiters, and the fact that "you can graduate as quickly as you finish your coursework" in the distance learning program really benefits the working professionals that attend Ball State. The administration "focuses on helping you meet any academic needs you have."

ADMISSIONS CONTACT: REBECCA L. BAER
ADDRESS: WB 147, MUNCIE, IN 47306
PHONE: 765-285-5329 • FAX: 765-285-8818
E-MAIL: MBA@BSU.EDU • WEBSITE: WWW.BSU.EDU/MBA

Student Life and Environment

Many of the program's enrollees are also Ball State graduate assistants; perhaps it naturally follows that this "friendly," "outgoing" bunch is always "willing to offer assistance and advice." All in all, the student body here is very diverse, representing many countries, ages, and backgrounds. "From the recently laid off exec trying to better himself, to the house wife that wants to have a one up on the competition when re-entering the work force," all bases are covered. Although it is situated in the Midwest, "we seem to have a large amount of foreign students," as well.

While Muncie itself "is not a very nice city," the school is "heavily involved in the local community." Ball State has a strong reputation for maintaining high tech facilities especially in media, education, and business departments. A recent total overhaul of facilities has only further benefitted the school: "the entire campus has been updated including new buildings, roads, landscapes, etc." Everything is very student-friendly, "minus the parking." "Free internet EVERYWHERE on campus, all sporting events are free, most speakers and events on campus are also free." "I've had a VERY positive experience with BSU," says one student.

Admissions

Ball State is nothing if not amenable to all types of students, and the school's application reflects as much. The two primary criteria are your cumulative undergraduate GPA and GMAT scores; a minimum GPA of 2.75 is required (recent entering students had an average GPA of 3.4), as is a minimum GMAT of 450 (recent entering students had an average composite GMAT score of 531). Students must also submit a transcript, application, and a one- or two-page business resume or curriculum vita for use by the Admissions Selection Committee, in which they must portray their work and educational history in a professional style. Students must also submit GMAT or GRE scores from within the past five years; this requirement is waived for anyone who has a JD, PhD, PharmD, or MD. Students must be fully admitted and receive letters of acceptance from both the Graduate School and the MBA program before they can begin classes.

FINANCIAL FACTS

Annual tuition (in-state/ out-of-state)	$7,344/$14,220
Fees	$2,511
Cost of books	$1,000
Room & board	$8,340

ADMISSIONS

Admissions Selectivity Rating	80
# of applications received	90
% applicants accepted	90
% acceptees attending	80
Average GMAT	557
Range of GMAT	450–710
Accepts GRE scores	Yes
Average Verbal GRE	154
Range of Verbal GRE scores	147–163
Average Quantitative GRE	154
Range of Quantitative GRE scores	150–160
Average Writing GRE	3.8
Range of Writing GRE scores	3.0–5.0
Average GPA	3.3
TOEFL required of international students	Yes
Minimum TOEFL (paper/web)	550/79
Application fee	$60
International application fee	$60
Deferment available	Yes
Maximum length of deferment	1 semester
Transfer students accepted	Yes
Transfer application policy Up to 9 credit hours may be considered for transfer from an accredited institution.	
Non-fall admissions	Yes
Need-blind admissions	Yes

EMPLOYMENT PROFILE

Career Rating	82	Grads Employed by Function% Avg. Salary	
Percent employed at graduation	55	Marketing	(11%) $50,000
Percent employed 3 months after graduation	11	Finance	(33%) $85,333
		HR	(22%) $68,250
Average base starting salary	$82,643	Other	(22%)
Primary Source of Full-time Job Acceptances			
School-facilitated activities	5 (5%)		
Graduate-facilitated activities	22 (24%)		
Unknown	64 (70%)		

BAYLOR UNIVERSITY
HANKAMER SCHOOL OF BUSINESS

GENERAL INFORMATION
Type of school   Private
Affiliation   Baptist
Academic calendar   Semester

SURVEY SAYS...
Friendly students, Good peer network, Conservative students, Happy students
Solid preparation in:
Finance, General management, Teamwork, Communication/interpersonal skills, Presentation skills, Quantitative skills, Computer skills, Social responsibility

STUDENTS
Enrollment of parent
  institution   16,787
Enrollment of MBA Program   95
% male/female   68/32
% out-of-state   27
% part-time   4
% underrepresented minority   16
% international   12
Average age at entry   26
Average years work
  experience at entry   3

ACADEMICS
Academic Experience Rating   93
Profs interesting rating   90
Profs accessible rating   95
Student/faculty ratio   15:1
% female faculty   35

Joint Degrees
MBA/MSIS is 2 years; MBA/Master of Engineering is 3 years for both degrees; JD/MBA, JD/MTax, and MBA/Master of Social Work are 4 years for both degrees.

Prominent Alumni
Paul Foster, Western Refining; Drayton McLane, McLane; Mark Hurd, Oracle; Godfry Sullivan, Splunk; Bob Simpson, Texas Rangers

Academics

Baylor University, a popular Southern institution located halfway between Dallas and Austin, appeals to those looking for "a small program" with "a cozy atmosphere" and "a lot of emphasis on ethics." With both a concentration and a dual degree program in healthcare administration, Baylor is also a strong draw for those looking to make their mark in the nation's transforming healthcare sector. Those students have high praise for the program, asserting that "it will be ranked among the top programs" soon. "Hospital CEOs speak to our class approximately nine times per semester," writes one student, extolling the "incredible healthcare administration speaker series." The program includes a placement experience during which students "work directly with a CEO and become an actual hospital administrator for seven months."

There's more than healthcare to Baylor, though. MBAs call the strategy and organizational behavior courses here "some of the best in the country." Students also tell us that the program provides "the freedom and opportunity to engage in any activity that would benefit your personal development." "Whether it's spending an entire day with Warren Buffett, working in China for a semester with top global firms, traveling to Austin every Friday to learn and explore capital investment analysis, or going to a local prison to decrease the recidivism rate by going over business plans with inmates, you can do it at Baylor," one student writes. Another cites an MBA class devoted to inter-program case competition, for which Baylor not only offers a course but also pays participants' cost of participation, including "room, entry fee, flight, etc." (The team took third prize at the competition hosted by George Washington University in 2010.) Business education neophytes praise the Integrated Management Seminar, "a semester specifically designed for non-business undergrads to provide a fabulous foundation before the core MBA program begins."

Career and Placement

Baylor employs career placement professionals who work exclusively with the school's approximately ninety MBA students as well as with alumni. Students tell us that "the career professionals are planning to take the case to businesses more aggressively than bringing the businesses to Baylor (although...some of that will [still] take place)." Students say this strategy makes sense considering that "Baylor is not competing right now with Texas, Rice, and SMU" when it comes to on-campus recruiting, in part due to the small size of the program. Some complain that "the [placement office's] focus is on Texas, and if you're not looking in Texas, good luck!"

Employers who most frequently hire Baylor MBAs include: Accenture, American Express, Anadarko Petroleum, Bank of America, Baptist Health Center, Bearing Point, CITGO, CNA Insurance, Comerica, Community Bank And Trust, ConocoPhillips, Deloitte & Touche, Echostar Communications, Edward Jones, Ernst & Young, ExxonMobil, FBI, First City Financial, First Preference Mortgage, Hatteras Yachts, H.E.B. Grocery Company, Intecap, Internal Revenue Service, Johnson & Johnson, JP Morgan Chase Bank, Keller Williams, Kersher Trading, KPMG, Merck, Microsoft, Middleton, Burns & Davis, Occidental Services, Inc., Perot Systems, Perryman Consulting, PricewaterhouseCoopers, Protiviti, Quala-T, Steak 'n Shake Operations, Inc., Sterling Bank, Sungard Consulting, TXU, Texas Farm Bureau, U.S. Department of Labor, UBS Financial Services, Inc., and Wal-Mart.

Student Life and Environment

"Student life in the MBA program is excellent," with "ample opportunity to meet interesting business leaders outside of the classroom, attend case competitions, and participate in intramural sports. Additionally, many students find that there is a healthy work-life balance at Baylor's MBA program." The university "gives free tickets to all sporting events for graduate students, which is a big deal in the Big 12 Conference, and that includes football and basketball games. Business school students often attend the games together." Some students say Baylor is "a conservative Baptist school" that "does not encourage…drinking or partying," so those unaccustomed to a more conservative setting may find the extracurricular scene here "limited."

The Baylor campus features "several resources available for use [by] graduate students only, including a graduate lounge and breakout rooms with access restricted to grad students, which facilitates the ease of group work." When there are "breaks during the day, students usually hang out in the graduate lounge playing ping pong or talking and catching up on each other's weekend."

Admissions

Those seeking admission to Baylor's Hankamer School of Business must submit the following materials: a completed application (online application preferred); two letters of recommendation from individuals who know you professionally and can assess your skills and potential; official undergraduate transcripts (international students who attended a non-English-speaking school must provide professionally translated and interpreted academic records); a GMAT score report; a current resume; and personal essays detailing qualifications, experiences, and objectives in pursuing a Hankamer MBA. International students whose first language is not English must also submit a score report for the TOEFL or the IELS. Hankamer processes applications on a rolling basis; candidates are notified of their admission status as soon as a decision is made.

FINANCIAL FACTS

Annual tuition (in-state/ out-of-state)	$36,360/$36,360
Fees	$6,238
Cost of books	$2,000
Room & board (on/off-campus)	$10,000/$10,000
% of students receiving aid	75
% of first-year students receiving aid	75

ADMISSIONS

Admissions Selectivity Rating	91
# of applications received	194
% applicants accepted	36
% acceptees attending	67
Average GMAT	634
Range of GMAT	590–668
Accepts GRE scores	Yes
Average Verbal GRE	158
Range of Verbal GRE scores	155–160
Average Quantitative GRE	156
Range of Quantitative GRE scores	152–160
Average GPA	3.3
Minimum TOEFL (paper/web)	600/100
Application fee	$50
International application fee	$50
Early application deadline	11/15
Early notification date	12/1
Regular application deadline	4/15
Regular application notification	5/1
Application Deadline/Notification	
Round 1:	11/15 / 12/1
Round 2:	2/15 / 3/1
Round 3:	4/15 / 5/1
Round 4:	6/15 / 7/1
Deferment available	Yes
Maximum length of deferment	1 year
Transfer students accepted	Yes
Transfer application policy	

A student who has been admitted to a graduate program at another university, and who desires admission to Baylor, must present a transcript that presents the student's active, satisfactory work toward the same degree. Only 6 hrs may be transferred into the MBA program.

Non-fall admissions	Yes
Need-blind admissions	Yes

EMPLOYMENT PROFILE

Career Rating	93	**Grads Employed by Function% Avg. Salary**	
Percent employed at graduation	87	Marketing	(9%) $109,500
Percent employed 3 months after graduation	96	Operations	(22%) $67,750
		Consulting	(1%) $80,000
Average base starting salary	$77,900	Management	(17%) $80,000
Primary Source of Full-time Job Acceptances		Finance	(35%) $80,000
School-facilitated activities	17 (77%)	MIS	(4%) $63,000
Graduate-facilitated activities	5 (23%)	Other	(9%) $77,900
Unknown	0 (0%)	**Top 5 Employers Hiring Grads**	
		Baylor Scott and White (4), Essilor (3), USAA (2), HP (2), Tenet (1)	

BELLARMINE UNIVERSITY
W. FIELDING RUBEL SCHOOL OF BUSINESS

GENERAL INFORMATION

Type of school	Private
Affiliation	Roman Catholic

SURVEY SAYS...

Classmates have diverse work experience, Friendly students, Good peer network, Cutting-edge classes, Happy students, Students love Louisville, KY
Solid preparation in:
Accounting, General management, Teamwork, Communication/interpersonal skills, Presentation skills, Entreprenurial studies

STUDENTS

Enrollment of parent institution	3,800
Enrollment of MBA Program	140
% male/female	64/36
% part-time	64
% underrepresented minority	15
% international	1
Average age at entry	24

ACADEMICS

Academic Experience Rating	87
Profs interesting rating	93
Profs accessible rating	93
% female faculty	33
% underrepresented minority faculty	7

Prominent Alumni

Joseph P. Clayton, In 2001, was the CEO and now is the Chairman of the Board of Directors, Sirius Satellite Radio; Dr. James Heck, Inventor of the drug, Cancidas. Honored by the National Science Foundation for research.; Susan M. Ivey, Chairman, President/CEO Reynolds American Inc.; Angela Mason, Co-founder of ITS Services. Sold in 2003, with over 600 employees. One of America's top Aftrican-American Enterprises.; Leonard P. Spalding, Retired, CEO Chase Mutual funds Corp/Retired, Pres. & CEO Vista Capital Mgmt.

Academics

A cozy business school in Louisville, Kentucky, Bellarmine University offers individual attention and personal growth within a practical MBA curriculum. The "small-school atmosphere and small classroom sizes" are a huge benefit of this program, allowing students to build close relationships with their professors and classmates. Academically, collaboration is a key aspect of the Bellarmine experience, and from the beginning of the program, "everything is team based." To encourage group problem solving, networking, and interaction, "Bellarmine groups its students into cohorts of four or five," and they take all core courses together. In fact, the program is designed to help students round out their qualitative abilities, and the curriculum places a strong "emphasis on improving student's writing, speaking, presentation, and teamwork skills." In the classroom setting, professors are "good at facilitating meaningful class discussions," which bring each student's experience to light. A current student agrees, "The cohort design and grouping throughout the weekend program has increased my team-building skills."

Bellarmine's faculty comprises "published and scholarly professors," who have a strong understanding of business theory. Nonetheless, real world skills are emphasized over academic analysis, and students are pushed to "learn through case studies in a team-oriented environment." Don't expect to lean back and snooze through a lecture; courses are discussion based and, often, small groups "lead case study discussions for the entire class." Bellarmine has deep ties in the local metropolis. "One of Bellarmine's advantages is that a majority of its professors have great career experience, and some are still working in the Louisville area." A student recounts, "We have accounting teachers who have headed departments for Deloitte; IRS Tax Attorneys teaching tax and business law; and a lawyer/econ Ph.D. who teaches economics and how to do business in non-capitalist countries." Although the school "could offer a wider variety of MBA electives," students appreciate the varied experience faculty members bring to the classroom. Class work is often augmented by the invitation of special "speakers and contributors, who are able to share more recent 'real world' experiences" with the student body.

For working professionals, the Bellarmine MBA program is flexible, allowing students to tailor coursework to fit their busy schedules. Depending on the pace in which you complete coursework, the MBA can take anywhere from two to five years to complete. Classes are held in the evenings and on weekends. "The convenience is great for someone looking to go to school part time." Overall, the program is "very well run, with minimal red tape." When it comes to planning your schedule or paying your bills, "the administration is wonderful to work with, very helpful, and makes things easier on students." A "personal touch" distinguishes the experience, and "staff, faculty, and administration care about the students and their success."

Career and Placement

Preparation for the real world begins in the Bellarmine classroom. Professors "know what is going on in the job market today and how it will affect us when we leave." As such, teaching is geared toward practical applications, which students can take directly back to their jobs. Those looking to make a career change after the MBA have access to the campus Career Center, which maintains online job and internship boards and hosts a series of job development events on campus. Though many of these events are directed at the undergraduate community, MBA students can benefit from campus-wide career fairs or make appointment with career counselors for a resume and cover letter review.

Working full-time as they attend the program, most students will stay at their current company after graduation. Therefore, career services aren't as robust at Bellarmine as they are at other full-time MBA programs. There are "a lot of internship opportunities" offered through the career center, but an MBA student admits, "I have not seen a lot of recruiting, except for accounting or finance."

Student Life and Environment

Bellarmine students come from "a wide variety of race, social, and educational backgrounds," and join the program "experienced in various fields of business." In the classroom, students are "very supportive and collaborative," and most enjoy the heavy emphasis on group work. To facilitate student interaction, there is a "very nice computer lab and library study area" in the business school facilities. "Students normally gather at common areas on campus" before attending classes. Overall, "the facility is very safe and excellent," and comfortably located on a "beautiful" campus.

With laudable time management skills, most students at Bellarmine "can balance class loads with their professional duties quite well." Nonetheless, Bellarmine graduate students have a lot on their plates, and most are "not very social outside of class." A student explains, "Most all of us have full-time jobs, so we have limited time to spend at school." Socializing, when it happens, is mostly low-key. For example, "many [students] try to go out after Friday class to have fun for a couple of hours."

Admissions

To apply to Bellarmine's MBA program, students must submit a completed application form, personal essays, two letters of recommendation, academic transcripts from all college coursework, and official GMAT scores. Test scores and previous academic performance are the two most important factors in an admissions decision, though work experience is also weighted strongly. For last year's entering class, the average GMAT score was 470, and the average GPA was 3.2 on a 4.0 scale.

ADMISSIONS	
Admissions Selectivity Rating	82
# of applications received	59
% applicants accepted	68
% acceptees attending	100
Average GMAT	460
Range of GMAT	390–540
Accepts GRE scores	Yes
Average GPA	3.2
TOEFL required of international students	Yes
Minimum TOEFL (paper/web)	550/80
Application fee	$40
International application fee	$40
Deferment available	Yes
Maximum length of deferment	5 Years
Transfer students accepted	Yes
Transfer application policy Accept up to 12 graduate credits from an accredited University.	
Non-fall admissions	Yes
Need-blind admissions	No

BELMONT UNIVERSITY
THE JACK C. MASSEY GRADUATE SCHOOL OF BUSINESS

GENERAL INFORMATION
Type of school   Private
Affiliation   Christian
                        (Nondenominational)
Academic calendar   Trimester

SURVEY SAYS...
Classmates have diverse work experience, Friendly students, Good peer network, Conservative students, Happy students, Students love Nashville, TN
Solid preparation in:
General management, Teamwork, Communication/interpersonal skills, Presentation skills, Doing business in a global economy, Entreprenurial studies

STUDENTS
Enrollment of parent institution	7,351
Enrollment of MBA Program	143
% male/female	54/46
% out-of-state	29
% part-time	83
% underrepresented minority	20
% international	4
Average age at entry	26
Average years work experience at entry	5

ACADEMICS
Academic Experience Rating	**86**
Profs interesting rating	92
Profs accessible rating	96
Student/faculty ratio	6:1
% female faculty	32
% underrepresented minority faculty	9
% part-time faculty	18

Joint Degrees
Dual MBA/MACC - 2.5 to 3 years

Prominent Alumni
Damon Hininger, CEO, Correction Corporation of America; Claire M. Gulmi, EVP/CFO, AmSurg; Charles Hagood, CEO, Healthcare Performance Partners, Inc.

Academics

For Nashville-area professionals looking to jump-start their career, Belmont University's graduate business programs offer a "great value." The professional MBA for working adults—Belmont's flagship program—offers a "great classroom-based education that is flexible enough for a working student." With all classes held at night, most Belmont students are juggling career and studies; fortunately, "educators understand [students'] work/life demands" and "are consistently flexible when [students need] to balance work and life with academics." Belmont's core curriculum covers a wide breadth of business areas, including basics like finance, business law, and technology, as well as more innovative topics in entrepreneurship and leadership. Neither highly qualitative nor quantitative, "the program is balanced between verbal, interpersonal, and mathematical reasoning abilities." Overall, the program is challenging, but "the pace is so fast that sometimes we are not able to cover some subjects in enough detail." If you do want to delve into details, the MBA offers the "flexibility to customize [your] degree" through areas of concentration in accounting, entrepreneurship, finance, business intelligence, healthcare, marketing, or music business. Of particular note, every Belmont student must also participate in an international trip as a requirement of graduation; destinations range from Amsterdam to Beijing to Cape Town.

Working professionals want to learn skills they can apply in the workplace, and Belmont caters to that goal. Here, "the classes are focused on real world topics" and "the learning style is hands-on." In the classroom, "the program is largely case-based, encouraging students to use critical thinking skills and sharpen interpersonal skills," and across disciplines, "the professors encourage classroom discussion." The faculty further promotes Belmont's practical perspective by bringing their extensive business experience to the classroom. Like the students, most Belmont professors were "working professionals and therefore experts in the field they are teaching." At this friendly school, faculty members "give great practical advice" and are "truly interested in helping students learn and grow."

At Belmont, classes are uniformly small, with about twenty students in the average classroom. Students love the mix of big-name resources and intimate atmosphere, saying "Belmont has the feel of a small school with the professors and reputation of a top university." A student adds, "It is big enough to offer amenities and benefits of a large school, but small enough to still be a tight-knit group." On this community-oriented campus, "fellow students, the professors, and the school staff seem to sincerely care about me and each other."

Career and Placement

The Massey College of Business Career Development Center serves undergraduate and graduate business students through individualized career coaching, interview training, resume preparation, and job and internship listings. After graduation, the vast majority of Massey graduates (about 85 percent) stay in the Middle Tennessee area, contributing to the school's strong alumni network in greater Nashville. While praising their school's deep ties in the region, students feel that "Belmont could improve more in getting more companies to recruit their students" and by drawing new employers from some of Nashville's largest industries, such as healthcare. In recent years, companies that have hired graduates of the Massey College of Business Administration, include AT&T, Dell, Deloitte & Touche, Ernst & Young, HCA, Pfizer, Morgan Stanley Smith Barney, Marriott, Sony/ATV, and WebMD.

ADMISSIONS CONTACT: TONYA HOLLIN, ADMISSIONS ASSISTANT
ADDRESS: 1900 BELMONT BOULEVARD, NASHVILLE, TN 37212
PHONE: 615-460-6480 • FAX: 615-460-6353
E-MAIL: MASSEYADMISSIONS@BELMONT.EDU • WEBSITE: MASSEY.BELMONT.EDU

Belmont MBA candidates are predominantly working professionals, and many aren't looking for a new position after graduation (rather, they are hoping to assume new responsibilities at their existing organization with the help of an MBA). However, should they someday be looking to make a change, Massey graduates can count on lifelong loyalty: All alumni have access to services offered through the Center for Career Development including a job posting site, career counseling, and various online tools.

Student Life and Environment

With its evening course schedule, accommodating staff, and practical approach to business, Belmont attracts many "young professionals up on current events and looking to advance their careers." At this school, "people are smart and hard workers, and have big, diverse goals [in] life," offering great opportunities to network in different industries. Between students, "the culture is professional but fun without being too rigid," and, though there is a mix of cultures and viewpoints, "everyone feels comfortable and gets to express their personal views." "There are numerous activities and clubs to take part in" through the business school, including honor societies and volunteer work. Even if they don't participate in campus activities, "everyone is still very social and friendly," and networking opportunities abound. A student explains, "Courses are structured with many group work requirements, which somewhat supercedes the need for student activity groups, as we are all meeting together regularly."

Located on seventy-five acres in southeast Nashville, Belmont University has a "great urban location" and a comfortable campus environment, boasting modern classrooms and "beautiful flower gardens." Although most Belmont MBA students don't have extra time to take advantage of the resources on campus, they do appreciate the school's "convenient location." At the same time, Belmont has a growing reputation, and students say it's time to "significantly update some of [its] facilities and technologies to keep up with the expansion." Based on feedback, the Massey Business Center is currently in the midst of a $12 million complete renovation to improve the quality and delivery of educational services.

Admissions

To apply to Massey, students must submit an application, an undergraduate transcript, GMAT scores, a current resume, and at least two professional recommendations. In recent years, the average Belmont MBA candidate was about twenty-eight years old, had over six years of professional work experience, and scored around 526 on the GMAT. To be eligible for the program, students must have an undergraduate degree in any field. For those without a degree in business, Belmont will help a student determine which basic business courses they should take before matriculation.

FINANCIAL FACTS

Annual tuition (in-state/ out-of-state)	$52,330/$52,330
Fees	$1,125
% of first-year students receiving aid	86

ADMISSIONS

Admissions Selectivity Rating	78
# of applications received	59
% applicants accepted	95
% acceptees attending	68
Average GMAT	527
Range of GMAT	460–570
Accepts GRE scores	Yes
Average GPA	3.3
TOEFL required of international students	Yes
Minimum TOEFL (web)	550
Application fee	$50
International application fee	$50
Regular application deadline	7/1
Deferment available	Yes
Maximum length of deferment	One year
Transfer students accepted	Yes
Transfer application policy Application process is the same for all students. May transfer up to 6 hours from an accredited university.	
Non-fall admissions	Yes
Need-blind admissions	Yes

EMPLOYMENT PROFILE

Career Rating	86	**Grads Employed by Function% Avg. Salary**
Percent employed at graduation	42	**Top 5 Employers Hiring Grads**
Percent employed 3 months after graduation	68	Xtend Healthcare (2), UBS (2), HCA (1), Warner Music Group (1), Tractor Supply (1)
Average base starting salary	$45,572	
Primary Source of Full-time Job Acceptances		
School-facilitated activities	(85%)	
Graduate-facilitated activities	(15%)	
Unknown	(0%)	

BENTLEY UNIVERSITY
GRADUATE SCHOOL OF BUSINESS

Academics

Students in the MBA program at Bentley University brag that their program combines "the most modern technology available" with "real-world work experience" to provide "the best mix of price, location, and quality." Bentley's impressive resources include a 3,500-square-foot facility complete with a trading floor with two Trans-Lux data walls, sixty work stations, an adjacent business suite, and a marketing center that features numerous state-of-the-art research and analysis labs. "Some [of the technology] is accessible from home, too," a boon to the school's many commuting part-timers.

Bentley's cutting-edge approach extends to its academics. Students pursue "the most unique and interesting concentrations" in addition to "all the traditional areas of study." Unique offerings include Human Factors in Information Design, Business Analytics, and Marketing Analytics, programs that students argue "are in line with what is needed in the real world." Bentley's "accounting program is the best around," excelling in both general accounting and taxation. Information technology, unsurprisingly, is also an area of strength.

Bentley's many part-time students appreciate the program's flexibility ("You can take two courses in one night, and there are some online offerings," a student explains), but warn that "it is hard to connect with other students" because "there are no real cohorts." The Bentley MBA and Bentley Emerging Leaders MBA, in contrast, "is comparatively small and becomes tight-knit" over the course of the program. For all students, the program is "intense," but fortunately, "the professors and administration are very helpful." One student points out that "many workshops and information sessions exist outside of class," and as a result students enjoy "a very engaging academic experience." MBAs also appreciate that "professors teach course work in a practical manner. I always leave feeling like I have something I can use the next day."

Career and Placement

Bentley's Nathan R. Miller Center for Career Services (CCS) "offers a great deal of support in finding career opportunities" for the school's MBAs. Career Advisors receive a strong assist from Bentley's solid "reputation among Boston-area employers" as well as from professors who "use their networks" to help their students. Students here also benefit from the Job Search Skills (JSS), a program designed to help them better position themselves in the battle for top jobs. JSS programs vary by area of concentration, meaning students receive plenty of field-specific assistance. The CSS provides lifetime service to alumni, another huge plus.

Top employers of Bentley MBAs include: Boston Scientific, Converse Inc., Covidien, Deloitte Consulting, Federal Reserve Bank of Boston, Ernst & Young, Fidelity Investments, EMC, Genzyme Corporation, JPMorgan Chase & Company, KPMG, Morgan Stanley, PricewaterhouseCoopers, Microsoft, National Grid USA, Nuance Communications, Raytheon, Staples, and State Street Corporation.

Student Life and Environment

The majority of Bentley MBA students attend the part-time evening program. The full-time program is comprised of 10 percent of the student body. Bentley typically draws "academically capable people with many diverse backgrounds," although some here "wish there were fewer people coming straight out of a four-year program," even though such students "are still surprisingly able to contribute to conversations. However, they lack a certain perspective."

Bentley MBAs enjoy "a beautiful campus and buildings." Grad classes "are concentrated in a couple of buildings near each other," a blessing during the cold Massachusetts winters. So too are the "shuttles around campus." Even so, some feel that the space dedicated to graduate students needs to be expanded. One writes that the school "should have more options for dining on campus and more places suitable for graduate students to study either individual[ly] or in groups." Most part-time students must balance "a heavy course load" with work and family responsibilities, leaving little or no time for extracurricular and other campus activities. Those not so burdened report that "campus activities are in abundance, from professional to entertainment. There is usually at least one club or association hosting an event open to the whole school body" at any time. Campus organizations "cater to different educational paths and cultures," with a number representing various international student constituencies.

Off-campus entertainment is also readily accessible, as Bentley is located in Waltham, a mere ten miles from downtown Boston. Both Boston and Cambridge are easily accessible by train. The school also runs a regular shuttle between the Bentley campus and Harvard Square.

Admissions

Applicants to the Bentley MBA program must submit all of the following materials to the Admissions Committee: a completed application form; official copies of all transcripts for all post secondary academic work; an official GMAT score report; two letters of recommendation; essays (topics detailed in application); and a resume. Applicants to the Bentley MBA, Emerging Leaders MBA, or the MS + MBA program must sit for an interview; interviews are optional for all other applicants. In addition to all of the above, international applicants must also submit an international student data form and confirmation of financial resources; a copy of their passport name page; and TOEFL score. International applicants are strongly encouraged to use a transcript evaluation service. Bentley admissions officers pride themselves on personalizing the admissions process by looking at the whole person when making admissions decisions. Work experience is strongly preferred but not required.

Prominent Alumni

Chris Lynch '91 MBA, Partner, Accomplice, LLC; Charles Nickerson '85, MBA '89, Senior VP Fidelity Shared Services; Daniel Farley '95 MBA, Executive Vice President of State Street Global Advisors, and CIO of the Investment Solutions Group; Theresa Bresten '87 MBA, Vice President and Treasurer, HP Hood Inc.

FINANCIAL FACTS

Annual tuition (in-state/ out-of-state)	$37,410/$37,410
Fees	$455
Cost of books	$1,400
Room & board (on/off-campus)	$16,730/$16,730
% of students receiving aid	48
% of first-year students receiving aid	61
% of students receiving grants	34
Average award package	$27,260
Average grant	$23,671
Average loan	$19,915
Average student loan debt	$36,844

ADMISSIONS

Admissions Selectivity Rating	82
# of applications received	167
% applicants accepted	74
% acceptees attending	44
Average GMAT	573
Range of GMAT	510–640
Accepts GRE scores	Yes
Average GPA	3.3
TOEFL required of international students	Yes
Minimum TOEFL (paper/web)	600/100
Application fee	$50
International application fee	$50
Early application deadline	11/1
Early notification date	12/15
Application Deadline/Notification	
Round 1:	12/1 / 1/15
Round 2:	1/20 / 3/5
Round 3:	3/15 / 5/1
Round 4:	5/1 /
Deferment available	Yes
Maximum length of deferment	Up to 1 year
Transfer students accepted	No
Non-fall admissions	Yes
Need-blind admissions	Yes

EMPLOYMENT PROFILE

Career Rating	89	Grads Employed by Function	% Avg. Salary
Percent employed at graduation	66	Marketing	(26%) $58,143
Percent employed 3 months after graduation	80	Operations	(5%)
		Consulting	(10%) $68,125
Average base starting salary	$60,223	Management	(8%) $70,000
Primary Source of Full-time Job Acceptances		Finance	(21%) $54,724
School-facilitated activities	20 (43%)	MIS	(21%) $65,750
Graduate-facilitated activities	20 (43%)	Other	(8%) $45,000
Unknown	7 (14%)	**Top 5 Employers Hiring Grads**	

Top 5 Employers Hiring Grads
Deloitte Consulting (2), Ernst & Young (2), KPMG (2), PwC (1), athenahealth (1)

Berry College
Campbell School of Business

Academics

Berry College is a small private school, located on a beautiful and expansive wooded campus in Rome, Georgia. This setting provides a unique backdrop for the Campbell School of Business, which unites a savvy MBA curriculum with a friendly and intimate atmosphere. Within the greater Rome area, Berry College is a "convenient and reputable" choice for an MBA, with all classes offered in the evenings (classes meet one night per week throughout the fall, spring, and summer terms). Located fewer than 100 miles from Atlanta and Chattanooga, the program is designed for working professionals, as well as early-career students. For full-time students, the school offers the opportunity to take on a graduate assistantship position, which offsets the cost of tuition in exchange for hours worked on campus.

Along with the master of education, the MBA is one of two graduate programs offered at Berry, and the atmosphere reflects the intimate atmosphere of the undergraduate college. With a low enrollment, the "small class sizes and the relationships students have with professors" are the best parts of the educational experience. Here, professors "are always willing to help and seem happy to be there, teaching the courses." Bringing strong educational and professional backgrounds to the program, "the faculty at Berry [is] surprisingly accomplished," and students note a "professional commitment to academic excellence" throughout the faculty and staff. Berry is an interactive environment where students are encouraged to participate in class discussions, and those who have already entered the workforce often "have interesting stories and work experience to contribute to class." While the benefits are manifold, the low enrollment also has some drawbacks. For example, course scheduling can be difficult because "the school does not offer all required classes at all times. Just once every two years." In addition, the elective offerings are more limited at Berry than at larger institutions; some feel it would be a benefit to have "more classes, more options" within the MBA curriculum.

Overseen by a competent administration, "the school is run well," and the curriculum is well-designed, emphasizing a holistic approach to business. The MBA begins with a series of proficiency requirements in accounting, marketing, statistics, economics, finance, and management—but these can be waived for students who have an undergraduate degree in business. Thereafter, all students must complete twenty-one credit hours of core courses and nine credit hours of business electives (students may also earn course credit for internships), which cover a range of topics including written and oral communication skills, leadership, and ethics. Typically, students complete the program in two years, though the college allows up to six years of study.

Career and Placement

The Berry College Career Center offers career counseling, resume and cover letter assistance, online job boards, and an online database of job tips and resources. These services are open to all undergraduates and graduate students, as well as alumni (alumni may even request login information to access online job boards); however, the Career Center's efforts are principally aimed at the undergraduate community.

Graduates of the Campbell School of Business, students have taken jobs with companies including CFA, Georgia Pacific, Walton Communications, Industrial Developments International, Wiser Wealth Management, and Anheuser Busch. While the school has a strong reputation in the region, students admit that, "Berry College could improve in connecting its grad students with jobs outside of the Rome metropolitan and Atlanta areas."

ADMISSIONS CONTACT: DR. GARY WATERS, ASSOCIATE VP OF ENROLLMENT MANAGEMENT
ADDRESS: 2277 MARTHA BERRY HWY NW, PO BOX 490159, MOUNT BERRY, GA 30149-0159
PHONE: 800-BERRY-GA • FAX: 706-290-2178
E-MAIL: ADMISSIONS@BERRY.EDU • WEBSITE: BERRY.EDU

Student Life and Environment

Taking a cue from Berry's pastoral campus environment, Berry students are "friendly and down-to-earth," yet also take their studies seriously. At Berry, students "work hard all day and work hard during their classes," and many are "goal-oriented" and "driven." A tribute to the Berry College's pleasant atmosphere and academic excellence, many MBA candidates are returning Berry students who also received their undergraduate degree from the school. In fact, many come to the graduate program directly after college. Therefore, "the majority of students are fairly young and inexperienced," with limited experience in the real world. As a result, the older, working students who "come from outside of the school add a great deal of value" to the program.

Berry is located on an enormous wooded campus (one of the world's biggest) on the outskirts of Rome, Georgia. If you would like to get involved in extracurricular pursuits, "the school has a great campus with many activities to participate in," and "there is always an activity or cultural event" at school. At the same time, students observe, "The graduate program isn't as active in the school community but the opportunity is there if the student wanted to be involved." Even so, "gym and library facility access is fully granted" to graduate students, and many take advantage of these resources.

Admissions

To apply to Berry College's MBA program, students must submit undergraduate transcripts, two letters of reference, official GMAT scores, a current resume, and a 500-word goals statement. To be eligible for the program, students must have a GMAT score of at least 400; an undergraduate GPA of 3.0 or better is preferred. To be considered for a position, students should submit their application materials at least 30 days before the start of a new semester.

ADMISSIONS

Admissions Selectivity Rating	79
# of applications received	17
% applicants accepted	94
% acceptees attending	81
Average GMAT	558
Range of GMAT	430–630
Accepts GRE scores	No
Average GPA	3.0
TOEFL required of international students	Yes
Minimum TOEFL (paper/web)	550/
Application fee	$0
International application fee	$0
Regular application deadline	7/1
Deferment available	Yes
Maximum length of deferment	One semester
Transfer students accepted	Yes
Transfer application policy The curriculum committee may grant transfer credit for appropriate graduate-level course work completed at other AACSB-accredited institutions to a maximum of two 3-semester-hour courses, for a total of 6 semester hours. Transfer credit is not granted for Strategies of World-Class Organizations (BUS 685).	
Non-fall admissions	Yes

BOSTON COLLEGE
CARROLL SCHOOL OF MANAGEMENT

GENERAL INFORMATION

Type of school	Private
Affiliation	Roman Catholic-Jesuit
Academic calendar	Semester

SURVEY SAYS...

Classmates have diverse work experience, Friendly students, Good peer network, Good social scene, Happy students, Students love Chestnut Hill, MA
Solid preparation in:
Finance, Accounting, General management, Teamwork, Presentation skills, Quantitative skills

STUDENTS

Enrollment of parent institution	14,100
Enrollment of MBA Program	545
% male/female	64/36
% part-time	67
% international	32
Average age at entry	28
Average years work experience at entry	4

ACADEMICS

Academic Experience Rating	92
Profs interesting rating	92
Profs accessible rating	95
Student/faculty ratio	22:1
% female faculty	35
% part-time faculty	41

Joint Degrees

MBA/MSF; MBA/MSA; MBA/JD; MBA/MSW; MBA/MSN; MBA/MEd.; MBA/MS Biology, Chemistry, Geology, Geophysics; MBA/MA Math, Slavic Studies, Russian, Linguistics; MBA/MA Pastoral Studies.

Prominent Alumni

Robert Manning, '87, Chairman, President & CEO, MFS Investment Management; Dennis J. O'Brien, '82, Chairman, Digicel; Fay Donohue, '80, CEO & President, DeltaQuest (Delta Dental)

Academics

Boston College's Carroll School of Management's "brand reputation" is second to none, especially "in the Boston area." "People around here think that it's Harvard," one student proudly reports. Boston College has everything an MBA student could want, including "[its] Boston location, small class size, great culture, strong alumni network, [a] mix of theoretical and practical learning, affordable tuition, [and] good scholarships." "Boston College offered me the best combination of ranking and scholarship," an Oil and Energy student explains. "Additionally, Boston is a great city and the campus is awesome." The "opportunities provided by the city of Boston" are ample, and the Carroll School of Management has a "strong influence" in the city's thriving business community.

The "reputation and quality of professors" is a big draw for Boston College. Professors wield "a diverse array of learning tools (lecture, cases, group exercises, etc.)" and "make themselves entirely available and are supportive of personal goals in addition to classroom objectives." The "excellent" administration also gets high marks from students. "They work hard to get you registered and setup [and] support the learning experience." Basically, at Boston College the faculty "care about the student's success and the administration is there to make it happen." The school is responsive to student feedback too, taking it "very seriously and implement[ing] changes accordingly." Although some students did wish the school would "offer [more] online courses."

The "small class sizes" provide intimate learning environments of business students and an "emphasis on hands-on learning." However, being housed in Boston College means students at the Carroll School of Management get "the perfect blend of a small program with large resources from a major academic institution." A financial services student sums their decision to attend thusly: "After talking to alumni, the pride they had in BC was something I knew I wanted to be a part of."

Career and Placement

Boston College boasts "the best alumni network in Boston" and "influential alumni" abound in the area. The school's career placement office "really goes above and beyond to help students find their way." Although some students say that the school has a harder time finding student work outside of Boston, others say "there are MANY opportunities presented by career services for students looking for jobs outside of the Boston area." The school's award winning "TechTrek West" combines classroom learning on the BC campus with a week-long field study to Silicon Valley. It is "a perfect way to both study the industry and network with some great people in the [tech] industry." Students within 12 months of graduation can apply through the MBA job posting system, and on-campus recruiting activities are scheduled later in the day to accommodate part-time students.

Last year's graduating class had an average total compensation (salary plus signing bonuses) of over $98,408. Seventy-five percent of those found placement in the Northeast. The top five employers from the most recent class were Liberty Mutual Insurance Co., Credit Suisse, EMC, Adidas, and Santander.

ADMISSIONS CONTACT: SHELLEY BURT, DIRECTOR OF GRADUATE ENROLLMENT
ADDRESS: FULTON HALL 315, 140 COMMONWEALTH AVENUE, CHESTNUT HILL, MA 02467-3808
PHONE: 617-552-3920 • FAX: 617-552-8078
E-MAIL: BCMBA@BC.EDU • WEBSITE: WWW.BC.EDU/MBA

Student Life and Environment

Boston College boasts an "unbelievably beautiful" campus, and the location in the bustling city of Boston has many obvious benefits. Carroll School of Management's students tend to be "motivated and outgoing" men and women in their "late twenties to early thirties." The student body is "focused because they are balancing work and school, but are friendly and want to network." The nature of the business program can make some students "competitive," yet most students are "willing to help" and "interested in advancing their careers and those of their peers." The environment is unlike "the cut-throat and pretentious culture that is infamous at other schools." "Everyone knows one another because it is a small class," and there are always events going on both on campus and off.

Admissions

Admission to the Carroll School of Management's renowned program is understandably competitive. For a recent entering class, the average GPA was 3.35 and the average GMAT was 666. The school does pride itself on a diverse and accomplished student body, so other factors, such as work experience come into play. While the school only recommends two years of work experience before applying, the average student had 4.4 years of professional experience before beginning their MBA.

FINANCIAL FACTS

Annual tuition (in-state/ out-of-state)	$45,520/$45,520
Fees	$150
Cost of books	$1,500
% of students receiving aid	45
% of first-year students receiving aid	45
% of students receiving grants	45
Average student loan debt	$63,080

ADMISSIONS

Admissions Selectivity Rating	89
# of applications received	595
% applicants accepted	38
% acceptees attending	39
Average GMAT	664
Range of GMAT	620–700
Accepts GRE scores	Yes
Average Verbal GRE	155
Range of Verbal GRE scores	150–159
Average Quantitative GRE	154
Range of Quantitative GRE scores	150–157
Average Writing GRE	4.0
Range of Writing GRE scores	3.5–4.5
Average GPA	3.3
TOEFL required of international students	Yes
Minimum TOEFL (paper/web)	600/100
Application fee	$100
International application fee	$100
Application Deadline/Notification	
Round 1:	11/1 / 1/15
Round 2:	1/15 / 3/15
Round 3:	3/15 / 5/1
Round 4:	4/15 / 6/1
Deferment available	No
Transfer students accepted	Yes
Transfer application policy	
4 courses are accepted (with a grade of B or higher) from other AACSB MBA Programs.	
Non-fall admissions	No
Need-blind admissions	Yes

EMPLOYMENT PROFILE

Career Rating	94	Grads Employed by Function	% Avg. Salary
Percent employed at graduation	71	Marketing	(18%) $89,000
Percent employed 3 months after graduation	88	Operations	(3%)
		Consulting	(22%) $84,714
Average base starting salary	$94,963	Management	(24%) $106,033
Primary Source of Full-time Job Acceptances		Finance	(30%) $90,579
School-facilitated activities	42 (60%)	Other	(3%)
Graduate-facilitated activities	28 (40%)		
Unknown	0 (0%)		

BOSTON UNIVERSITY
QUESTROM SCHOOL OF BUSINESS

Academics

The "well-rounded and comprehensive" MBA program at Boston University Questrom School of Business offers students the opportunity to tailor their MBA program experience to their life and their career.

In the two-year full-time MBA program (an "interactive learning experience addressing the dynamics of global business"), students spend their first year in a fifty or so person cohort (second year classes are generally held in the evenings with part time students); the school also offers a popular dual-degree MS-MBA program in which students can earn a traditional MBA with a Master of Science in Digital Innovation (MSDi), an "excellent" Health Sector MBA, and a Public & Nonprofit MBA. The Evening program, which takes longer to complete but is designed for working students, is taught by the same professors as found in the full-time two-year program and offers the same electives.

The traditional MBA courses are typically case-based and are partnered with additional seminars in Ethics and Business Law, as well as Executive Communications and Executive Presentations that help to "really refine students' 'soft' business skills." "The administration does a good job getting speakers and industry connections to come on campus," says a student. Some professors "are really good," others are "just so-so," but the top ones "bring out the best out of the student in the class discussions." There are a good number of team projects throughout the semester ("truly the strength of the school"), and students appreciate the "ample opportunities...to work collaboratively."

The administration (helmed by a well-liked Dean) "really demonstrates their interest and commitment to the [Questrom] MBA student experience": "Daily through pre-term, and progressively throughout classes and individual lectures and projects, [Questrom] MBA administration and faculty consistently surveys students for feedback, ratings and potential changes." "I have compared it to friends in other graduate programs at other schools. It is remarkable how few headaches I have as a result of the well-managed administration," says one student.

Career and Placement

The Career Center boasts good hire rates and a "gigantic" and "active" alumni network, and the office's facilities and services were overhauled in summer 2013 to provide a slew of new offerings. Students praise the interview readiness programs as top notch.

The company recruiters that the school draws "tend more toward finance, health care and consulting" (in particular health care), and "could be more diverse" to accommodate those students with other focuses. "If you, as a student, want to find a job at TOP companies, you need to make a lot of efforts on your own," says one student. "The few well-known recruiters on campus get their pick of the litter," says another.

Recent employers of BU students are PricewaterhouseCoopers, Cognizant, Liberty Mutual, AT&T, and Deloitte.

Student Life and Environment

The "friendly and helpful" crew here is "antithetical to the expected cutthroat nature of business/business school." Life at BU is "incredibly social"; there are "school council dances, cohort parties, and classmates always putting together nights out to sporting events, bars, clubs, and fun places in Boston." From basketball tournaments to bake offs to bowling nights, the cohort competitions also "really bring the MBA class together." The student body has a large international component (particularly Asia).

BU is located centrally in an "amazing city," (also the epicenter of a healthcare hub), and does a great job of effectively leveraging the numerous surrounding schools. Students "have many places to meet and often participate in a lot of off-campus activities thanks to the incredible learning environment the city creates." Networking among Boston local professional groups is a huge benefit to getting a degree here.

Admissions

Admissions to BU's MBA programs are highly competitive, with only around 30 percent of applicants receiving an offer of admission each year. The mean GMAT score for last year's entering class was 682 (with a 50 percent mid-range of 640 to 720), the average GPA was 3.35, and students had an average of around five years of work experience.

FINANCIAL FACTS

Annual tuition (in-state/out-of-state)	$47,422/$47,422
Fees	$760
Cost of books	$5,944
Room & board	$12,620
% of students receiving aid	94
% of first-year students receiving aid	96
% of students receiving grants	92
Average award package	$39,561
Average grant	$28,252
Average loan	$32,027
Average student loan debt	$71,000

ADMISSIONS

Admissions Selectivity Rating	93
# of applications received	1,094
% applicants accepted	35
% acceptees attending	39
Average GMAT	682
Range of GMAT	640–720
Accepts GRE scores	Yes
Average Verbal GRE	158
Range of Verbal GRE scores	154–161
Average Quantitative GRE	158
Range of Quantitative GRE scores	155–162
Average GPA	3.3
TOEFL required of international students	Yes
Minimum TOEFL (paper/web)	600/95
Application fee	$125
International application fee	$125
Application Deadline/Notification	
Round 1:	10/17 / 12/20
Round 2:	1/4 / 3/3
Round 3:	3/22 / 4/28
Deferment available	No
Transfer students accepted	Yes
Transfer application policy Classes must be from an AACSB-accredited institution.	
Non-fall admissions	Yes
Need-blind admissions	Yes

EMPLOYMENT PROFILE

Career Rating	95
Percent employed at graduation	76
Percent employed 3 months after graduation	93
Average base starting salary	$100,010
Primary Source of Full-time Job Acceptances	
School-facilitated activities	24 (23%)
Graduate-facilitated activities	25 (23%)
Unknown	57 (54%)

Grads Employed by Function	%	Avg. Salary
Marketing	(13%)	$91,165
Operations	(5%)	$92,000
Consulting	(31%)	$112,375
Management	(23%)	$102,214
Finance	(14%)	$90,600
HR	(2%)	
MIS	(5%)	$89,000
Other	(7%)	$103,333

Top 5 Employers Hiring Grads
PricewaterhouseCoopers (6), Collaborative Consulting (5), Deloitte Consulting (5), Biogen (4), Liberty Mutual (4)

BOWLING GREEN STATE UNIVERSITY
COLLEGE OF BUSINESS ADMINISTRATION

Academics

Whether you choose to enter the full-time, part-time, or Executive MBA program at Bowling Green State University you will experience efficient, practical, instruction at a great value. Offering a crash course in business, Bowling Green's full-time MBA "is only twelve months long," and is comprised of a series of foundation, core, and capstone courses. Tuition is reasonable and, for highly qualified students, graduate assistantships can cover a portion of "the cost of tuition, and [pay] an additional living stipend." Given the program's accelerated time frame, low cost, and scholarship options, students say, "It is probably [a] much better bang for the buck than most two-year programs (even at Ivy League schools.) " Similarly, the school's twenty-three-month Professional MBA is "perfect for busy, working professionals." Designed for students with a minimum of three years in the workforce, "the location and times are extremely convenient and the cost is very reasonable," making it an affordable way to boost your career prospects in Bowling Green.

While convenience and value are large part of the equation, students assure us that practicality isn't the only reason they chose BGSU. For many, the school's small size and community atmosphere is a major draw. Here, the administration is accessible, and the school is "very well-run and very user-friendly." A current student shares: "I have had a very positive experience working with everyone in the college from the secretaries to the dean." Thanks to uniformly small class sizes, students are "encouraged to work with our fellow students through group projects and presentations." A current student adds, "We have a well-rounded cohort and the class spends a lot of time debating all kinds of issues relating to the material." No matter which program you enter, you'll benefit from friendly professors, who "share a love and enthusiasm for teaching as well as helping their students to [achieve] success." Providing both rigor and support, "the program is challenging (as it should be), but the professors are encouraging, treat us as professionals, and make themselves available outside of class and office hours to aid in our success." Successful in the real world—not just the ivory tower—Bowling Green's "knowledgeable and friendly" faculty "consistently incorporate[s] useful information and real-life scenarios into their instruction, making each class valuable to my future career." A student in the Professional MBA program agrees: "Even though I've been working for over twenty-five years, I have taken away a good deal of information to apply on the job." Despite the strength of the curriculum, some would like the school to offer "more areas of specialization." (Currently, BGSU offers three areas of concentration in accounting, finance, and supply chain management.)

In addition to the full-time and part-time programs at Bowling Green, the Executive MBA Program gets top marks from seasoned professionals, who say "the course work is very challenging and stimulating" and "professors are extremely knowledgeable and friendly." To make everything smooth and simple, "all course registration and book purchases are handled by the staff for the Executive MBA program, easing the burden on working professionals." While EMBA students "only spend Friday, Saturday and Sunday on campus once a month," they say, "Subjects are taught on task and time is used wisely."

Career and Placement

Most students in the Professional and Executive MBA programs are already working full time when they begin the program at Bowling Green, and therefore, many are not actively seeking employment. For full-time students, career planning is woven into the curriculum at Bowling Green State University through practical courses in leadership, technology, and other applied skills, as well as a series of professional development seminars. Through the business school, students may also contact career development specialists to help them with their job search.

In addition to the assistance they receive within the business school, the Bowling Green State University Career Center assists the undergraduate and graduate community with their job search through career counseling, job and internship fairs, campus recruiting, and career development workshops.

Student Life and Environment

For Professional MBA students, "classes are not held on the main campus, but rather at a newly renovated, state-of-the-art complex that is approximately twenty-five miles north of the main campus." This facility is "convenient, well-maintained," and offers "full access to all technology (wireless web access, software, printers, etc.) to ensure success." Even though they attend school off-site, part-time students say, "The administration office does a good job of keeping us informed of what is happening on campus." Unfortunately, most part-time students agree that between "working full time and going to school two nights a week, plus homework and reading, there is no time left for other club activities."

On the main campus, "the business school has made great strides in improving facilities," though some would like the school to improve the "building appearance and technology amenities" in the classrooms. Full-time students benefit from "an active student body" and "a diverse array of activities on campus such as sporting events that we can access for free." On campus and in the surrounding town, there are "a lot of students to socialize with." On that note, students say Bowling Green "is very much a college town, with a good bar scene" and an affordable cost of living.

Admissions

To apply to BGSU's graduate business programs, students must submit an application form, an official undergraduate transcript, GMAT scores, a resume, and two professional recommendations. The school also requests a personal statement, outlining the applicant's objectives in pursuing an MBA and explaining how they might contribute to the program. In some cases, applicants to the Executive MBA who have extensive work experience (ten years or more) may be exempt from submitting GMAT scores.

FINANCIAL FACTS

Annual tuition (in-state/ out-of-state)	$15,252/$26,214
Fees	$2,745
Cost of books	$1,500
% of students receiving aid	46
% of first-year students receiving aid	46
% of students receiving grants	46
Average award package	$15,126
Average grant	$10,545

ADMISSIONS

Admissions Selectivity Rating	87
# of applications received	270
% applicants accepted	50
% acceptees attending	94
Average GMAT	531
Range of GMAT	460–598
Accepts GRE scores	Yes
Average GPA	3.3
TOEFL required of international students	Yes
Minimum TOEFL (paper/web)	550/80
Application fee	$45
International application fee	$75
Early application deadline	2/1
Regular application deadline	3/1
Deferment available	Yes
Maximum length of deferment	1 year
Transfer students accepted	Yes
Transfer application policy Students in the MBA programs (full-time, professional, and executive) are limited to a maximum of nine graduate credit hours of transfer credit from AACSB accredited institutions.	
Non-fall admissions	Yes
Need-blind admissions	Yes

EMPLOYMENT PROFILE

Career Rating	77	Grads Employed by Function% Avg. Salary
Average base starting salary	$51,500	Top 5 Employers Hiring Grads
Primary Source of Full-time Job Acceptances		Marathon Petroleum Corporation (4)
School-facilitated activities	3 (%)	
Graduate-facilitated activities	19 (%)	
Unknown	57 (%)	

BRANDEIS UNIVERSITY
BRANDEIS INTERNATIONAL BUSINESS SCHOOL

GENERAL INFORMATION
Type of school	Private
Affiliation	Nonsectarian
	Jewish-sponsored college
Academic calendar	Semester

SURVEY SAYS...
Friendly students, Liberal students, Abundant mentors available, Happy students, Abundant clubs and activities
Solid preparation in:
Marketing, Finance, General management, Teamwork, Communication/interpersonal skills, Presentation skills, Quantitative skills, Doing business in a global economy, Environmental sustainability

STUDENTS
Enrollment of parent institution	336
Enrollment of MBA Program	57
% male/female	63/37
% part-time	2
% international	82
Average age at entry	27
Average years work experience at entry	4

ACADEMICS
Academic Experience Rating	89
Profs interesting rating	94
Profs accessible rating	92
Student/faculty ratio	11:1
% female faculty	26
% part-time faculty	54

Joint Degrees
BA/MA

Prominent Alumni
Yoni Balan, Global Business Development at Kronos; David Katsnelson, Director, Macroeconomics at RISI; Varun Seth, Account Director at Ogilvy & Mather, New Delhi

Academics

At Brandeis International Business School (IBS), "learning is not limited to theoretical concepts. Keeping education connected to the real world of business and policy is an integral part of the IBS experience." The University offers students a "strong foundation in economics and finance." Moreover, Brandeis is renowned for its "global focus," and MBA candidates here are privy to "a truly global platform for professionals who seek advancement in international business." Indeed, many people here greatly appreciate that the school "has students from more than seventy countries." It provides an "excellent cultural mix" and "terrific exposure [to other] cultures." Overall, the "academic rigor can be quite high, but it, in part, depends on what course load you choose to take and how much you want to challenge yourself."

Importantly, Brandeis students are full of praise for their professors. Certainly, they "are well respected in their fields" and are "always available to provide further guidance." And one content second year student adds, "The professors are very friendly, extremely smart, and are concerned that we graduate with a great job. The open-door policy is very true." This admiration also extends to Brandeis' administration. As a first year student happily shares, "The administration is very proactive in organizing the events at the college and making sure that everyone participates in these events." And another second-year student quickly follows up stating, "Whatever you want to get done, the school's administration will help you achieve it."

Career and Placement

Brandeis' IBS Career Center strives to help their students land plum internships and employment opportunities. The office provides a number of services, from access to online libraries and databases to career education and advising. Students frequently take advantage of mock interview lessons, company information sessions, and panel presentations. Additionally, there are a handful of networking events, the culmination of which is the school's annual on-campus career fair. Of course, despite the Career Center's best efforts, many students wish they would be more proactive about attracting more companies. As one first-year student shared, "Although the Career Services Office does a great job, the possibilities to get paid internships are limited. From my point of view, most local and small companies recruit here." Additionally, a second-year student chimes in that he'd like to see "job placement increase for international students in the United States." However, an optimistic and hopeful student counters, "It is definitely a young school, but the rate that we are growing with the intelligent people graduating from here, in a few years we will have a larger alumni network of extremely successful professionals, who will carry the Brandeis IBS name throughout the world as a premier education in international business."

Companies which have recruited at Brandeis IBS include: Apple, Accenture, BlackRock, Bloomberg LP, Care.com, comScore, Inc, Cornerstone Research, Dassault Systemes, Deloitte, EMC, Ernst & Young, Facebook, Fidelity, Goldman Sachs, Google, HSBC, IBM, Infor, JP Morgan, Chase, Kimberly-Clark, KPMG, Moody's Analytics, NERA Economic Consulting, PricewaterhouseCoopers, Santander, State Street, Takeda Pharmaceuticals, UBS, Wilson Sporting Goods, World Bank.

Student Life and Environment

If pressed to describe their peers in one word, most MBA candidates at Brandeis would define their fellow students as "diverse." Indeed, the program is "hugely international," and "everyone here is open to new experiences." By and large, people find their classmates "cooperative" and "collaborative." And one second year breathes a sigh of relief explaining, "They are friendly, and the environment is encouraging as opposed to competitive." One slightly chagrined student does note that "the average student age is younger than I had expected." Another student concurs, adding that some classmates are "a bit too young and a bit too inexperienced to be in business school." Others disagree and quickly assert that their fellow students "bring interesting perspectives" and argue that there are plenty of "people with different professional backgrounds [to] enrich discussions." Perhaps this student sums up his peers best: "They are people I want to spend time with outside of the school."

Life at Brandeis moves "very fast." Students are "constantly multi-tasking between class work, group projects, and club events." Certainly there is much to participate in. As one MBA candidate highlights, "There are lots of clubs, and importantly, lots of opportunities of opening ones on your own. TGIFs and group activities at the International Business School are a good time to get together and relax after pretty stressful and hectic (although rewarding and energizing at the same time) study weeks at Brandeis." Additionally, students love to take advantage of Brandeis' proximity to Boston. As one student reveals, "Access to Boston is great. The school helps out on the weekend by providing busses, which run later than public transportation."

Admissions

Though Brandeis' MBA program is relatively new, competition for that coveted acceptance letter is still fierce. The admissions committee is on the hunt for applicants who can demonstrate both a keen analytical ability and proven leadership skills. Additionally, admissions officers will carefully assess your undergraduate record and expect strong GMAT or GRE scores. Further, given the curriculum and the makeup of the student body, it's important to display an interest in international issues. It is recommended that applicants have at least two years of work experience. Finally, international students will need to take the TOEFL exam. A score of 100 on the iBT TOEFL is required.

FINANCIAL FACTS

Annual tuition	$49,841
Fees	$132
Cost of books	$1,400
Room & board	$13,632
% of students receiving aid	83
% of first-year students receiving aid	80
% of students receiving grants	83
Average award package	$20,619
Average grant	$19,457
Average loan	$11,152
Average student loan debt	$22,876

ADMISSIONS

Admissions Selectivity Rating	84
# of applications received	95
% applicants accepted	64
% acceptees attending	29
Average GMAT	613
Range of GMAT	500–690
Accepts GRE scores	Yes
Average Verbal GRE	156
Range of Verbal GRE scores	150–157
Average Quantitative GRE	156
Range of Quantitative GRE scores	149–162
Average GPA	3.3
TOEFL required of international students	Yes
Minimum TOEFL (paper/web)	600/100
Application fee	$100
International application fee	$100
Application Deadline/Notification	
Round 1:	11/1 / 12/11
Round 2:	1/15 / 2/26
Round 3:	3/15 / 4/26
Round 4:	5/1 / 5/31
Deferment available	Yes
Maximum length of deferment	1 year
Transfer students accepted	Yes
Transfer application policy	
Transfer applicants are considered for admission but transfer credit is not awarded for courses taken at other institutions.	
Non-fall admissions	No
Need-blind admissions	Yes

EMPLOYMENT PROFILE

		Grads Employed by Function	% Avg. Salary
Career Rating	83		
Percent employed at graduation	20	Marketing	(25%) $58,750
Percent employed 3 months after graduation	47	Operations	(6%)
		Consulting	(31%) $67,000
Average base starting salary	$64,357	Finance	(19%)
Primary Source of Full-time Job Acceptances		Other	(19%) $50,000
School-facilitated activities	4 (17%)	**Top 5 Employers Hiring Grads**	
Graduate-facilitated activities	12 (52%)	PWC (3), Apple (1), Capital One (1), Kronos	
Unknown	7 (31%)	(1), Santander (1)	

BRIGHAM YOUNG UNIVERSITY
MARRIOTT SCHOOL OF MANAGEMENT

Academics

BYU's Marriott School of Management "boasts one of the strongest brands among MBA programs in the nation." And it's easy to understand why! From the moment future MBAs saunter onto the campus, it's evident that the school "is dedicated to the development of its students." What's more, it has "a great reputation for producing leaders who are ethical [and] competent" and individuals who will surely make a difference. And while the "courses are academically rigorous" students appreciate that they're "not filled with busy work or pointless repetitive exercises." Instead, there's a healthy "blend of cases and lectures" which we're told "works very well."

Of course, Marriott School also provides stellar instruction. Indeed, "the professors are drawn from top universities and businesses from around the world." And as one grateful student reveals, "Most of them are making significant sacrifices to teach at BYU over more lucrative private sector options. That means they care deeply about their students and will do almost anything to help each one succeed. A fellow MBA agrees adding, "This afternoon I was in an adjunct professor's office, who also works as a CEO, who spent over an hour connecting me to his network, polishing my job-hunt strategy and more." Perhaps this content student sums up the Marriott School experience best, "There are few people that I respect in the world as much as the professors and administrators that I have met here at BYU. They are considerate of our interests, extremely intelligent, and great role models in both academia and family life."

Career and Placement

Students are certainly drawn to BYU for its phenomenal job placement rates. A graduating MBA immediately concurs boasting, "I chose this school because it has stellar placement; I knew that I could get a job at a Fortune 500 after coming out." And it's clear that the administration strives to ensure this continual success. For example, there are a myriad of "programs in place for student mentoring to ensure the highest quality internships." A Marriott School student further explains, "Career services has an amazing program called the Sherpa Program where they hire forty second-years to help and mentor first years on their internship search." Moreover, MBA hopefuls fortunate enough to become part of the BYU family join "an amazing network of alumni who have successful careers and are [always] willing to lend a hand." As another astonished student concludes, "Months before I started business school, students began to reach out to me to help me prepare for school, networking, and the job search."

ADMISSIONS CONTACT: YVETTE ANDERSON, MBA PROGRAM ADMISSION COORDINATOR
ADDRESS: W437D, TANNER BUILDING, PROVO, UT 84602
PHONE: 801-422-3500 • FAX: 801-422-0513
E-MAIL: MBA@BYU.EDU • WEBSITE: MBA.BYU.EDU

Student Life and Environment

Marriott School manages to attract "smart, hard working and business savvy people that you can trust." Indeed, students here describe their peers as "people you would want to go into business with." Importantly, though they strive for success "students do not try to achieve…at the expense of their fellow classmates. Much to the contrary, we will help each other and thereby elevate the success of all in the program. It's truly amazing to see." A second year student agrees stating, "Students are very collaborative and willing to help each other whether it's studying or finding a job."

Just as important to Marriott School MBAs, "family is definitely central to the student life at BYU." Indeed, "clothing exchanges, family dinners, sporting events, parties, etc. are all available for families." Fortunately, we're assured that "activities are well-balanced between families, couples, and singles." And there's plenty of which to take advantage. For example, "the MBA program threw a tailgate party for the big BYU/U of U football game, the international students have held a Chinese New Years celebration, we've had a Indian Holi festival off campus, gone sledding, [etc.]." Additionally, there's "an event called Tanner Thursday where we are encouraged to network with students and faculty in the program to get to know them better and also have set up lunch with the director of the program." All in all, "there is never a week where an MBA student or their family would want for things to do."

Admissions

When it comes to assessing applicants, admissions officers at the Marriott School of Management take a holistic approach. Indeed, they consider both academic and professional accomplishments and weigh those against a candidate's potential to contribute to the Marriott School community. Admissions officers are also on the lookout for individuals who possess both strong leadership and teamwork skills. All in all, they want students who will fit in with and benefit from BYU.

FINANCIAL FACTS

Annual tuition	$11,970
Cost of books	$1,772
Room & board	
(on/off-campus)	$12,088/$12,088
% of students receiving grants	80
Average grant	$7,430
Average loan	$14,478

ADMISSIONS

Admissions Selectivity Rating	90
# of applications received	420
% applicants accepted	48
% acceptees attending	80
Average GMAT	674
Range of GMAT	640–710
Accepts GRE scores	No
Average GPA	3.5
TOEFL required of	
international students	Yes
Minimum TOEFL	
(paper/web)	590/94
Application fee	$50
International application fee	$50
Early application deadline	12/1
Regular application deadline	5/1
Application Deadline	
Round 1:	12/1
Round 2:	1/15
Round 3:	3/1
Round 4:	5/1
Deferment available	Yes
Maximum length of	
deferment	2 years
Transfer students accepted	Yes
Transfer application policy	
15 credit hours of approved grad-	
uate-level courses, no pass/fail	
grades, and a minimum grade of B	
Non-fall admissions	No
Need blind admissions	Yes

EMPLOYMENT PROFILE

Career Rating	96	Grads Employed by Function% Avg. Salary	
Percent employed at graduation	84	Marketing	(28%) $103,866
Percent employed 3 months		Operations	(15%) $103,100
after graduation	92	Consulting	(6%) $127,143
Average base starting salary	$102,793	Management	(9%) $104,982
Primary Source of Full-time Job Acceptances		Finance	(16%) $101,292
School-facilitated activities	85 (69%)	HR	(21%) $95,863
Graduate-facilitated activities	38 (31%)	Other	(4%) $95,580
Unknown	0 (0%)	Top 5 Employers Hiring Grads	

Top 5 Employers Hiring Grads
Amazon.com Inc. (10), Adobe Systems Incorporated (8), Microsoft Corporation (8), Intel Corporation (6), PwC LLP (6)

BROCK UNIVERSITY
GOODMAN SCHOOL OF BUSINESS

GENERAL INFORMATION
Type of school	Public
Affiliation	No Affiliation
Academic calendar	Semester

SURVEY SAYS...
Friendly students, Students love St.
Catharines, ON
Solid preparation in:
Accounting, Teamwork,
Communication/interpersonal skills,
Presentation skills

STUDENTS
Enrollment of parent institution	18,512
Enrollment of MBA Program	94
% part-time	36
% international	11
Average age at entry	26
Average years work experience at entry	4

ACADEMICS
Academic Experience Rating	**72**
Profs interesting rating	68
Profs accessible rating	67
% female faculty	27

Academics

Boasting "an excellent reputation for its business degree, especially in accounting," Ontario's Goodman School of Business offers "a great learning environment with many opportunities" to a youngish student body. Because it's a relatively new program, the Brock MBA is especially open to innovation; students praise the curriculum for "encouraging fresh ideas" and the faculty for its "innovative approaches to teaching."

MBAs also love Goodman's "small class sizes, which enable professors to recognize students' strengths and weaknesses and permit students to approach professors when they need help. It is a relaxed learning environment" in which "an atmosphere of trust between students and school personnel" prevails. Goodman profs "are knowledgeable and well-respected in their fields" and "do an exceptional job of presenting the material in an attention-grabbing style." Students appreciate how their instructors "always have time to talk outside of class and are extremely helpful."

The Goodman MBA includes a sequence of required courses and an option for specialization in one of seven "streams": accounting, CPA/MBA, business analytics, finance, human resource management, marketing, or operations management. Students may also opt for a general MBA. Students may choose to replace up to three of their specialization courses with independent research projects; such projects are subject to the approval of the dean and the MBA Committee. Students may attend on a full-time or part-time basis. The full-time degree can be completed in two years; the part-time degree must be completed within six years. Part-timers who adhere to the suggested schedule—two courses during each of the Fall and Winter terms, one course during the Spring term—can finish the program in four years.

Career and Placement

The Goodman School of Business at Brock University maintains a Career Development Office to serve all undergraduates and graduates enrolled at the faculty. The office manages the Graduate Recruitment Program for MBA students; through this program, students have access to employer information sessions and on-campus interviews. A Career Expo in the fall brings employers to campus for recruiting purposes. The office also offers resume review, interviewing and job search workshops, online job search tools, and assistance with international job placement. Brock offers a co-op MBA to students who are at the university for at least two semesters of study (beginning in the fall term) and who maintain at least a 75 average in the program. The co-op provides access to additional workshops, seminars, and a speaker series in addition to co-op placement. The program is open to international students.

Student Life and Environment

Goodman's student body "is extremely diverse," with "many international students [who arrive] through the International Student Program and through exchanges." Students also bring "a diverse set of experiences" to the program: "Some students come to the program with many years of experience, while others bring a more academic perspective to the program." Some feel the balance needs to shift in this area, reporting that "way too many students have no work experience and are straight out of undergrad." Everyone agrees that "some here, especially the part-time students, have great work experience and input to contribute."

Brock's student-run Graduate Business Council "does an excellent job of giving us opportunities to connect outside of the classroom. They organize pub nights and socials as well as organize us to compete in business case competitions." Campus amenities include "state-of-the-art" gymnasiums, fitness centers, an Olympic size swimming pool, squash and tennis courts, outdoor fields, and a hiking trail system that runs through campus and beyond, leading to the Niagara Escarpment. Students report that school facilities "are great for athletics, food, and study areas."

Hometown St. Catharines, located a mere twelve miles from Niagara Falls and just seventy miles from Toronto, "has a great lifestyle," with "tons of trendy nightclubs in St. Catharines and Niagara Falls." Students describe the overall vibe as "easy-going" with "not too much hustle and bustle," which they ascribe to "the nature of being located in St. Catharines." The city is accommodating enough that "many students spend a lot of time off campus."

Admissions

Admission to the MBA program at Goodman is based on five main criteria. The quality of one's undergraduate education is most important; Brock seeks students with at least a 3.0 undergraduate GPA. A minimum GMAT score of 550 is required, as are three letters of recommendation from professors and/or supervisors at work; a personal statement; and a resume. Applications are assessed holistically; strength in one area may be sufficient to compensate for weaknesses elsewhere, according to the school's website. Professional experience, though preferred, is not required. Those whose first language is not English must demonstrate English proficiency through the TOEFL or IELTS.

FINANCIAL FACTS

Annual tuition (in-state/ out-of-state)	$11,255/$21,978
Fees	$345
Cost of books	$1,000
Room & board (on/off-campus)	$10,000/$10,000
% of students receiving aid	15
% of first-year students receiving aid	15
% of students receiving grants	15

ADMISSIONS

Admissions Selectivity Rating	86
# of applications received	133
% applicants accepted	60
% acceptees attending	63
Average GMAT	603
Range of GMAT	540–680
Accepts GRE scores	No
Average GPA	3.5
TOEFL required of international students	Yes
Minimum TOEFL (paper/web)	620/105
Application fee	$125
International application fee	$125
Regular application deadline	8/1
Regular application notification	8/15
Deferment available	Yes
Maximum length of deferment	One year.
Transfer students accepted	Yes
Transfer application policy All transfer applications must submit the same documentation as regular applicants. Their transcripts are assessed for transfer credits (up to 10) during the admissions review process.	
Non-fall admissions	Yes
Need-blind admissions	Yes

EMPLOYMENT PROFILE

Career Rating	93	Top 5 Employers Hiring Grads
Percent employed at graduation	60	Royal Bank of Canada, CIBC, ScotiaBank,
Percent employed 3 months after graduation	93	Hydro One, Loblaw Co.
Average base starting salary	$78,500	

BRYANT UNIVERSITY
GRADUATE SCHOOL OF BUSINESS

Academics

Bryant University's MBA program is "designed with working professionals in mind," according to the school, and students report that the school definitely lives up to this reputation. The "structured part-time program [makes] it easy to balance the rigors of graduate study with the reality of maintaining a full-time job," one student explains.

The part-time MBA at Bryant is structured as a cohort program, "where students are accepted to the school as a class and move through the entire program together." Students complete all core courses as part of a single team (although "some professors allow teams to change members") before "becoming separated in electives." Most students find the cohort system a huge plus, saying it promotes "a lower dropout rate, better student interaction, and deeper relationships and networks with students." One writes, "The cohort approach is excellent. I have built great relationships with my fellow students, and teachers are in tune with where classes stand in the learning process, making the flow from semester to semester seamless."

Bryant recently added a full-time one-year program. The first class graduated in 2010, and some members say of their experience, "Being the first year there were some kinks, but they have tried to put together a program that is not only academically beneficial but also gives us some real-world exposure."

Students note that "Bryant has a very good reputation" in the region. Professors "have industry experience, they are not only theoretical or academic," and most "are enthusiastic...the passion they exude filters throughout the class." Administrators "are very open and approachable. We recently voted on electives, and there is one that wasn't selected. Instead of being stuck, the dean is setting aside time to consider how we might be able to add the course. I've been very pleased that this type of response has been the norm [for] any issues that arise and not just a glowing example." Academically, "the environment is challenging, yet fair, and [students are] well-supported. It is a great investment." As one student sums up, "Overall Bryant is probably the best value MBA in New England outside of Cambridge/Boston. The campus is very clean and safe, the professors are all gray hairs with decades of experience in the real world, and the library and gym facilities are exceptional."

Career and Placement

The Amica Center for Career Education serves the undergraduate students, graduate students, and alumni of Bryant University. The office provides counseling services, assessment instruments, and workshops on resume writing, interviewing, and job-search skills. The Center maintains a career services library and facilitates contact with alumni through the school's Alumni Career Network. It should be noted that the Bryant MBA is designed for working professionals, many of whom are looking to improve their positions with their current employers rather than seeking new jobs. The school draws students from a number of local employers, including Amgen, Amica Mutual Insurance, Citizens Bank, Davol, Fidelity Investments, Gilbane Building Company, Perot Systems, Rogers Corporation, Stanley Bostich, Tyco Healthcare, and Zebra Technologies.

Student Life and Environment

Located in "a safe rural setting," Bryant's campus is "beautiful and inviting, not too big but not too small." "All the buildings and grounds are maintained impeccably," one student reports. The campus is also "on the cutting edge of technology," with "every room completely equipped." Bryant has an active undergraduate campus life, but opinion is mixed on the extent to which Bryant MBAs take advantage. Some students observe that "Students in the graduate program are very removed from the undergraduate programs and students. For the most part, graduate students are not involved in campus life, although attendance is high at 'graduate only' events. Most graduate students do not get involved with campus organizations," though all this may change in coming years as the full-time, one-year MBA program expands. On the other hand, a student in the one-year program notes that "Life at Bryant is very community-focused. The school tries to involve all students in all activities, such as on-campus presenters, homecoming activities, etc."

Though the extent of graduate student involvement on campus might be up for debate, the on-campus diversity is not. There's "a really strong multicultural element" at Bryant. In the part-time program, "students range in age from early twenties to late fifties," and many have "more than ten years of business experience. The diversity of professional backgrounds brings an added element to the class, as we have many engineers in the program." Students tend to be "competitive" and "like to challenge one another to promote and foster positive results. It's a very team-orientated program."

Admissions

Applicants to graduate programs at Bryant University must provide the Admissions Department with the following materials: a completed application form; a personal statement of objectives (no less than 500 words long); a current resume; one letter of recommendation from a professional who can evaluate your skills and potential; official transcripts for all previous undergraduate and graduate work (regardless of whether it resulted in a degree); and an official GMAT score report. In addition to the above, international students must also provide a statement of finances, professional translation and interpretation of any foreign language transcripts, and, for those whose first language is not English and who did not earn an undergraduate degree from an English-speaking institution, an official TOEFL score report. An interview is "strongly encouraged."

FINANCIAL FACTS

Annual tuition (in-state/ out-of-state)	$37,304/$37,304
Cost of books	$1,200
Room & board	$13,200
% of students receiving aid	33
% of first-year students receiving aid	56
% of students receiving grants	3
Average award package	$29,093
Average grant	$9,624
Average loan	$19,501
Average student loan debt	$30,415

ADMISSIONS
Admissions Selectivity Rating 60*

BUTLER UNIVERSITY
COLLEGE OF BUSINESS

GENERAL INFORMATION
Type of school	Private
Affiliation	No Affiliation
Academic calendar	Semester

SURVEY SAYS...
Classmates have diverse work experience, Friendly students, Conservative students, Happy students, Students love Indianapolis, IN
Solid preparation in:
Marketing, Finance, General management, Teamwork, Communication/interpersonal skills, Quantitative skills, Doing business in a global economy

STUDENTS
Enrollment of parent institution	4,500
Enrollment of MBA Program	155
% male/female	75/25
% out-of-state	0
% part-time	98
% underrepresented minority	0
% international	0
Average age at entry	29
Average years work experience at entry	7

ACADEMICS
Academic Experience Rating	89
Profs interesting rating	92
Profs accessible rating	95
Student/faculty ratio	25:1
% female faculty	17
% underrepresented minority faculty	6
% part-time faculty	44

Joint Degrees
PharmD/MBA

Prominent Alumni
Lynda Smirz, VP & Chief Med Officer, Acute Care Div, Universal Health Services; Hugh Lytle, President & CEO, Univita Health; Dennis Bassett, CEO, Indiana, Ohio & Kentucky region, JP Morgan Chase

Academics

Boasting a "broad program to introduce students to all business specialties," Butler's focus on "applying real world experiences to the classroom" provides an MBA experience that makes it "very popular" for residents of the region. Flexibility is key here. As one student notes, "If you want a concentration that is not offered, professors will work with you to tailor your education needs/wishes." Concentrations are offered in finance, international business, leadership, entrepreneurship and innovation, and marketing, though students must also take a core curriculum. This is launched by the Gateway Experience, a full day foray into the operations of a local business followed by student analysis. That sort of experience is typical of what students at Butler will enjoy; "executive mentors (are) provided," and professors "have been around the block a time or two," ensuring that this program "attracts a diversely experienced student body."

If flexibility is a hallmark of Butler's education, so is balance. Expect a "good balance of difficult and moderately easy classes." As one student noted, in some classes, "I didn't need to open the book but in some courses I read every page of the book." A helpful, "responsive" administration is a frequent target for praise among students. Administrators here "don't ignore you and always try to be helpful," ensuring they "work with students on every aspect. A large school wouldn't do that, but Butler does." This school's leadership "is very willing to make integrating the learning experience with busy careers and family lives" a priority, and it shows in the number of students who juggle active careers and busy class schedules. "They work with students to make sure they are successful while considering students' personal lives."

"Real life business application in the classroom is integral to learning at Butler," an approach led by "both adjunct and tenured professors who offer a balance of real world work experience as well as strong academic thought." Some students, whose comments largely focused on fill-in teachers, note that there are "one or two bad apples," but overall educators here "will really push you to learn stuff practical to the modern business world."

Career and Placement

For students in the Midwest in particular, Butler provides good inroads to a career. "Being in the program is helpful for networking with people in other companies (big and small) around Indianapolis," one student commented. When Forbes recently ranked the 200 largest metropolitan areas in the United States to determine which were the best places for business and careers, Indianapolis ranked in the top ten. That is a major help with job prospects. "There are thousands of top companies right in our backyard," a student noted. With opportunities to get hands-on experience with many of these companies and "guests that bring relevant speakers to class," Butler students enjoy good exposure to strong employers.

Butler's MBA graduates have gone on to work for companies such as Eli Lilly and Company, Roche, M&I Bank, Regions Bank, Firestone, and the NCAA.

ADMISSIONS CONTACT: STEPHANIE JUDGE, DIRECTOR OF MARKETING
ADDRESS: COLLEGE OF BUSINESS, 4600 SUNSET AVENUE, INDIANAPOLIS, IN 46208-3485
PHONE: 317-940-9221 • FAX: 317-940-9455
E-MAIL: MBA@BUTLER.EDU • WEBSITE: WWW.BUTLERMBA.COM

Student Life and Environment

Students who want to be surrounded by those with real life experience will find Butler to be a welcoming environment. Butler attendees are "generally about thirty years old and at the experienced or manager status in their careers," though they can "range from just out of undergrad to sixty years old." Working full-time while also attending classes is common. As one student noted, "Nearly all of my classmates had full time careers, so life at school was typically limited to class." Professions, ethnicities, and educational backgrounds vary, but a consistent trait is that students here are "committed, smart and friendly." Even though "most of the people have families and outside lives that are a priority when they aren't at work or in class," Butler students will still "get together for group projects, and occasionally socially." For those interested in connecting with their school in a way that extends beyond the classroom, "the MBA Association does a good job providing for opportunities to connect with peers, faculty, staff, business professionals and alumni."

Though there can be a competitive streak among some on campus—hardly unusual for an MBA program— "fellow students are more supportive than competitive; people are down to earth and have a good sense of humor." The "personable and great classmates" students work alongside come from "very different backgrounds and experiences, yet everyone has an incredibly strong work ethic." Students, especially those in the night programs, may have much to deal with outside the classroom, but in the classroom "we enjoy working in groups together." Some graduates say they "have developed some great lifelong friendships."

Admissions

Expect your undergraduate GPA, GMAT score, letters of recommendation, and work experience to be important when it comes to what the Admissions Committee for Butler's MBA program considers. What you have accomplished outside the classroom or work environment is not weighed at all; extracurricular activities are not taken into account in the admissions process. Residency is not a factor—Butler is a private institution—though most students are from the Midwest. The average GPA of recently admitted students was 3.32/4.0 and their GMAT score ranged from 510-680. Most students had seven or more years of work experience.

FINANCIAL FACTS

Fees	$0
Cost of books	$1,000
% of students receiving aid	0
% of first-year students receiving aid	0
% of students receiving grants	0
Average award package	$13,644
Average grant	$10,890
Average loan	$14,719
Average student loan debt	$25,176

ADMISSIONS

Admissions Selectivity Rating	84
# of applications received	49
% applicants accepted	69
% acceptees attending	94
Average GMAT	578
Range of GMAT	500–680
Accepts GRE scores	No
Average GPA	3.3
TOEFL required of international students	Yes
Minimum TOEFL (paper/web)	550/79
Application fee	$0
International application fee	$0
Regular application deadline	8/1
Regular application notification	8/10
Application Deadline/Notification	
Round 1:	8/1 / 8/10
Round 2:	12/1 / 12/15
Round 3:	4/1 / 4/15
Deferment available	Yes
Maximum length of deferment	1 year
Transfer students accepted	Yes
Transfer application policy	
Up to 12 credit hours may transfer - applicant must be transferring from an AACSB accredited institution with a letter of good standing from program.	
Non-fall admissions	Yes
Need-blind admissions	Yes

CALIFORNIA POLYTECHNIC STATE UNIVERSITY, SAN LUIS OBISPO
ORFALEA COLLEGE OF BUSINESS

Academics

Poised at the intersection of business and technology, California Polytechnic State University's graduate business programs are a great choice for students with a background in applied science or architecture. As a state school, Cal Poly is "less expensive" than comparable private institutions, yet its AACSB-accredited business programs are rigorous, current, and intimate, enrolling fewer than fifty students each year. The MBA comprises sixty to sixty-four total credits for graduation; depending on your schedule, availability, and academic goals, students have "the option for one- or two-year completion" of the MBA, with an academic focus in general management, agribusiness, or graphic communication document systems management. The chance to complete a specialized MBA in just one year—even without an undergraduate degree in business—is a huge advantage to this program. At the same time, students must be prepared to work hard: not only is coursework challenging and accelerated, "the program requires students [to] maintain a 3.0 GPA" throughout. For working students who want to pursue a degree part-time, or for those who'd like to explore concurrent employment or internship opportunities, Cal Poly also allows students to take fewer than the full-time 16 units per quarter, through a secondary MBA track.

For many, the major benefit of Cal Poly is its strength in technical fields, which students can exploit through technology-oriented electives, or through formal dual degree programs with other academic departments. Of particular note, the school offers joint MS and MBA degrees in engineering management and engineering fields (including aerospace, civil and environmental, computer science, and more). Almost 40 percent of current MBA candidates are concurrently enrolled in a master's program, telling us that, "the dual degree program is fantastic" at Cal Poly. A current student adds, "The MBA/EMP dual degree program they offer was exactly the type of program that I was looking for, and Cal Poly has a tremendous reputation in the world of engineering."

A hallmark of the Cal Poly MBA program is the "learning-by-doing teaching style," which encourages students to develop applicable skills through coursework. To that end, classes and assignments include teamwork, case studies, and presentations. Additionally, the "international business course"—a unique offering within an accelerated program—gives students the opportunity to study a foreign economy and business practices during a two-week trip overseas. In recent years, the program took students to India and China. Students can also tailor their education by pursuing research projects in conjunction with Cal Poly faculty, or by competing with other business students in national case study and strategy competitions. When it comes to Cal Poly's faculty and administration, it's a mixed bag. Here, "there are some professors that are outstanding, and some that are good in their field, but not good at teaching." A student summarizes, "It's a cliché, but the more effort you put into the program, the more you will get out of the program."

Career and Placement

At Cal Poly, Career Services hosts career fairs and networking events for the entire school community. They also offer career preparation assistance, including resume revisions and interview skills workshops. While graduate students are free to participate in these offerings, "the career services are more geared towards undergrads" at Cal Poly. Fortunately, the school boasts an excellent reputation and strong ties to the local community. Even without extensive assistance, around 85 percent of Cal Poly students have accepted a job offer by graduation; three months out, 100 percent of MBA alumni are employed.

Top employers of Cal Poly MBA graduates include Northrup Grumman, Raytheon, Rantec, General Dynamics, Sun MicroSystems, Deloitte Consulting, Qualcomm, IBM, Agilent Technology, Amgen Inc., Lawrence Livermore Labs, Pacific Gas & Electric, USDA, Dept of Veterans Affairs, KPMG, Pratt & Whitney, Morgan Stanley, Boston Scientific, PriceWaterhouseCoopers, Sandia National Lab, Lam Research, Columbia Sportswear, Adelaida Cellars. The mean base salary for MBA graduates is $100,000.

Student Life and Environment

Life is good at Cal Poly. Located on a hilltop overlooking San Luis Obispo, "the college campus is gorgeous" and the surrounding town is beautiful, friendly, and student-oriented. No wonder many students say "the location" is among the Cal Poly's greatest assets. Graduate students have access to the school's excellent recreation center, health center, and library, and they may even choose to live on campus. Within the business school, the Graduate Students in Business Association (GSBA) organizes social gatherings for students and faculty, as well as fundraisers and professional development events.

Cal Poly offers just a few graduate programs; therefore "the undergrads overwhelmingly outnumber the graduate students" on campus. Fortunately, "the Graduate School of Business students have their own Room/Lounge with a fridge, microwave, tables, computers, and whiteboards"—a nice enclave for the more mature crowd. At Cal Poly, most MBA candidates are "young, career-driven" professionals, principally from technical or engineering backgrounds.

Admissions

To be eligible for admission to Cal Poly's Orfalea College of Business graduate programs, students must possess an undergraduate degree from an accredited university, and a competitive undergraduate GPA and GMAT scores. For accepted applicants, the mid-80 percent GPA range was 2.8 to 3.75; for GMAT scores, the mid-80 percent range was 580 to 750. To be eligible for dual degree programs, students must meet the eligibility requirements for both programs.

Prominent Alumni

Robert Rowell, President, Golden State Warriors; Linda Ozawa Olds, Founder, Jamba Juice; Bill Swanson, Chairman & CEO, Raytheon Company; Burt Rutan, Pres., Scaled Composites, designer SpaceShipOne; Gary Bloom, CEO, Veritas

FINANCIAL FACTS

Annual tuition (in-state/ out-of-state)	$7,356/$19,260
Fees	$9,897
Cost of books	$1,638
Room & board (on/off-campus)	$9,846/$9,846
% of students receiving aid	40
% of first-year students receiving aid	40
% of students receiving grants	30
Average award package	$18,776
Average grant	$6,713
Average loan	$16,690

ADMISSIONS

Admissions Selectivity Rating	97
# of applications received	181
% applicants accepted	20
% acceptees attending	86
Average GMAT	640
Range of GMAT	580–750
Accepts GRE scores	Yes
Average GPA	3.4
TOEFL required of international students	Yes
Minimum TOEFL (paper/web)	550/80
Application fee	$55
International application fee	$55
Regular application deadline	7/1
Deferment available	No
Transfer students accepted	Yes
Transfer application policy Maximum of 8 units transfer	
Non-fall admissions	No
Need-blind admissions	Yes

EMPLOYMENT PROFILE	
Career Rating	94
Percent employed at graduation	90
Percent employed 3 months after graduation	95
Average base starting salary	$95,000

CALIFORNIA STATE POLYTECHNIC UNIVERSITY, POMONA
COLLEGE OF BUSINESS ADMINISTRATION

GENERAL INFORMATION
Type of school	Public
Affiliation	No Affiliation
Academic calendar	Quarter

SURVEY SAYS...
Students love Pomona, CA
Solid preparation in:
General management, Teamwork,
Communication/interpersonal skills,
Presentation skills, Computer skills

STUDENTS
Enrollment of parent institution	22,501
Enrollment of MBA Program	107
% part-time	53

ACADEMICS
Academic Experience Rating	**79**
Profs interesting rating	73
Profs accessible rating	75

Academics

The College of Business Administration at California Poly Pomona parlays the university's strengths in engineering and technology into a unique MSBA in Information Systems Auditing, a program that prepares students for careers in computer forensics and information systems security. "It's a nationally-recognized program," students here remind us while insisting we feature it prominently in the school's profile. Consider it done.

Cal Poly also offers a more conventional MBA program, with concentrations available in accounting, finance, marketing, operations management, human resources, hospitality management, entrepreneurship, information management, and international business. Even in its more conventional pursuits, however, the school forges a unique tack. A Cal Poly MBA, students inform us, is a "hands on MBA" with "a technical emphasis" that encourages a "learning-by-doing philosophy." One student explains: "Very few professors will stand in the front of the room and lecture for four hours. Classes are very interactive and students are provided with plenty of opportunities to present their opinions and put learning points to use." Students also report that "all classes require students to work on group projects, which prepares you well to work in teams in real world." Cal Poly also offers a Professional MBA at its Metro in Downtown Los Angeles (minimum two years' supervisory work experience mandatory for entry).

Cal Poly is "one of the few state universities using the quarter system," which "makes things fly by. When you are starting the quarter, you already have to start studying for mid-terms; when mid-quarter arrives, you already have to start seeking for affordable books for the next quarter." Fortunately, the program has "exceptional instructors" who "are mostly young (in their forties) and provide access to modern management principles and practices while at the same timing give information about classical management principles." Good instruction helps ease the academic burden some, but students warn that many here "reduce their work responsibilities to cope with the heavy course load. It's not an easy place for full-time/part-time working professionals."

Career and Placement

Career services for MBAs here are provided by the Cal Poly Pomona Career Center (CPPCC), a central office serving all undergraduate and graduate students at the university. The CPPCC provides all standard counseling and placement services. Many students do not even use the service; they already have jobs that they hope to advance in by earning a graduate degree. One who does complains unequivocally: "The career placement is terrible at Cal Poly for MBA students. Ninety-five percent of companies come in looking for engineers, accountants and some hospitality, and most are only interested in undergrads for entry-level positions. I'm considering crashing a UCI career day just to get referrals." Employers who frequently recruit at Cal Poly include: Bank of America, Boeing, Deloitte, Disneyland Resort, Ernst and Young LLP, IBM, Kaiser Permanente, KPMG International, Merrill Lynch, PricewaterhouseCoopers, Proctor & Gamble, Southern California Edison, and Wells Fargo Bank.

ADMISSIONS CONTACT: HILARY BREEZE, GRADUATE PROGRAMS ADVISOR
ADDRESS: GRADUATE BUSINESS PROGRAM, 3801 WEST TEMPLE AVENUE, POMONA, CA 91768
PHONE: 909-869-2363 • FAX: 909-869-4559
E-MAIL: GBA@CSUPOMONA.EDU • WEBSITE: CBA.CSUPOMONA.EDU

Student Life and Environment

The Cal Poly student body consists of "smart working professionals" who are "very diverse both ethnically and professionally." Their professions "range anywhere from human resources managers to information technology managers to production line managers," and "several *Fortune* 500 companies" are represented here. Academically, the group includes "students who graduated with degrees in engineering, psychology, liberal arts, science, etc." The quality of students has "a significant impact on the class [because they] have plenty of experience to draw from" and "have a lot to say about the subjects that we are learning." Students "raise the bar [for each other] by being very competitive in studies and overall creativity and innovation."

Because most students are "full-time workers and commuters to classes," they typically "do not get too involved with on-campus activities." "MBA students here are more focused on their careers and families then on being connected to the school," one student explains. That's too bad, because the Cal Poly Pomona campus is "beautiful. It's nestled in between mountains and is full of trees," and students tell us that makes it a "good place to study and lead a stress-free life." Perhaps things will change in the years to come; some here already detect a campus that is "transferring from a commuter school to a school with a lot of campus activities. All of the events are getting bigger and better. The exposure of the campus is being seen in the size and popularity of the events."

Admissions

Cal Poly Pomona operates on a quarterly academic schedule; the school accepts MBA applications for each quarter. All of the following components of the application are carefully considered: complete post-secondary academic record as reflected in official transcripts; GMAT scores (must be no more than five years old); two letters of recommendation from current or former employers; and a resume. Applicants who attended an undergraduate institution at which English is not the primary language of instruction must provide official TOEFL scores. Applicants must meet the following criteria to be considered for admission: an overall undergraduate GPA of at least 3.0; a minimum GMAT score of 450; and, if required, TOEFL scores of at least 580 on the paper-and-pencil test, 237 on the computer-based test, or 92 on the Internet-based test. Meeting minimum requirements does not guarantee admission to the program.

FINANCIAL FACTS

Annual tuition (in-state/ out-of-state)	$11,696/$17,648
Room & board (on/off-campus)	$17,226/$15,053

ADMISSIONS

Admissions Selectivity Rating	91
# of applications received	188
% applicants accepted	19
% acceptees attending	50
Average GMAT	547
Range of GMAT	502–580
Accepts GRE scores	No
Average GPA	3.2
TOEFL required of international students	Yes
Minimum TOEFL (paper/web)	580/92
Application fee	$55
International application fee	$55
Deferment available	No
Transfer students accepted	Yes
Transfer application policy Candidates must meet our admission criteria.	
Non-fall admissions	Yes
Need-blind admissions	Yes

CALIFORNIA STATE UNIVERSITY, CHICO
COLLEGE OF BUSINESS

Academics

California State University, Chico offers a practical and personable MBA program, well suited to Northern California professionals. With a "great regional reputation," Chico students feel confident they can leverage their education in the workplace. Above all else, professors have "a lot of relevant industry experience" and offer "good insight into the business world." Across disciplines, Chico professors "keep up with current events," and class content is constantly "changing according to the news today." Chico distinguishes itself academically through a focus on project management, information technology and business information systems. Chico State's innovative Center for Information Systems Research involves students in a variety of hands-on projects in the business technology sector, and the school has been "a member of the SAP alliance" since 1996.

While academics are strong, the environment is remarkably supportive, too. When a student needs extra assistance, professors are "easily accessible" and "always available outside of class." A current student shares, "I have met many professors through independent projects, and they have been very helpful and guided me to the right resources." Throughout the curriculum, there is an "emphasis on teamwork, interpersonal skills, and both qualitative and quantitative learning." Students are encouraged to engage with the work, and "most professors try to create an environment that promotes active discussions." The focus on group work, as well as real world applications, make for a "very practical learning experience," which is immediately applicable to the real world. A small business owner tells us, "Classes are at night, and my real-life laboratory is my business during the day."

Working students appreciate the balance at Chico, saying, "The atmosphere is focused, but there is not too much pressure on the students." "Overall, the program is consistent and organized," and the "staff is flexible and understanding" with students who work full-time. On the other hand, some feel the Chico experience "might be better if we had a more competitive environment," noting that there is a noticeable "lack of rigor in some classes." In addition to the value offered to professionals, Chico also offers a "3+2" program for business undergraduates from partner schools, which offers the "opportunity to get a masters degree one year after your bachelor degree." Several international universities also participate in the school's 3+2 program, which brings "a large number of international students" to campus. For many, the international community is an unexpected plus of a Chico education, helping them to develop "cultural skills in a business environment that is less cutthroat than the real business world."

Career and Placement

As a part of California State University, Chico, business students have access to the University's Career Center, where they can sign up for individual consultations with a career counselor. Students can also attend the Career Center's workshops and career development events throughout the year. Located in Northern California, Chico State maintains a "strong relationship with the San Francisco business community," and, every year, "CSU Chico brings in various companies at the career fair." International students, however, feel the school could do a better job helping them score internships and jobs, while locals say it is "very difficult to find employment" in surrounding Chico, which was affected by the economic downturn.

ADMISSIONS CONTACT: DR. MATT MEUTER, MBA DIRECTOR,
ADDRESS: 321 TEHAMA HALL, CSU, CHICO, CA 95929-0051
PHONE: 530-898-5880 • FAX: 530-898-6360
E-MAIL: MBA@CSUCHICO.EDU • WEBSITE: WWW.CSUCHICO.EDU/MBA

Around forty percent of Chico's MBA candidates are already employed when they begin the program, and most plan to stay at their current position after graduation. For those taking new positions, the mean base salary for graduates was $71,588 in 2010, with close to 80 percent of students remaining in the western United States. Chevron USA, KPMG, and Deloitte are among the school's top employers.

Student Life and Environment

Chico State is a vibrant and bustling university, located in a pretty town in the Sierra Nevada foothills. The "beautiful campus" makes a wonderful backdrop to the business school, and "there are always people hanging out on campus" before and after class. There are "lots of things happening around campus" for those who want to partake, including "great cultural activities" and plenty of "volunteer opportunities" in the local community. While "most MBAs don't have time to participate in the many activities offered by the school," others say they make a concerted effort to get involved.

At this medium-sized public school, graduate students are "close-knit," yet diverse culturally, socially, and academically. Some students are "fresh out of undergraduate school with no experience" in the workplace, while others are seasoned professionals, who continue to work full-time throughout the duration of the program. Many students are "very passionate about learning," while "others are not very serious about the program." Because the school operates a partner program with several international universities, there are numerous students from overseas. With regards to the international community, a current student tells us, "Getting to know them on a collegial, friendly level during my MBA has been one of the most important experiences so far."

Admissions

To be eligible for a graduate program at Chico, prospective students must have an overall undergraduate GPA of 2.75, and a GPA of at least 3.0 for the final thirty hours of coursework. To apply to the MBA program, students must submit standardized test scores in addition to their academic transcripts, though the GRE may be substituted for the GMAT. The most recent entering class had an average GMAT score of 569 and an average GRE score of 302. The average work experience for entering students is more than three years.

FINANCIAL FACTS

Annual tuition (in-state/ out-of-state)	$8,268/$8,268
Fees	$4,572
Cost of books	$1,000
Room & board (on/off-campus)	$0/$10,000
% of students receiving aid	40
% of first-year students receiving aid	40
% of students receiving grants	40
Average award package	$16,279
Average grant	$4,470
Average loan	$11,743
Average student loan debt	$17,473

ADMISSIONS

Admissions Selectivity Rating	86
# of applications received	66
% applicants accepted	62
% acceptees attending	100
Average GMAT	570
Range of GMAT	535–595
Accepts GRE scores	Yes
Average GPA	3.2
TOEFL required of international students	Yes
Minimum TOEFL (paper/web)	550/80
Application fee	$55
International application fee	$55
Regular application deadline	3/1
Deferment available	No
Transfer students accepted	Yes
Transfer application policy A maximum of 9 semester units of post-baccalaureate transfer and /or CSU, Chico Open University coursework may be included in a master's degree program, provided that the courses are from an AACSB accredited institution.	
Non-fall admissions	Yes
Need-blind admissions	Yes

EMPLOYMENT PROFILE			
Career Rating	**79**	**Grads Employed by Function**	**% Avg. Salary**
Average base starting salary	$71,588	Marketing	(15%) $41,000
Primary Source of Full-time Job Acceptances		Consulting	(15%) $65,000
School-facilitated activities	3 (38%)	Management	(15%) $132,000
Unknown	5 (63%)	Finance	(25%) $46,000
		MIS	(30%) $67,500
		Top 5 Employers Hiring Grads	
		IGT Company, Cap Gemini, IBM, Deloitte, KPMG	

CALIFORNIA STATE UNIVERSITY, EAST BAY
COLLEGE OF BUSINESS AND ECONOMICS

GENERAL INFORMATION
Type of school   Public
Affiliation   No Affiliation
Academic calendar   Quarter

SURVEY SAYS...
Liberal students
Solid preparation in:
Accounting, Presentation skills

STUDENTS
Enrollment of parent
  institution   14,527
Enrollment of MBA Program   345
% male/female   51/49
% out-of-state   1
% part-time   12
% underrepresented minority   12
% international   36
Average age at entry   28
Average years work
  experience at entry   3

ACADEMICS
Academic Experience Rating   91
Profs interesting rating   89
Profs accessible rating   90
Student/faculty ratio   24:1
% female faculty   30
% underrepresented
  minority faculty   12
% part-time faculty   35

Prominent Alumni
Mark Mastov, Founder of 24 Hour
Fitness; Bill Lockyer, State Treasurer
of California; Mike Abary, Senior VP
, Sony IT Products Division; Mahla
Shagfi, Senior VP and Regional
Director, Union Bank of California;
Judy Belk, Senior VP Rockefeller
Philanthropy Advisors

Academics

Located in the San Francisco Bay Area, California State University, East Bay's College of Business and Economics offers an "excellent curriculum and professors," "great location," as well as flexible schedule for working students. The college also boasts a "very inclusive and diverse culture" without the "cut-throat" mentality found at so many other business schools. Instead, CSUEB encourages a "collaborative/helpful approach to get to the finish line whether that be to survive a tough class or to reach graduation."

Students say the greatest strength of CSUEB's College of Business and Economics is "the instructors." Professors here are "excellent in all areas," and "really knowledgeable, skillful, and kind." They "are invested in the learning and growth of their students," notes one student. The professors "take extra time and give great advice" and "want to facilitate real learning and instill long-lasting knowledge." Many professors are "established in their fields and careers so they have a very strong knowledge around what they teach." Because of this they are "able to provide a practical look at things and how what you're learning in class will help you in the real world." "It is nice to learn about how things should be," says one student, "and as a business owner, I strive to push my business objectives using the ideals that I learn in my academic life." Furthermore, the "professors in the MBA program treat students like colleagues rather than students and that is very much appreciated." While students gave glowing reviews to their professors overall, some students noted that there were "more male professors than female," and that they "would love to see/hear about women in business more often." In fall 2015, the College says it will maintain a 3:2 (male to female) faculty ratio with 39 percent female faculty in the regular faculty body, up 6 percent from fall 2014.

Overall, students say their professors "are easy to access and are generally prompt with email responses." They are "very helpful and make time for students before and after class." And students also find the administration "accessible" and "helpful." One students notes: "The administration has been very accommodating to ensure that I am able to graduate on time by offering additional classes that meet my needs." CSUEB is a great fit for students looking for a flexible, supportive, and challenging learning environment in a beautiful setting.

Career and Placement

Students find the administration at CSUEB is "very helpful." CSUEB has a dedicated career placement office that hosts "seminars, workshops, career fairs, counseling, and job boards." And there is "a dedicated career counselor for business students." There are "plenty of events provided by the CSUEB specifically for the business students," including "mixers, networking events, résumé workshops, business card printing, photo shoots for LinkedIn, and other opportunities." As far as "career placement, it is up to the student to reach out if they need help," notes one student, but if "someone asks for help, the school will provide that support." Overall, the students say the administration is "responsive, enthusiastic, communicative, and caring about the student body!"

ADMISSIONS CONTACT: DR. JOANNA LEE, DIRECTOR OF GRADUATE PROGRAMS
ADDRESS: 25800 CARLOS BEE BLVD, HAYWARD, CA 94542
PHONE: 510-885-2419 • FAX: 510-885-2176
E-MAIL: JOANNA.LEE@CSUEASTBAY.EDU • WEBSITE: CBEGRAD.CSUEASTBAY.EDU

Student Life and Environment

Students praise CSUEB's "beautiful campus." And can you blame them? The main campus overlooks the San Francisco Bay, hills, and mountains and the Concord campus sits amidst the picturesque foothills of Mt. Diablo. Off campus, there is no shortage of things to do from enjoying the natural scenery to nightlife, restaurants, and cultural institutions in the greater SF Bay area. On campus, there is a "beautiful dining commons and other great eateries," "excellent computer labs and study facilities," "academic clubs," and "fraternities."

The student body overall is "multicultural," "intelligent," "competitive," "team-oriented," "helpful," "hard-working," and "friendly." Many students attend part-time, and "most of them are working in the daytime, have families," and come from "diverse backgrounds personally and professionally." In addition, "many are international" and "bilingual." Students feel their classmates are "very cooperative" and "eager to help one another succeed." The school is "very diverse with varying ages, cultures, races, life stages, experiences, and occupations."

Admissions

Applicants to CSUEB must submit an application including an official undergraduate transcript; letters of recommendation; GMAT score; and a GRE score if available. The average GPA and GMAT score of applicants admitted to the program varies from year to year. GMAT score may be waived for applicants with five or more years of professional work experience.

FINANCIAL FACTS

Fees	$11,886
Cost of books	$3,000
Room & board	
(on/off-campus)	$15,000/$15,000
% of students receiving aid	29
% of first-year students	
receiving aid	29
% of students receiving grants	14
Average award package	$12,761
Average grant	$5,542
Average loan	$12,630
Average student loan debt	$31,890

ADMISSIONS

Admissions Selectivity Rating	89
# of applications received	648
% applicants accepted	31
% acceptees attending	62
Average GMAT	540
Range of GMAT	460–590
Accepts GRE scores	Yes
Average Verbal GRE	148
Range of Verbal	
GRE scores	146–154
Average Quantitative GRE	152
Range of Quantitative	
GRE scores	145–155
Average Writing GRE	4.5
Range of Writing	
GRE scores	3.5–5.0
Average GPA	3.4
TOEFL required of	
international students	Yes
Minimum TOEFL	
(paper/web)	550/79
Application fee	$55
International application fee	$55
Regular application deadline	6/30
Regular application notification	8/30
Deferment available	No
Transfer students accepted	No
Non-fall admissions	Yes
Need-blind admissions	Yes

CALIFORNIA STATE UNIVERSITY, FRESNO
CRAIG SCHOOL OF BUSINESS

Academics

A member of the California State University System, California State University—Fresno's Craig School of Business offers "an education that rivals the top universities at a fraction of the cost." Many, if not most of those who attend Craig are working professionals, and the school's curriculum "works well with a full-time work schedule," including night and weekend classes. Fresno State employs world-class educators who have real world experience working with/managing companies, such as: HP, Rug Doctor and dozens more, and "many of the professors have owned their own companies and have experience outside of just their focus."

The "absolutely outstanding" faculty gives "consistently solid instruction" and brings "an incredible amount of work experience and knowledge in regards to their respective business fields." Many were "very successful business people who teach because who love it," and "it is wonderful to hear their life lessons shared with the students." "My experience has exceeded my expectations before I started the program," says one student. Everybody is willing to learn, "even the professors," whose genuine excitement about what they do rubs off on the student body. The "very astute" professors have "crystal clear and inspirational instructions" and leave memorable impressions on students. "I have encountered some professors I plan to keep in contact with for years to come," says one.

The "well-run" administration is more than understanding of how busy its students' lives are; at one point, "the program staff handled all of the paperwork so that we students didn't need to worry about them." Class sizes are small, so "you can get as much personal attention as you want," and it's "easy to get classes" of your choice. "I've learned a lot of interesting, applicable concepts at Fresno State," says a student.

Career and Placement

The prestige and recognition of the CSU Fresno name in the business world is a huge boon to graduates, and the school's "pay to tuition ratio is among the best." The Career Services Office "gives the students ample opportunity to find great jobs as well as overseas experience." Most already have jobs when they choose to attend Fresno State, but there are many group projects that are required, so students find that a great deal of natural networking occurs throughout the course of the program. Students are required to take three elective courses, and one of their internships may be used as an upper division elective towards their degrees. Specializations are available in agribusiness, entrepreneurship, finance, general management, human resource management, information systems, and marketing. Alumni are also especially useful to Craig graduates, and job offers are frequently posted for graduates via Craig's various social networking sites.

Student Life and Environment

Virtually every student here "is working full-time and going to school full-time," which "makes it easier to relate to one another." This "ethnically diverse" group is all "at different phases of their careers," and ranges from "professionals with young families up to people in their forties with already established careers," including "VPs of companies, HR managers, entrepreneurs, stay-at-home moms, sales executives, and more." All are "willing to learn and want to learn along with you" and are "open to meeting new people and making new friends." Each "very eclectic" class represents "right, left and middle political points of view," making for a "fun mixture."

Life is "very busy" when classes are in session, with many local people swarming about and "a lot of activities available." A lot of the MBA students went to undergrad at CSU Fresno and live locally. There are "many social and health wellness fairs throughout the semester," and there is also "a pub that serves wine and beer" for students who "enjoy mingling socially with their classmates" over a drink.

Admissions

Applicants to the Craig MBA program must submit the following materials: official GMAT score report (minimum score of 550 with ranking at or above the first quartile on verbal and mathematics portions); a completed online application; two letters of recommendation; a statement of purpose/essay; and official transcripts for all post-secondary academic work. International non-English-speaking students who did not graduate from an English language institution must also submit an official TOEFL score report. Admissions decisions are based primarily on GMAT scores and academic performance over the last sixty semester credits of undergraduate work; applicants must have earned at least a 2.5 GPA over that period to merit consideration. Work experience, demonstrated management potential, and the applicant's statement of purpose are also considered.

FINANCIAL FACTS

Annual tuition (in-state/ out-of-state)	$12,172/$18,868
Average grant	$10,000
Average loan	$21,000

ADMISSIONS

Admissions Selectivity Rating	87
# of applications received	136
% applicants accepted	36
Average GMAT	600
Range of GMAT	500–710
Accepts GRE scores	Yes
Average GPA	3.4
TOEFL required of international students	Yes
Minimum TOEFL (paper/web)	550/80
Application fee	$55
International application fee	$55
Regular application deadline	4/1
Application Deadline	
Round 1:	4/1
Round 2:	10/1
Deferment available	Yes
Maximum length of deferment	1 year
Transfer students accepted	Yes
Transfer application policy	
Transfer must be from and AACSB accredited school, 9 units may be transfer on an approved basis and applicant must meet standard admittance requirements (same as a new applicant).	
Non-fall admissions	Yes

CALIFORNIA STATE UNIVERSITY, FULLERTON
MIHAYLO COLLEGE OF BUSINESS AND ECONOMICS

GENERAL INFORMATION

Type of school	Public
Affiliation	No Affiliation
Academic calendar	Semester

SURVEY SAYS...
Friendly students
Solid preparation in:
General management

STUDENTS

Enrollment of parent institution	38,414
Enrollment of MBA Program	330
% male/female	66/34
% part-time	89
% underrepresented minority	15
% international	34
Average age at entry	28
Average years work experience at entry	5

ACADEMICS

Academic Experience Rating	**89**
Profs interesting rating	89
Profs accessible rating	90
Student/faculty ratio	10:1
% female faculty	27
% underrepresented minority faculty	41
% part-time faculty	16

Prominent Alumni
Steve Charton, President and CEO, Hospitality; Kevin Costner, Businessman and Actor; Steve G. Mihaylo, President & CEO, Telecommunications; Jim Woods, Chairman Emeritus & CEO (Retired), Aerospace; RIchard Davis, President, CEO & Chairman, Banking

Academics

"A reputable state university with an excellent business school," Cal State Fullerton runs the largest accredited business school in the State of California. For current and future Southern California professionals, CSUF is a great way to get an edge in the business world, without breaking the bank. With a strong faculty and ties in the local business community, this school offers a "quality program at an affordable price." Whether you choose to go to school full time or part time, the Flex MBA is entirely "customizable," and "can be moderated in difficulty, depending on course choice and workload." Taking two classes per semester, flex students can complete the program in fewer than three years. Taking four classes per semester, full-time students can complete the program in sixteen months.

For both full-time and part-time students, the Mihaylo MBA program consists of ten foundation courses, four electives, and a capstone course. Through electives, students can pursue an academic concentration in one of thirteen different fields; there is "great accounting faculty," as well as a strong finance department at CSUF. In addition to academic programs, the school operates fifteen "Centers of Excellence," like the Small Business Institute, where faculty and students conduct research and case studies within a real business environment. Across departments, "professors are all very knowledgeable in terms of both theory and real-world experience," and many "use their lifetime experiences to spice up the class discussions." While "most professors are outstanding and inspiring," students admit that the overall quality of the teaching staff can be "inconsistent," especially when it comes to tenured faculty.

Since many students are balancing work, school, and personal life, most CSUF professors are "sympathetic to the many demands facing graduate students, who have full-time jobs and families." Overall, CSUF is a "warm environment, with professors who care about students" and an administration that is "supportive and helpful" to its ample student body. "Some admin mix-ups" in the past with regards to books and scheduling have been addressed by a new and expanded staff. All things considered, an MBA at Cal State Fullerton is an "excellent value." Armed with both academic and practical experience, graduates leave the program "ready to work and lead in the workforce."

Career and Placement

For those who love the surf and sand in Southern California, "CSUF has excellent ties to the local Orange County business community." Throughout the program, "the professors and administration work as partners in helping us achieve our career goals." Students are encouraged to visit the Business Advising Center to meet with career path advisors, who help them choose a concentration, plan their education, and develop a career search strategy. In addition, students can make an appointment with the business career specialist at the Mihaylo Career Center, who helps place graduates in accounting, finance, international business, information systems, and marketing positions.

Though the programs are strong, career development could be improved with the addition of "more networking activities within the program, outside the program, and with other schools that have similar programs." Students would also like to see Cal State Fullerton continue to build "relationships with higher quality employers and recruiters." A student explains, "We have a good program, but our career center is geared for undergraduates, and they do no have that much to offer for graduate students." The school has listened to its students, though, and an expanded career center staff includes a dedicated adviser for MBA students.

ADMISSIONS CONTACT: PRE-ADMISSION ADVISOR
ADDRESS: 800 N. STATE COLLEGE BLVD, SGMH 4210, FULLERTON, CA 92831-3599
PHONE: 657-278-3622 • FAX: 657-278-7101
E-MAIL: MBA@FULLERTON.EDU • WEBSITE: MBA.FULLERTON.EDU

After graduating from Cal State Fullerton, MBA candidates join a "large alumni network" of more than 55,000 former students in Southern California and beyond. Currently, Mihaylo graduates are employed at Ford Motor Company, Hewlett Packard, Merrill Lynch, Morgan Stanley, Nestlé, Fox Sports, KPMG, Warner Brothers, PricewaterhouseCoopers, Paramount, Boeing, Deloitte & Touche, US Bank, Verizon, Walt Disney Company, Kaiser Permanente, and Toshiba, among others. In recent years, the mean base salary reported by Cal State Fullerton MBA graduates was over $62,000 annually.

Student Life and Environment

CSUF is a large MBA program, which attracts a wide variety of students at any level of their career, but still brings the average class size to less than 30 students. Here, students are "very diverse in terms of ethnicity, race, ideas, background, and ages," though "most are in their mid- to late twenties and have two to five years of work experience." As a "very diverse and professional environment," CSUF caters to students "looking to move up in their careers." In the classroom, students keep the bar high, but competition low. Generally, students are "very sociable people," who are "pleasant to study with."

Collegiate activities are generally "geared toward undergraduate students," so most MBA candidates are "only at the business school for class or to study." Nonetheless, CSUF offers a nice school environment on their main campus, where the business school building offers "plenty of nice, quiet, clean study areas." Caffeine-fueled students add, "The Starbucks in the business school is a definite plus," and there is a "state-of-the-art gym provided to students, free of charge." Most students are quick to praise their campus experience.

Admission

Admission to Cal State Fullerton is competitive. Incoming students in last year's class had an an average GMAT score 566 and a 3.26 GPA. To best prepare for admission, students should attend an information session on the Cal State Fullerton campus. These sessions regularly fill to capacity, so prospective students should register online in advance to secure a spot.

FINANCIAL FACTS

Annual tuition (in-state/ out-of-state)	$12,279/$18,975
Cost of books	$3,720
Room & board (on/off-campus)	$34,828/$34,720
Average award package	$4,000
Average grant	$4,000

ADMISSIONS

Admissions Selectivity Rating	85
# of applications received	353
% applicants accepted	52
% acceptees attending	48
Average GMAT	551
Range of GMAT	530–580
Accepts GRE scores	Yes
Average Verbal GRE	152
Range of Verbal GRE scores	148–156
Average Quantitative GRE	155
Range of Quantitative GRE scores	152–157
Average Writing GRE	3.8
Range of Writing GRE scores	3.0–4.5
Average GPA	3.1
TOEFL required of international students	Yes
Minimum TOEFL (paper/web)	570/88
Application fee	$55
International application fee	$55
Early application deadline	4/1
Regular application deadline	4/1
Deferment available	No
Transfer students accepted	Yes
Transfer application policy Students must apply as a new student and courses will be evaluated. Students may transfer in up to 9 units.	
Non-fall admissions	Yes
Need-blind admissions	Yes

California State University, Long Beach
College of Business Administration

GENERAL INFORMATION

Type of school	Public
Affiliation	No Affiliation
Academic calendar	Semester

SURVEY SAYS...
Students love Long Beach, CA
Solid preparation in:
General management

STUDENTS

Enrollment of parent institution	33,579
Enrollment of MBA Program	232
Average age at entry	27
Average years work experience at entry	3

ACADEMICS

Academic Experience Rating	**88**
Profs interesting rating	87
Profs accessible rating	91
Student/faculty ratio	25:1

Joint Degrees
MFA/MBA, 3 years FT (including two summer sessions) offered jointly between the Theatre Arts Department and the Graduate School of Business.

Academics

Students looking for the biggest "bang for the buck" will appreciate California State University, Long Beach. Although "tuition and fees have gone up every semester, what we are getting in return is still a great deal," at least "compared to other universities." There are many reasons to choose Cal State in addition to its affordability. "The campus is conveniently located, parking is good and the resources (database subscriptions, computer equipment) provided are excellent." Also popular with students are the small program and class sizes, which make it "easy to get to know many of your classmates throughout your stay." At CSULB, "classmates are invested in the education experience." "Fellow students are fun to work with and bring different experiences helping to enrich discussion." There are "many foreign students" in the graduate program who help to provide an "international business focus" during classroom discussions. International students appreciate the opportunity to "take advantage of their experiences" at Long Beach.

Finding a program that meets individual needs at CSULB is easy to do. There are "many options for working folk," including a "Saturday only program" which is a twenty-three-month long lock-step cohort. The three basic options include the Saturday MBA, the Self-Paced Evening MBA, and the eighteen-month Daytime Accelerated MBA. A good majority of students fit into the part-time category, and these commuters appreciate the school's ample parking and location in the "convenient" city of Long Beach. A current student describes it as "one of the most beautiful and diverse cities in the country."

Generally, students attend CSULB for its "smaller classes, good choice of different programs, [and] great location." One student says the school and its programs are "definitely growing by leaps and bounds." Another student who is a military veteran says, "The VA program here is the best of any school I have seen." Overall, students should come away from the school with "strong academics" as well as a "great sense of a real life business experience."

Many students also find the cohort system as one of the school's "greatest strengths." Although at times it may create some "isolation" from the rest of the campus, it does a great job of unifying peers within one's group, allowing students "time to develop relationships and strengthen our network," which is "almost impossible when your classmates change every session."

Getting help on campus is a positive experience as well. "The administration and faculty are very accessible and diverse." Students say that administrators "are fantastic in keeping students informed and getting them involved." Students' opinions about the faculty vary, yet many feel that "professors are very helpful and always have open lines of communication." Some say that although their academic and professional knowledge is well respected, their ability to teach effectively covers a "wide range." Also, some students consider it a disadvantage that not all professors "have extensive real-world experience."

Career and Placement

CSU's MBA Career Management Services "is very interactive and helpful with networking for future careers." Besides maintaining an MBA job board and hosting on-campus recruiting events in a variety of business disciplines, they also maintain contact with alumni to encourage networking opportunities. Attending one of the large, campus-wide career fairs hosted by the Career Development Center affords yet another opportunity to meet potential employers. In recent years, large companies have visited campus, including Alaska Airlines, Accountants Incorporated, American Capital Group, California National Bank, CVS/Carmark Pharmacy, First Investors, Kelly Scientific Resources, Ameriprise Financial, Boeing, Northrop Grumman, and Comerica Bank.

Student Life and Environment

The MBA program combines a mix of students from several different countries, some who come directly from an undergraduate program and others that have "fifteen-plus years of work experience." This "diverse, friendly" student body consists of a solid group of classmates who "are invested in the education experience."

Although the school provides "ample opportunities to get into clubs and programs," graduate students with busy lifestyles may not have the opportunity to be "as involved as [they] would like to be." They do say, however, that they appreciate the "beautiful" campus and the surrounding area is "very nice." Long Beach is a thriving community that "gives access to so many different activities and different cultures." Students feel "safe" in this environment. They welcome the comfortable surroundings that are not only motivating, but also provide "a great atmosphere to study."

Students looking for off-campus housing will find selections that are "organized" with "a lot of affordable options." Weekend students remark that Saturdays are "quiet and uneventful" and that "not all of the services are open that day." Having a full-time job means that they miss out on "attending training during the week."

Admission

GMATs, GREs and undergraduate GPAs carry the most weight when applying to CSU's graduate school. Work experience is a plus but is not required. Solid letters of recommendations and a strong personal statement can be helpful but involvement in extracurricular activities is not considered.

Applications are accepted on a rolling basis with deadlines for fall admissions being 6/1 and spring admissions being 10/30. Students enrolling in CSU's MBA program have an average age of twenty-nine and with five years of work experience. Average GMAT scores were 570 and GAP was 3.4, with a 2.75 minimum requirement.

FINANCIAL FACTS

Annual tuition (in-state/ out-of-state)	$12,290/$18,986
Average grant	$0
Average loan	$0

ADMISSIONS

Admissions Selectivity Rating	87
# of applications received	308
% applicants accepted	49
% acceptees attending	77
Average GMAT	570
Range of GMAT	480–650
Accepts GRE scores	Yes
Average GPA	3.4
TOEFL required of international students	Yes
Minimum TOEFL (paper/web)	550/80
Application fee	$55
International application fee	$55
Regular application deadline	6/1
Deferment available	Yes
Maximum length of deferment	One semester.
Transfer students accepted	Yes
Transfer application policy Must meet admissions criteria	
Non-fall admissions	Yes
Need-blind admissions	Yes

CALIFORNIA STATE UNIVERSITY, LOS ANGELES
COLLEGE OF BUSINESS AND ECONOMICS

GENERAL INFORMATION

Type of school	Public
Affiliation	No Affiliation

SURVEY SAYS...
Friendly students
Solid preparation in:
General management, Presentation skills

STUDENTS

Enrollment of parent institution	21,755
Average age at entry	27
Average years work experience at entry	6

ACADEMICS

Academic Experience Rating	**90**
Profs interesting rating	88
Profs accessible rating	90
Student/faculty ratio	15:1
% female faculty	30
% underrepresented minority faculty	37
% part-time faculty	10

Academics

The MBA program at California State University, Los Angeles College of Business and Economics is mainly designed to serve the needs of working professionals through flexible scheduling (meaning predominantly night classes are offered). This state recognized university is "affordable and practical" and the subject matter of the courses is "up-to-date with what's going on in the industry."

CSULA is staffed with "many amazing, knowledgeable and experienced professors," each of whom "brings their own flavor to the school and the program." Professors all demonstrate "commitment and accessibility to provide students with guidance not only in the classroom but also outside of it," and "provide great real world examples of both current and past models." They "are able to teach at a fast pace or slow pace depending on how quickly the class is retaining the information." Not only are the professors expecting to be wowed by projects and analytical results delivered by students, but "there is a fierce competition among MBA students to outshine one another" and "deposit more creativity and innovation in to the project and final executions."

Although students are pleased with surrounding the program, some say that the administration and formalities "make it very difficult for a student to efficiently progress through the minutia of the program." Little things such as "navigating through the required steps or other non-academic items can be very time consuming and very irritating." Still, "the overall academic experience is positive."

Career and Placement

Although many of the students already have jobs, those that are looking to change careers or are coming straight from undergrad wish that the school would help them "connect more with job market/placement after graduation." Many feel that CSULA doesn't broadcast the MBA program as loudly as other graduate majors in the college of business and economics, despite its quality. "The value of CSULA MBA program is the next big secret," says a student. That being said, career fairs are held every two months, and "entrepreneurship is totally encouraged out here and ideas are really heard and guided." MBA students have a dedicated staff member to assist with placement and connecting with companies after graduation. There "are enough activities and resources to help students succeed at CSULA," and "the staff here try to help students with any questions and needs."

ADMISSIONS CONTACT: EDWARD HSIEH, ASSOCIATE DEAN
ADDRESS: COLLEGE OF BUSINESS AND ECONOMICS, 5151 STATE UNIVERSITY DRIVE
LOS ANGELES, CA 90032 UNITED STATES • PHONE: (323) 343-2800 • FAX: (323) 343-5462
E-MAIL: MBACBE@CALSTATELA.EDU • WEBSITE: CBE.CALSTATELA.EDU

Student Life and Environment

The campus is centrally located in Los Angeles ("a great place for living and studying"), making it easy for students to come directly from work, and is "very friendly and definitely has an academic feel to it." Life at school is dependent on the type of student, the breakdown being: "Half of the students are here for career advancement and the other half are here to begin a career after graduation." Many are international students (primarily from Asia), and many also received their undergraduate degrees from CSULA as well. For the most part, "most graduate students are commuters and are only on campus for class or class activities and homework," and undergraduates without jobs "tend to be the ones who are actively engaged in school activities and clubs." Regardless, there are "many opportunities for social interactions," including the group projects and case studies that are "the essential part of the MBA program." "There are many working students here which makes it easier to work together during school projects and study groups." "Working in groups is like a simulation that prepares to for the actual job," says a student.

Admissions

It's not difficult to make it through the gates at CSULA; students just need an overall GPA of at least 2.5, a GMAT score higher than 500 (or a GRE score of above 300), three letters of recommendation, and a resume. Admission is based upon comparison against the rest of the applications received in a quarter, so students who are not admitted may simply repay the application fee and try again the next quarter. A TOEFL score of at least 80 (internet), 213 (computer) or 550 (paper) is required for those applicants who earned a bachelors degree from a school where English was not the principal language of instruction.

FINANCIAL FACTS

Annual tuition (in-state/ out-of-state)	$7,600/$13,600
Fees	$4,080
Cost of books	$1,800
Room & board (on/off-campus)	$12,000/$17,000

ADMISSIONS

Admissions Selectivity Rating	89
# of applications received	437
% applicants accepted	12
% acceptees attending	100
Average GMAT	550
Range of GMAT	510–570
Accepts GRE scores	Yes
Average GPA	3.3
TOEFL required of international students	Yes
Minimum TOEFL (paper/web)	550/80
Application fee	$55
International application fee	$55
Regular application deadline	4/26
Deferment available	No
Transfer students accepted	Yes
Transfer application policy At most 13 units (3 courses) can be transfered.	
Non-fall admissions	Yes
Need-blind admissions	No

CALIFORNIA STATE UNIVERSITY, NORTHRIDGE
DAVID NAZARIAN COLLEGE OF BUSINESS AND ECONOMICS

Academics

If you're a California resident looking for a great MBA program in the San Fernando Valley, it would behoove you to consider California State University, Northridge. For starters, the university's "strong local reputation" can't be beat. It also comes with a "reasonable" price tag which connotes a "great value" and ensures that graduate school is actually "financially feasible."

The program itself is "designed for fully-employed professionals" and classes are "offered [in the] evenings and/or [on] weekends." And the curriculum is geared towards enhancing "leadership" skills, aiming to leverage "real work scenarios" for teaching purposes. Cal State Northridge also places a premium on "experiential learning," the cornerstone of which is the "MBA Consulting Project." This project grants students the opportunity to apply the theories they've learned in a practical setting.

Many Cal State Northridge MBAs would describe their "very qualified" professors as a highlight of the program. Generally, these instructors marry "academic[s] with real life application." More specifically, professors frequently "share their consulting experience and [information about] projects they are working on." And many Cal State Northridge professors are exceedingly supportive. As one grateful student shares, "My first year I needed academic support and my professors helped me find resources that aided in my success. I had to work very hard, but my professors were sensitive to making sure I got the help I needed." Lastly, students tend to find the administration "helpful" as well. And they appreciate that administrators strive to make themselves readily "available for advice and planning."

Career and Placement

In the past, Cal State Northridge's career services were seen as lacking. Thankfully, the tide is beginning to turn. A relieved second-year informs us, "The school is making tremendous progress toward building career services on campus of the business school and now provides a career support exclusively to MBA students." The Career Center helps students navigate the complex corporate environment and today's competitive job market. Cal State Northridge MBAs can now tap into amazing resources that sharpen their networking and social media skills. And they can easily tweak their résumés and receive tips on how to launch a creative and effective job search.

ADMISSIONS CONTACT: DIRECTOR OF GRADUATE PROGRAMS
ADDRESS: 18111 NORDHOFT ST., NORTHRIDGE, CA 91330-8380
PHONE: 818-677-2467 • FAX: 818-677-3188
E-MAIL: MBA@CSUN.EDU • WEBSITE: CSUN.EDU/MBA

Student Life and Environment

Cal State Northridge MBAs happily report that their "fellow students are very diverse and very friendly." The vast majority are also "very team oriented and possess strong leadership skills and a strong acumen for business overall." Of course, this business savvy likely stems from the fact that most students are "working professionals," a detail which definitely serves to "elevate class discussions." As a satisfied second-year shares, "I've greatly appreciated almost every single one of my classmates' contributions and feel like I benefit from their experience and perspective."

While the academics at CSNU are "fast paced," we're told that the school still manages to foster a "friendly environment." However, be warned that "class hours are intense with debates and preparation is the key to success." Moreover, the social life is limited since "it is an evening program and the classes run till 10:00 P.M. at night." Many students also "have families with children and prefer to leave after class." Though, when time permits, students enjoy taking advantage of the university's "state of the art sports facility. . . [which has] a fabulous pool for swimming." It's a great way to work out some of those tough business decisions!

Admissions

Cal State Northridge is one of the most affordable programs in Southern California, but also rather small. Therefore, admission to the MBA program is competitive. To be eligible for graduate study, students must have at least a 3.0 GPA from their last 60 hours of undergraduate coursework and score within the 50th percentile on the GMAT. In reality, the average GPA for the most recent incoming class was 3.1 and the average GMAT score was 568. One year of professional work experience is a requirement of the program, though the school favors applicants with three to five years in the workforce.

FINANCIAL FACTS

Annual tuition (in-state/ out-of-state)	$7,830/$7,830
Fees	$4,572
Cost of books	$1,826
Room & board (on/off-campus)	$10,980/$13,050
% of students receiving aid	43
% of first-year students receiving aid	67
% of students receiving grants	26
Average award package	$14,645
Average grant	$3,999
Average loan	$16,171
Average student loan debt	$35,379

ADMISSIONS

Admissions Selectivity Rating	88
# of applications received	115
% applicants accepted	47
% acceptees attending	67
Average GMAT	583
Range of GMAT	535–635
Accepts GRE scores	No
Average GPA	3.1
TOEFL required of international students	Yes
Minimum TOEFL (paper/web)	550/79
Application fee	$55
International application fee	$55
Regular application deadline	5/1
Deferment available	Yes
Maximum length of deferment	one semester
Transfer students accepted	Yes
Transfer application policy 9 units max transfer credit	
Non-fall admissions	Yes
Need-blind admissions	Yes

CALIFORNIA STATE UNIVERSITY, SAN BERNARDINO
COLLEGE OF BUSINESS AND PUBLIC ADMINISTRATION

Academics

The MBA program at CSU San Bernadino provides its students with notable flexibility and value in addition to reliable educational quality. Students, many of whom are California locals, often choose CSUSB for its "affordability and location," and always for its "good reputation" within an established university. Professors are "helpful" and relevant; they "incorporate and acknowledge changing academic and business trends" within their curricula. "Our school's greatest strengths are its faculty, staff, and professors. These folks do everything they can to develop school pride." Similarly, CSUSB students find their classmates to be "professional, active in class, participatory, challenging" people with whom they share "quality interactions." Though many students find CSUSB's quarter system to be a "short time period to get a good grasp of a subject," they also report that "as long as you go with the flow and do the work," the MBA program is "outstanding." "My class sizes have been small to manageable, and my professors have been helpful and available." The faculty and CSUSB's "very strong entrepreneurial program" are called out by students as particular assets of the program, as well as the "good library." "The workload is very heavy," to be sure, but students feel they get "great value for [their] money" out of the intensity of a CSUSB MBA experience.

Career and Placement

CSUSB offers an "accelerated traditional MBA program" that can prove worthwhile for students who don't have time to wait to get to the next phase of their careers, and the school's "low cost" can also certainly help students reach their desired income bracket faster. But CSUSB's real impact on its students' futures often comes in the form of relationships with professors and administrators: "It was a shock to get such good educators and mentors along my journey. I am very pleased with my education and my career opportunities have doubled in availability and salary." It's equally true that, as an MBA student, your classmates will become your colleagues, and CSUSB students appreciate these "outgoing and supportive" classmates, who are "eager to succeed and [to] take on new challenges, self-motivated," and "talented in their respective fields." Some "big employers of CSUSB graduates" include "the County of San Bernardino, Omnitrans, ESRI, and Stater Bros."

Student Life and Environment

For many students, CSUSB is a "commuter school with students working as well as attending school," meaning that the school may seem to have an "older [than] average student body" and that some students "do not stay on campus once classes are done." However, this flexibility is essential for working "professionals, change-of-career students," those who "have families," and "foreign students." "Balancing work and school is tough," but "a student can do as much or as little as they wish to get as much from their education as possible." Students find their educational environment enriched by their peers, who are "pleasant," "helpful, and concerned about being good colleagues," and "good people overall." They appreciate having diversity as a part of their MBA experience: "My fellow students come from a diverse set of backgrounds such as China, Asia, India, and Saudi Arabia. They also have far-ranging career fields from pastors to former bankers." And it can't be denied that Southern California's climate and beauty appeal to students, who call the university's "natural setting" a strength: "When people come to campus it feels you are in touch with nature."

Admissions

As an AACSB-accredited program (afforded to less than 5 percent of MBA programs), CSUSB has high standards for its applicants. Read the "Choose The Right MBA" page on its website carefully to choose whether you'll apply for its Traditional MBA, Online MBA, or Executive MBA Program, all of which have specific application requirements. For the Traditional, a minimum GMAT score of 470 or GRE score of 298 (with a 3.0 GPA) is required from within the last five years; the Online MBA Program requires 5 years of professional work experience; the Executive track is by invitation only. For students seeking financial aid, CSUSB offers very competitive grants, scholarships, teaching assistantships, and other opportunities to defray tuition.

FINANCIAL FACTS

Annual tuition (in-state/ out-of-state)	$7,860/$7,860
Fees	$6,084
Cost of books	$3,000
Room & board (on/off-campus)	$10,940/$21,000
% of students receiving aid	46
% of first-year students receiving aid	23
% of students receiving grants	34
Average award package	$16,515
Average grant	$6,744
Average loan	$15,306
Average student loan debt	$21,633

ADMISSIONS

Admissions Selectivity Rating	85
# of applications received	219
% applicants accepted	53
% acceptees attending	62
Average GMAT	526
Range of GMAT	590–560
Accepts GRE scores	Yes
Average Verbal GRE	153
Range of Verbal GRE scores	149–157
Average Quantitative GRE	152
Range of Quantitative GRE scores	148–156
Average Writing GRE	3.3
Range of Writing GRE scores	3.0–4.0
Average GPA	3.3
TOEFL required of international students	Yes
Minimum TOEFL (paper/web)	550/79
Application fee	$55
International application fee	$55
Early application deadline	2/1
Early notification date	3/1
Regular application deadline	7/15
Regular application notification	8/15
Application Deadline/Notification	
Round 1:	2/1 / 3/1
Round 2:	4/1 / 5/1
Round 3:	7/15 / 8/15
Deferment available	No
Transfer students accepted	Yes
Transfer application policy	
Only three approved graduate courses may be transferred into our MBA Program from approved U.S. Universities.	
Non-fall admissions	Yes
Need-blind admissions	No

EMPLOYMENT PROFILE

Career Rating	71
Primary Source of Full-time Job Acceptances	
Unknown	104 (100%)

CARNEGIE MELLON UNIVERSITY
TEPPER SCHOOL OF BUSINESS

Academics

The Carnegie Mellon name is synonymous with excellence in technology, math, and applied science, so it's no surprise that the Tepper School of Business is known for its "analytical rigor" and "tech focus." The school's unique MBA covers topics like finance, marketing, operations, entrepreneurship, and consulting in consecutive "seven-and-a-half-week minis"—short, immersive semesters. Students say the curriculum "incorporates quantitative analysis into almost every class as a complement to the typical qualitative approach." A dual emphasis on leadership and analytics is integrated into the course work and student experience. Plus, for anyone interested in tech, Tepper will really give you the cutting edge: "Research and collaboration from across the entire [Carnegie Mellon] campus is often implemented into lectures and readings." Business courses are further augmented by "fantastic interdisciplinary opportunities across campus," including joint degree programs in computational finance, software engineering, law, and health care policy, among other fields.

While analytics are the Tepper hallmark, soft skills, particulary leadership and teamwork, are heavily emphasized. Of particular note, classes almost all include a collaborative component, and "most professors assign work for groups of three to six students at a time." Through the Accelerate Leadership Center, students receive one-on-one coaching. In addition to the academic focus on organizational behavior, the "skills that you learn at this school prepare you to manage and lead teams in organizations." "Coursework is tough, demanding, and challenging" (in fact, some would like to see the workload reduced), but the "outstanding faculty" makes the effort worthwhile. Plus, "the professors have an open door policy and are very accessible," so students are never left to fend for themselves while tackling hard material. The student to faculty ratio is 5:1. A student exclaims, "I am quite surprised by how willing most of the professors can be to be helping outside of classes, even on Fridays!"

A model of efficiency, Tepper's administration is quick in implementing changes proposed by both students and faculty, and there is an effort to "constantly improve student experience and academic curriculum." For example, "a new class this semester was thought of by a professor, approved, and added to the offered courses list in under forty-eight hours." A student adds, "Administration is more than willing to help students with specific problems and due to the small size of our program, they're rarely overwhelmed with requests."

Career and Placement

Through both curricular and extracurricular offerings, Tepper "faculty and administration do a great job preparing students for future careers." Working with Tepper School's Career Opportunities Center, students have access to corporate presentations, on-campus interviews, career and internship counseling, and networking trips to cities like New York, Silicon Valley, and Boston. The school maintains strong "relationships with specific tech and consulting firms" on the East and West Coasts, yet recruiting comes from a range of sources: "Companies come here for all disciplines from all over the country/world," offering "quite a variety of opportunities." A current student shares, "I've had a great experience at Tepper. I was able to land a full-time offer at a prestigious consulting firm and I'm confident that I have learned the proper business tools to excel there once I graduate."

In recent years, Tepper students have taken diverse jobs at corporations including Amazon.com, Deloitte, GlaxoSmithKline, Accenture, Booz and Company, McKinsey & Company, KPMG Consulting, PwC, General Mills, Unilever, AOL, Google, Intel Corporation, Morgan Stanley, and Wachovia. The class of 2014 had a mean base salary of nearly $110,000. Technology and consulting services were the most popular industries, capturing almost 33 percent and 27 percent of the class, respectively, with financial services coming in third, with about 16 percent of graduates.

Student Life and Environment

At this "very prestigious" business school, "everyone is extremely career driven and most people really want to get value out of their education." At the same time, Tepper MBAs manage to be "ambitious without being obnoxious," balancing a dedication to their studies with a friendly and collaborative attitude. "There are no competitive undertones in classes or with career search" on this friendly campus. When interacting with their classmates, most students are "happy to help out with everything from careers to homework."

"Academic and social clubs and activities are diverse and well-funded" at Tepper, and most MBA candidates find time to get involved in extracurricular activities. One student tells us, "I spend at least as much time on extracurricular activities (case competitions, clubs, events, etc.) as I do on class work." Socially, "most people will go out at least one or two nights a weekend, if they do not have families," often congregating at one of the "central watering holes within walking distance of where most students live." There are also "weekly social events on campus," which are particularly fun because "everyone knows each other" in this small program.

A great environment for graduate students professionals, and families, the Carnegie Mellon campus is located near downtown Pittsburgh, "a beautiful city and very affordable on a student budget." A student adds, "As someone with a family, there is definitely a lot in the Pittsburgh area to keep everyone busy and happy."

Admissions

Tepper evaluates prospective students on a range of factors, and the school encourages students to look beyond the medians and means when considering their eligibility for admission. That said, admission is selective. For the past three years, over 50 percent of the incoming class has submitted GMAT scores of 700 or higher. The average GPA for entering students was 3.24 for 2015.

Prominent Alumni

David A. Tepper, CEO & Founder, Appaloosa Management; David Coulter, Vice Chairman and Managing Director, Warburg Pincus LLC; Francisco D'Souza, CEO, Cognizant Technology Solutions

FINANCIAL FACTS

Annual tuition (in-state/ out-of-state)	$60,000/$60,000
Fees	$746
Cost of books	$7,440
Room & board	$14,612
% of students receiving aid	75
% of first-year students receiving aid	75
% of students receiving grants	54
Average award package	$80,198
Average grant	$23,518
Average loan	$55,820
Average student loan debt	$93,440

ADMISSIONS

Admissions Selectivity Rating	94
# of applications received	1,701
% applicants accepted	31
% acceptees attending	40
Average GMAT	690
Range of GMAT	640–740
Accepts GRE scores	Yes
Average Verbal GRE	159
Range of Verbal GRE scores	156–164
Average Quantitative GRE	162
Range of Quantitative GRE scores	160–163
Average Writing GRE	4.1
Range of Writing GRE scores	3.5–4.5
Average GPA	3.3
TOEFL required of international students	Yes
Minimum TOEFL (paper/web)	600/100
Application fee	$200
International application fee	$200
Application Deadline/Notification	
Round 1:	10/5 / 12/15
Round 2:	1/4 / 3/23
Round 3:	3/15 / 5/16
Round 4:	5/1 / 6/1
Deferment available	No
Transfer students accepted	No
Non-fall admissions	No
Need-blind admissions	Yes

EMPLOYMENT PROFILE

Career Rating	97	Grads Employed by Function% Avg. Salary	
Percent employed at graduation	82	Marketing	(17%) $112,580
Percent employed 3 months after graduation	90	Operations	(7%) $109,182
		Consulting	(32%) $127,621
Average base starting salary	$115,253	Management	(15%) $105,308
Primary Source of Full-time Job Acceptances		Finance	(23%) $104,828
School-facilitated activities	139 (82%)	MIS	(5%) $131,875
Graduate-facilitated activities	30 (18%)	Other	(1%)
Unknown	1 (1%)	**Top 5 Employers Hiring Grads**	
		Amazon, Inc. (20), PwC Advisory (20), IBM Corp. (5), A.T. Kearney (5), Eaton Corp. (4)	

CASE WESTERN RESERVE UNIVERSITY
WEATHERHEAD SCHOOL OF MANAGEMENT

GENERAL INFORMATION
Type of school	Private
Affiliation	No Affiliation
Academic calendar	Semester

SURVEY SAYS...
Classmates have diverse work experience
Solid preparation in:
Environmental sustainability

STUDENTS
Enrollment of parent institution	11,340
Enrollment of MBA Program	294
% male/female	64/36
% out-of-state	15
% part-time	35
% underrepresented minority	13
% international	30
Average age at entry	28
Average years work experience at entry	4

ACADEMICS
Academic Experience Rating	**90**
Profs interesting rating	88
Profs accessible rating	93
Student/faculty ratio	4:1
% female faculty	33
% underrepresented minority faculty	3
% part-time faculty	38

Joint Degrees
MBA/MD; MBA/JD; MBA/Master of Global Management; MBA/MPH; MBA/MS Biochemistry; MBA/MS Social Administration; MBA/MS Medical Physiology; MBA/MS in Management

Prominent Alumni
Mark Weinberger, Global Chairman & CEO, Ernst & Young; Donald Washkewicz, Chairman, Parker Hannifin Corporation; Chuck Fowler, Chariman, Fairmount Santrol; Arthur Anton, President & CEO, Swagelok Company; David Lingafelter, President, Moen Corporation

Academics

There's no doubt that Case Western Reserve's Weatherhead School is an academic powerhouse, especially within the Cleveland area. And, considering its "good reputation," "great financial aid package[s]" and "intimate class size[s]," it's an amazing option for any future MBA. Students are always eager to highlight Weatherhead as a leader in "organizational behavior" and "a world pioneer in establishing a design & innovation department within a management school." It's certainly a strong program for those looking "to gain exposure to the healthcare industry" as well. After all, "Weatherhead is surrounded [by] and has strong connections to MetroHealth, University Hospitals, and Cleveland Clinic."

Inside the classroom, students are greeted by "fantastic" professors who "have loads of academic and real world experience." A first-year MBA further explains, "Some of them give us insights we would not find in any textbook." They are also "easily approachable and [frequently] involve . . . students in their research." Additionally, we've been assured that most Weatherhead instructors are "very willing to take time to explain concepts and receive feedback about their lectures." This same care and concern for the student body can be found amongst Weatherhead administrators as well. They often "go the extra mile to help a student in need" and strive to get to "know each student."

Career and Placement

The employment outlook for Weatherhead MBAs is pretty strong. For starters, we're told that "networking within the local community is fantastic." A grateful first-year provides more concrete evidence sharing, "The Career Management Office was able to help me get in contact with several businesses in the area. This lead to several interviews and internship offers." And students can also tap into an "alumni base [that is] very loyal and helpful."

Companies that tend to recruit and/or hire Weatherhead MBAs include: Amazon, GE Lighting, MetroHealth System, Sherwin Williams, JP MorganChase, Century Federal Credit Union, Ernst and Young, Hyland Software, and University Hospitals.

Student Life and Environment

MBA candidates at Weatherhead hail from "very diverse educational, geographical and professional backgrounds." Students say that their peers' "[work] experience range[s anywhere] from zero to fifteen years, [with] the average [being] around five years." Naturally, this helps ensure that "class discussions are rich with insights." Looking beyond their résumés, many students here describe their peers as "friendly," "outgoing," and "very willing to help if you need it with classes or other issues." Perhaps this second-year puts it best: "Honestly we're a huge group of friends. We study together and we play together. It's a great group to be around. I've made some lasting friendships here."

As the aforementioned student quote suggests, the atmosphere at Case is "more convivial and collaborative than competitive." This can likely be attributed, at least partially, to "the large amount of MBA social events which have high levels of participation." A knowledgeable second-year further explains, "On a daily basis, different groups at Weatherhead host events of all sorts, such as networking (hosted by Career Management Office), club based (e.g. Finance Club does a "Training the Street" workshop or Women in Business a dinner and panel discussion with female local leaders) and others. I would say we as students can keep ourselves busy easily and it is possible to select a mix of events that fit everyone's preferences." And, if that doesn't satisfy you, we're told that "there is lots to do in Cleveland if you are willing to explore on your own!"

Admissions

Gaining admission to Case's MBA program is certainly a competitive process and solid academic credentials are definitely required. The admissions office offers three application rounds—one with a November deadline, one with a January deadline and one with a March deadline. Applications received after the March deadline will be considered on a rolling basis (assuming space is still available) . The school requires applicants to have an undergraduate degree from an accredited institution and a minimum of two years (preferred) of full-time work experience. Mandatory application materials include academic transcripts, GMAT (preferred) or GRE score, English proficiency exam for non-native speakers (minimum score of 100 on the IBT version of the TOEFL required), two essays, current résumé, two letters of recommendation and, of course, an application fee.

FINANCIAL FACTS

Annual tuition (in-state/ out-of-state)	$38,250/$38,250
Fees	$200
Cost of books	$1,980
Room & board	$18,350
% of students receiving aid	94
% of first-year students receiving aid	95
% of students receiving grants	89
Average award package	$28,024
Average grant	$18,359
Average loan	$29,795
Average student loan debt	$23,653

ADMISSIONS

Admissions Selectivity Rating	88
# of applications received	387
% applicants accepted	45
% acceptees attending	37
Average GMAT	642
Range of GMAT	600–700
Accepts GRE scores	Yes
Average Verbal GRE	154
Range of Verbal GRE scores	147–158
Average Quantitative GRE	152
Range of Quantitative GRE scores	143–154
Average Writing GRE	4.2
Range of Writing GRE scores	3.5–4.5
Average GPA	3.2
TOEFL required of international students	Yes
Minimum TOEFL (paper/web)	600/100
Application fee	$100
International application fee	$100
Application Deadline/Notification	
Round 1:	11/16 / 12/21
Round 2:	1/11 / 3/7
Round 3:	3/21 / 5/9
Round 4:	5/30 / 6/27
Deferment available	No
Transfer students accepted	Yes
Transfer application policy	
Maximum number of transferable credits is 6 semester hours from an AACSB-accredited program.	
Non-fall admissions	No
Need-blind admissions	Yes

EMPLOYMENT PROFILE

Career Rating	90	Grads Employed by Function	% Avg. Salary
Percent employed at graduation	50	Marketing	(21%) $71,833
Percent employed 3 months after graduation	83	Operations	(15%)
		Consulting	(27%) $92,504
Average base starting salary	$79,641	Management	(12%) $63,121
Primary Source of Full-time Job Acceptances		Finance	(15%) $88,754
School-facilitated activities	27 (82%)	HR	(6%)
Graduate-facilitated activities	6 (18%)	MIS	(3%)
		Other	(0%)

Top 5 Employers Hiring Grads
American Greetings (1), Cleveland Clinic (1), Deloitte Consulting (1), Goodyear (1), KeyBank (1)

CENTRAL MICHIGAN UNIVERSITY
COLLEGE OF BUSINESS ADMINISTRATION

GENERAL INFORMATION

Type of school	public
Affiliation	No Affiliation
Academic calendar	semester

SURVEY SAYS...

Friendly students, Happy students
Solid preparation in:
General management, Teamwork,
Communication/interpersonal skills,
Quantitative skills, Doing business in
a global economy

STUDENTS

Enrollment of MBA Program	113
% male/female	64/36
% out-of-state	34
% part-time	49
% international	34
Average age at entry	28
Average years work experience at entry	3

ACADEMICS

Academic Experience Rating	67
Profs interesting rating	69
Profs accessible rating	75
Student/faculty ratio	23:1
% female faculty	20
% underrepresented minority faculty	10

Prominent Alumni

Roger L. Kesseler, Retired, VP
& Controller, The Dow Chemical
Company; Jerry D. Campbell, Pres.
& CEO, Community National Bank of
the South; Michael Fred O'Donnell,
Retired, Managing Director, Protiviti
Inc.; Robert I. Noe, CEO, 1 Sync;
Michael J. Bowen, Chairman & CEO,
Westwood Development Group

Academics

Central Michigan University offers a comprehensive MBA program with a focus on general management. Students appreciate the fact that "the program is affordable, and offers flexible scheduling though weekend classes and night classes." CMU's "well-structured...flexible" curriculum begins with a set of foundational and core courses, taught in a series of quick, eight-week terms. While the core is "very broad," students can later pursue a concentration in one of many fields, including accounting, business economics, general management, management consulting, and management information systems. Emphasizing real-world business skills, CMU "allows students to learn through practical applications of techniques," including case studies, simulations, and consulting projects. "Faculty is the greatest strength" here. Well-versed in contemporary business topics, "the graduate level professors in the business school contribute well-researched concepts with real-world practices to provide students with a relevant, practical skill set."

CMU offers the complete full-time MBA on its main campus in Mount Pleasant, as well as at its auxiliary facilities in Midland, Michigan. "All MBA classes are in the evenings [and] some on weekends," which makes the program a "great fit for full-time employees." At the same time, the program is appropriate for early career professionals who want to make a move into management positions, and many complete the program on a full-time basis. No matter what your previous professional preparation, the small class size "fosters communication through insightful dialogue between students and faculty" and "really allow[s] students to become more involved in the learning process." In most classes, "students are willing to engage in thoughtful conversation and challenge the view points of both other students and faculty." With a low graduate enrollment and a patently "friendly atmosphere," CMU's environment is student-centered and supportive. While the workload in some classes can be "very heavy," the teaching staff is "down-to-earth and easy to talk to," comprised of caring professors who "truly want what's best for the student." Similarly, "the administration at CMU is very competent and willing to help with an open-door policy to its students."

Career and Placement

Thanks to the school's flexible schedule and convenient evening classes, a large percentage of CMU students are working professionals—many of whom may not be looking for a new position after graduation. For those starting a new career (or those who want to make a career change), Central Michigan University's MBA program is designed to prepare students for a position in management, with numerous real world and practical experiences woven into the curriculum.

The university Career Services department maintains a job vacancy bulletin and hosts campus career fairs; however, students in the MBA program say the school could improve if they "spread more awareness of their programs." With such a strong academic program, students admit that, "CMU could improve how they market themselves as a business school. The quality of the MBA program is an aspect they should take greater steps to express to the nation."

ADMISSIONS CONTACT: PAMELA STAMBERSKY, MBA ADVISOR
ADDRESS: 252 ABSC-GRAWN HALL, MOUNT PLEASANT, MI 48859
PHONE: 989-774-3150 • FAX: 989-774-1320
E-MAIL: MBA@CMICH.EDU • WEBSITE: WWW.CBA.CMICH.EDU

Student Life and Environment

Attracting a mix of "international students, professionals, and full-time students," you might be "surprised at the diversity" on CMU's small, Midwestern campus. "There are a lot of foreign students and it is so cool to get to know people from around the world. You see many of the same faces as you move through the program so you are able to get to know people and make good friendships and networking connections." Across the board, students are "driven and striving for success in the program" and "willing to lend a hand."

"There is definitely a small-class, small-school feel" at CMU. The campus is "intimate, friendly, [and] safe," and "it is very easy to feel comfortable and welcome here." "People are very friendly, and good team players." While academics (and professional life) keep students on the go, there is more to CMU than classes and homework. "There are a multitude of clubs and activities for students to join," both through the business school, as well as the university at large. Juggling work and school, some part-timers don't have time to participate in extracurricular activities; others take full advantage of the school's lively atmosphere. A current MBA agrees, "As a married graduate student with a full-time career, I still find CMU to be engaging both in the classroom and on campus in general. There are plenty of student organizations, activities, and professional networking opportunities to take advantage of."

Most part-time students commute to school, while many full-time students live on campus. Unfortunately, campus residents without a car can feel a bit stranded. Happily, the CMU campus provides the necessary amenities, with "plenty of facilities like computer labs, libraries, [and a] student activity center." As its name implies, Mount Pleasant makes a nice backdrop to campus life; "the campus is located in a safe town, so students can freely walk around the beautiful campus and enjoy themselves." During the summer, students also enjoy "kayaking down the Chippewa River, bicycle trails, and events such as home shows and boat shows that are hosted on campus."

FINANCIAL FACTS

Annual tuition (in-state/ out-of-state)	$13,303/$23,746
Cost of books	$1,600
Room & board (on/off-campus)	$7,947/

ADMISSIONS

Admissions Selectivity Rating	80
# of applications received	93
% applicants accepted	86
% acceptees attending	89
Average GMAT	513
Average GPA	3.6
TOEFL required of international students	Yes
Minimum TOEFL (paper/web)	550/
Application fee	$35
International application fee	$45
Deferment available	Yes
Maximum length of deferment	one semester
Transfer students accepted	Yes
Transfer application policy	
Limit of 12 credit hours from an accredited institution	
Non-fall admissions	Yes
Need-blind admissions	No

CHAPMAN UNIVERSITY
THE GEORGE L. ARGYROS SCHOOL OF BUSINESS AND ECONOMICS

Academics

Chapman University, a "small," "beautiful" private university in Orange County, California, has a "very strong MBA program" that offers students a great education. But "it's not just about the classes," at Chapman. "It is about the relationships, the networking, and the experience. It is a comprehensive, 360-degree program." Chapman is "a research-intensive university" that offers "entrepreneurship incubators" and many other unique opportunities to its enthusiastic students. This is just one of the many reasons students are convinced that Chapman "will become one of the top business schools in the nation."

Chapman's distinguishing features include its programs in Entrepreneurship and Financial services, a dual MBA/MFA in Film and Television Producing, a "good study-abroad program" and its popular Flex MBA, which allows working students to attend full- or part-time during the evening. Chapman's traditional full-time MBA program has a strong focus on student career campaign. Students in both programs receive the majority of their credits from Chapman's core curriculum, which provides a solid foundation in business and finance. Electives include entrepreneurship, international business, corporate entrepreneurship, and marketing.

Students say they receive a "very personalized education" from the "outstanding faculty." Chapman's small classes are taught by "Ph.D.s and established professionals," who are "dedicated," "highly accessible," and "expect a lot." Academic and professional development is complimented by mentoring programs and contests run by the Ralph W. Leatherby Center for Entrepreneurship and Business Ethics, and research opportunities, conferences, and workshops hosted by the A. Gary Anderson Center for Economic Research, The Walter Schmidt Center for International Business, and Larry C. Hoag for Real Estate and Finance. Beyond the campus, the school has strong ties to the local business community, which gives students the chance to forge "lasting business relationships." Chapman students say the school does an excellent job preparing them to deal with "current economic conditions" and whatever else they may face in the future.

Career and Placement

Chapman's MBA program "has only become stronger with the addition of a highly visible office (Career Management Center) on campus," which employs "three full-time career placement specialists" to assist and support students in reaching their career goals. The center provides lots of specialized opportunities through individual career counseling and its many networking events, including the "Dinner for Eight" program, where eight students are selected to have an intimate dinner with a local business leader. One student says that the greatest strength of Chapman isn't the Career Management Center but "the people associated with the school," who provide "strong contacts, great jobs, networking, and lasting business relationships." The majority of graduates accepting new jobs took positions in the consumer products field, or in media or entertainment. The top five employers last year were Standard Pacific Homes, Ingram Micro, Experian, ADP, Commerce National Bank, and Lanes Capital Partners.

Student Life and Environment

Life at Chapman is filled with opportunities for networking and academic enrichment. The Entrepreneur Speaker Series and the Distinguished Speaker series regularly host influential business leaders, and each of the four research institutes offer additional lectures, panel discussions, and even book signings. The MBA association, run by a group of students elected by their peers, organizes lots of social and professional events, such as "Pizza and Beer Night," which "gives students the opportunity to eat and have some drinks with a high profile executive in a relaxed, non-pretentious atmosphere."

Many Chapman students attend part-time, and students tend to be on the younger side, so there is a wide-range of work experience and perspectives in classrooms. Though many students come from work in business attire, others sport "flip-flops and board shorts," though they "clean up nice, when they have to." Students are "friendly" and "smart," and are "very willing to collaborate and help one another succeed." They're "not at all competitive about grades, so study groups are very common." "There are a lot of sports and community events" for students who need a break from homework or networking, and "plenty of nearby restaurants and bars that support a small community vibe."

Admissions

Students entering Chapman have three years of work experience on average, and though the school prefers students to have spent at least two years in a professional field, they do accept strong applicants with experience. The GMAT or GRE is required for all programs except the Executive MBA. In addition to GMAT scores, the application package must also include two recommendations from people who know the student "in either a professional or academic setting." Students must have a minimum undergraduate GPA of 2.5, but the average undergraduate GPA of the entering class is considerably higher. Interviews are required for the full-time and Executive MBA program, while interviews for the Flex program "are by request or invitation." International students must take the TOEFL and have minimum scores of 600 for the paper-based portion, 213 for the computer-based, and 87 for the Internet-based portion or IELTS with a minimum score of 7. Applications for the full-time and Executive MBA programs are accepted for the fall semester only. Applications for the Flex Program are accepted for the fall and spring.

FINANCIAL FACTS

Annual tuition (in-state/ out-of-state)	$36,750/$36,750
Cost of books	$1,000
Room & board (on/off-campus)	$20,100/$20,100
% of students receiving aid	86
% of first-year students receiving aid	86
% of students receiving grants	73
Average award package	$31,000
Average grant	$15,811
Average loan	$36,042
Average student loan debt	$100,518

ADMISSIONS

Admissions Selectivity Rating	82
# of applications received	198
% applicants accepted	72
% acceptees attending	55
Average GMAT	579
Range of GMAT	528–640
Accepts GRE scores	Yes
Average Verbal GRE	148
Range of Verbal GRE scores	143–155
Average Quantitative GRE	150
Range of Quantitative GRE scores	146–152
Average Writing GRE	3.8
Range of Writing GRE scores	3.0–4.1
Average GPA	3.1
TOEFL required of international students	Yes
Minimum TOEFL (paper/web)	/87
Application fee	$60
International application fee	$60
Regular application deadline	6/1
Application Deadline	
Round 1:	11/1
Round 2:	2/1
Round 3:	6/1
Deferment available	Yes
Maximum length of deferment	1 year
Transfer students accepted	Yes
Transfer application policy	
Transfer up to six units of course work	
Non-fall admissions	Yes
Need-blind admissions	Yes

EMPLOYMENT PROFILE

Career Rating	80	Grads Employed by Function	% Avg. Salary
Percent employed at graduation	67	Marketing	(28%) $46,300
Percent employed 3 months after graduation	22	Finance	(22%) $53,750
Average base starting salary	$55,947	**Top 5 Employers Hiring Grads**	
Primary Source of Full-time Job Acceptances		Ingram Micro (2), PriceWaterhouseCoopers	
School-facilitated activities	6 (33%)	(1), United Entertainment Partners (1), Colliers	
Graduate-facilitated activities	8 (44%)	International (1), Amobee (1)	
Unknown	4 (22%)		

THE CHINESE UNIVERSITY OF HONG KONG
FACULTY OF BUSINESS ADMINISTRATION

Academics

In 1966, The Chinese University of Hong Kong became the first school in China to offer a full-time MBA program. Today, the university boasts one of the most reputable business schools in Asia and the Pacific, attracting students for its "international recognition, good academic reputation, and diverse teacher and student pools." A great entryway for those seeking a professional position in Hong Kong, the school boasts a "strong alumni network" in the city and an excellent reputation in the region. In particular, the school is touted for its programs in finance and marketing, with a special emphasis on Chinese business. Through lecture, case studies, group work, directed research, and discussion, classes are a balance of "individual and group efforts that cultivate teamwork among students that is important for business." Group work is particularly gratifying at CUMBA, where students comprise "a very diverse group from just about every continent. Their combined work experience and life experiences has really contributed to the program."

Maintaining a working relationship with various universities in mainland China and Taiwan, the school's "administration is very dedicated and efficient." The school attracts faculty from all over the world, and the current teaching staff includes professors from Australia, Hong Kong, Europe, New Zealand, mainland China, Southeast Asia, Taiwan, and the United States. Despite their varied origins, CUMBA faculty are deeply engaged in the Hong Kong business culture. A student attests, "Teaching staff are actively involved in the business community in areas of research and consulting. So there are lots of first-hand findings and . . . information [on] local business trends." On the whole, students appreciate the school's progressive outlook, saying professors "stay abreast of the real-life market and keep up to date with their own knowledge."

While Cantonese is the dominant language spoken in Hong Kong, courses at CUMBA are taught in English, with the exception of a few elective courses whose unique nature demands instruction in Chinese. The fifty-four-unit curriculum consists of required core course work, followed by electives. Through electives, students have the option to pursue a concentration in one of four areas: China business, finance, marketing, or entrepreneurship. The full-time curriculum can be completed in sixteen months of study, including internships. Without an internship, the program can be completed as quickly as twelve months. Either way, the program is intense, with a "busy workload and no breaks in between terms." In addition to the traditional MBA programs offered through the school, students may choose to pursue a joint-degree with partner universities in Mainland China or the HEC School of Management in France or the University of Texas at Austin.

Career and Placement

As part of the MBA experience, students at The Chinese University of Hong Kong are expected to develop career goals and design a plan of action to meet those goals. The Career Management Centre facilitates students looking for summer internship placements, as well as students looking for permanent positions after graduation. The centre also hosts an executive development series on presentation, communication, and influencing skills project management, and a series of career talks and job search workshops.

The Asian market continues to be a popular work location for CUMBA graduates. An over-whelming 92 percent have taken up career opportunities in this region. The ever growing Greater China market has attracted 72 percent of the class to continue to pursue their career development (47 percent in Hong Kong, 21 percent in China and 4 percent in Taiwan). Twenty percent are spilt among other Asian countries including India, Singapore, Japan, Korea and Thailand—truly reflecting the diversity of the students in contributing to the growth of this ever important continent.

ADMISSIONS CONTACT: MR. LAWRENCE CHAN, ADM DIRECTOR
ADDRESS: RM. G01, LEUNG KAU KUI BUILDING, CUHK SHATIN, NT
PHONE: 011-852-2609-7783 • FAX: 011-852-2603-6289
E-MAIL: CUMBA@CUHK.EDU.HK • WEBSITE: WWW.CUHK.EDU.HK/MBA

Nearly 91 percent of these graduates have been successfully undergoing career changes, either in job function (86 percent) or work location (46 percent), or both (34 percent). The Chinese University of Hong Kong's comprehensive MBA curriculum with a strategic focus in China and Asia plays an essential part in equipping career changers in facing the challenges of transformation and enabling them to explore new ventures in their targeted industries and locations.

Graduates have successfully moved from non-business and/or technical background to front line business development, consulting, or finance function. These career changers have proved their abilities to bring transferrable skill sets and strategic insights to their new roles.

Student Life and Environment

CUMBA boasts a "beautiful campus" environment, and its daytime and weekend-mode students take classes on the main campus. In 2010, the business school moved into a state-of-the-art new teaching building near its main campus, and classes from then on will be given there. Evening-mode students attend classes in the school's MBA Town Centre, a modern and spacious 900-square-meter facility located in downtown. In addition to the extensive computer facilities available via the larger university, MBA students have access to over 100 microcomputers in the Town Centre, connected via LAN network. MBA students have the option of living on campus in the graduate residence halls; they also have access to the school's sports facilities, including three indoor gyms and an Olympic-sized swimming pool.

One of the major attractions of CUMBA is its diverse student population, who bring experience "from a variety of professions and cultures." Totally student-run, the MBA Student's Association sponsors a broad range of social and professional events, including executive seminars, company visits, and study tours to mainland China. The school also sponsors various social and recreational events, such as charity and fund-raising activities and sports teams, although some students say, "Campus life is not adapted to international students at all." Even part-timers enjoy a sense of community. One says, "I am a part-time student. Fellow students usually have dinner gatherings after school."

Admissions

To be considered for admission to CUMBA, prospective students must hold an undergraduate degree (with at least a B average), have at least three years of relevant work experience post-graduation, and submit current GMAT scores. The average GMAT score for accepted applicants changes every year; however, the class average usually hovers between 620–640. Interviews are required for all short-listed applicants, either in person or via telephone, as determined by the selection committee.

FINANCIAL FACTS

Annual tuition (in-state/
  out-of-state) $61,700/$61,700
Room & board
  (on/off-campus) $5,700/$11,500

ADMISSIONS

Admissions Selectivity Rating	74
Average GMAT	650
Accepts GRE scores	No
Recommended	
Application fee	$100
International application fee	$100
Early application deadline	10/31
Regular application deadline	3/31
Regular application notification	5/31
Application Deadline/Notification	
Round 1:	11/30 / 1/31
Round 2:	1/15 / 3/15
Round 3:	3/31 / 5/31
Deferment available	Yes
Maximum length of	
deferment	1 year
Transfer students accepted	No
Non-fall admissions	No
Need-blind admissions	Yes

EMPLOYMENT PROFILE

Career Rating	64	Grads Employed by Function% Avg. Salary	
Percent employed at graduation	66	Marketing	(36%)
Percent employed 3 months		Consulting	(13%)
after graduation	23	Management	(4%)
		Finance	(27%)
		Other	(7%)

Top 5 Employers Hiring Grads
Google, PricewaterhouseCoopers Consulting, Bank of China International, BlackRock, Bulgari

THE CITADEL
SCHOOL OF BUSINESS ADMINISTRATION

Academics

If there is one word students at The School of Business Administration at The Citadel keep repeating, it's "reputation," "reputation," "reputation," with "location," "prestige" and "affordability" all coming in at a close second. The Citadel's long-standing record for "building leaders and sound decision-makers," educating "quality students," and having "by far the best MBA reputation in South Carolina" make the School a universally respected institution worldwide. What's more, just saying you go to The Citadel "gets a reaction from people." Students can also benefit from "in-state tuition" and "excellent professors"—forty-one in all—"with incredible work and academic histories," most of whom "are working professionals, some with military backgrounds." According to one sales management major, the "administration and professors are flexible, encouraging, and easily accessible. The MBA program has challenged me in many ways, and the overall educational experience has been very rewarding." Another like-minded student tells us, "All professors consider the global perspective and tailor their classes" accordingly.

The MBA program at The Citadel is roughly a two to six year program, depending on students' work status and class load, totaling thirty-six credit hours. Other dual-degree programs, such as the PharmD/MBA and MD/MBA will often require the same amount of time from students. Candidates have the option to pursue areas of study in sports management, financial services, supply chain management, and project management. In their course of study, all enrolled students are required to take classes that specifically emphasize cooperative learning and experiential learning, while internships and entrepreneurship courses are both offered but not required.

One unique co-curricular offering at The Citadel is the Mentors Program, which matches MBA students with leaders in the local business community. Students who choose to participate in this program will be matched with a prominent business leader based on common interest and career path. Students also have the option to pursue study abroad, which offers programs in Ireland, Spain, France, and the UK.

Career and Placement

The Citadel's Career Services Center maintains an online job and resume database for current students and alumni. The Center also has working relationships with several online job boards, which give students a wide breadth of places to begin their job hunts. In addition, the Center organizes several career fairs, which are open to the entire school community. As one "of the most highly recognized business schools" in the area, recruiters and companies will be on the lookout for recent graduates, but overall "career training and placement" are areas in need of attention from the administration. One student enrolled in a dual-degree PharmD/MBA pointed out, "Boeing is expanding into Charleston, and a lot of opportunities are passed along to the Citadel MBA students." Another student, a childcare administration major, tells us, "There is a very active MBA Association that is always organizing activities." Additionally, the School will often receive "many interesting speakers," and "alumni visit often," all of which offer unique and abundant networking opportunities for MBA candidates on the job-hunt.

ADMISSIONS CONTACT: KATHY JONES, DIRECTOR OF MBA PROGRAM AND BUSINESS SCHOOL OPERATIONS
ADDRESS: 171 MOULTRIE STREET, CHARLESTON, SC 29409
PHONE: 843-953-5257 • FAX: 843-953-6764
E-MAIL: CGC@CITADEL.EDU • WEBSITE: CITADEL.EDU/CSBA

Student Life and Environment

Among the reasons many students give for wanting to earn their MBA at The Citadel, it's often as simple as, "it's in Charleston." Much celebrated for its relaxed pace, friendly residents, and pristine ocean-front locale, Charleston, South Carolina, is a major draw for just about anyone. Thanks to the city's bucolic setting and old world charm, some students have cited the School's "old world study environment," consisting of leather couches and chairs, high ceilings, and old paintings." For prospective MBA students, The Citadel's status as a military academy can be somewhat misleading. One student reminds us that, while there "a lot of ex- or current military students, which is kind of to be expected at a military school, I was actually surprised at the number of non-military affiliated classmates." Another student touches on a similar point, offering that The Citadel is "much more diverse than one would expect at a conservative Southern military school."

On par with this sentiment, The Citadel does offer a wide range of activities for students, in addition to increasingly flexible scheduling options for commuters and part-time students with full-time jobs. "I'm very happy that the School is introducing more and more online courses," says a music business major. Many other students are taking advantage of The Citadel's night school program, which accommodates those who "work all day, then come straight to school" and will often take only "two classes per semester."

Admissions

Applicants to the MBA program at The Citadel must submit the following materials: GMAT scores, essay/personal statement, official undergrad transcript, resume, and at least two letters of recommendation. Other materials, such as proof of state residency, list of extracurricular activities, and an interview, are all optional but recommended. GRE scores will be taken into consideration, and proof of US residency or immigration form if an international student. Interestingly enough, while GMAT scores are given due attention, The Citadel places greater emphasis on an applicant's undergraduate GPA and essay/personal statement, indicating the school's vested interest in working with students who show exceptional aptitude, work ethic, and sincere desire to attend The Citadel.

FINANCIAL FACTS

Cost of books	$500
% of students receiving aid	28
% of students receiving grants	2
Average award package	$9,335
Average grant	$17,229
Average loan	$9,109
Average student loan debt	$24,379

ADMISSIONS

Admissions Selectivity Rating	79
# of applications received	47
% applicants accepted	89
% acceptees attending	95
Average GMAT	506
Range of GMAT	410–638
Accepts GRE scores	Yes
Average GPA	3.1
TOEFL required of international students	Yes
Minimum TOEFL (paper/web)	550/79
Application fee	$40
International application fee	$40
Regular application deadline	7/15
Regular application notification	7/15
Deferment available	Yes
Maximum length of deferment	12 Months
Transfer students accepted	Yes
Transfer application policy	A maximum of six hours credit for graduate courses from an AACSB-accredited institutions may be approved for transfer.
Non-fall admissions	Yes
Need-blind admissions	Yes

CITY UNIVERSITY OF NEW YORK—BARUCH COLLEGE
ZICKLIN SCHOOL OF BUSINESS

GENERAL INFORMATION
Type of school   Public
Affiliation   No Affiliation
Academic calendar   Semester

SURVEY SAYS...
Liberal students, Students love New York, NY, Classmates have diverse work experience
Solid preparation in:
Teamwork, Communication/interpersonal skills

STUDENTS
Enrollment of parent
  institution   16,500
Enrollment of MBA Program   1,531
% male/female   60/40
% part-time   87
% underrepresented minority   11
% international   22
Average age at entry   28
Average years work
  experience at entry   5

ACADEMICS
Academic Experience Rating   **88**
Profs interesting rating   86
Profs accessible rating   89
Student/faculty ratio   35:1
% female faculty   23
% underrepresented
  minority faculty   5
% part-time faculty   27

Joint Degrees
JD/MBA, 4.5 years (full-time)

Prominent Alumni
Larry Zicklin, Former Managing Partner, Neuberger Berman; Marcel Legrand, Sr. Vice President, Monster.com; JoAnn Ryan, President, ConEdison Solutions; William Newman, Founder & Chairman New Plan Excel Realty Trust; Hugh Panero, President & CEO, XM Satellite Radio

Academics

Baruch College's Zicklin School of Business sits at the intersection of quality, affordability, and opportunity. Students universally praise the school's cost and location, calling Zicklin the "best value in the greatest city" and rave about their access to "powerful resources and alumni." The school's "flexibility" and part-time study options make it is especially valuable for students who need to keep their full-time jobs (or take care of their full-time families). "It allowed me to continue working full-time and obtain my MBA in the evenings," one MBA student specializing in healthcare and government explains. Because of Baruch's "diversity, great curriculum, practical lessons, [and] on-campus recruitments," students consistently judge it to be "one of the top schools for 'return on investment.'"

While Baruch may not have the cachet of other New York City business schools, the "teachers are excellent, [the] curriculum is tough, and [it] will prepare you for the workplace." Baruch boasts top programs in accountancy, which students describe as "the #1 program for accountancy in New York State," as well as "international business and entrepreneurship programs with great success rates." The rigorous academics are challenging, and some first-year students find it "hard to keep up," especially when the material is unfamiliar. "Academics are tough especially in the first semester," one full-time student and former attorney comments. "Teachers are available, but sometimes the amount of work makes it hard to go for help. Those students [without a quantitative] background or [undergraduate] business degrees do find the work exceedingly challenging, and it's hard to keep up." Another student believes the curriculum needs "better class balance in the first semester" and that the program could benefit from "early start for non-business majors/background."

But students say those challenges are mitigated by "consistently good faculty and customer service." Accessible faculty "allow us to email them," rather than strictly relying on office hours, "because they understand that most of us have full-time jobs and families to take care of," one accounting student explains. Students say they take away a lot from these "great professors with real-life experience in building businesses or holding executive positions in large institutions." "Some faculty are amazingly good," and most "are top-notch, very well known in their respective fields, highly educated, and very accomplished."

Career Placement

Baruch's location offers great access to one of the world's major financial hubs along with "an innumerable amount of internships and professional development opportunities." Students say that the school's "excellent reputation around Wall Street" means that it "consistently ranks as a top school for Wall Street firms." Some students complain about Baruch's administration, describing it as "a huge bureaucracy," where "it is sometimes difficult to reach some of the administrative offices by phone." But those same students say the "the MBA advisors are great," and remind prospective students that "all comparisons for Baruch need to be made with the very affordable tuition in mind." Students also get career exposure from their professors, who "have great careers in great companies, share their experiences with students, and arrange for other top business leaders in various industries to speak with and motivate students."

ADMISSIONS CONTACT: THOMAS LO, ASSOCIATE DIRECTOR OF GRADUATE ADMISSIONS
ADDRESS: ONE BERNARD BARUCH WAY, BOX H-0820, NEW YORK, NY 10010
PHONE: 646-312-1300 • FAX: 646-312-1301
E-MAIL: ZICKLINGRADADMISSIONS@BARUCH.CUNY.EDU
WEBSITE: WWW.BARUCH.CUNY.EDU/ZICKLIN

Student Life and Environment

Business students at Baruch are "diverse, successful, [and] driven." The "different professional backgrounds" and the cultural diversity represented in the student body make for "stimulating conversations during lecture." Everyone is "friendly and eager to learn and network," "open to discussions and debates," and "work together well as a team." Students "often meet together outside of school" and generally describe each other as "good friends and great people to work with." The school provides "various student activities and clubs that are beneficial to students of diverse backgrounds," and "the school provides a lounge and a locker, so it makes it easier to relax between classes."

Admissions

An accredited bachelor's degree with official transcripts must be submitted along with either GRE or GMAT scores, letters of recommendation, undergraduate GPA, and a personal statement describing career goals and your reasons for obtaining a graduate degree. A résumé with evidence of professional work experience is required as are TOEFL scores for international students. The first round of applications is due 11/01; the second round is due 01/31; the third round is due 4/15; and applications for the part-time MBA are due 06/01.

FINANCIAL FACTS

Annual tuition (in-state/ out-of-state)	$12,770/$24,795
Fees	$2,269
Cost of books	$1,337
Room & board	$21,450
% of students receiving aid	80
% of first-year students receiving aid	95
% of students receiving grants	60
Average grant	$4,000
Average loan	$16,300
Average student loan debt	$30,000

ADMISSIONS

Admissions Selectivity Rating	88
# of applications received	1,146
% applicants accepted	47
% acceptees attending	62
Average GMAT	591
Range of GMAT	550–640
Accepts GRE scores	Yes
Average Verbal GRE	151
Average GPA	3.3
TOEFL required of international students	Yes
Minimum TOEFL (paper/web)	610/102
Application fee	$135
International application fee	$135
Early application deadline	1/15
Early notification date	3/31
Regular application deadline	5/31
Application Deadline/Notification	
Round 1:	1/15 / 3/31
Round 2:	4/15 / 6/30
Deferment available	Yes
Maximum length of deferment	1 year
Transfer students accepted	Yes
Transfer application policy	
Same application process as all applicants; up to 12 credits from an AACSB-accredited institution may be transferred.	
Non-fall admissions	Yes
Need-blind admissions	Yes

EMPLOYMENT PROFILE

Career Rating	81	Grads Employed by Function	% Avg. Salary
Percent employed at graduation	39	Marketing	(7%)
Percent employed 3 months after graduation	13	Operations	(11%) $83,833
		Consulting	(14%) $105,000
Average base starting salary	$81,678	Management	(4%)
Primary Source of Full-time Job Acceptances		Finance	(50%) $84,615
School-facilitated activities	12 (43%)	HR	(4%)
Graduate-facilitated activities	15 (54%)	MIS	(4%)
Unknown	1 (4%)	Other	(7%)

Top 5 Employers Hiring Grads
PwC (5), Ernst & Young (3), JPMorgan Chase (2)

CLAREMONT GRADUATE UNIVERSITY
THE PETER F. DRUCKER AND MASATOSHI ITO GRADUATE SCHOOL OF MANAGEMENT

GENERAL INFORMATION
Type of school	Private
Affiliation	No Affiliation
Academic calendar	Semester

SURVEY SAYS...
Friendly students, Liberal students, Happy students, Students love Claremont, CA
Solid preparation in:
General management, Teamwork, Social responsibility

STUDENTS
Enrollment of parent institution	2,200
Enrollment of MBA Program	109
% male/female	69/31
% part-time	27
% underrepresented minority	9
% international	50
Average age at entry	27
Average years work experience at entry	3

ACADEMICS
Academic Experience Rating	**84**
Profs interesting rating	93
Profs accessible rating	94
Student/faculty ratio	3:1
% female faculty	31
% underrepresented minority faculty	27
% part-time faculty	62

Joint Degrees
Dual-degree programs in Human Resources, Biosciences, Information Sciences, Economics, Art Business, Law, Industrial Design, Education, Psychology, Public Policy, and by special arrangement in other disciplines.

Academics

The Peter F. Drucker and Masatoshi Ito Graduate School of Management operates a distinctive MBA program in general management, which "embeds both business and social values into its curriculum." The school's "unique management philosophy" is largely inspired by the eponymous Peter F. Drucker, a pioneer writer and thinker in the field of management theory and practice. Particularly interesting is the school's Drucker-inspired concept of "management as a liberal art," which "gives students the opportunity to gain insights into management from various perspectives." In addition to "classes that focus on leadership, sustainability, organizational development, and effective management," every student must "take a class solely based on Drucker's philosophies as a core requirement." Of particular note, the Drucker MBA focuses on "developing ethical leaders," with class materials constantly emphasizing "the importance of social responsibility in business."

Drucker offers a number of graduate-level business degrees, including an MA in Arts Management as well as three options for the MBA: a full-time MBA in the day, a fully employed MBA for working professionals, and an executive MBA in the evenings and weekends. Students in all three programs have access to intensive overseas courses, offered during semester breaks, as well as semester-long exchange programs. While students are not required to complete an internship, "There are plenty of opportunities for students to get access to various companies through the many extracurricular clubs offered like the Entrepreneur & Venture Capital Club that visits businesses and entrepreneurs in Southern California." Most Drucker instructors are "excellent teachers," who are "very talented [and] well trained in their fields." While most have PhDs in business, the program is not overly academic; "material feels very up to date and applicable." While some students would like to see more academic rigor, they also appreciate the school's "good reputation" as a member of the Claremont Consortium of Colleges, which includes such well-known institutions as Pomona College and Claremont McKenna.

A "boutique" school with intimate class sizes, Drucker students benefit from "small classes and extremely close and personal interaction with professors." In addition to office hours, "it's not uncommon to be invited to lunch or coffee with a professor." When it comes to participating in this management-focused school, students are not let down: "The MBA Administration at Claremont Graduate University is amazing," consistently demonstrating accessibility, as well as "a willingness to accommodate the various needs of students." Despite incorporating a number of distinct degree programs, "there is a very good culture of communication between the administration, professors and students."

Career and Placement

The Career Management office at Drucker works with students on career planning, skills development, and networking. They also oversee an alumni mentor program, which connects current students with graduates of the MBA. Nonetheless, students would like to see "better relations with alumni" across the board. Unlike at larger business programs, "recruiters do not come on campus" for interviews, though students notice that there has been a recent push to bring more companies to Drucker for interviews and networking events. Though still slightly beleaguered, "recruitment has increased and the effort is noticeable, but [it is] a work in progress."

ADMISSIONS CONTACT: NOLA WANTA, SENIOR DIRECTOR OF ADMISSIONS AND MANAGEMENT PROFILES
ADDRESS: 1021 NORTH DARTMOUTH AVENUE, CLAREMONT, CA 91711
PHONE: 909-607-7811 • FAX: 909-607-9104
E-MAIL: DRUCKER@CGU.EDU • WEBSITE: WWW.DRUCKER.CGU.EDU

For the class of 2013, at least 75 percent of graduates were employed within three months of graduation, with an average starting salary of almost $61,333. There are Drucker graduates living in all fifty states, and recent graduates have accepted positions at a range of companies, including Bank of NY Mellon, Barclays Capital, Northwest Airlines, Ernst & Young, Deutsche Bank, General Motors, Goldman Sachs, International Monetary Fund, KPMG, Mattel, and Risk Management Solutions, among many others.

Student Life and Environment

Maybe it's all that Southern California sunshine, but students at Drucker say the school's "atmosphere is light and harmonious." Attracting MBA candidates from across the country, as well as internationally, "the student body is very diverse." In the full-time program, students "generally skew younger and less experienced," but they are nonetheless "friendly and eager to learn." Friendships blossom easily, and collaboration is more common than competition among classmates. A student explains, "We are competitive on a friendly level, for example in case competitions we get very competitive, yet we can also go grab a beer at the end of the day and have a good time."

When they are not hitting the books, Drucker students are eager to socialize with their colleagues. Among other campus events, the school hosts "regular student mixers," of which the biweekly Thursdays on Drucker Way are particularly popular. It's hard to dispute the fact that "beer, food, and table tennis is a nice way to end the week." Located in the small town of Claremont, just north of Pomona, California, and east of Los Angeles, "Claremont is known as the city of trees and PhDs." Around the business school, "the landscape is beautiful," and it is located "close to the village (downtown) so we can easily walk there if we need anything that isn't on campus." A current student enthuses, "I'm having the time of my life here!"

Admissions

To apply to Claremont Graduate University, prospective MBA candidates must submit a completed application, academic transcripts from all college-level coursework, current GMAT or GRE scores, three letters of recommendation, a personal statement, and a resume. Qualified candidates are invited to interview on campus; a current student warns, "The interviewing process to be admitted to the program was not easy." Students entering the full-time program had an average undergraduate GPA 3.29 and an average GMAT score of 609, with a range of 580-660. Students applying to the EMBA must have at least five years of experience in a senior-level position.

Prominent Alumni

Tawni Cranz, Chief Talent Officer, Netflix, Inc.; Junro Ito, Executive Officer and Director, Seven & i Holdings Co., Ltd.; Sirena Liu, Managing Director, China, 20th Century Fox; Mark Hatch, CEO & Co-Founder, TechShop

FINANCIAL FACTS

Annual tuition (in-state/ out-of-state)	$59,104/$59,104
Fees	$500
Cost of books	$800
Room & board (on/off-campus)	$8,100/$8,100
% of students receiving aid	71
% of first-year students receiving aid	76
% of students receiving grants	56
Average grant	$10,361
Average loan	$20,500
Average student loan debt	$28,097

ADMISSIONS

Admissions Selectivity Rating	72
# of applications received	153
% applicants accepted	49
% acceptees attending	47
Accepts GRE scores	Yes
TOEFL required of international students	Yes
Minimum TOEFL (paper/web)	/75
Application fee	$80
International application fee	$80
Early application deadline	11/1
Early notification date	12/1
Regular application deadline	2/1
Regular application notification	3/1
Application Deadline/Notification	
Round 1:	11/1 / 12/1
Round 2:	2/1 / 3/1
Round 3:	7/1 / 8/1
Round 4:	8/15 / 8/25
Deferment available	Yes
Maximum length of deferment	1 year
Transfer students accepted	Yes
Transfer application policy	
The maximum number of transferable credits is 10 units.	
Non-fall admissions	Yes
Need-blind admissions	Yes

EMPLOYMENT PROFILE

Career Rating	76	**Grads Employed by Function% Avg. Salary**	
Average base starting salary	$66,587	Marketing	(19%) $66,500
		Operations	(7%)
		Consulting	(19%) $118,333
		Management	(19%)
		Finance	(19%)
		Other	(19%) $49,500

Top 5 Employers Hiring Grads
IEHP (2), Northrop Grumman (2), Gartner Consulting, Inc. (1), Accenture (1), Blizzard Entertainment (1)

CLARK UNIVERSITY
GRADUATE SCHOOL OF MANAGEMENT

Academics

A small graduate business program strong in finance (so strong, in fact, that it offers both an MBA with a finance concentration and a Master of Science in Finance), the Graduate School of Management at Clark University provides a "collaborative atmosphere" to a student body drawn from both the immediate region and halfway around the globe. As a result, Clark is "very diversified, which brings many different perspectives to the classroom."

Finance and accounting are standout disciplines here ("Many of the finance professors have impressive concurrent careers, running hedge funds by day and teaching courses by night; they typically have highly recognized professional certifications in addition to their PhDs," one student notes), but MBAs report other curricular strengths as well, including concentrations in sustainability and and in social change, "which allow students to take elective courses in the International Development, Community and Environment (IDCE) Department at Clark . . . There is also a three-year dual-degree program (MBA/MA in CD or ESP) between these two departments." Clark's forward-looking, green-leaning proclivities are further revealed in "the dual-degree program offered in environmental science and policy and the MBA" as well as in the course Accounting and Finance for Sustainability. The School of Management also offers a full-time and part-time MSA program.

Clark's professors are "demanding but fair." Some "are outstanding. They come from experienced fields and they help you live the experience of the new material in all its aspects. Suddenly statistics and finance become easy and enjoyable with them." Others, however, "are dull and give you tedious work that takes hours but is not interesting." Students appreciate that "the school makes sure to take the student's opinion into account when re-enlisting a professor to teach for the upcoming semesters." The program also offers "many opportunities to help real businesses in the city" in order to gain "real life experience." More of this sort of thing could be on the way; as one student observes, "I have seen a steady progression in Clark's course offerings that indicates that they understand the 'real-world' challenges facing students and are adapting appropriately. I am particularly encouraged by the apparent increase in courses addressing innovation, social sustainability, entrepreneurship, and management leadership."

Career and Placement

Many Clark students say the Stevenish Career Management Center at Clark's GSOM "does a good job of helping students prepare for their career search. They edit resumes and cover letters, provide interview coaching, and give students information on nearby career fairs."

The Center provides a range of services including individual advising, resume and cover letter assistance, workshops, career fairs, on-campus recruiting events, alumni networking events, alumni professional seminars, internship placement, and job and internship postings. Although internships are required of students with fewer than three years of professional experience, some students consider that "it shouldn't be a requirement to attain an internship as a graduate student." Others state the office does "not do a sufficient job of getting employers interested in Clark's students." Employers who have recently hired Clark GSOM graduates include Ernst & Young, PwC, Deloitte, JP Morgan Chase, and Macy's.

Student Life and Environment

Clark University's location in the urban setting of Worcester, Massachusetts, provides the same opportunities and challenges of any urban campus. There is easy access to job and internship opportunities as well as to travel to Boston, Hartford, Providence and New York City. Clark's University Park Partnership brings together the University and Main South communities to help create a safe and vibrant neighborhood for all. However, students must take the usual safety precautions. Some report that there are "no real student bars and the like in the Clark area and that the neighborhoods surrounding the school have been allowed to fall into poverty by the town of Worcester." Students quickly note that "Clark has a world-class police force whose mission to protect the students is paramount" and that policing on campus includes a "good and very, very helpful" escort service though "there have been cases of students being mugged from time to time."

About 60 percent of Clark's MBAs are full-time students. Many spend a lot of time on and around campus. While "undergraduate student groups are closed to graduate students," MBAs enjoy "fun social events that the business school's student council puts on, and an interesting stock market activity that happens each semester." Some report that graduate student life "feels very disconnected from the rest of the school" and that it can "get boring at times because we are a very small community." Others state that the school "provides some networking alumni activities to help us to search jobs, and for international students, they organize some specific activities, such as Asian New Year, to make students [come] together and feel [at] home."

Clark's part-time students "are mostly native[s of] Worcester or Massachusetts, with different ages and backgrounds." Full-timers typically "come from different Asian countries," with India and China especially well-represented. International students "add a richness in perspective," although some "are weak in English."

Admissions

Clark requires the following of applicants: a completed admissions application; a personal essay; a current resume; two letters of recommendation; an official score report for either the GMAT or the GRE (an uncommon option); and official transcripts from all undergraduate and graduate programs previously attended. Interviews are optional. International applicants must submit all of the above as well as an official score report for the TOEFL or IELTS (if their native language is other than English) and proof of the financial support while attending the program. The school strongly encourages, but does not require, an online application.

FINANCIAL FACTS

Annual tuition (in-state/ out-of-state)	$32,743/$32,743
Fees	$2,080
Cost of books	$2,000
Room & board (on/off-campus)	$10,000/$10,000

ADMISSIONS

Admissions Selectivity Rating	82
# of applications received	122
% applicants accepted	65
% acceptees attending	35
Average GMAT	546
Range of GMAT	530–660
Accepts GRE scores	Yes
Average Verbal GRE	152
Range of Verbal GRE scores	144–160
Average Quantitative GRE	165
Range of Quantitative GRE scores	148–165
Average Writing GRE	3.0
Range of Writing GRE scores	3.0–5.0
Average GPA	3.2
TOEFL required of international students	Yes
Minimum TOEFL (paper/web)	577/90
Application fee	$75
International application fee	$75
Early application deadline	12/1
Regular application deadline	4/1
Application Deadline/Notification	
Round 1:	12/1 / 1/15
Round 2:	2/1 / 3/1
Round 3:	4/1 / 5/15
Round 4:	6/1 / 7/15
Deferment available	Yes
Maximum length of deferment	12 months
Transfer students accepted	Yes
Transfer application policy A maximum of two graduate courses from an AACSB accredited school can be transferred into the program. Foundation courses can be waived for undergraduate business majors.	
Non-fall admissions	Yes
Need-blind admissions	Yes

EMPLOYMENT PROFILE

Career Rating	76	Grads Employed by Function	% Avg. Salary
Average base starting salary	$55,940	Marketing	$53,067
		Consulting	$53,000
		Management	$64,000
		Finance	$52,050
		MIS	$90,000

Top 5 Employers Hiring Grads
Ernst & Young (1), EMC (1), Fidelity (1), JPMorgan Chase (1), Apple, Inc. (1)

CLARKSON UNIVERSITY
SCHOOL OF BUSINESS

Academics

Clarkson University, located in Potsdam New York, is a private university known "first and foremost as an undergrad engineering school"; however, many students look to its burgeoning business program to help them get a foothold in the business world. Its MBA program allows many of its students to finish in fewer than twelve months, even though many believe they could receive their degree in around "nine months." The "speed and reputation" of the program are just two of the good aspects of the program that many students enjoy. The school tends to use its engineering acumen to teach students about innovations in the engineering sector that may affect business and its own Institute for a Sustainable Environment, which helps to foster "green business."

The main focus of the curriculum, however, is the use of the "supply chain" style of management. While many find this especially "helpful" in the workplace, some students wish the curriculum were a little broader and that the school "cater a little more to marketing and sales students." One thing all students can agree on is that they love the size of the school and praise that, "[it] is very small [and] gives each student a very personalized experience." The faculty are a huge part of the experience and each takes "the time to get to know" the students. Those enrolled in the program think that most professors are "absolutely wonderful" and have taught them a great deal about various facets of business, yet the professors are occasionally hindered by an administration that is not exactly "unified," leaving some to re-teach material that students have already learned. Some subjects may also be under taught. Despite this, they say that the faculty is more than "willing to help students with schoolwork and find jobs." If the faculty is not available, many students love the team-oriented courses and say they "love working at school as [their] fellow students are always available if [they] need help."

Career and Placement

Clarkson University boasts that former graduates that have become CEO, president, or vice-president of a company. A large reason for this owes to the Graduate Career Services office, which helps all students find jobs after graduation. While some would like "more opportunities to network for jobs," all agree that the Career Services office is invaluable to students with assets like KnightLink which allows prospects to find job, co-op and internship listings, as well as career workshops. Students also take advantage of the alumni-mentoring program, which allows them to connect with graduates who will help and guide them through the process of finding a job.

Clarkson MBAs most frequently find work with IBM, Accenture, Lockheed Martin, GE, Cooper Industries, Frito-Lay, HSBC, Knowledge Systems and Research, Texas Instruments, and Whiting Turner. While the majority of graduates remain in the Northeast, students are placed throughout the country.

ADMISSIONS CONTACT: JOSHUA LaFave, ASSOCIATE DIRECTOR, GRADUATE BUSINESS PROGRAMS
ADDRESS: 8 CLARKSON AVE., CU BOX 5770, POTSDAM, NY 13699
PHONE: 315-268-6613 • FAX: 315-268-3810
E-MAIL: BUSGRAD@CLARKSON.EDU • WEBSITE: WWW.CLARKSON.EDU/GRADUATE

Student Life and Environment

Potsdam is located in rural New York, so "there isn't a whole lot to do unless you know where to find activities." The upside of an isolated campus is that students have fewer distractions: "You learn that business work is not always going to be a forty-hour work week"; weekends are often "straight work days where most group meetings and homework for the next week are done." Though some students note problems with "administration not always taking care of small issues immediately," "because it is a one-year program…problems are not an issue for very long before a new class comes in."

"Almost all [students] are what you'd traditionally picture as 'MBA' students: white, upper middle class, financially and socially moderate to slightly conservative," and "they are very good at quantitative analysis." "Everyone is accepting of what you believe. They may disagree but it is done in a way that allows for intelligent and thought-provoking conversation." And some students note "the pleasure to meet, interact with and become friends with students from other countries."

Admissions

The admissions department at Clarkson University requires that applicants submit an undergraduate transcript, GMAT or GRE scores, TOEFL scores (if necessary), and a Test of Spoken English (TSE) (for international students whose native language is not English; the TSE can be administered via telephone), a detailed resume, two one-page personal essays, and three letters of reference. Awards of merit-based scholarships are determined during the admissions process; no separate application is required. Those requiring foundation course work prior to commencing their MBAs "may enroll in the courses at Clarkson during the summer Business Concepts Program before entering the advanced MBA program. For students doing graduate work at another university, they may be allowed to transfer in nine credit hours of graduate work."

FINANCIAL FACTS

Annual tuition (in-state/ out-of-state)	$37,590/
Fees	$440
Cost of books	$2,000
Room & board	$7,500
% of students receiving aid	85
% of first-year students receiving aid	85
% of students receiving grants	85
Average award package	$26,476
Average grant	$6,500
Average loan	$34,000
Average student loan debt	$31,932

ADMISSIONS

Admissions Selectivity Rating	83
# of applications received	121
% applicants accepted	60
% acceptees attending	55
Average GMAT	525
Range of GMAT	480–580
Accepts GRE scores	Yes
Average GPA	3.6
TOEFL required of international students	Yes
Minimum TOEFL (paper/web)	550/80
Application fee	$25
International application fee	$35
Deferment available	Yes
Maximum length of deferment	1 year
Transfer students accepted	Yes
Transfer application policy May transfer in up to 9 credit hours of graduate work from another AACSB accredited institution.	
Non-fall admissions	Yes
Need-blind admissions	Yes

EMPLOYMENT PROFILE

Career Rating	87	**Grads Employed by Function% Avg. Salary**	
Percent employed at graduation	36	Operations	(50%) $58,833
Percent employed 3 months after graduation	75	Consulting	(17%) $50,000
		Management	(8%) $58,000
Average base starting salary	$57,000	Finance	(17%) $55,000
Primary Source of Full-time Job Acceptances		MIS	(8%) $50,000
School-facilitated activities	12 (44%)	**Top 5 Employers Hiring Grads**	
Graduate-facilitated activities	4 (14%)	IBM (3), Frito Lay (1), Cooper Industries (1),	
Unknown	11 (42%)	Bechtel (1), J&J/Duracell (1)	

CLEMSON UNIVERSITY
COLLEGE OF BUSINESS AND BEHAVIORAL SCIENCE

GENERAL INFORMATION
Type of school	Public
Affiliation	No Affiliation
Academic calendar	Aug-May

SURVEY SAYS...
Students love Clemson, SC, Friendly students, Good peer network, Smart classrooms
Solid preparation in:
General management

STUDENTS
Enrollment of parent institution	22,698
Enrollment of MBA Program	417
% male/female	67/33
% out-of-state	39
% part-time	67
% underrepresented minority	33
% international	22
Average age at entry	31
Average years work experience at entry	7

ACADEMICS
Academic Experience Rating	**68**
Profs interesting rating	69
Profs accessible rating	65
Student/faculty ratio	5:1
% female faculty	34
% underrepresented minority faculty	10
% part-time faculty	11

Joint Degrees
MBA + master's or PhD in a variety of fields. Students must be accepted by both degree programs.

Prominent Alumni
J. Strom Thurmond, U.S. Senator (died 2003); Kristie A. Kenney, U.S. Ambassador to the Phillipines; Robert H. Brooks, President, Naturally Fresh Foods; Nancy Humphries O'Dell, Access Hollywood co-anchor; Mark Richardson, President, Carolina Panthers

Academics

The College of Business & Behavioral Science at Clemson University offers a combination of daytime and evening classes to its full-time MBAs as well as a full slate of evening classes to part-timers at the school's satellite campus in Greenville. Clemson MBAs tout the program's "rigorous curriculum" and excellent value; "The value of this degree vs. the cost of the degree appears to be very high," one student tells us.

Clemson's MBA offers concentrations in innovation and entrepreneurship, services science, supply chain management, health services, and marketing analysis. Full-timers are enthusiastic about "the entrepreneurial focus of the program." One writes, "It is rare to find relevant assistantships in an MBA program, and Clemson University provides some [of the] best opportunities for entrepreneurs to learn necessary business skills while working closely with start-up companies in South Carolina. They also do a marvelous job of bringing technologies developed by Clemson's Research Institutes to a forefront and finding their commercial value."

The program boasts "some very good professors and interesting class topics," and students praise professors for "their willingness to help outside of class" and for being "generally reasonable when it comes to grades and making changes if the general class population is not grasping the material well." Students also note that "the administration here at Clemson University is very helpful. Any time I have asked for help regarding admission, enrollment, or financial aid they have always been able to answer my questions." Finally, they report that "Clemson's study abroad programs are attractive and meaningful."

Career and Placement

Clemson University maintains an Office of MBA Career Development dedicated to its business graduates. For those who seek out the service, the Office of Career Development office offers career placement support including one-on-one professional coaching and personalized placement assistance as well as a range of self-assessment instruments, job-search counseling, interviewing and resume-writing workshops, and recruiting and networking events. Students also report that "the alumni base and networking opportunities" here are "a great strength." Companies hiring recent Clemson MBAs include Blackbaud, Bausch & Lomb, CapGemini, Colonial Life, Disney, GE, Home Depot, Lockheed Martin, Michelin, Milliken, Nestle, Northwestern Mutual, Resurgent Capital Service, Schneider, and Target. About one-third of Clemson MBAs wind up in marketing and sales; about as many find work in general management.

Student Life and Environment

The full-time and part-time degree programs are now located in downtown Greenville, South Carolina, about forty-five minutes away from the main university campus. The Greenville campus, known as Clemson at the Falls, is located at Falls Park—an urban park featuring hiking and jogging paths, landscaped gardens, and an architecturally distinctive suspension bridge linking the Clemson campus building to Main Street. Students tell us that life here involves "hectic course work with case studies, quizzes, midterms, discussions, presentations and projects. Apart from the course work, we have regular MBA Student association meetings . . . to discuss and organize events related to community work, organizing events with alumni, etc. Then we have regular discussions and talks by guest speakers, which are compulsory to attend as part of our course work. We have regular social gathering with MBA alumni and with faculty also." Reflecting upon all this activity, one student observes that "Clemson has a great tradition of merging academia with life. You feel like you're a part of the school and the community."

ADMISSIONS CONTACT: ADMISSIONS DIRECTOR, MBA PROGRAMS
ADDRESS: 55 E. CAMPERDOWN WAY, GREENVILLE, SC 29601
PHONE: 864-656-3975 • FAX: 864-656-0947
E-MAIL: MBA@CLEMSON.EDU • WEBSITE: WWW.CLEMSON.EDU/MBA

Beyond the classroom, the new location strategically places college faculty and students at the center of the Greenville business community, allowing full-time students to attend classes and simultaneously hold internships or part-time positions in local businesses.

The Clemson MBA program attracts students who "are very competitive in most facets of life: sports, academics, job-search, etc. However, this competitive spirit does not manifest itself in pettiness, but rather in a collective effort to elevate the performances of both ourselves and our peers."

Admissions

Applicants to the MBA program at Clemson must submit a current resume (two years of work experience is required for students w/undergraduate degree in business); one official transcripts representing all undergraduate work; two letters of recommendation; a one- to two-page personal statement; interview (full-time applicants only); and, an official GMAT score report (score of at least 600 preferred for applicants to the full-time program). Non-native English speakers applying to the full-time program must also submit TOEFL scores (score of 600 paper-based or 237 computer based preferred), an International Student Financial Certification Form, and translations of transcripts not in English.

FINANCIAL FACTS

Annual tuition (in-state/ out-of-state)	$18,666/$30,672
Fees	$500
Cost of books	$1,300
Room & board (on/off-campus)	$13,500/$13,500

ADMISSIONS

Admissions Selectivity Rating	81
# of applications received	346
% applicants accepted	84
% acceptees attending	79
Average GMAT	583
Range of GMAT	530–625
Accepts GRE scores	Yes
Average GPA	3.2
TOEFL required of international students	Yes
Minimum TOEFL (paper/web)	600/100
Application fee	$80
International application fee	$90
Regular application deadline	6/1
Regular application notification	6/30
Deferment available	Yes
Maximum length of deferment	one year
Transfer students accepted	Yes
Transfer application policy Must meet all admission requirements. Can transfer a maximum of 12 semester hours of acceptable coursework.	
Non-fall admissions	Yes
Need-blind admissions	Yes

EMPLOYMENT PROFILE

Career Rating		76	Grads Employed by Function	% Avg. Salary
Percent employed at graduation		61	Marketing	(11%) $70,000
Percent employed 3 months after graduation		33	Operations	(11%) $75,000
			Management	(33%) $57,617
Average base starting salary		$60,353	Finance	(22%) $47,800
Primary Source of Full-time Job Acceptances			HR	(11%) $80,000
School-facilitated activities	9 (53%)		MIS	(11%) $49,724
Graduate-facilitated activities	8 (47%)		**Top 5 Employers Hiring Grads**	
Unknown	0 (0%)		Michelin (1), Milliken and Co. (1), Sempra Us Gas and Power (1), ScanSource (1), Chicago Bridge and Iron (1)	

THE COLLEGE OF WILLIAM & MARY
RAYMOND A. MASON SCHOOL OF BUSINESS

Academics

The College of William & Mary is "the second oldest college in the Nation." Its "placement in the historic triangle offers students the opportunity to learn where Thomas Jefferson studied" as well as walk "the streets where the ideas of America were founded." MBAs appreciate the "amazing history" of the Raymond A. Mason School of Business at the College of William & Mary, "the quality instructors, the scope of the courses that are taught" and "the quality connections the school has in the business community." Many students are first dawn to the program because of its strong reputation and "high prestige" but stay because of the "strong academics," "collaborative culture" and the "focus on leadership development." In addition, the program is military-friendly and features a flexible schedule for part-time and non-traditional students, including weekend and night classes, as well as a newly launched online MBA program.

MBAs call the quality of professors "absolutely phenomenal" and appreciate the "small class size, collaborative environment, and opportunity for guided professional work and mentoring with professors, Executive Partners, fellow classmates, and alumni." The faculty is "enthusiastic and easily accessible to students," and most of them "live within walking distance." "The college itself is perfect in size," which leads to a "[v]ery personal program with lots of involvement from professors and staff."

William & Mary provides excellent opportunities for advancement through programs like the MBA Executive Partners Program. The Executive Partners are "over 100 retired high ranking executives in their industry that bring a vast amount of knowledge and experience to the MBA program." These "top-level business executives mentor students," and give them an insight into the job market "like none other." The program provides each student with her or his "own 'coach' who is a retired executive." As one student notes these "retired executives [are] willing to meet with you at any time to help you advance in your career goals." The program "encourages team-projects whenever possible, which creates a very collaborative atmosphere in many classes." With its emphasis on collaboration and strong ties to the business community, it's clear that "this program is excellent at developing leaders and team players—not just teaching subjects."

Students also note the invaluable experience and connections gained from the "global business immersions, the student-managed investment fund[s] (Batten Fund and Dittrick Fund), field consultancies, Career Acceleration Modules (CAM)," and the "MBA Association." Students feel "well prepared to pursue" their "entrepreneurial goals in the future as a result of the networks, the mentoring, and the lessons gained through the Entrepreneurship CAM." Military and non-traditional students appreciate the "outstanding program" that fits their "full-time work schedule, with no online classes," as well as the "highly competitive" and highly selective program for the U.S. Army Training and Doctrine Command. The flexibility of the program doesn't diminish the quality of the education because as one student notes, "the faculty set the standards of success and the students uphold them and even surpass the expectations of the faculty."

Students say the "program has a 'small school' feel but [the] degree has a 'big school' impact." It is easy to see the appeal of a program that many students call a "private-school experience" without having to pay "private-school level tuition." MBAs agree that the "price, location and reputation" make this a great program.

Career and Placement

William & Mary is known for providing "a great career network" and students note that there are "many opportunities to build your professional network with alumni, executive partners, and fellow students." Students appreciate the "great graduate resources," "great career center," and "huge alumni network." Alumni "are positioned in great places, with good access to job networks," but there could stand to be more "female networking with alumni" and more "recruiting specifically in marketing fields—the focus is typically finance, consulting, and operations." Several students expressed a desire for a larger "diversity of potential employers."

The base salary for full time MBA graduates averaged $77,990. Within three years of graduating, students averaged a 50 percent increase in salary. At least 33 percent of Executive MBAs go on to start their own business, and an additional 26 percent of graduates were offered promotions after graduating. The majority of MBAs went into consulting, followed by the financial services industry and commercial and professional services.

Student Life and Environment

Students note that the "town of Williamsburg is beautiful and filled with history, as are the grounds of this amazing school." "There is plenty to occupy yourself [with] inside and outside the business school." In addition, students say the community is "friendly" and note that "the town heavily supports the college." The proximity to D.C. is also appreciated.

They find their fellow students to be "goal oriented, professional, and diverse," as well as "eager to learn and challenge themselves, and unafraid to challenge the status quo." "It is a wonderful learning environment," where the "sense of community is very strong." Since many of the Flex MBA students are working professionals they "understand the difficulty in balancing work, school, and personal responsibilities. This creates a very supportive environment where students are quick to help others and pull their own weight." Students consider the student body a major strength and appreciate that "admissions and recruitment have done a phenomenal job selecting the talent entering the college." In addition, the "large international and military enrollment provides a lot of unique perspectives."

Admissions

The Raymond A. Mason School of Business at the College of William & Mary offers four types of MBAs: Full-time MBA Program, Flex MBA Program, Executive MBA Program, and a new online MBA program. Admission requirements vary by program, but all applicants to Mason must submit: an official academic transcripts for all undergraduate and graduate work; an official GMAT or GRE score report; three personal essays; letters of recommendation; and a resume. Interviews are required and are by invitation of the school only. International applicants whose first language is not English must submit official score reports for the TOEFL, the IELTS, or the PTE (applicants scoring in at least the 60th percentile on the verbal section of the GMAT and at least a 5.0 on the AWA section of the GMAT are exempted from this requirement).

FINANCIAL FACTS

Annual tuition (in-state/ out-of-state)	$31,058/$41,514
Fees	$950
Cost of books	$1,545
Room & board (on/off-campus)	$10,334/$10,334
% of students receiving aid	68
% of first-year students receiving aid	72
% of students receiving grants	59
Average award package	$30,745
Average grant	$17,493
Average loan	$38,595
Average student loan debt	$66,947

ADMISSIONS

Admissions Selectivity Rating	86
# of applications received	329
% applicants accepted	58
% acceptees attending	53
Average GMAT	611
Range of GMAT	570–670
Accepts GRE scores	Yes
Average Verbal GRE	151
Range of Verbal GRE scores	147–155
Average Quantitative GRE	150
Range of Quantitative GRE scores	146–158
Average Writing GRE	4.0
Range of Writing GRE scores	3.5–4.0
Average GPA	3.3
TOEFL required of international students	Recommended
Minimum TOEFL (paper/web)	600/100
Application fee	$100
International application fee	$100
Application Deadline/Notification	
Round 1:	11/16 / 1/22
Round 2:	1/18 / 3/11
Round 3:	3/7 / 4/22
Round 4:	5/16 / 6/10
Deferment available	Yes
Maximum length of deferment	1 year
Transfer students accepted	No
Transfer application policy Transfer credits are not accepted.	
Non-fall admissions	No
Need-blind admissions	Yes

EMPLOYMENT PROFILE

Career Rating	91	Grads Employed by Function	% Avg. Salary
Percent employed at graduation	60	Marketing	(23%) $73,444
Percent employed 3 months after graduation	86	Operations	(16%) $79,776
		Consulting	(28%) $99,382
Average base starting salary	$80,742	Management	(9%) $62,167
Primary Source of Full-time Job Acceptances		Finance	(16%) $72,344
School-facilitated activities	24 (56%)	HR	(1%)
Graduate-facilitated activities	19 (44%)	MIS	(5%) $67,500
		Other	(2%)

Top 5 Employers Hiring Grads
Deloitte Consulting (4), IBM (3), Pantheon (3), Ernst & Young (2), Capital One (1)

COLORADO STATE UNIVERSITY
COLLEGE OF BUSINESS

GENERAL INFORMATION
Type of school   Public
Affiliation   No Affiliation
Academic calendar   August-July

SURVEY SAYS...
Classmates have diverse work experience, Friendly students, Good peer network, Cutting-edge classes, Happy students
Solid preparation in:
Finance, Accounting, General management, Teamwork, Communication/interpersonal skills, Quantitative skills, Computer skills, Doing business in a global economy, Social responsibility

STUDENTS
Enrollment of parent institution	32,236
Enrollment of MBA Program	1,020
% male/female	50/50
% out-of-state	52
% part-time	90
% underrepresented minority	10
% international	39
Average age at entry	33
Average years work experience at entry	7

ACADEMICS
Academic Experience Rating	86
Profs interesting rating	92
Profs accessible rating	91
% female faculty	30

Joint Degrees
Doctor of Veterinary Medicine and Master of Business Administration: MBA/DVM, 5 years.

Prominent Alumni
James Iacino, President, Seattle Fish Co.; Trevor Armstrong, President, Timken Motors and Cranes, LLC - dba Wazee; Kelly Green, Owner and Chairman of the Board, Birko; Kent Anderson, President, Macys.com; Trang Tran, CEO and Co-Founder of Fargreen

Academics

The College of Business at Colorado State University offers a solid mid-tier program for an "an amazing value" at a well-respected institution that is ideal for working students looking to progress or diversify their careers. There are multiple program options for career advancement (including Online, Professional, and Early Career), and eight-week classes terms, scheduling flexibility, online courses, and course layout all add to forward-thinking approach to the education model we move into an increasingly digital world. "I would not have been able to pursue an MBA had the option of online education not been available," says a student. Courses are "fast-paced and challenging" and provide a wealth of applicable skills for students to immediately begin putting into practice, and the staff in general is "very helpful and enthusiastic" about students' education.

The "go at your own pace" curriculum is lock-step, where each class builds on previous classes, and student admit that some of the classes can be extremely time intensive in terms of heavy reading and multiple assignments on top of class hours. Professors all have real world experience and "have experienced a magnitude of business success in their respective fields." Thanks to the staggering diversity of the students in any given class (both in-person and online), faculty makes sure that "there is a lot of insight as to how topics are handled in specific industries." "We have very lively discussions in our classes," says a student.

Online students have access to the same lectures as on-campus students (these can be attended live, or downloaded at a later date), but a few say that there is a "lack of resources and help for distance MBA students." "While I have had some interaction with a couple professors, typically the only interaction online students have is with their assigned Teacher's Assistant, called Section Coordinators or SCs," says one student (do note that "section coordinators are knowledgeable and helpful"). In addition, the distance students tend to represent much more of a variable in terms of devotion to the studies, so "random group assignments are often a gamble and it can be nerve wracking." Still, the program "does a good job of connecting us through discussion forums and group projects, and making us feel like we're part of the university."

Career and Placement

Most of the students in both the online and on-campus programs already have jobs, so the school places less of a focus on traditional career services. "This is a very good program, especially for working professionals," says an older student. "Being in an environment of other working professionals, as opposed to people in their early 20s, has also been a very helpful and satisfying part of my experience so far." The career center staff is "attentive" to requests and "giving of their time"—"We even practiced online interviewing," one student tells us—and while the large career fairs they host are catered toward undergraduates, MBAs "are treated individually to the networking opportunities that the CSU staff can provide." There is even a one credit career management staff that is "stellar, and is appropriate and valuable for on campus as well as online students."

Student Life and Environment

Many of the "very intelligent and hardworking students" here are well into their careers and have families, so the professional program tends to skew older (in the 30-45 range). The popular online MBA program is understandably quite different, and interaction between the two groups is limited to "lively" in-class discussions (on both the virtual and real space sides) and group work. Many students are in the military and work full-time, and professors understand that "you have a job/family/life and they bend over backward to accommodate that."

Admissions

To be eligible for admission to CSU, students must have maintained a 3.0 GPA or better from an accredited undergraduate college, or they must have completed a graduate degree and have at least four years of professional work experience. Students with a lower GPA must include a statement explaining their academic performance. Students with significant professional work experience may apply for a GMAT waiver. Applicants are advised of their admission status within three weeks of the application deadline.

FINANCIAL FACTS

Annual tuition (in-state/ out-of-state)	$9,348/$22,916
Fees	$8,154
Cost of books	$1,000
Average student loan debt	$41,373

ADMISSIONS

Admissions Selectivity Rating	**81**
# of applications received	505
% applicants accepted	78
% acceptees attending	70
Average GMAT	538
Range of GMAT	415–660
Accepts GRE scores	Yes
Average Verbal GRE	152
Range of Verbal GRE scores	150–154
Average Quantitative GRE	152
Range of Quantitative GRE scores	143–161
Average Writing GRE	3.9
Range of Writing GRE scores	3.0–4.5
Average GPA	3.2
TOEFL required of international students	Yes
Minimum TOEFL (paper/web)	565/86
Application fee	$60
International application fee	$70
Regular application deadline	6/1
Regular application notification	7/1
Deferment available	Yes
Maximum length of deferment	1 year
Transfer students accepted	No
Non-fall admissions	Yes
Need-blind admissions	Yes

COLUMBIA UNIVERSITY
COLUMBIA BUSINESS SCHOOL

Academics

As Sinatra says, if you can make it to graduation here, you can make it anywhere. The Columbia Business School offers one of the best finance educations in the country, capitalizing on its location to provide exposure to various leading financial institutions. While the school has been heavily focused on finance and consulting in the past, the school has shifted its programming to a more diverse focus (technology, social enterprise, retail and luxury goods, private equity and venture capital) to meet the career aspirations of its students. Everyone agrees that "the CBS culture is incredibly strong both in the classroom and out."

The "academic burden is very moderate" here (getting in is perhaps the hardest part); "people take academics seriously but will not kill themselves studying." Students looking to go into finance and consulting "are very career driven and knew what it takes to land good jobs," but this intelligent community of students "are willing to work together to achieve big goals." and some are "surprised at how collaborative it is academically, and how many resources professors make available to help you perform in class (particularly core classes)."

Professors get good marks all around, and some are "off-the-charts inspiring." "It's definitely a game changer when you can discuss with your professors real life business problems outside of the classroom," says a student. As pretty much everyone at CBS has several years of work experience under their belt, it helps to have some idea what you are looking to get out of the MBA experience in order to best take advantage of the education here. Once you have figured that out, "there are a ton of student groups and professors who are willing to help you achieve your goal." The elective offerings are "fantastic," class discussions are "high quality," and the curriculum offers "hands-down the best mix of practice and theory with access to the leaders of every major industry." Overall, a "diverse array of courses and strong class participation among student body translates to a great learning environment."

Career and Placement

A strong careers team, vast alumni network, and "superior access to prospective employers" provides instant access to summer and regular term internships and post-graduation jobs. "Being in the heart of NYC is a HUGE advantage that you don't understand until you get here and realize how easy it is to network with alumni and meet with companies," says one student. Similarly, the number and caliber of speakers that come to school for class visits and night panels is "amazing," and the location makes it very easy for C-suite execs and startups to visit. "It brings a great perspective to the topics we discuss in class, and careers students are considering," says a student. Columbia also provides excellent resources for students conducting "enterprise" job searches (those not participating in on campus recruiting), for those students going into start-ups, tech companies, social enterprise, and other sectors that predominantly hire just-in-time.

ADMISSIONS CONTACT: AMANDA CARLSON, ASSISTANT DEAN, ADMISSIONS
ADDRESS: 3022 BROADWAY, URIS HALL, ROOM 216, NEW YORK, NY 10027
PHONE: 212-854-1961 • FAX: 212-662-6754
E-MAIL: APPLY@GSB.COLUMBIA.EDU • WEBSITE: WWW.GSB.COLUMBIA.EDU

Student Life and Environment

CBS students are a diverse bunch in every way possible: "highly international, [with] different backgrounds from banking to non-profit, etc." What brings them together is the energy they put into the CBS community, where you have the option to do pretty much whatever you want: "If you want to hang out with people from school there are plenty of activities every single day, but since this is NYC you can also find your own plan." Indeed, the school is "very well integrated with the city," students "are involved in one hundred and one activities and love every moment of it," from Thursday happy hours to club events "at the city's best venues," and classmates are "super sociable and wonderful people and opportunities to meet those people abound." The Office of Student Affairs also "has its ears to the ground" and is constantly implementing new strategies to make school better for students, and "the administrators are as much of the student community as the students." "Students have the power to make any change they wish." Also of note: the business school is "very welcoming of spouses and significant others."

Admissions

A serious record of leadership and achievement is what distinguishes Columbia MBA candidates from other graduate business students. To determine a candidate's eligibility for the program, the admissions committee reviews academic transcripts, test scores, recommendations, personal essays, and background. Admission to Columbia is highly competitive, with only about 18 percent of applicants receiving an offer of admission. In recent years, incoming students had an average GMAT score of 716, with a range from 690–730.

FINANCIAL FACTS

Annual tuition (in-state/ out-of-state)	$65,988/
Fees	$2,736
Cost of books	$904
Room & board (on/off-campus)	$20,700/$20,700

ADMISSIONS

Admissions Selectivity Rating	**99**
# of applications received	5,829
% applicants accepted	18
% acceptees attending	73
Average GMAT	715
Range of GMAT	700–740
Accepts GRE scores	Yes
Average GPA	3.5
TOEFL required of international students	Yes
Application fee	$250
International application fee	$250
Early application deadline	10/7
Regular application deadline	4/13
Deferment available	No
Transfer students accepted	No
Non-fall admissions	Yes
Need-blind admissions	Yes

EMPLOYMENT PROFILE

Career Rating	99	Grads Employed by Function	% Avg. Salary
Percent employed at graduation	77	Marketing	(11%) $106,781
Percent employed 3 months after graduation	93	Operations	(4%) $116,200
		Consulting	(32%) $133,496
Average base starting salary	$127,637	Management	(2%) $129,727
Primary Source of Full-time Job Acceptances		Finance	(41%) $132,025
School-facilitated activities	259 (51%)	MIS	(1%) $105,500
Graduate-facilitated activities	109 (22%)	Other	(10%) $116,094
Unknown	136 (27%)	**Top 5 Employers Hiring Grads**	

Top 5 Employers Hiring Grads

McKinsey & Company (55), Bain & Company (35), Boston Consulting Group (29), Deloitte Consulting (28), JPMorgan Chase & Co. (14)

CORNELL UNIVERSITY
SAMUEL CURTIS JOHNSON GRADUATE SCHOOL OF MANAGEMENT

Academics

Even in the midst of numerous top-notch graduate programs, Cornell University's reputation for producing strong business leaders stands out. The school's strong brand name ("especially in Asia"), varied approach to teaching and learning, and the "wealth of interdisciplinary course offerings" are just some of the many things that students love, not to mention the "regular opportunities to collaborate closely with students from other prestigious graduate departments, located just steps from the business school." Johnson has a "fantastic, collaborative culture" that draws people in from the get-go and turns them into helpful alumni. "My academic experience at Johnson has encouraged me to refer other colleagues to this program," says a student.

Professors here go the extra mile for students and are "engaged and enthusiastic inside the classroom and extremely available for outside meetings with students." They're "obviously experts in their respective fields," and "they will push you, and sometimes frustrate you, but they care most about helping you succeed." Other unique aspects of Johnson include: a dual degree program between with the top HR program in the country, a strong focus on sustainability, and the student-run hedge fund (currently valued at $10 million), where "students pitch stocks and vote to decide whether or not to investment in a stock." The school's immersion program, which many students cite as their main reason for attending, is an intense, hands-on semester of integrated course and field work in a specific industry or career interest.

The administration is "pretty responsive to student needs," and it thinks of the little things that make students happy "like having bagels and coffee for finals." It "goes out of its way to garner feedback from students and constantly improves the curriculum." Most core subjects are condensed into the first semester, creating "occasional strains," but "the school works hard to schedule exams and deliverables to avoid overwhelming students." Being part of Cornell also "creates opportunities in multiple related disciplines, from engineering to city planning to agriculture."

Career and Placement

The recruiting opportunities at Johnson are "incredible," and the teaching and professional staff encourages students to challenge themselves, providing support "every step of the way." A "superior international network" means that alumni are "happy to speak with you and many take on the role of career coach, connecting you to unusual internship and job opportunities or helping with interview prep." "If you ever reach out to a Johnson alum, they will always get back to you," says a student. There is no cutthroat mentality here: "We work together to compete with students from other schools for jobs, not students within our school."

Career Services stands out "as a place that will go out of their way to help any student." The school has "the best system to prepare students for the summer internships, which is arguably the most important aspect of career switching." Its "tremendous" track record of placement in consulting internships and careers allows students "to gain hands-on experience in [their] field of interest as well as leadership impact."

Student Life and Environment

One student calls the Johnson crowd "some of the most intelligent, driven, passionate people I have ever been around." Each class brings "diverse perspectives from past work experiences and cultural backgrounds," and "there is a strong environment of collaboration"; despite "healthy competition," the majority of students "study together in Sage" and "informally tutor others for exams." When free time can be found, students enjoy spending it with each other" at local bars, playing on one of our many intramural teams, participating in a club event or going to hockey games," such as those of the Frozen Assets, the women's ice hockey team.

The community is "as tightly knit as can be," partly "because we're so far from a major city, but also because faculty and second-year students stress mutual support and collaboration." The somewhat remote location in Ithaca is "a gift," as "it forces you create new social circles with your classmates." Johnson students have access to the entire Cornell campus, including its facilities and other student clubs and activities. With so much to do, some life planning can be in order. One student advises, "Choose one to two professionally-focused club (s), one socially-focused club, and one sports-focused club. I find most students follow this 2-1-1 approach and are incredibly invested in their activities." Every Thursday, the whole Johnson community comes together for the "well-attended" Sage Social (which provides food and drinks for everyone, and sometimes themed events); social circles are "fluid," with many activities attended by students of all backgrounds and interests. The best way to describe a Johnson student is this: "they take their work seriously but not themselves."

Admissions

The Johnson application is online only and includes three 250-word essays—two mandatory, one optional. Mandatory topics cover professional achievement and career goals, and the optional essay may be used to detail extenuating circumstances or provide additional bolstering information. Johnson initially reviews applicants through a two-reader system; those who make the cut receive an interview, and only disputed files go to committee. As with other systems, this simply means that it pays to present an extremely strong case for admission. Last year's entering class reported a median GPA of 3.33, median GMAT score of 700, and five years of work experience.

FINANCIAL FACTS

Annual tuition (in-state/ out-of-state)	$61,584/$61,584
Fees	$3,000
Cost of books	$1,100
Room & Board	$16,760

ADMISSIONS

Admissions Selectivity Rating	99
# of applications received	1,833
% applicants accepted	15
Average GMAT	697
Accepts GRE scores	Yes
Average GPA	3.4
TOEFL required of international students	Yes
Minimum TOEFL (paper/web)	600/100
Application fee	$200
International application fee	$200
Application Deadline/Notification	
Round 1:	10/1 / 12/15
Round 2:	11/17 / 2/15
Round 3:	1/15 / 3/15
Round 4:	3/17 / 4/15
Deferment available	No
Transfer students accepted	No
Non-fall admissions	Yes
Need-blind admissions	Yes

EMPLOYMENT PROFILE

Career Rating	97	Grads Employed by Function	% Avg. Salary
Percent employed at graduation	00	Marketing	(13%) $104,500
Percent employed 3 months after graduation	88	Operations	(2%) $111,000
		Consulting	(25%) $126,300
Average base starting salary	$119,100	Management	(13%) $118,400
Primary Source of Full-time Job Acceptances		Finance	(38%) $118,100
School-facilitated activities	186 (83%)	Other	(8%) $132,200
Graduate-facilitated activities	37 (17%)	**Top 5 Employers Hiring Grads**	
Unknown	1 (0%)	Amazon (10), Deloitte Consulting (9),	
		Citigroup (9), J.P. Morgan Chase (9), Ernst &	
		Young (7)	

DARTMOUTH COLLEGE
TUCK SCHOOL OF BUSINESS

Academics

There is no rest for the weary at Tuck, where the "intensive academic core for first-years is accelerated and rigorous." During the elongated (thirty-two-week) school year, students take eighteen courses, two of which are electives. One of these is Tuck's trademark First-Year Project, a course in which student teams develop new business ventures or act as consultants in existing ventures, and in which grades rest on the final presentation and other outcomes. This method reflects Tuck's emphasis on "academic deliverables, such as group papers, projects, and presentations." The second year consists of 12 elective courses, which may reflect well-rounded interests or a specialization. For example, Tuck recommends that a student interested in nonprofit and sustainability management take Corporate Social Responsibility, Entrepreneurship in the Social Sector I and II, Ethics in Action, the Tuck Global Consultancy international field study, and Strategic Responses to Market Failure. One student reports, "I feel completely prepared to take on my career post-Tuck. The school does a fantastic job of working students hard in the first year, teaching them the core fundamentals of business, and letting them craft their own paths during the second year." One student notes, "Tuck could update its core curriculum and case study assignments to reflect the current business environment, i.e., more standard courses to better understand the private-market investment climate, corporate ethics, digital media/entertainment, and emerging economies."

Tuck operates through "full immersion." Students "do a lot of work in study groups, which are assigned and required for first-years." Mandatory team rotation forces each student to work closely with a wide swath of his or her peers during the first year. The small class size and rural location reinforces class cohesiveness and fosters intimacy between MBA students and Tuck faculty and staff. Professors host social "gatherings at their homes and get involved with student organizations." "I have had lunches, dinners, or drinks with the majority of my professors," reports one second-year, "and I am treated with a respect that goes beyond [typical] teacher-student interactions." Administrators are "the nicest people on Earth." Some have even been known to "come in on a Sunday evening and bring food and coffee for us when we have exams." The overall "quality" of faculty and administration alike is "extraordinary."

Career and Placement

Tuck is "very focused on helping students land the jobs they came here to get." "The Career Development Office works tirelessly on behalf of students," though this benefit is most useful for students pursuing "traditional career paths (i.e., consulting, finance, general management)." However, "students interested in other opportunities (i.e., marketing, retail) may need to do more work outside the Career Development Office." Dartmouth is a magnet for recruiters, and "one of the best parts of Tuck is that visiting executives spend meaningful time with us. They don't stop by on their way to another meeting; rather, they have lunch and/or dinner with us, hold individual office hours, and make an effort to share their experiences with members of the class." Recruitment is Northeast focused, but the career office "is continually trying to reach out to West Coast firms"—the ones who often "recruit locally at Stanford and UCLA"—"and does a couple of treks for students interested in returning to the West." The tides may be turning; one student reports seeing "Google, Microsoft, and PG&E on campus this year," a possible "indication that a more diverse lineup of firms [is] coming to Tuck."

ADMISSIONS CONTACT: DAWNA CLARKE, DIRECTOR OF ADMISSIONS
ADDRESS: 100 TUCK HALL, HANOVER, NH 03755
PHONE: 603-646-3162 • FAX: 603-646-1441
E-MAIL: TUCK.ADMISSIONS@DARTMOUTH.EDU • WEBSITE: WWW.TUCK.DARTMOUTH.EDU

Students seeking jobs in "nontraditional" vocations and regions will have better luck with Tuck's extremely strong, supportive alumni network. One student told this story of success: "I emailed a Tuck alum who is a managing director at a bulge-bracket investment bank in London, and he called me five minutes later to talk. He arranged a personal office visit… and actually talked HR into sending me straight to second round interviews, because the firm's London office didn't recruit on campus…all because I put 'Tuck' in the subject line."

Tuck's most recent graduating class reports a median total annual compensation of $179,000.

Student Life and Environment

Students call posh, pretty Hanover "the quintessential small, New England, Ivy League town," "within a short drive of many great ski resorts" and far removed "from the hustle and bustle of a big city." Unlike at many schools, most first-years live on campus. Couples and families live in the Dartmouth-owned Sachem Village housing complex or elsewhere off-campus. The environment is extremely "intimate" and "supportive." Tuckies consider their school very family-friendly, telling us that partners are an integral part of the social scene, and note that "classmates who have children while at Tuck" are surrounded by a "phenomenal support network." Tuck is very inclusive of gay and lesbian students and partners.

The isolated location and clustered housing contribute to "a great deal of school spirit" and "strong camaraderie" in a "work-hard, play-hard environment." "Tuck students really transplant their lives to be here…we make friends quickly here and socialize a lot with our classmates." Students belong to more than sixty clubs, teams, and publications, and attend numerous social functions every week. "The end of the week is typically characterized by social mixers (Tuck Tails), small group dinners…and the occasional full-blown party (winter and spring formals, Tuck Vegas, beach party)." Students report that "sports are very much a part of life at Tuck."

No one gripes about the intimacy, which results in great friendships and means close business ties in the future. "I have had a substantive conversation with each of my 240 classmates and will feel very comfortable calling any of them after graduation for career advice and/or business counsel," reports one Tuckie. The class of 2013 was 34 percent international and an additional 14 percent minority, however, sometimes students note they wish there was a bit more diversity.

Admissions

Like many other schools, Tuck wants to know that you love it for what it is, not only for what it can do for you; show that you have researched the school thoroughly. The class of 2016 reports an average GPA of 3.5 and GMAT score of 716.

Prominent Alumni

Elyse Allan, President & CEO, General Electric Canada; Roger McNamee, Co-Founder & Advisory Director, Elevation Partners; Thomas McInerney, COO, ING Insurance; Debi Brooks, Co-Founder, Michael J. Fox Foundation

FINANCIAL FACTS

Annual tuition	$64,200/
Fees	$4,665
Cost of books	$1,465
Room & board (on/off-campus)	$13,050/
% of students receiving aid	68
% of first-year students receiving aid	71
% of students receiving grants	40
Average award package	$64,362
Average grant	$22,974

ADMISSIONS

Admissions Selectivity Rating	98
# of applications received	2,437
% applicants accepted	22
% acceptees attending	52
Average GMAT	716
Range of GMAT	670–750
Accepts GRE scores	Yes
Average GPA	3.6
TOEFL required of international students	Yes
Application fee	$225
International application fee	$225
Application Deadline/Notification	
Round 1:	10/8 / 12/18
Round 2:	11/5 / 2/13
Round 3:	1/6 / 3/13
Round 4:	4/1 / 5/15
Deferment available	Yes
Maximum length of deferment	case by case basis
Transfer students accepted	No
Non-fall admissions	No
Need-blind admissions	Yes

EMPLOYMENT PROFILE

Career Rating	98
Percent employed at graduation	84
Percent employed 3 months after graduation	94
Average base starting salary	$117,860

DELAWARE STATE UNIVERSITY
COLLEGE OF BUSINESS

GENERAL INFORMATION
Type of school	Public
Affiliation	No Affiliation
Academic calendar	Rolling Basis

SURVEY SAYS...
Liberal students
Solid preparation in:
Presentation skills

STUDENTS
Enrollment of MBA Program	70
% male/female	53/47
% out-of-state	40
% underrepresented minority	31
% international	64
Average age at entry	29
Average years work experience at entry	4

ACADEMICS
Academic Experience Rating	**82**
Profs interesting rating	85
Profs accessible rating	84
Student/faculty ratio	8:1
% female faculty	30
% underrepresented minority faculty	60
% part-time faculty	20

Academics

Most of the students enrolled in the MBA program at Delaware State University's College of Business choose the program for its "convenient location" and for its attention to the needs of the "working professionals and aspiring managers" who attend here (classes are held exclusively during evening hours and weekends). The school describes its MBA as "an accelerated program geared towards working adults" that can be completed in eighteen months by those taking two courses per eight-week term and in just twelve months by those taking three courses per term. Even those shouldering a lighter workload can complete the program in two years by attending at least one summer session.

The DSU MBA program is designed to promote integrative learning in a functional context so that students can build important managerial and organizational skills. The program requires students to complete twenty-one credit hours of core courses, one capstone course, and nine credit hours of electives, which can be used to pursue a concentration in a single subject. Students lacking corresponding undergraduate coursework may be required to take some or all of eighteen credit hours in foundation courses. Foundation courses cover the following subjects: accounting, economics, finance, management information systems, marketing, and quantitative methods. Students may attempt to place out of any of these courses by passing a comprehensive exam, developed by the College of Business faculty, in the subject.

DSU's required core courses cover advanced economics, marketing management, business law and ethics, financial management, organizational leadership and behavior, operations analysis and management, and information and technology management. The capstone course is entitled Applied Strategic Management. Electives are offered in finance, information systems, and general management; concentrations are available in finance and information systems. Students may also participate in a case project in order to fulfill one of their elective requirements. According to the school's website, the case project "tests the student's strategic thinking and analytic skills" by requiring students either to (1) assess a company's income statement, balance sheet, annual reports, and other such documentation and provide recommendations; (2) manage an investment portfolio; or, (3) analyze "a series of general management cases that cover a broad range of strategic issues facing companies."

In order to graduate, students must earn a minimum grade point average of 3.0 with no more than six credit hours with a grade of C. Students who receive a grade of D or F during a course will be dismissed from the program; the school has procedures in place for students to appeal dismissal and/or academic probation. Students are required to complete the program in no more than five years.

Career and Placement

According to the school's website, the DSU Career Services office provides "technological and practical resources to provide students with the talent to conduct job searches, to become proficient in effective interviewing and presentation, and understanding the fit between their competencies and occupational requirements. Students also gain marketable experience through on- and off-campus collegiate activities, campus and community service, research projects, cooperative education, and internships to prepare them to manage their careers pre- and post-graduation." The service is designed primarily for the benefit of undergraduates, although graduate students and recent alumni may also utilize it.

Student Life and Environment

Students in the DSU MBA program form "a very culturally and ethnically diverse" group. Most are "hard-working students with full-time jobs" and "many have families to support," but there are also "some fresh college grads" in the mix. These "dedicated and helpful" students contribute to an intellectually challenging atmosphere."

DSU is located in Dover, the state capital. The state government and the United States Air Force are among the area's top employers; others include Playtex, Procter & Gamble, and General Mills, all of which have manufacturing facilities in or around Dover. The city is conveniently located, with fairly easy access to Philadelphia, Washington D.C., and Baltimore.

Admissions

Applicants to the Delaware State MBA program must submit the following documentation to the Admissions Committee: a completed application; official transcripts for all previous undergraduate and graduate work; an official score report for the GMAT; two letters of recommendation from individuals capable of assessing the candidate's ability to succeed in a graduate business program; a resume; and, a personal statement of career objectives and personal philosophy. In order to earn unconditional admission, applicants must have completed all foundations courses at the undergraduate level, and they must show an undergraduate GPA of at least 2.75, a minimum GMAT score of 400, and earn a score of at least 975 under the formula [(undergraduate GPA x 200) + GMAT score]. Applicants failing to meet these requirements may be admitted conditionally if they have an undergraduate GPA of at least 2.5 and a minimum GMAT score of 400; or, have an undergraduate GPA of at least 3.0 or an upper-division GPA of at least 3.25; or, meet all requirements except for the foundations requirement. Students admitted conditionally will have their status changed to "unconditional admission" once they have completed three MBA-level courses with a grade of at least B; they must submit a satisfactory GMAT score before being allowed to register for a fourth MBA-level course. Applicants with significant work experience (at least five years) in management may apply for admission as non-traditional students; the school may waive GPA and GMAT requirements for such applicants.

FINANCIAL FACTS

Annual tuition (in-state/ out-of-state)	$12,000/$24,000
Fees	$400
Cost of books	$1,200
Room & board (on/off-campus)	$7,500/$4,800
% of students receiving aid	20
% of first-year students receiving aid	40
% of students receiving grants	20
Average award package	$5,000
Average grant	$6,000

ADMISSIONS

Admissions Selectivity Rating	78
# of applications received	48
% applicants accepted	92
% acceptees attending	100
Average GMAT	450
Accepts GRE scores	No
Average GPA	3.0
TOEFL required of international students	Yes
Minimum TOEFL (paper/web)	/75
Application fee	$50
International application fee	$50
Deferment available	Yes
Maximum length of deferment	unlimited
Transfer students accepted	Yes
Transfer application policy They must complete the application process and provide the official transcripts.	
Non-fall admissions	Yes
Need-blind admissions	No

EMPLOYMENT PROFILE

Career Rating	77	**Grads Employed by Function% Avg. Salary**	
Percent employed at graduation	2	Marketing	(20%)
Percent employed 3 months		Operations	(5%)
after graduation	3	Management	(20%)
Average base starting salary	$55,000	Finance	(20%)
Primary Source of Full-time Job Acceptances		**Top 5 Employers Hiring Grads**	
School-facilitated activities	(40%)	Bank of America (13), Chase (15), JP Morgan	
Graduate-facilitated activities	(20%)	(25)	
Unknown	(40%)		

DREXEL UNIVERSITY
LeBow College of Business

Academics

Academics at Drexel University encompass a breadth of Colleges and Schools whose programs are designed to provide the foundation of study enriched by experiential learning to produce the next generation of scholars, professionals, and leaders. LeBow College of Business fits squarely into that tradition. Noted strengths of the MBA program include "a pragmatic approach to real-world application." Offering a "strong and dynamic curriculum" that "stresses practical education," LeBow offers "a solid emphasis on business analysis processes with a strong technology background as well." Practical application is delivered through "case studies and other real-life simulations" that "help in applying concepts and attaining a better understanding of how to approach a given situation." Students in the full-time MBA program also benefit from a three-month summer co-op program that provides hands-on experience while "helping students learn more about the industries in which they might wish to pursue a career."

Part-time and full-time students will find numerous options at LeBow. The school offers a one-year full-time MBA. Those unable to attend daytime classes will likely prefer the two-year evening cohorted Accelerated MBA offered in the Philadelphia campus and in the suburban Malvern, PA location. LeBow also offers a more traditional part-time At-Your-Own-Pace MBA and two online part-time MBAs. The online MBA is a conventional part-time cohort MBA delivered online over twenty-four months (one on-campus residency and a midpoint online consulting residency is required). The second is the Online Flex MBA, with a 3.5 year degree completion time to allow for a lighter course schedule. All programs operate on a fast-paced quarterly academic calendar that allows "more chances to take courses during a year," and all programs place "a strong emphasis on leadership."

Students praise the LeBow administration, reporting that the school "appears to be pouring a lot of money into the marketing of the LeBow brand. That will likely produce more of a return for [us] upon graduation." One MBA happily tells us, "The administration could not make the process any easier to prevent any type of potential distraction from your academics. If you wish to pursue further study in a discipline or make local contacts in a discipline they are always there to help." Likewise, professors "are really open to meeting with students and discussing classroom ideas in a different context. They enjoy getting to know their students and sharing their own experiences." Faculty members "bring real-world issues to classroom for discussions and potential problem solutions. Some even share their consultancy experiences with the students. Overall, it is highly stimulating and excellent learning experience."

Career and Placement

LeBow's Office of MBA Career Services offers "excellent career services," according to students. Through "various career service events and networking opportunities," career counselors "really make an effort to involve as many students as possible and showcase their events in a professional way. Just in the last few months I have attended several Employer of the Week sessions that have [piqued] my interest in industries I had not previously considered. Also the Mentor Match program has been pivotal in honing my networking skills and [giving me the opportunity to interact] with alumni in both formal and informal settings." Drexel's alumni network represents another "great opportunity to see how Drexel positively impacted the careers of so many professionals who were once in our position years ago." Finally, "regular job fairs...are often good opportunities for networking."

Top employers of recently graduated Drexel MBAs include: eBay, Agilent Technologies, Independence Blue Cross, Booz Allen, SAP, PwC, Deloitte Consulting, Comcast, IBM, SEI.

ADMISSIONS CONTACT: JOHN ADAMSKI, DIRECTOR GRADUATE ADMISSIONS
ADDRESS: 3220 MARKET STREET, GERRI C. LEBOW HALL, PHILADELPHIA, PA 19104
PHONE: 215-895-6804 • FAX: 215-895-1725
E-MAIL: MBA@DREXEL.EDU • WEBSITE: WWW.LEBOW.DREXEL.EDU/

Student Life and Environment

"Drexel provides plenty of professional and social networking opportunities" for its MBAs, although full-time students benefit the most (since they are on campus most frequently). Full-timers report "an overwhelming range of opportunities available," with "clubs and competitions for every interest" that include "networking events for women in business, video game clubs, consulting groups, music labels, etc. Academics are always number one priority, but there are plenty of outside opportunities for fun." Philadelphia is an asset in that regard. It's "a city that has a ton of opportunities" and provides a "great local business and government network." Overall, students enjoy a "good life/school/work balance," with "plenty of opportunities to pursue other school-related activities without having to overcommit yourself."

LeBow has a diverse population in its MBA programs with 21 percent of students having undergrad degrees in liberal arts, 19 percent in sciences, another 20 percent in engineering, tech, or other subjects, and 40 percent in business. Students say this mix results in "a nice balance between very intelligent and a lot of fun." The different programs draw different types of students, of course. The full-time program tends to be younger and less experienced, while the Executive MBA draws students who "have extensive work experience and understand the importance of a business graduate degree."

Admissions

Applicants to the Drexel LeBow MBA program must submit all of the following: transcripts for all undergraduate work and for any graduate study; an official GMAT score report; letters of recommendation; a personal essay; and a resume. Applicants are assessed based on academic performance, professional experience, career goals, extracurricular record, and potential to contribute positively to the Drexel MBA program. International applicants must also submit an official score report for the TOEFL if English is not their first language, unless they hold an undergraduate degree from an institution at which instruction is in English.

FINANCIAL FACTS

Annual tuition (in-state/ out-of-state)	$25,000/$25,000
Fees	$800
Cost of books	$1,200
Room & board	$15,000
% of students receiving aid	76
% of first-year students receiving aid	76
% of students receiving grants	42
Average award package	$29,890
Average grant	$16,246
Average loan	$21,050
Average student loan debt	$48,981

ADMISSIONS

Admissions Selectivity Rating	91
# of applications received	1,934
% applicants accepted	57
% acceptees attending	29
Average GMAT	620
Range of GMAT	580–680
Average GPA	3.2
TOEFL required of international students	Yes
Minimum TOEFL (paper/web)	600/95
Application fee	$50
International application fee	$50
Early application deadline	10/15
Regular application deadline	8/1
Deferment available	Yes
Maximum length of deferment	12 months
Transfer students accepted	Yes
Transfer application policy	Completed application and all supporting materials to be reviewed by Admissions Committee. Only non-cohorted programs allow for transfer credits from an AACSB accredited school.
Non-fall admissions	Yes
Need-blind admissions	Yes

EMPLOYMENT PROFILE

Career Rating	86	Grads Employed by Function	% Avg. Salary
Percent employed at graduation	26	Marketing	(15%) $87,400
Percent employed 3 months after graduation	59	Operations	(12%) $53,250
		Consulting	(24%) $55,875
Average base starting salary	$63,691	Management	(12%) $82,000
Primary Source of Full-time Job Acceptances		Finance	(29%) $61,402
		Other	(6%)

Top 5 Employers Hiring Grads
TYCO Electronics, PNC, Deliotte, Campbell's Soup, South Jersey Industries

DUKE UNIVERSITY
THE FUQUA SCHOOL OF BUSINESS

GENERAL INFORMATION

Type of school	Private
Affiliation	No Affiliation
Academic calendar	Terms

SURVEY SAYS...

Classmates have diverse work experience, Friendly students, Good peer network, Good social scene, Abundant mentors available, Helpful alumni, Happy students, Abundant clubs and activities, Students love Durham, NC
Solid preparation in:
Finance, Accounting, General management, Teamwork, Communication/interpersonal skills, Presentation skills, Quantitative skills, Doing business in a global economy

STUDENTS

Enrollment of parent institution	14,950
Enrollment of MBA Program	894
% male/female	65/35
% part-time	0
% underrepresented minority	17
% international	40
Average age at entry	29
Average years work experience at entry	5

ACADEMICS

Academic Experience Rating	**98**
Profs interesting rating	94
Profs accessible rating	97
Student/faculty ratio	8:1
% female faculty	18
% underrepresented minority faculty	5
% part-time faculty	22

Joint Degrees

MBA/JD, 4 years; MBA/MPP, 3 years; MBA/Master of Forestry, 3 years; MBA/Master of Environmental Management, 3 years; MBA/MS Engineering, 3 years; MBA/MD, 5 years; MBA/MSN, 3 years.

Academics

Name and reputation aside, what really differentiates Duke University's Fuqua School of Business is its "unbelievable culture, collaborative environment, focus on consequential leadership," and an administration that actively seeks opportunities to improve and respond to student feedback "like no organization I have ever witnessed," according to a student. The cohort-based Daytime MBA begins with the month-long Global Institute, an introduction to Fuqua that features three core classes designed to lay a foundation for business acumen. These courses and the quarter term system make academics across the first three quarters very demanding, and "combined with recruiting and a desire to establish and maintain a social life . . . make for a very time-consuming experience." With that said, "the immersion is a great element, and the culture and supportive nature of those that self-select into Fuqua creates the feeling of a family."

The school knows exactly the intellectual wringer it is putting students through, and offers total support, striking "a perfect balance between learning and development." Deans are incredibly visible, and there is an understanding that "that there is so much more value to an MBA than just the curriculum." The school's unique schedule with no classes on Wednesdays is "a huge contributor to the way that Fuqua operates." First, the classes on Fridays keep students around Durham on the weekends, which reinforces the social and community-focused environment. Second, "the midweek break allows time for students to properly prepare for the second half of the week."

The environment mimics that of the real business world: "collaboration-heavy, with tons of competing priorities, in a fast-paced, dynamic, challenging environment." The school does not specialize in any one career track and has very developed and strong programs across all sectors; there is "a real focus on staying relevant" with new course additions like Project Finance, and a wide variety of concentrations help students to arm themselves against the working world. "I have never been part of an organization where the administration cares as much as they do here at Fuqua," says a student.

Career and Placement

The Fuqua brand name certainly does well within companies that hire MBAs, and an "unparalleled network" of alumni is at the ready to help get students into work. "Without question, I will pick up the phone for any Fuqua grad that calls me ten years from now, and then some," says a student. Some here claim that the Career Management Center is stronger in some areas than others, with an excellent track record placing finance, CPG marketing, and consulting candidates. Extracurricular activities are an excellent way for students to hone their skills, and "between workshops, club mentors and peer interviewing, the clubs ensure that first years are well prepared for interview season." The Consulting Club, for instance, "prepares an eight-week interview prep course for first years that is taught by second years and a number of panels to help address any recruiting questions or concerns, as well as helping to organize case interview sessions." In recent years, top recruiters have included Deloitte, Boston Consulting Group, Microsoft, McKinsey, and PricewaterhouseCoopers.

ADMISSIONS CONTACT: LIZ RILEY HARGROVE, ASSOCIATE DEAN FOR ADMISSIONS
ADDRESS: 100 FUQUA DRIVE, DURHAM, NC 27708-0120
PHONE: 919-660-7705 • FAX: 919-681-8026
E-MAIL: ADMISSIONS-INFO@FUQUA.DUKE.EDU • WEBSITE: WWW.FUQUA.DUKE.EDU

Student Life and Environment

The set of "engaging, passionate people" that make up Team Fuqua bring a range of interests to help to create a "convivial student culture on campus." Students here "are intrinsically motivated to do their best, but never at someone else's expense." Clubs and organizations run rampant throughout campus, and "a large part of the social experience is trying new things and getting the opportunity to interact with people you've never met before." Fuqua Fridays are a popular pastime, in which all students and families are invited to a free dinner and drinks, helping to "foster the broadest community possible."

The facilities are fantastic, and the community is "thoroughly engaged in all aspects of MBA life." Partners and children are welcomed at many events ("the Partners club does a great job connecting partners with each other, the outside community, and with jobs in the area"), and Duke basketball remains the universal key to all students' interests. Among the best qualities at Duke is the tremendous flexibility in how you focus your time. "Across academics, career, and extra curricular/social activities, each student identifies what they want most out of their experience and the school provides the resources to take full advantage," says a student.

Admissions

Admission to Fuqua is highly competitive; you will have the best chance of acceptance if you apply as early in the admissions cycle as possible. The admissions committee does not have any minimum GMAT scores or GPA requirements. However, for the 2014 entering class, the GMAT range for students in the 25th to 75th percentile was 660–720, while the average GPA range was 3.2–3.7.

Prominent Alumni

Timothy D. Cook, CEO, Apple, Inc.; Melinda French Gates, co-chair and trustee, Bill & Melinda Gates Foundation; Michael W. Lamach, chairman & CEO, Ingersoll-Rand; David B. Snow, Jr., chairman & CEO, Cedar Gate Technologies, LLC; Joseph R. Swedish, president & CEO, Anthem, Inc.

FINANCIAL FACTS

Annual tuition (in-state/ out-of-state)	$60,600/$60,600
Fees	$3,356
Cost of books	$7,014
Room & board	$12,394
% of students receiving aid	76
% of first-year students receiving aid	80
% of students receiving grants	47
Average award package	$59,157
Average grant	$21,469
Average loan	$61,508
Average student loan debt	$114,759

ADMISSIONS

Admissions Selectivity Rating	96
# of applications received	3,424
Average GMAT	696
Range of GMAT	670–720
Accepts GRE scores	Yes
Average GPA	3.4
Application fee	$225
International application fee	$225
Application Deadline/Notification	
Round 1:	9/15 / 10/26
Round 2:	10/14 / 12/17
Round 3:	1/5 / 3/15
Round 4:	3/22 / 5/6
Deferment available	Yes
Maximum length of deferment	1 year, decided case by case
Transfer students accepted	No
Non-fall admissions	No
Need-blind admissions	Yes

EMPLOYMENT PROFILE

Career Rating	98	Grads Employed by Function	%	Avg. Salary
Percent employed at graduation	85	Marketing	(16%)	$109,509
Percent employed 3 months after graduation	94	Operations	(4%)	$117,077
		Consulting	(35%)	$130,374
Average base starting salary	$119,056	Management	(17%)	$109,911
Primary Source of Full-time Job Acceptances		Finance	(20%)	$117,229
School-facilitated activities	273 (77%)	HR	(2%)	$120,400
Graduate-facilitated activities	72 (20%)	MIS	(4%)	$107,814
Unknown	10 (3%)	Other	(2%)	$129,167

Top 5 Employers Hiring Grads
McKinsey (24), Deloitte (21), Microsoft (19), Boston Consulting Group (17), Amazon (15)

DUQUESNE UNIVERSITY
JOHN F. DONAHUE GRADUATE SCHOOL OF BUSINESS

Academics

Duquesne University's Donahue School of Business is unique because of its emphasis on sustainability and business ethics. Duquesne's award-winning, full-time, one-year MBA Sustainability is its star program, drawing students who understand sustainability is "a global business imperative." One student in this "outstanding" program says it will "open a lot of doors as the business world continues to evolve." Duquesne's other MBA programs are also strong. Its professional evening MBA allows students to work and participate in various academic and professional enrichment activities. All students are required to take a foundational core of classes but can take electives or add a concentration in the following areas: Finance, Management, Marketing, and Supply Chain Management. The school also offers master's programs in Accounting, Information Systems Management, Management, and Sports Business, along with joint-MBA degree programs.

Duquesne is devoted to teaching and supporting ethical business practices, and all students are required to take an "Applied Business Ethics" course. The Institute for Ethics in Business promotes "business ethics, responsible financial management, and sustainability in the global marketplace," and hosts the Distinguished Ethics Speaker Series. The "varied work backgrounds of [my fellow] students" and the presence of international students ensure everyone is exposed to global viewpoints.

Teamwork is a big part of academic life at Duquesne, where "small class sizes" allow students to work with each other on rewarding projects "that collaborate across all classes." Professors are "enthusiastic" and "knowledgeable in their respective fields," and bring "real-world application to the material." They are "friendly" and "accessible," and "show a genuine interest in the success of their students." Students looking to enrich their academic experience or become more involved in the school can apply for a graduate assistantship. These competitive appointments employ students in one of three areas: assisting with faculty research; tutoring in accounting, economics, finance, or statistics; or working in administrative offices. Students are not eligible for these positions until they are accepted, and they must maintain a 3.5 GPA while holding them.

Career and Placement

The Donahue School of Business does not have its own student career office, so students use the University's Career Services Center, which serves the rest of the school. The center hosts career fairs, networking events, and on-campus interviews for students at all levels. It also provides resume help and career counseling. However, some students would like to see "better alumni networking and career services for graduate students."

Duquesne's "excellent reputation" means it is able to attract a wide range of companies to its events. Employers who recently visited campus include Allegheny Technologies, Alcoa, Bank of New York Mellon, Deloitte, PNC Bank, PricewaterhouseCoopers, T. Rowe Price, US Steel, Westinghouse.

Student Life and Environment

"The greatest strengths of Duquesne are the students," who are "enthusiastic, innovative, hard working, competitive and very smart." One student described his peers as "young professionals" who want to take their careers "to the next level."

Many students commute and work part- or full-time, which means classes are filled with

ADMISSIONS CONTACT: PATRICIA MOORE, MANAGING DIRECTOR OF GRADUATE PROGRAMS
ADDRESS: 600 FORBES AVENUE, PITTSBURGH, PA 15282
PHONE: 412-396-6276 • FAX: 412-396-1726
E-MAIL: GRAD-BUS@DUQ.EDU • WEBSITE: WWW.BUSINESS.DUQ.EDU/GRAD

people with "interesting and diverse" professional experience. "I appreciate the varied work backgrounds of my fellow students," one student says. "It helps to provide insight to other industries and fields."

Despite its large commuter population, the school still manages to provide a "close-knit community" and a "personal" educational experience. One commuter says that even students who live off campus feel like they live on campus because they're "constantly in the buildings." Students love Duquesne's location in downtown Pittsburgh, which makes the school "convenient for working professionals" and puts students in "close proximity to downtown Pittsburgh's business and professional climate." The school is also "close to some of the most popular entertainment districts" of Pittsburgh "as well as within a five-mile radius of four other colleges," so there are lots of opportunities for socializing and meeting people.

Admissions

All students applying to Duquesne's MBA programs must take the GMAT or GRE (waivers are available for work experience, advanced degrees, or academic performance), and international students must also take the TOEFL or the IELTS. The full- and part-time MBA program admits students for the fall, spring, and summer semesters, but students in the MBA Sustainability program may only enter in the fall. Applications require official transcripts, letters of recommendation, a resume, and a personal statement on what strengths you will bring to the program. Students seeking admission to the Sustainability program have different personal essay options. Interviews are not required, but personal or phone interviews can positively supplement applications. Four-year bachelor degrees are required for admission, and international students who received a degree after three years of study may enroll in Duquesne's MBA Bridge Program, which allows them to take the necessary year of classes at the undergraduate level and apply those credits toward their MBA.

FINANCIAL FACTS

Annual tuition (in-state/ out-of-state)	$54,831/$54,831
Fees	$0
Cost of books	$3,400
% of students receiving aid	89
% of first-year students receiving aid	94
% of students receiving grants	87
Average award package	$10,584
Average grant	$5,439
Average loan	$18,485
Average student loan debt	$37,308

ADMISSIONS

Admissions Selectivity Rating	78
# of applications received	81
% applicants accepted	89
% acceptees attending	40
Average GMAT	545
Range of GMAT	500–580
Accepts GRE scores	Yes
Average Verbal GRE	149
Range of Verbal GRE scores	140–154
Average Quantitative GRE	147
Range of Quantitative GRE scores	145–147
Average Writing GRE	3.5
Range of Writing GRE scores	2.8–4.0
Average GPA	3.4
TOEFL required of international students	Yes
Minimum TOEFL (paper/web)	577/90
Application fee	$0
International application fee	$0
Application Deadline/Notification	
Round 1:	12/1 / 1/15
Round 2:	3/1 / 4/1
Round 3:	4/15 / 5/15
Deferment available	Yes
Maximum length of deferment	One year
Transfer students accepted	Yes
Transfer application policy	
The Donahue School will accept up to 10.5 transfer credits from an accredited college or university.	
Non-fall admissions	Yes
Need-blind admissions	Yes

EMPLOYMENT PROFILE

Career Rating	**87**	**Grads Employed by Function% Avg. Salary**	
Percent employed 3 months after graduation	75	Marketing	(25%) $45,000
		Consulting	(50%) $57,250
Average base starting salary	$57,375	Other	(25%) $70,000
Primary Source of Full-time Job Acceptances		**Top 5 Employers Hiring Grads**	
Graduate-facilitated activities	4 (100%)	Bank of New York Mellon, University of Pittsburgh Medical Center (UPMC), Pittsburgh Plate Glass (PPG), PNC Bank, American Eagle Outfitters	

EAST CAROLINA UNIVERSITY
COLLEGE OF BUSINESS

Academics

East Carolina is a medium-sized public school, but it seems like a smaller, more expensive one. Its MBA program provides students with lots of "individual attention" and allows them to tailor the program to their needs. "ECU has an intimate feel," one student says. "Professors know students' names," and the campus has a "friendly atmosphere." Students can take classes on campus, online, or both. It's common for distance education programs to feel alienating, but students say "very little of the East Carolina spirit is lost over the Internet." "There is still a lot of communication that goes on" in the online program, and the interactive media "makes up for the lack of face time" and means students still "get a chance to know people pretty well." Students may attend full or part time, and can change the number of classes they take and the method through which they take them every semester. One student explains, the school "is set up to meet students' needs, not the students having to work around the school."

East Carolina requires a number of foundation classes, such as Financial and Managerial Accounting and Financial Management, but students who studied business as an undergraduate can have these requirements waived if they took similar courses and received a B or higher. All students must take eight common body of knowledge courses that provide a solid foundation in business and three elective courses that allow them to focus on areas of their choice. Students may choose to take four electives toward a certificate in an area they want to specialize in. Current offerings include Business Analytics, Health Care Management, Finance and Management Information Systems, Marketing, and Project Management.

Professors at East Carolina get high marks. The "strong" and "challenging" faculty members are "genuinely concerned with their students' success in the program," and really "push them to get better." They are accessible outside of class, and students can "build real relationships with them." One student explains that a "professor put me in touch with professional networking organizations. Another put me in touch with a professor outside my program, who had insight into an aspect of business I am interested in." Professors definitely "expect hard work and high professionalism from each student," and those interested in East Carolina should be prepared to devote themselves to their studies. One online student who also works full time says, "My life revolves around class assignments, cases, group work, and other obligations. This program is not for the faint of heart!" East Carolina's combination of a demanding, but flexible academic program, dedicated professors, and enthusiastic students make for a great experience and is why so many people think the school offers a great "bang for the buck."

Career and Placement

East Carolina University's Center for Student Success offers students a wide-range of individualized support for their academic and professional needs. The College of Business Career Center assists students with internship and job searches, conducts mock interviews, and provides help with resumes. In addition to providing networking opportunities, the Center hosts career fairs and on-campus interviews. Companies that visited campus in the past year include Credit Suisse, BB&T, Ferguson/Wolseley, PIE Event,

ADMISSIONS CONTACT: DR. SHANAN GIBSON, ASSOCIATE DEAN
ADDRESS: 3203 BATE BUILDING, GREENVILLE, NC 27858-4353
PHONE: 252-328-6970 • FAX: 252-328-2106
E-MAIL: GRADBUS@ECU.EDU • WEBSITE: WWW.BUSINESS.ECU.EDU

FINANCIAL FACTS

Annual tuition (in-state/ out-of-state)	$6,480/$18,790
Fees	$2,119
Cost of books	$800

ADMISSIONS

Admissions Selectivity Rating	**79**
# of applications received	166
% applicants accepted	88
% acceptees attending	79
Average GMAT	520
Range of GMAT	470–560
Accepts GRE scores	Yes
Average GPA	3.3
TOEFL required of international students	Yes
Minimum TOEFL (paper/web)	550/80
Application fee	$70
International application fee	$70
Deferment available	Yes
Maximum length of deferment	1 year
Transfer students accepted	Yes
Transfer application policy Maximum of 9 semester credit hours from AACSB accredited institution accepted	
Non-fall admissions	Yes
Need-blind admissions	Yes

Sinclair Broadcasting, and McGladrey & Pullen.

Student Life and Environment

The flexibility offered by East Carolina attracts a wide-range of students. You'll find students, who are "young and old, single and married, career changers, and professionals seeking to enhance their status within their current career tracks." Though people may be different, one student says "everybody is here to learn." Students are "excited about learning, and this energy comes through." Students who have "been in the professional world for several years, bring a wealth of knowledge and experience" into classroom discussions. The large number of distance learners does not diminish the school's spirit; in fact, the online students are some of the program's biggest champions.

The campus itself is nice and has "great places to study and to wind down" and offers lots of "great extracurricular activities." The football games are popular and "always a whole lot of fun." However, as many students work full time and have family obligations, not everyone has time to participate in campus life, so those looking to actively socialize may have to look beyond the MBA program. Luckily, the Graduate Business Association organizes a lot of activities, such as networking programs with local business leaders and recruiters, as well as professional development seminars and social nights. Many departments, such as Accounting, Finance, and Management, have their own student organizations, and the school also has chapters of two national honor societies, Beta Gamma Sigma, and Phi Kappa Phi.

Admissions

East Carolina University does not require applicants to have previous professional experience and does not ask for recommendations or a personal statement. To be eligible for admission, students must have a degree from an accredited institution. Admissions for all programs are on a rolling basis, and students may begin classes in the fall, spring, or summer. Admission is based off of a student's "admission index number," which is calculated from the student's GMAT or GRE score and undergraduate GPA. International students must take the TOEFL and score at least 550 on the written exam, 213 on the computer exam, and 80 on the Internet portion of the exam.

EAST TENNESSEE STATE UNIVERSITY
COLLEGE OF BUSINESS AND TECHNOLOGY

GENERAL INFORMATION

Type of school	Public
Affiliation	No Affiliation
Academic calendar	Semester

SURVEY SAYS...

Good social scene, Good peer network

Solid preparation in:
Accounting

STUDENTS

Enrollment of parent institution	12,156
Enrollment of MBA Program	71
% male/female	55/45
% out-of-state	10
% part-time	70
% underrepresented minority	10
% international	10
Average age at entry	28
Average years work experience at entry	3

ACADEMICS

Academic Experience Rating	**70**
Profs interesting rating	77
Profs accessible rating	71
Student/faculty ratio	7:1
% female faculty	10
% underrepresented minority faculty	2
% part-time faculty	0

Prominent Alumni

Pal Barger, Food Services

Academics

There aren't many choices at the College of Business and Technology at East Tennessee State University—the small program maintains only three business and three technology departments (accounting, economics/finance, management/marketing)—but for those who are interested in a general purpose business degree, ETSU delivers.

In addition to the traditional MBA, the school also offers an MAcc (master's of accounting), and a graduate certificate in business administration for "those who seek a basic understanding of business administration but who may not be able to make the commitment of time, effort, and money required to seek a master's degree."

MBAs at ETSU feel that "the administration and faculty here are very student-oriented. Most have set times when they are available outside of class; others excel and really go the extra mile both in class presentation and in their availability to those students that require extra instruction." Overall, "the program is very well-organized and runs smoothly. The program has been staffed administratively to be a success. Everyone is focused on their customer—the student." Professors are regarded as "very knowledgeable in their fields, and many of them are widely recognized as great scholars." One student writes, "Most of them have a work background that can lead to some very good discussions in class, and [the professors present] the applications of the concepts in the real world through their stories." Faculty members are also "easy to work with and understanding about personal matters that can arise." ETSU students are "a very diverse and accepting group. All of us have different ideals and political and social backgrounds." Another student concurs: "We are like a family at ETSU. You go through the same classes with pretty much the same group of students. We are all interested in each other's success. There is low competition." Most students agree that the school does "a very good job of getting the student prepared with the knowledge that is needed in the workplace, but there is just so much that can be taught in the classroom setting." Many students have full-time jobs, and say "true learning from the classroom is applied to the jobs that are obtained after school." Across the board, students love that "the school is large enough to offer remote-learning facilities, and classes are generally available at convenient times for working adults." Most of all, however, students appreciate that professors "show a major interest in students' ability to understand the work."

Career and Placement

The Career Placement and Internship Services Office at East Tennessee University serves the school's entire undergraduate and graduate student body. The office hosts recruitment visits from various companies, sponsors and participates in career fairs, maintains online job boards and resume books, and offers counseling in interview skills, job search, career match, and resume writing. Recent on-campus recruiters included New York Life, Norfolk Southern, Wachovia, and Wells Fargo. Students are aware that "Johnson City is a small town, which limits the amount of recruiting that is done on campus." Even so, many "believe that [the] school could improve by really showing students what is available out there and helping them find jobs when they get done. It is there right now [at the Career Placement and Internship Services Office], but a student really has to push to find it."

Student Life and Environment

East Tennessee State University is located in Johnson City, a small Appalachian city close to both the North Carolina and Virginia borders. The surrounding area, dubbed the Tri-Cities region, also includes Bristol and Kingsport; the charming town of Abingdon, Virginia, is also not too far afield. The area is an outdoor enthusiast's paradise, offering plenty of opportunities for hiking, climbing, skiing, and nature walks. The Tri-Cities area is a rising force in the health care industry, with a developing biotech industry that could bring big players to the region.

With more than 14,000 students (about 2,200 of whom are graduate students), the ETSU campus has the population to support a busy social scene. MBAs report, "There is a very good social scene, with Thursday nights being the night that most students go out to the clubs. There are not a lot of clubs in the area, but there are many places that one can go and have a beer if they so choose." Students try to find time to support their men's basketball team, the ETSU Bucs.

ETSU has expanded in recent years, adding several new buildings, including a fitness center (students love the "fully-equipped athletic facility"). Not all MBAs take the time to enjoy the ETSU campus, however; they note that "the school is a high commuter school. This leads to a low participation level in on-campus clubs" and other activities. Those who do participate recommend the school's several national honor societies. One student touts "the university organization called 'President's Pride.' Through this organization, I am able to socialize with other students, faculty, administrators, and [members of the] community by volunteering for university/community functions."

Through its Adult, Commuter, and Transfer Services (ACTS) Office, ETSU assists its many nontraditional students in adapting to student life. ACTS staff advises students on the nuts and bolts of registration, direct them to the campus's various tutoring services, and help parents find child-care services. This last one can be a problem for MBAs, who typically attend evening classes.

Admissions

Applications to the College of Business and Technology at East Tennessee State University are considered on a rolling basis. Applicants must submit the following to the Graduate Admissions Office: official copies of transcripts for all undergraduate and graduate work; standardized test scores (GMAT for the MBA or MAcc; TOEFL scores (where applicable); a personal statement; and a resume. All applicants are presumed to be competent with computers and math literate through calculus.

FINANCIAL FACTS

Annual tuition (in-state/ out-of-state)	$5,446/$15,722
Fees	$1,100
Cost of books	$1,000
Room & board (on/off-campus)	$5,000/$6,000
% of students receiving aid	25
% of first-year students receiving aid	25
% of students receiving grants	25
Average award package	$6,000
Average grant	$6,000
Average loan	$4,000
Average student loan debt	$10,000

ADMISSIONS

Admissions Selectivity Rating	82
# of applications received	70
% applicants accepted	77
% acceptees attending	85
Average GMAT	535
Range of GMAT	450–700
Average GPA	3.3
TOEFL required of international students	Yes
Minimum TOEFL (paper/web)	550/
Application fee	$25
International application fee	$35
Regular application deadline	6/1
Deferment available	Yes
Maximum length of deferment	one year
Transfer students accepted	Yes
Transfer application policy Up to 9 approved hours MAY be accepted.	
Non-fall admissions	Yes
Need-blind admissions	Yes

EMPLOYMENT PROFILE

Career Rating	74	Grads Employed by Function	% Avg. Salary
Average base starting salary	$38,000	Marketing	(10%) $38,000
		Management	(50%) $30,000
		HR	(10%) $30,000
		Top 5 Employers Hiring Grads	
		Eastman Chemical (2)	

EASTERN MICHIGAN UNIVERSITY
COLLEGE OF BUSINESS

Academics

With its convenient location, "experienced professors," and "low tuition," the MBA program at Eastern Michigan University's College of Business offers a great return on investment. "Designed for working professionals," EMU's courses are offered in the evenings, on the weekends, via the Internet, and through hybrid online/classroom delivery. The format is totally flexible, and students can take as little as one class per semester and up to a full course load. While balancing a career and an education can be tricky business, students say EMU "provides great support for students and overall great atmosphere of learning."

At EMU, "most of the professors are amazing," with close to 100 percent of the school's faculty holding the highest degree available in their field. Students admit that "you get a couple bad professors/classmates along the way, but there is little if anything to complain about." Graduate class sizes average fewer than twenty, which gives students the opportunity to "work directly with professors who provide PhD-level class time, rather than having to work through a teaching assistant." The result is a dynamic classroom environment, in which discussion is encouraged and "professors challenge you to develop your own opinions regarding global business and economies." In addition to the professors, there is "lots of diverse work experience among the students," adding even more depth to the academic environment. Real-world applications are stressed in the classroom, though students would like to see coursework incorporate "more up-to-date case studies" and hands-on instruction. One student suggests, "EMU needs to strengthen their program with real business partnerships where students can apply what they learn and gain real job experience."

The MBA curriculum is comprised of foundation coursework (which can be waived for students with previous education in business), core coursework, electives, and an area of specialization, which combine for a program of study between thirty-six–fifty-four credit hours. Catering to its diverse student body, EMU offers specializations in a variety of business fields, including business analytics, e-business, entrepreneurship, internal auditing, international business, management, and nonprofit management, as well as the opportunity to pursue a general MBA with no particular specialization (in that case, students can take a range of elective coursework to meet the units required for graduation).

Career and Placement

EMU students love the fact that their school caters to full-time working professionals. Unfortunately, the flip side of this arrangement is that there is more limited career support and recruiting programs at EMU than you'd find at a traditional full-time MBA. For those looking to expand their network in Detroit and Ann Arbor, "there are several clubs that have outstanding connections to our alumni and important people in the area." In addition, the College of Business maintains updated listings of internships and full-time jobs available in the area, and occasionally invites recruiters to campus to meet with current students and alumni.

ADMISSIONS CONTACT: MICHELLE HENRY, DIRECTOR, GRADUATE BUSINESS PROGRAMS
ADDRESS: 300 W. MICHIGAN AVENUE, STE. 306, YPSILANTI, MI 48197
PHONE: 734-487-4444 • FAX: 734-483-1316
E-MAIL: COB.GRADUATE@EMICH.EDU • WEBSITE: WWW.COB.EMICH.EDU

FINANCIAL FACTS

Annual tuition (in-state/ out-of-state)	$10,926/$19,980
Fees	$851
Cost of books	$700
Room & board (on/off-campus)	$6,008/
% of students receiving aid	52
% of first-year students receiving aid	36
% of students receiving grants	16
Average award package	$13,505
Average grant	$6,428
Average loan	$14,613

ADMISSIONS

Admissions Selectivity Rating	86
# of applications received	174
% applicants accepted	44
% acceptees attending	60
Average GMAT	498
Accepts GRE scores	Yes
Average Verbal GRE	153
Average Quantitative GRE	152
Average GPA	3.3
TOEFL required of international students	Yes
Minimum TOEFL (paper/web)	550/80
Application fee	$45
International application fee	$45
Deferment available	Yes
Maximum length of deferment	one year
Transfer students accepted	Yes
Transfer application policy 6 credits may be accepted for the core if from an AACSB accredited school, and/or 6 credits may be accepted towards the elective area upon approval	
Non-fall admissions	Yes
Need-blind admissions	Yes

In complement to the resources at the business school, the University Advising and Career Development Center has a COB office that can assist with career planning and job-search skills. They also organize on-campus recruiting events with local companies. Prospective students should note, however, that the Career Development Center's services are chiefly directed at undergraduates, and "many of the recruiting companies are hiring retail managers, rather than looking for candidates for higher-quality positions." A student adds, "Our Career Services Center has little help for those outside of accounting and finance."

Student Life and Environment

Eastern Michigan University is a large public school with more than 20,000 students, a vibrant athletics program, and more than 300 active student organizations on campus. In the business school's sizable graduate programs, most students "work full-time and enroll in school part-time," making it difficult to also get involved with extracurricular campus activities. Nonetheless, students say it's "great to interact with other professionals" at the College of Business, describing their classmates as "career-oriented" and ambitious, yet "easy to get along with." For students on the main campus who'd like to branch out socially, there are "a number of clubs available for those who have time," including an MBA Association.

Located in the suburban community of Ypsilanti, the EMU campus is "very convenient" to both Ann Arbor and Detroit, and theses two cities provides endless cultural, entertainment, food, and nightlife options. Drawing from the greater metropolitan area, EMU's College of Business is incredibly "multicultural," with students from a range of backgrounds and levels of experience.

Admissions

To be considered for admission to Eastern Michigan University's MBA program, students must have a minimum undergraduate GPA of 2.75, and a score of at least 450 on the GMAT (with a score of 20 or better in the verbal section and 24 or better in the quantitative section). The school will also accept the GRE in lieu of the GMAT; a score of 297 or higher is required for admission. The GMAT/GRE may be waived for high achieving students from AACSB-accredited undergraduate programs. Prospective students must also submit a personal statement detailing their educational goals and professional experience, a résumé, and, for students whose first language isn't English, TOEFL or IELTS scores.

EASTERN WASHINGTON UNIVERSITY
COLLEGE OF BUSINESS AND PUBLIC ADMINISTRATION

GENERAL INFORMATION
Type of school	Public
Affiliation	No Affiliation
Academic calendar	Quarter

SURVEY SAYS...
Students love Spokane, WA
Solid preparation in:
Teamwork

STUDENTS
Enrollment of parent institution	12,361
Average age at entry	31
Average years work experience at entry	4

ACADEMICS
Academic Experience Rating	**82**
Profs interesting rating	88
Profs accessible rating	88
Student/faculty ratio	25:1
% female faculty	37
% underrepresented minority faculty	2
% part-time faculty	0

Joint Degrees
MBA/MPA 80 Credits 2 Years MBA/HSAD Certificate 70 Credits 1 1/2 Years

Academics

Current and future Spokane professionals choose Eastern Washington University's MBA program for its blend of affordability, convenience, and quality. The curriculum consists of forty-eight credit hours, with elective concentrations in accounting or finance. In addition to the traditional MBA, the school offers "a dual master (MBA/MPA) option" for those interested in the public or nonprofit sector. Taking a full course load, the MBA "program can be finished within one year," though the flexible schedule is highly accommodating to working professionals too. "Night classes fit well within a typical eight to five working schedule," and the campus in central Spokane is "easily accessible from in or slightly out of town." Most importantly, the school's instructors are "very understanding when you have personal circumstances interfering with class, and will do everything they can to work with you while still maintaining the highest academic standards for their students."

At this small public school, students speak highly of the MBA faculty, describing their professors as "knowledgeable, professional, personable, down-to-earth, accessible, and reasonable." Many instructors are "very highly regarded in the academic community," staying active in business research and regularly publishing scholarly articles. They are not only academics though. With strong ties to the local business community, professors "bring significant professional experience to the classroom, which helps tremendously in understanding and applying models and theories taught in class." Plus, with students ranging in age from twenty-one to fifty-nine, "The diversity of students and faculty significantly enhances the learning environment and challenges you to think more critically." Nonetheless, some students would like to see the program take an even more practical approach, saying the coursework contains "very few case studies" and skips over some essential skills, like business-plan writing.

While rigor varies by course, most "professors are tough" and classes are time-consuming. According to a current student, "We all work our tails off together to get through this program." Fortunately, professors are "all very accessible outside the classroom, even when you don't come knocking during office hours," and most "go out of their way to explain things in a way that you can understand." Likewise, "the administration is very helpful and patient" and the "easy enrollment process" makes it easier for working students to consider a degree. In addition to kindness and convenience, cost is a major reason students choose the program; EWU is "considerably less expensive than its neighboring competitors, yet it has the same AACSB accreditation."

Career and Placement

Eastern Washington University's Office of Career Services provides counseling and job placement assistance to the entire student body. The office organizes occasional career fairs, on-campus interviews, and other recruitment events, in addition to maintaining an online career management system, which matches potential employers with current students and alumni. Career Services is mostly focused on the school's large undergraduate population, so recent graduates in the MBA program are the most likely to benefit from their services.

Within the business school, students would like to see more contact with the local community: "The MBA program director does what she can as far as generating job leads for us, but it would really help if the business school were to develop partnerships with businesses." The good news is: no matter what your career plans, counting yourself among the many EWU alumni is a huge benefit in the real world. At EWU, "the network you gain access to is by itself worth the cost of the program."

ADMISSIONS CONTACT: CYNTHIA PARKER, PROGRAM COORDINATOR
ADDRESS: 668 NORTH RIVERPOINT BLVD., SPOKANE, WA 99202-1677
PHONE: 509-358-2248 • FAX: 509-358-2267
E-MAIL: CPARKER@MAIL.EWU.EDU • WEBSITE: WWW.EWU.EDU/MBA

Student Life and Environment

Though it is a small program, there is quite a bit of diversity within Eastern Washington University's MBA class. The affordable in-state price tag draws many locals, but the program also attracts "students from all over the world, so there is a high percentage of international people" on campus. In terms of life experience, "many students come straight from undergraduate into [the] MBA program," while others enroll mid-career. Overall, the mix of people and personalities creates a positive learning environment wherein "each student brings a wealth of personal and professional experiences" to the classroom.

Eastern Washington University's main campus is located in the small town of Cheney, Washington, whereas MBA classes are taught on a satellite campus in downtown Spokane. With no direct link to the school's large undergraduate community, there is not much action at the small business school facility. A student admits, "The campus I am on does not have many student activities; it would be nice if some could be added." Nevertheless, there is "a very positive, supportive atmosphere" throughout the business school as well as "an increasing sense of students working together to achieve similar goals." Up-to-date facilities, including a 200-seat auditorium, create a great learning environment, and there is plenty of nearby parking in addition to numerous public transportation options for commuters.

Admissions

To be eligible for admission to Eastern Washington University's MBA program, students must have a GPA of at least 3.0 from the last sixty semester hours of undergraduate coursework and a GMAT score of at least 450. In-person interviews are also required for admission to the program. Applications are accepted on a rolling basis; for domestic applicants, there are no application deadlines for any quarter.

FINANCIAL FACTS

Annual tuition (in-state/ out-of-state)	$21,600/$30,785
Fees	$610
Cost of books	$1,600
Room & board (on/off-campus)	$8,248/$8,248
% of students receiving aid	25
% of first-year students receiving aid	25
% of students receiving grants	5
Average grant	$0
Average loan	$0

ADMISSIONS

Admissions Selectivity Rating	79
# of applications received	73
% applicants accepted	82
% acceptees attending	65
Average GMAT	489
Range of GMAT	220–740
Accepts GRE scores	Yes
Average GPA	3.3
TOEFL required of international students	Yes
Minimum TOEFL (paper/web)	580/92
Application fee	$100
International application fee	$100
Regular application deadline	1/1
Regular application notification	1/1
Deferment available	Yes
Maximum length of deferment	1 Year
Transfer students accepted	Yes
Transfer application policy We will accept up to 12 quarter based transfer credits.	
Non-fall admissions	Yes
Need-blind admissions	Yes

ELON UNIVERSITY
MARTHA AND SPENCER LOVE SCHOOL OF BUSINESS

GENERAL INFORMATION

Type of school	Private
Affiliation	No Affiliation
Academic calendar	Trimester

SURVEY SAYS...

Classmates have diverse work experience, Friendly students, Happy students
Solid preparation in:
General management, Teamwork, Communication/interpersonal skills, Presentation skills

STUDENTS

Enrollment of parent institution	6,631
Enrollment of MBA Program	122
% part-time	100
Average age at entry	32
Average years work experience at entry	9

ACADEMICS

Academic Experience Rating	**87**
Profs interesting rating	93
Profs accessible rating	94
Student/faculty ratio	21:1
% female faculty	48
% underrepresented minority faculty	17
% part-time faculty	4

Prominent Alumni

Allan Davis, CEO, AllFab Solutions; Kathleen Galbraith, President, Duke Regional Hospital; Danielle Hoversten, Executive VP & CFO, Senn Dunn Insurance; Bernadette Spong, Sr. VP for Finance of UNC Health Care + CFO of Rex Healthcare; Dr. Andre Valcour, VP and Laboratory Director, Center for Esoteric Testing, Lab Corp

Academics

Elon University's Martha and Spencer Love School of Business has a "great reputation" as "a specialized MBA for full-time working professionals." Students praise Elon's "leadership philosophy," "learning culture," and "great program flexibility." A small university in a small town, Elon offers "small class and program size" in which the "average class is fifteen, and large classes are thirty." Elon focuses "on engaged learning, top quality of content taught, [and] values-based leadership. . . . It's why their reputation is growing so rapidly," one student notes.

There is nothing that students rave about more than the "top-notch" and "amazing" administration who "all work very well together and make you feel at home." "The program is administered with the touch of a five-star hotel," one happy student reports. Especially singled out for praise is "student liaison extraordinaire" Judy Dulberg, the MBA Program Coordinator who is "the glue for the whole operation." Everyone here is "super friendly" and "always there to help any time of day." As at many universities, the "professors vary" but most "are understanding and helpful." The professors are "open with their time and always willing to meet outside of class," and most of them "have over twenty years experience in their fields." Professors bring this "real business experience" to class, and courses themselves are "largely current event and real world driven." Professors "offer challenging work, but are also always there to help."

All in all, Elon offers "a special, tight knit community" in central North Carolina. "The greatest strengths of Elon include the culture, the people, the campus cleanliness, and overall safety." This is a school where "professors know students by name. Even Deans know students by name." As one student says, "Elon fosters an atmosphere deeply rooted in supporting one another through team building activities."

Career and Placement

Elon is largely made up of students who are currently employed, and some say the school could "improve in career placement." "We receive occasional job opportunities emailed to us, but the majority of student are currently employed since this is a part time program and therefore there isn't a lot of emphasis placed on career placement," one student elaborates. That said, Elon offers many career services to students who seek them out including employer networking, self-assessment exercises, and résumé and cover letter assistance. Top employers for Elon graduates include Cisco, IBM, LabCorp, Fresh Market, Oracle, Volvo, Wells Fargo Bank, Ralph Lauren, General Dynamics, Johnson Controls, Progress Energy, Inc., Cone Health, American Express Corporation, and BB&T.

ADMISSIONS CONTACT: ARTHUR W. FADDE, DIRECTOR OF GRADUATE ADMISSIONS
ADDRESS: 2750 CAMPUS BOX, ELON, NC 27244
PHONE: 800-334-8448 EXT. 3 • FAX: 336-278-7699
E-MAIL: GRADADM@ELON.EDU • WEBSITE: WWW.ELON.EDU/MBA

Student Life and Environment

Students at Elon are "ambitious," "cooperative," "young professionals" who are "all excited about learning and sharing their experiences and ideas." The population is "diverse," but the average student is "mid-twenties to mid-thirties, white, middle-class, and male." A large number of students—"too many" according to one—are "alumni and employees" of Elon. The peer group here is "competitive but supportive." "We all want to better ourselves and to better our lives, and can do so by pushing each other in the classroom," one student says. "The mix of students that are working and attending school simultaneously is roughly fifty-fifty with full-time students." Those who are employed tend to work "in the Greensboro and Raleigh/Durham area." As a "part-time program" filled with students with "day jobs," most "MBA students don't spend much time on campus." But there is a "subset" that is "very active" on the "beautiful" campus. "There are also regular activities outside of class like trips to minor league baseball games, golf outings, and barbecues." One student suggests, "More social activities should be available for people with small children." Another says, "thus far, my experience with my cohorts has been well worth the price of the MBA."

Admissions

Elon enrolls students in March and September, and the deadlines for applications are February 15th and August 15th. The admissions committee looks specifically for "outstanding students who have demonstrated academic ability, professional leadership and managerial promise." Students should make sure to highlight their leadership experience on their resume when applying. Otherwise, the school requires GMAT or GRE scores, undergraduate transcripts, any graduate school transcripts, two letters of recommendation, and a minimum of two years professional work experience.

FINANCIAL FACTS

Annual tuition (in-state/ out-of-state)	$17,892/$17,892
Fees	$0
Cost of books	$600
% of students receiving aid	51
% of first-year students receiving aid	41
% of students receiving grants	16
Average award package	$14,692
Average grant	$9,467
Average loan	$15,753
Average student loan debt	$37,275

ADMISSIONS

Admissions Selectivity Rating	81
# of applications received	68
% applicants accepted	84
% acceptees attending	88
Average GMAT	562
Range of GMAT	470–620
Accepts GRE scores	Yes
Average Verbal GRE	155
Range of Verbal GRE scores	152–157
Average Quantitative GRE	150
Range of Quantitative GRE scores	147–151
Average Writing GRE	3.9
Range of Writing GRE scores	3.5–4.5
Average GPA	3.3
TOEFL required of international students	Yes
Minimum TOEFL (paper/web)	550/79
Application fee	$50
International application fee	$50
Deferment available	Yes
Maximum length of deferment	1 year
Transfer students accepted	Yes
Transfer application policy	A student may transfer up to 9 semester hours of credit from another AACSB accredited school
Non-fall admissions	Yes
Need-blind admissions	Yes

EMORY UNIVERSITY
GOIZUETA BUSINESS SCHOOL

GENERAL INFORMATION
Type of school   Private
Affiliation   No Affiliation
Academic calendar   Semester

SURVEY SAYS...
Classmates have diverse work
experience, Friendly students, Good
peer network, Good social scene,
Abundant mentors available
Solid preparation in:
Marketing, Finance,
General management

STUDENTS
Enrollment of parent institution	14,724
Enrollment of MBA Program	595
% male/female	69/31
% out-of-state	87
% part-time	42
% underrepresented minority	19
% international	39
Average age at entry	29
Average years work experience at entry	6

ACADEMICS
Academic Experience Rating	**97**
Profs interesting rating	94
Profs accessible rating	98
Student/faculty ratio	5:1
% female faculty	25
% underrepresented minority faculty	8
% part-time faculty	27

Joint Degrees
Master of Business Administration/
Doctor of jurisprudence (MBA/JD),
Master of Business Administration/
Master of Public Health (MBA/
MPH) (five semesters), Master of
Business Administration/Master
of Divinity (MBA/MDIV), Master of
Business Administration/Doctor of
Physical Therapy (MBA/DPT)

Prominent Alumni
Chris Federico, MBA 2007, SVP;
Senior Relationship Manager of
Bank of America

Academics

With its "small class sizes, intimate learning environment" and amazing Atlanta location, there's no doubt that any MBA student would count themselves fortunate to attend Emory's Goizueta School of Business. The program is extremely "community oriented" and tends to place "a strong emphasis on collaboration." And, considering how "rigorous" the curriculum is, all that teamwork will surely be appreciated. Moreover, MBA students here value the fact that there are "a lot of opportunities to gain leadership experience." Perhaps even more importantly, the "programs also provide tremendous flexibility in terms of electives, independent research projects, and international travel." And there's a "huge focus on real world learning."

Inside the classroom, MBA candidates are greeted by professors who are "approachable and easily accessible." What's more, it's quite evident that they are "very invested in truly knowing their students and helping them succeed." They also have a lot of professional experience from which students can greatly benefit. As a second-year MBA explains, "Most [professors] do significant consulting on the side and can bring in fabulous guest speakers, take us on company site visits, or apply a real world case to the topic." Lastly, the "administration has open door policies that actually mean something, and they go out of their way to keep constantly improving." And a grateful first-year adds, "They lead trips, host book clubs, and frequently walk around common areas just to see what we're up to. It really feels like a family."

Career and Placement

MBA candidates will be delighted to learn that Emory consistently reports "great job placement statistics." Of course, given Goizueta's "strong investment banking recruiting record" this isn't too surprising. Additionally, the school maintains numerous "connections to major businesses in Atlanta," a fact that's supported by the "100 percent internship placement rate." A thrilled first-year explains in more detail, "Emory's location in Atlanta gives it a significant advantage . . . It is located in a major business hub without any significant competitors close by. As a result students can [really] take advantage of many local resources and companies." Lastly, beyond the recruiting opportunities, students here also love to sing the praises of the alumni. As another grateful first-year shares, "The alumni network has also been fantastic. [They] have been very willing, if not eager, to assist in any way possible."

Admissions Contact: Julie R. Barefoot, Associate Dean and Director of MBA Admissions
Address: 1300 Clifton Road, Atlanta, GA 30322
Phone: 404-727-6311 • Fax: 404-727-4612
E-mail: Admissions@bus.emory.edu • Website: www.goizueta.emory.edu

Student Life and Environment

Students at Goizueta seem to have genuine affection for their peers. Indeed, they rush to describe their fellow MBAs as "intellectually curious," "hardworking," and "very friendly." Best of all, they are the kind of individuals who "go out of their way to help each other." And while some students can be "competitive," we're assured that it's "[never] to the detriment of others." Indeed, a second-year student insists, "Teamwork and an overwhelming sense of community is always felt."

Additionally MBA candidates insist that Emory is a "very fun place to be." After all, "networking and being involved with more than academics is highly encouraged." As a first-year student interjects, "KEGS on Thursdays (Keeping Everyone at Goizueta Social) is the highlight of everyone's week. It's the perfect time to have a beer, relax, and catch up with friends after a stressful week." And an impressed second-year shares, "Last week alone we had a women's networking event, our fifty days till graduation party and a holi festival. There are always many things to do on top of your studies and classmates truly take advantage of what Emory and the Atlanta environment have to offer."

Admissions

Applicants to the Goizueta MBA program must submit the following materials: a completed online application; official transcripts for all undergraduate and graduate schools attended; an official GMAT score report; a résumé containing both your employment and educational background; application essays which allow candidates to reveal a little more about who they are and two letters of recommendation that are of a professional nature (choose at least one individual who knows you well in your current job). An interview is also required before an offer of admission is extended. International students whose first language is not English must also submit official score reports for the TOEFL, PTE, or IELTS. Candidates for the one-year program must have an undergraduate degree in a business-related discipline or a strong quantitative background and "solid business experience."

FINANCIAL FACTS

Annual tuition (in-state/ out-of-state)	$49,600/$49,600
Fees	$540
Cost of books	$5,702
Room & board (on/off-campus)	$17,932/$17,932
% of students receiving aid	75
% of first-year students receiving aid	80
% of students receiving grants	67
Average award package	$49,477
Average grant	$27,127
Average loan	$39,490
Average student loan debt	$79,415

ADMISSIONS

Admissions Selectivity Rating	94
# of applications received	1,460
% applicants accepted	29
% acceptees attending	40
Average GMAT	678
Range of GMAT	640–710
Accepts GRE scores	Yes
Average Verbal GRE	161
Range of Verbal GRE scores	157–164
Average Quantitative GRE	159
Range of Quantitative GRE scores	156–164
Average Writing GRE	4.4
Range of Writing GRE scores	4.0–5.0
Average GPA	3.3
TOEFL required of international students	Yes
Minimum TOEFL (paper/web)	600/
Application fee	$150
International application fee	$150
Application Deadline/Notification	
Round 1:	10/9 / 12/3
Round 2:	11/13 / 1/28
Round 3:	1/8 / 3/11
Round 4:	3/11 / 4/29
Deferment available	Yes
Maximum length of deferment	1 year
Transfer students accepted	No
Non-fall admissions	No
Need-blind admissions	Yes

EMPLOYMENT PROFILE

Career Rating	97	**Grads Employed by Function% Avg. Salary**	
Percent employed at graduation	79	Marketing	(18%) $98,691
Percent employed 3 months		Operations	(3%) $97,767
after graduation	94	Consulting	(38%) $130,857
Average base starting salary	$113,295	Management	(11%) $106,164
Primary Source of Full-time Job Acceptances		Finance	(29%) $104,028
School-facilitated activities	87 (86%)	HR	(1%)
Graduate-facilitated activities	14 (14%)	**Top 5 Employers Hiring Grads**	
Unknown	0 (0%)	PwC (11), EY (8), Accenture (5), UPS (4), Delta Air Lines (4)	

ESSEC BUSINESS SCHOOL
THE ESSEC MBA PROGRAM

GENERAL INFORMATION

Type of school	Private
Affiliation	No Affiliation
Academic calendar	Trimester

SURVEY SAYS...
Good social scene
Solid preparation in:
Finance, General management,
Teamwork

STUDENTS

% male/female	51/49
% international	20
Average age at entry	24
Average years work experience at entry	1

ACADEMICS

Academic Experience Rating	**59**
Profs interesting rating	62
Profs accessible rating	65
% female faculty	23

Joint Degrees
China: Peking University; Germany: Mannheim University; Korea: Seoul National University; Singapore: Nanyang Technological University; Mexico: EGADE Tec de Monterrey; India: IIM Ahmedabad; Japan: Keio University

Prominent Alumni
Christian BALMES, President Director General, Shell France; Charles BOUAZIZ, General Manager, Pepsico Europe; Emmanuelle MIGNON, President Sarkozy's Chief of Staff; Dominique REINICHE, President Europe, The Coca Cola Company; Serge VILLEPELET, President, PriceWaterHouseCoopers

Academics

If you're looking for a "flexible" MBA at "a major player on the international level among European business schools" and one of "the top business schools in France," ESSEC is a school you should consider. After completing eight management fundamentals courses, ESSEC MBAs fashion their own curricula, choosing from more than "200 electives" each semester. Students love the freedom, telling us that "each quarter, we can basically choose to take classes at ESSEC Business School in Paris or Singapore, do an internship with a company in France or abroad, or go on an exchange program abroad with one of ESSEC MBA's eighty academic partners," whose ranks include many prestigious names in the United States and around the world. The school's administration "does a great job of managing this 'a la carte' system," allowing students to "choose almost any courses we want in order to create our specialization and formation."

Because ESSEC believes that students should make "a constant connection between work and the classroom," all students must have at least eighteen months of validated professional experience prior to graduation. These internships are easy to find thanks to ESSEC's "great relationship with the business world." The school "has strong links with international finance and consulting companies"; and a campus in Singapore means that opportunities to intern in Southeast Asia are constantly developing. ESSEC's practical philosophy permeates the classroom as well; here "courses are not just theory. We have a lot of business cases given by corporate partners, and we have a lot of work every week to prepare other business cases in groups (teamwork is very important here)." Throughout the program, there is a "prominent international dimension" bolstered by "the school's ever-increasing partnerships overseas."

The faculty includes "outstanding professors recognized in their fields of specialization, people who publish a lot. They help us get most prepared for our chosen profession and they are also very available and most willing to give us useful insights." Part-time faculty are drawn from "top-notch businesswomen and men and successful entrepreneurs. In any case, they always have a great experience and very useful insights to share."

Career and Placement

Students report that "ESSEC is the best passport to great job opportunities in France and worldwide. The school administration and students are really eager to keep in very close contact with firms. There is a constant exchange between the academic, student, and business world. Companies are often involved in student projects too." The school's "excellent relations with European businesses" help students procure the internships required to complete their MBAs. While ESSEC's connections are strongest in France, "many foreign companies also recruit (largely for their French subsidies), such as the consulting companies McKinsey, BCG, etc. ESSEC is part of their main target schools for recruiting."

Employers most likely to hire ESSEC MBAs include: PricewaterhouseCoopers, L'Oréal, Renault, Societe Generale, Deloitte Touche Tohmatsu, Danone, Michelin, BNP Paribas, Capgemini, Accenture, EDF-GDF, Pinault Printemps Redoute, Procter & Gamble, Deutsche Bank, 3 Suisses International, Pfizer, LVMH, Ernst & Young, Boston Consulting Group, A.T. Kearney, SC Johnson, and Bain.

ADMISSIONS CONTACT: JOSIANE STIRLING, GLOBAL MBA PROGRAM ASSISTANT
ADDRESS: AVENUE BERNARD HIRSCH, B.P. 50105 CERGY-PONTOISE, 95021 FRANCE
PHONE: +33 1 34 43 37 13 • FAX: +33 1 34 43 37 12
E-MAIL: STIRLING@ESSEC.EDU • WEBSITE: WWW.ESSEC.EDU/GLOBALMBA

FINANCIAL FACTS

Annual tuition (in-state/ out-of-state)	$32,500/$45,500
Cost of books	$500
Room & board	$10,000

ADMISSIONS

Admissions Selectivity Rating	**74**
# of applications received	5,117
Average GMAT	675
Range of GMAT	600–730
TOEFL required of international students	Yes
Minimum TOEFL (paper/web)	600/100
Application Deadline/Notification	
Round 1:	10/10 / 12/5
Round 2:	1/26 / 3/23
Round 3:	4/29 / 6/9
Deferment available	Yes
Maximum length of deferment	1 year
Transfer students accepted	No
Non-fall admissions	No
Need-blind admissions	Yes

Student Life and Environment

ESSEC encourages students to participate in extracurricular life, and students respond, forming "about eighty different clubs" that encompass not only business activities but also "theater, a choir, painting, photography, sports, and social groups." The area surrounding ESSEC, Cergy Pontoise, is "Parisian suburb" located "about an hour from the center of the city by commuter train." Some describe it as "a modern city with very good amenities, including an artificial lake for sailing or rowing and other water sports, a nearby skating rink, and very good town libraries." Others tell us that "living in Cergy can be a little bit disappointing for those who would prefer the dense atmosphere of Paris to ESSEC school life." Local housing "is pretty easy to find" and "not too expensive."

ESSEC is "undergoing immense changes," students tell us, reporting that new professors are being recruited at an international level. The school is going global and will become internationally known very soon." Some here tell us that "you can stay all day long at ESSEC, and there's always something to do and somewhere to go." Though in the past students have noted that "facilities here could improve," recent renovations have been completed including several new buildings.

Admissions

Students are admitted to ESSEC either as traditional MBAs (this is the way international students enter the program), French MBAs, or as "grande école" students (French students who have attended two years of postsecondary school and are now ready for intensive, focused study in a discipline such as business). Students applying to the traditional MBA program must provide the school with an official GMAT or TAGE-MAGE score report, official transcripts for all postsecondary academic work, an interview, and a resume. Applicants must be under the age of thirty-two; one or two years of professional experience is highly recommended. French MBA students follow the "French MBA" admissions path. "Grande école" applicants must meet a variety of requirements, including completion of the undergraduate period and completion of at least one six-month internship.

EMPLOYMENT PROFILE

Career Rating	76	Grads Employed by Function% Avg. Salary	
Average base starting salary	$07,000	Marketing	(21%)
Primary Source of Full-time Job Acceptances		Operations	(5%)
School-facilitated activities	(50%)	Consulting	(36%)
Graduate-facilitated activities	(4%)	Management	(5%)
Unknown	(46%)	Finance	(20%)
		HR	(1%)
		Other	(12%)

Top 5 Employers Hiring Grads
Cap Gemini (10), BNP Paribas (6), Ernst & Young (5), KPMG (5), McKinsey & Company (5)

FAIRFIELD UNIVERSITY
CHARLES F. DOLAN SCHOOL OF BUSINESS

GENERAL INFORMATION

Type of school   Private
Affiliation   Roman Catholic-Jesuit
Academic calendar   Semester

SURVEY SAYS...

Friendly students, Happy students, Students love Fairfield, CT
Solid preparation in:
Finance, General management, Teamwork, Communication/inter-personal skills, Presentation skills, Quantitative skills

STUDENTS

Enrollment of parent
  institution   4,600
Enrollment of MBA Program   79
% part-time   71
Average age at entry   25
Average years work
  experience at entry   2

ACADEMICS

Academic Experience Rating   89
Profs interesting rating   93
Profs accessible rating   93
Student/faculty ratio   19:1
% female faculty   39

Prominent Alumni

William C. Crager, President, Envestnet, Inc.; Sheila Kearney Davidson, Executive VP, Chief Legal Officer, New York Life Insurance Co.; Patricia E. Glassford, Vice President and CFO, GE Energy Management; Brian P. Hull, Chairman, Strategic Clients and Partnerships, UBS Group- Americas; Gavin G. O'Connor, Partner and COO, Investment Management Division, Goldman Sachs

Academics

Armed with a "strong reputation" coupled with a "strong commitment to the Jesuit ideals of serving others," it's no surprise that students flock to attend Fairfield University's MBA program. Students here greatly appreciate that the school "caters to people who work full time." Moreover, Fairfield offers "small class sizes," "an extensive alumni network," and "great business contacts." Although the school offers a "challenging curriculum," some students feel that it is time for an overhaul or update. As one slightly chagrined student explains, "The University should take the time to conduct a thorough overview of its curriculum and concentrations. It could use some refreshing."

Fortunately, students are ebullient when it comes to describing their professors. They are truly "dedicated and experienced professionals" who are "very knowledgeable, accessible and open-minded." They "encourage students to think for themselves, even if that means challenging the professors in class." Additionally, they are highly accessible. Another highly content student shares, "many of them will go out to lunch or coffee and explain concepts or help with networking." Though the vast "majority of the school's professors care a lot about the quality of their teaching" some students feel that there's room for improvement. A second-year student clarifies, "Newer, younger professors with more current experience would be a welcome improvement to the program. I would like to have more women professors, as well." However, she does conclude by stating, "Overall I am very happy with my academic experience at Fairfield University and have learned a lot."

Career and Placement

Fairfield University's Career Center is truly focused on helping students find coveted internship and employment opportunities. The office endeavors to take advantage of the school's prime location between Boston and New York, developing relationships and connections with companies in both cities. Of course, some students wish they would also focus on opportunities within their own backyard. As one graduating student shares, "Fairfield should actively seek to build relationships with financial institutions based in Stamford (RBS, UBS, etc.)." The career center continually offers resume workshops and practice interview sessions. It also provides access to a number of local career fairs. Another student adds that Fairfield has "an extensive alumni network and great business contacts." However, some begrudge the fact that the office serves the entire university and feel this detracts from specific MBA prospects. As one student states, "It seems to me career placement is geared more toward undergraduates than graduate students; while Fairfield has addressed the career needs of graduate students lately, I think the efforts should be on par with the undergraduates."

Employers that frequently hire Fairfield graduates include General Electric, People's Bank, American Skandia, United Technologies, Pitney Bowes, The Common Fund, Bayer Corporation, UBS Warburg, Gartner, Unilever, and Pfizer.

ADMISSIONS CONTACT: DR. MARK LIGAS, ASSOCIATE DEAN/DIRECTOR OF GRADUATE PROGRAMS
ADDRESS: 1073 NORTH BENSON ROAD, FAIRFIELD, CT 06824
PHONE: 203-254-4000 • FAX: 203-254-4029
E-MAIL: MLIGAS@FAIRFIELD.EDU • WEBSITE: WWW.FAIRFIELD.EDU/MBA

FINANCIAL FACTS

Annual tuition	$19,560
Fees	$500
Cost of books	$1,000

ADMISSIONS

Admissions Selectivity Rating	**85**
# of applications received	55
% applicants accepted	55
% acceptees attending	67
Average GMAT	515
Range of GMAT	470–570
Accepts GRE scores	Yes
Average Verbal GRE	150
Average Quantitative GRE	153
Average GPA	3.3
TOEFL required of international students	Yes
Minimum TOEFL (paper/web)	550/80
Application fee	$60
International application fee	$60
Deferment available	Yes
Maximum length of deferment	1 Year
Transfer students accepted	Yes
Transfer application policy Up to 6 credits from another graduate program. We also have a reciprocity agreement with the other JESUIT institutions.	
Non-fall admissions	Yes
Need-blind admissions	Yes

Student Life and Environment

Fairfield University manages to attract a "wide variety of student," ensuring the MBA program is an eye-opening experience. While students do admit that their peers can be "competitive," they quickly stress that they are also incredibly "friendly." Moreover, they are "hardworking," "creative," and "dedicated." There is also a healthy mix of students in their twenties, thirties, and forties. The older MBA candidates tend to "work full-time, have families, and go to school at night." These students tend to limit their interaction to "night and weekend classes" and "don't spend much time on campus other than for class." However, the younger MBA crowd is eager to move the discussion outside of the classroom. As one student says, "The social atmosphere is one of my favorite parts of the school. Group discussions and projects are obviously very fun, but so is grabbing a drink with a few students after class and even having professors tag along! We all have a great time talking about our current jobs, and grabbing tips from each other. I cannot say enough about how much I have loved getting to know the other students and professors." Another student continues, "The University has formed an office of graduate students, which has been doing a much better job of offering specific programs and services for graduate students of all schools." By and large, students appreciate Fairfield's "great" location, which is "not too rural, but not too urban either." They also enjoy the fact that it is "close enough to some of the major metro NY companies (IBM and Pepsi) without being in the hustle and bustle of it all." When students want to unwind, they frequently take advantage of downtown Fairfield "for dinner, drinks, and hanging out."

Admissions

Admission to Fairfield University's business school is certainly competitive. All facets of the application, from professional resume and personal statement to transcripts and GMAT scores, are thoroughly considered and evaluated. Applicants must have successfully completed undergraduate coursework in college-level mathematics, microeconomics, macroeconomics, and statistics. Typically, accepted students have at least a 3.0 GPA and earned a GMAT score of 500, at minimum. Additionally, students from non-English speaking countries must take the TOEFL. To secure admission, it is strongly recommended that applicants earn a composite score of 550 for the paper test, 213 for the computer-based, or 80 on the Internet-based test. Applications are accepted on a rolling basis. Those candidates supremely interested in attending Fairfield should submit their application as early as possible.

FAIRLEIGH DICKINSON UNIVERSITY
SILBERMAN COLLEGE OF BUSINESS

GENERAL INFORMATION
Type of school	Private
Affiliation	No Affiliation
Academic calendar	Academic Year

SURVEY SAYS...
Happy students, Students love Teaneck, NJ
Solid preparation in:
Doing business in a global economy

STUDENTS
Enrollment of parent institution	12,247
Enrollment of MBA Program	536
% part-time	60
% underrepresented minority	10
% international	20
Average age at entry	29

ACADEMICS
Academic Experience Rating	**86**
Profs interesting rating	88
Profs accessible rating	89
Student/faculty ratio	20:1
% female faculty	21
% underrepresented minority faculty	41
% part-time faculty	40

Joint Degrees
PHARMD/MBA, 5 years; MBA in Management/MA in Corporate and Organizational Communications, 72 credit program.

Prominent Alumni
Cheryl Beebe, VP & CFO, Corn Products International, Inc.; Dennis Strigl, President & COO, Verizon Communications (retired); Robert Huth, President & CEO, David's Bridal; Joseph Mahady, President, Wyeth Pharmaceuticals; Dick Sweeney, VP, Keurig

Academics

Fairleigh Dickinson University, or FDU, attracts students from around the world, especially those looking for a strong faculty and a vicinity to New York City. Another highlight for the University is its AACSB accreditation, which many students cite as another factor in their decision to attend the school. FDU offers MBAs with nine different specializations including accounting, finance, international business, and marketing, among others. Another option for those looking to speed up their education is the Accelerated MBA that allows their liberal arts or business undergraduate students a chance to earn an MBA in fifteen months. They also have a shortened study abroad program that allows their busier students to travel to another country for two weeks in the summer, giving them a taste of what international business is like.

This kind of drive is prevalent throughout the student body with many saying that both "competition" and an "eagerness to learn" are the norms. Many say that "work and studies tend to be heavy," but that the experience is worth it with most raving that the "classroom atmosphere is spectacular." Many find that they learn how to "prioritize time very quickly." The school tries to keep each class small and the students realize this fact explaining that they feel like they are getting "individual attention." While a small minority wishes there was "more emphasis" on teacher evaluations, most students are more than happy with their teachers raving that the school's professors are its "greatest strength," and that the students are "proud" to have them as instructors.

The majority of the faculty is "a mix of global businessmen and local success stories" but have earned a great reputation with the students and are considered "very attentive and helpful." This mix helps give classes "every possible view of business and provides students with insight from different points of view." The diversity is much appreciated as participants feel it gives them "a strong global business education." Students have a desire to be involved in their classes through the teachers "encouraging class participation [and] linking new events with class materials." They are known for their willingness to offer an abundance of support in that they "spend an extraordinary amount of time outside of the classroom helping and guiding students."

Career and Placement

The Career Development Services Center helps students in a variety of ways by providing different help such as assessment testing, career fairs, workshops, internship opportunities, on-campus recruiting, and an online job search website, among others. Occasionally students say they wish there was "more focus on internships" from the University, but that they find the "proximity to companies and New York" to be a "distinct advantage," when looking for job opportunities. The professor's experience does not hurt either, with many of them having "strong ties to local businesses."

Graduates have a Average base starting salary of $70k per year with the top five employers being Verizon, Deloitte, Johnson & Johnson, ADP, and Credit Suisse.

ADMISSIONS CONTACT: SUSAN BROOMAN, DIRECTOR OF GRADUATE RECRUITMENT & MARKETING
ADDRESS: FAIRLEIGH DICKINSON UNIVERSITY GRADUATE ADMISSIONS, METROPOLITAN CAMPUS
1000 RIVER ROAD (T-KB1-01), TEANECK, NJ 07666 • PHONE: 201-692-2554
FAX: 201-692-2560 • E-MAIL: GRAD@FDU.EDU • WEBSITE: WWW.FDU.EDU

Student Life and Environment

FDU has two campuses in New Jersey, one in Teaneck and one in Madison. One of the things that many students love about both campuses is the fact that the college "attracts a number of different students with highly diverse backgrounds." A significant portion of the student body includes international students who describe FDU as a "truly global school." In fact some think it's wonderful that "in a room of ten to twelve people … no two people [might] be from the same country." Despite any cultural differences, the students show great respect and label each other "helpful, enthusiastic, [and] smart." The student body is also "fairly young" for those seeking an MBA, but part of that may be the aforementioned ability for undergraduates to gain an MBA as well.

FDU succeeds in striking "a balance between academic, social and recreational aspects of student life." Many students bond not only in the classroom, but also in one of the many activities the campus puts together. The school often "organizes various trips outside the classroom to get [us] acquainted with various places" and with New York City nearby, there is no shortage of things for students to see and do. And, unlike a lot of other schools, students have no issues with the administration saying they find it "very helpful," to their learning experience and course registration.

Admissions

Those seeking to apply can do so in two ways, online or via printed out form. Applications are accepted on a rolling basis. Those applying online will have the forty dollar application fee waived. Domestic students need to make sure to send proof of their bachelor's degree, official college transcripts, their official score report for the GMAT taken within the last five years, and a current resume. International students will also need to send in their TOEFL, IELTS, or Pearsons PTE-A as well as two letters of recommendation and a completed and notarized affidavit of financial support if they are applying for a student visa.

Those looking for help on the GMAT can enroll in the Sexton Preparation Course. Upon completion of the course, a full credit will be applied to the student's tuition charge.

FINANCIAL FACTS

Annual tuition (in-state/ out-of-state)	$23,720/$23,720
Fees	$418
Cost of books	$1,000
Room & board (on/off-campus)	$10,202/
% of students receiving aid	56
% of students receiving grants	33
Average award package	$20,500
Average grant	$5,225
Average loan	$14,670

ADMISSIONS

Admissions Selectivity Rating	82
# of applications received	824
% applicants accepted	59
% acceptees attending	45
Average GMAT	478
Accepts GRE scores	Yes
Average GPA	3.4
TOEFL required of international students	Yes
Minimum TOEFL (paper/web)	550/79
Application fee	$40
International application fee	$40
Deferment available	Yes
Maximum length of deferment	one year
Transfer students accepted	Yes
Transfer application policy Foundation courses can be waived by meeting FDU waiver policy. 6 graduate level credits can be transferred from other AACSB schools with a grade of B or higher.	
Non-fall admissions	Yes
Need-blind admissions	Yes

EMPLOYMENT PROFILE		
Career Rating	71	**Top 5 Employers Hiring Grads** Verizon, Deloitte, Johnson & Johnson, ADP, Credit Suisse

FAYETTEVILLE STATE UNIVERSITY
SCHOOL OF BUSINESS AND ECONOMICS MBA PROGRAM

Academics

Fayetteville State University's Business School offers students the unbeatable combination of "low cost" coupled with a "great reputation." Students here truly appreciate that the "core curriculum is not repetitive and boring" and that the "small class sizes make learning easy and interactive." The program caters to individuals who are employed full-time and promises a "flexible" course schedule. Moreover, students can opt to either take classes online or on campus, and many courses are offered in the evening.

Students at Fayetteville are full of admiration for their professors. An impressed first-year student shares, "All my professors are top notch. Not only are they proficient in their fields, they have a true desire to see each and every student succeed." Additionally, students here truly appreciate the unparalleled access professors seem to grant them. As one MBA candidate reveals, "Professors are also extremely helpful. They are willing to give you their cell phone numbers, so that you can call anytime with questions, and they make themselves available on weekends, throughout the day." Perhaps almost as impressive is that "e-mails for the most part are answered immediately. Professors also ensure that each class is recorded via Panopto, so if you are unable to attend you can still see them lecture on blackboard."

Praise is also extended to the "outstanding" administration. As another student shares, "They are all tremendously helpful and quick to assist students with anything from advising to outside competitions, opportunities, and internships." "The MBA office's open-door policy created an atmosphere of nurturing support for its students. My experience in the MBA program not only taught me the necessary skills to be successful in the business world, but also how to think logically in a stringently growing global enterprise."

Career and Placement

Fayetteville State's Career Services Center works diligently to ensure that students and alumni have a myriad of employment opportunities. Advocating on behalf of its students, Career Services has partnered with a number of organizations and services to guarantee that students have access to a variety resources. The office provides a number of workshops, and MBA candidates can receive help honing their resume, practice with mock interviews, and learn tips about refining their job search. The University also hosts several career fairs throughout the year. These events attract a wide variety of companies and organizations, such as Rite Aid, The Hershey Company, Lowe's, WalMart, Internal Revenue Service, Social Security Administration, BB&T, and Altria. While the Career Services Center does offer assistance, some MBA students feel as though the office could do more. As one student states, "From my experience, the career placement is more geared to undergrads. Specific emphasis should be placed on MBA students."

Student Life and Environment

MBA candidates at Fayetteville State definitely agree that their fellow students truly enrich their academic experience. They are "very friendly" and "concerned with grasping the material verses simply going through the motions." As one student elaborates, "My fellow classmates are excited to learn new and interesting things, and they are always willing to work together to make sure that everyone is on the same page." Indeed, despite sometimes letting their "competitive" natures shine through, most students are "helpful and promote teamwork and team building." Fortunately, Fayetteville's Business School manages to attract a "diverse" group of students. As one graduating student shares, "My fellow classmates are a diverse group from all walks of life. I enjoy each class because of the stimulating class discussions and rigorous debate. I look forward to building a valuable network, because they all are leaders within their respective fields."

While some students occasionally grumble that "parking is not always easy," most agree that life at Fayetteville is "great." And though a number of students enroll in online or evening classes, many find the campus "full of life." A large number of students are busy with families and full-time jobs, so socializing is often kept to a minimum. However, there are opportunities for extracurricular activities. As another student recounts, "There are several organizations available that give students an opportunity for national recognition. FSU has provided opportunities for me to compete in national business plan competitions, where I have won cash prizes and gained powerful connections."

Admissions

Admissions officers at Fayetteville State take a holistic approach to their evaluation process, assessing undergraduate transcripts, GMAT scores, and letters of recommendation. Additionally, international applicants hailing from non-English speaking countries are required to take the TOEFL exam. It should be noted that students who have not yet taken the GMAT will be allowed to enroll in a maximum of twelve credit hours before gaining full admission to the program. If the student earns a minimum of a "B" in each course, the classes will count toward fulfilling requirements upon full admission. Further, current Fayetteville undergraduates studying accounting, business administration, or economics, and finance may apply for admission during their junior year. Upon acceptance, they can begin taking graduate level courses as a senior. The remaining MBA courses can be completed in one additional year.

FINANCIAL FACTS

Annual tuition (in-state/ out-of-state)	$3,281/$14,129
Fees	$4,159
Room & board (on/off-campus)	$7,000/$8,000

ADMISSIONS

Admissions Selectivity Rating	85
# of applications received	57
% applicants accepted	58
% acceptees attending	100
Average GMAT	471
Range of GMAT	430–520
Accepts GRE scores	Yes
Average Verbal GRE	149
Range of Verbal GRE scores	144–153
Average Quantitative GRE	150
Range of Quantitative GRE scores	145–153
Average Writing GRE	3.9
Range of Writing GRE scores	3.3–4.0
Average GPA	3.2
TOEFL required of international students	Yes
Minimum TOEFL (paper/web)	550/
Application fee	$40
International application fee	$40
Early application deadline	4/15
Regular application deadline	7/1
Deferment available	Yes
Maximum length of deferment	Normally One Year
Transfer students accepted	Yes
Transfer application policy	Up to six credit hours can be transferred from an AACSB accredited program.
Non-fall admissions	Yes
Need-blind admissions	Yes

FLORIDA GULF COAST UNIVERSITY
LUTGERT COLLEGE OF BUSINESS

Academics

Opened in 1997, the Lutgert College of Business at Florida Gulf Coast University offers a part- or full-time traditional MBA and executive MBA program, as well as an MS in accounting and taxation and an MS in Information Systems. Students may attend the traditional MBA on campus or online, but the other programs require on-campus and full-time attendance. As of August 2015, the traditional MBA requires all students to take nine hours of foundation courses and thirty-six core/elective hours. Those who studied business as an undergraduate may waive many or all of the nine foundation hours. Students in the traditional MBA program must choose a concentration in Finance, General Management, Information Systems, or Marketing, though students may opt for an interdisciplinary concentration with the approval of their academic advisor. Those taking courses online may only do an interdisciplinary concentration from the above areas. Pursued full-time, the MBA may completed in less than 18 months online or on-campus. All of FGCU's MBAs receive solid training in systems orientation and relevant technology. Additionally, students in all programs leave with strong analytical and creative thinking skills, communication, and interpersonal skills. They appreciate that the program is newer than most and that they are a part of a "growing institution" and "community," with a "beautiful" and "expanding campus" and "state-of-the-art infrastructure and classrooms with highly integrated technology."

The program's strengths are its "flexibility and the professors," as well as the small classes that allow people to know their "professors and other classmates on a more personal level." The faculty has lots of "real-world work experience," and "draw from their experience and teach you real-world applications of the academics." They're "engaging, accessible, and interested in your personal and professional development." Classes range from "exceedingly demanding" to "easy," but either way it can be tough for those working full time or who've been out of school for a while to "adjust to the course load." Students report that "course selection and availability is somewhat limited," which can make it difficult to get all the classes needed to complete a degree in a shortened timeframe." Electives are also offered less consistently than students would like.

FGCU has forged relationships with many international business schools and has an international student exchange program known as the "Second Circle." The program allows students from universities in France, Germany, New Zealand, and Sweden to study at FGCU for up to two semesters. FGCU students with a GPA of 3.0 or higher may spend up to two semesters at designated partner universities in these countries. Second Circle is an impressive and rewarding program for students seeking to deepen their understanding of international business and who want to gain experience abroad and work on their language skills.

Career and Placement

FGCU's Career Development Services office serves the entire undergraduate and graduate population, and some students in the MBA program would like to see "more resources for graduating MBA students for professional/career positions and internship opportunities." However, the office does host career fairs and on-campus recruiting events, as well as workshops and seminars. Students can also receive help with their job searches, resumes, and business etiquette. Employers who visited the campus in 2015 included General Electric, Northwestern Mutual Financial Network, Marathon Engineering Corp, Prudential, Primerica Financial Services, Scotlynn Commodities, Hertz Corporation, Siemens Energy, Allyn International Services, AXI International, Gartner, Inc., Target,

ADMISSIONS CONTACT: ANA HILL, ADMISSIONS-REGISTRAR OFFICER-GRADUATE ADMISSIONS
ADDRESS: 10501 FGCU BOULEVARD SOUTH, FORT MYERS, FL 33965
PHONE: 239-590-7408 • FAX: 239-590-7843
E-MAIL: GRADUATE@FGCU.EDU • WEBSITE: WWW.FGCU.EDU

and Algenol Biofuels, though these companies are not necessarily looking to hire graduates of the MBA program.

Student Life and Environment

Students at FGCU are busy. Many who attend on campus work full time, and many of them also have families, so their ability to enjoy the campus or extracurricular activities is limited, if it exists at all. FGCU undergrads who entered the program directly and international students tend to have far fewer obligations and, therefore, have a larger presence outside of class. People at FGCU say their peers are "dedicated, hard-working, knowledge driven, enjoyable to work with, and dependable." Many students "have had professional work experience, which translates into richer class discussions that help to make material covered in class more practical, rather than theoretical."

The Business & Entrepreneurship Club coordinates many different professional growth opportunities for students. It arranges for graduate and undergraduate students from various majors to interact with the local business community and share information.

Admissions

Applicants to FGCU's MBA program do not need to have professional experience. The admission committee focuses on student's undergraduate GPA and GMAT or GRE scores when evaluating applications. Students must have either a minimum GPA of 3.0 for their final sixty credit hours of undergraduate work or a minimum GMAT score of 500 or GRE equivalent; and a formula score of at least 1,050 under the formula [(undergraduate GPA X 200) + GMAT score], with a minimum GMAT score of at least 450. International students from countries where English is not the primary language must also submit TOEFL scores. The school requires a minimum of 550 for the written portion of the test, 213 for the computer based, and 79 for the Internet-based portion.

FINANCIAL FACTS

Annual tuition (in-state/ out-of-state)	$6,974/$28,170
Fees	$1,987
Cost of books	$1,200
Room & board (on/off-campus)	$8,359/$8,250
% of students receiving aid	47
% of first-year students receiving aid	3
% of students receiving grants	44
Average award package	$10,052
Average grant	$3,196
Average loan	$10,634
Average student loan debt	$26,621

ADMISSIONS

Admissions Selectivity Rating	85
# of applications received	94
% applicants accepted	39
Average GMAT	528
Range of GMAT	470–550
Accepts GRE scores	No
Average GPA	3.4
TOEFL required of international students	Yes
Minimum TOEFL (paper/web)	550/79
Application fee	$30
International application fee	$30
Early application deadline	5/1
Regular application deadline	6/1
Regular application notification	7/1
Deferment available	Yes
Maximum length of deferment	1 Semester
Transfer students accepted	Yes
Transfer application policy 6 credits of approved graduate-level coursework may be transferred from a regionally accredited institution.	
Non-fall admissions	Yes
Need-blind admissions	Yes

FLORIDA INTERNATIONAL UNIVERSITY
ALVIN H. CHAPMAN GRADUATE SCHOOL OF BUSINESS

GENERAL INFORMATION
Type of school	Public
Affiliation	No Affiliation
Academic calendar	Varies

SURVEY SAYS...
Classmates have diverse work experience, Happy students, Students love Miami, FL
Solid preparation in:
General management, Operations, Teamwork, Communication/interpersonal skills, Presentation skills, Quantitative skills, Doing business in a global economy

STUDENTS
Enrollment of parent institution	47,959
Enrollment of MBA Program	427
% male/female	65/35
% out-of-state	0
% part-time	80
% underrepresented minority	53
% international	41
Average age at entry	30
Average years work experience at entry	6

ACADEMICS
Academic Experience Rating	90
Profs interesting rating	92
Profs accessible rating	90
Student/faculty ratio	11:1
% female faculty	31
% underrepresented minority faculty	44
% part-time faculty	23

Joint Degrees
MBA/MS Finance; MBA/MS Management Information Systems; MBA/MS Int'l Real Estate; MBA/MS Human Resource Management; MBA/Master Int'l Business.

Academics

As its moniker suggests, Florida International University offers MBAs that are "more internationally-oriented" than your standard graduate business program. This emphasis is especially pronounced in the school's one-year International Business program, but it applies to all the graduate degrees offered here. The school parlays its location in Miami, "the gateway to the Americas," to focus particular attention on Latin America and the Caribbean, regions well-represented on the faculty and among the student body.

No matter your academic interests and scheduling needs, FIU probably has an MBA program to suit you. Its twenty-month Executive MBA "is an excellent program for managers with over twelve years of work experience." For less experienced professionals, the eighteen-month Downtown MBA or the Evening MBA on FIU's campus may be good fits. For those unable to get away from the office, the Corporate MBA delivers the program to the workplace. And if you're looking for a specialized MBA in healthcare, FIU offers that as well.

Students praise FIU's "excellent reputation in the south Florida business community," its affordability, and the "top-notch" professors and administration. Students report approvingly that "the school has a team of administrators assigned to the MBA program. They handle everything for us, and I mean everything: enrollment, books, materials, copies, meals, etc." One MBA notes, "It is especially appealing that the business program is run somewhat independently from the rest of the university to ensure higher quality services and resources." Overall, students find the program "very well-organized," led by "extremely competitive and prepared" professors who "are all known leaders in their field and have great experiences to share with us." "The faculty have provided real insight into their industr[ies] and created stimulating learning environments for the most part," one student explains. Classroom discussion is enhanced by a "very international" and diverse student body. "You get investment bankers [and people in] rank and file jobs trying to get ahead, all working together" here. With all these assets, no wonder students call an FIU MBA "a superb investment at a very low price."

Career and Placement

Chapman's Career Management Services office provides graduate students and alumni with counseling and placement assistance. The office works closely with the university's general Career Services Office to coordinate career fairs, on-campus interviews, and other career-related events. Students tell us that FIU's alumni network is large and very helpful.

Top employers of FIU MBAs (including currently employed students attending one of the part-time programs) include: PricewaterhouseCoopers, B/E Aerospace, Commerce Bank, P&G, FPL, Fitch Ratings, Brightstar Corporation, Bank of America, Caterpillar, GE, and Choice Hotels International.

Student Life and Environment

FIU's MBA program is housed "in a brand-new building with extremely comfortable and high-technology resources," with "many locations for classmates to gather and work in a comfortable environment." "The resources you need for research and completing assignments are readily available" here, and the school even "makes ample provision for students who are without computers; for example, access to computers whether in the computer room or the library." Full-time students report that they experience "a fast-paced environment" driven by classes, extracurriculars, and an active Student Government Association. They also tell us that "the sports program is up and coming, so the students are very excited and try hard to get the rest of us motivated to cheer for the Golden Panthers!" Part-timers tend to visit campus only for classes and schoolwork, and as a result are less engaged in campus life.

The FIU MBA program is "like the United Nations. We come from many nations: Germany, France, [United States], Central America, and South America. When they say 'Florida International University'—they mean it." Students are drawn from an equally impressive array of industries "including banking, healthcare, pharmaceutical, automotive, logistics, insurance, etc." There are a lot of "strong A-type personalities, which in my book means we 'Ace' in everything we do, be it group assignments, weekly tests, heated arguments over project submissions, or a chilled beer to commemorate the end of a quarter."

Admissions

Admissions requirements to FIU's MBA programs vary somewhat from program to program. As a general rule, students with the best combination of grade point average, applicable test scores, and pertinent work experience who also meet specific program requirements will have the first opportunity to enter the programs, according to the school's website. Applicants to the school's popular International MBA program must submit the following materials: an official copy of an undergraduate transcript, with a GPA of at least 3.0 in upper-division course work strongly preferred; official proof of undergraduate degree; a current resume; a personal statement; and an official GMAT or GRE score report. In addition to the above documents, international students whose primary language is not English must also provide an official score report for the TOEFL or the IELTS. They must also submit their transcripts to a translation agency to be forwarded to FIU, and they must provide the following documents: Declaration of Certification of Finances (DCF); a bank letter; a sponsor letter if applicable; and an F-1 transfer if they already have an F-1 Visa.

Prominent Alumni

Carlos Alvarez, Mayor, Miami Dade County; Tony Argiz, Partner, Morrison Brown Argiz & Farra CPA; Manny Medina, Chairman, Terremark; Dennis Klinger, VP & Chief Info. Off., Florida Power & Light Com.; Carlos Migoya, Regional Pres., Wachovia Bank, N.A.

FINANCIAL FACTS

Annual tuition (in-state/ out-of-state)	$34,000/$39,000
Cost of books	$2,000
Room & board (on/off-campus)	$12,000/$18,000
% of students receiving aid	79
% of first-year students receiving aid	82
% of students receiving grants	4
Average award package	$21,080
Average grant	$5,000
Average loan	$8,000
Average student loan debt	$40,000

ADMISSIONS

Admissions Selectivity Rating	85
# of applications received	1,094
% applicants accepted	56
% acceptees attending	69
Average GMAT	551
Range of GMAT	510–580
Accepts GRE scores	Yes
Average GPA	3.3
TOEFL required of international students	Yes
Minimum TOEFL (paper)	550
Application fee	$30
International application fee	$30
Deferment available	Yes
Maximum length of deferment	1 year
Transfer students accepted	Yes
Transfer application policy A student may receive permission to transfer up to 6 semester hours of graduate credit towards his or her degree program.	
Non-fall admissions	Yes
Need-blind admissions	Yes

EMPLOYMENT PROFILE

Career Rating	77	Grads Employed by Function	%	Avg. Salary
Percent employed at graduation	11	Marketing	(14%)	$46,000
Percent employed 3 months after graduation	2	Operations	(14%)	$60,000
		Management	(14%)	$70,000
Average base starting salary	$45,571	Finance	(43%)	$37,000
Primary Source of Full-time Job Acceptances		HR	(0%)	$49,250
School-facilitated activities	3 (43%)	MIS	(0%)	$52,000
Graduate-facilitated activities	4 (57%)	Other	(14%)	$60,000
Unknown	0 (0%)			

Top 5 Employers Hiring Grads
Price Waterhouse Coopers (13), Burger King Corp. (11), Grant Thornton (4), Cherry Bekaert & Holland CPA's (2), Marriot International (1)

FLORIDA STATE UNIVERSITY
COLLEGE OF BUSINESS

GENERAL INFORMATION
Type of school   Public
Affiliation   No Affiliation
Academic calendar   Semesters

SURVEY SAYS...
Good peer network
Solid preparation in:
Communication/interpersonal skills,
Presentation skills

STUDENTS
Enrollment of parent
  institution   41,000
Enrollment of MBA Program   74
% male/female   87/13
% out-of-state   14
% part-time   56
% underrepresented minority   16
% international   0
Average age at entry   27
Average years work
  experience at entry   5

ACADEMICS
Academic Experience Rating   71
Profs interesting rating   73
Profs accessible rating   72
Student/faculty ratio   30:1
% female faculty   31
% underrepresented
  minority faculty   16

Joint Degrees
JD/MBA, 109 credit hours, 4 years.

Prominent Alumni
John Thiel, Head of U.S. Wealth
Management for Merrill Lynch;
Cinny Murray, Brand President of
Chico's; Judy Schmeling, COO &
CFO of HSN, Inc.; Todd Combs,
Investment Manager for Berkshire
Hathaway; John Culver, Group
President of Starbucks Coffee China
& Asia Pacific

Academics

The College of Business at Florida State University offers a variety of options to suit the diverse needs of its MBA student body. Students straight out of college and anxious to earn a graduate degree typically find their way to the school's one-year full-time MBA program. Busy professionals can choose between an on-campus part-time program and an online program with "an asynchronous, totally web-based curriculum." The super-ambitious can pursue joint degrees in business and law or business and social work. In all programs, the reasonable tuition ("It's a prestigious school at a great value," writes one student) and "the growing reputation of the business school" are compelling factors in bringing students aboard.

Florida's full-time MBA is a cohort-based lockstep curriculum, with students remaining in the same work group throughout the twelve-month program. Students in the program may concentrate in finance or marketing and supply chain management, or they may earn a general MBA. Part-time students complete the same core courses and study with the same professors as do their full-time counterparts; however, they are not divided into cohorts and they cannot pursue a concentration. The online MBA can be completed in its entirety remotely. Again, students complete the same core courses with the same professors as do other FSU MBAs. The online MBA allows for concentrations in real estate and analysis or hospital administration. Students may also complete a general MBA.

FSU faculty members receive strong grades overall. Students tell us, "The professors in the business department are amazing. They are very congenial and well-spoken. They are helpful at all times. Most teachers are older and contain a strong sense of experience. They know how to teach a class that is entertaining, interactive, and fun." Some warn that "there are quite a few professors here with heavy accents that may take a little concentration to understand," but even they concede that "their willingness to help you outside the classroom and brilliance far outweigh this drawback." Teachers also "do a very good job of keeping class interesting by incorporating technology, group assignments, etc."

Career and Placement

Because FSU's MBA program is small and largely part time, the school does not maintain a separate career services office for graduate students in business. It does, however, sponsor an MBA Internship Program in which "carefully structured project work" allows both students and employers to "realize the benefits of this program." The school also offers coaching and career-related resources in order to help students plan their job search and marketing of their skills. The school hosts semi-annual MBA Networking Night events and on-campus and videoconference interviews. It also provides students access to a host of job-posting resources. Students report, "Our career center is great about creating internship opportunities. However, as far as full-time positions after graduation, the focus is more on undergrads. There are few recruiters [who] come specifically for MBAs." In the plus column, "networking seems to be one of the biggest strengths of Florida State. Through the College of Business, my sorority, and all the amazing staff, the opportunities are endless."

Employers most likely to hire FSU MBAs include BB&T, CSX, Harris, JP Morgan, Protiviti, and Wachovia Bank.

ADMISSIONS CONTACT: LISA BEVERLY, ADMISSIONS DIRECTOR
ADDRESS: GRADUATE PROGRAMS, COLLEGE OF BUSINESS, FSU, TALLAHASSEE, FL 32306-1110
PHONE: 850-644-6458 • FAX: 850-644-0588
E-MAIL: GRADPROG@COB.FSU.EDU • WEBSITE: WWW.COB.FSU.EDU/GRAD

Student Life and Environment

Full-timers at FSU basically get to extend their college years by one, albeit with a heavier workload. Students tell us: "Life is relaxed and challenging. We have a lot of work but ample time to complete it. Everyone wants to have a good time, but it's about priorities. If you go to class, you will succeed." Campus life offers "the perfect balance of challenging schoolwork, amazing social groups, and fun nightlife," and "the School of Dance and Music puts on (sometimes free) performances for the community. FSU energizes Tallahassee," a city that is "a great place to be" although "it is a small town and can get boring quick." One student suggests "picking up a hobby that you can do around town in all the parks and woods—Frisbee, mountain biking, kayaking, football, whatever— just stay involved in a physical activity."

Part-time students engage mostly in class and study groups. One observes: "It's nice being able to see the same people semester after semester. That gives us all a sense of warmth when we get into new classes. Life here is pretty busy, people running around trying to get things done on time...not much different from in the real world." Part-timers regard themselves as "more adaptable and friendly" than their full-time peers, whom they regard as "still a bit immature."

Admissions

The Admissions Office at Florida State University requires all of the following from applicants to its MBA program: two official copies of transcripts for all post-secondary academic work; an official GMAT score report; three letters of recommendation from former professors and/or employers; a current resume; a personal statement; and a Florida Residency affidavit, if appropriate. Students must have proficiency working with PCs. International students whose first language is not English must also submit an official score report for the TOEFL (minimum score: 550 paper-based test, 250 computer-based test, or 100 Internet-based test). All test scores must be no more than five years old. The school lists the following programs designed to increase recruitment of underrepresented and disadvantaged students: the FAMU Feeder Program, FAMU Graduate & Professional Days, GradQuest, MBA Advantage, Minority Student Orientation Program, Leslie Wilson Assistantships, the Delores Auzenne Minority Fellowship, and the University Fellowship.

FINANCIAL FACTS

Annual tuition (in-state/ out-of-state)	$11,544/$26,698
Cost of books	$800
Room & board (on/off-campus)	$11,178/$11,178
% of students receiving grants	34
Average award package	$21,000
Average grant	$5,700

ADMISSIONS

Admissions Selectivity Rating	86
# of applications received	146
% applicants accepted	58
% acceptees attending	88
Average GMAT	569
Range of GMAT	540–620
Accepts GRE scores	No
Average GPA	3.4
TOEFL required of international students	Yes
Minimum TOEFL (paper/web)	550/
Application fee	$30
International application fee	$30
Regular application deadline	2/1
Deferment available	Yes
Maximum length of deferment	12 months
Transfer students accepted	Yes
Transfer application policy Transfer applicants must complete the same application process as all other applicants.	
Non-fall admissions	Yes
Need-blind admissions	Yes

EMPLOYMENT PROFILE

Career Rating	70	Top 5 Employers Hiring Grads
Percent employed at graduation	26	CSX, Protiviti, Harris Corp, Deutsche Bank,
Percent employed 3 months after graduation	10	Lockheed Marting
Average base starting salary	$57,250	

FORDHAM UNIVERSITY
GABELLI SCHOOL OF BUSINESS

GENERAL INFORMATION

Type of school   Private
Affiliation   Roman Catholic-Jesuit
Academic calendar   Trimester

SURVEY SAYS...

Happy students, Students love New York, NY
Solid preparation in:
Finance, Teamwork, Presentation skills

STUDENTS

Enrollment of parent institution	15,693
Enrollment of MBA Program	448
% male/female	61/39
% out-of-state	31
% part-time	79
% underrepresented minority	6
% international	45
Average age at entry	28
Average years work experience at entry	5

ACADEMICS

Academic Experience Rating	**89**
Profs interesting rating	90
Profs accessible rating	92
Student/faculty ratio	14:1
% female faculty	30
% underrepresented minority faculty	30
% part-time faculty	29

Joint Degrees

MBA/JD, 42 months; MBA/MS Information Systems, 24 months; MBA/MST, 24 months

Prominent Alumni

Nemir Kirdar, Founder/President, Investcorp Bank; James N. Fernandez, former EVP and CFO, Tiffany & Co.; Patricia Fili-Kruschel, former Chairman NBC Universal News Group; Darcy Antonellis, CEO of Vubiquity; Tom Locastro, Director, Oppenheimer & Co.

Academics

It's easy to see why MBA candidates are drawn to Fordham. After all, the program's fantastic "location and reputation" within New York are a huge asset. Students also truly value the "positive environment" that's fostered here and quickly assert that it's a great institution at which to "grow and learn." Certainly, some of that sentiment can be attributed to both "small classes sizes and [the] family-like atmosphere" that permeates the campus. Additionally, students greatly appreciate that both "the faculty and course work . . . focus on business as a force for social responsibility and strong moral ethics"; it's not a program that's solely about "how to grow your profit margin."

Moreover, prospective applicants interested in the part-time program will be delighted to hear that there's "very little distinction between full-time and part-time students." Indeed, "part-time students [have] all the same access to classes, teachers student clubs and resources as the full-time students." Additionally, the program "offer[s] excellent flexibility, and the ability to switch to full-time if necessary."

Further, Fordham professors are "all very knowledgeable on their subject matter" and "amazing at giving us real life examples of what they are teaching." They also continually prove themselves to be both "very accessible" and "supportive." A fortunate first-year shares, "I was nervous about a job interview and got the best pep talk from my management professor, the kind of motivation that I thought could only exist in the movie Remember the Titans." We should all be so lucky to find such a mentor!

Career and Placement

Fordham MBAs delight in revealing that the school is "the best place to build a professional network." After all, the "majority of MBA students work for high profile firms in finance, the arts, media, accounting, etc. . . . And they bring their real world knowledge and connections to class. For example, a fellow student who works for Land Rover emailed an enviable job opportunity to our entire class." Of course, plenty of success can also be attributed to Fordham's amazing career center. One thankful MBA shares, "As an international student I was able to adapt to American business culture fast through career center workshops and events." Indeed, the "school provides resources to improve each student's skills (soft skills and technical skills) as well as help with recruiting process (résumé reviews, mock interviews, career counseling) which makes each individual ready for successful job search."

Fordham MBAs can be found working for companies such as: Bravo TV, Goldman Sachs, Google, Condé Nast, Hearst Corporation, MetLife, KPMG, Northwestern Mutual, UBS and Ogilvy & Mather.

Student Life and Environment

Fordham definitely excels at creating "a strong sense of community, [both] across programs (MBA and MS) and between full- and part-time students." As one delighted first-year student explains, "You walk down the hallway and you most likely know everyone." Importantly, there are "weekly social events hosted by a variety of clubs that are located close to campus." And students here really relish the opportunity to mingle with their peers "outside of class." Moreover, we're told that these clubs "are a great way to meet people who started the program at different times or who are in different specialties." It's also quite common for students to take advantage of the weekly "networking [events]" Fordham sponsors.

Of course, there's also plenty of which to take advantage beyond school sanctioned events. After all, "the campus is located in Lincoln Center in the heart of New York City." As a first-year student boasts, "Within walking distance there are plenty of bars and restaurants for students to meet up at and socialize and network after class. We are also just blocks away from some of the most prestigious employers in the world."

Admissions

Students looking to enroll in Fordham's Gabelli School of Business MBA program will need to have an up-to-date resume of their work experience. Most average about six years of previous work. Although test scores are important, they are not the deciding factor. The admissions office looks more closely at undergraduate GPA, good letters of recommendation, and a well-written essay. Ninety countries are represented at Fordham; 33 percent of full-time graduate students are international. The average age at enrollment is twenty-eight, average GPA is 3.2, and average GMAT is 604. Rolling applications need to be received by June 1 (May 1 for international students).

FINANCIAL FACTS

Annual tuition (in-state/ out-of-state)	$46,644/$46,644
Fees	$1,019
Cost of books	$1,500
Room & board (on/off-campus)	$20,700/
% of students receiving aid	71
% of first-year students receiving aid	56
% of students receiving grants	40
Average award package	$13,750
Average grant	$8,468
Average loan	$18,341
Average student loan debt	$45,853

ADMISSIONS

Admissions Selectivity Rating	85
# of applications received	383
% applicants accepted	57
% acceptees attending	42
Average GMAT	610
Range of GMAT	560–640
Accepts GRE scores	Yes
Average Verbal GRE	156
Range of Verbal GRE scores	153–159
Average Quantitative GRE	154
Range of Quantitative GRE scores	151–155
Average Writing GRE	4.1
Range of Writing GRE scores	3.5–4.5
Average GPA	3.3
TOEFL required of international students	Yes
Minimum TOEFL (paper)	100
Application fee	$130
International application fee	$130
Application Deadline	
Round 1:	11/1
Round 2:	2/1
Round 3:	5/1
Deferment available	Yes
Maximum length of deferment	1 Year
Transfer students accepted	No
Non-fall admissions	Yes
Need-blind admissions	Yes

EMPLOYMENT PROFILE

		Grads Employed by Function	% Avg. Salary
Career Rating	89		
Percent employed at graduation	63	Marketing	(11%) $102,500
Percent employed 3 months		Operations	(5%) $95,000
after graduation	70	Consulting	(5%) $95,000
Average base starting salary	$84,357	Finance	(68%) $76,222
Primary Source of Full-time Job Acceptances		HR	(5%) $100,000
School-facilitated activities	13 (68%)	Other	(5%)
Graduate-facilitated activities	4 (21%)	**Top 5 Employers Hiring Grads**	
Unknown	2 (11%)	PricewaterhouseCoopers (3), KPMG (2), Citigroup (1), Johnson & Johnson (1), Pfizer (1)	

FRANCIS MARION UNIVERSITY
SCHOOL OF BUSINESS

GENERAL INFORMATION

Type of school	Public
Affiliation	No Affiliation
Academic calendar	Semester

SURVEY SAYS...

Friendly students
Solid preparation in:
Presentation skills, Quantitative skills,
Computer skills

STUDENTS

Enrollment of parent institution	3,947
Enrollment of MBA Program	56
% male/female	50/50
% out-of-state	0
% part-time	25
% underrepresented minority	20
% international	7
Average age at entry	12
Average years work experience at entry	0

ACADEMICS

Academic Experience Rating	**64**
Profs interesting rating	63
Profs accessible rating	62
Student/faculty ratio	10:1
% female faculty	40
% part-time faculty	0

Academics

The School of Business at South Carolina's Francis Marion University offers "excellent preparation for real-world business decision-making" in a "convenient" MBA program "scheduled in the evening to accommodate working students." Since FMU is a state school, it does so at a price that doesn't break the bank.

This small school—one of the smallest state universities to earn AACSB accreditation, according to the university's public relations materials—offers a "challenging learning environment" in which "professors are easy to approach" and, consequently, the almost exclusively part-time student body "gets to know professors one on one." FMU offers a general MBA that is designed to serve the general business population of the Pee Dee region and beyond.

All FMU MBAs must complete courses in accounting for management control, managerial economics, financial theory and applications, strategic management, management science and statistics, and marketing theory and application. Students in the general MBA program must also complete classes in financial accounting, information systems, international business, management theory and applications, production management, and entrepreneurship.

MBAs praise the program's faculty, noting that "professors with real-world experience are integrated into active businesses and graduate programs." Primarily, they appreciate the convenience afforded by the school's location and scheduling, as well as the low cost of attending to Palmetto State natives.

Career and Placement

FMU's MBA program is too small to support career services dedicated exclusively to its students. MBAs receive career assistance from the university's Office of Career Development, which serves undergraduates and graduates in all divisions. Students here also benefit from an active Alumni Association, whose newest chapter is the MBA Alumni Chapter.

ADMISSIONS CONTACT: BEN KYER, DIRECTOR
ADDRESS: BOX 100547, FLORENCE, SC 29501-0547
PHONE: 843-661-1436 • FAX: 843-661-1432
E-MAIL: ALPHA1@FMARION.EDU • WEBSITE: ALPHA1.FMARION.EDU/~MBA

FINANCIAL FACTS

Annual tuition (in-state/ out-of-state)	$4,890/$9,568
% of students receiving aid	8

ADMISSIONS

Admissions Selectivity Rating	**81**
# of applications received	15
% applicants accepted	67
% acceptees attending	100
Average GMAT	400
Accepts GRE scores	Yes
Average GPA	3.0
TOEFL required of international students	Yes
Minimum TOEFL (paper/web)	550/
Application fee	$37
International application fee	$37
Deferment available	Yes
Transfer students accepted	Yes
Non-fall admissions	Yes
Need-blind admissions	No

Student Life and Environment

FMU draws a "driven and goal-oriented" student body that is "culturally diverse and career diverse." Life here is hectic, with most students juggling career and family obligations in addition to school responsibilities. Because of the many demands on their time, most students have little inclination to join in extracurricular activities. The program offers "many organizations" to those interested, but students warn that "they aren't as organized or publicized as well as they should be."

The school does a better job with its cultural and entertainment offerings to the general student population, hosting a wide range of performances, exhibits, and lecture series. The school houses an art gallery that displays student and faculty work as well as traveling exhibitions, film series, a planetarium and observatory, concerts, and festivals. FMU's Patriots are successful enough that the school plans to move its entire athletic program to Division I in the coming years; two teams already compete at that level, with the other ten currently competing in Division II.

FMU is located just outside of Florence, SC, a city with nearly 70,000 residents within its borders and its suburbs. Florence offers a number of movie theaters, malls, restaurants, a symphony orchestra, and professional hockey (the Pee Dee Pride skate in the East Coast Hockey League). The city is located at the intersections of I-95 and I-20, making travel in all four cardinal directions a snap. Columbia, Charleston, Myrtle Beach, and Fayetteville, NC, are all within 100 miles.

Admissions

Applicants to the FMU MBA program must submit a completed application; official transcripts for all postsecondary academic work, in a sealed envelope addressed to the applicant from the awarding school; official GMAT scores; two letters of recommendation; and a personal statement of purpose. All materials must be delivered to the school in a single envelope or package. In addition, international applicants must submit official TOEFL scores and a Confidential Financial Statement form demonstrating their ability to pay all expenses related to an FMU MBA. All successful applicants meet the following minimum guidelines: a score greater than 950 under the formula [(undergraduate GPA x 200) + GMAT score] or a score greater than 1000 under the formula [(GPA for final 60 hours of undergraduates work x 200) + GMAT score]. Also, they must earn at least a score of 400 on the GMAT. Applicants with non-business undergraduate degrees are generally required to complete the business foundation sequence prior to beginning work on their MBA. The sequence is three-course curriculum covering the basics of information systems, finance, and marketing. Students with undergraduate business degrees typically have this requirement waived.

THE GEORGE WASHINGTON UNIVERSITY
SCHOOL OF BUSINESS

GENERAL INFORMATION

Type of school	Private
Affiliation	No Affiliation
Academic calendar	Semester

SURVEY SAYS...

Classmates have diverse work experience, Liberal students, Students love Washington, DC
Solid preparation in:
General management, Teamwork, Doing business in a global economy

STUDENTS

Enrollment of parent institution	26,396
Enrollment of MBA Program	817
% male/female	59/41
% out-of-state	87
% part-time	78
% underrepresented minority	9
% international	53
Average age at entry	28
Average years work experience at entry	6

ACADEMICS

Academic Experience Rating	**89**
Profs interesting rating	86
Profs accessible rating	92
Student/faculty ratio	14:1
% female faculty	31
% underrepresented minority faculty	6
% part-time faculty	52

Joint Degrees

MBA/JD degree; MBA/MA International Affairs; MBA/MS Finance; MBA/Project Management; MBA/Information Systems Technology; MBA/MS Business Analytics.

Prominent Alumni

Colin Powell, MBA, Former US Secretary of State; Henry Duques, BBA & MBA, Former President & CEO, First Data Corp.; Michael Allen Balmuth, MHSA, Vice Chairman & CEO, Ross Stores

Academics

If you're on the hunt for a prestigious business school in a fantastic location, you might want to consider George Washington University. Certainly, being situated in the heart of Washington D.C., the program has a strong "focus on international business" and plenty of opportunities for working and studying abroad. As one thrilled second-year student chimes in, "I studied in Israel & Rwanda while pursuing my MBA." Moreover, given that many students here lead busy lives, they fully appreciate that it's easy to create a "flexible schedule." Indeed, we're told that it's common to take a "mix of online and in-person courses." What's more, this flexibility extends beyond just scheduling. Students thankfully have a lot of opportunity to " take courses outside of the business school that relate to [their] career interests."

Inside the classroom, MBA candidates are greeted by "polished," "professional" and "brilliant" professors who typically "maintain an open door policy." One impressed student volunteers, "Most of my professors have exceeded my expectations in terms of making their subject matter relevant and engaging." Unfortunately, MBAs aren't as kind when it comes to GW's administrators. Many bluntly assert that they "are poor at their jobs." However, as one optimistic student explains, "We went through three different deans since I've started a couple years ago, but again, things are picking up and changing for the better."

Career and Placement

Job prospects for George Washington MBAs are pretty sunny. As you might have already guessed, given GW's location, the school maintains many "connection[s] to public sector opportunities." More specifically, the school has strong "relationships [with] organizations such as [the] World Bank and IMF." Additionally, we're told that "consulting firms are recruiting here constantly, specifically for federal consulting." A lot of this success is due in no small part to the hardworking efforts of the Career Center. Students can swing by the office for interview tips and résumé help. The center also coordinates numerous on-campus recruiting sessions throughout the academic year.

Companies that tend to hire George Washington MBAs include Bank of America, Booz Allen Hamilton, Google, Deloitte, Federal Reserve, U.S. Department of the Interior, Macy's, Merrill Lynch and the World Wildlife Fund.

Student Life and Environment

George Washington MBAs are definitely a diverse bunch. Indeed, the program manages to net "a broad spectrum of [students] from around the country and around the world, with very diverse backgrounds and interests." And though at times they can be "competitive," we're also assured that these MBAs are "very social and friendly." Students also define their peers as "ambitious and open-minded" and while they are "driven to succeed," they are "not cut-throat." And, perhaps most important, many really want to "make a difference in the world."

Outside of the classroom, GW's b-school provides "a number of networking opportunities, both professional and social, to help create a strong sense of community among [students]." Many MBAs also like to take advantage of the numerous student clubs, which continually prove to be "very effective at hosting weekly activities including alumni panels [and] workshops. Lots of students also get together to collaborate on and participate in "business plan competitions [and] case competitions." Of course, most students point to the "unofficial post class happy hours" as a personal highlight. In fact, they are so popular that "faculty frequently join" as well. Lastly, students are fortunate enough to have D.C. as their playground. It's a "trendy" city that is "easy to get around" and features some of the finest restaurants, museums and cultural activities in the world. What more could you possibly desire?

Admissions

Admission to GW's School of Business is competitive. The school tends to take a well-rounded approach so academic performance, test scores, work experience, personal statements and recommendations will all be closely analyzed. GW prides itself on the diversity of its student body so applicants of all backgrounds are welcomed and encouraged to apply. Finally, interviews will be granted by invitation only.

FINANCIAL FACTS

Annual tuition (in-state/ out-of-state)	$48,907/$48,907
Fees	$68
Cost of books	$1,000
Room & board (on/off-campus)	$20,742/$20,742
% of students receiving grants	45
Average grant	$15,656

ADMISSIONS

Admissions Selectivity Rating	88
# of applications received	611
% applicants accepted	43
% acceptees attending	34
Average GMAT	646
Range of GMAT	610–690
Accepts GRE scores	Yes
Average Verbal GRE	158
Range of Verbal GRE scores	153–163
Average Quantitative GRE	158
Range of Quantitative GRE scores	155–162
Average Writing GRE	4.0
Range of Writing GRE scores	3.0–5.0
Average GPA	3.2
TOEFL required of international students	Yes
Minimum TOEFL (paper/web)	600/100
Application fee	$75
International application fee	$75
Application Deadline/Notification	
Round 1:	10/26 / 12/18
Round 2:	1/6 / 2/26
Round 3:	3/7 / 4/22
Round 4:	5/2 / 5/27
Deferment available	No
Transfer students accepted	Yes
Transfer application policy Standard Application Procedures. Transfer credits accepted only from AACSB accredited schools, pending department approval.	
Non-fall admissions	Yes
Need-blind admissions	Yes

EMPLOYMENT PROFILE

Career Rating	94	Grads Employed by Function	% Avg. Salary
Percent employed at graduation	62	Marketing	(13%) $98,667
Percent employed 3 months after graduation	93	Operations	(9%) $92,500
		Consulting	(38%) $99,950
Average base starting salary	$98,055	Management	(12%) $111,750
Primary Source of Full-time Job Acceptances		Finance	(16%) $86,300
School-facilitated activities	27 (40%)	HR	(3%)
Graduate-facilitated activities	29 (42%)	Other	(9%) $92,800
Unknown	12 (18%)	Top 5 Employers Hiring Grads	

Top 5 Employers Hiring Grads
Deloitte Consulting LLP (5), IBM (3), Bank of America Merrill Lynch (2), General Electric (1), Microsoft (1)

GEORGETOWN UNIVERSITY
MCDONOUGH SCHOOL OF BUSINESS

GENERAL INFORMATION
Type of school   Private
Affiliation   Roman Catholic-Jesuit
Academic calendar   Semesters are
     divided into 2 modules

SURVEY SAYS...
Classmates have diverse work experience, Friendly students, Good peer network, Good social scene, Happy students, Abundant clubs and activities, Students love Washington, DC
Solid preparation in:
General management, Teamwork, Communication/interpersonal skills, Presentation skills, Doing business in a global economy

STUDENTS
Enrollment of parent institution	17,858
Enrollment of MBA Program	914
% male/female	68/32
% out-of-state	89
% part-time	42
% underrepresented minority	7
% international	37
Average age at entry	28
Average years work experience at entry	5

ACADEMICS
Academic Experience Rating	93
Profs interesting rating	90
Profs accessible rating	95
Student/faculty ratio	5:1
% female faculty	24
% underrepresented minority faculty	13
% part-time faculty	44

Joint Degrees
MBA/MSFS, 3 years; MBA/JD, 4 years; MBA/MPP, 3 years; MBA/MD, 5 years

Prominent Alumni
Ann Sarnoff, President, BBC North America; Laurence Tosi, CFO, Airbnb; Bob Steers, CEO, Cohen & Steers; Craig Walker, CEO, Switch Communications Inc.

Academics

Located in Washington, D.C., Georgetown's access to international interests in both business and policy make it a desirable choice for career-minded students. The school offers an MBA with "a global approach," with the second year ending in a nine-day international consulting experience. Due to this and other factors, students are "impressed with their global focus and their emphasis on using business to help society." Because the business program "is not focused on any one particular aspect of business," Georgetown "gives its students a true understanding of business from many points of view around the world, allowing for international opportunities for growth."

Those hoping for a foundation in ruthless business practices will not find it here. McDonough fosters a "collaborative spirit when it comes to both learning and practicing business." In fact, "the Georgetown MBA program was the first institution to implement a business ethics course as a requirement for graduation." The school "pushes integrity across all levels," the result being a "high caliber of business professionals" among the graduates. Some students hope to see more "emphasis on sustainability/green trends in coursework."

Georgetown has "an excellent reputation for being academically rigorous, diverse, and high quality," and regarding the business school specifically, students consider McDonough the "highest caliber school in the region," a school that will "afford me better opportunities than other programs in this area." Students enjoy that the "smaller program size is more intimate compared to other large business schools."

A newly designed MBA Curriculum launched in the Fall of 2012 to replace the former modular system; it is filled with both classroom and experiential learning, and provides greater rigor, greater emphasis on quantitative and analytical skills, and a focus on principled leadership. One student in particular recognizes this fact yet remarks that "at the end of a course, I still come out learning more than what I bargained for."

Career and Placement

Career-minded students should find no shortage of post-school opportunities thanks to a "strong alumni network," "great networking connections," and "good access to recruiters." Some suggest that "due to its smaller size (compared to other business schools), some employers do not spend as much time as they might at other institutions," but because McDonough boasts "proximity to power sources in D.C.," hard-working graduates can expect a "great upward trajectory" provided they take advantage of the "great recruiting sessions" and "strong career connections in the business world." Though "the administration is relatively new," students say they are "dedicated to improving the school." An integral part of that is a new Director of Career Management, who works to be "extremely helpful in providing advice and consultation."

Employers who have hired McDonough graduates include: Citigroup, Booz Allen Hamilton, Credit Suisse, Merrill Lynch, AES, America Online, International Finance Corporation (IFC), 3M, American Express Company, Avaya, Bank of New York, Deloitte Touche Tohmatsu, Ford Motor Company, and JPMorgan Chase.

ADMISSIONS CONTACT: SHARI HUBERT, ASSOCIATE DEAN & DIRECTOR OF ADMISSIONS
ADDRESS: RAFIK B. HARIRI BUILDING, 37TH & O STREETS, NW, WASHINGTON, DC 20057
PHONE: 202-687-4200 • FAX: 202-687-7809
E-MAIL: GEORGETOWNMBA@GEORGETOWN.EDU • WEBSITE: MSB.GEORGETOWN.EDU

Student Life and Environment

Life at the McDonough School of Business at Georgetown University is one of constant challenge, with academics the focus of most days. "Georgetown's MBA is all-consuming," students say, but "in a good way." Indeed, "it is often difficult to find a group study room or classroom not filled with students studying on an evening or weekend." Students feel they are encouraged to work hard, "especially when [they] see [their] peers working just as hard." The school's collaborative, often non-competitive environment helps foster an atmosphere in which the "intense" workload is not overwhelming; it is just a fact of life. "Life at McDonough is rigorous and community-driven," attendees insist. "Students work extremely hard and take great pride in the Georgetown brand."

However, McDonough students do find time to relax. There is a "very social atmosphere with many social activities planned for students." "Post-class happy hours" take place, though most say that school activities are preferred, including "clubs, student government associations, and community service projects." Living in or around the D.C. Metro area offers ample things to do outside of school. "Wine tours, sports and activities on Capitol Hill" and more are regularly on the agenda, as well as volunteering with school and local organizations, music clubs, museums, and more. Even with all those opportunities, the "intense school spirit" present throughout the Georgetown student body means that for many it is school first, even when it comes to leisure time.

One student sums it up: "Students are engaged in campus life, however [they are] mostly focused on business school events and activities."

Admissions

If you do not have a minimum of two years of post-collegiate professional experience, do not apply. At least two years, with three or more preferred, is required prior to admission. Prospective students should be prepared with the including documents: an online application form (required), a resume, one essay (required), official transcripts for all postsecondary academic work, at least one recommendation from professional relationships, and an official GMAT or GRE score report. International students take note: an official score report for the TOEFL, IELTS, or Pearson Test of English is required in addition to the above materials. Interviews are invitation-only and come after the first application deadline; accepting interview invitations is strongly encouraged.

FINANCIAL FACTS

Annual tuition (in-state/ out-of-state)	$53,850/$53,850
Fees	$2,839
Cost of books	$2,646
Room & board	$20,306
% of students receiving aid	61
% of first-year students receiving aid	65
% of students receiving grants	35
Average award package	$55,860
Average grant	$23,418
Average loan	$62,067
Average student loan debt	$47,202

ADMISSIONS

Admissions Selectivity Rating	89
# of applications received	2,034
Average GMAT	692
Range of GMAT	660–710
Accepts GRE scores	Yes
Average GPA	3.4
TOEFL required of international students	Yes
Minimum TOEFL (paper/web)	600/100
Application fee	$175
International application fee	$175
Application Deadline/Notification	
Round 1:	10/1 / 12/15
Round 2:	1/5 / 3/20
Round 3:	4/1 / 5/15
Deferment available	Yes
Transfer students accepted	No
Non-fall admissions	No
Need-blind admissions	Yes

EMPLOYMENT PROFILE

		Grads Employed by Function	%	Avg. Salary
Career Rating	95			
Percent employed at graduation	73	Marketing	(16%)	$99,233
Percent employed 3 months after graduation	86	Operations	(6%)	$110,818
		Consulting	(30%)	$118,208
Average base starting salary	$108,789	Management	(5%)	$92,111
Primary Source of Full-time Job Acceptances		Finance	(33%)	$110,496
School-facilitated activities	133 (68%)	HR	(1%)	
Graduate-facilitated activities	53 (27%)	MIS	(2%)	
Unknown	9 (5%)	Other	(7%)	$93,375

Top 5 Employers Hiring Grads
PricewaterhouseCoopers (9), Ernst & Young (9), Deloitte (9), Citigroup Inc. (8), IBM Corp. (7)

GEORGIA INSTITUTE OF TECHNOLOGY
SCHELLER COLLEGE OF BUSINESS

Academics

No doubt Georgia Tech boasts "a great brand name," but that's hardly all this school has to offer its MBAs. With a "curriculum designed to integrate management and technology," Georgia Tech positions its grads well in the increasingly technologically-focused world of business. Furthermore, the school's Atlanta location means access to some of the best business minds—and some of the top business employers—in the Southeast. In addition, the school "provides great value for the money."

Students find Georgia Tech's many assets in surprising places. One writes, "before coming to school, I would have said our greatest strength was our technology focus and proximity to one of the premier engineering schools in the world. Now...I would say that our professors and career services are tied for greatest strengths. I will put either up against any top-ten business school any day." MBAs here report that Georgia Tech has "a great faculty in accounting, IT, and operations," and identify entrepreneurship, finance, and international management as other standout areas. Across disciplines, an "innovative curriculum keeps pace with the rapidly changing business and technology environment."

Georgia Tech's full-time program offers "strong networks and personal attention." "Small class sizes mean that students can have a high degree of impact in clubs, research assistantships, and special, self-initiated projects," one student observes (Of course, it also means that "not all electives that you may want will be offered.") The program places "an emphasis on teamwork and collaborative relationships" that students embrace, describing "a positive yet challenging work environment." The "workload can be overwhelming at times," but "the heavy emphasis on group projects means we have strong and reliable classmates to lean on if we need it."

Career and Placement

The Jones MBA Career Center provides "outstanding" support to assist students in developing a successful career strategy and plan. Each student is assigned a career advisor "who helps us find internships and jobs in our preferred fields," a service students deem "invaluable." Other resources include an in-depth career course, job search tools, and individual career coaching.

Atlanta's big-city locale is a plus for students in their job search, because the school "can get business heads and leaders from the city of Atlanta" to visit campus, meet with and mentor students, assist in networking, and provide internships and jobs. As one student sums up, "The program is very much oriented toward the job market, and the school is known to get [strong] job placement. From the time you are accepted, you begin evaluating employers and job hunting. You are given exceptional tools and resources (however, you are also under a great deal of pressure to secure a high-paying job)."

Among the top employers of Georgia Tech MBAs are North Highland, Bank of America, Deloitte Consulting, Emerson, Delta Air Lines , KPMG, Amazon, Capgemini Consulting, The Home Depot, and IBM.

Student Life and Environment

There's a "friendly atmosphere" in the Georgia Tech MBA program, where "social networking events and clubs are an integral part of [the] business school experience." The b-school facility "has several common areas, comfortable lobbies, and group work areas," so "no one is ever by himself. Even if working diligently on different homework assignments, we tend to cluster together and have a social environment." Classrooms "are all equipped with a computer-managed multimedia system, which includes double projectors and screens, document camera, laptop hookups and DVD," and "faculty offices are easily accessible in the building. The facilities are very clean and updated."

Because the program holds "no classes on Fridays," Thursday night is a time for socializing. "Every Thursday there is a social event either at a restaurant, atrium in the academic building, or elsewhere where current students, alumni, and professors interact in a relaxed environment," students tell us. Fridays aren't for hangovers, though; students "have two or three group meetings every Friday." The "Fridays off" policy, students explain, "is the only thing that makes group work possible" in this busy program.

Georgia Tech's "midtown Atlanta location" "offers numerous educational, professional, and social opportunities," although some warn that the surrounding neighborhood "has some safety issues." Most everyone agrees that the Atlanta location is a huge advantage overall, both in terms of "keeping outside 'real world' connections with professionals in our industry of choice" and culturally. "It is an exciting and vibrant life at Georgia Tech," one student reports.

Georgia Tech "attracts many people from the engineering fields, but also from financial services as well. This makes for a strong competition between teams in case reports and presentations." The program is home to lots of "Type-A driven people who are very engaging in class discussion and projects." Even so, "the culture is not over-competitive or cut-throat. We are like a family pushing each other to learn and to accomplish great things."

Admissions

GMAT or GRE scores, undergraduate GPA, work experience, and the results of a personal interview (scheduled by invitation only) are the factors that weigh most heavily with those who evaluate applicants for Georgia Tech's MBA program. Personal essays and recommendations are also important. TOEFL scores are required of applicants whose first language is not English or who have not successfully completed a year of college/university level study in the United States or another English-speaking country. Applications are processed on a rolling basis, a system that typically favors those who apply early.

FINANCIAL FACTS

Annual tuition (in-state/ out-of-state)	$28,896/$39,484
Fees	$2,192
Cost of books	$1,200
Room & board	$12,840
% of students receiving aid	65
% of first-year students receiving aid	69
Average award package	$28,929
Average student loan debt	$49,332

ADMISSIONS

Admissions Selectivity Rating	97
# of applications received	444
% applicants accepted	22
% acceptees attending	65
Average GMAT	678
Range of GMAT	610–720
Accepts GRE scores	Yes
Average Verbal GRE	163
Range of Verbal GRE scores	160–167
Average Quantitative GRE	160
Range of Quantitative GRE scores	156–167
Average GPA	3.3
TOEFL required of international students	Yes
Minimum TOEFL (paper/web)	600/100
Application fee	$75
International application fee	$75
Application Deadline/Notification	
Round 1:	10/15 / 12/15
Round 2:	1/15 / 3/15
Round 3:	3/15 / 5/1
Round 4:	5/15 / 6/15
Deferment available	Yes
Maximum length of deferment	1 year
Transfer students accepted	No
Non-fall admissions	No
Need-blind admissions	Yes

EMPLOYMENT PROFILE

Career Rating	97	Grads Employed by Function% Avg. Salary	
Percent employed at graduation	82	Marketing	(16%) $96,452
Percent employed 3 months after graduation	93	Operations	(9%) $101,333
		Consulting	(37%) $113,261
Average base starting salary	$105,029	Management	(17%) $100,636
Primary Source of Full-time Job Acceptances		Finance	(10%) $100,000
School-facilitated activities	42 (65%)	MIS	(5%) $110,000
Graduate-facilitated activities	17 (26%)	Other	(6%) $96,232
Unknown	6 (9%)	**Top 5 Employers Hiring Grads**	
		Bank of America (9), North Highland (8),	
		AT&T (4), Deloitte Consulting (3), EY (2)	

GEORGIA SOUTHERN UNIVERSITY
COLLEGE OF BUSINESS ADMINISTRATION

GENERAL INFORMATION
Type of school	Public
Affiliation	No Affiliation
Academic calendar	Semester

SURVEY SAYS...
Friendly students, Conservative students
Solid preparation in:
Teamwork, Communication/inter-personal skills, Presentation skills, Quantitative skills

STUDENTS
Enrollment of parent institution	20,459
Enrollment of MBA Program	93
% male/female	61/39
% out-of-state	14
% part-time	45
% underrepresented minority	39
% international	14
Average age at entry	28
Average years work experience at entry	0

ACADEMICS
Academic Experience Rating	**85**
Profs interesting rating	89
Profs accessible rating	91
Student/faculty ratio	30:1
% female faculty	37
% underrepresented minority faculty	19
% part-time faculty	8

Joint Degrees
MBA with a concentration in Health Services Administration or Information Systems, 2 yrs evening/part time

Prominent Alumni
Dan Cathy, President/CEO, Chick-fil-A; James Kennedy, Director, NASA John F. Kennedy Space Center, retired; Elizabeth Cook, Singer/Songwriter; Luke Bryan, Singer/Songwriter; Mike Davis, Executive Director, USGA

Academics

Uniting an "excellent academic reputation" with a "reasonable cost," Georgia Southern University has been conferring graduate business degrees for more than forty years. Today, a Georgia Southern MBA isn't only for those in the Savannah-Statesboro area. In addition to the college's long-standing MBA program for professionals, Georgia Southern's popular "WebMBA program has a good reputation," as well as AACSB accreditation. Students who need the convenience of an online diploma choose Georgia Southern because the "flexible online format" makes it easy for them to complete their courses from anywhere in the world. For those seeking a more traditional MBA experience, Georgia Southern is also a "well known brick-and-mortar school," which specifically caters to part-time students.

Whether you choose to attend in person or online, there is a "heavy workload" throughout the program. Live classes are generally interactive, and "you have to stay on your toes" during discussions. Fortunately, "professors genuinely want to see students learn and succeed." If you need extra assistance, "the majority of professors are very accessible" and "willing to answer questions and address concerns" during office hours or via email. As instructors, Georgia Southern professors are "helpful and knowledgeable" about the topics they teach and always "stay on top of current business trends." In fact, "many of them are actively researching in their field," while others bring strong real-world credentials to the classroom. Of particular note, "many of the professors are professionals and consultants, so their experience is invaluable to classroom instruction." At the same time, students say the program would be improved if the curriculum included "more real-life classes, such as entrepreneurship and negotiation," as well as "more managerial applications" in coursework.

Currently, Georgia Southern offers two official MBA specialties—health services administration and information systems—as well as an SAP certification. For students who choose to concentrate their studies in health services administration, the school "just opened a new College of Public Health building." The administration is efficient and generally "runs things in the background without any problems." "The faculty and staff at Georgia Southern are very helpful and available to answer any questions" students have. Student concerns are listened to and addressed. For example, in the past, there were problems with regards to taking required classes, but "the school is already taking steps to streamline the enrollment process." As a part of Georgia's public school system, the MBA is offered at a "very reasonable price." Overall, for convenience, quality, and cost, this program is "worth every penny."

Career and Placement

Students in Georgia Southern's part-time and web-based programs are generally working in a professional capacity at the time they start their MBA program. As a result, there are rather limited career services for these students. In fact, many web students say they have very little interaction with the Georgia Southern campus or administration.

ADMISSIONS CONTACT: GORDON N. SMITH, PHD, DIRECTOR OF GRADUATE BUSINESS PROGRAMS
ADDRESS: P. O. BOX 8050, STATESBORO, GA 30460-8050
PHONE: 912-478-5767 • FAX: 912-478-7480
E-MAIL: GRADSCHOOL@GEORGIASOUTHERN.EDU • WEBSITE: COBA.GEORGIASOUTHERN.EDU/MBA

For students considering a career change, there is a dedicated career counselor assigned to the College of Business through the university's Office of Career Services. Students can meet with the counselor for help creating a job search strategy. Students and alumni from the College of Business also have access to all the services offered by the greater Office of Career Services, which include conferences, career development seminars, campus recruiting programs, and internship placements. For those with limited career experience, "many of the programs offered have internships and co-ops built into the curriculum." Overall, "the university does an excellent job of making resources available to students, particularly given the anemic job market." However, students would still love to see "more job opportunities at career services."

Student Life and Environment

The largest higher-learning institution in the Savannah area, "Georgia Southern is a wonderful school located in a great, slow-paced part of Georgia." The charming campus is situated in the small city of Statesboro, and the university's "proximity to Savannah" makes it easy for students to commute to work, while also offering access to all the rich cultural life of Georgia's coastal city. The vast majority of Georgia Southern students are "working professionals with diverse backgrounds and busy lives outside of school." They join the program "from all walks of life" but share a passion for their careers and education. Academically, the program can get "competitive among classmates," yet students are "very cooperative" when working together on group projects.

Web students have little to no contact with life at Georgia Southern, and "students who use the satellite campus aren't able to enjoy Georgia Southern's beautiful campus." Fortunately, those who crave camaraderie will find a "strong network of alumni and student organizations," which host "ongoing activities" on the larger campus, from athletics to performances. On occasion, the College of Business will also host special events "for graduate students to mingle." Some students would welcome the addition of family-friendly activities on campus, while younger MBA candidates would like to see "more activities on the graduate student level" in general. A student laments, "There are some of us who do not have families and would like to socialize in an adult atmosphere in our free time."

Admissions

To be considered for a spot at Georgia Southern University, students must submit a completed application to include a resume, an essay, transcripts from all undergraduate colleges and universities, and official GMAT scores. Admissions are determined using a comprehensive review of all application materials. In recent years, incoming MBA students had an average undergraduate GPA of 3.4 and average GMAT scores of 487. Students are enrolled biannually, fall and spring.

FINANCIAL FACTS

Annual tuition (in-state/ out-of-state)	$9,824/$29,712
Fees	$2,098
Cost of books	$1,200
Room & board (on/off-campus)	$9,800/$9,800
% of students receiving aid	61
% of first-year students receiving aid	76
% of students receiving grants	30
Average award package	$13,012
Average grant	$7,456
Average loan	$11,884

ADMISSIONS

Admissions Selectivity Rating	81
# of applications received	65
% applicants accepted	75
% acceptees attending	63
Average GMAT	491
Range of GMAT	430–570
Accepts GRE scores	No
Average GPA	3.3
TOEFL required of international students	Yes
Minimum TOEFL (web)	213
Application fee	$50
International application fee	$50
Regular application deadline	8/1
Deferment available	Yes
Maximum length of deferment	1 year
Transfer students accepted	Yes
Transfer application policy	

No more than 6 semester hours of graduate credit may be transferred to a graduate program at Georgia Southern. Only grades of "B" or higher will be accepted for transfer.

Non-fall admissions	Yes
Need-blind admissions	Yes

GEORGIA STATE UNIVERSITY
J. MACK ROBINSON COLLEGE OF BUSINESS

Academics

"One of the top business schools in Atlanta," Georgia State University offers a cosmopolitan MBA to a diverse student body. Catering to a range of urban professionals, the school offers several distinct MBA tracks. For those with busy careers, the Flexible MBA is an evening and weekend program, which allows up to five years for completion. Another popular choice, the PMBA, is also designed for working professionals; however, this program is a two-year cohort-based degree, which moves quickly and maximizes networking opportunities with classmates. In addition to these two programs, the school offers an Executive MBA for seasoned managers, as well as a full-time program with major overseas components, called the Global Partners MBA. With evening classes at "multiple locations" in Atlanta, the majority of Georgia State's MBA programs give students "the flexibility to remain employed full time throughout the curriculum."

Georgia State's MBA provides a "strong background in general business areas, while allowing you to focus on your area of interest" through electives and study abroad. "Professors are a mix of experienced professionals and long-tenured educators," who are "extremely knowledgeable" and able to "make complicated concepts understandable and relevant." Teaching working professionals, professors excel at "staying up to date with current business trends, from global to local." Just as importantly, "the business school learning environment depends heavily on your classmates' experiences." Since "many of the students have ten-plus years of relevant work experience," students are pleased to find that their "classmates bring good industry knowledge to discussions."

Keeping up with classes and professional life is definitely a challenge for many MBA students, as "the program moves at a very fast pace." At the same time, the "PMBA isn't as intense or competitive as some full-time programs because everyone is working full time." Helping to streamline the experience, "the administration is very involved" with students, and it "has perfected making the process easy" on busy working professionals. Staff handles most of the paperwork, so "students don't have to do any of the 'administrative' tasks, like registering or ordering books." "PMBA facilities are top notch," located on a number of convenient satellite campuses in Atlanta.

Career and Placement

Throughout Georgia State, there is a strong "focus on getting the MBA student where they want to go" in their career. While many part-time students aren't necessarily seeking a new job after graduation, they are nonetheless pleased that "the school leverages its location in a vibrant business city and its connections to business leaders to give students access to reputable companies for academic and career purposes." "Individual career counseling is made available as part of the program," and students have access to myriad services through the Robinson Career Management Center in the business school. There are frequent career development workshops on campus, as well as a few recruiting events. At the same time, "the job selection through the career placement center is limited," as the program lacks a large community of job seekers. A student explains, "We don't have a full-time program, so companies don't recruit at GSU like they do at Emory and GT."

ADMISSIONS CONTACT: TOBY MCCHESNEY, ASSISTANT DEAN
GRADUATE RECRUITING AND STUDENT SERVICES
ADDRESS: SUITE 625, 35 BROAD STREET, ATLANTA, GA 30302-3988
PHONE: 404-413-7167 • FAX: 404-413-7162
E-MAIL: MASTERSADMISSIONS@GSU.EDU • WEBSITE: WWW.ROBINSON.GSU.EDU

In recent years, many important companies have hired MBA grads from Georgia State, including Hewitt Associates, Tauber & Balser PC, KPMG LLP, Coca-Cola Enterprises, Deloitte Consulting, Towers Perrin, Federal Reserve Bank of New York, McKesson Corporation, UPS, Wells Fargo, GE Healthcare, KPMG UNUM Corporation, Frazier & Deeter LLC, Ernst & Young LLP, and Wachovia Securities. The average starting salary for PMBA graduates is $75,000, with a range between $45,000 and $150,000 annually. Flexible MBA students earn an average salary of about $65,000.

Student Life and Environment

Drawing from Atlanta's large urban population, the MBA program at GSU is "very diverse." One of the program's major benefits is making connections and networking with "student peers from major corporations." Fortunately, social interactions are, to some extent, built into the curriculum. Group work is included in most classes, and students say you should expect to attend "team meetings and phone conferences at least two hours weekly." On the whole, students are "competitive in their work lives but more collaborative in the academic environment."

Georgia State students are "surrounded by countless opportunities in downtown Atlanta," and, when time permits, "students enjoy each other's company in and out of the classroom." Spread across several satellite facilities, many students rarely come to the main campus downtown. However, "the program tries to host mixers" for business students, and "the Graduate Business Association puts on a Leadership Speaker Series and several networking/happy hours throughout the year." As expected for marketing mavens, "events are generally held at trendy, popular venues and executed flawlessly." In addition to blowing off steam, these events are "excellent opportunities for networking and making new friends." At the same time, students with families note that most student activities are "geared at single, younger students."

Admissions

Admissions requirements vary for each of Georgia State's MBA programs, specifically with regards to work experience. For the executive MBA, students should have at least seven years of experience (with five in a management position), while the PMBA is designed for students with a minimum of four years full-time in the workforce. The Flexible MBA requires at least one year of work experience. Georgia State prefers that students have spent two or three years in the real world before beginning the program. The average GMAT score for the entering class was 611.

Prominent Alumni

Kat Cole, President, Cinnabon; James E. Copeland, Former CEO, Deloitte Touche Tohmatsu; Richard H. Lenny, Former Chairman, Hershey Foods; Kenneth Lewis, Former Chairman & CEO, Bank of America; William H. Rogers, CEO and President of Sun Trust Banks

FINANCIAL FACTS

Annual tuition (in-state/out-of-state)	$7,866/$22,482
Fees	$2,128
Cost of books	$2,000
Room & board (on/off-campus)	$13,148/$11,195

ADMISSIONS

Admissions Selectivity Rating	86
# of applications received	261
% applicants accepted	55
% acceptees attending	55
Average GMAT	613
Range of GMAT	588–643
Accepts GRE scores	Yes
Average Verbal GRE	155
Range of Verbal GRE scores	150–159
Average Quantitative GRE	154
Range of Quantitative GRE scores	151–157
Average GPA	3.2
TOEFL required of international students	Yes
Minimum TOEFL (paper/web)	610/101
Application fee	$50
International application fee	$50
Early application deadline	2/1
Regular application deadline	5/1
Deferment available	Yes
Maximum length of deferment	Two semesters
Transfer students accepted	No
Non-fall admissions	Yes
Need-blind admissions	Yes

GONZAGA UNIVERSITY
GRADUATE SCHOOL OF BUSINESS

GENERAL INFORMATION

Type of school	Private
Affiliation	Roman Catholic-Jesuit

SURVEY SAYS...
Friendly students
Solid preparation in:
General management, Presentation
skills

STUDENTS

Enrollment of parent institution	7,614
Enrollment of MBA Program	220
% male/female	62/38
% out-of-state	20
% part-time	65
% underrepresented minority	24
% international	13
Average age at entry	30
Average years work experience at entry	5

ACADEMICS

Academic Experience Rating	**91**
Profs interesting rating	92
Profs accessible rating	95
Student/faculty ratio	5:1
% female faculty	40
% underrepresented minority faculty	15
% part-time faculty	15

Joint Degrees
MBA/MAcc, 2 yrs FT. MBA/JD,
MAcc/JD 3-3.5 years.

Prominent Alumni
Ezra Eckhardt, Executive Vice
President at Umpqua Bank; Jerome
Conlon, Former Sr. VP at NBC, for-
mer VP at Starbucks, Current Chief
Marketing of Open Source Global;
Stuart McKee, Chief Technology
Officer - Microsoft; Katherine
Morgan, Greater Spokane Valley
Chamber of Commerce president &
CEO; Michael R. Coleman, Retired
VP of IBM

Academics

Gonzaga University is about "teaching students life lessons through a Jesuit educa-tion," which appeals to the MBA students in its Graduate School of Business. A "great reputation in the business community," especially for its "accounting program," and an "awesome flexible curriculum structure" that "is designed with working individuals in mind (with evening and online classes) " also draw area business grads to the program, which can be completed full-time in three semesters (including summer, fall, and spring).

Gonzaga's MBA curriculum consists of twenty-two credits in core courses (eleven two-credit classes) and eleven credits in electives, and students are given the option for a "core-trailer," which gives them "a very unique opportunity to focus in on a subject that they enjoyed during the core part of the semester." Students report that the curriculum is "broad and covers many aspects of the modern business environment" and is "a tough workload that stresses excellence. Classes may run from 7:30 A.M. to 8:00 P.M. at night," with break hours in between. Professors "integrate course material throughout the pro-gram" and "rarely present contradicting information" as "the material in the program is well-planned," though "some tenured professors don't seem to care about updating their courses anymore." Students also appreciate that the program allows for a "flexibility of coursework." "Students need to have more opportunities to simulate complex projects and the teamwork needed to solve them," one student notes. Luckily, "Gonzaga's School of Business is always looking for students' input to make those improvements."

At Gonzaga, both faculty and the business administration "stress the importance of personal connections. As a result, students are able to easily build a strong alumni net-work." This close-knit culture "really adds to the MBA experience." "For those who are entrepreneurial...classes such as business consulting enable students to try their hand at consulting for a local business." "I learned more practical skills in Gonzaga's MBA program than I ever expected in an academic setting," says one student.

Career and Placement

The Gonzaga Career Center and the School of Business Administration staff and faculty "do a great job of trying to provide students with as much planning help and advice that they can possibly give," including: self-assessment, career planning, resume writing, and conducting a successful job search; mock interviews and interview critiques; on-campus recruiting and interviewing; a career-resources library; alumni events; and internship placement assistance. Students complain, "Despite its great instructors and faculty, the school needs to do a better job in connecting students with careers." Due to the small size of both the city of Spokane and the University, not a lot of major companies recruit at Gonzaga, and "a lot more legwork is needed on behalf of the student to find his or her post-graduation path." Thus, despite its "great reputation" in the Northwest, "the MBA program may best benefit those who already know where they want to go after they graduate."

Employers of Gonzaga business graduates include Avista, Bank of America, Boeing, Deloitte, Ernst & Young, Honeywell, Itron, KPMG, Microsoft, PricewaterhouseCoopers, and Starbucks. Fifty percent of Gonzaga MBAs go into finance and accounting.

Student Life and Environment

Gonzaga's MBA candidates are broken down to recent undergrad graduates who immediately started their MBAs and working individuals who are returning to get an MBA after starting a career. Some feel that many students "have little to no work experience, which makes getting an MBA a real disservice to themselves." The culture is "more collaborative than competitive," and students tend to be "friendly and willing to help their peers," down-to-earth, "dependable" and "can pull their own weight." "Being taught from the Jesuit perspective and a student population in which you get to know most of the other students quite well" is a positive at Gonzaga, one student says.

Students are "fairly isolated from the campus in that our classes start at the end of the traditional day, and our building is on one edge of the campus," though you "can tell that administration has made great efforts to try to improve the camaraderie of all students." Luckily, the building is "amazing, has everything in one place, and the lounge has a fantastic view of a lake beneath and downtown in the distance." Evening classes "allow working professionals to attend classes." One student notes, "I cannot say enough about the flexibility and responsiveness of the MBA program team. From professors to the administrative staff, this experience has been outstanding."

Those who choose to engage in campus life tell us that it is "full of opportunities to get involved in fun activities and helpful charities," though not many of these apply to the family-oriented. "A few attempts have been made to encourage students to socialize, but nothing really applies to families, so I do not participate," says one student. The basketball games are free for students and are "full of excitement" and, as an added bonus, revenue "generated by the basketball team is used to improve the school and the school's reputation." Local charities "love the help from grad students and rely on them for help in creating business plans, conducting market research, and planning marketing activities." Hometown Spokane is in eastern Washington, is "cold during the winter, and not all that exciting compared to Seattle, which is four hours away."

Admissions

Applicants to the MBA program at Gonzaga must submit one official copy of all postsecondary academic transcripts, official GMAT/GRE scores, resume, two letters of recommendation, and a completed application (which includes three short essays). International students must also submit official TOEFL scores (if English is not their first language) and a financial declaration form. An interview may be required of some international applicants. Work experience is not required, "but is strongly encouraged," and "the majority of students who enter the program have four or five years of prior work experience."

EMPLOYMENT PROFILE

Career Rating	78	Grads Employed by Function	% Avg. Salary
Average base starting salary	$66,500	Marketing	(7%)
		Operations	(13%)
		Consulting	(5%)
		Management	(5%)
		Finance	(35%)
		HR	(5%)
		MIS	(5%)
		Other	(25%)

Top 5 Employers Hiring Grads
Itron, Boeing, WA Trust Bank, Providence Health, Avista

Grand Valley State University

Seidman College of Business

GENERAL INFORMATION

Type of school	Public
Affiliation	No Affiliation
Academic calendar	Semester

SURVEY SAYS...

Friendly students, Students love
Grand Rapids, MI
Solid preparation in:
Teamwork

STUDENTS

Enrollment of parent	
institution	23,857
Enrollment of MBA Program	229
% male/female	62/38
% part-time	73
% underrepresented minority	67
% international	4
Average age at entry	31
Average years work	
experience at entry	8

ACADEMICS

Academic Experience Rating	**84**
Profs interesting rating	86
Profs accessible rating	89
Student/faculty ratio	25:1
% female faculty	20
% underrepresented	
minority faculty	30
% part-time faculty	0

Joint Degrees

Dual JD/MBA w/ MSU Law, 4 yrs

Prominent Alumni

Laurie Beard, Pres/CEO Founders
Trust Personal Bank; John Bultema,
Pres Fifth Third Bank Western
Michigan; Curt Pullen, EVP Herman
Miller, Pres Herman Miller NA;
Robert Bockheim, Pres/COO Nucraft
Furniture; Mark Olesnavage, Pres
Hopen Therapeutics

Academics

Tucked away in western Michigan, Grand Valley State University promises both "affordability" and a celebrated reputation. Indeed, the MBA program at Grand Valley offers "a great education in a great location." The MBA program is geared toward working professionals, but experience is not required.

The traditional MBA offers a balance of both business theory and practical application. There is a heavy emphasis on applied research and group projects, helping students hone their problem-solving abilities. Moreover, MBA candidates are required to take a large number of core courses, ensuring they have a breadth of knowledge and a strong foundation in business fundamentals. These courses range from Contemporary Managerial Accounting and Marketing Management to Global Competitiveness, Strategy and Operations, and Supply Chain Management. Additionally, MBA students may choose to focus in finance, innovation and technology management, or health sector management.

MBA students at Grand Valley truly appreciate their "smart" and "efficient" professors. They work diligently to "instill real-world principles" in their students and know how to demonstrate "solutions to everyday business problems." A pleased student shares, "Professors all have real-world experience, which makes a very big difference in the quality of education. They aren't just talking about what they think it is like in the business world; they can honestly say 'when I worked on a project like this' or 'when I was Project Manager/CFO.' It makes a big difference not only in quality but the amount of respect they are given from the student body." Students are also full of praise for the "incredible" administration, which "seems to run fairly smoothly." They always appear "well prepared," and it is very clear that they "truly care about the students."

Careers and Placement

The Seidman MBA is a program primarily for working professionals. Most students are employed when they begin their MBA studies and remain employed by the same firms when they graduate. However, there are a handful of students interested in pursuing new career options and professional opportunities, and they do feel that Grand Valley's career services can be lacking. Many would appreciate if the office became "more visible and helpful." As one somewhat frustrated student expounds, "Career Services should help expose students to jobs and internships and to business people in the community in order to help us get better jobs. They need to foster introductions with those companies that strongly value a MBA from GVSU."

ADMISSIONS CONTACT: CLAUDIA BAJEMA, GRADUATE BUSINESS PROGRAMS DIRECTOR
ADDRESS: 401 W. FULTON, GRAND RAPIDS, MI 49504
PHONE: 616-331-7400 • FAX: 616-331-7389
E-MAIL: GO2GVMBA@GVSU.EDU • WEBSITE: WWW.GVSU.EDU/BUSINESS

Student Life and Environment

Grand Valley manages at attract a "great mix of personalities" who hail "from different backgrounds." Most agree that their peers are "friendly and easy to approach." Moreover, they are "intelligent" and quite focused on "pursuing success inside and outside of the classroom." A graduating student adds that she has found her fellow students to be "encouraging and supportive and always willing to lend a hand to a friend." Further, the vast majority of Grand Valley MBA students maintain full-time employment while enrolled, and they manage to successfully incorporate their work experience into class discussions. Many students truly appreciate this facet and find it adds to their "market knowledge" and certainly "helps to expand horizons."

Though many MBA candidates are busy juggling their jobs and families, they are quick to assert that "there is always something fun to do" around campus. Students also love hometown Grand Rapids, Michigan's second largest city. Located between Detroit and Chicago, Grand Rapids is a vibrant city in its own right. Students can take advantage of a myriad of cultural events and opportunities. Entertainment options include the Grand Rapids Symphony, Broadway Theater Guild, Grand Rapids Ballet, and Opera Grand Rapids. Sports enthusiasts will also find their appetite satiated. Grand Rapids features several professional sports teams including the Griffins (AHL hockey), and the Whitecaps (baseball).

Admissions

The admissions officers at Grand Valley State are looking for applicants who want to strengthen their business acumen and learn how to tackle today's business challenges. Successful candidates demonstrate that they have keen analytical skills, strong problem-solving abilities, and proven leadership experience. Applicants' academic records, GMAT scores, and work history are all thoroughly evaluated. The admissions committee does not require or request any particular undergraduate major. Lastly, applicants who are not native English speakers must also submit scores for the TOEFL.

FINANCIAL FACTS

Cost per credit hour	
(in-state/out-of-state)	$608/$798
Fees	$0
Cost of books	$2,500
Room & board	
(on/off-campus)	$9,600/$7,000

ADMISSIONS

Admissions Selectivity Rating	80
# of applications received	120
% applicants accepted	93
% acceptees attending	91
Average GMAT	575
Range of GMAT	450–720
Accepts GRE scores	Yes
Average GPA	3.65
TOEFL required of	
international students	Yes
Minimum TOEFL	
(paper/web)	80/6.5
Application fee	$30
International application fee	$30
Regular application deadline	8/1
Regular application notification	8/10
Deferment available	Yes
Maximum length of	
deferment	1 year
Transfer students accepted	Yes
Transfer application policy	
Up to 9 credits of MBA equivalent course work from another AACSB-accredited university, grade of B or better, and course (s) taken within past 5 years.	
Non-fall admissions	Yes
Need-blind admissions	Yes

EMPLOYMENT PROFILE		
Career Rating	71	**Top 5 Employers Hiring Grads**
		Amway Corporation, Steelcase Corporation, Gordon Food Service, Mercantile Bank, X-Rite Corporation

HARVARD UNIVERSITY
HARVARD BUSINESS SCHOOL

GENERAL INFORMATION
Type of school   Private
Affiliation   No Affiliation
Academic calendar   September-May

SURVEY SAYS...
Classmates have diverse work experience, Friendly students, Good peer network, Good social scene, Cutting-edge classes, Helpful alumni, Happy students, Abundant clubs and activities, Students love Boston, MA
Solid preparation in:
Finance, General management, Teamwork, Communication/interpersonal skills, Doing business in a global economy, Entreprenurial studies

STUDENTS
Enrollment of MBA Program	1,872
% male/female	59/41
% part-time	0
% underrepresented minority	26
% international	35
Average age at entry	27
Average years work experience at entry	4

ACADEMICS
Academic Experience Rating	99
Profs interesting rating	96
Profs accessible rating	94
% female faculty	25
% underrepresented minority faculty	29
% part-time faculty	19

Joint Degrees
JD/MBA, 4 years; MPP/MPA/MBA, 3 years; MD/MBA, 5 years; DMD/MBA, 5 years

Prominent Alumni
Michael Bloomberg, Former Mayor, New York City; Founder, Bloomberg L.P.; Jamie Dimon, Chairman & CEO, J.P. Morgan Chase & Co.; Jeff Immelt, CEO of General Electric; Sheryl Sandberg, Chief Operating Officer, Facebook; Michelle Zatlyn, Cofounder, CloudFlare

Academics

It can't be denied that the Harvard Business School name speaks for itself, or that its students, who are often "heavily recruited," speak about it in a parade of superlatives. They chose HBS because it has the "best global reputation," or for its "amazing facilities, highest paid alumni, strong alumni network," or for its "high-quality professors." Indeed, "prestige," "reputation" and "brand" all loom large in students' depictions of HBS, as do its "culture," "case-based curriculum," "location," and "unique learning opportunities both inside and outside the classroom." "Professors are engaged, available, and the best in their field," and they "push and pull to test opinions," meaning "real discussion and debate occurs." The "case method is incredible at teaching a broad-based, multifaceted approach to leadership," and HBS's "administration is trying to address the lack of female case protagonists," with "some work left to go." Students definitely take their work seriously: they "come on time and (mostly) prepared," and "there is a strong culture against using electronics in the room, so everyone is actually focused on the classroom experience." Administratively, "the school runs like clockwork," so smoothly that one student jokes it's "like it was built by and for German/Swiss first-born children." Students can't praise their classmates highly enough: "Wonderful. Accomplished. Charismatic. Leaders making a difference in the world." "Going to school with fellow HBSers is a dream come true."

Career and Placement

An HBS MBA comes at a hefty price tag, but students near-unanimously feel it "has a brand that make[s] it worth a large investment." HBS's "reputation, job placement, alumni network, geographic reach," and "world-renowned professors" all aid its graduates' desirability to employers, and students feel especially well-prepared for the workforce in "general management and leadership," as well as in "the case method and how it teaches you to stand by what you believe." While New York and Boston have long been meccas for the ambitious MBA grad, current students "note that San Francisco is beginning to displace the East Coast as the most popular post-grad destination," though it's wise to remember that often "start-ups . . . aren't going to go through campus career services" for recruiting. Luckily, HBS's "connections, access, and alumni reach" are second to none, and its "brand name will get you an interview anywhere."

Student Life and Environment

At HBS, "students are always doing something—be it traveling, starting a company, leading a conference." Due in part to the fact that "an unconventional grading system decreases the need to be cutthroat," students find each other "surprisingly nice, humble, helpful, and non competitive" as well as "the highest density of smart, successful, and motivated people you can find." The atmosphere is "cooperative and collaborative, with "very active social and industry clubs," and "the section experience here gives everyone a group of close-knit friends who you can bond with over shared social experiences or things that happened in the classroom." For many, business school is a kind of "two-year vacation from their stressful, high-performance lives," so there's definitely "lots of fun. Lots of parties." "People here are serious and highly capable, but at the same time know how to relax and have fun." Students prize the ability to share their MBA experience with "amazing people coming from all around the world, from so many different backgrounds, with very strong views and different perspectives," who "make the conversation really interesting!"

Admissions

HBS hosts three annual application rounds for prospective students in September, January, and April. The school explicitly states three priorities for incoming students: Habit of Leadership, Analytical Aptitude and Appetite, and Engaged Community Citizenship. Application requirements include the standard GMAT/GRE, TOEFL if applicable, essay, résumé, and two letters of recommendation, as well as an invitation-only interview and post-interview reflection. Current undergraduates or master's students may want to take note of the 2+2 Program, which consists of two years of professional work experience followed by two years in the HBS MBA Program.

FINANCIAL FACTS

Annual tuition	$61,225/
Fees	$11,087
% of students receiving aid	62
% of first-year students receiving aid	62
% of students receiving grants	46
Average award package	$69,200
Average grant	$35,100
Average loan	$48,000
Average student loan debt	$79,667

ADMISSIONS

Admissions Selectivity Rating	**99**
# of applications received	9,686
% applicants accepted	11
% acceptees attending	91
Range of GMAT	710–790
Accepts GRE scores	Yes
Average GPA	3.7
TOEFL required of international students	Yes
Minimum TOEFL (web)	109
Application fee	$250
International application fee	$250
Application Deadline/Notification	
Round 1:	9/9 / 12/9
Round 2:	1/6 / 3/30
Round 3:	4/4 / 5/11
Deferment available	No
Transfer students accepted	No
Non-fall admissions	No
Need-blind admissions	Yes

EMPLOYMENT PROFILE

Career Rating	99	Grads Employed by Function	% Avg. Salary
Percent employed at graduation	81	Marketing	(19%) $123,719
Percent employed 3 months after graduation	91	Operations	(2%) $117,822
		Consulting	(31%) $129,945
Average base starting salary	$131,646	Management	(14%) $118,923
		Finance	(29%) $146,993
		Other	(4%) $128,729

HEC Montréal
MBA Program

Academics

HEC Montréal is an internationally recognized business school that offers two program options: a renowned one-year full-time program in English or French, or a two-year part-time evening program in French only (though students may take some electives in English in order to improve their language capacity). Many permanent residents take advantage of the intense, cost-effective full-time program to get the "best bang for the buck" and then re-enter the work force with a HEC Montréal degree under their belts and a network of alumni to tap into.

This being an "extremely strenuous" one-year intensive program, "life is hectic." The school makes "excellent use of available slots to schedule seminars, meetings and workshops." The administration is "very available, well-run and supportive of student life." They are very clearly "there to make things easier for us," according to a student. Professors are similarly outstanding; faculty members are "almost 100 percent PhDs, with solid work experience" to boot, and are "very accessible and have a lot of business experience."

Career and Placement

A HEC Montréal MBA is a highly visible degree to have (particularly in the international business world). The school's ties with leading companies make for excellent recruiting options resulting in 88 percent of graduates finding employment within six months of graduation. The school's ties with leading companies make for excellent recruiting options, and there are many opportunities to take part in networking events and clubs—it's just a matter of "finding time around class and other work to do all the activities desired." "It is do-able, it just requires a lot of motivation and time," says an exhausted student. Top recent employers of HEC Montréal graduates include Bombardier, Deloitte, RBC Financial Group, Fidelity investment, and Telefilm Canada.

ADMISSIONS CONTACT: JULIE BENOIT, ADMINISTRATIVE DIRECTOR, MBA PROGRAM
ADDRESS: 3000, CHEMIN DE LA CÔTE-SAINTE-CATHERINE, MONTREAL, QC H3T 2A7
PHONE: 514-340-6957 • FAX: 514-340-7327
E-MAIL: MBA@HEC.CA • WEBSITE: WWW.HEC.CA

Student Life and Environment

This is a highly international group that "comes from all the continents." "I believe we do speak...more that fifteen to twenty different languages," says a student. People are "friendly" and "their experiences are very relevant," so "contribution is very important" and people always "work together and help each other." The life stages of each "very culturally diverse" class runs the gamut—some are married and well-entrenched in careers, some are single and just starting out—but there is "a great social life" and a "collegial atmosphere amongst fellow students and the facilities." The cafeteria, library, and classrooms are "very high quality," which "makes day-to-day life as comfortable as possible," and Montréal is "a great place to live" and spend time in the few free hours a student can squeak out.

Admissions

Admission to the MBA program at HEC Montréal is competitive; the school reports that it is "unable to accept all eligible candidates who apply" because class space is limited. Admissions decisions are based on academic record, professional experience (three years minimum required), standardized test scores (TAGE-MAGE or GMAT), letters of recommendation, interviews, and candidates' career objectives. Applicants must provide the school with official transcripts for all post-secondary academic work, a curriculum vitae, and an official score report for standardized tests. The application includes supplementary questions, to be answered in essay form. Applicants to the English-language fulltime intensive program must demonstrate English proficiency via testing (TOEFL, IELTS, or HEC Montréal's own HECTOPE) if their native language is not English. Non-native French speakers applying to the French-only program must complete the Test de français international (an ETS-administered exam). Applicants who are not citizens of Canada must obtain a certificat d'acceptation du Québec (C.A.Q.) and a document attesting to their right to reside in Canada (Student Authorization or Ministerial Permit). The school recommends that accepted students apply for these documents as soon as they receive confirmation of their admission to the program.

FINANCIAL FACTS

Annual tuition (in-state/ out-of-state)	$7,027/$29,150
Cost of books	$2,280
Room & board (on/off-campus)	$11,625/$16,250
% of students receiving aid	50
% of first-year students receiving aid	50
% of students receiving grants	50
Average award package	$330,000
Average grant	$5,000

ADMISSIONS

Admissions Selectivity Rating	**74**
# of applications received	477
% applicants accepted	38
% acceptees attending	90
Accepts GRE scores	Yes
TOEFL required of international students	Yes
Minimum TOEFL (web)	100
Application fee	$83
International application fee	$258
Early application deadline	6/1
Early notification date	8/15
Application Deadline/Notification	
Round 1:	6/1 / 8/15
Round 2:	9/1 / 10/15
Round 3:	10/15 / 11/30
Round 4:	1/15 / 2/15
Deferment available	Yes
Maximum length of deferment	1 year
Transfer students accepted	No
Non-fall admissions	Yes
Need-blind admissions	Yes

EMPLOYMENT PROFILE

Career Rating	90	Grads Employed by Function	% Avg. Salary
Percent employed at graduation	33	Marketing	(28%) $73,300
Percent employed 3 months after graduation	76	Operations	(12%) $74,700
		Consulting	(19%) $81,000
Average base starting salary	$75,000	Management	(22%) $79,900
Primary Source of Full-time Job Acceptances		Finance	(10%) $67,900
School-facilitated activities	(43%)	Other	(9%) $68,900
Graduate-facilitated activities	(27%)	**Top 5 Employers Hiring Grads**	
Unknown	(30%)	Deloitte (4), TD Bank Financial Group (3), Air Canada (2), Bombardier Aerospace (2), Pratt & Whitney Canada (2)	

HEC PARIS
HEC MBA PROGRAM

Academics

With a reputation in Europe that is "second to none," HEC Paris (located just outside the city) boasts a "stellar" faculty, a world class reputation, a double degree option, and a significant presence in niche areas such as Luxury and Sustainable Business that is not commonly found in other MBA programs. Following a curriculum overhaul, a truly "global and well-rounded view" of business is presented with a strong emphasis on case studies and group work.

The full-time HEC MBA lasts for twelve or sixteen months and is divided into two phases. During the Fundamental Phase, students gain a solid foundation in the core business subjects; in the customized phase, students choose to complete either a specialization or an international exchange (based upon their personal career objectives), and either a fieldwork project or "a wide range" of electives. HEC also offers other degrees and programs, and "the entire campus is well integrated," with an interconnection between Masters, MBAs, and Grande École students via the sharing of "a lot of activities" such as sports, clubs, and parties.

The MBA administration team is drawn from various nationalities and "reflects the school's international character"; it is "unlike usual French administrations" in that it is "quick, effective and listens to demands promptly." The school helps students in making visa and other travel arrangements, and "class representatives meet the administration on a regular basis." The dean's office is also "wide open," with specific time slots made available for students.

Career and Placement

The administration has "excellent outreach" to the "vast alumni network" (more than 50,000 graduates worldwide), calling upon them to meet with current students and act as guest speakers and ambassadors for the school. Companies come "from all over" to recruit at HEC, and the school has "one of the most widespread and global networks available." "I have contacted lots of alumni with an 80 percent plus response rate and willingness to help," says a student. Soft skills are highly stressed here, and "professors are very talented at ingraining the skills into the pupils," and there are also career management activities every Friday, which include presentation skills, mock interviews, and CV writing sessions.

A large number of students go on to work outside of France; many students are "multi-lingual, not just bi-lingual," but English is the only language required to attend HEC, as students say that "with intermediate French you can work almost everywhere." "You need French just to joke around with colleagues. Business is all English," says one. The much-appreciated duration of the program is "the perfect timing for a career change," and many students here have taken a pause from a former job in order to gain international exposure before going back into the work force.

Recent employers of HEC Paris graduates include Amazon, Goldman Sachs, McKinsey, Shell, and L'Oréal.

Student Life and Environment

This is a "very serious and career oriented" group, but the overall climate is "very friendly" and "the level of respect is very high among the participants in the program." Program participants are divided into "intakes" (read: season of admission), and with fifty countries represented at the school, the student body is "very diverse in experience and ethnicity." "The term minority doesn't apply at this school since students from every country/region are a minority." "It is really amazing how much we learn from other students by the simple fact the work teams are made, on purpose, of people whose background have nothing to do with each other's," says another.

The campus is located near the foothills of Jouy-en-Josas and has "a very large green area, a lake and plenty of [open space]." Coupled with "good and affordable" family housing, the school is a "great place to raise kids in a quiet and healthy environment." "Overall the quality of life here is outstanding if you enjoy living in a 'student bubble' type environment," says a student. Perhaps this accounts for the "great social life" between students, many of whom take weekend trips to other European destinations.

Admissions

The HEC Paris MBA admissions process is rigorous. First, each candidate is evaluated based on their standardized test scores and undergraduate performance, as well as quantitative factors as evidenced in their personal recommendations and work experience. After candidates have passed the first stage of review, they must attend two in-person interviews with HEC Alumni, HEC professors, or other HEC community members. Each of these interviews begins with a ten-minute presentation by the MBA candidate, followed by a question- and-answer session. Last year's entering class had an average GMAT score of 690, with a range between 640 and 730.

FINANCIAL FACTS

Annual tuition (in-state/ out-of-state)	$62,525/$62,525
% of students receiving grants	52
Average grant	$12,029

ADMISSIONS

Admissions Selectivity Rating	93
# of applications received	1,994
% applicants accepted	19
% acceptees attending	62
Average GMAT	690
Range of GMAT	660–710
Accepts GRE scores	Yes
Range of Quantitative GRE scores	1–1
TOEFL required of international students	Yes
Minimum TOEFL (paper/web)	600/100
Application fee	$200
International application fee	$200
Deferment available	Yes
Maximum length of deferment	Case-by-case basis
Transfer students accepted	No
Non-fall admissions	Yes
Need-blind admissions	Yes

EMPLOYMENT PROFILE			
Career Rating	**86**	**Grads Employed by Function% Avg. Salary**	
Average base starting salary	$121,080	Marketing	(15%)
		Operations	(13%)
		Consulting	(22%)
		Management	(17%)
		Finance	(14%)
		Other	(33%)
		Top 5 Employers Hiring Grads	
		Amazon, Apple, AT Kearney, Uber, Schneider Electric	

HHL Leipzig Graduate School of Management

Academics

According to the ecstatic students we spoke with, HHL Leipzig is "the best business school in Germany." While "best" might be difficult to qualify, the school certainly offers a stellar reputation along with an affordable price tag. MBA candidates here greatly appreciate the program's entrepreneurial focus and are also quick to highlight the "great strategy and finance departments." While the vast majority of professors are German, one graduating student assures us that he has "had visiting professors from all over the world." Students also find their teachers "very friendly, helpful, and competent." Additionally, many assert that professors are "flexible" and very "student oriented."

The HHL curriculum is interdisciplinary, focusing on leadership and global experience and takes an integrated management approach. Students must complete a core group of courses to gain a foundation in basic management concepts. They then select a number of electives of their choosing, ensuring expertise in a field of interest. Their education is capped by a master's thesis. Finally, students can either opt to complete the program in fifteen months or extend their studies up to twenty-one months.

Career and Placement

Graduates of HHL's MBA program find themselves privy to a great number of career opportunities. Many land employment with a myriad of prominent international consulting, commercial, industrial, and financial firms. A large range of companies regularly recruit at HHL for both internships and permanent positions. Impressively, 100 percent of German students, and 95 percent of international students find employment within three months of graduation. The Career Services Department facilitates this process by providing a variety of resources to their MBA candidates. Students can attend company presentations, interview trainings, and CV and cover letter writing workshops. They can also take assessment tests and receive assistance with career path modeling. There are also a handful of on-campus recruiting events, along with career fairs.

Employers that frequently hire HHL Leipzig graduates include Allianz AG, Amazon, Henkel KgaA, KPMG, Porsche, Roland Berger, eBay, adidas, Schott, Vorwerk, Kienbaum Management Consultants, PUMA, Carl Zeiss, Deloitte, Infosys, Robert Bosch, Deutsche Bank, A.T. Kearney, Rehau, Samsung, Intel, Triumph, Bertelsmann, Capgemini, and RWE.

Student Life and Environment

MBA students at HHL are generally fairly impressed with their classmates. Although they can be "competitive," they show a high level of "intellectual curiosity" and are "eager to contribute to team work." Not surprisingly, the school manages to net a "diverse" student body and one that is "open to different people and cultures." Additionally, students define their peers as "motivated" and "flexible" and people who "seek a challenge." The program yields a wide age range, and students are generally anywhere from twenty-four to forty years old. However, the average age is twenty-nine, and most have around five years of work experience. Despite the diversity, most agree that a "family environment" permeates the campus.

ADMISSIONS CONTACT: RALUCA MODOIU, STUDENT RECRUITMENT MBA
ADDRESS: JAHNALLEE 59, LEIPZIG, GERMANY 04109
PHONE: +49 341 - 9851 889 • FAX: +49 341 - 9851 615
E-MAIL: RALUCA.MODOIU@HHL.DE • WEBSITE: WWW.HHL.DE

Academics at HHL are demanding, and students "spend many hours at school." If they aren't in class, students can often be found attending "lectures, networking in the cafeteria, or slaving over group work." Of course, even these industrious souls need to kick back every now and again, and many classmates frequently "gather to have some drinks and share thoughts on business, economics, and politics."

Beautiful Leipzig also provides great distractions from business theory. A mere hour from Berlin by train, Leipzig is a cosmopolitan city in its own right. Considering that Bach, Mendelssohn, Wagner, and Goethe all lived there, it's no surprise that there is still a thriving arts scene. The city is home to the Gewandhaus Orchestra; the world famous St. Thomas Choir; and a variety of museums, cafes, restaurants, and nightclubs. And with more than 40,000 students, it's no wonder that this is a great place to study.

Admissions

Admissions officers at HHL Leipzig Graduate School of Management are on the hunt for applicants who demonstrate a global outlook and international experience. Exposure to other cultures will be paramount for any successful candidate. Applicants should have an undergraduate degree or the equivalent academic qualification and three years of professional experience prior to starting the program. In addition to transcripts, the admissions committee also closely examines GMAT scores, curriculum vitae (maximum three pages), documents confirming employment, a motivation letter, and two letters of recommendation. Applicants who reside in countries that do not offer the GMAT may instead submit GRE scores as a substitute. Further, students who hail from non-English speaking countries must prove proficiency through either the TOEFL or IELTS. However, there are exceptions. Non-native English speakers do not have to submit test scores if they either earned an undergraduate or postgraduate degree from an English-speaking program or if they have lived or worked in an English speaking country for more than six months in the last two years. Finally, it should be noted that some non-EU residents face an earlier application deadline due to visa requirements. This does not affect applicants from Australia, Israel, Japan, the United States, Canada, and New Zealand.

FINANCIAL FACTS

Annual tuition (in-state/ out-of-state)	$16,000/$16,000
Fees	$180
Cost of books	$150
Room & board	$8,000
% of students receiving aid	30
% of first-year students receiving aid	55
% of students receiving grants	15
Average award package	$20,500
Average grant	$11,000
Average loan	$30,000

ADMISSIONS

Admissions Selectivity Rating	84
# of applications received	150
% applicants accepted	49
% acceptees attending	45
Average GMAT	630
Range of GMAT	550–780
Accepts GRE scores	Yes
TOEFL required of international students	Recommended
Minimum TOEFL (paper/web)	580/96
Application fee	$0
International application fee	$0
Early application deadline	1/31
Early notification date	2/20
Regular application deadline	6/30
Regular application notification	7/20
Application Deadline/Notification	
Deferment available	Yes
Maximum length of deferment	One intake
Transfer students accepted	Yes
Transfer application policy Double Degree agreements with international partners	
Non-fall admissions	Yes
Need-blind admissions	Yes

EMPLOYMENT PROFILE

Career Rating	74	Grads Employed by Function% Avg. Salary	
Percent employed at graduation	76	Marketing	(19%)
Percent employed 3 months after graduation	19	Operations	(10%)
		Consulting	(19%)
Primary Source of Full-time Job Acceptances		Management	(14%)
School-facilitated activities	5 (24%)	Finance	(14%)
Graduate-facilitated activities	21 (76%)	HR	(5%)
		MIS	(5%)
		Other	(14%)
		Top 5 Employers Hiring Grads	
		PwC (2), Bombardier (1), Sandoz (1), Allianz (1), Metro (1)	

HOFSTRA UNIVERSITY
FRANK G. ZARB SCHOOL OF BUSINESS

GENERAL INFORMATION
Type of school	Private
Affiliation	No Affiliation
Academic calendar	Semester

SURVEY SAYS...
Liberal students, Happy students
Solid preparation in:
Marketing, General management,
Presentation skills, Doing business in
a global economy

STUDENTS
Enrollment of parent institution	10,814
Enrollment of MBA Program	875
% male/female	55/45
% out-of-state	77
% part-time	92
% underrepresented minority	10
% international	75
Average age at entry	26
Average years work experience at entry	6

ACADEMICS
Academic Experience Rating	**85**
Profs interesting rating	89
Profs accessible rating	91
Student/faculty ratio	8:1
% female faculty	23
% underrepresented minority faculty	26
% part-time faculty	50

Joint Degrees
JD/MBA, 4 yrs; BBA/MBA, 5 yrs;
BBA/MS, 5 yrs.

Prominent Alumni
Kathryn Marinello, CEO & Chairman
- Stream Global Services Inc.;
Director - General Motors; Steven
Freiberg, Senior Advisor - The
Boston Consulting Group; Shawn
Matthews, CEO - Cantor Fitzgerald;
Daniel Henry, American Express
Foreign Exchange - Executive VP
& Chief Financial Officer; Michael
Roberge, President and Chief
Investment Officer - Massachusetts
Financial Services Co.

Academics

Located just a hop and skip away from New York City, the Hofstra University Frank G. Zarb School of Business provides a well-regarded degree that benefits from proximity to a thriving industry center and the student population that works within it. Individuals can choose from a Part-Time, Full-Time, Online, or Executive MBA, and the school now offers an accelerated hybrid online-onsite MBA program in Manhattan. Resources are plentiful and growing; the school has one of the nation's largest academic trading rooms, equipped with thirty-four Bloomberg terminals, and a partnership with Northwell Health feeds its strong health care program (and is a major working student source).

Students admit that "diverse backgrounds . . . enhance the learning experience," and faculty and administrators "are very responsive to any issues which students present." As far as faculty makeup, the school "has done a great job in blending high quality full-time faculty with excellent high profile leaders from the private sector in part-time adjunct roles." This has given classes a great balance of academic and real-world knowledge, and students receive "an unparalleled opportunity for a window into the current business environment at a high level and also a great chance for networking." "I feel such arrangements with the private sector provide for a tremendous learning experience as well as exposure for potential future employment," says one. "Participation is an essential component to each and every class," and professors "are very friendly and treat students as adults."

Career and Placement

New York is the unspoken co-captain of the Frank G. Zarb School of Business, and access to the city's leaders, jobs, and internships is an automatic leg up for all Hofstra students. The Career Services department provides a great deal of support for job seekers and holders, including counseling, job and internship search coaching, career development workshops, résumé and cover letter critiques, and salary negotiation. The Graduate Executive Speakers Series offers students opportunities to network and "is a definite plus that allows students to listen and interact with business leaders." There is "a constant invitation to participate in school-sponsored activities," and the administration is "organized and collaborative" for all requests for career assistance. The average starting salary for a Zarb graduate is $55,714, with the majority of students going into the financial services industry. Recent employers of Zarb graduates include Cablevision, Charles Schwab, KPMG, the MTA, Viacom, and UPS.

ADMISSIONS CONTACT: SUNIL SAMUEL, ASSISTANT VICE PRESIDENT OF ADMISSION
ADDRESS: 126 HOFSTRA UNIVERSITY, 105 MEMORIAL HALL, HEMPSTEAD, NY 11549
PHONE: 800-463-7672 • FAX: 516-463-4664
E-MAIL: GRADUATEADMISSION@HOFSTRA.EDU • WEBSITE: WWW.HOFSTRA.EDU/BUSINESS

Student Life and Environment

This group of "ambitious, self motivated business professionals" is clearly "looking to enhance their skill sets in all aspects of business and networking." The majority of students are professionals who work full-time while also taking on a full course load, so socializing outside of classroom projects is not common, and no one really has an issue with it. "Most of the American students tend to work together in groups" (as do the Chinese students), but all are "dedicated and supportive." "Students recognize that cultural competency and diversity are essential to success in the global business environment," and interactions between students are all friendly and positive.

Admissions

Most of Hofstra's graduate business programs begin accepting applications in the fall or spring term. Students are evaluated based on their undergraduate academic performance, professional experience, leadership potential, letters of recommendation, and GMAT or GRE scores. The 25th to 75th percentile range of GPA scores for admitted students was 3.05 to 3.60, and the range for GMAT scores was 530 to 600. High-achieving students (having a minimum GMAT score of 600 and an undergraduate GPA of 3.3 or above as well as having maintained a 3.3 GPA or higher every semester they are in the program) have the option of applying as an Honors Scholar, a title that will be conferred at graduation.

FINANCIAL FACTS

Annual tuition (in-state/ out-of-state)	$21,924/$21,924
Fees	$970
Cost of books	$4,375
Room & board (on/off-campus)	$17,930/$17,830
% of students receiving aid	85
% of first-year students receiving aid	88
% of students receiving grants	76
Average award package	$10,237
Average grant	$6,231

ADMISSIONS

Admissions Selectivity Rating	80
# of applications received	1,604
% applicants accepted	75
% acceptees attending	27
Average GMAT	563
Range of GMAT	530–600
Accepts GRE scores	Yes
Average GPA	3.3
TOFFL required of international students	Yes
Minimum TOEFL (paper/web)	550/80
Application fee	$75
International application fee	$75
Application Deadline/Notification	
Deferment available	Yes
Maximum length of deferment	1 year
Transfer students accepted	Yes
Transfer application policy	
Number of transferable credits is limited to a maximum of 9 credits.	
Non-fall admissions	Yes
Need-blind admissions	Yes

EMPLOYMENT PROFILE

Career Rating	80	Grads Employed by Function% Avg. Salary	
Percent employed at graduation	29	Marketing	(8%) $50,000
Percent employed 3 months after graduation	19	Finance	(38%) $55,484
		MIS	(46%) $59,167
Average base starting salary	$55,571	Other	(8%) $40,000
Primary Source of Full-time Job Acceptances		Top 5 Employers Hiring Grads	
School-facilitated activities	4 (27%)	Cablevision (1), Nassau University Medical	
Graduate-facilitated activities	9 (60%)	Center (1), OpenLink Financial LLC (1),	
Unknown	2 (13%)	Janover LLC (1), WeiserMazars LLP (1)	

HONG KONG U. OF SCIENCE AND TECHNOLOGY
HKUST BUSINESS SCHOOL

Academics

Business students looking to catch a ride on the Asian economic boom would do well to consider The Hong Kong University of Science and Technology (HKUST), the "top MBA school in Asia" with a "strategic location at the heart of Asia." "The focus of the program is on the region," and the program is in "a perfect location to leverage Asia's booming economy." "Ever since my studies, I have had the ambition to prepare myself for a career in the Asian region," one student says, explaining the decision to attend HKUST. HKUST employs a "very strong teaching facility in finance" and an "intense academic atmosphere." "The MBA office has some major gaps to cover, but it is clearly trying to improve itself to better serve the MBA students."

Academics at HKUST can be intense, and the "workload is a killer." "We need 100+ hours a week" to complete homework, classes, group projects, discussion, and club activities, according to one student. Although students also note that "the school is very supportive." The Administration "must be the friendliest and [most] helpful bunch of people I have ever met."

Despite the problems students have with the MBA office, they are much happier with the professors. "Overall the school has brilliant teachers that are balanced between academia and business experience," offering a "nice blend of practitioners from the East, business professionals from the West, and academics." "I was initially worried about joining a business school based in Hong Kong because of perceived language barriers," one student explains. "Thankfully, I never faced such a challenge because all the professors were educated from the top business schools in the United States, and as a result, their communication skills are exceptionally good." Some of the "business leaders in Asia" who the school boasts as faculty include WalMart China's former president, PepsiCo Asia's former president, and the GM of Hutchinson Whampoa's Investment and Head Legal Counsel.

Career and Placement

"Hong Kong is the best transition point to the China market," and HKUST provides lots of help for students to get in on the action. "As a European with work experience in North America, I wanted to become part of the Asian growth story," one student says. "What better place could there be than the leading Asian business school!" HKUST takes students on trips to different cities and even countries in the region, such as Beijing or Singapore, to get students acquainted with the Asian style of business. The business school also stations representatives in Beijing, Shanghai, and Shenzhen. The HKUST career team constantly offers workshops, networking opportunities, one-on-one career coaching sessions, and many other services to help students begin careers.

HKUST is best "known for finance," and 45 percent of graduates accept a job in finance or accounting. Some students say HKUST "needs to improve on other career tracks." For example, there are "very few courses on marketing." Students also wish the school had a better brand recognition outside of Asia. "I really think the key for the school is to build a stronger brand," one student says. "I heard from exchange students from U.S. top schools that our classes are comparable." Eighty-one percent of students found employment within three months of graduation, and their average base salary was $93,500 in U.S. dollars. Some companies that have recruited from HKUST include ANZ, Banco Santaner, Barclays, Cisco, Citi, DuPont, Google, IMS Consulting, J.P. Morgan, Li & Fung, LinkedIN, Microsoft, Nomura, Samsung, and Walmart.

ADDRESS: CLEARWATER BAY, HKUST KOWLOON, HONG KONG
PHONE: 852-2358-7539 • FAX: 852-2705-9596
E-MAIL: MBA@UST.HK • WEBSITE: WWW.MBA.UST.HK

Student Life and Environment

HKUST boasts a very diverse student body, as the school "attracts students from all over the world. "On any given day, we have at least around fifteen to twenty nationalities represented in class." "Ninety-seven percent of students are from overseas," and the school is a veritable "United Nations." This means students approach school in different ways. "Westerners are very liberal" at HKUST, while "there are many students from China, who have a somewhat more conservative approach." The school has "more than ten clubs and often has different activities," which makes "life at HKUST really interesting and fascinating." Students like to "participate in different social events, like doing charity work, mingling with students of other schools, and having dinner with alumni." "Half of the students are more into social networking, and half are not very sociable," suggests one student. Students spend most of their time doing work, and "sleeping fewer than five hours is common" in the fall.

"The campus is amazing" and "located next to the bay," offering great views from dorm room windows. "Sports facilities available are great, including soccer pitch, track, in/outdoor pools, in/outdoor basketball, tennis, ping pong, squash, weight lifting, wall climbing, volleyball, and badminton." Some students say dorm "facilities are worn out," and business students should try to live off campus. "The student housing is meant for undergraduates. There are only two bathrooms shared by the whole floor." MBA students will begin to move to a larger and nicer dorm in 2014.

Admissions

Students applying to HKUST need to have an undergraduate degree and at least two years of work experience. The average GMAT score for accepted students is between 610 and 736. Having an interest in Asian culture and Asian business markets doesn't hurt either.

FINANCIAL FACTS

Annual tuition (in-state/ out-of-state)	$69,900/$69,900
Cost of books	$1,300
Room & board (on/off-campus)	$9,500/$20,000

ADMISSIONS

Admissions Selectivity Rating	83
# of applications received	610
% applicants accepted	58
% acceptees attending	65
Average GMAT	636
Range of GMAT	590–690
Accepts GRE scores	Yes
TOEFL required of international students	Yes
Minimum TOEFL (paper/web)	600/100
International Application Deadline/Notification	
Round 1:	11/13 / 2/6
Round 2:	1/13 / 4/10
Round 3:	3/13 / 6/5
Deferment available	Yes
Maximum length of deferment	1 year
Transfer students accepted	No
Non-fall admissions	No

EMPLOYMENT PROFILE

Career Rating	80	Grads Employed by Function% Avg. Salary	
Percent employed 3 months after graduation	71	Marketing	(10%)
		Consulting	(18%)
		Management	(14%)
		Finance	(34%)
		HR	(2%)
		MIS	(2%)
		Other	(20%)

HOWARD UNIVERSITY
SCHOOL OF BUSINESS

Academics

Students at Howard University School of Business feel confident that their degree will earn them the right position after graduation. Job placement is one of the school's greatest strengths, and "with the economy in the state that it is, it is imperative that you attend a university that will help you get employment." An education at Howard provides students with "access to top-level managers within the business world and... out-of-class preparedness for the real world of business." "The school has a far-reaching network and reputation, and also provides opportunities to its students that are on par with top 20 MBA programs."

Many know Howard University as the "most prestigious African American University in the country." Being a part of the school's "strong legacy" is important to many and also a source of pride to carry the Howard "brand name." The School of Business "provides a wealth of opportunities to students," and perhaps some of the "best opportunities for minority students." "From CEO lectures, Fortune 500 companies recruiting daily on campus, and various opportunities abroad, the program is able to provide a well-rounded MBA experience."

"Howard University School of Business is a very unique learning environment." "Everyone in the program is striving for excellence." A student explains the value of her classmate's energy and excitement towards learning. "I look forward to every class because it's...intellectually stimulating." Intimate classes add to the quality of learning and overall strength of the program. "Due to the size of the program the students are extremely close and supportive." High quality learning is possible thanks to professors that are "extremely personable and more than willing to go out of their way to assist students." Outside of classes, professors "are always approachable and are actively interested in how their subject directly relates to the students internships and future career goals so they can do their best to prepare students for their bright futures."

Thankfully, the obstacle of cost is surpassed for many here as "Howard provides a significant amount of financial assistance to its students." "When you consider that some high-performing students are able to earn half or full tuition coverage, there is even more value added to the degree." "The academic experience can be difficult to balance at times as most students are involved in some form of extracurricular activities." What makes all the hard work and money Howard students spend worthwhile are the "high returns expected from the investment." With all the "access to networks and recruiters, and global travel opportunities, the program does deliver considerable value for an MBA."

Although students would mostly agree that "school administration have an invested interest in our success," several opined that they "could be more efficient." Other areas that students thought could use improvement include, "technology capabilities of classroom[s] and aging buildings."

Career and Placement

Many students appreciate career services for their "outstanding program" and "great networking opportunities." One student says these services are "the best I've seen around, they create opportunities after opportunities." Not only do they do "a fantastic job placing their students with internships and careers," they also have in place a "strong alumni network." Students receive "tons of emails from the University staff about internship and full-time employment opportunities." They report "plenty of social and networking opportunities," and appreciate the "several programs [organized] by the school to develop [their] leadership skills." These include required monthly leadership development workshops "that help with job preparation, search, placement, and achievement," as well as "an executive lecture series every semester where the CEOs of large corporations come and speak with us and we are able to network with them."

Besides Howard's "corporate connections" and "resources available in Washington, D.C.," students are "impressed with the variety of recruiters that visit the school with a sincere interest in the MBA students (particularly in the Supply Chain Management program)." Top Businesses recently hiring Howard graduate students include UTC, Dell, AT Kearney, DuPont, General Motors, and JP Morgan Chase. "The recruitment here for minority talent is unparalleled." This student definitely agrees and declares, "I am confident that I will secure the job that want when I graduate."

Student Life and Environment

"The life as a graduate student in Howard University is filled with work as well as fun." The school offers a good amount of "student activities and community involvement." The student body consists of a "creative, organized, and motivated" bunch who are eager to "change the future of business." This dedication shows by their commitment to serve "on Boards and associations throughout DC, MD and VA"; and even though, "there is a healthy competition among classmates," it does not deter from the "family" environment that exists around the school. "We are all focused on being successful but just as interested in doing what we can to ensure our classmates are making the right connections and prepared to succeed as well. We all want our class to continue Howard's legacy of producing competent and successful minority students."

Admissions

Along with an application, prospective students must submit GMAT or GRE scores, official transcripts for all undergraduate and graduate course work, three letters of recommendation from at least one academic and one professional supervisor, a personal statement describing the applicant's abilities, experiences, and goals in pursuing the MBA, undergraduate GPA, and proof of at least two years of significant post-collegiate professional or managerial experience. Applicants must have completed business or applied calculus at the undergraduate college level in order to be admitted. International applicants must also submit a Statement of Financial Resources.

FINANCIAL FACTS

Annual tuition (in-state/ out-of-state)	$33,166/$33,166
Fees	$1,233
Cost of books	$5,000
Room & board (on/off-campus)	$21,518/$21,518
% of students receiving aid	95
% of first-year students receiving aid	83
% of students receiving grants	58
Average award package	$48,643
Average grant	$26,548
Average loan	$29,459
Average student loan debt	$47,661

ADMISSIONS

Admissions Selectivity Rating	85
# of applications received	94
% applicants accepted	47
% acceptees attending	75
Average GMAT	494
Range of GMAT	410–590
Accepts GRE scores	Yes
Average GPA	3.28
TOEFL required of international students	Yes
Minimum TOEFL (paper/web)	550/79
Application fee	$75
International application fee	$75
Early application deadline	11/15
Early notification date	1/1
Regular application deadline	4/1
Regular application notification	5/1
Application Deadline/Notification	
Round 1:	11/15 / 1/1
Round 2:	2/1 / 3/1
Round 3:	4/1 / 5/1
Deferment available	Yes
Maximum length of deferment	2 semesters
Transfer students accepted	Yes
Transfer application policy Must meet Howard's MBA Program Admission Criteria; can only transfer a maximum of 6.0 credit hours from an AACSB-accredited Graduate Business Program.	
Non-fall admissions	Yes
Need-blind admissions	Yes

EMPLOYMENT PROFILE

Career Rating	94	**Grads Employed by Function% Avg. Salary**	
Percent employed at graduation	87	Marketing	(18%) $96,667
Percent employed 3 months after graduation	96	Operations	(40%) $103,580
		Finance	(5%) $90,000
Average base starting salary	$95,824	HR	(14%) $97,333
Primary Source of Full-time Job Acceptances		MIS	(9%) $90,000
School-facilitated activities	17 (77%)	**Top 5 Employers Hiring Grads**	
Graduate-facilitated activities	5 (23%)	American Airlines, General Motors (3), Technologies (2), Dupont (2), Accenture (2), Raytheon (2)	

IAE BUSINESS SCHOOL
MANAGEMENT AND BUSINESS SCHOOL

GENERAL INFORMATION
Type of school   Private
Affiliation   No Affiliation

SURVEY SAYS...
Good peer network, Happy students
Solid preparation in:
Finance, General management

STUDENTS
Enrollment of MBA Program	48
% male/female	69/31
% underrepresented minority	15
% international	35
Average age at entry	28
Average years work experience at entry	5

ACADEMICS
Academic Experience Rating	**72**
Profs interesting rating	77
Profs accessible rating	62
% female faculty	9
% underrepresented minority faculty	16

Academics

Located in Pilar, Argentina, IAE Business School's intensive MBA programs maintain an "excellent reputation in Argentina and throughout Latin America," a strong global focus throughout the curriculum, and "regionally-related" course material for those interested in Latin American business. The rigorous, multicultural, bilingual program (classes are taught in Spanish and English) has been honed over time to provide a quality education to its students. As the school's website states, the one-year MBA program "is the result of the thirty-five-year experience IAE has acquired in providing part-time Executive MBA programs and the contributions of many years.

IAE's one-year MBA has a daily schedule that runs from 9:00 A.M. to 6:00 P.M. The program begins with a leveling course, during which students are reacquainted with fundamental quantitative skills in statistics, mathematics, and accounting. After completing these basic proficiencies, students begin the core curriculum, which focuses on three areas: technical skills; critical thinking skills that teaches you new ways to approach both professional and personal problems; and teamwork skills. The school also offers several elective courses, as well as a Team Building and Outdoor Activities module, designed to promote problem-solving skills in a playful environment. Throughout the MBA, international business and Latin American business context are emphasized. The school's international student body adds depth and perspective to the discussion on global issues.

Students speak highly of the program, describing their professors as "excellent, friendly and student-oriented." "Most of them have PhDs, and they have a lot of patience. They always are able to help you inside and outside the class." A student adds, "They are always available to answer the questions or [have] meetings to study specific and interesting topics." The program runs smoothly, and this ease is especially important given the amount of work that the MBA requires. As one MBA notes, "The administration provides exceptional service. It is well prepared for the needs of its classmates: Everything we need is available for us." Perhaps most important, "IAE has very good contacts with businesses in Latin America, and a very important aspect is that it provides us with academic and executive mentors."

Career and Placement

The Career Services Department at IAE works with students and companies to facilitate recruitment and placement. Among other services, they offer mentoring programs, on-campus interviews, individual and group career counseling, and career development workshops. Despite the school's international focus, students report that "the department is underdeveloped, especially in the international job market." The alumni network, on the other hand, "is unbelievable," according to students; one reports, "I could speak to many important executives from the best companies in country because they were alumni." Today, IAE graduates are working in diverse countries, including Germany, Malaysia, the United States, Mexico, and Puerto Rico. Employers who have worked with IAE include Eli Lilly, Glaxo Smithkline (GSK), Kimberly Clark, Halliburton, Philips, Grupo Assa, Novo Nordisk, Thomson Reuters, Mapfre, Johnson & Johnson, Maersk, entre otras.

FINANCIAL FACTS	
Annual tuition	$17,000/

ADMISSIONS	
Admissions Selectivity Rating	83
# of applications received	111
% applicants accepted	57
% acceptees attending	76
Average GMAT	618
TOEFL required of international students	Yes

Student Life and Environment

IAE's campus "is located in Pilar, fifty kilometers from Buenos Aires" the capitol of Argentina, in a beautiful setting with a lot of trees, flowers, and greenery everywhere. The campus building and facilities are incredible, providing all the technical resources needed and, in the surrounding community, you can find everything near the campus: a mall, restaurants, supermarkets, movies, gas stations, etc. Campus facilities include areas where students "can play soccer, tennis, and rugby during the two-hour lunch break." Big-city life isn't too far off, as "the campus is one hour away from Buenos Aires." Students note, however, that "since IAE's program is a one-year MBA, the workload is so heavy that there is very little time to do activities outside the classroom." Classes convene from 9:00 A.M. to 6:00 P.M.; most students "study until 9:00 P.M., then have some dinner with friends," and stop for the day. Despite the rigors of the program, "the nice environment, people, and landscape make you enjoy every moment."

Drawing a largely international student body, only about 54 percent of IAE's MBA students are Argentine; the remaining 46 percent of students come from other parts of Latin America, Europe, and the United States. Students are drawn from all sectors, including marketing, banking, consulting, engineering, services, and even agriculture. Students are "very different but open-minded," and universally described as "very supportive" of their classmates. In addition to their professional prowess, most "have great senses of humor, don't hesitate to help one another, and enjoy hanging out."

Admissions

Experience is very important to IAE Business School, Universidad Austral. Applicants to the full-time MBA program at IAE Business School must have at least three years of post-undergraduate work experience and be at least twenty-five years old. The admissions department requires all of the following materials: official transcripts for all post-secondary academic work; an official GMAT score report with a minimum score of 550; a resume; personal essays; letters of recommendation; a completed application form; and, for students whose first language is not English, a minimum TOEFL score of IBT 88, CBT 230 and PBT 570. IAE also offers its own skills exam, the IAE Test, which can be taken in lieu of the GMAT and is only scheduled by previous appointment on campus or online.

EMPLOYMENT PROFILE			
Career Rating	61	Grads Employed by Function% Avg. Salary	
Average base starting salary	$17,000	Marketing	(13%)
		Operations	(6%)
		Consulting	(11%)
		Finance	(4%)
		HR	(4%)

IDAHO STATE UNIVERSITY
COLLEGE OF BUSINESS

GENERAL INFORMATION
Type of school   Public
Affiliation   No Affiliation
Academic calendar   Semester

SURVEY SAYS...
Friendly students, Happy students
Solid preparation in:
Accounting, General management

STUDENTS
Enrollment of parent
  institution   13,977
Enrollment of MBA Program   110
% male/female   74/26
% part-time   52
% underrepresented minority   8
% international   15
Average age at entry   30
Average years work
  experience at entry   0

ACADEMICS
Academic Experience Rating   **66**
Profs interesting rating   71
Profs accessible rating   71
Student/faculty ratio   23:1
% female faculty   20
% underrepresented
  minority faculty   2
% part-time faculty   0

Academics

The College of Business at Idaho State University offers MBA classes in two locations: on its main campus in Pocatello and at a satellite location in Idaho Falls. Students love the convenience and the cost of the program; many laud the "great return on investment" represented by an ISU MBA. One student notes that the Idaho Falls location is "very convenient for professionals working for or with Idaho National Laboratory." Evening-only classes at the location make the program even more convenient (the school notes that some emphasis areas require students to take some daytime classes).

"Class sizes are small and the professors are always available outside of class" at ISU, where "everyone is on a first-name basis with the professors and the atmosphere is laid back yet still professional." One student writes, "I have been pleasantly surprised with the quality of teachers and students that are a part of this program. I feel that the teachers genuinely care about the success of the students and their understanding and application of the material. The students come with years of experience and willingly and benefi-cially contribute to the material taught." The curriculum here, while "challenging, is backed by a supportive network of professors and students. Relying on help outside of class in the way of face-to-face meetings and study groups makes the experience much more successful."

ISU offers a general MBA as well as MBAs with emphasis areas in accounting, computer information systems, management, marketing, finance, and health care administration. Students tell us that "finance and accounting are very strong at Idaho State University." As for the future, students report that the administration is "doing a good job of moving the university towards a good goal—a medical school—which is what they were hired to do." Look for the health care administration segment of this program to grow as the school continues in this direction.

Career and Placement

MBAs at Idaho State University receive career services from the Career Development Center, which serves all undergraduates, graduates, and alumni at ISU. The office pro-vides career counseling, career testing, internship referrals, student employment oppor-tunities, alumni connections, workshops in job search skills, resume review, on-campus interviews, and job fairs. Students tell us that the school needs to "attract recruiters from world-class companies for all areas of emphasis. It seems like the accounting depart-ment does well but that other areas of emphasis are lacking these contacts." One MBA observes: "There are not that many recruiters from outside of southeast Idaho at job fairs. This is especially a problem for the MBA students who most likely will be looking for jobs prior to and immediately after graduation."

Student Life and Environment

Idaho State University's main campus is located in Pocatello, a city with a population of about 50,000. ON Semiconductor, Alliance Title and Escrow, and the university are among the city's largest employers. Students tout the "small-town feel of the town," noting the "low crime rate and conservative values." The location provides easy access to outdoor recreation, and "most people enjoy outdoor activities on the weekend such as skiing, snowmobiling, hiking, etc." The school also offers MBA classes in Idaho Falls, a city whose motto "Where Great Adventures Begin" highlights its proximity to such attractions as Grand Teton National Park and Yellowstone National Park. Idaho National Laboratory is by far the city's biggest employer with about 7,500 employees. Healthcare, education, government, and retail are the city's other primary employers.

ADMISSIONS CONTACT: SAM PETERSON, MBA DIRECTOR
ADDRESS: STOP 8020, 921 S 8TH AVE, POCATELLO, ID 83209
PHONE: 208-282-2966 • FAX: 208-236-4367
E-MAIL: PETESAM@ISU.EDU • WEBSITE: COB.ISU.EDU

Students appreciate that "ISU is very facilitating to married families," with "an incredibly family-friendly campus. There's plenty of family housing on campus and a huge day care center." Their only complaint is that "facilities are outdated." "The building is slightly in need of renovation," one student explains. Another points out that "the university has taken steps to modernize the college's building and its miscellaneous resources such as computer labs and information networks," but even she concedes that a facilities overhaul is in order.

"Most students are non-traditional students" here. This "is true of the undergraduate classes and the graduate ones. Since most students have spouses and children, college life is not as exciting as one may expect." MBA candidates "generally have at least two or three years of work experience since receiving their undergraduate degree" and are "focused and serious about learning." They tend to be typically conservative Idahoans, but "a politically liberal transplant from a West Coast city" in their midst assures that "it was easy to form great relationships with my conservative classmates."

Admissions

Applicants to the CoB MBA program at Idaho State University must apply for admission to the university Graduate School and must also meet additional CoB admissions requirements. A completed application includes: official transcripts for all post-secondary academic work; an official GMAT score report; a current resume; and two letters of recommendation. A score of at least 1150 under the formula [(200 x GPA for final 60 semester hours of undergraduate work) + GMAT score] is required for consideration; those meeting this requirement are not guaranteed admission. Applicants holding a master's degree from an accredited institution may have the GMAT requirement waived. International applicants must also submit a statement of financial support and an official score report for either the TOEFL or the IELTS. Minimum required scores: 80, Internet-based test; 213 with a 21 on Section 1, computer-based test; 550 with a score of at least 55 on Section 1, paper-based test; or 6.5, IELTS.

FINANCIAL FACTS

Annual tuition (in-state/ out-of-state)	$5,848/$15,650
Cost of books	$1,000
Room & board (on/off-campus)	$7,500/$7,500
Average grant	$0
Average loan	$0

ADMISSIONS

Admissions Selectivity Rating	**81**
# of applications received	73
% applicants accepted	75
% acceptees attending	60
Average GMAT	540
Range of GMAT	480–580
Average GPA	3.5
TOEFL required of international students	Yes
Minimum TOEFL (paper)	550
Application fee	$55
International application fee	$55
Regular application deadline	7/1
Regular application notification	7/7
Application Deadline/Notification	
Deferment available	Yes
Maximum length of deferment	2 yrs
Transfer students accepted	Yes
Transfer application policy 9 credits max, from an AACSB program.	
Non-fall admissions	Yes
Need-blind admissions	No

EMPLOYMENT PROFILE

Career Rating	69
Percent employed at graduation	47
Average base starting salary	$59,000

ILLINOIS INSTITUTE OF TECHNOLOGY
STUART SCHOOL OF BUSINESS

Academics

The Stuart School of Business at Chicago's Illinois Institute of Technology (Illinois Tech) recognizes the diverse needs of its students and "focuses on innovation" in order to accommodate them all. While the full-time MBA is typically completed over three years, working professionals with a minimum of five years of work experience that are looking to expedite their MBAs can enroll in the school's part-time Accelerated MBA. Those who want to pursue their degrees while continuing to work can take their MBA part-time in the evenings at the Downtown campus.

Illinois Tech is a world-class research institution, and, not surprisingly, Stuart MBAs benefit from the presence of the high-powered academics here and the "excellent research opportunities." Three research centers—the Center for Financial Innovation, the Center for Strategic Competitiveness, and the Center for Strategic Finance—offer unique options to adventurous MBAs. There is even an optional specialization in sustainability that trains students "to identify, develop, communicate, and help implement practical and equitable business strategies that advance the ecological sustainability of the Chicago area, while fostering current and future economic viability." Stuart was recently ranked among the world's leaders in incorporating sustainability management.

Many here, however, prefer more traditional fare. Stuart MBAs laud the School's entrepreneurship program, as well as offerings in finance and marketing. Quite a few full-time students take advantage of dual-degree programs in law, design, finance, or public administration. Throughout the curriculum, students praise the use of technology and real-life examples, and the fact that "presentation skills and teamwork are highly celebrated and nurtured." The "superb" Stuart professors "are always willing to help and provide out-of-the-classroom tutorials and further explanations." Plus, they always "challenge students to do their best." "I have never met another group so willing to teach," says a student. However, at this level, "there is no 'spoon feeding'; students have to do their research on their own and learn the skills to do so." Similarly, administrators "are extremely helpful and go out of their way to get to know each student personally and help anyone."

With Illinois Tech's small cohorts, there is no crowding in the school's computer labs or the "vast library," which offers a "very huge online research library and article access and excellent infrastructure." For many, though, "the school's greatest strength is its strategic location," as downtown Chicago is "an amazing place to study and grants access to businesses around the school and access to socialize, not only with fellow students, but with professionals in the vicinity." About the only weakness here, students tell us, is that "the school should do more marketing of itself, and Career Services should do more on its networking with employers."

Career and Placement

The Career Management Center at the Stuart School provides students with one-on-one career counseling, workshops in interviewing and resume preparation, and research on companies and opportunities appropriate to each student's goals. Student self-assessment tools help the office tailor its services to the individual needs of each MBA, and for the part-timers, "the course work flows very easily with full-time work obligations." The university at large conducts career fairs through its Career Services.

Employers who most frequently hire Stuart MBAs include Northern Trust, Bank of America, ABN-Amro, Lucent Technologies, JPMorgan, Navistar, Johnson & Johnson, Capital One, Vankampen, US EPA, Reuters, Motorola, Inc., and CME Group. About half of all Stuart MBAs remain in the Midwest after graduation.

Student Life and Environment

Illinois Tech's main MBA programs are located "in a separate building in downtown Chicago. That building houses law, design, and business school students only, so there isn't much activity there really, just serious-looking students walking to and fro." Still, "the open-space layout of the building and the open-minded students allow for students to be able to talk, ask questions or even ask one another to watch their stuff while they go use the restroom." The main campus has more life, including "amenities for kids and spouses," and there is a free shuttle to transport students between campuses. MBA students participate in "lots of study groups, there are socials many Wednesdays and "there is plenty of time for students to be involved in extracurricular activities." The way that Stuart is designed, there are also "many opportunities to network both inside and out of school through events," and a "high level of trust, cooperation, and communication among students."

The student body includes many "young, hardworking, and individualistic" students, who have considerable work experience, and it is "highly diverse," meaning that students are "very accepting of different cultures and backgrounds." One student observes, "The diverse population aids in creating a learning experience unlike any other. Students learn as much (if not more) outside the classroom than in the classroom, just by interacting with everyone around them." When they can find the time, students love to take advantage of "the world's biggest financial city," which also offers plenty in the way of culture, entertainment, fine dining, and nightlife. Again, it comes back to location. "Stuart is located near the Chicago Loop in the midst of big-name business companies, allowing for excellent networking and job opportunities. It's also very close to public transportation."

Admissions

The Illinois Tech Stuart School of Business requires applicants to submit GMAT scores (the School's minimum is 500, though a few exceptions are allowed), official undergraduate transcripts for all schools attended, one letter of recommendation from individuals "who are able to assess your academic and/or career achievements and potential," one personal statement, and a resume. International students must also submit TOEFL scores no more than two years old. Undergraduate transcripts in languages other than English must be accompanied by an English translation.

FINANCIAL FACTS

Annual tuition (in-state/ out-of-state)	$31,050/$31,050
Fees	$1,350
Cost of books	$820
Room & board	$10,800
% of students receiving aid	95
% of first-year students receiving aid	80
% of students receiving grants	95
Average award package	$12,108
Average loan	$37,671

ADMISSIONS

Admissions Selectivity Rating	**85**
# of applications received	133
% applicants accepted	47
% acceptees attending	15
Average GMAT	553
Range of GMAT	520–640
Accepts GRE scores	Yes
Range of Verbal GRE scores	143–143
Average Quantitative GRE	166
Range of Quantitative GRE scores	166–166
Average GPA	3.3
TOEFL required of international students	Yes
Minimum TOEFL (paper/web)	600/85
Application fee	$75
International application fee	$75
Regular application deadline	Rolling
Application Deadline/Notification	
Deferment available	Yes
Maximum length of deferment	1 year
Transfer students accepted	Yes
Transfer application policy	
With advisor approval, may transfer up to 6 semester credits hours or equivalent.	
Non-fall admissions	Yes
Need-blind admissions	Yes

EMPLOYMENT PROFILE

Career Rating	69	Top 5 Employers Hiring Grads
Primary Source of Full-time Job Acceptances		Northern Trust Corporation (2), Walgreens (1),
School-facilitated activities	1 (%)	McGraw Hill Education (1)
Graduate-facilitated activities	2 (%)	
Unknown	47 (%)	

ILLINOIS STATE UNIVERSITY
COLLEGE OF BUSINESS

GENERAL INFORMATION
Type of school	Public
Affiliation	No Affiliation
Academic calendar	Semester

SURVEY SAYS...
Friendly students, Happy students,
Abundant clubs and activities,
Students love Normal, IL
Solid preparation in:
General management, Teamwork,
Presentation skills, Quantitative skills

STUDENTS
Enrollment of parent	
institution	20,807
Enrollment of MBA Program	114
% male/female	56/44
% out-of-state	13
% part-time	66
% underrepresented minority	8
% international	44
Average age at entry	24
Average years work	
experience at entry	3

ACADEMICS
Academic Experience Rating	**87**
Profs interesting rating	91
Profs accessible rating	96
Student/faculty ratio	1:1
% female faculty	38
% underrepresented	
minority faculty	21
% part-time faculty	1

Joint Degrees
MPA

Prominent Alumni
Jack Hartung, Vice President
and CFO, Chipotle and its Partner
Brands Group; LaVerne Council,
Asst. Secretary for Information
Technology and CIO, Office of
Information and Technology,
U.S. Department of Veterans
Affairs; Dave Magers, Retired CFO
COUNTRY Financial; Jeff Stempora,
CEO, Evogi Group; Benjamin
Hart, President and CEO, Heritage
Enterprises Inc.

Academics

Price, flexibility, and reputation are the cornerstones of Illinois State University's College of Business. Led by professors who "provide the students with learning experiences that effectively prepare us for the business world" and an administration which gives students "a strong foundation for the program by frequently communicating school objectives, supplying valuable resources, and assisting students outside the classroom," this is a school that offers "big school resources and ranking at a budget price."

The MBA program at ISU is geared towards flexibility to meet the needs of both full and part-time students. One student is glad to be provided with "the flexibility to increase or decrease my workload as best fits my situation." Professors here are "willing to go the extra mile to help out" and accommodate a student's work schedule. Some students complain that "research is not a large priority," indicating that "finding sponsorship for optional thesis study is nearly impossible." Others say the College of Business should invest in new technology in order to keep pace with changes in the business world. "Direct application to corporate (and public sector) business settings should be a focus in the classroom. This will better prepare students for their next job."

Students say ISU has "the right combination of location, cost, reputation, and challenging coursework," making it so that they feel "there was no other choice for me in terms of graduate schools." The five academic departments of ISU's College of Business and the highly-focused centers of study within each—the Institute for Entrepreneurial Studies and the International Business Institute within the department of Management and Quantitative Methods, for instance—allow students to refine job skills relevant to their field. The "challenging coursework" here is offset by professors who "challenge students to critically think and are genuinely enthusiastic to teach us."

Career and Placement

Along with Hire-A-Redbird and other services provided by ISU's Career Center, "corporate partnerships" and general networking help move students into the next phase of their life in the business world. "Strong cooperation between companies and the business school through internships and classroom instruction from practitioners in various fields of business," along with large job fairs, places students in close contact with companies such as State Farm, Caterpillar, Growmark, Sprint, Archer Daniels Midland, Country Financial, and Sherwin-Williams Company.

Student Life and Environment

At ISU's College of Business, full-time students will work side-by-side with "older individuals with families and twenty-plus years of full-time professional experience." As many as half the attendees are part-time students, juggling the burdens of work, home, and family on top of a challenging body of academics. According to one student, "Coming to school is a quiet break from reality where I get to interact with many diverse and interesting people." One might think this mix would divide classrooms, but "the atmosphere... promotes interaction amongst all the sections of students," with both longtime professionals and younger students learning from one another. The small size of ISU's MBA program means it has "a close-knit student population," a group of "friendly, helpful" classmates who make sure "the atmosphere is always positive."

Diversity among the student population extends to the student body's place of origin. A large portion of the student population "are either international or have a strong international background." The positive atmosphere extends to this portion of the student body, too. "The students are friendly and there is a shared culture of learning for growth opportunity—professionally and personally—not just to acquire the degree."

For those whose primary daily responsibilities revolve around school, there is no shortage of things to do when class is over. "There is always something going on over the weekend, especially during the summer," students enthuse, indicating that "overall, quality of life is good and a good stress-buster from the hectic study schedules." Athletics, a wealth of student organizations, and a campus with easily accessible facilities make filling downtime simple.

Admissions

Applications to ISU's MBA program must go through the Graduate School. Fall semester applications are due by July 1; spring semester applications by December 1; and summer semester applications by April 1. Though work experience is not required, it is considered beneficial and is "strongly encouraged." Ensure all applications include two official copies of transcripts for all academic work completed beyond high school, along with GMAT scores, a resume, personal essays, and two letters of recommendation. All must be attached to the online Graduate School application. Applicants will want a strong GPA for their final sixty credit hours of undergraduate work and excellent GMAT scores, as those are the biggest factors in admissions decisions. Successful applicants have posted an average GPA of 3.40 and an average GMAT score of 535. TOEFL or IELTS scores are required for international students whose first language is not English. Be prepared to meet a minimum score of 600 on the paper-and-pencil TOEFL, 250 on the computer-based TOEFL, 90 in the Internet-based TOEFL, or 7.5 on the IELTS. Prospective students interested in Graduate Assistantship appointments must apply for a position prior to March 1st. The application is separate from the Program application and can be found via the "employment" link on the university's homepage. The benefits include a tuition waiver and monthly stipend.

FINANCIAL FACTS

Annual tuition (in-state/ out-of-state)	$6,246/$13,986
Fees	$1,422
Cost of books	$991
Room & board (on/off-campus)	$9,754/$8,460
% of students receiving aid	57
% of first-year students receiving aid	68
% of students receiving grants	47
Average award package	$9,943
Average grant	$7,117
Average loan	$15,246
Average student loan debt	$24,660

ADMISSIONS

Admissions Selectivity Rating	80
# of applications received	64
% applicants accepted	77
% acceptees attending	51
Average GMAT	535
Range of GMAT	500–555
Accepts GRE scores	No
Average GPA	3.4
TOEFL required of international students	Yes
Minimum TOEFL (paper/web)	600/90
Application fee	$50
International application fee	$50
Regular application deadline	7/1
Application Deadline/Notification	
Deferment available	Yes
Maximum length of deferment	1 year
Transfer students accepted	Yes
Transfer application policy Must be in good academic standing and complete all regular application requirements, maximum 9 hours transfer credit accepted	
Non-fall admissions	Yes
Need-blind admissions	Yes

IMD INTERNATIONAL
INTERNATIONAL INSTITUTE FOR MANAGEMENT DEVELOPMENT

Academics

Situated in Lausanne, Switzerland, IMD International is "a life changing experience" for business students who want an "intense one year program with special focus on leadership." This "very prestigious" program offers "international exposure," "diversity," and a "focus on soft skills and leadership capability." IMD has a reputation as the "best" of one-year MBA programs, and it is "famous for hard work." "With ninety students we have a small but strong community at the beautiful shores of Lake Geneva," one student says. The "convenient location" in central Europe provides "access to local network in a still growing country" as well as proximity to France, Germany, and other major European economies.

IMD students "come from multicultural backgrounds and most [have] experience in industry, not financial markets." Most have "an average of six years working experience" and bring "that level of successful work history with them into lively and constructive dialogues between fellow students and professors." This is an "amazing opportunity to spend time with a small group from thirty-nine different nationalities." The "very high quality" and "really top-notch" faculty come "with extensive experience and fit the school profile." "The professors not only taught us in class, they also led us on real business projects with real companies that had real problems," one student attests. Professors tend to have a "close relationship" with students, and are "responsive, easy to access and have a coffee chat, and well prepared for the classes." As one student raves, "It seems that every member of the faculty is an extraordinary pillar in their industry."

"Family" is the way students at IMD describe their relationship with professors and administration. Students quickly get to know the faculty and staff "on a personal level." This is "probably driven by [the] small size" of the program. The administration "does the job" and is "always helpful." IMD requires very "intensive study," but that only brings everyone closer: "The mood at the school is one of camaraderie and bonding through hard work." "Class size is ninety, which makes it a very intimate experience." Applicants should note that this is "a rather expensive program," but, if you can pay the "hefty sum," "it is one of the fastest MBAs to pay back the investment."

Career and Placement

Although the school has a small class size, students say there is a "strong alumni network." One student notes that despite a small alumni body, "they are very active/proactive and occupy very high positions with lots of recruiting and networking power." That said, many students wish the school would "provide more networking opportunities" and say that "improving the career services offering" should be a priority. Students do love the "discovery expedition" where students travel to "a different location such as Singapore, New York or Sao Paulo to learn about the specifics of doing business in those areas." Seventy-five percent of recent graduates work in Industry, 22 percent in Manufacturing, and 14 percent in Consumer Goods. Ninety-three percent of grads "changed function, industry, or geography" within three years of graduating. The Top Ten hiring companies were Amazon, DuPont, Google, Johnson & Johnson Services, McKinsey & Company, Nestlé, Royal Dutch Shell, Samsung, Siemens, The Boston Consulting Group.

Student Life and Environment

The "highly intelligent," "experienced," and "international" students can be summed up as "amazing unicorns." Students here are unique, but if you have to generalize, the student body is "mostly competitive and have pretty open . . . and liberal mind[s]." As an international program located in Europe, the student body is very "ethnically diverse students (thirty-nine nationalities in a class of ninety)." Many students have "worked in different countries" and "speak several languages." Life on campus tends to revolve around work: "We work or are in class from 8:00 A.M. to 10:00 P.M., six days per week." While "workload leaves little time for activities," "when we party, we party very hard and had a lot of fun." Students enjoy "hiking trips, sporting activities, wine classes, parties, cultural activities, [and] museum visits." Overall, this is "an extremely rigorous and high-pressure experience that bonds us like family."

Admissions

Only ninety students are accepted each class, so competition is stiff. Applicants must have a bachelor's degree or equivalent, a strong command of the English language, a second language, a minimum of three years of work experience, and GMAT scores. The vast majority of IMD students scored between 600 and 730 on the GMAT. While only three years of work experience is required, the majority of students have four to nine years of experience.

FINANCIAL FACTS

Annual tuition (in-state/ out-of-state)	$60,604/$60,604
Fees	$25,252
Cost of books	$0
Room & board	$36,362
% of students receiving aid	50
% of first-year students receiving aid	50
% of students receiving grants	26
Average award package	$37,139
Average grant	$26,576
Average loan	$31,177

ADMISSIONS

Admissions Selectivity Rating	82
Average GMAT	663
Range of GMAT	640–690
Accepts GRE scores	Yes
Application fee	$353
International application fee	$353
Early application deadline	2/1
Regular application deadline	9/1
Application Deadline	
Round 1:	2/1
Round 2:	4/1
Round 3:	6/1
Round 4:	8/1
Deferment available	No
Transfer students accepted	No
Non-fall admissions	Yes
Need-blind admissions	Yes

EMPLOYMENT PROFILE

Career Rating	**97**	**Grads Employed by Function% Avg. Salary**	
Percent employed 3 months		Marketing	(21%)
after graduation	87	Operations	(11%)
Average base starting salary	$127,744	Consulting	(30%)
Primary Source of Full-time Job Acceptances		Management	(31%)
School-facilitated activities	(65%)	Finance	(16%)
Graduate-facilitated activities	(35%)	Other	(1%)

Top 5 Employers Hiring Grads
BCG (6), Accenture (3), Hilti (3), Dow Chemical (2), Cisco (2)

INDIANA STATE UNIVERSITY
SCOTT COLLEGE OF BUSINESS

GENERAL INFORMATION
Type of school	Public
Affiliation	No Affiliation
Academic calendar	Semester

SURVEY SAYS...
Friendly students, Happy students
Solid preparation in:
General management, Teamwork,
Doing business in a global economy

STUDENTS
Enrollment of parent institution	13,584
Enrollment of MBA Program	86
% male/female	83/17
% out-of-state	13
% part-time	73
% underrepresented minority	0
% international	39
Average age at entry	32
Average years work experience at entry	8

ACADEMICS
Academic Experience Rating	**67**
Profs interesting rating	70
Profs accessible rating	64
Student/faculty ratio	23:1
% female faculty	27
% underrepresented minority faculty	0
% part-time faculty	0

Academics

Designed primarily for students early in their business careers, the MBA program at Indiana State University offers graduate-level preparation to aspiring managers and business professionals. "Small classes, great teachers, good assistantships" and an affordable tuition add up to excellent value for students here.

Size is both a major asset and an occasional drawback at ISU. With fewer than sixty students in the entire program, students enjoy "individual attention that better prepares the students in a hands-on manner." Small class sizes also mean great faculty accessibility; one student points out, "All of my classes have been taught by senior professors, department chairs, etc. The mentors and connections I'm gaining are fantastic." The size of the program also helps foster a "friendly environment inside and outside the classroom." On the downside, "Class scheduling can be difficult since limited classes are offered each semester." Also, small programs often suffer from neglect in some areas, and ISU's is no exception. For example, ISU "needs to continually update case studies," an area in which students say the program is deficient. "Especially during these economic times, we need very current cases."

The Indiana State MBA consists of thirty-three semester units (students seeking a specialized concentration must complete an additional three semester units), which can be completed in one year and four months of full-time study. Students wishing to continue to work while they earn their MBAs may also choose to study part-time. Through core course work and electives, the program emphasizes strategic thinking, problem-solving skills, organizational change, international business, and group dynamics. Hands-on learning occurs through opportunities to assist faculty in real-world research projects in programs such as the Small Business Development Center (SBDC), which provides business planning assistance to start-up companies, and through consulting services to existing small businesses.

Career and Placement

Since 2004 when the College of Business opened the Meis Student Development Center (MSDC), students have had a dedicated facility where they can research positions using the Sycamore CareerLink electronic database, attend career-building workshops, and prepare for interviews. One student writes the following: "My experience with the Career Center is that they only provide the website for assistance in job searches and two career fairs per year. The staff does not provide any other help." Employers interviewing on the ISU campus during a recent recruiting year included: AFLAC, AmSouth, Caterpillar, Dauby O'Connor & Zaleski CPA, Federated Mutual Insurance Company, Marathon Oil, Travelers, and West Point Financial/Mass Mutual.

ADMISSIONS CONTACT: JEFF HARPER, EXECUTIVE DIRECTOR, MBA PROGRAM
ADDRESS: INDIANA STATE UNIVERSITY, 30 N. 7TH STREET, TERRE HAUTE, IN 47809-BUS
PHONE: 812-237-2002 • FAX: 812-237-8720
E-MAIL: ISU-MBA@INDSTATE.EDU • WEBSITE: WWW.INDSTATE.EDU/MBA

Student Life and Environment

"There is always something to be involved in for anyone who wants to get involved" in ISU's MBA community, students tell us. "Whether they are activities organized by the MBA Association (MBAA) or seminars and conferences hosted by leaders of industries, the ISU business school contributes positively towards a student's personality and mentality," a student observes. Students are particularly impressed with MBAA, whose events "allows students from all cultures to come together." Students also appreciate "a lounge for MBA students to study, eat, socialize, and plan," and it should be noted that the College of Business has moved to a new, state-of-the-art building.

Hometown Terre Haute "has the most amazing public parks," facilitating "all [sorts] of outdoor activities. We are also very close to Indianapolis, Chicago, Louisville, and St. Louis, so we have been to Pacers games, Rams games etc. There is so much to do in this area and the cost of living is so low that you have money to enjoy life, even while in b-school."

The ISU MBA program attracts a mix of full timers—typically "young and busy," with some continuing directly from undergraduate study—and part timers adding school to a busy calendar that also includes a full-time job and family obligations. There is a large international contingent here, which makes for a "culturally diverse" campus. Students are "friendly and helpful," even when there are language barriers, and "work together on projects to make sure everyone understands." One writes: "As an international student I have never felt like a foreigner at ISU…[My classmates] always contribute positively in the classroom environment as well as outside." Academically, students describe their peers as "moderately competitive, with the occasional outstanding scholar."

Admissions

In considering applicants for the MBA program, Indiana State University considers the following criteria: acceptance to the College of Graduate and Professional Studies; successful completion of undergraduate degree; GPA of at least 2.7, or a GPA of at least 3.0 over the final sixty semester hours of undergraduate study; basic computing skills; GMAT scores; and prerequisite competency. Prerequisite course work for the program includes statistics; additionally, marketing and production and operation management are "strongly recommended."

FINANCIAL FACTS

Annual tuition (in-state/ out-of-state)	$5,958/$12,690
Fees	$3,548
Cost of books	$1,200
Room & board (on/off-campus)	$7,800/$7,800
% of students receiving aid	86
% of first-year students receiving aid	95
% of students receiving grants	14
Average award package	$12,606
Average grant	$2,838
Average loan	$15,835
Average student loan debt	$21,394

ADMISSIONS

Admissions Selectivity Rating	81
# of applications received	75
% applicants accepted	76
% acceptees attending	67
Average GMAT	528
Range of GMAT	505–560
Accepts GRE scores	No
Average GPA	3.1
TOEFL required of international students	Yes
Minimum TOEFL (paper/web)	550/
Application fee	$45
International application fee	$65
Application Deadline/Notification	
Deferment available	Yes
Maximum length of deferment	2 years
Transfer students accepted	Yes
Transfer application policy Will only accept 6 credit hours from AACSB accredited Universities.	
Non-fall admissions	Yes
Need-blind admissions	Yes

INDIANA UNIVERSITY—BLOOMINGTON
KELLEY SCHOOL OF BUSINESS

GENERAL INFORMATION

Type of school	Public
Affiliation	No Affiliation
Academic calendar	Semester

SURVEY SAYS...

Classmates have diverse work experience, Friendly students, Good peer network, Good social scene, Abundant mentors available, Helpful alumni, Happy students, Abundant clubs and activities
Solid preparation in:
Marketing, Finance, Accounting, General management, Teamwork, Communication/interpersonal skills, Presentation skills, Quantitative skills

STUDENTS

Enrollment of parent institution	48,514
Enrollment of MBA Program	372
% male/female	70/30
% out-of-state	90
% part-time	0
% underrepresented minority	8
% international	34
Average age at entry	28
Average years work experience at entry	5

ACADEMICS

Academic Experience Rating	96
Profs interesting rating	96
Profs accessible rating	98
Student/faculty ratio	20:1
% female faculty	24
% underrepresented minority faculty	4
% part-time faculty	0

Joint Degrees

MBA/JD; MBA/MA (area studies); MBA/MA (Telecommunications); MBA/JD

Prominent Alumni

Cheryl Bachelder, BS 77, MBA 78, CEO, Popeyes Louisiana Kitchen, Inc.; Jeff Fettig, BS 79, MBA 81, Chairman & CEO, Whirlpool Corporation

Academics

An administration that is "extremely student-focused and works hard to enhance (their) experience" is a hallmark of Indiana University—Bloomington's Kelley School of Business. This "well run" school "responds very quickly to the problems of students," with an administration and educators who "do all that they can to enhance students' experiences." In fact, students say the administrators at Kelley are "on par with any top ten program."

Part of that comes from teachers who are "are incredible at making textbook problems become real-world applicable." The "incredibly qualified and smart" professors "are passionate about making our experience a positive one." There is no question that "academics are taken seriously at Kelley. Professors care about students learning—not just about grades, but understanding concepts." The "rigorous curriculum" here "prepares a student to compete with the best," key to helping students "grow personally and professionally." Faculty recognize that the world of business is not a solo sport, and the education here reflects that. "Students become very dynamic in team settings because of it."

Students here will begin with an integrated fifteen-week core curriculum before plunging into an education that will ask you to "continuously strive to keep up with change and improvement." Even with challenging academics, few students will find roadblocks at Kelley, in large part thanks to the "excellent faculty" being on hand to help. "The administration and faculty of the Kelley School are second to none. Any administration issues are dealt with quickly and the professors are very interested in preparing you for success by making themselves available after class."

Career and Placement

The Academy structure at Kelley "leads to better interview preparation and therefore more companies being interested in coming to campus." Couple that with the "broad Hoosier network" and a "top marketing program with fantastic companies coming on campus" and it's easy to see why Kelley has "unrivaled exposure to best-in-class CPG companies (General Mills, P&G, Nestle, ConAgra)." Add to that a "strong entrepreneurship program and international experience opportunities," as well as faculty who will "bend over backwards to help you land that job/internship," and opportunities abound. Students don't need to rely solely on the faculty, either. They can also rely on the career services team and one another. "Many students find internships and full time offers because their classmates helped them make the right connections."

The biggest recruiters here include EY, Intel, PwC, Deloitte, AT&T, Amazon, Target, General Mills, Microsoft, and those MBAs went to a wide range of positions. In 2015 about 22 percent took positions in manufacturing, 19 percent went into consulting, 15 percent were in healthcare, 14 percent found financial services gigs, 10% ended up in consumer products, 7 percent went into technology and 7 percent found roles in retail.

Admissions Contact: James Holmen, Director of Admissions and Financial Aid
Address: 1275 East Tenth Street, Suite 2010, Bloomington, IN 47405-1703
Phone: 812-855-8006 • Fax: 812-855-9039
E-mail: IUMBA@indiana.edu • Website: http://kelley.iu.edu/mba

Student Life and Environment

If you want an opportunity to slow down, you won't get it here. "Life at the Kelley School is very busy, but it is very gratifying because you are able to apply what you're learning to projects that the professors have spent time developing." Students here tend to be "busy with lot of learning," but expect "inclusion and collaboration" rather than classmates who only look out for themselves. "Graduate school is difficult enough without having a cut-throat culture or a miserable environment. The Kelley environment supports students to achieve and to help one another." Just be ready to remain motivated. "The pace is fast, and you feel like a slacker if you are not actively involved with activities and projects keeping you busy all the time. It's a great environment for staying sharp and competitive."

That is not to say there aren't opportunities for fun. "Bloomington offers a lot for a smaller town—great restaurants, museums and shows. At the same time, things are easy to get to and relatively cheap, which is a great combination for a busy student." You'll be on your feet most of the time, as students "often walk to school, walk to the gym and walk to go out," but that only serves to enhance the "one big family" atmosphere at Kelley. If you don't want to hit the town, "there are many clubs and groups for different interest groups which are all student-led under the student-elected MBA Association," as well as "many weekend social/networking opportunities."

Admissions

Many hope to be part of the Kelley MBA program, but because it is highly selective, competition to get in is fierce. Expect the Admissions Office to consider your academic record, including cumulative grade point average; area of concentration; balance of electives and trend of grades; GMAT scores; work experience (two or more years strongly recommended); evidence of leadership ability; one letter of reference; and personal essays. You don't need to have majored in business as an undergraduate, but you should understand algebra and statistics and have some facility with spreadsheets. There are separate screenings for each of the program's four separate application deadlines. Regardless, your chances are better if you apply early; however, it is better to wait for a later deadline if doing so will improve your application. If you are seeking merit scholarships, try to apply by the January 5th deadline.

FINANCIAL FACTS

Annual tuition (in-state/ out-of-state)	$25,500/$44,460
Fees	$2,101
Cost of books	$1,950
Room & board (on/off-campus)	$12,150/$12,150
% of students receiving aid	90
% of first-year students receiving aid	90
% of students receiving grants	81
Average award package	$43,320
Average grant	$25,757
Average loan	$34,208
Average student loan debt	$63,065

ADMISSIONS

Admissions Selectivity Rating	94
# of applications received	1,471
% applicants accepted	29
% acceptees attending	43
Average GMAT	668
Range of GMAT	620–710
Accepts GRE scores	Yes
Average Verbal GRE	161
Range of Verbal GRE scores	155–164
Average Quantitative GRE	156
Range of Quantitative GRE scores	144–163
Average Writing GRE	3.9
Range of Writing GRE scores	3.0–4.5
Average GPA	3.4
TOEFL required of international students	Yes
Minimum TOEFL (paper/web)	600/100
Application fee	$75
International application fee	$75
Application Deadline/Notification	
Round 1:	10/15 / 12/20
Round 2:	1/5 / 3/15
Round 3:	3/1 / 4/30
Round 4:	4/15 / 5/31
Deferment available	Yes
Maximum length of deferment	1 year
Transfer students accepted	No
Non-fall admissions	No
Need-blind admissions	Yes

EMPLOYMENT PROFILE

Career Rating	96	**Grads Employed by Function**	**% Avg. Salary**
Percent employed at graduation	77	Marketing	(28%) $99,277
Percent employed 3 months after graduation	89	Operations	(6%) $104,904
		Consulting	(22%) $126,164
Average base starting salary	$107,006	Management	(12%) $99,026
Primary Source of Full-time Job Acceptances		Finance	(26%) $105,045
School-facilitated activities	133 (82%)	MIS	(4%) $96,002
Graduate-facilitated activities	30 (18%)	Other	(2%)

Top 5 Employers Hiring Grads
EY (10), Deloitte Consulting (7), Whirlpool (5), Eli Lilly (4), 3M (3)

INDIANA UNIVERSITY—KOKOMO

SCHOOL OF BUSINESS

GENERAL INFORMATION
Type of school — Public
Academic calendar — Semester

SURVEY SAYS...
Friendly students, Happy students
Solid preparation in:
Accounting, General management, Operations, Communication/interpersonal skills, Quantitative skills, Computer skills

STUDENTS
Enrollment of parent
institution — 4,100
Enrollment of MBA Program — 85
% male/female — 80/20
% out-of-state — 1
% part-time — 63
% underrepresented minority — 1
% international — 85
Average age at entry — 31

ACADEMICS
Academic Experience Rating — **63**
Profs interesting rating — 61
Profs accessible rating — 62
Student/faculty ratio — 6:1
% female faculty — 40
% underrepresented
minority faculty — 1
% part-time faculty — 0

Academics

The School of Business at Indiana University—Kokomo (IU Kokomo) capably serves area professionals seeking to advance their careers through an MBA degree, offering a "great education at an affordable price." Students praise the program's "excellent reputation" with area employers, as well as its "convenient location" and small class sizes that "make for an intimate setting." "Students are people, not numbers here." A public school that is one of only a dozen AACSB-accredited MBA programs in the state of Indiana, Kokomo provides a compelling option to business people seeking an affordable career-advancement opportunity in and around this city of 50,000.

IU Kokomo's program is "attuned to the regional industry base" of north-central Indiana, but is also flexible enough to "foster effective management of resources in diverse organizational units and settings," according to the school's promotional material. Because nearly all its students work full time, the program offers flexible scheduling. All required classes are held during the week in the evening hours; electives are offered either during the day or in the evenings. Classes are alternately offered in eight- and sixteen-week formats, accommodating both those in a hurry to complete course work and those who wish to learn at a less frantic pace. Except for a capstone course, classes may be taken in any order, another accommodation for the convenience of IU's busy students. Such convenience comes with a tradeoff, however, making it impossible for the school to fully integrate the curriculum, and some wish that there were "more electives" and more real-world learning experiences "where we actually get to use what the professor is stressing in lectures." For example, it would be helpful to have, "an integrated case study that encompasses at least two courses per semester," an impossibility under the current system. Some think that a few of the professors overcompensate for this lack of opportunities for practical demonstration by developing trickier and more "complex exams."

Part-time students typically complete Kokomo's thirty-credit MBA program in four years. The program is small, facilitating student-teacher interaction, and professors here are accessible, willing, and "brilliant, for the most part." The downside of the school's size is that it limits options. Some students complain that some courses are not offered frequently enough.

Career and Placement

IU Kokomo does not aggressively promote its career services for MBA students. Because most students in the program "are employed full time in positions of responsibility," few actually require placement services or career counseling, and those who do generally rely on the assistance of their professors. MBAs may take advantage of the University's Office of Career Services, which maintains job boards, a Career Library and Resource Center, and online career-related databases.

Top employers in Kokomo include Delphi Electronics & Safety, Howard Regional Health, Saint Joseph Hospital, Haynes International, Meijer, and the University.

ADMISSIONS CONTACT: GLORIA L. PREECE, MBA DIRECTOR
ADDRESS: PO BOX 9003, KOKOMO, IN 46904-9003
PHONE: 765-455-4249 • FAX: 765-455-9348
E-MAIL: GPREECE@IUK.EDU • WEBSITE: WWW.IUK.EDU/MBA

Student Life and Environment

IU Kokomo attracts a "larger population of older students" of "all forms and fashions," with "many women and minorities" filling out the ranks. MBAs here tend to be "normal, everyday people trying to better themselves in tough economic times," and most often have a full-time job. They have "multiple demands on their time" in addition to school, including careers and, quite often, family obligations, so the school is usually "close to home" for all who attend. "My teammates for group work have been strong contributors, leaving no one person with a disproportionate work load. Our work groups are committed to getting as much done as possible just before or just after classes meet, as we are all busy otherwise, and that works well for everyone." Though most are "very friendly and helpful," some "tend to stick together with fellow students from the same employer" and are "not always welcoming to outsiders."

IU Kokomo is "strictly a commuter campus" where students "come in, go to class, and leave," so "there are relatively few gatherings as with other traditional campuses." Despite the lack of socializing, there are few complaints, as this is specifically what most students are here for. "The format of the classes is set up in a way that it's possible to have a life while earning your degree. The value of the program is amazing." It is worth highlighting the efforts of the MBA Association (MBAA), which organizes social and intellectual events for those students who do spend time on campus. The school invites business leaders as part of its distinguished lecture series, enabling students to learn from some of the business world's top players. Some here feel that "the safety of students attending night classes is an issue. I never see security at night, and the lighting could be better." Statistics indicate that the city of Kokomo has a below average rate of crimes, such as assault, robbery, and automobile theft.

Admissions

Admission to the MBA program at IU Kokomo requires a bachelor's degree from an accredited college or university (business major not required), a completed application to the program, a personal statement of career goals, and official transcripts for all postsecondary academic work. Most applicants must also submit GMAT scores; those already holding graduate degrees from accredited institutions, however, may be exempted from this requirement. Successful completion of undergraduate-level courses in calculus, statistics, and composition, and a background in microcomputer applications are prerequisites to beginning the MBA program. These courses can be completed after admission to the program, however. Some qualified applicants may be denied admission due to space and resource constraints. Admissions decisions are made on a rolling basis, so it pays to apply as early as possible. International applicants must meet the aforementioned requirements and must also submit proof of English proficiency. The MBA program admits students for fall, spring, and summer semesters. IU Kokomo accepts students with deficiencies in their business education background, but these students are required to complete up to 18 credit hours of foundation courses in business.

FINANCIAL FACTS

Annual tuition (in-state/ out-of-state)	$8,700/$19,770
Fees	$535
Cost of books	$2,000
Room & board	$10,000
Average grant	$0

ADMISSIONS

Admissions Selectivity Rating	**80**
# of applications received	27
% applicants accepted	89
% acceptees attending	100
Average GMAT	512
Accepts GRE scores	No
Average GPA	3.3
TOEFL required of international students	Yes
Minimum TOEFL (paper/web)	550/73
Application fee	$40
International application fee	$60
Regular application deadline	6/15
Application Deadline/Notification	
Deferment available	Yes
Transfer students accepted	Yes
Transfer application policy	
6 credits from AACSB accredited schools	
Non-fall admissions	Yes
Need-blind admissions	Yes

Indiana University of Pennsylvania
Eberly College of Business and Information Technology

GENERAL INFORMATION
Type of school	Public
Affiliation	No Affiliation
Academic calendar	Semester

SURVEY SAYS...
Friendly students, Liberal students, Happy students
Solid preparation in:
Marketing, General management, Operations, Teamwork, Communication/interpersonal skills, Doing business in a global economy, Environmental sustainability

STUDENTS
Enrollment of parent institution	13,775
Enrollment of MBA Program	387
% male/female	68/32
% out-of-state	91
% part-time	39
% underrepresented minority	1
% international	91
Average age at entry	25

ACADEMICS
Academic Experience Rating	**86**
Profs interesting rating	92
Profs accessible rating	94
Student/faculty ratio	12:1
% female faculty	14
% underrepresented minority faculty	48
% part-time faculty	3

Prominent Alumni
Richard B. Clark, '80, President & CEO, Brookfield Financial Properties LP; Terry L. Dunlap, '81, General Manager, Allegheny Ludlum; Florence Mauchant, '85, Partner, HT Capital Advisors LLC; Timothy W. Wallace, '79, CEO, FullTilt Solutions; Jeffrey R. DeMarco, '81, Partner, KPMG LLP

Academics

With a broad-based curriculum, affordable in-state tuition, and uniformly small class sizes, the MBA program at Indiana University of Pennsylvania is suitable to both recent graduates and mid-career professionals. With many courses taught in the evenings, the program can be tailored to fit your schedule, as well as your educational goals. For those who want to complete the degree quickly, the school offers "a fast-paced one-year completion opportunity" (open to students with an undergraduate degree in business). However, there are also "options for doing concentrations/ specialization for those who want a longer program," or for those who wish to concentrate their studies on a field like international business, human resources, supply chain management, marketing, finance, and accounting. Offering a great return on investment, this public school "is not expensive compared to another MBA programs, and the quality is still very good." Despite the attractive price tag, the curriculum is well-designed, the administration is efficient, and "everything is done to allow students to work as smoothly as possible, [and] we have easy access to all resources needed."

Eberly's MBA curriculum strives to stay current with business trends, and practical business applications are constantly incorporated into class work. Drawing on their real-world credentials, "professors are constantly reinforcing what is being taught with real life experiences or with what is going on in the world today." The school has made strides in integrating industry trends into the business curriculum. For example, it has recently introduced an elective in social media marketing to augment traditional marketing coursework. Another feature that stands out about the Eberly MBA is its focus on international business. This focus is reflected in both the staff and the students, as Eberly recruits "professors and students who are from all different parts of the world, as well as who have been to all different parts of the world." Here, "it is a pleasure to work in an intercultural group and we learn more about other cultures and our globalized world economy!"

Uniting intimacy with opportunity, "the greatest strength of the school is the small campus feel mixed with a big college feeling." Thanks to the relatively small graduate enrollment, Eberly students enjoy "small class sizes" and the opportunity to work directly with their professors, while still benefiting from the larger campus environment as well as the big, state-of-the-art Eberly College of Business complex. Within the business school, "professors are always willing to give an extra hand, and are always available during office hours." Likewise, the "school administration is very helpful and reacts very quickly to all our inquiries and demands!"

Career and Placement

The Indiana University of Pennsylvania Career Development Center assists all undergraduates, graduate students, and alumni with career preparation, internships, and job placement. The Career Development Center offers help with resume writing, interviewing skills, and job-hunting techniques, and it offers one-on-one counseling by appointment. In addition, the Career Development Center organizes job fairs and campus recruiting programs, while also maintaining an updated list of job opportunities online. While their services are open to MBA candidates, some say the Center "could use some overhauling," with a greater focus on "attracting good companies for internships and placements."

In recent years, the mean base salary for IUP graduates was over $50,000, and over 70 percent of students had accepted a job within three months of graduation. Companies that recruit on the IUP campus include American Express, Bristol-Myers Squibb Co., Cigna, DuPont Company, EDS, Exxon Company, Federated Investors, General Motors, Georgia Pacific, Deloitte & Touche LLP; Ernst & Young LLP; PricewaterhouseCoopers LLP, Sun Microsystems, Inc., Wal-Mart, Walt Disney World Company, and Westinghouse.

Student Life and Environment

A "very diverse" student body, over 66 percent of Eberly students are international, with more than twenty countries represented on campus. This diversity is a blessing to the academic experience, as "everyone comes to class with a clear mind, ready to share their background [and] experiences" and most "find it very interesting to learn about their cultures and societies."

Despite their different backgrounds, students at this program get along well. In fact, "being in the MBA school at IUP is like having a small group of friends.... It's easy to get together with fellow students to study and go over things or just hang out." A student exclaims, "I've always enjoyed IUP for the vast social networking I'm able to do. Even though the town is small, I always have something to do, whether it's participating in a club, or just relaxing on weekends." An hour northeast of Pittsburgh, IUP is near a major city, yet the small-town atmosphere makes it a "peaceful place for studying" and ensures "affordable" cost of living. On that note, hometown Indiana, Pennsylvania isn't everybody's cup of tea. In fact, Indiana "is a very tiny town, so you can either enjoy it or hate it."

Admissions

To be eligible for admission to IUP, students must have a minimum undergraduate GPA of at least 2.6 (for those who graduated from college fewer than five years ago) or 2.4 (for those who graduated from college more than five years ago.) Prospective students must also present GMAT scores of 450 or better. In addition to test scores and undergraduate transcripts, students must also submit a one-page personal statement, at least two letters of recommendation, and an updated resume. High-achieving national and international applicants are eligible to apply for graduate assistantships after completing the first part of the core curriculum.

FINANCIAL FACTS

Annual tuition (in-state/ out-of-state)	$8,906/$13,358
Fees	$2,781
Cost of books	$1,100
Room & board (on/off-campus)	$11,560/$11,560
% of students receiving aid	69
% of first-year students receiving aid	93
Average award package	$12,187
Average grant	$12,899
Average loan	$15,446

ADMISSIONS

Admissions Selectivity Rating	81
# of applications received	253
% applicants accepted	75
% acceptees attending	83
Average GMAT	492
Range of GMAT	460–535
Accepts GRE scores	Yes
Average GPA	3.4
TOEFL required of international students	Yes
Minimum TOEFL (paper/web)	540/76
Application fee	$50
International application fee	$50
Regular application deadline	8/1
Application Deadline/Notification	
Deferment available	Yes
Maximum length of deferment	1 year
Transfer students accepted	Yes
Transfer application policy Written request for transfer required of transfer applicants. Maximum of six credits transfer. Credits requested for transfer must carry a grade of "B" or Its equivalent or better and must have been completed within the last five years.	
Non-fall admissions	Yes
Need-blind admissions	Yes

EMPLOYMENT PROFILE

Career Rating	84	**Top 5 Employers Hiring Grads**
Percent employed 3 months		BNY Mellon, IBM, Prudential, BNP Paribas,
after graduation	51	Ernst & Young
Average base starting salary	$55,600	
Primary Source of Full-time Job Acceptances		

INDIANA UNIVERSITY—SOUTH BEND
JUDD LEIGHTON SCHOOL OF BUSINESS AND ECONOMICS

GENERAL INFORMATION

Type of school	Public
Affiliation	No Affiliation
Academic calendar	Semester

SURVEY SAYS...
Happy students
Solid preparation in:
Quantitative skills

STUDENTS

Enrollment of parent institution	7,574
Enrollment of MBA Program	91
% male/female	49/51
% out-of-state	18
% part-time	81
% underrepresented minority	12
% international	15
Average age at entry	29
Average years work experience at entry	7

ACADEMICS

Academic Experience Rating	**87**
Profs interesting rating	88
Profs accessible rating	93
Student/faculty ratio	24:1
% female faculty	21
% underrepresented minority faculty	0
% part-time faculty	21

Joint Degrees
MBA/MSA (total of 54 credits) .

Academics

Indiana University South Bend's Leighton School of Business and Economics is a "value provider" when it comes to getting an exceptional business education. The school offers working professionals a "cost effective" and convenient means to advance their careers or switch industries. The flexible schedule (including night classes), "great business school credentials," and the part-time MBA program make for a "good reputation," and "the in-state-residence tuition is attractive."

Most of the professors "know present and past students by name," and are "engaged" and accessible to students. "I am able to get questions answered expeditiously," says one. The cultural and ethnic diversity of professors is a huge plus, and though "some are better than others," all are "extremely well-versed in the subjects they teach." There is an "ease of contact" with teachers, and "all professors have a sincere interest in working with students." The administration is also well run, and "when we contact the Dean of the program directly, he is very responsive."

Students who have taken specific business classes within the last five years may qualify for automatic exemption from Foundation classes to save time and money. MBA candidates have three optional concentrations from which to choose: Finance, Human Resources, and Marketing. As most people here have already tasted the world of full-time employment, the commitment to work is high, and these students "always turn in their assignments and give really impressive presentations."

Career and Placement

Since the majority of those who attend IU South Bend are currently employed and whose degrees are frequently paid for by their employers, Career Services is not as necessary as at some other business schools; the typical candidate enters the program because their present or future position requires increased managerial competence. The one exception includes younger students or those who are looking to change their careers. A few students say that IU South Bend "needs more connections to businesses" so that graduates can have more ease to "transition from [an] MBA program into a job that requires the specific concentration of the MBA." Most who attend apply for the business degree and are normally not disappointed by the program or their results. "The experience has been everything I expected," says one student.

ADMISSIONS CONTACT: TRACY P. WHITE, ASST. DIRECTOR/ACADEMIC ADVISOR
ADDRESS: 1700 MISHAWAKA AVENUE, P O BOX 7111, SOUTH BEND, IN 46634-7111
PHONE: 574-520-4138 • FAX: 574-520-4866
E-MAIL: GRADBUS@IUSB.EDU • WEBSITE: GRADUATEBUSINESS.IUSB.EDU

Student Life and Environment

The business school is "well laid out," most of the buildings are close together, and parking is not overly difficult. IU South Bend is mostly a commuter school composed of "local people wanting to get their MBA while at a full-time job," so the school "doesn't offer many outside activities," and "there is limited student-student interaction." Though most interactions do center on classes and professional organizations, students are always "social and eager to exchange ideas." One student comments, "They have helped me see different sides of issues and solutions." This "friendly and down to earth, intelligent and unpretentious" group is "evenly split between males and females," and made up of mostly "older students…with families," and "younger students [who] are international." All around, students are "very motivating and inspiring." "Everyone has interesting side stories and business ventures," says a student.

Admissions

The MBA program at IU South Bend requires applicants to submit all of the following: an online application; official transcripts of all postsecondary academic work; two recommendations (completed online); a personal statement; current resume; and an official GMAT score report (a GMAT waiver is possible, under certain conditions). International students whose native language is not English must submit all of the above as well as an official score report for the TOEFL; minimum required score for consideration is 550 (paper-based test), 213 (computer- based test) or 79 (internet-based test). Applications are accepted for Fall, Spring, or Summer semesters. IU South Bend admits students at two levels: full admission and probationary admission. Full admission requires a minimum GMAT score of 450. Probationary admission is granted to applicants "whose GPA does not quite meet minimum standards." All students must maintain a cumulative GPA of at least 3.00 to remain in, and to graduate from the program.

FINANCIAL FACTS

Average grant	$0
Average loan	$0

ADMISSIONS

Admissions Selectivity Rating	83
# of applications received	82
% applicants accepted	66
% acceptees attending	85
Average GMAT	526
Range of GMAT	450–680
Accepts GRE scores	Yes
Average GPA	3.2
TOEFL required of international students	Yes
Minimum TOEFL (paper/web)	550/79
Application fee	$40
International application fee	$60
Regular application deadline	7/1
Application Deadline/Notification	
Deferment available	Yes
Maximum length of deferment	one year
Transfer students accepted	Yes
Transfer application policy	
Contact the office for a determination of which classes might transfer. In general, max is 12 credits from AACSB school only with min course grade of B	
Non-fall admissions	Yes
Need-blind admissions	No

INDIANA UNIVERSITY SOUTHEAST
SCHOOL OF BUSINESS

Academics

"The value is wonderful and the classes are small" at the Indiana University Southeast School of Business, which provides a great (and inexpensive) opportunity for students, particularly those who are working full-time, to pursue an MBA. The evening classes and curriculum lets students pace themselves according to their availability and work schedules, and the course work is "engaging" with challenging material that "forces us to think about things in different ways and apply that material to our current jobs or see how it would apply to someone in a different role." A few students say that some of the classes seem a bit rote, but "the school is actively reassessing its courses and seeks to improve in those areas."

The "dedicated" professors "bring a wealth of personal business experience to class," "are passionate about what they teach," and implement real-life examples at every turn of the page. "Professors make all of the difference in the world," says a student. "They understand that most of us have jobs and families are flexible with our schedules." They stay after class and "give attention to any topic, small or large that is of concern to their students." "The fact that our classroom sizes are roughly fifteen to twenty students gives us a great opportunity to get to know both the students and professors on a more personal level," says a student.

Career and Placement

The IUS Career Development Center provides all students in the MBA programs with career counseling, internships, résumé reviews, mock interviews, and job fairs. However, most students at IUS are looking to move ahead in their current positions, so job searches are not the main concern so much as job skills. Students have the option to call and schedule one-on-one appointments with counselors, or take advantage of the extensive alumni network that IUS provides; the School of Business also conducts a number of CEO Roundtables per year. The school is located near both Indianapolis and Louisville, so there is a wide range of industries and job markets from which students can draw from. Some students do wish that the school would add more alumni guest speakers from the business community, who could "talk about how they have used what they learned in the MBA program in solving real world problems."

Student Life and Environment

The Graduate Center is located off of the main campus, which "preserves the culture and level of maturity that is needed." As most people here are working professionals, life is busy and it is "very much a commuter campus" (IUS also happens to have a large crowd of students from Louisville), so "there is little connection between students and the school outside of class." This doesn't mean that people are brusque: Students "are extremely helpful and conduct themselves in a way that is very friendly" and "usually socialize with each other and professors." There is certainly a variety of ages and backgrounds—students "tend to be a mix of mid-career professionals and some younger millennials" and most students are married, many with children—but "everyone works together to achieve the ultimate goal of MBA degree."

Admissions

For the IUS admissions committee, the most important factors in an admissions decision are a student's previous academic performance, the quality of his or her undergraduate degree program, standardized test scores, and previous work experience. The average GMAT score for this year's class was 540, with a range between 470–670 for the 25th to 75th percentile. Students generally receive a response from the University within three weeks of the application deadline. Any applications post-marked after the deadline will be considered on a space-available basis.

FINANCIAL FACTS

Annual tuition (in-state/ out-of-state)	$6,150/$12,870
% of students receiving aid	27
% of first-year students receiving aid	9
% of students receiving grants	12
Average award package	$9,466
Average grant	$2,343
Average loan	$12,668
Average student loan debt	$21,047

ADMISSIONS

Admissions Selectivity Rating	79
# of applications received	60
% applicants accepted	92
% acceptees attending	87
Average GMAT	530
Range of GMAT	470–670
Accepts GRE scores	Yes
Average GPA	3.3
TOEFL required of international students	Yes
Minimum TOEFL (paper/web)	550/81
Application fee	$35
International application fee	$35
Early application deadline	6/15
Early notification date	7/15
Regular application deadline	7/20
Regular application notification	8/15
Application Deadline/Notification	
Deferment available	Yes
Maximum length of deferment	1 semester
Transfer students accepted	Yes
Transfer application policy	

Students may transfer a maximum of 6 graduate credit hours (with no grades below B) from another AACSB-accredited MBA program to count toward the 37 credit hour MBA curriculum at IU Southeast. Students may request that graduate credit not meeting this criterion be reviewed for transfer approval. The final disposition of all transfer course work is determined by the Director.

Non-fall admissions	Yes
Need-blind admissions	Yes

INSEAD

Academics

INSEAD brands itself as "the business school for the world," and it can provide hard facts to support its claim. Students tell us the program is "is incredibly international, unrivaled by any other school," with a broad international student population and campuses in France, Abu Dhabi, and Singapore. One student observes: "My fellow students come from 70 countries. My study group is an epitome of globalization: a Mexican investment banker, a Taiwanese accountant, a French Navy officer, an American diplomat, and a Bulgarian marketer, all exchanging knowledge in INSEAD. How much better could it be?" Further driving the point home is the fact that INSEAD is "the only prestigious MBA program that requires three languages upon exit."

Students, grateful for a program that "is not only US-centric," love the international focus at INSEAD. At the same time, students may augment their time in Asia, Europe, and/or the Middle East with a semester in the United States through the school's partnership with the Wharton School at University of Pennsylvania and the Kellogg School of Management at Northwestern University. They also appreciate the fact that it's a ten-month program that "gives quicker return on investment" than longer, more expensive MBA programs. INSEAD has "a strong reputation in consulting and general management" that translates into "placement success with top-tier consulting firms." The school also offers "exceptional private equity and investment courses (private equity, realizing entrepreneurial potential, leveraged buyouts, etc.)." Perhaps the school's greatest strength, though, is the quality of its student body; one MBA tells us, "The work experience of all candidates is extremely high, which creates in-depth, dynamic discussions and learning in the classroom." Another adds: "At this point, any question I have about any country or industry can be solved by simply asking the right classmate."

As in most accelerated programs, "academics are extremely challenging" at INSEAD, especially "for someone completely new to business or on topics for which you have no knowledge. " However, "at the same time there is a stress toward making sure that students understand the basics and all that is necessary for business. What's more, other students who have had experience or who studied business in undergrad are always open to help and encourage each other." The large size of the program, coupled with the speed at which it is completed, "sometimes makes it feel as though you are passing through an MBA factory." Even so, "the administration is generally prompt and receptive, especially with regards to clubs, network and career activities," and is also very efficient.

Career and Placement

INSEAD maintains a Career Development Centre on both its campuses in France and Singapore. The offices promote students to employers around the globe while providing MBAs with one-on-one counseling and coaching, job search strategies, and on-campus recruiting events. Some students complain that Career Development Centre counselors are "used to a specific way of working and don't think outside the box. The focus is all on consulting, finance, and maybe a little industry." Others say, Career Development Centre "is doing a good job, but there is room for improvement, as the school has a lot to offer on the job market." Nearly all agree that the school's substantial alumni network is "very helpful and intent on seeing current graduates succeed."

The diversity of the student body is reflected in the global career prospects; in recent years, INSEAD graduates took jobs at more than 345 companies in sixty-four different countries. Employers most likely to hire INSEAD MBAs include McKinsey & Company, Google, LVMH, Credit Suisse, The Boston Consulting Group, Samsung, Barclays Capital, Bain & Company, Amazon, Microsoft, Standard Chartered Bank, Rocket Internet/Groupon, Shell, and Siemens. Nearly 34 percent of INSEAD MBAs wind up in consulting functions, 17 percent take jobs in financial services, and 49 percent take jobs in industry.

Student Life and Environment

"The INSEAD year is a very intense period," students tell us, noting, "As there are classes every day, we have to study just like in high school and more or less all the time. There is a lot of group work...But, we all understand the quality of the people around us and the need for social interaction," and most here find time for fun.

INSEAD's Fontainebleau campus "is extremely dynamic. There's always something going on, but at the same time depends on the intake. At the end of the day, activities are driven by students. Sometimes, the one-year nature of the program makes keeping activities and clubs continuous a bit challenging." Weekends often feature "fantastic parties at chateaus in the French countryside. The school even provides shuttle buses. Can you beat that?" The Singapore campus "is superb" and "quite relaxed because of the setting."

Admissions

INSEAD has two intake points, in September and January. Students may apply to begin the program at either time; application is online only. All applicants must provide a personal profile, five personal essays (with a sixth optional essay), two recommendations attesting to leadership potential and management capacity, a photograph, a statement of integrity, an official GMAT or GRE score report, and official transcripts for all post-secondary academic work. In addition, all students must enter the program with proficiency in English and a second language. Non-native English speakers may submit results from the TOEFL, TOEIC, PTE Academic, CPE, or IELTS; English speakers must provide certification of a second language. A third commercially useful language (sorry, no Latin!) is required to graduate; while language instruction is available through INSEAD, the intensity of the MBA program is such that the school recommends students get a start on their third language before the program begins. The applicant's choice of campus is not taken into account in the admission decision. However, if the program at their first-choice campus is full, candidates will be offered a spot at the other campus or on the wait list.

FINANCIAL FACTS

Annual tuition (in-state/ out-of-state)	$77,355/$77,355
% of students receiving grants	20

ADMISSIONS

Admissions Selectivity Rating	75
Average GMAT	700
Range of GMAT	650–740
TOEFL required of international students	Yes
Minimum TOEFL (paper/web)	620/105
Application Deadline/Notification	
Round 1:	3/2
Round 2:	4/20
Round 3:	6/15
Round 4:	7/27
Deferment available	No
Transfer students accepted	No
Non-fall admissions	Yes
Need-blind admissions	Yes

IONA COLLEGE
HAGAN SCHOOL OF BUSINESS

GENERAL INFORMATION
Type of school   Private
Affiliation   Roman Catholic
Academic calendar   Trimester

SURVEY SAYS...
Happy students
Solid preparation in:
Teamwork, Presentation skills, Doing
business in a global economy

STUDENTS

Enrollment of parent institution	3,977
Enrollment of MBA Program	332
% male/female	61/39
% out-of-state	8
% part-time	46
% underrepresented minority	20
% international	43
Average age at entry	26
Average years work experience at entry	2

ACADEMICS

Academic Experience Rating	**77**
Profs interesting rating	92
Profs accessible rating	91
Student/faculty ratio	8:1
% female faculty	26
% underrepresented minority faculty	13
% part-time faculty	44

Prominent Alumni
Robert Greifeld, President and CEO,
NASDAQ OMX Group; Don McLean,
an American singer-songwriter,
most famous the songs "American
Pie" and "Vincent"; Laurence
Downes, Chairman of the Board and
CEO, New Jersey Resources; Robert
LaPenta, Chairman, President and
CEO of L-1 Identity Solutions; major
owner of champion thoroughbred
racehorses; Alfred Kelly, former
President of American Express and
President/CEO of the NY/NJ Super
Bowl Host Committee, current CEO
of Intersection

Academics

The Hagan School of Business fully capitalizes on its proximity to New York City, offering MBA and FastTrack MBA programs that lets professionals learn and apply with alacrity. Eight different concentrations help students to hone and build their skill sets to service their personal career goals, and a slew of advanced and Post-Masters Certificates (including in health care information systems, long term care services management, and sports and entertainment management) sweeten the deal. Distance learning and hybrid courses, as well as two programs locations (in Westchester and Rockland counties) help accommodate working students; this relative ease creates a "nurturing learning environment," in which students "can develop personally and academically in comfort." For the traditional MBA, courses are scheduled once a week in the evening on a trimester basis and twice a week during two summer sessions.

The school has "a bright and cheerful atmosphere," mostly due to "the diverse student body and courteous professors," and "classes are challenging in a way that makes learning exciting." Significant emphasis is placed upon participation, and small classes facilitate this greatly. The professors are "very knowledgeable, friendly, courteous and always willing to help understand the material." "I love the fact that I can ask as many questions or more examples and they will be able to explain in detail until I understand the topic," says a student. Faculty members are always available for additional hours, and "all have 'real-world' experience, and they share their experiences with the [students]." Some say that the administration "is a little out of date, and could do with being more efficient," but they are "very responsive to emails."

Career and Placement

All career support is provided by the Gerri Ripp Center for Career Development, which offers résumé and cover letter critiques, job and internship search tools via GAELlink, Iona's online career management system, mock interviews, fall and spring job fairs, and career advising (though there is only one adviser for the entire MBA program, "which makes seeing all of the students extremely difficult"). The location near New York can't help but place opportunities close at hand via professors and the extensive alumni network, and students are easily able to transfer their class work to their experiences on the job experience. "I was able to connect my career to just about everything I was learning in my classes," says a student.

ADMISSIONS CONTACT: BEN FAN, DIRECTOR OF MBA ADMISSIONS
ADDRESS: 715 NORTH AVENUE, NEW ROCHELLE, NY 10801
PHONE: 914-633-2256 • FAX: 914-637-7720
E-MAIL: SFAN@IONA.EDU • WEBSITE: WWW.IONA.EDU/HAGAN

Student Life and Environment

As anyone will tell you, "the greatest strength is the students in the MBA." They are "engaging, willing to help and easy to establish relationships," "self-motivated and focused on acquiring new skills and knowledge to advance their careers," and bring a "diverse set of backgrounds" to the table. In addition to current professionals, Hagan has a surprising number of younger students with only a couple years of work experience, and many come directly from Iona undergrad, completing the spectrum of working individuals. "I had the pleasure to meet people from all over the world," says a student. All are "willing to help each other towards a common goal, whether it be completing an assignment or through forming a study team." The "traditional campus setting" of both locations is also a nice boon to students of all stages, who have a place to centralize themselves and coordinate meetups.

Admissions

Applicants to the Hagan MBA program must submit the following materials: a completed Hagan School of Business application form, along with a $50 application fee; copies of official transcripts from each undergraduate and graduate institution attended; two letters of recommendation; and an official score report for the GMAT reflecting a score no more than five years old (the GMAT requirement may be waived for applicants with at least seven years of post-undergraduate professional experience). Interviews are optional. International applicants must submit all of the materials listed above, as well as an official score report for the TOEFL. Applications are processed on a rolling basis and are valid for one full year from the day they are received by the school. Applicants may request an interview, which the school recommends but does not require.

FINANCIAL FACTS

Cost of books	$1,500
% of students receiving aid	60
% of first-year students receiving aid	65
% of students receiving grants	38
Average award package	$22,640
Average grant	$6,576
Average loan	$24,852
Average student loan debt	$36,233

ADMISSIONS

Admissions Selectivity Rating	65
# of applications received	199
% applicants accepted	97
% acceptees attending	32
Accepts GRE scores	No
Average GPA	3.1
TOEFL required of international students	Yes
Minimum TOEFL (paper/web)	580/80
Application fee	$50
International application fee	$50
Application Deadline/Notification	
Deferment available	Yes
Maximum length of deferment	1 year
Transfer students accepted	Yes
Transfer application policy	

In addition to the eight core classes that can be waived based on undergraduate or graduate credit, one or two classes may be accepted as transfer credit at the discretion of the Director of the Program. All students must complete a minimum of 33 credit hours within the MBA Program to have a degree conferred at Iona.

Non-fall admissions	Yes
Need-blind admissions	Yes

ITHACA COLLEGE
SCHOOL OF BUSINESS

GENERAL INFORMATION
Type of school	Private
Affiliation	No Affiliation

SURVEY SAYS...
Friendly students, Liberal students, Students love Ithaca, NY
Solid preparation in:
Finance, Accounting, Teamwork, Communication/interpersonal skills, Presentation skills, Quantitative skills, Environmental sustainability, Social responsibility

STUDENTS
Enrollment of parent institution	6,769
Enrollment of MBA Program	36
% male/female	58/42
% part-time	14
% underrepresented minority	13
% international	6
Average age at entry	22
Average years work experience at entry	0

ACADEMICS
Academic Experience Rating	**75**
Profs interesting rating	88
Profs accessible rating	97
% female faculty	31
% underrepresented minority faculty	12
% part-time faculty	15

Academics

MBA students in Ithaca College's small graduate program may choose between an MBA in business administration and an MBA in professional accountancy. Both degrees require thirty-six credit hours and can be completed by full-time students in twelve months—and this is the selling point of the program. As one student explains, "A one-year program offered me a faster track to my post-MBA life."

The curriculum for Ithaca's Business Administration MBA includes 8 required courses, which build up to a comprehensive capstone experience. In addition, students choose four elective courses. Classes emphasize "a balance between building technical and interpersonal skills," and students praise professors for their "hands-on teaching philosophy." "The faculty is always willing to bend over backwards to meet students' academic and professional needs," says one student. "While the professors remain rather rigid in their expectations of students, most will work tirelessly with students to ensure they succeed." Another student notes, "The school does a good job offering elective courses that are in line with students' career aspirations. Since the program is small, faculty surveys students prior to each semester. The result is a course offering that honestly reflects the interests of students. I see this adaptability as Ithaca's greatest strength because it can help overcome the obstacles often associated with a smaller business school."

Ithaca's Professional Accountancy MBA primarily functions as the culmination of a five-year undergraduate/graduate program for students in the college's undergraduate accounting program, although candidates from other schools can gain admission. Most here agree that although "many students that graduated from Ithaca as undergrads" are now part of the MBA program, there are also "older" or "married" students in attendance.

The curriculum includes a thorough review of principles of business administration as well as advanced instruction in financial accounting and reporting, managerial and cost accounting, auditing, taxation, and principles of business law. Students in both programs are full of praise for the school. "Overall, I think the school is really starting to take off. Ithaca worked hard to receive AACSB accreditation, [and] since that happened the school has retained high standards for both students and faculty." Another adds, "Tuition is high, but you can definitely see where the money went. Everything from the smart boards in the classrooms—which help make articulating difficult accounting concepts much easier—to the trading room is state-of-the-art."

Students note that the one-year duration of the program helps offset the relatively high cost of attending. That said, while it had been a "little pricey" in the past, "prices have come down." They also appreciate the fact that the business school administration "welcome(s) comments and suggestions from the grad students on what could help better the program. If you have any problems, they do their best to help you solve the issues." The future's looking bright here, so bring your shades.

Career and Placement

The Ithaca College Career Services Office provides self-assessment inventories, e-Recruiting tools, one-on-one advising, mock interviews, workshops, a library, and on-campus recruiting. The school also hosts a graduate school job fair and other special recruiting events. Though despite all this, some students find that "Ithaca could do a better job attracting recruiters from upper-tier businesses." While they appreciate the "many local recruiters on campus" and "ample alumni network and mentoring program," some still find a dearth of businesses at which they're "trying to get [their] foot in the door."

Employers who recruit on the Ithaca campus include Lockheed-Martin, Merrill Lynch, PricewaterhouseCoopers, Ernst & Young, Deloitte, KPMG International, and an active alumni recruiting network.

Student Life and Environment

MBA students at Ithaca College enjoy "a great community atmosphere" at a school that "is just the right size, so that you can go anywhere and know somebody, and meet somebody new." One student writes, "All students are easygoing and approachable. The small size of the program means that many people have identical course schedules. This makes for a tight-knit group of students and strong, long-lasting friendships."

The demands of the program keep MBA students "pretty detached from the rest of the campus. You never deal with grad students from any of the other programs (unless they happen to take a business elective)." However, "students work hard and play hard" when their schedule allows. "Most weekends I find myself in one or more bars or restaurants eating and drinking with classmates," says one student. Ultimately, "Life at Ithaca is good."

Admissions

Applicants to Ithaca's MBA program must have completed either a bachelor's program in business or accounting, or a bachelor's program in any non-business field plus undergraduate business coursework equivalent to Ithaca's pre-MBA minor.. Post-undergraduate work experience is not required; in fact, many students enter the program immediately after completing work on their bachelor's degree. Successful applicants typically have "an undergraduate GPA of 3.0 or higher and a minimum GMAT score of 500. All applications must include official undergraduate transcripts, official GMAT scores, and two letters of recommendation in addition to the essay. Merit-based academic scholarships are also available from the program.

FINANCIAL FACTS

% of students receiving grants	40

ADMISSIONS

Admissions Selectivity Rating	67
# of applications received	40
% applicants accepted	95
% acceptees attending	79
Accepts GRE scores	No
Average GPA	3.4
TOEFL required of international students	Yes
Minimum TOEFL (paper/web)	550/80
Application fee	$40
International application fee	$40
Early application deadline	3/1
Early notification date	4/1
Regular application deadline	5/1
Regular application notification	6/1
Application Deadline/Notification	
Deferment available	Yes
Transfer students accepted	Yes
Transfer application policy Transfer credits from AACSB-accredited institutions accepted on case-by-case basis.	
Non-fall admissions	Yes
Need-blind admissions	Yes

JOHN CARROLL UNIVERSITY
THE BOLER SCHOOL OF BUSINESS

GENERAL INFORMATION
Type of school   Private
Affiliation   Roman Catholic-Jesuit
Academic calendar   Semesters

SURVEY SAYS...
Friendly students, Conservative students
Solid preparation in:
Teamwork, Communication/interpersonal skills, Presentation skills

STUDENTS
Enrollment of parent institution	3,673
Enrollment of MBA Program	77
% male/female	63/37
% out-of-state	20
% part-time	47
% underrepresented minority	2
% international	5
Average age at entry	28
Average years work experience at entry	1

ACADEMICS
Academic Experience Rating	**83**
Profs interesting rating	88
Profs accessible rating	91
Student/faculty ratio	14:1
% female faculty	25
% underrepresented minority faculty	8
% part-time faculty	15

Prominent Alumni
Tim Russert, Senior VP & Washington burea chief for NBC; Don Shula, Former NFL Coach; John Boler, Chairman & Founder of The Boler Company; Richard Kramer, President & CEO of Goodyear Tire; John Breen, Retired CEO of Sherwin Williams

Academics

The Boler School of Business at John Carroll University offers a part-time MBA program for working professionals with at least two years of work experience and a full-time one year accelerated program (fifth-year) for recent graduates. Unlike traditional MBA programs, the part-time "MBA is focused around solving real business problems" and learning about the decisions business leaders have to make. Every class starts with a real problem, posed by a regional company, and "over the semester, students learn tools to help solve the company's problem." These unique courses "are designed to challenge students to leverage all business disciplines" and learn about project management, leadership, innovation, and resource allocation, instead of separating knowledge fields by theme or topic. This helps students "absorb relevant knowledge" and learn "to solve problems from a multi-discipline perspective" and approach them "from a holistic point of view." This is particularly helpful to "those who work full time" because they can "immediately put into practice theories they've learned in their current profession."

Students think the majority of professors are great and appreciate that they "are connected to community business leaders." Professors "tend to have real-world experience" and are "knowledgeable in their fields." Additionally, they are "friendly" and "helpful," and are willing to "go the extra mile to ensure a great education and comprehension of material." Students appreciate the flexibility of the program and the "convenient scheduling" that allows them to vary the number of classes they take each semester. John Carroll is really about putting students first, and with its affordable tuition and "stellar" local reputation, it's no surprise students are so "impressed" with the program.

Career and Placement

The Boler School of Business does not have its own career office, so students must rely on the Center for Career Services that is used by all graduate and undergraduate students. The Center hosts career fairs and on-campus interviews that are well attended thanks to Boler's strong reputation for producing excellent students. "Career Services does a great job bringing companies to campus for interviews and helping students find jobs," one student says. The Center also provides career coaching and help with fundamentals like resumes. Boler does offer a lot of networking events, and local business leaders are always speaking on campus. One student says that "John Carroll business students are viewed as extremely competent, hard-working, and ethical. With many Fortune-500 firms located in Cleveland, John Carroll students are strong contenders for any position within them." A dedicated internship coordinator provides assistance to fifth year MBA students to complete their professional development requirement.

Still, students think there is "room for improvement" in the school's career programming. One of Boler's best resources is its professors, who "move in the spheres of influence and can be a catalyst to professional growth." Additionally, other students in the program are "invaluable resources and serve as internal referral sources to help students in search of new careers get a foot in the door." Organizations that recently visited the campus include GE Capital, Avery Dennison, Ernst & Young LLP, Progressive, PricewaterhouseCoopers LLP, PolyOne Corporation, and Sherwin Williams, although these organizations were not specifically looking for MBA grads.

ADMISSIONS CONTACT: KRISTOPHER TIBBS, ASSISTANT DEAN—GRADUATE BUSINESS PROGRAMS
ADDRESS: 1 JOHN CARROLL BOULEVARD, UNIVERSITY HEIGHTS, OH 44118-4581
PHONE: 216-397-4391 • FAX: 216-397-1833
E-MAIL: GRADBUSINESS@JCU.EDU • WEBSITE: WWW.JCU.EDU/MBA

Student Life and Environment

Like many universities with a large commuter student population, student life at Boler is a little lacking. But while some wish there were more activities or options for socializing, others say "there is no reason any John Carroll student should ever be bored." "John Carroll's sports teams are always competing on campus and provide high-level sports entertainment." Additionally, "there is plenty to do in the area socially," and "downtown is within fifteen minutes of campus." Perhaps some of the 5th year MBA students find themselves with time to socialize, but plenty of part-time students say that between their jobs, classes, schoolwork, and families, they don't have time for anything else anyway. Students say that despite this, they've "formed several relationships within their cohort" and are in "constant e-mail communication" with other students. There is a lot of "camaraderie" among students, who describe their peers as "friendly," "supportive," "professional," and "intelligent." Students are competitive but are still "very open and willing to help each other."

Admissions

Boler requires a minimum of two years of professional experience to be admitted to the part-time MBA program. No work experience is required for students applying to the fifth-year MBA program. Students applying to Boler must submit official transcripts from all colleges attended, GMAT scores, one letter of recommendation, a resume, and a personal statement entitled "Graduate Business Education: Enabling Me to Achieve My Personal Goals and Become a Leader." The MBA program requires a minimum GPA of 2.8. The average GPA of the entering class is 3.23 and an average GMAT score of 520. International applicants, whose primary language is not English must take the TOEFL and score a minimum of 550 on the paper portion, 215 on the computer portion and 79 on the Internet portion. They must also have their "non-US credentials" evaluated by an independent organization.

FINANCIAL FACTS

Annual tuition (in-state/ out-of-state)	$15,390/$15,390
Fees	$0
Cost of books	$1,000
% of students receiving aid	46
% of first-year students receiving aid	52
% of students receiving grants	10
Average award package	$15,152
Average grant	$9,367
Average loan	$13,450
Average student loan debt	$24,217

ADMISSIONS

Admissions Selectivity Rating	77
# of applications received	44
% applicants accepted	98
% acceptees attending	72
Average GMAT	520
Range of GMAT	470–590
Accepts GRE scores	Yes
Average Verbal GRE	151
Range of Verbal GRE scores	145–152
Average Quantitative GRE	152
Range of Quantitative GRE scores	150–153
Average Writing GRE	3.8
Range of Writing GRE scores	3.5–4.0
Average GPA	3.4
TOEFL required of international students	Yes
Minimum TOEFL (paper/web)	550/79
Application fee	$0
International application fee	$0
Application Deadline/Notification	
Deferment available	Yes
Maximum length of deferment	1 year
Transfer students accepted	Yes
Transfer application policy Applicants from Jesuit MBA Network memebers will have all MBA credits transferred. Otherwise, applicants are reviewed on a case-by-case basis.	
Non-fall admissions	Yes
Need-blind admissions	Yes

EMPLOYMENT PROFILE

Career Rating	76	Grads Employed by Function% Avg. Salary	
Percent employed at graduation	80	Operations	(20%)
Average base starting salary	$41,875	Finance	(40%)
Primary Source of Full-time Job Acceptances		Other	(40%)
School-facilitated activities	1 (20%)	**Top 5 Employers Hiring Grads**	
Graduate-facilitated activities	2 (40%)	Deloitte (1), Sherwin-Williams (1), Kenan	
Unknown	2 (40%)	Advantage Group (1), Lake Erie Energy Development Corporation (1)	

KENNESAW STATE UNIVERSITY
MICHAEL J. COLES COLLEGE OF BUSINESS

GENERAL INFORMATION

Type of school	Public
Affiliation	No Affiliation
Academic calendar	Semester

SURVEY SAYS...

Classmates have diverse work experience, Friendly students, Happy students, Students love Kennesaw, GA
Solid preparation in:
General management, Teamwork, Communication/interpersonal skills, Presentation skills, Quantitative skills

STUDENTS

Enrollment of parent institution	33,000
Enrollment of MBA Program	170
% part-time	100
Average age at entry	31
Average years work experience at entry	9

ACADEMICS

Academic Experience Rating	94
Profs interesting rating	92
Profs accessible rating	93
Student/faculty ratio	7:1
% female faculty	37
% underrepresented minority faculty	24
% part-time faculty	5

Joint Degrees

MBA/MPA, 51 credit hours; MBA/Masters of Conflict Management, 53 credit hours; MBA/Masters of Information Systems, 51 credit hours.

Prominent Alumni

Tom Hughes, President and CEO (retired), National Electronic Attachment; Wiliam Hayes, CEO, Northside Hospital-Cherokee; Kerstin Valdes, Vice President of Finance-Consumer, Georgia Pacific; Brad Kehm, Global Sales Director-Tennis, Nike; Keith Schroeder, CEO and Founder, High Road Craft Ice Cream

Academics

One of the largest business programs in the state of Georgia, Kennesaw State University also has "the lowest cost out of all good schools in the Atlanta area." The "affordable" tuition means a "cost effective" education that doesn't skimp on quality. "Why pay a lot more for education when KSU offers great value for the cost?" one student muses. One notable feature of the school is its unique "Returned Peace Corps Fellows" program that waives tuition for Peace Corps volunteers. The school's "physical location" is a big strength for students. The campus is located "right off two highways," making it easy for students to balance family, life, jobs, and school. A related benefit of Kennesaw is its "amazing flexibility in its program" that, one student explains, means "I can base my course load on what's going on at work and in my life." This part-time program allows students to get their MBA in as little as one and a half years or as many as six, depending on the student's needs.

"At Coles College of Business, the opportunities are near infinite and the caliber of professors, staff, and education is more than enough to groom the next leaders of business and society," one happy student proclaims. "Teachers recognize that most students work full time," although that sometimes means that classes could use "a little more rigor." Students give mixed reviews to the professors. "I've had phenomenal professors who are engaging and really care about the students and I've had the opposite as well," one student says. "Some of the professors seem to be here only for the research and publication opportunities." However, most teachers are "outstanding human beings and intellectuals" who "truly are engaged with their students." "My professors are excellent and they have given me the opportunity to truly discover myself," one student declares. Classes at Kennesaw "are conducted in a very open forum," which promotes "a culture of engagement at the University." "Students are encouraged to participate and contribute to the learning process," leading students to feel "as challenged by" their peers as by their instructors. Students feel that the "facilities are great" and that the administration is "easily accessible and very helpful." One business student compares the Kennesaw experience to previous colleges they attended and declares that "Kennesaw State is a ten out of ten on a scale for administration."

Career and Placement

Kennesaw State University works hard to help students find work. Students "frequently receive emails from faculty about job/internship opportunities," and the school's "career fairs have an excellent range of companies represented." "It is true that there has been little in the way of targeted career placement efforts of MBA students," although this may be improving with "the inclusion of guest lectures from various Atlanta based companies." Many students at Kennesaw are already working and not necessarily actively looking for new work. Instead, they use their MBA to increase their career opportunities and skill set.

ADMISSIONS CONTACT: TIMOTHY ISLES, MBA RECRUITER
ADDRESS: 1000 CHASTAIN ROAD, #9109, KENNESAW, GA 30144
PHONE: 470-578-4470 • FAX: 470-578-9088
E-MAIL: TISLES@KENNESAW.EDU • WEBSITE: WWW.COLESMBA.COM

Student Life and Environment

Students at Kennesaw are "very busy" "working professionals" who come "from all walks of life." These are "friendly, smart, helpful, driven," and "high-achieving" workers "trying to better themselves while working full time." There is great "diversity" in the student body all around, including "age, race, and backgrounds." One student says that even being only "eight classes into my degree, I have already met many fellow students with whom I hope to stay in touch with for the rest of my life."

"The MBA campus is segregated from the rest of campus," which has the benefit of making "parking very easy for classes." "There are many graduate programs on campus to address the social aspects of college life," but most students are balancing their education with careers and family and have little time to socialize. Still, "there is always something going on at the Campus Green" and "Kennesaw State offers a wide variety of in-class and out of class opportunities to be involved with the campus, alumni, and outside activities."

Admissions

Admission to Coles MBA program is based on three required items: professional work experience, academic transcripts, and GMAT score. In addition, students can request an optional interview. The school offers complimentary GMAT prep sessions to all applicants who desire them.

ADMISSIONS	
Admissions Selectivity Rating	**91**
# of applications received	131
% applicants accepted	29
% acceptees attending	76
Average GMAT	595
Range of GMAT	540–610
Accepts GRE scores	Yes
Average GPA	3.1
TOEFL required of international students	Yes
Minimum TOEFL (web)	80
Application fee	$60
International application fee	$60
Early application deadline	6/1
Regular application deadline	7/1
Application Deadline/Notification	
Deferment available	Yes
Maximum length of deferment	1 year
Transfer students accepted	Yes
Transfer application policy Transfer credit from AACSB International accredited universities is possible. Limits and restrictions apply.	
Non-fall admissions	Yes
Need-blind admissions	Yes

KENT STATE UNIVERSITY
THE COLLEGE OF BUSINESS ADMINISTRATION

GENERAL INFORMATION
Type of school | Public
Affiliation | No Affiliation
Academic calendar | Semester

SURVEY SAYS...
Friendly students, Liberal students
Solid preparation in:
Teamwork

STUDENTS
Enrollment of parent
  institution | 41,005
Enrollment of MBA Program | 122
% male/female | 67/33
% out-of-state | 10
% part-time | 50
% underrepresented minority | 5
% international | 44
Average age at entry | 24
Average years work
  experience at entry | 2

ACADEMICS
Academic Experience Rating | **85**
Profs interesting rating | 85
Profs accessible rating | 91
Student/faculty ratio | 30:1
% female faculty | 40
% underrepresented
  minority faculty | 9
% part-time faculty | 5

Joint Degrees
MBA/MSN, 3 yrs; MBA/MLS, 2
yrs; MBA/Master of Architecture,
2 yrs; MBA/MA Translation, 2 yrs;
MBA/MA Communication Studies,
2-3 yrs.

Prominent Alumni
Drew A. McCandless, SVP Global
Excellence Initiatives, Sherwin-
Willliams; Virginia Albanese, CEO,
Fedex Custom Critical; Andrew
Traicoff, VP Consumer Sales &
Customer Development, Goodyear;
Dennis Cuneo, Managing Partner,
Fisher & Phillips, LLP; MR
Rangaswami, Managing Director,
Sand Hill Group

Academics

A big name in Ohio education, Kent State University serves the Midwest with a range of high-quality MBA programs. Here, young professionals can jump-start their careers through an "enjoyable and enlightening" academic curriculum, offered at "a value price." Catering to students at every stage of life, the college operates a full-time MBA on the main campus and part-time MBA. Seasoned managers can apply for the fast-paced Executive MBA and the Executive MBA for Healthcare Professionals, and "Kent is one of a few schools in the nation that has a dual-masters degree with architecture and business." Cost effective and convenient, "Kent State is in the heart of northeast Ohio, which makes it possible to have a career in one of the surrounding cities, while going to graduate school part-time."

Kent State maintains an accomplished team of business professors, who often come to the college from impressive executive and managerial positions. On the whole, "professors are extremely knowledgeable and eager to teach," and they usually "stay up-to-date on current events and issues related to their fields in business." To encourage networking and build soft skills, the program "promotes group work," and classroom discussions are encouraged. A current student adds, "In the part-time MBA program, everyone is working, so we are able to share real-world experiences in the classroom. There is something every night in class that I can take and apply to my job."

Whether they attend in the evenings or full-time, MBA students can expect a "fairly heavy workload" throughout the program. Fortunately, they'll receive plenty of support from the faculty and staff. At Kent State, "the professors are incredibly interested in the students' success," and they are "almost always available for individual consultation on topics not necessarily related to class work." A student shares, "I am very comfortable meeting with professors during office hours, even when I am not enrolled in one of their courses." Administrators are also "very helpful," and make it clear that they "really care about your future success as an individual." Finally, Kent State is an excellent value. As a state school, "the tuition is relatively low," while the regional reputation is excellent.

Career and Placement

Most students in the Part-time MBA are already employed when they enter the program, and may even be receiving tuition reimbursement from their employer. As a result, the majority of these students are not actively seeking employment. However, Kent State makes an "effort to prepare students for life after graduation," even if they aren't looking for a new job. Across the curriculum, "the classes are well integrated into real-world business careers," and practical applications are emphasized.

While completing an MBA, students have access to various professional development opportunities, including networking events, career planning workshops, and a mentorship program, through which students are paired with executives in their field of interest. Students can also "consult advisors and a career manager to know more about how to draft a career plan and get fully prepared." With a strong reputation throughout the state, the college maintains "good contacts with potential employers" in the region. After completing the MBA program, Kent State graduates earn an average base salary of $54,167.

Admissions Contact: Louise Ditchey, Administrative Director
Address: P.O. Box 5190, 475 Terrace Drive, Kent, OH 44242-0001
Phone: 330-672-2282 • Fax: 330-672-7303
E-mail: gradbus@kent.edu • Website: www.business.kent.edu

Student Life and Environment

On the main campus, as well as the auxiliary facilities, Kent State offers a "great atmosphere and learning environment for its students." Students are able to maintain a balanced lifestyle, as "the workload is enough to keep busy, but not so busy that you cannot have a life outside of school and work." Plus, "the business school encourages students to stay involved with extracurricular activities," like case competitions and academic clubs. "Full-time students are more apt to be involved" in campus life than busy part-time students. Nonetheless, "the camaraderie among part-time students is very strong" at Kent State. Drawing students from across the globe, The College of Business Administration benefits from "rich diversity in student culture and ethnicity." Classroom discussion can become rather lively, and "even if we don't agree on political or social issues, there is always room for intellectual debate."

Beyond the business college, the greater Kent State University is "large enough to offer any club or activity students are interested in." Off campus, Kent is "a college town" that offers "opportunities for community service and professional practice," as well as good old-fashioned fun.

Admissions

If you are considering Kent State University for your MBA, you'll get your first taste of the college's charms through the "friendliness of the recruiting staff." Full-time students can only apply for fall admission, and there are several priority application deadlines during the winter and spring. The school also offers graduate assistantship programs to help full-time students pay for their education. To be considered for an assistantship or scholarship, students must submit an additional application form and should apply as early as possible. The average test scores, work experience, and GPA of incoming students vary by program. However, the average GPA and GMAT scores for the entire program were 3.29 and 556, respectively.

FINANCIAL FACTS

Annual tuition (in-state/ out-of-state)	$10,864/$18,380
Fees	$1,200
Cost of books	$1,200
Room & board (on/off-campus)	$10,400/$9,000
% of students receiving aid	30
% of first-year students receiving aid	15
% of students receiving grants	0
Average award package	$21,457
Average grant	$0
Average loan	$0

ADMISSIONS

Admissions Selectivity Rating	85
# of applications received	77
% applicants accepted	61
% acceptees attending	66
Average GMAT	568
Range of GMAT	530–630
Accepts GRE scores	Yes
Average GPA	3.3
TOEFL required of international students	Yes
Minimum TOEFL (paper/web)	550/80
Application fee	$45
International application fee	$70
Regular application deadline	4/1
Regular application notification	4/15
Application Deadline/Notification	
Deferment available	Yes
Maximum length of deferment	one year
Transfer students accepted	Yes
Transfer application policy -AASCB accredited program -Less than 6 years old by the time Kent degree is conferred–12 credit hours maximum -Approved by graduate committee and dean	
Non-fall admissions	Yes
Need-blind admissions	Yes

EMPLOYMENT PROFILE

		Grads Employed by Function	% Avg. Salary
Career Rating	81		
Percent employed at graduation	32	Finance	(24%) $67,500
Percent employed 3 months after graduation	37	HR	(12%) $52,500
		MIS	(6%) $47,500
Average base starting salary	$54,167	Other	(58%) $40,500
Primary Source of Full-time Job Acceptances		**Top 5 Employers Hiring Grads**	
		Eaton (1), Nestle Purina (1), EY (1), Exact Holding North America (1), E-Waste (1)	

La Salle University

School of Business

Academics

For Philadelphia-area professionals looking to jump-start their careers, La Salle University School of Business "is a city school with a suburban feel." The MBA program maintains "high expectations" while creating a "class setting [that] is intimate and inviting." La Salle's professors and administrators truly "understand the working student who is trying to balance work, life, and schooling." "La Salle University offers an excellent program with great flexibility for working family members," one part-time MBA student explains. "Satellite schools conveniently located around the suburbs of Philadelphia," so students can attend class close to work or home. Evening and Saturday classes along with intersession and summer courses "help students complete their degrees in a reasonable amount of time." Online and hybrid classes can provide students with full-time jobs or other obligations with greater flexibility as well.

La Salle offers students "small class sizes with professors [who are] willing to help." Students appreciate that their professors "are also practitioners, so their real-life experiences are great resources," and they "are very good at integrating real-life business situations into our classwork." As one student explains, La Salle professors "make every project or assignment team-oriented and simulate a true business environment." In addition to "teamwork or group projects in every single class," "presentation skills" are also an important part of the curriculum and "almost every class makes you get up and present." Overall, La Salle students report that their professors are "amazing," "[dedicated] and eager to help."

Career and Placement

La Salle students boast about their "strong job placement record," including a 100% job placement rate among recent graduates from its one-year MBA program. Many MBA students at La Salle have already begun their careers, and "most of them [are] working with 3 to 10 years of experience." Students say that they come to La Salle for "increased income or better job opportunities." Students benefit from belonging to a cohort of business professionals who are "serious about getting an MBA and advancing in business" and who represent various industries, from "large firms like Amazon, KPMG, and Ace Insurance" to "local non-profits." There are "ample" opportunities for "networking with classmates and professors" and for students "to take concepts from the classroom and immediately implement them at the office." La Salle's "great reputation in the area" and the diverse business and educational backgrounds of its students create an "opportunity for continued learning and career advancement."

ADMISSIONS CONTACT: ELIZABETH SCOFIELD AND DENISE SAURENNANN, DIRECTORS
ADDRESS: 1900 WEST OLNEY AVENUE, PHILADELPHIA, PA 19141 UNITED STATES
PHONE: 215-951-1057 • FAX: 215-951-1886 • E-MAIL: MBA@LASALLE.EDU
WEBSITE: WWW.LASALLE.EDU/ACADEM/SBA/GRAD/INDEX.SHTML

Student Life and Environment

Students find La Salle to be "warm and welcoming," and they are " impressed with the way the business school tries to engage its students" through "basketball games, happy hours, and other social events" that "get students together outside of the classroom and networking." The main campus has recently completed "a new state-of-the art business building" that provides students "with food stands, computer/printer labs, MBA lounge, and [. . .] an environment to gather together to study, work on projects, collaborate, set up meetings, and socialize." The student body is "mostly working adults, many managing families, with school and full-time jobs." This "very diverse group of students, many from different countries and different industries," are all "friendly," "driven, and willing to work hard in their classes." Students rave about their classmates and find it "a pleasure to attend class after working all day with such good people."

Admissions

La Salle requires applicants for their full-time MBA to have obtained a four-year undergraduate degree and to submit official transcripts, résumé or personal statement, and test scores from the GMAT or GRE. Applicants who have earned a graduate degree already or who have an undergraduate business degree from an AACSB-accredited program and at least a 3.2 GPA may be able to have the GRE or GMAT requirement waived. International students will need to take the TOEFL, IELTS unless their undergraduate degree is from an US college or university. International students also need to submit a statement of financial responsibility form. The admissions committee weighs each applicant's interest, aptitude, and potential to succeed, but no prior work experience is required. Applicants for the more intensive one-year MBA who do not have an undergraduate degree or a minor in business must complete a pre-MBA foundations class before beginning the program.

FINANCIAL FACTS

Annual tuition	$22,350
Fees	$570
Cost of books	$1,000
Room & board	$8,260

ADMISSIONS

Admissions Selectivity Rating	**75**
% acceptees attending	50
Average GMAT	450
Accepts GRE scores	Yes
Average Verbal GRE	146
Average Quantitative GRE	144
Average Writing GRE	3.3
TOEFL required of international students	Yes
Minimum TOEFL (paper)	573
Application fee	$0
International application fee	$0
Regular application deadline	8/15
Deferment available	Yes
Transfer students accepted	No
Non-fall admissions	Yes
Need-blind admissions	No

EMPLOYMENT PROFILE

Career Rating	86	Grads Employed by Function	% Avg. Salary
Percent employed at graduation	82	Marketing	(11%) $51,000
Percent employed 3 months after graduation	90	Consulting	(2%)$64,000
		Management	(9%) $47,500
Average base starting salary	$53,625	Finance	(70%) $54,887
Primary Source of Full-time Job Acceptances		HR	(5%) $52,000
School-facilitated activities	3(7%)	Other	(2%) $45,000
Graduate-facilitated activities	41(93%)		

LAMAR UNIVERSITY
COLLEGE OF BUSINESS

Academics

The College of Business at Lamar University offers affordable, respected MBA and leadership programs and a flexibility of scheduling (including a full-time evening program) that makes this a go-to for regional professionals looking for an advanced business degree. Classes place an emphasis on ethics and social responsibility as core element in the business environment, and the curriculum is designed in a way that all students have an opportunity to succeed, meaning "the onus of success lies squarely with the student."

Small class sizes are "very helpful" in allowing the students to forge strong relationships with both the professors and other students ("a good student teacher interface"), and most professors are "inspiring, encouraging [and] have good humor." "You feel you want to come to class because you learn and enjoy the subject at the same time," says a student. Most professors have in-field work experience and "give you some of the 'you won't learn this in that book' education." They are all "understanding, hold everyone to the same high standards, and truly want you to succeed if you want to." The MBA administrative staff "works very well with the students and professors" and is "more than available to the students on a regular basis."

Career and Placement

The Dean, professors, and staff are "unbelievably helpful" and "go out of their way to accommodate the students." Many students here are established working professionals; they appreciate the administration's understanding of their outside commitments and "[do] all that is reasonable for a working individual" to help them uphold their requirements for classes, grades, and a diploma. Students who aren't "feel like something should be available for those of us in this category," such as career fairs.

Lamar has an excellent reputation in Texas and "the school...has very strong roots in the community and outside of it." The "well-organized" MBA Advisement Office is "very attentive, friendly, and helpful."

Student Life and Environment

Students at Lamar are "friendly, intelligent, and bring challenges to each class." This "diverse student base" brings skills sets from "engineering, banking, retail, manufacturing, law, and finance to the program" and contributes well through questions, answers, and support. Students come "from many cultures, experiences and age levels., religions, and countries." For the most part, "everyone embraces the southern hospitality of Texas."

Beaumont is a "very nice city," and is "really good for students to focus on their studies because it does not have a lot of entertainment places." The food, gym, library, and computer labs are "outstanding," and "the campus is large, but not cumbersome." While some wish that there were more group social gatherings and organized events, people say that "it is not the depressing night school crowd that you would normally assume night classes might attract." "My peers all seem to be highly motivated and successful professionals who are pursuing an advanced degree for more specialized credentials in their career field," says a student.

Admissions

Lamar University requires all applicants to provide GMAT scores, undergraduate transcripts, essays, and TOEFL scores (for students whose native language is not English). An interview, letters of recommendation, personal statement, resume, and evidence of computer experience are all recommended but not required; all are taken into account in rendering an admissions decision. Applicants must earn a score of at least 1000 under the formula (200 multiplied by GPA plus GMAT score) or a score of 1000 under the formula (200 multiplied by GPA for final sixty semester hours of undergraduate work plus GMAT score). International applicants must provide proof of financial support.

FINANCIAL FACTS

Annual tuition (in-state/ out-of-state)	$8,910/$19,440
Fees	$4,452
Cost of books	$1,741
Room & board (on/off-campus)	$10,558/
% of students receiving aid	78
% of first-year students receiving aid	77
% of students receiving grants	55
Average award package	$5,814
Average grant	$1,553
Average loan	$9,135
Average student loan debt	$37,674

ADMISSIONS

Admissions Selectivity Rating	83
# of applications received	65
% applicants accepted	57
% acceptees attending	62
Average GMAT	474
Range of GMAT	408–558
Accepts GRE scores	No
Average GPA	3.3
TOEFL required of international students	Yes
Minimum TOEFL (paper/web)	550/79
Application fee	$25
International application fee	$75
Early application deadline	4/15
Regular application deadline	8/8
Application Deadline/Notification	
Deferment available	Yes
Maximum length of deferment	1 year
Transfer students accepted	Yes
Transfer application policy Accept 6 hours from another AACSB MBA program	
Non-fall admissions	Yes
Need-blind admissions	Yes

EMPLOYMENT PROFILE

Career Rating	76	**Grads Employed by Function**	**% Avg. Salary**
Percent employed at graduation	11	Management	(4%) $42,500
Average base starting salary	$58,000	Finance	(2%) $40,000
Primary Source of Full-time Job Acceptances		Other	(4%) $82,500
School-facilitated activities	1 (20%)	**Top 5 Employers Hiring Grads**	
Unknown	4 (80%)	Mead Westvaco (1), Cook Parker (1), First Financial Bank (1)	

LONG ISLAND UNIVERSITY—POST
COLLEGE OF MANAGEMENT

GENERAL INFORMATION
Type of school	Private
Affiliation	No Affiliation
Academic calendar	Trimester

SURVEY SAYS...
Happy students
Solid preparation in:
Presentation skills, Doing business in
a global economy

STUDENTS
Enrollment of parent institution	14,708
Enrollment of MBA Program	164
% male/female	52/48
% out-of-state	2
% part-time	40
% underrepresented minority	3
% international	36
Average age at entry	27
Average years work experience at entry	5

ACADEMICS
Academic Experience Rating	85
Profs interesting rating	88
Profs accessible rating	87
Student/faculty ratio	15:1
% female faculty	29
% underrepresented minority faculty	54
% part-time faculty	0

Joint Degrees
JD/MBA: JD, 3 yrs, MBA 1.5 yrs;
BS Business/MBA: BS 4 yrs, MBA
1 yr; BS Accountancy/MBA: BS 4
yrs, MBA 1 year; BA Economics/
MBA: BS 4 yrs, MBA 1 yr; BFA Arts
Management/MBA: BS 4 yrs, MBA
1 yr; BA International Studies/MBA:
BS 4 yrs, MBA 1 yr.

Prominent Alumni
Bill Nuti, CEO of NCR Corp.;
Howard Lorber, CEO of Nathan's
Famous; Peter Gibson, CEP of
Knowledgent Group; Rosemary
Roser, VP&Controller of Nat'l
Football League; Sara Beth Levine,
Chairman of Sarabeth's Kitchen

Academics

Long Island University—Post offers an AACSB-accredited MBA through "the flexibility of a Saturday program" or through a series of night classes, which occur weekly, Monday through Thursday. The Saturday program takes anywhere from fifteen to twenty-three months to complete and features all-day classes held only on Saturdays. Additionally, those who opt for weekly night classes may supplement them with Saturday classes, as well. There is also an advanced certification program in which students may opt to specialize in one of four areas, including finance and international business. The requirement for this program is four additional electives. Most students choose a part-time schedule because it allows them to comfortably continue leading lives off campus. "I attend night classes, which do not interfere with my daily schedule. As a full-time student I am enrolled in three courses of study, which are highly relevant and have real-world applications." Another student says, "I would truly recommend others for this program. Flexibility is key when you have a full-time job."

Enrolled students come from various business backgrounds, such as medical communications, construction, and technology. "The differing perspectives at Post help to broaden the overall attitude of students and faculty alike. You learn something new every day." Some "students are looking to kick start their own careers and help contribute to Long Island communities," while others have little or no experience. Students who attended LIU for their undergraduate studies say they have no problem adapting to the graduate curriculum. And of those with no prior training, one claims to have quickly gained an "excellent" grasp on the material because of the program's professors. "They are always willing to clarify content and go the extra mile." "The faculty are all Ph.D. holders from prestigious business schools." "Most or all have considerable real-world experience" as well. Students are pleased with the professors' ability to follow current global events and economic shifts. One student says the program "makes you become more creative and competitive. I can see the big difference between my friends in other colleges. I feel gifted for being educated in this school." Some students feel differently, suggesting that not all professors measure up. They also argue that there aren't enough options. "The range of courses could be a lot better and wider." Some classes that are listed are not offered every year.

As far as the administration is concerned, students had little to say. One complimented the librarians who help with projects and papers, and another says, "All the departments have very good employees and are always willing to help you." The B. Davis Schwartz Memorial Library houses 2.3 million volumes.

Career and Placement

The Office of Career Services offers a variety of services to the students at LIU including the following: career counseling, mock interviews, recruiting events, and self-assessment diagnostics. Students, however, find real job assistance lacking. One describes it as "nonexistent," while another suggests, "Get better companies to come to job fairs." However, many students at LIU are professionals already working in the field, and the student services do not apply to them.

Student Life and Environment

Students praise each other as "smart" and "dedicated." "There is a good mix ranging in age, ethnic background, educational background, and career background. All are friendly and we work well together." They also describe each other as "intelligent," "ambitious," "outgoing," and "cooperative." Students "bring a lot of ideas to class discussion," probably because they are a part of a "very diverse population." LIU has many international students. There is a high percentage of locals in the student body as well. They choose the school precisely for that reason—it's close to home.

Post's "breathtaking campus" spans a few hundred acres of green lawns and dense woods. It's near the beaches on the North Shore of Long Island, and students "love the location," as well as its proximity to New York City. Most are commuters and find that aside from academics, there isn't much to keep them on campus. They do mention, however, that "class times are set up to provide ample time for commuters." One thing they do complain about is the lack of parking on campus, although a few students suggest it's nicer to have the trees and a longer walk, than sacrifice the natural beauty. As far as balancing home and work life with a part-time MBA, one student says confidently, "I am very busy with work and a family, and I have been able to accomplish everything that will ensure my success."

Admissions

The admissions committee at LIU requires candidates to submit official GMAT/GRE scores, undergraduate GPA, two letters of recommendation, a personal essay, and a resume. Other elements the committee takes into consideration are extracurricular activities, work experience, and an interview. Students must also be competent in business communications, mathematics, and computers and be able to pass a waiver exam. TOEFL scores are necessary for those students whose first language is not English.

FINANCIAL FACTS

Annual tuition (in-state/ out-of-state)	$20,790/$20,790
Fees	$484
Cost of books	$2,300
Room & board (on/off-campus)	$14,000/
Average grant	$3,000

ADMISSIONS

Admissions Selectivity Rating	**82**
# of applications received	136
% applicants accepted	62
% acceptees attending	49
Average GMAT	470
Range of GMAT	420–520
Accepts GRE scores	Yes
Average Verbal GRE	150
Range of Verbal GRE scores	151–151
Average Quantitative GRE	153
Range of Quantitative GRE scores	149–154
Average Writing GRE	2.5
Range of Writing GRE scores	2.5–2.5
Average GPA	3.2
TOEFL required of international students	Yes
Minimum TOEFL (paper/web)	563/85
Application fee	$50
International application fee	$50
Regular application deadline	8/15
Regular application notification	8/15
Application Deadline/Notification	
Deferment available	Yes
Maximum length of deferment	One Year
Transfer students accepted	Yes
Transfer application policy	
A maximum of 12 business credits may be waived, if coursework was taken within the last five years with a grade of "B" or better from an AACSB accredited School (reducing program to 36 credits) .	
Non-fall admissions	Yes
Need-blind admissions	Yes

LOUISIANA STATE UNIVERSITY
E. J. OURSO COLLEGE OF BUSINESS

GENERAL INFORMATION

Type of school	Public
Affiliation	No Affiliation
Academic calendar	Fall/Spring/ Summer

SURVEY SAYS...

Friendly students, Good peer network, Good social scene, Conservative students, Happy students, Abundant clubs and activities, Students love Baton Rouge, LA
Solid preparation in:
Finance, Teamwork, Communication/ interpersonal skills, Presentation skills, Quantitative skills

STUDENTS

Enrollment of parent institution	31,527
Enrollment of MBA Program	108
% male/female	52/48
% out-of-state	17
% underrepresented minority	14
% international	17
Average age at entry	24
Average years work experience at entry	2

ACADEMICS

Academic Experience Rating	**88**
Profs interesting rating	88
Profs accessible rating	93
Student/faculty ratio	28:1
% female faculty	27
% underrepresented minority faculty	3
% part-time faculty	0

Joint Degrees

Dual JD/MBA, 4 years

Prominent Alumni

James C. Flores, Joseph Herring, CEO/Chairman of the Board/ Director, Covance, Inc.; David P. Steiner, President and CEO, Waste Management; Emmet Stephenson, CEO of Stephenson and Company and Stephenson Ventures.

Academics

Louisiana State University's E. J. Ourso College of Business unites "a great quality curriculum, impressive career placement, and low tuition costs" in a single prestigious program. This large public school serves the needs of a diverse business community by offering four tracks to an MBA: full-time, Professional MBA (part-time), Executive MBA, and online, while maintaining an "outstanding reputation on a national level." For all students, the MBA begins with a core curriculum in business fundamentals, including accounting, marketing, and finance. After completing the core, "students get a lot of freedom in choosing their electives," which range from entrepreneurship to IT management. Of particular note, the school distinguishes itself with "one of the best internal audit programs in the country." Special academic programs further compliment coursework; for example, the entrepreneurship programs offers "real-world coursework that allows students to work with local business upstarts in obtaining venture capital."

At LSU, the classroom experience is top notch. "Classes are well structured and academically challenging," and "the small class size makes getting access to professors easy." Professors are generally "well accomplished in their careers," but never look down their noses at students. On the contrary, they are "open to new ideas and shape lectures based on student input, student interest, and current events." Incorporating lots of discussion and group work, classes are "structured in a way that resembles a work environment rather than a normal classroom." Through case studies and presentations, students are called upon to "discuss real-world applications in all classes instead of just learning the theories behind the topics." By encouraging a deeper involvement with the material, professors "really create a learning and participatory environment that encourages thinking."

The real world is never far from the classroom, and LSU makes a point of "connecting us with area business leaders and exposing us to opportunities with local companies." As a result, "LSU is known around the South for having one of the best MBA programs," as well as a loyal alumni base.

Career and Placement

The LSU Flores program knows that MBA candidates want to land choice jobs after graduation, and "all levels of administration are focused on placing students into their jobs of choice by rigorous career management and a high level of academics." Real-world skills are taught throughout the program, and students "get lessons on everything from dinner etiquette to attire and interviewing." "The fact that LSU has such a strong connection with Louisiana companies and businesses from the surrounding local areas, really provides benefit to students." LSU also connects students with "a vast network of alumni that come back to the school to speak and recruit." For full-time students, "the internship program is remarkable," offering the opportunity to get their feet wet in the real world. In addition to business school programs, graduate students can make use of LSU's Career Services. There is an annual career fair, which serves the entire campus, as well as a special career reception for just the business college.

Finance and accounting are the two most popular fields for LSU graduates, capturing more than 35 percent of the student body. Operations and marketing follow, together comprising more than a third of the students. The average salary for LSU graduates is about $60,000, with offers ranging from $45,000 to $100,000, depending on a student's field and industry. JPMorgan Chase, Capital One, Deloitte, Ernst and Young, Albemarle, ExxonMobil, Goldman Sachs, Entergy Corporation, PwC, and Chevron are among LSU's recent employers. By graduation, 70 percent of MBA students had already accepted an offer, and another 24 percent joined them three months later.

Student Life and Environment

For LSU Flores MBA candidates, the lifestyle at LSU is well-rounded and rewarding. Coursework is very time consuming, but "there is a strong sense of camaraderie among students, which is fueled by long hours spent working on group projects." Plus, "the curriculum is challenging, but is beautifully balanced by constant social opportunities." Among the many options within the business school, "The LSU Flores MBA Association has made great efforts to sponsor social events, so students get a chance to meet their classmates." In addition, students are involved in numerous philanthropic projects around Baton Rouge, and "regularly partner with Toys for Tots, Habitat for Humanity, and Boys Hope Girls Hope." Even those who rarely participate in campus activities are quick to admit that, "LSU athletic events are the experience of a lifetime, especially football games at Tiger Stadium."

"Baton Rouge is easily one of the top college towns in the country," offering a plethora of inexpensive, student-oriented fun. In their free time, classmates "get together to participate in amateur sports leagues, foreign movie night, charity events, Mardi Gras, Baton Rouge Art Melt, and marathons." Those who love the South are particularly happy here, noting that, "Louisiana State University is fueled by deep southern traditions, rooted in cultures and customs that cannot be duplicated anywhere else in the nation."

Admissions

Admission to the LSU Flores MBA Pprogram is competitive. To be considered eligible for the program, students must have a GPA of at least 3.0 from undergraduate coursework. Although there is no minimum GMAT score required for admission, the school favors applicants with scores in the 600s, or better. In 2015, the average GMAT score was 626. LSU encourages students seeking scholarships to apply early in the admissions cycle.

FINANCIAL FACTS

Annual tuition	$8,239
Fees	$5,972
Cost of books	$1,850
Room & board	
(on/off-campus)	$8,000/$10,000
% of students receiving aid	43
% of first-year students	
receiving aid	53
% of students receiving grants	21
Average award package	$12,370
Average grant	$7,861
Average loan	$16,614
Average student loan debt	$6,351

ADMISSIONS

Admissions Selectivity Rating	86
# of applications received	137
% applicants accepted	42
% acceptees attending	77
Average GMAT	626
Range of GMAT	570–740
Accepts GRE scores	Yes
Average Verbal GRE	151
Range of Verbal	
GRE scores	144–160
Average Quantitative GRE	155
Range of Quantitative	
GRE scores	144–166
Average GPA	3.3
TOEFL required of	
international students	Yes
Minimum TOEFL	
(paper/web)	550/79
Application fee	$50
International application fee	$70
Early application deadline	12/6
Early notification date	12/23
Regular application deadline	5/15
Regular application notification	6/1
Application Deadline/Notification	
Round 1:	12/6 / 12/23
Round 2:	2/7 / 2/28
Round 3:	4/4 / 4/30
Round 4:	5/15 / 6/1
Deferment available	Yes
Maximum length of	
deferment	One year
Transfer students accepted	Yes
Transfer application policy	
Applicants must have attended	
an accredited school and meet	
the entrance requirements for the	
Flores MBA Program.	
Non-fall admissions	No
Need-blind admissions	Yes

EMPLOYMENT PROFILE

Career Rating	90	Grads Employed by Function	%	Avg. Salary
Percent employed at graduation	70	Marketing	(11%)	$47,667
Percent employed 3 months		Operations	(7%)	$50,667
after graduation	90	Consulting	(11%)	$66,750
Average base starting salary	$57,601	Management	(16%)	$60,480
Primary Source of Full-time Job Acceptances		Finance	(36%)	$56,348
School-facilitated activities	22 (49%)	HR	(7%)	$64,500
Graduate-facilitated activities	23 (51%)	MIS	(2%)	$70,000
		Other	(9%)	$62,467

Top 5 Employers Hiring Grads
Capital One (2), Deloitte (3),
PricewaterhouseCoopers (2), Postlethwaite &
Netterville (2), KPMG (2)

LOYOLA MARYMOUNT UNIVERSITY
COLLEGE OF BUSINESS ADMINISTRATION

GENERAL INFORMATION

Type of school	Private
Affiliation	Roman Catholic-Jesuit
Academic calendar	Semester

SURVEY SAYS...

Classmates have diverse work experience, Friendly students, Good peer network, Good social scene, Happy students, Students love Los Angeles, CA
Solid preparation in:
General management, Teamwork, Communication/interpersonal skills, Presentation skills, Quantitative skills, Doing business in a global economy, Environmental sustainability

STUDENTS

Enrollment of parent institution	9,661
Enrollment of MBA Program	208
% male/female	56/44
% part-time	100
% underrepresented minority	37
% international	20
Average age at entry	27
Average years work experience at entry	5

ACADEMICS

Academic Experience Rating	**90**
Profs interesting rating	92
Profs accessible rating	95
Student/faculty ratio	7:1
% female faculty	20
% underrepresented minority faculty	29
% part-time faculty	38

Joint Degrees

JD/MBA, 4 yrs; Master of Systems Engineering/MBA, 4 yrs.

Academics

Students rule the school at Loyola Marymount University. At this private Southern California institution, each MBA candidate can pursue an education that uniquely fits his or her lifestyle, professional commitments, and educational goals. Designed for individuals with at least two years of professional or internship experience, the LMU MBA program holds classes in the evenings. Students take core coursework in the first year, and choose electives and courses based on area of emphasis in their second year. The "versatile and flexible schedule" is designed with the busy student in mind. For their required global study component, students choose between two "shorter two-week international [programs], which are ideal for fully employed students who want to study abroad." "Getting required courses is always easy," and if students aren't sure exactly how to shape their experience, Loyola will help. Throughout the program, "professors and advisers will work with students to craft a program that meets their needs without taking over their life."

Loyola maintains a new "very challenging and well-rounded curriculum," offered as a cohort core, an area of concentration, and an international experience all included in a bundled price. Loyola is a Jesuit school, and, as a result, "social entrepreneurship and ethics are hot topics throughout all the classes." The school is also "a leader in green business and has very strong connections to technology, aerospace, and defense industries." The academic experience is defined by "small class sizes and personal attention." When students need extra assistance with coursework—or even just to chat—"professors are easily accessible via phone, email, or during office hours." "Professors publish work regularly" and "are tremendously knowledgeable and up to date" on the business world. While a number of classes are extremely current, some students feel that "the school could do a much better job integrating current business and economic trends into the coursework."

Business students are keen to evaluate an organization's efficiency, and most give high marks to Loyola's operations. From class registration to scheduling, "the school's administration is a well-oiled machine that keeps everything running very smoothly and efficiently." "The new library is exceptional and helps facilitate on-campus studies and group work." The school also employs a "business librarian, who can help us do research." Unlike most commuter campuses, "parking on campus is a breeze, with free valet service during peak hours." Loyola maintains a reputation as "one of the best schools in the Los Angeles area," and it continues to improve its rank and services. Among other factors, "the competitiveness and caliber of student has also increased significantly in just the past few years, improving the overall value of the experience."

Career and Placement

LMU students and alumni have full access to the MBA Career Services Office (CSO). The CSO provides access to several online job boards, provides resume and interview preparation advice, and offers individual career counseling. Students praise the career services staff that is "willing to provide extensive one-on-one time to students and will connect them with alumni across the nation." On that note, "alumni have been extremely helpful in career advice, opportunities, and placement."

Students love Loyola's fabulous Los Angeles location, which keeps them close to a plethora of great job opportunities. With L.A. at their fingertips, students "would like to see more networking events and employers on campus" and more aggressive career placement. Loyola Marymount is constantly bettering its services in response to student requests. Many note that, "The CSO has improved drastically over the past year with an increase in staff and response to student feedback." During the last few semesters, the "frequency of seminars and workshops has increased," while "job postings specifically recruiting LMU students have begun to rise." There is also a push to create "joint programming with the Alumni Association."

Student Life and Environment

"Perched atop the bluff overlooking Marina Del Rey, the LMU campus is lush and beautiful," boasting an excellent environment and great resources for students. "The library is state of the art with phenomenal technology," and there is an "excellent gym and pool facility, which is also open to spouses." In the business school, students can take advantage of "an amazing new library, more computer and study rooms, an on-campus bar, and lounges and restaurants."

At Loyola, the school year kicks off with the "Annual Welcome Back BBQ to bring current students and new students together." For those who want to get involved in campus life, "the Student Association is very active and plans many events and volunteering programs throughout the year." Community service is popular with the business school, as are "happy hours, soccer matches, softball games, BBQs, and tailgating at University sports events." Since all students attend classes part-time, "grad students mostly just come and go and don't really stay on campus between classes." However, "LMU has started organizing activities for married students with families," which may attract a new group of participants.

Admissions

Applicants are accepted to Loyola Marymount's MBA program on a rolling basis. Once all materials have been submitted, the admissions committee can render a decision in just two weeks. With limited space in the program, early applicants will have an advantage over those who apply late in the admissions cycle. Students are evaluated on their previous academic performance, work experience, GMAT scores, personal essay, and recommendations. The average GMAT for last year's entering class was 596, but the school accepted students with a wide range of test scores.

FINANCIAL FACTS

Annual tuition	$88,500
% of students receiving aid	69
% of students receiving grants	73
Average award package	$19,940
Average student loan debt	$29,670

ADMISSIONS

Admissions Selectivity Rating	**85**
# of applications received	193
% applicants accepted	59
% acceptees attending	47
Average GMAT	596
Range of GMAT	560–640
Accepts GRE scores	Yes
Average GPA	3.4
TOEFL required of international students	Yes
Minimum TOEFL (paper/web)	600/100
Application fee	$50
International application fee	$50
Application Deadline	7/15
Deferment available	Yes
Maximum length of deferment	1 year
Transfer students accepted	Yes
Transfer application policy Students from other Jesuit MBA Programs may transfer core and electives through the Jesuit Transfer Network. Students who attend an AACSB accredited MBA Program (non-Jesuit) with equivalent course work of B or better may ONLY transfer in 6 units of upper division course credits.	
Non-fall admissions	No
Need-blind admissions	Yes

LOYOLA UNIVERSITY CHICAGO
GRADUATE SCHOOL OF BUSINESS

GENERAL INFORMATION
Type of school   Private
Affiliation   Roman Catholic-Jesuit
Academic calendar   Quarter

SURVEY SAYS...
Friendly students, Students love Chicago, IL
Solid preparation in:
Teamwork

STUDENTS
Enrollment of parent institution	16,437
Enrollment of MBA Program	400
% male/female	63/38
% out-of-state	33
% part-time	78
% underrepresented minority	22
% international	31
Average age at entry	30
Average years work experience at entry	7

ACADEMICS
Academic Experience Rating	**89**
Profs interesting rating	90
Profs accessible rating	94
Student/faculty ratio	18:1
% female faculty	25
% underrepresented minority faculty	11
% part-time faculty	11

Joint Degrees
MBA/JD; MBA/MSIMC; MBA/MSSCM; MBA/MS Nursing; MBA/MS Pharmacology; MBA/MSHR; MBA/MSA; MBA/MSF.

Prominent Alumni
Michael Quinlan, Former Chairman & CEO, McDonald's; Robert Parkinson, Chairman and CEO of Baxter International Inc.; Mark Satkiewicz, President and CEO of SmartWool Inc.; Robin Fern, Manager of Strategic Alliances, Water.org; Kaye Ceille, President, Zipcar

Academics

A university founded in the Jesuit tradition, "Loyola is a school that is focused on developing the entire individual," and business ethics is a mainstay of the MBA program. While MBA course content resembles other graduate business programs, Loyola distinguishes itself in a number of ways. In particular, "success is not measured in dollars, but rather [in] how one can contribute to society in a meaningful and productive way." To that end, "every class incorporates ethics and ethical situations and relates them to real-world business issues." At the same time, the curriculum focuses on practical business, and "is very relevant and applicable." Through coursework, students work in teams, analyze case studies, or work on live projects in cooperation with a partner business or organization. A current student enthuses, "I take advantage of student organizations and outside consulting projects, and often feel that these have more value than my classes." To add an international perspective to the MBA, "the study abroad program is fantastic," offering numerous two-week summer courses overseas. Another student tells us, "I will be afforded wonderful study abroad opportunities through this program and will be traveling to China, India, and Rome."

Combining expertise with excellence, the majority of Loyola professors are "highly experienced and make the learning experience worthwhile." While there are some "pure academics" on staff, they are outnumbered by current and former business leaders, who bring real-world content to the coursework. In fact, Loyola's adjunct professors "are among the best at bringing a 'real-world' perspective into the classroom." Most importantly, professors are "very enthusiastic about their subject and classes, and they all very much love teaching." As a result, "the classroom experience is dynamic and engaging," and the "thought-provoking course content" inspires discussion and critical thinking. A student remarks, "I have enjoyed many of my classes so much, I am actually somewhat disappointed when the quarter comes to an end!" At the same time, Loyola is a large school, so it's easier to get lost in the crowds. A current student admits, "It's difficult to have good, thoughtful discussions in classes with fifty people in attendance."

Loyola's "flexible class schedule" is great for part-time students, and "the course load is perfect for a professional who has a full-time job." In addition, the "ability to switch between full-time and part-time status" gives students the opportunity to complete their degree at their own pace. Full-timers, on the other hand, sometimes feel "the course work doesn't seem as challenging as it could be." A school on the move, "The GSB has grown considerably just within the last year," and students admit, "The administration seems a little overwhelmed by the number of students currently enrolled." Fortunately, a student writes, "The school is committed to providing students with an exceptional experience. When there are hurdles to overcome, the administration is quick to identify how things might improve."

Career and Placement

Loyola's downtown "location in a world class city" brings students within a stone's throw of many reputable employers. This private university maintains a great local reputation, and the focus on practical skills throughout the MBA curriculum helps to prepare students for the workplace. A current student agrees, "In this time of economic crisis, I feel incredibly prepared and optimistic that my MBA degree will make me stand out from the competition."

Loyola University's Career Management Services assists job seekers through resume critiques, career workshops, and advising. They also operate an online recruiting program, which allows students to research employers, post their resumes, and sign up for campus interviews via the web. Despite these services, "the school could do a much better job attracting more quality employers to recruit at Loyola." A current MBA candidate laments, "The school is in a sweet spot for business in the country but doesn't take full advantage of the networking possibilities." On the other hand, "there are students who have found great jobs through Career Management and have received excellent coaching from the staff....It all depends on what a person expects."

Student Life and Environment

Loyola is a large, urban university, which attracts "all different backgrounds, ages, interests, career paths (if working), intelligence levels, and points of life." While some students are too busy to participate in extracurricular activities, others find time to "belong to a number of clubs that meet before class once or twice a month." More informally, there are "plenty of opportunities to mingle after class and on weekends," and students attend "social events at bars or restaurants after class every month." Still, you won't get the social atmosphere you'd find on a residential campus: "Although the social life is improving, the school definitely feels like a commuter school."

"Located in the heart of downtown Chicago," Loyola's well-placed campus is a major benefit of the program. Academic resources are good, and "the library is excellent." "Getting information from any source at the school has been easy." Unfortunately, many business school classrooms lack modern technology and suffer from "a poor layout, not conducive to class discussion." A student adds, "More than 30 percent of assignments are group related, yet less than 5 percent of computers in the library cater toward group work. Options like LCD projectors (or mounted televisions with a monitor input) in group rooms would be greatly appreciated."

Admissions

At Loyola, the academic calendar is divided into quarters. Accordingly, there are four start dates each year, so the school is continuously accepting and enrolling new students. To apply, prospective students must submit an application form, two letters of recommendation, a statement of purpose, a current resume, undergraduate transcripts, and official GMAT test scores.

FINANCIAL FACTS

Fees	$888
Cost of books	$1,200
Room & board	$17,030
% of students receiving aid	52
% of first-year students receiving aid	56
% of students receiving grants	10
Average award package	$27,833
Average grant	$10,786
Average loan	$30,271

ADMISSIONS

Admissions Selectivity Rating	86
# of applications received	536
% applicants accepted	49
% acceptees attending	53
Average GMAT	542
Range of GMAT	500–590
Accepts GRE scores	Yes
Average Verbal GRE	150
Range of Verbal GRE scores	146–157
Average Quantitative GRE	151
Range of Quantitative GRE scores	147–156
Average Writing GRE	3.6
Range of Writing GRE scores	3.0–4.0
Average GPA	3.3
TOEFL required of international students	Yes
Minimum TOEFL (paper/web)	577/90
Application fee	$50
International application fee	$50
Regular application deadline	7/15
Deferment available	Yes
Maximum length of deferment	1 year
Transfer students accepted	Yes
Transfer application policy	Up to 9 hours of B or better coursework can transfer from AACSB-accredited institutions. In order to assist students who are transferred to other cities before graduation, the MBA program at Loyola University Chicago participates in the Multilateral Jesuit MBA Agreement with a number of other MBA programs at Jesuit universities.
Non-fall admissions	Yes
Need-blind admissions	Yes

EMPLOYMENT PROFILE

Career Rating	70	Grads Employed by Function	% Avg. Salary
Primary Source of Full-time Job Acceptances		Marketing	(18%)
School-facilitated activities	(12%)	Operations	(14%) $172,166
Graduate-facilitated activities	(64%)	Consulting	(5%)
Unknown	(24%)	Management	(18%)
		Finance	(14%)
		HR	(5%)
		MIS	(5%)
		Other	(18%)

Top 5 Employers Hiring Grads

Accretive Health (2), Ariel Investments (1), Robert Bosch LLC (1), Cancer Treatments Centers of America (1), ComEd (1)

Loyola University Maryland
Sellinger School of Business and Management

Academics

Loyola's Sellinger School of Business and Management is anchored by core Jesuit beliefs. It offers a "value-based" education that emphasizes "reflective learning" and the importance of ethical behavior and leadership skills. All students must take two courses in the Law and Social Responsibility department: one on legal and regulatory compliance and another on ethics and social responsibility. The department also offers electives, such as legal and managerial issues in not-for-profit organizations and intersections among power, privilege, and professional identity for those wanting to further specialize in the area. Students say they "appreciate the Jesuit influence" and name the Jesuit "commitment to excellence" and "strong belief in business ethics" as reasons for picking the school.

Loyola is dedicated to its students and offers four different MBA programs, at two locations, with varying delivery methods. This ensures that students' needs are met, and that they are not forced into a cookie-cutter program. The most popular program is the part-time Professional MBA, which offers evening classes and the freedom to vary the number of credits students take each semester. The MBA Fellows program is designed for professionals with managerial experience and has Saturday classes only. The Executive MBA is a cohort program for seasoned professionals that meets all day Friday and Saturday every other weekend. Loyola's Emerging Leaders MBA is a full-time, twelve-month accelerated program for early career students. The school also offers an MS in finance and a certificate in accounting and cyber security. All of these programs have a "great reputation" and a reasonable price.

Loyola's part-time programs "cater to working individuals" and give them "flexibility and greater control" over the curriculum. Classes are offered at convenient times in locations close to the Baltimore area. All programs require a set of core classes to ensure students have a wide and strong understanding of the business world, but some professional MBA students may find requirements waived if they graduated from college in the past few years and received high grades in similar courses. After completing these courses, professional MBA students may concentrate in accounting, finance, information systems, international business, management, or marketing. Classes are challenging and require group projects. While theory is taught, the program emphasizes "where business and the country are headed, and how to be a part of that." One student loves that "many of the concepts taught can be applied as both an entrepreneur and corporate executive." Loyola's professors fall at "both ends of the spectrum." Students find the full-time faculty is "incredible" and "very effective and encouraging." Some of the adjunct professors, however, should "simply stick with their day jobs." The administration also gets mixed reviews, but most find them "fantastic to work with." When you consider Loyola's "great reputation," price, and willingness to support student success, it's no wonder students say going there is a "great experience."

Career and Placement

The Sellinger School of Business does not have its own career office, so students must use the Career Center that serves the rest of the undergraduate and graduate students. Loyola's Career Center is still able to provide personal and relevant help to graduate business students, however. Experienced advisors offer career counseling, and the center holds various workshops, mock interviews, and resume critiques. Sellinger has a very strong alumni network that provides valuable networking and mentoring opportunities for students. Career fairs and on-campus recruiting events help students make connections to future employers. Businesses that attended the most recent career fair include ING Financial Partners, Liberty Mutual, State Farm, Primerica, The Central Intelligence Agency, Financial Management Service, Morgan Stanley, and The Neilson Corporation.

Student Life and Environment

All of Sellinger's programs attract high-caliber individuals. Students are "very motivated and intelligent," and while they can sometimes be "competitive," almost everyone is "helpful and friendly." Most students work full time, and many are married and have families. Students say their peers' different personal and professional backgrounds really "add to the learning environment." "Everyone brings something unique," one student explains, and this creates an "innovative, challenging, and intellectually stimulating culture." Students are "opinionated and interested in the topics covered in classes," which makes for "engaging" and "active discussions."

Most students at Loyola are incredibly busy and generally don't have time to socialize with other students. Some students would like to see "more opportunities for socializing and networking outside of the classroom," as "it would help strengthen the program and build upon the teamwork and morale already present."

Admissions

Students applying to Loyola must submit their undergraduate transcript, GMAT scores, recommendations, resume, and personal statement. Students applying to all programs except the Emerging Leaders MBA and the Accounting Certificate Program must have previous work experience. The average undergraduate GPA for the entering class was 3.3, and the average GMAT score was 551. Applicants with a 3.25 undergraduate GPA and five years of work experience may request a waiver for the GMAT requirement, as may students with an advanced degree in another discipline. International students whose first language is not English must submit TOEFL scores. Additionally, applicants who hold degrees from non-U.S. institutions must have their academic record evaluated by an independent service.

FINANCIAL FACTS

Annual tuition (in-state/ out-of-state)	$63,000/$63,000

ADMISSIONS

Admissions Selectivity Rating	75
# of applications received	142
Average GMAT	551
Range of GMAT	483–600
Accepts GRE scores	Yes
Average Verbal GRE	55
Range of Verbal GRE scores	47–62
Average Quantitative GRE	34
Range of Quantitative GRE scores	23–45
Average GPA	3.3
TOEFL required of international students	Yes
Minimum TOEFL (paper/web)	550/80
Application fee	$60
International application fee	$60
Application Deadline/Notification	
Deferment available	Yes
Maximum length of deferment	1 year
Transfer students accepted	Yes
Transfer application policy Only classes from another AACSB accredited school will be counted, total 6 credits.	
Non-fall admissions	Yes
Need-blind admissions	Yes

EMPLOYMENT PROFILE

Career Rating	88	Grads Employed by Function	% Avg. Salary
Percent employed at graduation	25	Marketing	(13%) $60,000
Percent employed 3 months after graduation	69	Operations	(13%) $67,500
		Consulting	(19%) $77,333
Average base starting salary	$66,000	Management	(13%)
Primary Source of Full-time Job Acceptances		Finance	(19%) $66,666
School-facilitated activities	3 (19%)	Other	(25%)
Graduate-facilitated activities	9 (52%)	**Top 5 Employers Hiring Grads**	
Unknown	3 (19%)	CareFirst BlueCross Blue Shield (3), Amazon (1), American Express (1), Faugle Pratt Company (1), Yajje and Company (1)	

LOYOLA UNIVERSITY NEW ORLEANS
JOSEPH A. BUTT, S.J. COLLEGE OF BUSINESS

Academics

Loyola's "small, flexible MBA program" "really caters to each and every student," a fact appreciated by the predominantly part-time student body in the College of Business' graduate programs. MBAs here also love the "Jesuit tradition," which encourages "involvement in the New Orleans community." "I appreciate being at a place that not only educates my mind, but gives me social awareness as well," one student writes.

Loyola offers a general "professional" MBA as well as a "fast-track" MBA designed to be completed within one year. Furthermore, the MBA program offers specialization tracks allowing students to select three elective courses in a specific concentration including: Finance, Entrepreneurship, Marketing, and Operations. The MBA culminates in a Capstone Consulting Project where students are required to conduct research and produce an in-depth report of a company applying all major topics covered in all required courses taken throughout the student's tenure in the MBA program.

Both programs are comprised of 40 credit hours; 12 (3 credit hour) courses separated by 4 (1 credit hour) immersion weeks that offer more intensive seminars on topics vital to an MBA program such as orientation and launch, venture and start-up entrepreneurship, career development, and ethics and social justice.

Loyola professors "are very involved with the students. The classes are small and the faculty care about the students' well being and learning." One student writes, "I was shocked to learn how easily accessible my professors were. They really are interested in your education and your life and they want you to succeed! In fact, they will put in extra hours to make sure you do just that. The business school here is more like a family, which makes it that much easier to learn." Administrators are "excellent." Indeed, the administration seems intent on exploring all opportunities to improve the program. "The quality and experience of the new students has improved each year as admission standards have become tougher," MBAs here report approvingly.

Career and Placement

Loyola maintains a Career Development Center to serve all undergraduate and graduate students of the university. Services include self-assessment instruments, career counseling, internship and job placement services, and guidance in resume writing, interviewing, job search, and salary negotiation skills. The office organizes on-campus recruiting events. One student "is not sure how much other students utilize" the CDC, but she does use the office's service and finds it "extremely helpful, especially because I recently moved to the area." The MBA Association also contributes by organizing networking events.

In recent years, Loyola MBAs have been placed with Chevron, Children's Hospital, Fidelity Homestead Savings Bank, General Electric, Shell Trading, US Department of Treasury, UNITY of Greater New Orleans, John Besh Restaurant Group, Postlethwaite and Netterville.

ADMISSIONS CONTACT: ASHLEY FRANCIS, DIRECTOR OF GRADUATE PROGRAMS
ADDRESS: 6363 ST. CHARLES AVENUE, CAMPUS BOX 15, NEW ORLEANS, LA 70118
PHONE: 504-864-7953 • FAX: 504-864-7970
E-MAIL: MBA@LOYNO.EDU • WEBSITE: BUSINESS.LOYNO.EDU/MBA

Student Life and Environment

Designed to "keep your attention," "classes are interactive and fun" at Loyola, where "professors expect your best and highest quality work, but go above and beyond to provide the support you need in order to succeed. Coming to class is like meeting with friends and family every night." Students tell us that "life at school is stressful" but worth the hard work. "I do feel like I am learning more than I ever have," one writes.

Loyola classes meet once a week on weekday evenings. While most students are part-timers with full-time jobs, "there are [also] many full-time students that have part-time jobs. Everybody knows everyone. You have many of the same classes with the same people." "Significant effort has been made recently to improve the cohesiveness among students" at Loyola, with "MBA functions almost every week to bring the students closer together." One student reports, "The MBA program does a good job of organizing social events within as well as outside of the school."

Loyola is located in the fashionable uptown section of New Orleans, just next door to Tulane University. The area is known for its fine restaurants and upscale shopping. The city's Central Business District, Garden District, and French Quarter are all easily accessible from campus via the city's picturesque streetcar line.

Most MBAs at Loyola "are just out of [their] four-year degree [programs], but there are some that have been in the workforce for a while." It's not just locals in attendance here. One student told us he was "very surprised to discover how many students are from every part of the country and so many different backgrounds." Across the board, students tend to be "very friendly and willing to help each other out. The MBA association facilitates this atmosphere by scheduling meet and greets and other social events throughout the semester."

Admissions

Loyola requires the following of applicants to its MBA program: a complete application, official transcripts for all past postsecondary academic work; an official score report for the GMAT or an official GRE score; two letters of recommendation; a 400-word personal statement of purpose; and a resume. International students whose first language is not English must also submit TOEFL scores; all international students must provide an affidavit demonstrating sufficient financial resources to support themselves during their tenure at the university. Interviews are optional; work experience is not required. Application fees can be waived for those attending an Open House.

FINANCIAL FACTS

Cost of books	$1,200

ADMISSIONS

Admissions Selectivity Rating	**80**
# of applications received	61
% applicants accepted	82
% acceptees attending	76
Average GMAT	505
Range of GMAT	370–650
Accepts GRE scores	Yes
Average GPA	3.1
TOEFL required of international students	Yes
Minimum TOEFL (paper/web)	580/92
Application fee	$50
International application fee	$50
Regular application deadline	6/30
Application Deadline/Notification	
Deferment available	Yes
Maximum length of deferment	1 academic year
Transfer students accepted	Yes
Transfer application policy	
With the exception of courses taken at Jesuit consortium schools, a maximum of 6 credit hours of transfer work may be applied to 700- and 800-level courses in the M.B.A. program curriculum. Only courses taken within 7 years prior to enrollment will be considered. Prior written permission must be obtained.	
Non-fall admissions	Yes
Need-blind admissions	Yes

EMPLOYMENT PROFILE

Career Rating	79	**Top 5 Employers Hiring Grads**
Percent employed at graduation	67	Shell Oil Company (1), Southern Theatres,
Average base starting salary	$57,301	LLC (1), Ochsner Health System (2),
		Crestmark Bank (1), Cigna (1)

MARQUETTE UNIVERSITY
COLLEGE OF BUSINESS ADMINISTRATION

GENERAL INFORMATION
Type of school	Private
Affiliation	Jesuit
Academic calendar	Semester

SURVEY SAYS...
Friendly students, Happy students
Solid preparation in:
Teamwork, Presentation skills,
Quantitative skills

STUDENTS
Enrollment of parent institution	11,745
Enrollment of MBA Program	297
% part-time	84
Average age at entry	30
Average years work experience at entry	6

ACADEMICS
Academic Experience Rating	88
Profs interesting rating	90
Profs accessible rating	93
Student/faculty ratio	3:1
% female faculty	38
% underrepresented minority faculty	12
% part-time faculty	36

Joint Degrees
MBA/JD, 4 yrs; MBA/JD in sport business, 4 yrs; MBA/MSN, 4-6 yrs; MBA/MS Political Science, 3-6 yrs.

Academics

A respected MBA program in downtown Milwaukee, Marquette University provides a balanced perspective on business education. The strength of the program stems from the top-quality teaching staff, comprised of experienced academics with long careers in the classroom. Many have distinguished themselves through "very good published research and a strong reputation for teaching modern theories of economics." At the same time, "the academic experience is a good mix of high-level thinking and actual financial, economic, and accounting knowledge." Tenured staff is augmented with adjunct faculty, so you get a good "mixture of full-time professors and working professors." The school furthers real-world instruction by regularly "inviting guest speakers from prominent local businesses" to address classes or speak to the MBA community.

Designed for working professionals, Marquette classes are held in the evenings and weekends on three campuses in metropolitan Milwaukee. One thing that separates Marquette from other graduate business programs is that "it is not a program that is split between full-time and half-time students, but rather, its night classes cater to anyone and everyone." "Smaller class sizes allow for more discussion and interaction," so Marquette students really benefit from the fact that the "best and brightest young professionals in Milwaukee are sitting next to you in class." It can even be a great way to network, as "classes are full of students who work for Fortune-500 companies." Across disciplines, the education is "consistent in quality" with "good professors throughout the program." Beyond the core, however, "class offerings may be a bit light," making it more difficult to specialize your coursework through electives. Some would love to see a concentration in public health, while others say, "a larger selection of finance classes would be nice."

While Marquette is "very accommodating to part-time students," MBA candidates are quick to remind us that "classes are rigorous" and the program is time-consuming. If the workload gets overwhelming, "professors are always welcoming and willing to spend time during office hours and after class to help." Likewise, the administration is highly accessible and helpful. A current student shares, "I can easily schedule time with my advisor, there have been no billing or schedule mistakes, and when I call with questions, the people are knowledgeable and quick to respond."

Career and Placement

For current and future Midwest professionals, "a Marquette MBA makes a statement in the Milwaukee, Madison, Chicago, and Minneapolis areas." Most students plan to leverage this excellent reputation at their current positions. However, some students attend the program full-time or plan to make a career change after completing graduate school. For these students, Marquette operates the Business Career Center, where students can seek individual career counseling, resume and interview preparation, and help with networking strategies. The Career Center can also help career changers set up informational interviews and research local companies.

ADMISSIONS CONTACT: DR. JEANNE SIMMONS, ASSOCIATE DEAN
ADDRESS: PO BOX 1881, STRAZ HALL SUITE 275, MILWAUKEE, WI 53201-1881
PHONE: 414-288-7145 • FAX: 414-288-8078
E-MAIL: MBA@MARQUETTE.EDU • WEBSITE: WWW.MARQUETTE.EDU/GSM

In addition to the Business Career Center, graduate students have access to Marquette University's online job boards and are welcome to attend campus-wide career fairs and networking events. Since few students are actively applying for a new position after the MBA, job seekers feel that the school could "improve job search counseling" for those who want to start a new career, and ramp up its "internship placement for full-time students."

Student Life and Environment

The MBA program at Marquette attracts students from a range of backgrounds: "Some students are liberal, some conservative, some entrepreneurial, some corporate." Nonetheless, there is a strong community on campus, and even new students feel well-integrated into the program. A current MBA relates, "As a full-time student [who] entered the MBA program straight from my undergrad career, I never felt like I have been treated differently by the more experienced students and professors." In class, students are commendably "hardworking, task-oriented, and committed to contributing to class and group work." Outside the classroom, group projects usually go smoothly and "everyone is helpful and accommodating" to each other's ideas and schedules.

Although the school operates two satellite facilities, "the downtown campus is part of what defines the Marquette experience" for many students. Not only are they "close to the business center of the city," Milwaukee is "a nice place to live and work." Convenience is also a large factor, as "the proximity of Marquette's campus to downtown Milwaukee, where many students live and work, allows for a quick and easy commute." When feeling social, Marquette students might "meet for a drink after class or after a test to talk about school, work, and life." However, because the program is largely part-time, most students admit that, "school life is limited to attending class, team project activities, and the occasional MU basketball game."

Admission

To be considered for admission to Marquette, students must have a minimum GPA of 3.0 from their undergraduate coursework, and a total score of 500 or better on the GMAT. Students who fall below these guidelines may be admitted provisionally to the graduate program. Though work experience is not a requirement, an applicant's resume is also strongly weighed; currently, the average Marquette student has over seven years of professional experience. Students can apply to begin their coursework any semester. There are special deadlines for those who want to study on the satellite campuses in Waukesha or Kohler.

FINANCIAL FACTS

Annual tuition (in-state/ out-of-state)	$18,900/$18,900
Fees	$0
Cost of books	$1,200

ADMISSIONS

Admissions Selectivity Rating	83
# of applications received	131
% applicants accepted	76
% acceptees attending	80
Average GMAT	562
Accepts GRE scores	Yes
Average GPA	3.4
TOEFL required of international students	Yes
Minimum TOEFL (paper/web)	580/90
Application fee	$50
International application fee	$50
Application Deadline/Notification	
Deferment available	Yes
Maximum length of deferment	usually one year
Transfer students accepted	Yes
Transfer application policy	
We accept transfers from other Jesuit Schools (JEBNET agreement - see WWW.jesuitmba.ORG). We will also accept up to 6 approved credits from AACSB schools.	
Non-fall admissions	Yes
Need-blind admissions	Yes

MASSACHUSETTS INSTITUTE OF TECHNOLOGY
SLOAN SCHOOL OF MANAGEMENT

Academics

The MIT Sloan MBA Program has "both the best entrepreneurial program of any business school in the world and the most fantastic technology available," students insist. And that's hardly all the school offers; on the contrary, students tell us that MIT Sloan is "the best all-around program in allowing students to learn about innovative endeavors while still teaching and offering the most academically challenging traditional MBA curriculum of all schools."

MIT expertly exploits the synergies of its location in a great city and its affiliation with a great university. Students brag about "Sloan's ties to the real business world. In the last week alone, I listened to three *Fortune 500* CEOs speak on campus and had dinner with a partner from a local VC firm and a partner from a local law firm. Many of the professors have incredibly deep experience and connections to industry and bring great insight along those dimensions." They are especially impressed with "how connected MIT Sloan is with companies in a non-recruiting season," which they justly see as "a real point of differentiation" for the program. MIT's Herculean status in the worlds of math, engineering, and science contribute substantially to the MBA program. "There are very low barriers between schools; interdisciplinary work and entrepreneurship are actively encouraged between business and engineering," one student writes. MIT's many strengths make possible such programs as the Leaders for Global Operations Program—"an operations and logistics-focused program" that students call "the best dual-degree program in business and engineering in the country."

Throughout the program, MIT Sloan emphasizes "a strong hands-on approach to learning" and cooperative work. "At MIT Sloan, practically everything is done in teams," students tell us. The workload "is what you expect of MIT: rigorous and quantitative." Most don't mind the challenge; as one explains, "Although the workload is heavy, people actually want to prepare just for the opportunity to participate in discussions in where faculty are posing questions to the most pressing business issues. A place like MIT Sloan is a reason why people want to continue their education." The cherry on the sundae is global travel; "everyone travels on trips or treks, both foreign and domestic. I am headed to Japan for ten days with 200 of my classmates. These are student-planned trips that are excellent ways to get to see other cultures and get business exposure around the world."

Career and Placement

MIT Sloan's Career Development Office provides MBAs with a range of career management resources, including seminars, self-assessment tools, library materials, and online databases and services. Students tell us that "the CDO is great for traditional MBA jobs such as banking, [and] consulting and the major corporations and tech companies." Some report the office is "not as good with smaller and tougher markets such as private equity and venture capital," although students interested in those fields can make use of the "career trek" program, which offers trips around the globe to job-hunt and learn about a variety of industries. "The focus on entrepreneurship means that a lot of MIT Sloan students are starting companies or working at early-stage startups right after school," and are thus less inclined to make use of the CDO. Supplementing the CDO, "clubs have a huge impact on career choices, setting up relationships, bringing in speakers, etc. Alumni are also a great resource, and a fantastic channel for connecting. Many Sloanies are looking to work for startups, tech, or smaller firms without traditional recruiting seasons, and alumni are very helpful in this regard."

ADMISSIONS CONTACT: ROD GARCIA, ADMISSIONS DIRECTOR
ADDRESS: 50 MEMORIAL DRIVE, SUITE 126, CAMBRIDGE, MA 02139
PHONE: 617-258-5434 • FAX: 617-253-6405
E-MAIL: MBAADMISSIONS@SLOAN.MIT.EDU • WEBSITE: MITSLOAN.MIT.EDU/MBA

Employers most likely to hire MIT Sloan MBAs include Bain & Company, Booz & Co., The Boston Consulting Group, Citi, Amazon.com, Fidelity, Goldman Sachs, Google, IBM, and McKinsey & Company.

Student Life and Environment

MIT Sloan keeps students plenty busy with work, but they still somehow find time to "participate in clubs and set up the many conferences we host. For example, the Sports Analytics Conference this spring had general managers from each of the top four professional sports (basketball, hockey, baseball, and football) sit on a panel. How cool is that?" Students tell us that MIT Sloan "provides more opportunities than anyone could expect. I find that I spend about 50 percent of my time on academics and the other 50 percent working with clubs and local companies, a perfect balance that allows me to take what I've learned in the classroom and apply it in a real-world setting." It's easy to get overwhelmed; according to one student, "School is a blur with so many classes, activities, guest speakers, etc. In terms of social activities, I think you have to pick your spots. Otherwise you will fall behind in your coursework and job search, but the options are pretty limitless here."

Admissions

Completed applications to the MIT Sloan MBA program include two letters of recommendation, post-secondary transcripts (self-reported prior to interview; if called for an interview, applicants must provide official transcripts), a current resumé, two personal essays, supplemental information, and GMAT or GRE scores. The school requires additional materials from applicants to the Leaders for Global Operations Program (LGO). The nature of the program favors candidates with strong quantitative and analytical skills, as well as those with strong personal attributes including leadership, teamwork, and ability to make decisions and pursue goals.

FINANCIAL FACTS

Annual tuition (in-state/ out-of-state)	$61,440/$61,440
Cost of books	$1,926
Room & board (on/off-campus)	$14,363/$14,363
% of students receiving aid	82
% of first-year students receiving aid	82
% of students receiving grants	4
Average award package	$66,355
Average grant	$25,502
Average loan	$60,061
Average student loan debt	$92,937

ADMISSIONS

Admissions Selectivity Rating	99
# of applications received	4,133
Average GMAT	710
Range of GMAT	660–760
Accepts GRE scores	Yes
Average GPA	3.6
Application fee	$250
International application fee	$250
Application Deadline/Notification	
Round 1:	9/24 / 12/20
Round 2:	1/7 / 4/1
Deferment available	No
Transfer students accepted	No
Non-fall admissions	No
Need-blind admissions	Yes

EMPLOYMENT PROFILE

Career Rating	97	Grads Employed by Function% Avg. Salary	
Percent employed at graduation	85	Marketing	(6%) $106,646
Percent employed 3 months after graduation	95	Operations	(10%) $118,996
		Consulting	(35%) $126,537
Average base starting salary	$118,406	Management	(10%) $112,366
Primary Source of Full-time Job Acceptances		Finance	(24%) $110,980
School-facilitated activities	(81%)	Other	(1%) $0
Graduate-facilitated activities	(18%)	**Top 5 Employers Hiring Grads**	
Unknown	(1%)	McKinsey & Company (30), Bain & Company (12), Boston Consulting Group (16), Citi (8), Amazon (20)	

MERCER UNIVERSITY—ATLANTA
EUGENE W. STETSON SCHOOL OF BUSINESS AND ECONOMICS

GENERAL INFORMATION
Type of school   Private
Affiliation   No Affiliation
Academic calendar   Evening MBA:
2-8wk sessions per semester

SURVEY SAYS...
Classmates have diverse work experience, Friendly students, Happy students
Solid preparation in:
Marketing, Finance, Accounting, General management, Operations, Teamwork, Presentation skills, Quantitative skills, Doing business in a global economy

STUDENTS
Enrollment of parent institution	8,603
Enrollment of MBA Program	234
% male/female	49/51
% out-of-state	17
% part-time	39
% underrepresented minority	63
% international	11
Average age at entry	30
Average years work experience at entry	9

ACADEMICS
Academic Experience Rating	88
Profs interesting rating	92
Profs accessible rating	93
Student/faculty ratio	17:1
% female faculty	38
% underrepresented minority faculty	53
% part-time faculty	7

Joint Degrees
DMBA/Doctor of Pharmacy; DMBA/Master of Divinity; MBA/MAcc; MBA/DPT

Prominent Alumni
Griffin B. Bell, Former U.S. Attorney General; Budge Huskey, President & CEO, Coldwell-Banker Real Estate, LLC; Bob Sauerburg, President, Conde Nast; Nathan Deal, Governor of Georgia

Academics

One of Georgia's premiere higher-learning institutions, Mercer University offers several business degree options on its graduate-focused Atlanta campus: a flexible evening MBA, an Executive MBA, professional MBA, virtual MBA, a master of accountancy (MAcc), and a one-year full-time MBA (the only of Mercer's various campuses that offers a full-time option). The school is also home to "one of the only pharmacy programs in the country to offer a dual MBA/PharmD degree." Mercer's flexible MBA is popular with local professionals, who call it "Atlanta's most accommodating MBA program for working students." For part-timers, "classes meet one night a week for eight weeks, so it's possible to take classes even when you have a full-time job and other commitments." On top of that, professors "understand we work full-time and have family obligations, so the workload is moderate but challenging." How challenging is up to the student: "Some take their time with one class per session, others overload to finish early." The full-time MBA is likewise efficient, covering business fundamentals in an intense, cohort-based program that spans less than one calendar year (though students who did not study business as an undergraduate must take additional four-week Business Foundations courses before matriculation).

Known for "academic excellence in finance and accounting," Mercer's curriculum covers business fundamentals from economics to communications. After completing the core, students take electives, including a required international business class or an overseas trip. Throughout disciplines, Mercer employs "strong professors with real-world experience," who are able to offer an "in-depth understanding of what we were learning in class and how it applied to the business world." On top of that, Mercer's "small class size" lends itself to "team-oriented projects and a lot of class interaction," giving students a chance to collaborate, network, and develop their communication skills. Students dole out praise for Mercer's "extremely dedicated professors," who balance top-notch business skills with a true desire "to help students succeed." In fact, "everyone at Mercer is committed to enhancing the student's experience." Like the faculty, "the administrative offices are also helpful," ensuring the program runs smoothly.

Career and Placement

Many MBA candidates at Mercer are attending the program part-time and are not looking for a new job after graduation. Instead, they plan to leverage the practical skills they've acquired in the classroom to gain a better position and higher salary at their current job. To that end, a Mercer education is effective. One student attests, "I was able to secure my current position prior to graduation as a direct result of my then-current graduate enrollment at Mercer. I graduated in December, have earned an 18 percent increase in salary and am currently searching for a more significant managerial position within my firm and outside."

Those in the full-time program (or looking to make a career change after completing the degree part-time) have access to the school's Office of Career Services, which offers career counseling and workshops on résumé preparation and interviewing, in addition to hosting career fairs on campus. (Note that career fairs are often aimed at a certain industry, like pharmacy.) While students certainly benefit from Mercer's "good reputation" in Atlanta, they say their school could improve its career-development offerings by promoting "more involvement from alumni," as well as "a stronger link to the Atlanta business community."

Student Life and Environment

Mercer's Atlanta campus is focused on graduate programs, with advanced students of medicine, education, and theology, among other disciplines, sharing 300 tree-filled acres inside the Atlanta Perimeter. The business school attracts students from "diverse age ranges and backgrounds," as well as at different points in their careers. In the evening programs, "MBA students are mostly part-time students with full-time jobs (and some are effectively full-time students with full-time jobs)." As a result, there is "little emphasis on social or extracurricular activities"; for most, "school life consists of classes, group project meetings and studying." Nonetheless, Mercer's emphasis on collaboration means students frequently work together and build relationships, even if they don't socialize outside of class.

For full-timers, "Mercer is a thriving campus during the day," offering students access to myriad clubs and activities, as well as recreational facilities and fitness classes. At the business school, there are frequent career-related special events, like guest speakers and alumni networking events, as well as "festivities such as a "cook outs" (free to students) to celebrate the end of the semester." "The library and the library's website are also great resources for research," and students appreciate the "nice meeting rooms available for students to reserve in order to study, work on projects, [and] have meetings." Plus, the school's "suburban campus" offers a central Atlanta location that is both "outstanding and safe."

Admissions

For Mercer's Evening and Full-time MBA programs and the MAcc, a prospective student's GRE or GMAT scores and previous academic record are the most important factors in an admissions decision. A résumé is also required as a part of the application package. Though no work experience is required for the full-time program, the average student has four years of professional experience before matriculation. For full consideration, applications should be submitted to the full-time program by May 15; there are five entry points for part-time students, who are admitted on a rolling basis.

FINANCIAL FACTS

Annual tuition (in-state/ out-of-state)	$25,416/$25,416
Fees	$450
Cost of books	$1,683
Room & board (on/off-campus)	$14,265/$14,265
% of students receiving aid	71
% of first-year students receiving aid	74
% of students receiving grants	6
Average award package	$16,141
Average grant	$8,871
Average loan	$16,681
Average student loan debt	$33,363

ADMISSIONS

Admissions Selectivity Rating	83
# of applications received	184
% applicants accepted	66
% acceptees attending	78
Average GMAT	533
Range of GMAT	490–585
Accepts GRE scores	Yes
Average Verbal GRE	152
Range of Verbal GRE scores	150–155
Average Quantitative GRE	151
Range of Quantitative GRE scores	148–155
Average GPA	3.2
TOEFL required of international students	Yes
Minimum TOEFL (paper/web)	550/80
Application fee	$50
International application fee	$100
Early application deadline	7/1
Early notification date	7/15
Regular application deadline	7/15
Application Deadline/Notification	
Deferment available	Yes
Maximum length of deferment One calendar year, then student must reapply	
Transfer students accepted	Yes
Transfer application policy Will consider up to two courses (6 sem. hrs.) in transfer within past five years, from AACSB accredited institutions.	
Non-fall admissions	Yes
Need-blind admissions	Yes

EMPLOYMENT PROFILE

Career Rating	85		
Percent employed at graduation	16		
Percent employed 3 months after graduation	63		
Average base starting salary	$60,000		
Primary Source of Full-time Job Acceptances			
School-facilitated activities	3 (16%)		
Graduate-facilitated activities	9 (47%)		
Unknown	7 (37%)		

Grads Employed by Function	%	Avg. Salary
Marketing	(33%)	$37,500
Operations	(8%)	$40,000
Management	(8%)	$50,000
Finance	(25%)	$60,000
Other	(25%)	$55,000

Top 5 Employers Hiring Grads
Federal Reserve (1), Spanx (1), Athena Health (1), Enterprise Rental Car (1), Digitec Media (1)

MERCER UNIVERSITY—MACON

EUGENE W. STETSON SCHOOL OF BUSINESS AND ECONOMICS

GENERAL INFORMATION

Type of school	Private
Affiliation	Baptist

SURVEY SAYS...

Good peer network
Solid preparation in:
Marketing, Accounting,
Communication/interpersonal skills

STUDENTS

Enrollment of parent institution	40
Enrollment of MBA Program	40
% male/female	45/55
% out-of-state	0
% part-time	99
% underrepresented minority	0
% international	0
Average years work experience at entry	4

ACADEMICS

Academic Experience Rating	61
Profs interesting rating	71
Profs accessible rating	66
Student/faculty ratio	20:1
% female faculty	55
% part-time faculty	0

Joint Degrees

JD/MBA 3 YEARS

Academics

A long-standing Georgia institution with a "great reputation" and a strong "community feeling," Mercer University offers a friendly and convenient evening MBA program, specially designed for working professionals. Based at the school's main campus in Macon (though the university also operates several MBA programs in other Georgia cities, including Atlanta), this program is divided into two parts: foundational courses and core courses. For those with previous academic experience in business, the foundation courses may be waived. All students, however, must complete the core, a series of advanced courses in business fundamentals, including applied microeconomic analysis, management and leadership, and business ethics. With a focus on the relationship between business and society, the Mercer curriculum is current and contemporary. According to current students, "The administration goes to great lengths to offer courses relevant to our career goals and interests." An "outstanding offering of seminars and lecture series" augment the core, and students can take advantage of "faculty-led study abroad opportunities each year." While students generally praise the academic program, some say the school should offer a greater variety of electives, as well as coursework that is "more applicable to small business and entrepreneurs."

Mercer maintains a "low student-to-faculty ratio" and "optimal" class sizes, encouraging interaction and discussion between students and teachers. In the classroom, "lectures are loosely structured to provide ample opportunities to contribute and share real-world perspectives." A student details, "Everyone has different educational, ethnic, and social backgrounds. Everyone likes to add to classroom discussion where they can." Fortunately, collaboration is more common than competition, and "most people work toward each person succeeding as oppose to the "cut-throat" environment some business students experience." Since most Mercer students are balancing their education with a career (and personal lives), it can definitely be challenging to keep pace with the program. Fortunately, the school is known for its decidedly "friendly atmosphere." If schoolwork proves challenging, "professors are willing to take extra time for those who need it and to lend advice in projects inside the classroom or in work life outside the classroom." Like the faculty, "the administration generally cares about students, and there is an overall open-door policy for students." Exclaims a student, "My academic experience has been hard work and time consuming, but it is worth every moment!" Another agrees, "There is a lot of work involved, but it's not impossible to get everything done. The administration is very helpful. The majority of the professors are easily accessible."

Career and Placement

The Office of Career Services at Macon serves the undergraduate and graduate communities of the main Macon campus, as well as the Eastman Center. Among other student services, the Office of Career Services hosts career fairs and campus recruiting events. At a recent career fair, Frito Lay, GEICO, Geotechnical & Environmental Consultants, Honeywell Technology Solutions, Inc, Support Systems Associates, Inc., and Universal Avionics Systems Corp. were among the employers that came to interview MBA candidates. However, for those hoping to change careers, Mercer students admit that, "Because most students are employed, emphasis on career services is not present. More energy towards helping students with career decisions would be appreciated." A current student adds, "As an MBA student, I would definitely like to see the Career Placement services improve for MBA students. The school currently tailors this program to mainly

ADMISSIONS CONTACT: ROBERT HOLLAND JR, DIRECTOR OF ACADEMIC ADMINISTRATION
ADDRESS: 1400 COLEMAN AVENUE, SSBE, MACON, GA 31207
PHONE: 478-301-2835 • FAX: 478-301-2635
E-MAIL: HOLLAND_R@MERCER.EDU • WEBSITE: WWW.MERCER.EDU

undergraduate students." Nonetheless, students know that they will be able to cash in on the Mercer name during their career, as well as benefit from the school's "established network with leaders in many fields of business and economics." A student agrees, "I chose Mercer because it has a great reputation."

Student Life and Environment

According to most MBA students, it's strictly business at Mercer University. While Mercer's undergraduate college is lively and social, most MBA students "work and live off campus" and "don't seem to be involved in other organizations on campus." A current MBA candidate (and undergraduate alumni) laments, "There was a lot more to do while I was getting my undergraduate degree." At the same time, some note that the MBA student population is beginning to change as the school admits younger students, especially through the school's joint degree and work-study programs. A student explains, "There is a good mix of full-time working adults from the community, and young adult graduate assistants and law students." No matter what their age, experience, or career goals, most Mercer MBAs are "driven individuals pursuing skills that will increase their performance in their current career or make them more marketable for a future career."

Located in downtown Macon, "the campus is quiet and safe-feeling and fosters an environment for learning." However, some say they'd like to see "more parking and more convenient food options for night class students." Others mention that "campus security could be better." A current student elaborates, "Students live in what they call the Mercer Bubble, protected by patrolling campus police, who do a very good job, but can't stop everything."

Admissions

Students are accepted to Mercer University based on a combination of their GMAT scores, prior academic performance, and, in some cases, previous professional experience in a management position. Mercer admits students three times a year for the fall, spring, and summer terms. In recent years, the average student was twenty-nine years old, and 15 percent of the student body was international.

ADMISSIONS	
Admissions Selectivity Rating	**75**
# of applications received	12
% applicants accepted	100
% acceptees attending	100
Average GMAT	530
TOEFL required of international students	Yes
Minimum TOEFL (paper/web)	550/
Application fee	$50
International application fee	$100
Application Deadline/Notification	
Deferment available	Yes
Maximum length of deferment	1 YEAR
Transfer students accepted	Yes
Transfer application policy	
Can't transfer more than 6 semester hours from AACES accredited program	
Non-fall admissions	Yes

Miami University (OH)
School of Business

GENERAL INFORMATION
Type of school	Public
Affiliation	No Affiliation
Academic calendar	Semesters

SURVEY SAYS...
Classmates have diverse work experience, Friendly students, Good peer network, Conservative students, Happy students, Students love West Chester, OH
Solid preparation in:
Finance, Accounting, General management, Teamwork, Quantitative skills

STUDENTS
Enrollment of parent institution	23,983
Enrollment of MBA Program	107
% out-of-state	0
% part-time	100
Average age at entry	35
Average years work experience at entry	11

ACADEMICS
Academic Experience Rating	89
Profs interesting rating	93
Profs accessible rating	91
Student/faculty ratio	6:1
% female faculty	11
% underrepresented minority faculty	16
% part-time faculty	21

Academics

Students at Miami University's School of Business say their efficient program is "the best option in the Cincinnati area for working professionals with families to get their MBA." Before they even enroll, the school of business makes it easy for fully employed professionals to consider a graduate degree, offering prerequisite coursework online (as well as proficiency exams for students who want to test out of foundational classes) and a GMAT prep course right on campus. Once they have been accepted, students find the MBA program is "designed to be convenient for the working professional," with classes offered two evenings per week over the course of two years. The school's administration makes every effort to streamline the experience, offering "concierge-level" services for students. Among other conveniences, the all-inclusive tuition includes all fees and materials; at the beginning of each semester, the administration will "register you for class" and "buy all your books." They even have dinner service for evening classes, which "is a significant help to make the day easier." A current student enthuses, "They understand that we are working full time and make every effort to cater to us so all we have to do is study and attend class."

"A very focused professional MBA," the curriculum includes thirty-six credit hours of upper-level business courses, of which twenty-seven are core courses in economics, accounting, marketing, management, and other key business areas. With the remaining nine elective credits, students may choose to pursue a concentration in marketing or finance. Throughout the curriculum, there is an emphasis on collaboration, with a "cohort-based" program that maintains students within the same small academic community during the full MBA. Note that the program does not allow flexibility in the academic calendar; "the classes are prescheduled to keep the cohort together." Throughout the program, professors rely on case-based instruction, encouraging students to use critical thinking skills and real-world experience to solve business problems in the classroom. This interactive approach to education is particularly effective at Miami University, as students are "extremely intelligent with a lot of work experience," making them valuable contributors to class discussion. In fact, students range from "very early in their career to executives that have owned multiple companies." Staying on top of the coursework is not always a breeze, but it is rewarding: "Academically, the work is a challenge to keep up with, but it is that challenge that keeps it engaging."

Many students choose the School of Business for its excellent regional reputation, telling us that the school lives up to its strong credentials: The professors are "all very smart and challenge students to excel." In the classroom, "some teachers are outstanding and some are not so great." However, the vast majority are "approachable and seem to care about doing a good job." Plus, any time the program falls short, students feel they have the full attention of the school's administration and staff. As they continue developing the part-time MBA, "the administration is open to suggestions on how the program or any given course can be improved."

Career and Placement

The School's MBA program is specifically designed for working professionals, with a curriculum focused on increasing business acumen and problem-solving skills. To that end, the program is effective in promoting a student's long-term career goals. A current student attests, "I received my undergraduate degree from Miami University's School of Business and was well-prepared to enter the workforce. I knew that this program would afford that same high-caliber education."

While they are looking to advance their career, most students aren't actively looking for a new job after graduation. At the same time, "Miami is well known in the Cincinnati area," so the degree is a good investment in the future.

Student Life and Environment

The Miami University graduate business program is located in the Voice of America Learning Center (VOALC) a special satellite campus located just off the I-75 in West Chester, Ohio. "The facility is state of the art," with classrooms specially designed for business instruction and discussion. The VOALC is also "centrally located and close to Cincinnati and Dayton," making it convenient for students in either city to get to campus in the evenings. Several of Miami's undergraduate programs, as well as the graduate education department, share the VOALC campus with the MBA.

There are no residential facilities on campus; "everyone in the program lives in the greater Cincinnati Area" and commutes to school in the evenings. As a result, "the concept of student life in a classical sense does not apply" to the experience. Nonetheless, the atmosphere at the business school is consistently friendly and professional. Most Miami students are "highly motivated professionals," who are always "intelligent, professional, and pleasant" in dealing with their classmates. The cohort structure encourages networking and relationships among MBA candidates, to good effect. A current student tells us, "The forty people that are in my class are like family to me now after two years."

Admissions

Applications for the fall semester are accepted through June 15. Once you have submitted all your application materials, including GMAT scores and undergraduate transcripts, the admissions committee will make a decision within two to three weeks. A recent incoming class had an average GMAT score of 556 and an average undergraduate GPA of 3.3, as well as an average of ten years professional work experience before matriculation. While almost half of incoming students hold an undergraduate degree in business, the other half join the program from liberal arts or technical fields.

FINANCIAL FACTS

% of students receiving aid	24
% of first-year students receiving aid	16
Average loan	$22,377
Average student loan debt	$22,377

ADMISSIONS

Admissions Selectivity Rating	83
# of applications received	75
% applicants accepted	71
% acceptees attending	60
Average GMAT	593
Range of GMAT	557–662
Accepts GRE scores	Yes
Average GPA	3.2
TOEFL required of international students	Yes
Minimum TOEFL (web)	95
Application fee	$50
International application fee	$50
Application Deadline/Notification	
Deferment available	Yes
Maximum length of deferment	2 years
Transfer students accepted	Yes
Transfer application policy Transfer.Org will be used to evaluate whether your coursework is equivalent to the standard.	
Non-fall admissions	Yes
Need-blind admissions	Yes

MILLSAPS COLLEGE
ELSE SCHOOL OF MANAGEMENT

Academics

A cozy place to get an MBA, Else School of Management at Millsaps College maintains a friendly "small-college feel" alongside a "strong reputation for academic excellence" throughout the South. With its pleasant, liberal arts atmosphere, "you feel welcome no matter where you are on campus, and the size gives you a warmth you wouldn't expect" from a top-rated business program. The intimate environment really distinguishes the Else School experience, in which "faculty and staff always take a personal interest in helping students reach their goals." Thanks to the low MBA enrollment, students can also count on having "smaller class sizes" throughout the graduate business program, giving them a chance to interact closely with their professors, as well as their classmates. From economics to marketing, "the atmosphere of class is always full of discussion and open-minded conversation."

The only Millsaps department to confer graduate-level degrees, Else offers a Masters in accounting, as well as a full-time MBA program for traditional students and an Executive MBA for mid-career managers. The full-time MBA is comprised of foundation, core, and elective courses; foundation courses may be waived for students with an undergraduate degree in business. Depending on their previous preparation, students entering the program post-college can finish the MBA in anywhere between one to three years, though "there is a fast track" for current Millsaps undergraduates, which allows them to obtain an MBA with just one additional year of study. For EMBA students, it can be a challenge to balance work, family life, and academics. Fortunately, busy part-timers feel supported by the school's faculty, and say the "administration is very personal and helpful" in response to student concerns.

Boasting both real-world know-how and a genuine dedication to teaching, Else School professors are "insightful, experienced, and entertaining." Throughout the program, professors "do all they can to make the classroom experience worthwhile," and the academic experience is "engaging and very interactive." Most importantly, students feel their education has immediate real-world applicability. The professors are "experts in their fields "and" stay on top of current events and trends. Academically, "courses are tough, but you will definitely learn through rigorous application of theory." Plus, "instructors that take time to make sure the students understand the material," and they are very "approachable" outside of class. Not only do they maintain office hours, professors "enthusiastically give their time to support students, even after the semester is over."

Career and Placement

The Else School Career Center assists undergraduate and graduate business students in their internship or job search; they are also available to Else School alumni. The Career Center organizes networking events and career fairs on campus, offers resume and interview assistance, and runs career-related workshops throughout the year. Through the Career Center, business students also have access to numerous online job boards. While students say their career prospects look good, they also say the school could "make sure that working students (older students) are aware of career fairs, career opportunities," which are generally directed at recent graduates.

Not only is a Millsaps education "highly regarded in the region," it is the "only accredited MBA in Jackson," so students have a serious advantage in the local job market. Plus, the school's faculty has strong ties in the local area, so "communication and networking are easily facilitated here." Outside the Jackson area, there may be fewer opportunities to translate a Millsaps MBA into a top-notch job offer. Almost all of Millsaps business graduates take positions in the South.

ADMISSIONS CONTACT: MELISSA MEACHAM, DIRECTOR OF GRADUATE BUSINESS ADMISSIONS
ADDRESS: 1701 NORTH STATE STREET, JACKSON, MS 39210
PHONE: 601-974-1253 • FAX: 601-974-1260
E-MAIL: MBAMACC@MILLSAPS.EDU • WEBSITE: WWW.MBA.MILLSAPS.EDU

Student Life and Environment

A "warm and welcoming" environment permeates the business school at Millsaps, where students say, "It's very easy to make friends" and get involved in the campus community. Most MBA candidates are "very intelligent but also have great social skills," making them ideal companions both inside and outside the classroom. Within this "close-knit" community, the "business school clubs always have different activities that keep a strong cohesiveness within the student body throughout the semesters." Millsaps is a residential college, where "most undergraduates live on campus, while most MBAs live off campus." Even if they don't shack up in the dorms, full-time MBA candidates may still be highly involved with the school community. Here, both undergrads and graduate students "are able to participate in IM activities and other functions the school puts on (plays, concerts, varsity games etc.)"

By contrast, there is "not a great deal of campus life" for part-time MBA candidates. Balancing schoolwork with professional and family commitments, older students would love to see "more resources for parents with children." At the same time, "Millsaps has gone to lengths to make the EMBA students feel welcome and as much a part of other Business School activities as we are able to or wish to participate in." A part-time student assures us, "Even with our really busy schedules with work and school, we are still able to enjoy every aspect of life."

Admissions

To apply to Millsaps, prospective MBA candidates must submit undergraduate transcripts, GMAT scores, an admissions essay, and two letters of recommendation. In addition to regular application materials, applicants to the graduate business programs are also required to interview with the Director or Associate Director of Graduate Admissions. The recent entering class had an average undergraduate GPA of 3.4 and an average GMAT score of 560. The GMAT is not required for EMBA applicants.

FINANCIAL FACTS

Annual tuition	$26,400
Cost of books	$550
% of students receiving aid	85
% of first-year students receiving aid	100
% of students receiving grants	90

ADMISSIONS

Admissions Selectivity Rating	81
# of applications received	48
% applicants accepted	85
% acceptees attending	90
Average GMAT	560
Range of GMAT	500–730
Accepts GRE scores	Yes
Average GPA	3.4
TOEFL required of international students	Yes
Minimum TOEFL (paper/web)	550/
Application fee	$25
International application fee	$25
Early application deadline	4/1
Application Deadline/Notification	
Round 1:	4/1 / 4/25
Deferment available	Yes
Maximum length of deferment	1 year
Transfer students accepted	Yes
Transfer application policy Student in Good Standing. 6 hours from a non-AACSB program; 12 hours from a AACSB accredited program	
Non-fall admissions	Yes
Need-blind admissions	Yes

EMPLOYMENT PROFILE			
Career Rating	74	Grads Employed by Function% Avg. Salary	
Percent employed at graduation	5	Marketing	(2%)
Percent employed 3 months		Finance	(2%)
after graduation	8	MIS	(2%)

MINNESOTA STATE UNIVERSITY, MANKATO
COLLEGE OF BUSINESS

GENERAL INFORMATION
Type of school   Public
Affiliation   No Affiliation
Academic calendar   Semester

SURVEY SAYS...
Friendly students, Good peer network, Cutting-edge classes, Happy students, Smart classrooms
Solid preparation in:
General management

STUDENTS
Enrollment of parent institution	15,000
Enrollment of MBA Program	54
% male/female	86/14
% out-of-state	50
% part-time	86
% underrepresented minority	14
% international	50
Average age at entry	32
Average years work experience at entry	7

ACADEMICS
Academic Experience Rating	**66**
Profs interesting rating	69
Profs accessible rating	67
Student/faculty ratio	10:1
% female faculty	40
% underrepresented minority faculty	0
% part-time faculty	2

Academics

A completely affordable price tag, a Twin City area satellite campus located in Bloomington at the Normandale Partnership Center, and a "powerful track record for delivering quality education," not to mention one of the few accredited MBA programs in the state make the College of Business at Minnesota State University—Mankato "a big part of the community as a whole, and held in high regard." There have been recent capital improvements to the "beautiful campus," including "great visual and technological facilities."

The program is "quite well run," especially considering "it is naturally difficult to balance each course's difficulty considering the different background experiences of the students." The activities that accompany the academic work are "up to date, current, and not from the old books," giving students something they "can see and work with in…real life." The statistics/financial courses in particular are "beneficial and challenging," as are "innovative courses like the Executive seminar and Strategic Management."

Though the "excellent" professors get mostly high marks all around—a few "put only a small amount of work into class or are unprepared"—some would like to see more "come from business and not academia," so they might bring more practical applications to the classrooms. "I feel like those of us who are currently working have much more relevant experience to share than the instructors," says a student. The majority of the professors who are adjunct are "awesome and have great real world experience."

The difficulty and workload differs greatly from course to course, but the "flexible program structure" allows students to match their workload with their personal responsibilities and time. Courses are "more hands-on than theoretical," "very content and knowledge driven, and are updated real time based on the trends." Classes usually "use case analysis and team-based projects to present the course work," and many students meet on weekends. "The knowledge gained from my course mates cannot be overemphasized," says one student. Evening classes are a plus and a two-month semester is also "a plus." Some students do wish there were more courses available and "more options with regards to MBA concentrations."

Career and Placement

The MNSU MBA is "definitely directed toward people who are working full-time." The huge international student and full-time working population reduces the burden on the Career Development Center, which offers "very little help" for those who are looking for jobs after graduation, but "this is not a big issue as most students are employed." "The value of MSU-Mankato's MBA program is higher than that of most programs because costs are relatively cheap," and most students are mainly looking for the degree rather than the placement. There are plenty of experience opportunities as well as excellent career networking for international students, and "the way the program is designed makes it easy…to learn and understand the concepts in a better way." Students also benefit from "a strong focus on leadership throughout the program."

ADMISSIONS CONTACT: LINDA MEIDL, STUDENT RELATIONS COORDINATOR
ADDRESS: MORRIS HALL 151, MINNESOTA STATE UNIVERSITY, MANKATO, MN 56001
PHONE: 507-389-5425 • FAX: 507-389-1318
E-MAIL: LINDA.MEIDL@MNSU.EDU • WEBSITE: COB.MNSU.EDU

Student Life and Environment

This "friendly, social" group is "overall pretty great." "We all get along and work together to solve problems that arise," says a student, "[we're] a great group of new friends." One student says that "there are not as many working students as I expected, so much of the work situation discussion comes from a small number of us," but "many of them are very engaging with worldly views and experience." This is still "a good mix of students. There are people fresh out of college, people looking for a career change, and people looking to advance in their current career." Minnesota also draws a sizeable international student population.

Life at school is pretty "stress free." "I go twice a week, meet with classmates before class for supper, then go to class," says one student. Many will also meet with classmates on weekends to study. The campus is in "a great area that showcases the school—housing is close, businesses are nearby and support students, public transportation is available, but it is also a ped/bike friendly area too." There is a "well set up" daycare available (although a long waitlist exists) for working parents to use during the day.

Admissions

Applicants to the MBA program at MSU Mankato's College of Business must submit all of the following materials to the College of Graduate Studies: a completed application form; two official transcripts from one's degree-granting institution(s); a completed immunization form; and official score reports for the GMAT and, if applicable, the TOEFL. International applicants must also complete a Financial Statement Form demonstrating that they have sufficient funds to pay for the program. Most international applicants are required to have their undergraduate transcripts evaluated by a well-regarded credential evaluation service. All applicants must submit a resume, and two letters of reference to the College of Business. Admission to the MBA program is competitive. Students earning a score of 1000 or higher under the formula [(200 × undergraduate GPA) + GMAT score] and scoring at least 500 on the GMAT will be admitted to the program.

FINANCIAL FACTS

Annual tuition (in-state/ out-of-state)	$12,451/$12,451
Fees	$454
Cost of books	$1,200
% of students receiving grants	4

ADMISSIONS

Admissions Selectivity Rating	78
# of applications received	29
% applicants accepted	83
Average GMAT	532
Range of GMAT	440–630
Accepts GRE scores	No
Average GPA	3.2
TOEFL required of international students	Yes
Minimum TOEFL (paper/web)	500/61
Application fee	$40
International application fee	$40
Regular application deadline	6/1
Application Deadline/Notification	
Round 1:	6/1 / 6/15
Round 2:	11/1 / 11/15
Deferment available	Yes
Maximum length of deferment	1 year
Transfer students accepted	Yes
Transfer application policy Upon evaluation, would accept a maximum of 8 credits from another MBA or graduate program.	
Non-fall admissions	Yes
Need-blind admissions	Yes

MONMOUTH UNIVERSITY
LEON HESS BUSINESS SCHOOL

Academics

Monmouth University, located in West Long Branch, New Jersey, was founded in 1933 "to provide opportunity for higher education to area high school graduates who, in those Depression-era days, could not afford to go away to college." This tradition of accessibility remains a cornerstone of Monmouth University's mission. Many students in the MBA program also received their undergraduate degrees from Monmouth University, and listed location, convenience, competitiveness, and good professors as the primary strengths of Monmouth University's Leon Hess Business School.

The university's MBA program offers specialized concentrations for accounting, finance, marketing, management, and real estate. MBAs in these programs take core business classes as well as subject-specific electives. The program features a flexible schedule that encourages enrollment of mid-career, non-traditional, and part-time students. Classes are held, for the most part, on weekday evenings, with some additional classes meeting on Saturdays. Many students are drawn to the MBA at Monmouth because "they offer an accelerated program that allows students to earn the degree in one year" and students consider the school "well run" with "generous grants and scholarships."

Students note that "[s]ince Monmouth University is a smaller institution …the administrators and professors get to know their students on a more personal level, and are very interested in helping them achieve their academic goals." "Professors are easy to gain access to" and "[w]illing to help." The small campus setting "allows each student to get one-on-one time with professors and administrators." They "are always there whether …via email, phone call, or meeting up at a time that is convenient."

Professors are "very knowledgeable in their fields" and their real life work experience "gives them the chance to share real-life business scenarios with students" and discuss "how particular topics were handled." Students found this much more helpful than "just reading case studies or chapters in a text book." Monmouth offers "vast course offerings and times," and students say that the administration "will add classes if multiple students need them" and that both professors and the administration are "very accommodating to working professionals." One student found the professors helpful, but thought the material they taught was "dated," and the classes "easy and unchallenging."

In addition, students have access "to a variety of 'real world' experts," including the "H.R. Young Lecture Series, the Accounting Club Speakers, the Finance Club Speaker, the S.B. Siegel Lecture Series."

Career and Placement

"The connections the university creates are wonderful," says one student, and "they allow so much opportunity for employment." "Since it is a smaller school, most administrators and professors know students by name and even know some of their personal and academic goals," says another. Many students found their professors helpful in getting internships and jobs. Graduates have gone on to fill a wide range of positions from accountant to senior executive in various industries, and the university counts among its alumni a three-time Olympic Gold Medalist and captain of the U.S. Soccer team as well as a US federal judge.

ADMISSIONS CONTACT: LAURIE KUHN, ASSOCIATE DIRECTOR OF GRADUATE ADMISSION
ADDRESS: 400 CEDAR AVENUE, WEST LONG BRANCH, NJ 07764-1898
PHONE: 732-571-3452 • FAX: 732-263-5123
E-MAIL: GRADADM@MONMOUTH.EDU • WEBSITE: WWW.MONMOUTH.EDU

Student Life and Environment

The Monmouth University campus is a National Historic Landmark, as well as the former site of U.S. President Woodrow Wilson's summer home. Students say the 158-acre campus is "beautiful" and "very active." There are "many things to do on and off campus" and "they are constantly holding events, groups, clubs, and opportunities for employment." Past activities have included "trips to the beach, Broadway plays, and even a tour of the NYSE." Noting its close proximity to the Jersey Shore, one student states: "When you study near the beach there is never a downfall!"

Students "seem genuinely interested in being there and participating, which makes the experience enjoyable," though some found their fellow students lacking in "work experience" and "immature." A few students noted that there wasn't much interaction with fellow students outside of classes since so many students commute or work full-time, but a portion of the younger students are "local to the area, so it's easy to get together outside of class or see one another in public places, which helps create positive relationships." Students appreciate that due to the small size of the school "a lot of students are in the same classes together" and this allows students to "get comfortable working in groups and also enables them to take away more from each class."

Admissions

All applicants to Monmouth University must submit: an official academic transcripts for all undergraduate and graduate work; an official GMAT or GRE score report, an essay, and a resume are required; two letters of recommendation are optional. Interviews are not required.

Prospective students with a CPA or CFA license or master's degree may waive the admissions tests altogether. Merit-based scholarships are awarded to master's students based on their academic achievement upon acceptance by the Graduate Admission Office and are renewable throughout enrollment assuming preset academic minimums are met. International applicants whose first language is not English must submit official score reports for the TOEFL (the minimum score eligible is 550 on the paper-based test; 213 on the computer-based test; 79 on the web-based test).

FINANCIAL FACTS

Annual tuition	$19,764
Fees	$700
Cost of books	$740
Room & board	$11,320
% of students receiving aid	71
% of first-year students receiving aid	65
% of students receiving grants	65
Average award package	$11,473
Average grant	$5,911
Average loan	$14,555
Average student loan debt	$27,094

ADMISSIONS

Admissions Selectivity Rating	79
# of applications received	134
% applicants accepted	81
% acceptees attending	69
Average GMAT	469
Range of GMAT	440–550
Accepts GRE scores	Yes
Average Verbal GRE	153
Range of Verbal GRE scores	149–155
Average Quantitative GRE	153
Range of Quantitative GRE scores	148–154
Average Writing GRE	4.4
Range of Writing GRE scores	4.0–5.0
Average GPA	3.4
TOEFL required of international students	Yes
Minimum TOEFL (paper/web)	550/79
Application fee	$50
International application fee	$50
Regular application deadline	7/15
Application Deadline/Notification	
Deferment available	Yes
Maximum length of deferment	1 year
Transfer students accepted	Yes
Transfer application policy must complete at least 36 cr at Monmouth Transfer crds must be within 7yrs and with acceptable grade	
Non-fall admissions	Yes
Need-blind admissions	Yes

MONTCLAIR STATE UNIVERSITY
FELICIANO SCHOOL OF BUSINESS

GENERAL INFORMATION
Type of school   Public
Affiliation   No Affiliation
Academic calendar   Year-round

SURVEY SAYS...
Friendly students
Solid preparation in:
Accounting, General management,
Presentation skills, Quantitative skills

STUDENTS
Enrollment of parent institution	20,465
Enrollment of MBA Program	299
% male/female	56/44
% out-of-state	3
% part-time	68
% underrepresented minority	38
% international	25
Average age at entry	30

ACADEMICS
Academic Experience Rating	**78**
Profs interesting rating	87
Profs accessible rating	89
Student/faculty ratio	25:1
% female faculty	26
% underrepresented minority faculty	36
% part-time faculty	23

Prominent Alumni
Dr. Steve Adubato, Anchor, WNET NY, PBS; Dr. Paul Weber, Senior Director, Medical Affairs at Enzon Pharmaceuticals; Annette Catino, President & CEO, QualCare, Inc.; Thomas P. Zucosky, CIO, Discovery Capital Management; A. J. Khubani, President & CEO, Telebrands

Academics

Graduate students get a good return on their investment at Montclair State University, an "affordable" public school with an "up-and-coming business program" near New York City. Having recently reworked their graduate curriculum, Montclair's Feliciano School of Business offers several distinct MBA options on its New Jersey campus: an evening program, an Executive MBA and a Hybrid Saturday MBA. For all three programs, the school has introduced a "redesigned cohort-based MBA," through which students complete a comprehensive core curriculum in tandem with a small group of classmates. The structure encourages greater interaction and networking between MBA candidates—a huge asset to the experience, given that "fellow students are competent, pleasant to work with, and provide an engaging atmosphere in the classroom." A new online MBA is offered beginning in Fall 2016.

Beyond classroom instruction, the Montclair MBA curriculum provides a "complete educational experience," from the ongoing executive speaker series to the "foundations toolbox," an online resource to help students prepare for the MBA. For a global perspective, students participate in a nine to ten day "international [study] trip," an intensive course taught overseas, which focuses on the political and cultural aspects of global business. While the program offers a range of excellent resources, prospective students should carefully review the course offerings before enrolling, to ensure a cohort structured program is the correct fit for them. On the whole, "the administration for the MBA has been very receptive to students." Whenever a problem arises, "the MBA office is very quick in their responses and follow up."

Thanks to the small class size, "you do not get lost in the crowd" at Montclair, and "the professors do seem to offer a lot of assistance outside of class." The majority of the "professors are outstanding," though students admit that while there are "rock stars," a few professors can be lacking. In particular, finance and accounting professors get good marks from students, and "the economics professors are above average." Essential to working adults, practical education is a focus in the coursework; in the classroom, professors "use their real life experiences to teach us and get us up to date."

Career and Placement

The majority of Montclair students are already employed when they begin the program, using the MBA to advance in their current position. Those looking for new jobs will benefit from the school's proximity to New York City, one of the largest and most diverse job markets in the world. Currently, graduates of Montclair School of Business hold jobs at companies including Northwestern Mutual, Market Analytics, Enterprise RAC, Disney World, New York Life, Deloitte, Citigroup, CH Robinson, Estee Lauder, Merrill Lynch, KPMG, MTV, Prudential, The Hampton Inn, Bayer Healthcare, Party City, Target, Ernst & Young, and others.

The School of Business Career Services office is available to help undergraduate and graduate students explore careers and prepare for the job hunt through workshops, speakers, Internet resources, and individual career counseling sessions. With regards to the assistance offered by Career Services, a current student explains, "You basically post your resume, which they pass on to employers involved in in-campus recruiting. They call you for interviews, when they feel you are a match for a position." While this system does produce opportunities, students would love to see more networking events on campus.

ADMISSIONS CONTACT: MS. LYNN DAVIS, ASSISTANT DIRECTOR OF ADMISSIONS AND RECRUITING
ADDRESS: COLLEGE HALL, ROOM 203, ONE NORMAL AVENUE, MONTCLAIR, NJ 07043
PHONE: 973-655-5147 • FAX: 973-655-7869
E-MAIL: GRADUATE.SCHOOL@MONTCLAIR.EDU • WEBSITE: WWW.MONTCLAIR.EDU/MBA

Student Life and Environment

Montclair's graduate business programs principally attract students from the local area, in addition to a smaller population of international students. Within the student body, there is a "very diverse mix ethnically, and many different professions represented." No matter what their background, students are generally "hard-working professionals that are attending the MBA program at night." A student in the Saturday program attests, "My fellow students within the cohort are very intelligent, hard working, reliable, and goal oriented."

Outside the classroom, the business school hosts networking events and frequent business speakers for the benefit of the MBA program, and it recently began hosting case competitions as well. While most students cannot find the time for extracurricular activities, others take advantage of the collegial atmosphere. "On campus, life is pretty rich. You get to meet lots of people, interact, network and have fun." A current student adds, "I have always been a commuter in my studies. Montclair is the first school that I felt truly encouraged [to have] an on campus social life."

The School of Business moved into a new building in summer 2015, and overall, the school's 250-acre campus is "very nice with many improvements in the past few years." Only fourteen miles from New York City, it's easy to take advantage of the big city's recreational, professional, and entertainment options, while enjoying the more tranquil, suburban atmosphere in Montclair and the surrounding area.

Admissions

Applications for Montclair's MBA programs are accepted on a rolling basis year-round. Usually, an admissions decision will be rendered within two to three weeks after the school receives a completed application packet. To be considered, students must submit undergraduate transcripts, official GMAT or GRE scores, a personal essay, and one letter of recommendation. Students may be eligible for admissions without taking the GMAT or GRE if they have a 3.0 GPA or higher from a Bachelor's or Master's degree program. Successful applicants to the Executive MBA program usually have at least five years of full-time work experience before matriculation.

FINANCIAL FACTS

Annual tuition (in-state/ out-of-state)	$12,083/$12,083
Fees	$1,595
Cost of books	$1,749
Room & board (on/off-campus)	$14,010/$10,442
% of students receiving aid	48
% of first-year students receiving aid	52
% of students receiving grants	7
Average award package	$16,731
Average grant	$3,869
Average loan	$16,523
Average student loan debt	$32,472

ADMISSIONS

Admissions Selectivity Rating	71
# of applications received	157
% applicants accepted	73
% acceptees attending	78
Accepts GRE scores	Yes
Average GPA	3.2
TOEFL required of international students	Yes
Minimum TOEFL (paper/web)	380/83
Application fee	$60
International application fee	$60
Application Deadline/Notification	
Deferment available	Yes
Maximum length of deferment	1 year
Transfer students accepted	Yes
Transfer application policy	
Students who have completed prior academic coursework in business, may be waived from up to 12 credits of foundation courses.	
Non-fall admissions	Yes
Need-blind admissions	Yes

MONTEREY INSTITUTE OF INTERNATIONAL STUDIES
FISHER INTERNATIONAL MBA PROGRAM

GENERAL INFORMATION

Type of school	Private
Affiliation	No Affiliation
Academic calendar	Semester

SURVEY SAYS...

Good social scene, Liberal students,
Happy students, Students love
Monterey, CA
Solid preparation in:
Presentation skills, Doing business
in a global economy, Environmental
sustainability

STUDENTS

Enrollment of parent institution	798
Enrollment of MBA Program	82
% male/female	51/49
% part-time	8
% underrepresented minority	37
% international	45
Average age at entry	27
Average years work experience at entry	3

ACADEMICS

Academic Experience Rating	86
Profs interesting rating	89
Profs accessible rating	95
Student/faculty ratio	7:1
% female faculty	15
% underrepresented minority faculty	12
% part-time faculty	44

Joint Degrees

MBA/MA International
Environmental Policy Joint
Degree; MBA/MA International
Policy Studies with focus on
Trade,Investment and Development,
or Human Security and
Development; MBA/MPA Non-rofit
Management; MBA/MA Translation;
MBA/MA Translation & Localization
Management

Academics

The Fisher International MBA program at MIIS offers students just what it says it does, an MBA in international business. Not only that, but the campus itself, located in central California, has an international feel. "Half the students in every class are international students," and all are required to be proficient in a second language. Students are also "encouraged to study abroad." "I came here to avoid being around the traditional business school student wanting to go make millions and maximize profit without caring about social or environmental impact." There is an emphasis on green business strategies, as well as an understanding of what the future of business will actually look like. "The school itself is entrepreneurial. This year, it launched an innovative program in partnership with social impact investment firms to send students out to emerging countries like Vietnam, India, Nigeria, and Tanzania. The students work with the venture firms directly." The program's focus is on language studies, environmental issues, corporate responsibility, and cross-cultural negotiation. "Last year as a part of the sustainability lecture series, business leaders from interesting new ventures like Revolution Foods and Numi Tea came to lecture weekly." Students appreciate the "cross-sector focus, specifically international development and environmental policy." They also like the "accessibility to other disciplines." At MIIS students have the opportunity to specialize or opt for a dual degree. They can work toward an MBA, as well as an MA in fields, such as environmental policy, public administration, and translation.

Students love "the international perspective, the size (for its adaptability, personal attention, etc.), the innovative nature of the curriculum, and the focus on sustainability." "The school is small but packs a punch. In the same week, students could see guest lecturers on Nuclear Proliferation in Iran, and representatives from Denmark talk about how the country achieved a 100 percent growth rate without an increase in petroleum use." Because of its small size, "everything is personalized. The administration has designed the program, so that no two students' experience is the same, each being custom tailored to the student's professional goals." "If we want to see something happen, we can make it happen." "The administration is forward-thinking and proactive in finding new and exciting directions for the school; there is an ability to adapt quickly to new trends in education and business." Some professors are "excellent" and "frequently engage with students" outside of class. Students say professors are on a first-name basis with many students. One suggests "the academic rigor could be more standardized. Some courses are highly rigorous, while others are not." Others worry that "a couple really good professors retired this term." They hope they will be replaced "with equally talented professors."

Career and Placement

The Center for Advising and Career Services (CACS) for the Fisher International MBA program "acts as an 'executive search firm'," helping students "target potential employers and enhance their value." Students are assigned advisors during the admissions process, and career planning starts from day one. They offer personal consultations, as well as a multitude of workshops covering topics, such as salary negotiation, how to interview, and networking. Students admit the office "is slowly pulling things together." What hampers this process is the school's size and location. Not many recruiters are coming to campus, and one student reports you can "expect to get a job and an internship on your own." However, there is an online job resource for both students and alumni, and the school hosts an annual career fair, which draws more than 100 employers to campus.

ADMISSIONS CONTACT: CAROLINE LATORRE, ENROLLMENT MANAGER
ADDRESS: 460 PIERCE STREET, MONTEREY, CA 93940
PHONE: 831-647-4123 • FAX: 831-647-6405
E-MAIL: ADMIT@MIIS.EDU • WEBSITE: FISHER.MIIS.EDU

The top five employers who hired graduates last year were the following companies: PriceWaterhouse Coopers, Veritas Wealth Advisors, Ernst & Young, LeCroy Corp, Foundation for Community Development.

Student Life and Environment

At MIIS "students are responsible, well rounded, and honest." They are also "aware of international issues," "socially conscious," and "culturally sensitive." Students are "motivated by new and creative ideas" and "have a desire to operate outside of their comfort zones." They have "a great combination of international experience and curiosity. Many students have been in the Peace Corps or are going. Many are bilingual or multilingual." Most have lived and worked abroad or are international students visiting from other countries.

"You can't ask for a more beautiful area than the Monterey Bay peninsula." Monterey is located on the coast in central California about two hours south of San Francisco. It has a population of about 30,000 residents, making it "fairly quiet." There are "wonderful restaurants in town and in surrounding areas." However, there is "not much variety in night life." The school sponsors a monthly happy hour during which students mingle with faculty and staff, and students also interact with students in other programs through various activities. There is a scuba club, a golf club, as well as a Women in Business club, just to name a few. There are also "many opportunities for outdoor activities in the surrounding area."

Admissions

The committee requires from its applicants the following materials for admission: an official GMAT score report; a personal essay; undergraduate GPA and transcripts from all post-secondary institutions previously attended; letters of recommendation; work experience; and two years of foreign language study. Most students average three to four years of work experience. A GRE score will suffice in lieu of the GMAT. Second language proficiency (which is also required), can be acquired through an intensive language immersion program offered by the school the summer prior to entrance.

Prominent Alumni

Fumio Matsushima, Head of Private Banking, HSBC Japan; Laurent-Gabriel Vinay, CEO/President, Hugo Boss Japan; Elizabeth Powell, Vice President of Customer Service, Motorola; Naoko Yanaghara, Vice President of AT&T Japan

FINANCIAL FACTS

Annual tuition	$33,950
Fees	$56
Cost of books	$900
Room & board	$17,111
% of students receiving aid	95
% of first-year students receiving aid	100
% of students receiving grants	95
Average award package	$25,967
Average grant	$10,163
Average loan	$26,396
Average student loan debt	$33,165

ADMISSIONS

Admissions Selectivity Rating	83
# of applications received	107
% applicants accepted	73
% acceptees attending	71
Average GMAT	567
Range of GMAT	490–640
Accepts GRE scores	Yes
Average GPA	3.4
TOEFL required of international students	Yes
Minimum TOEFL (paper/web)	550/80
Application fee	$50
International application fee	$50
Early application deadline	12/1
Early notification date	12/15
Regular application deadline	3/15
Regular application notification	5/1
Application Deadline/Notification	
Deferment available	No
Transfer students accepted	Yes
Transfer application policy	
Credits must be from an AACSB accredited college or university, must be with a B or better. Possible to transfer up to 25% of total program. Dean makes final determination.	
Non-fall admissions	Yes
Need-blind admissions	Yes

EMPLOYMENT PROFILE

Career Rating	76	Grads Employed by Function	% Avg. Salary
Percent employed at graduation	21	Marketing	(14%)
Percent employed 3 months after graduation	43	Operations	(5%)
		Consulting	(9%)
		Management	(18%)
		Finance	(9%)
		MIS	(5%)
		Other	(9%)

NATIONAL UNIVERSITY OF SINGAPORE

BUSINESS SCHOOL

GENERAL INFORMATION

Type of school	Public
Affiliation	No Affiliation
Academic calendar	August

SURVEY SAYS...

Classmates have diverse work experience, Friendly students, Good peer network, Liberal students, Abundant clubs and activities, Students love Singapore
Solid preparation in:
Finance, General management, Teamwork, Quantitative skills

STUDENTS

Enrollment of parent institution	3,687
Enrollment of MBA Program	152
% male/female	60/40
% out-of-state	92
% part-time	38
% underrepresented minority	0
% international	92
Average age at entry	32
Average years work experience at entry	6

ACADEMICS

Academic Experience Rating	96
Profs interesting rating	89
Profs accessible rating	94
Student/faculty ratio	8:1
% female faculty	32
% underrepresented minority faculty	0
% part-time faculty	28

Joint Degrees

NUS MBA w/ Peking University; NUS MBA w/ HEC Paris; NUS MBA/ MPP w/ Lee Kuan Yew School of Public Policy; NUS MBA/MPA with Lee Kuan Yew School of Public Policy; NUS MBA/Master of Real Estate with The Department of Real Estate; NUS MBA/Masters of Advanced Management Programme w/ Yale School of Management; NUS PhD/MBA; S^3 Asia MBA w/ Fudan University & Korea University; UCLA-NUS Executive MBA.

Academics

For students who choose the National University of Singapore's (NUS) MBA for its strategic location, they make the choice to be in the heart of Asia, in cosmopolitan Signapore: One student says simply of NUS, "It is the best school in Asia about Asia." Indeed, NUS' "good reputation as a premier Asian school" is sharply enlivened by its location "in a center of finance." Students value NUS' ability to "combine academic studies with practical experience" in their MBA education, as well as the fact that some of their professors are "practitioners from the professional world." "The finance, accounting, and economics professors" get especially high ratings from students.

"The size of each class is also small—about fifty students in one class," which encourages "every student to participate in class." Students also appreciate the intellectual variety of participating in "classroom studying, study groups, study trips, networking sessions and social activities," experiential learning, and say that, through a synthesis of all these experiences, their "understanding of global business, sustainability, team work and life skills has [been] enhanced." NUS' "School administration is very supportive and takes feedback," and indeed, students participate in "platforms such as town hall events and other formal and informal meetings" to help administrators "understand and improve areas where students are facing difficulty." As a whole, one students sums up the NUS MBA as "a great learning experience, especially for developing insights into Asian business environments."

Career and Placement

NUS' "location in Singapore, the heart of Asia, has provided the school great connections to a lot of international companies," and those connections benefit its students' upward mobility immensely. "The NUS MBA is top-ranked in Asia," and the school facilitates "lots of programs and networking events to help expand network and job search opportunities" for students. Students report that NUS boasts a "large group of adjunct professors who . . . bring us hands-on industry experience and exposure," so that their MBA education keeps one eye on the future. "Singapore is a hub for the energy industry," as well as the finance industry, in particular, but for students with different career aspirations, "the school has an excellent infrastructure and resource center." NUS "attracts diversity," and its students find "can learn a lot from people coming from different parts of the world."

ADMISSIONS CONTACT: CHUA NAN SZE, MARIE-ANTONIE, DIRECTOR (GRADUATE STUDIES)
ADDRESS: NUS BUSINESS SCHOOL, MOCHTAR RIADY BUILDING, 15 KENT RIDGE DRIVE, LEVEL, 4
SINGAPORE, 119245 • PHONE: 011-65-651-8763 • FAX: 011-65-68724423
E-MAIL: MBA@NUS.EDU.SG • WEBSITE: MBA.NUS.EDU

Student Life and Environment

NUS students love both Singapore and their campus. "Singapore is one of the most friendly countries in the world," and it "guarantees a high standard of living. The city and university is so safe that you can walk on your own even at midnight." It's a "beautiful city to live in," as well as a "perfect studying and living environment on campus." "We live on a beautiful campus. The rent is lower than living off campus and married students are welcome with their spouses. We have a pool, gym, food courts and study rooms." Most NUS students "are living on-campus" during their education, which means "students are pretty close to each other," and also encourages a greater sense of cohesiveness and teamwork. "We have an amazing cohort with people from twenty-six nationalities," many of whom have "some connection with Asia," and students find each other "energetic, friendly and competitive," as well as "very diverse both culturally" and in terms of "work experience." "There are a lot of activities to keep one busy," and students take advantage of them. In terms of work-life balance, "the workload is tough but manageable," partially because "NUS definitely has a 'high challenge-high support' environment."

Admissions

The NUS MBA program "seeks individuals who have integrity, strong leadership capabilities and the desire to achieve academic and management excellence." Admission requirements include a strong undergraduate academic record, at least two years of full-time work experience, the GMAT/GRE, and where applicable, the TOEFL/IELT. Short-listed applicants will be interviewed and may be asked for additional materials.

Prominent Alumni

Ms. Grace Fu Hai Yien, Minister for Culture, Community and Youth & Leader of the House

FINANCIAL FACTS

Annual tuition (in-state/ out-of-state)	$44,851/$44,851
Fees	$292
Cost of books	$800
Room & board (on/off-campus)	$8,487/$8,704
% of students receiving aid	50
% of first-year students receiving aid	50
% of students receiving grants	50
Average award package	$9,602
Average grant	$9,602
Average loan	$0
Average student loan debt	$0

ADMISSIONS

Admissions Selectivity Rating	96
# of applications received	2,258
% applicants accepted	7
% acceptees attending	96
Average GMAT	656
Range of GMAT	600–700
Accepts GRE scores	Yes
TOEFL required of international students	Yes
Minimum TOEFL (paper/web)	620/100
Early application deadline	1/31
Early notification date	3/1
Regular application deadline	3/31
Regular application notification	5/31
Application Deadline/Notification	
Round 1:	1/31 / 3/1
Round 2:	3/31 / 5/31
Deferment available	Yes
Maximum length of deferment	1 year
Transfer students accepted	Yes
Transfer application policy Admission and credit transfer applications are evaluated on a case-by-case basis, and depend on the student's record and performance within the MBA program, the quality of the program and School.	
Non-fall admissions	No
Need-blind admissions	Yes

EMPLOYMENT PROFILE

Career Rating	90	Grads Employed by Function% Avg. Salary	
Percent employed 3 months after graduation	90	Marketing	(22%)
		Operations	(9%)
Average base starting salary	$67,181	Consulting	(22%)
Primary Source of Full-time Job Acceptances		Management	(14%)
School-facilitated activities	95 (100%)	Finance	(24%)
		HR	(3%)
		Other	(6%)

Top 5 Employers Hiring Grads
Microsoft (3), HP (2), DBS (2), Priceline.com (2), A.T. Kearney (1)

NEW JERSEY INSTITUTE OF TECHNOLOGY
SCHOOL OF MANAGEMENT

GENERAL INFORMATION

Type of school	Public
Affiliation	No Affiliation
Academic calendar	Semester

SURVEY SAYS...
Friendly students, Liberal students
Solid preparation in:
General management, Teamwork,
Presentation skills, Quantitative skills

STUDENTS

Enrollment of parent institution	11,325
Enrollment of MBA Program	166
% male/female	67/33
% out-of-state	58
% part-time	76
% underrepresented minority	18
% international	55
Average age at entry	34

ACADEMICS

Academic Experience Rating	**87**
Profs interesting rating	89
Profs accessible rating	88
Student/faculty ratio	17:1
% female faculty	17
% underrepresented minority faculty	8
% part-time faculty	50

Academics

One of the things that really sets the New Jersey Institute of Technology, or NJIT, apart from other schools is its emphasis on understanding how technology and science intersect within the business sector. The school promotes the notion that business is not a "separate entity" from technology and that the two are more intertwined than ever. A great number of students say they chose to attend NJIT for their MBA so that they, having received a degree in an area such as Technology Management, could be "unique" among their colleagues in the business sector. The school also boasts an impressive Executive MBA, or EMBA, program and most classes take place on weekends or Fridays allowing the "flexibility [they] require to work and obtain an MBA at the same time." The EMBA takes it's philosophy of "relevance, practicality, and innovation" to heart and this "the curriculum is geared towards the job market." The program focuses on knowledge that can be directly applied in the workplace, which many of the students find not only helpful, but also "very interesting." This focus on practical knowledge is refreshing, and most students say that it's a "more valuable emphasis" than if the school were only "focused on finance" or other areas of a similar ilk. There are also online courses, in addition to weekend courses, for those that may still have trouble getting to and from each class.

The school has also built up quite a "strong reputation in the Northeast region." With its AACSB accreditation for both its graduate and undergraduate programs, and the fact that the MBA program costs "considerably less than other programs" of its kind, it is no wonder that so many students are singing its praise.

The classes at the NJIT School of Management tend to be "very small," which is fine for most students as they find the faculty to be "excellent." The school has thirty faculty members and approximately 700 students. While there are, of course, issues with the occasional professor, such as prolonged responses "to emails or requests for office hours," most of the professors are said to be "very accessible and willing to help," and they come to the classroom with "good field experience [from] corporate America."

Career and Placement

The Career Resource Center of NJIT helps students through a variety of ways, including resume review, job search, students write resumes, search for jobs, find career fairs, and locate online job postings. They also have a section that assists students in finding jobs with "Green" companies. In keeping with their focus on technology, the center also has a career podcast that keeps students up-to-date with career tips and thoughts on the job market. Employers seeking MBAs during a recent NJIT Career Fair included the Air Force, Alcatel-Lucent, Apex Technology, Associated Press, AT&T, Broadridge Financial Solutions, Census 2010, CIGNA, Makro Technologies, Maquet Cardiovascular, McKesson, MMC Systems, New York State Department of Transportation, Public Service Enterprise Group, QPharma, Schindler Elevator Corporation, Softnice, Verizon, and Vonage.

Student Life and Environment

One of the first things that students seem to mention is the school's location. Located in New Jersey, the campus is "conveniently close" to New York City. While the school, located in downtown Newark, is in the middle of "museums [with] plenty of restaurants in the area," most tend to focus on the proximity of New York due to the "quick access by public transportation." This quick access is also helpful since NJIT is largely a commuter school, and many of the students have jobs during the day. For those who have time, trips to places like Washington D.C. and other various locales are available, which provide "educational value" and allow students to expand their knowledge and visit various companies and landmarks in each city.

People get along with their fellow classmates and identify the student body as being "very diverse and friendly." Since many of those attending classes have jobs, they "all contribute their work experiences" to each classroom and team function, which gives everyone a chance to learn from each other's unique experience set. This type of shared understanding helps students learn to respect each another's views and to hold each other "in great esteem and with great affection." In fact, even in the distance-learning program, students say their fellow classmates are, "more helpful and supportive than [they] would have expected from a distance learning program." The administration maintains this mutual respect as well. Some say that there are "miscommunications" at the administrative level, but the majority believes that "student feedback is truly listened to and evaluated carefully," and that level of attention helps students. They believe the administration is both "accommodating and helpful."

Admissions

As with most MBA programs, applicants must provide proof of their earned bachelor's degree and submit their Graduate Management Admissions Test or GRE; although, applicants who already hold a master's or doctoral degree from an accredited university are exempt from the GMAT/GRE requirement. International students may submit their TOEFL score in addition to the GMAT. Students can also submit a personal statement, a resume of their work experience and up to three letters of recommendation. although optional, these submissions are recommended by the school.

FINANCIAL FACTS

Annual tuition (in-state/out-of-state)	$18,500/$27,340
Fees	$2,652
Cost of books	$3,200
Room & board (on/off-campus)	$13,296/$10,300
% of students receiving aid	44
% of first-year students receiving aid	48
% of students receiving grants	9
Average award package	$18,611
Average grant	$5,448
Average loan	$20,022
Average student loan debt	$40,211

ADMISSIONS

Admissions Selectivity Rating	**83**
# of applications received	208
% applicants accepted	54
% acceptees attending	49
Average GMAT	580
Range of GMAT	560–620
Accepts GRE scores	Yes
Average Verbal GRE	150
Range of Verbal GRE scores	145–156
Average Quantitative GRE	160
Range of Quantitative GRE scores	159–160
Average Writing GRE	3.5
Range of Writing GRE scores	3.0–4.0
TOEFL required of international students	Yes
Minimum TOEFL (paper/web)	550/79
Application fee	$65
International application fee	$65
Application Deadline/Notification	
Deferment available	No
Transfer students accepted	No
Non-fall admissions	Yes
Need-blind admissions	No

New Mexico State University

College of Business

GENERAL INFORMATION

Type of school	Public
Affiliation	No Affiliation
Academic calendar	Semester

SURVEY SAYS...

Cutting-edge classes, Happy students
Solid preparation in:
Accounting, General management

STUDENTS

Enrollment of parent institution	15,490
Enrollment of MBA Program	161
% male/female	51/49
% out-of-state	35
% part-time	60
% underrepresented minority	57
% international	18
Average age at entry	27
Average years work experience at entry	4

ACADEMICS

Academic Experience Rating	64
Profs interesting rating	62
Profs accessible rating	69
% female faculty	31
% underrepresented minority faculty	14
% part-time faculty	0

Joint Degrees

Dual B Sc Engr/MBA, 5 yrs.

Prominent Alumni

John J. Chavez, Mng Dir. Phase One Ventures/NM Startup Factory; Robert D. Chelberg, Lt. General, U.S. Army (Retired); John M. Cordova, Sports Mgt Group Dir., Coca Cola; Andres Gutierrez, CIO, Family Health Centers of San Diego, Inc.; James Hawkins, CFO, Canon National Bank, Colo Springs

Academics

The College of Business at New Mexico State University is "extremely technologically savvy," a quality that serves it well in a state that is home to several air force bases, major NASA operations, two national laboratories, Spaceport America, and several big tech players (Intel, for one, has a large manufacturing plant in Albuquerque).

NMSU incorporates technology in all disciplines, and has developed several specialized degrees. The school also "concentrates on entrepreneurs because of its abundant resources" such as NMSU's Arrowhead Center, which provides assistance to clients on- and off-campus in the areas of intellectual property, technological commercialization, and entrepreneurship education.

Many students simply appreciate the convenience of the program, praising its "wonderfully-located campus with a very unique and culturally-diverse academic program." The school serves both full-time and part-time MBAs, and fully understands and meets the needs of traditional and nontraditional students when it comes to education. In the past 10 years, NMSU has even "created an MBA cohort program for the Los Alamos National Laboratory. Laboratory," and for employees at the White Sands Missile Range near Las Cruces. Those programs are now being replaced with a cohort-based distance MBA which is online with a synchronous online component and one evening per week. A school that comes to you—you can't beat that for convenience.

Instructors at NMSU "are well-respected in their fields and apply real-world applications to their lectures and assignments," while "the administration is always very responsive whenever a conflict arises." A "socially and ethnically diverse student population" informs class discussion. One student sums up, "I have had a very positive overall academic experience. Every single administrator and faculty member has treated me with the utmost respect and professional courtesy."

Career and Placement

NMSU's Placement and Career Services Office provides university students with on-campus employment, internship listings, career listings, workshops, advising, job fairs, and online research tools. The school holds a number of job fairs and other recruiting events throughout the year, but all are primarily targeted toward undergraduates. As a result, relatively few of the many companies that visit campus specifically seek MBAs.

Recent employers of NMSU MBAs include: Accenture, ElPaso Electric, Ernst & Young, Agilent Technologies, ConocoPhilips Company, General Motors, Hewlett-Packard, IBM, Intel, KPMG International, NASA, Los Alamos National Laboratories, Sandia National Laboratory, TXU Energy, and Wells Fargo.

Student Life and Environment

NMSU "is a great place to continue your education and the Las Cruces area is second to none," students report, adding that "Las Cruces is a very slow-paced, small-town type environment. It is, however, slowly changing due to this area being designated as one of the top-ten places to retire in the nation." The school is located "in its own private corner of the city, and it is very safe, clean, and spirit-oriented."

Many who attend the MBA program work at least part time as well; one such student writes, "This is a focused and relevant MBA that meets my needs as a nontraditional student who holds down a full-time civil engineering job." When they can manage to take a break from their responsibilities, they "enjoy attending college sporting events and special events at the Pan American Center on campus. The campus is also a nice place to take a long walk for exercise or leisure, strolling from pond to pond." The campus includes excellent facilities for workouts and for study. Some here point out that "NMSU could definitely improve in how it caters to students with families. Child care is only available to students with very low incomes, or at the standard child care rates in this city." There are a number of activities for children at the NMSU Museum, the Las Cruces Natural History Museum, the Farm and Ranch Heritage Museum, as well as youth sports teams.

The NMSU MBA population includes "a large portion of international students, who come because of the affordability and friendly environment. [Students] with widely diversified cultures and nations contribute to the discussions related to international trade and global business management." Students "have diverse work experience, which makes interaction between students interesting and useful" and results in "a very professional approach to problem-solving case studies or application of curriculum covered in course material."

Admissions

Applicants to the NMSU MBA program must apply for admission to the university's graduate school before they can be admitted to the MBA program. Admission to the graduate school requires that the applicant hold a four-year undergraduate degree from an accredited institution with a GPA of at least 3.0 (some exceptions to the GPA requirement are possible; contact school for details). International applicants must earn at least a 550 on the paper-based TOEFL or a 79 on the IBT; NMSU also accepts the IELTS with a 6.5 score. Applicants to the MBA program must meet one of the following criteria: an undergraduate GPA of at least 3.5 from an institution with a business program accredited by AACSB or ACBSP; a minimum GMAT score of 400 and a minimum score of 1050 under the formula (GPA multiplied by 200 plus GMAT); possession of a graduate degree from a U.S. regionally accredited institution; or completion of at least four years of full-time professional work and an undergraduate GPA of at least 3.25 from an institution with a business program accredited by AACSB or ACBSP.

FINANCIAL FACTS

Annual tuition (in-state/ out-of-state)	$4,941/$15,107
Fees	$306
Cost of books	$1,200
Room & board (on/off-campus)	$6,914/$8,550

ADMISSIONS

Admissions Selectivity Rating	**85**
# of applications received	101
% applicants accepted	51
% acceptees attending	71
Average GMAT	470
Range of GMAT	430–510
Accepts GRE scores	Yes
Average GPA	3.6
TOEFL required of international students	Yes
Minimum TOEFL (paper/web)	550/
Application fee	$40
International application fee	$50
Regular application deadline	7/15
Regular application notification	8/4
Application Deadline/Notification	
Deferment available	Yes
Maximum length of deferment	1 yr
Transfer students accepted	Yes
Transfer application policy A maximum of 9 semester credits from an AACSB International accredited school.	
Non-fall admissions	Yes
Need-blind admissions	Yes

NEW YORK UNIVERSITY
LEONARD N. STERN SCHOOL OF BUSINESS

GENERAL INFORMATION
Type of school   Private
Affiliation   No Affiliation
Academic calendar   Semester

SURVEY SAYS...
Classmates have diverse work experience, Friendly students, Good peer network, Good social scene, Happy students, Abundant clubs and activities, Students love New York, NY
Solid preparation in:
Finance, Teamwork, Presentation skills, Quantitative skills

STUDENTS
Enrollment of parent institution	50,027
Enrollment of MBA Program	2,339
% male/female	64/36
% part-time	66
% underrepresented minority	10
% international	33
Average age at entry	28
Average years work experience at entry	5

ACADEMICS
Academic Experience Rating	**99**
Profs interesting rating	93
Profs accessible rating	93
Student/faculty ratio	7:1
% female faculty	21
% underrepresented minority faculty	3

Joint Degrees
MD/MBA, with the School of Medicine; JD/MBA, with the School of Law; MA/MBA, with the Institute of French Studies (GSAS); MPA/MBA, with the Wagner School of Public Service; MBA/MFA, with the Tisch School; MBA/MS in Mathematics in Finance; MS in Biology/MBA; Dual MBA with HEC School of Management.

Academics

Smack dab in the middle of New York City, NYU's Stern School of Business couldn't have a better location, location, location. From finance to the arts, "New York delivers every opportunity imaginable," and Stern is "well integrated into NYC, both physically and in the people it brings in as faculty, guest speakers, and partners." Best suited to ambitious students with well-honed career goals, "you can do anything you want to do at Stern." Over half of the credit hours required for the MBA are electives, and "Stern is able to offer a very broad range of courses and activities for students with any business interest." A dream school for future bankers, Stern has deep ties on Wall Street and is ranked "among the top schools in the world for people working or hoping to work in finance." At the same time, it is known for its excellent programs in luxury retail, marketing, technology, and media and entertainment; those with an interest in social enterprise work or creative fields also note that "Stern has a great support system for alternative career goals," including partnerships with the Wagner School of Public Service and Tisch School of the Arts. In fact, Stern "is fully integrated within the university," and business students can take up to a quarter of their classes at other NYU schools, allowing for a truly individualized education. To top it all off, "most students take advantage of opportunities to study abroad" through Stern's one- and two-week "Doing Business In..." international programs, spring-break trips, or semester-long exchange programs.

Despite Stern's historic strength in finance, there's "less corporate/institutional mind-set" here; instead you'll find "an emphasis on thinking creatively," as well as a "dedication to solving real-world problems through business." On campus, "the culture is extremely collaborative," and "students don't just care about their own success; they care about their classmates' as well." Likewise, "professors make it a point to be accessible and often make it mandatory to meet students one-on-one." In the classroom, "the faculty is exceptional," including a number of well-known business personalities. Though there are some academics on staff, most instructors "have vast real-world experience in the fields they teach," bringing a practical perspective into the classroom. While students admit there is "some bureaucracy at the administrative level," administrators are "always addressing our needs, eager for our feedback and putting that feedback into action."

Career and Placement

Thanks to its stellar reputation, wide-ranging career-development opportunities, and aggressive campus recruitment programs, Stern boasts an impressive track record helping MBA candidates achieve prestigious, high-paying positions. Through the Office of Career Development, students have access to myriad services, from career panels to résumé reviews, as well as industry-specific training. The school maintains deep ties with many companies and "incredible access to recruiters"; plus, the "location in the heart of New York makes networking with alumni and companies all the easier." With so much in their favor, Stern graduates hit the ground running—in fact, most have made major strides long before graduation day. A current student enthuses, "With no finance experience, I have already secured my summer internship offer at a top investment bank."

In recent years, the following companies hired multiple Stern graduates: Accenture, Amazon.com, Bain & Company, Barclays Capital, Bayer Healthcare, Citi, Colgate Palmolive, Credit Suisse, Deutsche Bank, Disney, Estée Lauder, Goldman Sachs, Google, IBM Consulting, JPMorgan, Kraft, L'Oréal, McKinsey & Company, Morgan Stanley, PepsiCo, PricewaterhouseCoopers, Sony, and Strategy&, UBS, and Yahoo!. The class of 2015 had a salary range of $30,000-$160,000, with an average base salary of over $114,863 (the average signing bonus was an additional $30,410). Impressively, more than 73 percent of the

ADMISSIONS CONTACT: PAULA STEISEL GOLDFARB, ASSUSTANT DEAN, MBA AND EXECUTIVE MBA ADMISSIONS AND GRADUATE FINANCIAL AID
ADDRESS: 44 WEST 4TH STREET, SUITE 6-70, NEW YORK, NY 10012 • PHONE: 212-998-0600
FAX: 212-995-4231 • E-MAIL: STERNMBA@STERN.NYU.EDU • WEBSITE: WWW.STERN.NYU.EDU

class found their position through on-campus recruiting and interviews, or other Stern-supported professional development activities.

Student Life and Environment

"There is a strong sense of community" at Stern, where students are hard working and competitive, but also "very outgoing, collaborative, and inquisitive." As soon as you step on campus, "you have a great support network in all parts of your life, and it's easy to make friendships that will last long past graduation." There's never a dull moment on this "vibrant" campus, where "everyone is on their hustle, all the time, with incredibly varied interests." Every day, there are "an abundance of social activities and networking opportunities" at the school, from club meetings and "guest speakers" to the well-attended weekly Beer Blasts. A current student exclaims, "The hardest part is knowing how to pick one activity over another! There are frequently too many enticing conferences, programs, and activities going on to make an easy decision."

"Located in one of the most exciting cities in the country," Stern is a great place to go to school "both because of the opportunities and activities available here and the wide range of people you meet." A reflection of the city that surrounds it, Stern draws students from many backgrounds and industries; the "professional diversity" among students enriches the academic experience, while "a high percentage of international students" brings a global perspective to the community. Without exception, everyone loves the urban location, saying, "You can't beat New York City." However, they do mention one well-advertised detractor: "Cost of living overall is very high in New York."

Admissions

Admission to Stern is highly selective. Most recently, the school received close to 3,700 applications for 340 spots in the entering class. Entering students had an average undergraduate GPA of 3.51 and an average GMAT score of 720. Note that Stern accepts either the GRE or the GMAT; there is no minimum test score needed to apply. Close to 35 percent of the class is international or a dual-citizen.

Prominent Alumni

John Paulson, President, Paulson & Co., Inc.; Ken Langone, Founder, Chairman and CEO, Invemed Associates LLC; Robert Greifeld, President & CEO, The NASDAQ Stock Market, Inc.; George Barrett, Chairman and CEO, Cardinal Health, Inc.; Leonard Stern, Chairman and CEO, The Hartz Group, Inc.

FINANCIAL FACTS

Annual tuition (in-state/ out-of-state)	$63,720/$63,720
Fees	$2,472
Cost of books	$1,980
Room & board (on/off-campus)	$25,200/$25,200
Average award package	$62,340
Average student loan debt	$107,458

ADMISSIONS

Admissions Selectivity Rating	98
# of applications received	3,696
% applicants accepted	20
% acceptees attending	46
Average GMAT	720
Range of GMAT	700–740
Accepts GRE scores	Yes
Average GPA	3.1
TOEFL required of international students	Yes
Application fee	$250
International application fee	$250
Application Deadline/Notification	
Round 1:	10/15 / 12/15
Round 2:	11/15 / 2/15
Round 3:	1/15 / 4/1
Round 4:	3/15 / 6/1
Transfer students accepted	No
Non-fall admissions	No
Need-blind admissions	Yes

EMPLOYMENT PROFILE

Career Rating	96	Grade Employed by Function	%	Avg. Salary
Percent employed at graduation	79	Marketing	(16%)	$98,722
Percent employed 3 months after graduation	89	Operations	(3%)	$87,714
		Consulting	(33%)	$125,396
Average base starting salary	$114,863	Management	(5%)	$106,077
Primary Source of Full-time Job Acceptances		Finance	(38%)	$115,495
School-facilitated activities	222 (73%)	MIS	(2%)	$102,000
Graduate-facilitated activities	66 (22%)	Other	(3%)	$121,500
Unknown	18 (6%)	**Top 5 Employers Hiring Grads**		

Top 5 Employers Hiring Grads
Amazon, Deloitte Consulting, IBM, JPMorgan, PricewaterhouseCoopers

North Carolina State University

Poole College of Management

GENERAL INFORMATION

Type of school	Public
Affiliation	No Affiliation
Academic calendar	Semester

SURVEY SAYS...

Classmates have diverse work experience, Friendly students, Happy students, Students love Raleigh, NC
Solid preparation in:
Operations, Teamwork, Communication/interpersonal skills, Presentation skills, Quantitative skills

STUDENTS

Enrollment of parent institution	34,015
Enrollment of MBA Program	538
% male/female	58/42
% out-of-state	18
% part-time	85
% underrepresented minority	10
% international	29
Average age at entry	27
Average years work experience at entry	4

ACADEMICS

Academic Experience Rating	93
Profs interesting rating	90
Profs accessible rating	95
Student/faculty ratio	5:1
% female faculty	33
% underrepresented minority faculty	3
% part-time faculty	21

Joint Degrees

MS Microbial Biotechnology/MBA; DVM/MBA; MAcc/MBA; JD/MBA; MIE/MBA.

Prominent Alumni

Tony O'Driscoll, Executive Director & Regional Managing Director - Asia, Duke Corporate Education; Joydeep Ganguly, VP and Head, Corporate Engineering, Facilities & Operations, Gilead Sciences; Stephanie Trunzo, COO, Chief Digital Officer & Partner, PointSource

Academics

The Jenkins MBA at NC State University's Poole College of Management places a large emphasis on skills that will tie directly into the strengths of the region. With its main campus located in the state capital of Raleigh and a satellite location in Research Triangle Park, "a focus on technology and innovation" with "a strong emphasis on hands-on experiences." For future-oriented students, the "emphasis on real world projects and technology focus in many classes" makes NC State "one of the best values for a full-time MBA in the country." This "emphasis on real world, hands-on learning differentiates it from the other programs in the area," especially the "focus on technology and innovation." Indeed, one student notes, "This is a program for people who want to lead teams and stay on the cutting edge of technology."

A discipline helping this MBA program "dramatically increase in ranking and reputation" despite the program being less than 20 years old is its Supply Chain curriculum. "They are able to provide real projects with real companies allowing students to apply knowledge they learn to real life situations." Other programs of note include a lauded Biosciences Management program, which fits well with the regional presence of several major pharmaceutical and bioengineering corporations, and the Entrepreneurship and Technology Commercialization program that enables graduate business students to develop startups right from the classroom..

Though high achievement is expected, cutthroat academics are not. Here the "atmosphere is congenial but focused," and "teamwork is highly emphasized." Because most classes take place in the same building, "there is a great deal of interaction with other students." Students who are "focused on career success and money" may be disappointed that "that is not the case at NC State," but others will be pleased to find that educators here "care a lot about sustainability" and showcasing how business fits into the larger world. School administration shows "an almost fanatical focus on improvement and a willingness to experiment." The result is that despite its relative newness, "some elements of the program are already receiving national attention (Supply Chain, the Entrepreneurship Program) and some will soon (the Consumer Behavior initiative)."

Career and Placement

"The promise of working on real world projects for companies in co-ordination with normal academic activities" is not only a major draw for students here, it gives them an opportunity to get hands-on experience with many of the same corporations that may later recruit them. There is a "long-term culture of industry partnerships that is expanding to startups" at NC State which helps the school "stay abreast of events and networking opportunities." MBAs will benefit from the services of a dedicated Career Resources Management which not only aids in networking and recruitment, but which also provides workshops on resume writing and cover letters, interviewing skills, and job search strategies.

During the course of their study, students can expect to work hand-in-hand with entities such as Caterpillar, Lenovo, IBM, Bank of America and Lenovo. Graduates from NC State's Graduate School of Management have in recent years been recruited by firms such as American Airlines, BB&T, Chevron, Cisco Systems, Deloitte, Eaton Corporation, Ericcson, Glaxo Smith Kline, Lab Corp, Net App, Novartis Animal Health, Novozymes, Progress Energy, Red Hat, Research Triangle Institute, SAS, and Siemens Medical.

Student Life and Environment

Those accepted to NC State should expect to find an "extremely diverse" group of "intelligent, friendly people who work hard during the day and still have energy and enthusiasm to continue learning and make class fun in the evenings." Those hoping to immerse themselves in ambition will find it among the student body. Attendees say it is "great to work with other students committed to their goals and aspirations." Students at NC State are in the business of learning about business, and they are serious about it. "They push us in our studies, and encourage us to work hard."

Life here centers around a "very collaborative environment," one in which objectives, either within or outside of the classroom, are "based centrally around team activities." Those who see business as a ruthless, individual pursuit will instead find a "program … trying to develop a different mindset from traditional MBA programs." This is aided by the MBA Student Association, which "works to provide social activities and community service projects for the students outside of class." The goal is to provide both full-time and part-time students an opportunity "to network with each other, as well as providing opportunities to positively impact the community."

Outside of class and class projects, MBA students spend a lot of time brainstorming. One student explains, "There's always a few of us throwing plans at each other. These aren't all Silicon Valley plans either—we've got fashion designers, textile inventors and others all listening to each other. It's a very stimulating environment." There are also many clubs, cultural activities, and of course Raleigh's nightlife to distract from the relentless pursuit of knowledge and experience typical among those in the MBA program.

Admissions

Academic record, GMAT scores, essays, letters of reference all come into play, as do work and volunteer experience, when weighing one's application to NC State's Jenkins MBA Program. The competitive admissions process will take into account your management potential, as well as prior employment, or volunteer and/or military experience. Though not required of full-time students, two years of full-time employment is "strongly recommended." Such experience is, however, required of part-time students. One's background should include coursework in either calculus or statistics. Applicants whose primary language is not English must submit TOEFL or IELTS scores; a minimum TOEFL score of 250 on the computer-based test or 100 on the Internet-based test or a minimum IELTS score of 7.5 is required. Interviews are also required, and potential candidates will be contacted directly once all of their documents are reviewed and accepted.

FINANCIAL FACTS

Annual tuition (in-state/ out-of-state)	$19,977/$34,561
Fees	$2,372
Cost of books	$854
Room & board (on/off-campus)	$10,785/$13,039
% of students receiving aid	90
% of first-year students receiving aid	93
% of students receiving grants	85
Average award package	$29,150
Average grant	$23,847
Average loan	$19,664
Average student loan debt	$36,759

ADMISSIONS

Admissions Selectivity Rating	90
# of applications received	224
% applicants accepted	40
% acceptees attending	56
Average GMAT	640
Range of GMAT	570–710
Accepts GRE scores	Yes
Average Verbal GRE	159
Range of Verbal GRE scores	149–166
Average Quantitative GRE	159
Range of Quantitative GRE scores	154–164
Average Writing GRE	3.9
Range of Writing GRE scores	3.0–4.5
Average GPA	3.6
TOEFL required of international students	Yes
Minimum TOEFL (paper/web)	600/100
Application fee	$75
International application fee	$85
Early application deadline	10/15
Early notification date	11/15
Regular application deadline	3/1
Regular application notification	4/1
Application Deadline/Notification	
Round 1:	10/15 / 11/15
Round 2:	1/15 / 2/15
Round 3:	3/1 / 4/1
Deferment available	Yes
Maximum length of deferment	1 year
Transfer application policy The NC State MBA Program can accept up to 12 hours of transfer credit from another AACSB-accredited MBA program	
Need-blind admissions	Yes

EMPLOYMENT PROFILE

		Grads Employed by Function%	Avg. Salary
Career Rating	92		
Percent employed at graduation	72	Marketing (30%)	$86,700
Percent employed 3 months after graduation	92	Operations (27%)	$84,951
		Consulting (6%)	$81,250
Average base starting salary	$82,389	Management (6%)	$80,000
Primary Source of Full-time Job Acceptances		Finance (9%)	$78,001
School-facilitated activities	21 (58%)	Other (22%)	$73,200
Graduate-facilitated activities	15 (42%)	**Top 5 Employers Hiring Grads**	
Unknown	0 (3%)	Red Hat (5), Cisco (4), USAA (3), Caterpillar (3), Patheon (2)	

NORTHEASTERN UNIVERSITY
COLLEGE OF BUSINESS ADMINISTRATION

Academics

Northeastern offers both full-time and part-time MBA tracks, as well as online MBA options. The part-time program has three options: an Evening MBA, an Executive MBA, and a High Tech MBA. The biggest perk of a part-time MBA is "flexibility." Students can keep their full-time jobs and organize their class schedules around them. The full-time program is two years long and includes the famous "Corporate Residency" in which students are given paid internships for six months with a business in the Boston area. Most students admit this is why they chose Northeastern for their MBA. "The opportunity to work with a company for six months will allow me to learn more about the company, be involved in a project from start to finish, and impress hiring managers." Also, the program "has a great reputation." Students who enter the school hoping for a career change find the internship indispensable. In addition to the opportunity to gain tangible field experience and get paid for it, many mention "Northeastern also provided more scholarship funds than any other school." Other highlights of the program are "the required international field study" and the "manageable class sizes of around thirty-five students." Also, "the quality of professors is very high." "Northeastern has done an excellent job recruiting professors from top-tier schools." "All of them have Ph.D.s, and the Boston area has such an academic wealth that many teachers are of very high quality." Professors are "easy to approach" and incorporate a "great teaching style" in their classrooms. "Courses are designed to allow students to understand each discipline in a managerial/decision-making way." Professors also "coordinate projects and exams with each other" and are "very available outside of class."

Students do notice that some courses aren't as engaging as others. "There is a noticeable difference in energy between the first-year, full-time classes and the second-year, evening classes (not nearly as strong)." Still, most students feel the school "deserves a better ranking."

Career and Placement

"There is a great deal of emphasis placed on each student's career development. The career center team makes sure that every student has the opportunity to get placed in a six-month paid corporate residency position." Students also praise the "variety of businesses" participating in the program. "You are given an executive-level mentor and even participate in six executive networking lunches during your first year." The luncheons are limited to six students, so each gets "individual attention" from the executives, who are from "top companies." In addition to the Executive Luncheon Series, there are "Insider Insight Sessions, guest speakers, and an alumni database." These opportunities are why most students say they chose Northeastern. The career center doesn't stop at internships; it also places students in full-time positions. Students say Northeastern has "high placement rates."

Of the past year's graduating class, 71 percent had accepted job offers by graduation, and 95 percent had accepted offers three months after graduation. Students were hired by the following companies: IBM Corporation, Raytheon, Staples, Inc., W.R. Grace & Co., and Ernst & Young.

ADMISSIONS CONTACT: EVELYN TATE, DIRECTOR, RECRUITMENT AND ADMISSIONS
ADDRESS: 350 DODGE HALL, 360 HUNTINGTON AVENUE, BOSTON, MA 02115
PHONE: 617-373-5992 • FAX: 617-373-8564
E-MAIL: GSBA@NEU.EDU • WEBSITE: WWW.MBA.NEU.EDU

Student Life and Environment

"The NEU MBA program is very social." "There is a sense of friendly competition, but at the end of the day, everyone wants to see each other succeed." "The students in my program opened up quickly to each other." "Our class became one large group of friends by the end of the first year." Students describe each other as "easy going, intelligent, spirited, inspirational, and fun." Another says fellow classmates are "outgoing, realistic, pragmatic, and down to earth." Some students did mention a social gap between those entering fresh from undergrad and more experienced students. However, they all tend to be "supportive of each other." The small class size "leads to very strong bonds."

Most students mention location as one of the main reasons why they chose Northeastern. "The location of the school within Boston cannot be better. It is next to the Museum of Fine Arts. It has its own stop on the subway and is connected to the greater Boston area via public transportation." "Most students stay on campus all day." The school is located in what is known as the Fenway Cultural District. Even though it's in an urban setting, it has trees, green quads, and is a beautiful space.

Admissions

The admissions committee at Northeastern University requires the following materials from its applicants: copies of official transcripts from all post-secondary schools attended; a current resume; three essays; two letters of recommendation; an official GMAT score report; and the online application form. An interview is also important, as is work experience. The school prefers its entrants to have at least two years of professional work experience. International students whose first language is not English must send TOEFL or IELTS scores. Roughly one in four candidates is selected.

FINANCIAL FACTS

Annual tuition (in-state/ out-of-state)	$44,280/$44,280
Fees	$325
Room & board	$25,350
% of students receiving aid	83
% of first-year students receiving aid	100
% of students receiving grants	78
Average award package	$37,456
Average grant	$31,192
Average loan	$21,944

ADMISSIONS

Admissions Selectivity Rating	95
# of applications received	596
% applicants accepted	22
% acceptees attending	54
Average GMAT	644
Range of GMAT	600–690
Accepts GRE scores	Yes
Average Verbal GRE	155
Range of Verbal GRE scores	151–158
Average Quantitative GRE	159
Range of Quantitative GRE scores	157–162
Average Writing GRE	3.8
Range of Writing GRE scores	3.3–4.5
Average GPA	3.3
TOEFL required of international students	Yes
Minimum TOEFL (paper/web)	600/100
Application fee	$100
International application fee	$100
Early application deadline	11/1
Early notification date	12/20
Regular application deadline	4/15
Regular application notification	6/1
Application Deadline/Notification	
Round 1:	11/1 / 12/20
Round 2:	1/15 / 2/28
Round 3:	3/15 / 5/1
Round 4:	4/15 / 6/1
Deferment available	No
Transfer students accepted	Yes
Transfer application policy	
We may award a limited number of transfer credits for MBA courses taken at AACSB-accredited institutions.	
Non-fall admissions	No
Need-blind admissions	Yes

EMPLOYMENT PROFILE

		Grads Employed by Function	% Avg. Salary
Career Rating	94		
Percent employed at graduation	71	Marketing	(10%) $71,725
Percent employed 3 months after graduation	95	Operations	(36%) $82,385
		Consulting	(10%) $93,750
Average base starting salary	$81,797	Management	(5%) $75,000
Primary Source of Full-time Job Acceptances		Finance	(14%) $83,333
School-facilitated activities	27 (68%)	Other	(2%) $55,000
Graduate-facilitated activities	13 (32%)	**Top 5 Employers Hiring Grads**	
		EMC (4), Raytheon (4), National Grid (2), IBM (2), Wellington (2)	

NORTHERN ARIZONA UNIVERSITY
THE W.A. FRANKE COLLEGE OF BUSINESS

GENERAL INFORMATION
Type of school   Public
Affiliation   No Affiliation
Academic calendar   August-May

SURVEY SAYS...
Friendly students, Students love
Flagstaff, AZ
Solid preparation in:
Accounting, Teamwork,
Communication/interpersonal skills,
Presentation skills

STUDENTS
Enrollment of parent institution	29,031
Enrollment of MBA Program	36
% male/female	58/42
% out-of-state	25
% part-time	0
% underrepresented minority	11
% international	6
Average age at entry	25
Average years work experience at entry	2

ACADEMICS
Academic Experience Rating	**82**
Profs interesting rating	85
Profs accessible rating	94
Student/faculty ratio	3:1
% female faculty	27

Academics

Efficiency is the name of the game at the Franke College of Business at Northern Arizona University. This school's AACSB accredited accelerated MBA program is just "ten months from start to finish," cramming a full MBA curriculum into less than a year of coursework. Not surprisingly, the result is an "intense course load," tons of homework, and a "fast-paced, invigorating environment." A current student admits, "I'm lucky if I get more than a couple of hours on the weekends to go grocery shopping. This place will get you in and out in a hurry, but you certainly won't have time for anything else while you're doing it." At the same time, the breakneck format affords students a number of important benefits. In particular, it's a great deal: Here, students only leave the workforce for a year and tuition is "significantly lower" than at a traditional two-year program. In addition, for students who plan to take the CPA exam, NAU offers the opportunity to complete their accounting courses and earn an MBA in just two years. A popular choice, "over half the program is enrolled in the MBA-ACC offering, while the other half navigates the traditional MBA." On that note, accounting classes get top marks, while students say "the management and finance courses add value and the principles learned will be handy going forward."

Despite the program's rigor, the Franke College of Business is a surprisingly cooperative and down-to-earth place. Throughout the business school, "the environment is one of learning and collaboration where the majority of teachers are interested in helping students achieve success." With few exceptions, "the teachers are extremely approachable," and, due to the limited graduate enrollment, "the small class sizes means we receive more individual attention from professors." Teamwork is encouraged across the curriculum, which builds soft skills while also helping to ease the stress of coursework. A student agrees, "The academic experience at NAU is demanding and high-pressured, although the group nature of a lot of our work allows students to use their best skills when contributing within this environment." Like the faculty, "the school's administration goes that extra mile" to assist students, and it truly works "to make the MBA program as stress-free as possible." The school generally runs smoothly and the curriculum is well-designed; however, some students tell us, "There does not appear to be a lot of communication between the professors" when it comes to planning and evaluating courses.

Career and Placement

The ten month program allows students to enter the workforce sooner. In some cases, students don't even need to look for a new job after graduation. A current student explains, "I left my job to be in this program, but given that I will be applying back with them within a year, I don't need to go through the same hiring process." For those students looking for a new position, the Career Development Office provides undergraduate and graduate students with various career and professional development programs. Through the Career Development Center, employers recruit students for entry-level and full-time positions, as well as for internships. Companies that recently participated in one of the Career Development Office's recruiting events include Vanguard, Equity Methods, McGladrey, Grant Thornton, PFSweb, CliftonLarsonAllen, Target, Lohman Company, Deloitte & Touche, KPMG, Eide Bailly, and Ernst & Young. Still, students feel the MBA would improve with the addition of "more job placement opportunities." In particular, students would like to see more recruiting companies from Phoenix and other big cities.

ADMISSIONS CONTACT: KATIE POINDEXTER, COORDINATOR
ADDRESS: BUSINESS GRADUATE PROGRAMS, P.O. BOX 15066, FLAGSTAFF, AZ 86011-5066
PHONE: 928-523-7387 • FAX: 928-523-7996
E-MAIL: FCB-GRADPROG@NAU.EDU • WEBSITE: WWW.FRANKE.NAU.EDU/GRADUATEPROGRAMS

Student Life and Environment

Located in the beautiful mountain town of Flagstaff, NAU offers "outstanding" facilities, a professional atmosphere, and a scenic backdrop. The W.A. Franke College of Business building is LEED-certified. All classrooms "overlook a green retention area" where students can be seen "playing Frisbee, sitting and reading under the perimeter trees, or just relaxing." In addition, students have access to a "great MBA lounge that offers students a place to complete course work as well as eat lunch and socialize." "Most students are laid-back and easygoing" with their classmates, though "hardworking" and competitive in the classroom. A younger crowd, many MBA candidates are "recent graduates with no actual work experience," though you'll also meet some mid-career professionals in class.

While the atmosphere is laid-back, MBA students are definitely busy. One admits, "Honestly, in a ten-month accelerated program, I haven't much of an opportunity to have much of a life outside of school." When they want to relax, there are plenty of "outdoor activities" in the surrounding area, from local hikes and skiing, to the nearby Grand Canyon. On campus, the larger university also offers social, recreational, and cultural events. MBA students can be as involved in the school as they'd like; "some students take full advantage of everything NAU has to offer, while others do not."

Admissions

Students who have completed foundation business coursework can complete the accelerated MBA in ten months. Those lacking one or more foundation courses can complete needed coursework at NAU in the summer before the MBA program begins. To apply, prospective students must submit their undergraduate transcripts, official GMAT or GRE scores, a current resume, two references, and a set of personal essays. After submitting their application materials, prospective students are invited to interview. Interviews begin in the fall and students are admitted on a rolling basis. Complete applications are accepted until July 10, or until the class reaches capacity of fifty students.

FINANCIAL FACTS

Annual tuition (in-state/ out-of-state)	$10,977/$22,617
Fees	$7,000
Cost of books	$1,500
% of first-year students receiving aid	94

ADMISSIONS

Admissions Selectivity Rating	78
# of applications received	50
% applicants accepted	98
% acceptees attending	73
Average GMAT	559
Range of GMAT	490–608
Accepts GRE scores	Yes
Average Verbal GRE	154
Range of Verbal GRE scores	151–158
Average Quantitative GRE	152
Range of Quantitative GRE scores	149–156
Average Writing GRE	3.8
Range of Writing GRE scores	3.5–4.1
Average GPA	3.5
TOEFL required of international students	Yes
Minimum TOEFL (paper/web)	550/83
Application fee	$65
International application fee	$65
Application Deadline/Notification	
Deferment available	Yes
Maximum length of deferment	1 year
Transfer students accepted	No
Non-fall admissions	Yes
Need-blind admissions	Yes

EMPLOYMENT PROFILE

Career Rating	79
Percent employed at graduation	70
Percent employed 3 months after graduation	23
Average base starting salary	$55,151

NORTHERN KENTUCKY UNIVERSITY
HAILE/US BANK COLLEGE OF BUSINESS

GENERAL INFORMATION

Type of school	Public
Affiliation	No Affiliation
Academic calendar	Semester

SURVEY SAYS...

Classmates have diverse work experience

Solid preparation in:
General management, Teamwork, Presentation skills

STUDENTS

Enrollment of parent institution	15,000
Enrollment of MBA Program	200
% part-time	90
Average age at entry	28
Average years work experience at entry	5

ACADEMICS

Academic Experience Rating	**84**
Profs interesting rating	89
Profs accessible rating	92
Student/faculty ratio	22:1
% female faculty	27
% underrepresented minority faculty	13
% part-time faculty	33

Joint Degrees

JD/MBA, minimum 5 years

Academics

Its location "ten minutes from downtown Cincinnati, Ohio" and "affordable [overall cost] relative to other AACSB-accredited schools in the area" draws enthusiastic students to Northern Kentucky University's College of Business. About 85 percent of the students here attend part-time, and those who do appreciate that "classes are offered in the evenings"—most courses meet from 6:00 to 9:00 P.M. once a week—"so that [students] can attend all required classes without cutting into [their] work schedules." While class times are convenient, students say that NKU's "greatest strength" is "the course work itself. NKU is very challenging and very strict with academics. Although it is not so easy to prepare for class at times, this has helped prepare me well for my professional career by pushing me to the limit." Class sizes are "small," and professors are "passionate about their subject areas" and "always willing to stay [after class] with you and meet whenever you need to." They're also, for the most part, "flexible and understand that most graduate students also work full time and have a family." Many have "very relevant real-life experience to impart," and their ranks "include the former director of human resources of a major public utility, a former Oracle executive, and a finance professor who works as a Certified Financial Planner on the side. No, Jack Welch does not teach here, but those [who] do are knowledgeable and do a good job." Students love that NKU "allows specialization of the MBA" and cite its Entrepreneurship Institute, International Business Center, and finance programs as major strengths.

Overall, students find NKU to be a place where "the student is the top priority." "The staff has always been quick [when] answering my questions and available when I need them," a student writes.

Career and Placement

"There is a wonderful Career Center on campus, but it is primarily focused on meeting the needs of undergraduates," NKU business students tell us. That being said, students admit that, for the most part, they "already have jobs, so career placement is not a large need." Most are looking to move up the ranks with their current employer; those looking to jump ship turn to their fellow students for job leads. Which isn't to say there aren't those who'd like a little more help in the area of job placement: "I think we need more career counselors within the MBA program for those of us who do not come from a traditional business background," one student tells us. To answer these concerns, NKU created a designated career counselor and a college of business alumni office to assist graduate students with career guidance and placement.

ADMISSIONS CONTACT: JIM BAST, DIRECTOR, MBA PROGRAM
ADDRESS: 363 BC, NUNN DRIVE, HIGHLAND HEIGHTS, KY 41099
PHONE: 895-572-7695 • FAX: 859-572-7694
E-MAIL: MBUSINESS@NKU.EDU • WEBSITE: WWW.NKU.EDU/~COB/GRADUATE/MBA

Student Life and Environment

Many at NKU are "on the 'slow' track to finish because of the demands of family and jobs." As such, the school differs from institutions that "have the same students begin and end the program together"; most here "meet different students each semester." Despite this, students report that their "classmates are great people who, through this MBA program, have become real friends." Such friendships are forged largely without the assistance of clubs or activities geared toward graduate students: "I'm a commuter, so most of my time at school is in class, in the library, or meeting to do group work," a typical student writes. While NKU's campus "has food/coffee stands in almost every building" and "computers everywhere with free printing," drawbacks include a "mostly concrete" aesthetic and difficult parking "at certain times of the day."

Students describe their "hardworking" peers as "friendly" but "competitive." NKU strongly recommends that potential applicants obtain two years of work experience before applying, and, by all accounts, its student body is "very diverse" in employment backgrounds. "Most [students here] are mid-twenties to mid-thirties," but "age ranges from twenty to fifty." "Quite a few are married with children" and "Most have significant work experience." When students seek common ground, they need look no further than their objective: "We are all here for the same reason: to get an MBA," one student writes. That being said, most students are "eager to learn and get the most from their MBA experience, not just a credential."

Admissions

To gain admission to NKU, applicants must obtain a bachelor's degree from a regionally accredited institution and possess a cumulative undergraduate GPA of at least 2.75 on a 4.00 scale; he or she must also obtain a score of at least 525 on a GMAT taken within the last five years and, if applicable, obtain a score of at least 550 on the paper version of the TOEFL (or at least 213 on the computer version of the test). Exceptions to the GMAT include: GRE score within the last 5 years, possession of a Master degree, MD, or PhD, or similar advanced degree.

FINANCIAL FACTS

Cost of books	$0

ADMISSIONS

Admissions Selectivity Rating	78
# of applications received	84
% applicants accepted	88
% acceptees attending	59
Average GMAT	513
Range of GMAT	440–760
Accepts GRE scores	No
Average GPA	3.2
TOEFL required of international students	Yes
International Regular application deadline	6/1
Application Deadline	
Round 1:	6/1
Deferment available	Yes
Maximum length of deferment	1 year
Transfer students accepted	No
Non-fall admissions	No
Need-blind admissions	Yes

NORTHWESTERN UNIVERSITY
KELLOGG SCHOOL OF MANAGEMENT

Academics

At the Kellogg School of Management at Northwestern University, you can almost feel the cooperation in the air. "It's the kind of atmosphere that even if you don't know people, you will say 'hi' in the halls," reports one student. This "collaborative," "collegial," and "student-led environment" at Kellogg means that students' input is always sought, and their voices and desires have a huge impact on the course the school takes both academically and socially. Students agree that this crash-course in democracy is "the best way to train tomorrow's business leaders" and note that it also lends the school "a certain energy around the campus that brings excitement to each and every day."

One facet of the collaborative spirit is that professors receive regular performance evaluations. However, it seems the results are rarely negative as the majority of students here praise them as "bright, accomplished, fair, and engaging."

Another major draw to the program is the school's One-Year MBA Program that allows students to earn their MBAs in just twelve months. "Kellogg's One-Year Program is one-of-a-kind," one student says. "It's the best return on investment and offers great flexibility combined with small classes and highest quality students." There is, of course, the traditional Two-Year Program available as well. In addition to the One-Year MBA Program, another unique facet at Kellogg is the MMM Program, a dual-degree in conjunction with the McCormick School of Engineering at Northwestern University and designed to aid students who wish to pursue "management roles in product and/or service driven companies." In addition, the MMM program integrates management, operations, and design.

Kellogg offers seven majors in which students can specialize. In particular, students single out the "breadth of the marketing, strategy, and finance departments." In addition to majors, students can select "pathways" to build expertise in particular areas or industries including: Data Analytics, Entrepreneurship & New Ventures, Health Care Enterprise Management, Real Estate, Scaling Businesses, and Social Impact.

Overridingly, students feel confident in regards to their prospective futures thanks to the Kellogg School's "overall atmosphere, solid reputation and ranking, [and] strength across academic disciplines."

Career and Placement

Recent recruiters with a presence at Kellogg include Abbott, McKinsey & Company; Microsoft Corporation, Google and Target; most students are confident that their school has a "sterling reputation among corporate recruiters." It helps, too, that professors are "student-focused" and fellow students are "willing to go out on a limb to help . . . with recruiting, career advice, and schoolwork." Students agree that the team-focused environment ensures that "networking at Kellogg is tremendous."

ADDRESS: DONALD P. JACOBS CENTER, 2001 SHERIDAN ROAD, EVANSTON, IL 60208
PHONE: 847-491-3308 • FAX: 847-491-4960
E-MAIL: MBAADMISSIONS@KELLOGG.NORTHWESTERN.EDU
WEBSITE: WWW.KELLOGG.NORTHWESTERN.EDU

Student Life and Environment

Kellogg is situated in Evanston, Illinois, along the shores of Lake Michigan, with only a short commute on the El (elevated train) to downtown Chicago. While most here appreciate the city's proximity to campus "There is [also] a lot going on [at] school." One student explains, "There are dozens, maybe hundreds of clubs at school—special interest, sports, academic, career, spouse/children, politics and government, nonprofit, gay and lesbian, etc." The student body on the whole is "alive and energetic."

In addition, the Kellogg School is in the process of building a new facility on its Evanston campus. It will be the first educational building of its kind for the 21st century—a one-of-a-kind lakeside structure designed to maximize flexibility in teaching, leverage the use of technology, foster creativity and community building, convene conversations that matter and inspire global interconnections.

Admissions

Admissions Officers at Kellogg have the unenviable job of whittling a pile of approximately 4,300 applications down to an admitted class of about 492. During this process, they look for work experience, academic excellence, and personality. The school's Admissions Board conducts thousands of interviews each fall. For a recent entering class, the average GMAT score was 724. In addition, 40 percent of Kellogg students hail from outside of the United States, and for those applicants, TOEFL scores are required.

FINANCIAL FACTS

Annual tuition (in-state/ out-of-state)	$64,059/$64,059
Fees	$1,225
Cost of books	$1,647
Room & board (on/off-campus)	$15,711/

ADMISSIONS

Admissions Selectivity Rating	**98**
# of applications received	6,086
Accepts GRE scores	Yes
TOEFL required of international students	Yes
Application fee	$250
International application fee	$250
Application Deadline/Notification	
Round 1:	9/22 / 12/16
Round 2:	1/6 / 3/23
Round 3:	4/6 / 5/11
Deferment available	Yes
Maximum length of deferment	case by case
Transfer students accepted	No
Non-fall admissions	Yes
Need-blind admissions	Yes

EMPLOYMENT PROFILE

Career Rating	97	Grads Employed by Function% Avg. Salary	
Percent employed at graduation	84	Marketing	(20%) $107,218
Percent employed 3 months		Operations	(3%) $115,833
after graduation	02	Consulting	(39%) $130,767
Average base starting salary	$121,274	Management	(8%) $113,517
Primary Source of Full-time Job Acceptances		Finance	(18%) $125,361
School-facilitated activities	(80%)	MIS	(4%) $122,525
Graduate-facilitated activities	(20%)	Other	(8%) $109,485

Top 5 Employers Hiring Grads

McKinsey & Company (34), Bain & Company (28), The Boston Consulting Group (26), Deloitte Consulting LLP (20), PwC Strategy& (18)

OAKLAND UNIVERSITY
SCHOOL OF BUSINESS ADMINSTRATION

GENERAL INFORMATION
Type of school   Public
Affiliation   No Affiliation
Academic calendar   Semester

SURVEY SAYS...
Friendly students
Solid preparation in:
Teamwork

STUDENTS
Enrollment of parent institution	20,711
Enrollment of MBA Program	301
% part-time	100
Average age at entry	29
Average years work experience at entry	6

ACADEMICS
Academic Experience Rating	**66**
Profs interesting rating	60*
Profs accessible rating	65
Student/faculty ratio	8:1
% female faculty	20
% underrepresented minority faculty	0
% part-time faculty	30

Joint Degrees
MS Safety Management, 2-6 yrs; MS Engineering Management, 2-6 yrs

Prominent Alumni
Rob Manilla, Vice President and Chief Investment Officer, The Kresge Foundation; Mark Mendola, Vice Chairman, US Tax Leader, PwC; Linda Voss, Chief Financial Officer & Chief Operating Officer, Ally Corporate Finance; Michael Novak, Vice President, Controlling, Chrysler; Rob Dutkiewicz, President, Clayton & McKervey

Academics

Prospective MBAs, especially those with undergraduate ties to Oakland University, or roots in Michigan, feel that OU's combination of "accreditation, prestige, location," and "number of graduates working in Michigan" are second to none. Indeed, at OU, "First and foremost, the quality of education is the greatest strength." MBA students report that the "school is run very well," and they appreciate its "balance of disciplines," "the opportunity to earn a concentration with my degree," and opportunities for "employment as a graduate research assistant." OU's "smaller class sizes allow for more meaningful interaction with professors," "the school feels small and personal," and "everyone contributes to engaging conversations on current business applications of the lessons we're being taught." "Classroom discussions on real life events are employed regularly and challenge the students to think and reflect on . . . how they would handle different situations." Similarly, evaluation of students is also skewed towards these real-life applications: "Grades are more heavily based on projects and presentations rather than exams," and often "professors use case studies coupled with group discussions and assignments to facilitate a critical analysis of best business practices." Students say they have "many professors that [they] consider role models," who "significantly improved [their] understanding of business dynamics through a practical, hands-on approach which will help advance [their] career[s]." In particular, one student says, "My operations and computer-based business analytic courses were amazing."

Career and Placement

Oakland University's "strong correlation between academics and real life experiences make this a robust program," as does the fact that its "faculty and administration care deeply about the value of the program to the graduate." Students value having individual "person to person contact with advisor[s]," and also flourish in collaboration with professors, who "are very enthusiastic about the subject matter that they teach, and they encourage students to excel in the business world beyond academia." OU MBAs are eager to take advantage of OU's "events, workshops, career fairs, and many other opportunities to aid us in our professional development." OU's "strong reputation" certainly helps with job placement, and it enjoys an especially "strong connection to the automotive industry surrounding the university." OU's "convenient location and class times" make the program manageable for students who need to keep their current jobs, and to help land students' next jobs, the university excels at identifying "what the employers needs are, and aligning partnerships to incorporate those lessons within the educational experience."

Student Life and Environment

Oakland University MBAs see themselves as "career-minded individuals with common goals of bettering themselves and helping society." Demographically, many students are "full-time workers, commuters, intelligent, diverse, professional, older," and "half of the MBA students are engineers and many are married with children." Students of international backgrounds "find the people are friendly and open to other cultures." For working students, OU has an accessible "evening program that enabled me to work full-time while attending class in the evening." Indeed, OU MBA students actively appreciate their classmates' work experience: "Most MBA students have full time jobs, which is good because it helps to learn from other students' real world experiences." Despite surface-level differences, OU MBA "students love learning, are highly professional and work well together."

Admissions

The application staples for admission to Oakland University's MBA program are standard: an undergraduate degree, GMAT scores, two recommendation forms, and, for international students, a transcript evaluation and TOEFL. OU also requires a supplemental School of Business Administration application for prospective MBAs. Students seeking to specialize their degree are well-advised to examine OU's many options: the MBA has two partner programs in Engineering Management or Safety Management, and optional concentrations in Accounting, Business Analytics, Business Economics, Entrepreneurship, Finance, Human Resource Management, International Business, Marketing, Management Information Systems, Product/Operations Management, and Supply Chain Management. For highly experienced professionals, Oakland's Executive MBA Program provides an opportunity to "further develop their leadership skills and advance their business knowledge in a concentrated format."

FINANCIAL FACTS

Annual tuition (in-state/ out-of-state)	$11,790/$18,486
Fees	$0
Cost of books	$1,716
Room & board (on/off-campus)	$9,250/$6,204
% of students receiving aid	27
% of first-year students receiving aid	34
% of students receiving grants	9
Average award package	$13,249
Average grant	$8,963
Average loan	$13,945
Average student loan debt	$31,488

ADMISSIONS

Admissions Selectivity Rating	77
# of applications received	85
% applicants accepted	91
% acceptees attending	71
Average GMAT	454
Range of GMAT	420–488
Accepts GRE scores	Yes
Average GPA	3.3
TOEFL required of international students	Yes
Minimum TOEFL (paper/web)	550/79
International Regular application deadline	7/15
Application Deadline/Notification	
Deferment available	Yes
Maximum length of deferment	1 year
Transfer students accepted	Yes
Transfer application policy Up to nine credits of relevant course work may be transfered (3.0 or better)	
Non-fall admissions	Yes
Need-blind admissions	Yes

EMPLOYMENT PROFILE

Career Rating	76	Grads Employed by Function	% Avg. Salary
Percent employed at graduation	64	Marketing	(25%) $83,333
Percent employed 3 months after graduation	21	Operations	(17%) $59,000
		Consulting	(8%) $65,000
Average base starting salary	$78,000	Finance	(17%) $80,500
Primary Source of Full-time Job Acceptances		HR	(17%) $70,000
School-facilitated activities	4 (33%)	Other	(8%) $138,000
Graduate-facilitated activities	5 (42%)	**Top 5 Employers Hiring Grads**	
Unknown	3 (25%)	Chrysler Group LLC, Volkswagen Group, Kelly Services, Inc, General Motors, Comerica	

THE OHIO STATE UNIVERSITY
MAX M. FISHER COLLEGE OF BUSINESS

GENERAL INFORMATION
Type of school | Public
Affiliation | No Affiliation
Academic calendar | Semester

SURVEY SAYS...
Classmates have diverse work experience, Friendly students, Good peer network, Good social scene, Abundant mentors available, Happy students, Abundant clubs and activities, Students love Columbus, OH
Solid preparation in:
Finance, General management, Operations, Teamwork, Communication/interpersonal skills, Presentation skills, Quantitative skills, Doing business in a global economy

STUDENTS
Enrollment of parent
institution | 65,184
Enrollment of MBA Program | 562
% male/female | 72/28
% out-of-state | 33
% part-time | 60
% underrepresented minority | 7
% international | 32
Average age at entry | 27
Average years work
experience at entry | 4

ACADEMICS
Academic Experience Rating | 98
Profs interesting rating | 92
Profs accessible rating | 96
Student/faculty ratio | 6:1
% female faculty | 22
% underrepresented
minority faculty | 23
% part-time faculty | 13

Joint Degrees
MBA/JD, 4 yrs; MBA/MHA, 3yrs; MBA/MD, 5 yrs; MBA/PharmD, 5 yrs; MLHR/HESA in Education, 3 yrs; MBA/MENR, 3 yrs; MBA/MS Ag Dev, 3 yrs; MBA/MPA, 3 yrs; MAcc/BSBA, 5 yrs.

Academics

Despite being a part of a large sports and research university, the intentionally small size of Fisher College of Business allows the school to create a high quality and personalized program focused on results and excellence. Fisher offers an Executive MBA, an MBA for Working Professionals, and a full-time program, and boasts top-notch Operations and Logistics and Marketing programs that attract recruiters from top companies each year. Students in the Working Professional MBA program and the full-time MBA program can customize a specialized niche of study to complement their general MBA degree, and students from all programs can cull from more than 100 elective courses to create an individualized degree.

"Everyone is willing to support the student experience," and "learning takes place on many levels, from in the class, to around the pizza box, to having a lunch appointment with a local business executive who serves as your mentor." "The administration, professors, and academic experience exceed the high expectations I set," says a student. "I have been blown away by the quality of the professors," says another. Most come from top-rated business schools and offer "an outstanding mix of industry experience and academic integrity." "I wake up every day excited to attend school," says a student. The administration offers students many options for electives.

Most of the assignments are dynamic group projects which "equates to many hours with fellow students," and "the pace is quick and often times we'll have a VERY heavy case/work load in a short period of time." This "frustrates many students, but keeps them sharp." The work load "strikes a good balance of class work with external networking events and social functions."

Career and Placement

"Career services are excellent" at Fisher, which attracts top national employers with ease and "will work hard to help you get a job with a company with whom they already have connections." "They will help you land a job at your dream company, but they won't do it for you." The thorough business education provided by the school has given it a leading reputation across the country, and students are even able to take on "real consulting projects with paying clients" during their program. "The mix of industry executives with high profile academics as well as the extraordinarily wide breadth of resources that comes with Ohio State and the Big Ten creates the perfect mixture for an MBA student to become a future industry executive," says a student. "Although we technically compete for the same jobs everyone is extremely friendly and helpful," says a student of the annual job hunt frenzy. "Fisher students can enjoy all the resources from Ohio State."

Top employers of recent Fisher graduates include Deloitte, Ernst & Young (EY), Nationwide Insurance, Emerson, and Amazon.

Student Life and Environment

"We all know each other, and everyone is willing to help others out for the sake of individual and group success," says a student of this highly collaborative group, who are "around one another frequently." Columbus is "a very lively city," and is a "fun environment for married or single students." There is a good community of people who regularly socialize outside of school at bars, restaurants, houses, or events, and, of course, everyone is "actively engaged in the Ohio State sports culture." Students have a variety of associations to choose from, based on business focus area, service to the community, and other common interests, to connect with students.

As for the logistics of life, "off campus housing is outstanding," there is an "excellent… day care" for those with kids, and "the best part is, you can live well on a student budget."

Admissions

The Admissions Office at Fisher requires applicants to provide one official copy of transcripts for each undergraduate and graduate institution attended, GMAT or GRE scores, two letters of recommendation, essays, and a resume (work experience required). In addition to the above, international applicants whose first language is not English must provide proof of English proficiency (the school accepts several standardized tests, including the TOEFL and IELTS) and admitted international students must provide an affidavit of financial support. Admissions interviews are conducted only at the request of the Admissions Department.

Prominent Alumni

Leslie Wexner, Chair & CEO, L Brands; Lisa Ingram, President & CEO, White Castle; Jesse J. Tyson, President & CEO, National Association of Black MBAs; Paula Bennett, President & CEO, J.Jill Group, Inc.; Mark R. Goldston, Executive Chairman, Pulse Health

FINANCIAL FACTS

Annual tuition (in-state/ out-of-state)	$30,120/$49,592
Fees	$1,019
Cost of books	$1,234
Room & board (on/off-campus)	$12,142/$12,142
Average award package	$33,715
Average grant	$22,352
Average loan	$31,863
Average student loan debt	$56,171

ADMISSIONS

Admissions Selectivity Rating	97
# of applications received	594
% applicants accepted	24
% acceptees attending	81
Average GMAT	664
Range of GMAT	635–690
Accepts GRE scores	Yes
Average Verbal GRE	155
Range of Verbal GRE scores	150–161
Average Quantitative GRE	156
Range of Quantitative GRE scores	153–159
Average Writing GRE	4.4
Range of Writing GRE scores	4.0–4.5
Average GPA	3.5
TOEFL required of international students	Yes
Minimum TOEFL (paper/web)	600/100
Application fee	$60
International application fee	$70
Early application deadline	10/15
Application Deadline/Notification	
Deferment available	Yes
Maximum length of deferment	1 year
Transfer students accepted	No
Non-fall admissions	No
Need-blind admissions	Yes

EMPLOYMENT PROFILE

Career Rating	97	Grads Employed by Function	% Avg. Salary
Percent employed at graduation	72	Marketing	(15%) $98,597
Percent employed 3 months after graduation	96	Operations	(18%) $101,434
		Consulting	(19%) $111,147
Average base starting salary	$98,388	Management	(5%) $92,333
Primary Source of Full-time Job Acceptances		Finance	(21%) $95,300
School-facilitated activities	86 (%)	Other	(22%) $86,711
Graduate-facilitated activities	12 (%)	**Top 5 Employers Hiring Grads**	
Unknown	2 (%)	Nationwide Insurance (7), Ernst & Young (5), IBM Corp. (5), Emerson (3), Procter & Gamble (2)	

OLD DOMINION UNIVERSITY
COLLEGE OF BUSINESS AND PUBLIC ADMINISTRATION

Academics

Old Dominion University offers its MBA students a unique "flexibility with a combination of on campus and online classes." Students highly value this adaptability: "The program has met and exceeded all my expectations, and fits perfectly in with my work and personal family life." ODU's location in Norfolk, Virginia, long an American shipping and military hub as a major port, provides an especially valuable array of contacts and opportunities for returning veterans in the university's "shipping program," and ODU is also "accommodating to the requirements/needs of international students." MBA students say "the staff at the University, everyone involved from the program office to the classroom, is committed to strengthening the program and supporting students." Administrators "are very supportive and quick responders," and professors tend equally to be "reachable and up-to-date with trends and fads," as well as to have "strong research credentials." "Professors at Old Dominion University try their best to help students excel not only in classroom, but also in the workplace." "The Strome Entrepreneurial Center is amazing," and ODU's "reputation in the local community" is also strong. Students perceive their classmates as people who "take the MBA courses and grades very seriously." "Affordability and convenience" rank among Old Dominion's students' highlights of their MBA experience: "The value is unparalleled. I get an excellent degree for a reasonable price."

Career and Placement

Old Dominion enjoys a "good reputation in the Hampton Roads area," home to an ever-growing network of business opportunities, and its "in-state tuition" helps to keep MBA costs reasonable for Virginians. The school excels in facilitating "networking for military/veterans," and "Old Dominion University is a great place to launch a career at the Port of Virginia or as a defense contractor." ODU students feel well-prepared for a "competitive business world" no matter their particular field: "The MBA program organizes evening socials every month, and students get to network with current MBA students or alumni." In addition, "there is an Entrepreneurial Center on campus that helps students with business ideas." Another student reports, "I go to an Economics luncheon twice a year for free, it includes a lunch and we get to listen to the economic forecast being presented by distinguished faculty and guest speakers." ODU provides "so many organizations to join" and "speakers from big companies" to hear that students can't help but get involved.

ADMISSIONS CONTACT: MS. SHANNA WOOD, MBA ASSOCIATE DIRECTOR
ADDRESS: 1026 CONSTANT HALL, NORFOLK, VA 23529
PHONE: 757-683-3585 • FAX: 757-683-5750
E-MAIL: MBAINFO@ODU.EDU • WEBSITE: HTTP://ODU.EDU/MBA

Student Life and Environment

Old Dominion's hybrid online/on-campus MBA program brings together "a great combination of commuter and resident students," and one student finds that "the commuter aspect works flawlessly for me." Since so many students maintain full-time jobs while in school, students describe their classmates as "office workers who have strong intellectual curiosity." "Military vets" are a strong presence in the school's fabric, and there's a wide range of walks of life represented at ODU: students are "friendly, busy, working, some married, some with kids, some just starting out, others who have been working for a long time." Classmates describe each other as "hardworking, ambitious," "open minded, friendly, competitive, intelligent," "studious and cooperative."

Admissions

As previously mentioned, Old Dominion University offers students both online and in-person MBA experiences: the Online MBA, On-campus MBA, and Blended MBA all have the same requirements and application processes. Working and traveling professionals, military veterans, and those raising a family may appreciate the flexibility of the Online or Blended MBA option while students who prefer an immersive face-to-face educational experience, are seeking financial aid or teaching assistantships, or hail from international backgrounds might benefit most from the On-campus MBA. GMAT scores, transcripts, a letter of recommendation, a personal statement, and a résumé (as well as a TOEFL, if applicable) are requested from all prospective MBA applications, and for those wishing to determine in-state tuition eligibility, a tuition-rate-determination form is also required. Some applicants may qualify for GMAT/GRE waver, contact the program for details.

FINANCIAL FACTS

Annual tuition (in-state/ out-of-state)	$9,280/$23,200
Fees	$297
Cost of books	$2,500
Room & board (on/off-campus)	$12,474/$10,100
% of first-year students receiving aid	48
Average grant	$9,110
Average loan	$11,212

ADMISSIONS

Admissions Selectivity Rating	**85**
# of applications received	105
% applicants accepted	55
% acceptees attending	50
Average GMAT	557
Range of GMAT	530–600
Accepts GRE scores	Yes
Average Verbal GRE	154
Range of Verbal GRE scores	153–156
Average Quantitative GRE	152
Range of Quantitative GRE scores	150–154
Average Writing GRE	3.9
Range of Writing GRE scores	4.0–4.0
Average GPA	3.2
TOEFL required of international students	Yes
Minimum TOEFL (paper/web)	550/80
Application fee	$50
International application fee	$50
Application Deadline/Notification	
Deferment available	Yes
Maximum length of deferment	1 year
Transfer students accepted	Yes
Transfer application policy We accept up to 12 credit hours from AACSB accredited MBA programs only.	
Non-fall admissions	Yes
Need-blind admissions	Yes

PACIFIC LUTHERAN UNIVERSITY
SCHOOL OF BUSINESS

GENERAL INFORMATION
Type of school	Private
Affiliation	Lutheran
Academic calendar	4-1-4-3

SURVEY SAYS...
Classmates have diverse work experience, Friendly students, Happy students
Solid preparation in:
General management, Teamwork, Communication/interpersonal skills, Presentation skills, Doing business in a global economy, Social responsibility

STUDENTS
Enrollment of parent institution	3,191
Enrollment of MBA Program	69
% male/female	61/39
% out-of-state	10
% part-time	54
% underrepresented minority	23
% international	7
Average age at entry	32
Average years work experience at entry	9

ACADEMICS
Academic Experience Rating	**85**
Profs interesting rating	90
Profs accessible rating	95
Student/faculty ratio	15:1
% female faculty	42
% underrepresented minority faculty	0
% part-time faculty	0

Joint Degrees
MSN/MBA, 30 months

Prominent Alumni
Brad Tilden, CEO Alaskan Air Group; Morten Nordstad, CEO, Pharmaq; Sandra Cochran, President & COO, Cracker Barrel; Dr. William Foege, former Director, Center for Disease Control; Joyce Barr, Former U.S. ambassador to Namibia

Academics

Offering a "globally-focused program" that's "well-known in the area," the School of Business at Pacific Lutheran University satisfies South Puget Sound area locals, who appreciate "the convenience offered to working professionals" here. With "small class sizes" facilitating plenty of "one-on-one interactions," the PLU MBA program employs a "customer service approach" that keeps students happy. This part-time program, "designed for working professionals," can be completed in less than two years.

Standout features of the PLU MBA include an emphasis in technology and innovation management, mentioned by several students as the main draw to the school; PLU also offers areas of emphasis in entrepreneurship and closely-held enterprises, as well as in health care management. A general MBA without concentration is also available. All students must complete a "ten-day international trip requirement," which grateful MBAs note is "included in the cost of tuition." Recent destinations include France, Spain, China, Dubai, Taiwan, Germany, Switzerland, Ireland, and Peru. Students describe the experience as "amazing" and cite it as a major asset to the program.

Most agree, however, that the faculty and program administrators are PLU's primary selling points. The "excellent professors" at the School of Business are "experienced, flexible, always available, and professional." They go out of their way to utilize their students' professional experiences in class. As one student explains, "Professors try very hard to learn about each student and cater lessons/lectures to our professional backgrounds." Small classes mean lots of student participation. "As a student you are challenged to learn, and you are a part of the class. It's expected that the students are active in the classes," one MBA warns. The administration of PLU's MBA program "is handled almost exclusively by the program administrator/director," a great arrangement for students, who report that administrative services in their program are among the best on campus.

Career and Placement

The Career Development Office at PLU provides placement and counseling services for all undergraduates, graduate students and alumni. The office assists students with internship and career placement. The PLU Business Network is an alumni group who schedules networking events to help alumni and current BBA and MBA students connect. A significant networking opportunity open to PLU MBAs is the PLU MBA Executive Leadership Series, a series of addresses delivered by area executives. Recent speakers have included the President and CEO of Esterline, President and COO of Miligard Windows, and the CFO of 5.11 Tactical. But a "strong alumni network" is probably PLU's greatest placement service. Students note the "sustained good reputation of [PLU] graduates," and benefit from "having a larger number of them in key companies and industries, serving in positions of great importance and responsibility."

Employers who most frequently hire Pacific Lutheran MBAs include Boeing, Microsoft, Weyerhaeuser, State Farm Insurance, Intel, and Starbucks.

Student Life and Environment

A "new business building" and a "beautiful campus" are among the top amenities of the PLU MBA experience. The building boasts "state-of-the-art facilities [that] cater to the unique [challenges] of working students," including "Wi-Fi available throughout the entire building." Opportunities to connect with classmates are limited as a result of the part-time nature of the program and the busy schedules most students maintain. However, students have the opportunity to connect at monthly networking events for students and alumni as well as frequently interact though, "classroom-related team project activities" that one student describes as "exciting and promising, as well as offering distinct challenges." Despite the fact that many students' schedules prevent them from spending a lot of time on campus, a "very collegial atmosphere" still manages to pervade the program.

Students in the PLU MBA program bring "very diverse backgrounds and professional experiences" to the classroom. A great many are "hardworking, family-oriented professionals with a lot going on in their lives," ranging "from stay-at-home moms and dads to army surgeons and city managers." One student reports that "when working together, I felt in all cases that we were peers, that never did one person's experience make them better than another, that everyone was able to contribute."

Admissions

At PLU, applicants are "evaluated individually based on a presentation of factors indicating equivalence to admission standards, a promise of success in graduate school, qualities of good character, and potential contributions to the educational mission of the graduate program and university." Applicants must provide the school with the following materials: official transcripts covering all undergraduate and graduate work; an official GMAT or GRE score report; a current resume; a completed application form; two letters of recommendation; and a 300-word statement of personal goals. Candidates whose native language is other than English must also submit an official TOEFL or IELTS score report. International transcripts must be submitted to the Educational Perspectives transcript translation agency for evaluation. All international applicants are required to submit a Declaration of Finances prior to issuance of an I-20. Applicant may be eligible for a GMAT waiver.

FINANCIAL FACTS

Fees	$0
Cost of books	$1,800
Room & board	
(on/off-campus)	$9,230/$9,130
% of students receiving aid	51
% of first-year students	
receiving aid	56
% of students receiving grants	35
Average award package	$15,152
Average grant	$4,783
Average loan	$21,711
Average student loan debt	$49,332

ADMISSIONS

Admissions Selectivity Rating	79
# of applications received	53
% applicants accepted	83
% acceptees attending	61
Average GMAT	498
Range of GMAT	340–630
Accepts GRE scores	Yes
Average Verbal GRE	152
Range of Verbal	
GRE scores	147–161
Average Quantitative GRE	149
Range of Quantitative	
GRE scores	144–156
Average Writing GRE	3.9
Range of Writing	
GRE scores	3.5–4.5
Average GPA	3.3
TOEFL required of	
international students	Yes
Minimum TOEFL (paper)	573
Application fee	$55
International application fee	$55
Application Deadline/Notification	
Deferment available	Yes
Maximum length of	
deferment	1 year
Transfer students accepted	Yes
Transfer application policy	
In order to graduate, a student must complete a minimum of 24 semester hours in residence at PLU.	
Non-fall admissions	Yes
Need-blind admissions	Yes

EMPLOYMENT PROFILE

Career Rating	89	Grads Employed by Function	% Avg. Salary
Percent employed at graduation	0	Management	(18%)
Percent employed 3 months		Finance	(9%)
after graduation	80	Other	(73%)
Average base starting salary	$75,000	**Top 5 Employers Hiring Grads**	
		Boeing, Intel, Russell Investments, Weyerhaeuser, Microsoft	

PENNSYLVANIA STATE UNIVERSITY
SMEAL COLLEGE OF BUSINESS

Academics

The Penn State Smeal MBA is grounded in the university's longstanding tradition of excellence, and students are consistently attracted to its "strong community with a good reputation around the world." Indeed, a "strong alumni network," is one of the Penn State Smeal MBA's greatest benefits, along with "excellent academics, great career opportunities," and a "top-notch" faculty and administration. "The professors have a vast amount of experience," and students find them "excellent at integrating real-world experiences" and "new business trends to into its courses, such as sustainability business strategy." "Penn State Smeal MBA faculty have extensive consulting experience and are highly regarded researchers," and in particular, "the supply chain and finance professors are excellent and prepare students to be top tier talent coming out of the program." Penn State's "small class size makes access to faculty and administration extremely easy," and its "professors are very open to suggestion for improvement and regularly adjust class based on students' needs." The "administration is receptive to students' needs" as well. All of this academic and administrative force combines to ensure Penn State Smeal MBA students will succeed: "I've been pushed to limits I never thought were possible, and I'm a better person for their insistence on pushing us to perform and produce at the highest level."

Career and Placement

The "Penn State Brand" figures prominently both in students' reasons for choosing Penn State's Smeal MBA programs and in the value they'll take with them when they leave. Penn State Smeal MBAs have "no classes on Friday in an effort to give students time to work on job search and group projects," and this priority "make[s] it easy to focus on learning, personal development, and career strategy" during school. In terms of professional advancement, students name Penn State's "strong alumni network," "quality of professional recruitment," and "the alumni advisory board which mentors students" as among "the program's greatest strengths." The program hosts "many recruiting companies [to] come and spend the day" talking to students, including representatives from "Nike, Deloitte, and other Fortune 500 companies." "Penn State MBAs are friendly, hard working, and appreciative of the opportunities Penn State presents them," and students see their classmates as people who "performed well in their internships and will be a major part of my network post-graduation." The program's "professors expect a lot but truly prepare you to succeed in interviews and the workforce," and its "students are prepared to roll up their sleeves and get dirty."

Student Life and Environment

One student says of life at Penn State: "After living here for a year, I know why it is called Happy Valley. It might be cold in the winter, but the people here are warm and welcoming." Indeed, many other students echo this appreciation for feeling as though "The entire program is a huge, supportive family" in "a very safe college town." "Life is busy. But the people and the setting (a beautiful mountain valley) are good rewards for the times that aren't too busy." There's a "great sports atmosphere, developed downtown area just off of campus, strong commitment to the local community, and good social atmosphere of the student population" overall. "The camaraderie at Penn State is absolutely amazing," and students get close to each other: "We spend a lot of time in the business building whether it is for class, studying, or hanging out in the commons." "Spouses and families are actively invited to come to all activities," which facilitates "a positive MBA experience outside of the classroom" with events "such as football tailgates, Diwali celebration, and a Lunar New Year celebration." "Penn State has over 30 percent international students," and sees itself as "a community that embraces the diversity of our population." Comprised of "great team players with high IQs and EQs," the Penn State Smeal MBA program attracts and produces "compelling leaders who are highly intelligent."

Admissions

Penn State requires applicants to provide evidence of sufficient funds to cover its annual price tag, but one student notes that "the school does an outstanding job of financially supporting its students, with a large percentage receiving at least one year, if not both years, tuition free with insurance coverage and a stipend." Application requirements include an essay, résumé, transcripts, two letters of recommendation, and a brief, unique Video Application Questions application segment.

FINANCIAL FACTS

Annual tuition (in-state/ out-of-state)	$23,708/$38,068
Fees	$1,142
Cost of books	$3,500
Room & board	$17,400
% of students receiving aid	98
% of first-year students receiving aid	100
% of students receiving grants	97
Average award package	$24,325
Average grant	$18,515
Average loan	$22,775
Average student loan debt	$36,235

ADMISSIONS

Admissions Selectivity Rating	96
# of applications received	637
% applicants accepted	17
% acceptees attending	61
Average GMAT	636
Range of GMAT	582–690
Accepts GRE scores	Yes
Average Verbal GRE	156
Range of Verbal GRE scores	151–160
Average Quantitative GRE	159
Range of Quantitative GRE scores	153–164
Average Writing GRE	4.0
Range of Writing GRE scores	3.0–5.0
Average GPA	3.4
TOEFL required of international students	Yes
Minimum TOEFL (paper/web)	600/100
Application fee	$65
International application fee	$65
Early application deadline	10/1
Early notification date	12/1
Regular application deadline	4/1
Regular application notification	4/1
Application Deadline/Notification	
Round 1:	10/1 / 12/1
Round 2:	12/1 / 2/1
Round 3:	2/1 / 4/1
Round 4:	4/1 / 6/1
Deferment available	Yes
Maximum length of deferment	1 year
Transfer students accepted	Yes
Transfer application policy A maximum of six elective credits can be transferred.	
Non-fall admissions	No
Need-blind admissions	Yes

EMPLOYMENT PROFILE

Career Rating	95		
Percent employed at graduation	71		
Percent employed 3 months after graduation	86		
Average base starting salary	$101,072		

Primary Source of Full-time Job Acceptances

School-facilitated activities	51 (90%)
Graduate-facilitated activities	6 (11%)

Grads Employed by Function% Avg. Salary

Marketing	(26%) $92,346
Operations	(39%) $98,586
Consulting	(24%) $117,000
Management	(2%)
Finance	(7%) $100,500
MIS	(2%)

Top 5 Employers Hiring Grads

Dell Inc. (11), Deloitte Consulting LLP (8), A.T. Kearney Inc. (2), Apple Inc. (2), Johnson & Johnson (2)

PENNSYLVANIA STATE UNIVERSITY—ERIE, THE BEHREND COLLEGE
BLACK SCHOOL OF BUSINESS

Academics

The Black School of Business at Penn State Behrend College "provides the best value for a working student in the local area," one MBA here explains, adding, "You get the Penn State name, an outstanding general MBA education, and student-work flexibility." Behrend enjoys "an outstanding reputation" in the region, making it an excellent choice for students looking to build their careers in and around Erie.

A general degree that aims to develop the critical-thinking skills necessary for a career in mid- and upper-level management, the Behrend MBA curriculum consists of forty-eight units, or thirteen courses. Of these, eighteen units form the foundational core courses, which are comprised of three introductory classes: Costs, Competition, and Market Performance; Demand, Operations, and Firm Performance; and Integrated Business Analysis. After completing these courses, students must complete twenty-one credits of required advanced courses and nine credits of elective course work. For those who have already taken business courses, the program can be streamlined through the omission of certain foundation courses. Depending on their previous academic preparation, full-time students can usually complete the MBA curriculum in three semesters; part-time students usually require two to four years to complete the program.

Behrend works hard to keep its MBA program student-friendly with an "attractive and clean" campus (that includes "a new facility for the business school"), "small classes" and "accessible professors." Most faculty members "have extensive real-world experience that greatly adds to their lessons. Additionally, many are locals and have experience at the major companies in the area and understand the general job situation of the area." Students describe the curriculum as challenging, citing "tough courses" that "equate to well-educated students." Another reports, "The professors expect a lot. No class was easy. I consider myself to be an intelligent person, but have felt less so at times because of the difficulty of the work." Among the drawbacks of a Behrend MBA, "some courses are only offered one semester each year," making it "very difficult to have a consistent workload. Some semesters are much heavier than others due to course offerings." Even so, students here agree that Behrend is "the best school, academically, for the region."

Career and Placement

A high percentage of Penn State Behrend students are currently employed in professional positions and are pursuing an MBA with the intention of improving their career opportunities at their current companies. In fact, a considerable number of Penn State Behrend students receive tuition assistance from their employers. Some, however, see their MBAs as a stepping stone to a new career (or, for students pursuing MBAs straight out of college, simply a career). For those, the Penn State Behrend Academic Advising and Career Development Center serves both the undergraduate and graduate population at the college, including students in the MBA program. The CDC hosts career fairs, on-campus recruiting and interview events, seminars, and workshops. A growing number of organizations participate in Penn State Behrend career fairs each year. Employers who frequently hire Behrend MBAs include: Deloitte Consulting, Paradigm Wave, Ingentor, GE Infrastructure-Transportation Systems, IBM, Erie Insurance Group, National City Corporation, Graham Packaging, HealthAmerica, and the Pennsylvania State University.

Student Life and Environment

Behrend MBAs enjoy "state-of-the-art" classrooms that "allow us to utilize multimedia learning," which they very much appreciate. The campus itself is "very clean, safe, and attractive," "not so large that it is overwhelming but still offering most [of the] opportunities of a large school." And here's something you rarely hear at any school, much less a state institution: there's "plenty of parking" here.

Campus life offers "a number of clubs and organizations for students," and "the school also hosts a very wide array of speakers, and events," but most of these events seem planned primarily for undergraduates. "There are no solely business school programs of any kind. The most activity available is an unofficial happy hour at the end of the semester," one student writes.

Admissions

Students may apply to begin study at Penn State Behrend's Black College of Business in the fall, spring, or summer semester. Admissions decisions are made on a rolling basis. To apply, students must submit two official transcripts, official GMAT scores, a statement of purpose, an application fee, and three recommendation forms. Candidates with the highest GMAT scores and GPA are given priority in admissions. Candidates are evaluated based on the strength of their combined GMAT score and GPA; therefore, a lower GMAT score can be compensated for by a higher GPA, or vice versa. International applicants whose first language is not English must meet all of the above requirements and must also submit an official score report for the TOEFL or IELTS.

FINANCIAL FACTS

Cost of books	$1,848
Room & board (on/off-campus)	$0/$12,852
% of students receiving aid	38
% of first-year students receiving aid	31
% of students receiving grants	12
Average award package	$25,798
Average grant	$986
Average loan	$25,699
Average student loan debt	$29,730

ADMISSIONS

Admissions Selectivity Rating	82
# of applications received	51
% applicants accepted	80
% acceptees attending	85
Average GMAT	543
Range of GMAT	490–578
Accepts GRE scores	Yes
Average Verbal GRE	154
Range of Verbal GRE scores	152–156
Average Quantitative GRE	153
Range of Quantitative GRE scores	152–155
Average Writing GRE	4.0
Range of Writing GRE scores	4.0–4.0
Average GPA	3.4
TOEFL required of international students	Yes
Minimum TOEFL (paper/web)	550/80
Application fee	$65
International application fee	$65
Regular application deadline	6/27
Application Deadline/Notification	
Deferment available	Yes
Maximum length of deferment	two years
Transfer students accepted	Yes
Transfer application policy	
Up to 10 credits of relevant graduate work completed at an accredited institution.	
Non-fall admissions	Yes
Need-blind admissions	Yes

EMPLOYMENT PROFILE

Career Rating	77	Grads Employed by Function	% Avg. Salary
Percent employed at graduation	0	Marketing	(27%) $61,000
Percent employed 3 months after graduation	0	Operations	(18%) $94,000
		Management	(9%) $53,500
Average base starting salary	$64,000	Finance	(9%) $40,000
Primary Source of Full-time Job Acceptances		HR	(9%) $65,000
School-facilitated activities	3 (27%)	MIS	(9%) $46,000
Unknown	8 (72%)	Other	(9%) $72,000

Top 5 Employers Hiring Grads
PNC Financial Services (1), jKaiser Permanente (1), Erie Insurance (1), Department of Defense (1), Giant Eagle (1)

PEPPERDINE UNIVERSITY
GRAZIADIO SCHOOL OF BUSINESS AND MANAGEMENT

GENERAL INFORMATION
Type of school	Private
Affiliation	Church of Christ
Academic calendar	Trimester

SURVEY SAYS...
Classmates have diverse work experience, Friendly students, Good peer network, Good social scene, Cutting-edge classes, Happy students, Abundant clubs and activities, Students love Los Angeles, CA
Solid preparation in:
Marketing, Finance, General management, Teamwork, Communication/interpersonal skills, Presentation skills, Quantitative skills

STUDENTS
Enrollment of parent institution	7,632
Enrollment of MBA Program	1,225
% male/female	63/37
% out-of-state	20
% part-time	83
% underrepresented minority	13
% international	46
Average age at entry	28
Average years work experience at entry	5

ACADEMICS
Academic Experience Rating	**94**
Profs interesting rating	93
Profs accessible rating	95
Student/faculty ratio	13:1
% female faculty	29
% underrepresented minority faculty	17
% part-time faculty	35

Joint Degrees
BS/MBA, 5 yrs; BS/IMBA, 5 yrs; JD/MBA, 4 yrs; MBA/MPP, 4 yrs

Prominent Alumni
Lt. General Robert Neller, Commandant of the Marine Cops; Oscar Munoz, CEO United Airlines; Christos Christakos, Former Chairman &CEO of E-Trade

Academics

Hands-on learning, small class sizes, and easy access to faculty are typically what sell Pepperdine's MBA program to students, who say the Graziadio School of Business and Management is "unlike any other business school." "Going to school with a view of the ocean from your classroom window and study breaks on the beach is a grad school experience you can't get anywhere but Pepperdine," says a student. The Fully-Employed MBA program is designed for working professionals, and the Full-Time MBA program offers courses in an accelerated or traditional two-year format. Pepperdine Graziadio has five locations in Southern California, as well as programs in Santa Barbara, Silicon Valley, Dallas, TX, and through online and hybrid formats.

The "intellectually stimulating" faculty at Graziadio are easily accessible, and each is "committed to becoming a lifelong resource and mentor" for their students. As almost all professors work in the field, they "can give us real examples of how things can be used and applied" and are able to help with networking. "Having a practitioners' focus is a tremendous asset, since the work is not completely theoretical and aims for constant application," says a student. SEER (Socially, Environmentally, and Ethically Responsible) values are a focus of many of the entrepreneurship classes, and the emphasis on ethical business practices is a draw for many. Students also praise the opportunity to practice their skills in a "safe but very real setting" through the "truly unique" E2B (Education to Business) experiential learning program, where students work in groups with companies to solve real business issues. Often, students see their recommendations implemented at these companies when their projects are complete.

Career and Placement

Pepperdine has a strong reputation in California, and the school encourages networking events on- and off-campus, particularly where alumni can attend. That being said, many here say that the Career Management Center "could do a better job" in helping students find placement and prepare for interviews, as students have to be extremely proactive. "Nobody is going to help you fix up your résumé and find a job if you don't first show interest and ask," one student explains. Graziadio career services has recently added career staff to all campuses, including satellite campuses, and increased career services offered (individual consultations, events, etc.) to both current students and alumni. Typical companies that recruit Pepperdine MBA graduates include AT&T, Bank of America, Deloitte, Ernst & Young, and Mattel.

ADMISSIONS CONTACT: MARGO BELL, ASSISTANT DIRECTOR
ADDRESS: 6100 CENTER DRIVE, STE. 400, LOS ANGELES, CA 90045
PHONE: 310-568-5555 • FAX: 310-568-5727
E-MAIL: MBABSM@PEPPERDINE.EDU • WEBSITE: BSCHOOL.PEPPERDINE.EDU

Student Life and Environment

The main campus is "tucked into a quaint beach community only a short drive into the city," but given the geographic spread of students across campuses, "a commuter culture can develop or students cluster and spend time off-campus." Pepperdine students are "very friendly and approachable—it's the culture of the business school." Life at Graziadio is "very familial," and there are organizations and clubs for everyone from "concentration-specific organizations to spiritual clubs and organizations that help support like-minded causes." These welcoming groups are "great ways to interact beyond the classroom" and build a sense of community. A large international population means "many different worldly views are brought to the table [that] enhance the conversation," contributing to a "great group of intelligent, ambitious, and collaborative professionals who all work together to learn as much as possible."

Admissions

The admissions process for Pepperdine's MBA program is fairly by the book. The committee seeks successful professionals looking to enhance or develop their business management skills. It is the goal of the Pepperdine Graziadio admissions team to assemble a diverse group of students who bring strong leadership skills and unique experiences to classes. Applicants must have earned a bachelor's degree (complete with a solid GPA) from an accredited university. They are required to have a minimum of one or three years work experience, depending on the MBA program. Finally, applicants must submit an undergraduate transcript as well as GMAT (preferred) or GRE scores earned within the last five years. Pepperdine also offers many GMAT waiver opportunities for qualified individuals.

FINANCIAL FACTS

Annual tuition (in-state/ out-of-state)	$46,400/$46,400
Fees	$80
Cost of books	$1,000
Room & board (on/off-campus)	$13,800/$13,800
% of students receiving aid	79
% of first-year students receiving aid	73
% of students receiving grants	38
Average award package	$35,726
Average grant	$13,891
Average loan	$41,921
Average student loan debt	$83,183

ADMISSIONS

Admissions Selectivity Rating	91
# of applications received	379
% applicants accepted	32
% acceptees attending	51
Average GMAT	612
Range of GMAT	580–670
Accepts GRE scores	Yes
Average Verbal GRE	148
Range of Verbal GRE scores	143–153
Average Quantitative GRE	153
Range of Quantitative GRE scores	151–160
Average GPA	3.2
TOEFL required of international students	Yes
Minimum TOEFL (paper/web)	600/100
Application fee	$100
International application fee	$100
Application Deadline/Notification	
Round 1:	11/1 / 2/1
Round 2:	4/1
Round 3:	5/1
Deferment available	Yes
Maximum length of deferment	1 year
Transfer students accepted	Yes
Transfer application policy	
No more than 2 courses may be transferred, contingent upon policy committee approval	
Non-fall admissions	No
Need-blind admissions	Yes

EMPLOYMENT PROFILE

Career Rating	89	Grads Employed by Function	% Avg. Salary
Percent employed at graduation	50	Marketing	(24%) $78,594
Percent employed 3 months after graduation	70	Consulting	(17%) $71,214
		Management	(7%) $93,000
Average base starting salary	$75,821	Finance	(31%) $72,542
Primary Source of Full-time Job Acceptances		HR	(5%)
School-facilitated activities	21 (50%)	MIS	(1%)
Graduate-facilitated activities	20 (48%)	Other	(14%) $82,250
Unknown	1 (2%)	**Top 5 Employers Hiring Grads**	
		AT & T (4), Bank of America (2), Deloitte (2), Earnest & Young (1), Mattel (1)	

PITTSBURG STATE UNIVERSITY
GLADYS A. KELCE COLLEGE OF BUSINESS

Academics

Students looking for "a quality school located in a quiet area that is great for learning" are encouraged to check out Pittsburg State University's Gladys A. Kelce College of Business. This "top ranked" Kansas program has "an outstanding faculty, beautiful campus, and very friendly atmosphere." "At PSU, students come first" and the "student-centered mentality seems to permeate the entire system." Students love the cost, bragging about how "cheap [it is] to go here" despite having an "international reputation." Applicants might be surprised at the "global connections for such a small time Kansas school." This reputation seems prominent in Saudi Arabia, as several students said they came to PSU based on a "Government of Saudi recommendation" that commended the "family friendliness for married students."

"There is an excellent diversity of professors at PSU," one happy student says. "Even though I am a 'non-traditional' student, I feel that I have really grown academically and personally due to the guidance of the PSU professors." The professors are "excellent academics" "with real world experiences" who are "very dedicated to their students. These "consummate professionals" are "engaging" and illuminate students with their extensive "professional experience." That said, some students feel that some professors "are stuck in the dark ages" and "need to update their materials and 'real world' examples." "Classes are small" at PSU, and professors know their students by name. Students think that the "administration is great" and the staff as a whole is "friendly, helpful, and respectful to their students." The building itself "is old and could use some facelift," and the school as a whole is "getting too small for the growing student body," although an estimated $19 million renovation is in the works. "PSU offers a very diverse array of academic studies," one student says, "most notably: accounting, business administration, education, plastics engineering, construction management, and automotive engineering." "I love the professors of the management and marketing office of Pittsburg State," one student says. "I feel that they have honed my ability to think critically, speak in public, and work in a team."

Career and Placement

"PSU graduates enter the workforce with not only academic achievements," one student explains, "but with real-life experiences and information from knowledgeable professors, involved alumni, and participating employers." Career services provides a plethora of job help to students, such as on-campus recruiting, career fairs, and resume critiques. Over 200 organizations come to campus to conduct interviews at PSU each year. Some of the largest employers of PSU graduates are Sprint, Deloitte, and Walmart. Fully 90 percent of PSU MBA graduates find employment within six months of graduation.

ADMISSIONS CONTACT: BIENVENIDO CORTES, ASSOCIATE DEAN & MBA DIRECTOR
ADDRESS: 1701 SOUTH BROADWAY, PITTSBURG, KS 66762-7540
PHONE: 620-235-4594 • FAX: 620-235-4578
E-MAIL: MBA@PITTSTATE.EDU • WEBSITE: WWW.PITTSTATE.EDU/BUSINESS

Student Life and Environment

Your average MBA student at PSU is "around the age of twenty-five to thirty-five, mostly married or engaged," and comes to school with "at least a year of job experience." Students describe their peers as "friendly and helpful," "hardworking and disciplined," and "very diverse and liberal minded." It is "easy to talk to about anything" with a fellow PSU student as "the school's diverse and multi-national student population provides a great atmosphere where students are encouraged to get to know one another." One happy student describes his experience in glowing terms: "I am here with my wife and two kids and they love being here, we have made friends with a program PSU offers called host family and they have been so nice to us. They showed us the town when we arrived gave us support and especially their friendship."

Life here is "low key, relaxing and enjoyable." "All of the MBA students are very hard working to meet the high requirements" and do not necessarily have much free time to socialize. Still, there is a "friendly atmosphere" and "small town feeling" around campus. It is a "university town," meaning life here is "very conducive for academic work and raising a family." There are "lots of opportunity to socialize after classes and on weekends" if you have the free time, and the school conducts "tons of activities" on campus.

Admissions

PSU seeks a diverse student body. Roughly 20 percent of MBA are international and 50 percent are women or minorities. Applicants are required to have a minimum GMAT of 450 and to hold a four-year degree from an accredited university. For "unconditional admission," the school says you must accrue 1050 points according to this formula: "200 times the overall undergraduate grade point average plus the GMAT score." Students can submit an equivalent GRE score instead of a GMAT score.

FINANCIAL FACTS

Annual tuition (in-state/ out-of-state)	$7,288/$17,048
Cost of books	$1,000
Room & board (on/off-campus)	$6,734/$6,734
% of students receiving aid	50
% of first-year students receiving aid	25
% of students receiving grants	15
Average award package	$8,500
Average grant	$3,500
Average loan	$8,500

ADMISSIONS

Admissions Selectivity Rating	77
# of applications received	278
% applicants accepted	81
% acceptees attending	26
Average GMAT	456
Range of GMAT	290–710
Accepts GRE scores	Yes
Average GPA	3.3
TOEFL required of international students	Yes
Minimum TOEFL (paper/web)	550/79
Application fee	$60
International application fee	$60
Regular application deadline	7/15
Regular application notification	8/1
Application Deadline/Notification	
Round 1:	5/1 / 5/15
Round 2:	7/15 / 7/30
Round 3:	10/15 / 10/30
Round 4:	12/15 / 12/30
Deferment available	Yes
Maximum length of deferment	One year
Transfer students accepted	Yes
Transfer application policy	
Up to 9 semester hours may be transferred from another MBA accredited program.	
Non-fall admissions	Yes
Need-blind admissions	Yes

EMPLOYMENT PROFILE

		Grads Employed by Function% Avg. Salary	
Career Rating	81		
Percent employed at graduation	60	Marketing	(24%) $44,000
Percent employed 3 months after graduation	25	Management	(54%) $45,000
Average base starting salary	$46,000	MIS	(22%) $45,000
Primary Source of Full-time Job Acceptances		**Top 5 Employers Hiring Grads**	
School-facilitated activities	31 (66%)	Deloitte & Touche (2), Sprint (4), Koch	
Unknown	16 (34%)	Industries (2), Walmart (2), AllState (2)	

PORTLAND STATE UNIVERSITY
SCHOOL OF BUSINESS ADMINISTRATION

GENERAL INFORMATION
Type of school   Public
Affiliation   No Affiliation

SURVEY SAYS...
Liberal students, Students love
Portland, OR
Solid preparation in:
Teamwork, Environmental sustain-
ability, Social responsibility

STUDENTS
Enrollment of parent
   institution   28,076
Enrollment of MBA Program   180
% male/female   53/47
% out-of-state   45
% part-time   67
% underrepresented minority   21
% international   35
Average age at entry   30
Average years work
   experience at entry   7

ACADEMICS
Academic Experience Rating   88
Profs interesting rating   86
Profs accessible rating   89
Student/faculty ratio   35:1
% female faculty   9
% part-time faculty   61

Joint Degrees
Business Intelligence and Analytics
Certificate, PT 1 year.

Prominent Alumni
Gary Ames, former President/
CEO, U.S. West; Gerry Cameron,
retired Chairman of the Board, U.S.
Bancorp; Scott Davis, CEO, UPS;
Larry Huget, President/COO, ESCO
Corp; J. Greg Ness, President/COO,
StanCorp Financial Group

Academics

Taking a cue from its progressive environs in Portland, Oregon, Portland State University offers an MBA program with a "focus on sustainability" and an emphasis on "personal development as a leader." Offering more than your standard MBA, "this school is committed to the whole student," and "creativity, along with sustainable, equitable solutions, are promoted, even prized." Throughout the hefty seventy-four-credit curriculum, you'll never lose sight of the school's core values: "PSU also works hard to integrate sustainability into most aspects of the curriculum, from core classes to elective offerings." The MBA includes plenty of required coursework (as well as required hands-on projects), yet electives give students the opportunity to tailor their education. In fact, "the wide latitude given to students to pursue their studies in a multi-disciplinary manner" is a trademark of PSU's graduate program. SBA has several Graduate Certificates for students, including: Social Innovation, Global Supply Chain, and Business Intelligence & Analytics.

Thanks to its strong reputation and enviable Portland location, PSU can "attract and retain an extremely high-quality faculty roster." On the whole, "professors are informed, enlightened educators as well as experts in their respective fields." Despite overall excellence, students say there are a few instructors who "seem unprepared, disorganized, and unclear on what they're supposed to be teaching us." The local community also plays an important role in the PSU experience. "Portland is truly at the center of this nation's move toward sustainability," and therefore, "being in Portland is a huge plus—there's so much sustainable business thinking and practice here that it's easy to see in the field what I learn in school." A student adds, "I have been introduced to and met with many people that are driving regional and national movements on the cutting edge of sustainability."

PSU is a large school, but you won't get lost in the crowd. Despite its 400-plus enrollment, "The SBA manages by breaking up [its] graduate studies into discrete cohorts and providing a concrete plan of study for each. There's never much doubt what you should be doing, yet there is flexibility should you need it." Depending on your schedule, the school offers several program options. For full-time students, "MBA cohort classes are four hours long one day a week from about [noon] until four," while part-time students "typically go to class two to three evenings a week." Though students say the business school's classrooms could use a refresh, (a major renovation will be complete in September 2017), "the academic resources are great." For example, "the library has done a lot of work to make research as easy as possible, even for those of us who are only on campus a couple times a week."

Career and Placement

The largest business school in the state, the School of Business Administration maintains "powerful connections to the Portland-area business community." Within the business school itself, faculty and administrators are "are ultra-accessible and always willing to provide career advice or introduce you to people they know in the business community." In addition, PSU has "a good alumni network" throughout the state of Oregon. Drawing on its deep ties in the Portland community, the academic experience at PSU is augmented by various professional development activities, like expert panel discussions, alumni networking events, and a mentorship program. At the same time, students note that career services are not as robust as they'd like. While the school affords them many opportunities, "students are expected to leverage other offerings, such as mentoring programs, informational interviews, etc." Companies that have partnered with PSU through the mentor program, as student project partners, or as employers include Damier Trucks, N.A., Nike, Tektronix, Hitachi Consulting, Intel Finance, and Hanna Andersson. The average starting salary for full-time PSU students is about $65,320.

Student Life and Environment

Friendly and down-to-earth, PSU students "defy the typical business school stereotype of sharkish students dying to get ahead." A current student observes, "While I expected to enter B-school with a bunch of traders and bankers, I was surprised to find a group of students that shared my, and Portland's, sensibilities regarding the world, and who are looking forward to showing the world that businesspeople are not only out to bring down the financial system en route to earning billions." Although there is a general interest in sustainability and ethics, at PSU you'll meet students from a "wide range" of backgrounds. As such, there are "a variety of activities to participate in regardless of your industry," and, on campus, there are lots of resources for a diverse student body—including "several childcare centers."

In both the full-time and part-time MBA program, many "people come to class and then go home," without making time for clubs or student groups. However, most students are involved in school-related activities outside of class, such as "internships, networking opportunities, and even…regular community service." In addition, many students are "open to meet after class or on weekends to socialize." Thanks to PSU's "vibrant urban location" in downtown Portland, students enjoy everything the Pacific Northwest has to offer, including plenty of "good food and coffee locations close by."

Admissions

To be considered for the full-time MBA program, students must have a minimum undergraduate GPA of 2.75, or, alternately, 3.0 in nine units of graduate-level coursework. Prospective students should also have at least two years of professional work experience before entering the program. In the class of 2014, the average GMAT was 623 and the mean undergraduate GPA was 3.31.

FINANCIAL FACTS

Annual tuition (in-state/ out-of-state)	$23,049/$27,924
Fees	$2,394
Cost of books	$2,300
Room & board (on/off-campus)	$12,000/$12,000

ADMISSIONS

Admissions Selectivity Rating	87
# of applications received	224
% applicants accepted	51
% acceptees attending	61
Average GMAT	615
Range of GMAT	570–650
Accepts GRE scores	Yes
Average Verbal GRE	158
Range of Verbal GRE scores	155–165
Average Quantitative GRE	154
Range of Quantitative GRE scores	152–155
Average Writing GRE	4.3
Range of Writing GRE scores	4.0–4.5
Average GPA	3.3
TOEFL required of international students	Yes
Minimum TOEFL (paper/web)	550/80
Application fee	$67
International application fee	$67
Early application deadline	11/15
Early notification date	1/1
Regular application deadline	2/1
Regular application notification	3/15
Application Deadline/Notification	
Deferment available	Yes
Transfer students accepted	Yes
Transfer application policy	
Maximum of 1/3 of the total number of PSU credits may transfer from a US accredited university.	
Non-fall admissions	No
Need-blind admissions	Yes

EMPLOYMENT PROFILE

Career Rating	90	Grads Employed by Function% Avg. Salary	
Percent employed at graduation	45	Marketing	(31%) $71,600
Percent employed 3 months after graduation	85	Operations	(25%) $71,000
		Consulting	(19%) $80,500
Average base starting salary	$69,568	Finance	(25%) $64,600
Primary Source of Full-time Job Acceptances		Top 5 Employers Hiring Grads	
School-facilitated activities	6 (25%)	Daimler Trucks N.A. (2), Nike (1), Hitachi	
Graduate-facilitated activities	10 (42%)	Consulting (1), Deloitte (1), IBM (1)	
Unknown	8 (33%)		

PURDUE UNIVERSITY
KRANNERT SCHOOL OF MANAGEMENT

GENERAL INFORMATION

Type of school	Public
Affiliation	No Affiliation
Academic calendar	Semester

SURVEY SAYS...

Classmates have diverse work experience, Friendly students, Happy students, Abundant clubs and activities
Solid preparation in:
Finance, Accounting

STUDENTS

Enrollment of parent	
Institution	39,409
Enrollment of MBA Program	150
% male/female	74/26
% out-of-state	50
% part-time	0
% underrepresented minority	16
% international	49
Average age at entry	26
Average years work	
experience at entry	4

ACADEMICS

Academic Experience Rating	**96**
Profs interesting rating	94
Profs accessible rating	96
Student/faculty ratio	2:1
% female faculty	25
% underrepresented	
minority faculty	2
% part-time faculty	9

Joint Degrees

BS Management/MBA; BS Industrial Engineering/MBA; BS Mechanical Engineering/MBA; BS Electical Engineering/MBA; BS Health Science Pre-professional/MBA; BS Industrial Management/MBA; BA in Communications/MSHRM, BS in Management/MSHRM.

Prominent Alumni

Joseph Forehand, Retired Chairman, Accenture; Marshall Larsen, Chairman, President, CEO, Goodrich Corp.; Marjorie Magner, Managing Partner, Brysam Global Partners

Academics

Purdue University's Krannert School of Management is a heavyweight in the MBA universe, especially when it comes to its "areas of strength: quantitative methods, operations, finance, and economics." Those looking to develop a "strong analytical and quantitative background" can hardly go wrong with a Krannert MBA. Best of all, at state school prices, Krannert "provides a great return on investment." But it's not just the school's low tuition that lends Krannert a kinder bottom line. As one student explains, "Many of us are actually doing this program at almost no cost thanks to the number of scholarships and assistantships [on offer]. This is very unique for a top MBA program. My friends at Wharton, MIT, Tepper, etc. are paying way more!"

Krannert excels even outside its quantitatively-focused standout disciplines. Students encounter a faculty experienced "in every aspect of management, from operations and finance to marketing and HR" here. But Krannert's academic excellence comes with high expectations. Academics are tough; there's a "'no BS' atmosphere here. Here you are expected to 'work hard, work right, and work together.'" MBAs assure us that Krannert "will push everyone to the limits, truly creating upending experiences that develop the individual along several dimensions." This is true not merely in terms of in-class work; the program "also provides several experiential learning opportunities through [its] consulting projects and study abroad programs." "The experiential learning projects give us good exposure to real-world work before we actually take the plunge," students tell us.

In terms of size, Krannert is just right. The program "is small enough for each student to stand out and become a leader if they would like to," yet "large enough and diverse enough to really learn a lot from your classmates." Krannert keeps class sizes small, which "means that students have greater one-on-one time with professors and they remain closely knit even years after graduation." Krannert professors "work to continue to contribute to research and stay involved in their respective fields," yet remain "genuinely interested in helping their students and are open and available to them any time we need."

Career and Placement

Students can prepare for interviews, contact employers, research companies, and complete career counseling through the Krannert Graduate Career Services office. The office receives mixed reviews. Some praise career services staff as attentive and "very committed to the students." Others demur, complaining that "the school should do a better job at alumni networking and improve its career services." This problem is particularly acute, we're told, when it comes to career services for international students, no small issue at a school with a 43 percent international student enrollment.

Recent employers of Krannert MBAs include: Bank of America, Citibank, Cummins, Discover Financial, General Electric, Guidant, IBM, Intel, Pratt & Whitney, Procter & Gamble, Raytheon, Samsung, United Technologies, and Wyeth.

ADMISSIONS CONTACT: BRENDA KNEBEL, DIRECTOR OF ADMISSIONS
ADDRESS: RAWLS HALL, SUITE 2020, 100 S. GRANT STREET, WEST LAFAYETTE, IN 47907-2076
PHONE: 765-494-0773 • FAX: 765-494-9841
E-MAIL: KRANNERTMASTERS@PURDUE.EDU • WEBSITE: KRANNERT.PURDUE.EDU

Student Life and Environment

Krannert "had the best building of any school I visited," one student notes, referring to the "well-equipped facilities in ... Rawls Hall," which "is consistently rated the best building on campus. It is in the best location on campus, next to the student union building, and the main hill where all the shops and stores are, and only literally ten steps from the most popular bar in town." The building is a nexus of activity, hosting "classes, student club activities, social gatherings, coffee [houses], call outs, company presentations, guest speakers, team assignments, study groups, etc."

The school "really tries to make a community for all of its students," through campus "organizations that help new students, international students, and families become accustomed to life in West Lafayette. They host many cultural events to show the diversity of its student body and educate everyone [on the different] cultural background[s]." Campus life offers "a huge number of activities that one can take part in or lead. Be it clubs, the entrepreneurship center (Burton D. Morgan), international trips, club trips, case competitions, taskforces, GCSMI (Supply Chain Initiative), social activities, etc." Hometown West Lafayette has "plenty of restaurants to choose from and cost of living is very affordable." Purdue athletics is another big attraction, of course.

The student body includes "a truly international population that provides for diversity in culture, thoughts, and work styles." "It has truly been a melting pot experience," one student writes. Students are also diverse in age: "There are a number of students who are married [and some with] kids," while "at the same time, there are quite a few students that graduated from undergrad within a year of starting the MBA program."

Admissions

To apply to the Krannert School of Management, all candidates must submit an online application using the school's online application system. All candidates must submit an official undergraduate transcripts (8 semesters), GMAT scores, an updated resume, 2 letters of recommendations, one essay and a statement of purpose. The most recent entering class had a mean GPA of 3.38 on a 4..0 scale, and an average GMAT score of 635. Women comprised 26% of the entering class. Approximately one-third of the entering class arrived with undergraduate degrees in business with almost as many with engineering degrees at the undergraduate level.

FINANCIAL FACTS

Annual tuition (in-state/ out-of-state)	$22,418/$42,184
Fees	$794
Cost of books	$2,696
Room & board (on/off-campus)	$10,030/$10,030
% of students receiving aid	79
% of first-year students receiving aid	70
% of students receiving grants	68
Average award package	$26,565
Average grant	$13,451
Average loan	$28,323
Average student loan debt	$45,807

ADMISSIONS

Admissions Selectivity Rating	93
# of applications received	643
% applicants accepted	26
% acceptees attending	42
Average GMAT	635
Range of GMAT	583–698
Accepts GRE scores	Yes
Average Verbal GRE	157
Range of Verbal GRE scores	157–158
Average Quantitative GRE	157
Range of Quantitative GRE scores	152–163
Average GPA	3.4
TOEFL required of international students	Yes
Minimum TOEFL (paper/web)	600/93
Application fee	$60
International application fee	$75
Early application deadline	11/15
Early notification date	12/30
Regular application deadline	1/15
Regular application notification	2/20
Application Deadline/Notification	
Round 1:	11/15 / 12/30
Round 2:	1/15 / 2/20
Round 3:	3/1 / 4/15
Round 4:	4/15 / 5/30
Deferment available	Yes
Maximum length of deferment	1 year
Transfer students accepted	No
Non-fall admissions	No
Need-blind admissions	Yes

EMPLOYMENT PROFILE

Career Rating	92	Grads Employed by Function	% Avg. Salary
Percent employed at graduation	62	Marketing	(11%) $94,750
Percent employed 3 months after graduation	81	Operations	(40%) $92,588
		Consulting	(16%) $96,175
Average base starting salary	$92,546	Management	(6%) $101,833
Primary Source of Full-time Job Acceptances		Finance	(13%) $88,400
School-facilitated activities	62 (75%)	HR	(7%) $77,250
Graduate-facilitated activities	26 (25%)	MIS	(7%) $97,644

Top 5 Employers Hiring Grads
Amazon.com (4), UTC (4), Intel (3), Shell (2), Bank of America (2)

QUINNIPIAC UNIVERSITY
SCHOOL OF BUSINESS

GENERAL INFORMATION
Type of school	Private
Affiliation	No Affiliation

SURVEY SAYS...
Happy students
Solid preparation in:
General management, Teamwork,
Communication/interpersonal skills,
Presentation skills, Quantitative skills

STUDENTS
Enrollment of parent institution	8,803
Enrollment of MBA Program	306
% male/female	48/52
% out-of-state	39
% part-time	66
% underrepresented minority	10
% international	14
Average age at entry	28
Average years work experience at entry	5

ACADEMICS
Academic Experience Rating	**86**
Profs interesting rating	92
Profs accessible rating	95
Student/faculty ratio	17:1
% female faculty	36
% underrepresented minority faculty	15
% part-time faculty	3

Joint Degrees
JD/MBA, 4 yrs

Prominent Alumni
William Weldon '71, Chairman/CEO
Johnson & Johnson; Murray Lender
'50, Co-Founder Lender's Bagels;
Bruce Dumelin '71, CFO (retired)
Bank of America; Joseph Onorato
'71, CFO (retired) Echlin, Inc.; Terry
Goodwin '67, VP & Mgr./Equity
Trading (retired) Goldman Sachs

Academics

At Quinnipiac University, located in Hamden, Connecticut, a conventional MBA is offered along with options to specialize in Healthcare Management and Supply Chain Management. Students may also choose to pursue a CFA (Chartered Financial Analyst) certification. Quinnipiac also offers Internet classes to help students achieve these goals, as well as full online MBA program. The school of business is comprised of part-time professionals, as well as full-time students pursuing a joint BA/MBA or a joint BS/MBA. Part-time students can choose from evening classes or accelerated online courses, while the full-time program offers classes in the afternoons and evenings.

Students choose Quinnipiac because it's "strong in finance and accounting." It has an "excellent reputation," "hybrid MBA" program, and a "good teacher-student ratio." Students enjoy the small class sizes, claiming "the professors know all their students." Small class sizes translate into a "more personalized" educational experience. "Professors are very visible and very willing to help. They really invest their time in the students and understand the real-life issues (work, family obligations, etc.) that we face." Professors also bring "real-world experience" into the classroom, and "the courses keep up with current trends." Professors are "smart," "challenging," and "available." Students are often given group assignments, which culminate in a presentation. "This prepares you for presentations in the real world, as well as building your skills to work with others." Students emphasize the "practical" education they receive. Professors also take the time to "speak with students about their particular fields." Most agree they've had a "great experience" with Quinnipiac faculty.

The "classroom facilities are some of the best I've seen." The program has "high-tech equipment for presentations, a Financial Technology Center for real-time trading, and HD video monitors that constantly keep us up-to-date on current news." One student admits the facilities are what made Quinnipiac a top choice. "The administration has a solid strategy of how to make Quinnipiac a major university with many opportunities. Unfortunately, the MBA Director position has seen high turnover in recent years." Quinnipiac students admit its reputation is slowly growing. Still, they praise the administration's flexibility.

Career and Placement

Career services at the School of Business, include individual career counseling appointments, career fairs, on-campus recruiting, and mock interviews. If students need help writing resumes and cover letters, that is also provided. Additionally, there is an online tool called QU Career Connections where students can view job listings, add their resume, and sign up for interviews. The School of Business "has an extremely devoted team that works diligently to host network receptions, maintain the career website, assist with resumes, and regularly communicate with students." Also, there is "a new director of the business school who has worked very hard to make QU more competitive and to bring new employers to recruit." QU "has been great at providing work opportunities for all the students in many diverse fields in the business world." Part-time students are concurrently employed by some of the following organizations: Bayer, Yale New Haven Hospital, and United Technologies.

ADMISSIONS CONTACT: JENNIFER BOUTIN, ASSOCIATE DIRECTOR OF GRADUATE ADMISSIONS
ADDRESS: 275 MOUNT CARMEL AVE, N1-GRD, HAMDEN, CT 06518-1940
PHONE: 203-582-8672 • FAX: 203-582-3443
E-MAIL: GRADUATE@QUINNIPIAC.EDU • WEBSITE: WWW.QUINNIPIAC.EDU

Student Life and Environment

Quinnipiac is located in Hamden, Connecticut, a suburb of the city of New Haven. It has a population of just under 60,000 and is two hours north of New York City. Quinnipiac is "a beautiful campus located right outside of Sleeping Giant State Park." It's "safe and offers a great environment for learning and social life." Another student claims that "when you step foot on QU grounds, you just want to grab a book and start studying." The academic environment at Quinnipiac is described as "friendly, yet challenging" and "culturally diverse." "When working on a team project, students are very professional and contribute equally to the work." Students' ages vary somewhat. "There are older students, such as myself enrolled in the program (age 40+), but the majority are just starting their careers." They have a chance to mix by joining one of the "limited number of graduate clubs" available, but, "the graduate population is not very interested in participating in additional activities or socials." This may be because many older students have work and families. Due to their myriad obligations, "there is no time for life at school." However, some suggest that "all the students are connected and stay so through a variety of ways, like going out for dinners, meeting for classes, etc." Of those "'older students'" some hope for "more programs and options."

Admissions

In addition to the application, the admissions committee requires the following from its applicants: official transcripts for all post-secondary academic work; an official GMAT or GRE score report; a personal essay; undergraduate GPA; two letters of recommendation; and a current resume. The GMAT score and the undergraduate GPA are most important in the process. Also considered are work experience, extracurricular activities, and an interview. TOEFL scores are required for those whose native language is not English. The average GPA for admitted students is 3.36, and the average GMAT score is 523. There is a high acceptance rate at Quinnipiac, and the admissions process is rolling. The five-year BS/MBA program is open to Quinnipiac undergraduates only.

FINANCIAL FACTS

Annual tuition (in-state/ out-of-state)	$24,840/$24,840
Fees	$666
Cost of books	$2,500
Room & board (on/off-campus)	$12,990/$14,830
% of students receiving aid	49
% of first-year students receiving aid	58
% of students receiving grants	10
Average award package	$19,753
Average grant	$8,142
Average loan	$19,781
Average student loan debt	$41,406

ADMISSIONS

Admissions Selectivity Rating	81
# of applications received	225
% applicants accepted	80
% acceptees attending	81
Average GMAT	523
Range of GMAT	480–620
Accepts GRE scores	Yes
Average GPA	3.4
TOEFL required of international students	Yes
Minimum TOEFL (paper/web)	575/90
Application fee	$45
International application fee	$45
Application Deadline/Notification	
Deferment available	Yes
Maximum length of deferment	One year
Transfer students accepted	Yes
Transfer application policy	up to 9 graduate transfer credits allowed from regionally accredited schools. The grades must be a B or better.
Non-fall admissions	Yes
Need-blind admissions	Yes

RADFORD UNIVERSITY
COLLEGE OF BUSINESS AND ECONOMICS

GENERAL INFORMATION

Type of school	Public
Affiliation	No Affiliation

SURVEY SAYS...

Friendly students
Solid preparation in:
General management

STUDENTS

Enrollment of parent institution	9,743
Enrollment of MBA Program	46
% male/female	77/23
% out-of-state	46
% part-time	72
% underrepresented minority	38
% international	46
Average age at entry	28
Average years work experience at entry	7

ACADEMICS

Academic Experience Rating	87
Profs interesting rating	90
Profs accessible rating	91
% female faculty	15
% underrepresented minority faculty	20
% part-time faculty	1

Academics

Repeat business is one of the telltale signs of success in retail, and by that standard Radford University must be doing a pretty good job; a considerable number of students in our survey self-identified as former Radford undergrads, and nearly all cited their satisfaction during their first go-around as the reason for pursuing an MBA here. With an undergraduate population consisting of approximately 25 percent business majors, Radford has a large customer base from which to draw graduate students. You could say that business is booming at Radford's College of Business and Economics.

Radford now offers the MBA program as a full-time, part-time, and online. offering Radford MBAs tell us that their program "is general in nature" and that "students wanting to specialize in a specific segment of business, e.g., marketing, may be well-served to look elsewhere." They are quick to add, however, that the program "does prepare you for work in many areas of business and does not skimp on content or focus in doing so" and that "those who want the knowledge and skills to run an organization, even a global one, will be hard-pressed to find a better school, especially for the price." Part-time students also appreciate the way the program is "geared toward people who work full-time jobs." While describing the Radford MBA as "a challenging part-time program," they note that convenient scheduling and professors who will "work with your work schedule to [help you] get through the MBA program" make it "easy for a working professional to get an MBA" here.

Radford's thirty-six credit hour curriculum is divided in a two-thirds, one-third split between required courses and targeted electives in analytics and innovation (which constitute twelve hours). The program utilizes "a face-to-face presentation format" and includes a substantial writing component. "Small class sizes" and a faculty that "is very student-oriented (rather than concentrating on writing professional papers and books, they concentrate on teaching, which is a good thing)" make this a very student-friendly program. Professors "do an excellent job of tying in current events and international matters of interest," although some "don't seem to have much experience in the professional corporate world. Many seem to have spent most of their time in academia." MBA courses are offered in two locations: the main campus in Radford, Virginia, and the Roanoke Higher Education Center in Roanoke, Virginia. The program is now also offered online.

Career and Placement

The Career Services Office at Radford University offers a variety of resources to undergraduates, graduates, and alumni. These include a virtual resume, internship, and a jobs database "where students and employers come together to post and view resumes and position openings," as well as workshops in resume and portfolio development, career fairs, and career-assessment tools. On-campus recruiters include Ameriprise Financial, DMG Securities, Ferguson Enterprises, Northwestern Mutual, State Farm, Wachovia, and the federal government.

Student Life and Environment

The Radford University MBA program is "a mix of adult and young adult students." The latter group includes nearly all of the full-time students, a combination of recently mint-ed American undergraduates and international students. The student body tends to be "young, eager to get into a professional setting, worried about the job market," "friendly, hard-working, and intelligent." Working professionals constitute a substantial minority whose experience and insights are welcomed by their younger peers.

Full-timers describe campus life as being "like any typical college student's life," with the "majority of time spent studying and preparing for class." Part-time students typi-cally don't have time for the "many activities, clubs, and organizations that are at this school." Those who attend classes at the Roanoke Higher Education Center tell us that "the RHEC is a newly remodeled, high tech, and comfortable facility more suited to providing an appropriate atmosphere for educating older MBA students."

Hometown Radford is a small town in the Blue Ridge Mountains; Roanoke is about forty-five miles away. The area is most amenable to outdoor enthusiasts, as it provides easy access to the Appalachian Trail, the New River, and Claytor Lake. Shopping, restaurants, nightlife, and such are not in great supply, students warn, although the proximity of Roanoke helps to make up for this deficiency. Charleston, West Virginia, and Greensboro, North Carolina, are also within a reasonable driving distance.

Admissions

Admission to Radford's MBA program is considered via a full portfolio review. Application requires successful completion of an undergraduate degree with a preferred minimum GPA of 3.0. Applicants must also submit an official report of GMAT or GRE scores (applicants with five or more years of work experience can apply for a waiver of the GMAT or GRE requirement); two letters of recommendation; a resume of work experience; and statement of intent. Also, applicants must demonstrate business pro-ficiency through accredited collegiate preparation in the following foundation areas or equivalents: economics, accounting, finance, and statistics. Students can earn credit for some of these foundation areas through CLEP testing as well as online noncredit courses taught by RU faculty. In addition to meeting the above requirements, international stu-dents must also provide a certified letter of sponsorship and a bank statement proving sufficient finances to cover their first year of study. Those whose first language is not English must submit TOEFL scores.

FINANCIAL FACTS

Annual tuition (in-state/ out-of-state)	$7,632/$16,392
Fees	$3,504
Cost of books	$1,100
Room & board (on/off-campus)	$7,498/$7,498
% of students receiving aid	39
% of first-year students receiving aid	60
% of students receiving grants	15
Average award package	$9,000

ADMISSIONS

Admissions Selectivity Rating	87
# of applications received	54
% applicants accepted	44
% acceptees attending	63
Average GMAT	515
Range of GMAT	510–580
Accepts GRE scores	Yes
Average Verbal GRE	151
Range of Verbal GRE scores	151–151
Average Quantitative GRE	155
Range of Quantitative GRE scores	154–156
Average Writing GRE	3.8
Range of Writing GRE scores	3.5–4.0
Average GPA	3.1
Minimum TOEFL (paper/web)	550/
Application fee	$50
International application fee	$50
Application Deadline/Notification	
Deferment available	Yes
Maximum length of deferment	1 year
Transfer students accepted	Yes
Transfer application policy	
Transfer students complete the same application process as other students. They may transfer in a maximum of twelve credit hours. Individual decisions on transfer-ability of credits are made based on a syllabus review.	
Non-fall admissions	Yes
Need-blind admissions	Yes

RENSSELAER POLYTECHNIC INSTITUTE
LALLY SCHOOL OF MANAGEMENT

GENERAL INFORMATION
Type of school	Private
Affiliation	No Affiliation
Academic calendar	Semester

SURVEY SAYS...
Cutting-edge classes
Solid preparation in:
Entreprenurial studies

STUDENTS
Enrollment of parent institution	7,113
Enrollment of MBA Program	49
% male/female	62/38
% part-time	57
% underrepresented minority	19
% international	33
Average age at entry	25
Average years work experience at entry	2

ACADEMICS
Academic Experience Rating	**85**
Profs interesting rating	87
Profs accessible rating	93
% female faculty	28
% underrepresented minority faculty	2
% part-time faculty	28

Joint Degrees
MBA/MS, 2 yrs

Prominent Alumni
George M. Low '48, NASA administrator who headed the Apollo program; James Q. Crowe '72, Founder and Builder of telecom industry compaines; Denis Tito '64, Founder of Wilshire Associates; Ray Tomlinson '63, Inventor of email in 1971; Marcian E. "Ted" Hoff, Inventor of microprocessor

Academics

Rensselaer Polytechnic Institute's Lally School of Management and Technology offers numerous graduate business programs with a strong focus on technology and close ties to the Northeast business community. For hard-working students, Lally's MBA is fast-paced and efficient: taking a full course load, required credit hours can be completed in a mere twelve months. Those who want to tailor their degree or make a career change can pursue a specialization module in addition to core courses, but they'll still have a diploma within seventeen to twenty-four months. (Currently, the school offers optional specializations in entrepreneurship, finance, information systems, marketing, and new product development, business analytics, and supply chain management.) For local professionals, Lally also offers a flexible full-time MBA. In addition, the school operates numerous master's programs in related business fields, such as an MS in Quantitative Finance and Risk Analytics, an MS in Business Analyltics, an MS in Supply Chain, and an MS in Technology Commercialization and Entrepreneurship. These specialized programs "raise the level of the MBA program by exposing MBA students to other advanced disciplines and specializations so that MBA students, upon graduation, are already familiar with working with field specialists such as financial engineers."

While the delivery format differs, MBA programs at Lally comprise forty-five credit hours of coursework, with the option of extending the degree to sixty credits. The core curriculum takes a cross-disciplinary approach to business, and several courses are taught by teams of professors from different disciplines. As students point out, Rensselaer is a "world-class research institution," and the MBA program draws on the school's historic strength in technology and applied science. Here, students benefit from a "very good mix of technology management classes with traditional finance, marketing, and operations management classes." Business issues in fields like information technology or nanotechnology are often discussed in the classroom, and "many of the MBA students are working on commercializing technologies." A student elaborates, "The greatest strength of RPI is the interdisciplinary nature of all of the degree programs. For the Lally School specifically, its strength is the integration of technology into the classroom, preparing students to work in the high-tech 21st century workplace."

"The faculty is fantastic" at Rensselaer, and "small class sizes help [students] take advantage of their experience and research." While "professors and classes get an A-plus," students say Rensselaer's "administration gets a C-plus." Overseen by "a multi-layer bureaucracy," there can be plenty of red tape. Fortunately, the personnel at the business school are approachable and friendly. "The administrators understand the issues that students have and are very patient and understanding, and go above and beyond to help students."

Career and Placement

Lally's Career Services Team manages a comprehensive suite of workshops, professional development tools, and a portfolio of employment opportunities. The Career Team also oversees employer information sessions, MBA career panels, and trips to New York City and Boston to meet with alumni and provide career shadowing opportunities. Lally has a strong reputation in the local region, and students find that the "alumni [were] extremely helpful during my career search!"

ADMISSIONS CONTACT: GINA O'CONNOR, ASSOCIATE DEAN OF ACADEMIC AFFAIRS
ADDRESS: 110 EIGHTH STREET–PITTSBURGH BUILDING, TROY, NY 12180-3590
PHONE: 518-276-6565 • FAX: 518-276-8190
E-MAIL: LALLYMBA@RPI.EDU • WEBSITE: LALLYSCHOOL.RPI.EDU

Companies that have recently recruited at Lally include Accenture, American Express, Albany Molecular Research Corporation, Bank of America, Blue Slate Solutions, Boeing, Citigroup, Clorox, Deloitte, ECG Consulting Group, Foster Miller, General Electric, Honeywell, IBM, Microsoft, Mimeo.com, Phillips, Proctor & Gamble, United Technologies, and Xerox. More than 40 percent of graduates stay in the Northeast region.

Student Life and Environment

The full-time MBA program at Lally comprises "roughly fifteen hours per week in class," plus another twenty to twenty-five hours per week doing homework, projects, and readings. Stimulated by the team-oriented curriculum, "study groups emerge between students, and project teams learn to work with each other and spend time together outside of the classroom." Beyond academics, students also might get together for mingling and career development opportunities. In particular, "The Graduate Management Student Association does a great job organizing social and networking events."

The MBA program is targeted at those with work experience, but also considers those coming direct from RPI or other undergraduate programs. It is easy to participate in the multitude of activities on the larger Rensselaer campus. For example, a current MBA candidate tells us, "I am involved in multiple performing arts groups, including Sheer Idiocy, the improvisational comedy troupe; WRPI, the college radio station; and The Players, the traditional theater organization. I am also the Student Outreach Coordinator for the Admissions Office." Not everyone, however, gets so involved in campus life. At Lally, "some students are detached from the program, but others are very engaged and make the experience very good."

Admissions

To apply to Lally's graduate business programs, students must submit a completed application form, one personal essay, standardized scores, undergraduate transcripts, two letters of recommendation, and, if applicable, TOEFL scores. Candidates are also encouraged to schedule an interview with the admissions department. The school accepts both the GMAT and the GRE. A recent incoming class had a mean GMAT score of 625 and an average undergraduate GPA of 3.27, and more than 50 percent majored in a technical field as an undergraduate. Those far removed from school or a test-taking setting can submit the ETS Personal Potential Index(PPI) to supplement their application.

FINANCIAL FACTS

Annual tuition (in-state/ out-of-state)	$48,100/
Fees	$2,339
Cost of books	$2,841
Room & board (on/off-campus)	$13,320/$13,320

ADMISSIONS

Admissions Selectivity Rating	86
# of applications received	57
% applicants accepted	56
% acceptees attending	59
Average GMAT	608
Range of GMAT	500–750
Accepts GRE scores	Yes
Average GPA	3.4
TOEFL required of international students	Yes
Minimum TOEFL (paper/web)	577/88
Application fee	$75
International application fee	$75
Application Deadline/Notification	
Round 1:	12/1 / 2/1
Round 2:	1/15 / 3/15
Round 3:	3/1 / 4/15
Round 4:	4/15 / 6/15
Deferment available	Yes
Maximum length of deferment	1 year, must reapply
Transfer students accepted	No
Non-fall admissions	No
Need-blind admissions	Yes

EMPLOYMENT PROFILE

Career Rating		Grads Employed by Function	% Avg. Salary
Percent employed at graduation	90		
Percent employed at graduation	43	Operations	(25%) $61,677
Percent employed 3 months		Consulting	(25%) $65,000
after graduation	86	Management	(8%) $101,000
Average base starting salary	$70,167	Finance	(25%)
Primary Source of Full-time Job Acceptances		MIS	(17%) $70,000
School-facilitated activities	3 (25%)	**Top 5 Employers Hiring Grads**	
Graduate-facilitated activities	5 (42%)	Citibank (1), GE (1), Johnson & Johnson (1),	
Unknown	4 (33%)	NXP Semiconductor (1), Textron Systems (1)	

RICE UNIVERSITY
JESSE H. JONES GRADUATE SCHOOL OF BUSINESS

GENERAL INFORMATION
Type of school	Private
Affiliation	No Affiliation
Academic calendar	Semester

SURVEY SAYS...
Friendly students, Good peer network, Good social scene, Abundant mentors available, Helpful alumni, Happy students, Abundant clubs and activities, Students love Houston, TX
Solid preparation in:
Finance, Accounting, General management, Teamwork, Presentation skills, Quantitative skills, Entreprenurial studies

STUDENTS
Enrollment of parent institution	6,623
Enrollment of MBA Program	617
% male/female	66/34
% out-of-state	51
% part-time	64
% underrepresented minority	9
% international	28
Average age at entry	28
Average years work experience at entry	5

ACADEMICS
Academic Experience Rating	97
Profs interesting rating	94
Profs accessible rating	96
Student/faculty ratio	5:1
% female faculty	24
% underrepresented minority faculty	4
% part-time faculty	44

Joint Degrees
MBA/MD; MBA/ME; MBA/ Professional Science Master

Prominent Alumni
James S. Turley, Retired Chairman & CEO of Ernst & Young (EY), and Honorary Director and former Chair of Catalyst's Board of Directors

Academics

It's safe to say that Rice University's Jones Graduate School of Business is "highly regarded." Armed with a "beautiful campus," "great electives" and overall "well-rounded program," it's easy to see why tomorrow's business leaders flock here. It also doesn't hurt that the school has a reputation for offering "hefty financial aid [packages]." Additionally, given its prime Houston location, it's probably not too surprising that the school's "reputation in the energy industry is unparalleled." Jones also posts "high ranking[s] in entrepreneurship" as well. And prospective students intending to enroll part-time will take heart in hearing that part-timers here "are seamlessly assimilated into the Rice student body." A grateful first-year shares, " I don't feel like a 'part time' student, but as full[y] an MBA candidate as those students who are enrolled in the daytime program."

Importantly, "small class sizes" help to ensure that strong relationships are forged with Jones' "smart, engaging" professors. "Highly respected in their fields," instructors here "are also excellent teachers that truly care about their students." Indeed, they "are very quick to help, and are available in person, on the phone, or by email." Students also give high marks to the "very responsive" administration that ensures that "Rice runs like clockwork."

Career and Placement

Rice MBAs certainly love to tout Jones' career services office. As one first-year student excitedly shares, "The career center has been phenomenal in helping me think through future options and connecting me to people that can help me achieve my goals." Overall, "the school is very well respected in the energy and investment banking industries." Of course, it also doesn't hurt that Rice's plum Houston location "places it in close proximity to a large number of Fortune 500 companies." An ecstatic second-year explains, "the Houston economy is exploding and we are the best school in the area and have our pick of most of the best jobs." It's also important to note that plenty of opportunity arises from other Jones graduates. As a thankful second-year student concludes, "Alumni are incredibly helpful and willing to meet. I have met with more than twenty alumni for coffee/drinks and never once been turned down."

Companies that tend to hire Rice MBAs include EY (Ernst & Young), Deloitte, ExxonMobil, HP, and Infosys.

ADMISSIONS CONTACT: SUE OLDHAM, DIRECTOR OF ADMISSIONS
ADDRESS: MBA ADMISSIONS, PO BOX 2932-MS 531, JONES SCHOOL, HOUSTON, TX 77252-2932
PHONE: 888-844-4773 • FAX: 713-348-6147
E-MAIL: RICEMBA@RICE.EDU • WEBSITE: WWW.BUSINESS.RICE.EDU/

Student Life and Environment

Jones manages to consistently attract "thoughtful, engaging, smart [and] driven" students. Perhaps even more importantly, MBA candidates here tend to be "very friendly" as well. As one first-year student happily shares, "Everyone is looking out for each other." Many individuals also report that their peers seem to have "a well defined work/life/study balance." This can likely be attributed to the fact that a large number of students are "married or married with children." Thankfully, you'll also find "a broad range of personalities and backgrounds." However, we are warned that while Jones is "internationally diverse" there's a "very low number of African American students."

It's quite common for Rice MBAs to spend a good deal of time in their academic building. Hence, they relish the fact that "many study rooms and resources are available" and greatly appreciate that there are loads of "on campus food options." MBA candidates also love the fact that the "university gym is across the street" making it "convenient to get some exercise in before or after class." Best of all, the facilities are "in good condition," "accessible" and "eco friendly."

Finally, socially speaking, students proudly boast that " there are more opportunities to get involved and network than you can take advantage of." Indeed, there's "an event every night if you can make the time." As one content student explains in further detail, "We have a class party every Thursday where free food and beer is provided. Everyone brings their spouses and kids." All of these activities help to affirm the conviction that the friendships and connections forged at Jones "will endure long after graduation."

Admissions

Rice looks for well-rounded students with an excellent academic track record. The Rice MBA Full Time program competitively seeks top students by offering over 40 named merit-based scholarships to each incoming class. Accepted students have an average GMAT score of 676 and an average GPA of 3.34. Work experience, résumé, and interview skills are equally important with students averaging four years of work upon enrollment. Letters of recommendations and well-written essays can serve to bolster one's application. Admission applications to the Full Time MBA program are accepted in three rounds in October, January, and April.

FINANCIAL FACTS

Annual tuition (in-state/ out-of-state)	$53,000/$53,000
Fees	$3,093
Cost of books	$2,600
Room & board (on/off-campus)	$13,275/$15,075
% of students receiving aid	90
% of first-year students receiving aid	85
% of students receiving grants	86
Average award package	$43,218
Average grant	$31,204
Average loan	$27,578
Average student loan debt	$55,156

ADMISSIONS

Admissions Selectivity Rating	95
# of applications received	775
% applicants accepted	27
% acceptees attending	55
Average GMAT	676
Range of GMAT	640–710
Accepts GRE scores	Yes
Average GPA	3.3
TOEFL required of international students	Yes
Minimum TOEFL (paper/web)	600/100
Application fee	$200
International application fee	$200
Application Deadline/Notification	
Round 1:	10/5 / 12/15
Round 2:	1/9 / 4/5
Round 3:	4/7 / 5/10
Round 4:	4/4 / 5/6
Deferment available	Yes
Maximum length of deferment	one year
Transfer students accepted	No
Non-fall admissions	No
Need-blind admissions	Yes

EMPLOYMENT PROFILE

Career Rating	96	Grads Employed by Function	%	Avg. Salary
Percent employed at graduation	82	Marketing	(14%)	$95,455
Percent employed 3 months after graduation	91	Consulting	(24%)	$124,600
		Management	(6%)	$112,500
Average base starting salary	$109,901	Finance	(38%)	$107,018
Primary Source of Full-time Job Acceptances		Other	(18%)	$108,923
School-facilitated activities	60 (69%)	**Top 5 Employers Hiring Grads**		
Graduate-facilitated activities	25 (29%)	EY (Ernst & Young) (5), Deloitte (3),		
Unknown	2 (2%)	ExxonMobil (3), HP (3), Infosys (3)		

ROCHESTER INSTITUTE OF TECHNOLOGY
SAUNDERS COLLEGE OF BUSINESS

GENERAL INFORMATION
Type of school   Private
Affiliation   No Affiliation
Academic calendar   Semester

SURVEY SAYS...
Liberal students
Solid preparation in:
General management, Teamwork

STUDENTS
Enrollment of parent
  institution   18,606
Enrollment of MBA Program   145
% male/female   57/43
% out-of-state   66
% part-time   34
% underrepresented minority   12
% international   40
Average age at entry   25
Average years work
  experience at entry   3

ACADEMICS
Academic Experience Rating   89
Profs interesting rating   90
Profs accessible rating   91
Student/faculty ratio   6:1
% female faculty   27
% underrepresented
  minority faculty   10
% part-time faculty   0

Joint Degrees
MS in Computational Finance;
MBA w/ concentrations (2 years):
Communication and Media
Technologies; Health Systems
Administration; Human Resource
Development; Industrial and
Systems Engineering Management;
Print Media; Public Policy

Prominent Alumni
James Salzano, CEO, Easy Spirit,
Inc.; Betty Noonan, Chief Marketing
Officer and General Manager, Cree,
Inc.; Donald James Truesdale,
Partner, Managing Director,
Goldman Sachs; Frank S. Sklarsky,
EVP and CFO, PPG Industries, Inc.

Academics

Located in upstate New York, Rochester Institute of Technology is known for its academic excellence in technology and applied science. Accordingly, RIT's MBA programs provide a "great blend of management and technical education," preparing students for the realities of the workplace through practical instruction, teamwork, and applied learning. Within the MBA curriculum, "courses are updated frequently to allow for new events, technologies, and information." (In recent years, "sustainability is growing in importance," as is entrepreneurship.) A major benefit of the program is the "the wide array of concentrations offered," including such unique offerings as digital marketing, quality and applied statistics, and environmentally sustainable management—as well as more traditional business fields like accounting, operations management, and supply chain management. In addition to established concentrations, students can tailor their education through elective courses in eight other RIT colleges, like computer science, fine arts, sustainability, and engineering.

The MBA can be completed on a full-time or part-time basis, with classes offered in the daytime and the evening, as well as online. Course work is "fast-paced" and challenging." Despite the "vigorous schedule," "professors are extremely flexible if students need to miss class for work." On that note, most RIT instructors "know students' names and take interest in the students' personal lives." With an average class size of just twenty-three students, "professors go out of their way to be sure concepts are well understood and topics are relevant and beneficial to us." Even in the classroom, RIT emphasizes practical skills, and most professors "have significant corporate experience and tie it well with the academics to offer an enriched experience." In fact, many RIT instructors "still work as consultants for major companies." All classes are taught by faculty, not teaching assistants.

Students who received an undergraduate business degree from RIT and 4+1 MBA Partner schools can "waive some classes" in the MBA program, or complete a BS and MBA through on accelerated five-year schedule. Taking advantage of this attractive opportunity, many "students seem to come directly from undergrad," though "each class tends to have at least some students who have been in the workplace." Furthermore, RIT undergraduates "are required to have a good deal of co-op (internship) experience before they graduate (usually between six months to one year or more.)" For those who want to build on their real-world credentials, RIT offers plenty of "hands-on, experiential, practical learning" experiences. Here, students can participate in optional internships or co-op work experiences, business plan and case competitions, and team-based projects both on and off campus. Among other offerings, the school's "Innovation Center is a new-business incubator, and they are always asking for the business students to come and consult for them."

Career and Placement

Serving the undergraduate and graduate community, RIT's Cooperative Education and Career Services offers robust career preparation services, including an executive-in-residence program, mentorship program, online job resources, career fairs, and networking events. While the campus maintains a robust recruiting program," based on the school's strength in engineering, technology, and science, "Most of the companies at the career fair are looking to hire tech students with very few hiring management students." As such, "the campus is still trying to get more interest from the business community to send companies here for new talent."

In recent years, full-time MBA candidates reported a median starting salary of more than $58,000, with a range between $40,000 and $130,000. They took jobs at AXA Advisors, Cleveland Cavaliers, Discover Financial Services, Goldman Sachs, Google, Harris Corporation, IBM, JP Morgan Chase, Insero & Company, Key Bank, Kinex Pharmaceuticals, Ortho Clinical Diagnostic, Paychex, PWC, Toyota, United Technologies Corp., Wegmans, and Xerox.

Student Life and Environment

Part of a large, private, comprehensive university, Saunders College of Business offers a well-rounded student experience, which appeals to both part-time and full-time students. Here, "the facilities are good and campus activities are diversified," and there are plenty of "great resources available"—including an "outstanding" gym. As you'd expect from a technical school, business students enjoy contemporary technology in the classroom and "have access to amazing equipment" to prepare their "group presentations."

On this large campus, students "come from about twenty different countries," creating a "very diverse and global environment." While they enthusiastically participate in class, "it is hard for graduate students to be more involved due to the late night classes and other obligations." Still, even these students acknowledge that "there are lots of opportunities on campus for fun and Rochester is a great place to live." Among full-timers, "the students are friendly and very focused when it comes to school, but don't shy away from playing the occasional poker game now and then."

Admissions

To be considered for admission to RIT's graduate business programs, RIT not only considers academic record and test scores, but evaluates a student based on his or her letters of recommendation, resume, and personal statement. While many full-time students join the program directly after undergraduate work, most part-time students have three to five years of professional experience before starting the program.

FINANCIAL FACTS

Annual tuition (in-state/ out-of-state)	$20,902/$20,902
Cost of books	$2,026
Room & board (on/off-campus)	$12,274/$12,274
% of students receiving aid	75
% of first-year students receiving aid	75
% of students receiving grants	65
Average award package	$23,000
Average grant	$13,500
Average loan	$26,200
Average student loan debt	$36,600

ADMISSIONS

Admissions Selectivity Rating	85
# of applications received	290
% applicants accepted	52
% acceptees attending	35
Average GMAT	526
Range of GMAT	460–590
Accepts GRE scores	Yes
Average Verbal GRE	147
Range of Verbal GRE scores	142–152
Average Quantitative GRE	150
Range of Quantitative GRE scores	146–155
Average Writing GRE	3.4
Range of Writing GRE scores	3.0–4.0
Average GPA	3.5
TOEFL required of international students	Yes
Minimum TOEFL (paper/web)	580/92
Application fee	$60
International application fee	$60
Regular application deadline	8/1
Application Deadline/Notification	
Deferment available	Yes
Maximum length of deferment	1 year
Transfer students accepted	Yes
Transfer application policy	
Transfer up to 3 courses if relevant to program. Grade of B or better. Credits must be earned within 5 years of transferring to RIT.	
Non-fall admissions	Yes
Need-blind admissions	Yes

EMPLOYMENT PROFILE

Career Rating	79	Grads Employed by Function	% Avg. Salary
Percent employed at graduation	85	Marketing	(19%) $46,333
Percent employed 3 months after graduation	96	Operations	(7%) $81,667
		Consulting	(5%) $60,500
Average base starting salary	$58,315	Management	(19%) $40,000
Primary Source of Full-time Job Acceptances		Finance	(36%) $52,800
School-facilitated activities	32 (76%)	MIS	(10%) $95,000
Unknown	10 (24%)	Other	(5%) $0

Top 5 Employers Hiring Grads
PWC (1), IBM (1), Google (1), Goldman Sachs (1), Cleveland Cavaliers (1)

ROLLINS COLLEGE
CRUMMER GRADUATE SCHOOL OF BUSINESS

Academics

The Crummer Graduate School of Business offers three MBA programs which each cater to professionals at different stages in their career. The Executive MBA meets only on Saturdays and is designed for mid- to senior-level professionals, while the other two options draw individuals with less than a decade of work experience. The Early Advantage program draws recent college grads looking to get a head start on their career, while the Professional MBAs work during the day and then take evening classes two nights a week. Knowing that most people are working and busy, "everybody in the administration is always available to you" and the "students are truly the customers." "Everybody knows your name. We see the dean everywhere and he always participates in activities with us," says a student.

Professors are top notch, bringing "a wealth of real world experience to the classroom." They "represent a wide range of cultures, industry experience, and research expertise in different fields," and "repeatedly publish in renowned journals." The curriculum is "very methodical," and follows an order of classes that build on each other, preparing you for the next courses. "We are thoroughly trained, challenged everyday, [and] exposed to real-life situations," says a student. "They understand what we are wanting to do upon graduation and are very helpful to teach us the tools to apply our knowledge in the business world." Due to the small size of the school there are somewhat "limited class offerings, and some of the niche classes do no occur due to limited registrations."

Career and Placement

The Rollins MBA reputation is strong within Florida (particularly nearby Orlando), and the Career Resource Center understands that their students' reasons for attending Crummer and their job aspirations are different across its three programs. All Early Advantage students are required to complete a one-on-one career strategy session, mock interview, and an MBA-level internship. Career aid given to Professional and Executive MBA students tends to be more toward job strategy development, networking, and assessment. Both Early Advantage and Professional MBA students may participate in Rollins MBA Global Consulting projects (which include a one-week trip abroad to conduct field research). Crummer "offers a wide variety of things for students to do that involved every aspect of business—from finance to consulting to entrepreneurship," and "really help[s] you learn more about what you are interested in through firsthand experience." Top employers of Rollins grads include The Walt Disney Co., SAP, Siemens Energy, Fidelity Investments, and CNL Financial Group, Inc.

ADMISSIONS CONTACT: JACQUELINE BRITO, ASSISTANT DEAN
ADDRESS: 1000 HOLT AVE. - 2722, WINTER PARK, FL 32789-4499
PHONE: 407-646-2405 • FAX: 407-646-2522
E-MAIL: MBAADMISSIONS@ROLLINS.EDU • WEBSITE: WWW.ROLLINS.EDU/MBA

Student Life and Environment

The "beautiful campus" is situated in the historic city of Winter Park in sunny Florida, knocking a level of stress off of life immediately. As ages of students range from mid-twenties to early forties, "this brings many different perspectives" and there is an "even mix of competitive students and 'average' students" who "can all communicate openly." Cohorts tend to be tight-knit, and, as each program is team-centric and presentation-based, students continue with the same team throughout their entire tenure at the school and "form a family-like bond."

Many of the Executive MBA students are only present on Saturdays, while the other two programs tend to spend more time with classmates in both work and social environments when projects allow. "The quality of life and balance between my work and personal life is fantastic," says one student of the workload. "It's very comparable to anine to five workload, which is good preparation for the business world." There are "so many clubs that you want to be a part of, there just aren't enough hours in the day."

Admissions

Applicants to Crummer's MBA program must provide the school with the following: official transcripts for all undergraduate, graduate, and professional schoolwork; an official GMAT or GRE score report; statement of purpose; two confidential evaluations; and a résumé. Interviews are conducted only at the school's invitation. Applicants to the Executive MBA program must meet all of the above requirements (though GMAT scores are only needed conditionally for some), in addition to a required interview and a proof of support from their employers is strongly encouraged.

FINANCIAL FACTS

Annual tuition (in-state/ out-of-state)	$35,600/$35,600
Fees	$240
Cost of books	$1,310
Room & board (on/off-campus)	/$18,010
% of students receiving aid	65
% of first-year students receiving aid	64
% of students receiving grants	58
Average award package	$26,082
Average grant	$26,128
Average loan	$27,855
Average student loan debt	$54,744

ADMISSIONS

Admissions Selectivity Rating	85
# of applications received	269
% applicants accepted	57
% acceptees attending	73
Average GMAT	552
Range of GMAT	480–600
Accepts GRE scores	Yes
TOEFL required of international students	Yes
Minimum TOEFL (paper/web)	600/100
Application fee	$0
International application fee	$0
Application Deadline/Notification	
Round 1:	2/1 /
Round 2:	5/1 /
Round 3:	8/1 /
Deferment available	Yes
Maximum length of deferment	One year
Transfer students accepted	Yes
Transfer application policy	
The school accepts up to 6 credits transferred from an MBA program that is accredited by the AACSB.	
Non-fall admissions	Yes
Need-blind admissions	Yes

EMPLOYMENT PROFILE

Career Rating		80	Grads Employed by Function	% Avg. Salary
Percent employed at graduation		47	Marketing	(32%) $43,375
Percent employed 3 months after graduation		24	Operations	(3%) $41,000
			Consulting	(14%) $58,900
Average base starting salary		$51,191	Management	(11%) $47,667
Primary Source of Full-time Job Acceptances			Finance	(24%) $54,333
School-facilitated activities	21 (57%)		HR	(5%) $66,250
Graduate-facilitated activities	14 (38%)		Other	(11%) $60,000
Unknown	2 (5%)		**Top 5 Employers Hiring Grads**	
			Pearso Online Learning Services (4), Merrill Lynch Bank of Smerica (2), Gartner, Inc. (1), Intel (1), Siemens Energy (1)	

ROTTERDAM SCHOOL OF MANAGEMENT
ERASMUS UNIVERSITY

Academics

Future international business moguls choose Rotterdam School of Mangement, Erasmus University (RSM) for two simple reasons: The school provides "the most international MBA" experience in the world, and Rotterdam is in the heart of the EEC, with "easy access" to Germany and the "EU labor market." RSM provides a "very challenging, positive learning environment," but its intensive twelve-month MBA program is not for the faint of heart. The "workload is heavy," and the curriculum is front-loaded (students take eleven general management courses in the first two semesters). During this period, the day "starts at 9:00 A.M. with classes and ends at 7:00 P.M. with some group work or . . . [an] assignment." Overworked students take comfort in the fact that their professors are "excellent! They clearly enjoy teaching their subject matters, and because they are from all over the world, we get different perspectives in class." Students also point out that "the small class size means we have more opportunities to form close relationships with the program staff." During the third semester, students choose an advanced course from one of four areas of specialization (finance, marketing, or strategy). The final semester is an elective curriculum. All academic work in residency at RSM is conducted in English.

With one eye trained on the executive job market and the other on skill development and business knowledge, Rotterdam is what "b-school should be"; that is, "practical and academic at the same time." The Personal Leadership Development program, a mandatory twelve-month experiential course, adds additional value. One student sums it up: "In hindsight I would not have gone to any other business school. RSM offers the right balance of soft and hard skills." "The school [also] has a strong sense of social responsibility." "I am now equipped to be a stronger and more sensitive businessperson," writes one satisfied student.

Career and Placement

RSM MBAs can look forward to bright and lucrative careers. While the school is responsible for connecting students with optional internships and half of post-MBA jobs, students also find significant career opportunities within an ever growing alumni network and elsewhere. Companies recruiting at RSM include ING Bank, ABN Amro, Johnson & Johnson, Deloitte, Amazon, AT Kearney. Top recruiters of 2014 are FMO, Microsoft, Cargill, Heineken, D.E. Master Blenders , Shell, Emerson, IBM, Tata Consultancy Services, and Philips. The main goal of career services is to facilitate progress towards the best suitable job after graduation.

Student Life and Environment

RSM "students form a strong and very connected group," students say. "Everyone is automatically a member of every club. It's your responsibility to contribute as much or as little to the events. For example, though you may not be in any entrepreneurial courses, you are automatically invited to [hear] every entrepreneurial speaker on campus. And once you arrive, you are welcome in the room." The collegial atmosphere is "perfect and wonderful," says one MBA candidate. "I'd like to go back to the first semester and to start again." Even so, students are "extremely driven." "Almost half want to be entrepreneurs or have owned businesses." RSM's "inspiring and challenging" students don't shrink from competition or from giving "positive and constructive criticism."

Diversity is no afterthought here—it's the reason MBA candidates choose RSM. Students say that the "international perspective was a big draw. Several other [schools] claimed to be international, but mostly had over 50 percent from one or two backgrounds." RSM, on the other hand, "has fifty nationalities and only small clusters from the same backgrounds." This means that students learn "a lot from classmates," and "there is no ruling racial group in our class." "It is just great!" enthuses one student. "A mix of cultures brings so many good things out of each student that it is almost like magic. The amount of kindness that I've experienced is just overwhelming." Demographically speaking, a preponderance of the students are European and Asian, with large Indian and Taiwanese communities; the average student is in his or her late twenties, with an undergraduate background in business or economics and more than five years of pre-MBA work experience. A quarter of MBA candidates are women. Partners and spouses "have banded together" to form "a supportive network," "and routinely have nights out on the town."

Admissions

RSM follows a personal approach to admissions which means they only encourage candidate with potential to apply—good news to the self-selected pool of MBA candidates whose passion for international business and culture brings them to RSM. Admission is no cakewalk—successful applicants report an average GMAT score of 655 and a minimum of three years' work experience—but the numbers give good reason for optimism. The most recent application requires essays on career goals, hobbies and interests, and difficult decisions—slightly more personal topics than appear on American applications. Submit translations of your academic transcripts if they are written in languages other than English, and prepare for an interview if you make the first cut. Admission is rolling.

FINANCIAL FACTS

Annual tuition	$50,750/
Fees	$65
Cost of books	$1,600
Room & board	$18,000
% of first-year students receiving aid	51
Average award package	$25,167
Average grant	$12,368
Average loan	$35,379
Average student loan debt	$48,882

ADMISSIONS

Admissions Selectivity Rating	74
Average GMAT	655
Accepts GRE scores	Yes
Deferment available	No
Transfer students accepted	No
Non-fall admissions	Yes
Need-blind admissions	Yes

EMPLOYMENT PROFILE

Career Rating	91	Grads Employed by Function% Avg. Salary	
Percent employed at graduation	61	Marketing	(32%) $81,596
Percent employed 3 months after graduation	82	Operations	(4%) $50,688
		Consulting	(28%) $94,926
Average base starting salary	$86,163	Management	(10%) $71,884
Primary Source of Full-time Job Acceptances		Finance	(23%) $113,379
School-facilitated activities	47 (68%)	Other	(4%) $119,469
Graduate-facilitated activities	22 (32%)		

Top 5 Employers Hiring Grads
Deloitte (3), Tata Consultancy Services (3), Stanley Security Solutions Europe & Black and Decker (3), Philips (2), Shell (2)

ROWAN UNIVERSITY
THE ROHRER COLLEGE OF BUSINESS

GENERAL INFORMATION
Type of school   Public
Affiliation   No Affiliation

SURVEY SAYS...
Cutting-edge classes
Solid preparation in:
Communication/interpersonal skills,
Presentation skills

STUDENTS
Enrollment of parent
    institution   14,778
Enrollment of MBA Program   107

ACADEMICS
Academic Experience Rating   **73**
Profs interesting rating   62
Profs accessible rating   64
Student/faculty ratio   17:1

Joint Degrees
MBA/DO 5 years

Academics

Offering "a good location, good tuition, and good environment" in the Philadelphia area (and, thanks to the recent addition of online classes, beyond), Rowan University's Rohrer College of Business MBA program delivers what local students want. As one such student explains, "The school has a good ranking within schools in the Northeast and has a tuition rate that could not be matched by comparably ranked schools. Short of someone else paying for my education, it was the best value, period."

Part-time students love the flexible scheduling at Rowan. Classes meet for three hours once a week (typically on a weeknight, although some courses meet on Saturday mornings). The program is available online, further enhancing the convenience of the program. The curriculum commences with twenty-seven hours of required core courses covering fundamental general management skills. The curriculum also leaves room for nine hours of electives; students may choose to take a variety of courses that match their career needs or may use these courses to specialize in finance, accounting, management, marketing, supply chain and logistical systems, or management information systems. Part-time students typically take between three to six years to complete their MBAs here. Those enrolled full-time have the option of completing the program in a single year.

Students love "the small size" of Rowan's MBA program, reporting that it increases "the accessibility of the professors." As one student tells us, "Every professor I have had you could email them a question about the course, and get a solid answer within a day usually." Administrators earn similarly high marks. One student notes, "I have had nothing but a pleasant experience at Rowan, even when I had a family emergency. The faculty and staff were very understanding and accommodating and allowed me to work around the days I needed to provide care for a relative."

Career and Placement

Rowan maintains a Career Management Center "to provide developmental advising" to all students in their pursuit of academic and professional goals. The CMC serves the entire school; there is no office dedicated specifically to MBAs or to business students on the undergraduate and graduate levels. CMC Services include one-on-one counseling, workshops, online self-assessment and job databases (like Experience), career publications, and employer directories. Services are available to alumni as well as to current students. It should be noted that most current students are full-time workers looking to advance within their current places of work; relatively few students seeking MBAs at Rowan are actively searching for new jobs. Those in the job market tell us that Rowan's small size "is a strength" when it comes to academics, "while at the same time it is a weakness when it comes to companies that recruit at the school."

ADMISSIONS CONTACT: JAMES JORDAN, MBA PROGRAM DIRECTOR
ADDRESS: BUNCE HALL, 201 MULLICA HILL ROAD, GLASSBORO, NJ 08028
PHONE: 856-256-4024 • FAX: 856-256-4439
E-MAIL: GLOBALADMISSIONS@ROWAN.EDU • WEBSITE: WWW.ROWAN.EDU/MBA

Student Life and Environment

Rowan's MBA program "is meant for both part-time and full-time students," with the majority attending part time, usually while also managing full-time jobs. On-campus activities "are meant for people who live on campus," which means that they are directed at undergraduates. "On-campus stuff [does not apply] to most MBAs at Rowan, since they are for the most part commuters or from the South Jersey area." Residents and non-residents alike warn that parking on or near campus can be a challenge.

Rowan's suburban New Jersey hometown of Glassboro is a mere half-hour's drive from Philadelphia; the Jersey shore is less than an hour to the east, and Atlantic City is only 50 miles away. New York, Washington, D.C., and the Chesapeake are all within easy commuting distances. All of this adds up to opportunity. To prove it, the Rowan campus is in the midst of an ambitious expansion program, with makeovers planned for most facilities and several new buildings going up, including a new building for the College of Business. Students praise the new athletic center and enjoy watching Rowan's excellent Division III men's and women's basketball teams.

Most Rowan MBAs "are in their upper twenties to upper thirties with very diverse backgrounds and experience[s]."

Admissions

Rowan's graduate business school students are required to complete nine foundation courses in accounting, statistics, principles of finance, principles of marketing, calculus, operations management, and economics. Students who have successfully completed equivalent courses at the undergraduate level may place out of these foundation classes. Applicants to the MBA program must submit official transcripts for all undergraduate work (with a minimum GPA of 2.5 overall), GMAT or GRE scores, two letters of recommendation, a personal statement of career objectives, and a resume. International students whose first language is not English must also provide TOEFL scores (minimum required score: 79 iBT, 550 written exam, 213 computer-based exam).

FINANCIAL FACTS

Cost of books	$1,000

ADMISSIONS

Admissions Selectivity Rating	**81**
# of applications received	61
% applicants accepted	61
Average GMAT	522
Accepts GRE scores	Yes
Average GPA	3.3
TOEFL required of international students	Yes
Minimum TOEFL (paper/web)	550/79
Application fee	$65
International application fee	$65
Application Deadline/Notification	
Deferment available	Yes
Maximum length of deferment	1 year
Transfer students accepted	Yes
Transfer application policy Students may transfer up to 9 credit hours.	
Non-fall admissions	Yes
Need-blind admissions	Yes

RUTGERS, THE STATE UNIVERSITY OF NEW JERSEY
RUTGERS BUSINESS SCHOOL—NEWARK AND NEW BRUNSWICK

GENERAL INFORMATION

Type of school	Public
Affiliation	No Affiliation
Academic calendar	trimester

SURVEY SAYS...
Cutting-edge classes
Solid preparation in:
Teamwork, Communication/interpersonal skills, Presentation skills

STUDENTS

Enrollment of parent institution	50,000
Enrollment of MBA Program	1,239
% male/female	61/39
% out-of-state	12
% part-time	81
% underrepresented minority	8
% international	27
Average age at entry	28
Average years work experience at entry	5

ACADEMICS

Academic Experience Rating	**80**
Profs interesting rating	73
Profs accessible rating	72
Student/faculty ratio	3:1
% female faculty	34
% underrepresented minority faculty	62
% part-time faculty	174

Joint Degrees
BA/MBA, 5-6 yrs; BS/MBA, 5-6 yrs; MPH/MBA, 3 yrs; MD/MBA, 5 yrs; JD/MBA, 4 yrs; MS/MBA in Biomedical Sciences, 2.5 yrs; MPP/MBA, 3 yrs; MCRP/MBA, 3 yrs.

Prominent Alumni
Thomas A. Renyi (MBA '68), Chairman & CEO, The Bank of New York Mellon; Gary M. Cohen (MBA '83), President, BD Medical (Becton, Dickinson and Co.); Irwin M. Lerner, Retired Chairman of the Board, Hoffmann-La Roche; Nicholas J. Valeriani, Worldwide Chairman, Johnson & Johnson; Ralph Izzo, President & CEO, PSEG

Academics

With campuses in New Brunswick and Newark, many choose Rutgers Business School because it offers "the very best combination of quality and cost." The fact that it is "more affordable than private schools in the NY area" makes it attractive to many when coupled with its "solid reputation." Strengths include the top ranked Supply Chain Management and Pharmaceutical Management programs (the pharmaceutical industry is thriving in New Jersey, so job prospects abound), as well as strong Marketing and Finance programs. "Some Finance professors are even better than those at Ivy Leagues," one student enthused. "I'm pleasantly surprised and thankful not to get into any Ivy League, where the cost-benefit tradeoff would have been negative."

Professors are described as "hit or miss," but most agree that their teachers fall under the category of "hit," with students praising their "engaging, challenging, and thought provoking curriculum." They are happy to find their professors "have real hands-on experience in the class they teach and are very interested in educating us on their material" and describe them as educators who "do not simply teach, [but also] mentor, offer career advice, and share career opportunities that match with students interests." However, while professors are generally praised, many students complain about a "sorely understaffed" administration, which "can be a red tape nightmare." Overall though, students find them to be "accessible and genuinely concerned with [their] success"

Career and Placement

The MBA program is seen as offering strong inroads to a post-school career. The Supply Chain Management and Pharmaceutical Management programs at Rutgers not only win high praise; they draw in "guest speakers from the pharmaceutical industry" among many others. It is "pretty well known and a lot of companies do recruit from the school, such as Johnson and Johnson," as well as Newark-based Prudential. Some students suggest the school "should make more connections with the large financial institutions in the New York City area," claiming a lack of strong recruitment. The same criticism is aired about opportunities coming out of their marketing department.

Students will not have to work alone in making connections. An "excellent" career services department will "help you with resumes, cover letters and mock interviews," along with soliciting feedback from companies after your interviews. The Office of Career Management will "go to great lengths to bring top companies to recruit on campus and readily go to bat for students who seek positions at companies that would normally only recruit from Ivy League schools." Add to that a "strong alumni network" and a Small Business Development Center, which "helps entrepreneurs prepare business plans and start their own businesses," and students are given excellent preparation for post-school success.

Student Life and Environment

Campus life is rarely relevant for MBA students; for them, "it's a commuter's lifestyle." Though Rutgers boasts "a very large campus with a lot of activities," offering "many clubs and organizations to join and ... a lot of career fairs where companies will recruit," MBA students will find that the commuter lifestyle "doesn't lend well to a strong social network, because people tend to be on campus only for classes." That said, for those on campus, "Rutgers Business School has a congenial environment where everyone is very approachable." Even part-time students "still feel a part of the community." Whether full-time or part-time, "both groups are professional and competitive," a group who are "very driven and are very inspired academically." Working students come from varied career backgrounds—and that is seen as a positive. "As we have different professional backgrounds the contributions made during class are very informative." That said, some complain that the school's curved grading policy "does not encourage the sharing of ideas and help" since "everyone is competing for the same grade of A and the rest of just placed on the curve."

Part-time students are "usually focused on their current careers and applying classroom learning to work situations (and vice versa)," while full-time students "have more time to socialize and to network." This gives the latter "more opportunities to meet people from the industry or recruiters, and to apply for internships, Leadership Development Programs etc." Some say students here "do not team well, they are only concerned with collecting a grade and degree," but that is a minority opinion. Most suggest the student body is "respectful" and "friendly," even "when we have disagreement within class discussions. We respect each other."

Admissions

The programs admissions office resides on the Newark campus. However, students can chose their home campus as either Newark, New Brunswick, Madison, or Jersey City. Students are required to finish their degree at either Newark or New Brunswick. Students must apply to the campus at which they hope to attend—but take note that the full-time program is available only at the Newark campus. There are no minimum GMAT score requirements or GPA requirements, and a specific academic background is not required, but at least two years of professional work experience is strongly recommended. Interviews are not always part of the admissions process, but they may be requested of MBA candidates.

FINANCIAL FACTS

Annual tuition (in-state/ out-of-state)	$23,630/$40,628
Fees	$2,545
Cost of books	$5,000
Room & board (on/off-campus)	$14,000/$15,000
Average award package	$42,500
Average grant	$10,683
Average student loan debt	$42,500

ADMISSIONS

Admissions Selectivity Rating	89
# of applications received	352
% applicants accepted	42
% acceptees attending	52
Average GMAT	637
Range of GMAT	580–710
Accepts GRE scores	Yes
Average Verbal GRE	157
Range of Verbal GRE scores	152–160
Average Quantitative GRE	155
Range of Quantitative GRE scores	152–159
Average GPA	3.3
TOEFL required of international students	Yes
Minimum TOEFL (paper/web)	600/100
Application fee	$73
International application fee	$73
Application Deadline/Notification	
Round 1:	1/20 / 2/20
Round 2:	3/15 / 4/15
Round 3:	5/1 / 5/29
Deferment available	Yes
Maximum length of deferment	1 Year
Transfer students accepted	Yes
Transfer application policy	
Flex students may transfer a maximum of 12 applicable core credits earned at an AACSB-accredited MBA program, with a grade of "B" or better, taken within 5 years	
Non-fall admissions	Yes
Need-blind admissions	Yes

EMPLOYMENT PROFILE

Career Rating	92	**Grads Employed by Function**	**%**	**Avg. Salary**
Percent employed at graduation	75	Marketing	(36%)	$96,658
Percent employed 3 months after graduation	95	Operations	(26%)	$78,871
		Consulting	(11%)	$77,833
Average base starting salary	$86,647	Finance	(25%)	$81,828
Primary Source of Full-time Job Acceptances		Other	(2%)	$100,000
School-facilitated activities	36 (60%)	**Top 5 Employers Hiring Grads**		
Graduate-facilitated activities	24 (40%)	Bayer (4), Johnson & Johnson Family of Companies (7), Panasonic (3), Dell (3), Quest Diagnostics (3)		

RUTGERS, THE STATE UNIVERSITY OF NEW JERSEY—CAMDEN
SCHOOL OF BUSINESS

GENERAL INFORMATION
Type of school   Public
Affiliation   No Affiliation
Academic calendar   Semester

SURVEY SAYS...
Happy students
Solid preparation in:
Finance, Operations, Presentation
skills

STUDENTS
Enrollment of parent
  institution   65,000
Enrollment of MBA Program   157
% male/female   36/64
% out-of-state   5
% part-time   88
% underrepresented minority   37
% international   3
Average age at entry   30
Average years work
  experience at entry   6

ACADEMICS
Academic Experience Rating   83
Profs interesting rating   92
Profs accessible rating   94

Joint Degrees
MBA/JD, 117 credits, 4-7 years;
MBA/MD, 5-6 years.

Prominent Alumni
Tony D'Alessandro, Vive President/
CIO, Avantor Performance; Thomas
Cellucci, Chief Commericalization
Officer, Dep tof Homeland Security;
David Tilton, President, Atlantic
Care Regional Medical center;
Arthur Hicks, President, Cybex
International; Stuart Hill, Vice
President, Hill International

Academics

Rutgers, The State University of New Jersey-Camden, or "Rutgers-Camden," boasts a "strong brand name through research literature," and "caters to part-time returning students" predominantly in South Jersey, Philadelphia and other parts of the Delaware Valley. In addition to enjoying a "good reputation," students at this business school repeatedly cite Rutgers-Camden's "location, location, location," owing to the school's "close proximity" to nearby cities like Philadelphia, New York, and Washington, D.C., not to mention its "proximity to home" for many working, part-time students. "This school has a good mix of students," one MBA student informs us. "Some are older and in professional careers— physicians, CPAs, lawyers, and engineers. Some are analysts looking to move into management, and some students are in the MBA/JD program going to school full-time." Among those students enrolled in the joint MBA/JD program, the general consensus is that Rutgers-Camden is "a respected institution in the legal community."

For students enrolled in the MBA program alone, they can expect to complete their twelve foundational and forty-two required credits within two to four years, while dual-degree students in the MBA/JD and MBA/MD joint programs can expect to complete their degree in three years. Degree programs and concentrations in the following are offered: finance, international business and operations, management, marketing, and entrepreneurs. Study-abroad programs in France, Brazil, and South Africa are also offered. The school also offers two new Masters programs: the Professional Master of Business Administration (PMBA), an accelerated twenty-one-month lock-step, cohort-based program for working professionals; and the Professional Master of Accountancy (PMAc) program, an accelerated sixteen-month lock-step, cohort-based program for participants with a broad background in accounting and business who want to develop their careers in other areas. The school also offers a fully online MBA degree—the Rutgers Online MBA.

The thirty-four faculty members at Rutgers-Camden are described as "knowledgeable," "flexible," and "responsive" to students' needs. Additionally, the professors "bring interesting life and work experiences to the classroom." One procurement specialist informs us that, "I attended Rutgers for my undergrad degree in Business Management," and "the professors are what brought me back" for the MBA program. As one student notes, "they are very good at using different teaching methods—group projects, in-class discussions, and resources beyond the text book." Considering that many students arrive at Rutgers-Camden with a solid resume in hand, it's particularly beneficial that, according to one accounting major, the professors "value your work experience." However, some students have informed us when it comes to the overall quality of faculty, it can be "hit or miss." While on the one hand, "some are engaging and have worked in the private sector before teaching, others are bookworms with no teaching ability or private sector experience." But this same student concedes, "I guess in a way it is good to have both types." According to one recent MBA graduate, "The caliber of this School's professors and administration help to make Rutgers-Camden an absolutely amazing value considering its relatively low tuition."

Career and Placement

The Career Services office at Rutgers-Camden, like that of any reputable business school, offers a wide array of resources for graduating students. In addition to the 100 plus companies who offer internships during the fall and spring, more than twenty or so companies regularly recruit summer interns each year, in addition to the twenty or so companies who regularly recruit summer interns each year. According to recent data, full-time students who found employment within 3 months of graduating enjoy a mean base salary of nearly $59,000. Although Rutgers-Camden has a favorable reputation among business schools, it very much remains a "local" institution, and "close to home" for most of its students. This is evidenced by the fact that approximately 80 percent of full-time MBA graduates accepted employment in the Northeast, and the remaining 20 percent went to Mid-Atlantic states. A vocal minority informs us that "Career Services are awful." However, not many students second this sentiment. More than adequate "job placement resources" are used by the student body, and as one satisfied student specializing in marketing research tells us, "marketing and database marketing are superior classes that offer hands-on learning and focus on the job market."

Student Life and Environment

The student body at Rutgers-Camden has been described as a "multicultural mix of both recent undergrads and very seasoned professionals." But one important thing for prospective students of Rutgers-Camden to keep in mind is that "many students enrolled in the MBA program are working professionals, and take classes part time." This factors in to how Rutgers-Camden caters to its student body. As one corporate communications major tells us, "classes are offered in the evenings, and occasionally on weekends or online," although the MBA program itself is not offered online. She continues, "I find that there is a lack of camaraderie among students, because many of us are only on campus one-two nights a week, have full-time jobs, and some also have families." By and large, "it is difficult for most of the MBA population to dedicate a lot of time to extracurricular activities," although "some students do socialize at a weekly 'Thirsty Thursday' event," and generally speaking, "there is availability to participate in clubs." Rutgers-Camden also happens to be situated in the heart of Camden, right "next to public transportation, so you have the option to drive or take the train," whether you are commuting to and from home, or looking to enjoy some of the night life in Philadelphia, which is just across the river from Camden.

Above all, students have informed us that this is a place to work and to be among "friendly, hard-working people trying to advance their careers and knowledge." Camden is a comfortable environment in which to do this, but for most students at Rutgers-Camden, clearly the work comes first. Diversity in the classroom is also important to many students, as they feel this translates well into the professional realm. As one JD-MBA student tells us, "My fellow students are a very a very diverse group, who run the gamut from single, foreign-exchange students, to single parents working full-time, to reservist, to the older married family-oriented types, employed and unemployed alike."

Admissions

Applicants to the Rutgers-Camden MBA program must submit the following: an online application (via the school's website), academic transcripts from undergrad and graduate (if applicable) institutions, essay/personal statement, two letters of recommendation, GMAT scores (this requirement is waived for applicants with a Ph.D., JD, or MD degree from an accredited U.S. institution), and a current resume (optional, but highly recommended for those applicants with work experience). Prospective students should keep in mind that, among the admissions requirements, Rutgers-Camden places great emphasis on GMAT scores, undergraduate GPA, and work experience. International applicants are required to submit a TOEFL score of 230 (computer based test) or 550 (written test). These applicants must also submit a Financial Statement Documentation (available on the school's website).

FINANCIAL FACTS

Annual tuition (in-state/ out-of-state)	$22,544/$38,239
Fees	$2,495
Room & board (on/off campus)	$12,750/$18,090
% of students receiving aid	70
% of first-year students receiving aid	75
% of students receiving grants	17
Average award package	$20,393
Average grant	$8,028
Average loan	$21,478

ADMISSIONS

Admissions Selectivity Rating	78
# of applications received	61
% applicants accepted	38
% acceptees attending	27
Average GMAT	560
Range of GMAT	460–669
Accepts GRE scores	Yes
Average Verbal GRE	150
Range of Verbal GRE scores	149–165
Average Quantitative GRE	152
Range of Quantitative GRE scores	148–165
Average GPA	3.2
TOEFL required of international students	Yes
Minimum TOEFL (paper/web)	550/79
Application fee	$65
Deferment available	Yes
Maximum length of deferment	1 semester
Transfer students accepted	Yes
Transfer application policy Students must complete at least 36 credits in our program. We will transfer courses from AACSB-accredited schools with a grade of B or better.	
Non-fall admissions	Yes
Need-blind admissions	Yes

EMPLOYMENT PROFILE

Career Rating	77	**Top 5 Employers Hiring Grads**
Average base starting salary	$58,812	Lockheed Martin (1), Campbells Soup (3), Deloitte & Touche (1), JP Morgan Chase (1), Computer Sciences Coporation (1)

SACRED HEART UNIVERSITY
JOHN F. WELCH COLLEGE OF BUSINESS

Academics

The imprimatur of Jack Welch, former CEO of General Electric, impresses many MBAs at Sacred Heart University. "I'm a big fan of Jack Welch," one current student tells us; "the name Welch being attached to the school will hopefully bring much more recognition," another adds hopefully. The GE connection isn't lost on students either; the fact that the program "is held in high regard by GE in Connecticut," where many of these graduates will eventually seek employment, is a key factor in their decision to pursue the Welch MBA.

Sacred Heart is not merely relying on a famous name to attract and satisfy students. In 2009, the school introduced a new curriculum that begins with a fixed integrated core curriculum that "is very applicable to the real world" and culminates in concentration work in accounting, finance, marketing, or management. Students note that "the new Welch MBA format has been a monumental task to get rolling" and commend "the staff and professors [who] go above and beyond to make sure each student is heard and prepared for the tasks at hand." They call the new curriculum "an interesting and exciting new take on the traditional MBA" with a "dynamic new format [that] is very interesting and keeps us on our toes!" The program "fully embraces the fast-paced changes of the modern world" and "trains students to be more than analytical" in order to produce "effective leaders and decision makers, ready to go."

Students commend "the breadth and depth of knowledge of the faculty" at Welch, calling their teachers an "outstanding group of professors with diverse backgrounds to teach various aspects of the business world. Their skills and knowledge in their particular subject is outstanding and…[set within] today's business world." Because "the school is not too large," students benefit from "the opportunity to get to know one another" and their teachers in the classroom. Through an international MBA in Luxembourg offering concentrations in finance and general management, Welch students have the opportunity to undertake internships in finance, marketing, international business and information technology in Luxembourg.

Career and Placement

SHU's Office of Career Development offers a range of services to MBA students. Staff members provide assistance with resume creation and critique; conduct seminars on interview skills; maintain online job postings; and organize on-campus job fairs and interview sessions. The office hired a full-time Assistant Director whose primary focus is on MBA student internships and job placement. During a recent academic school year, 105 employers attended the school's annual career fair and nineteen employers interviewed on campus, including PricewaterhouseCoopers, General Electric, Target, Ernst & Young, Sikorsky, KPMG, and Legg Mason.

Student Life and Environment

"Most students are commuters who hold jobs during the day" at Welch, although "the students who come directly from undergraduate work appear to do a lot together." MBAs agree that in its current manifestation, the school's extracurricular life "is mainly geared towards the full-time undergraduates (concerts, clubs, student activities, sports). The graduate schools tend to just focus on classes and not student life." However, they also note that "the business school is just starting to survey its students about how we want help: network with alumni and other community leaders [versus] speakers, etc." That bodes well for the future. For now, though, "if you are not already a part of the university via undergrad work or currently working at the school, there is a major gap between the university and its graduate students."

The student body is a mix of seasoned professionals and freshly minted BAs. The older students "are personable and knowledgeable without being 'know-it-alls.'" All students in the program enjoy a "strong sense of collegiality and collaboration."

Admissions

Applicants to the MBA program at SHU's Welch College of Business must submit the following materials: a completed online application; official transcripts from all undergraduate institutions attended (showing a minimum 3.0 cumulative GPA); a personal statement of career and academic goals and a summary of relevant business experience; two letters of recommendation; a current professional resume; and an official GMAT score report (applicants with at least two years professional work experience must score a minimum of 400; for all others, the minimum score is 500). International applicants, including applicants to the MBA program in Luxembourg, must submit transcripts in English; foreign language transcripts must be translated and analyzed by an approved professional service. Applicants whose first language is not English (except those with a degree from an English-language institution) must submit an official score report for the TOEFL or IELTS. Students should anticipate at least a three month wait in the issuance of student visas for the Luxembourg program. The Luxembourg program runs approximately nine six-week sessions per year; students may apply for admission and begin the program during any session. The Fairfield campus operates on a trimester calendar.

FINANCIAL FACTS

Cost of books	$1,500
Room & board	$15,900
% of students receiving aid	30
% of first-year students receiving aid	9
% of students receiving grants	0
Average award package	$17,257
Average grant	$0
Average loan	$17,257
Average student loan debt	$25,605

ADMISSIONS

Admissions Selectivity Rating	**86**
# of applications received	159
% applicants accepted	50
% acceptees attending	70
Average GMAT	501
Range of GMAT	440–530
Accepts GRE scores	Yes
Average GPA	3.3
TOEFL required of international students	Yes
Minimum TOEFL (paper/web)	570/80
Application fee	$75
International application fee	$75
Early application deadline	2/15
Application Deadline/Notification	
Deferment available	Yes
Maximum length of deferment	1 year
Transfer students accepted	Yes
Transfer application policy Transferred credits are reviewed by the Program Director.	
Non-fall admissions	Yes
Need-blind admissions	Yes

SAGINAW VALLEY STATE UNIVERSITY

COLLEGE OF BUSINESS AND MANAGEMENT

GENERAL INFORMATION

Type of school	Public
Affiliation	No Affiliation
Academic calendar	year round

SURVEY SAYS...

Happy students
Solid preparation in:
Teamwork, Presentation skills, Doing business in a global economy

STUDENTS

Enrollment of parent institution	10,245
Enrollment of MBA Program	131
% male/female	63/37
% out-of-state	0
% part-time	49
% underrepresented minority	8
% international	76
Average age at entry	29

ACADEMICS

Academic Experience Rating	**82**
Profs interesting rating	87
Profs accessible rating	86
Student/faculty ratio	12:1
% female faculty	13
% underrepresented minority faculty	13
% part-time faculty	0

Academics

Saginaw Valley State University, located in University Center, Michigan, just outside of Saginaw, appeals to many prospective students because of its "good reputation," "large number of international students," "fair tuition," and "accredited program." Factors such as "small class size" and the fact that SVSU is "close to home" are also received well by a large portion of the student body. According to one student, "I was looking for a different perspective than the one I received while getting my BBA at the University of Michigan—one that considers small business." A solid faculty and administrative staff help provide these different perspectives. Like any other accredited graduate institution, students' feedback indicates that some professors are "great," while "others are horrible." But as one sales and marketing students tells us, "the professors and administration staff continue to teach and learn business practices that shape the students of the MBA program. They have consistently encouraged effective teamwork, communication, entrepreneurialism, and globalization." "Administration has made things very easy for most MBA candidates," another student assures us, and overall are "pretty supportive when you have other work requirements," such as a full-time job in addition to your studies.

The online component, in combination with onsite classes (or "hybrid format"), is something many students consider beneficial for their learning needs. While SVSU has a "surrounding environment that is good for studying," the offering of "eight-week courses in hybrid format" is an "affordable" and "convenient" option for students who cannot commit to full-time, on-campus study. Additionally, all core courses are offered in the hybrid format. The hybrid format, however, is something several students have expressed hesitation toward. According to one student, "ninety-five percent of your time must be on campus." Another student has suggested that, "maybe weekend classes could be offered, and more fully online courses, as well."

SVSU offers degree programs and concentrations in accounting, economics, entrepreneurship, finance, international business, leadership/management, and marketing. An elective course in sustainability practices is also offered, which explores and analyzes the use, development, and implementation of alternate energy strategies for sustainable business projects.

Cost-effectiveness is also something many SVSU students praise and makes the school particularly appealing for recent undergrads looking to pursue graduate work without the hassle of relocating. One newly enrolled MBA candidate tells us, "I completed my undergraduate degree in electrical engineering at SVSU and had a good experience while there. Furthermore, the cost of the MBA at SVSU is significantly cheaper than elsewhere." Compared to the estimated "$80,000 to complete your degree at U of Michigan," a similar degree from SVSU will run you about "$20,000," and "both degrees are accredited."

ADMISSIONS CONTACT: DR. MARK MCCARTNEY, MBA DIRECTOR
ADDRESS: 7400 BAY ROAD, UNIVERSITY CENTER, MI 48710
PHONE: 989-964-4064 • FAX: 989-964-7497
E-MAIL: CBMDEAN@SVSU.EDU • WEBSITE: WWW.SVSU.EDU/CBM

Career and Placement

SVSU's Career Planning and Placement Office regularly hosts on-campus interviews, career fairs, and resume building workshops. A bevy of internships, available to SVSU students and graduates, are also coordinated through the Office. Among the provided services, students have noted the Office's concern with testing students' aptitude to gauge proper career placement, but as one science research major tells us, this practice should be lessened, and the administration should be more focused on "finding you gainful employment." The general consensus among the students who provided feedback is that career services at SVSU could do with significant improvement. Both "alumni relations and job placement" are particular areas that students have expressed concern over, and according to one student, the career fairs are attended by "companies that aren't hiring, or they won't talk to you and just direct you to their websites."

Student Life and Environment

As a relatively new school within the Michigan state college system, SVSU has a decent-sized campus (750 acres) and a surrounding area with much to offer. As one sales and marketing major puts it, SVSU has a "small-town feel mixed with big-town academics and accreditation." This does help cultivate an "atmosphere that is ideal for learning and developing professional business skills." On the whole, the school and its administration appear most concerned with catering to a working and career-oriented student body. One satisfied student informs us that, "SVSU MBA students are all working students; even the international students for the most part have jobs." While this type of environment is beneficial for most looking to juggle responsibilities and advance their careers, "this offers a challenge for group activities." For those students with the time and inclination, the school "provides an excellent gym and lots of extracurricular activities. There are also several clubs, such as the International Student Club, Chess Club, and Math Club."

For MBA candidates seeking a place where they can supplement their working lives with night classes, SVSU is very "accommodating." Some students have expressed a need for improvement when it comes to international students. One student in particular had this to say: "They should have a specific officer to help us international students to be easier involved in the University culture." On-campus support offices are also available for various students groups, including minorities, international students, women, and LGBT groups.

Admissions

Applicants to the MBA program at Saginaw Valley State University must submit the following: official undergraduate transcript, essay/personal statement, and two letters of recommendation. Students must provide GMAT scores or complete an alternative internal MBA entrance exam. The minimum acceptable GMAT score is 450. A resume is optional as well, but for those applicants with significant work experience and less than stellar test scores should consider off-setting one with the other. International students are required to submit TOEFL scores, with the following minimum scores: 550 for written test, 213 for computer-based test, and 79 for web-based test.

FINANCIAL FACTS

Annual tuition (in-state/ out-of-state)	$8,956/$16,847
Fees	$262
Cost of books	$1,220
Room & board (on/off-campus)	$9,538/$11,622
% of students receiving aid	53
% of first-year students receiving aid	62
% of students receiving grants	34
Average award package	$12,922
Average grant	$9,689
Average loan	$15,428

ADMISSIONS

Admissions Selectivity Rating	77
# of applications received	105
% applicants accepted	89
% acceptees attending	32
Average GMAT	475
Range of GMAT	465–490
Accepts GRE scores	Yes
Average GPA	3.2
TOEFL required of international students	Yes
Minimum TOEFL (paper/web)	550/79
Application fee	$30
International application fee	$80
Deferment available	Yes
Maximum length of deferment	7 semesters
Transfer students accepted	Yes
Transfer application policy may transfer 6 credits	
Non-fall admissions	Yes
Need-blind admissions	Yes

SAINT JOSEPH'S UNIVERSITY
ERIVAN K. HAUB SCHOOL OF BUSINESS

GENERAL INFORMATION
Type of school	Private
Affiliation	Roman Catholic-Jesuit
Academic calendar	Semesters

SURVEY SAYS...
Friendly students, Happy students
Solid preparation in:
Accounting, General management,
Teamwork, Presentation skills,
Quantitative skills

STUDENTS
Enrollment of parent institution	8,629
Enrollment of MBA Program	497
% male/female	57/43
% out-of-state	21
% part-time	80
% underrepresented minority	13
% international	38
Average age at entry	29
Average years work experience at entry	6

ACADEMICS
Academic Experience Rating	88
Profs interesting rating	89
Profs accessible rating	91
Student/faculty ratio	18:1
% female faculty	21
% underrepresented minority faculty	17
% part-time faculty	37

Joint Degrees
DO/MBA Program w/ Philadelphia
College of Osteopathic Medicine
(2 yrs for MBA component); MBA/
MS Financial Services; MBA/MS
Business Intelligence & Analytics;
MBA/MS Managing Human Capital

Prominent Alumni
Robert J. Caruso, Founder &
Chairman, the Impact Republic
Company; Mark A. Casale,
Chairman, CEO and President of
Essent Group, Ltd.; Michael F.
Erbick, Chief Information Officer &
Senior Vice President IT, Chick-fil-A

Academics

Saint Joseph University's proud "Jesuit tradition" challenges students "intellectual abilities" while providing "a holistic business education." "Saint Joseph's University has a solid academic reputation and offers scheduling flexibility for working students." The Finance program in particular has a "great reputation" especially in the Philadelphia area. SJU has "strong alumni ties in the region" and students love the location in one of America's most famous Eastern cities. Students are very pleased with the "fairly priced" and "reasonable" tuition. "The part time MBA is flexible and recognized," and the school offers the "freedom to attend classes online or on campus." The Jesuit tradition is infused in the culture of SJU, something many students love. "The idea of social responsibility and teaching individuals for the greater good of society is a real focal point," one student declares, "and I think that is something our country needs at the moment."

"Course offerings have been plentiful and variable (allowing the available times to easily fit your work/home schedules)," one Project Management student reports. "Professors and Faculty are excellent," although some complain the administration "sometimes makes questionable decisions related to the quality of students accepted into the program." Others say "the administration is extremely helpful particularly regarding picking classes." "Almost everyone is helpful and informative" and "you can tell the faculty and staff really care and are passionate about the school." Courses at SJU "[integrate] past and present business techniques and concepts." As at many schools, your academic experience "really comes down to which professors you have that make or break your experience." Still, "generally the Professors are well rounded" and "very supportive of students." "So far so good," reports a Business and Finance student. "I am about to begin my third semester and have only great things to say about Saint Joseph's University." Another likens SJU to "the picture of a well-oiled machine" and says "from the moment I showed up at an information session until now, my ninth week of my first semester, every experience has been a positive one."

Career and Placement

"SJU has a great reputation in the Philadelphia area and a strong alumni base," and does a great job of helping students find work in the area. The professors, who "have more than twenty years of industry experience," help create "a good base for a breadth of careers in business." The career development center "serves the entire university and has no department specifically for graduate students" and some students suggest they do not put enough work into placement. Still between the large alumni network, the location in Philadelphia, and "companies recruiting on campus," SJU students tend to find great work in Philadelphia and elsewhere.

ADMISSIONS CONTACT: JEANNINE LAJEUNESSE, MBA, ASSISTANT DIRECTOR
ADDRESS: 5600 CITY AVENUE, MANDEVILLE 284, PHILADELPHIA, PA 19131
PHONE: 888-SJU-MBA-1 • FAX: 610-660-1599
EMAIL: SJUMBA@SJU.EDU • WEBSITE: WWW.SJU.EDU/MBA

Student Life and Environment

SJU "is a warm friendly community" of "mainly working professionals that take class at night. Though some full-time younger students are also involved." Students are "kind," "friendly," "ambitious, and eager to learn something new." Because of this, "conflicts during group projects have been minimal." "As a foreign student with some trouble to understand the US culture and language," one international student says, "I get a lot of help with my patient fellow classmates and professors." The SJU experience will vary depending on if you are a full-time, part-time, or online student. "Life at school allows students to network however due to the part-time nature of the program students try to be as efficient as possible with their time on campus," one student reports. Although the "neighborhood is a little rough," students generally feel safe on campus. One student sums the SJU experience up thusly: "I find that I am comfortable on campus, I feel welcomed, and I absolutely enjoy studying at the library and Post Learning Commons."

Admissions

Saint Joseph's accepts rolling submissions and admits MBA students for spring, fall, and summer terms. Applicants will need to submit the following materials to the school: an official transcript from each undergraduate and graduate institution at which credits were earned; an official GMAT score report (not more than seven years old), GRE is also accepted; two letters of recommendation; a current resume; and a personal statement of 250 to 500 words outlining career objectives and the value of an MBA in reaching those objectives. International applicants must submit all of the following as well as a statement of financial support. International applicants who attended undergraduate institutions at which English was not the language of instruction may have their transcipts translated and interpreted by World Education Service or by SJU. Students whose first language is not English must submit an official TOEFL score report. IELTS or PTE exam are also accepted.

FINANCIAL FACTS

Annual tuition (in-state/ out-of-state)	$17,532/$17,532
Fees	$0
Cost of books	$800
% of students receiving aid	41
% of first-year students receiving aid	66
% of students receiving grants	23
Average award package	$12,559
Average grant	$4,148
Average loan	$17,773

ADMISSIONS

Admissions Selectivity Rating	84
# of applications received	244
% applicants accepted	63
% acceptees attending	68
Average GMAT	516
Range of GMAT	420–590
Accepts GRE scores	Yes
Average Verbal GRE	150
Range of Verbal GRE scores	148–152
Average Quantitative GRE	152
Range of Quantitative GRE scores	148–154
Average GPA	3.2
TOEFL required of international students	Yes
Minimum TOEFL (paper/web)	550/80
Application fee	$35
International application fee	$35
Deferment available	Yes
Maximum length of deferment	1 year
Transfer students accepted	Yes
Transfer application policy	Transfer applicants must provide a completed application including original test scores. A total of 6 credits may be transferred into the program provided the coursework is equivalent to the MBA coursework, a grade of B or higher was earned, and the school is AACSB accredited.
Non-fall admissions	Yes
Need-blind admissions	Yes

EMPLOYMENT PROFILE

Career Rating	72	Grads Employed by Function	% Avg. Salary
		Marketing	(11%) $80,000
		Management	(18%) $101,000
		Finance	(3%) $55,000
		MIS	(12%) $175,000
		Other	(12%) $85,000

SAINT LOUIS UNIVERSITY
JOHN COOK SCHOOL OF BUSINESS

Academics

If there's one pervasive reason that students choose Saint Louis University for their MBAs, it's the school's "impeccable reputation" in the local business community. In practice, students say the program lives up to its solid gold credentials. "The overall academic experience is both challenging and rewarding," combining business theory and real-world practice with a refreshing "ethical consciousness" for the modern workplace. Depending on a student's professional goals, SLU offers two different MBA options, as well as dual-degree programs in law, health administration, medicine, and education. Those who want a quick but professional degree can pursue an MBA through the school's new "full-time, one-year timeline," which runs students through a rigorous interdisciplinary business program over the course of one calendar year. For working professionals, the part-time MBA is "flexible enough to accommodate students with active careers," allowing them to "shape the classes to better fit their needs and interests." "Professors understand the difficulties in working full-time while pursuing an MBA," and administrators "provide outstanding services to part-time MBA students."

Both part-time and full-time students must complete a series of foundation, breadth, and required courses in advanced business topics. After that, the curriculum "allows students to choose an area of emphasis for their MBA" through elective coursework in accounting, economics, entrepreneurship, finance, international business, health industries, nonprofit organizations, real estate, management, information technology management, marketing, project management, or supply chain management. Business trends and world events are integrated into the curriculum, and students can expect to "spend a lot of time learning about current (and therefore extremely relevant) business issues." A student enthuses, "The John Cook School of Business at Saint Louis University has challenged me to think domestically and globally, both quantitatively and qualitatively, and with a sense of social responsibility, ethics, and morals." Even while attending the program part time, MBA candidates benefit from "the flexibility to customize the program," along with the "the opportunity to study abroad for a week or two."

SLU's business program is "competitive and academically challenging," but well balanced. Within the faculty, students find "a combination of full-time professors who are very knowledgeable in their fields, as well as adjunct, who are actually doing what they are teaching." At the same time, students admit that "faculty members are inconsistent in quality." Researching professors before signing up for classes can vastly improve the experience. The total graduate enrollment at the Cook School of Business is fewer than 400 students, making the school feel rather small and manageable. Students feel comfortable expressing their opinions, and "the administration is very approachable and willing to listen to feedback." A current student attests, "Everyone I have interacted with in the Graduate Business School office is friendly, knowledgeable, and quick to help resolve any question or problem you might have."

Career and Placement

The John Cook School of Business has its own dedicated Career Resource Center, which serves both undergraduate and graduate business students through one-on-one career counseling, job search strategies, and resume revisions. "The Career Resources Center is top-notch," and it "frequently holds seminars and networking sessions" for MBA candidates. Among other programs, the School hosts company information sessions and casual meet-and-greet events with local businesses. In addition, SLU has done "a great job integrating with the local business community and in connecting with alumni." However,

ADMISSIONS CONTACT: NANCY BISCAN, PROGRAM COORDINATOR
ADDRESS: 3674 LINDELL BLVD. SUITE 132, ST. LOUIS, MO 63108
PHONE: 314-977-6221 • FAX: 314-977-1416
E-MAIL: GRADBIZ@SLU.EDU • WEBSITE: GRADBIZ.SLU.EDU

students in the part-time program mention that the school might improve the process of "mentoring and advising those of us looking to change careers," though those who want individual attention can seek out the dedicated graduate career advisers.

Saint Louis University graduates work at companies that include Anheuser-Busch/ InBev, The Boeing Company, Express Scripts, Wells Fargo, Cintas Corp, Monsanto, and Emerson. Graduates have a mean base salary of $57,450, with a range from $40,000 to $82,000. Marketing and sales are the two most popular career fields for SLU graduates.

Student Life and Environment

No matter whether a student is in the part-time, full-time, or joint degree programs at SLU, the curriculum is challenging and time-consuming. At the same time, "the culture is very welcoming," and students in the business school enjoy a surprisingly "laid-back environment" amid group work and case studies. "There is a real sense of camaraderie" between students and a surprisingly bustling atmosphere around the business school building, where there are frequent regional, national, and international speakers. "There are a variety of study areas in the business school," and "there are always students hanging out in the common areas studying and eating." While the environment is comfortable, students say it isn't always functional. Fortunately, the University Library, located right next to the business school, is undergoing a large-scale renovation.

Unlike most professional or executive programs, "SLU makes the extra effort to make commuter and part-time students really feel at home on campus." For example, "the last week of every month, the Graduate Business office provides dinner each night during the part-time MBA courses." Students also point out the value of "the social events that are planned for the business school," through which "full-time and part-time students can meet and socialize."

Admissions

To apply to Saint Louis University, prospective students must submit official academic transcripts from undergraduate coursework, a current resume, GMAT scores, two letters of recommendation, a personal statement, and a completed application form and related fee. The full-time program enrolls students once a year, in May. Part-time students are reviewed and accepted on a rolling basis, all year long. In recent years, the average GMAT score for entering students was 581.

FINANCIAL FACTS

Annual tuition	$52,035/
Fees	$440
Cost of books	$1,500
Room & board (on/off-campus)	$0/$12,000
% of students receiving aid	90
% of first-year students receiving aid	90
% of students receiving grants	90
Average grant	$11,840

ADMISSIONS

Admissions Selectivity Rating	81
# of applications received	184
% applicants accepted	85
% acceptees attending	70
Average GMAT	581
Range of GMAT	520–620
Accepts GRE scores	Yes
Average GPA	3.2
TOEFL required of international students	Yes
Minimum TOEFL (paper)	570
Application fee	$90
International application fee	$90
Deferment available	Yes
Maximum length of deferment	1 year
Transfer students accepted	Yes
Transfer application policy Part-time MBA only; 6 credit hours from another AACSB accredited school. Also, member of Jesuit MBA Consortium.	
Non-fall admissions	Yes
Need-blind admissions	Yes

EMPLOYMENT PROFILE

Career Rating	88	Grads Employed by Function	% Avg. Salary
Percent employed at graduation	39	Marketing	(30%) $56,943
Percent employed 3 months after graduation	69	Operations	(13%) $60,000
		Consulting	(26%) $62,567
Average base starting salary	$57,435	Finance	(13%) $43,667
Primary Source of Full-time Job Acceptances		Other	(17%) $59,000
School-facilitated activities	8 (32%)	**Top 5 Employers Hiring Grads**	
Graduate-facilitated activities	17 (68%)	Anheuser Busch (1), The Boeing Company (1), Emerson (1), Monsanto (1), Cintas Corp (1)	

SAN DIEGO STATE UNIVERSITY
GRADUATE SCHOOL OF BUSINESS

GENERAL INFORMATION
Type of school   Public
Affiliation   No Affiliation
Academic calendar   Semester

SURVEY SAYS...
Students love San Diego, CA
Solid preparation in:
Teamwork

STUDENTS
Enrollment of parent institution	33,230
Enrollment of MBA Program	299
% male/female	61/39
% out-of-state	10
% part-time	51
% international	51
Average age at entry	28
Average years work experience at entry	5

ACADEMICS
Academic Experience Rating	**85**
Profs interesting rating	85
Profs accessible rating	89
Student/faculty ratio	38:1
% female faculty	31
% part-time faculty	33

Joint Degrees
MBA/MA in Latin American Studies, 3-4 yrs. MBA/JD, 4 yrs.

Prominent Alumni
Doug Collier, Founding CFO Volcom; Jim Sinegal, Co-founder; Costco; Neil Schloss, VP & Treasurer, Ford Motor Company; Mark Snell, President, Sempra Energy; Dennis Gilmore, CEO, President; 1st American Financial Corp

Academics

It is not difficult to sum up the qualities that draw students to San Diego State University's Graduate School of Business. One student explains, "[It's a] nice location for me, good class times, a competitive curriculum, and a good solid reputation for a great up-and-coming business program and full and part time MBA programs." Those views are consistent throughout the comments about this "quite affordable" local school that has "a great business reputation." Though some air complaints about a few "mostly uninterested" professors, the consensus is that SDSU's business program is the "best quality for the money." Couple a "flexible program" with a "large networking base" and attendees will find "a community with numerous opportunities to give back and share [one's] new skills in constructive ways."

What students walk away with will depend on their own focus and drive, since the "quality of professors is highly volatile and you can't be sure how well they will teach or lecture." However, when the professors are good, the classroom experience is very worthwhile. Business students are glad that "professors with long work experience are common." For example, one student boasts, "The two courses in my last semester consisted of a senior director and a CEO from Qualcomm (a Fortune 500) and biotech firm, respectively." That "large depth of experience and knowledge" these educators share with their students suggests "professors promote critical thinking in class, as opposed to just lecturing. More emphasis is placed on in-depth analysis than on test taking." One student without a strong background in business was glad to note, "This school made my transition from a non-business background to a business program very smooth."

Such experience extends to the students. "Fifty percent of people have their own business in my classes," one student notes. Even for those without a wealth of previous business experience, SDSU offers a "consistently [top] ranked" entrepreneurship program and a Sports MBA program that boasts "access to many higher-ups in the sports industry in the San Diego and Southern California area." It also takes part in a Venture Capital Investment Competition that gains big exposure for participants. Some students worry that "ridiculous budget cuts" will mar the MBA program, but for others the future looks bright. Current administrators are "transforming the program," and the school is "integrating lecturers into the courses," all of which indicates a program that is sometimes "flying by the seat of its pants" but is generally on the upswing.

Career and Placement

A "large alumni network," strong "career services assistance ... helpful MBA advisors, and the flexibility of the program" are the strengths of the program here. There are "excellent career counselors and job matching," along with "lots of alumni in the community" that make for good post-school career opportunities. With more than sixty years in operation, the school has amassed "a huge alumni base" which, some students note, "The program needs to utilize [more fully]." "The systems are in place, and as long as students tap into it," one student writes, "the resources the school provides are amazing."

Student Life and Environment

"The San Diego State Campus is full of life and activity," bustling with concerts, shows, and more. The San Diego area offers sports, a huge array of restaurants catering to every culinary desire, and of course, the students of SDSU. No matter your focus, and no matter whether full-or part-time, "there are many places where you can find your niche and be happy." The common ground for SDSU Graduate School of Business students is, unsurprisingly, San Diego itself. One student notes, "It is a beautiful location, with beautiful weather and happy people. It has the feel of a big city, with many small communities making up that big city, so you get the best of both worlds." Despite its cozy feel, San Diego is indeed a city—and urban areas often mean opportunities for education, recreation, and more. "The closer to campus you live, the more involved you can get, which ultimately leads to success in classes or building lasting relationships that will serve you into life beyond graduation."

Like the surrounding city itself, students here are "very outgoing and easy to interact and work with," a group of "high achievers with a strong competitive drive and interest in furthering their careers." SDSU keeps students "very busy with work," while the city offers ample opportunities for entertainment. Whether full-time students who are "hard-working, motivated individuals who want to improve their future career possibilities" or part-time students who are "busy, working professionals, mostly young in their careers," students here tend to be "diverse, friendly, knowledgeable, and very helpful."

Admissions

Prepare to compete against almost 1,500 other applicants to SDSU's MBA program. Taken into consideration will be your GMAT score; GPA or undergraduate academic work (a minimum of 2.85 for American students, 3.0 for international students is required, with an average GPA for admitted students of 3.3); letters of recommendation, a resume (work experience is not required but is preferred); and personal statement. The final three "can enhance an application" but are not required. Expect to submit official TOEFL scores if you are an international student whose first language is not English. Such students should expect to meet a minimum paper-and-pencil test score of 550, computer-based score of 213, or an Internet-based score of 80. Apply as early as possible; whether for the fall or spring terms, applications are processed on a rolling basis.

FINANCIAL FACTS

Annual tuition (in-state/ out-of-state)	$8,242/$17,170
Fees	$6,096
Cost of books	$1,804
Room & board	$12,706

ADMISSIONS

Admissions Selectivity Rating	86
# of applications received	575
% applicants accepted	48
% acceptees attending	51
Average GMAT	591
Range of GMAT	530–660
Accepts GRE scores	No
Average Verbal GRE	56
Range of Verbal GRE scores	25–89
Average Quantitative GRE	52
Range of Quantitative GRE scores	28–80
Average Writing GRE	3.8
Range of Writing GRE scores	3.0–4.5
Average GPA	3.2
TOEFL required of international students	Yes
Minimum TOEFL (paper/web)	550/80
Application fee	$55
International application fee	$55
Regular application deadline	3/1
Regular application notification	5/15
Deferment available	No
Transfer students accepted	Yes
Transfer application policy	Transfer applicants apply through the normal admissions process. A limited number of transfer credits may be accepted based on an evaluation of the applicant's transcripts.
Non-fall admissions	No
Need-blind admissions	Yes

EMPLOYMENT PROFILE

Career Rating		81	Grads Employed by Function% Avg. Salary	
Percent employed at graduation		29	Marketing	(17%) $59,800
Percent employed 3 months after graduation		27	Operations	(14%) $55,000
			Management	(21%) $69,167
Average base starting salary		$61,241	Finance	(21%) $55,500
Primary Source of Full-time Job Acceptances			Other	(27%) $63,625
School-facilitated activities	3 (10%)		**Top 5 Employers Hiring Grads**	
Graduate-facilitated activities	14 (48%)		HD Supply (3), Qualcomm Technologies Inc.	
Unknown	12 (42%)		(2), Mayflower Medical Group (2)	

SAN FRANCISCO STATE UNIVERSITY
COLLEGE OF BUSINESS

Academics

San Francisco State University's College of Business offers a contemporary MBA program, right in the middle of the Bay Area's business community. While SFSU's main campus is located in a residential neighborhood, the business school has its own building in "the heart of San Francisco's financial district." The curriculum is high quality and progressive, and the "flexible schedule and very convenient location" make this school a top choice for San Francisco professionals. "The opportunity to individually tailor an MBA to a specific job market is key," and many students choose SFSU to participate in the school's popular "sustainable business emphasis." In fact, there is a "focus on corporate responsibility and sustainability" throughout the program, which is well aligned with the Bay Area's forward-thinking business climate.

The faculty takes a varied approach to teaching, with mixed results. "There are some that read directly from slides and others that are extremely engaging. They take book concepts and translate them into real-life situations." Students admit that, "you need to be a little selective in the professors you choose," but reassure us that, "if you do your research, there are enough accomplished professors here to get a solid education." No matter who oversees classes, the curriculum is time consuming, as "courses require a lot of group work, a lot of reading, and several presentations." However, the rewards are worth the effort, and students benefit from "engaging classroom discussion" in their classes. Always current, SFSU "professors are teaching the latest trends" through contemporary case studies.

Due to "the state of California budget constraints," the program has experienced some recent limitations. For example, "they aren't always able to offer elective classes consistently." Fortunately, "the administration has done an excellent job communicating potentialities and schedule changes to the student body." In fact, the administration gets high marks all around, and the "program advisers and program coordinator are very easy to talk to and helpful." Both full-time and part-time students assure us, "If you plan out your schedule right, you won't really have any trouble getting the classes you need." And, even as the state raises student tuition and fees, an MBA from San Francisco State still comes at a "fairly low cost" for its quality.

Career and Placement

According to SFSU's happy grad students, "San Francisco is an amazing city to get an MBA in because so many companies are headquartered nearby, especially if you have an interest in entrepreneurship." On top of that, the school's close "proximity to Silicon Valley" opens up a world of options in high tech and computing. While there are several top-rated business schools in the greater Bay Area, SFSU students say you can't write off their strong, yet affordable public program. A current student elaborates, "a lot of students feel that SFSU doesn't have a name like Stanford or UC Berkeley, but the connections are there. We have people who work for Google and Yahoo! and, like myself, at Genentech, who, if you reach out, are connected and can help students."

Within the business school, students have access to ongoing career workshops and personalized career counseling. There is an annual career fair, as well as ongoing recruiting events at the business school and the main SFSU campus. MBA candidates may also take advantage of the online job boards managed by the University's Career Center. The mean base salary for last year's San Francisco State MBA graduates was about $85,000 annually, with 90 percent of students accepting a position within three months of graduation. Some of the biggest employers of SFSU graduates are Wells Fargo Bank, Genentech, PG&E, Autodesk, and Bank of America.

Student Life and Environment

The student body at SFSU reflects the Bay Area's interesting local culture, and "because nearly 50 percent of the school's students are international, the school ranks very high in diversity." Group projects tend to go well, and "most everyone is laid back," despite the pressures of business school. Some complain that students who "come straight from undergrad" are "uninterested and inexperienced" when compared to their older counterparts, but San Francisco's MBA candidates are "generally thoughtful, professional, and engaged" throughout the program.

Located downtown, the petite SFSU "campus is brand new and very nice," and "the surrounding area is, of course, awesome." Not only is the campus convenient for downtown professionals, there are "tons of restaurants and shops around" the neighborhood. On campus, the school augments the curriculum through "interesting events and presentations outside regular classes," and administrators "constantly send out emails about networking events and clubs." Among the more popular activities, "every Thursday, the social club meets at a bar after night class." Even so, "there is not a strong community aspect among SFSU students," as most maintain an active personal and professional life outside of school.

Admissions

Prospective SFSU students are evaluated on their undergraduate academic records, GMAT scores, current resumes, statements of purpose, and letters of recommendation. To be eligible for admission, students must have a 3.0 GPA and an undergraduate degree from an accredited university. While there is no minimum requirement, the University recommends at least three years of full-time work experience before matriculation. For more information about programs or to get help deciding which MBA is right for you, the business school hosts periodic open houses for prospective students.

FINANCIAL FACTS

Annual tuition (in-state/ out-of-state)	$12,834/$21,762
Fees	$3,404
Cost of books	$1,500
Average grant	$0
Average loan	$0

ADMISSIONS

Admissions Selectivity Rating	89
# of applications received	296
% applicants accepted	29
% acceptees attending	54
Average GMAT	562
Range of GMAT	520–620
Accepts GRE scores	Yes
Average Verbal GRE	154
Range of Verbal GRE scores	151–158
Average Quantitative GRE	154
Range of Quantitative GRE scores	149–159
Average Writing GRE	4.0
Range of Writing GRE scores	3.5–4.5
Average GPA	3.4
TOEFL required of international students	Yes
Minimum TOEFL (paper/web)	590/96
Application fee	$55
International application fee	$55
Early application deadline	1/15
Early notification date	2/15
Regular application deadline	5/15
Regular application notification	7/1
Application Deadline/Notification	
Round 1:	1/15 / 2/15
Round 2:	4/1 / 5/1
Round 3:	5/15 / 7/1
Deferment available	No
Transfer students accepted	Yes
Transfer application policy	
Transfer applicants will need to apply as a new applicant. Transfer applicants may he eligible to waive foundation courses.	
Non-fall admissions	Yes
Need-blind admissions	No

EMPLOYMENT PROFILE

Career Rating	72	Top 5 Employers Hiring Grads
		Wells Fargo Bank, Kaiser Permanente, Pacific Gas and Electric (PG&E), Cisco, Genetech

SAN JOSE STATE UNIVERSITY
LUCAS GRADUATE SCHOOL OF BUSINESS

GENERAL INFORMATION

Type of school	Public
Affiliation	No Affiliation
Academic calendar	Semester

SURVEY SAYS...
Friendly students
Solid preparation in:
Presentation skills, Doing business in
a global economy

STUDENTS

Enrollment of parent institution	32,773
Enrollment of MBA Program	162
% male/female	47/53
% out-of-state	0
% part-time	34
% international	31
Average age at entry	28

ACADEMICS

Academic Experience Rating	**88**
Profs interesting rating	85
Profs accessible rating	91
Student/faculty ratio	26:1
% female faculty	49
% underrepresented minority faculty	43
% part-time faculty	48

Joint Degrees
MBA/MS Engineering, 32 months

Academics

Located smack dab in the middle of the Silicon Valley, San Jose State University's business programs benefit from the energy and innovation of their famous surroundings. "No place on earth is more entrepreneurial or technology-centric" than SJSU, where the MBA programs boast an "innovative syllabus," a "global mindset," and a top-notch faculty from the region's prominent industries. For MBA candidates, SJSU offers several program options: the Early Career MBA program on the main SJSU campus which includes accelerated track, full-time, and part-time tracks (the accelerated program can be completed in just a year), and the MBA for Professionals, a "flexible program for working students," offering year-round classes in the evenings and some weekends. With accommodating teachers and a flexible schedule, the MBA for Professionals "is an ideal program for anyone who wants an MBA, but needs to keep working full-time while getting it." A current student attests, "When I needed to be out of town for work the week of a final, the professor was very willing to reschedule the test for me so it wouldn't interfere with my business trip."

Delivered by a team of "world-class teachers" and an "accommodating" administration, the "academic experience is positive, effective, and worthwhile" at San Jose State. Academically, the program balances "a good mix of lectures, case studies, and assignment[s]." On that note, you'll get a blend of theory and practice in the classroom, as "professors are very knowledgeable and have experience in both academics and industry." "Teachers here are experienced in Silicon Valley trends and do their best to incorporate them into class work." Coursework is interactive, and "discussions in class are lively, [and] periodically include [the] latest news and trends." Friendly as well as experienced, "professors are very easily approachable and always try to correlate classroom learning with real-world problems as closely as possible."

"Value" is another important factor in many students' decisions to attend SJSU. A state school, SJSU has a much lower price tag than other local programs, giving prospective MBA candidates an "affordable option at a respected school," without leaving the Bay Area. Unfortunately, like many public schools, budget cuts have affected San Jose State and there has been "an increase in tuition" in response. Core classes are offered on a cyclical schedule to ensure all students meet their requirements. Despite limitations, "the administration has been wonderful and very responsive to all concerns," and students say the program runs efficiently.

Career and Placement

The business school at San Jose State University is propitiously located "right in the middle of Silicon Valley, with access to all [the] big-shot companies, and their executives." In addition, "the majority of students in the program come from great high-tech companies," which makes networking as easy as attending class. The Career Center at SJSU helps the undergraduate and graduate student community make connections in the local job market through recruiting events and job fairs. While most SJSU grads score great post-grad positions, some full-time students would like to see Career Services provide "better help finding jobs after graduation," through the addition of new events like "job fairs specifically designed for MBA students." The Lucas School does employ a career advisor dedicated to working with all MBA students on skills such as resume writing, interviewing techniques, business etiquette and networking. Many students in the part-time program receive tuition assistance from their current companies and therefore aren't looking for new jobs after graduation. Currently, you'll find recent SJSU business school graduates working at diverse companies like Charles Schwab, City Bank, Apple, Applied Materials, Chevron Corporation, Cisco Systems, Ebay, E*TRADE,

ADMISSIONS CONTACT: MARGARET FARMER, ADMISSIONS COORDINATOR
ADDRESS: ONE WASHINGTON SQUARE, BUSINESS TOWER 350, SAN JOSE, CA 95192-0162
PHONE: 408-924-3420 • FAX: 408-924-3426
E-MAIL: LUCAS-SCHOOL@SJSU.EDU • WEBSITE: WWW.SJSU.EDU/LUCASSCHOOL

HSBC Group Holdings, IBM, Lockheed Martin, Intel Corporation, Hewlett-Packard, Sprint, Nortel, Genentech, Microsoft, Pepsico, Google, Starbucks Coffee, NASA, Texas Instruments, and Xerox.

Student Life and Environment

Students in SJSU's Early Career MBA program love life on their well-equipped urban campus. The school is located right in the middle of downtown San Jose, and "food at the Student Union is great and the campus is gorgeous." Diversity is a trademark of this large public school, and within the business program, "a lot of the students speak more than one language and have lived abroad." Despite cultural, ethnic, professional, and political diversity, "everybody makes an effort to get along, get to know each other. The teamwork required for projects is very good as it encourages intercultural interaction."

In the MBA for Professionals program, "classes are taught off campus" so many part-timers "feel very disconnected from the SJSU student body." Fortunately, the auxiliary facility is "centrally-located and well-equipped," and there is plenty of parking for commuters. While full-time cohorts are tight, socializing is more limited among part-timers, who are "very busy outside of class (since we are in an evening program, almost all of my classmates also have full-time jobs)." For most, that means a "get-in and get-out" attitude about school, and "class work outside of class is usually handled via teleconferences or face-to-face meetings when possible."

Admissions

For those considering SJSU's graduate business programs, the school offers the unique opportunity to schedule a pre-qualification interview, which allows prospective students to discuss their eligibility for the MBA program with admissions officials. In all cases, students must have an undergraduate degree with a GPA of at least 2.5 to be considered for the program. Competitive candidates will have a GPA of 3.3 or better and GMAT scores of 550 or above.

FINANCIAL FACTS

Annual tuition (in-state/ out-of-state)	$13,160/$16,508
Cost of books	$1,860
Room & board (on/off-campus)	$14,217/$13,434

ADMISSIONS

Admissions Selectivity Rating	88
# of applications received	355
% applicants accepted	34
% acceptees attending	55
Average GMAT	553
Range of GMAT	500–600
Accepts GRE scores	Yes
Average Verbal GRE	151
Range of Verbal GRE scores	147–154
Average Quantitative GRE	152
Range of Quantitative GRE scores	148–154
Average Writing GRE	3.8
Range of Writing GRE scores	3.5–4.5
Average GPA	3.3
TOEFL required of international students	Yes
Minimum TOEFL (paper/web)	/80
Application fee	$55
International application fee	$55
Regular application deadline	5/1
Regular application notification	7/1
Deferment available	No
Transfer students accepted	Yes
Transfer application policy Applicant must meet admission requirements. Up to 30% of units may be transferred from a regionally accredited institution.	
Non-fall admissions	Yes
Need-blind admissions	Yes

SANTA CLARA UNIVERSITY
LEAVEY SCHOOL OF BUSINESS

GENERAL INFORMATION

Type of school	Private
Affiliation	Roman Catholic-Jesuit
Academic calendar	Quarters

SURVEY SAYS...
Cutting-edge classes
Solid preparation in:
Finance, General management,
Teamwork, Doing business in a global economy, Entrepreneurial studies

STUDENTS

Enrollment of parent institution	9,015
Enrollment of MBA Program	555
% male/female	40/60
% part-time	76
Average age at entry	30
Average years work experience at entry	6

ACADEMICS

Academic Experience Rating	**67**
Profs interesting rating	73
Profs accessible rating	76
% female faculty	21
% underrepresented minority faculty	3
% part-time faculty	62

Joint Degrees
JD/MBA - 4 years JD/MSIS - 4 years

Academics

The Leavey School of Business at Santa Clara University combines "Jesuit values, primarily in the quality of education and the emphasis on high integrity," with a Silicon Valley location that draws "the cream of the crop to the faculty, such as the former 3Com CEO." The result is a unique MBA program—available in either an evening, accelerated, or Executive MBA format—that "caters to part-time students," but also has plenty to offer full-timers, all within the confines of an "environment that is very supportive." Depending on the MBA track, classes are either offered in cohort or regular class format and on evenings or weekends, which allows students to maintain their current positions in the workplace.

Customer service is the name of the game at Leavey, where administrators "do everything they can to keep up with the changing trends in business and business schools." For example, the programs include opportunities for international exposure for the student. Every summer, one or two student groups visit another country to meet with business leaders and financial institutions to understand how business is done in that country. Students recently went to Vietnam and Chile. Professors all "know the subject of their teachings and are very professional" and take a similar student-first approach as the administration. They are "eager to help students in the classroom and to introduce them to colleagues for future employment opportunities. They are always available for personal/professional consultation."

Leavey's curriculum employs "a great case-study approach" that "is structured to maximize teamwork abilities." Students find this pedagogical approach immediately applicable to their professional lives. MBAs also "love the 'experimental' classes that students can choose as electives, such as Spirituality and Leadership, which really gets you to focus on your inner self and become a better, less stressed person." Students tell us the school excels in accounting, general management, and marketing. Asked where the school should improve, one student comments, "For some reason, the school is not as well-recognized as other schools in the area, namely Stanford and Berkeley. I think the school will stand to gain if marketed better." Another adds, "I wanted something that was going to challenge me as well as help me get a jump start in the business world. As of so far, the business school has surpassed all expectations."

Career and Placement

Students appreciate the "great Bay-Area network" connected to SCU. MBAs benefit from "a terrific level of interaction with leaders and innovators in Silicon Valley." The Graduate Business Career Management Office capitalizes on these connections to help students procure internships. "The quarter system allows for some interesting internship opportunities in the area because local employers know some students can be available part-time or full-time for a quarter or two," explains one student. Though the Office does offer recruitment events, individual consulting services, and workshops exploring topics—such as personal branding and business etiquette—students feel the service isn't all it could be. As one observes, "Since most students are working, there are limited resources devoted to the internship/career placement program. Also, SCU does not do enough promotion of the program out in the business community. Its reputation is only good regionally, despite its high ranking as a part-time business program." However, many changes have been implemented in career management in the past few years.

Employers of graduates are Cisco, Deloitte & Touche, Wells Fargo, Lockheed Martin, Johnson & Johnson, Hewlett-Packard, VMWare, and Intel.

ADMISSIONS CONTACT: TAMMY FOX, DIRECTOR, MBA ADMISSIONS
ADDRESS: 109 LUCAS HALL, 500 EL CAMINO REAL, SANTA CLARA, CA 95053-0001
PHONE: 408-554-4539 • FAX: 408-544-4571
E-MAIL: GRADBUSINESS@SCU.EDU • WEBSITE: WWW.SCU.EDU/BUSINESS

Student Life and Environment

MBAs report that SCU "provides a safe, clean study environment coupled with a very caring and personal staff. The school really treats students as 'customers' and caters to their needs, offering extended library hours during exams. The staff wants the students to succeed." Part-time students appreciate that "the schedule is really terrific and works for working folks as well as commuters."

SCU's "gorgeous and safe campus" offers a number of top amenities, including "a state-of-the-art gym and pool, great recreation areas, and a late-night venue called The Bronco with a pool table, a large television, and several couches." Also available are campus-wide wireless access, breakout rooms for private meetings/study, and case-style and collaborative classrooms. Although most students are part-time with numerous other commitments outside school, MBAs here do occasionally socialize. "It's easy to spot people you know everywhere; unfamiliar faces never stay that way." Another student points out that "life at school can be great for those who do the work to get involved. It can be a commuter school if that is all a student wants to get out of it. But there is always something social to do on the weekends, either sponsored by the school or just going out with other MBA students."

"Many students here have jobs," which "provide the best opportunity for networking and recruiting after graduation, as you have gained so many resources at numerous organizations," students tell us. MBAs range from the mid-twenties to the mid-forties. Their "backgrounds are extremely diverse; they come from such areas as financial services, banking, semiconductors, software, technology management, finance, and human resources, to name a few." Engineers from the Silicon Valley are the single most visible contingent.

Admissions

Applicants to Leavey MBA programs at SCU must provide the Admissions Office with all of the following: Official transcripts for all postsecondary academic work; official GMAT/GRE score reports reflecting scores no more than five years old; a completed online application; two letters of recommendation from individuals "who can speak directly to your professional strengths and areas of growth"; and a personal essay. A second essay is optional, and candidates will be contacted for interviews once all application materials are submitted. Candidates whose first language is not English must also submit official score reports for the TOEFL (minimum required score: 600 paper-based test, 100 on the new IBT test). Leavey also accepts IELTS to demonstrate English proficiency (minimum required score: 7.0). Work experience requirements vary by program. On average, admitted students have five years of post-undergraduate professional experience.

FINANCIAL FACTS

Fees	$150
% of students receiving grants	28
Average grant	$4,600

ADMISSIONS

Admissions Selectivity Rating	**77**
Average GMAT	630
Accepts GRE scores	Yes
Average Verbal GRE	154
Average Quantitative GRE	155
Average Writing GRE	4.0
Average GPA	3.2
TOEFL required of international students	Yes
Minimum TOEFL (paper/web)	600/100
Application fee	$100
International application fee	$150
Early application deadline	4/1
Regular application deadline	6/1
Application Deadline	
Round 1:	4/1
Round 2:	6/1
Deferment available	Yes
Maximum length of deferment	2 Quarters
Transfer students accepted	Yes
Transfer application policy Apply as all others; must be in good standing in the program they are transferring from.	
Non-fall admissions	Yes
Need-blind admissions	Yes

SEATTLE PACIFIC UNIVERSITY
SCHOOL OF BUSINESS AND ECONOMICS

GENERAL INFORMATION
Type of school	Private
Affiliation	Free Methodist
Academic calendar	Quarters

SURVEY SAYS...
Abundant mentors available,
Students love Seattle, WA
Solid preparation in:
Presentation skills

STUDENTS
Enrollment of parent institution	3,902
Enrollment of MBA Program	103
% male/female	70/30
% out-of-state	80
% part-time	87
% underrepresented minority	99
% international	99
Average age at entry	33
Average years work experience at entry	6

ACADEMICS
Academic Experience Rating	85
Profs interesting rating	85
Profs accessible rating	90
Student/faculty ratio	17:1
% female faculty	30
% underrepresented minority faculty	10
% part-time faculty	5

Academics

A small, Christian-affiliated college in a progressive Northwest city, Seattle Pacific University offers an MBA and Masters in Information Systems Management that considers "another way of doing business." At SPU, business education "really isn't just about the bottom line, but about sustainable, ethical business practices." "Christian values" are fundamental to the school's mission, and students note a "dedication to social issues" through the curricular and extracurricular offerings. In addition, the school's Center for Integrity in Business explores the intersection of faith and business, bringing plenty of experts, new research, and special events to campus. As a result, this MBA doesn't just introduce skills; it focuses on "building character to stand in the face of obstacles." A current student enthuses, "I believe there are some great leaders that come from the school, and will go on to affect their communities and the world in a powerful way."

The MBA at Seattle Pacific is a comprehensive general management degree comprising nine core courses, ten required advanced courses, and five elective courses. Teamwork and communication skills are emphasized throughout the curriculum, and there is a "focus on social ventures" in the coursework. To tailor the MBA, the school recently introduced another area of concentration in social and sustainable enterprise. In addition, SPU "offers a MS-ISM degree," which "incorporates the best of the technical IT world and the business world to create leaders who can excel, and most importantly, communicate in both worlds." Despite the emphasis on technology, students feel the curriculum could include "better teaching of quantitative subjects and less reliance on qualitative." While small in size, Seattle Pacific University boasts great "connections to [the] business community" and an active "mentorship program" with local business partners through the Center for Applied Learning. In addition, the school frequently invites "community leaders into class[es]...for live demonstration."

For working professionals, "flexibility" is a major advantage of SPU's programs, which include MBA classes in the evenings. Professional students also appreciate "the willingness of the staff and faculty to work with you to accommodate a busy work life." On that note, the atmosphere at SPU is very supportive, and "most of the professors are very receptive to extending help and want feedback on their classes." The program is small, so class sizes are reduced. In the MBA program, there are rarely more than thirty students in a class (and the average class size is just thirteen to fifteen students.) In addition to provoking students' comments and discussion, "the small class sizes have allowed [students] good access to [their] professors." The school employs both adjunct and full-time faculty. "Most of the professors are very good" and students, on the whole, are "very satisfied with the classes, professors, and classmates." Students are split on the administration, however. Some say the top brass should "be more responsive to their customers," while others assure us that "the administration is solid, wants the best for us, and works hard to get the best."

Career and Placement

At SPU, students are prepared for the workplace throughout their studies. Practical business applications are emphasized in MBA coursework, and the school's mentorship program is active and appreciated. At the same time, "there aren't very many internship opportunities for graduate business students" at Seattle Pacific University, as many students are already working when they start the program. Those who enter the MBA with more limited business experience say the program would improve if the "internships program integrated with the grad business program, so we can get some experience before graduating with a new degree."

Open to all MBA candidates, Seattle Pacific University serves the undergraduate, graduate, and alumni communities at the school. Through this office, graduate students can schedule one free career counseling appointment and one resume review, and also gain access to online job boards and research tools. Top employers of Seattle Pacific MBA candidates include Boeing, Microsoft, Starbucks, and Safeco.

Student Life and Environment

Seattle Pacific University is a small, private school, located on a forty-acre campus just ten minutes from downtown Seattle. Within the graduate business programs, SPU attracts a small but engaging student body. For many, "what has made the classroom so interesting [is] the diverse backgrounds and experiences of…student[s]." Teamwork is a mainstay of the program, and most students are "able to work well on small group projects, have good communication skills, [and] are inclusive." Overall, students are "friendly and helpful," and "the school has a great, positive atmosphere."

Thanks to the flexible course schedule, most MBA candidates are working "professionals with full-time jobs" in Seattle. For busy evening students, life consists of "work all day, school all night, and then homework the rest of the week."

Admissions

Prospective students with an undergraduate GPA of 3.0 and one year of full-time work experience can take up to three MBA courses or two ISM courses before officially applying to the program. SPU accepts applicants for the autumn, winter, spring, and summer terms. To be eligible for the MBA and MS-ISM programs, students must have an undergraduate degree with a 3.0 GPA and substantive work experience (at least one full year of post-undergraduate work experience). A GMAT score over 500 is preferred.

FINANCIAL FACTS

Fees	$0
Cost of books	$1,368
Room & board	
(on/off-campus)	$4,816/$12,800
% of students receiving grants	2
Average grant	$1,200

ADMISSIONS

Admissions Selectivity Rating	83
# of applications received	42
% applicants accepted	69
% acceptees attending	66
Average GMAT	547
Range of GMAT	430–660
Accepts GRE scores	Yes
Average GPA	3.3
TOEFL required of	
international students	Yes
Minimum TOEFL	90
Application fee	$50
International application fee	$50
Regular application deadline	8/1
Regular application notification	8/31
Deferment available	Yes
Maximum length of	
deferment	2 quarters
Transfer students accepted	Yes
Transfer application policy	
Regular Admission Process	
Non-fall admissions	Yes
Need-blind admissions	Yes

SEATTLE UNIVERSITY
ALBERS SCHOOL OF BUSINESS AND ECONOMICS

Academics

The Albers School of Business and Economics at Seattle University is a "unique" and "well-structured" program with a strong "Jesuit tradition" on a "beautiful campus in an economically thriving city." In short, it is a "diamond in the rough." Located "in the heart of Seattle Metro Area," Albers "has a diverse cultural set of faculty, students, and staff." The Seattle location is especially attractive for MBA students as many major American companies like Amazon, T-Mobile, Microsoft, and Starbucks are based here. The Albers MBA program builds a "strong sense of community," and its unique "focus on social justice" and "strong core values" are baked into "every aspect of the school."

Students praise the "convenience and flexibility" of the program and call it a "great program for working professionals." For example, "classes [are] offered at night in two locations" and students are allowed "up to five years to finish coursework (which helps for students that work full time & have families)." The school also has a new "Bridge MBA" program that "has classes during the day." The Bridge MBA is a twelve-month program aimed at helping non-business undergraduates get a jumpstart on their business careers.

The professors at SU "are amazing" and "willing to spend time with you so that you understand the materials." "I have been happy with every professor I have had, and many of them have been outstanding," one student attests. Most of the teachers here "have worked in business so can relate real world experiences to classroom work." Students say that the administration is "very open and willing to help," and provide "abundant" "opportunities to tweak the program" to student needs. Students also praise the school's efforts "helping students network." "They often host events outside of school and off campus to help students get together and network and socialize," one student explains. Another sums up his experience at Albers: "The actual academic program at Seattle U has exceeded my expectations, and I truly believe I'm getting a great return on my investment."

Career and Placement

Students say that "the placement center at Albers is exceptional" and "holds numerous events for networking and career advancement." A huge advantage of Seattle University is the location. Seattle is an economic powerhouse of the West Coast, and the school uses those connections to help students. "I participated in the mentoring program for two years and it was absolutely fantastic to network with executives from Nordstrom and Starbucks," one student says. Some notable alumni include William Foley, Jr., the Chairman of Fidelity National Financial; Mohamed Ali Alabbar, Chairman of Emaar Properties; and Gary Brinson, founder of The Brinson Foundation. Top employers of Seattle MBA grads include Amazon, Microsoft, Boeing, Ernst & Young, T-Mobile, KPMG, and Starbucks.

ADMISSIONS CONTACT: JANET SHANDLEY, DIRECTOR, GRADUATE ADMISSIONS
ADDRESS: 901 12TH AVENUE, PO BOX 222000, SEATTLE, WA 98122-1090
PHONE: 206-296-2000 • FAX: 206-296-5656
E-MAIL: GRAD-ADMISSIONS@SEATTLEU.EDU • WEBSITE: WWW.SEATTLEU.EDU/ALBERS

Student Life and Environment

Students are described as "driven," "hard-working," "open-minded," "fun," "eager," and "entrepreneurial." The peer group really helps "develop the learning environment" at Seattle U. Many are already "accomplished leaders within their organizations." SU students are "very dedicated to the work that they do and have a great sense of self and social awareness." "I am impressed at the intelligence, capability and varied experience my classmates bring to the table," one student says.

As SU is "an evening program," "people come do their thing, then go." "Night classes and working during the day makes it difficult to participate in club or activities on campus" for many students, but for those who have the time "life at school is incredibly fun, engaging and exciting." Campus life is "definitely geared more toward a younger student (without spouse or children)," and "there are always activities and clubs meeting." Most people are in "pretty tight cohorts," and "the socials are fun as well as it allows us to relax and at times connect with other years and cohorts." But no matter how much time students spend on campus, they all love "the community." As one student put it, "My fellow students are people I would like to work with in the 'real world.'"

Admissions

The Albers School of Business and Economics allows students to enter during any of the four quarters, so applicants have four potential deadlines each year. The school requires GMAT or GRE scores, undergraduate transcripts, and transcripts from any post-baccalaureate academic work. International students whose first language is not English must also submit TOEFL or IELTS scores (minimum IELTS score is 7.0). The school also requires a résumé documenting at least two years of professional work experience for most programs.

FINANCIAL FACTS

Annual tuition	$22,545
Fees	$870
Cost of books	$900
Room & board	$20,000
% of students receiving aid	65
% of first-year students receiving aid	65
% of students receiving grants	28
Average award package	$16,484
Average grant	$10,041
Average loan	$19,630
Average student loan debt	$19,442

ADMISSIONS

Admissions Selectivity Rating	82
# of applications received	174
% applicants accepted	43
% acceptees attending	88
Average GMAT	560
Range of GMAT	530–610
Accepts GRE scores	Yes
Average Verbal GRE	156
Range of Verbal GRE scores	147–159
Average Quantitative GRE	153
Range of Quantitative GRE scores	150–164
Average Writing GRE	3.8
Range of Writing GRE scores	3.0–4.1
Average GPA	3.2
TOEFL required of international students	Yes
Minimum TOEFL (paper/web)	580/92
Application fee	$55
International application fee	$55
Regular application deadline	8/20
Deferment available	Yes
Maximum length of deferment	1 year
Transfer students accepted	Yes
Transfer application policy Applicants must meet standard admission requirements. University will accept 9 quarter credits from AACSB accredited schools. Students transferring from an accredited Jesuit MBA program (JEBNET) may transfer up to 50% of credits.	
Non-fall admissions	Yes
Need-blind admissions	Yes

SETON HALL UNIVERSITY
STILLMAN SCHOOL OF BUSINESS

GENERAL INFORMATION

Type of school	Private
Affiliation	Roman Catholic
Academic calendar	Semester

SURVEY SAYS...

Classmates have diverse work experience, Friendly students, Happy students
Solid preparation in:
General management, Teamwork, Communication/interpersonal skills, Presentation skills, Quantitative skills, Doing business in a global economy

STUDENTS

Enrollment of parent institution	10,100
Enrollment of MBA Program	177
% male/female	65/35
% out-of-state	14
% part-time	66
% underrepresented minority	17
% international	33
Average age at entry	30
Average years work experience at entry	7

ACADEMICS

Academic Experience Rating	**88**
Profs interesting rating	90
Profs accessible rating	93
Student/faculty ratio	7:1
% female faculty	15
% underrepresented minority faculty	20
% part-time faculty	43

Joint Degrees

MBA/JD; MBA/MSN; MBA/MA Diplomacy & International Relations.

Prominent Alumni

James O'Brien, CEO Napier Park Global Capital; Gerald P. Buccino, Chairman and CEO of Buccino & Associates; David B. Gerstein, President Thermwell Products Co., Inc.

Academics

Located just outside the hustle and bustle of New York City, Seton Hall University offers a convenient, suburban alternative for city professionals looking to pursue an MBA. At Seton Hall, "the MBA program is designed for students who work full time," and features evening classes and a "convenient location" near major New Jersey roadways and rail system. Efficiency is a key advantage of the Seton Hall MBA, which offers "a streamlined program of forty-two credits, compared to other schools with sixty credits." Even with lower credit requirements, the program can be "taxing" and students warn, "The commitment, perseverance, and dedication one has to make while working a demanding job in NYC or on the NJ business coastline across from NYC must not be underestimated." Fortunately, Seton Hall makes every effort to accommodate busy professionals. Here, professors are highly accommodating and accessible, and "even if they can't meet for special office hours, personal cell phone calls or emails are not uncommon."

"Seton Hall University is one of the most prestigious universities in the area," and the MBA program lives up to the school's strong reputation. Throughout the MBA core curriculum, the "subject material is made very relevant to modern business," with a focus on finance, economics, and behavioral and quantitative sciences. After the core, students can tailor their coursework through academic concentrations in fields like finance, marketing, information technology management, supply chain management, and sports management. The academic experience is hands-on, so be prepared to roll up your sleeves and get busy: "Presentations, in-class discussions, and group assignments are [a] vital part of every course." In addition, every student must conceive and complete a service project before graduation. Students really appreciate the fact that Seton Hall "incorporates core values in its program: integrity, diversity, social responsibility."

In the classroom, "professors can be hit or miss but, for the most part, they are good at what they do and teach well." A current student enthuses, "I am very impressed with how lively my professors are...even the ones teaching stats and heavy quants." In addition to tenured staff, Seton Hall can "attract excellent adjunct professors from nearby corporations in New York City and Northern New Jersey." Most are "demonstrated leaders in the field," ranging from the "CEO of a public company" to a "lawyer for the Vatican." Things run smoothly at Seton Hall and, throughout the business school, "the offices are always well-staffed with knowledgeable employees." An important compliment to the academic experience, students appreciate that "the facilities are modern and the use of technology aids with learning during a full-time work lifestyle." For example, "the trading room is equipped with a Bloomberg terminal which is also a nice touch."

Career and Placement

The Seton Hall University Career Center assists graduate students with their job search through career assessment and career counseling, mock interviews, online job boards, and networking events. For MBA candidates, the Career Center maintains several counselors who are specially designated to help graduate business students find a job or internship. While many Seton Hall students are already working when they enter the program, they say, "The school has been working towards providing more support for career transition, such as networking events and career fairs."

Seton Hall alumni work at a wide range of companies, including Johnson & Johnson, Deloitte, Ernst & Young, Merrill Lynch, New York Life Insurance Company, Booz Allen Hamilton, New Jersey Nets, New York Mets, New York Yankees, Madison Square Garden, Masterfoods USA, Mercedes-Benz, Prudential Financial, PricewaterhouseCoopers, and Tiffany & Co.

Student Life and Environment

Located on a "very safe and clean" campus "just ten miles from New York City," Seton Hall University offers a pleasant environment with excellent facilities. The MBA program is largely part-time, so most students "drive in for class and leave" directly afterwards. However, others tell us that they "love spending time on the green terrace anytime between or after classes," or often "grab food at the dining hall/food court, which has a diverse selection of restaurants." Housed in Jubilee Hall—"the new business building with numerous resources inside it for class"—business students enjoy a comfortable and modern facility, with "state-of-the art" resources, wireless Internet, and web-based classroom technology.

The largely part-time student population can "create difficulties in creating and sustaining clubs on the school campus"; however, the upshot is that you get a "great mix of industry experience among students" which contributes to class discussion and "creates a stimulating learning environment." Most students have work experience before entering the program, but "the age range and experience is dramatic—from fifth years to [those seeking] career transitions, as well as dual-degree students from the Whitehead School of Diplomacy." the School of Law, and the College of Nursing. Despite their differences, "everyone is eager to learn and help out the others around them," and, in general, group work goes smoothly and everyone pulls their weight.

Admissions

To apply to Seton Hall's Stillman School of Business, prospective graduate students must submit transcripts from their undergraduate studies, GMAT scores, a resume of work experience and credentials, a two-paragraph personal statement, and a letter of recommendation. Every applicant is evaluated individually; however, Seton Hall generally requires admits to have a minimum undergraduate GPA of 3.0 on a 4.0 scale, and a minimum GMAT score of 500. Applications are reviewed and admissions decisions are rendered on a rolling basis.

FINANCIAL FACTS

Annual tuition (in-state/ out-of-state)	$30,264/$30,264
Fees	$644
Cost of books	$1,500
Room & board	$15,000
% of students receiving aid	47
% of first-year students receiving aid	51
% of students receiving grants	11
Average award package	$20,593
Average grant	$10,660
Average loan	$18,383
Average student loan debt	$12,998

ADMISSIONS

Admissions Selectivity Rating	83
# of applications received	148
% applicants accepted	72
% acceptees attending	82
Average GMAT	555
Range of GMAT	530–580
Accepts GRE scores	Yes
Average Verbal GRE	148
Range of Verbal GRE scores	142–152
Average Quantitative GRE	158
Range of Quantitative GRE scores	155–161
Average Writing GRE	3.4
Range of Writing GRE scores	2.5–4.3
Average GPA	3.2
TOEFL required of international students	Yes
Minimum TOEFL (paper/web)	607/102
Application fee	$75
International application fee	$75
Regular application deadline	5/31
Deferment available	Yes
Maximum length of deferment	1 year
Transfer students accepted	Yes
Transfer application policy Students must submit a formal application and satisfy requirements for admission. Students are eligible to transfer/waive up to a maximum of 12 credits.	
Non-fall admissions	Yes
Need-blind admissions	Yes

SHIPPENSBURG UNIVERSITY
JOHN L. GROVE COLLEGE OF BUSINESS

GENERAL INFORMATION
Type of school	Public
Affiliation	No Affiliation
Academic calendar	Aug–Aug

SURVEY SAYS...
Happy students
Solid preparation in:
Accounting, Teamwork, Presentation skills, Doing business in a global economy, Entreprenurial studies

STUDENTS
Enrollment of parent institution	7,355
Enrollment of MBA Program	420
% male/female	71/29
% out-of-state	68
% part-time	93
% underrepresented minority	0
% international	64
Average age at entry	30
Average years work experience at entry	6

ACADEMICS
Academic Experience Rating	**85**
Profs interesting rating	88
Profs accessible rating	89
Student/faculty ratio	19:1
% female faculty	21
% underrepresented minority faculty	8
% part-time faculty	0

Prominent Alumni
Dean Kootz, Author; Jeanne Shaheen, U.S. Senator; Rob Davis, Retired Professional Football Player - Green Bay Packers; General Tommy Franks, USA Retired Former Commander-in-Chief; ,

Academics

Founded in 1971, Shippensburg University's John L. Grove College of Business is one of the premier business schools in the Mid-Atlantic, offering three different options for its MBA program: a part-time night program for working professionals (93 percent of students are part time), a full-time cohort program for recent college graduates and young professionals, and an entirely online program. The school's numerous satellite campuses in Harrisburg, York, and East Stroudsburg offer the convenience and proximity that many of those who attend Shippensburg rank highest on their list of priorities, and the administration is "very flexible with class scheduling and seem to try and accommodate everyone within the three different branch campuses." "From what I know, they are doing a good job running the program," says a student.

Overall, students come here because "Shippensburg offers a great curriculum for the cost." Though the student body is "sometimes challenged with students lacking 'real-world' experience," the conversation and discussion is "animated and good when properly facilitated and creates a great learning environment." The faculty are "good—some are great," but their grading standards are sometimes too forgiving: "they pass everyone," according to one student. One plus that students commend is the faculty's willingness "to be available for contact almost all the time." Small class sizes and a "good use of technology" also facilitate "an intimate learning experience between professor and student."

Career and Placement

The school's reputation proceeds it within the central Pennsylvania area, and a Shippensburg MBA usually serves the intended purpose of the student, which is to receive an accredited MBA; whether they are trying to switch careers or advance within a current one, most students will take care of their professional development goals on their own. There are no options for students to focus on one area in the MBA program, which a few do regret, but students agree that they "would highly recommend the program to prospective students." "I have been impressed and thoroughly pleased," says one.

ADMISSIONS CONTACT: MELANIE LUGO, SECRETARY
ADDRESS: 1871 OLD MAIN DRIVE, GROVE HALL 324, SHIPPENSBURG, PA 17257
PHONE: 717-477-1483 • FAX: 717-477-4132
E-MAIL: MLLUGO@SHIP.EDU • WEBSITE: WWW.SHIP.EDU/BUSINESS

Student Life and Environment

It's a busy life for most of those who attend Shippensburg, who are often "older, non-traditional students" who come to campus just for classes—the part-time program is two classes a night, one night a week—and then duck out to attend to personal responsibilities. "I work nine to ten hours a day, then take two classes away from the main campus. I don't have time to become involved in much else," says a student, who is one of many who prefer to keep their experience "simple and basic." Students are "accepting, caring, and helpful" and range from fresh-out-of-school grads to veterans of the working world, with a fair number of "mid-level employees of government or local companies" enrolling in the part-time program.

Those who attend classes at the satellite campuses, mainly "working professionals from a diverse range of businesses," "do not have the interactions that people from the main campus do." Most clubs and activities meet in the late afternoon and so are reserved for full-time students, and part-time students do wish that the school was better at "making the business clubs more accessible to working professionals." Within class, people find a "very good camaraderie" and fellow students that are "open-minded in group situations and overall supportive and collaborative."

Admissions

The Admissions Office at Shippensburg University requires applicants to submit official copies of transcripts for all undergraduate work and a current resume. GMAT scores are required for applicants that have fewer than five years of work experience from the date of their undergraduate degree; students required to take the GMAT must submit an official GMAT score report of 450 or higher. In addition, applicants must either have work experience or undergraduate credits in computer usage, oral and written communication, and quantitative analysis. A personal statement and letters of recommendation are both optional. International applicants must not only meet all of the above requirements but must also submit: an international student application; an evaluation of their transcripts by a professional evaluating service (either Educational Credential Evaluators (ECE) or World Education Services (WES)); an official score report for the TOEFL; and an affidavit of support accompanied by a current bank statement. Applicants who do not meet Shippensburg's admissions requirements may seek special consideration. Some such students do receive provisional admissions status, which allows them to enter the program and continue contingent upon success in their initial MBA course work.

FINANCIAL FACTS

Annual tuition (in-state/ out-of-state)	$8,172/$12,258
Fees	$2,394
Cost of books	$1,015
% of students receiving aid	42
% of first-year students receiving aid	53
% of students receiving grants	21
Average award package	$10,320
Average grant	$6,884
Average loan	$12,117

ADMISSIONS

Admissions Selectivity Rating	**80**
# of applications received	118
% applicants accepted	86
% acceptees attending	97
Average GMAT	490
Range of GMAT	460–560
Accepts GRE scores	Yes
Average GPA	3.2
TOEFL required of international students	Yes
Minimum TOEFL (paper/web)	500/68
Application fee	$45
International application fee	$45
Deferment available	Yes
Maximum length of deferment	Up to one year
Transfer students accepted	Yes
Transfer application policy If applicable can transfer up to nine credits.	
Non-fall admissions	Yes
Need-blind admissions	Yes

SOUTHEAST MISSOURI STATE UNIVERSITY
DONALD L. HARRISON COLLEGE OF BUSINESS

GENERAL INFORMATION
Type of school	Public
Affiliation	No Affiliation
Academic calendar	Semester

SURVEY SAYS...
Friendly students
Solid preparation in:
Finance, Accounting, General management, Teamwork, Communication/interpersonal skills, Presentation skills, Computer skills

STUDENTS
Enrollment of parent institution	11,987
Enrollment of MBA Program	154
% male/female	36/64
% out-of-state	9
% part-time	64
% underrepresented minority	4
% international	67
Average age at entry	29

ACADEMICS
Academic Experience Rating	90
Profs interesting rating	91
Profs accessible rating	92
Student/faculty ratio	19:1
% female faculty	42
% underrepresented minority faculty	10
% part-time faculty	

Joint Degrees
Joint MBA and Masters in International Business and Economics offered with University of Applied Sciences, Schmalkalden, Germany.

Academics

For a "top-notch education at an affordable price," Missouri residents recommend the business school at Southeast Missouri State University. An inexpensive public school, "the university provides an excellent bang for your buck," yet doesn't skimp on a quality education. Catering to current and soon-to-be professionals in the Cape Giradeau area, all classes are held in the evenings. However, SEMO's MBA programs can be completed either part time or full time (the former is the more popular option), and the school operates an entirely online program for students whose schedules do not accommodate classroom work. The program begins with the common core, which covers key business areas ranging from accounting and finance to quantitative and qualitative research methods. After completing the core, students can focus their studies in a single business area, such as finance, industrial management, health administration, or sports management. In addition to coursework, full-time students often augment their coursework with for-credit internships, with teaching assistant positions through the ample "graduate assistantship opportunities" (which also include tuition assistance), or through one of the school's numerous short-term overseas programs. As one appreciative student exclaims, "Their international programs were the best experience of my life!"

Appealing to mature students, "the class environment is unique, in that is very professional, as if you were going to work." Likewise, "the teachers expect all students to come prepared and [they] develop helpful but strenuous assignments." A current student adds, "They give us the responsibility to learn and take on the role as a facilitator of learning rather than keeping it very structured, letting the students do a lot on their own." The teaching staff gets strong reviews from current students, who say their instructors add "very helpful and relevant insight into what we are studying." A current student enthuses, "the professors at Southeast are wonderful. Not only are they experienced in their field, but their teaching styles are excellent."

Despite the emphasis on professionalism, the environment at SEMO is incredibly down-to-earth and friendly. Here, "class sizes are small, so professors get to know you pretty well" and in-class discussions are encouraged. For those who need extra guidance, "the teachers do a great job of making themselves available to the students outside of the classroom for one-on-one help." The small size also facilitates networking between students; "having a smaller campus helps you connect with a wide variety of people in a variety of fields," which makes "classroom discussions very interesting and relevant to the real world."

Career and Placement

As a graduate student enrolled in the MBA program, SEMO students may take advantage of the various services offered through the university's Career Services office. Career Services offers free career advising, salary projections, resume and cover letter revisions, career testing, and interview preparation by appointment. The Career Services office also organizes both job fairs and campus recruiting programs, free of charge. For a fee, students may also access a list of current job opening listings in the region. Because their efforts serve the entire school community, MBA candidates feel, "The Career Center could be greatly improved in order to better serve graduate students."

ADMISSIONS CONTACT: DR. KENNETH HEISCHMIDT, DIRECTOR, MBA PROGRAM
ADDRESS: MBA PROGRAM; SOUTHEAST MISSOURI STATE UNIVERSITY,
1 UNIVERSITY PLAZA, MS 5890, CAPE GIRARDEAU, MO 63701
PHONE: 573-651-5116 • FAX: 573-651-5032
E-MAIL: MBA@SEMO.EDU • WEBSITE: WWW.SEMO.EDU/MBA

While Career Service does not work exclusively with graduate business students, students say, "The MBA office does a great job of making MBA students aware of job opportunities that come to its attention." In fact, many students say, "The school puts a great deal of effort [into helping] students get jobs after graduation and organizes various networking events throughout the semester." Students enrolled in the program full-time can also lay the foundation for their career through for-credit internships.

Student Life and Environment

Located in the riverside city of Cape Giradeau, the SEMO campus is a "peaceful and safe place" to work and study. Just over 100 miles from St. Louis, Cape Giradeau is a small city of 35,000, yet provides "everything that we need as students, and…is a great place to live as well." With classes held in the evenings, most SEMO students work during the day and commute to school in the evenings; therefore, they aren't actively involved in campus life. However, if you're interested in some campus camaraderie, students assure us that "there are a ton of things going on all the time, if people just look around."

On the whole, "Students at SEMO are very diverse and intelligent" joining the business program "from many different work environments." The atmosphere is more collaborative than competitive, and, for group assignments, everyone is "very helpful and work great together." Students say, "The moderately-sized student body is also a strength." At this school, "it's big enough that you can meet plenty of new people, but small enough that you can walk across campus and run into several people you know on the way."

Admissions

To be eligible for admission to Southeast Missouri State University's graduate business program, students must have an undergraduate degree in business from an accredited college or university. Students who do not have an undergraduate degree in business must take a series of prerequisite coursework before they can begin the MBA. Successful applicants will generally have a minimum GMAT score of over 430 and a minimum GPA in foundational (prerequisite) coursework of a C or better. To be considered for a graduate assistantship position, applicants must have a minimum undergraduate grade point average of 2.7.

FINANCIAL FACTS

Annual tuition (in-state/ out-of-state)	$6,259/$11,683
Fees	$809
Room & board (on/off-campus)	$8,285/$8,285
% of students receiving aid	44
% of first-year students receiving aid	58
% of students receiving grants	34
Average award package	$5,621
Average grant	$4,361
Average loan	$7,887

ADMISSIONS

Admissions Selectivity Rating	86
# of applications received	131
% applicants accepted	42
% acceptees attending	45
Average GMAT	520
Range of GMAT	455–570
Accepts GRE scores	Yes
Average Verbal GRE	155
Range of Verbal GRE scores	152–156
Average Quantitative GRE	153
Range of Quantitative GRE scores	152–155
Average Writing GRE	3.8
Range of Writing GRE scores	3.5–4.0
Average GPA	3.3
TOEFL required of international students	Yes
Minimum TOEFL (paper/web)	550/79
Application fee	$30
International application fee	$40
Regular application deadline	8/1
Deferment available	Yes
Maximum length of deferment	1 year
Transfer students accepted	Yes
Transfer application policy	Up to twelve credit hours of appropriate coursework may be transferred into the program
Non-fall admissions	Yes
Need-blind admissions	Yes

SOUTHERN ILLINOIS UNIVERSITY—CARBONDALE
COLLEGE OF BUSINESS

GENERAL INFORMATION
Type of school	Public
Affiliation	No Affiliation
Academic calendar	Semester

SURVEY SAYS...
Good social scene, Helpful alumni, Happy students
Solid preparation in:
Teamwork, Communication/interpersonal skills, Computer skills

STUDENTS
Enrollment of MBA Program	145
% male/female	85/15
% out-of-state	3
% part-time	64
% underrepresented minority	10
% international	10
Average age at entry	27
Average years work experience at entry	9

ACADEMICS
Academic Experience Rating	**65**
Profs interesting rating	67
Profs accessible rating	69
Student/faculty ratio	4:1
% female faculty	19
% underrepresented minority faculty	17
% part-time faculty	0

Joint Degrees
MBA/JD, 105 credits, 3-4 years; MBA/MS in Agribusiness Economics, 51 credits, 1-2.5 yrs; MBA/Master of Arts in Mass Communication (MBA/MA), 51 credits, 12 months to 2.5 year; MBA/BA of Science in Computer Science

Academics

With its affordable tuition and strong academic programs, Southern Illinois University is a smart pick for professionals from the Midwest. Through the College of Business, SIU offers a traditional MBA, a masters of accountancy, and a PhD in business administration, as well as an AACSB-accredited online MBA. Students in the campus program dole out praise for the business school. "The MBA program is outstanding and the professors are well-educated in their particular fields." Students are also quick to point out that the faculty boasts "a lot of well-established names," including a number of professors who are "recognized worldwide for their research." Small class sizes and a friendly atmosphere ensure that students have close contact with their talented professors. Coming from a "wide variety of academic and professional backgrounds," professors not only offer deep "insight and knowledge" in their subject area, they also encourage debate and discussion between students. Classes are "full of intellectual conversation," and students "contribute valuable information to class discussion and always make you strive to outperform your peers." A current student enthuses, "Classes can actually be enjoyable because I know I'm going to learn something each day." Outside the classroom, collaboration is encouraged, and frequent "group work is also time consuming, but very educational."

Speaking to the quality of the program, a large number of current MBA candidates received their undergraduate degree from SIU's College of Business and decided to stay on or return to the school for the graduate program. Particularly attractive to early-career MBA candidates, the school offers the opportunity to apply for a graduate assistantship, which pays a monthly stipend in return for twenty hours a week of work with a full-time faculty member. These positions are valuable, but challenging; a current student with a graduate assistantship explains, "Most of the day is spent on campus, with some days lasting from 8 A.M. to 10 P.M." On that note, the MBA workload is intense, "but not impossible," and students "are encouraged to learn how to work more efficiently" in order to keep up with the demands of the curriculum. While instructors are often "very strict and demanding," they "typically have an open door policy for students." When you take the time to visit professors in their offices, "they are really good at answering questions and make sure that you have a full understanding of everything before [you leave]."

SIU offers "very competitive tuition rates for an excellent program." Regardless of affordability, students are pleased to report that the school maintains a "very professional environment" with "efficient operations" and "good communication" with the student body. At SIU, "weekly if not daily emails are sent to business students informing them of upcoming events." SIU attracts many recent grads and early-career professionals, who would like to see "more interaction with employers (internships, recruiting, projects)" to prepare them for the real world. At the same time, the school offers a number of programs "that help prepare students for the real world. For example, "Saluki Student Investment Fund manages the SIU foundation portfolio worth over 1 million dollars." SIU also offers a month-long overseas program for students who would like to add an international focus to their studies.

ADMISSIONS CONTACT: DR. SUZANNE ALTOBELLO, MBA PROGRAMS DIRECTOR
ADDRESS: REHN HALL 133, 1025 LINCOLN DRIVE, MAIL CODE 4625, CARBONDALE, IL 62901
PHONE: 618-453-3030 • FAX: 618-453-2832
E-MAIL: COBGP@BUSINESS.SIU.EDU • WEBSITE: MBA.BUSINESS.SIU.EDU

Career and Placement

The College of Business Placement Center at Southern Illinois University serves undergraduate and graduate students, alumni, and online MBA candidates. The center provides individual career counseling services and conducts mock interviews, maintains online job listings, and organizes campus career fairs. Through the center, students also have access to a number of online job boards, as well as the "Digital Kiosk," a collection of career-related articles and resources for job seekers. Those who have attended career events say, "The employers at career fairs are substantial, including CAT, Boeing, etc." At the same time, graduate students feel "career development is a little weak" for MBA graduates. The Placement Center does "have contacts with the big four accounting firms," but most hiring managers come to campus in search of undergraduate students and accounting majors.

Student Life and Environment

While there are more than 20,000 students on the greater SIUC campus, there is a collegial atmosphere within the business school. Enrolling around 100 graduate students, "The College of Business is not huge and we quickly get to know everyone." Students at SIU are "mostly from the Midwest"; however, the school attracts a number of international students, bringing "very diverse cultures" to the small campus environment. Students are "high achievers for the most part," who take their studies seriously. When the semester is thoroughly underway, MBA candidates are "slightly insane from [a] lack of sleep." Fortunately, most manage to be both "friendly and competitive at the same time." Some say they "like to catch drinks together after class."

Nestled within the Shawnee National Forest, "Carbondale is a college town, hence life here is very peaceful." Students really appreciate "the small town feel that normally doesn't go along with such a large university." In their free time, Carbondale residents can "go to the wineries, hike in the beautiful state parks, or just enjoy the beautiful weather." When in search of more cosmopolitan pleasures (as well as a larger job market), the city of St. Louis is fewer than 100 miles to the west of SIUC's campus; both Chicago and Kansas City are also within striking distance, fewer than 300 miles away.

Admissions

To be eligible for admission to SIU's graduate programs, students must have a minimum GMAT score of 550 and a GPA of at least 2.7 for the last two years of undergraduate coursework. While these are the required minimums, the median GPA for students admitted MBA program was much higher, at 3.5. Students with a business-related degree from an AACSB-accredited school and a GPA of 3.5 or higher may qualify for a GMAT waiver.

FINANCIAL FACTS

Annual tuition (in-state/ out-of-state)	$7,767/$17,897
Fees	$2,798
Cost of books	$1,100
Room & board (on/off-campus)	$12,712/$0
% of students receiving aid	72
% of first-year students receiving aid	74
% of students receiving grants	37
Average award package	$22,283
Average grant	$8,233
Average loan	$25,559
Average student loan debt	$21,045

ADMISSIONS

Admissions Selectivity Rating	82
# of applications received	118
% applicants accepted	86
% acceptees attending	87
Average GMAT	594
Range of GMAT	550–628
Accepts GRE scores	Yes
Average GPA	3.4
TOEFL required of international students	Yes
Minimum TOEFL (paper/web)	550/80
Application fee	$50
International application fee	$50
Early application deadline	3/1
Early notification date	3/15
Regular application deadline	6/15
Regular application notification	6/30
Deferment available	Yes
Maximum length of deferment	1 year
Transfer students accepted	Yes
Transfer application policy	We will accept a maximum of 6 hours of transfer credit from an AACSB- accredited school. Courses that meet our foundation requirements are not transferred, they are merely accepted. as fulfilling the requirement.
Non-fall admissions	Yes
Need-blind admissions	No

SOUTHERN ILLINOIS UNIVERSITY—EDWARDSVILLE
SCHOOL OF BUSINESS

Academics

Located just thirty minutes away from downtown St. Louis, the School of Business at Southern Illinois University Edwardsville offers an "exceptional and...convenient" MBA program with courses in evening and weekend formats on the Edwardsville campus. This "up and coming school" offers "a well-rounded program" that is "taught by professors with real world experience." The school's curriculum, which includes condensed eight week courses, tends to be more general, meaning that students "take a wide variety of classes" and follow a pretty standard structure. Though some wish that there were "more possible concentrations" and the program was less geared towards "non-business undergrads," most are quite pleased with the degree they obtain here since the school is "in the midst of an expansion."

Students love most of their "exceptional" professors and feel that "they relate the coursework to everyday life." They "seem to truly care about students learning and being able to apply information in the real world," and "know how to communicate their information to their students effectively." "Their ability to answer questions from their experience in the field has earned my respect," says one admiring student. "Most of my professors still consult in their respective industries. They are very current on business trends and developments," says a student.

Though the overall satisfaction level is quite high, people agree that the school could stand to "weed out some of the less effective professors"; while most "are readily available for appointments or have preset office times," a handful "could not be inconvenienced with meeting with students outside normal class time." The school's administration is known for being "easily accessible and friendly," "has made planning classes easy," and has "a great concept of real-world work life [that they] implement . . . in the classroom." Classes here place a great deal of emphasis on group work, which is furthered by the "ease of communication through online resources (great e-presence)."

Career and Placement

Most students at SIUE "seem to be working professionals pursuing their MBA in order to enhance their income or receive a promotion," and "SIUE has the best value for the level of accreditation of all St. Louis area schools." Some wish that the school would "align coursework with skills needed for upper management"; the more experienced students are pretty much in agreement that classes are a breeze. "The instructors are good, but anyone who breathes gets a B," says one. A couple of students who are looking to get placed into a new job directly after graduation wish that the school would "add more networking and recruiting efforts aimed specifically at MBA students," but others have lauded the school for its "helpfulness when acquiring an assistantship," among other things. Its base efforts are also appreciated: "I went to a mock interview at the CDC, and I was treated seriously and went away from the experience pleased that I'd spent the time. Plus, they've always offered (organized) career fairs, resume services, and other professional events to the MBA students, as well as the undergraduate students."

ADMISSIONS CONTACT: SCHOOL OF BUSINESS STUDENT SERVICES, ADMISSIONS OFFICER
ADDRESS: CAMPUS BOX 1186, EDWARDSVILLE, IL 62026
PHONE: 618-650-3840 • FAX: 618-650-3979
E-MAIL: MBA@SIUE.EDU • WEBSITE: WWW.SIUE.EDU/BUSINESS/MBA

Student Life and Environment

The students at SIUE are "a near equal mix of recent undergraduate graduates and returning adults," all of whom are "very competitive, yet helpful and friendly." Everybody "is nice," and "it helps that everybody is working on their MBA for similar reasons." Though many in the MBA program just drop in for classes (one student says that "social life is not existent among MBA students"), there are "many various clubs, sports, Greek life, and volunteer options at SIUE" on this "vibrant and active campus" for those who do choose to participate.

Aside from its extremely convenient location near St. Louis, the campus is located on its own 2600 acres, "making it non-commercialized, which is another plus." Furthermore, "the size is perfect and the accommodations are excellent."

Admissions

Applicants to the SIUE MBA program must apply for admission to the university Graduate School, which includes submitting official transcripts for all post-secondary academic work and an official GMAT score report (applicants holding a PhD, MD, or equivalent degree need not submit GMAT scores, and graduates of SIUE do not need to have official transcripts sent). Admissions decisions are based primarily on undergraduate performance and GMAT scores (a recent entering class had an average GPA of 3.2 and average GMAT score of 510). The school recommends at least two years of work experience prior to entering the program. Entering students must demonstrate proficiency (typically through undergraduate coursework) in statistics and computer software; students lacking these proficiencies will be required to complete non-degree courses in the subjects in order to gain proficiency. International applicants must meet all the above criteria and submit an official TOEFL score report (minimum score of 550 paper-based test or 213 computer-based test). Rejected applicants may appeal the admissions decision to the MBA program director. Applicants with undergraduate GPAs of at least 2.8 may be admitted conditionally, pending subsequent successful completion of six credit hours of coursework in the program.

FINANCIAL FACTS

Annual tuition (in-state/ out-of-state)	$7,038/$17,596
Fees	$1,919
Cost of books	$2,963
Room & board	$9,052
Average award package	$9,241
Average grant	$4,866
Average loan	$10,979

ADMISSIONS

Admissions Selectivity Rating	79
# of applications received	113
% applicants accepted	88
% acceptees attending	82
Average GMAT	505
Range of GMAT	420–610
Accepts GRE scores	Yes
Average GPA	3.3
TOEFL required of international students	Yes
Minimum TOEFL (paper/web)	550/
Application fee	$31
International application fee	$31
Deferment available	Yes
Maximum length of deferment	1 year
Transfer students accepted	Yes
Transfer application policy From an AACSB accredited school and up to 9 hours.	
Non-fall admissions	Yes
Need-blind admissions	Yes

SOUTHERN METHODIST UNIVERSITY
COX SCHOOL OF BUSINESS

GENERAL INFORMATION
Type of school   Private
Affiliation   Methodist
Academic calendar   Mod/Semester

SURVEY SAYS...
Classmates have diverse work experience, Friendly students, Good peer network, Good social scene, Conservative students, Cutting-edge classes, Abundant mentors available, Helpful alumni, Happy students
Solid preparation in:
Finance, Accounting, General management, Operations, Teamwork, Communication/interpersonal skills

STUDENTS
Enrollment of parent institution	11,272
Enrollment of MBA Program	438
% male/female	67/33
% part-time	53
% underrepresented minority	6
% international	27
Average age at entry	27
Average years work experience at entry	4

ACADEMICS
Academic Experience Rating	94
Profs interesting rating	95
Profs accessible rating	96
Student/faculty ratio	37:1
% female faculty	20
% underrepresented minority faculty	3
% part-time faculty	15

Joint Degrees
JD/MBA; MA Arts Administration/MBA; MSSM (Master of Science in Sport Management)

Prominent Alumni
Beth E. Mooney, Chair and CEO - KeyCorp; Thomas Horton, Former Chairman - American Airlines Group, Inc. and American Airlines; Martin L. Flanagan, President and CEO - Invesco; Robert Dudley, Group CEO - BP

Academics

Southern Methodist University's Cox School of Business has one of the country's premier business programs, offering challenging academics, small classes, and excellent networking and travel opportunities for all. The professors and the administration are "fantastic in providing support in a timely fashion, answering questions over email, and being available to meet when students need them." Modernity and applicability are valued here; classes often deal with real-life situations, so students "can tease out how we could translate [them] to our own industries," and many members of the adjunct faculty are currently executives in industry today. The school looks to enhance learning via new technologies, such as collaboration tools and distance learning, and the optional Business Leadership Center workshops and networking opportunities outside of the classroom complement the curriculum. The introduction of new classes as a result of the changing economic environment has been a major advantage of the program; for example, "an accounting-based valuation class was offered and conducted by a professional leader who is changing the way in which people think about valuation." In addition, professors are "very involved with keeping their course content up to date."

The school's dual degree options and flexibility were big draws for current students (courses are the same in the evening and daytime), who say the administration at SMU "works hard to balance the needs of Part-Time, Full-Time and Executive MBAs and overall does a fantastic job." Students love the freedom to choose electives and concentrations over a fixed-course plan, and all students spend two weeks abroad for a global business course. "The business climate in Dallas, Texas is bustling as companies continue to relocate their headquarters to the area," and the school has a unique mentoring program (The Associate Board) through which "students have the opportunity to select a Dallas professional as a mentor." Most of the administrators "know each full-time MBA student personally."

Career and Placement

The "local network is very powerful," and connections to the Dallas business community yield plenty of internships and job opportunities, though a few students wish that the school would "expand recruitment process to be more national." Plenty of well-positioned alumni are more than eager to "open doors for graduates." The administration is "very willing to help each and every student regardless of class standing" and the student-led advisory board "does a great job of providing plenty of networking opportunities." SMU has a unique tailgate called The Boulevard, which "has companies come to campus in an atmosphere where networking is a breeze." The Cox Career Center has recently reorganized and re-staffed and "has done a tremendous job at providing access to high-income careers that aren't posted on any other job board." The school's partnership with The Disney Institute is a particular favorite, where Cox students are given the chance "to learn about how the Disney Company creates and maintains culture within their large organization." "The opportunity to meet with high level executives is unparalleled," says a student. Some companies that have recently recruited out of SMU include Deloitte, 7-Eleven, Hilton Worldwide, Vanguard, and General Mills.

Student Life and Environment

The size of the student body guarantees intimacy (most students live close to one another on this "beautiful campus"), and students "have weekly happy hours and constant club meetings" to help bolster community. "We all want each other to succeed. There's very much a feeling of 'rising tide lifts all boats' here," says a student. "I feel like I've gained a hundred new friends," says another. Classmates "definitely feel like colleagues, not competition." Plenty of social activities are available to students, including traditions such as the Cox Cup where first years compete with second years in events like flag football, tennis, basketball, trivia night, and a canned food drive. "There is no shortage of fun stuff to do. The real challenge is finding ways to do everything you want to do and still get your work done," says a student. This group is "mostly single, but certainly a few married people [are] in the program"; all are "fun, smart, and often quite accomplished" and come from all walks of life, so "you can't help but get interesting perspectives all the time." While the school is historically conservative, "there is a good sized population of liberal-minded students."

Admissions

Successful applicants to SMU have leadership experience, a strong academic record, and competitive scores on the GMAT. Last year, the range of GMAT scores for accepted applicants was 600–690, and the average undergraduate GPA was 3.28. Personal qualities are also heavily weighed, and Cox admits students with a history of professional and personal growth, demonstrated achievements, proven academic abilities, and leadership potential. Although an academic background in business is not a requirement for admission, SMU recommends students enter the program with a working knowledge of calculus, accounting, statistics, and microeconomics.

FINANCIAL FACTS

Annual tuition (in-state/ out-of-state)	$45,975/$45,975
Fees	$5,420
Cost of books	$3,200
Room & board	$18,300
% of students receiving aid	80
% of first-year students receiving aid	76
% of students receiving grants	70
Average award package	$43,876
Average grant	$27,360
Average loan	$45,626
Average student loan debt	$81,298

ADMISSIONS

Admissions Selectivity Rating	92
# of applications received	580
% applicants accepted	36
% acceptees attending	61
Average GMAT	656
Range of GMAT	590–710
Accepts GRE scores	Yes
Average Verbal GRE	156
Range of Verbal GRE scores	152–161
Average Quantitative GRE	159
Range of Quantitative GRE scores	158–162
Average GPA	3.4
TOEFL required of international students	Yes
Minimum TOEFL (paper/web)	600/100
Application fee	$0
International application fee	$0
Early application deadline	10/15
Early notification date	12/1
Regular application deadline	1/11
Regular application notification	3/1
Application Deadline/Notification	
Round 1:	10/15 / 12/1
Round 2:	1/11 / 3/1
Round 3:	3/1 / 4/15
Round 4:	5/2 / 6/1
Deferment available	Yes
Maximum length of deferment	1 year
Transfer students accepted	No
Non-fall admissions	No
Need-blind admissions	Yes

EMPLOYMENT PROFILE

Career Rating	95	Grads Employed by Function% Avg. Salary	
Percent employed at graduation	67	Marketing	(15%) $97,182
Percent employed 3 months after graduation	82	Operations	(2%)
		Consulting	(10%) $104,333
Average base starting salary	$100,304	Finance	(54%) $101,291
Primary Source of Full-time Job Acceptances		MIS	(1%)
School-facilitated activities	45 (%)	Other	(18%) $99,250
Graduate-facilitated activities	27 (%)	**Top 5 Employers Hiring Grads**	
Unknown	17 (%)	AT&T (7), American Airlines (5), Sabre (5), JP Morgan (4), Toyota (4)	

ST. JOHN'S UNIVERSITY
THE PETER J. TOBIN COLLEGE OF BUSINESS

Academics

St. John's University's business school, the Peter J. Tobin College of Business, enjoys quite a reputation, and deservedly so. Many students say they applied to the school on its "good reputation," in addition to many unique perks offered throughout its program. One of the main academic draws to the school is its Risk Management Program. The School of Risk Management is housed in a state-of-the-art building located in the East Village, Manhattan. In addition to their "very strong curriculum," the School of Risk Management building also houses the Center for Professional Education, the division that provides custom and non-degree granting programs, the Insurance Hall of Fame and the world famous Kathryn and Shelby Cullom Davis Library.

One of the true hallmarks of any good university includes its professors, and St. John's follows this precedent. While there are some teachers at SJU that the occasional student identifies as, "not helpful and stressful," the vast majority of professors here "convey a true commitment and investment in the university and the students," and provide "excellent lectures." Many teachers are "experienced in the fields they teach or oversee," which allows them to "provide the latest information" from the business world and "apply [the] concepts in class [to] real world examples." This kind of teaching provides "valuable insight" into the business world, which is useful since most students either work full-time or are looking for a job. By offering real world experience, instead of only tests, the school demonstrates that it is "more focused on [the] growth of its students than it is on what grade they get at the end of the year."

Career and Placement

St. John's Career Center helps students in a variety of ways: it offers them assistance in writing a resume, searching for jobs, internship placement and evaluating potential job offers. In addition, St. John's promotes an on-campus group called Career Peers, which connects students to a group of other students their own age who are trained to answer job search questions they might have. The school personalizes the center so students do not have to search through an answer database for help. There are four major campuses: one in Rome, Italy and three in New York City (Queens, Manhattan, and Staten Island), and students find ample job opportunities in both. There are "good connections" in New York, "specifically in finance," and in Rome many students intern with the UN'S World Food Program, which "offers an incredible resume boost." Indeed the university is "very up-to-date with the job market," and it helps it students make themselves some of the "most marketable" graduates in the tri-state area.

Student Life and Environment

As with most MBA programs, many people commute to class since they have full-time jobs, but since the four campuses are located in major cities those who do attend find the commute "very convenient." In New York there are campuses in Queens, Manhattan, and Staten Island and students love that they can choose classes in all three boroughs. This option makes it "easier to fit trips to campus" in students' schedules. There are also plenty of opportunities to study abroad and students can sign up to visit, or even attend classes, at the Rome campus as well. Many find this opportunity to be "a truly amazing experience." It is also easier for students studying abroad since all of the classes are taught in English, but foreign students still get the flavor of living in a new city with other students who have "come from all over the world." All campuses have plenty to do for those living on or near campus, or just looking to hang around after class since there are "lots of different kinds of organizations." In addition, the "random activities that take place here are great ways to battle the stress of an MBA."

Students tend to be a fairly mixed group of people; their personalities and backgrounds are all quite unique. "Some students are extremely competitive, while others are a bit more relaxed," but the mixing of different groups really makes class discussions 'vibrant.' Despite any differences, students still greatly respect one another and define the student body as "independent, hard-working, and smart." As far as school administration goes, there seems to be a "requisite amount of difficulty when it comes to doing basically anything," but the "administrators are accessible and generally helpful" as well as "very accommodating" to many of the students' needs. With the convenient locations and "hard-working" students, many find a "very fulfilled life" at SJU.

Admissions

For those looking to apply, keep in mind that fall semester applications are usually due at the beginning of May and spring semester applications are usually due near the beginning of November. Applicants must submit evidence of a baccalaureate degree, two letters of recommendation, and their official GMAT score. GPA is not "exclusively" taken in to consideration, but the current average GPA of accepted students is 3.2 on a 4.0 scale.

FINANCIAL FACTS

Annual tuition (in-state/ out-of-state)	$20,790/$20,790
Fees	$340
Cost of books	$610
Room & board (on/off-campus)	$19,700/$14,288
% of students receiving aid	54
% of first-year students receiving aid	56
% of students receiving grants	39
Average award package	$25,331
Average grant	$19,911
Average loan	$28,161
Average student loan debt	$58,073

ADMISSIONS

Admissions Selectivity Rating	79
# of applications received	210
% applicants accepted	83
% acceptees attending	51
Average GMAT	524
Range of GMAT	490–570
Accepts GRE scores	No
Average GPA	3.3
TOEFL required of international students	Yes
Minimum TOEFL (paper/web)	550/213
Application fee	$50
International application fee	$50
Regular application deadline	5/1
Deferment available	Yes
Maximum length of deferment	One Year
Transfer students accepted	Yes
Transfer application policy	Must use regular application. Individual review of transfer credits. Maximum of six credits from another AACSB accredited program. Courses must be identical in content to a course(s) we offer.
Non-fall admissions	Yes
Need-blind admissions	Yes

EMPLOYMENT PROFILE

Career Rating	79	Grads Employed by Function	% Avg. Salary
Percent employed at graduation	58	Marketing	(16%) $52,820
Percent employed 3 months after graduation	20	Management	(7%) $60,333
		Finance	(44%) $53,643
Average base starting salary	$54,093	Other	(21%) $54,700
Primary Source of Full-time Job Acceptances		**Top 5 Employers Hiring Grads**	
School-facilitated activities	17 (14%)	Ernst & Young (4), PricewaterCoopers (2),	
Graduate-facilitated activities	17 (14%)	BNY Mellon (1), Deloitte (1), Protiviti (1)	
Unknown	90 (73%)		

ST. MARY'S UNIVERSITY
GREEHEY SCHOOL OF BUSINESS

GENERAL INFORMATION
Type of school	Private
Affiliation	Roman Catholic
Academic calendar	Semester

SURVEY SAYS...
Classmates have diverse work experience, Friendly students, Cutting-edge classes, Happy students
Solid preparation in:
Marketing, Accounting, General management, Teamwork, Communication/interpersonal skills, Presentation skills, Doing business in a global economy, Environmental sustainability, Social responsibility

STUDENTS
Enrollment of parent institution	3,625
Enrollment of MBA Program	53
% male/female	69/31
% part-time	8
% international	9
Average age at entry	27

ACADEMICS
Academic Experience Rating	**89**
Profs interesting rating	89
Profs accessible rating	94
Student/faculty ratio	10:1
% female faculty	36
% underrepresented minority faculty	4
% part-time faculty	5

Joint Degrees
JD/MBA, 108 hrs JD/24 hrs MBA, 3 yrs.

Prominent Alumni
Bill Greehey, CEO, Nustar; Stuart Parker, CEO, USAA

Academics

The MBA program at St. Mary's University's Bill Greehey School of Business offers innovative programs designed to graduate conscientious global business leaders. The program includes a JD/MBA dual degree option, as well as an additional dual degree with The University of Applied Sciences in Schmalkalden, Germany. The MBA program advances the University's Marianist tradition of community service through "a wealth of classes" in ethical leadership, corporate social responsibility, sustainability, and social entrepreneurship. It is also home to a unique host of real-world experiential learning opportunities, such as the chance to be a volunteer federal income tax preparer for area residents through St. Mary's Volunteer Income Tax Assistance (VITA) program or to study abroad in places like Brazil, Denmark, South Korea, and France. In addition, the curriculum is based on a Marianist focus on the education and development of the total person. This includes modules on Advanced Behavioral Skills dealing with conflict resolution, innovation and creativity, interpersonal communication and other skills that differentiate top performers at work.

Students complete a thirty-three semester-hour program consisting of eleven courses which include a Rapid Innovation Social Business Prototyping, an International Field Study, and a capstone project. The program requires three full semesters and a summer to complete and new cohorts are launched each fall. With the help of "the friendly administration," students are able to take advantage of specialized programs such as the accoutancy track for students working toward their CPA certification.

Students praise faculty for "focusing on teaching and understanding" and providing "real-life cases that the professors experienced in their former occupations," including the wisdom of "some exceptional standouts, who are nationally competitive." St. Mary's has always been known for its personal touches and small class sizes, and students confirm that faculty "spend a lot of time working with students on the nuances that can't be conveyed in an hour" and help "mentor them on career decisions." Students appreciate that this small program is not overly bureaucratic, which is derived from an administration-faculty union that "works hand-in-hand to ensure that students receive the best education and support both inside and outside the classroom as possible."

Career and Placement

The Career Services Center at St. Mary's University provides one-on-one career counseling to both students and alumni; a library of career-related materials, including hard-copy and online job-search databases; special events (Resume Drive, Business Etiquette Dinner, Mock Interview Day); a career fair; and connections to an alumni mentoring program. Many wish that the Center engaged in more than just "passive marketing" and had "more connections to different industries," and most agree that St. Mary's is "primarily a San Antonio school." "Many of the students are from the area and intend to stay in the area following graduation." For this reason, students tell us that "the strong alumni network" is one of the biggest attractions of a St. Mary's degree. Employers interviewing on the St. Mary's campus include such organizations as USAA; HEB; The San Antonio Spurs; Union Pacific; Culinary Institute of America; Fisher, Herbst &Kemble; Enterprise Rent-A-Car; The American Red Cross; Tesoro Corporation; Valero; and NuStar Energy.

ADMISSIONS CONTACT: JEREMY M. GRACE, DIRECTOR, MASTER OF BUSINESS PROGRAMS
ADDRESS: ONE CAMINO SANTA MARIA, SAN ANTONIO, TX 78228-8507
PHONE: 210-436-3101 • FAX: 210-431-2220
E-MAIL: JMGRACE@STMARYTX.EDU • WEBSITE: WWW.STMARYTX.EDU/MBA

Student Life and Environment

St. Mary's student body is "extremely varied in terms of background, education, and experience," and most are there "to further their career or gain a competitive edge in their respective industries." The school has traditionally served the Hispanic community well; over half of all undergraduates here are Hispanic. On the whole, students "are clearly proud of this university," and this shows in the "strong interaction between undergraduate and graduate students." Most "usually work full-time" or have a family. Classmates describe each other as a "team-oriented, hard-working, and friendly" group that "converges on campus and brings a wealth of information and context to class discussions and group projects," providing a "'been-there' context, which solidifies the theory taught in class." This willingness to share is also demonstrated through the numerous "clubs, activities, festivals and academic events," as "there is always something taking place on campus for students, athletes, and the community."

With over one million residents within city limits and almost as many living in the metropolitan area, San Antonio is the second-largest city in Texas and one of the larger cities in the country. The military and petroleum industries both have major presences here. With nearly 20 million visitors every year, San Antonio (and its "excellent weather") is also a major player in the nation's tourism trade.

Admissions

Applicants to the MBA program at St. Mary's must apply to the graduate school for admission. There is no cost associated with the application process. Applications are reviewed by the MBA program director, who makes admissions recommendations to the Dean of the business school. Candidates must submit the following materials to the office of admissions: a completed on-line application form; an official score report for the GMAT or the GRE (contact the program director for minimum acceptable scores); an LSAT score for students pursuing the JD/MBA option; two sets of official transcripts for all postsecondary academic work; two letters of recommendation from individuals well acquainted with the applicant's academic/professional ability; and a completed health form (required by Texas State Law). A telephone or on-campus interview is required. International applicants must provide all of the above materials, as well as a signed financial statement, and an official score report for the TOEFL (minimum acceptable score: 570 paper-based, 230 computer-based, 80 Internet or a minimum score of 6.5 on the IELTS English-language proficiency test (Academic or General); students with lower TOEFL or IELTS scores may be allowed to attend an English language program or classes at St. Mary's in order to meet minimum language proficiency requirements. Students may receive regular admission, which is unconditional. Conditional admission under certain circumstances is permitted, allowing students to enroll in no more than nine hours of classes after which their admission status is reappraised. International students are not eligible for conditional admission.

In addition, students may receive special admission as non-degree seeking students for the MBA Professional Accountancy track or under other special circumstances approved by the Program Director.

FINANCIAL FACTS

Annual tuition	$19,920
Fees	$4,555
Cost of books	$1,900
Room & board	
(on/off-campus)	$7,500/$11,915
% of students receiving grants	71
Average grant	$4,740

ADMISSIONS

Admissions Selectivity Rating	84
# of applications received	57
% applicants accepted	60
% acceptees attending	71
Average GMAT	542
Range of GMAT	500–580
Accepts GRE scores	Yes
Average Verbal GRE	0
Range of Verbal	
GRE scores	0–0
Average GPA	3.1
TOEFL required of	
international students	Yes
Minimum TOEFL	
(paper/web)	570/80
Application fee	$0
International application fee	$0
Early application deadline	7/1
Early notification date	7/30
Deferment available	Yes
Maximum length of	
deferment	1 year
Transfer students accepted	Yes
Transfer application policy	
On recommendation of the	
Graduate program director may	
accept a maximum of 6 semester	
hours for the those seeking an	
MBA with a concentration in	
Professional Accountancy from	
AACSB-accredited programs.	
However, no transfer hours	
are accepted into the lock-step	
Greehey MBA.	
Non-fall admissions	Yes
Need-blind admissions	Yes

STANFORD UNIVERSITY
STANFORD GRADUATE SCHOOL OF BUSINESS

GENERAL INFORMATION

Type of school	Private
Affiliation	No Affiliation
Academic calendar	Quarter

SURVEY SAYS...

Classmates have diverse work experience, Friendly students, Good peer network, Good social scene, Liberal students, Cutting-edge classes, Abundant mentors available, Helpful alumni, Happy students, Abundant clubs and activities, Students love Stanford, CA
Solid preparation in:
Finance, Accounting, General management, Teamwork, Communication/interpersonal skills, Presentation skills, Quantitative skills, Doing business in a global economy, Entreprenurial studies

STUDENTS

Enrollment of MBA Program	824
% male/female	60/40
% part-time	0
% underrepresented minority	20
% international	31
Average years work experience at entry	4

ACADEMICS

Academic Experience Rating	99
Profs interesting rating	90
Profs accessible rating	97
Student/faculty ratio	6:1
% female faculty	19
% underrepresented minority faculty	14
% part-time faculty	52

Joint Degrees

It is possible to earn dual degrees with any other Stanford University department. CS-MS in Computer Science/MBA, EE-MS in Electrical Engineering/MBA, JD/MBA, MA in Education/MBA, MBA/MS in Environment and Resources, and MBA/MPP (public policy).

Academics

For those that are let through its hallowed doors, the Stanford University Graduate School of Business gives them "unmatched exposure to the best of what the business world has to offer." An exceptional focus on leadership development, experiential learning, and soft skill development dovetails neatly with the well-known quantitative analysis curriculum, and the school offers numerous lab environments designed to help students "grow interpersonally, try new leadership styles, and give and receive honest and read time feedback." The GSB is truly a student-led school, and the administration "constantly asks for feedback and quickly and actively responds to and incorporates" it. The flexibility of the curriculum leaves "lots of time for electives" and classroom discussions are engaging, thanks to the fact that "students are not afraid to challenge the status quo." Community is king here, and the weekly event TALK—where a student shares their life story—is "a perfect representation of the community."

The "unreal" professors "strive exceptionally hard to be strong teachers and often solicit feedback to improve the courses." Admittance here includes "access to superstars" that include many "world-class professors who are not only gold-standard researchers, but also dedicated and skillful instructors." They "put a lot of effort into classes" and want to make sure that it sticks: "Every professor I asked [has] made himself/herself available outside of class multiple times."

"Someone once put it best when they said the worst part of GSB is the 'agony of options.' At any given moment there are at least half a dozen amazing things you could be doing," says a student. From the Global Management Immersion Experience (GMIX) program to Leadership Labs to the fellows coaching program (which is "outstanding for receiving coaching as a first year and learning to coach as a second year"), students here do not lack for experiences and learning opportunities with which to "reflect on who you are/who you want to be."

Career and Placement

The Career Management Center (CMC) is one of the most comprehensive career services departments out there; simply finding students jobs is not their main concern. The Career and Life Vision Program stresses self-reflection through small peer groups and one-on-one coaching sessions; the Industry Insider Advising Program connects students with leaders in a variety of areas; things like "Meet the Company" Presentations and "Fewer Than 300" small- and medium-sized company networking events only further drive home the center's goal of helping students realize their potential.

Indeed, the career search at Stanford "weights much more heavily toward networking" (as facilitated by the CMC), and students here are handshake soldiers by the time they depart. The proximity to Silicon Valley and the "links with tech/start up communities" are huge pluses for many who are looking to jump off here, though finance is the biggest destination. More than 350 organizations hired up Stanford grads last year (almost all of them hiring multiple people), culled down from the list of thousands of employers who recruited at the GSB, including Amazon.com, Apple, Bain & Company, Booz & Company, Boston Consulting Group, Cisco Systems, Dell, Education Pioneers, Genentech, General Mills, Goldman Sachs, Johnson & Johnson, Intel, Google, Hulu, IDEO, NBC Universal (GE), U.S. Government, Nike, VMware, Warner Bros., and many more.

Student Life and Environment

This group comes from "incredible backgrounds" all over the world, creating a gumbo of "unbelievably smart and driven, yet incredibly humble and kind" individuals. The majority of students are unmarried and live on-campus, and hence "are exceptionally out-going and interested in getting to know other students." Social life revolves around "small group dinners and coffee chats," and most "believe it is possible to get to know everyone of their classmates." There is plenty to do on campus to suit all academic and extracurricular interests, given the size of Stanford campus overall; and though Palo Alto itself "doesn't have much, it's feasible to go up to San Francisco weekly, particularly if you have a car." The campus itself "looks like paradise." "I caught myself in telling a friend in February: 'I just walked through the sunny courtyard, smelling orange blossoms, lilacs, and honeysuckle. I'm wearing shorts and contemplating a run in the hills, or going to the meditation center,'" says a student. Competition is not in the nature of a GSB student, who are "much more focused on building collaborative, long term relationships with each other than trying to finish at the top of the academic rank." "In many ways, alumni of the GSB have the same attachment to the GSB that they do to their undergraduate schools," says one impressed student.

Admissions

Stanford being Stanford, admission is selective. Applicants will be evaluated in three areas: intellectual vitality, demonstrated leadership potential, and personal qualities and contributions. That means grades are not enough. Stanford is looking for outstanding candidates who will fit into the school's history of accomplishment and innovation. Admissions, according to school officials, is an art, not a science. There are no minimum GMAT score or GPA requirements. Current students have a GMAT range from 550–790, with a mean score of 732. In other words, there is no magic formula. Excel, succeed, and stand out from the crowd in all aspects of your life to improve your chances.

Prominent Alumni

Phil Knight, Founder and Chairman, Nike Inc.; Mary Barra, CEO, General Motors; Charles Schwab, Founder and Chairman, Charles Schwab & Co.; Jacqueline Novogratz, Founder and CEO, Acumen Fund; Jeffrey Bewkes, CEO and Chairman, Time Warner

FINANCIAL FACTS

Annual tuition (in-state/ out-of-state)	$64,050/$64,050
Fees	$0
Cost of books	$2,787
Room & board (on/off-campus)	$29,202/$29,202
% of students receiving aid	64
% of first-year students receiving aid	67
% of students receiving grants	53
Average award package	$66
Average grant	$35,343
Average loan	$41,781
Average student loan debt	$83,762

ADMISSIONS

Admissions Selectivity Rating	99
# of applications received	7,899
Average GMAT	733
Accepts GRE scores	Yes
Average GPA	3.8
TOEFL required of international students	Yes
Minimum TOEFL (paper/web)	600/100
Application fee	$275
International application fee	$275
Deferment available	Yes
Maximum length of deferment	Only for college seniors
Transfer students accepted	No
Non-fall admissions	No
Need-blind admissions	Yes

EMPLOYMENT PROFILE

Career Rating	99	**Grads Employed by Function% Avg. Salary**		
Percent employed at graduation	72	Marketing	(27%)	$121,466
Percent employed 3 months		Operations	(3%)	$131,714
after graduation	86	Consulting	(18%)	$128,278
Average base starting salary	$133,406	Management	(12%)	$123,043
Primary Source of Full-time Job Acceptances		Finance	(31%)	$157,449
School-facilitated activities	97 (46%)	Other	(8%)	$110,529
Graduate-facilitated activities	114 (54%)	**Top 5 Employers Hiring Grads**		
Unknown	1 (0%)	Bain & Company, BCG, Facebook, Google, McKinsey & Co.		

STATE UNIVERSITY OF NEW YORK AT BINGHAMTON
SCHOOL OF MANAGEMENT

GENERAL INFORMATION

Type of school	Public
Affiliation	No Affiliation
Academic calendar	2 Semester

SURVEY SAYS...

Liberal students, Cutting-edge classes, Happy students, Abundant clubs and activities
Solid preparation in:
General management, Teamwork, Communication/interpersonal skills, Presentation skills, Quantitative skills, Computer skills, Doing business in a global economy

STUDENTS

Enrollment of parent institution	16,913
Enrollment of MBA Program	82
% male/female	64/36
% out-of-state	8
% part-time	2
% underrepresented minority	8
% international	33
Average age at entry	24
Average years work experience at entry	2

ACADEMICS

Academic Experience Rating	**92**
Profs interesting rating	90
Profs accessible rating	94
Student/faculty ratio	8:1
% female faculty	19
% underrepresented minority faculty	6
% part-time faculty	50

Joint Degrees

Watson (School of Engineering)/ MBA Fast Track-5 years (Bachelors+MBA); Harpur (College of Arts & Sciences)/MBA Fast Track-5 years (Bachelors+MBA)

Academics

"Close proximity to New York City," an excellent "reputation for quality" (particularly in New York), "one of the best accounting programs in the nation," and a small program size that ensures students won't get lost in the crowd, are among the top reasons students give for choosing the MBA program at Binghamton University. It also doesn't hurt that it "all comes with an extremely reasonable price tag," with "cheap tuition" even for out-of-state students.

The four-semester MBA program at Binghamton University (BU) employs "an extremely team-based approach" to education "that replicates real-world business in a way many other business programs do not," students inform us. This is especially true in the first year, during which the program covers core essentials. One student explains, "The first year of the program requires students to stick with a set group of students to work on projects, presentations, papers, and cases. It can be difficult at times, but the lessons learned are crucial for the real world." Full-time MBA students are also required to obtain an internship during the course of the program, which may be used toward fulfilling an elective course requirement. The school also offers a Fast Track Professional MBA in New York City (with classes taking place on Saturdays over the course of a year), and a Fast Track MBA to Binghamton undergraduates. The program allows them to earn both a BA and an MBA in five years, no small feat considering that a Binghamton MBA requires sixty-nine credits, "more than any other university."

For a state school, BU provides excellent service and a "smart organizational system." Students tell us that "the school really tries to adapt to the latest management concepts and ideals" and that administrators are "are diligent and available to help students with interviews and networking opportunities." Most of the professors have been practitioners in their respective fields at one point or another, which means "the tone of the course matches the tone of the discipline and serves to address the gap between theory and practice that plagues weaker business programs." The only knock on teachers is that "many are foreign," so that "sometimes it is difficult to understand what is being said due to accents." Most often, however, instructors "can communicate easily with the students." Another asset to the program is that "the alumni that are in highly respected companies are great, and everyone really tries to pull for other Binghamton students." "I have also interfaced with alumni on many occasions, gaining insights into investment banking and asset management," says one student.

Career and Placement

For a small program, Binghamton does a good job of bringing some major recruiters to its relatively remote location. One student informs us that "we have powerhouse recruiters from Credit Suisse, Goldman Sachs, the big four accounting, all the engineering firms, as well as many others. Without question, the recruiting at this school is on an incredible climb upwards. More and more powerhouse companies are coming to Binghamton." Still, those here would like to see the school's reputation grow at a faster rate, as "most rankings underestimate the potential on campus." The Career Development Center offers counseling services, career workshops, resume-development services, resume-referral services, a career-resource library, and access to the alumni network.

Top employers of Binghamton MBAs include Ernst & Young, Deloitte, KPMG, Lockheed Martin, and Target.

Student Life and Environment

Many classes for the fall are held in the evenings at Binghamton's "centralized campus," which "leads to very long days, especially for those who also have part-time jobs" and hampers extracurricular involvement. As these "motivated" students progress through the program, however, the school offers "plenty opportunities to get involved on campus," from the Finance Society to stock pitch and M&A competitions that allow students to "apply coursework to real-world topics and compete with fellow students in a constructive manner." The latter "implements various activities throughout the year including coffee hours, open bars, networking events," "horseback riding, bowling, etc." There is also a wide range of work experience among students, which benefits those at all stages of their careers. "The breadth of industry knowledge in the program is very impressive and fosters meaningful class discussions that drive home course material," says a student.

The city of Binghamton "has lots of things going for it besides the downtown bar scene. For one thing, there is a hometown hockey team and baseball team, an opera house, numerous playhouses, and theaters, too. We are also the carousel capital of the United States. Binghamton is ethnically diverse as well, and there are often ethnic festivals going on throughout the Southern Tier." Also, "living expenses here are not much," especially when compared to the cost of living in much of the rest of the state. The university also "has a great Division-I athletic department that provides exciting competitions for the students to attend," and many do.

Admissions

Applicants to the Binghamton MBA program must submit two copies of official undergraduate transcripts for all college work, two letters of recommendation, a personal statement, a resume, and GMAT scores. Work experience, while preferred, is not required. Additionally, international students must submit a certified statement of financial responsibility and TOEFL scores (minimum acceptable score is 590 for the paper version, 243 for the computer version, or 96 for the internet version). A basic understanding of calculus is "strongly recommended" for all incoming students; strong calculus skills are necessary for those interested in studying finance or operations management.

Prominent Alumni

Mark Deutsch, Partner/Private Equity; Matthew Singer, Partner/Accounting; Gary Meltzer, US Advisory Leader/Investment Mgmt & Real Estate; Howard Elsen, Managing Director/Business Development; Allen Zwickler, Managing Director/Finance

FINANCIAL FACTS

Annual tuition (in-state/ out-of-state)	$14,410/ $24,390
Fees	$2,101
Cost of books	$1,000
Room & board (on/off-campus)	$0/$18,122
% of students receiving aid	45
% of first-year students receiving aid	41
% of students receiving grants	12
Average award package	$16,554
Average grant	$2,963
Average loan	$20,396
Average student loan debt	$12,678

ADMISSIONS

Admissions Selectivity Rating	87
# of applications received	176
% applicants accepted	53
% acceptees attending	51
Average GMAT	621
Range of GMAT	583–658
Accepts GRE scores	Yes
Average Verbal GRE	151
Range of Verbal GRE scores	149–153
Average Quantitative GRE	153
Range of Quantitative GRE scores	148–158
Average Writing GRE	3.8
Range of Writing GRE scores	3.8–4.0
Average GPA	3.5
TOEFL required of international students	Yes
Minimum TOEFL (paper/web)	590/96
Application fee	$75
International application fee	$75
Regular application deadline	3/1
Deferment available	Yes
Maximum length of deferment	1 year
Transfer students accepted	No
Non-fall admissions	No
Need-blind admissions	Yes

EMPLOYMENT PROFILE

Career Rating	87	Grads Employed by Function	% Avg. Salary
Percent employed at graduation	62	Marketing	(13%) $55,000
Average base starting salary	$62,136	Operations	(13%) $57,000
Primary Source of Full-time Job Acceptances		Consulting	(38%) $67,000
		Management	(4%)
		Finance	(25%) $58,600
		MIS	(4%) $80,000
		Other	(4%) $55,000

Top 5 Employers Hiring Grads
Protiviti(3), EY (2), Bloomberg LP (1), DayNine Consulting (1), HSBC (1)

STATE UNIVERSITY OF NEW YORK—OSWEGO

SCHOOL OF BUSINESS

GENERAL INFORMATION

Type of school	Public
Affiliation	No Affiliation
Academic calendar	Semester/year round

SURVEY SAYS...

Good peer network, Cutting-edge classes
Solid preparation in:
Accounting, General management

STUDENTS

Enrollment of parent institution	7,937
Enrollment of MBA Program	239
% male/female	68/32
% out-of-state	7
% part-time	65
% underrepresented minority	25
% international	4
Average age at entry	28
Average years work experience at entry	5

ACADEMICS

Academic Experience Rating	**66**
Profs interesting rating	71
Profs accessible rating	69
Student/faculty ratio	19:1
% female faculty	33
% underrepresented minority faculty	20
% part-time faculty	29

Joint Degrees

BS Accounting/MBA,5 yrs;
BA Psychology/MBA, 5 yrs;
BA Broadcasting and Mass
Communications/MBA, 1 yr FT (for graduate work).

Prominent Alumni

Al Roker, NBC Today Show
weather anchor; Alice McDermott,
National Book Award Winner and
best-selling novelist; Ken Auletta,
New Yorker Columnist & critically
acclaimed author; Robert Moritz,
Chairman and Senior Partner,
PricewaterhouseCoopers

Academics

Students who enroll in the School of Business at SUNY Oswego can expect several things: excellent value for their money, intimate classes, knowledgeable professors, state-of-the-art facilities, and an excellent hockey team. As one student puts it, "In most areas, the school of business is at the top of its class. The classes are challenging and worthwhile. Most professors are really good at their areas. They are also widely available to help students both inside and out of class," and "really want to see the students succeed." According to most of the students, the "very small classes promote learning and student-professor interaction." The program "provides a lot of hands-on work and team activities to help form a strong work ethic" among students.

Designed as a degree in general management, an MBA from SUNY Oswego provides a solid grounding in the basics of modern business organization. The school says that "this program is intended to be equally applicable to private, public, and governmental sectors of management." The foundation subjects required of students include management, accounting, marketing, organization, law, and finance. In addition, students can choose to specialize in a specific field such as international management, manufacturing management, organizational leadership, or financial services. Foundation course requirements include management information systems, managerial finance, marketing management, management science I, international business, global perspectives on organizational management, and management policy. Students have a choice of taking classes at the Oswego Campus, at the Metro Center in downtown Syracuse, and online. In addition to general management electives, students can also specialize in accounting. Students in the accounting track can gain professional experience by participating in the Volunteer Income Tax Assistance (VITA) program. Students interested in finance can spend a semester at the Levin Institute's International Finance and Global Banking in New York City.

Students find their coursework both rigorous and exciting. As one puts it, "the professors are excellent and the classes are fun and challenging." Another says, "the course load is challenging, requiring solid communication and organization skills." Fortunately, the student body as a whole is "reliable and helpful." "We help each other out in our classes. I think the students in the graduate program really create a bond with one another."

Career and Placement

Although Oswego has a lot to offer—lovely campus, low cost, quality education, intimate program—most students wish it would go further in strengthening its Career Services department. There is little aid specifically for prospective MBAs, and the job search is often directed almost entirely by the student. As one puts it, "Connecting with employers is a difficult task. Linking up with quality employers looking for graduates with postgraduate degrees needs to be addressed." The exception is accounting, which has numerous national and regional public accounting firms actively recruiting throughout the year.

Student Life and Environment

Students say their "classmates are very intelligent. They provide a lot of feedback to one another, work well together, and create a competitive environment which prepares people for the job market." All rave about their "beautiful campus," which, they proudly point out, is also extremely "technologically-advanced and mostly wireless." The typical MBA's social life is strong, and there are "plenty of bars around for an active nightlife." As one student says, "At Oswego, I had the opportunity to make new friends from all over the world. The social life is active and I consider myself lucky." For the most part, students claim to be "very active on campus. There is a multitude of clubs and organizations to choose from." Students enjoy their "great gyms to work out in or play a game of racquetball." Plus—as is typical in upstate New York—the school's athletic life centers on their "excellent hockey team, instead of football." As one student puts it, "what's excellent about living on campus here is that there is every resource that you could possibly need available on campus. There are new buildings and renovations, from a new student center to the newly renovated freshman residence hall and new business center with technology classrooms."

Admissions

To be considered for admission to the small MBA program at the School of Business at SUNY Oswego, a candidate must have a minimum GPA of 2.6 out of 4.0. The minimum required score for the GMAT is 490. Taking the TOEFL test is also required for students whose native language is not English.

FINANCIAL FACTS

Annual tuition (in-state/ out-of-state)	$14,410/$24,390
Fees	$1,045
Cost of books	$800
Room & board	$12,990
% of students receiving aid	63
% of first-year students receiving aid	68
% of students receiving grants	4
Average award package	$12,462
Average grant	$1,712
Average loan	$12,686
Average student loan debt	$12,761

ADMISSIONS

Admissions Selectivity Rating	**80**
# of applications received	124
% applicants accepted	81
% acceptees attending	67
Average GMAT	506
Range of GMAT	330–610
Accepts GRE scores	Yes
Average GPA	3.3
TOEFL required of international students	Yes
Minimum TOEFL (paper/web)	560/83
Application fee	$65
International application fee	$65
Deferment available	Yes
Maximum length of deferment	five years
Transfer students accepted	Yes
Transfer application policy Six credits may be accepted for transfer into the program.	
Non-fall admissions	Yes
Need-blind admissions	Yes

State University of New York—University at Albany
School of Business

GENERAL INFORMATION

Type of school	Public
Affiliation	No Affiliation
Academic calendar	September-May

SURVEY SAYS...
Friendly students
Solid preparation in:
General management, Teamwork

STUDENTS

Enrollment of MBA Program	349
% male/female	62/38
% part-time	76
% underrepresented minority	10
% international	19
Average age at entry	31

ACADEMICS

Academic Experience Rating	**67**
Profs interesting rating	67
Profs accessible rating	68
Student/faculty ratio	4:1
% female faculty	28
% underrepresented minority faculty	0
% part-time faculty	10

Joint Degrees
JD/MBA (4 years)

Prominent Alumni
Joan Solotar, Managing Director, Blackstone; Dean C Backer, Partner, Goldman Sachs; Elda DiRe, Partner, E&Y; Jeff Black, Vice Chairman, Deloitte; Michael Carmen, Partner, Wellington Management

Academics

Since 1970, the School of Business at the University at Albany has "the best combination of education quality and value." Many who attend, having already been undergrads, are familiar with the State University of New York system, and it is well known that the School of Business offers solid academics at an incredibly affordable price. Even though the University at Albany is a larger research institution, the "small size of the school dictates easy accessibility to the administration and instructors," so "graduate students are treated well here."

The "great professors" of UA really "know their subjects" and are "available outside of class to discuss class and other materials." Class sizes are small, yet the projects are "challenging but not impossible." The full-time program offers six concentration paths: Cyber Security, Entrepreneurship, Finance, Human Resources Information Systems, Information Technology Management, and Marketing. Each student takes part in a cornerstone, integrative project at the end of their first year called "G3"; it applies the various functional aspects of business learned throughout the first year to the sustainability issues facing a real organization in today's competitive, global economy.

The school's administration "provides support to students who need resources for business plan competitions and the like"; students are also easily able to gain experience through internships in the school's Small Business Development Center, which supports small startup companies, family-owned enterprises, entrepreneurial ventures, among others, by offering free personal counseling in developing strategic business plans, identifying appropriate sources of funding, and providing market research, management information, and financial analysis. Other experience building opportunities can be found through the Center for Institutional Investment Management, which actively promotes institutional investment management research among faculty and students through research grants, travel support, and the acquisition of relevant academic and practitioner databases—not to mention the Center's dedicated Bloomberg terminals.

Career and Placement

As already mentioned, the greatest strength of the School of Business is its small size. "This drives the administration and faculty to go out of their way to try to place students in jobs," even if students are not able to land their first choice of a position and must start lower on the totem pole. For those who work hard, the school's name and reputation for "an incredibly competitive education" bring in enough recognition and recruitment to land top jobs (the school has a particularly strong relationship with the Big 4 accounting firms). "I have been able to land a job in a Fortune 500 company due to the excellent career placement services," says one. One intangible quality that students gain from UA's many projects includes the invaluable practice of presenting themselves "without fear," and the school is very good at putting students "into the organizations that will hire them."

ADMISSIONS CONTACT: ZINA LAWRENCE, DIRECTOR, GRADUATE STUDENT SERVICES
ADDRESS: MASSRY CENTER FOR BUSINESS 1400 WASHINGTON AVE, ALBANY, NY 12222
PHONE: 518-442-4961 • FAX: 518-442-4975
E-MAIL: ZLAWRENCE@ALBANY.EDU • WEBSITE: WWW.GRADUATEBUSINESS.ALBANY.EDU

Student Life and Environment

Students here "tend to be younger and less experienced than [students at] other schools, and this is reflected in their behavior and thoughts," says one member of the student body. "They are bright and willing to learn, but I was surprised by the lack of work experience," says another. The "diverse range of backgrounds makes it hard to generalize," but overall students here "are outgoing, smart, and socially active." "Very few" are married or have children. "Everyone is friends, and there is shared camaraderie with the entire class," according to one. "They will help when needed and are always available to help [one] another out."

Coursework typically fills up the week, and "after class, we usually meet with our teams to work on assigned projects" or business plan competition entries. As for extracurricular fun, there are plenty of friends to be found in the school's other graduate programs, and the state capital of Albany "has a lot to offer in terms of restaurants, parks, and museums if you know where to look."

Admissions

Applicants to the MBA program at the State University of New York at Albany School of Business must provide the graduate admissions department with all of the following: official copies of transcripts for all postsecondary academic work, an official score report for the GMAT, a resume, three letters of recommendation, a personal statement of purpose, and a completed application. International applicants whose undergraduate degrees were earned at non-English language institutions must provide all of the above plus an official score report for the TOEFL (minimum acceptable score: 600 paper-based; 450 computer-based); a financial affidavit accompanied by appropriate supporting documentation to demonstrate the applicant's "ability to meet all educational and living expenses for the entire period of intended study"; and they must past a SPEAK test during orientation. Furthermore, international academic transcripts in languages other than English must be accompanied by a certified English translation.

FINANCIAL FACTS

Annual tuition (in-state/ out-of-state)	$14,410/$24,390
Fees	$1,550
Cost of books	$1,600
Room & board	$11,986

ADMISSIONS

Admissions Selectivity Rating	**86**
# of applications received	219
% applicants accepted	55
% acceptees attending	85
Average GMAT	570
Range of GMAT	510–690
Accepts GRE scores	No
Average GPA	3.4
TOEFL required of international students	Yes
Minimum TOEFL (paper/web)	600/100
Application fee	$75
International application fee	$75
Early application deadline	3/1
Early notification date	4/1
Regular application deadline	5/1
Regular application notification	6/1
Deferment available	Yes
Maximum length of deferment	1 Year
Transfer students accepted	Yes
Transfer application policy We may accept up to 50% transfer credit in each program of study.	
Non-fall admissions	Yes
Need-blind admissions	Yes

EMPLOYMENT PROFILE

Career Rating	**85**	**Grads Employed by Function%**	**Avg. Salary**
Percent employed at graduation	62	Marketing	(3%)
Percent employed 3 months after graduation	88	Consulting	(41%) $68,000
		HR	(4%) $60,000
Average base starting salary	$60,000	MIS	(45%) $68,000
Primary Source of Full-time Job Acceptances		Other	(7%) $62,500
School-facilitated activities	18 (63%)	**Top 5 Employers Hiring Grads**	
Graduate-facilitated activities	1 (3%)	E&Y (6), Collaborative Solutions (2), General	
Unknown	10 (34%)	Electric (1), KPMG (1), Metaformers (1)	

STATE UNIVERSITY OF NEW YORK—UNIVERSITY AT BUFFALO
SCHOOL OF MANAGEMENT

GENERAL INFORMATION

Type of school	Public
Affiliation	No Affiliation
Academic calendar	Semester

SURVEY SAYS...
Friendly students, Cutting-edge classes, Abundant mentors available, Happy students, Abundant clubs and activities, Students love Buffalo, NY
Solid preparation in:
Finance, General management, Teamwork, Communication/interpersonal skills, Presentation skills, Quantitative skills, Computer skills

STUDENTS

Enrollment of parent institution	30,000
Enrollment of MBA Program	447
% male/female	67/33
% out-of-state	36
% part-time	3
% underrepresented minority	8
% international	33
Average age at entry	25
Average years work experience at entry	2

ACADEMICS

Academic Experience Rating	**88**
Profs interesting rating	80
Profs accessible rating	95
% female faculty	28
% underrepresented minority faculty	3
% part-time faculty	10

Joint Degrees
JD/MBA; MD/MBA; Architecture/MBA; Pharmacy/MBA; BS/MBA Business or Engineering; MBA/MSW; AuD/MBA; MBA/MPH; DDS/MBA

Academics

Offering AACSB-accredited graduate programs since the 1930s, the University at Buffalo School of Management has a long history of excellence, operating both a full-time and part-time MBA, as well as a twenty-month executive MBA for seasoned professionals. The academic programs are "very well-organized" and "the school does a great job of emphasizing 'management' as an underlying factor in each course" in the core curriculum. While covering business fundamentals like finance and marketing, the curriculum moves ahead with the times, and "courses are constantly updated and altered to reflect real-world experience based on current events," and integrated ethics. Getting a strong practical perspective isn't a problem: UB complements the academic offerings with "great opportunities outside the classroom," including "professional speakers, networking events, country forums, [and] community service," as well as case competitions and special offerings, like business projects with corporate partners. To further augment the curriculum, UB operates several formal exchange programs with business schools overseas, as well as shorter "trips to China for international business classes."

Along with affordable tuition, UB offers a "smaller, more intimate MBA experience" with an "emphasis on teamwork and leadership skills" throughout the curriculum. Within each incoming class, full-time students are divided into fixed cohorts then assigned to a fixed study group of five to six students. "Group meetings outside of class require a lot of time and commitment" and can be among the most challenging aspects of the program. A student elaborates, "The curriculum is difficult and pushes students to their limits in all realms, especially in regards to working in a team environment with people you may not know to start out or who have very different perspectives than you." Despite the challenges, the focus on teamwork "simulates the real world" and "provides for a great learning environment." A student admits, "I have created a great network here, both with the students, professors, alums and other community members." Adds another, "The students are all very close and the faculty and administration are extremely involved." While the environment is friendly, the teaching staff can be "hit and miss" in the classroom, and some professors are universally disliked. Fortunately, "professors are very good overall" and "many are leaders in [their] fields." Even more importantly, "the professors have been great and are always accessible if needed, whether...after class, during weekly office hours, or by setting up a special time to meet."

Career and Placement

At UB, career planning begins—quite literally—before you even step on campus. As a requirement of graduation, all students must complete MBA Advantage, a comprehensive professional development program in August before your first year (with additional sessions in January and September). In addition to MBA Advantage, the Career Resource Center (CRC) helps students prepare for the job hunt through career development workshops, practice interviews, career advising and more. The CRC also hosts various networking and recruiting events to link current students with local employers and alumni. UB is "very well-known in Western New York," and students benefit from the school's "great reputation and strong regional recruiting" program. For those who plan to stay in the area, UB has a "strong alumni network, especially locally."

In recent years, MBA graduates report an average base salary of more than $63,000, with a range between $35,000 (internationally) and $115,000 (U.S.). Eighty-six percent of students were employed within three months of graduation. More than 45 percent of the class took positions in Western New York. Over the past few years, the top employers of MBA graduates have included M&T Bank, Citi, PricewaterhouseCoopers, Ernst & Young, Mattel (Fisher-Price), Deloitte, IBM, New Era Cap, and Rich Products.

Student Life and Environment

Group work is an integral part of the UB curriculum and for many, "the variety of students from varying backgrounds/majors" and "the great presence of international students from all around the world make this academic experience tremendous both in and out of class." While teamwork can be challenging, "Everybody gets along well and builds great relationships." Throughout the MBA, "classes are all in one building," a recently completed facility, complete with high-tech classrooms, conference rooms, breakout rooms, and a cafe. With everything concentrated into one space, "it has become like a family atmosphere." While MBAs share facilities with the undergraduate population, a newly-renovated graduate lounge provides them with their own exclusive space.

Outside of course work, many full-time students are involved in extracurricular activities, like case competitions, student clubs, and special programs like "alternative spring break." The most active campus club, the Graduate Management Association hosts happy hours and daytrips, among other activities. On campus, "frequent student-focused events are held, including a formal dinner with students and faculty [at] the end of each semester, in addition to charity drives and social events." A great place to call home, "Buffalo is a small city, but many of the students are from the area and know where the hangouts are."

Admissions

There are no minimum standardized test score requirements for entry into UB's MBA program; a student's full background is considered when making an admission's decision.

Prominent Alumni

Millard "Mickey" S. Drexler, Chairman and CEO, J.Crew Group, Inc.; John R. Alm, Retired President & CEO Coca Cola Enterprises; Mitchell S. Klipper, CEO, Barnes & Noble, Inc.; Judy Vredenburgh, President and CEO, Girls Inc.; Robert Swan, CFO & Senior Vice President of Finance, eBay Inc.

FINANCIAL FACTS

Annual tuition (in-state/ out-of-state)	$14,410/$24,390
Fees	$4,264
Cost of books	$1,438
Room & board (on/off-campus)	$11,639/$14,621
% of students receiving aid	29
% of students receiving grants	16

ADMISSIONS

Admissions Selectivity Rating	86
# of applications received	343
% applicants accepted	57
% acceptees attending	58
Average GMAT	611
Range of GMAT	570–650
Accepts GRE scores	Yes
Average Verbal GRE	153
Average Quantitative GRE	153
Average GPA	3.4
TOEFL required of international students	Yes
Minimum TOEFL (paper/web)	570/95
Application fee	$100
International application fee	$100
Early application deadline	10/1
Early notification date	12/1
Regular application deadline	2/1
Regular application notification	3/15
Application Deadline/Notification	
Round 1:	10/1 / 12/1
Round 2:	2/1 / 3/15
Round 3:	4/1 / 5/1
Round 4:	5/15 / 6/1
Deferment available	Yes
Maximum length of deferment	one year
Transfer students accepted	No
Non-fall admissions	Yes
Need-blind admissions	Yes

EMPLOYMENT PROFILE

Career Rating	90	Grads Employed by Function	% Avg. Salary
Percent employed at graduation	51	Marketing	(13%) $50,060
Percent employed 3 months after graduation	81	Operations	(17%) $62,600
		Consulting	(9%) $63,750
Average base starting salary	$60,168	Management	(7%) $66,000
Primary Source of Full-time Job Acceptances		Finance	(30%) $55,697
School-facilitated activities	23 (50%)	HR	(4%)
Graduate-facilitated activities	23 (50%)	MIS	(13%) $75,680
		Other	(7%)

Top 5 Employers Hiring Grads
Citi (5), Deloitte (3), IT America (3), HSBC (2), Rich Products (2)

STETSON UNIVERSITY
SCHOOL OF BUSINESS ADMINISTRATION

GENERAL INFORMATION
Type of school	Private
Affiliation	No Affiliation
Academic calendar	Semesters

SURVEY SAYS...
Happy students, Students love DeLand, FL
Solid preparation in:
Finance, Accounting, General management, Teamwork, Communication/interpersonal skills, Presentation skills, Quantitative skills, Computer skills

STUDENTS
Enrollment of parent institution	4,333
Enrollment of MBA Program	136
% male/female	64/36
% out-of-state	11
% part-time	32
% underrepresented minority	21
% international	13
Average age at entry	30

ACADEMICS
Academic Experience Rating	**86**
Profs interesting rating	92
Profs accessible rating	95
Student/faculty ratio	15:1
% female faculty	26
% underrepresented minority faculty	16
% part-time faculty	5

Joint Degrees
JD/MBA, 3 yrs; MSP/MBA, 8 semesters

Prominent Alumni
Max Cleland, Secretary of the American Battle Monuments Commission; George Winston, Recording Artist; Jacob DeGrom, Pitcher for the New York Mets; J. Craig Crawford, Congressional Quarterly columnist; Jim Haskins, NHL Vice President

Academics

Stetson University offers fast-paced MBA programs for working professionals on three of its four central Florida campuses. In broad strokes, the Stetson MBA is divided into the following areas: foundational course work (or prerequisite courses), advanced course work, and electives. Stetson's is a general MBA, and students can tailor their education through elective courses in fields like decision science, finance, management, information technology, and marketing. In addition, the EMBA International Field experience program combines business visits with a consulting project and presentations to corporate leadership. Throughout the MBA course work, professors emphasize case studies and real world applications, giving students important skills they can take back to the workplace.

Stetson offers the MBA degree on their main campus in DeLand, as well as on their campuses in Celebration (Orlando) and Gulfport. In all locations, the school offers a "great class schedule" for working professionals, with MBA courses offered once a week in the evenings. While Stetson's Professional MBA allows students to take as many courses as fit their schedule, the Accelerated MBA is both fast and efficient. Students who have already fulfilled the prerequisites can complete the program in just over a year by attending full-time. Even part-time students often finish the entire MBA in just two years of study. (Stetson will review an applicant's undergraduate transcript to estimate how many prerequisite courses are required; often, students with an undergraduate degree in business are required to complete fewer courses.) In addition to the traditional MBA, Stetson offers a challenging, cohort-based, fifty-one-credit hour Executive MBA on the school's Celebration campus that includes leadership courses and executive coaching. More than four years of work experience is required for this program. The school also offers a joint JD/MBA at Gulfport, which can be completed at lightening speed: just three years for both degrees, start to finish.

A recommendation in itself, many students come to Stetson's graduate business program after completing their undergraduate degree at the college. Indeed, Stetson's graduate programs retain many of the qualities—like intimacy and friendliness—that define the undergraduate experience. A particular advantage, the Stetson MBA is a relatively small program, giving students excellent access to their professors, and an emphasis on "one-on-one discussions." Even more importantly, "the professors are excellent and outstanding mentors on campus," providing insight and support to their students. While many professors are accomplished professionals, they are "dedicated to the educational services, not busy with their own research." Course delivery is in-person (not online), but professors incorporate technology, using Blackboard software to post syllabi, assignments, grades, and, occasionally, discussion forums online.

ADMISSIONS CONTACT: OFFICE OF GRADUATE ADMISSIONS
ADDRESS: 421 NORTH WOODLAND BOULEVARD, UNIT 8289, DELAND, FL 32723
PHONE: 386-822-7100 • FAX: 386-822-7112
E-MAIL: GRADADMISSIONS@STETSON.EDU • WEBSITE: WWW.STETSON.EDU/PORTAL/GRADUATE

Career and Placement

Stetson's campuses are located throughout central Florida, keeping students close to the job markets in Orlando, Daytona Beach, and St. Petersburg. The university operates a Career and Professional Development Office on the main campus, open to current students and alumni. Students can sign up for individual counseling appointments, or they may attend career-related events, such as skills presentations, expert speakers, or on-campus interviews. Though the Career and Development Office promotes all events to undergradute and graduate students, some MBA students feel that services are mainly directed to the undergraduate community.

Student Life and Environment

With a convenient evening course schedule and several campus locations, Stetson attracts many "working professionals who are striving to advance their careers." On the whole, these students comprise a "very driven group," who are "goal-oriented" and "serious about academics." At the same time, the atmosphere is collaborative, as most students are also "interested in diversifying their skills in both business and networking." For professionals the atmosphere is supportive, and students find they "can relate with classmates, since many also have full-time jobs."

Located in central Florida, students at Stetson enjoy proximity to both local businesses and the beach—and everyone loves Florida's year-round sunny weather. On the main campus, the Lynn Business Center is equipped with high-speed Internet and numerous computer terminals. Despite the nice campus environment, prospective students should be aware that Stetson's MBA is principally designed for working professionals. Accordingly, some students would like to see "more of a sense of community" at Stetson, as "the campus is a ghost town on the weekends." However, the school has placed great emphasis on student life and student activities in recent years.

Admissions

Stetson accepts new students to the MBA program on a rolling basis. Once all application materials are received, students can expect a reply from the university immediately. To be considered for the joint JD/MBA on the Gulfport campus, students must first be admitted to Stetson's College of Law. Undergraduate GPA and test scores are typically the two most important factors in an admissions decision in Stetson's MBA.

FINANCIAL FACTS

Annual tuition (in-state/ out-of-state)	$17,658/$17,658
Fees	$0
Cost of books	$1,500
% of students receiving aid	35
% of first-year students receiving aid	36
% of students receiving grants	13
Average award package	$16,939
Average grant	$10,582
Average loan	$17,834
Average student loan debt	$29,960

ADMISSIONS

Admissions Selectivity Rating	81
# of applications received	106
% applicants accepted	77
% acceptees attending	71
Average GMAT	513
Range of GMAT	465–550
Accepts GRE scores	Yes
Average Verbal GRE	147
Range of Verbal GRE scores	141–154
Average Quantitative GRE	147
Range of Quantitative GRE scores	140–154
Average GPA	3.2
TOEFL required of international students	Yes
Minimum TOEFL (web)	90
Application fee	$50
International application fee	$50
Regular application deadline	8/1
Deferment available	Yes
Maximum length of deferment	1 year
Transfer students accepted	Yes
Non-fall admissions	Yes
Need-blind admissions	Yes

EMPLOYMENT PROFILE

Career Rating	79	**Top 5 Employers Hiring Grads**
Percent employed at graduation	78	Disney (1), Deloitte (1), Charles Schwab (1),
Percent employed 3 months after graduation	22	Houghton Mifflin Harcourt (1), University of North Carolina at Chapel Hill (1)
Average base starting salary	$46,751	

SUFFOLK UNIVERSITY
SAWYER BUSINESS SCHOOL

GENERAL INFORMATION

Type of school	Private
Affiliation	No Affiliation
Academic calendar	Semester

SURVEY SAYS...

Classmates have diverse work experience, Friendly students, Liberal students, Students love Boston, MA
Solid preparation in:
General management, Teamwork, Communication/interpersonal skills, Presentation skills, Doing business in a global economy

STUDENTS

Enrollment of parent institution	8,046
Enrollment of MBA Program	359
% male/female	49/51
% out-of-state	22
% part-time	76
% underrepresented minority	22
% international	43
Average age at entry	28
Average years work experience at entry	4

ACADEMICS

Academic Experience Rating	88
Profs interesting rating	88
Profs accessible rating	90
Student/faculty ratio	3:1
% female faculty	42
% underrepresented minority faculty	12
% part-time faculty	34

Joint Degrees

MBA/MS Accounting, 18-24 months FT, 20-32 months PT; MBA/MS Finance, 18-24 months FT, 20-32 months PT; MBA/MS Taxation, 18-24 months FT, 20-32 months PT; JD/MBA, 4 yrs FT; 5 yrs PT; JD/MPA, 4 yrs total FT; 5 yrs PT; JD/Masters in Finance, 4 yrs FT; 5 yrs PT

Academics

Located in Boston, Suffolk University's Sawyer Business School offers a conventional MBA; specialized MBA programs in health administration and nonprofit management; a Global MBA with a focus on international finance; "an Executive MBA program where everyone in the class has more than ten years of real world experience"; as well as a "combination JD/MBA program." The school is known for its "quality program," "great reputation," "amazing location," and for providing the "best opportunity for the cost." It is ideal for working students who appreciate the "flexible schedule" that allows them to work fulltime, go to school fulltime, and still "be done in two years."

The school boasts a "good mix of career academics and professors who have practical experience in the corporate world." Overall, "professors are very knowledgeable and create positive learning environments." The faculty "has very real knowledge of the subjects they teach" and "typically have very good networks."

Professors are "very current with the changes in the business world and are very informative." Courses center "around teamwork and case analysis," which "contribute to the real working environment." And "the diverse student population contributes towards classroom discussions." The diverse "age groups and work experiences that are shared provide excellent insight into the business topic discussed," notes a student from the Class of 2015. "It makes the material come alive as we share our experiences with what we are learning," says another. "Small class size is a big plus," and the "professors and administration are amazing." Professors are "accessible" and "helpful," and students feel they "can go to them with anything and be treated respectfully."

Students praise the specialized programs and global MBA, saying "the international business aspects in the classroom, the ability to travel to other countries as a grad student, and the diversity of the student body" greatly enhance their overall education. Students praise "how well integrated the global and international aspect is incorporated into the program." In short, Sawyer is a great fit for students looking for an affordable, high-quality education, in a diverse environment, with a focus on global business.

Career and Placement

Since Sawyer has "strong alumni connections," students "feel confident" about their "career prospects." Students say Sawyer "is very good with helping students network with professionals and companies." The student "business association is active and plans wonderful events."

And the school administration "also helps students get access to job search portals that we would otherwise not have access to." Though some say the administration is "very good at helping students develop skills outside of the classroom setting through networking events and workshops," others say career services could be improved.

Student Life and Environment

Some students say that what they like most about Sawyer "is its vibrant culturally diverse environment," while others say "location, location, location." Since Sawyer is located in Boston, students have access to a wealth of resources off campus, from nightlife and restaurants, to museums, libraries and other cultural institutions. A "majority of the students work full time," and students come and go as they please, availing themselves of the resources they need. As one full-time student notes: "I am working so I don't have much time for much besides studying and school work but I am involved in two student-run organizations." One is "dedicated to MBA students and the other is a female MBA organization." Both "organizations put a lot of effort into networking and hosting networking events for all graduate students."

Students find their classmates to be "hardworking," "diligent," "friendly," and "proactive." They are "quite professional and personable." And the "large population of international students" adds to a welcome "global mindset." Students like the campus and say "study areas are plentiful and students are often willing to help one another succeed."

Admissions

Applicants to Suffolk are encouraged to apply online. Applicants must submit an application including official undergraduate transcripts; a goal statement; a current résumé summarizing academic qualifications, appropriate work and volunteer experience, relevant skills, and any honors or awards received; two letters of recommendation; GMAT score (see individual programs for program dependent codes); and a GRE score. In addition, an interview is required for the Executive MBA and Global MBA. International students must have a TOEFL score of 550 on the paper version or 213 on the web-based version.

Prominent Alumni

Robert Mudge, New England Region President, Verizon; Tara Taylor, VP, State Street Global Advisors; Patrick Callaghan, President Pepperidge Farms; Peter Gicheru, Finance Controller, Coca-Cola South Africa

FINANCIAL FACTS

Annual tuition	$41,440
Fees	$26
Cost of books	$1,200
Room & board	$20,400
% of students receiving aid	62
% of first-year students receiving aid	66
% of students receiving grants	40
Average award package	$20,145
Average grant	$10,587
Average loan	$21,203
Average student loan debt	$48,525

ADMISSIONS

Admissions Selectivity Rating	**83**
# of applications received	379
% applicants accepted	62
% acceptees attending	47
Average GMAT	486
Range of GMAT	310–620
Accepts GRE scores	Yes
Average GPA	3.3
TOEFL required of international students	Yes
Minimum TOEFL (paper/web)	550/80
Application fee	$50
International application fee	$50
Early application deadline	3/15
Regular application deadline	6/15
Deferment available	Yes
Maximum length of deferment	1 year
Transfer students accepted	Yes
Transfer application policy same as for regular applicants	
Non-fall admissions	Yes
Need-blind admissions	Yes

EMPLOYMENT PROFILE

Career Rating	84	Grads Employed by Function	% Avg. Salary
Percent employed at graduation	22	Marketing	(32%) $120,667
Percent employed 3 months after graduation	44	Operations	(16%) $109,667
		Finance	(26%) 74,125
Average base starting salary	$75,000	General Management	(16%) $181,667
Primary Source of Full-time Job Acceptances		**Top 5 Employers Hiring Grads**	
Unknown	6 (100%)	Deloitte (1), Partners Health Care (1), EMC Corporation (1), Genetech (1), Microsoft (1), KIMS Global Hospital (1), Even3 (1)	

SYRACUSE UNIVERSITY
MARTIN J. WHITMAN SCHOOL OF MANAGEMENT

GENERAL INFORMATION
Type of school	Private
Academic calendar	Semester

SURVEY SAYS...
Friendly students, Liberal students, Happy students, Abundant clubs and activities
Solid preparation in:
Marketing, Accounting, General management, Operations, Teamwork, Presentation skills, Doing business in a global economy, Entreprenurial studies

STUDENTS
Enrollment of parent institution	21,789
Enrollment of MBA Program	81
% male/female	69/31
% out-of-state	10
% part-time	0
% underrepresented minority	3
% international	63
Average age at entry	25
Average years work experience at entry	3

ACADEMICS
Academic Experience Rating	90
Profs interesting rating	91
Profs accessible rating	93
Student/faculty ratio	4:1
% female faculty	29
% underrepresented minority faculty	24
% part-time faculty	23

Joint Degrees
MBA/Juris Doctorate (4 years) MBA/Master of Public Administration (3 years) With any other degree-bearing graduate program offered at Syracuse University

Academics

The small MBA program at Syracuse University's Whitman School of Management is a good fit for new graduates and early career professionals hoping to ramp up their business acumen and gain valuable experience in the real world. Academically, the MBA curriculum is well rounded, covering a wide breadth of subject areas, while also placing "emphasis on finance, supply chain, entrepreneurship" and accoutning. A great place to get your feet wet in the world of business, there is an "experiential component featured in many of the classes," as well as myriad "opportunities given to MBA students to participate within different organizations, whether as an intern or as a consultant to a large reputable firm." A current student adds, "These academic consulting engagements added depth to many of the courses through projects that provided and often required innovative and hands-on approaches."

Whitman professors are generally "productive and efficient," with "excellent academic backgrounds" in their fields of specialization. When it comes to leading a class, however, students say their skill set varies: "There are professors who are great, know their fields, and can quickly apply lessons to what is going on around the world." On the other hand, "many of the older faculty lack presentation skills. Lectures can be very dry." The upshot is that, across the board, professors are supportive and "willing to help on projects outside of the classroom." In fact, thanks to the "very small class size," "you can get to know your classmates and your professors on a personal level." At the same time, students love the fact that Syracuse offers all the "resources of a large institution," including a "beautiful new building" for business students, replete with "up-to-date technology."

In addition to the traditional MBA, busy professionals have the option of enrolling in MBA@Syracuse, the well-regarded online MBA program (formerly known as iMBA) "which combines actual on-campus learning via weeklong residencies, along with online course work." Residencies are also hosted off-campus in major business centers around the world, and weekly live classes are hosted online. The online MBA program has been re-launched as in partnership with 2U, Inc., a leading provider of cloud-based software as-a-service solutions for leading nonprofit colleges and universities. According to those in the program, it "provides the same educational experience as the full-time MBA (same curriculum, professors, etc.), but has a much more flexible format." In addition, the school offers a "great JD/MBA program with lots of connections in NYC," as well as a joint MBA/MPA program in conjunction with the U.S. Army.

Career and Placement

Whitman's emphasis on experiential learning is a boon to students looking to jump-start their career after the MBA. Plus, the school's individualized focus makes it easier to prep for a successful job hunt. Here, faculty and staff "go above and beyond to ensure you are well prepared for your career, and customize plans to place you in your dream company." Specifically, via the Whitman Career Center, students have access to professional-development workshops, personal coaching, and "strong networking events" with local companies. Particularly advantageous for those looking locally, "Alumni are set on creating successful opportunities for current students."

While everyone agrees that "Syracuse's MBA program is on the rise," students would like to see more on-campus recruitment opportunities for MBA candidates, suggesting the school could improve by opening a "career center focused specifically and only on graduate students, (MBAs, master's, and PhD students)." Fortunately, improvement is already in the works: students note that, this year, the school is "doing a great deal to bring more business recruiters and alumni onto campus for networking opportunities." In 2013, Syracuse graduates had an average base salary of $70,769, with a range between $50,000 and $92,000. Top hiring companies include Ernst & Young, Publics, AXA Equitable, Phillips Healthcae, and Norvartis.

Student Life and Environment

Students at Whitman are a "very diverse group" of people, who "all come from different industries," as well as varying academic backgrounds. With long-term goals and plenty of ambition, these "highly intelligent" students are "competitive and driven" when it comes to coursework and careers. Fortunately, that competitiveness does not negatively affect the academic environment. On the contrary, the atmosphere at Whitman is "very collegial and collaborative," and students are "friendly, extremely helpful, and supportive" of their classmates.

"Syracuse's full-time MBA group is very close," described by some as "one big extended family." On campus, "there is hardly ever a day that goes by when there isn't an event, speaker, or sports activity that students can attend," and "there are plenty of clubs and groups to join where you can mentor, lead, participate in the community and more." In addition to events at the business school, MBA candidates can also take advantage of the resources on the greater campus, like "attending sold-out sports games and events featuring figures such as Hillary Clinton or the Dalai Lama." Though "winter is long" and very cold, the medium-sized city of Syracuse is a comfortable hometown, with plenty of recreation and cultural events for students. For example, "the city of Syracuse has different events going on every weekend in the summer. They have blues festivals, Irish festival, and several others." On top of that, the school is "near New York City," allowing students to take advantage of the many social and professional opportunities in the Big Apple.

Admissions

To apply to the full-time program, students must submit academic transcripts, GMAT scores, two essays, and two letters of recommendation. In 2014, incoming students had an average GMAT score of 626 and average pre-MBA work experience of thirty months. More than 65 percent of incoming students had undergraduate degrees in fields other than business. The GMAT is waived for the MBA@Syracuse if the applicant has at least five years of professional work experience. Pre-MBA work experience for the MBA@Syracuse averages eleven years.

Prominent Alumni

Martin J. Whitman, Founder of Third Avenue Value Fund; Dick Clark, Chairman and CEO of Dick Clark Productions; Dan D'Aniello, Founding Partner of the Carlyle Group; The Honorable Alfonse D'Amato, Former U.S. Senator; Arthur Rock, Venture capitalist, Arthur Rock & Company

FINANCIAL FACTS

Annual tuition (in-state/ out-of-state)	$38,064/$38,064
Fees	$480
Cost of books	$2,500
Room & board (on/off-campus)	$13,870/$13,870
% of students receiving aid	100
% of first-year students receiving aid	100
% of students receiving grants	100
Average grant	$26,212
Average student loan debt	$65,890

ADMISSIONS

Admissions Selectivity Rating	86
# of applications received	135
% applicants accepted	59
% acceptees attending	43
Average GMAT	626
Range of GMAT	610–640
Accepts GRE scores	Yes
Average GPA	3.5
TOEFL required of international students	Yes
Minimum TOEFL (paper/web)	600/100
Application fee	$75
International application fee	$75
Early application deadline	11/30
Early notification date	12/21
Regular application deadline	4/19
Regular application notification	5/17
Application Deadline/Notification	
Round 1:	11/30 / 12/21
Round 2:	1/1 / 2/1
Round 3:	2/15 / 3/15
Round 4:	4/19 / 5/17
Deferment available	Yes
Maximum length of deferment	1 year
Transfer students accepted	No
Non-fall admissions	No
Need-blind admissions	Yes

EMPLOYMENT PROFILE

Career Rating	89	Grads Employed by Function	% Avg. Salary
Percent employed at graduation	21	Marketing	(37%) $62,520
Percent employed 3 months after graduation	70	Operations	(21%) $73,125
		Consulting	(11%)
Average base starting salary	$73,881	Finance	(21%) $75,869
Primary Source of Full-time Job Acceptances		Other	(10%)
School-facilitated activities	11 (58%)	**Top 5 Employers Hiring Grads**	
Graduate-facilitated activities	8 (42%)	Ernst & Young (1), Deloitte Consulting (2), Amazon (1), JPMC (1), Publicis (1)	

TEMPLE UNIVERSITY
THE FOX SCHOOL OF BUSINESS AND MANAGEMENT

Academics

Temple University's reputation has been growing exponentially in the business world. Naturally, this notion is certainly not lost on current students who praise the school's "high-end new facilities, rising rankings, and strong brand equity." Additionally, Temple's Philadelphia location guarantees "proximity to major companies;" companies with which the school has forged strong relationships. Students also benefit from "small class sizes" which "provide a one-on-one experience with the opportunity to collaborate with award-winning faculty." However, opinion on academic rigor is definitely divided. Students find the caliber for most courses to be "world class," but some feel that the professional development course "seems tailored more toward an undergrad population" and the international population. But these skills must be useful with the corresponding rise in placement rates.

For the most part, professors "truly care about each individual student and keep classes fresh with ideas and topics that are timely in today's business world." Students also eagerly report that they are great at fostering "meaningful discussion." Just as essential, it's apparent that Temple professors are "dedicated to teaching" and they really do their utmost to make themselves "accessible."

Moreover, the administration makes a concerted effort to "seek student input." They frequently ask MBA candidates to "evaluate [their] classes, courses and overall experience." And the school truly utilizes this feedback to ensure the program "constantly stays up on trends." Indeed, "The Fox School is on the road to continuous improvement; the program is continually evolving to help meet student needs."

Career and Placement

The Fox School of Business provides students with many avenues for job placement. For starters, Temple MBAs truly value that they can turn to their teachers for career advice and assistance. As a second-year student proudly shares, "With some exception, most professors have fantastic real-world experience and are happy to share themselves and their networks with any willing student." Additionally, MBA candidates can take advantage of Temple's "strong...web application[s] that help students find internships and jobs." Though a demoralized second-year laments that "job postings are not always indicative of the industries students are looking to enter." Fortunately, due to Temple's growing stature, students have noticed "more prominent recruiters showing up at career fairs."

The vast majority of Temple MBAs seek employment within the Northeast and Mid-Atlantic regions. Of course, the program does attract an international crowd and graduates can be found around the globe from England and France to Nigeria and India. Employers who frequently hire Fox students include Accenture, Deloitte Consulting LLP, Ernst & Young, JP MorganChase, Campbells Soup, SAP, Vanguard, GlaxoSmithKline, KPMG, G.E., Comcast, and Boenning and Scattergood.

ADMISSIONS CONTACT: WILLIAM M. RIETH, DIRECTOR GRADUATE ENROLLMENT MANAGEMENT
ADDRESS: 1801 LIACOURAS WALK, ALTER HALL, SUITE 701, PHILADELPHIA, PA 19122-6083
PHONE: 215-204-5890 • FAX: 215-204-1632
E-MAIL: FOXINFO@TEMPLE.EDU • WEBSITE: FOX.TEMPLE.EDU/GRAD

Student Life and Environment

Temple MBAs speak quite highly of their peers. One student tells us, "My fellow students are what I love most about Temple—they are cooperatively competitive. Students are there to help one another with class work, internship/job searches, networking, etc. This has been one of the most collaborative environments I've enjoyed thus far." Moreover, many also describe their fellow students as "wonderful, interesting, intelligent people." And a content first-year further explains, "My fellow students are a diverse mix of both domestic and international students with a variety of professional backgrounds. We have a great sense of community and associate with the members of our cohort both inside and outside of the classroom."

"With few exceptions," Temple MBAs are "busy from 7:00 A.M. to midnight." Of course, that's completely understandable considering "there is always something to do here, and there is always somebody to do it with." The school "consistently offers speakers and events that we can attend for free—these include C-Suite individuals, athletic coaches, various politicians, etc." And when students are looking to unwind in a less academic manner, they can "always go out to bars and house-parties in Philadelphia." All in all, "it is a work hard play hard environment and the learning experience is outstanding."

Admissions

We won't mince words; gaining admission to Temple's MBA program is competitive. When assessing applicants, admissions officers look for individuals with solid business exposure, strong interpersonal skills, academic aptitude and potential. A candidate's personal goals are also considered. To apply, you'll be required to submit college transcripts, a current resume, two letters of recommendation, two essays (and an optional statement) and a GMAT score from within the last five years. Non-native English speakers will also be required to submit a TOEFFL score from within the last two years (unless a previous degree was acquired from an English speaking university). Finally, admission interviews are conducted on an invitation only basis.

FINANCIAL FACTS

Annual tuition (in-state/ out-of-state)	$30,375/$42,579
Fees	$1,165
Cost of books	$1,300
Room & board (on/off-campus)	$17,796/$18,660
% of students receiving aid	60
% of first-year students receiving aid	66
% of students receiving grants	39
Average award package	$19,155
Average grant	$16,314
Average loan	$28,812
Average student loan debt	$78,994

ADMISSIONS

Admissions Selectivity Rating	92
# of applications received	626
% applicants accepted	39
% acceptees attending	77
Average GMAT	632
Range of GMAT	610–660
Accepts GRE scores	Yes
Average GPA	3.6
TOEFL required of international students	Yes
Minimum TOEFL (paper/web)	600/100
Application fee	$60
International application fee	$60
Early application deadline	12/10
Early notification date	1/15
Regular application deadline	3/1
Regular application notification	3/31
Application Deadline/Notification	
Round 1:	12/10 / 1/15
Round 2:	3/1 / 3/31
Round 3:	5/31 / 6/15
Round 4:	6/30 / 7/15
Deferment available	Yes
Maximum length of deferment	1 Calendar year
Transfer students accepted	Yes
Transfer application policy	
Reviewed on a case by case basis.	
Non-fall admissions	Yes
Need-blind admissions	Yes

EMPLOYMENT PROFILE

Career Rating	93	Grads Employed by Function% Avg. Salary	
Percent employed at graduation	79	Marketing	(13%) $80,750
Percent employed 3 months after graduation	97	Operations	(20%) $75,000
		Consulting	(40%) $78,708
Average base starting salary	$75,473	Management	(10%) $64,567
Primary Source of Full-time Job Acceptances		Finance	(13%) $71,250
School-facilitated activities	30 (79%)	MIS	(3%) $68,000
Graduate-facilitated activities	8 (21%)	**Top 5 Employers Hiring Grads**	

Top 5 Employers Hiring Grads
Deloitte Consulting LLP (4), JP Morgan Chase (2), Herspiegel Consulting (2), Merck (2), Bristol Myers Squibb (2)

TEXAS A&M INTERNATIONAL UNIVERSITY
A.R. SANCHEZ, JR. SCHOOL OF BUSINESS

GENERAL INFORMATION

Type of school	Public
Affiliation	No Affiliation
Academic calendar	Semester

SURVEY SAYS...

Friendly students
Solid preparation in:
General management

STUDENTS

Enrollment of parent institution	7,213
Enrollment of MBA Program	140
% male/female	46/54
% out-of-state	0
% part-time	83
% underrepresented minority	54
% international	46
Average age at entry	27
Average years work experience at entry	5

ACADEMICS

Academic Experience Rating	**83**
Profs interesting rating	89
Profs accessible rating	91
Student/faculty ratio	23:1
% female faculty	20
% underrepresented minority faculty	36
% part-time faculty	4

Academics

Texas A&M International University (TAMIU) is conveniently "located in an area with a strong international trade industry" and offers a "normal work environment" that has "grown much" in recent years. TAMIU's Sanchez School of Business has, according to one student concentrating in international trade, "a strong international business focus and a faculty from diverse educational, professional, and cultural backgrounds." The school's "relatively small classes" also help cultivate "an excellent learning environment" in which to earn an accredited MBA. The course load has been described as "intense and demanding," and even "too much if you are a student who works full-time." But overall, as one student tells us, "The effort gone into this coursework is greatly compensated by the knowledge attained. It takes practice and hands-on projects to learn what is expected of my career."

In addition to a diverse faculty of thirty-six, who specialize in international taxation, accounting, banking and finance, and trade theory, among other disciplines, TAMIU's student body also covers a broad spectrum of experience and background. "Most of my fellow classmates," one student notes, "are older and wiser with experience from different business backgrounds. It is very interesting to learn about their experiences. We get to hear about real-life scenarios and how they are handled or should have been handled." TAMIU also benefits from a "relaxed" and "peaceful" learning environment, which complements the school's intense academic workload. There are also "great computer labs and library," and the "food retailers are excellent."

Among the advanced degrees offered by TAMIU, the list includes an onsite MBA, an online MBA, as well as MPACC, MS-IS and a Ph.D. in International Business Administration. On average, the approximate length of each master's program for full-time students is one and a half years of study. Specific degree programs and concentrations at TAMIU include international banking and finance, international business, international trade and logistics, and management. Given the impressive offerings at TAMIU, not many students find cause for complaint, but some students have expressed concern that members of the local business community are unable to audit classes.

Career and Placement

The Texas A&M International Career Services Office provides counseling and placement services to the entire undergraduate and graduate student body. The office organizes on-campus recruiting events, career expos, and job fairs. It also offers one-on-one counseling, workshops, library services, and resume review. Many TAMIU students have professed a need for improvement in some areas of career placement. For instance, the complete lack of available internships and scarce opportunities for "job networking" and "training" are areas of concern, while other students have noted the need for greater recruiting services and better "alumni relations."

Student Life and Environment

Campus life at TAMIU has been described as "very diverse," comprised of "dedicated individuals who help promote and improve clubs and organizations." Among the more popular organizations, and in particular those active in assisting students "figure out a future career," are the "Enactus, Association of International Students (AIS), and Student Government." These organizations are instrumental in coordinating timely lecture series, so that students can remain up to date on current practices and concerns in the business community. Adding to the diverse flavor of campus life at TAMIU, the student body is made up of a vast international body, including students from "China, India, Russia, Spain, Italy, Mexico, Kenya, Jordan, Nepal," and several other countries.

"Life here is awesome," says one student. "I have great communities like AIS, and the recreational center helps me" release the stress of an "exhaustive and hectic" course load. Another student majoring in business administration had this to offer: "The student body is a close family group. TAMIU is my school family, from professors to the students." Another noted perk for much of the student body, particularly those with full-time jobs, is the availability of evening courses. "I am able to take courses in the evening and work full-time during the day," says one student attending school part-time.

Located in the southern Texas town of Laredo, also known as "The Gateway City" due to a shared border with Mexico, the city's location makes it a hub for international trade and manufacturing, and thus in many respects, an ideal place for business students. On the TAMIU campus itself, extracurricular activities are available but by no means abundant. As one student puts it, "While school life is somewhat budding, the school does little to promote campus life in general; most of the 'campus life' exists off campus."

Admissions

Applying to the TAMIU MBA program is a two-step process, as applicants must be admitted to both the University and the A.R. Sanchez, Jr. School of Business in order to enroll in the MBA program. All applicants to the MBA program must submit the following materials: GMAT or GRE scores, essay/personal statement, official undergraduate transcript, two letters of recommendation, and resume/CV, all of which will be given great and equal consideration by the Graduate Admissions Committee. TOEFL scores are required from all international applicants, with minimum scores of 550 for the written test, 213 for the computer-based test or 79 for the internet-based test. An IELTS score of 6.5 or higher may be used in lieu of the TOEFL. Eligible Mexican students can benefit from in-state tuition fees, which are much lower than those paid by other international students.

FINANCIAL FACTS

Annual tuition (in-state/ out-of-state)	$1,386/$8,406
Fees	$4,200
Cost of books	$1,092
Room & board (on/off-campus)	$8,259/$7,065
% of students receiving aid	38
% of first-year students receiving aid	37
% of students receiving grants	15
Average award package	$7,317
Average grant	$4,050
Average loan	$6,880
Average student loan debt	$20,316

ADMISSIONS

Admissions Selectivity Rating	77
# of applications received	32
% applicants accepted	97
% acceptees attending	87
Average GMAT	460
Accepts GRE scores	Yes
Average Verbal GRE	144
Range of Verbal GRE scores	140–147
Average Quantitative GRE	143
Range of Quantitative GRE scores	137–147
Average Writing GRE	2.8
Range of Writing GRE scores	2.5–3.0
Average GPA	3.0
TOEFL required of international students	Yes
Minimum TOEFL (paper/web)	550/79
Application fee	$50
International application fee	$50
Regular application deadline	4/30
Deferment available	Yes
Maximum length of deferment	1 year
Transfer students accepted	Yes
Transfer application policy	Application process is the same as new applicants; transfer students may request to transfer up to six hours of graduate credit
Non-fall admissions	Yes
Need-blind admissions	Yes

TEXAS A&M UNIVERSITY—COLLEGE STATION
MAYS BUSINESS SCHOOL

GENERAL INFORMATION
Type of school — Public
Affiliation — No Affiliation
Academic calendar — Semester

SURVEY SAYS...
Good peer network, Smart class-rooms
Solid preparation in:
Accounting, General management, Operations

STUDENTS
Enrollment of parent institution	58,920
Enrollment of MBA Program	123
% male/female	69/31
% out-of-state	23
% part-time	0
% underrepresented minority	9
% international	33
Average age at entry	28
Average years work experience at entry	5

ACADEMICS
Academic Experience Rating	**83**
Profs interesting rating	82
Profs accessible rating	79
Student/faculty ratio	7:1
% female faculty	17
% underrepresented minority faculty	6
% part-time faculty	0

Joint Degrees
MMBA/MS Finance; MBA/MS Management Information Systems; MBA/DVM; MBA/JD (with South Texas College of Law); MBA/MD; MBA/MS Biomedical Engineering

Academics

Business-minded MBA candidates say you get a "great return on investment" at Texas A&M University. While tuition at this public university is "relatively inexpensive," the business school offers a "high-quality education," spearheaded by an "unmatched teaching staff." The "academically-challenging and quantitatively-focused" curriculum is incredibly intense, compressing the equivalent of a two-year fulltime MBA into just eighteen months. Students praise the efficiency of the school's accelerated schedule, which reduces costs and career interruption while nonetheless providing "well-rounded" business training. In fact, "the ability of the professors and the program to crunch so much information into that time is outstanding." On the flip side, some students feel the program's speed isn't necessarily an advantage, as "we never have to time to prepare sufficiently and then discuss it in depth." Fortunately, those who'd like to extend their education may decide to stay at Texas A&M for an extra semester, during which time they can specialize in accounting, consulting, e-commerce, finance, marketing, and real estate, among others.

Teaching is taken seriously Texas A&M, and the school's "excellent" faculty are truly involved with the educational process. In class, "the teachers are engaging and concerned about student learning," and "try hard to make sure everybody understands the course material." Outside of class, "professors and administration are extremely helpful. They have open-door policies and are easily accessible." In addition, the school's administration is friendly and student-oriented. From top to bottom, "everybody in the MBA office goes out of their way to make sure we have great opportunities to learn outside the classroom, hear great speakers, and succeed in the program."

Every Texas A&M business school class is small, allowing plenty of individual attention while simultaneously encouraging interaction and discussion in (and outside) the classroom. Explains a student, "The classes are a perfect size to harness great discussions—a lot of opinions and viewpoints, but not so many that it's difficult to be heard in a single class period." At the same time, the intimate classroom environment means no one can slack off or slip through the cracks; "the classes are discussion-intensive, so every day requires a good bit of preparation." On the whole, students admit that Mays is a "very, very competitive environment," and, to keep up with the program's demands, students "often spend weekends studying and preparing for the upcoming week."

If Mays students didn't already have enough on their plate, the program includes a plethora of curricular and extracurricular activities that are designed to add depth and practical experience to the program. Of particular note, the MBA includes a required consulting project, which gives students the opportunity to apply classroom principals to a real-world business environment. Beyond curricular offerings, the program incorporates enrichment features like the "MBA Venture Challenge" case competition, a "Dean's Leadership Speaker Series" and opportunities for executive coaching and leadership development and training.

Career and Placement

With an excellent 94 percent job placement rate, it's no surprise that students sing the praises of the Career Management Center. The CMC staff is "professional, respectful, and wonderful to work with," and is lauded for coming up with "creative ideas in a challenging internship/job market." Another unique advantage of the school's eighteen-month format is that A&M students graduate in December, making them "available for that recruiting period when there is not a large supply of MBA students attempting to be recruited."

In addition to the business school's job placement services, the school's active alumni network is another benefit of attending Texas A&M. With graduates all over Texas and beyond, "the Aggie network is famous for how in-touch alumni are to students." In a recent academic year, the majority of Texas A&M graduates (84 percent) took jobs in the southwest, and most students went on to work in the technology, consulting, and energy industries. Last year, the mean starting salary was $100,675.

Student Life and Environment

Between classes, homework, lectures, and social life, there is "never a dull moment" at Texas A&M. Though most MBA candidates say their coursework keeps them supremely occupied, they also appreciate the openness and camaraderie that exists between the students at Mays Business School. While students are "determined to succeed," "everybody in the class is very social and works together." Within the Mays community, "friendliness and professionalism abound."

The business school is located on Texas A&M's main campus, home to nearly 59,000 students. Politically and socially, "A&M is a very conservative school and the students, for the most part, are very conservative" in the business school as well. A&M is a large, research university, so "it is very easy to get involved in Texas A&M's culture. Football games and other outside activities are a 'must see' and current students make it a point to take new students to these events." School spirit surges—even in the graduate programs—and students tell us, "The Aggie Spirit is something one ought to experience." Surrounding College Station is a "quiet, largely safe" town of 107,000, which grew alongside the university. If you're craving something a little more urban, the campus is just a few hours drive from Austin, Dallas/Fort Worth, Houston, and San Antonio.

Admissions

Texas A&M deliberately limits the size of each incoming class, and admissions are competitive. Prospective students must have fulltime post-baccalaureate work experience to be considered for the program; however, Peace Corps, missionary work, or military service is counted as work experience, even if it took place before the college degree. Select applicants may be invited to interview with the Admissions Committee.

FINANCIAL FACTS

Annual tuition (in-state/ out-of-state)	$11,616/$25,510
Fees	$16,000
Cost of books	$2,522
Room & board (on/off-campus)	$14,772

ADMISSIONS

Admissions Selectivity Rating	96
# of applications received	489
% applicants accepted	24
% acceptees attending	57
Average GMAT	654
Range of GMAT	580–710
Accepts GRE scores	Yes
Average Verbal GRE	157
Range of GRE	153-163
Average Quantitative	157
Average Writing GRE	3.9
Range of Writing GRE scores	3.5-4.3
Average GPA	3.5
TOEFL required of international students	Yes
Minimum TOEFL (paper/web)	600/100
Application fee	$175
International application fee	$200
Application Deadline	
Round 1:	10/26
Round 2:	1/25
Round 3:	3/1
Round 4:	4/19
Deferment available	Yes
Maximum length of deferment	1 year
Transfer students accepted	No
Non-fall admissions	No
Need-blind admissions	Yes

EMPLOYMENT PROFILE

Career Rating	94	Grads Employed by Function	% Avg. Salary
Percent employed at graduation	75	Marketing	(16%) $101,857
Percent employed 3 months after graduation	94	Operations	(11%) $91,200
		Consulting	(27%) $115,833
Average base starting salary	$100,675	Management	(18%) $90,333
Primary Source of Full-time Job Acceptances		Finance	(24%) $93,000
School-facilitated activities	76%	Human Resources	(4%) $91,000
Graduate-facilitated activities	20%	**Top 5 Employers Hiring Grads**	
Unknown	4%	Dell (6), HP (5), Deloitte Consulting (4), Amazon (3), Infosys (3)	

TEXAS A&M UNIVERSITY—CORPUS CHRISTI
COLLEGE OF BUSINESS

GENERAL INFORMATION

Type of school	Public
Affiliation	No Affiliation
Academic calendar	Semester

SURVEY SAYS...

Happy students
Solid preparation in:
Teamwork

STUDENTS

Enrollment of parent institution	10,510
Enrollment of MBA Program	163
% male/female	52/48
% part-time	38
% underrepresented minority	21
% international	61
Average age at entry	27

ACADEMICS

Academic Experience Rating	**82**
Profs interesting rating	88
Profs accessible rating	90
% female faculty	34
% underrepresented minority faculty	25
% part-time faculty	

Academics

Students at Texas A&M University—Corpus Christi (TAMUCC) say that in order to truly appreciate their school's stellar MBA programs, you must first put them in proper geographical perspective. TAMUCC "is a regional school, so comparing it with the experience of [students] at Top-25 schools is not fair," one such student points. However, "given its status as a regional school and the mission of the university as it relates to the regional approach, the TAMUCC MBA program is excellent." Indeed, most here want a program that is first and foremost convenient, affordable, and flexible enough to accommodate students with full-time jobs. In these areas and more, students here tell us, TAMUCC delivers.

Case in point: TAMUCC "has a great core foundation and the potential to become a great public university." MBAs here benefit from the "wide variety of students [from] different countries" which broadens their educational experience. There is a particularly strong Hispanic student presence and a concurrent focus on business matters of interest to the American-Hispanic community. And then, of course, there's the "affordable tuition," the "small size of most classes"—the program is "not...too congested while still being large enough to have good facilities"—and the "easy-to-deal-with university administration," which works hard to ease the burdens of the school's overtaxed students. One student took special note of the program's "flexibility for working parents. I'm a single parent and have felt supported and encouraged by all of my professors and my advisor."

Similarly, professors "take the students' welfare into consideration" and "will always create extra time outside the class to answer questions to help make the learning process easy." Most instructors here "are very passionate about their work and it shows in their lecturing. They have relevant experience in their disciplines that they can relate to students showing real-life applications of the material." As one student explains, "I believe that the professors are the greatest strengths [of the program]. The passion and experience that they bring to the classroom is great. There are a couple who are not so great, but the majority are fantastic. Their enthusiasm makes you want to learn, and the material is challenging." TAMUCC offers its MBAs two areas of concentration: international business, and health care management.

Career and Placement

The TAMUCC Career Services office provides counseling and placement services for all undergraduates, graduate students, and alumni of the university. Frequent seminars and presentations are offered on such topics as "How to Job Search in the 'Hidden Market,'" "The Second Interview and Salary Negotiation," and "How to Get a Federal Job." The office also provides career counseling, computer-based self-assessments, job search advisement, online and hard-copy job postings, a career resource library and computer lab, videotaped mock interviews, and job fairs and on-campus recruiting events.

Top employers in the area include the Naval Air Station Corpus Christi, Christus Spohn Health System, the Corpus Christi Army Depot, H-E-B Grocery Co., Bay Limited, SSP Partners/Circle K, Driscoll Children's Hospital, APAC, First Data, and Gulf Marine Fabricators.

ADMISSIONS CONTACT: SHARON POLANSKY, DIRECTOR OF MASTERS PROGRAMS
ADDRESS: 6300 OCEAN DRIVE UNIT 5808, CORPUS CHRISTI, TX 78412-5808
PHONE: 361-825-2655 • FAX: 361-825-2725
E-MAIL: SHARON.POLANSKY@TAMUCC.EDU • WEBSITE: WWW.COB.TAMUCC.EDU

Student Life and Environment

"There is a very diverse population from a multitude of cultures" within the TAMUCC MBA program, and "this is very important…in South Texas, [where] the majority of the population is either Hispanic or white." Students here are "very ambitious and amiable," and while "discussions in class are heated, there is a mutual respect." The student body "is about 30 percent international," "which gives a very diverse, unique experience in the classroom." A sizeable group of military personnel further adds to the diverse backgrounds and perspectives. Except for the international students, most here are "balancing a full work load, course load, family life and other extracurricular activities."

TAMUCC's "attractive campus by the ocean" engenders a "laid-back, casual, 'feels like island time'" atmosphere. "Don't let people wearing flip flops fool you," though; these are "very hardworking/studying individuals." The program forces them to be actively involved in class, as the classroom "is very participation-oriented rather than the professor only lecturing." Fortunately TAMUCC students are up to the challenge.

Admissions

All applicants to the TAMUCC MBA program must submit the following materials: official transcripts for all undergraduate and graduate work; an official score report for the GMAT (test score can be no more than five years old); two letters or recommendation; a current resume or curriculum vitae; a personal essay stating your reasons for pursuing the MBA; and a completed application form. In addition, international students whose first language is not English must submit an official score for the TOEFL and an evaluation of non-English language transcripts executed by Education Credential Evaluators, Inc., International Education Research Foundation, Inc., or World Education Services. All international applicants must submit an I-34 form or other notarized confirmation of adequate financial support, a copy of their current visa, and proof of medical insurance.

FINANCIAL FACTS

Annual tuition (in-state/ out-of-state)	$3,522/$9,840
Fees	$2,110
Cost of books	$792
Room & board (on/off-campus)	$11,448/$10,087

ADMISSIONS

Admissions Selectivity Rating	**81**
# of applications received	55
% applicants accepted	78
% acceptees attending	88
Average GMAT	484
Range of GMAT	438–523
Accepts GRE scores	No
Average GPA	3.3
TOEFL required of international students	Yes
Minimum TOEFL (paper/web)	550/80
Application fee	$50
International application fee	$70
Regular application deadline	7/15
Deferment available	Yes
Maximum length of deferment	1 year
Transfer students accepted	Yes
Transfer application policy Possibility of transferring in 6 credits from accredited school with grade of B or above.	
Non-fall admissions	Yes
Need-blind admissions	Yes

TEXAS CHRISTIAN UNIVERSITY
NEELEY SCHOOL OF BUSINESS

Academics

Texas Christian University's Neeley School of Business offers the best of both worlds, uniting a "small-school atmosphere with big business ties." Located in the heart of the Dallas–Fort Worth metropolitan area, the school has "access to and relationships with many top companies." "Networking opportunities are second to none," and career and internship prospects look particularly positive in this vibrant business-oriented city. At the same time, "personalized attention" is a hallmark of the TCU Full-time program. With fifty to sixty students in each incoming class, the "small and accessible size" of the school guarantees that students benefit from plenty of interaction with the "world-class faculty." Here, "it is easy to reach professors and ask questions." In addition to the faculty, "every TCU employee involved with the MBA program has a clear and unwavering passion for growing the program and graduating successful students." Administrators are "very accommodating, know all of the students well, and are very accessible."

Depending on your needs and your career experience to date, Neeley offers a range of MBA options, including a part-time evening program, an executive MBA, a twenty-one-month full-time program, and an accelerated twelve-month full-time program. In the full-time program, students are assigned to small project teams during the first year, a great way to get to know your classmates. While the atmosphere is close-knit, the curriculum is rigorous. There is an "extremely heavy workload in the beginning" of the full-time MBA, and "all of the students in the program hold each other to a high standard." Described as "outstanding," Neeley professors bring "a ton of practical industry experience" to the classroom. Students point out that "the professors in supply chain are really good," and the school offers the opportunity to pursue a functional concentration in that field, as well as in marketing, finance, and accounting. MBA candidates may further tailor their studies through elective courses in a specific industry, like health care or real estate; the school's "up-and-coming" MBA for Energy Professionals is particularly suited to its Texas location.

A Neeley education "focuses more on experiential learning" than strict academics. In this "applicable career-focused program," there is an emphasis on developing a practical perspective, and professors are committed to "pushing our limits and growing our skills in communication, presentations, etc. from the moment classes begin." Throughout the MBA, class work is "supplemented with a great deal of real-world work experiences, though programs like Neeley & Associates Consulting," a specialized class in which students review and evaluate real-world clients with the guidance of faculty experts. Students can further augment their education through study abroad, frequent "networking events," and special trips and events, like "going to meet Warren Buffet."

Career and Placement

In addition to the many real-world projects incorporated into the Neeley MBA curriculum, the school offers a robust suite of job-related resources for MBA candidates, including individualized career coaching, internship placement, interview prep, and annualcareer-oriented trips to places such as New York City, Chicago, or San Deigo. There are also ample networking events on campus, including roundtables and special dinners with national and regional business leaders. Students say the school has deep ties in the local business community, and "the alumni are fiercely loyal to their own and most will go out of their way to help."

ADMISSIONS CONTACT: PEGGY CONWAY, DIRECTOR OF MBA ADMISSIONS
ADDRESS: P.O. BOX 298540, FORT WORTH, TX 76129
PHONE: 817-257-7531 • FAX: 817-257-6431
E-MAIL: MBAINFO@TCU.EDU • WEBSITE: WWW.MBA.TCU.EDU

Eighty-five percent of students graduating from TCU in May 2013 had a job within three months of graduation, with starting salaries averaging $85,367. Students recently took jobs or internships at Accenture, AT&T, Deloitte Consulting, Ericsson, Ernst & Young, Frito-Lay, Galderma, Halliburton, Healthpoint LTD, Hewlett-Packard, Intel Corp., JCPenney, Johnson & Johnson, Kellogg's, Kimberly-Clark, Merrill Lynch, Sherwin Williams, Texas Instruments, and Verizon. The school has a "great reputation in DFW," but students do note that the school "tends to place best at companies in DFW. For students looking for jobs elsewhere, that can be difficult."

Student Life and Environment

Despite its modest size, you'll find plenty of diversity on the TCU campus. The school attracts a unique group of students whose collective "experience crosses the globe and many different industries." An ambitious and "capable" group, MBA students are also collaborative: Here, "students are often found working and studying together" as they try to keep up with group projects and assignments. Despite the program's demands, TCU is a "welcoming" environment, where "people know each other well and easily become friends."

"The community is very vibrant" at TCU, with ongoing extracurricular activities and social events taking place on campus. For example, "there are multiple networking opportunities every week," as well as "free movies, speeches from famous professors from other schools, festivals for minority communities," and more. In addition to school-related activities, students meet up for "happy hours, meals, working out at the Rec, or other fun activities as the occasion arises." Students can also take advantage of the multitude of recreational activities, arts, and entertainment in the Dallas–Fort Worth area, where they'll find everything from "honky-tonk" to "golfing" to world-class museums in addition to the thriving professional and collegiate athletic teams and events.

Admissions

Neeley seeks to admit highly motivated and academically talented students who will succeed in a graduate-level program. That said, there is no minimum GPA nor minimum test scores required for admission; the range of GMAT scores for admitted students is usually very broad, spanning from the mid 500s to the mid 700s. (If they want to edge up their numbers, applicants to the program can take a free GMAT prep course via the Neeley website.) In the full-time program, students typically have about four to five years of professional experience before starting the MBA. In the professional MBA, five to seven years is the norm.

FINANCIAL FACTS

Annual tuition	$38,208
Fees	$6,400
Cost of books	$2,000
Room & board	$16,500
% of students receiving aid	96
% of first-year students receiving aid	95
% of students receiving grants	96
Average award package	$44,530
Average grant	$33,975
Average loan	$24,247
Average student loan debt	$48,048

ADMISSIONS

Admissions Selectivity Rating	88
# of applications received	210
% applicants accepted	49
% acceptees attending	46
Average GMAT	642
Range of GMAT	570–700
Accepts GRE scores	Yes
Average Verbal GRE	155
Range of Verbal GRE scores	145–162
Average Quantitative GRE	160
Range of Quantitative GRE scores	152–164
Average Writing GRE	4.0
Range of Writing GRE scores	3.0–4.0
Average GPA	3.3
TOEFL required of international students	Yes
Minimum TOEFL (paper/web)	600/100
Application fee	$100
International application fee	$100
Early application deadline	11/1
Early notification date	12/15
Regular application deadline	3/1
Regular application notification	4/1
Application Deadline/Notification	
Round 1:	11/1 / 12/15
Round 2:	1/15 / 2/15
Round 3:	3/1 / 4/1
Round 4:	4/15 / 5/15
Deferment available	Yes
Maximum length of deferment	1 year
Transfer students accepted	Yes
Transfer application policy	
Nine semester hours may be transferred from an AACSB accredited institution.	
Non-fall admissions	Yes
Need-blind admissions	Yes

EMPLOYMENT PROFILE

Career Rating	95	Grads Employed by Function	% Avg. Salary
Percent employed at graduation	71	Marketing	(18%) $87,333
Percent employed 3 months after graduation	89	Operations	(15%) $83,752
		Management	(10%) $87,625
Average base starting salary	$89,579	Finance	(49%) $90,726
Primary Source of Full-time Job Acceptances		Other	(8%) $98,333
School-facilitated activities	33 (85%)	**Top 5 Employers Hiring Grads**	
Graduate-facilitated activities	6 (15%)	Alcon (4), AT&T (3), American Airlines (2), Michaels (2), Elevate (2)	

Texas Southern University
Jesse H. Jones School of Business

Academics

Located in Houston, Texas Southern University's Jesse H. Jones School of Business is known for its "strong faculty" and "great connections," as well as "flexible class schedules," "small classroom sizes," and affordable price. The school boasts "one of the most diverse faculties in the nation," and the U.S. government recently designated Texas Southern University "as a National Transportation Security Center of Excellence (NTSCE)." "The greatest strength of my school," says one student, "is that it is a well known university with competitive programs such as Pharmacy, Business, and Law."

Students at TSU enjoy a good "student-to-professor ratio" and find that "professors are really helpful inside and outside class." Students praise the "high quality of experienced professors who are always willing to share their knowledge and experiences," and note that the "curriculum forces you to use your critical thinking ability," a valuable skill that endures long after graduation. "This program forces you to look at situations objectively," says ones student, and the diversity of the program encourages students to consider "multiple viewpoints" and "be educated on different cultures." The business school invites "various speakers to come and speak" regularly. Professors and staff take "the time out to help you and point you in the right direction" and "don't let you give up." They want to "see you succeed and will bend their backs to help you do so," notes a student from the Class of 2016. The "professors are tough, but it aids us into becoming successful in the future," notes a student in the healthcare industry. Students consider their fellow classmates to be as important to their education as their professors. Classroom debates encourage students to show their "individual strength," and teamwork encourages students to help each other and network among the student body. "Everyone that I have worked with in group assignments is very friendly and helpful," notes one student. They are a "great groups of individuals to work with!!" Students roundly praise not only their professors and fellow students, but also the "group-oriented" nature of the school. TSU is a great fit for students looking for an affordable MBA in a diverse and supportive environment.

Career and Placement

Students choose TSU not only "because it has a great business school," but also because of the "great relationships with many businesses" that will help "catapult" students' careers. They appreciate the "strong connection with the corporate and government society," as well as "having easy access to the Dean." "The greatest strength of TSU is helping students prepare for the life after school," notes one student. The "school administration is very helpful" and they "go above and beyond when helping their students." There are "great business partners/companies who are ALWAYS recruiting on this campus."

ADMISSIONS CONTACT: MAHESH VANJANI, DIRECTOR, GRADUATE PROGRAMS IN BUSINESS
ADDRESS: GRADUATE PROGRAMS IN BUSINESS, JHJ SCHOOL OF BUSINESS, HOUSTON, TX 77004
PHONE: 713-313-7786 • FAX: 713-313-7725
E-MAIL: VANJANIM@TSU.EDU • WEBSITE: WWW.TSU.EDU/EMBA

Student Life and Environment

Many students praise the close-knit quality of the student body and the "family-like environment." The school works "hard to help everyone feel comfortable and at home." Students at TSU are ethnically and socioeconomically diverse. And as one student says, the administration is "understanding" and "accommodating to all races and ready and willing to work with all." "The greatest strength of our school is the camaraderie," notes another.

Students find their classmates to be "friendly," "sociable," "eager," "ambitious," and "willing to learn." They are "hard working," "competitive," and "always striving to be better." "I couldn't ask for more from a student body," says one student. Most students are "really into their studies" and "take this program seriously." Being around such dedicated classmates "really helps other students who want to succeed." "My fellow students are energetic and happy to be attending TSU," says one student. "They show respect for one another and are very helpful." Many "students are in their early thirties and are into their careers already," which add networking opportunities as well as a diversity of experience. And student organizations like the GSA are a big "help for social networking."

Admissions

Applicants must submit an undergraduate transcript with a minimum GPA of 2.5 (C+) or better or a grade point average of 3.0 on the last sixty semester hours of undergraduate course work, GMAT score, and an Analytical Writing score of 3.5 or above on GRE or GMAT exam to fulfill the English proficiency requirement. Individual programs may have additional standards and requirements. For international students, a score of at least 550 on the paper-based test is required, 213 on the computer-based test, or 79 on the internet-based test of the TOEFL.

FINANCIAL FACTS

Annual tuition (in-state/ out-of-state)	$4,896/$10,368
Fees	$1,757
Cost of books	$1,400
Room & board (on/off-campus)	$6,500/$13,980

ADMISSIONS

Admissions Selectivity Rating	80
# of applications received	181
% applicants accepted	56
% acceptees attending	60
Average GMAT	371
Range of GMAT	250–520
Accepts GRE scores	Yes
Average GPA	3.0
TOEFL required of international students	Yes
Minimum TOEFL (paper/web)	550/79
Application fee	$50
International application fee	$75
Regular application deadline	7/15
Deferment available	Yes
Maximum length of deferment	1 year
Transfer students accepted	Yes
Transfer application policy	

Apply similar to regular applicants For traditional MBA a maximum of 6 credit hours can be transferred subject to approval. No Transfer Credits accepted for the online Executive MBA (EMBA) program.

Non-fall admissions	Yes
Need-blind admissions	Yes

EMPLOYMENT PROFILE		
Career Rating	71	**Top 5 Employers Hiring Grads** Sysco, Citgo, Chevron, City of Houston, State of Texas

TEXAS TECH UNIVERSITY
JERRY S. RAWLS COLLEGE OF BUSINESS ADMINISTRATION

GENERAL INFORMATION
Type of school   Public
Affiliation   No Affiliation
Academic calendar   rolling

SURVEY SAYS...
Friendly students, Conservative students, Happy students
Solid preparation in:
Finance, Accounting, General management, Teamwork, Communication/ interpersonal skills, Presentation skills, Social responsibility

STUDENTS
Enrollment of parent
  institution   35,859
Enrollment of MBA Program   447
% male/female   70/30
% out-of-state   8
% part-time   3
% underrepresented minority   31
% international   5
Average age at entry   36
Average years work
  experience at entry   6

ACADEMICS
Academic Experience Rating   **90**
Profs interesting rating   92
Profs accessible rating   93
Student/faculty ratio   12:1
% female faculty   25
% underrepresented
  minority faculty   16
% part-time faculty   0

Joint Degrees
Dual MBA programs with: MD/MBA 4 years; JD/MBA 3 years; PharmD/ MBA 3 years; MA Architecture/MBA 2 1/2 years; MA foreign language/ MBA 2 years; Biotechnology/MBA 3-4 years

Prominent Alumni
Jerry V. Smith, President/J. V. Smith Professional Corporation- CPA; Joshua T. Robertson, Healthcare Entrepreneur, Executive; Mike Kehoe, V.P. International Mkt. Bloomin' Brands

Academics

Busy West Texas professionals seeking an MBA program with "affordable tuition, friendly professors, and a broad curriculum" may find a home at the Rawls College of Business at Texas Tech. Rawls' MBA program offers evening courses to part-time and full-time students. In addition, Executive-style MBA programs offer the option of a convenient block scheduling system that students like ("We meet twice a year for six days straight, eight hours a day") or a one-weekend-a-month calendar. Rawls has custom designed a number of combined degrees and Executive-style MBA programs to fit the needs of professionals of all stripes. A combined MD/MBA "is a unique opportunity providing the experience and preparation for a future in healthcare administration or private practice." Dual business degrees are also available in architecture, foreign languages, law, personal financial planning, pharmacy, and environmental toxicology.

Students praise the Rawls MBA for "the flexibility it offers to working professionals" and for a "benefit/cost ratio much greater than similar programs" in the area. They are especially effusive about the administration, which "takes care of everything for the students. They register us for classes, feed us, and provide us with all of the materials and resources needed for our classes." As one student puts it, "The administration is a joy to work with. If you have any questions about courses, registration, etc. they respond quickly to emails and have an open-door policy." Likewise, students are "especially impressed by the willingness of the professors to accommodate students with full-time jobs and families. As a group, they have been very helpful in making sure that my workload is effective in the curriculum and works with my schedule."

Tech, one student observes, is "not so large and accomplished that everyone has a sense of entitlement and arrogance, yet it's not small and struggling to keep its head above water." It is large enough to offer a broad selection of offerings, including STEM MBA, MBA for Working Professionals, and Dual MBA Programs. Instructors in these programs "are beyond knowledgeable in their fields and are also easy to access for questions about course work or the job market in their particular field. I have never met anyone within the program that was not willing to help the students succeed," one student writes.

Career and Placement

Texas Tech serves a full-time and part-time student body. Many of the students in the MBA for Working Professionals Program attend at the expense of their employers and intend to remain with those employers after graduation. Companies likely to employ Texas Tech MBAs include Accenture, Amegy Bank, Bank of America, BNSF Railway, C.H. Robinson Worldwide, CB Richard Ellis, Comerica, Conoco Phillips, Deloitte, Enterprise Rent-a-Car, Ernst & Young, Exxon Mobil, FDIC, Frito Lay, Frost Bank, Geico, General Motors, Goldman Sachs, ISNetworld, JPMorgan Chase, KPMG, Lockheed Martin, National Instruments, Northrop Gruman, ORIX USA, PlainsCapital, PricewaterhouseCoopers, Ryan, Pioneer Natural Resources, Protiviti, Sherwin-Williams, Target, USAA, WalMart, and Wells Fargo Bank.

ADMISSIONS CONTACT: MARY FRANCES WEATHERLY, DIRECTOR, GRADUATE & PROFESSIONAL PROGRAMS
ADDRESS: RAWLS COLLEGE OF BUSINESS, GRADUATE SERVICES CENTER, LUBBOCK, TX 79409-2101
PHONE: 806-742-3184 • FAX: 806-742-3958
E-MAIL: RAWLS.MBA@TTU.EDU • WEBSITE: TEXASTECHMBA.COM

Student Life and Environment

The Texas Tech campus "has excellent facilities overall." The Rawls Building, which was completed in December 2011, achieved LEED Gold certification for energy use, lighting, water and material use. The classrooms are state of the art with billboard size projection and sophisticated wi-fi.

The rest of the "beautiful" Tech campus is "filled with art from around the world," and "its Spanish-style architecture is unique and beautiful." Campus amenities include "a gym [that] has outstanding equipment and a library [that] has an extensive availability of resources, including media resources and things through interlibrary loan (the staff is very helpful with this)." It's a welcoming atmosphere on campus, according to one student: "I have always felt comfortable on Tech campus, especially walking around at night." It's a busy place; "there are always sporting events to attend on the weekends and the Center for Campus Life and Student Government Association [is] always hosting free events for students. The graduate association also makes sure students are involved with monthly socials, philanthropy events (especially during the holidays), and campus-wide events, like tailgating before football games. The Rawls Graduate Association works especially hard to connect students in the program together, making classes more comfortable and provides more networking overall."

Admissions

Texas Tech requires applicants to submit undergraduate transcripts, GMAT scores, and a resume. Other optional elements of the application considered by the school include research experience, awards, leadership positions held in college and/or industry, civic and volunteer activities, motivation, evidence of past success, letters of recommendation, and the admissions office's assessment of the applicant's potential to provide a unique perspective within the program.

FINANCIAL FACTS

Annual tuition (in-state/ out-of-state)	$11,298/$27,678
Fees	$5,998
Cost of books	$1,200
Room & board	$10,043
% of students receiving aid	70
Average award package	$20,500
Average grant	$2,500
Average student loan debt	$20,500

ADMISSIONS

Admissions Selectivity Rating	86
# of applications received	235
% applicants accepted	54
% acceptees attending	81
Average GMAT	564
Range of GMAT	481–680
Accepts GRE scores	Yes
Average GPA	3.1
TOEFL required of international students	Yes
Minimum TOEFL (paper/web)	550/79
Application fee	$60
International application fee	$60
Early application deadline	3/1
Deferment available	Yes
Maximum length of deferment	one year
Transfer students accepted	Yes
Transfer application policy Up to six credit hours of graduate level work from an AACSB accredited school may transfer. Final approval granted by Graduate Dean.	
Non-fall admissions	Yes
Need-blind admissions	Yes

EMPLOYMENT PROFILE

Career Rating	90	**Grads Employed by Function% Avg. Salary**	
Percent employed 3 months		Marketing	(12%) $58,333
after graduation	88	Consulting	(8%) $69,167
Average base starting salary	$59,224	Management	(20%) $56,563
		Finance	(8%) $61,000
		MIS	(4%) $48,000
		Other	(31%) $60,625

Top 5 Employers Hiring Grads
Wells Fargo, Ernst & Young, National Oilwell Varco, Target, Protiviti

TULANE UNIVERSITY
FREEMAN SCHOOL OF BUSINESS

GENERAL INFORMATION
Type of school   Private
Affiliation   No Affiliation
Academic calendar   Semester

SURVEY SAYS...
Classmates have diverse work experience, Friendly students, Good social scene, Happy students, Abundant clubs and activities, Students love New Orleans, LA
Solid preparation in:
Finance, Accounting, Teamwork, Presentation skills, Quantitative skills, Computer skills, Doing business in a global economy, Entreprenurial studies

STUDENTS
Enrollment of parent
  institution   13,462
Enrollment of MBA Program   234
% male/female   33/67
% part-time   42
% underrepresented minority   10
% international   41
Average age at entry   28
Average years work
  experience at entry   4

ACADEMICS
Academic Experience Rating   89
Profs interesting rating   89
Profs accessible rating   95
Student/faculty ratio   15:1
% female faculty   33
% underrepresented
  minority faculty   5
% part-time faculty   10

Joint Degrees
MBA/MD - 5 years, MBA/JD - 4 years; MBA/Master of Arts in Latin American Studies - 2 1/2 years; MBA/Master of Health Administration - 3 years; MACCT/ MBA ,- 2.5 years; MBA/ MGM 2 years; MBA/ MNRG 2.5 years

Academics

A number of outstanding features distinguish the Freeman School of Business at Tulane University, particularly in the area of finance, where enrolled students enjoy "one of the best finance programs in the country." The program is equipped with an "unmatched" trading floor; a portfolio management program (Fenner Fund) where students manage over $2.5 million in real funds; and an investment analysis program (Burkenroad Reports) where students capture stocks-under-rocks.

Finance has such a "well-deserved great reputation" at Freeman that other strengths of the program are sometimes overlooked. Marketing "continues to grow here, while the energy specialization "is very smart for this area of the country." Freeman also excels in entrepreneurial studies; as one student explains, "I chose Tulane because of the ability to focus on entrepreneurship and the school's access to successful entrepreneurs, through whom I could learn to be a more effective business owner." Finally, the school recognizes the speed at which all business is becoming international through its "strong experiential Global Management program," which "sends the entire class on three trips abroad," thereby "emphasizing the global business curriculum in a truly hands-on environment."

The sum is greater than the considerable parts at Freeman, students tell us. One writes, "The greatest strengths of Tulane are its abilities to integrate the different segments of business and make them relevant, not just to corporate America, but also to small business and global business. Tulane also facilitates discussion on how your business or company can align its operations to take into consideration all stakeholders, thus becoming an organization that creates both profit and social good." An "excellent" relationship with the local community means that "business leaders around the community are accessible and supportive." Students also appreciate how the "school administration has done a great job in the recovery efforts since Katrina." Be forewarned that the program operates on seven-week terms that can fly by; "the first is by far the most intense, and they get gradually easier," one student explains.

Career and Placement

Tulane's Career Management Center earns mixed reviews from students. Several complain that "on campus recruiting is weak. We miss almost all of the big companies due to our location. We only get energy companies or a few other random companies based in Texas or the rest of the South to come to Tulane." Some simply wish the office would be "more proactive," but some go further, calling it the school's "weakest area" and asserting that "students are practically on their own when it comes to acquiring an internship or employment." Several acknowledged that the down economy was certainly a factor in the Center's disappointing outcomes.

Companies most likely to hire Freeman MBAs include BearingPoint, Capital One, Citibank, Daymon Worldwide, Deloitte & Touche, Entergy, Federal Express, First Albany Capital, Hibernia, Johnson & Rice, JPMorgan Chase, Latitram, Piper Jaffray & Co., RBC, & Company, Teracore Consulting, Tidewater Marine, TXU, Verizon, and Wachovia.

ADMISSIONS CONTACT: MELISSA BOOTH, DIRECTOR OF GRADUATE ADMISSIONS AND FINANCIAL AID
ADDRESS: 7 MCALISTER DRIVE, SUITE 401, NEW ORLEANS, LA 70118
PHONE: 504-865-5410 • FAX: 504-865-6770
E-MAIL: MBOOTH3@TULANE.EDU • WEBSITE: FREEMAN.TULANE.EDU

Student Life and Environment

Tulane is in New Orleans, so it should come as no surprise that life here can be "a lot of fun." "Many people socialize heavily on the weekends (we go out a lot). New Orleans literally has events every weekend. If you can't find something to do here, you're not looking at all," is how one student sums things up. The city is so focused on socializing that "school slows down during busy periods, such as Mardi Gras." Accordingly, many here enjoy a "very good mix of school and entertainment. New Orleans is the best place to go to school. Mardi Gras, Jazz Fest, and the food [all add up to] a once-in-a-lifetime experience."

Within the program, "the numerous clubs are mostly strong. The strongest is [the] entrepreneurship club, [which] is very good with matching people [with] local small business owners who can be mentors/potential employers." The local business community "truly embraces the MBA students, with leaders often speaking on campus and offering to meet with us individually on our own time. People are simply friendly here and take an interest in Tulane students. It makes networking locally incredibly easy." Freeman classes "are hard but not impossible," and for many, "juggling so many opportunities… is probably the hardest part of attending grad school [at Tulane]."

Tulane MBAs "are a diverse group from all over the world, many with different political views and worldviews." "One-third of our class is made up of international students, so it makes everything—discussion, group work, assignments—much more interesting," one student tells us.

Admissions

Freeman reviews applications to its graduate programs in three separate rounds, and the school encourages students to apply as early as possible to maximize their chances of gaining admission. The following is required to apply: an undergraduate transcript, an affidavit of support, an official GMAT/GRE score report, TOEFL/IELTS/PTE scores (for international students whose first language is not English), two letters of recommendation, a current resume, personal statement, and interview. Minority recruitment efforts include Destination MBA, the National Black MBA Association Career Fair, targeted GMASS searches, and minority fellowships. For the incoming class of 2015, entering students earned a median GMAT score of 676 and boasted a median 3.2 undergraduate GPA.

Prominent Alumni

Ricardo Salinas Pliego, President and CEO of Grupo Salinas and Grupo Elektra; Regina Benjamin, Surgeon General of the United States; Mark Bostick, President, Comcar Industries; Larry Gordon, Film Producer, former President of 20th Century Fox; Haibo Dai, Exec. Director, Shanghai Lingang New Town

FINANCIAL FACTS

Annual tuition (in-state/ out-of-state)	$46,147/$46,147
Fees	$5,280
Cost of books	$1,600
Room & board	$15,900
% of students receiving aid	88
% of first-year students receiving aid	100
% of students receiving grants	78
Average award package	$45,674
Average grant	$30,736
Average loan	$43,532

ADMISSIONS

Admissions Selectivity Rating	84
# of applications received	219
% applicants accepted	73
% acceptees attending	48
Average GMAT	676
Range of GMAT	650–710
Accepts GRE scores	Yes
Average GPA	3.2
TOEFL required of international students	Yes
Minimum TOEFL (paper/web)	610/102
Application fee	$125
International application fee	$125
Application Deadline/Notification	
Round 1:	11/1 / 12/1
Round 2:	1/1 / 2/1
Round 3:	3/1 / 4/1
Round 4:	5/1 / 6/1
Deferment available	No
Transfer students accepted	No
Non-fall admissions	No
Need-blind admissions	Yes

EMPLOYMENT PROFILE

Career Rating	91	Grads Employed by Function% Avg. Salary	
Percent employed at graduation	49	Marketing	(16%) $70,000
Percent employed 3 months after graduation	88	Consulting	(29%) $81,400
Average base starting salary	$80,300	Management	(5%)
Primary Source of Full-time Job Acceptances		Finance	(34%) $75,000
School-facilitated activities	24 (55%)	Other	(16%) $100,000
Graduate-facilitated activities	18 (41%)	**Top 5 Employers Hiring Grads**	
Unknown	2 (4%)	APTIFY (5), iGate Technologies, Inc. (2), L'Oreal (1), Ipsos (1), Dow Chemical Company (1)	

THE UNIVERSITY OF AKRON
COLLEGE OF BUSINESS ADMINISTRATION

Academics

The University of Akron's College of Business Administration offers flexible programs with both full-time and part-time options, including an evening MBA program which qualifying students can complete in as few as twelve months if they meet the required undergraduate course work. An orientation session at the start of the first semester will allow students to get acquainted with the program. From there, it is on to a program devoted to "preparing you for your future." Concentrations include finance, international business, management, strategic marketing, supply-chain management, health care, interdisciplinary, and business analytics.

Through a diverse student body, "high competition" among classmates, and an administration willing to "change curriculum to better serve students," the University of Akron "really prepare[s] its students to excel in the marketplace." However, one student believes the work is "much less difficult than I had anticipated." Still others say that "some professors are difficult to approach and to schedule time with," with the most disgruntled of students claiming a few professors are "arrogant and really don't want to help students." This is in sharp contrast to those who find educators at Akron to be "friendly and accessible" and a group that "make[s] sure that we learn through discussions and active participation."

In fact, many students are "amazed" at the qualifications of the "fantastic" MBA professors here and are pleased to find "an outstanding staff and members of faculty that know what is best for their students to be the future cadres of the worldwide village." Educators who "bring real world, practical knowledge that is second to none" not only help provide a "rewarding" educational experience, they also "inform you of job opportunities, workshops, internships, clinics, etc." But do not expect your hand to be held. "It is up to you to follow up. If you do follow up you have all of their resources at your disposal."

Career and Placement

Akron is located near Cleveland's job market, which is an immediate plus, as is the school's "local connections with reputable companies." The school's Center for Career Management offers career services for all undergraduates, graduate students, and alumni. Through this office, students and alumni will have access to help with career planning, summer internships, job searching, interviewing, and resume writing. With Akron's "strong network," and "companies in both public accounting and industry heavily recruiting here, it helps make it very easy to land a job in whichever area you prefer." School-organized career fairs give students a "chance to meet some prominent businesses" and "build [their] professional network." Employers who have hired from the Akron MBA pool include Goodyear Tire & Rubber Company, Delloite & Touche, Babcock & Wilcox, Dominion, FirstEnergy, Enterprise, Progressive, National City Bank, and J.M. Smuckers.

Student Life and Environment

As is typical with MBA programs, Akron's program is peopled with a mix of full-time and part-time students, along with the "vast array of career backgrounds" one expects from such a mix. "Some have just finished undergraduate school," one student writes, "and some are returning to school after twenty years of work experience." The group is "as intellectually diverse as we are ethnically. For every one of our students who are truly interested in learning this material and gaining these experiences, there are an equal number who are clearly trying to put in as little work as possible to achieve a passing grade." Overall, most are "hard-working" and "friendly" students interested in "obtaining a degree to enhance their career."

There is no great divide between full-time and part-time students. "Even though the majority of the students are part-time, they are interested in working with and giving back to the university. This provides for an interactive environment that sparks interesting discussion both inside and outside of the classroom." Those accepted to Akron's MBA program will find that their classmates "are strong academically with important experience that contributes to classroom discussion." Most students here "honestly enjoy the process of learning and take pride in what we accomplish, regardless of what letter winds up on our transcripts." In addition to students with diverse work backgrounds, "we also have students from different countries that bring an interesting perspective to discussions."

Outside the classroom "there is always something fruitful that you can hook yourself up with." When not utilizing the library or the resources of the Center for Career Management, students can check on weekly emails sent to Zipline that "update us on the events that will happen the week to come." The urban setting of Akron may not compare to a major city's—students admit, "the surrounding areas are not that great"–but "there is a pretty good nightlife." The school itself features athletics, a free bowling alley, recreation center, and other amenities, along with the clubs and students organizations one expects from a major college. As one student sums it up, "The bottom line is you can do a lot of useful things every day. The only thing that keeps us from contributing to these activities is our classes."

Admissions

While weighing your application Akron's admissions committee will consider your undergraduate GPA (minimum GPA of 2.75 required), GMAT scores (minimum score of 500 required), and TOEFL scores (international applicants). In addition, they will seek two letters of recommendation; a letter of purpose; a resume; a review of graduate and post-baccalaureate performance; and professional association and student organization memberships. International applicants must apply at least three months prior to their intended date of entry into the program. The school also sponsors a diversity program to enhance minority recruitment to the MBA program.

FINANCIAL FACTS

Room & board (on/off-campus)	$13,000/$13,000
% of students receiving aid	28
% of students receiving grants	13
Average award package	$15,881
Average grant	$23,838
Average loan	$9,349
Average student loan debt	$16,989

ADMISSIONS

Admissions Selectivity Rating	83
# of applications received	239
% applicants accepted	61
% acceptees attending	37
Average GMAT	558
Range of GMAT	530–600
Accepts GRE scores	Yes
Average Verbal GRE	150
Range of Verbal GRE scores	145–154
Average Quantitative GRE	152
Range of Quantitative GRE scores	145–162
Average Writing GRE	3.7
Range of Writing GRE scores	3.0–4.0
Average GPA	3.4
TOEFL required of international students	Yes
Minimum TOEFL (paper/web)	550/79
Application fee	$45
International application fee	$70
Regular application deadline	7/15
Regular application notification	8/1
Deferment available	Yes
Maximum length of deferment	one year
Transfer students accepted	Yes
Transfer application policy	Gateway courses may be waived based on comparable coursework or proficiency testing. Nine credits of advanced course work may transfer from AACSB accredited schools if approved by the Director.
Non-fall admissions	Yes
Need-blind admissions	Yes

EMPLOYMENT PROFILE

Career Rating	72

Grads Employed by Function% Avg. Salary

Marketing	(15%)	$81,667
Operations	(40%)	$86,875
Management	(10%)	$51,500
Finance	(30%)	$58,333
MIS	(5%)	$70,000

Top 5 Employers Hiring Grads

The Goodyear Tire and Rubber Co. (2), Timken Steel Company (1), General Electric (1), Bridgestone America (1), Alcoa (1)

THE UNIVERSITY OF ALABAMA AT BIRMINGHAM
SCHOOL OF BUSINESS

GENERAL INFORMATION
Type of school   Public
Affiliation   No Affiliation
Academic calendar   Semester

SURVEY SAYS...
Conservative students
Solid preparation in:
Presentation skills

STUDENTS
Enrollment of parent institution	18,568
Enrollment of MBA Program	380
% male/female	70/30
% out-of-state	5
% part-time	78
% underrepresented minority	25
% international	11
Average age at entry	29
Average years work experience at entry	6

ACADEMICS
Academic Experience Rating	84
Profs interesting rating	88
Profs accessible rating	89
Student/faculty ratio	30:1
% female faculty	18
% underrepresented minority faculty	9
% part-time faculty	0

Joint Degrees
Master of Business Administration/ Master of Public Health (MBA/ MPH); Master of Business Administration/Master of Science in Health Administration (MBA/MS).

Prominent Alumni
John Bakane, CEO, Mills; Daryl Byrd, CEO and President, Iberia Bank; Susan Story, CEO and President, Gulf Power Company; James Woodward, Chancellor, UNC; Stephen Zelnak, CEO and President, Martin Marietta Materials

Academics

The Collat School of Business at the University of Alabama at Birmingham is designed for current working professionals looking to advance their careers at a reasonable price, and to balance their professional and personal lives against school. Students can choose between a One-Year or Two-Year MBA, with concentrations available in four areas (finance, information technology management, healthcare management, and marketing) and dual degree options available (the MBA-Master of Science in Health Administration is a popular option). Most classes are held in the evening and on weekends, and many are also available online for blended learning, and true to modern form, "most students prefer to coordinate activities and communications by utilizing cloud-based systems."

Professors are "experienced professionals with a significant amount of published research." They are "relatable and knowledgeable" and "make themselves accessible" to any student that seeks help. Thanks to a newly streamlined curriculum, courses themselves "are designed to be challenging and are geared toward real world application" and integrate "an atmosphere of collaboration and learning" via group work and group studying. However, there are some professors that "simply assigned reading and gave tests" and are "only good for strict book learners."

The school administration "has always been transparent and open about policy changes and available to meet when needed." The Dean of the Business School is "very receptive to the needs of students and has a great strategic plan for the school"; recently, a plan was approved to construct a new business school building and innovation center.

Career and Placement

As the only accredited MBA program in the Birmingham area, the school has prominence among local businesses, many of which already employ UAB students. Students say that one of the school's greatest strength is its relationships with businesses outside of the university, and the Career Services office "does a great job of helping students find jobs after graduation they are there for anyone who wants one." The office holds regular career fairs, resume prep sessions, workshops, and luncheons to help move students down their career paths; as most at UAB are simply looking to move further in a current career, the focus is more on advancement than starting out. Employers who frequently hire UAB graduates include Regions Bank, Southern Company, Southern Progress, UAB, and Wells Fargo.

Student Life and Environment

The MBA program is "very separate from the rest of the school" with "large common areas to study, relax or do homework" and "a nice little restaurant within the school that is popular." Most students in the "very ethnically diverse student body" at UAB "are in their mid-twenties to early thirties and are married," and have a wide variety of business backgrounds ("from full-time students right out of undergraduate studies to surgeons seeking exposure to a business education"). Since most students are older and have a career or family needs, "they do not spend much time together outside of class and group project related functions" and "you must get to know your classmates through case studies and other group activities." Still, "people are friendly and there is an excitement in the air at the business school."

Admissions

Work experience, academic GPA, and scores on the GMAT are considered very important by those making admissions decisions for the graduate business programs at UAB. Personal essays, and letters of recommendation also receive consideration. Applicants to the program must submit an official GMAT score report, official transcripts from all colleges and universities attended, two letters of reference, and a current résumé. Students must demonstrate aptitude in calculus with a grade of C or better in a calculus course completed within the previous five years. The admissions committee may request an interview, but otherwise interviews are not required. Non-native English speakers must score at least 550 on the TOEFL and provide an ECE report to accompany their transcripts. It is recommended that international applicants apply six months in advance of the application deadline to ensure adequate time to process appropriate visas.

ADMISSIONS

Admissions Selectivity Rating	**81**
# of applications received	227
% applicants accepted	81
% acceptees attending	70
Average GMAT	558
Range of GMAT	480–680
Average GPA	3.3
TOEFL required of international students	Yes
Minimum TOEFL (paper/web)	550/80
Application fee	$60
International application fee	$75
Regular application deadline	7/1
Regular application notification	8/1
Deferment available	Yes
Maximum length of deferment	1 year
Transfer students accepted	Yes
Transfer application policy Must meet UAB MBA admission requirements, transfer courses must be from AACSB accredited program and equivalent to our required courses.We will accept up to 25% of the degree program in transfer work with a minimum "B" grade.	
Non-fall admissions	Yes
Need-blind admissions	Yes

THE UNIVERSITY OF ALABAMA AT TUSCALOOSA
MANDERSON GRADUATE SCHOOL OF BUSINESS

Academics

With collaborative learning a mandatory part of the curriculum, students at Manderson will find that they will rarely be facing the challenges of this small business program alone. That spirit of collaboration extends to the staff, too. Here "administration is very involved and helpful," working to "send out daily emails relating to various business related activities including career fairs, job/internship offers, and helpful hints/ tools for interviews, resumes, and cover letters." What difficulties students face are overcome through "easy to access professors who foster individual relationships with students both in and outside of the classroom." Another student notes that "the MBA Administration has faced some turnover as far as personnel," but these changes "did not keep the MBA Administration from focusing on students."

Manderson graduates say they have "had the honor to learn from some of the best teachers I have ever had here in the program," a group who are also "great mentors" who "love for the students to come meet with them and ask them for advice, even if it has nothing to do with class." Drawing from their real world experiences allows professors here to equip students for the challenges they will face. "They want students to do well, and don't just preach from a textbook. The professors at Alabama use everyday examples and demonstrate how integrity is the most important." Some students say professors can be "a mixed bag," but overall they are seen as "very experienced and knowledgeable, so they have a lot to offer to the students and expect students to be prepared, dedicated, and ambitious throughout their education in the program."

Evolution is part of the process here. "The administration inside the MBA program has been going through major changes through our first year, but they have done everything in their power to make the transition as smooth as possible." The "helpful administration, good professors, and a tough but fair academic experience" show that educators here "work hard and honestly care about helping the students reach their goals." As one student says, "Entering the MBA/MSCE program here at The University of Alabama was one of the best things to happen for my life and hopefully my career."

Career and Placement

Manderson students have ample opportunities for career advancement, and those opportunities are rich in part "because of a strong department of finance with excellent faculty and opportunities to network with alumni." The "well-developed entrepreneurship and innovation program" will sway many Manderson's way, especially since the school has "great relationships with large companies for internship and employment opportunities." For outgoing students, those shots at great positions won't take long to arise. "The Manderson staff has great corporate connections and the teachers try to make class assignments as similar as possible to real life situations."

In a recent year, 77 percent of the graduating class had accepted a job offer by the time of graduation. Some 91 percent accepted an offer within three months of graduation. The median base salary was about $65,000, with a range between $22,500 and $120,000. The career coordinators that are part of the Manderson Graduate School of Business program arrange individual advising sessions, resume revisions, skills workshops, alumni career panels, and on-campus recruiting programs for both jobs and internships. There are countless opportunities. Over the last few years, students here took internships at companies like Alabama Power, Compass Bank, Sterne Agee, PriceWaterhouseCoopers, Chesapeake Consulting, BMW, Red Cross, Wal-Mart, Hewlett Packard, Procter & Gamble, and St. Vincent Hospital.

ADMISSIONS CONTACT: PATRICIA "TUT" WILSON, DIRECTOR OF MBA RECRUITING & ADMISSIONS
ADDRESS: MANDERSON GRADUATE SCHOOL OF BUSINESS, BOX 870223, TUSCALOOSA, AL 35487
PHONE: 205-348-6517 • FAX: 205-348-4504
E-MAIL: MBA@CBA.UA.EDU • WEBSITE: MANDERSON.CBA.UA.EDU

Student Life and Environment

"Life at school is essentially super-undergraduate," with a workload that is "intense but manageable." The collaborative environment means "there is a lot of interaction with teams and groups." Indeed, "you can often find many students in the lounge provided for MBA students. It also usually involves a panel or information session from a company or business." What downtime students get is often used for career advancement, "researching internships and jobs and filling out many applications. Additionally, there's also constant work to be done on one's resume and cover letter, etc."

None of this is to say that students are working twenty-four hours a day. Both students and the school work together to create meaningful distractions from your studies. "Outside of class, there are plenty of opportunities to get involved with groups that involve your interests as well as social groups that meet once a week," and "organizations within the MBA program also provide opportunities to gather with fellow classmates for a variety of activities." The "unique and pretty cool atmosphere" and attractive location mean that "outside of school and work activities, the campus is full of things to do to add a little fun when you need a break." Indeed, "Tuscaloosa is a great city that affords the small college feel with the amenities of a larger city," offering plenty to do on weekends. Happy hours, intramural games, community service projects, outdoor activities, and more provide ways to wind down from the "very busy" week.

Admissions

Fewer than 100 students are admitted to the program each year, with classes beginning in the fall. To apply, students must submit a current resume, GMAT or GRE scores, three letters of recommendation, and official undergraduate transcripts. Decisions on admissions are made on a rolling basis; those seeking financial assistance should apply by the priority deadlines. About 40 percent of those in the program enter directly from college; applicants are not required to have significant professional experience before matriculation.

FINANCIAL FACTS

Annual tuition (in-state/ out-of-state)	$9,826/$24,950
Fees	$2,500
Cost of books	$1,000
Room & board	$6,000
% of students receiving aid	47
% of first-year students receiving aid	55
Average award package	$9,450
Average grant	$6,583

ADMISSIONS

Admissions Selectivity Rating	**89**
# of applications received	194
% applicants accepted	50
% acceptees attending	84
Average GMAT	658
Range of GMAT	580–740
Accepts GRE scores	Yes
Average Verbal GRE	153
Range of Verbal GRE scores	150–155
Average Quantitative GRE	154
Range of Quantitative GRE scores	152–156
Average GPA	3.5
TOEFL required of international students	Yes
Minimum TOEFL (paper/web)	550/80
Application fee	$50
International application fee	$60
Early application deadline	1/5
Early notification date	1/15
Regular application deadline	4/15
Regular application notification	4/30
Deferment available	Yes
Maximum length of deferment	One year.
Transfer students accepted	Yes
Transfer application policy Applicants may transfer up to 12 hours of elective credit from another AACSB-accredited graduate program. However, the MBA core must be taken in our program.	
Non-fall admissions	No
Need-blind admissions	Yes

EMPLOYMENT PROFILE

Career Rating	90	Grads Employed by Function	% Avg. Salary
Percent employed at graduation	64	Marketing	(5%) $50,667
Percent employed 3 months after graduation	91	Operations	(30%) $59,078
		Consulting	(14%) $69,000
Average base starting salary	$64,893	Management	(2%)
Primary Source of Full-time Job Acceptances		Finance	(35%) $67,098
School-facilitated activities	32 (56%)	MIS	(11%) $60,500
Graduate-facilitated activities	22 (39%)	Other	(4%)
Unknown	3 (5%)	**Top 5 Employers Hiring Grads**	

Top 5 Employers Hiring Grads
PricewaterhouseCoopers (6), Regions (4), Georgia-Pacific (2), Cigna HealthSpring (2), The University of Alabama (2)

UNIVERSITY OF ALBERTA
SCHOOL OF BUSINESS

Academics

The first business school in Canada to receive accreditation from the American Assembly of Collegiate Schools of Business, University of Alberta operates a full-time and part-time MBA on its Edmonton campus, an accelerated executive MBA, and a part-time program in Ft. McMurray. Integrating quantitative know-how with important qualitative skills, University of Alberta offers a "well-balanced education" through a mix of core course work and electives. Lectures are enhanced by "up-to-date case analyses," and throughout the curriculum there is a "focus on interpersonal skills and relationships." "There is a lot of group work in the MBA program," and therefore, "who you choose to work with, identifying your working style, and how to work with others are all vital components of a success strategy for the MBA." In complement to course work, students can participate in co-curricular opportunities, like the annual International Study Tour and MBA mentorship program. Students also note that the school's excellent lecture series is "worth attending" and "case competitions are fantastic."

"Since it's a research university, most professors have PhDs"; however, the Alberta faculty comprises a "good mix of academics and professionals." The classroom experience is generally rewarding, and "most professors are well-prepared and appropriate for their specific classes." At the same time, some professors "deliver a better course than others and who you get is simply the luck of the draw." Fortunately, the administration is receptive to student input, and "feedback is given from students to professors at the end of each term regarding the class and their teaching." A current student assures us, "They truly care and listen to suggestions on how to make things better."

When it comes to the nuts and bolts, things run smoothly at Alberta. "The MBA Programs Office does a great job behind the scenes," and, for the most part, the "registration process for class is well-run, smooth, and easy." At the same time, there is a bit of a divide between full-time students and their part-time counterparts. In many cases, "the part-timers do not feel as connected to the administration as the full-timers as we are not at school during the day." On the flipside, part-timers praise the fact that the "part-time program is excellent—flexible around work schedules and amenable to work-life balance." When it comes to the bottom line, students agree that the University of Alberta is an "excellent value." "Highly-regarded" in the Edmonton area, tuition is inexpensive, the area offers an "affordable cost of living," and the program is efficient (the full-time program can even be completed in as little as sixteen months).

Career and Placement

Through the MBA Career Services Office, students have access to professional career coaching and myriad career management resources. For first-year students, Career Services also offers the workshops, "Business 504," a crash course in career management. With 20,000 Alberta alumni, the school maintains a strong local network, and many corporate speakers, recruiters, and representatives visit campus. In fact, some students say "the network[ing] opportunities that are made available" are the program's greatest strength. Unfortunately, part-time students often feel they weren't invited to the party. A part-time student complains, "If there are company info sessions they are held during the day, so it is hard for part-time students to attend a lot of the sessions."

Over the past five years, 90 percent of Alberta graduates had accepted a position within three months of graduation. Alberta graduates have been hired by Accenture, Alberta Economic Development, ATB Financial, Bell, Bearing Point, CEMEX, China Zheshang Bank, Deloitte, Ernst & Young, Edmonton Airports, Direct Energy, HSBC Bank Canada,

Intuit, KPMG, Newell Rubbermaid, Parks Canada, Saudi Aramco, Sierra Systems, TD Canada Trust, and TEC Edmonton, among many others. Full-time graduates had an average starting salary of over $75,000 annually, and part-time students reported an average salary of over $95,000.

Student Life and Environment

With a broad-based core and numerous areas of specialization, Alberta attracts students from "many different business and non-business backgrounds"—as well as from many countries across the world. While students are "very diverse in every aspect," most agree that Alberta students are generally "knowledgeable, hard-working, respectful, and intelligent." In the part-time program, "most classmates are busy people, majority married and working," and they rarely have time to participate in extracurricular activities on campus. Spare time is squeezed even tighter because "all collaboration [has] to take place outside of normal business hours and outside of class time." (Fortunately, the business school is well equipped, and "there is an MBA specific lounge and study area that is very useful for group work and activities.")

Full-time students have a different take on life at Alberta. For them, "school life is filled with a multitude of opportunities, movies, social events, case competitions, [and] athletics." In the evenings, "there are numerous social events put on by the MBA association, which includes high-ranking guest speakers, free food, and great information." A second-year student tells us, "Life at school is a lot of fun. I spend more time in group meetings and extra-curricular activities (e.g., case competitions) than in class." Another student chimes in: "From the courses offered to the students in the program (55 percent international) to the social events and clubs to join, there is truly something here for everyone."

Admissions

To be considered for admission to the University of Alberta, students must have a minimum undergraduate GPA of 3.0, a minimum GMAT score of 550, and at least two years of professional work experience. Students must also submit two letters of recommendation and a personal statement. In the part-time and full-time programs, the recent incoming class had an average undergraduate GPA of 3.4 and average work experience of more than four years.

FINANCIAL FACTS

Annual tuition (in-state/ out-of-state)	$12,220/$12,220
Fees	$1,500
Cost of books	$1,000
Room & board (on/off-campus)	$7,500/$9,500
% of students receiving grants	100
Average grant	$5,000

ADMISSIONS

Admissions Selectivity Rating	92
# of applications received	333
% applicants accepted	31
% acceptees attending	58
Average GMAT	627
Range of GMAT	600–660
Accepts GRE scores	Yes
Average GPA	3.4
TOEFL required of international students	Yes
Minimum TOEFL (paper/web)	600/100
Application fee	$100
International application fee	$100
Regular application deadline	6/1
Deferment available	Yes
Maximum length of deferment	1 year
Transfer students accepted	Yes
Transfer application policy Transfer students are reviewed on an individual basis. Transfer credit is normally limited to 18-credits and must be from an AACSB accredited school.	
Non-fall admissions	No
Need-blind admissions	Yes

EMPLOYMENT PROFILE

Career Rating	81	Grads Employed by Function	%	Avg. Salary
Percent employed at graduation	56	Marketing	(20%)	$83,033
Percent employed 3 months after graduation	78	Operations	(36%)	$96,500
		Consulting	(14%)	$77,000
Average base starting salary	$81,420	Management	(3%)	
Primary Source of Full-time Job Acceptances		Finance	(9%)	
School-facilitated activities	(40%)	Info Tech	(7%)	$80,000
Graduate-facilitated activities	(16%)	Other	(11%)	$63,000
Unknown	(44%)	**Top 5 Employers Hiring Grads**		
		Deloitte (2), Government of Alberta (2), Scotiabank (2), TD (2), University of Alberta (2)		

UNIVERSITY OF ARIZONA
ELLER COLLEGE OF MANAGEMENT

GENERAL INFORMATION

Type of school	Public
Affiliation	No Affiliation
Academic calendar	Semester

SURVEY SAYS...

Classmates have diverse work experience, Friendly students, Happy students
Solid preparation in:
Finance, General management, Teamwork, Communication/interpersonal skills, Presentation skills

STUDENTS

Enrollment of parent institution	42,236
Enrollment of MBA Program	41
% male/female	59/41
% out-of-state	24
% part-time	0
% underrepresented minority	22
% international	46
Average age at entry	26
Average years work experience at entry	3

ACADEMICS

Academic Experience Rating	94
Profs interesting rating	87
Profs accessible rating	94
Student/faculty ratio	3:1
% female faculty	34
% underrepresented minority faculty	17
% part-time faculty	26

Joint Degrees

JD/MBA 3 and 4 years; MD/MBA- 5 years; MS MIS/MBA- 2.5 years; MBA/PharmD- 5 years; MBA/MSF- 2.5 years; MBA/MS in Engineering and Optical Science: 3 years; MBA/MPH: 3 years; MBA/Marketing 2.5 years

Academics

The Eller College of Management at the University of Arizona is "recognized as one of the nation's leading business schools" in MIS and entrepreneurship, many students here report. And "the weather doesn't hurt, either" adds one happy student.

Experiential learning plays an important part in the Eller curriculum; students identify this as "one of the greatest strengths" of the program. One MBA explains how it works: "In the spring semester, MBAs work in teams with local businesses to assess real-world problems, make strategic recommendations, and ultimately assist the businesses in solving those problems." Another tells us, "The experiential learning is more than just a resume builder. It's a very real, very challenging experience, designed to prepare students for future leadership positions." The school's strong "relationship with key businesses" in the area plays a key role in making the experiential learning component a success.

Students also appreciate that class sizes at Eller "are small enough that the students have easy access to professors…. Students are able to develop relationships and personal bonds with professors." These personal touches permeate the program's administration as well. One student reports, "The administrative staff adds great value to the student experience…[and] goes out of its way to help students find whatever they need. Cross-discipline courses, job opportunities, highly tailored informational interviews—the administration works hard to provide students with any resources they need." At the other end of the size spectrum is the university-at-large. It is huge, and this too is seen as an asset; "With a large campus, the business students can take advantage of wonderful resources for the entire school," one student explains.

Eller professors "are very engaging and add significant value. The tenured staff places a strong emphasis on real-world experiences, ranging from case competitions judged by working professionals to company site visits." Instructors "are also very available for office hours and discussion outside of class. This creates an atmosphere of 'twenty-four-hour learning.'"

Career and Placement

The Office of Career Management aims to provide highly personalized service to each individual student, in the process of helping them plan and achieve their career goals. The office organizes five annual job fairs on campus, networking events with alumni, company visits, and financial support for students who want to go to national MBA job fairs. The office further supports students in their job search through professional development workshops, interview preparation, resume preparation, and professional mentoring.

Companies most likely to hire Eller MBAs include Emerson, Deloitte, Discover, AT&T, Intel, Henkel, Bard, Roche, PetSmart, US Airways, Raytheon, Sandia National Labs, APS, Solon, PricewaterhouseCoopers, and WalMart.

Student Life and Environment

"Great weather and a very nice campus" soften the edges of Eller's intense program in graduate business study. Those who want to do better than scrape by will need to exert themselves, however; "excelling in all classes and electives requires an intense work week," students report. Program cohesion is enhanced through group work (the program requires "continuous case competitions, group projects, and presentations") and "lots of networking activities (e.g., happy hours, philanthropy, coed intramural sports teams)." Eller hosts "numerous guest speakers and [provides] chances to learn more with outside class activities." Students "work very hard but play hard as well. Everyone knows everyone else and there is a standing invite to any social events." Eller's "friendly, conservative, helpful, hard-working, social, busy" students form "a small group" who as a result are "very close. Everyone works together and helps others succeed while remaining competitive with people from other schools (instead of walking over people from the same program)." It's "a very diverse [group] with backgrounds ranging from Peace Corps workers to former hedge fund traders. We have military officers and students with private consulting backgrounds."

Admissions

Eller admissions officers seek candidates with a strong academic background, professional experience that demonstrates progress and the desire for challenges, leadership potential, and integrity. All applicants must submit one copy of unofficial transcripts for all post-secondary academic work, an official GMAT score report, a professional resume, two professional letters of recommendation, and two comprehensive essays (and a third for scholarship applicants). Interviews are required but are scheduled at the request of the school only; in other words, only those who make the first cut are asked to interview. International applicants must meet all the criteria above and submit TOEFL scores (if English is not their first language), official transcripts and a copy of their diploma (translated by a recognized service if not granted by an English-language institution), and a statement of financial self-sufficiency.

In its efforts to maximize the presence of underrepresented groups, the Eller MBA Program attends regional and national job/recruiting fairs organized by National Society of Hispanic MBAs (NSHMBA), Society of Hispanic Professional Engineers (SHPE) and National Society of Black Engineers (NSBE). In addition, the Eller MBA program is listed in Hobsons' Black MBA and Hispanic MBA Students' Guides. It also participates in on-campus recruitment fairs geared toward underrepresented minority students.

Prominent Alumni

Gregory Boyce, CEO, Peabody Energy; Brian Gentile, CEO, Jaspersoft; Terry Lundgren, CEO, Macy's; Richard Carmona, President, Canyon Ranch; Charles Nelson, Owner, Sprinkles Cupcakes

FINANCIAL FACTS

Annual tuition (in-state/ out-of-state)	$24,100/$43,300
Fees	$4,500
Cost of books	$4,800
Room & board (on/off-campus)	$8,400/$8,400
% of students receiving aid	95
% of first-year students receiving aid	99
% of students receiving grants	93
Average award package	$24,683
Average grant	$18,708
Average loan	$20,642
Average student loan debt	$30,797

ADMISSIONS

Admissions Selectivity Rating	92
# of applications received	160
% applicants accepted	39
% acceptees attending	66
Average GMAT	654
Range of GMAT	640–690
Accepts GRE scores	No
Average GPA	3.4
TOEFL required of international students	Yes
Minimum TOEFL (paper/web)	600/100
Application fee	$100
International application fee	$100
Application Deadline/Notification	
Round 1:	12/1 / 1/15
Round 2:	2/15 / 3/15
Round 3:	3/15 / 4/15
Round 4:	5/1 / 6/1
Deferment available	Yes
Maximum length of deferment	1 year
Transfer students accepted	No
Non-fall admissions	No
Need-blind admissions	Yes

EMPLOYMENT PROFILE

Career Rating	90	Grads Employed by Function	% Avg. Salary
Percent employed at graduation	46	Marketing	(25%) $84,100
Percent employed 3 months after graduation	85	Consulting	(15%) $80,000
		Management	(10%)
Average base starting salary	$78,009	Finance	(5%)
Primary Source of Full-time Job Acceptances		MIS	(25%) $70,739
School-facilitated activities	9 (41%)	Other	(20%) $91,250
Graduate-facilitated activities	9 (41%)	**Top 5 Employers Hiring Grads**	
Unknown	4 (18%)	Pricewaterhouse Coopers (3), Microsoft (2), Vantage West Credit Union (2), General Electric (1), Humana (1)	

UNIVERSITY OF ARKANSAS—FAYETTEVILLE
SAM M. WALTON COLLEGE OF BUSINESS

Academics

Just thirty miles from Walmart headquarters, the "top-ranked public business college" at the University of Arkansas—Fayetteville gets more than just its name from the world-famous retailer. "Walmart's extensive involvement" in the school pays off in a thousand different ways, from fantastic internship opportunities to the "cutting edge" supply chain and retail management program—not to mention, the world-class business environment in Fayetteville. Thanks to the school's famous benefactor, "Northwest Arkansas is a business epicenter," with "over 1,500 suppliers based locally." Without jetting off to New York or Tokyo, "students are given opportunities to interact with Fortune 500 CEOs on a regular basis"—often without leaving campus. Here, "You'll rarely find a day when there is not a CEO or other successful alumni coming back to contribute."

Walton operates two MBAs: a traditional full-time program and a part-time Executive MBA. With classes held "once a month on Saturdays," the part-time program "offers a lot of flexibility for working professionals." Students praise the "blended delivery," which "incorporates both in-class and distance learning." On top of that, "the administration ensures that the students lives are easy when it comes to enrollment and degree requirements"—they even provide all the materials (and meals!) on class day. For full-timers, the experience is likewise fast-paced, packing a full academic program—including an internship or overseas trip, independent projects, and case competitions—into just sixteen months of study.

Students in both full-time and part-time programs are bowled over by the quality of the academic experience. With a name like Walton, it's hardly a surprise that "the retail and supply chain management is highly recognized," drawing many students already working in the field. Yet professors across departments are "experienced professionals with real-world knowledge," who are "incredibly gifted in their field of research" and "truly excited about the material they teach." Professors are also willing to provide "additional instruction beyond class time," both to help with class material and to "answer any questions we have related to application of learned material in the workplace."

The MBA is "very, very well run," overseen by an administration that is "second to none." A boon to busy students, "the administration ensures that the students lives are easy when it comes to enrollment and degree requirements." They also "take steps to "improve the MBA program every year according to students' feedback." Icing on the cake, "the cost of the program is relatively inexpensive compared to their national rankings," making a Walton education a rather savvy venture.

Career and Placement

The future looks bright for Walton graduates. Not only are there "a huge amount of new jobs in this area per capita," students say they "have a leg-up" with local employers through the school's corporate partnerships. Walton offers a host of "great resources, like the career center, the writing center, and professional development classes," which all contribute to the school's excellent placement rate. One student raves, "The career services office has to be one of the best in the nation." Not only do they provide career advice but they "will happily make calls on your behalf and are constantly engaging you in the process of finding a job." For full-timers, "the Walton school does a great job of setting students up with internships," and better yet, it's "extremely easy to get a job after graduation at a great company."

ADMISSIONS CONTACT: MARION DUNAGAN, ASSISTANT DEAN
ADDRESS: 310 WILLARD J. WALKER HALL, UNIVERSITY OF ARKANSAS, FAYETTEVILLE, AR 72701
PHONE: 479-575-2851 • FAX: 479-575-8721
E-MAIL: GSB@WALTON.UARK.EDU • WEBSITE: GSB.UARK.EDU

In recent years, over 141 companies recruited on the Walton campus, with students taking jobs at companies including Axion Corporation, Deloitte & Touche, General Mills, IBM, KPMG, J.B. Hunt Transport Services, NBC Universal, Newell Rubbermaid, Tyson Foods, Shell Oil, Spectrum Brands, USA Truck, and, of course, Walmart. The 2014 graduating class had an average starting salary of $65,406, with a range between $50,000 and $92,500.

Student Life and Environment

University of Arkansas—Fayetteville provides a "rich cultural and academic atmosphere" in which to study, including "excellent facilities for MBA students." Full-timers usually "spend a significant amount of time on campus," studying, hanging out with friends, or, on game day, cheering on the Razorbacks; "As a part of the SEC, sports are a major event on campus." Students in the EMBA program admit that they are "not that involved in school activities," but they do make some time for networking: "A majority of the first and second year executive MBA students will all gather together at a local bar for food and drinks after our Saturday classes."

The school draws students from "very diverse backgrounds," though "the majority of us work with or for Walmart in some fashion." Walton does an excellent job fostering friendships and networking between MBA candidates. A student shares, "By the end of orientation, I knew my way around the town, fun places to go, and the names and backgrounds of my entire class as well as my faculty/administration." Of the warm atmosphere, another student adds, "As a woman, I feel incredibly welcomed into this business environment. Our class is fifty-fifty—a huge reason I chose U of A."

Overall, "Northwest Arkansas is a very nice area to live and work." With a population of around 75,000, "Fayetteville is the perfect size for a college town. It offers everything a student needs with reasonable costs."

Admissions

For students applying to Walton's full-time MBA, GMAT scores and academic record are the most important factors in an admissions decision, though previous work experience is also recommended. The school prefers a score of 600 or better on the GMAT and an undergraduate grade point average of 3.3 or above. For part-time students, GMAT scores and previous work experience are the two most important factors in evaluating an application, with a minimum of two years' professional experience required to apply. GMAT waivers are available to Executive MBA applicants with exceptional work experience.

FINANCIAL FACTS

Annual tuition (in-state/ out-of-state)	$17,986/$44,438
Fees	$2,074
Cost of books	$1,750
% of students receiving aid	46
% of first-year students receiving aid	30

ADMISSIONS

Admissions Selectivity Rating	88
# of applications received	423
% applicants accepted	45
% acceptees attending	78
Average GMAT	596
Range of GMAT	490–760
Accepts GRE scores	Yes
Average GPA	3.6
TOEFL required of international students	Yes
Minimum TOEFL (paper/web)	550/79
Application fee	$40
International application fee	$50
Early application deadline	4/1
Early notification date	5/1
Regular application deadline	9/15
Regular application notification	10/15
Deferment available	Yes
Maximum length of deferment	1 year
Transfer students accepted	Yes
Transfer application policy 6 hours may transfer from AACSB Institutions	
Non-fall admissions	Yes
Need-blind admissions	Yes

EMPLOYMENT PROFILE

Career Rating	92	Grads Employed by Function	% Avg. Salary
Percent employed at graduation	72	Marketing	(38%) $66,188
Percent employed 3 months after graduation	88	Operations	(3%)
		Consulting	(6%)
Average base starting salary	$65,406	Management	(21%) $60,429
Primary Source of Full-time Job Acceptances		Finance	(6%)
School-facilitated activities	16 (76%)	MIS	(6%)
Graduate-facilitated activities	5 (24%)	Other	(2%)

Top 5 Employers Hiring Grads
Walmart (2), Henkel (1), Kellogg (1), Land O'Lakes (1), Nielsen (1)

THE UNIVERSITY OF BRITISH COLUMBIA
SAUDER SCHOOL OF BUSINESS

Academics

The Sauder School of Business at the University of British Columbia offers both a fifteen-month full-time and twenty-eight-month part-time MBA in the Robert H. Lee Graduate School. The full-time program convenes at the school's 100-acre campus west of Vancouver's downtown core; the part-time program meets at the school's downtown campus in Robson Square.

Sauder's full-time program commences with a fully integrated core curriculum that "integrates eleven subjects to create one hectic but excellent learning environment." Students describe this intensive thirteen-week sequence, which imposes a heavy workload and requires a high level of complex analysis, as a boot camp-like experience. The remainder of the program is devoted primarily to specialization electives and professional development. Students tell us that finance is one of the school's strongest areas, although supply chain management, entrepreneurship, and international business also earn praise. An "option to partake in international exchange and an internship" during the final six months of the program means students can leave UBC with two unique and valuable experiences; the former reinforces the international focus of the curriculum as a whole.

Part-time students at Sauder experience the same faculty and curriculum as do full-timers, including the rigorous Integrated Core. The chief difference is scheduling; the part-time program is offered on Friday evenings and on weekends to accommodate students' work schedules. Students in both the full-time and part-time programs describe professors as "a mixed bag. Some are excellent scholars, some are accomplished business leaders, but others don't seem fit to teach master's level courses. Thankfully this last group is a minority." They also tell us that "the support the MBAs receive from the dean, the library staff, the career center, and the MBA office is unbelievable" and that "UBC also has excellent research facilities."

Career and Placement

UBC's Hari B. Varshney Business Career Centre offers "both personal consultation and a structured program" to help students identify goals and develop strategies to meet those goals. Self-assessment, coaching sessions, skills-training programs in resume-writing, interviewing, and networking, recruiting events that bring "corporate recruiters from prominent companies" to campus to interview job candidates, and job postings all figure into the mix here. Some here tell us that "the career center is also very helpful when it comes to finding internships, preparing for interviews or just researching industries," while others complain that the office still needs to improve its performance "if the school wants to be taken seriously at a global level."

Employers likely to hire UBC MBAs include Accenture, BC Hydro, Bell Mobility, Best Buy/Future Shop, BP, Business Objects, Cadbury, Elecronic Arts, Elli Lilly, Fraser Health Authority, GE, Health Canada, Hilti, Honeywell, HSBC, Intrawest, Kodak, Kraft, L'Oreal, Lululemon Athletica, Nike Inc, Nokia, Pepsi Bottling Group, Pivotal Corporation, PMC-Sierra, PricewaterhouseCoopers, Royal Bank Canada, Teekay Shipping Corporation, Telus, Terasen, Vancity, Vancouver Coastal Health, Vancouver International Airport Authority, Vancouver Port Authority, VANOC, and Weyerhauser.

ADMISSIONS CONTACT: MBA & ECM PROGRAMS OFFICE
ADDRESS: #111 - 2053 MAIN MALL, VANCOUVER, BC V6T 1Z2
PHONE: 604-822-8422 • FAX: 604-822-9030
E-MAIL: MBA@SAUDER.UBC.CA • WEBSITE: WWW.SAUDER.UBC.CA/MBA

Student Life and Environment

The Sauder School "treats the MBA students extremely well. We're spoiled, in fact," with loads of opportunities for career-building extracurricular clubs, recreation, and study-related travel. One student reports: "I have traveled to Nashville and Hamilton, and before this degree is completed I will have been to London (Ontario), Harvard, Philadelphia, and Porto Fino, Italy. Each of these trips is heavily subsidized by our dean. It is his mission to get as many students involved in activities that help promote the Sauder name." The full-time program also has "an excellent social rep who is constantly creating new excuses for us to take a night off from studying." Hometown Vancouver "is amazing," students tell us. "There is always a group of students going for a run, a bike, a hike or a sail," and skiing is accessible during much of the year, thanks to the proximity of Whistler Mountain.

The full-time program at Sauder draws "a very diverse group" that is "nearly 60 percent international, bringing to the classroom "diverse backgrounds of experience and culture." While "quite competitive," students here are quite willing to "help each other with course issues." The school has "a great MBA office to assist students with any problems. It also has a language center to help international students edit their papers and improve their proficiency in English."

Admissions

Admission to the Sauder MBA program is extremely competitive. All applicants must submit official transcripts for undergraduate work (students who attended schools where English was not the primary language must arrange for a certified translation of their transcripts to be delivered to UBC), official GMAT score reports, evidence of English proficiency (TOEFL scores for students whose first language is not English) essays, a resume, and three letters of reference. Interviews are by invitation only; the school interviews roughly half its applicant pool. The school's brochure notes, "Competitive applicants generally have more than two years of full-time post-baccalaureate work experience for admission to the program." On average, students enter the program with six years' full-time professional experience. Applications are processed on a rolling basis; the process favors those who apply early. Admitted students may not defer admission.

FINANCIAL FACTS

Annual tuition (in-state/ out-of-state)	$32,450/$32,450
Cost of books	$2,200

ADMISSIONS

Admissions Selectivity Rating	**88**
# of applications received	512
% applicants accepted	48
% acceptees attending	51
Average GMAT	642
Range of GMAT	570–730
Accepts GRE scores	No
Average GPA	3.3
TOEFL required of international students	Yes
Minimum TOEFL (paper)	600
Application fee	$125
International application fee	$125
Regular application deadline	4/30
Application Deadline	
Round 1:	12/15
Round 2:	2/28
Round 3:	4/30
Deferment available	No
Transfer students accepted	No
Non-fall admissions	No
Need-blind admissions	Yes

EMPLOYMENT PROFILE

Career Rating	89	Grads Employed by Function	% Avg. Salary
Percent employed 3 months after graduation	83	Marketing	(20%) $78,700
		Operations	(9%) $73,000
Average base starting salary	$77,500	Consulting	(20%) $98,000
		Management	(15%) $66,100
		Finance	(20%) $75,500

UNIVERSITY OF CALGARY
HASKAYNE SCHOOL OF BUSINESS

Academics

Located in Canada's "second business center (behind Toronto)," University of Calgary's Haskayne School of Business "has close connections with local business." That's a big deal when you're in "the heart of the energy sector of Canada" and those connections forge a "link to the oil and gas business environment and high-level executives." Students note that "the integration into the oil and gas community is very evident here (e.g., speaker panels with oil execs, etc)." Haskayne's energy-related specialization is in global "energy management and sustainable development."

Energy isn't the sole focus of a Haskayne MBA, though; on the contrary, "there is a good emphasis on bringing in execs from a wide range of industries," with finance and accounting among the program's other strengths. Across the curriculum, Haskayne employs "a mix of both...cases and structured lectures...and methods even beyond the two...to provide all the learning that's essential to make good leaders for tomorrow." "In some courses, the guest speakers alone provided the ROI in the course," one student exclaims. "Really, really interesting" electives include "entrepreneurship and new venture courses that are so much fun." "Leadership panel discussions and other networking and learning events for students" add further value. Speaking of value, "the cost of living as well as the tuition rates are reasonable" here, meaning that Haskayne "offers an outstanding graduate education at a fairly affordable price." Students also see, and appreciate, the program's "willingness to be innovative and [administrators'] willingness to receive student input." Haskayne offers a twenty-month daytime MBA, an executive MBA, an evening MBA at its downtown campus, a Global Energy Executive MBA offered in five locations around the world, and a thesis-based MBA for those interested in pursuing business research.

Career and Placement

Students are very enthusiastic about the career opportunities afforded by Haskayne's "close connections with local businesses," and the Career Center earns praise for "providing access to new job opportunities." In surveys, the school's location is consistently listed as one of its major benefits. As one student explains, the program "takes advantage of being located in an energy industry hub to provide relevant courses of study and integrat[ion] with the local business community." Some feel there's too much focus on the energy sector; one student tells us that "the Career Center is great, but a lot of the companies they bring in are oil- and gas-focused. It would be nice if they also engaged other industries."

Companies that frequently hire graduates include Enmax Corporation, Nexen Inc., Enbridge Inc., Suncor Energy, Bell Canada, CIBC World Markets Inc., Scotia Bank, SMART Technologies Inc., TransCanada, TELUS Communications Ltd., Devon Canada, Shell Canada, Imperial Oil LTD, ATB Financial, Mercer Management, and Deloitte Consulting.

ADMISSIONS CONTACT: MICHELINE CAMPANARO, ADMISSIONS COORDINATOR
ADDRESS: 2500 UNIVERSITY DRIVE, NW, CALGARY, AB T2N 1N4
PHONE: 403-220-3808 • FAX: 403-282-0095
E-MAIL: MBAREQ@UCALGARY.CA • WEBSITE: WWW.HASKAYNEMBA.CA

Student Life and Environment

Life at Haskayne "allows each student to be as involved or uninvolved as we want to be. Those who want to get involved can join the MBA Society. Those who don't have time to get involved...simply go to classes and that's it." Involvement is strongest among full-time students, one of whom reports "that following great classes and group meetings there is a large proportion of students that get together and go out for drinks. We have great networking and social events planned throughout the year such as 'Iron Chef MBA,' curling, ski trips, etc. Just a great relaxing break from the busy schoolwork." Those in the part-time program, on the other hand, usually "do not get the benefit of experiencing school life to its fullest." School, work, and family obligations typically leave them little time for networking events.

Haskayne MBAs "range in age from twenty-two to forty-two, single to married and having five kids, limited experience to amazing experience. Despite my classmates coming from different regions of the planet and different regions of Canada, we have a strong sense of camaraderie and good communication." The program includes "a lot of creative people and well-rounded people...just the kind of people that you wouldn't expect to run into in an MBA program." Students represent "a broad range of industries...but many are experienced professionals from the oil and gas sector."

Admissions

Applicants to Haskayne must submit the following materials: two sets of official transcripts for all post-secondary work (minimum undergraduate GPA of 3.0 over final two years of course work required), an official GMAT score report, two letters of reference, two copies of a current resume (two years appropriate professional experience is preferred), and two copies of a personal statement explaining their purpose in pursuing a Haskayne MBA and detailing any special attributes they can contribute to the program. College transcripts in a language other than English must be translated by a recognized translation service. Applicants for whom English is a second language must submit an official score report for either the TOEFL or IELTS.

FINANCIAL FACTS

Annual tuition (in-state/ out-of-state)	$16,231/$28,808
Fees	$1,696.21
Cost of books	$2,000
Room & board (on/off-campus)	$12,000/$12,000
% of students receiving grants	37
Average grant	$4,858

ADMISSIONS

Admissions Selectivity Rating	86
# of applications received	218
% applicants accepted	47
% acceptees attending	50
Average GMAT	635
Range of GMAT	560–750
Accepts GRE scores	No
Average GPA	3.8
TOEFL required of international students	Yes
Minimum TOEFL (paper/web)	600/100
Application fee	$125
International application fee	$145
Early application deadline	1/15
Regular application deadline	6/1
Deferment available	Yes
Maximum length of deferment	one year
Transfer students accepted	Yes
Transfer application policy We can accept up to nine courses (5 exemptions and 4 higher standing)	
Non-fall admissions	Yes
Need-blind admissions	Yes

EMPLOYMENT PROFILE

Career Rating	83	**Grads Employed by Function% Avg. Salary**		
Percent employed at graduation	69	Marketing	(22%)	$82,117
Percent employed 3 months after graduation	25	Operations	(31%)	$107,110
		Consulting	(13%)	$74,530
Average base starting salary	$88,379	Management	(4%)	
Primary Source of Full-time Job Acceptances		Finance	(17%)	$88,142
School-facilitated activities	21 (50%)	MIS	(4%)	
Graduate-facilitated activities	18 (44%)	Other	(9%)	$73,191
Unknown	2 (6%)	**Top 5 Employers Hiring Grads**		
		Ernst &Young (2), Weatherford (1), Stantec (1), Trans Alta (1), City of Calgary (1)		

UNIVERSITY OF CALIFORNIA—BERKELEY
HAAS SCHOOL OF BUSINESS

GENERAL INFORMATION
Type of school   Public
Affiliation   No Affiliation
Academic calendar   Semester

SURVEY SAYS...
Friendly students, Good social scene,
Good peer network, Happy students
Solid preparation in:
Teamwork, Entrepreneurial studies,
Environmental sustainability

STUDENTS
Enrollment of parent institution	37,581
Enrollment of MBA Program	1,435
% male/female	63/37
% out-of-state	71
% part-time	65
% underrepresented minority	13
% international	38
Average age at entry	29
Average years work experience at entry	5

ACADEMICS
Academic Experience Rating	**86**
Profs interesting rating	87
Profs accessible rating	87
% female faculty	22
% part-time faculty	64

Joint Degrees
MBA/MPH in Public Health: 5
semesters MBA/JD: 8 semesters
MBA/MIAS: 6 semesters

Prominent Alumni
Patrick Awuah, '99, Founder &
President, Ashesi University, Ghana
/ Education; Barbara J Desoer, '77,
CEO, Citibank / Financial Services;
Kristen Groos Richmond, '06,
Co-founder & CEO, Revolution
Foods / Education; Kirsten Saenz
Tobey, '06, Co-founder & CIO,
Revolution Foods, / Education; Joe
Jimenez, MBA 84, CEO, Novartis,
Switzerland

Academics

The Haas School of Business at the University of California—Berkeley is a "top school for academics and recruitment opportunities," especially "on the West Coast." Students here note that the MBA program is "outstanding on all levels: professionally, academically, and socially." Thanks to an environment that encourages student involvement and input, most here "feel like they have a real role in shaping their own academic experiences." As one student explains, there are "a million ways to get involved and really make a difference. Experiential learning opportunities everywhere you turn." Things "move fast here" thanks to the structure of the courses, but students find themselves supported by "fantastic" and "accessible" professors who "sincerely care" about these future entrepreneurs. "We learn from professors who not only are recognized as top academics in their respective fields, but also professionals who shape the direction of the industry," explains one student. Additionally, Haas' administration "seems to have a singular focus on improving the experience for students." According to students, "They go to great lengths to take in, process, and change the program per student recommendations."

Students praise the "small, intimate program" for being exactly that: "small" and "intimate." "We only have 240 students per class (at least officially...sometimes one or two more get added)," says one student. This "tight-knit" environment creates a distinctly "collaborative culture" that forges lasting connections (which come in handy after graduation). The "caliber of students, faculty, administration, and career services staff" are all "top-notch," which provides a solid base for development. "Haas excels at entrepreneurship (not just social entrepreneurship)," explains one student. "Its heavy involvement and leadership in the Berkeley Energy Resources Collaborative (BERC) provides great opportunities in alternative/green energy entrepreneurship." The school also offers a "health care and international business focus." Another key component of the program is its "close ties" and proximity "to Silicon Valley." Students also single out their "excellent" dean, Richard Lyons, for praise. As one student says, "He's an energetic, reputable professor who spent time in the real world on Wall Street."

Career and Placement

After graduation, Berkeley MBAs breathe easy knowing that their program's high profile and sound reputation go a long way in providing job opportunities for them—not to mention that it also has "an alumni network that spans the globe." As is often the case at such schools, the Haas Career Center provides a broad range of excellent services. Students here benefit from one-on-one advisement, access to numerous online job databases, industry clubs, workshops, seminars, and a mentoring program in which second-year students counsel first years in their search for internships. Employers most likely to hire Berkeley MBAs include Google, Amazon, Apple, Bain & Company, Deloitte Consulting LLP, Pacific Gas and Electric, McKinsey, Genentech.

Student Life and Environment

According to students, life at Haas is "extremely busy and involved." "Beyond schoolwork—which is the focus—almost every student is involved in at least one if not two or three extracurricular activities, most of which are student-run," says one student. "There are often symposiums, speakers, new clubs forming, and conferences to attend." The extracurricular activities, just like the school, are largely "student-driven," meaning that "if a student can dream of an activity, club, or academic venture...it can be done, and in fairly easy fashion." "Life at school is a whirlwind," explains one student. "There are so many clubs, speakers, and events to check out—but never enough time in the day. Last week, I was involved in organizing a panel on sustainable design with speakers from IDEO, Patagonia, and Nike, while also participating in a chili cook-off!"

Needless to say, "life at Haas is rich and very intensive." Despite being "very active and busy between academic and social opportunities," students find time for the "important things in life." "Dodgeball on Mondays, softball on Tuesdays, and bar of the week on Thursdays—I love b-school!" says one student. Berkeley is "a great college town" with "amazing access to San Francisco, Napa Valley, and Lake Tahoe" (no surprise that the student body reports an "overall appreciation for the outdoors"). In addition, the location in the Bay Area "provides a wealth of opportunity for networking."

Thanks to the school's "small class size" Haas has "a very strong sense of community." "People are trustworthy and helpful," says one student. "Friendly," "easygoing," and "international" are all words that could be used to describe the student body here. The "collaborative" environment means that there "isn't the typical cutthroat competition apparent at other business schools." The "diverse" and "welcoming" students here are "keen to support each other." As one student explains, "Life at Haas is unique to every individual, and yet there are so many opportunities for shared experiences."

Admissions

Applicants to Haas graduate programs must submit all the following materials to the admissions department: official copies of transcripts for all postsecondary academic work, an official GMAT score report, letters of recommendation, a personal statement, and a resume. Interviews are conducted on an invitation-only basis. In addition to the above materials, international applicants whose first language is not English must also submit official score reports for the TOEFL or IELTS. The school considers all of the following in determining admissions status: "demonstration of quantitative ability; quality of work experience, including depth and breadth of responsibilities; opportunities to demonstrate leadership, etc.; strength of letters of recommendation; depth and breadth of extracurricular and community involvement; and strength of short answer and essays, including articulation of clear focus and goals."

FINANCIAL FACTS

Annual tuition (in-state/out-of-state)	$0/$12,245
Fees	$53,907
Cost of books	$1,162
Room & board (on/off-campus)	$26,274/$24,324
% of students receiving aid	67
% of first-year students receiving aid	69
% of students receiving grants	57
Average award package	$50,487
Average grant	$27,660
Average loan	$49,641
Average student loan debt	$77,826

ADMISSIONS

Admissions Selectivity Rating	99
# of applications received	3,497
Average GMAT	717
Range of GMAT	700–730
Accepts GRE scores	Yes
Average GPA	3.6
TOEFL required of international students	Yes
Minimum TOEFL (paper/web)	570/90
Application fee	$200
International application fee	$200
Application Deadline/Notification	
Round 1:	10/1 / 1/15
Round 2:	1/7 / 3/26
Round 3:	3/11 / 5/14
Deferment available	No
Transfer students accepted	No
Non-fall admissions	No
Need-blind admissions	Yes

EMPLOYMENT PROFILE

Career Rating	98	Grads Employed by Function% Avg. Salary	
Percent employed at graduation	72	Marketing	(16%) $121,423
Percent employed 3 months after graduation	94	Operations	(5%) $114,856
		Consulting	(25%) $131,833
Average base starting salary	$123,403	Management	(24%) $120,648
Primary Source of Full-time Job Acceptances		Finance	(21%) $121,572
School-facilitated activities	107 (59%)	HR	(3%) $109,968
Graduate-facilitated activities	70 (39%)	MIS	(3%) $128,333
Unknown	4 (2%)	Other	(3%) $112,100

Top 5 Employers Hiring Grads
Amazon (4), McKinsey & Company (8), Google (7), Adobe Systems (6), Deloitte Consulting LLP (9)

UNIVERSITY OF CALIFORNIA—DAVIS
GRADUATE SCHOOL OF MANAGEMENT

GENERAL INFORMATION
Type of school   Public
Affiliation   No Affiliation
Academic calendar   Quarters

SURVEY SAYS...
Classmates have diverse work experience, Friendly students, Good peer network, Liberal students, Happy students, Students love Davis, CA
Solid preparation in:
General management, Teamwork, Communication/interpersonal skills, Presentation skills, Quantitative skills

STUDENTS
Enrollment of parent institution	35,186
Enrollment of MBA Program	511
% male/female	74/26
% out-of-state	59
% part-time	83
% underrepresented minority	6
% international	36
Average age at entry	29
Average years work experience at entry	6

ACADEMICS
Academic Experience Rating	**99**
Profs interesting rating	93
Profs accessible rating	94
Student/faculty ratio	7:1
% female faculty	29
% underrepresented minority faculty	4
% part-time faculty	56

Joint Degrees
JD/MBA, 4 years; MD/MBA, 6 years; Engineering/MBA, 2 years; Ag Econ/MBA, 2 years; MS/MBA, 3 years

Prominent Alumni
Michael Picker, President, CA Public Utilities Commission; Sue Miller-Sylvia, IBM Fellow; Gordon C. Hunt, Jr., M.D., Chief Medical Officer (Retired), Sutter Heatlh; Cathinka Wahlstrom, Senior Managing Director, Accenture

Academics

The well-regarded MBA program Graduate School of Management at the University of California, Davis offers three different options and a strong quantitative background for students with work experience under their belts. Whether enrolled in the full-time program at Davis, or the part-time night and weekend programs at the campuses in the Bay Area and Sacramento (which teach all of the same material as the full-time program), students are afforded a "great combination" of challenging and rewarding classes, "very supportive atmosphere," and "many opportunities to expand our experiences well beyond the classroom."

The "stellar faculty" is "very well-informed" and offers "a variety of interesting current world topics." They "are willing to talk to you about anything and will spend as much time as you want discussing how to use things from class at work," and even "sit with the students at meals and will join in at happy hours." The school is also "doing a really good job bringing in experienced business people to teach electives"; the curriculum is a "great mix of classes" that also provides multiple opportunities to apply theoretical knowledge in practical setting, including "study trips, projects with actual companies, individual and group studies, internships and much more." Additionally, classes are up-to-date and provide both historical and recent cases and business examples that allow students to gain a better understanding of the concepts and curriculum.

The administration is similarly "student-oriented." It "works very hard to listen to and communicate with the students," and the Dean's Student Advisory Board meets once a quarter ("The Dean is impressive and obviously on a diehard mission to put our school in the top ten"). However, given the unique nature of the part-time schedule (i.e. Friday/Saturday classes), scheduling of classes can be messy, and "it is often difficult to pair core classes with popular electives."

Career and Placement

This program "has a reach into many regions beyond Sacramento" thanks to the Career Development Office's ability to reach out into markets that students are most interested in and their "willingness to develop something to further student's success." Most everyone attending Davis part-time is already employed, but the networking opportunities across students in different industries and the ability to work with classmates in consulting projects outside of school are "amazing." "We have people from San Jose, Oakland, Pleasanton, and as far as Ukiah commuting to the program, which makes it a large network of students in Fortune 500 companies," says a student. "We all study together, we eat together, and we bond together, which builds a strong student network of trust and accountability." Some students do think that the school's efforts to facilitate networking with actual companies themselves could be stepped up; in the past three years, the students themselves "have put together an alumni networking event that has successfully facilitated job and career changes."

Student Life and Environment

This bunch is "willing to learn and help each other out." Most also have lives outside of school and work so are quite busy, so at times "they can appear stressed." But, they are all "good-natured, friendly, and approachable people." There are "a ton of activities and clubs" that can help "to improve your business acumen," and across all of the programs, students "interact, work on projects, socialize outside of class." "My classmates quickly became a tight-knit group," says one student. Lunch and/or dinner is provided for the Bay Area weekend program (during which time announcements are made), which "promotes a cohort model that closely replicates the total-immersion experience offered by full time programs." "With three campuses offering very similar courses at different times of the day and week, you can work around your professional schedule," says a student.

For those who can carve time our of their academics, life, and extracurriculars, it is worth noting that the city of Davis "is an amazing jewel in the Central Valley...there is an amazing offering of athletics and healthy living businesses, and boasts a very large proportion of small businesses, as opposed to chains."

Admissions

Admissions Officers for the MBA program at UC Davis consider the following factors in assessing candidates: academic potential, professional potential, and personal qualities. Full-time work experience is not required for admission, but students average five years of work experience. Applicants must submit the following materials: a completed application form (online or hard copy); a current resume; a list of outside activities and honors; two short personal essays; official transcripts from each undergraduate and graduate institution attended; two letters of recommendation; and an official GMAT/GRE score report. Applicants whose native language is not English must submit an official TOEFL score report or IELTS reflecting a score no more than two years old. Applications to the MBA program are accepted for the fall only.

FINANCIAL FACTS

Annual tuition (in-state/ out-of-state)	$37,711/$49,956
Fees	$1,986
Cost of books	$1,771
Room & board	$15,030
% of students receiving aid	100
% of first-year students receiving aid	100
% of students receiving grants	100
Average award package	$45,038
Average grant	$9,901
Average loan	$35,137
Average student loan debt	$70,273

ADMISSIONS

Admissions Selectivity Rating	98
# of applications received	343
% applicants accepted	18
% acceptees attending	70
Average GMAT	683
Range of GMAT	640–730
Accepts GRE scores	Yes
Average Verbal GRE	159
Range of Verbal GRE scores	155–163
Average Quantitative GRE	160
Range of Quantitative GRE scores	157–166
Average Writing GRE	3.8
Range of Writing GRE scores	3.0–4.0
Average GPA	3.3
TOEFL required of international students	Yes
Minimum TOEFL (paper/web)	600/100
Application fee	$125
International application fee	$125
Early application deadline	11/2
Early notification date	12/14
Regular application deadline	3/15
Regular application notification	4/26
Application Deadline/Notification	
Round 1:	11/2 / 12/14
Round 2:	1/11 / 2/15
Round 3:	3/15 / 4/26
Round 4:	5/10 / 6/21
Deferment available	Yes
Maximum length of deferment	1 year
Transfer students accepted	Yes
Non-fall admissions	No
Need-blind admissions	Yes

EMPLOYMENT PROFILE

Career Rating	95	Grads Employed by Function	% Avg. Salary
Percent employed at graduation	51	Marketing	(34%) $108,100
Percent employed 3 months after graduation	94	Operations	(6%)
		Consulting	(18%) $106,000
Average base starting salary	$101,867	Management	(3%)
Primary Source of Full-time Job Acceptances		Finance	(27%) $98,750
School-facilitated activities	16 (48%)	MIS	(3%)
Graduate-facilitated activities	17 (52%)	Other	(9%) $103,333

Top 5 Employers Hiring Grads
Intel (3), Wells Fargo (3), UC Davis Health System (2), Deloitte (1), Tesla Motors (1)

UNIVERSITY OF CALIFORNIA—IRVINE
THE PAUL MERAGE SCHOOL OF BUSINESS

GENERAL INFORMATION
Type of school	Public
Affiliation	No Affiliation
Academic calendar	Sept-June

SURVEY SAYS...
Classmates have diverse work experience, Friendly students, Good peer network, Good social scene, Abundant mentors available, Helpful alumni, Happy students, Abundant clubs and activities, Students love Irvine, CA
Solid preparation in:
Marketing, Finance, Teamwork, Communication/interpersonal skills, Presentation skills, Quantitative skills

STUDENTS
Enrollment of parent institution	28,000
Enrollment of MBA Program	635
% male/female	64/36
% out-of-state	10
% part-time	66
% international	40
Average age at entry	29
Average years work experience at entry	5

ACADEMICS
Academic Experience Rating	93
Profs interesting rating	89
Profs accessible rating	96
% female faculty	29
% underrepresented minority faculty	21
% part-time faculty	61

Joint Degrees
MD/MBA: Five or Six year program
JD/MBA: Four year program

Prominent Alumni
Lisa Locklear, Vice President, Ingram Micro; Darcy Kopcho, Executive Vice President, Capital Group Companies; George Kessinger, Pres. and CEO, Goodwill Industries International; Norman Witt, Vice President Community Development, The Irvine C

Academics

The combination of academic innovation, strong industry ties, and a relaxed California environment make UC Irvine's Paul Merage School of Business a top pick for future SoCal professionals. The school's first-year MBA curriculum covers business fundamentals like finance and marketing while maintaining "a strong emphasis on innovation and international business" throughout disciplines. In the second year, students tailor their education through an impressive selection of elective courses in areas ranging from brand management to new product development. A student tells us, "I started with an interest in finance, and gradually discovered an affinity for strategy and technology. Because Merage does not put you on a track, I had the chance to get exposure to finance but the freedom to switch my focus late in my first year." Class work is augmented by ample hands-on "opportunities outside of the classroom," including business-plan competitions and nonprofit consulting projects, as well as the ten-week field project course, through which students consult for a regional company. Study abroad programs also receive top marks. A current MBA candidate attests, "My four months living in Budapest, Hungary was life changing and gave me an incredible perspective on international business and cultural differences in the workplace."

With only 100 students in each incoming class, the "intimate learning environment" is a signature of the Merage program. The small class size makes it easy to "build personal relationships with everyone at the school, including professors and staff." At Merage, "the professors really want to see us succeed and make themselves available to all students to answer questions or talk about their research." The staff and administration is also "world-class": "The career center and programming support staff are excellent and always available to meet," and administrators are "extremely quick to respond and act to just about anything." Of particular note, the dean is "outstanding," "communicating his vision for our school and supporting students through has vast connections and experience in business." Between students, "the program requires a lot of group work," which encourages networking both in and out of the classroom. Fortunately, Merage maintains an unwaveringly "cooperative environment." Here, "students want to see each other succeed, as evidenced by the large groups that study together prior to tests, or the peer feedback we receive in preparing for group presentations."

Career and Placement

"The major business program in all of Orange County," Merage has the edge in the local job market, where students benefit from direct "access to some of the top companies in the country: Taco Bell, Blizzard, Pimco, the list goes on and on." In addition to the old standbys, "there are a lot of new companies moving to the area and have established recruiting efforts with the school." On top of that, "the school has a very strong alumni base which is very interested in helping current students in their search for employment." Merage may not be as famous as some of L.A.'s big business schools, but students assure us that the "companies that know our school love us."

Merage's "excellent career center" makes the most of the school's strong local connections, maintaining a "great track record" with graduating MBAs. Career Center programs start right at the beginning of the MBA, guiding student through every step in the career-search process, from defining their career goals to landing a choice internship. Top hiring companies at Merage include AT&T, Deloitte, AERS, Deloitte Consulting, Experian, General Electric, IBM, Johnson & Johnson, JP Morgan, KPMG, Niagara Bottling, Pacific Life, Roth Capital Partners, and the Walt Disney Company, among many others. Finance and accounting, consulting, and sales and marketing were the most popular job functions for a recent class.

ADMISSIONS CONTACT: ELISA LEE, ASSISTANT DIRECTOR, RECRUITMENT AND ADMISSIONS
ADDRESS: SB 220, IRVINE, CA 92697-3125
PHONE: 949-824-4622 • FAX: 949-824-2235
E-MAIL: MBA@MERAGE.UCI.EDU • WEBSITE: MBA.MERAGE.UCI.EDU

Student Life and Environment

"Life at Merage is very dynamic." Beyond the classroom, there are frequent "networking events, volunteer events, interviewing, seminars, academic group meetings, and many other opportunities for professional and personal growth." Though the administration creates a lot of these opportunities, you'll also find that student-run "clubs are very active and organize a mix of social and career focused events like executive panels, mixers, trips, speaker series, and tours." Socially, "there is a business school student mixer at a nearby bar or restaurant" every week, as well as "a few mixers that take place between different schools every quarter."

Located on the Southern California coast, life in Orange County is "fantastic." With its "gorgeous beaches" and sunny weather providing the perfect backdrop, "students are always organizing outdoor activities (beach BBQs, intramural sports, etc)." There's "great food and nightlife in Irvine and Newport"; not to mention, the school is "close enough to L.A. that many people visit on the weekends." At the same time, the suburban atmosphere keeps things low-key; many mention that it's "very safe here."

Admissions

To apply to UC Irvine's Merage School of Business, students must submit an online application form, official transcripts from college, GMAT or GRE scores, two letters of recommendation, a résumé, and two essays. Qualified candidates will be invited to interview as a further requirement for admission. The current MBA class had an average GPA of 3.37 and average GMAT scores of 657 (with a middle 80 percent range of 600-720). Though the average work experience for entering students is five years, incoming students have prior professional experience ranging from zero to fifteen years.

FINANCIAL FACTS

Annual tuition (in-state/ out-of-state)	$38,450/$47,089
Cost of books	$2,400
Room & board (on/off-campus)	$12,720/$17,803

ADMISSIONS

Admissions Selectivity Rating	**95**
# of applications received	916
% applicants accepted	22
% acceptees attending	52
Average GMAT	657
Accepts GRE scores	Yes
Average GPA	3.4
TOEFL required of international students	Yes
Minimum TOEFL (paper/web)	600/80
Application fee	$150
International application fee	$150
Early application deadline	11/1
Early notification date	12/1
Regular application deadline	2/1
Regular application notification	4/1
Application Deadline/Notification	
Round 1:	11/1 / 1/15
Round 2:	12/1 / 3/1
Round 3:	2/1 / 4/1
Round 4:	4/1 / 6/15
Deferment available	No
Transfer students accepted	No
Non-fall admissions	No
Need-blind admissions	Yes

EMPLOYMENT PROFILE

Career Rating		93	Grads Employed by Function	% Avg. Salary
Percent employed at graduation		68	Marketing	(31%) $84,901
Percent employed 3 months after graduation		89	Operations	(12%) $81,714
			Consulting	(19%) $93,364
Average base starting salary		$84,857	Management	(7%) $90,000
			Finance	(17%) $81,550
			HR	(7%) $74,750
			MIS	(3%)
			Other	(3%)

Top 5 Employers Hiring Grads
Toyota, Deloitte Consulting, Niagara Bottling, Experian, AT&T

UNIVERSITY OF CALIFORNIA—LOS ANGELES
UCLA ANDERSON SCHOOL OF MANAGEMENT

GENERAL INFORMATION
Type of school	Public
Affiliation	No Affiliation
Academic calendar	Quarters

SURVEY SAYS...
Classmates have diverse work experience, Friendly students, Good peer network, Good social scene, Liberal students, Cutting-edge classes, Abundant mentors available, Helpful alumni, Happy students
Solid preparation in:
Marketing, Finance, General management, Operations, Teamwork

STUDENTS
Enrollment of parent institution	43,301
Enrollment of MBA Program	1,696
% male/female	69/31
% out-of-state	33
% part-time	57
% underrepresented minority	8
% international	29
Average age at entry	28
Average years work experience at entry	5

ACADEMICS
Academic Experience Rating	99
Profs interesting rating	94
Profs accessible rating	96
Student/faculty ratio	9:1
% female faculty	21
% underrepresented minority faculty	6
% part-time faculty	54

Joint Degrees
MBA/JD; MBA/MD; MBA/DDS; MBA/MPH; MBA/MURP; MBA/MPP; MBA/MLIS; MBA/MN; MBA/Master of Computer Science; MBA/Master of Latin American Studies

Prominent Alumni
Mr. Jim Moffatt, Global CEO & Deputy U.S. CEO; Deloitte Consulting LLP; Ms. Susan Wojcicki, CEO; YouTube; Mr. Laurence D. Fink, Chairman & CEO; BlackRock Inc.

Academics

UCLA's Anderson School of Management takes great pains to ensure the curriculum offered is "very practical" and that it continually reflects "emerging business trends." This success can partially be attributed to the fact that many classes "bring in renowned industry professionals to speak and give real world context to the course content." Though the majority of students find the coursework "challenging," they also say their classes are "rewarding" and issue assurance that "you will learn a lot."

Students speak glowingly of their "engaged" professors who are "all without a doubt incredibly intelligent and masters of their fields of study." Moreover they truly "understand the rigors and time challenges of an MBA program so they are very helpful in making sure we are successful." Additionally, these "outstanding" teachers "have a genuine concern that we learn; they ask for feedback a third- to half-way through the term to ensure that students are learning all the material and that the pace and style are well balanced." Another highly content student chimes in, "My professors have the kind of industry experience that make my jaw drop, they challenge me every day in class but at the end of the year I can go out with them." That camaraderie is "simply the best!"

Additionally, MBA candidates at UCLA Anderson are quick to note that the administration is "always available" and "very responsive to student suggestion and inquiry." A first-year student shares, "I feel as though I can meet with anybody at school." Perhaps more importantly, the administration is highly respected for being "transparent about [their] operations and strategies." Finally, a fellow first-year eloquently asserts, "The leadership team at Anderson is like the Showtime Lakers: just a set of all-stars that each brings something unique to the table."

Career and Placement

The opportunities for career placement and training at UCLA Anderson are plentiful. Students are happy to report that the school does "a great job of harnessing the formidable L.A. business community." Further, many deem the Parker Career Management Center to be "excellent." As one student on the brink of graduation gratefully shares, "They connected us with plenty of good companies. Interview preparation and resume/cover letter advice were also outstanding. [And they] prepared us well for the toughest interviews." Indeed, career services strives to offer "the best opportunity to land a top tier job markedly superior to the one we had before business school." This success also stems from "an institutionalized process whereby first-year students have 'Alumni Career Transition Coaches' and a 'Parker Career Management Series' which serves to spend months on interview and networking prep during the first and second quarters. Second-year students spend countless hours helping to ensure first-year students are engaged and will be successful in their job search."

ADMISSIONS CONTACT: ALEX LAWRENCE, ASSISTANT DEAN & DIRECTOR OF MBA ADMISSIONS
ADDRESS: 110 WESTWOOD PLAZA, GOLD HALL, SUITE B201,
LOS ANGELES, CA 90095-1481 • PHONE: 310-825-6944 • FAX: 310-825-8582
E-MAIL: MBA.ADMISSIONS@ANDERSON.UCLA.EDU • WEBSITE: WWW.ANDERSON.UCLA.EDU

Student Life and Environment

UCLA Anderson MBAs happily reveal that their program provides a "fantastic balance between school and social life." By and large, students love living in LA. And how can you not when "it's sunny all year"? Of course beyond weather, the city has "an impressive mix of large corporations and entrepreneurial ventures" ripe with internship opportunities. The school is continually hosting events which offer a great "mix of professional focus, student get-togethers, alumni networking and conferences." And one excited second-year even brags, "We [were] the first B-school to have a partnership with TED!" Overall, students embrace an "active lifestyle" which often means "hikes discussing case studies, beach visits with text books and a positive attitude across the school that mirrors the great weather."

Importantly, a congenial atmosphere permeates UCLA Anderson's campus. Across the board, students find their peers to be "extremely friendly and open." Fortunately, there "are no egos here." Instead, students approach everything with a "collaborative" mindset. And many truly appreciate that their fellow students "have incredibly different backgrounds, from all industries, countries and cultures and are willing to share and use that experience in their work and interactions."

Admissions

A top MBA program, competition for admission to UCLA Anderson is certainly stiff. Anderson is looking for candidates with strong communication skills who have a clear vision for their professional future. They want students who understand how they'll benefit from this particular MBA program. All applicants are required to have an undergraduate degree from an accredited four-year university (or international equivalent). Additionally, they must submit GMAT (highly preferable) or GRE scores, TOEFL or IELTS (for students who did not attend an English speaking university), two letters of recommendation, and one required essay. Work experience is recommended but not required. Finally, interviews will be conducted on an invitation only basis.

FINANCIAL FACTS

Annual tuition (in-state/ out-of-state)	$50,517/$54,644
Fees	$3,200
Cost of books	$1,494
Room & board (on/off-campus)	$17,719/$17,719
% of students receiving aid	80
% of first-year students receiving aid	77
% of students receiving grants	65
Average award package	$51,056
Average grant	$28,901
Average loan	$49,463
Average student loan debt	$88,654

ADMISSIONS

Admissions Selectivity Rating	97
# of applications received	3,533
% applicants accepted	20
% acceptees attending	53
Average GMAT	713
Range of GMAT	700–730
Accepts GRE scores	Yes
Average Verbal GRE	162
Range of Verbal GRE scores	160–165
Average Quantitative GRE	159
Range of Quantitative GRE scores	156–161
Average Writing GRE	4.8
Range of Writing GRE scores	4.5–5.0
Average GPA	3.5
TOEFL required of international students	Yes
Minimum TOEFL (paper/web)	560/87
Application fee	$200
International application fee	$200
Early application deadline	10/6
Early notification date	12/15
Regular application deadline	4/12
Regular application notification	5/24
Application Deadline/Notification	
Round 1:	10/6 / 12/15
Round 2:	1/5 / 3/29
Round 3:	4/12 / 5/24
Deferment available	No
Transfer students accepted	No
Non-fall admissions	No
Need-blind admissions	Yes

EMPLOYMENT PROFILE

Career Rating	07
Percent employed at graduation	73
Percent employed 3 months after graduation	87
Average base starting salary	$114,392
Primary Source of Full-time Job Acceptances	
School-facilitated activities	201 (76%)
Graduate-facilitated activities	63 (24%)

Grads Employed by Function	%	Avg. Salary
Marketing	(28%)	$106,110
Operations	(4%)	$101,300
Consulting	(21%)	$128,800
Management	(10%)	$109,308
Finance	(25%)	$115,795
Other	(12%)	$114,293

Top 5 Employers Hiring Grads
PwC (11), Deloitte (11), Adobe Systems Inc. (8), Bank of America Merrill Lynch (8), Microsoft (8)

UNIVERSITY OF CALIFORNIA—RIVERSIDE
A. GARY ANDERSON GRADUATE SCHOOL OF MANAGEMENT

GENERAL INFORMATION
Type of school	Public
Affiliation	No Affiliation
Academic calendar	quarter

SURVEY SAYS...
Friendly students, Liberal students
Solid preparation in:
Finance

STUDENTS
Enrollment of parent institution	21,539
Enrollment of MBA Program	117
% male/female	54/46
% out-of-state	9
% part-time	0
% underrepresented minority	54
% international	73
Average age at entry	25
Average years work experience at entry	3

ACADEMICS
Academic Experience Rating	86
Profs interesting rating	87
Profs accessible rating	94
Student/faculty ratio	7:1
% female faculty	19
% underrepresented minority faculty	62
% part-time faculty	41

Academics

Combine the Southern California climate with a "fantastic school" offering "generous financial aid, and it's easy to understand why the A. Gary Anderson Graduate School of Management at UC—Riverside gets such high marks from students. One raves, "I am having the time of my life [and]...feel very privileged to be here." Many MBA candidates here are taking their first steps in the business world, as applicants are not required to have work experience—which can be a good or bad thing depending on who you talk to. Some feel that the program only offers a "surface-level understanding of business." Other students laud the "challenging" classes, bolstered by the "very accessible" professors who "care very much about their students' learning and understanding of the course material." However, some gripe that a few seem "more focused on research, and not curriculum."

The six components of an MBA from AGSM are the core courses, an internship, the communication workshop, the electives, a "capstone course," and a case project or thesis.

Though the core courses take up more time than any other single component, students are most enthusiastic about the "wide diversity of electives," which are all seminar size and designed to "encourage participative learning." One student explains, "I love coming to a small school like UCR's AGSM. You get real interaction with professors, and all of the students know each other, which allows for tighter bonds and networks." There are ten areas of electives, and students are allowed to take up to nine courses from any area, such as accounting, entrepreneurial management, finance, general management, human resources management/organizational behavior, international management, management information systems, management science, marketing, and production and operations management.

Most students agree that "discussion is greatly encouraged" in class. A fair number of courses "require presentation with business formal attire" and some "even require group debate." One student notes, "It gives you some pressure, but it's fun." Some lament the feeling that the university "does not attach [enough] importance to our business school," and hope for this to change in the near future. Others, though conscious that the school is a "research-oriented university," wouldn't mind getting more "attention from some professors" who they find to be "mostly researchers and not lecturers."

Career and Placement

Aside from recent budget cuts, the thing that has most students at AGSM up in arms is the Career Resources Center. As one student says, "The school desperately needs a stronger Career Counseling Center designed just for the MBA students." Another adds, "I really think the school should begin to target the school's alumni more. There are many UCR MBAs in the industry and they could be a real resource and asset to the school." The MBA now has its own Career Services, which should help alleviate many of the students' concerns regarding "job placement," "internships," and "professional networking."

Student Life and Environment

In recent years, Riverside, California has undergone both something of a renaissance and an influx of people. Gone are the days of quiet orange groves, and in their place resides the veritable capital of the Inland Empire. Whether your tastes run to the great outdoors or to great shopping, students find "plenty of unique hangouts, interesting shopping, and a wide variety of eats to fit anyone's desires (and budget)." Some MBA students feel that they "lack social activities" within the program, though in many instances this could be blamed on the large amount of "homework" these students undertake. That said, as the university (and those that surround it) continue to grow, students can expect more avenues to their social outlets to open.

The school itself is housed in a 30,000-square-foot building that features "state-of-the-art research and teaching facilities." MBA students agree that their "computer lab is very nice" and relish that they, as MBAs, "have priority over all computers in the lab." Other students gripe that they're stuck in "a small building that consists of one lecture room and one classroom. Our school has suffered greatly from the previous budget cuts." Still, the building must have something going for it because "MBA students rarely venture onto the main campus at [UC Riverside], unless it's to go to the library or bookstore."

Students report that "most people are very nice, and it is easy to meet new people if you try." These "very laid-back and friendly" students have formed "a tight-knit community here because our graduate program is so small." "I pretty much know and am friends with every other MBA student," says one. Due to the proximity of students, there is "a level of competition between students during academic competitions and presentations," but most happily note that "it is healthy and in good fun."

Admissions

At AGSM, students from all undergraduate majors and levels of business experience are eligible for admission. In fact, more than 30 percent of all incoming students come from a background other than business and have little—if any—experience in the business world. According to the school, "There is no minimum GPA or GMAT requirement for MBA admission consideration." However, they also say, "Satisfying minimal standards does not guarantee admission, since the number of qualified applicants far exceeds the number of places available," meaning that you'd best do your best. It is worth noting that because the school doesn't require prior work experience, all prospective MBAs must complete an internship "to ensure your success upon graduation."

FINANCIAL FACTS

Annual tuition (in-state/ out-of-state)	$11,220/$23,463
Fees	$29,436
Cost of books	$2,000
Room & board (on/off-campus)	$10,890/$15,045
% of students receiving aid	39
Average award package	$24,404
Average student loan debt	$81,116

ADMISSIONS

Admissions Selectivity Rating	82
# of applications received	216
% applicants accepted	69
% acceptees attending	35
Average GMAT	587
Range of GMAT	555–620
Accepts GRE scores	Yes
Average Verbal GRE	152
Range of Verbal GRE scores	148–154
Average Quantitative GRE	160
Range of Quantitative GRE scores	159–164
Average Writing GRE	3.0
Range of Writing GRE scores	3.0–4.0
Average GPA	3.2
TOEFL required of international students	Yes
Minimum TOEFL (paper/web)	550/80
Application fee	$100
International application fee	$125
Regular application deadline	9/1
Application Deadline/Notification	
Round 1:	12/15 / 2/1
Round 2:	1/15 / 3/15
Round 3:	3/1 / 4/25
Round 4:	6/1 /
Deferment available	No
Transfer students accepted	Yes
Transfer application policy A maximum of 8 graduate units taken in residence may be transferred from qualifying institutions and courses.	
Non-fall admissions	No
Need-blind admissions	Yes

EMPLOYMENT PROFILE

Career Rating	85	Grads Employed by Function	% Avg. Salary
Percent employed at graduation	43	Marketing	(6%) $0
Percent employed 3 months after graduation	45	Operations	(4%) $0
		Consulting	(1%) $0
Average base starting salary	$71,382	Management	(8%) $92,000
Primary Source of Full-time Job Acceptances		Finance	(14%) $64,818
Unknown	47 (100%)	HR	(2%) $0
		MIS	(3%) $0
		Other	(9%) $0

Top 5 Employers Hiring Grads
Technicolor (2), CITIC (2), University of California Riverside (2), Kia Motors America (1), PwC (1)

University of Central Arkansas
College of Business

GENERAL INFORMATION

Type of school	Public
Affiliation	No Affiliation
Academic calendar	Semester

SURVEY SAYS...
Happy students
Solid preparation in:
General management

STUDENTS

Enrollment of parent institution	11,754
Enrollment of MBA Program	24
% male/female	67/33
% part-time	33
% international	33
Average age at entry	24

ACADEMICS

Academic Experience Rating	**80**
Profs interesting rating	90
Profs accessible rating	93
% female faculty	17
% underrepresented minority faculty	0
% part-time faculty	6

Prominent Alumni
Marisia Geraci, Executive Director, Heifer Intl., South Africa; Johnny Adams, CEO - First Security Bank; David Grimes, Financial Analyst - American Management Company; Gary Reifess, Vice Presient of Marketing - Producer's Rice Mill; Lori Ross, Director of Marketing - Conway Regional Medical Center

Academics

The University of Central Arkansas's College of Business is located in the city of Conway, just north of Little Rock. The college offers both full- and part-time programs, as well as online classes in major fields of study including accounting, economics, finance, information systems, management, and marketing. UCA is known for being "cost efficient" and for its "diversity," "high academic standards," and "smart and easygoing professors." For those looking to learn from home, students say, "UCA has made huge strides with online courses." Most "MBA course are now offered online making it more convenient for those students that work full-time." Many MBA candidates received their undergraduate degrees from UCA and returned, a testament to the quality of education. On such returning student notes: "The college is growing constantly" and the "MBA program is improving." "We got a new building and facility for business program right when I completed my undergraduate, so now during my MBA I am able to utilize those facilities and technologies."

The professors are "quite knowledgeable of the materials they teach" according to recent students, and "the school has good equipment, and a lot of resources." "The professors help make the school great," notes another. "I would argue they are as good as any in the area." Professors are "helpful" and "accessible for additional assistance if needed." All the "professors are really nice and try to help," say one student. The "information presented is academically sound and very relatable to real world life." Students feel that their input is welcomed in class and appreciate the use of "work experience" and real-world "examples to help teach the class." While some students laud the "interactive" nature of their classes, others say that though they learn and discuss "real life situations and cases," "UCA is still very traditional in how it teaches and tests." Overall students find their professors "very easy to work with." The course work may be "very hard, but because students and professors are friendly," students "still enjoy going to this school."

Career and Placement

Second only to the quality of the professors is the "ability to get a job," notes one student in the class of 2015. "Since the school is in a small and upcoming town, the community is very tight knit," notes another, and "they are very appreciative of graduates and work well with our University to hire recent grads." They are also "very helpful in assisting in finding employment and internships through our career services department." The accounting program at UCA "does an amazing job at bringing employer to campus and helping students network and prepare for interviews." Most students "receive a job offer before they even graduate."

ADMISSIONS CONTACT: DR. MICHAEL RUBACH, MBA DIRECTOR
ADDRESS: COLLEGE OF BUSINESS, UNIVERSITY OF CENTRAL ARKANSAS, CONWAY, AR 72035
PHONE: 501-450-5316 • FAX: 501-450-5302
E-MAIL: MRUBACH@UCA.EDU • WEBSITE: WWW.UCA.EDU/MBA

Student Life and Environment

Students say there is a "happy campus life," and most students are "laid back and relaxed." Though "UCA is located in a dry county," "there are bars and food places where you can get drinks" and the "closest wet county is fifteen to twenty minutes away." The school is "very safe" so there is not much to worry about. Students say their classmates are "motivated," "hardworking," and "cooperative." "People here are generally friendly," notes one student. "It's like a family." Overall they are "well-rounded" and come from "diverse backgrounds." Many "MBA students are athletes or former athletes and are still heavily involved in their teams." A significant percentage of students work full time while completing a part-time MBA. According to one part-time student, "the school has been great as far as including me in events and entertainment on-campus." The UCA "business building has a room on the third floor dedicated to MBA students to study, eat, or lounge," which the students appreciate, and the campus has "comfortable areas to sit and study throughout."

Admissions

Applicants must submit a GMAT score (minimum of 500), undergraduate transcripts, a personal essay, two letters of recommendation, and a current résumé. In certain cases a GRE score may also be accepted. Last year's entering class had an average GMAT score of 475 and an average undergraduate GPA of 3.23. International students must have a TOEFL score of 550 on the paper version or 79 on the web-based version.

FINANCIAL FACTS

Annual tuition (in-state/ out-of-state)	$4,375/$8,749
Fees	$1,269
Cost of books	$1,200
Room & board (on/off-campus)	$5,982/$5,982

ADMISSIONS

Admissions Selectivity Rating	**75**
# of applications received	30
% applicants accepted	90
% acceptees attending	89
Average GMAT	475
Range of GMAT	410–530
Accepts GRE scores	No
Average Verbal GRE	0
TOEFL required of international students	Yes
Minimum TOEFL (paper/web)	550/79
Application fee	$25
International application fee	$50
Regular application deadline	7/15
Deferment available	Yes
Maximum length of deferment	3 years
Transfer students accepted	Yes
Transfer application policy A maximum of 6 graduate hours is transferrable from a accredited institution.	
Non-fall admissions	Yes
Need-blind admissions	Yes

UNIVERSITY OF CENTRAL FLORIDA
COLLEGE OF BUSINESS ADMINISTRATION

Academics

If you're on the hunt for an MBA program with both great value and a great reputation, you might want to consider University of Central Florida. To begin with, the curriculum offered is geared to ensure that UCF MBAs are "competitive in today's work environment." UCF MBAs also have access to some "tremendous" professors. Indeed, instructors here frequently prove themselves to be "both informative and engaging." And though their "lectures are based on textbook topics" they typically "reach much further than a textbook could go."

Perhaps the greatest praise is reserved for the "outstanding" administration for the PMBA and EMBA. An appreciative and astonished first-year shares, "They send email[s] on a regular basis making us aware of events near business school that might affect parking. They provide snacks and drinks during breaks outside the classroom. They order in lunch when we have meetings during lunch. . . . They really make an effort to relieve as much of the stress as possible."

Students here are also quick to note that the EMBA really "cater[s] to working adults with a schedule of [three] Saturdays per month and one Friday." As a grateful second-year student explains, "This [makes] the program manageable [to] attend without [worrying about] having to miss an excessive amount of work." In addition, the "concierge service for registration and materials . . . [allows] working professional[s] to concentrate on the course work and . . . [avoid the headache of administrative tasks]." More importantly, since "the program is cohort based," students are really able to interact with their peers and hear "perspectives from other executives in various industries and fields."

Career and Placement

MBA students at UCF clearly benefit from the university's "partnerships with local industry and deep engagement with the Central Florida community." And, considering that hometown Orlando is a major tourist destination with a fast-growing economy, you can rest assured that opportunities abound. Companies that hire University of Central Florida MBAs include Walt Disney World Resort, Lockheed Martin, Morgan Stanley, NAVAIR and Charles Schwab.

ADMISSIONS CONTACT: KELLEY RASGAITIS, DIRECTOR OF GRADUATE ADMISSIONS
ADDRESS: 36 WEST PINE STREET, ORLANDO, FL 32801
PHONE: 407-235-3917
E-MAIL: MBA@UCF.EDU • WEBSITE: WWW.BUSINESSUCF.EDU

Student Life and Environment

UCF's College of Business Administration consistently manages to fill its classes with "bright," "engaging" and "collaborative" students. Many who choose to attend are already "established in their careers" but "looking for an MBA as a way to stand out amongst their peers." Fortunately, they all "bring different experiences to the table, allowing for strong discussions about every topic." For the most part, UCF MBA candidates are also "self motivated and dedicated to their school work, careers, and companies." And, perhaps most crucial, students are "sincere, welcoming, and desire to see everyone in the class succeed." The campus for the PMBA and EMBA programs is "located in downtown Orlando" which proves to be a "conducive environment for working professionals." As a first-year explains, "We don't have to drive around trying to find parking on campus." And, more importantly, the "environment [is] quiet, clean, and [meets our] needs." Overall, the main UCF campus manages to foster a "very laid back atmosphere," and students can sometimes be found "lounging around various spots on campus." However, the vast majority of MBAs are "busy [with] families [and] full time jobs." Therefore, it's quite common for students to attend classes and then depart soon after. Of course, when they want to take a break from studying, Orlando has plenty to offer. From great shops and restaurants to the Disney theme parks, you'll never get bored in this "multicultural" city!

Admissions

Applicants to the UCF College of Business MBA program must submit an online application to the UCF College of Graduate Studies. Additionally, applicants must submit official transcripts for each university or college previously attended, a personal essay, a current résumé, and letters of recommendation. The average GMAT score and undergrad GPA for last year's class were 570 and 3.3, respectively.

FINANCIAL FACTS

Cost of books	$2,000
Room & board	
(on/off-campus)	$9,000/$15,000
% of students receiving aid	53
% of first-year students	
receiving aid	57
% of students receiving grants	1
Average award package	$12,889
Average grant	$886
Average loan	$15,079
Average student loan debt	$39,960

ADMISSIONS

Admissions Selectivity Rating	**74**
# of applications received	310
% applicants accepted	56
% acceptees attending	92
Accepts GRE scores	No
Average GPA	3.3
TOEFL required of	
international students	Yes
Minimum TOEFL	
(paper/web)	575/92
Application fee	$31
International application fee	$31
Regular application deadline	7/15
Deferment available	No
Transfer students accepted	Yes
Transfer application policy	
Transfer applicants must be from a regionally or nationally accredited university. May transfer in up to 9 hours.	
Non-fall admissions	No
Need-blind admissions	Yes

THE UNIVERSITY OF CHICAGO
BOOTH SCHOOL OF BUSINESS

GENERAL INFORMATION

Type of school	Private
Affiliation	No Affiliation
Academic calendar	Quarter

SURVEY SAYS...

Students love Chicago, IL, Good peer network, Happy students, Smart classrooms
Solid preparation in:
Finance, Accounting, Quantitative Skills

STUDENTS

Enrollment of MBA Program	2,509
% part-time	
Average age at entry	27
Average years work experience at entry	5

ACADEMICS

Academic Experience Rating	**82**
Profs interesting rating	73
Profs accessible rating	76

Joint Degrees

MBA/MA Area Studies and Business MBA/MA International Relations and Business MBA/ JD Law and Business MBA/MD Medicine and Business MBA/ MPP Public Policy Studies and Business MBA/MA Social Service Administration and Business

Prominent Alumni

William Conway, Managing Director, The Carlyle Group; Brady Dougan, CEO Investment Banking, Credit Suisse; Gene Fama, Nobel Laureate; Satya Nadella, CEO, Microsoft; Sue Wagner, Co-Founder, BlackRock Financial Management

Academics

"The emphasis on [students] learning the basics rather than some predigested goo" along with "an unbeatable faculty" are "what make The University of Chicago's Booth School of Business one of the best, especially in hard-core areas such as finance and accounting," students tell us. A "rigorous quantitative program that compels students to think critically and analytically" is the hallmark of a Chicago Booth MBA, although students hasten to add that Booth also "emphasizes persuasion, communication, and negotiation skills."

Chicago Booth offers a full-time, part-time evening, part-time weekend, and executive MBA program. All four tracks share "top-notch" faculty, wide-ranging academic options, and an approach that "doesn't chase new trends in business but instead relies on teaching sound fundamentals that can then be applied to any situation." The programs differ in some details; full-time students, for example, enjoy a student-enacted grade nondisclosure policy that creates a conducive environment for "teamwork and sharing of ideas." Students must also complete the Leadership Exploration and Development (LEAD) program, which "provides analytic frameworks for leadership that are very helpful in determining the best way to use [one's] strengths and where to improve." Part-timers enjoy "great flexibility," noting that "most classes have several sessions taught by the same professor during the same quarter, enabling students to make up class sessions if for some reason they cannot attend their normal session." Booth's weekend MBA and Executive MBAs have "students flying to Chicago from across the U.S. and world to attend classes," which "connects a much broader and more diverse group of people than other MBA programs can."

Chicago Booth's faculty includes Nobel laureates and cutting-edge researchers "who also excel in the classroom." One accounting student reports, "Both my corporate tax strategy professor and my M&A accounting professor consult for corporate and government clients, so they have intimate knowledge of how to apply what they teach in the real world." Booth is best known for its faculty in finance, economics, and accounting, but students note that the school should work to "increase awareness of its excellence in marketing, entrepreneurship, and general management disciplines." Many students also "do a one-term or full-year exchange program at a foreign business school," and "these international career development opportunities are a big part of the experience for many Booth students."

Career and Placement

The Booth Career Services Office doesn't have to work hard; as one student explains, "The network and doors that open up to a graduate from Chicago Booth are outstanding. Gaining an MBA from this school carries a lot of weight and in the job market no one will question your education." That doesn't mean that Career Services slacks off, however; on the contrary, it "is an excellent resource and deserves praise," and does a good job attracting recruiters in consulting, accounting, and finance including McKinsey & Company, Citigroup, The Boston Consulting Group, UBS, A.T. Kearney, Credit Suisse, Goldman Sachs, Bank of America/Merrill Lynch, and Booz and Company.

Chicago Booth also excels at "preparing career changers. You learn from the best faculty in the world to attain the skills you need to succeed in your given career. The alumni, and especially second-year students at the school, are available to answer any questions. Career Services does an excellent job of helping you identify your transferable skills to your new targeted career. . . . I would highly recommend the school for people looking to change careers."

FINANCIAL FACTS

Annual tuition	$66,540
Fees	$1,128
Cost of books	$1,200
Room & board	$14,520

ADMISSIONS

Admissions Selectivity Rating	**98**
# of applications received	4,284
Average GMAT	726
Accepts GRE scores	Yes
Average GPA	3.6
TOEFL required of international students	Yes
Minimum TOEFL (paper/web)	600/104
Application fee	$250
International application fee	$250
Application Deadline/Notification	
Round 1:	9/17 / 12/10
Round 2:	1/5 / 3/17
Round 3:	4/5 / 5/19
Deferment available	Yes
Transfer students accepted	No
Non-fall admissions	No
Need-blind admissions	Yes

Student Life and Environment

"The social aspect of University of Chicago is often overlooked," students in the full-time program tell us, reporting that "there are all kinds of opportunities to get together with other students in social or more formal settings, including school-sponsored happy hours, etc." Although "MBAs here work as hard as students at any other b-school, we know how to have fun too." One student writes, "If anything, there are too many programs and opportunities to be involved. You need to carefully consider them all to properly juggle [your] schedule." And with "the great city of Chicago is at our doorstep," students don't have to look far to find a wide range of fun diversions.

The school is located on Chicago's South Side in the Hyde Park neighborhood, which "is too often made out to be a scary place when, in fact, it's not. There is a pretty unique mixture of socioeconomic groups here, so you can drive by a building with three poor families living in it and four blocks later be at a stop sign next to a million-dollar (or more) home. The fact is that it's on the South Side of Chicago so people automatically say, 'bad, scary neighborhood.'" Part-time students attend classes at the Gleacher Center, "a beautiful building" in downtown Chicago, just off the Magnificent Mile. For students whose activities keep them in the Hyde Park area, Booth's Charles M. Harper Center boasts a "winter garden," a "dramatic foyer in the center of the building" where "people can catch up, do work, or just relax for a moment."

Admissions

Admission to the Chicago Booth School of Business is extremely competitive. Admissions Officers scrutinize a wide array of qualifications, including academic record (quality of curriculum, scholarships, special honors, etc.), work experience (quality as well as quantity), and overall "fit"(interpersonal skills, unique experiences, philanthropic activity). Applicants must provide the Admissions Office with transcripts for all post-secondary academic work, an official GMAT score report, letters of recommendation, personal essays, and TOEFL/IELTS scores (for international students only). Interviews are required for all candidates. Applicants to the full-time program interview on a "by invitation only" basis.

EMPLOYMENT PROFILE

Career Rating	**96**	**Top 5 Employers Hiring Grads**
Percent employed at graduation	87	McKinsey & Company, Inc. (44), The Boston
Percent employed 3 months		Consulting Group, Inc. (29), Bain & Company,
after graduation	95	Inc. (18), Amazon.com, Inc. (14), Bank of
Average base starting salary	$123,561	America Merrill Lynch (12)

UNIVERSITY OF CINCINNATI
CARL H. LINDNER COLLEGE OF BUSINESS

GENERAL INFORMATION
Type of school   Public
Affiliation   No Affiliation
Academic calendar   Semester

SURVEY SAYS...
Happy students
Solid preparation in:
Accounting, General management,
Teamwork, Presentation skills,
Quantitative skills, Doing business in
a global economy

STUDENTS
Enrollment of parent
   institution   44,251
Enrollment of MBA Program   263
% male/female   60/40
% out-of-state   7
% part-time   56
% underrepresented minority   15
% international   25
Average age at entry   27
Average years work
   experience at entry   4

ACADEMICS
Academic Experience Rating   90
Profs interesting rating   89
Profs accessible rating   90
Student/faculty ratio   8:1
% female faculty   25
% underrepresented
   minority faculty   14
% part-time faculty   42

Joint Degrees
MBA/JD; MBA/MA in Arts
Administration; MBA/MD; MBA/
Nursing; MBA/MS in Accounting,
Information Systems, Finance,
Marketing, Business Analytics, or
Taxation (distance learning only);
MBA/MA in Applied Economics or
Human Resources - 2 years.

Prominent Alumni
Paul Polman, CEO, Unilever; John
F. Barrett, President & CEO, Western
& Southern Financial Group; Myron
E. Ullman, III, CEO, JCPenney

Academics

Part of the University of Cincinnati business behemoth, the Carl H. Lindner College of Business MBA Program is "equally flexible as it is respected," offering both a part-time (completed in as little as 18 months) and a full-time option (completed in as little as twelve months), with classes held at its Clifton Heights and Blue Ash campuses, as well as online. The "affordable" school will even waive foundational courses if a student has an undergraduate business degree. "I needed a program that could adapt to my unpredictable work schedule while still challenging me as well as being known beyond this region," says a student.

The program focuses "heavily on project-team based work and less on outdated traditional classroom instruction/testing." "[It] has challenged me to think out of the box and I have gained a great deal of respect for the school and its faculty in the past year," says a student. Professors are "loaded with experience" and a "passion to teach" and "can relate that knowledge in class." All classes are put online as podcasts, which "is great if you have to work late or are traveling," and the school also uses programs like Aplia and Connect to supplement lectures.

The school administration is "always looking to grow and adapt to the changing economy. They're focused on building for the future." "At the end of the day you can find good people who will help you get what you need," says one student. The school is "very accommodating" to working professionals' schedules, and "encourages students to be creative and find creative ways to challenge ourselves and change our communities." "As an MBA student at UC, I feel like I am an important part of the program. My ideas are heard; I am connected with my fellow students and faculty," says a student. "I was very skeptical at first but now I've realized what a brilliant business school it really is, and how relevant the courses are," says another.

Career and Placement

Students do wish that the UC name were a little further out there, in terms of getting recruiters to come to campus. "UC's business college sometimes seems to be like a well-kept secret," says one. Recent strides have been made in bringing top tier companies to campus. The university does a decent job of accessing "a great network of companies to interact with students and provide career opportunities." The school is fortunate to be located in a city with several Fortune 500-headquartered companies, so "the learning and employment opportunities are great."

Top employers hiring graduates are Proctor & Gamble, Google, IBM, Kroger, and KPMG.

ADMISSIONS CONTACT: JASON DICKMAN, ASSOCIATE DIRECTOR, ADMISSIONS
ADDRESS: CARL H. LINDNER HALL, SUITE 606, P.O. BOX 210020, CINCINNATI, OH 45221-0020
PHONE: 513-556-7024 • FAX: 513-558-7006
E-MAIL: GRADUATE@UC.EDU • WEBSITE: WWW.BUSINESS.UC.EDU/MBA

Student Life and Environment

"Parking is easy" and the "beautiful" campus is small enough that you "don't ever feel rushed." The MBA students are "instantly put into groups that we meet with outside of class, led by a faculty member," so all students are connected to one another, and "are willing to give you a hand if you have questions or help work together through a particular topic."

Students in the evening classes "have a little more age and more experience in the field." There are many clubs to help students relieve stress and have fun on and off campus, regardless of age, and everyone "is always doing something" whether it's "going to the school's sports games, hanging out in the courtyard, [or] just having fun." A great deal of UC students are commuters, and quite a few also attended the university for undergrad.

Admissions

The Admissions Committee requests the following from candidates seeking admission: an official GMAT or GRE score report; personal essay; resume; sealed copies of official transcripts for all post-secondary schools previously attended; and letters of recommendation. TOEFL or IELTS score report is required for international students. Interviews are required for the majority of candidates.. Both GMAT/GRE scores and GPA are very important to the committee. The average GPA is 3.5, while the average GMAT score is 646.

FINANCIAL FACTS

Annual tuition (in-state/ out-of-state)	$28,920/$40,677
Fees	$2,517
Cost of books	$4,500
Room & board	$19,000
% of students receiving aid	71
% of first-year students receiving aid	83
% of students receiving grants	63
Average award package	$12,476
Average grant	$6,975
Average loan	$17,948
Average student loan debt	$31,037

ADMISSIONS

Admissions Selectivity Rating	87
# of applications received	216
% applicants accepted	60
% acceptees attending	71
Average GMAT	646
Range of GMAT	582–712
Accepts GRE scores	Yes
Average Verbal GRE	156
Range of Verbal GRE scores	151–161
Average Quantitative GRE	151
Range of Quantitative GRE scores	141–157
Average Writing GRE	4.5
Range of Writing GRE scores	3.5–5.0
Average GPA	3.5
TOEFL required of international students	Yes
Minimum TOEFL (paper/web)	600/90
Application fee	$65
International application fee	$70
Early application deadline	1/1
Early notification date	2/1
Regular application deadline	8/1
Regular application notification	8/15
Application Deadline/Notification	
Round 1:	1/1 / 2/1
Round 2:	3/15 / 4/15
Round 3:	8/1 / 8/15
Deferment available	Yes
Maximum length of deferment	1 year
Transfer students accepted	Yes
Transfer application policy	
Transferring from an AACSB accredited institution, no more than 16 credit hours	
Non-fall admissions	Yes
Need-blind admissions	Yes

EMPLOYMENT PROFILE

Career Rating	92	Grads Employed by Function% Avg. Salary	
Percent employed at graduation	53	Marketing	(18%) $51,500
Percent employed 3 months after graduation	88	Operations	(11%) $64,600
Average base starting salary	$62,646	Consulting	(13%) $66,000
Primary Source of Full-time Job Acceptances		Management	(16%) $46,472
School-facilitated activities	7 (16%)	Finance	(20%) $77,000
Graduate-facilitated activities	14 (31%)	Other	(22%)
Unknown	24 (53%)	**Top 5 Employers Hiring Grads**	
		Procter & Gamble (2), GE Aviation (2), Toyota Motor Corporation (1), Pricewaterhouse Coopers (1), Dow Chemical (1)	

UNIVERSITY OF CONNECTICUT
SCHOOL OF BUSINESS

Academics

A great place to develop real-world credentials, the University of Connecticut's MBA program teaches business fundamentals while maximizing students' access to practical learning experiences. UConn's full-time MBA curriculum was recently redesigned to give students a highly personalized MBA experience, while drawing on the program's traditional strengths. UConn is "highly-regarded in the areas of finance and risk analytics," but the first-year core covers all functional areas of business in an integrated fashion. In the second year, students develop an individualized plan of study, taking a range of classes within business concentrations like finance, marketing, or real estate, among others. In addition to an active internship program, "UConn's MBA program [is] unique in that it offers numerous experiential learning accelerators," which are practice-based programs, often operated in conjunction with a corporate partner. While first-year full-time MBA classes are held in Storrs, second-year courses are offered in Hartford, Stamford and Waterbury, so they can easily coordinate with the experiential learning centers. Examples of accelerator programs include: innovation, a student managed investment fund, and a Sustainable Community Outreach and Public Engagement program. A current student elaborates, "I've been able to complete three semester-long consulting projects for real companies and non-profits, and have participated in two study abroad programs." In addition to the full-time program, working professionals can complete the MBA part-time program in Waterbury, Hartford, or Stamford.

A relatively small program, the full-time MBA "intimate class size" makes it easier for UConn students to build relationships with both their teachers and classmates. With roughly sixty to seventy students in each full-time class, "being part of this small cohort allows for personal attention and focused learning." In general, professors are "receptive to any type of question" in class, and many are "extremely motivated and genuinely interested in the academic success of their students." However, students admit that when it comes to teaching style, "professors run a wide gamut," including some highly-skilled instructors, and professors who seem more focused on their own projects.

For Connecticut residents, "the price of attending a state school was more reasonable" than attending a similar, private institution. On the downside, "the effects of state budget cuts can be seen throughout UConn as a whole, as well as the business school." Currently, "UConn is undergoing a great deal of change under the leadership of a new Dean," and there have been some bumps in the road as the program changes course. However, optimistic students observe, "The dean and the MBA director are very responsive to students' concerns, and changes have been made and continue to be made to improve the value of the school."

Career and Placement

While UConn enjoys great "local brand recognition" and "very good connections in the state of Connecticut," many students are disappointed with their school's career center. Drawing the majority of its business contacts from the immediate region, many feel that the "career center perhaps needs to widen its focus," and try "digging deeper into Wall Street or Boston" to make contact with more recruiters. On the flipside, a current student counters, "I have had interviews with Covidien, Pitney Bowes, General Electric, and Travelers Insurance, and I know UConn has a strong presence when I see that I am competing in the second round interviews with students from Yale and Cornell."

ADMISSIONS CONTACT: RAJENDRA SHIROLE, DIRECTOR
ADDRESS: 100 CONSTITUTION PLAZA, HARTFORD, CT 06103
PHONE: 860-486-2872 • FAX: 860-486-5222
E-MAIL: UCONNMBA@BUSINESS.UCONN.EDU • WEBSITE: WWW.BUSINESS.UCONN.EDU

In a recent year, 69 percent of UConn graduates were working, negotiating a job offer, or pursuing further study within three months of graduation. By six months, that number had jumped to 94 percent of students. The mean salary for recent UConn grads was $90,827 in the previous year, with a high of $160,000. Companies hiring UConn graduates include AC Nielsen, Aetna, Atlantic Records, Barclays, CIGNA, Citigroup, CVS Caremark, Deloitte Consulting, ESPN, General Electric, Hasbro Hewitt, Hubbell, Inc, IBM, ING, Liberty Mutual, Nestle, Nasdaq, PepsiCo, Pitney Bowes, Prudential Financial, Siemens, Sun Products Corporation, Travelers, Webster Bank, and XL Global Insurance.

Student Life and Environment

The entire MBA program will be moving from Storrs, Connecticut to the state's Capitol, Hartford. The program's new home will be at the Graduate Business Learning Center (GBLC). Attracting a "diverse group from all over the world," almost 40 percent of University of Connecticut's full-time MBA candidates are international. A collaborative cohort environment, "team activities are an integrated part of our school culture," and students are generally "smart, cheerful, [and] enthusiastic."

For first-year students, "school days are treated similar to a nine to five job," with class in the morning and homework to complete in the evening. Within this small program, everyone knows everyone, and students "typically socialize with the entire MBA class in-between classes." On campus, "mixers with students are fairly regular" and "some people are very motivated and active in clubs and networking events." However, "the full-time MBA is comprised of mostly commuter students, so we do not generally stay on campus when we are not in class."

Admissions

To be considered for UConn's MBA program, students must have at least two years of professional work experience, strong GMAT scores (usually between 560 and 710), and a solid undergraduate academic record. In recent years, the UConn incoming class had an average undergraduate GPA of 3.48 and an average GMAT score of 654. Full-time students had an average of five and a half years in the work force, while part-time students had seven years of professional experience.

FINANCIAL FACTS

Annual tuition (in-state/ out-of-state)	$13,026/$33,812
Fees	$826
Cost of books	$4,000
% of students receiving aid	52
% of first-year students receiving aid	47
% of students receiving grants	42
Average award package	$24,564
Average grant	$20,786
Average loan	$22,000
Average student loan debt	$58,767

ADMISSIONS

Admissions Selectivity Rating	89
# of applications received	268
% applicants accepted	42
% acceptees attending	47
Average GMAT	625
Range of GMAT	580–660
Accepts GRE scores	Yes
Average Verbal GRE	160
Range of Verbal GRE scores	152–168
Average Quantitative GRE	152
Range of Quantitative GRE scores	149–157
Average Writing GRE	4.3
Range of Writing GRE scores	3.5–5.5
Average GPA	3.4
TOEFL required of international students	Yes
Minimum TOEFL (paper/web)	575/90
Application fee	$75
International application fee	$75
Early application deadline	11/1
Regular application deadline	2/1
Application Deadline	
Round 1:	11/1
Round 2:	2/1
Round 3:	6/1
Deferment available	Yes
Maximum length of deferment	12 months
Transfer students accepted	No
Non-fall admissions	No
Need-blind admissions	Yes

EMPLOYMENT PROFILE

Career Rating	90	Grads Employed by Function	% Avg. Salary
Percent employed at graduation	63	Marketing	(16%) $86,667
Percent employed 3 months after graduation	79	Operations	(21%) $84,825
		Consulting	(16%) $101,667
Average base starting salary	$89,232	Management	(16%) $95,000
Primary Source of Full-time Job Acceptances		Finance	(26%) $83,832
School-facilitated activities	17 (89%)	MIS	(5%) $90,000
Unknown	2 (11%)	**Top 5 Employers Hiring Grads**	
		Prudential Retirerment (1), Gartner (1), T-Mobil (1), Aetna (1), PricewaterhouseCooper (1)	

UNIVERSITY OF DAYTON
SCHOOL OF BUSINESS ADMINISTRATION

GENERAL INFORMATION
Type of school   Private
Affiliation   Roman Catholic
Academic calendar   Semester

SURVEY SAYS...
Cutting-edge classes, Happy students, Smart classrooms
Solid preparation in:
Teamwork

STUDENTS
Enrollment of parent institution	11,368
Enrollment of MBA Program	179
% male/female	96/4
% part-time	86
% underrepresented minority	8
% international	28
Average age at entry	25
Average years work experience at entry	5

ACADEMICS
Academic Experience Rating	**73**
Profs interesting rating	70
Profs accessible rating	72
Student/faculty ratio	7:1
% female faculty	20
% underrepresented minority faculty	5
% part-time faculty	8

Joint Degrees
Joint Juris of Doctor of Law (JD) and Master of Business Administration (MBA) 3-4 years (combined JD and MBA degrees)

Prominent Alumni
Keith Hawk, Vice President, LexisNexis; Phil Parker, President & CEO, Dayton Area Cham. of Commerce; Mike Turner, US Congressman, OH; Linda Berning, Berning Investments

Academics

Students tell us that UD's integrated curriculum "is one of...the program's biggest strengths. It is unlike what any school in the region is offering, and it results in a more thorough educational experience." The school's program typically include an emphasis on "new management techniques. The Toyota Way and Lean Manufacturing are very popular" here. Students also boast of UD's "Marianist identity and values, which leads to a great sense of family. Students, staff and faculty are really close to one another. People help each other a lot." As one MBA explains, "If I get a B, someone is asking me what they can do to help. If I get an A, someone is asking me if I can help them, and I always agree. We're a team, no doubt."

One student reports that he is "really impressed by all the opportunities UD provides its students with outside classes. Its entrepreneurship program is supported by out-of-class valuable experiences. For example, the Business Plan Competition...offers us the possibility to create a real business plan and to receive funds to implement it. I also heard finance students telling me that they can't believe that they are allowed to manage millions of dollars on behalf of UD at the Davis Center. I really like being able to turn my theoretical knowledge into practical experience at UD, because now, I feel more confident that I will be able to apply what I learned to real-life situations."

The University provides students with numerous chances to broaden their business resumes. One student reports that he is "really impressed by all the opportunities UD provides its students with outside classes.... For example, the Business Plan Competition offers...us the possibility to create a real business plan and to receive funds to implement it...I really like being able to turn my theoretical knowledge into practical experience at UD, because now, I feel more confident that I will be able to apply what I learned to real-life situation."

UD also offers a very popular Bachelor's Plus Master's Program in which University of Dayton undergraduates are "able to achieve 150 hours for the CPA exam and get an MBA degree." The school's "administration is good and getting better" and "cares about what the students think," professors are "passionate and well-prepared leaders who are engaging and challenging," and students enjoy "many opportunities to gain experience in your particular field, whether with student organizations, access to alumni, or career/academic development programs and workshops." With all that going for the school, it's no wonder students tell us that "UD's MBA program is probably one of the best-kept secrets in Ohio."

Career and Placement

MBAs at the University of Dayton are served by the Career Services Office, which assists undergraduates, graduates, and alumni in their development and placement needs. The office provides graduate students with the following services: career advisement; job search and résumé critiquing workshops, career fairs, online résumé referral, on-campus recruiting events, mock-interviews, and contact with the alumni career network. Students tell us that the school "has an excellent reputation and a great relationship with local/regional employers." Top employers of U Dayton MBAs include Wright Patterson Air Force Base, Emerson Climate Technologies, Fifth Third Bank, Reynolds & Reynolds, and LexisNexis. Other employers include AK Steel, AT&T, Greene Memorial Hospital, Honda, IBM, Kettering Medical Center, and Premier Health Partners.

Admissions Contact: Mandy Schrank, MBA Program Manager
Address: 300 College Park Avenue, Dayton, OH 45469-7020
Phone: 937-229-3733 • Fax: 937-229-3882
E-mail: mba@udayton.edu • Website: business.udayton.edu/mba

Student Life and Environment

Students brag that UD is a collegial campus, the sort of place where "every time you pass someone, whether that be a student, professor, or even the custodial staff, a pleasant 'Hello, how is your day?' is exchanged. This allows for a comfort in the classroom that, in turn, allows for education beyond the text to flourish." This open dialogue is equally available to international students; writes one from France, "UD is reputed for taking care of its international students. I knew before my arrival here that faculty and staff would be very accessible and helpful, and that I would be individually recognized by them."

SBA accommodates "a lot of MBA social events and opportunities as well as seminars for career and professional skill development," while the university at large offers "plenty of activities organized by the students and university-sponsored events that give the students plenty of options to take a break and get away from school work for a while."

While "there is an overwhelming majority of Caucasian students" here, there are also "students from France, Germany, China, and various racial minorities as well. Age covers the vast spectrum from recent graduate to retired. Non-traditional students mix well with young professionals."

Admissions

All applications to the University of Dayton MBA program must include a resume, official transcripts for all postsecondary academic work, a completed application, and an official GMAT score report; the GMAT entrance requirement may be delayed for students with strong academic records, allowing them to enroll conditionally for one semester before submitting GMAT scores. A cover letter, current resume, and letters of recommendation from employers or professors are recommended but not required. International applicants must meet all of the above requirements and must also provide a translation of any non-English language transcripts and official scores for the TOEFL (minimum score of 550 paper exam, 213 computer exam, or 80 Internet-based exam required for unconditional admission. Alternatively, international students may submit an IELTS score of 6.5 or higher in lieu of the TOEFL requirement.

FINANCIAL FACTS

Annual tuition	$27,690
Fees	$75
Cost of books	$800
% of students receiving aid	50
% of students receiving grants	20

ADMISSIONS

Admissions Selectivity Rating	**96**
# of applications received	331
% applicants accepted	16
% acceptees attending	87
Average GMAT	546
Range of GMAT	540–610
Accepts GRE scores	Yes
Average GPA	3.3
TOEFL required of international students	Yes
Minimum TOEFL (paper)	550
Application fee	$0
International application fee	$50
Deferment available	Yes
Maximum length of deferment	1 year
Transfer students accepted	Yes
Transfer application policy Students may request up to 6 semester hours of approved graduate transfer credit of course work of "B" or better graded quality completed in acceptable time frame.	
Non-fall admissions	Yes
Need-blind admissions	Yes

EMPLOYMENT PROFILE

Career Rating	73	**Top 5 Employers Hiring Grads**
		Wright Patterson Air Force Base, Emerson Climate Technologies, Fifth Third Bank, Reynolds & Reynolds, LexisNexis

UNIVERSITY OF DENVER
DANIELS COLLEGE OF BUSINESS

Academics

The University of Denver's Daniels College of Business is known for its "great history," "dedication to ethics" and "outstanding reputation for quality of education." It has a strong "commitment to Ethics, Sustainability, Globalization" and "International Business" that "sets it apart from other MBA programs." In addition, the small size of the program allows for "more intimate relationships between students and professors."

The program is built to be flexible for both the Full-time and Part-time cohorts yet still "conducted in a classroom setting" rather than online. The "professors understand that they are teaching people with current and in some cases long-term business experience and the way they teach and interact with [students] reflects that." The "administrators have all had real jobs beyond just being in academia which makes a difference in how they interact with [students] as well as teach." The university uses a "cohort system" that allows the students to remain with the same group of classmates throughout the program. In so doing, MBAs are able "to develop relationships with classmates over the one-and-a-half year lockstep program." The cohort system is "[r]un like a close-knit family." The "[c]ohort leader enrolls students in classes and keeps [them] informed of all upcoming events and career opportunities." This is especially helpful for busy, working professionals. And since "everyone in the part-time program is working full-time," it "positively impacts the cohort by keeping everyone focused on accomplishing tasks in a timely manner."

"Most of the staff know us on a first name basis," one student notes, which is "[v]ery rewarding." "The professors are very outgoing and you can tell that they love what they teach. They make you want to succeed in the classroom." MBAs "get real world applicability and experience. No longer are the lessons out of a book, studying business theory. Lessons are from key business leaders in the community." "They clearly have their eye on the future," one student notes. Professors are known for their "keen ability to teach as well as write academically. They also relate personably and are approachable outside of class." Professors are even "willing to come in on weekends to hold study sessions and increase learning."

The university "encourages group work and leadership training. MBAs take "personality tests at the beginning of the program" to "help students to recognize their strengths and weaknesses." "There is one trip at the beginning of the course that allows classmates to bond" and an "international trip at the end of the program to allow for international business education." "Through DU's MBA program," one student notes, "I was able to transform from a middle-of-the-road employee to an outstanding one with much more confidence and skills that are valuable to employers. This can all be attributed to the administration, professors, and my academic experience."

Career and Placement

The program is known for its "great sense of community, where alumni engage and support graduates and undergraduates" and "notable alumni list," especially for those interested in working in Denver. "The career center offers assistance with resumes, cover letters, general job search information, among various other resources and services." MBAs found "the career center very helpful" as well as the "career events and resources for finding jobs." MBAs go on to work at companies like Goldman Sachs, Charles Schwab, and IBM.

Student Life and Environment

University of Denver "is located close to many great attractions such as downtown Denver and the Rocky Mountains." Students call the location "amazing." "Denver is one of the best cities to live in and the University of Denver plugs students into the great parts of living here."

Since students are "grouped by cohorts" it creates a sense of community." "Life at Daniels feels like a big high school," one student notes. "Everyone is recognizable and is collaborative. There is very little competition among students." The university provides space for students to "meet together before classes and right after work so that if [they] want to eat, finish up last minute projects, interact with other PMBA students or just decompress [they] can." "Classmates are close and often go to happy hour immediately following class." They often "become friends outside the program—going to dinner, golf outings, concerts, game watches, etc." and some join intramural and case competition teams together.

In general, students found their classmates to be "working professionals that are extremely driven, high performing, high achievers, high energy," and "good socially." Though some note that the student body could be more diverse.

Admissions

Admission is selective and officials consider each student's whole package including the candidate's personal, professional, and intellectual background. An undergraduate degree, GMAT or GRE scores, resume, statement of purpose, and two letters of recommendation are required. In addition, a minimum of four years of work experience is recommended for the Full-time MBA program and five years for the PMBA. Admission to the executive MBA program requires 10 or more years of work experience. Interviews are offered on an invitation-only basis for the full-time program and required for the part-time and Executive MBA programs. A recent the matriculating class had an average undergraduate GPA of 3.27 and an average GMAT of 599.

FINANCIAL FACTS

Annual tuition (in-state/ out-of-state)	$44,160/
Fees	$855
Cost of books	$1,925
% of students receiving aid	95
% of first-year students receiving aid	98
% of students receiving grants	94
Average award package	$26,824
Average grant	$14,440
Average loan	$28,978

ADMISSIONS

Admissions Selectivity Rating	**81**
# of applications received	154
% applicants accepted	74
Average GMAT	585
Range of GMAT	540–640
Accepts GRE scores	Yes
Average Verbal GRE	182
Range of Verbal GRE scores	151–161
Average Quantitative GRE	192
Range of Quantitative GRE scores	150–158
Average Writing GRE	3.9
Range of Writing GRE scores	3.5–4.4
Average GPA	3.2
TOEFL required of international students	Yes
Minimum TOEFL (paper/web)	570/88
Application fee	$100
International application fee	$100
Early application deadline	11/15
Early notification date	12/15
Regular application deadline	3/15
Regular application notification	5/1
Application Deadline/Notification	
Round 1:	11/15 / 12/15
Round 2:	1/15 / 2/15
Round 3:	3/15 / 4/15
Round 4:	5/15 / 6/15
Deferment available	Yes
Maximum length of deferment	1 year
Transfer students accepted	Yes
Transfer application policy 8 quarter hours (6 semester hours) toward electives	
Non-fall admissions	Yes
Need-blind admissions	Yes

EMPLOYMENT PROFILE

Career Rating	**86**	**Grads Employed by Function**	**% Avg. Salary**
Percent employed at graduation	30	Marketing	(49%) $59,058
Percent employed 3 months after graduation	59	Operations	(3%)
		Consulting	(6%) $75,000
Average base starting salary	$61,400	Management	(9%) $80,000
		Finance	(30%) $57,888
		HR	(3%) $80,000

Top 5 Employers Hiring Grads
Apple (1), Bank of America (1), Deloitte (1), Medtronic (1), Samsung (1)

UNIVERSITY OF FLORIDA
HOUGH GRADUATE SCHOOL OF BUSINESS

GENERAL INFORMATION
Type of school	Public
Affiliation	No Affiliation
Academic calendar	Semester

SURVEY SAYS...
Classmates have diverse work experience, Friendly students, Good peer network, Good social scene, Happy students
Solid preparation in:
Finance, General management, Teamwork, Communication/interpersonal skills, Presentation skills, Quantitative skills, Doing business in a global economy

STUDENTS
Enrollment of parent institution	52,286
Enrollment of MBA Program	572
% male/female	66/34
% out-of-state	29
% part-time	81
% underrepresented minority	20
% international	13
Average age at entry	26
Average years work experience at entry	4

ACADEMICS
Academic Experience Rating	**99**
Profs interesting rating	93
Profs accessible rating	95
Student/faculty ratio	2:1
% female faculty	31
% underrepresented minority faculty	33
% part-time faculty	2

Joint Degrees
MBA/JD); MBA/MS in Medical Sciences, Biotechnology; MBA/Ph.D in Medical Sciences, Biotechnology; MBA/Doctor of Pharmacy; MBA/PhD in Medical Sciences; MBA/MD

Academics

The University of Florida MBA is designed specifically towards professional success, with three full-time program options that allow students to personalize their experience based on their academic and work history and a part-time program that meets just one weekend a month. Students find the caliber of opportunities "to be on par with schools that charge substantially higher tuition." They say that opportunity partnered with low cost of living expenses and "a ton of resources" make UF an exceptionally good investment. The same expectations of curriculum and academic achievement are in place for all programs whether you attend full time or part time, and this "level of integrity of the students is . . . a great strength."

The overall academic experience is "enriching and rigorous, yet manageable for a working professional," so "the only thing students have to worry . . . about is showing up and completing their assigned work." "Lunch is always taken care of . . . semester and this program runs as smooth as butter!" says a happy working student. The school administration is "very well-organized, with consistent communication and availability," and "all events and semester requirements are managed well in advance." Given the small class size, the administration, career services team, and professors are all able to give personal attention to each student. "This makes it easier for all students not only in the academic side, but also in the recruiting season when it is crucial to be well-prepared to land a job."

While the atmosphere is competitive, there is "still a great sense of teamwork and desire to increase our knowledge collectively." Concisely, the UF MBA has "a superior reputation in Florida regarding the quantitative and qualitative MBA coursework, rigorous standards, and excellent outlook for opportunities on graduation."

Career and Placement

The "extremely proactive" career resource office is "far and away the best aspect of UF MBA." "They have provided constant networking and career search opportunities in many different fields" and "put us in front of alumni and recruiters" at every corner using personal connections to set up meetings and interviews. "The amount of preparation they give us on interviewing, STAR stories, [and] case questions is above and beyond," says a student. Many here "have extensive work experience and are looking to leap forward in their careers," so students also frequently meet outside of class and look for opportunities to network. In addition, the school subsidizes a trip to a national MBA career fair for all its students, and the "outstanding case competition coaches" have led the team to consecutive championships in different intercollegiate competitions. Recent companies hiring UF grads include ExxonMobil, Johnson & Johnson, McKinsey & Company, Microsoft, and Wells Fargo.

Student Life and Environment

The "vibrant community" of Gainesville is a fantastic town to live in, "centrally located to both beach communities and to large cities." The facilities are "new and stunning," and students have access to all the resources of the large university (such as a sports complex, intramurals, several libraries, and the UF incubator). There are "official and unofficial social events pretty much every week," making for "a very friendly, community oriented atmosphere." This being Florida, game days are great events for bonding with "nearly everyone in town coming out to tailgate." Especially active are "a robust student government and student-run business," with student programming that is "high quality and frequent." With such accommodating options for programs, the business school comprises a "very diverse selection of students: international, doctors, lawyers, pharmacists, [and] bankers," in which "everyone in the program feels a sense of community and is willing to go out of their way to assist other students."

Admissions

The first step in the admissions process is to decide which of the many UF MBA programs is the right fit for you and your career goals. UF MBA has a streamlined online application process. You can only apply to one MBA program at a time; however, after reviewing an application, the admissions staff may recommend a student for another MBA program. Full-time applicants are automatically considered for scholarships when they apply, so no extra paperwork is needed. For traditional full-time students, the average GMAT score is about 670. In the executive, online, and professional programs, the average GMAT score for entering students is about 600. All UF MBA programs admit students on a rolling basis.

Prominent Alumni

Mr. Rob Cornella, CFO, The Coca-Cola Company, Germany, BSBA '93, MBA '95; Ms. Valerie Insignares, Senior Vice President, Chief Restaurant Operations Officer, Darden Restaurants, Inc., MBA 1999; Mr. William Muir, Jr., Executive Vice President, Chief Operating Officer, Jabil Circuit, Inc., BSISE '92, MBA '92

FINANCIAL FACTS

Annual tuition (in-state/ out-of-state)	$12,737/$30,130
Fees	$1,000
Cost of books	$1,950
Room & board	$11,900
% of students receiving aid	93
% of first-year students receiving aid	94
% of students receiving grants	88
Average award package	$22,960
Average grant	$13,593
Average loan	$24,656
Average student loan debt	$30,549

ADMISSIONS

Admissions Selectivity Rating	98
# of applications received	529
% applicants accepted	18
% acceptees attending	71
Average GMAT	663
Range of GMAT	640–700
Accepts GRE scores	No
Average GPA	3.4
TOEFL required of international students	Yes
Minimum TOEFL (paper/web)	600/80
Application fee	$30
International application fee	$30
Early application deadline	12/1
Regular application deadline	2/15
Deferment available	Yes
Maximum length of deferment	1 year
Transfer students accepted	No
Non-fall admissions	Yes
Need-blind admissions	Yes

EMPLOYMENT PROFILE

Career Rating	97	Grads Employed by Function	% Avg. Salary
Percent employed at graduation	85	Marketing	(20%) $112,760
Percent employed 3 months after graduation	96	Operations	(11%) $87,375
		Consulting	(13%) $106,000
Average base starting salary	$99,241	Management	(9%) $83,750
Primary Source of Full-time Job Acceptances		Finance	(36%) $99,000
School-facilitated activities	33 (73%)	HR	(4%) $0
Graduate-facilitated activities	12 (27%)	MIS	(2%) $0
		Other	(2%) $0

Top 5 Employers Hiring Grads
ExxonMobil (7), IBM (3), Ryder Systems (3), Microsoft (2), Cognizant Consulting (2)

UNIVERSITY OF GEORGIA
TERRY COLLEGE OF BUSINESS

GENERAL INFORMATION

Type of school	Public
Affiliation	No Affiliation
Academic calendar	Semester

SURVEY SAYS...
Classmates have diverse work experience, Friendly students, Good peer network, Good social scene, Conservative students, Helpful alumni, Happy students, Abundant clubs and activities
Solid preparation in:
Finance, Teamwork, Communication/ interpersonal skills

STUDENTS

Enrollment of parent institution	36,130
Enrollment of MBA Program	98
% male/female	72/28
% out-of-state	29
% part-time	0
% underrepresented minority	14
% international	38
Average age at entry	35
Average years work experience at entry	4

ACADEMICS

Academic Experience Rating	**94**
Profs interesting rating	91
Profs accessible rating	95
Student/faculty ratio	1:1
% female faculty	27
% underrepresented minority faculty	24
% part-time faculty	0

Joint Degrees
JD/MBA; MBA/MPH; LLM/MBA; MD/MBA

Prominent Alumni
Debbie Storey, EVP Mobility Customer Service, AT&T; Jay Ferro, Chief Information Officer, American Cancer Society; Wes Rogers, President & CEO, Landmark Properties

Academics

Located in beautiful Athens, Georgia, the Terry College of Business's "world class" MBA program offers a little bit of everything: a "strong alumni base," "phenomenal town, Southern charm, [low] cost of living, affordable tuition, and proximity to Atlanta." This "small program" allows for small class sizes and "provides better interaction with faculty" than many other MBA programs. That does not mean that there are not a "vast number of courses available to pick from." "I also liked its focus on leadership and the fact that Terry requires volunteer hours to graduate," one student says. There are "many scholarships and assistantships offered" for students who qualify. UGA is a merit "school that was focused on building well-rounded business leaders (plenty of field trips and business dinners)" Explaining their decision to attend, one student says: "As a career changer, I was drawn to the fact UGA has an extremely dedicated career services team, a strong alumni network, and a great reputation with companies."

Perhaps due to its small size, the Terry College of Business has a "very personable administrative staff" and "down-to-earth admissions." "The commitment of the administration to improve and partner with the students is phenomenal," and both the administration and faculty are "very accessible." The small size of the program "offers absolute accessibility to any class and professor." The "knowledgeable and passionate" professors "are leaders in their field." "They teach skills that will be extremely useful in a work setting, and they utilize real-world business cases to prepare us for management roles." As with anything, "you can work as little or as much as you want, but at the end of the day you get out of it what you put into it." "The doors always seem to be open" at UGA, and the professors "encourage you to reach out to them with questions outside of class."

Career and Placement

Placement for UGA students is helped by the fact "that all the professors have had extensive real business experience beyond academia" and that the "MBA Director and admissions staff are excellent." "The career center does everything in their power to help you land a job," although "our career management center staff could provide students with a more well-rounded and customized career search." There are some issues with placement, such as the "small number of companies that recruit on campus," but that is directly related to "the program's small size." The most recent graduating class found an average mean base salary of about $84,364. Nearly 75 percent earned placement in the Southern region of the United States.

Student Life and Environment

Students love Athens, declaring "this town is great!" "There is plenty to do" in town such as "live music, outdoor activities, intramural sports, good people, [and] great city events." In addition, this "great college town" is "nearby Atlanta." "We're close to a big city, yet far enough away to have a small town feel," one student explains.

The typical MBA student is "energetic, supportive, friendly, [and] ambitious," and students "have a diverse set of backgrounds and future ambitions." Although one student cautions that the student body is "not very diverse in the sense of ethnicity/race." The students here "have personalities as well as brains," although at times they can be "fiercely competitive." "My fellow students roll up their sleeves without hesitation but are still willing to kick back when the work is done," one student says. While "the workload is demanding" students still are "left with enough time to get to know each other, and the town, outside of the academic setting." "We have a focus on academic work during the week and enjoy our weekends, especially during football season," a Financial student states. Students "all have fun together" and develop a "strong identity" as proud Bulldogs.

Admissions

UGA's strong reputation and small size—52 students were enrolled last year—make it competitive to get into. The 2015 class had an average GPA of over 3.4 and an average GMAT of 643. The school looks most closely at applicants GPA, GRE or GMAT scores, work experience and interview. Because interpersonal skills are highly important to the program, a personal interview with admissions staff is mandatory prior to acceptance.

FINANCIAL FACTS

Annual tuition (in-state/ out-of-state)	$13,192/$31,510
Fees	$2,270
Cost of books	$1,650
Room & board (on/off-campus)	$11,300/$14,750
% of students receiving aid	97
% of first-year students receiving aid	98
% of students receiving grants	41
Average award package	$30,481
Average grant	$7,953
Average loan	$17,415
Average student loan debt	$22,284

ADMISSIONS

Admissions Selectivity Rating	92
# of applications received	329
% applicants accepted	31
% acceptees attending	51
Average GMAT	643
Range of GMAT	600–690
Accepts GRE scores	Yes
Average Verbal GRE	154
Range of Verbal GRE scores	149–158
Average Quantitative GRE	155
Range of Quantitative GRE scores	151–158
Average GPA	3.4
TOEFL required of international students	Yes
Minimum TOEFL (paper/web)	600/100
Application fee	$100
International application fee	$100
Application Deadline/Notification	
Round 1:	10/5 / 12/1
Round 2:	12/1 / 1/20
Round 3:	1/10 / 3/3
Round 4:	3/15 / 5/1
Deferment available	Yes
Maximum length of deferment	1 year; 2 years for 2+2 Program
Transfer students accepted	No
Non-fall admissions	No
Need-blind admissions	Yes

EMPLOYMENT PROFILE

Career Rating	91	**Grads Employed by Function**	**% Avg. Salary**
Percent employed at graduation	69	Marketing	(11%) $94,000
Percent employed 3 months		Operations	(4%)
after graduation	80	Consulting	(18%) $78,250
Average base starting salary	$84,364	Management	(14%) $82,667
Primary Source of Full-time Job Acceptances		Finance	(50%) $83,800
School-facilitated activities	18 (64%)	HR	(4%)
Graduate-facilitated activities	10 (36%)	**Top 5 Employers Hiring Grads**	

AT&T (5), Cox Enterprises (4), Delta Air Lines (2), The Home Depot (1), Coca-Cola (1)

University of Hartford
Barney School of Business

GENERAL INFORMATION
Type of school   Private
Affiliation   No Affiliation

SURVEY SAYS...
Happy students
Solid preparation in:
General management

STUDENTS
Enrollment of parent institution	6,992
Enrollment of MBA Program	386
% male/female	53/47
% out-of-state	17
% part-time	86
% underrepresented minority	7
% international	8
Average age at entry	31
Average years work experience at entry	7

ACADEMICS
Academic Experience Rating	88
Profs interesting rating	86
Profs accessible rating	89
Student/faculty ratio	10:1
% female faculty	31
% underrepresented minority faculty	18
% part-time faculty	13

Joint Degrees
E2M (MBA & ME Engineering) - (2 - 4 years MBA/MSAT (2 - 3 years)

Prominent Alumni
David Cordani, CEO, CIGNA Corporation; Patrick Tannock, President, XL Insurance Bermuda; Donald Allan, CFO, Stanley Black & Decker; Elizabeth Gagne, VP, Travelers; Joseph Zubretsky, President & CEO, Hanover Insurance; Mark Lieb, President & CEO Spectrum Asset Management

Academics

One student says of the decision to get an MBA from the University of Hartford: "I needed a place that saw my time as a two-way street." UH distinguishes itself in its "good reputation in insurance," "dual degree master's in mechanical engineering and MBA," and its location in the job-rich Northeast corridor. Its "small classes" make it "easy to get into the classes you want," while the program's format and schedule offers "flexibility and accommodation to students who work full time." The "Barney School of Business faculty are a group of highly respected individuals because of their teaching skills and business experience," as well as their "excellent comprehension of future trends" and their ability to "adapt to the needs of up and coming young professionals." "Most of the professors are outstanding, experienced and updated in recent changes, and motivated." The "administration is helpful and prompt," and "takes pride in the experience its students have during their matriculation here." UH students themselves are "experienced in their respective fields," as well as "intelligent and participative in discussions." "There is . . . a good mix of professional backgrounds in the student body itself, which lends itself to applying the lessons to the real world, no matter what industry is represented in the class." Overall, the learning "atmosphere is very good" and the "instructors have great experience." But don't expect UH academics to be easy: "Students do not get a free pass if they aren't up to the challenge."

Career and Placement

UH's location in Hartford puts it within a stone's throw of some very large and influential employers—United Technologies Corporation, The Hartford, Aetna, and more. "Cigna has a partnership with the University," and UH is considered "very credible especially in the Hartford area." As such, many local students choose UH because "their company is paying for it," but whether your employer can invest in your education or not, the UH "MBA program is affordable and has great recognition in the area." UH's faculty is another asset to students' job searches past graduation: "The professors—all PhDs—have the actualized knowledge because all of them do research work and are involved with practical projects in different companies of diverse industries." Both UH students and faculty comprise "a globe-representing swath of backgrounds, positions, and experiences." UH's MBA program may be especially attractive to undergraduate business students: "The University of Hartford allowed me to expedite my graduate studies by allowing me to waive certain core courses which I had shown skill in (the undergraduate equivalents). "

ADMISSIONS CONTACT: MANAGER, GRADUATE STUDENT SERVICES
ADDRESS: 200 BLOOMFIELD AVENUE, CENTER FOR GRADUATE & ADULT SERVICES, CC231 WEST
HARTFORD, CT 06117
PHONE: 860-768-4444 • FAX: 860-768-4821
E-MAIL: MBAINFO@HARTFORD.EDU • WEBSITE: BARNEY.HARTFORD.EDU

Student Life and Environment

The University of Hartford "seems very much like a commuter school" because its students are balancing many different things. UH MBAs "come from varied backgrounds and stages in life" to comprise "a diverse mix, representing the globe." The "casual, close-knit" student atmosphere fosters camaraderie between classmates who are "always willing to support" each other "academically and professionally." Many students are "middle aged, have family or familial responsibilities, in a full time job and looking to improve themselves," and others are "young professionals trying to improve themselves." Either way, UH's "flexible study schedule and relatively lower cost of tuition" is widely appealing to its students of all ages and stages. "Sports, arts and entertainment activities are available for different kinds of expectations. There are several restaurants on the campus and the grounds are green and maintained." Even though it's commuter-heavy, "life is social here," and there are "lots of good free lectures on campus" for students to enjoy.

Admissions

The University of Hartford is popular for its relatively flexible GMAT requirement: Students with prior business education and professionals with at least three years of work experience may apply and interview for a GMAT waiver, which the university says "may be granted in appropriate circumstances." UH undergrads, and business majors from other undergraduate programs, should read the fine print of UH's MBA course requirements to see if they qualify for any other waivers in required courses. All MBA applications must include an online application form, official transcripts, two letters of recommendation, a résumé, and a letter of intent, as well as, in most cases, GMAT results.

FINANCIAL FACTS

Annual tuition (in-state/ out-of-state)	$11,520/$11,520
Fees	$327
Cost of books	$800
% of students receiving aid	22
% of first-year students receiving aid	65
% of students receiving grants	9
Average award package	$15,555
Average grant	$5,423
Average loan	$16,165
Average student loan debt	$25,934

ADMISSIONS

Admissions Selectivity Rating	88
# of applications received	206
% applicants accepted	43
% acceptees attending	85
Average GMAT	535
Range of GMAT	490–720
Accepts GRE scores	Yes
Average GPA	3.3
TOEFL required of international students	Yes
Minimum TOEFL (web)	80
Application fee	$50
Deferment available	Yes
Maximum length of deferment	1 year
Transfer students accepted	Yes
Transfer application policy	Based on Individual Cases.
Non-fall admissions	Yes
Need-blind admissions	Yes

UNIVERSITY OF HOUSTON
C.T. BAUER COLLEGE OF BUSINESS

Academics

University of Houston's MBA program is perfect for "experienced professionals seeking a respected degree [yet unwilling to] break the bank." The program's curriculum affords students the "ability to customize [their] degree to [their] interests." A grateful student clarifies, "They have set up the Bauer MBA Program to be much more like an undergrad program where you have all sorts of choices on how you want to pursue your MBA." Of course, perhaps "the greatest strength of Bauer is [its] celebration of diversity." Another thrilled student explains, "Each student/professor/faculty member brings a unique perspective from their own personal experience[s] and Bauer capitalizes on it." Many are also quick to take advantage of the "great study abroad options [as well as] developmental organizations like the Red Lab, Cougar Venture club, Society for HR Management, etc."

Students here are generally quite pleased with their "knowledgeable" professors. And they truly value the fact that their professors have "lots of real world experience to share." Just as important, it's also quite evident that Bauer professors are wholly invested in their students. As one impressed future MBA interjects, "I've taken a statistics course where the professor offer[ed] study review sessions on Sundays to ensure students who need[ed] additional help [had] the access." Moreover, "professors routinely volunteer their time to host 'Bauer Boot Camps' on topics ranging from Excel mastery, introductory statistics, to understanding case methodology." And while some students gripe about the administration, calling them "indifferent," others assure us that "overall, the school is run very well."

Career and Placement

Students at Bauer greatly appreciate that "the school has a large alumni [network]," which they eagerly tap into when it comes time to job hunt. Moreover, they can also easily leverage the university's "strong connections with major oil and gas companies within Houston." And, perhaps most importantly, students have access to the "extraordinary" Rockwell Career Center. Indeed, Rockwell provides students with a range of indispensible services. The office organizes a number of workshops, career fairs and information sessions specifically tailored to MBAs. Bauer students are also granted access to the MBA Resume Book, a premier recruiting tool wherein students can market their talents and experience through an online resume book. And many MBA candidates benefit from On-Campus Recruiting (OCR), which helps connect students with potential employers.

Student Life and Environment

The MBA students at University of Houston are a busy lot. After all, many either "work part-time [or] are full-time [professionals]." Therefore, they appreciate the fact that Bauer makes "resources...readily available on weekends [and] late into the evening. This helps "to ensure that evening students have the same accommodations as the day time students." Fortunately, we're told that despite the workload "the social life is good." On the other hand, we are also cautioned that "it's up to you to mingle and make friends." Thankfully, that shouldn't prove too difficult. Indeed, "there's a lot of camaraderie" amongst these MBAs. That's certainly understandable given that Bauer students find their peers to be "encouraging and supportive." And they do manage to occasionally find time to kick back. For example, "many students attend the football and basketball games since [they] get free admission and discounted guest tickets." Additionally, as one might expect, "Saturdays in the fall [you can find] tailgating going on all over campus." Lastly, MBA students here rave about their location. As one satisfied student regales us, "Houston is a great place to be whether it is you want to walk in the park, music festivals, or going out to eat. Not to mention, [the city] is the energy capital of the world along with having one of the world's finest medical centers. Everything is very accessible."

Admissions

Admissions officers at Bauer take a fairly straightforward and traditional approach. Therefore, applicants should anticipate that their undergraduate transcript, GMAT scores, recommendations, resume and personal statement will all be thoroughly vetted. Candidates with GMAT scores and GPAs lower than the average admitted student will face an uphill battle. Finally, the earlier you submit an application, the better.

Prominent Alumni

Jack Moore, Chairman, President and CEO, Cameron International Corp.; Marvin Odum, President, Shell Oil Company; Karen Katz, President and CEO, Neiman Marcus Stores; David Callender, President, University of Texas Medical Branch; Elizabeth Killinger, Senior Vice President and Retail Regional President, Texas Reliant

FINANCIAL FACTS

Annual tuition (in-state/ out-of-state)	$22,650/$37,350
Fees	$954
Room & board (on/off-campus)	$13,569/
% of students receiving aid	77
% of first-year students receiving aid	71
% of students receiving grants	70
Average award package	$21,546
Average grant	$9,119
Average loan	$24,993

ADMISSIONS

Admissions Selectivity Rating	88
# of applications received	383
% applicants accepted	47
% acceptees attending	72
Average GMAT	609
Range of GMAT	570–640
Accepts GRE scores	Yes
Average Verbal GRE	156
Range of Verbal GRE scores	153–158
Average Quantitative GRE	154
Range of Quantitative GRE scores	150–156
Average Writing GRE	3.8
Range of Writing GRE scores	3.5–4.0
Average GPA	3.4
TOEFL required of international students	Yes
Minimum TOEFL (paper/web)	603/100
Application fee	$75
International application fee	$150
Regular application deadline	6/1
Deferment available	Yes
Maximum length of deferment	1 year
Transfer students accepted	No
Non-fall admissions	Yes
Need-blind admissions	Yes

EMPLOYMENT PROFILE

Career Rating	90	Grads Employed by Function	% Avg. Salary
Percent employed at graduation	44	Marketing	(8%)
Percent employed 3 months after graduation	75	Operations	(17%) $71,100
		Consulting	(8%)
Average base starting salary	$67,800	Management	(4%)
Primary Source of Full-time Job Acceptances		Finance	(33%) $66,150
School-facilitated activities	16 (67%)	HR	(17%) $70,000
Graduate-facilitated activities	8 (33%)	MIS	(8%)
		Other	(4%)

Top 5 Employers Hiring Grads
ExxonMobil (1), Schlumberger (1), Calpine Corporation (1), Apache (1), Stout Risius Ross (1)

University of Houston—Victoria

School of Business Administration

GENERAL INFORMATION

Type of school	Public
Affiliation	No Affiliation
Academic calendar	Academic

SURVEY SAYS...

Cutting-edge classes
Solid preparation in:
General management, Doing business in a global economy

STUDENTS

Enrollment of parent institution	4,569
Enrollment of MBA Program	1,139
% male/female	52/48
% out-of-state	5
% part-time	76
% underrepresented minority	75
% international	18
Average age at entry	35

ACADEMICS

Academic Experience Rating	**57**
Profs interesting rating	64
Profs accessible rating	87
% female faculty	31
% underrepresented minority faculty	91
% part-time faculty	

Academics

The University of Houston—Victoria (UHV) School of Business Administration "has excellent accreditations and is also one of the most cost effective schools available." The "high-quality programs are convenient and affordable." UHV offers many different ways for students to earn their degree. One may enroll full-time or part-time, choose on-line courses or a traditional classroom setting, or a combination of both. With so many options and so much flexibility, many can take advantage of the opportunity to earn a graduate business degree. Students can choose from the Strategic MBA, which can be completed full-time in sixteen months or part-time over the course of three years; the Global MBA, which can be completed full-time in eleven to twenty-one months and provides a specialized curriculum for students interested in international business; or the MS-Economic Development/Entrepreneurship, which takes nearly twenty-four months to complete on a part-time schedule. There is also a program designed especially for international students: the Fourth Year Bridge (Strategic or Global) MBA.

According to current students, "The education is great, challenging, and affordable," and the school's excellent reputation is well deserved. The professors at UHV are an excellent resource and are "very helpful, professional, [courteous], caring, fair, and highly knowledgeable in their areas of study." They understand what a suitable workload is for graduate students who most likely work full-time and may have a family besides. "While they show mercy they do push us to become the best that they can train us to be." Diversity exists both in the student body as well as in the faculty. This variety of experiences that come from a global classroom enriches all of the courses, especially those conducted in a classroom setting. "The professors are experts in their fields, and encourage real-world, practical applications of the concepts discussed in class." Students attest that "the quality of the curriculum is very high" and courses do a great job at staying relevant so that they "relate to current events around us."

The University of Houston—Victoria has auxiliary facilities at Sugar Land and Cinco Ranch. Courses at these locations, as well as at Victoria, include comprehensive coursework in economics, management, finance, marketing, and leadership. One student describes the courses as "very challenging," yet feels that "the academic experience is priceless." Administration at each facility is "helpful," and they "care about ensuring a quality educational experience for the students."

Career and Placement

Career services here are not so predominant as at other graduate schools. Rather than students hoping to land a new job after graduation, many are just looking for a "career boost," such as a promotion, to propel them upward at the job they already have. "Most students are currently employed in the professional field, and are married with children. They see the MBA program as a chance to improve their careers." Others, like this student comment, "It was suggested that I attend UH-Victoria by my manager."

ADMISSIONS CONTACT: TRUDY WORTHAM
ADDRESS: OFFICE OF ADMISSIONS/RECORDS, 3007 N BEN WILSON ST VICTORIA, TX 77901
PHONE: 361-570-4848 • FAX: 361-580-5500
E-MAIL: ADMISSIONSANDREGISTRATION@UHV.EDU • WEBSITE: WWW.UHV.EDU

Although the school provides the "best courses and professors," they tend to provide "[fewer] opportunities for graduate students in the job market." One student notes that the University provides fewer internship opportunities to graduate students than expected. Help is available for those who are looking for a new career, and "the campus always has career fairs and resume workshops." In addition, "the school sends out many emails with job, internship, and special training opportunities." However, students who are working full-time may find it hard to attend these events. An alumni network might better serve these students who could network on their own schedules. Regardless of what the career center provides to graduate students, students profess that just being a part of the program promotes continuous "opportunities to network and build professional relationships."

Student Life and Environment

Student life varies greatly, depending on where, when, and how classes are taken. Since taking classes online "doesn't leave much interaction," these students will miss some of the diversity and bonding experiences traditional classroom-learners experience. Fellow students are described as "very diverse," with a "wide variety of ages, experience levels, and backgrounds." They are also noted as being "very creative," and they do their best to "support each other in achieving goals."

UHV students are proud of their school. They take classes seriously and expect a high degree of professionalism from not only their professors and administration but from their fellow students as well. Therefore, it is not surprising that they are not only "friendly" but "great to work with." The busy life of most students allows for some activities outside of class but not many. Most commuters simply "attend class and get back home." Others are able to find time to "arrive early to talk and [to review] questions on class and mingle."

The Houston area is very conducive to jobs in the energy industry. Here, students are surrounded by multinational global energy companies so "the location is perfect."

Admissions

Students enroll at the University of Houston—Victoria School of Business Administration from a wide range of ages, with the average age being thirty-five. GMAT scores and undergraduate GPAs are required and hold the most weight in the admissions office. Letters of recommendation, essays, extracurricular activities, and work experience are not considered for enrollment.

ADMISSIONS	
Admissions Selectivity Rating	63
# of applications received	196
% applicants accepted	99
% acceptees attending	85
Accepts GRE scores	Yes
TOEFL required of international students	Yes
Minimum TOEFL (paper/web)	550/79
Application fee	$0
International application fee	$0
Deferment available	Yes
Maximum length of deferment	1 year
Transfer students accepted	Yes
Transfer application policy Graduate business students may transfer up to 6 hours of graduate-level business coursework from an AACSB-accredited program with the approval of the Assistant Dean.	
Non-fall admissions	Yes
Need-blind admissions	Yes

UNIVERSITY OF ILLINOIS AT CHICAGO
LIAUTAUD GRADUATE SCHOOL OF BUSINESS

Academics

The Liautaud Graduate School of Business offers students an unbeatable combination of academic rigor and affordability. The school's "flexibility" is another huge deciding factor for many students. A second-year quickly explains, "I started off part-time while working full-time. I then switched to working part-time and going to school full-time. The program allows for students to make course load adjustments as necessary." Academically, Liautaud excels in "finance and management information systems." And students love the fact that the program offers some "unique electives [such as] Negotiations [and] Business Analytics." Additionally, Liautaud provides "great opportunities for real life entrepreneurship and venture experiences." For example, the "Interdisciplinary Product Development course [allows] student teams from Business, Design and Engineering work to solve a real-world problem for a sponsoring firm." In general, "course offerings are in line with hot sectors that are in demand by both students and employers."

MBA candidates here report that the vast majority of professors are "smart, experienced . . . interesting and know their business." And while they certainly "don't take it easy on anyone," it's evident that they "genuinely want students to learn and succeed." To that end, UIC professors "are all highly communicative and have an open door policy that they actually enforce, enabling students to see them whenever there is academic difficulty." The same goes for the "nice" administration which is "very easy to contact" and seemingly "well organized."

Career and Placement

When it comes to the job hunt, there's no denying that UIC's "proximity to downtown Chicago" is a huge asset. Indeed, the city is overflowing with opportunity and students can capitalize on "local name recognition." Thankfully, the university is also full of "great connections." And the "career center is very active in getting students prepared for finding jobs." In fact, over the last academic year, more than 500 employers have visited UIC in their recruitment efforts. Beyond simply courting these organizations, career services works diligently to guarantee students will be prepared to knock their interviews out of the proverbial park. To that the end, the MBAs can take advantage of a variety of workshops featuring everything from mock interviews to resume writing.

Student Life and Environment

You can rest assured that UIC MBAs come "from multiple industries and all walks of life." Moreover, they "seek the greater good for those in the program and actively contribute to helping each other with potential job opportunities and homework." Indeed, there's "a real atmosphere of team work and 'having each others' backs'." And, overall, the majority of students here can be described as "extremely hard working, kind, funny, interesting and intelligent."

Not surprisingly, life at UIC is dictated by whether or not you attend the MBA program as a full-time or part-time student. Part-time MBAs are usually only campus for classes. However, full-time students reveal that there are "many different opportunities to interact with others through clubs, intramurals, and events." More specifically, "MBAA has monthly social events (they took over the planetarium, visit breweries, end of semester pizza parties, sporting events, etc.), but they also bring in top-notch companies for mentoring, advice, and the inside scoop on how they succeed." Finally, when students need to completely escape school life, they can explore all of the cultural and social opportunities Chicago offers.

Admissions

All applicants to the MBA program at the Liautaud Graduate School of Business must submit an online application, an application fee, two copies of official transcripts for all post-secondary academic work, two letters of recommendation, a personal statement, resume, and official GMAT or GRE score. Students who are non-native speakers of English must also submit a TOEFL score. A minimum of a B average is required in at least the last sixty hours of undergraduate course work (though provisional acceptance may be extended to promising applicants who fail to meet this benchmark). For the best results, applicants' GMAT scores should be at or above the average GMAT scores of the incoming class. The school also places emphasis on professional work experience. After submitting their materials for review, qualified applicants will be invited to interview with the admissions committee.

Prominent Alumni

Axel Strotbek, CFO, Audi AG; Terry Pfab, CIO, McKesson Medical Surgical; Ric Estrada, President & CEO, Metropolitan Family Services; Mary Szela, CEO, Melinta Therapeutics

FINANCIAL FACTS

Annual tuition (in-state/ out-of-state)	$19,954/$31,952
Fees	$4,004
Cost of books	$1,499
Room & board (on/off-campus)	$12,970/
Average loan	

ADMISSIONS

Admissions Selectivity Rating	93
# of applications received	237
% applicants accepted	30
% acceptees attending	97
Average GMAT	575
Range of GMAT	530–630
Accepts GRE scores	Yes
Average Verbal GRE	152
Range of Verbal GRE scores	140–163
Average Quantitative GRE	152
Range of Quantitative GRE scores	148–156
Average Writing GRE	3.9
Average GPA	3.2
TOEFL required of international students	Yes
Minimum TOEFL (paper/web)	570/80
Application fee	$60
International application fee	$60
Regular application deadline	6/15
Deferment available	Yes
Maximum length of deferment	One year
Transfer students accepted	Yes
Transfer application policy	

Applicants need to apply and be accepted to the Liautaud MBA Program. They can submit transcripts for previous coursework with a grade of B or better and a course description. The classes must be from an AACSB accredited institution. Maximum of 12 semester hours may transfer.

Non-fall admissions	Yes
Need-blind admissions	Yes

EMPLOYMENT PROFILE

Career Rating	91	Grads Employed by Function	%	Avg. Salary
Percent employed at graduation	15	Marketing	(33%)	$56,875
Percent employed 3 months after graduation	81	Operations	(10%)	
		Consulting	(33%)	$86,357
Average base starting salary	$74,941	Management	(5%)	
Primary Source of Full-time Job Acceptances		Finance	(14%)	
School-facilitated activities	(43%)	HR	(0%)	
Graduate-facilitated activities	(52%)	Other	(5%)	
Unknown	(5%)	**Top 5 Employers Hiring Grads**		

Huron Consulting (1), Infosys (1), Advisory Board Company (1), Epic Systems Corporation (1), Forsyth Solutions (1)

UNIVERSITY OF ILLINOIS AT URBANA-CHAMPAIGN
COLLEGE OF BUSINESS

GENERAL INFORMATION

Type of school	Public
Affiliation	No Affiliation
Academic calendar	Semester

SURVEY SAYS...

Classmates have diverse work experience, Friendly students, Good social scene, Happy students, Abundant clubs and activities
Solid preparation in:
Marketing, Finance, General management, Teamwork, Presentation skills, Quantitative skills, Doing business in a global economy

STUDENTS

Enrollment of parent institution	44,550
Enrollment of MBA Program	326
% male/female	74/26
% out-of-state	71
% part-time	51
% underrepresented minority	6
% international	43
Average age at entry	26
Average years work experience at entry	5

ACADEMICS

Academic Experience Rating	95
Profs interesting rating	92
Profs accessible rating	96
Student/faculty ratio	38:1
% female faculty	16
% underrepresented minority faculty	5
% part-time faculty	11

Joint Degrees

MBA/MA Architecture; MBA/MS Electrical & Computer Engineering; MBA/MS Civil and Environmental Engineering; MBA/MS Electrical Engineering; MBA/MS Industrial Engineering; MBA/MS Mechanical Engineering; MBA/MD Medicine; MBA/MS Journalism; MBA/JD Law; MBA/MS Human Resource Education; MBA/ILIR; MBA/MS Materials Science & Engineering.

Academics

The low in-state tuition and access to the resources of a large university have made the University of Illinois at Urbana-Champaign's MBA program a popular one. That means getting into popular courses can be difficult, especially highly desired electives seen as "much more interesting" than the sometimes "very elementary" basic business courses. These electives, which have "excellent professors and course material," is where UI shines. Students at UI are encouraged to tailor their MBA to their own career goals. In year two, students take sixteen credits of electives and sixteen credits towards a concentration in fields like marketing, finance, information technology, or general management. The "relentless coursework" —one student referred to it as "a proving ground" —is balanced by a "terrific staff" who "care about students doing well and make themselves available to everyone for additional support."

Developing not only your skills but also your ability to use those skills after school is a priority for many professors here. "Overall, the professors here take an interest in students beyond class work and will offer their support in a career search and personal learning and growth." Indeed, "the school provides ample opportunities for students to get as involved as they'd like. There are several out of the classroom opportunities to gain experience (case competitions, leadership roles, work experience, consulting)." That experience is not limited to working with business leaders in the region, either. "The international opportunities here for MBAs are outstanding. Every student is given the opportunity to do at least one global consulting project that includes travel to a foreign country. Some students are able to travel to two or more countries related to their studies."

Though professors here are almost universally praised, the administration "has a lot of room for improvement," especially with regard to "inefficient" communication with students—though others note that the administration is clearly "concerned about student needs." Overall, "in addition to peerless international immersion opportunities, the University of Illinois provides a close-knit, family-like atmosphere that is simply not matched by any other MBA program, public or private."

Career and Placement

The University of Illinois proves to be a draw in part because "it provides international opportunities that far exceed any other program" in the same price range. One student notes the school "gave me the chance to travel to five emerging economies and apply my media and consulting skill set to diverse clientele." Responding to student suggestions that the school improve its corporate ties in big cities, the MBA Career Services Organization has become part of a new college wide Business Career Services Organization aimed at increasing visibility for MBA students to companies that recruit at the college.

Prospects for graduates tend to be good. The media base salary for graduates of the Illinois MBA program is close to $90,000 annually, ranging from about $60,000 on the low end to $160,000 on the high end. General management and finance fields draw the highest number of graduates, about half of them taking jobs in the Midwest. The top hiring companies included AT&T, Cisco Systems, Ernst & Young, ExxonMobil, Hewitt Associates, LG, Peabody Energy, Procter & Gamble, Robert Bosch Corporation, and Sears Holdings Corporation.

Student Life and Environment

With peers who tend to be "young professionals who generally are more likely to spend a night in studying class material than go out socially or network," and who represent a diverse range of places, ages and experiences—some 40 percent come from overseas—it may be surprising that students here are "are easy to engage, very involved and supportive in each others' learning." There is a high level of competition to do well, but students are not overly competitive with one another. "Students are more concerned about seeing success in everyone than putting others down so they can rise to the top." One student noted, "I was pleasantly surprised that everyone has been really collaborative and not cut throat. Everyone wants to see one another succeed."

Students here stay busy. If not immersed in studies, they are involved with extracurricular activities, networking, or simply enjoying what this college town has to offer. "It's been a great place to try new things, meet new people, and figure out what my strengths are." It's easy to find the time to wind down from the grind if you're so inclined, such as on "Thursday nights for Mug Club, when the class goes out to a different bar every week and celebrates the survival of another seven days." Clubs and students organizations are numerous. "I feel that Illinois strongly encourages students to take on new challenges," one student notes, "and I've gained a lot from this."

Admissions

Though recent classes had median GMAT score of 650, with an 80 percent range between 620 and 700, there are no minimum GMAT scores required for entry to the program. However, at least two years of work experience are strongly recommended. Most admitted to the program have more; the average student had about four years of professional experience prior to acceptance. You can learn more about the Illinois MBA by chatting online with one of the school's admissions officers, or attending an admissions event in your area.

Prominent Alumni

Mike Tokarz, Chairman, The Tokarz Group; Tom Siebel, Founder, Chairman & CEO, Siebel Systems, Inc.

FINANCIAL FACTS

Annual tuition (in-state/ out-of-state)	$21,974/$32,974
Fees	$3,736
Cost of books	$2,429
Room & board (on/off-campus)	$14,193/$14,193
% of students receiving aid	82
% of first-year students receiving aid	83
Average grant	$10,621

ADMISSIONS

Admissions Selectivity Rating	96
# of applications received	670
% applicants accepted	23
% acceptees attending	52
Average GMAT	659
Range of GMAT	620–700
Accepts GRE scores	Yes
Average Verbal GRE	156
Range of Verbal GRE scores	152–163
Average Quantitative GRE	157
Range of Quantitative GRE scores	153–160
Average GPA	3.3
TOEFL required of international students	Yes
Minimum TOEFL (paper/web)	/79
Application fee	$70
International application fee	$90
Early application deadline	10/5
Application Deadline/Notification	
Round 1:	12/15
Round 2:	1/18
Round 3:	3/15
Round 4:	5/24
Deferment available	Yes
Maximum length of deferment	1 year
Transfer students accepted	No
Non-fall admissions	No
Need-blind admissions	Yes

EMPLOYMENT PROFILE

Career Rating	91	Grads Employed by Function	% Avg. Salary
Percent employed at graduation	65	Marketing	(12%) $85,400
Percent employed 3 months after graduation	78	Operations	(5%) $77,667
		Consulting	(22%) $95,750
Average base starting salary	$89,563	Management	(27%) $88,111
Primary Source of Full-time Job Acceptances		Finance	(13%) $85,904
School-facilitated activities	(31%)	HR	(12%) $85,500
Graduate-facilitated activities	(41%)	MIS	(5%) $104,667
Unknown	(28%)	**Top 5 Employers Hiring Grads**	

Top 5 Employers Hiring Grads
PricewaterhouseCoopers (4), Infosys (2), Deloitte Consulting (2), Accenture (2), James Hardie Building Products (2)

THE UNIVERSITY OF IOWA
HENRY B. TIPPIE SCHOOL OF MANAGEMENT

GENERAL INFORMATION
Type of school   Public
Affiliation   No Affiliation
Academic calendar   Semester

SURVEY SAYS...
Friendly students, Happy students,
Students love Iowa City, IA
Solid preparation in:
Finance, General management,
Teamwork, Presentation skills,
Quantitative skills

ACADEMICS
Academic Experience Rating   92
Profs interesting rating   90
Profs accessible rating   96
Student/faculty ratio   10:1
% female faculty   16
% underrepresented
  minority faculty   17
% part-time faculty   34

Joint Degrees
Joint-degree MBA programs
with Law, 4 years; Hospital and
Health Administration, 2.5-3 years;
Medicine, 5 years; Pharmacy, 5
years

Prominent Alumni
Christopher Klein, CEO, Fortune
Brands; Laura Desmond, CEO,
Starcom MediaVest; Jodi Taylor,
CFO, The Container Store; Steve
LaCroix, Executive VP and Chief
Marketing Officer, Minnesota
Vikings; Sheri Salata, President,
OWN

Academics

While some students extol the "wonderful experiential learning," and the "breadth of courses unmatched by most other institutions" that are offered at the Henry B. Tippie School of Management at The University of Iowa, others praise its "small class sizes along with the unique Academy structure." The Academy structure requires students to select "one of three academies based on their interests: Finance, Marketing, [or] Business Analytics." In 2009 the school revamped its curriculum from "two sixteen-week semesters to four eight-week modules. This allows students to take fewer classes at one time and focus all attention on the subject matter at hand."

Students generally laud the school's "high return on investment" and feel that "the greatest strengths of the University of Iowa are the [number] of opportunities that are available in academics, athletics, government, and volunteer work." They also highlight that "the association with the John Pappajohn Entrepreneurial Center is an outstanding resource whether you want to start or improve a business." The Entrepreneurial Center, in particular, is "a hidden gem" that "offers many business competition events throughout the year that provide funding for startups, access to successful entrepreneurs and business mentorship." Students also boast that "the school's Henry Fund"—a $3.1 million student managed investment fund—"has received the top honors for performance the past five years as well."

Classes at Tippie provide a "comfortable environment" where there is a "good mix of readings, lectures, simulations, and real-world applications" that helps to nurture "thought and healthy conversation." The small size of the program creates "opportunity for involvement, interviews, and faculty interactions" and "more personalized attention."

The students are also impressed by their "outstanding" and "top-notch" professors who are often "national experts [in] their subject area." These "approachable" professors "do a very good job getting to know the students and build a personal relationship with most." The school's administration also received kudos from the students who observe that "the administration and professors meet frequently to incorporate ideas that they have gained from other schools, their own insight, and feedback from students."

Career and Placement

Tippie students reveal, "We can do a little better with career services. As such, it is good but we have faced some challenges during the economic downturn." Another student says they feel "disappointed with the efforts given by the University of Iowa for career guidance." While this voice represents a concern amongst students, the University of Iowa did achieve a 98 percent placement rate in 2015. Other students offer a more positive view of the Career Services Office, saying that they "motivate you and they also are as demanding as our professors in doing things like mock interviews, networking events etc. Also there is a leadership course that offers help to prepare one to present in professional and personal setting[s]."

Although they long for "more geographically diverse recruiters" and feel that there needs to be more effort put into "attracting more companies to visit on campus," Tippie students have noticed some recent improvement in recruiting on campus. "During the past year we have begun attracting high-tech firms and investment banks due to the efforts of career services and alumni. We have recently had Amazon recruit on campus...and are seeking to expand Goldman-Sachs undergraduate recruitment to include MBAs. We are also seeing many mid-market investment banks and private equity groups recruit on campus."

ADMISSIONS CONTACT: DAVID DEYAK, ASSISTANT DEAN, MBA FULL-TIME PROGRAM
ADDRESS: C432 POMERANTZ CENTER, TIPPIE SCHOOL OF MANAGEMENT, THE UNIVERSITY OF IOWA
IOWA CITY, IA 52242-1000
PHONE: 319-335-1039 • FAX: 319-335-3604
E-MAIL: TIPPIEMBA@UIOWA.EDU • WEBSITE: TIPPIE.UIOWA.EDU/FULLTIMEMBA

Student Life and Environment

Students are enthusiastic in their praise of Iowa City's "vibrant atmosphere which helps you both learn and relax." The city's "night-life is great and there are also a lot of hole-in-the-wall restaurants that provide a lot of diversity in dining." Iowa City also "has easy access to Chicago, Minneapolis, St. Louis, and Kansas City, and is 20 minutes from the airport for longer journeys."

Students count their school's "friendly atmosphere from admissions to faculty and students" as one of its strengths. When not immersed in their studies, students can participate in "lots of social activities as well as many school-related activities" including "company presentations and speaker sessions every fortnight." One student gushes, "The guest speakers are phenomenal—John Rice [Vice Chairman of General Electric], Fred Whyte [President of Stihl] and Clay Jones [CEO of Rockwell Collins]—are just a snapshot of the leaders that spoke at our school while I was a student." For the more athletically-inclined students, "the football atmosphere is awesome and something that should be experienced."

The school's "small community of students" is self-described as "classic Midwest[ern] people—hardworking, fairly narrow life experience, super friendly, outcome-oriented, family people." "There is a strong moral compass, and you do not have to be worried about being stabbed in the back by a fellow student for an A." These "very friendly, welcoming, and supportive" students who are "top-of-the-line performers" include "motorbike racers, go-cart racers, triathlon/marathon runners, musicians, math geeks, entrepreneurs, ex-military men, etc."

Admissions

Applicants to Tippie's MBA programs must submit an online application, official transcripts of post-secondary work, essays, a professional resume, contact information for three references, an official GMAT or GRE score report, an admissions interview, and a TOEFL or IELTS score for international students. The school also strongly encourages applicants "to have a minimum of two years full-time, post-baccalaureate work experience."

FINANCIAL FACTS

Annual tuition (in-state/ out-of-state)	$19,936/$36,580
Fees	$1,645
Cost of books	$1,240
Room & board (on/off-campus)	$15,010/$15,010
% of students receiving aid	92
% of first-year students receiving aid	91
% of students receiving grants	75
Average award package	$41,716
Average grant	$17,953
Average loan	$21,621
Average student loan debt	$46,523

ADMISSIONS

Admissions Selectivity Rating 89

EMPLOYMENT PROFILE

Career Rating	95	Grads Employed by Function% Avg. Salary	
Percent employed at graduation	79	Marketing	(18%) $78,421
Percent employed 3 months after graduation	98	Operations	(5%)
		Consulting	(31%) $101,800
Average base starting salary	$94,088	Management	(5%)
Primary Source of Full-time Job Acceptances		Finance	(28%) $91,355
School-facilitated activities	28 (60%)	MIS	(3%)
Graduate-facilitated activities	19 (40%)	Other	(10%) $97,250

Top 5 Employers Hiring Grads
Booz Allen Hamilton (3), Amazon.com (2), CVS Caremark (2), Ford Motor Company (2), Capital One (1)

UNIVERSITY OF KANSAS
SCHOOL OF BUSINESS

GENERAL INFORMATION

Type of school	Public
Affiliation	No Affiliation
Academic calendar	Semester

SURVEY SAYS...
Happy students, Students love
Lawrence, KS
Solid preparation in:
General management, Doing busi-
ness in a global economy

STUDENTS

Enrollment of parent institution	27,983
Enrollment of MBA Program	220
% male/female	81/19
% part-time	75
% international	22
Average age at entry	29
Average years work experience at entry	35

ACADEMICS

Academic Experience Rating	**90**
Profs interesting rating	89
Profs accessible rating	93
Student/faculty ratio	14:1
% female faculty	24
% underrepresented minority faculty	17
% part-time faculty	45

Joint Degrees
MBA/JD; MBA/MA in Architecture;
MBA/Global Studies; MBA/
PharmD; MBA/Architecture; MBA
with concentration in Petroleum
Management

Prominent Alumni
Mark Heinrich (Retired RADM US
Navy), General Manager of Strategic
Sourcing and Supply Chain-
Microsoft; Dennis Depenbusch,
Director of New Ventures, Blue
Cross and Blue Shield of Kansas;
Blake Hawley, President & CEO at
Integrated Animal Health; Stanley
Lybarger, Retired CEO BOK Financial
Corporation; Cliff Illig, CEO &
Founder of Cerner Corporation

Academics

Students at the University of Kansas' School of Business describe their institution as "the best business school in the Midwest," and they have good reason to be so complimentary. "Positive, up-tempo, friendly, and lots of work," the Kansas program is "vastly under-rated" and a "truly wonderful" grad school experience. The students characterize the professors as "second to none" and are impressed with their academic and professional backgrounds." KU profs, who are "active in the business world within their fields," exhibit "a great blend of teaching skills and real-world experience."

Students are held to a high standard and are "expected to be well-prepared, well-read, and well-spoken in course discussions." The "fantastic" administration receives high praise as well. One MBA candidate reported that "if you want to try something different or want to attend a conference, they support you 100 percent of the time." Students also mention the administration's constant efforts "to improve facilities, encourage student involvement and input, and expand the faculty and curriculum."

On top of the full-time MBA offered at KU, the school also offers a Working Professional MBA, a Master's in Accounting, Master's in Finance, and several dual-degree MBAs, including a JD/MBA, MBA/MIM, MBA-PharmD, MBA/PM (petroleum management). KU also has an extensive PhD program in which students can concentrate in account-ing, information systems, finance, marketing, decision sciences, and management. KU's "focus on the global business environment" is a huge draw for many applicants, who feel that the school provides "an exceptional international business program for being in the middle of the United States and far from the coasts." Reasonable fees also are a major plus, and many students feel they're receiving a great deal of value for their money.

As one might expect from a school that focuses a great deal on international business, KU has an international program that allows students to obtain real-world experience in the global marketplace. The KU School of Business partners with the Center for International Business Education and Research to facilitate study abroad with an array of businesses across the globe. In the past few years students have traveled to India, China, Germany, France, Brazil, and Mexico as part of the program. With these types of experiences avail-able to students, it's no wonder they describe the KU program as a "good value for the money that offered many options in terms of international experience."

Career and Placement

On its website the school boasts that "KU Business alumni are chief officers and senior executives of dozens of *Fortune* 500 companies." Fortunately for KU students who aspire to such heights, Kansas City is home to many large corporations, including Sprint and Hallmark, and the metropolitan area has been named one of the "Top 20 Areas to Start and Grow a Company" by Inc.com. KU also has a second campus (Edwards Campus) located in nearby Overland Park, which was named one of the top ten cities for doing business by Business Development Outlook.

Students give glowing reviews to the school's Career Services Department, which does a "fantastic job of preparing students for the job-search process and facilitating that process through two massive career fairs, many interview and resume workshops, one-on-one counseling, and more." One student says, "I already have a job waiting for me when I complete the master's program, thanks to the business school's Career Services, and KU's strong reputation in the region."

ADMISSIONS CONTACT: DEE STEINLE, ADMINISTRATIVE DIRECTOR OF MASTERS PROGRAMS
ADDRESS: 206 SUMMERFIELD HALL, 1300 SUNNYSIDE AVENUE, LAWRENCE, KS 66045
PHONE: 785-864-7556
E-MAIL: MBA@KU.EDU • WEBSITE: WWW.BUSINESS.KU.EDU

Approximately 66 percent of Kansas students accepted job offers before graduating in a recent academic year, and by three months after graduation, that number had grown to 100 percent. The average salary for graduates was $58,000 (not including bonus). The majority of students accepted jobs in marketing and finance, although there were quite a few who went into operations and consulting. A range of companies recruit on campus, and the ones who hire graduates most frequently include Tradebot, MarketSphere, United Missouri Bank, and Sprint Nextel.

Student Life and Environment

KU students enjoy life on campus, which many describe as "great." The only complaint is that "there are really more things that I'd like to be able to participate in than I have time to do!" One student described life at KU as "filled with a variety of activities, including extracurriculars (Net Impact, [MBA Association]), social events put on by MBA student organizations, working for the MBA Admissions Office, and of course, course work."

Although the majority of the class is "ambitious and concentrated on their future," students are also "very fun people." There is diversity among the MBA candidates, and the students "vary from people straight out of undergrad to people thirty-five years old, and they all have different goals and lifestyles, but they communicate well and make the classes enjoyable by opening up discussion without judging others." Some say their classmates "are the very best part about my experience in the KU MBA program." Overall, students are more than satisfied with their experiences at KU. As one student said, "I cannot thank KU enough for preparing me to excel in my future endeavors."

Admissions

Applications are accepted at anytime, up until posted application deadlines. In a recently admitted class, students' average undergraduate GPA was around 3.3, and the average GMAT was approximately 573. Students had an average of three years of work experience.

FINANCIAL FACTS

Annual tuition (in-state/ out-of-state)	$9,075/$21,225
Fees	$7,025
Cost of books	$2,000
Room & board	$14,000
% of students receiving aid	80
% of first-year students receiving aid	85
% of students receiving grants	30
Average grant	$10,000

ADMISSIONS

Admissions Selectivity Rating	88
# of applications received	76
% applicants accepted	97
% acceptees attending	8
Average GMAT	608
Range of GMAT	540–640
Accepts GRE scores	No
Average GPA	3.2
TOEFL required of international students	Yes
Minimum TOEFL (paper/web)	53/
Application fee	$65
International application fee	$85
Early application deadline	1/15
Regular application deadline	6/1
Deferment available	No
Transfer students accepted	No
Non-fall admissions	No
Need-blind admissions	Yes

EMPLOYMENT PROFILE

Career Rating	90	Grads Employed by Function	% Avg. Salary
Percent employed at graduation	58	Marketing	(16%)
Percent employed 3 months after graduation	877	Operations	(11%)
		Consulting	(11%)
Average base starting salary	$61,083	Management	(11%)
Primary Source of Full-time Job Acceptances		Finance	(16%)
School-facilitated activities	12 (46%)	Other	(11%)
Graduate-facilitated activities	13 (50%)	**Top 5 Employers Hiring Grads**	
Unknown	1 (4%)	Payless Shoe Source, Koch Industries, Hill's Pet Nutrition, Cerner, DST Systems	

UNIVERSITY OF KENTUCKY
GATTON COLLEGE OF BUSINESS AND ECONOMICS

Academics

The Gatton College of Business and Economics at the University of Kentucky offers both a part-time Professional Evening MBA designed for the needs of local professionals and a full-time One Year Accelerated MBA. Many students in our survey identified the accelerated pace of the full-time program as a major attraction. It's "a quick program that offers a more intense learning experience along with the opportunity to work with executives at some of the largest world corporations" through "Project Connect, a partnership between the university and industry to provide practical education via projects" with regional businesses.

Students in both programs appreciate that Gatton "is recognized [as] the best graduate business school in the state," which "is very helpful in getting a job." "Good professors" and the "relatively low" tuition is also appealing, of course. The Gatton curriculum "is broken into modules such as new product development, mergers and acquisitions, supply chain management, and financial analysis," and "all tools and skills (finance, accounting, ops) are taught around the basis of these modules." The program "stays on top of the latest trends and technologies in business," another plus. This "very structured" program requires "a lot of group work." "The whole program is team-based, which is going to be helpful in the future," one student writes.

The Professional Evening MBA emphasizes a foundation in economics, finance, marketing, management, accounting, and information systems. Cross-functional teams of five are created and work with companies on projects in each of the three areas of emphasis. This is complemented by professors who are generally "very good and have a fairly structured teaching style" and blend "theory and real-world experience." In recent years the school "has added many faculty with real-world experience and shaped the program and skill sets you learn around executives' requests for incoming employees. It is amazing how tailored this program is to real work experience." Part-timers appreciate how "the professors understand that their students are also working professionals and have other lives besides the classroom." As a result, "the course load has not been unbearable, but it keeps you busy."

Career and Placement

MBA students have access to comprehensive career services through Gatton College's Graham Office of Career Management, including a career development course, which is required for one-year students and optional for part-time students. They also host events such as a large, two-day career fair each semester, employer information sessions, and campus interviews. To help students prepare for these events, Career Management offers individualized coaching sessions on topics including: resume writing, job searching, networking, interviewing, salary negotiating, etiquette, and more.

Last year the average salary for a Gatton graduate was $56,980. Employers hiring Gatton MBAs include Aldi, Alltech, BB&T, Brown-Forman, Deloitte, Ernst & Young, Fifth Third, Humana, Lexmark, PricewaterhouseCoopers, Schneider Electric, Toyota, Wright-Patterson Air Force Base, CGI, GE, Target, Tempur-Sealy, Trane, UPS, 3M, Hitachi, Ashland, and LG&E.

ADMISSIONS CONTACT: BEVERLY KEMPER, MBA ACADEMIC COORDINATOR
ADDRESS: 145 GATTON COLLEGE OF BUSINESS AND ECONOMICS, LEXINGTON, KY 40506-0034
PHONE: 859-257-7722 • FAX: 859-323-9971
E-MAIL: KEMPER@UKY.EDU • WEBSITE: GATTON.UKY.EDU

Student Life and Environment

For full-time MBAs, "Life at UK is focused on school rather than extracurricular activities, largely because of the length and intensity of the program." Cramming two years' worth of learning into eleven months doesn't leave a lot of time for extracurriculars or socializing. Full-timers generally live in "nice...well-priced" housing located "relatively close" to campus, "which is nice considering we are all working with companies [on Project Connect projects] and we have to meet daily." The MBA group forms "a very strong community." On days we have class, nearly all students arrive forty-five minutes to an hour early to socialize and visit" in the "dedicated MBA lounge...Professors will stop by as well." When time permits, students enjoy getting out and about in Lexington, an "exciting" and "excellent city" with "plenty to do."

Gatton full-timers don't have "as much work experience as [students at] some schools," but they are "hard workers and add a certain competitive edge in the classroom which I feel improves the overall experience. Outside of class, many of us commonly get together to socialize and even discuss business-related topics/concerns that arise in our workplaces and in the economy." The part-time student body includes a substantial number of "engineer-schooled and extremely goal-oriented" professionals.

Admissions

Applicants to the Gatton MBA program must submit the following materials: official transcripts for all undergraduate study (minimum GPA of 2.75 on a 4.0 scale required); an official score report for either the GMAT or the GRE; three letters of recommendation from individuals who can objectively assess the applicant's character and capabilities; a current resume; and a completed application. International applicants who do not hold undergraduate degrees from a U.S. institution must also submit an official score report for the TOEFL or the TWE. Gatton admits MBAs to the One Year Accelerated option in the summer, while the Professional Evening option begins in the fall. Among those accepted to the most recent class, the average GMAT score was 617 and the average undergraduate GPA was 3.5.

FINANCIAL FACTS

Annual tuition (in-state/ out-of-state)	$12,070/$25,448
Fees	$10,662
Cost of books	$2,500
Room & board (on/off-campus)	$8,250/$9,100
% of students receiving aid	35
% of first-year students receiving aid	35
% of students receiving grants	35
Average award package	$18,985
Average grant	$18,985
Average loan	$0
Average student loan debt	$0

ADMISSIONS

Admissions Selectivity Rating	82
# of applications received	181
% applicants accepted	84
% acceptees attending	79
Average GMAT	617
Range of GMAT	590–670
Accepts GRE scores	Yes
Average Verbal GRE	155
Range of Verbal GRE scores	151–159
Average Quantitative GRE	160
Range of Quantitative GRE scores	150–159
Average GPA	3.5
TOEFL required of international students	Yes
Minimum TOEFL (paper/web)	550/
Application fee	$65
International application fee	$75
Early application deadline	4/1
Regular application deadline	5/11
Deferment available	Yes
Transfer students accepted	Yes
Transfer application policy File must be completed and applicant is considered as a regular applicant only for Evening program	
Non-fall admissions	Yes
Need-blind admissions	Yes

EMPLOYMENT PROFILE

Career Rating	87
Percent employed at graduation	48
Percent employed 3 months after graduation	71
Average base starting salary	$56,980
Primary Source of Full-time Job Acceptances	
School-facilitated activities	15 (38%)
Graduate-facilitated activities	16 (40%)
Unknown	9 (22%)

Grads Employed by Function% Avg. Salary		
Marketing	(30%)	$40,100
Operations	(19%)	$60,529
Consulting	(3%)	
Management	(14%)	$57,323
Finance	(8%)	$61,000
MIS	(11%)	$62,000
Other	(16%)	$55,717

Top 5 Employers Hiring Grads
Wright Patterson Air Force Base (3), Hitachi Automotive (2), LG&E KU (2), Humana (1), IBM (1)

UNIVERSITY OF LOUISIANA AT LAFAYETTE
B. I. MOODY III COLLEGE OF BUSINESS

GENERAL INFORMATION

Type of school	Public
Affiliation	No Affiliation
Academic calendar	Semester

SURVEY SAYS...

Friendly students, Conservative students, Happy students, Students love Lafayette, LA
Solid preparation in:
Marketing, General management, Teamwork, Communication/interpersonal skills, Presentation skills, Quantitative skills, Computer skills, Doing business in a global economy

STUDENTS

Enrollment of parent institution	19,033
Enrollment of MBA Program	196
% male/female	51/29
% out-of-state	1
% part-time	56
% underrepresented minority	15
% international	9
Average age at entry	25
Average years work experience at entry	4

ACADEMICS

Academic Experience Rating	85
Profs interesting rating	90
Profs accessible rating	94
Student/faculty ratio	3:1
% female faculty	42
% underrepresented minority faculty	13
% part-time faculty	10

Prominent Alumni

Phillip Burguieres, Oil and Gas/ VP Houston Texans Professional Football Team; Mike DeHart, Stuller Management Services, Inc.; John Breaux, Former U.S. Senator; Charles DeBellevue, Colonel, U.S. Air Force; Dr. Ross Judice, Former Acadian Ambulance and Air Med, EVP and CMO

Academics

University of Louisiana—Lafayette's strong regional reputation, convenient course schedule, and friendly staff make it a justifiably popular choice for ambitious local professionals. Although students may choose to take a full course load, this "MBA program caters to students who work full-time jobs" and attend classes in the evenings. According to the busy bees in the program, the "curriculum is challenging and relevant," consisting of core courses in advanced business fundamentals like accounting, management information systems, marketing, and finance, followed by two elective courses in a student's discipline of choice. In addition to the traditional program, the school operates a respected MBA in health care administration, which combines six specialized courses in that field with five core courses from the general MBA core.

Students are happy to report that the MBA at University of Louisiana—Lafayette is overseen by a team of "very knowledgeable" and "amazingly talented teachers." While "the faculty and staff have high expectations" for their students, they are always "willing to assist those who ask for help." Here, "professors are very approachable," and the "school is small enough for teachers to get to know all students." "Presentations and teamwork" are a fixture in almost every class, and the varying professional backgrounds of MBA candidates help to foster "rich, insightful classroom discussions and activities." One student agrees, "With a lot of hands-on group projects, MBA students learn a great deal from working with other students from different backgrounds." Likewise, the school's staff and administration "wants students to succeed and ensures all needs for MBA students are met." In terms of improvement, students would also love to see "more diverse classes" offered, with newer topics like social media incorporated into the instruction.

For exacting business students, one of the most attractive aspects of a University of Louisiana education is the great return on investment. As a public school, "the tuition is very low considering the quality of education and the many great facilities." Students also note that the program is on the up-and-up, having "gained national recognition/ honors in the last few years" and, under the vigilant leadership of the current administrators, constantly improving. Of particular note, the program director and the administrative assistant who oversee the program receive top marks from students. A current MBA declares, "Dr. Viguerie, and Mrs. Jan are AMAZING!!! They are in constant communication with anybody that has questions, and they actually encourage students to come to them with any and every question that they might have!" Similarly, "professors are a great support system"; they "really care about teaching the students and want to provide any help they can." In fact, professors "go out of their way to work with your work schedule should issues arise," making it easier to balance work, school, and family life.

Career and Placement

Univeristy of Louisiana—Lafayette's MBA is geared toward working professionals (some of whom receive tuition assistance from their current employer), so very few MBA candidates are actively looking for a new job at graduation. Instead, most plan to leverage their education for a better position in their current company. As a result, professional development activities are somewhat limited on campus.

ADMISSIONS CONTACT: DR. MARY FARMER-KAISER, DEAN OF THE GRADUATE SCHOOL
ADDRESS: MARTIN HALL, ROOM #332, P. O. BOX 44610, LAFAYETTE, LA 70504-4610
PHONE: 337-482-6965 • FAX: 337-482-1333
E-MAIL: GRADSCHOOL@LOUISIANA.EDU • WEBSITE: GRADSCHOOL.LOUISIANA.EDU

Those who are looking for a new job or hoping to switch careers after graduation can get help at the campus Career Services center. Though principally aimed at the undergraduate community, Career Services organizes campus career fairs, hosts on-campus interviews and recruiting sessions, offers professional-development seminars, and keeps an updated list of open positions in the area. In addition, the school has a "great alumni base" and an active MBA Association, both of which can assist with local networking.

Student Life and Environment

Although it draws the majority of its students from the local community, "there is a very diverse age range, as well as diversity in ethnicity and fields of interest" at University of Louisiana—Lafayette. Most students have at least a few years of professional experience before coming to the MBA program, and even recent college graduates are likely to be working full-time when they join the program. Though there is a considerable group of single students, many are "married and have children," often balancing family life alongside school and career. Striking a good balance, almost everyone here is "motivated and achievement oriented, while at the same time being extremely open and friendly."

Though many students are busy with work obligations and family life, others are "very conscientious and involved" in the campus community. In their free time, MBA students can participate in social and networking events put on by the MBA Association, or sign up for volunteer projects with other MBA candidates. Located in the "little city" of Lafayette, the overally environment is low-key and student-friendly. According to UL students, "Lafayette is a great college town," with ample outdoor activities, great Cajun and Creole restaurants, and plenty of live music and nightlife.

Admissions

To be considered for admission to the University of Louisiana—Lafayette's MBA program, students must have an undergraduate degree from an accredited university, with a grade point average of 2.75 or better. Prospective students are also required to submit GMAT scores, three letters of recommendation, a professional résumé, and a statement of purpose.

FINANCIAL FACTS

Annual tuition (in-state/ out-of-state)	$8,554/$22,282
Fees	$0
Cost of books	$1,200
Room & board (on/off-campus)	$5,700/$10,200
Average award package	$12,765
Average grant	$3,000

ADMISSIONS

Admissions Selectivity Rating	77
# of applications received	95
% applicants accepted	97
% acceptees attending	74
Average GMAT	473
Range of GMAT	420–580
Accepts GRE scores	Yes
Average Verbal GRE	148
Range of Verbal GRE scores	142–156
Average Quantitative GRE	145
Range of Quantitative GRE scores	143–147
Average Writing GRE	3.3
Range of Writing GRE scores	3.0–4.0
Average GPA	3.2
TOEFL required of international students	Yes
Minimum TOEFL (paper/web)	550/81
Application fee	$25
International application fee	$30
Regular application deadline	6/30
Deferment available	Yes
Maximum length of deferment	12 months
Transfer students accepted	Yes
Transfer application policy Can transfer a maximum of 9 credit hours. Must apply through regular process. All transfer credits must be approved by MBA Director.	
Non-fall admissions	Yes
Need-blind admissions	Yes

UNIVERSITY OF LOUISVILLE
COLLEGE OF BUSINESS

GENERAL INFORMATION
Type of school   Public
Academic calendar   Year-round program

SURVEY SAYS...
Classmates have diverse work experience, Friendly students, Good peer network, Happy students, Students love Louisville, KY
Solid preparation in:
Marketing, Finance, General management, Teamwork, Presentation skills, Quantitative skills

STUDENTS
Enrollment of parent institution	22,529
Enrollment of MBA Program	213
% male/female	73/27
% out-of-state	33
% part-time	79
% underrepresented minority	11
% international	2
Average age at entry	28
Average years work experience at entry	5

ACADEMICS
Academic Experience Rating	92
Profs interesting rating	90
Profs accessible rating	93
Student/faculty ratio	7:1
% female faculty	22
% underrepresented minority faculty	19
% part-time faculty	8

Joint Degrees
Joint degree oppurtunities are available with all graduate and professional programs, including the Law, Engineering, and Medical schools.

Prominent Alumni
David Jones, Founder/ Former Chairman, Humana; Terry Forcht, Owner, Forcht Group; James Patterson, Founder/Former Chairman, Long John Silver's, Rally's

Academics

The small MBA program at the University of Louisville College of Business is a gem that is "only getting brighter everyday." Professional, Full-time, and Entrepreneurship MBAs are available, and all classes are held in the evenings or on weekends. Full-time MBAs have 3.5-hour classes held three evenings a week, and most students take advantage of the eleven-month competitive paid internship program, which provides significant exposure to local business contacts and features an international trip that "provides global perspective for concepts learned in class"—not to mention it practically pays for the cost of tuition. Lectures are often case-driven and geared towards application of concepts and ideas, and case reviews use current events. While professors are gracious, "they also have high expectations of the students."

The cohort setup is "wonderful": "To share all your classes with the same fifty people really allows for great team-building and collaboration," testifies a student. Students come from all industry backgrounds and are "very outgoing and interactive in class debates," which "adds to the conversations and provides diverse outlooks on situations." "Each week has been very challenging, and I have learned material that I can immediately use at work," says a student. Courses are designed so that fundamental topics are reinforced throughout the program, and this cohesive curriculum "congeals the concepts so that strategic and technical thinking will persist beyond graduation."

The "fantastic administration" is "well-organized [with] good communication," which is especially impressive since most classes meet in the evenings when administration is not typically present. Class schedules are handled by the administration and all students need to do "is let them know which classes we are interested in, and they do the rest. It is a very conducive environment to learn in." That being said, "electives are somewhat limited."

Career and Placement

The alumni are very helpful and "willing to meet with anyone if they are interested in a career path and try to give them help, guidance, or contacts of how to pursue their future careers." "I have had many meetings with different alumni and finally I landed a great job in wealth management because of the alumni," says one student. A sizeable city like Louisville draws employers to campus, and there are similarly "great internship opportunities for MBA students." The paid internship for full-time MBAs is one of the school's greatest boons, and while this means almost everyone is already employed across all programs, the Ulmer Career Center is still available for résumé assistance, interview prep, career counseling, and recruiting events.

ADMISSIONS CONTACT: GRADUATE PROGRAMS OFFICE
ADDRESS: COLLEGE OF BUSINESS, LOUISVILLE, KY 40292
PHONE: 502-852-7257 • FAX: 502-852-4901
E-MAIL: MBA@LOUISVILLE.EDU • WEBSITE: BUSINESS.LOUISVILLE.EDU/MBA

Student Life and Environment

The University of Louisville "has a fine campus" and the College of Business building "provides students with great resources," though "the surrounding areas need work for students to feel safe after dark." Students are given amenities such as "free food, access to Wi-Fi throughout campus and designated MBA-only study rooms, computer labs, and lounge areas." As a whole, this is a relatively young group native to the area, and outside of class students "always invite anyone and everyone to come grab some food or drinks at local restaurants on/near campus." "We try to have fun, but we also make sure we get our work done," says a student of a cohort that is "very motivated to get as much out every class as possible, both individually and as a group."

Admissions

Students do not need to rush their applications into the University of Louisville College of Business. Rolling admissions are open for all MBA programs until July 1. But applying early does have a financial advantage. A $1,000 scholarship is available to Entrepreneurship MBA early admit students who meet the May 1 priority deadline. Student interviews, GMAT scores, and undergraduate GPAs are given the highest consideration for incoming students. College transcripts, a personal statement, letters of recommendation, and résumé are also required. Students average over six years of work experience before enrolling at UL and the average age of enrollees over the past several years has been twenty-eight. About fifty students make up the Professional MBA classes, about forty attend the Entrepreneurship MBA classes, and about thirty-five are in the full-time MBA class.

FINANCIAL FACTS

Annual tuition (in-state/ out-of-state)	$32,000/$32,000
Fees	$0
Cost of books	$1,500
Room & board (on/off-campus)	$10,500/$12,500
% of students receiving aid	62
% of first-year students receiving aid	22
% of students receiving grants	27
Average award package	$13,338
Average grant	$7,746
Average loan	$13,936
Average student loan debt	$32,625

ADMISSIONS

Admissions Selectivity Rating	88
# of applications received	341
% applicants accepted	47
% acceptees attending	87
Average GMAT	580
Range of GMAT	540–630
Accepts GRE scores	Yes
Average Verbal GRE	155
Range of Verbal GRE scores	152–158
Average Quantitative GRE	154
Range of Quantitative GRE scores	151–157
Average Writing GRE	4.2
Range of Writing GRE scores	4.0–4.5
Average GPA	3.3
TOEFL required of international students	Yes
Minimum TOEFL (paper/web)	550/79
Application fee	$50
International application fee	$50
Regular application deadline	5/1
Deferment available	Yes
Maximum length of deferment	case by case basis, generally one year
Transfer students accepted	Yes
Transfer application policy Up to 9 credits are accepted (grade B or better) from an AACSB accredited MBA program, reviewed on a case by case basis.	
Non-fall admissions	Yes
Need-blind admissions	Yes

EMPLOYMENT PROFILE

Career Rating	77	Grads Employed by Function	% Avg. Salary
Percent employed at graduation	40	Marketing	(20%) $52,624
Average base starting salary	$41,445	Operations	(8%) $57,961
Primary Source of Full-time Job Acceptances		Consulting	(9%) $58,214
School-facilitated activities	9 (20%)	Management	(11%) $54,591
Graduate-facilitated activities	12 (38%)	Finance	(21%) $55,454
Unknown	11 (34%)	HR	(5%) $38,500
		MIS	(5%) $70,000
		Other	(22%) $53,047

Top 5 Employers Hiring Grads
US Army (1), Hilliard Lyons (1), Merrill Lynch (1), Vitera Healthcare Solutions (1), Pernod Ricard USA (1)

UNIVERSITY OF MARYLAND, COLLEGE PARK
ROBERT H. SMITH SCHOOL OF BUSINESS

Academics

A longstanding and thriving relationship with the resources and business leaders of the nearby Washington, D.C., and Baltimore metropolitan areas and a highly collaborative environment helps elevate students of the Robert H. Smith School of Business at the University of Maryland, College Park to perform at their highest levels. The theme of "Terps Helping Terps" runs throughout the Smith School, which prides itself on having "a community of inclusiveness, support and encouragement, which can be seen in job search teams, clubs and professional networking events."

The Smith Experience offers five different focus areas—consulting, global, social value creation, investing, and entrepreneurship—and "there are a ton of opportunities for both leadership and experiential learning," some of which are available to students just weeks into the program. The New Markets Venture Capital Clinic lets students gain professional experience in venture capitalism, case competitions are hotly anticipated events, and the chance to help manage the $2 million Mayer Fund (managed by a select group of second-year MBAs) are all projects that are "unique and very enriching and allow us to really put our learnings, knowledge and skills to good use." The school's international study programs provide a close-up of business operations around the world (in countries such as India, China, Brazil, and Spain), and Smith is also home to one of the country's thirty-one Centers for International Business Education and Research (CIBER).

Lots of effort is put into creating a well-rounded experience, and professors "love to talk about current events and will come to our weekly socials to do so," according to students. They are "generous with their time," "open to feedback," and "continuously aim at improving all aspects for better performance as a group." This top faculty "brings their research directly into the teaching environment" and have access to special guest speakers that add to the MBA experience and potential career networks.

Career and Placement

Smith's focus on Career Services is evident in its strong relationships with federal employers and firms in the DC area and its high placement within the consulting industry. While students have one dedicated career adviser, they are encouraged "to use all of the advisors if they are relevant to their career search"; students also can rely on each other for support in their job searches. "There has not been a single situation where a fellow student did not make time to either connect me to a contact or prep for an interview or exam," says one student. The networking benefits of having over one thousand part-time students are also not to be taken lightly, and "alumni come back and give back often in form of time and support." Top recent employers of Smith grads include Deloitte Consulting, Campbell Soup Company, IBM, iGATE, and PepsiCo.

Student Life and Environment

Smith students "are very social with one another" and take an interest in each other's personal lives"; smaller class sizes also encourage students to become cohesive in just a short period of time, which "helps us to accomplish more in group settings such as team-based academic and consulting projects." "We are a team and see our success as a collective," says a student. "Everyone looks at the bigger goal: having successful careers," says another of "the most helpful and friendly group of people." Nearly all students live off campus in Washington, DC or the surrounding suburbs, but are able to socialize outside of class at activities such as weekly socials, the annual inter-class competition between first and second years, charity poker tournaments, basketball games, football tailgates, the charity auction. After the first semester, students can guide their schedule to fit their personal lifestyle (which is "good if you need flexibility for a start-up") and "allows each person to grow in their own rate."

Admissions

To apply to Smith, students must submit scanned official copies of their undergraduate transcripts, official GMAT or GRE scores, two recommendation forms and required essay responses per the online application system. In the full-time program, the current entering class had GMAT scores ranging from 617-690 and an average undergraduate GPA of 3.25. The part-time class submitted GMAT scores between 500 and 690. Students have an average of 5.0 years of professional work experience before beginning the MBA program.

Prominent Alumni

Kevin Plank, CEO and Founder, Under Armour; Carly Fiorina, Head of Carly Fiorina Enterprises; Richard Shaeffer, Chairman, NYMEX Holdings; Bob Basham, Co-Founder, Outback; Albert P. Carey, CEO, PepsiCo

FINANCIAL FACTS

Annual tuition (in-state/ out-of-state)	$43,470/$52,380
Fees	$2,029
Cost of books	$1,500
Room & board (on/off-campus)	$15,000/$15,000

ADMISSIONS

Admissions Selectivity Rating	92
# of applications received	902
% applicants accepted	31
% acceptees attending	35
Average GMAT	658
Range of GMAT	620–710
Accepts GRE scores	Yes
Average Verbal GRE	155
Range of Verbal GRE scores	153–157
Average Quantitative GRE	154
Range of Quantitative GRE scores	150–156
Average Writing GRE	4.0
Range of Writing GRE scores	3.5–4.5
Average GPA	3.4
TOEFL required of international students	Yes
Minimum TOEFL (paper/web)	600/100
Application fee	$75
International application fee	$75
Early application deadline	1/15
Early notification date	4/1
Regular application deadline	3/1
Regular application notification	5/1
Application Deadline/Notification	
Round 1:	11/1 / 1/15
Round 2:	12/15 / 2/15
Round 3:	1/15 / 4/1
Round 4:	3/1 / 5/1
Deferment available	Yes
Maximum length of deferment	1 year
Transfer students accepted	No
Non-fall admissions	No
Need-blind admissions	Yes

EMPLOYMENT PROFILE

Career Rating	82	Grads Employed by Function% Avg. Salary	
Average base starting salary	$96,479	Marketing	(%) $100,889
Primary Source of Full-time Job Acceptances		Operations	(%) $100,500
School-facilitated activities	55 (%)	Consulting	(%) $98,700
Graduate-facilitated activities	15 (%)	Management	(%) $92,241
		Finance	(%) $86,625
		Other	(%) $96,200

Top 5 Employers Hiring Grads
Deloitte Consulting (4), M&T Bank Corp. (3), IBM (3), Verizon Communications (3), PepsiCo (2)

UNIVERSITY OF MASSACHUSETTS AMHERST
ISENBERG SCHOOL OF MANAGEMENT

GENERAL INFORMATION

Type of school	Public
Affiliation	No Affiliation
Academic calendar	Semester

SURVEY SAYS...

Classmates have diverse work experience, Friendly students, Liberal students, Happy students
Solid preparation in:
Accounting, General management, Operations, Teamwork, Presentation skills

STUDENTS

Enrollment of parent institution	29,269
Enrollment of MBA Program	1,294
% male/female	65/35
% part-time	96
% underrepresented minority	22
% international	22
Average age at entry	28
Average years work experience at entry	4

ACADEMICS

Academic Experience Rating	**93**
Profs interesting rating	92
Profs accessible rating	97

Joint Degrees

MBA/MS in Sport Management - 2 years; MBA/Master of Public Policy & Administration - 2.5 years; MBA/MS in Industrial Engineering - 3 years; MBA/MS in Civil Engineering - 3 years; MBA/MS in Environmental Engineering - 3 years; MBA/MS in Mechanical Engineering - 3 years

Prominent Alumni

John F. "Jack" Smith, Former Chief Executive Officer General Motors; James Pallotta, Chairman and Managing Director of Raptor Group, and President A.S. Roma

Academics

For savvy business students, Isenberg School of Management unites convenience, quality, and value. Any way you slice it, Isenberg School of Management is an "exceptional value," boasting a low in-state tuition, yet all the prestige and resources you'd expect from the UMass name. All students who are accepted into the full-time MBA program are automatically enrolled in the graduate fellowship program. That deal is very sweet, covering tuition, fees, healthcare, and a stipend. A student enthuses, "The best business decision I've made so far is to get my MBA in the full-time program where all of my tuition and fees are waived and I get paid" to be a fellow working on strategic initiatives for the school. A comprehensive thirty-seven to fifty-two-unit program (depending on concentration), the full-time MBA at UMass is completed on the school's main campus over the course of two years, or little as one year plus two courses. For those already in the workforce, Isenberg "caters to part-time students who have to work full-time" by offering a convenient part-time MBA, which can be completed in class at Springfield, Shrewsbury, Boston, or online. In addition, UMass offers dual degree programs in many fields, including sports management, public policy and civil, environmental, industrial, and mechanical engineering.

Although the full-time MBA enrollment is usually under fifty students each year, UMass is a large, public university. Therefore, it can be "hard to get a hold of the administrators because they're very busy." A student continues, "The administration has been nearly invisible, which is exactly how it should be—there have been no hassles over courses or deadlines." In 2013, the administration was reorganized under one Associate Dean. In contrast, the academic experience is surprisingly intimate, boasting small class sizes and "very supportive" professors. In the classroom, "discussions are interesting and it's easy to participate," and professors "welcome discussion and feedback and are willing to let students run with ideas while still…keep[ing] us on track."

Uniting practical knowledge with academic savvy, "professors are very knowledgeable within their respective fields" and "very current" on industry trends. Students also get a taste of the real world through various experiential learning opportunities. After completing the core curriculum, students have "freedom to choose courses, practicum, and search for jobs." Among other offerings, the "Practicum" is a semester-long consulting project, which lets second-year students test their business acumen while working directly with for-profit and not-for-profit regional businesses. A current student enthuses, "The end-of-program practicum project is extremely well put together, and is valuable for both real-world experience and resume-building."

Career Placement

Isenberg's MBA Career Management Office helps MBA candidates prepare for their career through a variety of services and networking programs. Among other offerings, the office operates a fully funded mandatory first-year Orientation to prepare students for the internship and job search through participation in MBA conferences and connecting with recruiters. It also focuses on practical lifelong learning skills that will make graduates better leaders in their organizations. While "the career center is good if you have specific questions," students admit that, "you really need to go out there and work for yourself to get anywhere" with the job search. Speaking of classmates, one student tells us, "We rely on each other to bring our personal networks into the program." Here, "people know what you are looking to do and keep their ears open for opportunities to pass along."

ADMISSIONS CONTACT: MICHAEL FAMIGNETTE, DIRECTOR OF FULL-TIME MBA
MARYBETH KIMBALL, DIRECTOR OF ADMISSIONS & ADVISING, PROFESSIONAL PROGRAMS
ADDRESS: 305 ISENBERG SCHOOL OF MANAGEMENT, UMASS, AMHERST, MA 01003
PHONE: 413-545-5608 • FAX: 413-577-2234
E-MAIL: MBA@ISENBERG.UMASS.EDU • WEBSITE: WWW.ISENBERG.UMASS.EDU/MBA

On campus, students have access to career fairs and networking events; however, MBA candidates would also like to see more upper-level recruiting at UMass. In fact, companies "often come to campus to recruit undergrads but have no interest in the MBAs." A student adds, "Since the program is so small there are no visits from recruiters. While the career center has been infinitely useful for me, it would be more beneficial if they could interest recruiters in the MBA class." In recent years, Isenberg graduates have taken jobs at Ford, Lego, Google, Capital One, EMC, Goldman Sachs, United Technologies Corp., Bj's Wholesales, Treavelers, and Mars.

Student Life and Environment

Amherst, Massachusetts, is the quintessential college town, and students in the business program aren't immune to their lively surroundings. Here, the atmosphere is collegial and friendly, and "students are active in clubs, sports/healthy living, arts activities, and more." Moreover, "being a small program affords the majority of us to continue to practice our leadership skills in clubs, which provides a semblance of running a business and gives us high visibility in the university, with alumni, and in the broader community."

With only fifty students in the full-time program, Isenberg is "truly a community." During the challenging first-year curriculum, "the class gets very close, works hard together, and works to help each other." In addition, "second-years are very active in helping the first-years adjust to the workload." In their free time, MBA candidates get together for "hikes, pot-luck dinners, [or] ice skating," and many attend the "weekly Thursday Night Out event sponsored by the Graduate Business Association." On the school's satellite campuses, students rarely get involved in any activities beyond classes. Nonetheless, they "enjoy interacting with the other students," and tell us that, "the facilities function well for what we need to accomplish."

Admissions

Isenberg accepts students based on their demonstrated record of academic achievement, promise for success in graduate school, quality of professional experience, and clarity of career purpose. To be eligible for Isenberg's full-time or part-time programs, students must have at least three years of professional, post-undergraduate work experience. The school accepts either GMAT or GRE scores. The part-time program enrolls students three times a year; the full-time program begins once a year, in the fall. Check Isenberg's website for complete deadlines.

FINANCIAL FACTS

Annual tuition (in-state/ out-of-state)	$2,640/$9,937
Fees (in-state/ out-of-state)	$12,114/$20,037
Cost of books	$4,000
% of students receiving grants	100
Average award package	$31,580

ADMISSIONS

Admissions Selectivity Rating	94
# of applications received	136
% applicants accepted	34
% acceptees attending	50
Average GMAT	639
Accepts GRE scores	Yes
Average Verbal GRE	160
Average Quantitative GRE	159
Average GPA	3.36
TOEFL required of international students	Yes
Minimum TOEFL (paper/web)	600/100
Application fee	$75
International application fee	$75
Regular application deadline	12/1
Regular application notification	1/15
Application Deadline/Notification	
Round 1:	12/1 / 1/15
Round 2:	2/1 / 3/15
Round 3:	4/1 / 5/1
Deferment available	Yes
Maximum length of deferment	1 year
Transfer students accepted	No
Non-fall admissions	No
Need-blind admissions	Yes

EMPLOYMENT PROFILE

Career Rating	87	Grads Employed by Function% Avg. Salary	
Percent employed at graduation	43	Marketing	(19%)
Percent employed 3 months after graduation	76	Operations	(19%)
		Consulting	(19%)
Average base starting salary	$75,088	Management	(25%)
		Finance	(6%)
		HR	(6%)
		MIS	(6%)

Top 5 Employers Hiring Grads
KPMG, Morgan Stanley Smith Barney, MassMutual Financial Group, Macy's, Lean Enterprise Institute

UNIVERSITY OF MASSACHUSETTS BOSTON
COLLEGE OF MANAGEMENT GRADUATE PROGRAMS

GENERAL INFORMATION

Type of school	Public
Affiliation	No Affiliation
Academic calendar	Semesters

SURVEY SAYS...
Liberal students
Solid preparation in:
Teamwork

STUDENTS

Enrollment of parent institution	17,030
Enrollment of MBA Program	537
% male/female	48/52
% out-of-state	41
% part-time	52
% underrepresented minority	26
% international	54
Average age at entry	26
Average years work experience at entry	5

ACADEMICS

Academic Experience Rating	88
Profs interesting rating	87
Profs accessible rating	87
Student/faculty ratio	25:1
% female faculty	35
% underrepresented minority faculty	55
% part-time faculty	20

Joint Degrees
MS in Accounting - 2 years
MS in Finance - 2 years MS in
International Management 2 years
MS in Information Technology 2
years

Prominent Alumni
Thomas M. Menino, Mayor, City of
Boston; Joseph Abboud, Fashion
Designer; George Kassas, Founder,
Cedar Point Communications; Mark
Atkins, CEO, Invention Machine;
Joseph Kennedy, U.S. Congressman

Academics

The MBA program at the University of Massachusetts—Boston's College of Management (the only public MBA available in the area) combines strategically focused management curriculum with optional specializations, offering in-state residents one of "the best educational values in the Boston area." "The in-state tuition is a lot more reasonable than all of the local private business schools," says one resident student. "My overall experience has been very positive and I recommend the program to anyone," says another.

"The classes are tailored to meet the needs of working students," and students with a related degree may even be eligible to waive some of the business core courses. Classes are "small and personal," and many MBA classes have a major case component that provides insight into corporate, non-profit and small business issues, while others use real-world projects and simulations. For students interested in specializing beyond just general management, the college offers fourteen specializations, including Accounting, Business Intelligence, and Entrepreneurship.

As most here are working professionals, students are all "committed to bettering themselves," and "group work is mandatory." The "diverse working backgrounds" that students bring to the table makes for "engaged classes with a lot of interaction with professors." As far as guidance goes, there is "definitely no hand holding," "you have to seek out advisors and course scheduling on your own," and "you have to keep your responsibilities in check." Students also say "the professors are solid." Though some say they can be "hit and miss" with a "mix of teaching ability," overall the MBA professors "know their material." The Chancellor gets high marks; students say that "given time he can turn this university in to the shining jewel of the UMass system."

Career and Placement

Many members of this "laid back community" are already employed for the most part (though around forty percent of students have only one year or less of professional experience), but "there are good on campus jobs available for full-time students to support their education." "If you plan on staying in the same field and going part time, it makes financial sense with return on investment," says one student who did just so. Another benefit is the "possibility of networking due to the college being in Boston." Students who are on the job hunt do wish that the school brought in "more potential employers for career fairs," or perhaps would start "a job board/portal exclusively for students."

Recent employers of UMass-Boston graduates include State Street Corporation, Bank of America, Ernst & Young, Fidelity Investments, and PriceWaterhouseCoopers.

ADMISSIONS CONTACT: TARA NORTON, ASSOCIATE PROGRAM DIRECTOR
ADDRESS: 100 MORRISSEY BOULEVARD, MBA OFFICE, BOSTON, MA 02125-3393
PHONE: 617-287-7720 • FAX: 617-287-7725
E-MAIL: GRADCM@UMB.EDU • WEBSITE: WWW.UMB.EDU/CMGRAD

Student Life and Environment

It's a commuter school, so the community is less cohesive than others, but UMass Boston "has the most diverse campus imaginable" in "a beautiful location." Many students here are first generation immigrants and/or first generation college graduates (the program is "very diverse in race, age, nationality, socio economic class"), so "in many ways, it's the embodiment of the American Dream." This is truly "a working class of people with real world experience in both life and in the workplace."

The administration is "well in touch with day to day activities," and "there is constant information and updates" regarding lectures, opportunities, and the "many sports activities, clubs, and other events offered."

Admissions

To be eligible for the MBA program at UMass Boston's College of Management, prospective students must have an undergraduate degree from an accredited college or university, GMAT scores, three letters of recommendation, and completed essays. In addition to test scores and undergraduate record, the admissions department evaluates students based on their recommendations, personal essays, and interview with the admissions department.

FINANCIAL FACTS

Annual tuition (in-state/ out-of-state)	$2000/$7300
Fees	$11,800/$17,700
Cost of books	$1,000
Room & board	$15,000
% of students receiving aid	65
% of first-year students receiving aid	55
% of students receiving grants	21
Average grant	$17,000
Average student loan debt	$13,000

ADMISSIONS

Admissions Selectivity Rating	86
# of applications received	612
% applicants accepted	57
% acceptees attending	59
Average GMAT	560
Range of GMAT	520–600
Accepts GRE scores	Yes
Average GPA	3.3
TOEFL required of international students	Yes
Minimum TOEFL (paper/web)	600/90
Application fee	$60
International application fee	$100
Early application deadline	3/1
Early notification date	4/1
Regular application deadline	5/1
Regular application notification	6/1
Application Deadline/Notification	
Round 1:	3/1 / 4/1
Round 2:	5/1 / 6/1
Deferment available	Yes
Maximum length of deferment	1 year
Transfer students accepted	Yes
Transfer application policy Same applicant procedure. Transfer credits and waivers will be considered.	
Non-fall admissions	Yes
Need-blind admissions	Yes

EMPLOYMENT PROFILE

Career Rating		88	Grads Employed by Function	% Avg. Salary
Percent employed at graduation		94	Marketing	(13%)
Percent employed 3 months after graduation		75	Operations	(20%)
			Consulting	(13%)
Average base starting salary		$74,257	Management	(13%)
Primary Source of Full-time Job Acceptances			Finance	(53%)
School-facilitated activities		1 (100%)	MIS	(13%)

Top 5 Employers Hiring Grads
State Street Corporation (4), EMC Corporation (2), Ernst & Young (6), Genzyme (2), PriceWaterhouseCoopers (2)

UNIVERSITY OF MASSACHUSETTS DARTMOUTH
CHARLTON COLLEGE OF BUSINESS

GENERAL INFORMATION

Type of school	Public
Affiliation	No Affiliation
Academic calendar	Sep - May

SURVEY SAYS...
Solid preparation in:
Marketing, General management,
Communication/interpersonal skills,
Doing business in a global economy

STUDENTS

Enrollment of parent institution	8,916
Enrollment of MBA Program	286
% male/female	60/40
% out-of-state	75
% part-time	55
% underrepresented minority	4
% international	71
Average age at entry	31

ACADEMICS

Academic Experience Rating	**70**
Profs interesting rating	66
Profs accessible rating	69
Student/faculty ratio	4:1
% female faculty	37
% underrepresented minority faculty	3
% part-time faculty	32

Joint Degrees
JD/MBA in conjunction with
University of Massachusetts School
of Law Dartmouth

Prominent Alumni
Paul Martins, CFO and Partner of
Wainwright Investments Counsel
LLC and subsidaries; Craig Costa,
VP of Operations for American
Dryer Corp.; Jay Waring, Waring
Sullivan Funeral Home; Margaret
Xifaras, Senior Partner of Lang,
Xifaras and Bullard; ,

Academics

The University of Massachusetts Dartmouth's Charlton College of Business goes the extra mile to make its MBA program as convenient as possible. The student body, largely made up of busy young professionals, appreciates the effort. Online and face-to-face courses make it easier for students to attend classes; "the ability to take online/blended courses" means they can sometimes skip the classroom entirely. An accommodating curriculum also helps; as one student explains, "I love the flexibility in the program. I can choose my classes in any order. Although it will be a four-year period before I finish in total, the slower pace is flexible and the option to take one course at a time is the only way I could have done it."

Cost is also a factor; students declare the UMassD MBA "the least expensive AACSB-accredited business program in the area." Students also praise "a stellar international core of professors with a wide range of professional and academic experience," noting their instructors' "focus on group work and presentations," which they regard as "very realistic in the business world." They're less bullish on the administration, describing it as "disjointed." "The administration needs to work more diligently at ironing out some of the bureaucracy in the system," one student explains. "On more than one occasion, I have received multiple answers to the same question, depending on who I speak with."

Students also note "there is sometimes trouble with the offerings in certain concentrations." Class availability sometimes diminishes the convenience of the program; students wish the school would "rotate the elective course offerings and have courses available for all concentrations that are offered" in order to mitigate the problem. Even so, students' opinion of the program as a whole is favorable; one writes, "The overall academic experience is challenging and engaging, [leaving me] very optimistic about potential for more success after graduation."

Career and Placement

The MBA program at UMassD utilizes the university's Career Resource Center, which serves all undergraduates, graduate students, and alumni. The office provides a battery of career services, including workshops in resume-writing, interviewing, and salary negotiation; online job and resume listings; and on-campus recruiting events, including job fairs. Efforts here are primarily directed toward the undergraduate population. One MBA explains, "The majority of MBA students are usually using the MBA program to advance in their current occupation, with many large local corporations paying their tuition. The CRC is available and encouraged to be utilized for students seeking employment after graduation." Some students are less than satisfied with the situation; "They need to build their network of companies up badly. In so doing, they need to get more companies to come on campus and recruit," one such student writes.

ADMISSIONS CONTACT: DONNA SOTOMAYOR, INTERIM DEAN FOR GRADUATE STUDIES
ADDRESS: 285 OLD WESTPORT ROAD, NORTH DARTMOUTH, MA 02747-2300
PHONE: 508-999-8543 • FAX: 508-999-8776
E-MAIL: DONNA.SOTOMAYOR.UMASSD.EDU • WEBSITE: WWW.UMASSD.EDU/CHARLTON

Student Life and Environment

The business school facility on UMassD's main campus is of recent vintage; the ultra-modern building, funded by a three million dollar grant from the Earle P. Charlton Family Trust, opened in 2004. Students speak highly of the main campus.

Students describe the UMassD MBA program as "commuter-based," with students' involvement "mostly limited to evening courses, with little interaction on campus during the day unless attending a special lecture." "There's no mandatory participation" in extracurricular activities, "which is good for me," a typical student offers. That's because most here "are working full time and do not have time to get involved in other things outside of class."

The student body here "is a mixture of students that have just graduated from college and others who are working and raising a family." One reports, "Some are young—in their twenties—but there is a good mix of twenties, thirties, and forties. I'm fifty-two but feel comfortable in the environment." The program is "internationally diverse," with "people from all around the world. It is much more diverse than I would have expected," a locally based student observes. "The international students are extremely friendly and bright. I enjoy working with them on projects," one student notes.

Admissions

Applicants to the UMassD MBA program must submit the following materials to the Admissions Committee: official transcripts from all post-secondary academic institutions attended (transcripts from institutions outside the US must be translated when not in English and evaluated by a Credit Evaluation service where the grading system deviates from the standard American four-point system); an official GMAT score report; two letters of recommendation, preferably one reflecting academic ability and one reflecting professional experience; a personal essay; and a current resume. International applicants must submit all the above plus an official score report for the TOEFL (minimum scores are: 533 paper-based test, 200 computer-based test, and 72 internet-based test) and visa-related paperwork. Admissions are processed on a rolling basis, with decisions typically coming with a month after the completed application is received. International applicants must apply by June 1 for fall entry and by November 15 for spring entry.

FINANCIAL FACTS

Annual tuition (in-state/ out-of-state)	$2,071/$8,099
Fees	$12,628
Cost of books	$3,354
Room & board (on/off-campus)	$11,622/$10,000

ADMISSIONS

Admissions Selectivity Rating	**78**
# of applications received	192
% applicants accepted	84
% acceptees attending	59
Average GMAT	487
Range of GMAT	420–540
Accepts GRE scores	Yes
Average Verbal GRE	155
Range of Verbal GRE scores	152–158
Average Quantitative GRE	156
Range of Quantitative GRE scores	147–165
Average Writing GRE	3.4
Range of Writing GRE scores	2.8–4.0
Average GPA	3.2
TOEFL required of international students	Yes
Minimum TOEFL (paper/web)	533/72
Application fee	$60
International application fee	$60
Regular application deadline	7/1
Deferment available	Yes
Maximum length of deferment	1 year
Transfer students accepted	Yes
Transfer application policy Maximum 6 credits	
Non-fall admissions	Yes
Need-blind admissions	Yes

UNIVERSITY OF MASSACHUSETTS LOWELL
ROBERT MANNING SCHOOL OF BUSINESS

Academics

Providing a "good balance between reputation and affordability" to business grads in and around the northeast corner of Massachusetts, the University of Massachusetts—Robert Manning School of Business offers an MBA "tailored to meet the busy working person's schedules." With "evening classes," a "practical approach to tests and assignments," and, most conveniently of all, an "excellent online program" that "allows you to blend online with on-campus courses" (or even take all classes online, if you prefer), a Lowell MBA offers enough "freedom and flexibility" to suit its student body, which largely consists of professionals looking for an advantage for management positions.

The UML MBA commences with twelve hours of foundation courses. Students who have completed equivalent undergraduate classes within the last five years and have earned at least a B may receive a waiver for some or all of these courses. The curriculum also includes seven core courses in accounting, finance, analysis of customers and markets, MIS, operations, managing organization design and change, and strategy. The program concludes with three electives, which students may use to develop a concentration in accounting, finance, or information technology. They may also take an MBA in general business.

UML professors "are excellent and helpful," "not pretentious," and "demanding, which helps students do a better job." The school works hard on the service end; professors and administrators "are hands on, always follow up, and contact you regarding any questions." That said, UML is a state school, so naturally "sometimes there is non-applicable red tape, like when I was asked for proof of immunizations even though I take all my classes online." All in all, students appreciate what they have here, reporting that "administrators do the best they can on limited staff and resources." As one student sums up, "the campus lacks the glossy touch, but I guess most here would agree that it gives the best value for your money. You have to remember that you are paying less than a third of what you would have paid at any private college [and] you still get a highly accomplished and dedicated faculty [that] works hard to embed the right kind of morals and values into your brain. The course textbooks, HBR case studies, and other miscellaneous materials are mostly the same as the ones used by the Ivy Leagues. The discussions are intense, and many ideas are innovative. I really don't think therefore that there is anything lacking academically."

Career and Placement

The UML Career Services Office provides counseling and placement services to all undergraduates, graduates, and alumni of the university. The office organizes a variety of job fairs throughout the school year. It also provides mock interviews, counsels students on resume writing and job-search skills, schedules corporate information sessions on campus, and offers access to online job search engines such as MonsterTRAK. The office coordinates the efforts of the University Career Advisory Network, which is essentially an online community of alumni and current students. Employers who most frequently hire UMass Lowell MBAs include: Bank of America, TD Bank, Fidelity, Putnam Investments, Raytheon, Pfizer, Procter & Gamble, EMC, Cisco, US Air Force, and U.S. Government.

Student Life and Environment

Over the years, online course offerings at Lowell have steadily grown in popularity. Today, one MBA explains, "Students are commuters or online, so the experience is not intimate. You don't form personal relationships with mentors/instructors" to the extent that students do elsewhere. Connections can be made with effort, however. Some students report "great opportunities for building relationships with professional networks," and others note that "there are many clubs and organizations for students to join. The office of student activities does a great job in matching students with their activities." These options are only really pursued by the program's few full-time students or by part-timers who don't also hold demanding full-time jobs.

Most here don't fit those descriptions. They're "working professionals" who "have at least a few years of professional experience and are part-time students who work full-time jobs." Their experiences "help in discussions in the class, as most of the arguments given are very practical and time-tested, and there is a lot to learn from everyone's experiences."

Admissions

The MBA program at the University of Massachusetts Lowell admits new students for both the fall and spring terms and requires applicants to submit the following materials: an official transcript of undergraduate grades; an official GMAT score report; three letters of recommendation from "employment-related sources" demonstrating a minimum of two years of relevant work experience; a current resume; and a one-page essay describing academic and career objectives. Applicants must complete prerequisite courses in microeconomics and statistics prior to entering the program. According to the school's website, "An aptitude for management decision-making and demonstrated academic ability are the most important qualifications for admission." International students whose first language is not English must submit an official score report for the TOEFL. There is also a full-time one year accelerated program that requires no work experience of recent college graduates from the UMass System. A GMAT score is required for other applicants.

FINANCIAL FACTS

Annual tuition (in-state/ out-of-state)	$1,637/$6,425
Fees	$12,162
Cost of books	$1,200
Room & board (on/off-campus)	$11,670/$11,670
% of students receiving aid	14
% of first-year students receiving aid	20
% of students receiving grants	2
Average award package	$15,721
Average grant	$9,423
Average loan	$15,388

ADMISSIONS

Admissions Selectivity Rating	81
# of applications received	243
% applicants accepted	85
% acceptees attending	82
Average GMAT	580
Range of GMAT	500–580
Accepts GRE scores	Yes
Average GPA	3.4
TOEFL required of international students	Yes
Minimum TOEFL (paper/web)	600/100
Application fee	$50
International application fee	$50
Deferment available	Yes
Maximum length of deferment	1 year
Transfer students accepted	Yes
Transfer application policy	Must be fron an AACSB accredited institution. Maximum of 12 transfer credits for the advance core courses, with a grade of a "B" or better earned in each of these courses.
Non-fall admissions	Yes
Need-blind admissions	Yes

UNIVERSITY OF MEMPHIS
FOGELMAN COLLEGE OF BUSINESS AND ECONOMICS

Academics

Fogelman College of Business and Economics at the University of Memphis is a no-non-sense professional MBA program designed for working people "from all walks of business life" who are looking to further their careers but who don't have a lot of time or energy to waste. The school has a solid reputation among locally-based businesses like FedEx. One student holds Memphis in such high regard that she has two degrees from there: "The University of Memphis is where I received my BBA in accounting. I liked my experience there, and I knew that an MBA from there would open many doors in the company that I work for."

Students say their "very knowledgeable" professors "present concepts completely" and help them relate the course material to practice. "Each of them has done extensive research in their field and [is] noted to be among the best in the country for their area of expertise." Another student says: "Every professor is interested in the development of each student into future managers and business leaders." The administration does not receive the same ringing endorsement, however. Some take issue with the allocation of funds in certain areas. One student was succinct and blunt: "Solid professors, good academic experience, but really bad administration that spends money" excessively.

Some students also have difficulty with course selection and enrollment; many required or desired classes are offered only once per semester under limited enrollment, and these courses "often conflict with each other." Since pretty much all of the courses take place in the evenings to accommodate the vast majority of students who have day jobs, there's very little leeway in terms of scheduling. But these night classes also give part-time and full-time students the opportunity to interact with each other through "small classes and heavy teamwork," something not found in a lot of MBA programs. "A lot of projects are team-based, so you get to know classmates very well." One student takes away warm feelings about the camaraderie he felt at the school: "I have a new set of best friends. I never thought it was possible after reaching age forty."

In keeping with the no-frills approach to the program, however, the facilities tend toward the sparse side. Several students expressed disdain for the academic buildings and equipment and spoke of the need for "more technology in the classroom." One student said the classrooms "need better seating. The desks were made for 4th graders."

Career and Placement

Some students say the program needs better ties to "big industries" to provide those students seeking out new or nonlocal careers with better job prospects. Fortunately for the students looking to stay in the area (and there are many), "there are several excellent companies in the area, also, that recruit heavily," and since the student body is, as one student puts it, "not nearly as competitive as I expected," everyone is "very supportive" and happy to help each other land available positions. Another boon to the school's local reputation is the recently formed partnership with the Leadership Academy. The partnership, known as the Community Internship, gives MBA students the chance to team with Leadership Academy fellows on projects designed to benefit the community.

Student Life and Environment

The school is located in the midtown area of Memphis, which "is great for students because there are a lot of social establishments nearby" offering "a lot of things for students to do recreationally." Of course, there are the well-traveled destinations like Graceland (check out Elvis' gaudy yellow and black rec room), Sun Studios, and the famous Beale Street, with its string of live-music joints and soul food. And the National Civil Rights Museum, located at the old Lorraine Motel where Martin Luther King, Jr., assassinated in 1968, is a haunting must-see for tourists and locals alike. Overall, "the University of Memphis, like the city of Memphis, is greatly underrated," one student says.

Since "most graduate students work and commute," little time is left for a social life outside of the classroom, but there's a foundation for friendship and networking among the "outgoing" and "friendly" individuals that attend Fogelman. Though some think "the school could put more effort into organized activities for students outside of class," the "busy" nature of the student body doesn't lend itself to much free time anyway, so complaints are few. Everyone is in agreement over the variety of backgrounds provided by their classmates: "The graduate population is very diverse, which makes things more interesting." "You have a great opportunity to meet people from various backgrounds (educational and ethnic)," another student says.

Admissions

Admittance to the professional MBA program at the Fogelman College of Business and Economics is not terribly selective, and the admissions requirements are fairly standard. Applicants to the school's professional MBA program must submit the following materials: a completed application (either online or via mail); an official copy of undergraduate transcripts from all colleges and universities attended (even if you did not graduate); a copy of your current resume; a statement of personal interest; a 1,000-word essay answering one of the acceptable questions provided on the school's admissions website; two letters of recommendation; and an official GMAT or GRE score report. Interviews and previous work experience are optional. In addition to the above documents, international students whose primary language is not English must also provide an official score report for the TOEFL (minimum score: 550, paper-based test; 213, computer-based test).

FINANCIAL FACTS

Annual tuition (in-state/ out-of-state)	$11,064/$22,776
Fees	$840
Cost of books	$1,000

ADMISSIONS

Admissions Selectivity Rating	**87**
# of applications received	148
% applicants accepted	54
% acceptees attending	76
Average GMAT	595
Accepts GRE scores	Yes
Average GPA	3.3
TOEFL required of international students	Yes
Minimum TOEFL (paper/web)	550/80
Application fee	$35
International application fee	$60
Regular application deadline	7/1
Application Deadline/Notification	
Deferment available	Yes
Maximum length of deferment	1 year
Transfer students accepted	Yes
Transfer application policy	

Approved transfer credit may be accepted in the Fogelman Colletge for not more than 9 semester hours of course credit toward a master's degree. Grades earned at another institution will not be computed in the University cumulative grade point average, nor will they be accepted for transfer, unless they are "B" (3.0) or better. No credit will be transferred unless it meets with the approval of the major advisor or program graduate coordinator.

Non-fall admissions	Yes
Need-blind admissions	No

UNIVERSITY OF MIAMI
SCHOOL OF BUSINESS ADMINISTRATION

Academics

Its unique access to Latin America is a huge selling point for The School of Business Administration at the University of Miami, which offers a One-Year and Two-Year MBA program, as well as four Executive MBAs and Professional MBA. Both the One-Year and Two-Year programs are lockstep (only the Two-Year offers concentrations), and the Professional MBA offers "easy logistics to attend class for working professionals." The curriculum is "well-structured and [has] good balance between all the different concentrations," albeit "very fast-paced with lots of material and a moderate to heavy reading load." Though the programs are extremely career-focused, a wide range of electives is offered so that students who come to UM without specific objectives might find their paths, and the powers that be are "creative in the development of new programs that help the university expand and attract top talent."

Professors here are "well-established, knowledgeable, and willing to help," "are experts in their field," and "have very high standards for student performance." "As long as you put forth the effort, you can pass but you will only excel if you really put your mind to it," advises a student. The administration is "extremely responsive and sensitive to the needs of the students," and in light of recent evaluation there has been a large effort to support student interaction and socialization. Breakfast and supper are served each day of class to allow Professional MBA students to meet and network, and the school "has a lot of activities, guest speakers, and workshops for students to attend outside of class."

Career and Placement

"Career searches always give back what the students put into them," and at Miami there are "plenty of opportunities." The Ziff Graduate Career Services Center is "strongly connected to firms in the financial services industry and tech industry," and students looking to do business in South America are likewise in luck. Clubs are active networking and skill-building hubs at UM, and the Management Consulting club in particular "is extremely engaged in academic, organizational, and leadership activities." Many students are already entrepreneurs looking to run or enhance their own business, and so the alumni and classmate network is crucial to advancement. "I learn as much from classmates as I do my professors," says one.

Top employers of recent UM grads include Bayview Asset Management, BACARDI USA, Citrix Systems, Microsoft Corporation, and CITIGroup.

Student Life and Environment

According to some students, "there couldn't be a better school for quality of life." Located "in the heart of sleepy Coral Gables, but within striking distance of most of the sights in Miami," the business school sits along the river that runs through campus and "much of the studying time is spent at the tables by the water enjoying Miami's weather." Even for students without cars, "the Metrorail runs right to campus from downtown," and during football season part- and full-time students alike "all try to make it to games." There is a "real diversity of backgrounds, ethnicity, and career aspirations" to be found at UM, and "since the business school is so small, the students are very close." "We know almost every person in the program at a personal level," says one. "While having competitive personalities, everyone helps each other because they realize we are colleagues at the end of the day," says a student. The school is "almost always bustling with activity."

Admissions

Applications are received and reviewed on a rolling basis until the class is full; students are encouraged to apply by the Round 3 application deadline. Students who wish to be considered for merit-based scholarships, fellowships, or graduate assistantship are advised to apply early, as they are limited and available for fall applicants only. Deadline for fall applicants is May 1. The greatest factors used in determining admissions include GMAT and GRE scores, undergraduate GPA, work experience, and personal interview. Letters of recommendation, a personal essay, and a résumé are also required along with the student application.

FINANCIAL FACTS

Annual tuition (in-state/ out-of-state)	$45,600/$45,600
Fees	$948
Cost of books	$540
Room & board (on/off-campus)	$16,622/$16,622
% of students receiving aid	63
% of first-year students receiving aid	68
% of students receiving grants	52
Average award package	$36,653
Average grant	$20,332
Average loan	$39,856
Average student loan debt	$62,877

ADMISSIONS

Admissions Selectivity Rating	97
# of applications received	600
% applicants accepted	23
% acceptees attending	71
Average GMAT	643
Range of GMAT	600–660
Accepts GRE scores	Yes
Average Verbal GRE	152
Range of Verbal GRE scores	150–153
Average Quantitative GRE	152
Range of Quantitative GRE scores	150–155
Average Writing GRE	3.8
Range of Writing GRE scores	3.6–4.0
Average GPA	3.3
TOEFL required of international students	Yes
Minimum TOEFL (paper/web)	600/94
Application fee	$0
International application fee	$0
Early application deadline	10/1
Early notification date	1/15
Regular application deadline	1/15
Application Deadline/Notification	
Round 1:	11/15 /
Round 2:	1/15 /
Round 3:	3/15 /
Deferment available	Yes
Maximum length of deferment	one year
Transfer students accepted	No
Non-fall admissions	No
Need-blind admissions	Yes

EMPLOYMENT PROFILE

Career Rating	93	Grads Employed by Function	% Avg. Salary
Percent employed at graduation	74	Marketing	(11%) $71,833
Percent employed 3 months after graduation	93	Operations	(11%) $88,667
		Consulting	(9%) $93,800
Average base starting salary	$78,334	Management	(2%) $45,000
Primary Source of Full-time Job Acceptances		Finance	(42%) $77,974
School-facilitated activities	34 (60%)	HR	(7%) $74,000
Graduate-facilitated activities	21 (37%)	Other	(5%) $64,667
Unknown	2 (3%)	**Top 5 Employers Hiring Grads**	
		Citi (3), Microsoft (3), Vitas Healthcare (3), Goldman Sachs & Co. (2), Deloitte Consulting LLP (2)	

UNIVERSITY OF MICHIGAN—ANN ARBOR
STEPHEN M. ROSS SCHOOL OF BUSINESS

GENERAL INFORMATION
Type of school	Public
Affiliation	No Affiliation
Academic calendar	Semester

SURVEY SAYS...
Classmates have diverse work experience, Friendly students, Good peer network, Good social scene, Cutting-edge classes
Solid preparation in:
General management, Teamwork, Communication/interpersonal skills

STUDENTS
Enrollment of parent institution	43,651
Enrollment of MBA Program	1,528
% male/female	68/32
% out-of-state	89
% part-time	22
% underrepresented minority	10
% international	36
Average age at entry	27
Average years work experience at entry	5

ACADEMICS
Academic Experience Rating	**96**
Profs interesting rating	91
Profs accessible rating	96
Student/faculty ratio	15:1
% female faculty	24
% underrepresented minority faculty	4
% part-time faculty	0

Joint Degrees
Architecture; Asian Studies/Chinese; Asian Studies/Japanese; Asian Studies/South Asia; Asian Studies/Southeast Asia; Civil Engineering; Construction Engineering and Management; Health Services Admin (Public Health); Higher Education (Education); Industrial and Operations Engineering; Information; Law (JD); Management of Patient Care Services (Nursing); Manufacturing Engineering; Medicine (MD); Modern Middle Eastern and North African Studies; Natural Resources and Environment

Academics

Armed with a "stellar reputation," extensive alumni network and offering great "flexibility in career concentration," it's no wonder that Michigan has such a well regarded MBA program. Students truly value the focus Ross has placed on both entrepreneurship and "hands-on" "action-based" learning. Indeed, there's a strong "emphasis on learning by doing, rather than lecture or case." Additionally, students appreciate that the school works diligently to foster a "collaborative culture." Moreover, the "general management curriculum" and "leadership development" ensures that students will leave Ross as effective, well-rounded business professionals.

While the "academic experience is surprisingly rigorous," students can rely on professors who "are heavily invested in our success and understanding." They are also very "accessible," "passionate" and "down to earth." A handful have even been deemed "rock stars that push students beyond the usual MBA platitudes and really transform your thinking." As a second-year student gushes, "The professors at Ross are amazing; they take the time to help with anything along their subject lines for class and for outside projects. Not only that but they are always more than happy to help you connect with their own contacts and other professors at the school."

By and large, the administration is held in high esteem as well. Students feel fortunate that "administrators continue to push an academic environment and curriculum that produces MBAs well-equipped to thrive in real world business settings." Even better, "the school is open to new ideas, courses, and course content, and courses are constantly under review." In the end, it's certainly easy to understand why these business students are so content!

Career and Placement

Considering the high "recognition of [the] Ross brand across the country and world," it's no surprise that career opportunities abound for Michigan MBAs. For starters, a strong alumni network means that "graduates are very accessible and interested in helping current students." Ross also manages to attract a high number of recruiters. As one appreciative second-year tells us, "The quality of companies that recruit here are...extremely diverse and of high quality." Ross Career Services also does a great job of helping advise and guide students in their search. Individual counseling sessions and career workshops are continually available. Moreover, the office helps student manage both the on-campus interview process as well as their personal outreach efforts.

Michigan MBAs can be found everywhere from New York and San Francisco to Chile, China and Russia. Employers who frequently hire Ross grads include Amazon.com, Boston Consulting Group, Citigroup, Deloitte, Google, JP Morgan Chase, McKinsey & Co., Medtronic, Bain and Company Inc., American Express Co., Proctor & Gamble, Goldman Sachs Inc., and PepsiCo.

ADMISSIONS CONTACT: SOOJIN KWON, DIRECTOR OF ADMISSIONS
ADDRESS: 701 TAPPAN STREET, ANN ARBOR, MI 48109-1234
PHONE: 734-763-5796 • FAX: 734-763-7804
E-MAIL: ROSSMBA@UMICH.EDU • WEBSITE: WWW.MICHIGANROSS.UMICH.EDU

Student Life and Environment

Michigan MBA students strive to create a good work-life balance for themselves. And luckily, "Ross gives the freedom and flexibility to pursue what you want, whether that's academics, the job market, club activities, helping others, or having fun." Certainly, "what you get out of the experience is up to you, and between the collegial atmosphere and various sporting events in Michigan's rich history, it is highly enjoyable to be at Ross." Indeed, "life in Ann Arbor is highly social, whether it [involves] tailgating at football games, mingling at the weekly happy hour for business students, or catching up with friends at a local restaurant." And since Michigan is in a college town and not a booming metropolis, "you're constantly running into your fellow classmates, which is fantastic from a networking perspective. You can't help but hang out with classmates ALL THE TIME, which means they become your good friends instead of classmates."

Admissions

Admissions officers are on the lookout for candidates who will truly benefit from Ross' approach to business management. They seek applicants with keen intellectual ability who will bring strong interpersonal and leadership skills into the classroom. Due to the analytical rigor of the program, it is recommended that students have a working knowledge of college-level mathematics. However, a traditional business background is not necessary or required and there are no pre-requisite courses for admission.

(Erb); Naval Architecture and Marine Engineering; Public Health; Public Policy; Russian and Eastern European Studies; Social Work; Urban Planning

Prominent Alumni

Stephen M. Ross, Chairman, The Related Companies

FINANCIAL FACTS

Annual tuition (in-state/ out-of-state)	$54,450/$59,450
Fees	$328
Cost of books	$6,052
Room & board	$13,504
% of students receiving aid	67
% of students receiving grants	41
Average award package	$52,348
Average grant	$28,497
Average loan	$50,539
Average student loan debt	$99,610

ADMISSIONS

Admissions Selectivity Rating	95
# of applications received	3,207
% applicants accepted	28
% acceptees attending	45
Average GMAT	708
Range of GMAT	690–740
Accepts GRE scores	Yes
Average Verbal GRE	162
Range of Verbal GRE scores	157–166
Average Quantitative GRE	160
Range of Quantitative GRE scores	157–162
Average GPA	3.4
TOEFL required of international students	Yes
Application fee	$200
International application fee	$200
Application Deadline/Notification	
Round 1:	10/5 / 12/18
Round 2:	1/4 / 3/18
Round 3:	3/21 / 5/13
Deferment available	Yes
Maximum length of deferment	1 year; considered on a case-by-case basis
Transfer students accepted	No
Non-fall admissions	No
Need-blind admissions	Yes

EMPLOYMENT PROFILE

Career Rating	97	**Grads Employed by Function% Avg. Salary**	
Percent employed at graduation	66	Marketing	(21%) $106,271
Percent employed 3 months after graduation	92	Operations	(6%) $118,500
		Consulting	(36%) $132,235
Average base starting salary	$118,274	Management	(6%) $108,409
Primary Source of Full-time Job Acceptances		Finance	(21%) $112,498
School-facilitated activities	254 (69%)	HR	(1%) $110,000
Graduate-facilitated activities	100 (27%)	Other	(6%) $112,450
Unknown	16 (4%)	**Top 5 Employers Hiring Grads**	

Top 5 Employers Hiring Grads
Amazon (34), McKinsey & Company (22), Deloitte (20), The Boston Consulting Group (14), PwC (12)

University of Michigan—Dearborn
College of Business

GENERAL INFORMATION

Type of school	Public
Affiliation	No Affiliation
Academic calendar	Semester

SURVEY SAYS...

Friendly students, Happy students
Solid preparation in:
Finance, General management,
Operations, Quantitative skills,
Computer skills

STUDENTS

Enrollment of parent institution	10
Enrollment of MBA Program	119
% male/female	93/7
% out-of-state	3
% part-time	85
% underrepresented minority	1
% international	3
Average age at entry	29
Average years work experience at entry	5

ACADEMICS

Academic Experience Rating	92
Profs interesting rating	90
Profs accessible rating	93
Student/faculty ratio	15:1
% female faculty	41
% underrepresented minority faculty	6
% part-time faculty	13

Joint Degrees

MBA/MS-Finance (57-66 credits)
MBA/MS-Information Systems (57-66 credits) MBA/MS-Supply Chain
Management (57-66 credits) MBA/
MSE-Industrial Systems Engineering
(57-66 credits) MBA/Master of
Health Services Administration in
Ann Arbor (81 credits)

Academics

After comparing MBA programs, many students choose University of Michigan—Dearborn for the unbeatable triumvirate of "value, location, and name brand" its College of Business offers. The program is geared toward part-time students, and the combination of "evening and online MBA classes are perfect for professionals already in the workforce." Courses begin three times a year (in September, January, and May), and through the "flexible online program," students can take as many (or as few) classes as fit their schedule. Core courses cover all functional business areas and comprise more than half the forty-eight units of required course work; however, students with undergraduate business degrees may be eligible to waive core course work, thereby completing the program in less time. After the core, students can choose to take various electives, or complete a concentration in finance, international business, marketing, supply chain management, information systems, or accounting. But the program is definitely open to students of all undergraduate majors and all levels of professional experience. The college has long maintained a strong local reputation (not to mention, it boasts the excellent University of Michigan name). Even so, students say things are always improving: "In the last few years, the program has become increasingly relevant and well-suited for graduate studies."

Just as they praise the college's dean, UMD students are pleased to report that the administration is "very accommodating and helpful," assisting students with everything from scheduling to academic advising. With a fairly large student body, it "can be difficult to get into popular classes, but the college has offered several options to help students get the classes they need." For students who take their classes on campus, the facilities are modern, and the school "provides the variety and excellence expected of a satellite campus of a world-class university." And, like the academic offerings, facilities are consistently improving. For example, the school opened a trading floor on campus in 2010, which helps bring real-world capacities to finance and accounting courses, in addition to being open for general use.

In terms of faculty, "there is a wide range of professor capability at this school." Many "are clearly experts in their fields," while others are less prepared for their important posts. On the whole, however, professors are "friendly and easily approachable" and "lectures are well-organized, and there is plenty of opportunity provided for discussion on topics of current interest." With an average of sixteen students in each classroom, "small class sizes help the interaction between students and professors, as well as among our peers." If you'd like assistance outside of class, "most of the professors will give you their home telephone number to reach them if you can't make office hours. They are as committed to us as we are to learning."

ADMISSIONS CONTACT: BRAD MAKI MA, DIRECTOR OF GRADUATE ADMISSIONS
ADDRESS: COLLEGE OF BUSINESS, 19000 HUBBARD DR., DEARBORN, MI 48126-2638
PHONE: 313-593-5460 • FAX: 313-271-9838
E-MAIL: GRADBUSINESS@UMD.UMICH.EDU • WEBSITE: WWW.COB.UMD.UMICH.EDU

Career and Placement

A large percentage of UMD students are already working full-time, and many receive tuition assistance from their employers. For those who are looking for a new job (or to make a career change), the College of Business's Internship and Career Management Center (ICMC) assists graduate students with their job and internship search through resume critiques, online job and internship boards, and career fairs. On the ICMC website, students can get information about upcoming events and workshops, or peruse current job listings and links to local employment assistance. Students are often surprised to find that their professors can be a great way to get a foot in the door of the local job market. A current student attests, "They are quite supportive even when you're finished with their class—it is not uncommon for professors to help with networking or career searches."

Student Life and Environment

On this suburban campus, most students are "working professionals" with a "few full-time students" added to the mix. While many are busy with work and family, this professional group takes their studies seriously, and most students are "eager to participate in class and highly focused on their academics." "Being a commuter university, there is not much networking outside of class," and clubs and extracurricular activities are limited. Still, some part-time students say they use "the library, health club, and all of the business offices" while others get together for "study groups outside of class time to prepare for exams or group projects."

For those who'd like a bit more camaraderie, the "COB has worked hard to improve student life," and many full-time MBA candidates say, "I have made friends that I expect to have the rest of my life." In addition, the larger university is home to over 9,083 students. There, "you will always find clubs sponsoring and advertising activities to try and get other students engaged." Campus facilities get good reviews, and recently, "A new food court and study lounge was added" to the business school area. "Research and technologies are top notch and on par with other major business schools," and "The College of Business has its own computer lab" with Internet access and printers.

Admissions

Applications to University of Michigan—Dearborn are accepted on a rolling basis; however, students are encouraged to apply by the priority deadline. Usually, once the university has received all of a student's application materials, an admissions decision will be made in just a few days. Most accepted applicants have a GMAT score in the high-500s and an undergraduate GPA of 3.5 on a 4.0 scale.

FINANCIAL FACTS

Cost of books	$4,606
Room & board (on/off-campus)	$7,880/$7,880
% of students receiving aid	36
% of first-year students receiving aid	45
% of students receiving grants	10
Average award package	$16,977
Average grant	$3,527
Average loan	$19,868
Average student loan debt	$51,420

ADMISSIONS

Admissions Selectivity Rating	89
# of applications received	97
% applicants accepted	39
% acceptees attending	74
Average GMAT	580
Range of GMAT	548–620
Accepts GRE scores	Yes
Average Verbal GRE	154
Range of Verbal GRE scores	154–156
Average Quantitative GRE	159
Range of Quantitative GRE scores	158–161
Average GPA	3.4
TOEFL required of international students	Yes
Minimum TOEFL (paper/web)	560/84
Application fee	$60
International application fee	$60
Regular application deadline	8/1
Application Deadline/Notification	
Deferment available	Yes
Maximum length of deferment	One year
Transfer students accepted	Yes
Transfer application policy	
Waivers will be given for courses equivalent to MBA core courses. Up to six credits of transfer may also be awarded for other MBA courses.	
Non-fall admissions	Yes
Need-blind admissions	Yes

University of Michigan—Flint
School of Management

GENERAL INFORMATION

Type of school	Public
Academic calendar	Semesters

SURVEY SAYS...

Cutting-edge classes
Solid preparation in:
Operations

STUDENTS

Enrollment of parent institution	8,470
Enrollment of MBA Program	154
% male/female	62/38
% out-of-state	4
% part-time	90
% underrepresented minority	13
% international	14
Average age at entry	31
Average years work experience at entry	9

ACADEMICS

Academic Experience Rating	**73**
Profs interesting rating	76
Profs accessible rating	68
Student/faculty ratio	4:1
% female faculty	28
% underrepresented minority faculty	5
% part-time faculty	26

Joint Degrees

Dual-Degree Program
Requirements: http://www.umflint.
edu/graduateprograms/dual-de-
gree-programs MBA/MSA 45-60
Credits MBA/MS in Computer
Science and Information Systems
45-75 Credits DrAP/MBA 48-57
Credits DNP/MBA 66-138 Credits
DPT/MBA 144-153 Credits

Prominent Alumni

Clarence Sevillian, CEO at McLaren
Bay Region; Kim Horn, President
& CEO at Priority Health; Mike
Maizland, CIO Shanghai OnStar;
Rodney P. Wood, Detroit Lions
President

Academics

If you are looking for a "prestigious top school for management" that offers a great deal of "flexibility," then consider the University of Michigan—Flint School of Management. The MBA program is "very structured and organized." One student who is "a very busy mom, wife, and full-time employee," says, "I like that they take care of everything for me. I do not need to worry about what classes I am taking next, or how to obtain my books. The courses are relevant and ... [can be taken] on campus [or] online. They encourage networking and are available when you need them." Other students agree, saying that the school is "well-managed" and "the time to complete the program was far less restrictive than others."

Coursework at UM–Flint is "a rigorous academic experience." "The pace is quick and the work is challenging; within the structure provided, there is plenty of room for self-expression." There are no easy grades here. "You earn an A, it's never handed to you." The faculty does a great job of providing students with the help and guidance they need to achieve that A. Faculty members "have an excellent grasp of the knowledge needed to convey difficult concepts. They encourage interaction among both students and other faculty." The content studied in the MBA program is "interesting and incredibly applicable." Also, "many fields and industries are represented in the classroom, not only in people from Michigan, but from all over the country and even some from different countries. My classmates have had a very positive impact on my learning experience."

Besides the traditional on-campus courses, students can opt for "NetPlus!," an innovative program that combines both online and in-class offerings. Students choosing the NetPlus! format work according to their own, flexible schedule, and are only required to attend on-campus classes once every six weeks. This enables students to "pursue an MBA while [they] travel for work." It also helps many who are juggling school with a demanding work schedule or long commute to campus. As one student sums it up, this "mixed-mode format was very appealing. It offered the best of both worlds (online and in-class)." Students also give the administration high marks. "The MBA program has a very strong administrative staff. They are friendly, listen well, and work very quickly."

Career and Placement

Students at UM–Flint have the support of "a strong career development office." Students benefit from the school's fine reputation with employers in Michigan and beyond. The Student Success Center at University of Michigan–Flint offers career guidance and counseling to undergraduates, alumni, and graduate students. The center hosts career fairs and offers advising services, however these services cater principally to undergraduates. One student points out that they can "receive daily emails from the career department listing campus visits and recruitment sessions from major companies." Unfortunately, not all students "take advantage of the office, though, and one must sign up for the service."

FINANCIAL FACTS

Annual tuition (in-state/ out-of-state)	$11,583/$14,751
Fees	$432
Cost of books	$1,000
Room & board (on/off-campus)	$8,178/$8,178
% of students receiving aid	43
% of first-year students receiving aid	50
% of students receiving grants	16
Average award package	$12,232
Average grant	$1,906
Average loan	$14,808
Average student loan debt	$32,925

ADMISSIONS

Admissions Selectivity Rating	**87**
# of applications received	116
% applicants accepted	49
% acceptees attending	77
Average GMAT	548
Range of GMAT	460–710
Accepts GRE scores	Yes
Average Verbal GRE	145
Range of Verbal GRE scores	143–146
Average Quantitative GRE	146
Range of Quantitative GRE scores	144–148
Average Writing GRE	3.2
Range of Writing GRE scores	3.0–3.5
Average GPA	3.3
TOEFL required of international students	Yes
Minimum TOEFL (paper/web)	560/84
Application fee	$55
International application fee	$55
Early application deadline	5/1
Application Deadline/Notification	
Deferment available	Yes
Maximum length of deferment	1 year
Transfer students accepted	Yes
Transfer application policy AACSB accredited program, "B" or better in the last 7 years, grad level, 9 cr hrs only, not part of any other degree program	
Non-fall admissions	Yes
Need-blind admissions	Yes

Student Life and Environment

A "very friendly campus environment" helps create the sentiment in which "it is always pleasant to be at school." Classmates are "highly experienced and educated." "They have different academic backgrounds, work environments, home settings, ages, genders, and [ethnicities]." This diversity in the graduate program "is one of its biggest strengths," says a student. "When having discussions in class or outside of class, the multiple frames of reference help me understand how different concepts could be used in real world settings. It's great that this program is able to intertwine theory and practice." Strong bonds are commonplace among graduate students here. One student is astounded at the ease in which friendships form, saying, "I've made more friends in the two years of my Graduate [degree] than I did in the four years of my Undergraduate degree."

The downtown location of UM–Flint offers convenience in "a great location and parking is included in your tuition." "The downtown area offers places to meet with classmates after class as well." A commuter notes that there are plenty of study spaces available "that are open twenty-four hours a day. So, for group projects class-mates and I are able to meet late in the evening, after class. This is fantastic, because so many of us have busy family and work lives. We don't have to take time off during the day to use the library, or find an off campus meeting location."

The program recently had a huge boost in technology and now students enjoy a new "state-of-the-art facility." They can now experience its finance lab and "there are many high tech study rooms, and a state of the art computer lab, research center, and student organization offices." But many students worry about the surrounding environment. Some "do not feel safe when walking to and from [their] car." "The university has a wonderful alert system that you can sign up for to get emails or alerts via text message regarding school closures or crimes," but "it's frightening to get a text about a mugging in broad daylight." UM-Flint public safety alerts include tips to remain safe on campus and officers are available 24/7 to escort students around campus and to their vehicles.

Admissions

Prospective students must submit GMAT scores, or GRE scores, undergraduate GPA, essay, letters of recommendation, as well as a resume to be considered for enrollment at the University of Michigan—Flint. The most weight in the admissions decision process is based on GRE or GMAT, and GPA scores. The Traditional MBA program starts classes twice a year. NetPlus! MBA enrolls students four times a year.

UNIVERSITY OF MINNESOTA

GENERAL INFORMATION

Type of school — Public
Affiliation — No Affiliation
Academic calendar — Semester

SURVEY SAYS...

Classmates have diverse work experience, Friendly students, Good peer network, Happy students, Abundant clubs and activities, Students love Minneapolis, MN
Solid preparation in:
Finance, General management, Teamwork, Presentation skills, Doing business in a global economy

STUDENTS

Enrollment of parent institution	46,800
Enrollment of MBA Program	1,242
% male/female	73/27
% out-of-state	46
% part-time	84
% underrepresented minority	14
% international	23
Average age at entry	28
Average years work experience at entry	5

ACADEMICS

Academic Experience Rating	93
Profs interesting rating	91
Profs accessible rating	94
Student/faculty ratio	17:1
% female faculty	30
% underrepresented minority faculty	24
% part-time faculty	46

Joint Degrees

JD/MBA; MHA/MBA; MPP/MBA; MA-HRIR/MBA; MD/MBA; PHARMD/MBA; ApplEcon/MBA; MBA/MSBA

Academics

At the University of Minnesota Carlson School of Management, experiential learning, proximity to Fortune 500 companies, a "stellar" Career Center, and a "robust dual degree program" are just a few of the happy offerings on tap for those who take advantage of the school's various MBA tracks. The school "makes life very enjoyable for the student body," administrators are "passionate advocates" for the programs, and "staff members go out of their way to remove barriers to success for students." Both the administration and professors "are very receptive to student feedback" and "are willing to change their approach to best suit the students." This includes "updating, removing, and replacing required courses; and providing specific resources to students."

The workload at Carlson is well balanced. Students say course work is "challenging, but it doesn't take hours of your day up to get it done" (the exception being some of the core curriculum, which "can be brutal some weeks"). The academic rigor is "sufficient for most students, even those with a business background," and "enterprise experience . . . gives real world experience and legitimate projects from companies." Smaller cohort sizes "leverage wiggle space, and a more personalized MBA program is the outcome," which includes "lots of coaching and mentoring being offered." The beloved professors "can apply the principles they're trying to teach us in a real world example while at the same time getting us to laugh." "We have beers on occasion and it's nice to know that these people have other interests than just class," says a student. They "offer many options to help us balance both school and work," including includes the ability to choose which two or three cases students want to write an analysis on, and courses of varying lengths throughout the semester.

Career and Placement

The "highly diverse and outstanding business community in the Twin Cities area" is the primary goal (or current employer) of most who attend Carlson, and "opportunities to network and improve our marketability outside of the classroom are plentiful." Minneapolis boasts numerous Fortune 500 companies, as well as a robust nonprofit sector, which "allows you to pursue whatever direction you want with your MBA, all while being part of a vibrant metropolis." For those who are seeking to work outside of Minnesota, "Carlson is also expanding networking opportunities on the West Coast" and is incredibly helpful in facilitating the job search of students who wish to do so.

The Career Center has "phenomenal and flexible offerings for part-time MBA students," as well. "My personal favorite is the all-day Career Conference for part-time students held on a Saturday each April," says one. The alumni network is equally as helpful: "There's a pride from being from Carlson and alumni want to do what they can to help the next generation of graduates succeed." Recent employers of Carlson grads include 3M, Amazon, Best Buy, Boston Scientific, Cummins, Deloitte Consulting, Delta Airlines, Dish Network, and Eaton Corporation.

Student Life and Environment

The U of M is "fantastic about engaging all students both in the classroom and with social activities": "From events during class times or on off days, there is a strong sense of togetherness." The school is constantly trying to cater to its busy student components, introducing part-time clubs, "networking socials" before and during class, Friday evening casual dinners, and a couple of all-day career workshops over the weekend. The student body is "a great mix that includes a large group of veterans and international students," and many students come from all over the country. There is an incredibly active social scene, and "it is more or less an expectation [that] students participate in that social scene," though "you can get as involved as you have time for." This includes many family-friendly and spouse-friendly activities and events: "I like the fact that my family was able to come and see what I do on a typical day, eat lunch with them and then meet my classmates. It really made me feel like I was combining two families."

Admissions

Candidates will need to submit GMAT scores, undergraduate GPA, work experience, a personal statement, and professional references. All are highly factored into the decision process. Interviews for the Full-Time MBA are invitation only. The GPA median for the Full-Time program for the entering Class of 2014 was 3.45 and the median GMAT score was 690. The Multicultural Affairs and Diversity Education (MADE) outreach program works jointly with several organizations to bring qualified minority candidates to the school. These organizations include the National Black MBA Association (NBMBAA), the National Society of Hispanic MBAs (NSHMBA), as well as the Asian MBA (AMBA).

Prominent Alumni

Thomas O. Staggs, Chairman, Walt Disney Parks & Resorts, The Walt Disney Company; John G. Stumpf, Chairman, President and CEO, Wells Fargo & Company; John H. Hammergren, Chairman and CEO, McKesson Corp.; Thia Breen, Global President of Estee Lauder Brand, Estee Lauder Companies Inc.

FINANCIAL FACTS

Annual tuition (in-state/ out-of-state)	$36,140/$46,500
Fees	$4,267
Cost of books	$3,000
Room & board (on/off-campus)	$15,000/$17,000
Average student loan debt	$54,723

ADMISSIONS

Admissions Selectivity Rating	90
# of applications received	594
% applicants accepted	39
% acceptees attending	37
Average GMAT	680
Range of GMAT	650–710
Accepts GRE scores	Yes
Average Verbal GRE	160
Range of Verbal GRE scores	156–164
Average Quantitative GRE	160
Range of Quantitative GRE scores	157–163
Average Writing GRE	4.4
Range of Writing GRE scores	4.0–4.9
Average GPA	3.4
TOEFL required of international students	Yes
Minimum TOEFL (paper/web)	580/84
Application fee	$75
International application fee	$75
Application Deadline/Notification	
Round 1:	11/1 / 1/15
Round 2:	12/1 / 2/15
Round 3:	2/1 / 4/15
Round 4:	4/1 / 5/15
Deferment available	Yes
Maximum length of deferment	1 year
Transfer students accepted	No
Non-fall admissions	No
Need-blind admissions	Yes

EMPLOYMENT PROFILE

Career Rating	89	**Grads Employed by Function% Avg. Salary**	
Percent employed at graduation	75	Marketing	(30%) $95,600
Percent employed 3 months after graduation	89	Operations	(8%) $91,967
		Consulting	(33%) $120,313
Average base starting salary	$106,435	Management	(4%) $102,333
Primary Source of Full-time Job Acceptances		Finance	(16%) $103,333
School-facilitated activities	57 (69%)	MIS	(2%)
Graduate-facilitated activities	21 (25%)	Other	(7%) $109,871
Unknown	5 (6%)	**Top 5 Employers Hiring Grads**	
		Dish Network (5), Deloitte Consulting (5), General Mills (4), Ecolab, Inc. (4), Target Corporation (4)	

UNIVERSITY OF MISSISSIPPI
SCHOOL OF BUSINESS ADMINISTRATION

GENERAL INFORMATION

Type of school	Public
Affiliation	No Affiliation
Academic calendar	Semester

SURVEY SAYS...
Good social scene, Cutting-edge classes
Solid preparation in:
Finance, Accounting, Teamwork, Doing business in a global economy

STUDENTS

Enrollment of parent institution	21,500
Enrollment of MBA Program	100
% male/female	60/40
% out-of-state	60
% part-time	40
% underrepresented minority	8
% international	4
Average age at entry	24
Average years work experience at entry	2

ACADEMICS

Academic Experience Rating	**68**
Profs interesting rating	69
Profs accessible rating	62
Student/faculty ratio	7:1
% female faculty	30
% underrepresented minority faculty	12
% part-time faculty	0

Academics

The University of Mississippi—known affectionately as "Ole Miss" to its many students and supporters—offers students two MBA options. The first is an intensive, one-year full-time MBA, which does not require post-undergraduate professional experience for admission; the other is the two-year online MBA for working adults, which gives strong preference to students with at least two years of post-undergraduate business-related employment.

Ole Miss' one-year program runs eleven months, commencing in July and ending in May. The curriculum consists of thirteen prescribed courses, taught cohort-style with an emphasis on "the integration of subjects into real business applications." Students warn that the program is intense. As one explains, "Overall, you have to be very serious if you want to be in a one-year program. Don't let the kind recruiters fool you: You are in for hell if you are not 100 percent committed...There is hardly any time to breathe. This is only for the extremely serious." Instructors "expect a lot out of us," and even "the administration is concerned with our performance and takes measures to continually monitor our progression through the classes. Overall, the academic experience is rigorous." One student concurs, "The program could use more breaks. Or, they could lengthen it to ease the stress."

The part-time MBA at Ole Miss is more flexible, using "alternate methods of delivering course content" through internet tools. The online program delivers the same MBA content and degree as the on campus program. In both the part-time and full-time program, "professors all have business backgrounds and have been tenured for a long time, or they have short academic careers and long, successful business careers in the fields they teach." Instructors typically employ "real-world examples and tie your education from them into your own work experiences. Dictation seldom happens. Discussion of the assigned readings is the primary classroom focus."

Career and Placement

Ole Miss MBAs receive career support from the university's Career Center. Students report that many of the best career opportunities come via the alumni network, which is "very supportive. The Ole Miss 'brand' is well-respected in the Southeast." Employers that recruit on the Ole Miss campus include Axciom, Allstate, Bancorp South, FedEx, Harrah's, IBM, International Paper, Regions Bank, and the Tennessee Valley Authority.

Student Life and Environment

The swift pace of the full-time MBA program means that many students "study so much that it is hard to have a life. But when there are small breaks, the potential to have a great time is definitely there." First and foremost, is Ole Miss football and the requisite tailgate parties beforehand, but there's much more to the social scene than sports. The school "offers a wide variety of activities socially and academically that you can become involved in. This place has a lot of great traditions." Students appreciate the Ole Miss grounds, which one describes as "a walking campus that promotes and produces beautiful people!"

Hometown Oxford is a small, Southern college town distinguished by the university and the residences of several famous writers, including John Grisham. The town has become a travel destination for many, not only for Ole Miss sporting events but also for festivals such as the Double Decker Arts Festival and conferences as the Faulkner & Yoknapatawpha Conference (named after the author William Faulkner, who made his home in Oxford, and the fictional county in which much of his work is set). The city of Memphis is just seventy miles to the north.

Full-timers at Ole Miss tend to be "very young. The majority are twenty-two years old. Some have had internships, but none have actually worked. It's very difficult to have a discussion about business if you've never been involved in one. The few students with work experience talk 95 percent of the time." The student community is close. As one student explains, "One thing about going through an MBA 'boot camp' like this is that you come together very quickly. Because you're all suffering together, people are very friendly and quick to help you out."

Admissions

All applicants to the full-time MBA program at Ole Miss must provide an official transcript of undergraduate work showing a minimum 3.0 GPA for the final sixty semesters hours of academic work; an official GMAT score report (the school lists 550 as the cut-off for "acceptable" scores); two letters of recommendation; and a 400-word personal statement of purpose. Students who have not completed prerequisite course work in undergraduate business disciplines will be required to complete such courses successfully before commencing work on their graduate degrees. International students must meet all of the above requirements and submit TOEFL scores (minimum acceptable score is 600). Applicants to the professional MBA program "with two or more years of post-baccalaureate degree professional work experience" receive "particular consideration" from the Admissions Committee. The professional MBA program is "very competitive."

FINANCIAL FACTS

Annual tuition (in-state/ out-of-state)	$11,300/$27,700
Average grant	$3,600

ADMISSIONS

Admissions Selectivity Rating	**76**
Average GMAT	570
Accepts GRE scores	Yes
Average Verbal GRE	160
Average Quantitative GRE	153
Average GPA	3.4
TOEFL required of international students	Yes
Minimum TOEFL (paper/web)	600/79
Application fee	$50
International application fee	$50
Application Deadline/Notification	
Deferment available	Yes
Maximum length of deferment	1 Year
Transfer students accepted	No
Non-fall admissions	Yes
Need-blind admissions	Yes

UNIVERSITY OF MISSOURI—COLUMBIA
ROBERT J. TRULASKE, SR. COLLEGE OF BUSINESS

GENERAL INFORMATION
Type of school	Public
Affiliation	No Affiliation
Academic calendar	Semester

SURVEY SAYS...
Friendly students, Good peer network, Good social scene, Cutting-edge classes, Abundant mentors available, Happy students, Abundant clubs and activities
Solid preparation in:
Marketing, General management, Teamwork

STUDENTS
Enrollment of parent institution	35,448
Enrollment of MBA Program	135
% male/female	68/32
% out-of-state	53
% part-time	9
% underrepresented minority	5
% international	32
Average age at entry	24
Average years work experience at entry	2

ACADEMICS
Academic Experience Rating	93
Profs interesting rating	93
Profs accessible rating	97
Student/faculty ratio	4:1
% female faculty	27
% underrepresented minority faculty	14
% part-time faculty	34

Joint Degrees
MBA/Bachelors in Industrial Engineering; MBA/MS in Industrial Engineering; MBA/JD; MBA/Master of Health Administration; MBA/Bachelors in Information Technology

Prominent Alumni
Stan Kroenke, Real Estate, Sports Teams & Media; Ralph Babb, CEO, Comerica; Jon Hamm, Actor; Sam Walton, Founder, Walmart and Sam's Club

Academics

The University of Missouri-Columbia, commonly referred to as "Mizzou," is the central and most populous campus in the four-school University of Missouri system. The Crosby MBA program, named after Gordon E. Crosby, Jr., the former USLIFE CEO who made a $10 million donation to the program in 2002, has been described as a "versatile program" where "current business issues and trends are the core of many classes." Mizzou has a "great combination of cutting edge curriculum and facilities for a bargain." Point in fact, both the benefits of in-state tuition and "excellent financial aid" make Mizzou a draw for in- and out-of-state residents alike. Mizzou's "well-ranked" business school also boasts "excellent dual-degree programs," such as a dual JD/MBA, a popular MHA/MBA and the five-year IMSE/MBA program, which according to one student, "allows me to get an education in both engineering and business while on the same campus."

Other program offerings within the Trulaske College of Business include degrees or concentrations in accounting, economics, healthcare administration, finance, international business, investment banking, leadership/management, marketing, marketing analytics certification, and non-profit management/public administration. The Mizzou campus itself also has the advantage of size. One chemical engineering student tells us, "The campus has a medical school, law school, and veterinary school, within a few blocks, making it ideal for entrepreneurship and innovation." All MBA candidates are required to take a course focused on experiential learning and to personally consult with small business owners.

Since Mizzou does offer such a "broad curriculum" and a large number of "resources available for students," the student body covers a wide range of experience, both professional and academic. One thankful student tells us Mizzou "allowed me to pursue my MBA without prior professional experience." Another student has indicated, "The students with work experience tend to come more from management and marketing backgrounds and have stronger skill sets than the 'straight-through' students." This dichotomy, while beneficial in many ways, has also prompted one concerned student to plead for the business school to "increase the number of students with work experience."

Career and Placement

The Crosby MBA Program Career Services provides a broad range of services, including individualized career coaching, resume-building workshops, on-campus interviews, counseling, and a mentoring program. Companies are often invited to Mizzou to present themselves and recruit worthy candidates. While some students comment that networking opportunities with alumni and top employers are lacking, and "there doesn't seem to be a push to attract companies outside the Midwest," global companies, such as AT&T, Deloitte, and Edward Jones, Cerner, and Chevron have all made frequent visits to the school. One student tells us, "I just had coffee with one of our alums working for a major consulting firm in Philadelphia and that was just the start of my alumni search." The MBA program also offers a variety of school-facilitated internship opportunities, and post-graduate job placement data suggests that Mizzou MBAs are not pigeonholed into one or two industries, but several, from manufacturing to non-profit and healthcare.

Student Life and Environment

Columbia is a "great college town," with an abundance of restaurants, bars, music, culture, parks, and related activities. Even though Mizzou enjoys a large campus at the center of town, downtown Columbia is just a few steps away, and there's always something to do. Students have described the Crosby MBA program as a "close-knit community of students who are very willing to help one another and a great learning community where there are a multitude of opportunities for students to get involved on campus." This "open and friendly" atmosphere has helped foster a business program that students laud for being "cooperative" and "less competitive" than similarly sized MBA programs.

The MBA Association at Mizzou holds "weekly happy hours and other social events," where students have the chance to "play numerous intramural sports and even participate on club teams." Prospective students may also be pleased to learn that the Association pays close attention to the diversity of its student body. Several Association members are also members of the Crosby Analytics Society and the National Association of Women MBAs, while others serve on the College of Business Diversity Committee.

Admissions

Applicants to the Crosby MBA program at The University of Missouri-Columbia are required to submit the following materials: GMAT or GRE scores, essay/personal statement, official undergraduate transcript, and an updated resume. Particularly close attention is paid to applicants' employability, test scores, undergraduate GPA (3.5 is average), and personal statement. International applicants are required to submit TOEFL or IELTS scores, with a 550 minimum for written test, 213 for computer-based, and 79-80 for web-based. While substantive post-undergraduate work experience (two or more years) is strongly considered, it is not a requirement for admission. Prospective students with excellent educational backgrounds in technology, engineering, bio/life sciences, journalism, and social sciences are historically successful in the Crosby MBA Program.

FINANCIAL FACTS

Annual tuition (in-state/ out-of-state)	$9,975/$26,705
Fees	$3,813
Cost of books	$906
Room & board (on/off-campus)	$9,908/$9,908
% of students receiving aid	88
% of first-year students receiving aid	94
% of students receiving grants	89
Average award package	$23,462
Average grant	$22,016
Average loan	$8,067
Average student loan debt	$22,616

ADMISSIONS

Admissions Selectivity Rating	**89**
# of applications received	245
% applicants accepted	42
% acceptees attending	51
Average GMAT	648
Range of GMAT	610–680
Accepts GRE scores	Yes
Average Verbal GRE	157
Range of Verbal GRE scores	155–159
Average Quantitative GRE	161
Range of Quantitative GRE scores	158–163
Average GPA	3.5
TOEFL required of international students	Yes
Minimum TOEFL (paper/web)	550/80
Application fee	$65
International application fee	$90
Application Deadline/Notification	
Round 1:	11/1
Round 2:	1/15
Round 3:	3/1
Round 4:	4/15
Deferment available	Yes
Maximum length of deferment	One year
Transfer students accepted	Yes
Transfer application policy Students may transfer 6 credit hours from an AACSB-accredited MBA program.	
Non-fall admissions	Yes
Need-blind admissions	Yes

EMPLOYMENT PROFILE

Career Rating	92	Grads Employed by Function	% Avg. Salary
Percent employed at graduation	66	Marketing	(28%) $62,909
Percent employed 3 months after graduation	91	Operations	(12%) $75,083
		Consulting	(10%) $54,800
Average base starting salary	$61,972	Management	(16%) $67,929
Primary Source of Full-time Job Acceptances		Finance	(24%) $55,488
School-facilitated activities	31 (62%)	Other	(10%) $58,200
Graduate-facilitated activities	19 (38%)	**Top 5 Employers Hiring Grads**	

Ascension Health (3), Dish Network (3), Alight Analytics (2), 3M (2), Daymon Worldwide (2)

University of Missouri—Kansas City
Henry W. Bloch School of Business and Public Administration

GENERAL INFORMATION

Type of school	Public
Affiliation	No Affiliation
Academic calendar	Semester

SURVEY SAYS...

Solid preparation in:
Teamwork, Communication/interpersonal skills, Presentation skills

STUDENTS

Enrollment of parent institution	15,492
Enrollment of MBA Program	375
% male/female	61/39
% out-of-state	43
% part-time	63
% underrepresented minority	14
% international	10
Average age at entry	30
Average years work experience at entry	3

ACADEMICS

Academic Experience Rating	68
Profs interesting rating	68
Profs accessible rating	68
Student/faculty ratio	13:1
% female faculty	26
% underrepresented minority faculty	21
% part-time faculty	5

Joint Degrees

JD/MBA (81 law school credit hours + 42 MBA credit hours) JD/MPA (81 law school credit hours + 36-39 MPA credit hours)

Prominent Alumni

Gerald Kelly, CEO of Silpada Designs; Terry Dunn, President and CEO, Dunn Industries, Inc.; Bob Regnier, President, Bank of Blue Valley; Tom Holcom, President, Pioneer Financial Services, Inc.; Esther George, COO of Federal Reserve Bank of Kansas City

Academics

The "dynamic community" at the University of Missouri—Kansas City unites some of the brightest business minds in the region. Academically, the school's MBA is known for its "outstanding entrepreneurship and innovation program," which was developed to compliment the growing number of new ventures and technology companies in the local area. Kansas City, together with several other Midwestern cities, is sometimes dubbed the "Silicon Prairie," and "there is a feeling that everyone at the Henry W. Bloch School of Management is a part of a larger movement in Kansas City to be officially known as the entrepreneurship capital of the United States." Those ties to the community are a huge strength of the program, and students praise the "local business community and their willingness to contribute to classes and research." A current student shares, "My involvement with the UMKC Institute for Entrepreneurship and Innovation recently helped me win a business planning contest valued at $100,000. I now have the opportunity to connect with the leading business men and women in my city."

Aside from the school's noted strength in entrepreneurship, the MBA curriculum trains students in business fundamentals, beginning with twenty-four credit hours of core coursework in key topics like marketing, management, and economics. After completing the core, students take fifteen credits of electives, with the option of pursuing a concentration in entrepreneurship, finance, general management, international business, leading and managing people, management information systems, marketing, or supply chain and operations management. While the faculty includes some "world-class researchers," "UMKC is not as heavy on theory, but they are VERY strong on practical." Professional students can immediately take knowledge and skills back to the workplace, as coursework focuses on "activities applicable to real-world situations." Students explain that even their employers regard UMKC as "the best business school at preparing students for the job" in the Kansas City area.

On campus, "UMKC offers a big-city feel with a suburban community and attitude, meaning the faculty and students are down-to-earth and the quality of the education is up to Ivy League standards." Speaking of the Ivy League, students dole out praises for their experienced and well-educated faculty, saying instructors are "engaging, intelligent, and fair." Most have "great real world experience they can draw on," which makes their lectures more applicable. These professors ultimately serve as valuable "resources for future opportunities" as well. A student adds, "The Bloch School professors are a cut above the rest. They are always there when you need them, and [they] are practical in their project assignment." Convenience and affordability make the UMKC programs all the more attractive. "Most students are working while in the program," so they appreciate the school's flexible evening schedule, while the "affordable" in-state tuition is the icing on the cake.

ADMISSIONS CONTACT: W.C. VANCE, DIRECTOR OF ADMISSIONS
ADDRESS: 5100 ROCKHILL ROAD, KANSAS CITY, MO 64110
PHONE: 816-235-1111 • FAX: 816-235-5544
E-MAIL: ADMIT@UMKC.EDU • WEBSITE: WWW.BLOCH.UMKC.EDU

Career and Placement

Students generally start the Bloch MBA when their professional career is already underway. "Most work for large corporations and are participating in a tuition reimbursement program," in which they plan to remain with the same company after graduation. Other students join the program "to start a business as part of the Entrepreneurship initiative." While they are in the minority, students at the early stages of their careers also say they benefit from the school's strong, practical education. A current student details, "I chose UMKC because I honestly believed they would help me find myself and the career in which I would fit. I have not been let down. Each class I'm learning more about myself and what the future holds." No matter what their career goals, Bloch students benefit from "personal access to Kansas City's top business professionals," through faculty, speakers, and networking events.

The Bloch Career Network adviser plans career-related workshops and helps manage an online job board, though these resources are principally aimed at assisting undergraduates. MBA candidates can also access the Career Services Center at UMKC, which serves the entire school community. Among other services, they offer resume help, internship placements, career fairs, and campus recruiting for both undergraduate and graduate students.

Student Life and Environment

UMKC has specially designed their MBA program to appeal to local professionals. As a result, a majority of students are "married with children, or what you would consider 'nontraditional,'" though there is a small community of students who "come straight out of [their] undergraduate" schooling. The campus as a whole attracts students from "a large mix of careers," so you will share a classroom and a campus with "MBA students, engineers, lawyers, and MPA students." On the whole, Bloch business students are "highly intelligent, motivated and friendly."

Masters of time management, most students "take a balanced approach to life," splitting their time between career obligations, coursework, and personal life. There are "a lot of commuters" so there is "not a whole lot of socializing" between MBA students on campus. Most "people show up for their class and leave," though they occasionally linger in the "computer labs, study areas, and meeting with class team members." Home to almost over 14,000 students, UMKC's vibrant campus is located in the Rockhill area of Kansas City. In their free time, students can easily access the range of cultural, recreational, shopping, and dining options around town.

Admissions

In addition to GMAT scores and undergraduate transcripts, applicants for University of Missouri—Kansas City's evening MBA program must submit a one-page goals statement, a current resume, and information about their current employment, including any travel commitments. Applicants to the EMBA program are not required to take the GMAT, but they must have extensive upper-level work experience as evidenced by their resume, letters of recommendation, and personal statement. Applications are accepted year-round on a rolling basis.

FINANCIAL FACTS

Annual tuition (in-state/ out-of-state)	$5,522/$14,256
Fees	$888
Cost of books	$1,180
Room & board (on/off-campus)	$9,560/$8,320
% of students receiving aid	43
% of first-year students receiving aid	50
% of students receiving grants	12
Average award package	$17,209
Average grant	$4,947
Average loan	$18,657
Average student loan debt	$26,513

ADMISSIONS

Admissions Selectivity Rating	**85**
# of applications received	203
% applicants accepted	60
% acceptees attending	80
Average GMAT	546
Range of GMAT	500–600
Accepts GRE scores	Yes
Average GPA	3.3
TOEFL required of international students	Yes
Minimum TOEFL (paper/web)	550/79
Application fee	$35
International application fee	$50
Regular application deadline	5/1
Application Deadline/Notification	
Deferment available	Yes
Maximum length of deferment	1 year
Transfer students accepted	Yes
Transfer application policy	
We will accept up to 6 hours of grad credit from an AACSB accredited institution	
Non-fall admissions	Yes
Need-blind admissions	Yes

UNIVERSITY OF MISSOURI—ST. LOUIS
COLLEGE OF BUSINESS ADMINISTRATION

GENERAL INFORMATION

Type of school	Public
Affiliation	No Affiliation
Academic calendar	Semester

SURVEY SAYS...

Classmates have diverse work experience
Solid preparation in:
Communication/interpersonal skills,
Presentation skills

STUDENTS

Enrollment of parent institution	16,719
Enrollment of MBA Program	487
% part-time	100
Average age at entry	28
Average years work experience at entry	3

ACADEMICS

Academic Experience Rating	85
Profs interesting rating	87
Profs accessible rating	89
Student/faculty ratio	11:1
% female faculty	30
% underrepresented minority faculty	9
% part-time faculty	30

Academics

The University of Missouri—St. Louis is a smart choice for local professionals who want to complete an MBA without interrupting their career. One of four "AASCB-accredited schools in the St. Louis area," UMSL offers several MBA options: the traditional evening MBA, the professional MBA, and the international MBA, offered in conjunction with partner universities overseas. For students in the evening program, "convenient class schedules" make UMSL a great choice (though evening students also say, "there is a great need for online course options" to provide greater flexibility). While classes in the evening program generally meet once a week, the professional MBA is a hybrid program, which combines weekend course work with online communication. As these options illustrate, the school's programs are principally geared toward "working professionals that attend UMSL and come to class and go home." However, the student body seems to be "shifting to younger students as they recognize the education level being received...surpasses the minimal cost to attend." On that note, USML is an excellent value. This school maintains a "good reputation in the St. Louis area for providing a good, quality business education," while also maintaining a "very affordable" tuition price.

The curriculum in both the evening and professional format provides training in the functional areas of business (though students in the evening program may also pursue an area of emphasis through elective course work). By all accounts, the administration is very "well-organized" and the curriculum is "up-to-date on trends and technology." At the same time, some students would like to see the core courses more ably synched. In some cases, "courses are repetitive," and students feel the MBA "should encompass a more general/integrated look at business and manage[ment]." Throughout the MBA, there is an emphasis on "combining the practical knowledge with the theoretical knowledge" in the classroom. At UMSL, "The professors are almost all professionals in their field," who "teach about real-world work experience and tie current events into the curriculum." Here, talented professors "make the course work interesting by providing practical knowledge in addition to theoretical knowledge, and truly being engaged in the industry." In fact, in the rare case that a teacher doesn't excel in the classroom, they nonetheless are experts in their fields. A student remembers, "There have been a few that were poor teachers but were good technically on the subject matter." Despite their real-world credentials, faculty "all seem to teach for the love of teaching versus for the pay," and they are "readily available outside of class and are always willing to help."

Career and Placement

Most UMSL programs are designed for working professionals who are looking to advance in their current position, rather than find a new job. However, for those seeking a career change, the UMSL Office of Career Services helps undergraduate and graduate students prepare for the job search through career counseling and job preparation workshops. The Office of Career Services also connects the university with local employers through networking events and job fairs. (At recent UMSL job fairs, numerous prominent companies attended, including Aflac Insurance, AT&T, Bank of America, Boeing, Commerce Bank, FedEx, Maxim Healthcare Services, Mutual of Omaha, Northwestern Mutual, Sherwin-Williams, St. Luke's Hospital, Target, Walgreens, and many more.) Through Career Services, students can also post their resume online, where it can be electronically matched with recruiting companies.

ADMISSIONS CONTACT: KARL KOTTEMANN, DIRECTOR, GRADUATE PROGRAMS
ADDRESS: ONE UNIVERSITY BOULEVARD, 350 JC PENNEY NORTH, ST. LOUIS, MO 63121-4499
PHONE: 314-516-5885 • FAX: 314-516-7202
E-MAIL: MBA@UMSL.EDU • WEBSITE: MBA.UMSL.EDU

Student Life and Environment

With a convenient evening or weekend schedule, UMSL attracts a lot of working professionals, who are "busy juggling work, school, and home responsibilities." While they have worries outside the classroom, this is a "hardworking" bunch, and "students are focused on doing well in their classes while also working a full-time job." When course work requires collaboration between classmates, students are "friendly and professional," and they "work well together in groups." By and large, "UMSL is a commuter school" and most people "are there to learn and leave."

As a part of the largest research university in the St. Louis area, UMSL has an "ethnically diverse" and active student body. As graduate business students, MBA candidates have access to numerous facilities on this 350-acre campus. For example, "the campus houses the largest Performing Arts Center in the Saint Louis Area. There are weekly and sometimes nightly events on campus, available for free or at a discount to UMSL students." Within the business school, however, students would like the administration to "upgrade our facilities and buildings." Located in suburban St. Louis, this school offers excellent access to the largest metropolitan center in Missouri. However, some students feel the campus is "set in a rough part of St. Louis," so there aren't many options for recreation or nightlife in the local area.

Admissions

The traditional (evening) MBA enrolls students three times a year, in the fall, spring, and summer terms. For the professional MBA and the international MBA, classes only start once a year, in the fall term. To apply, all programs require undergraduate transcripts, two letters of recommendation, and GMAT scores. Admission is selective, with only about 60 percent of applicants receiving an offer of admission. To be competitive, students should have a GMAT score of 500 or better, and an undergraduate GPA of at least 3.0. Promising students who fall short of these minimum standards may be considered for restricted admission.

FINANCIAL FACTS

Room & board (on/off-campus)	$10,300/$10,300
% of students receiving aid	46
% of first-year students receiving aid	51
% of students receiving grants	20
Average award package	$12,741
Average grant	$7,390
Average loan	$14,527
Average student loan debt	$10,052

ADMISSIONS

Admissions Selectivity Rating	80
# of applications received	225
% applicants accepted	80
% acceptees attending	70
Average GMAT	513
Range of GMAT	490–540
Accepts GRE scores	No
Average GPA	3.4
TOEFL required of international students	Yes
Minimum TOEFL (paper/web)	550/79
Application fee	$35
International application fee	$40
Regular application deadline	7/1
Application Deadline/Notification	
Deferment available	Yes
Maximum length of deferment	1 year
Transfer students accepted	Yes
Transfer application policy	
Transcripts are evaluated for relevant course work. Maximum of nine hours of acceptable graduate credit allowed to transfer in.	
Non-fall admissions	Yes
Need-blind admissions	Yes

EMPLOYMENT PROFILE

Career Rating	78	Grads Employed by Function	% Avg. Salary
Average base starting salary	$57,200	Marketing	(100%) $45,000
Primary Source of Full-time Job Acceptances		Operations	(67%) $85,000
School-facilitated activities	17 (23%)	Management	(88%) $68,600
Graduate-facilitated activities	58 (77%)	Finance	(100%) $51,400
		HR	(100%) $39,000
		MIS	(83%) $48,600

UNIVERSITY OF NEVADA—LAS VEGAS

LEE BUSINESS SCHOOL

GENERAL INFORMATION
Type of school   Public
Affiliation   No Affiliation
Academic calendar   Semesters

SURVEY SAYS...
Happy students
Solid preparation in:
General management, Teamwork,
Presentation skills

STUDENTS
Enrollment of parent institution	28,600
Enrollment of MBA Program	154
% male/female	65/35
% out-of-state	21
% part-time	54
% underrepresented minority	17
% international	17
Average age at entry	28
Average years work experience at entry	6

ACADEMICS
Academic Experience Rating	**90**
Profs interesting rating	88
Profs accessible rating	93
Student/faculty ratio	25:1
% female faculty	13
% underrepresented minority faculty	12

Joint Degrees
MS Hotel Administration/MBA 2.5
years MS Management Information
Systems/MBA 2.5 years JD/MBA
4 years full time/ 5 years part time
MBA/DMD Dental Medicine

Prominent Alumni
Rossi Rolenkotter, President/CEO,
Las Vegas Convention and Visitors
Authority; Dave Rice, Head men's
basketball coach, UNLV; Darcy
Neighbors, Founder and CEO,
CIM Marketing Partners; Linda
Rheinberger, Owner, One Source
Realty and Management; Cass
Palmer, President/CEO United Way
of Southern Nevada

Academics

The Lee Business School at the University of Nevada—Las Vegas offers two MBA tracks. One is an evening MBA, which students can complete either full- or part-time, and the other is an Executive MBA, designed for working professionals who plan to continue working full-time while pursuing their MBA. "For working students or students, who need to balance family life, this is the perfect environment." The evening program can be completed in two to four years, and students may opt to concentrate in one of the following fields: finance, human resources management, marketing, management information systems and new venture management. Students must complete forty-eight credit hours, thirty-three of which are devoted to a core curriculum. An accelerated program is open to students in the evening program who have a minimum score of 600 on the GMAT. Students must also exceed the 50th percentile on both the verbal and quantitative skills portion of the GMAT. Another prerequisite for the Executive MBA is an undergraduate business degree from an AACSB-accredited university.

The Executive MBA is an eighteen-month program during which all students follow the same general course of study. Students should have seven years work experience prior to applying, and of those seven years, three must be in "a key decision-making role." Classes take place every Friday and Saturday from 8:30 a.m. to 5:30 p.m. There is an initial full-week intensive prior to the start of classes. UNLV also offers joint degrees. Students also have the option to pursue one of four dual programs: the MBA/JD (Juris Doctor), the MBA/DDM (Doctor of Dental Medicine), the MBA/MS in Hotel Administration and the MBA/MS in Management Information Systems. Students choose UNLV due to its "location, affordability, and flexibility." It's the "only school in the state with AACSB accreditation," and students say "UNLV has the best hotel program." Some wish UNLV offered an additional specialization, one which might help them better prepare for work in "green jobs."

"UNLV's best attribute is the willingness of its professors to help students. Because half the students work full-time, they are very flexible when it come to scheduling office hours or addressing questions through email." "Professors come prepared for lectures" and "treat MBA students like professionals." The curriculum is "well organized," and professors stay on top of pertinent issues. "I feel I have gotten a superb exposure to the current business environment from them." Professors are also equipped with bedside manner. They "are always friendly and willing to help further explain difficult topics." Students praise "the use of teamwork, in almost every aspect of class." As for the administration, they "promptly respond to requests by phone and email."

Career and Placement

The Lee Business School Career and Professional Development office at UNLV serves only the University's graduate students, providing them with guidance and strategies specific to their interests in local, national and international business careers. The center assists them in developing career goals and a career plan, as well as helping students market themselves and contact alumni for jobs. The office also acts as a liaison between students businesses and alumni. The center maintains an online job database and organizes recruiting events for students on campus. Students say they like how close the school is "to the thousands of jobs that are on the Las Vegas strip." However, others worry UNLV needs to develop its image. "Our school needs to be perceived as competition by other learning institutions. Potential employers should know that UNLV produces analytical, top-notch graduates."

ADMISSIONS CONTACT: LISA DAVIS, MBA PROGRAMS ASSOCIATE DIRECTOR
ADDRESS: 4505 MARYLAND PARKWAY BOX 456031, LAS VEGAS, NV 89154-6031
PHONE: 702-895-3655 • FAX: 702-895-3632
E-MAIL: LBSMBA@UNLV.EDU • WEBSITE: BUSINESS.UNLV.EDU

UNLV MBAs typically have an average of five years' work experience when they enter the MBA program. Local and national companies visit the Lee Business School for recruitment of leadership positions.

Student Life and Environment

"The atmosphere at UNLV is similar to a commuter school. Most students, even undergraduates, work full time and live off campus." Students "are business professionals in many different industries and are on average a few years out of undergrad." The average age is "late twenties." "They are a diverse group that come from a variety of backgrounds," "a mixing pot of international students and students from other states." Regardless of their differences, students seem to share "similar values and goals." They are "smart, outgoing, and welcome challenges." Students say they value their classmates' ability "to stimulate" their minds. They are also "great friends and very helpful."

Las Vegas is half an hour from the Hoover Dam, the Colorado River, and Lake Mead. There is skiing and hiking less than an hour northwest of the city. However, being in Las Vegas itself has its bonuses for business students. The "modern" campus is "very exciting considering it is only miles from the Las Vegas strip." The campus also regularly hosts a variety of entertainers and lecturers.

Admissions

The Admissions Committee requests the following from its applicants: official transcripts for all post-secondary institutions attended, an official score report for the GMAT, two letters of recommendation, a personal essay, and a resume. The GMAT score and the GPA are most important to the committee, as is work experience. The average GPA of entering students is 3.37 and the average GMAT score is approximately 585. All international students seeking admission are asked to supply financial certification documents.

FINANCIAL FACTS

Annual tuition (in-state/ out-of-state)	$8,736/$8,736
Fees	$3,000
Cost of books	$2,400
Room & board (on/off-campus)	$10,000/$12,000
% of students receiving aid	62
% of first-year students receiving aid	60
% of students receiving grants	42
Average award package	$11,260
Average grant	$2,599
Average loan	$19,883
Average student loan debt	$49,223

ADMISSIONS

Admissions Selectivity Rating	88
# of applications received	120
% applicants accepted	49
% acceptees attending	75
Average GMAT	585
Range of GMAT	550–640
Accepts GRE scores	No
Average GPA	3.3
TOEFL required of international students	Yes
Minimum TOEFL (paper/web)	550/80
Application fee	$60
International application fee	$95
Regular application deadline	7/15
Regular application notification	7/20
Application Deadline/Notification	
Deferment available	Yes
Maximum length of deferment	one year
Transfer students accepted	Yes
Transfer application policy Must meet our admission deadlines and requirements. A total of 12 credits from an AACSB accredited school with a grade of B or better	
Non-fall admissions	Yes
Need-blind admissions	Yes

UNIVERSITY OF NEVADA—RENO
COLLEGE OF BUSINESS

Academics

One of the state's top MBA programs, the extremely affordable Nevada MBA program accommodates the needs of full and part time students by offering all evening courses so that students can complete a degree at their own pace without interrupting their professional career. A heavy emphasis on group projects, the ability to waive core course requirements if comparable courses have been completed, and "ideal" flexibility only further endear this program to those who come here. "I wouldn't be able to work and get my MBA nearly as easily without the setup we have here," says a student.

Students may also choose an "Area of Emphasis," in which they take nine elective credits that have an industry or functional emphasis. Current areas of emphasis include accounting, entrepreneurship, finance, and information technology (students can also pursue other areas of emphasis by taking graduate courses of their choice outside of CB).

Professors are "readily available outside the classroom and are knowledgeable about the subject that they are teaching," and "the adaptability and overall performance of the administrative staff and professors is admirable." The faculty "not only have academic experience, but are able to share real world knowledge that is invaluable to students working in such competitive business environments." Since most every student is also working while getting their degree, the intensity of the classes is tailored to allow for the busy professional and personal lives of students, and professors "understand if we have to miss a class for a particular reason." "I feel as though the coursework is challenging enough to get the message across, while still being understanding of the fact that we do have a life outside of school," says a student.

Career and Placement

The CB "encourages students to work with other students," which makes for a built-in networking as most students are working professionals. "I have heard of several job opportunities from fellow students," says one. Though the majority of those who attend Nevada are already employed, "many people are in the program to move to a new career path or because they want to advance from their current position." A good deal of engineers and tech-oriented people are seeking MBAs, so recruitment from companies like Microsoft occurs frequently, although a couple of students wish the school would "partner with companies to give students more job opportunities."

ADMISSIONS CONTACT: VICKI KRENTZ, COORDINATOR OF GRADUATE PROGRAMS
ADDRESS: MAILSTOP 0024, RENO, NV 89557
PHONE: 775-784-4912 • FAX: 775-784-1773
E-MAIL: VKRENTZ@UNR.EDU • WEBSITE: WWW.COBA.UNR.EDU/MBA

Student Life and Environment

This group (mostly in their twenties or thirties, and often married) is "friendly, supportive, team oriented, hardworking, [and] driven," yet "still incredibly personable." They understand "that the MBA program requires a different level of focus than under grad classes, and most of them seem to really embrace the challenge." The campus has several new buildings, and "the library and Student Union are great places to study and do group work." There is "a great sense of community" all around the campus, as seen by attendance at major sporting events and fine arts or other activities on campus, and "class diversity is great."

Being that this is a part-time program, the school does "a very good job of socializing information about clubs and other social gatherings." Reno itself has tons of "amazing" outdoor activities: it is within an hour of around twenty ski resorts and hiking trails (including Lake Tahoe), there's a river flowing through downtown for rafting, and there are "plenty of lakes to camp and fish." "It has the benefits of a big city in a small town," says a student.

Admissions

Two or more years of work experience, a minimum GPA of 2.75 on a 4.0 scale, and a GMAT score of at least 500 are required for admission to the College of Business at UNR. A resume, three letters of reference, and a two- to three-page personal statement concerning background and goals are also needed. A minimum TOEFL score of 550 paper-based, 213 computer-based, or 79 iBT (or an IELTS score of at least 7.0) is required from nonnative English speakers. The average GMAT score for those admitted in a recent class was 528, the average GPA was 3.28, and the average length of work experience was seven years.

FINANCIAL FACTS

Annual tuition (in-state/out-of-state)	$264/credit hr / $100/credit hr
Fees	$100/credit hr
Room & board	$9,000
% of students receiving aid	10
% of students receiving grants	2
Average award package	$7,000
Average student loan debt	$10,000

ADMISSIONS

Admissions Selectivity Rating	81
# of applications received	65
% applicants accepted	86
% acceptees attending	100
Average GMAT	524
Range of GMAT	420–620
Accepts GRE scores	Yes
Average Verbal GRE	152
Range of Verbal GRE scores	143–158
Average Quantitative GRE	151
Range of Quantitative GRE scores	145–157
Average Writing GRE	4.0
Range of Writing GRE scores	3.0–4.8
Average GPA	3.2
TOEFL required of international students	Yes
Minimum TOEFL (paper/web)	550/79
Application fee	$60
International application fee	$100
Regular application deadline	3/15
Application Deadline/Notification	
Deferment available	Yes
Maximum length of deferment	1 year
Transfer students accepted	Yes
Transfer application policy	The university's graduate school will only accept 9 transfer credits from another graduate program.
Non-fall admissions	Yes
Need-blind admissions	No

EMPLOYMENT PROFILE			
Career Rating	77	Grads Employed by Function% Avg. Salary	
Average base starting salary	$50,000	Marketing	(20%)
		Operations	(10%)
		Management	(10%)
		Finance	(25%)
		HR	(10%)
		MIS	(20%)
		Other	(5%)

UNIVERSITY OF NEW HAMPSHIRE
PAUL T. PAUL COLLEGE OF BUSINESS AND ECONOMICS

GENERAL INFORMATION

Type of school	Public
Affiliation	No Affiliation
Academic calendar	Five Terms in one year

SURVEY SAYS...

Friendly students, Students love Durham, NH
Solid preparation in:
General management, Teamwork, Communication/interpersonal skills, Presentation skills, Quantitative skills

STUDENTS

Enrollment of parent institution	15,155
Enrollment of MBA Program	103
% male/female	69/31
% out-of-state	21
% part-time	63
% underrepresented minority	35
% international	6
Average age at entry	27
Average years work experience at entry	5

ACADEMICS

Academic Experience Rating	**90**
Profs interesting rating	88
Profs accessible rating	92
Student/faculty ratio	5:1
% female faculty	21
% underrepresented minority faculty	3
% part-time faculty	3

Joint Degrees

Combined J.D. and MBA in 3 1/2 years. J.D. comes from UNH Law School. Current UNH seniors can apply early admission to MS Accounting program and count one graduate course towards both degree requirements.

Academics

There's no doubt that University of New Hampshire offers future MBAs an unbeatable combination of "relatively low tuition" and a "great reputation." Students here truly value both the "flexibility" afforded by the part-time program and the opportunity to accelerate one's studies with the "full-time, one year program." Moreover, they greatly appreciate having the ability to take courses in "Durham, Manchester or online." UNH MBA students are also quick to laud the "challenging" curriculum, one that's wholly "relevant to today's world economy." They also point to the "diverse" course offerings as a major strength. As one delighted student shares, "I have an environmental science background and was excited to find many professors specializing in corporate sustainability."

Indeed, a lot of student satisfaction derives from "amazing" professors who tend to "come from very different backgrounds." Students love that instructors here "actively discuss current business events and help us to apply our classroom learning to real-life situations." Just as crucial, they are "approachable and knowledgeable about the subject matter [they teach.]" And, importantly, UNH professors are "accommodating and flexible with their office hours in order to provide extra help when needed."

Career and Placement

The Paul College of Business and Economics boasts "an incredible job placement rate." And it's easy to understand why. To begin with, current MBA students at UNH are quick to highlight an extensive alumni network that's "fantastic [when it comes to] assisting with job searches, informational interviews, advice, etc." Of course, they can also turn to the stellar Career Services Office. There they can work with career counselors who help ensure that students have the necessary tools for a successful search. Specifically, MBAs can use the office for everything from resume workshops to mock interviews. And the Career Services Office assists students in securing jobs and internships in New England, across the country and around the world.

Student Life and Environment

University of New Hampshire's b-school continually manages to net some "extremely intelligent, hard-working, insightful, friendly [and] competitive" students. Perhaps most essential to a positive and rewarding experience, students here "are always willing to help each other out in their respective studies." As a grateful first-year shares, "All of us want each other to succeed and will offer help when needed." And, importantly, they also bring a "diverse set of experiences to the program which [can be] very [useful]."

Overall, "UNH is a very vibrant campus." Indeed, there "are excellent resources available to all students, as well as exclusive resources for the MBA's." We're also told that "there is a fantastic social aspect here. Greek life, clubs, sports teams, and political associations are booming." In addition, the "NH Seacoast is full of awesome opportunities for work and play." However, these things are more likely the provenance of the full-time students; part-time MBAs typically go to work, go to class and then head home.

Admissions

Applicants to the MBA program at UNH's Paul College must provide the Admissions Department with all of the following: official copies of transcripts for all postsecondary academic work; an official score report for the GMAT; three letters of reference focusing on the candidate's "strengths, weaknesses, and potential for academic and managerial success"; responses to essay questions, which the school deems a "crucial" aspect of the application; a current résumé; and any evidence of leadership skills that the applicant wishes to provide. Applicants to the Executive MBA program must undergo an admissions interview. Applicants to other MBA programs may request an interview but are not required to do so. (It is, however, "strongly recommended" that applicants who have "one or more weak components in their profile" schedule an appointment.) Two years of work experience is "recommended but not required" for the full-time and part-time MBA programs; a minimum of five years of professional experience is required for the Executive MBA program. International applicants must meet all of the above requirements and must submit an official score report for the TOEFL (minimum required score: 550 paper-based test, 213 computer-based test).

Prominent Alumni

Ronald K. Noble, Secretary General, INTERPOL; Elisa Steele, CEO and President of Jive Software; Garrett Ilg, Senior Vice President, Head of World Wide Enterprise Sales & Field Operations at Adobe; David Cote, Chairman/President/CEO of Honeywell; Elizabeth Hilpman, Owner, Barlow Partners

FINANCIAL FACTS

Annual tuition (in-state/ out-of-state)	$28,000/$42,000
Fees	$817
Cost of books	$2,400
Room & board (on/off-campus)	$10,160/$11,608
% of students receiving aid	78
% of first-year students receiving aid	78
% of students receiving grants	24
Average award package	$2,557
Average grant	$3,151
Average loan	$20,889
Average student loan debt	$24,234

ADMISSIONS

Admissions Selectivity Rating	87
# of applications received	280
% applicants accepted	49
% acceptees attending	81
Average GMAT	550
Range of GMAT	490–700
Accepts GRE scores	No
Average GPA	3.3
TOEFL required of international students	Recommended
Minimum TOEFL (paper/web)	550/79
Application fee	$65
International application fee	$65
Early application deadline	4/1
Regular application deadline	7/1
Application Deadline/Notification	
Round 1:	12/1 / 1/1
Round 2:	4/1 / 5/15
Round 3:	6/2 / 6/15
Deferment available	Yes
Maximum length of deferment	1 year
Transfer students accepted	Yes
Transfer application policy	
A maximum of eight credits may be considered for transfer credit.	
Non-fall admissions	Yes
Need-blind admissions	Yes

EMPLOYMENT PROFILE

		Grads Employed by Function	% Avg. Salary
Career Rating	84		
Percent employed at graduation	56	Marketing	(28%)
Percent employed 3 months		Consulting	(6%)
after graduation	90	Management	(6%)
		Finance	(11%)
		MIS	(33%)
		Other	(16%)

Top 5 Employers Hiring Grads
Sprague Energy (1), ThermoFisher (1), State Street (1), BAE (1), Dartmouth Hitchcock (1)

THE UNIVERSITY OF NORTH CAROLINA AT CHAPEL HILL
KENAN-FLAGLER BUSINESS SCHOOL

GENERAL INFORMATION

Type of school	Public
Affiliation	No Affiliation
Academic calendar	Semester with modules

SURVEY SAYS...

Classmates have diverse work experience, Friendly students, Good peer network, Good social scene, Cutting-edge classes
Solid preparation in:
Marketing, Finance, Accounting, General management, Teamwork

STUDENTS

Enrollment of parent institution	23,000
Enrollment of MBA Program	559
% male/female	74/26
% out-of-state	77
% part-time	
% underrepresented minority	12
% international	31
Average age at entry	29
Average years work experience at entry	5

ACADEMICS

Academic Experience Rating	96
Profs interesting rating	95
Profs accessible rating	98
Student/faculty ratio	5:1
% female faculty	23
% underrepresented minority faculty	1
% part-time faculty	0

Joint Degrees

MBA/MD; MBA/PharmD; MBA/JD; MBA/Master of Regional Planning; MBA/Master of Health Care Administration; MBA/Master of Public Health; MBA/Master of Science in Information Science; MBA/Master of Public Policy; MBA/Master of Environmental Management

Prominent Alumni

Rolf Hoffmann, SVP, Amgen, Inc.; Julian Robertson, Founder, Tiger Management Corp.

Academics

The University of North Carolina at Chapel Hill Kenan-Flagler Business School has been on the rise for years, and it continues its ascent thanks to a resoundingly happy student body, stellar alumni base, and good connections to growing industries such as consulting, healthcare, life sciences. The first semester of the two-year program is front-loaded to teach the core business skills, and then students can select from more than 125 elective courses as the year progresses. There is also a summer sessions prior to the start of the academic year, and most students participate, enabling them "to start preparing for the recruiting process early."

The academic experience is "nothing short of fantastic." It is common for professors "to sit down with individual students for an hour or more to discuss classes and career goals." The "balanced curriculum" and focus on analytical skills, problem solving, and interpersonal skills give students a "fundamental skillset as a general manager." "I think the school is a powerhouse for teaching students practical skills to get them started on their post-MBA careers," says a student. UNC's outstanding merit scholarship program also attracts many students that are accepted to top ten schools, ensuring "that the high end of the class can compete with anyone" in the workforce. People are "very kind to each other here," and "it really helps that the admissions office screens for team players with strong values."

The school is "run very well" ("I have been in all the classes I have wanted without problems," says a student) and is "very flexible in responding to students' demands." For example, in response to students' concern about too heavy a workload during the job search season, the administration "made a quick decision to change the course schedule and to increase support for students in their job search process."

Career and Placement

The career center "does a phenomenal job bring recruiters on campus and preparing students for the recruiting process," especially in "bringing in well-renowned firms, particularly in finance." "I have never heard of a school which is more supportive than Kenan-Flagler," says a student. Students say that the alumni base is smaller than other B-schools, but "closer and more willing to help current MBAs as a result." "The Carolina Blue mafia, as they are called, go out of their way to help UNC grads get jobs in the industry," says a student. "I don't think you can overstate the strength of our alumni network." Alumni generously work to create opportunities for UNC Kenan-Flagler students at their firms, in addition to "acting as mentors, helping us to perfect our interview skills by acting as sounding boards, and helping us network to find the best fit for us in terms of our career searches."

The Career Management Center has also taken significant initiatives in building a network with new companies like A.T. Kearney, Chevron, Roland Berger and Salesforce. They have also "increased their commitment to help international students find a job in the United States." Recent employers of UNC Kenan-Flager graduates include Amazon, Bank of America, Goldman Sachs, Johnson & Johnson, and Pepsico.

Student Life and Environment

Chapel Hill is the quintessential college town and the MBA students take advantage of the great restaurants, nightlife, shopping, and athletics nearby. Every week there are "endless socials that are extremely fun and inclusive" that bring together first and second years students and alumni, and it pays off in the rapport that results: "[Students] really take care of each other." "I have had classmates help me prepare for a job interview that they were also interviewing for." As a result of sufficient social networking opportunities, this "healthy mix of singles and students with families" all "know the faces and names of most of all the first and second year students." A "diverse and growing number of clubs and organizations" also allows students to pursue common interests. "Everyone is genuinely happy to come to school and is excited to learn," though some agree that "facilities could use a bit of a facelift. A lot of the decor and architecture is clearly from at least a decade ago."

Admissions

UNC Kenan-Flagler admits students who demonstrate leadership and organizational skills, communication ability, interpersonal skills, teamwork ability, analytic and problem-solving skills, drive and motivation, prior record of academic excellence, and strong career progression and commitment to career goals. Though no specific coursework is necessary, students must have knowledge of financial accounting, statistics, macroeconomics, and calculus. The average undergraduate GPA for a recent entering class was 3.41, and the average GMAT was 701.

FINANCIAL FACTS

Annual tuition (in-state/out-of-state)	$37,015/$54,413
Fees	$3,081
Cost of books	$1,484
Room & board (on/off-campus)	$23,198/$23,198
% of students receiving aid	74
% of first-year students receiving aid	75
% of students receiving grants	38
Average award package	$56,720
Average grant	$32,967
Average loan	$49,635
Average student loan debt	$93,897

ADMISSIONS

Admissions Selectivity Rating	92
# of applications received	2,357
% applicants accepted	34
% acceptees attending	35
Average GMAT	701
Range of GMAT	680–730
Accepts GRE scores	Yes
Average Verbal GRE	160
Range of Verbal GRE scores	152–170
Average Quantitative GRE	157
Range of Quantitative GRE scores	148–167
Average Writing GRE	4.4
Range of Writing GRE scores	3.0–6.0
Average GPA	3.4
TOEFL required of international students	Yes
Application fee	$150
International application fee	$150
Early application deadline	10/16
Early notification date	12/14
Application Deadline/Notification	
Round 1:	10/16 / 12/14
Round 2:	12/4 / 2/1
Round 3:	1/15 / 3/14
Round 4:	3/11 / 4/25
Deferment available	Yes
Maximum length of deferment	Varies by reason
Transfer students accepted	No
Non-fall admissions	No
Need-blind admissions	Yes

EMPLOYMENT PROFILE

Career Rating	97	Grads Employed by Function	% Avg. Salary
Percent employed at graduation	81	Marketing	(21%) $102,620
Percent employed 3 months after graduation	94	Operations	(5%) $96,320
		Consulting	(28%) $114,470
Average base starting salary	$108,627	Management	(10%) $106,888
Primary Source of Full-time Job Acceptances		Finance	(31%) $110,600
School-facilitated activities	162 (75%)	Other	(5%) $98,167
Graduate-facilitated activities	50 (23%)	**Top 5 Employers Hiring Grads**	
Unknown	5 (2%)	North Highland (17), Amazon (9), Deloitte (8), IBM (6), Morgan Stanley (5)	

THE UNIVERSITY OF NORTH CAROLINA AT CHARLOTTE

BELK COLLEGE OF BUSINESS

GENERAL INFORMATION

Type of school	Public
Affiliation	No Affiliation
Academic calendar	Semesters

SURVEY SAYS...

Happy students, Students love Charlotte, NC
Solid preparation in:
Teamwork, Presentation skills, Quantitative skills

STUDENTS

Enrollment of parent institution	27,000
Enrollment of MBA Program	253
% part-time	66
Average age at entry	30
Average years work experience at entry	6

ACADEMICS

Academic Experience Rating	**88**
Profs interesting rating	90
Profs accessible rating	93
Student/faculty ratio	26:1
% female faculty	29
% underrepresented minority faculty	74
% part-time faculty	0

Joint Degrees

JD/MBA (4-5 years) MBA/MHA (3 years)

Prominent Alumni

Gene Johnson, retired Chairman & CEO, Fairpoint Communications; Robert Niblock, Chairman & CEO -Lowe's Home Improvement; Kelley Earnhardt, General Manager, JR Motorsports; Robert Hull, CFO, Lowe's Home Improvement; Bob Qutub, CFO, MSCI, Inc.

Academics

Students at The University of North Carolina at Charlotte love the "proximity to the financial district in Charlotte," which is a "financial hub" with "Fortune 500 and other reputable companies throughout the region." "The flexibility of the program allows you to customize your concentrations, so they are relative to your strengths and what you would like to do in a future career," remarks one happy student. There is a "focus on banking, as there are a lot of BofA, Wells Fargo, and TIAA-CREF students," and the school has a particularly strong finance faculty. "The work piles up and is demanding," one student says, "however, I'm getting used to the pace, and I feel that the extra work I put in is appreciated and noticed." UNC Charlotte "is known for its diverse background and for its high expectation of students, which helps set up a two-way benchmark establishing goals for both the business school and the students."

Students are very happy with the "very hands on" and "extremely flexible" administration. There is a "strong commitment from administrators to help students succeed at scholastic and career goals," and "administrators will bend over backwards to help you in any way they can," such as "constantly making you aware of internships and available jobs." The administration is particularly quick at "answering questions or fixing problems." "I have not had an issue yet that they haven't fixed quickly," one student says. "Overall they are friendly, responsive, and knowledgeable." "The business school staff is very helpful and always available." Students do feel the administration should do more for students outside of normal weekday work hours. There are "not many 'after-work-hours' networking opportunities" and not enough "night/weekend class offerings for graduate studies."

Students are also proud of their professors, who "really care about their students" and whose "doors are always open." "My professors for the most part seem engaged, very intelligent, and reasonably demanding. The professors don't want cookie-cutter answers and encourage depth in responses." "A majority of the professors are top-notch," and the ones who aren't are "subject matter experts at worst." Although most professors "are really great," others "miss the mark and just teach the syllabus." "Like any academic institution, it's bureaucratic, but not so much." One student explains the school "is accessible, and you can always be pointed in the right direction."

Career and Placement

The administration at the Belk College of Business is the school's "primary strength." They put in extra work to help students network and intern to improve future job prospects. "They helped me to create an exchange program with a top MBA program in the UK, even though no previous relationship existed," says one student. "UNC Charlotte offers great mentoring and career placement," and its location in the financial hub of Charlotte is very helpful for students. The school has "close ties to the Charlotte business community" and a "reputation for placement." The school claims a mean base salary of $83,000 for new graduates. Some prominent alumni include Susan DeVore, president and CEO of Premier; John P. Derham Cato, Chairman of the Board, president, and CEO of The Cato Corporation; and Kelley Earnhardt, General Manager of JR Motorsports.

Student Life and Environment

Students are very impressed with the diversity at UNC Charlotte. "We have students from all races, all different types of work backgrounds, etc. It is very beneficial for class discussions because of all the different types of opinions that are voiced." There is everyone "from students straight out of undergrad school to workers who have been in the field fifteen years, but everyone is friendly." "Students are heavily engaged in academics and current events." Still, "most are in their early thirties with careers and are married," and some students wish the school recruited younger students. Others enjoy the "experienced workers who see a benefit in taking time from their personal lives to invest in this program" and provide a "great mix of professionals from different industries."

Students do feel that the "social aspect of the school" is lacking. "I feel that there really isn't a strong connection with graduate students and campus life. There aren't many graduate-level activities and clubs, which is quite the opposite environment from what I am used to," explains one student. A stronger social aspect could also improve the "brand" and make it "even stronger in the surrounding areas." There could also be more "family involvement in the MBA program, such as weekend activities. This will allow spouses and children to feel good about their loved ones being away from home twice a week for two years." That said, "emphasis on student life has been increasing with the construction of the new Student Union and the fact that a new football program is coming to the school." "We know it's a business school," one student laments, "but a little less formality to actually make it fun and worthwhile would be great!"

Admissions

Students applying to the Belk College of Business are evaluated based on their undergraduate record, GMAT scores, resume, personal essays, and letters of recommendation. The average GMAT score for entering students is currently 585. Work experience is strongly recommended but not required. In the fall 2012, the program began accepting the GRE with a minimum score of 151 on the quantitative and verbal sections.

FINANCIAL FACTS

Annual tuition (in-state/ out-of-state)	$12,263/$24,550

ADMISSIONS

Admissions Selectivity Rating	84
# of applications received	189
% applicants accepted	69
% acceptees attending	69
Average GMAT	585
Range of GMAT	540–620
Accepts GRE scores	Yes
Average GPA	3.4
TOEFL required of international students	Yes
Minimum TOEFL (paper/web)	557/83
Application fee	$65
International application fee	$75
Early application deadline	1/15
Early notification date	3/15
Application Deadline/Notification	
Round 1:	1/15 / 3/15
Round 2:	3/1 / 5/1
Deferment available	Yes
Maximum length of deferment	1 year
Transfer students accepted	Yes
Transfer application policy	

All students have to complete the graduate application materials and submit official test scores. With permission, it may be possible to transfer graduate level work from an AACSB-accredited university. This will be considered when the application materials are officially reviewed. At least 30 hours of graduate level coursework must be completed in residence at UNC Charlotte.

Non-fall admissions	Yes
Need-blind admissions	Yes

EMPLOYMENT PROFILE	
Career Rating	81
Average base starting salary	$83,000

THE UNIVERSITY OF NORTH CAROLINA AT GREENSBORO
JOSEPH M. BRYAN SCHOOL OF BUSINESS AND ECONOMICS

GENERAL INFORMATION

Type of school	Public
Affiliation	No Affiliation
Academic calendar	Semester

SURVEY SAYS...

Classmates have diverse work experience, Friendly students, Happy students, Students love Greensboro, NC
Solid preparation in:
Accounting, Teamwork, Quantitative skills

STUDENTS

Enrollment of parent institution	19,398
Enrollment of MBA Program	145
% male/female	51/49
% out-of-state	13
% part-time	62
% underrepresented minority	37
% international	27
Average age at entry	28
Average years work experience at entry	5

ACADEMICS

Academic Experience Rating	88
Profs interesting rating	90
Profs accessible rating	94
Student/faculty ratio	6:1
% female faculty	33
% underrepresented minority faculty	37
% part-time faculty	12

Joint Degrees

MSN/MBA, 62 credits, 2-5 years
MS Gerontology/MBA, 58 credits, 2-5 years

Prominent Alumni

Jeff Kellan, VP Supply Chain Operations, Toys R Us; Nido Qubein, President, High Point University; Steve Strader, President Broward/Palm Beach Market, AutoNation, Inc; Gregory Walker, Managing Director, Citi Private Bank in Boca Raton; J. Berrye Worsham, President/CEO, Cotton, Incorporated

Academics

The University of North Carolina at Greensboro Bryan School of Business and Economics offers its students a rigorous program filled with "great courses." The graduate program at this "prestigious" school is "challenging," but not necessarily overwhelming. Students agree that with dedication and the help of "a very supportive MBA Office," a degree here is very achievable. "The academic value is excellent!" exclaims a current student. "The degree can be attained in two-years, costs less than any comparable program in Central NC, and is very highly rated." High praise goes to the "fantastic student services and administration," which are "immensely effective in helping students [achieve] their goals." "The entire school administration shows a care for the student body and a strong desire for them to do well."

The faculty also receives glowing reports from students for being "well versed in their disciplines and very enthusiastic about teaching." They are also noted for being "very diverse" and "approachable and have the students' best interest in mind." One student agrees by saying, "I absolutely love the professors in the MBA program. They inspire me to want more out of myself. They aren't teaching us how to pass a test, they are teaching us how to survive and thrive in the world." Another student appreciates how "professors are effective at integrating recent business trends into the curriculum." The "classes are set up to ensure dialogue versus a monologue from the professor" which creates an "academically stimulating environment." The school as a whole does an excellent job helping students stay on track. Administrators "strive to facilitate each student mapping out a plan of study to match their particular career and life goals. Professors make themselves available throughout the entire program, not just during their class."

"Affordability" and a positive experience at UNCG's undergraduate school are both popular reasons for attending the graduate program here. One student sums this up saying, "I attended UNCG for my undergraduate studies and greatly appreciated the quality of my education, especially with respect to the price of tuition." Studying abroad is yet another draw to the school. "Our study abroad program is superb. We have a special course for MBA's in the spring to learn about business in a given country and then visit that country and make business contacts as part of the course."

Career and Placement

The school's location in Greensboro, North Carolina has "plenty of employers" and "provides for good job opportunities." Bryan's unique targeted recruiting service works to actively partner with local employers and in doing so promotes current students to employers with specific needs. There are several on-campus recruiting events and many of the MBA social events include alumni, who tremendously help in networking. "UNCG has a solid reputation in the oldest MBA program in the Triad. Many of the top companies in the area recruit from UNCG." The administration is very good about sending "email communication and announcements to students regarding activities, job fairs, and other announcements."

Student Life and Environment

A broad mix of students, both full-time and part-time, attend UNCG. One student put it this way: "The students in the Bryan MBA program come from a range of different backgrounds. My cohort alone represents seven different countries. This allows for different perspectives on international business and global issues. The students are friendly, but are focused on their studies and internships so there is limited social time."

The University of North Carolina at Greensboro has "great spirit" in a "nice little town" on a "safe campus." "The school is very much a community where professors, students, athletes, and non-students are frequently passing each other on campus." There are "nice buildings, classrooms, and facilities." "The gym is in great condition and the student union center has plenty of food options with space to sit and eat while studying." "There is plenty of off-campus housing." For those driving to campus, "parking is easily accessible." Campus transportation is available and "runs rather late for those that commute or want to get off campus. There are plenty of restaurants nearby including a few on campus as well as downtown." "The city of Greensboro is wonderful and offers everything a graduate student could want."

Classmates "are all bright, motivated individuals" who are "very amiable and fun, great to work with in group assignments, and very dedicated to their education and work." Many "are working parents…who have chosen to reach for something more either within their chosen careers or in a new and exciting one." They "come from very diverse backgrounds, making in-class discussions very fruitful and enriching. Everyone is open to discussion and generally accepting of each other's differences in opinions." "Classes are all very discussion driven and students are very active in them and will debate respectfully. Everyone is willing to help each other." People here are very tolerant. "Race and sexual preference never are a problem at our school."

Admissions

Admission requirements include GMAT scores, which average 573; an essay; undergraduate GPA, which averages 3.32; three letters of recommendations, and a resume. Fellowships, scholarships, and graduate assistantships are available to help defray already low tuition costs. International students must also submit TOEFL or IELTS scores and an affidavit of financial support. Alternatively, the Bryan Prelude program enables students to take MBA courses before committing to a degree. To apply to Bryan Prelude, students must submit an application, undergraduate transcripts, a statement of purpose, and resume.

FINANCIAL FACTS

Annual tuition (in-state/ out-of-state)	$9,673/$23,122
Fees	$2,326
Cost of books	$2,727
Room & board (on/off-campus)	$10,729/$9,040
% of students receiving aid	44
% of first-year students receiving aid	51
% of students receiving grants	20
Average award package	$13,330
Average grant	$5,971
Average loan	$13,594

ADMISSIONS

Admissions Selectivity Rating	82
# of applications received	114
% applicants accepted	78
% acceptees attending	62
Average GMAT	573
Range of GMAT	510–625
Accepts GRE scores	Yes
Average Verbal GRE	151
Range of Verbal GRE scores	147–157
Average Quantitative GRE	151
Range of Quantitative GRE scores	148–155
Average Writing GRE	3.4
Range of Writing GRE scores	3.0–4.0
Average GPA	3.2
TOEFL required of international students	Yes
Minimum TOEFL (paper)	550
Application fee	$65
International application fee	$65
Early application deadline	3/1
Regular application deadline	7/1
Application Deadline/Notification	
Deferment available	Yes
Maximum length of deferment	1 Year
Transfer students accepted	Yes
Transfer application policy	
They must be in good standing at a fellow AACSB Accredited MBA Program and may transfer no more than 12 semester credit hours of approved coursework with grades of B or better.	
Non-fall admissions	Yes
Need-blind admissions	Yes

EMPLOYMENT PROFILE

Career Rating	79	Grads Employed by Function% Avg. Salary	
Percent employed at graduation	50	Marketing	(33%)
Percent employed 3 months after graduation	50	Finance	(66%)
Average base starting salary	$59,500	**Top 5 Employers Hiring Grads**	
Primary Source of Full-time Job Acceptances		Volvo Trucks (1), Volvo Financial (1),	
School-facilitated activities	3 (27%)	PricewaterhouseCoopers (1), BRIJ (1)	
Graduate-facilitated activities	1 (13%)		
Unknown	4 (50%)		

THE UNIVERSITY OF NORTH CAROLINA AT WILMINGTON
CAMERON SCHOOL OF BUSINESS

GENERAL INFORMATION
Type of school   Public
Affiliation   No Affiliation
Academic calendar   Semester

SURVEY SAYS...
Friendly students, Happy students,
Students love Wilmington, NC
Solid preparation in:
Finance, Teamwork, Presentation
skills, Quantitative skills

STUDENTS
Enrollment of MBA Program	122
% male/female	83/17
% out-of-state	27
% part-time	50
% underrepresented minority	3
% international	18
Average age at entry	31
Average years work experience at entry	7

ACADEMICS
Academic Experience Rating	**86**
Profs interesting rating	90
Profs accessible rating	92
Student/faculty ratio	15:1
% female faculty	16

Academics

Uniting a top-notch business faculty with an intimate campus atmosphere, getting an MBA at the University of North Carolina at Wilmington's Cameron School of Business is a "warm, rewarding experience." This small public school offers several graduate business programs, including the popular Professional MBA, as well as a full-time International MBA (conferred in conjunction with partner universities overseas). For working professionals in the PMBA program, convenience is a key factor in their decision to attend UNCW. "The campus is conveniently located in the center of Wilmington" and all classes are held in the evenings or on the weekends. The school offers a "lock-step program where all students take the same classes together," and the curriculum spans two years (twenty-one months if you were a business undergrad), with four courses per semester. While the course load is demanding (especially for those holding down a full-time job), "classes are...manageable" and professors are friendly, accessible, and "reasonable regarding student expectations."

With a competent administrative team at the helm, "the MBA program is well-designed and run," and many students say the "caliber of professors and course material has exceeded my expectations." Group work is encouraged, and through assignments, "[students] to learn to work with all different types of people—just like the real work force." Among many of the school's special programs, the Learning Alliance is a sixt to nine-month project through which "students are put into groups and assigned a [regional] company" where they study and consult on business problems and opportunities. A student elaborates on the Learning Alliance: "Rather than just writing a marketing report based on a case study, an actual marketing project will be performed where students work with local businesses on their particular marketing needs." On the flipside, students would like the curriculum to include a broader international perspective, while others would like to see more specialized course offerings, as well as "more freedom to choose classes within the program."

UNCW students are impressed with the teaching staff, describing them as "highly educated with a lot of 'hands-on' work experience." Drawing from a wide range of industries, Wilmington professors range "from economics teachers who have worked at the Fed for thirty years, to management teachers who have worked for large corporations in high positions globally, to significantly published authors and highly sought-after consultants." In the classroom, they are on top of their game; "Professors of UNCW exhibit strong, experienced leadership in preparing, teaching, and guiding students through the business program." Likewise, "the administration is very service-oriented and goes out of [its] way to make student administrative obstacles easy [to overcome]." "Affordability" is the cherry on top of the cake—here, in-state tuition runs less than 50 percent the price at comparable private schools.

ADMISSIONS CONTACT: KAREN BARNHILL, GRADUATE PROGRAMS ADMINISTRATOR
ADDRESS: 601 SOUTH COLLEGE ROAD, WILMINGTON, NC 28403-5680
PHONE AND FAX: 910-962-3903
E-MAIL: BARNHILLK@UNCW.EDU • WEBSITE: WWW.CSB.UNCW.EDU/GRADPROGRAMS

Career and Placement

The UNCW Career Center serves both the undergraduate and graduate student community, assisting with internships, as well as full-time and part-time job placements. The Career Center organizes annual career fairs and networking events on campus, and offers an online job board and resume posting service for UNCW students. However, the business school does not have graduate-specific resources for career planning, and students say, "There is very little discussion about various fields and ways in which to apply an MBA degree." At the same time, the school does provide opportunities for networking through speaker panels, alumni events, and special events with local executives.

For students who would like to make a career change after completing their MBA, career services at UNCW can be a disappointment. A current student admits, "UNCW needs to do a better job with attracting recruiters to hire their MBA students. With top-level faculty and a top-level business education, our MBA students should be given networking and interviewing opportunities with various businesses in different fields on a regular basis." On the other hand, students point out, "So many people's employers are paying for their MBA education, they feel it is a violation of ethics to strongly encourage us to find new jobs."

Student Life and Environment

While they come from diverse professional and educational backgrounds ("from engineers to business students"), MBA candidates at UNCW are generally "hard-working, funny, and willing to support and help others." Competitiveness is kept to a minimum, and within cohorts, "a tight-knit bond forms between classmates." On campus, business students have access to "quiet study lounges in each building" and a "well-equipped library;" however, the classroom experience could improve with the introduction of "more technology tools." In fact, some students think, "CSB could really use a new building" altogether.

In the professional MBA program, "most all of the students are working professionals, so they are not involved in the day-to-day campus activities." However, graduate students do have access to the facilities and resources on the greater campus, and "about 10 percent use the gym facilities and library during non-class hours." Nonetheless, the atmosphere is friendly and social, boasting "that homey feeling of a small town where everyone knows and cares about everyone else." While they may not go out every weekend, "most of the students belong to the MBA Association, and participate in social events with each other outside of class." Even in the classroom, the feeling is laid-back; "Because of the warm climate and laid back atmosphere, I believe some students have never worn footwear besides flip flops ever."

Admissions

At UNCW, the MBA Program Committee—a group of five faculty members—reviews applications and makes all admissions decisions. In recent years, the average incoming student had an undergraduate GPA of 3.26 and a GMAT score of about 531 (in most cases, the school only considers applicants with a GMAT or GRE equivalent of 500 or better). Most years, the school accepts about 75 percent of applicants annually.

FINANCIAL FACTS

Annual tuition (in-state/ out-of-state)	$5,622/$11,244
Fees	$11,928
Cost of books	$1,000
Room & board	$13.690
% of students receiving aid	80
% of first-year students receiving aid	80
% of students receiving grants	40
Average award package	$20,000
Average grant	$2,000
Average loan	$20,000

ADMISSIONS

Admissions Selectivity Rating	82
# of applications received	92
% applicants accepted	77
% acceptees attending	87
Average GMAT	531
Range of GMAT	475–570
Accepts GRE scores	Yes
Average GPA	3.3
TOEFL required of international students	Yes
Minimum TOEFL (paper/web)	550/79
Application fee	$60
International application fee	$60
Early application deadline	11/1
Regular application deadline	4/1
Deferment available	Yes
Maximum length of deferment	1 year
Transfer students accepted	No
Non-fall admissions	Yes
Need-blind admissions	

THE UNIVERSITY OF NORTH DAKOTA
COLLEGE OF BUSINESS AND PUBLIC ADMINISTRATION

GENERAL INFORMATION
Type of school	Public
Affiliation	No Affiliation
Academic calendar	academic

SURVEY SAYS...
Friendly students
Solid preparation in:
General management, Teamwork,
Quantitative skills

ACADEMICS
Academic Experience Rating	73
Profs interesting rating	88
Profs accessible rating	89
Student/faculty ratio	2:1
% female faculty	24
% underrepresented	
minority faculty	29
% part-time faculty	0

Joint Degrees
JD/MBA, 81 J.D. credit hours and
27 M.B.A. credit hours, 4 to 7 years.

Prominent Alumni
Neil Arnold, Executive Vice
President/CFO/Treasurer; Dave
Goodin, President and CEO; Randy
Newman, President/CEO/Chairman;
Major Gerald F. Perryman Jr., Vice
President/ISR/SBA; Steve Shirley,
President

Academics

The AACSB-accredited MBA program at the University of North Dakota is "focused on offering students the resources they need for a flourishing future." Classes are offered in the afternoon, evening, and long distance and "can easily be fit into your busy schedule." Many students earn their degrees remotely, through a "convenient online MBA program." The curriculum at UND focuses on business technology with an opportunity to concentrate in international business. Due to the unique location of the school in Grand Forks, the middle of a large agricultural zone, students are exposed to both rural and big-city business. They are pleased with the school's state-of-the-art facilities, including modern computer labs and a marketing research center.

Professors are "dedicated and caring." They "take interest in students and truly care about them." Students say they are helpful and knowledgeable, and the small classroom size allows for real relationships to develop. They are respectable of students' lives outside the classroom and help them balance school and life. Professors also "do a very good job connecting the real world to the classroom." Students believe this is due to their work involvement outside of school. Most professors "have great experiences prior to their professorships and do an excellent job of sharing them." "Professors are always accessible and have an open-door policy." Students say they are "great mentors and will be lifelong connections." "So far every one of them has been helpful and engaging."

"The administration is professional and very well organized. Overall, my academic experience at the University of North Dakota has been superior to any other university I have attended." Students also like "the online tutoring center and the outstanding tech support." Most students agree things run smoothly. Although one student suggests UND could improve "by offering more sections of classes taught during day hours, rather than focusing on night classes."

Career and Placement

"The greatest strength of the University is its commitment to its students. There is no doubt in my mind that UND does everything in its power to help its students succeed." Career services at UND assist both undergraduate and graduate students with internship and job placement. The office offers career counseling and hosts an annual career fair each fall. In the spring, it coordinates on-campus interview sessions. Some students wish there were a separate fair specifically for the College of Business and Public Administration. The three most popular career fields after graduation are manufacturing, the military, and financial services. "Life in Grand Forks is not as diversified as that in big cities. However, we have good social events and networks with the companies around the Midwest." The placement percentage for the business school (graduate and undergraduate) is 97.2 percent. UND alumni have high positions at some of the following companies: Bank of America, Coca-Cola, General Motors Defense, and Nodak Electric Cooperative.

ADMISSIONS CONTACT: MICHELLE GARSKE, ASSISTANT DIRECTOR OF GRADUATE PROGRAMS
ADDRESS: 293 CENTENNIAL DRIVE, STOP 8098, GRAND FORKS, ND 58202
PHONE: 701-777-2397 • FAX: 701-777-2019
E-MAIL: MBA@BUSINESS.UND.EDU • WEBSITE: BUSINESS.UND.EDU/MBA

FINANCIAL FACTS

Annual tuition (in-state/ out-of-state)	$5,895/$14,718
Fees	$450
Cost of books	$1,000
Room & board (on/off-campus)	$8,520/$8,520

ADMISSIONS
Admissions Selectivity Rating 60*

Student Life and Environment

"Everyone I have met through the program has been very nice and good to work with," one student says. Students describe fellow students as "charismatic, dedicated, and intelligent," as well as "helpful" and "eager to learn." They enjoy working together and say they can learn a lot from each other. Most students seem to be commuters or involved in Internet courses; however, those who do live on campus have the option of living in the school's apartments and dormitories. Commuters remark on the location's convenience, but admit they do not really engage in life on campus. There is an MBA Student Association that organizes weekly discussions and other social activities for those who wish to participate. Also, "many activities and student organizations cross the line between undergraduate and graduate, so there is never a problem networking with students from a variety of disciplines." If students seek further recreation, the North Dakota Museum of Art is located right on the UND campus. Also, the school has a hockey team, which students "take pride in." They also mention that the "gym facility is outstanding."

Grand Forks is a city with a population of roughly 53,000 people. It sits on the western banks of the Red River of the North, just seventy-five miles south of Canada. An international student says North Dakota is "a safe and easygoing place where foreign students can easily concentrate on their studies and become familiar with American culture."

Admissions

The admissions committee requests the following from its applicants: official GMAT scores, undergraduate GPA, personal essay, and letters of recommendation. The most important factors are GPA and GMAT score. The graduate business program desires candidates with GPAs higher than 3.0 and GMAT scores more than 500. That being said, students who show promise may be admitted on a provisional basis if one score is high enough to balance out the other. GRE scores may be submitted in lieu of a GMAT score. The average GRE score is 1233. Admissions at UND College of Business are rolling.

UNIVERSITY OF NORTH FLORIDA
COGGIN COLLEGE OF BUSINESS

GENERAL INFORMATION

Type of school   Public
Affiliation   No Affiliation

SURVEY SAYS...

Friendly students, Conservative students, Happy students
Solid preparation in:
Marketing, Accounting, General management, Teamwork, Presentation skills, Quantitative skills, Doing business in a global economy

STUDENTS

Enrollment of parent institution	15,882
Enrollment of MBA Program	272
% male/female	49/51
% out-of-state	3
% part-time	63
% underrepresented minority	20
% international	32
Average age at entry	28
Average years work experience at entry	0

ACADEMICS

Academic Experience Rating	**91**
Profs interesting rating	90
Profs accessible rating	93
Student/faculty ratio	6:1
% female faculty	24
% underrepresented minority faculty	24
% part-time faculty	2

Joint Degrees

GlobalMBA - 63 hours

Prominent Alumni

John McCalpin, Senior Executive, Accenture; Mark Vitner, Chief Economist, Wachovia; Elaine Johnson, Principal, Navigy; David Hayes, Founder & CEO, Tempus Software; Donna Harper, Founder & CEO, SystemLogics Co., LLC

Academics

The Coggin College of Business at the University of North Florida has quite a bit to offer young business students and working professionals, many of whom describe UNF as "the best school in Jacksonville." "Location," "reputation," and an "amazing logistics program" are just some of the reasons many students offer for this. "I went here as an undergrad," one student tell us, "and had the best experience with the teachers and students. It was an easy decision to continue my education at UNF." While UNF is a relatively large university, many current MBA students laud the "small classes" at Coggin, particularly the "online opportunities" and "evening classes" for those students with full-time jobs. We are told time and again that many of Coggin's students are "motivated, hard-working professionals looking to advance their skills and knowledge."

Inside the classroom, as one student puts it, "professors are eager to facilitate learning." Another student majoring in information technology in higher education says, "I appreciated the emphasis on group and project work, which resulted in greater camaraderie and cohesion with my fellow classmates." However, in a considerate counterpoint, this student said some professors tend to "gloss over critical issues that I would think would be foundational in the curriculum of any business school today: ethics, social responsibility, and sustainability." While courses with a sustainability and green jobs focus are not currently offered in the MBA program at UNF, other efforts are made to broaden the school's reach in the business community, including hosting Women in Business networking events and various support groups for women, minorities, and international students.

Coggin enrolls about 285 students in its MBA program, and roughly 80 percent of the student body works full time while attending school, which explains UNF's abundance of evening, weekend, and hybrid course offerings. However, those with more flexible schedules may take advantage of UNF's study abroad program, with partner universities in France, Germany, Poland, China, and India. The traditional MBA program at UNF offers degrees and concentrations in accounting, construction management, e-business, economics, finance, international business, logistics, management applications, and sports management. In addition to the MBA program, UNF offers a unique GlobalMBA, a sixty-three-hour program in which students earn a UNF MBA as well as a joint master's degree from the University of Warsaw and Cologne University of Applied Sciences. GlobalMBA participants join a cohort of about forty students who spend a residency at Cologne University of Applied Sciences (Germany), University of Warsaw (Poland), Dongbei University of Finance & Economics (China), and UNF.

Career and Placement

The Career Management Center offers specialized services, including a professional skills development program, to assist Coggin students in securing internships and full-time positions. The Center provides many of the services one expects from a large university, including student counseling, recruiting and networking events, resumé writing workshops, and internship programs. While some students consistently recruit Coggin students [to] stand out more to employers," the list of companies that have attended previous events at UNF is quite impressive. The list includes Bank of America, Bi-Lo Holdings, Black Diamond Performance Reporting, Black Knight Financial Services, CEVA Logistics, CIT, Citi, Crowley Maritime, CSX, Deloitte, Deutsche Bank, EverBank, EY, Fidelity Investments, FIS, Florida Blue, FNF, GE Capital, JEA, Johnson & Johnson Vision Care, KPMG, McGladrey, MECLABS, Medtronic, Merrill Lynch, PwC, Rayonier, State Farm, SteinMart, Web.com, Wells Fargo, Volkswagen USA, and many more. A large majority of graduating students (99 percent) accept employment in Florida or other southern states.

Student Life and Environment

Located in Jacksonville, a "great mid-sized city" that's "near the beach" and "surrounded by islands," UNF's "rapidly growing" 1,300-acre campus has been "designed for future expansion," which can only mean good things for this young university.

The Coggin Business School is mostly a school for "working adults" who "cannot afford to stop working for two years," and in many cases are "entrenched because they own homes." With this type of student body, one might not expect an abundance of social activities on campus, but they'd be wrong. "There are many clubs and activities on campus," one student informs us. "They have live concerts and movies for free . . . throughout the year. The new student union is very comfortable," and students can now enjoy wireless access from anywhere on campus. However, for such a young university as UNF, there is always room for improvement. One student explains that he "would like to see more green initiatives" on campus, like "green rooftops" and "water saving urinals" that can save up to "40,000 gallons of water each year."

Admissions

Applicants to the Coggin College of Business must submit the following materials for consideration: GMAT or GRE scores. The minimum score for the GMAT is 500, and for the GRE (after 7/1/11) a 145 verbal and 150 quantitative. Applicants must also submit an official undergraduate transcript (undergrad GPA of 3.0 or higher). Letters of reference and personal statement should not be submitted because these will not be taken into account. International students are required to submit TOEFL scores, with minimums of 550 paper, 213 computer and 80 internet. A limited number of small scholarships are offered on a first-come, first-served basis to students from Latin American countries, in addition to which these students receive a waiver on out-of-state tuition fees.

FINANCIAL FACTS

Annual tuition (in-state/ out-of-state)	$9,794/$22,383
Fees	$2,054
Cost of books	$1,200
Room & board (on/off-campus)	$9,204/$9,166
% of students receiving aid	45
% of first-year students receiving aid	42
% of students receiving grants	9
Average award package	$14,089
Average grant	$5,528
Average loan	$15,127
Average student loan debt	$26,318

ADMISSIONS

Admissions Selectivity Rating	88
# of applications received	257
% applicants accepted	63
% acceptees attending	45
Average GMAT	528
Range of GMAT	488–573
Accepts GRE scores	Yes
Average Verbal GRE	151
Range of Verbal GRE scores	146–155
Average Quantitative GRE	149
Range of Quantitative GRE scores	146–152
Average GPA	3.3
TOEFL required of international students	Yes
Minimum TOEFL (paper/web)	550/80
Application fee	$30
International application fee	$30
Regular application deadline	8/1
Regular application notification	Rolling
Deferment available	Yes
Maximum length of deferment	1 semester
Transfer students accepted	Yes
Transfer application policy On a case by case basis	
Non-fall admissions	Yes
Need-blind admissions	Yes

EMPLOYMENT PROFILE

Career Rating	81	Grads Employed by Function	% Avg. Salary
Percent employed at graduation	75	Operations	(25%) $39,000
Percent employed 3 months after graduation	100	Management	(13%) $40,000
		Finance	(38%) $52,667
Average base starting salary	$44,667	Other	(25%) $33,250
Primary Source of Full-time Job Acceptances		**Top 5 Employers Hiring Grads**	
School-facilitated activities	2 (25%)	Deutsche Bank (8), CSX Transportation (6), EverBank (4), Deloitte (5), Ernst & Young (4)	

University of Northern Iowa
College of Business Administration

GENERAL INFORMATION

Type of school	Public
Affiliation	No Affiliation
Academic calendar	trimester

SURVEY SAYS...

Classmates have diverse work experience, Friendly students
Solid preparation in:
Marketing, General management, Teamwork, Presentation skills

STUDENTS

Enrollment of parent institution	12,273
Enrollment of MBA Program	67
% male/female	68/32
% out-of-state	39
% part-time	92
% underrepresented minority	2
% international	39
Average age at entry	31
Average years work experience at entry	9

ACADEMICS

Academic Experience Rating	90
Profs interesting rating	90
Profs accessible rating	92
Student/faculty ratio	25:1
% female faculty	17
% underrepresented minority faculty	19
% part-time faculty	0

Prominent Alumni

Nancy Aossey, CEO, International Medical Corporation; Mark Baldwin, CEO, Iowa Laser Technology (retired); Kevin Lentz, Sr. VP, Cuna Mutual Insurance; Gary Rolling, President and CEO J-Tec Associates, Inc.; Kyle Selberg, VP Marketing, Principal Financial Group

Academics

It's not hard to understand why MBA students would be compelled to attend University of Northern Iowa. Indeed, it's a "well-respected business school" and offers "competitive tuition" rates. And, with a very accommodating class schedule, it's clearly a program that's designed to support individuals who are "working full-time." In fact, many of the "major businesses in the area send employees [to UNI]," which leads to some fabulous networking opportunities.

Academically, MBA candidates are privy to "small classes" that allow for individual attention. Moreover, courses tend to place "an emphasis on teamwork." Students especially rave about the capstone business consulting project which "takes everything the students have learned and challenges them to apply [that] knowledge to local businesses or nonprofits with the guidance of mentors." The capstone is a "fantastic" educational experience and these MBAs relish the "opportunity to solve a real business problem."

Additionally, UNI professors "bring a lot of experience and knowledge to the MBA program." For the most part, they are also "responsive to students' needs," and they "know [how to] present the material well." The "efficient" administration earns high marks as well. As one second-year gushes, "The amount of administrative . . . support is amazing relative to the number of students. Turnaround on questions is very fast and the administration can support an advising need in short-notice." And, finally, perhaps this first-year says it best by simply referring to the faculty and staff as "awesome."

Career and Placement

The career services office at University of Northern Iowa really helps students understand how to market their knowledge, training, professionalism and work ethic (attributes that the MBA students here have in spades). Importantly, the office hosts two massive career fairs every year, one in the fall and one in February. However, don't expect career services to rest on those impressive laurels. Throughout the year, the office works to arrange a number of on-campus interviews for students as well, which helps to explain how over 95 percent of University of Northern Iowa MBAs are employed within six months of graduation!

Companies and organizations that have recruited and hired University of Northern Iowa students include: Central State Bank, Deloitte, Enterprise-Rent-A-Car, ConAgra Foods, Inc., John Deere, Northwestern Mutual, Pella Corporation, Penske Truck Leasing, Renewable Energy Group and Toyota Financial Services.

ADMISSIONS CONTACT: NANCY L. HOFFMAN, MBA PROGRAM ASSISTANT
ADDRESS: COLLEGE OF BUSINESS ADMINISTRATION, CURRIS BUSINESS BUILDING 325, CEDAR FALLS,
IA 50614-0123 • PHONE: 319-273-6243 • FAX: 319-273-6230 • E-MAIL: MBA@UNI.EDU
WEBSITE: WWW.CBA.UNI.EDU/DBWEB/PAGES/PROGRAMS/GRADUATE-BUS-ADMIN.CFM

Student Life and Environment

The College of Business Administration at UNI manages to populate its classes and cohorts with individuals of varying "backgrounds, ages and experiences." Then again, that shouldn't be too surprising given that there's a large number of "international [students who hail] from different parts of the world." Thankfully, no matter their heritage, most UNI MBAs appear to be "mature, wise and thoughtful." What's more, they are "smart, driven people who are fun to be around." And the vast majority have proven to be "business savvy" and "family-oriented" people "who value their education and free time."

Further, UNI does an amazing job at fully integrating both part-time and full-time students, ensuring they have the [opportunity to work with [each other]." The university also strives to accommodate both working professionals and students with families. And it's clear their efforts are paying off. Indeed, the school "sponsor[s many] activities for the [entire] family including sporting events, seminars and concerts." These are all well attended, proving that there's plenty of fun to be had outside of the classroom.

Admissions

GMAT scores, a personal statement, undergraduate GPA, and previous work experience are all very important for enrollment consideration. Letters of recommendations and college transcripts are also required along with one's application to UNI's College of Business Administration. Communication skills are highly factored into the decision process, as well as the applicant's demonstrated leadership potential, intellectual capability, and academic success during undergraduate and graduate work. The average age of recent students is thirty-two, the average undergraduate GPA is 3.37, and the average GMAT score is 545.

FINANCIAL FACTS

Annual tuition (in-state/ out-of-state)	$9,634/$19,804
Fees	$1,169
Cost of books	$3,000
Room & board (on/off-campus)	$8,320/$8,320
% of students receiving aid	24
% of first-year students receiving aid	10
% of students receiving grants	19
Average award package	$9,872
Average grant	$7,559
Average loan	$15,268

ADMISSIONS

Admissions Selectivity Rating	**88**
# of applications received	56
% applicants accepted	41
% acceptees attending	91
Average GMAT	545
Range of GMAT	500–610
Accepts GRE scores	No
Average GPA	3.4
TOEFL required of international students	Yes
Minimum TOEFL (paper/web)	550/79
Application fee	$60
International application fee	$70
Early application deadline	2/1
Regular application deadline	7/20
Application Deadline/Notification	
Deferment available	Yes
Maximum length of deferment	1 year
Transfer students accepted	Yes
Transfer application policy Students may transfer up to 10 hours of AACSB-accredited, graduate credit	
Non-fall admissions	Yes
Need-blind admissions	Yes

University of Notre Dame
Mendoza College of Business

GENERAL INFORMATION

Type of school	Private
Affiliation	Roman Catholic
Academic calendar	Seven-week Module

SURVEY SAYS...

Classmates have diverse work experience, Friendly students, Good peer network, Good social scene, Conservative students, Cutting-edge classes, Abundant mentors available, Helpful alumni, Happy students, Abundant clubs and activities
Solid preparation in:
Finance, Accounting, General management, Teamwork, Communication/interpersonal skills, Presentation skills, Quantitative skills, Doing business in a global economy, Environmental sustainability

ACADEMICS

Academic Experience Rating	95
Profs interesting rating	95
Profs accessible rating	97
Student/faculty ratio	3:1
% female faculty	20
% underrepresented minority faculty	11
% part-time faculty	27

Joint Degrees

JD/MBA: 4 years; JD/MBA: 3 years accelerated; Science/MBA - 5 years; Engineering/MBA - 5 years

Prominent Alumni

Lloyd Adams, National Vice President, SAP for Utilities, SAP America; Don Casey, CEO, Medical Segment, Cardinal Health; Scott Malpass, VP and Chief Investment Officer, University of Notre Dame; Paul Reilly, CEO, Raymond James Financial; Brandon Solano, CMO, Papa Murphy's International

Academics

Students come to the University of Notre Dame to become part of the "Notre Dame family," and few leave disappointed; the MBA program at the Mendoza College of Business fosters a strong sense of community that, coupled with the campus-wide school spirit, quickly makes Notre Dame feel like home. Add "outstanding professor-student interaction" and "great potential for alumni networking" and you understand why student satisfaction levels are so high here.

The Mendoza MBA program "excels at providing an overall business understanding," students tell us. The school offers a two-year full-time program that "is perfect for non-business undergraduate majors to gain a well-rounded understanding of business fundamentals," as well as a one-year program for those with exceptionally strong business backgrounds. Students say, "Ethics is a hallmark of the school and it can be seen in every course," and "the school's reputation for producing ethical graduates is more important in recent years than ever before."

Mendoza employs a modular curriculum, and "the 2007 class was the first to complete our entire course work under the current 'module' system. The module system will allow Notre Dame MBAs to be better prepared than were previous classes. The faculty here "is top-notch." Their research, publications, work experience, and generally great personalities inspire confidence in their ability to prepare [students] for the business world."

Career and Placement

"The majority of recruiting is Midwest-based" at Notre Dame, and while some complain about the dearth of New York finance-sector recruiters, most students feel that "the Career Office does a good job of locating companies from various regions." Mendoza MBAs recognize that "our small class size hinders our ability to get a large selection of companies from each region, but they are represented." However, "the situation is greatly improving, with some bulge-bracket and many middle-market banks already recruiting on campus. This will improve over time as the school moves toward its long-term mission of improving rank."

Of course, Notre Dame's storied alumni network helps with placement. Students tell us that "the Career Development Office recently made it easier for current MBA students to get in contact with alumni. Prior to this, it was a very prolonged process that involved Career Development responding to individual student's requests for alumni contact information in their respective field." These contacts can be invaluable. As one student reports, "The alumni of the school are always willing to go the extra mile for you. I have met with alumni from my hometown to get resume and career search advice." No wonder students brag that "becoming a member of the alumni network is worth more than the cost of tuition."

Companies recruiting Mendoza MBAs include: Amazon, Inc., Capital One, Cisco Systems, Credit Suisse, Deloitte, Delta Airlines, Ernst & Young, Google, Intel, McKinsey & Company, Nationwide Insurance, PricewaterhouseCoopers, Procter & Gamble, The Walt Disney Co., USB Investment Bank..

Student Life and Environment

There's no doubt that Notre Dame is a very social campus, but the extent to which MBAs can partake in that social life depends on whether they're in their first or second year of the program. First year is "very difficult" with a massive workload. Many students "spend twice as much time on schoolwork" during their first year, and find it difficult to "juggle [classes] with career pursuits." Those who can carve out some leisure time agree that "Notre Dame has a culture that is contagious! It's not hard to keep yourself busy with a broad range of activities, whether it's class, a group meeting, intramural game, community-service event, or a football tailgate. There's never a dull moment." Football unites the campus and provides more than mere entertainment; it also "lures large corporations for networking events." Also, alumni return to campus for football games "for years after graduation and usually for life." Hometown South Bend is a small town, with only a "few good places to go out." The "students make up for it, though. We host a lot of social gatherings."

Mendoza MBAs benefit from "a strong esprit de corps" built on team projects and "an ethical foundation that is reinforced constantly so that it actually has an effect." Most are "married, with families and children." They represent "more diverse backgrounds than some of the 'big' schools back East, meaning we have folks from engineering, the public sector, and other nontraditional or non-business backgrounds. These are very sharp people who may have had the 'wrong' undergrad pedigree but are every bit as bright as those at any b-school anywhere."

Admissions

Applicants to Mendoza's two-year MBA program must provide all of the following: proof of an undergraduate degree from an accredited college or university; official transcript(s); GMAT or GRE scores; a current resume; one essay (topic provided by school); a four-slide presentation; and two letters of recommendation. International students must also provide TOEFL scores or IELTS. Applicants to the one-year program must present academic transcripts showing successful completion of three credit hours of financial accounting, and three credit hours of statistics. All applicants are expected to have at least two years of meaningful work experience.

FINANCIAL FACTS

Annual tuition (in-state/ out-of-state)	$50,326/$50,326
Fees	$1
Cost of books	$1,700
Room & board (on/off-campus)	$9,900/$9,900
% of students receiving aid	93
% of first-year students receiving aid	96
% of students receiving grants	88
Average award package	$47,769
Average grant	$30,970
Average loan	$40,566
Average student loan debt	$50,405

ADMISSIONS

Admissions Selectivity Rating	90

EMPLOYMENT PROFILE

Career Rating	96	Grads Employed by Function	% Avg. Salary
Percent employed at graduation	76	Marketing	(14%) $103,500
Percent employed 3 months after graduation	93	Operations	(3%) $106,500
		Consulting	(23%) $113,712
Average base starting salary	$108,219	Management	(7%) $104,000
Primary Source of Full-time Job Acceptances		Finance	(31%) $105,400
School-facilitated activities	70 (61%)	MIS	(1%)
Graduate-facilitated activities	29 (25%)	Other	(10%) $114,182
Unknown	15 (13%)	**Top 5 Employers Hiring Grads**	

Top 5 Employers Hiring Grads
Deloitte (10), PricewaterhouseCoopers (7), EY (6), Capital One (4), Nationwide Insurance (3)

University of Oklahoma
Michael F. Price College of Business

GENERAL INFORMATION
Type of school   Public
Affiliation   No Affiliation
Academic calendar   Semester

SURVEY SAYS...
Friendly students, Conservative students
Solid preparation in:
Finance

STUDENTS
Enrollment of parent institution	30,786
Enrollment of MBA Program	190
% male/female	74/26
% out-of-state	29
% part-time	73
% underrepresented minority	4
% international	15
Average age at entry	26
Average years work experience at entry	3

ACADEMICS
Academic Experience Rating	**89**
Profs interesting rating	86
Profs accessible rating	90
Student/faculty ratio	9:1
% female faculty	23
% part-time faculty	8

Joint Degrees
MBA/JD 3 to 4 years MBA/MS in MIT 2 to 3 years MBA/MAcc 2 to 3 years BS in IE/MBA 5 years BBA/MAcc 5 years Generic Dual (MBA and any other Masters program) length varies MBA/IFP (Master in Energy Economics) 1.5 years

Prominent Alumni
Michael F. Price, Mutual Fund Investor; Randall Stephenson, Chair/CEO of AT&T; Steve Moore, CEO/OG&E; Archie Dunham, Chairman - Chesapeake Energy; ,

Academics

Professors at the Price College of Business at the University of Oklahoma are "a combination of top-notch academics and industry leading executives-in-residence making for a dynamic learning and networking experience." The brand name school offers a Full-Time and Professional (part-time) options, both of which utilize the same faculty, curriculum, and resources and elective specializations in energy, finance, entrepreneurship, management information technology, and risk management. As most people here are "looking to move upward in their respective organizations," the flexibility of the program is designed to accommodate working professionals, and the curriculum is designed to emphasize the lessons that can be imparted by classmates and applied immediately. "Having professionals that are working in the prominent industries in Oklahoma makes the class conversation much more useful and relevant," says a student.

With cohorts of only forty students, personalization is a key focus of the MBA programs, and no one lacks for attention from the administration or faculty. "I have been very impressed, not only by the level of instruction, but . . . the one-on-one time that I have received as an MBA student from both professors and advisers," says a student. Though some students feel that "the core classes are text book only" and there is not enough real-life application is mixed in to those class models, they says that "once you start your specific emphasis it changes drastically." Text book material is introduced through case studies, speakers and projects: "It is fun to go to class and interact with teachers who can answer almost any question I can ask and then some." Several display "complete mastery of their particular subject area," and relate it to current events, lending perspective to both a domestic and global business setting. Entrepreneurship professors are "all businessmen who have made millions of dollars in the business world and concentrate on sharing the wealth of knowledge they have learned and sometimes even sharing contacts," confirms a student.

Career and Placement

Job placement (particularly for the Professional MBA) somewhat revolves around "a big willingness for current students who are happy with their company helping other students find new placement," and part-time students are happy to find "networking opportunities similar to a full time program." Furthermore, administrators "take an active role in tapping their networks to assist with career and internship placement in the metro area." The Student Support Center offers career assistance for all OU MBA students, and they "are readily accessible all days of the week." Staff here does "a great job of giving students a lot of individual attention" in landing internships and employment, offering international opportunities to both work and study abroad, and connecting them with relevant industry professionals that can give input regarding industries of interest.

Top employers of recent Price graduates include Williams Partners, L.P., AT&T, Hitachi Consulting, Sonic Industries, and Carter Healthcare.

Student Life and Environment

The "ease with which one can meet new people and interact in a friendly manner with literally anyone you come across on any given day" is one of the school's greatest strengths, and there are myriad "great social events which encourage significant others and networking." "I feel as though I can engage anybody, anytime (respectfully, of course) with questions or by introducing myself, and it will be well-received," says a student. "I have developed strong friendships with high character people I would happily work with now and in the future," says another. Professional MBA students are juggling especially busy schedules, and with such a diverse group of working students, "it can be extremely challenging to meet up to complete several group assignments along, in multiple classes." For those who can, "the graduate lounge is pretty amazing," and there is ample opportunity to engage with both other business students and students in non-business majors. A large percentage of the programs are international students, and a fair number have engineering backgrounds.

Admissions

Applicants to the Price MBA program must submit the following materials to the Office of Admissions and Records: an application for admission to the university; an official transcript from every undergraduate and graduate institution attended; and, for international applicants, a financial statement as well as an official TOEFL score report if English is not their first language. In addition, all applicants must also submit the following materials to the MBA Admissions Office: an official score report for the GMAT or GRE; a current résumé; and a personal statement of career and educational goals. Two years of work experience is preferred but not required.

FINANCIAL FACTS

Annual tuition (in-state/ out-of-state)	$6,102/$23,677
Fees	$10,127
Cost of books	$1,200
Room & board (on/off-campus)	$11,170/$11,170
% of students receiving grants	60
Average award package	$22,116
Average grant	$7,389

ADMISSIONS

Admissions Selectivity Rating	87
# of applications received	129
% applicants accepted	55
% acceptees attending	63
Average GMAT	628
Range of GMAT	605–660
Accepts GRE scores	Yes
Average Verbal GRE	156
Range of Verbal GRE scores	152–158
Average Quantitative GRE	158
Range of Quantitative GRE scores	152–161
Average GPA	3.4
TOEFL required of international students	Yes
Minimum TOEFL (paper/web)	600/100
Application fee	$50
International application fee	$100
Early application deadline	11/15
Regular application deadline	5/15
Application Deadline/Notification	
Round 1:	11/15
Round 2:	1/15
Round 3:	3/15
Round 4:	5/15
Deferment available	Yes
Maximum length of deferment	1 year
Transfer students accepted	Yes
Transfer application policy Requests for transfer credit are reviewed upon acceptance to the MBA program. Courses must be from an AACSB-accredited institution with an earned grade of B or higher, taken within the last five years, and approved by the MBA department.	
Non-fall admissions	No
Need-blind admissions	Yes

EMPLOYMENT PROFILE

Career Rating	93	Grads Employed by Function	% Avg. Salary
Percent employed at graduation	77	Marketing	(8%) $0
Percent employed 3 months after graduation	90	Operations	(15%) $70,165
		Consulting	(15%) $90,675
Average base starting salary	$82,335	Management	(4%)
Primary Source of Full-time Job Acceptances		Finance	(54%) $78,750
School-facilitated activities	18 (69%)	Other	(4%) $0
Graduate-facilitated activities	8 (31%)		

Top 5 Employers Hiring Grads
AT&T (2), Deloitte (1), Boston Consulting Group (1), Sonic Industries (1), JP Morgan Private Bank (1)

UNIVERSITY OF OREGON
CHARLES H. LUNDQUIST COLLEGE OF BUSINESS

Academics

The University of Oregon's Charles H. Lundquist College of Business is a relatively small, green-oriented school offering an "excellent program in sustainable business practices," a particularly "strong entrepreneurship tract," and a top-ranked sports marketing and business program that, according to many students, is the "premier" program of its kind in the nation. As one very satisfied student puts it, "I would not have even looked at Oregon as an option if it weren't for its renowned sports business program." The Warsaw Sports Marketing program also offers its students the "opportunity to combine studies in corporate finance with the sports industry." One student working toward an MBA in sustainable business praises the school's "interdisciplinary nature" and its "ability to work directly with companies to consult on real world issues." However, based on the feedback we have received, the administration and faculty don't do a lot of hand holding when it comes to the students. While students "benefit from personal attention from the teaching staff in terms of advice on courses, career paths, and general resources," MBA candidates are expected to take full ownership of their studies and be proactive in their job search.

The role sustainability plays in Oregon's MBA program cannot be overstated. The College of Business's MBA in sustainable business was established in 2008, and its popularity has only grown since then. Many students come to Oregon specifically to earn their MBA at the school's relatively new Center for Sustainable Business Practices housed in the Lillis Business Complex, a LEED silver certified facility and one of the most environmentally friendly buildings of its kind in the country. "Business schools are a dime a dozen," says one sports business student, "I knew I wanted a school that offered a top-flight entrepreneurship focus, and the University of Oregon was tops on my list, but, beyond that, there is substantial value in being surrounded by students who are also staunchly interested in entrepreneurship."

In addition to Oregon's lauded programs in sports management, sustainability, and entrepreneurship, a number of dual-degree programs are also available, including a JD/MBA and MS/MBA with varying concentrations, as well as individual programs in finance, supply chain management, accounting, and media/entertainment. An Executive MBA program, which is located in Portland, is also offered. There are almost 200 students in the graduate business programs, with approximately 100 of them pursuing an MBA.

The age range of students is mid twenties to early thirties, and many in the program tend to arrive with at least a couple years of work experience, with backgrounds ranging from large corporations to small non-profit firms. Most students feel this helps provide students with a "well-rounded view of issues" that isn't disconnected from "real-world experiences." During students' second year of study, full-time MBA students also participate in a strategic planning project over the course of two terms. Through this experiential learning program, small student groups work as consultants to major Northwest businesses, including Adidas, Amazon, Hewlett Packard, and Intel.

Career and Placement

The Lundquist College of Business boasts four different centers of excellence, dedicated to sports marketing, finance and security analysis, entrepreneurship and innovation, and sustainable business practices. Each of these centers aims to foster experiential learning to "provide [students with] opportunities to interface with the business community." Regarding the college's career services, they rely on a relationship development model to serve the niche industries within their centers. Some students have told us that, while the

ADMISSIONS CONTACT: JESSICA BROWN, ADMISSIONS COORDINATOR
ADDRESS: 1208 UNIVERSITY OF OREGON, 302 PETERSON HALL, EUGENE, OR 97403-1208
PHONE: 541-346-3306 • FAX: 541-346-0073
E-MAIL: MBAININFO@UOREGON.EDU • WEBSITE: WWW.BUSINESS.UOREGON/EDU/MBA

"center is always willing to proofread a resume or cover letter," many would like to see "increased on-campus recruiting" from businesses, both local and national, and overall improvements in "career service offerings." "MBA recruiting is essentially non-existent," one advertising and marketing student tells us. The school does arrange for "periodic visits to regional business centers" in San Francisco, Portland, and Seattle, New York and an annual global business trip to Asia to meet with key business leaders and alumni. With hundreds of key industry partnerships, Oregon MBA garner an average base salary of $71,831 for recently graduated MBAs, and 81 percent of students having either received or accepted a job offer by three months after graduation. Oregon MBA students appear to be pretty self-sufficient.

Student Life and Environment

"I work hard and play hard. I've never been so busy," says one first-year student. Situated in bucolic Eugene, Oregon, "a small and quirky town" just "two hours down the road from Portland," students assure us that while this is no "thriving city," "we all appreciate the surrounding natural beauty . . . and there are endless opportunities to stay fit and well." Despite Eugene's "laid-back culture," a microenterprise development student informs us, "When you're in the program you are BUSY, but it's a good kind of busy. You spend a lot of time working on group projects and participating in clubs." Many industry professionals and guest speakers are invited to speak at on-campus events "almost every night."

Eugene is also "an environmentally conscious town," which helps explain the draw and reputation of U of O's sustainability program. In short, few students have anything remotely negative to say about the area. The abundance of outdoor "recreational activities" and "local breweries" fills up much of the students' leisure time, although a good portion of MBA students have conveyed that many "don't have any downtime."

Admissions

All applicants to the Lundquist College of Business should first consider that all graduate business students are in full-time programs, and no part-time option is offered. Applicants are required to submit their GMAT scores (600 minimum), official undergrad transcript (minimum GPA of 3.0), essay/personal statement, at least two letters of reference, and a resume or summary of professional experience. Applicants with real-world business experience will be given particular attention. International applicants must submit TOEFL scores, with 600 minimum on the written test or 96 minimum on web-based. Interviews are a requirement for admission.

FINANCIAL FACTS

Annual tuition (in-state/ out-of-state)	$26,490/$36,660
Fees	$1,784
Cost of books	$1,068
Room & board	$11,118
% of students receiving aid	85
% of first-year students receiving aid	91
% of students receiving grants	74
Average award package	$21,790
Average grant	$4,551
Average loan	$32,672
Average student loan debt	$37,957

ADMISSIONS

Admissions Selectivity Rating	89
# of applications received	224
% applicants accepted	43
% acceptees attending	59
Average GMAT	621
Range of GMAT	590–650
Accepts GRE scores	Yes
Average Verbal GRE	162
Range of Verbal GRE scores	159–167
Average Quantitative GRE	157
Range of Quantitative GRE scores	153–159
Average Writing GRE	4.0
Range of Writing GRE scores	4.0–5.0
Average GPA	3.4
TOEFL required of international students	Yes
Minimum TOEFL (paper/web)	600/96
Application fee	$50
International application fee	$50
Early application deadline	11/15
Early notification date	12/15
Regular application deadline	4/15
Regular application notification	4/15
Application Deadline/Notification	
Round 1:	11/15 / 12/15
Round 2:	2/15 / 3/15
Round 3:	4/15 / 5/15
Deferment available	Yes
Maximum length of deferment	1 year
Transfer students accepted	Yes
Transfer application policy Students may request to transfer a maximum of 9 graduate credits in the MBA program.	
Non-fall admissions	No
Need-blind admissions	Yes

EMPLOYMENT PROFILE

Career Rating	86	
Percent employed at graduation	39	
Percent employed 3 months after graduation	61	
Average base starting salary	$63,300	
Primary Source of Full-time Job Acceptances		
School-facilitated activities	5 (36%)	
Graduate-facilitated activities	7 (50%)	
Unknown	2 (14%)	

Grads Employed by Function% Avg. Salary
Other (100%) $63,300

Top 5 Employers Hiring Grads
adidas (1), Bank of America (1), Intel (1), Oracle (1), Titleist (1)

UNIVERSITY OF OTTAWA
TELFER SCHOOL OF MANAGEMENT

GENERAL INFORMATION

Type of school	Public
Academic calendar	Aug-Aug

SURVEY SAYS...

Classmates have diverse work experience, Friendly students, Students love Ottawa, ON
Solid preparation in:
General management, Teamwork, Presentation skills

STUDENTS

Enrollment of parent institution	42,672
Enrollment of MBA Program	115
% male/female	72/28
% part-time	10
% international	13
Average age at entry	33
Average years work experience at entry	8

ACADEMICS

Academic Experience Rating	**87**
Profs interesting rating	88
Profs accessible rating	92
% female faculty	35

Joint Degrees

MBA/JD (MBA and Law) (40 months)

Prominent Alumni

Ian Telfer, Chairman of Goldcorp Inc.; Harley Finkelstein, Chief Operating Officer, Shopƒ®fy; Bernie Ashe, CEO, Ottawa Sports and Entertainment Group; Guy Laflamme, Head of 2017 Celebrations, City of Ottawa; Dominique DeCelles, General Manager Hispanic Zone - Active Cosmetics Division, L'Oreal Americas

Academics

Located in Ottawa, the capital of Canada, the Telfer School of Management offers "a great place for learning with such a dynamic environment." Students are drawn to the "triple accreditation" (AACSB, AMBA and EQUIS) and the fact that the school is "bilingual" meaning the "MBA [is] available in French." The program has a "strong focus on global environment," a "solid reputation relative to other schools in the area," and a "low cost of tuition." It's "location in the national capital region" offers many "connections with local industry and the federal government." Consequently, "a lot of government workers" attend the program. "Because of the triple accreditation the school has, we get a lot of international students," one student explains. "This allows us to work and interact with many diverse cultures that we would normally not be exposed to. In a global marketplace, this is invaluable and should serve me well."

The "dedicated professors" are "available and reliable" and a real "pillar of strength and wisdom." The majority of the faculty are "well versed in their areas" and "showcase some of the brightest in their respective fields." "There are some very knowledgeable professors at this school who go the extra mile to connect with students and," one happy student reports. The administration is also "available and courteous," making an overall "very well organized administrative support unit."

The MBA at University of Ottawa is an intensive "one-year program," which "means less time out of the workforce." Despite the short program, the program "still incorporates a large practical component (consulting project and international trip)." The school places students in teams "for the duration of the program" which lets students "combine our strengths to overcome our weaknesses." It is also worth noting that the University of Ottawa is "very good at supporting partners and acknowledging the toll of an MBA on families." One student sums up their experience succinctly: "I just have two words: 'NET AWESOME'!"

Career and Placement

Since the Telfer School of Management is "well connected to the local business community," many MBA students find work in Canada's capital. Seventeen percent of a recent graduating class found work in government. The average mean base salary for that class was a little over $77,500. Employers who most frequently hire Ottawa MBAs include Adobe Systems, Bank of Nova Scotia, Bank of Canada, Canada Mortgage and Housing Corporation (CMHC), Costco, Deloitte, L'Oréal, RBC Royal Bank, SwiftTrade Securities, TD Waterhouse Investment, and Xerox Canada.

Student Life and Environment

Since the student body at University of Ottawa is "such a unique blend of local, national and international students that it is very hard to pinpoint what my fellow students are 'like'." However, most students are "friendly, outgoing, and helpful," and "the average age is late twenties, early thirties." Students get along well, perhaps thanks to "the program's approach to team work" which "facilities this positive environment."

As "[the university] is in the heart of downtown Ottawa, Canada's capital city," there is plenty to do both on campus and off. "Day to day, there is freedom to do what you want," one student explains. "If you want to be very involved in the school, you can be. If you prefer to do your own thing, that's fine as well." As Canadians, "we celebrate winter (given the weather), and enjoy the summer." "Due primarily to its intensive, twelve-month nature," there may not be as much time for extracurricular activities as at other programs. As one student states, "The important thing to know going into this program, is that you are willing to give it your all for a full twelve months."

Admissions

The University of Ottawa requires GMAT scores, personal statement, undergraduate transcripts, two letters of recommendation, at least three years of work experience, and an interview. Last year's class had an average GPA of 3.0 and an average GMAT score of 625. As the program is bilingual, applicants can apply in either French or English but will need to establish proficiency in their desired language.

FINANCIAL FACTS

Annual tuition (in-state/ out-of-state)	$18,787/$30,634
Fees	$1,139
Cost of books	$1,136
Room & board (on/off-campus)	$8,010/$5,908
Average grant	$5,067

ADMISSIONS

Admissions Selectivity Rating	87
# of applications received	243
% applicants accepted	49
% acceptees attending	54
Average GMAT	625
Range of GMAT	590–650
Accepts GRE scores	Yes
Average GPA	2.9
TOEFL required of international students	Yes
Minimum TOEFL (paper/web)	600/100
Application fee	$100
International application fee	$100
Regular application deadline	5/15
Application Deadline/Notification	
Deferment available	No
Maximum length of deferment	
Transfer students accepted	Yes
Transfer application policy A maximum of 24 credits could be retained for graduate courses in management completed in a Canadian MBA program or AACSB accredited program.	
Non-fall admissions	No
Need-blind admissions	Yes

EMPLOYMENT PROFILE			
Career Rating	87	Grads Employed by Function% Avg. Salary	
Percent employed at graduation	54	Marketing	(24%)
Percent employed 3 months		Operations	(3%)
after graduation	65	Management	(18%)
Average base starting salary	$68,166	Finance	(12%)
		HR	(3%)
		MIS	(9%)
		Other	(31%)

UNIVERSITY OF THE PACIFIC
EBERHARDT SCHOOL OF BUSINESS

GENERAL INFORMATION
Type of school   Private
Affiliation   Non-denominational,
            Methodist founded
            and affiliated
Academic calendar   Semester

SURVEY SAYS...
Friendly students, Good social scene,
Smart classrooms
Solid preparation in:
Presentation skills, Entrepreneurial
skills

STUDENTS
Enrollment of parent institution	6,281
Enrollment of MBA Program	36
% male/female	42/58
% part-time	33
% underrepresented minority	79
% international	13
Average age at entry	26
Average years work experience at entry	3

ACADEMICS
Academic Experience Rating	70
Profs interesting rating	66
Profs accessible rating	68
Student/faculty ratio	10:1
% female faculty	30
% underrepresented minority faculty	15
% part-time faculty	10

Joint Degrees
PharmD/MBA- 4 years JD/MBA- 4
years

Prominent Alumni
A.G. Spanos, Real Estate
Development; Pete Carroll, Coach,
Seattle Seahawks; Dell Demps,
General Manager, New Orleans
Pelicans, NBA; David Gerber, MGM/
Columbia/20thCenturyFox - Film &
TV Production; Dave Brubek, Jazz
Composer/ Musician

Academics

Located in Stockton, California, University of the Pacific is a distinctive private college that boasts a "very high standing both academically and professionally throughout our local community and state." Ideal for early-career professionals, the school's full-time program allows students from a range of academic backgrounds "to obtain an MBA in a highly intensive and challenging program." Fast-paced and efficient, the first term is "an intensive phase seventeen-unit semester broken down into eight modules. This intensive phase allows students to learn the fundamentals necessary for a business degree and requires spending most of the students' time at school." During this time, students are placed "in a cohort . . . and share all required classes." Therefore, each entering class is incredibly tight-knit, creating a unique learning environment. A current student explains, "This cohort of students is a wide array of culturally- and educationally-diverse students coming from various countries and experience levels. These factors contribute to an intellectually challenging classroom experience [that] goes beyond traditional book- or case-based classes." In addition to traditional business students, the "MBA program offers joint programs with Pacific's PharmD and JD programs...having the interaction from the other schools is a great resource."

After the first term, Eberhardt School's MBA program follows a typical semester model, with a more "moderate workload." At that point, students can tailor their educational experiences by choosing a track in general management or healthcare management.. They also take advantage of "the unique opportunity to study abroad in another country," through the school's Global Business Competition, or specialize in international issues through the school's Master's International MBA Program in cooperation with the Peace Corps. Future finance mavens can also hone their skills through the school's $3.0 million Eberhardt Student Investment Fund. While University of the Pacific and the Eberhardt School boast many world-class opportunities, students are most impressed by the small and intimate feeling that pervades this intimate Northern California school. With a student-faculty ratio of 16:1, "the greatest strengths of this school are the small classroom sizes [and] the professors' willingness to help students and get to know them on a one-on-one basis." A current student agrees, "I have been pleased with the teacher's performance and one-on-one help outside of classrooms. Teachers really take the time to make sure students understand the material and frequently check to make sure everyone is on the same page." Another adds, "Students are always welcome to question or seek help from professors and the professors offer a more peer-to-peer interaction, rather than the typical student-teacher relationship, which further encourages a beneficial educational experience." In addition to their friendliness and accessibility, Pacific professors are strong class leaders. On the whole, students are "very impressed with the quality of the teaching," saying their professors are "professional and can apply the material to real-life situations."

Career and Placement

Career development is an important part of the Eberhardt School's curriculum. A Career Development module in the first term helps students build a job search strategy and prepare for the professional world. Students are also required to complete a summer business internship, which offers the opportunity to build real-world skills and contacts. In addition, the Career Management Center hosts various on-campus recruiting events and interviews. Located a stone's throw away from the San Francisco Bay Area, the Silicon Valley and the state capital of Sacramento, "the network of contacts built from attending is excellent." The average student interviews with about seven different companies and receives two job offers by graduation. Recent employers of MBA graduates include Clorox, E & J Gallo, Blue Shield of California, FDIC, KPMG, TStryker Endoscopy and Yelp.

Student Life and Environment

Pacific's enthusiastic students dole out praises for their diligent classmates, saying, "Fellow students are both driven and work as a team. Together, we hope to succeed and push past boundaries." Due to the intense cohort format, "each class that comes through is extremely close-knit and shares their experiences like a single unit." A current MBA candidate elaborates, "Students are very genuine and really look out for one another. Because we spend all week together, many students have found strong friendships and even business partners for future ventures." While the school draws a few students from further a field, "the MBA student population is predominantly local—though they may have originated from somewhere else."

Based in the city of Stockton, California, "the campus is like a world of its own within the community"—a place where students feel comfortable studying and relaxing. To burn off steam, MBA students can participate in "intramural sports like evening basketball and flag football that are played against other schools on campus." Thursdays are a popular night for gatherings, and "the MBAs also spend a lot of time together outside of campus at dinner and studying." Attracting a younger crowd, some say the school could "try to make more programs available for full-time working students and their families." One explains, "Being a father and husband, my time is very limited. There are several times that I would've liked to involve my wife and children in my school activities, but that seemed out of place."

Admissions

To be considered for admission to the Eberhardt School's MBA program, students must submit an acceptable GMAT or GRE score. International students must meet minimum guidelines for TOEFL or IELTS and submit a WES evaluation of all international coursework. Prospective students are evaluated based on their performance in prior coursework, recommendation letters, GMAT or GRE scores, and an admissions interview. Admissions decisions are made on a rolling basis, and a new cohort of students is admitted each fall.

FINANCIAL FACTS

Annual tuition	$44,068
Fees	$520
Cost of books	$1,764
Room & board (on/off-campus)	$15,000/$17,000
% of students receiving aid	89
% of first-year students receiving aid	95
% of students receiving grants	66
Average award package	$27,508
Average grant	$31,697
Average loan	$15,321

ADMISSIONS

Admissions Selectivity Rating	85
# of applications received	81
% applicants accepted	52
% acceptees attending	43
Average GMAT	535
Range of GMAT	470–610
Accepts GRE scores	Yes
Average Verbal GRE	165
Range of Verbal GRE scores	165–165
Average Quantitative GRE	155
Range of Quantitative GRE scores	155–155
Average GPA	3.3
TOEFL required of international students	Yes
Minimum TOEFL (paper/web)	550/80
Application fee	$50
International application fee	$50
Early application deadline	1/15
Regular application deadline	3/1
Application Deadline/Notification	
Round 1:	1/15 / 3/1
Round 2:	3/15 / 5/1
Round 3:	6/1 / 7/1
Deferment available	Yes
Maximum length of deferment	1 year
Transfer students accepted	Yes
Transfer application policy	

Students may transfer up to two Advanced courses (not foundation level) from another AACSB accredited MBA Program. No more than 6 units of the 51 required units will be transferred for the full-time program. Transfers are not accepted for Master of Accounting (MAcc) or Part-time MBA Programs.

Non-fall admissions	No
Need-blind admissions	Yes

EMPLOYMENT PROFILE

Career Rating	73	**Grads Employed by Function**	**% Avg. Salary**	
Percent employed at graduation	50	Marketing	(22%)	
Percent employed 3 months after graduation	75	Operations	(44%)	
		Management	(22%)	
Average base starting salary	$56,729	Finance	(12%)	
Primary Source of Full-time Job Acceptances		**Top 5 Employers Hiring Grads**		
School-facilitated activities	6 (67%)	Blue Shield of CA (2), Vision Service Plan		
Graduate-facilitated activities	3 (33%)	(VSP) (1), Stryker Endoscopy (1), Dignity Health (1), Yelp (1)		

University of Pennsylvania
Wharton School Graduate Division

GENERAL INFORMATION
Type of school   Private
Affiliation   No Affiliation
Academic calendar   Semester

SURVEY SAYS...
Good social scene, Good peer net-
work, Smart classrooms
Solid preparation in:
Finance, Accounting, Quantitative
Skills

STUDENTS
Enrollment of parent
  institution   24,107
Enrollment of MBA Program   1,691
% part-time   0

ACADEMICS
Academic Experience Rating   89
Profs interesting rating   83
Profs accessible rating   72
% female faculty   20
% part-time faculty   24

Joint Degrees
MBA/JD (3 yr); MBA/MD; MBA/
DMD; MBA/MSE; MBA/MArch;
MBA/MA-Lauder; MBA/MA-SAIS
at Johns Hopkins; MBA/MPA-
Harvard's Kennedy School of
Government; MBA/MSW; MBA/PhD;
MBA/VMD; MBA/MSN; MBA/MA in
Environmental Studies

Academics

The University of Pennsylvania's Wharton School, one of the premier MBA programs in the world, is best known for its "strong finance reputation," but the curriculum's "strong emphasis on quantitative analysis" extends "across many disciplines, not just finance but marketing, entrepreneurship, operations, international business, real estate, etc." as well. All areas present a "holistic program with a mix of case studies, traditional lecture formats, experiential learning opportunities, and strong co-curricular programs."

Students brag that Wharton "provides all the resources necessary for us to succeed, and then some," reporting that "the difficult part here is deciding between which resources—lectures, seminars, simulations, clubs, special events—one can fit into one's schedule." Writes one student, "The breadth and depth of the academic curriculum and the extra-curricular activities is so huge that I would need at least six MBA years to experience 20 percent of it all." A heavy workload, described as "difficult for everyone but the most brilliant to manage," makes those choices even tougher. But what impresses students most here is the degree to which students themselves contribute to the learning experience. Wharton uses a "co-production model of learning" that "requires engagement from all participants in the Wharton community." One MBA observes, "Students sometimes add more value than assigned readings. Students make Wharton. 'Student-run' is an understatement." Another agrees, "The 'co-production model' is not just a buzz word; it really exists here."

Under the Wharton pedagogic system, "classes build on each other. Professors are known to coordinate timing of discussing certain topics to ensure that the student has mastered the concept in another class." Much work here is done in teams. To promote cooperation and reduce competitiveness, Wharton policy currently forbids grade disclosure to recruiters. Students report that the policy "fosters an environment of helping at the school." Nondisclosure apparently has little impact on students' motivation to work. One notes, "The school has high expectations for each admit, and the overall performance of the students rises to that expectation."

Career and Placement

Wharton is a brand that pretty much sells itself, so it's no surprise that the school's career services are highly regarded and widely appreciated by students. Each year brings the following career placement services to the campus: over 200 employer information sessions; almost 300 recruiting companies; and, more than 5,000 job-board postings. Wharton's Career Management Services Office also offers resume review and distribution, mock interviews, internship placement, one-on-one counseling, and over twenty-five career treks both in and outside the U.S. No wonder students praise the "fantastic career opportunities and resources." About 55 percent of Wharton MBAs take jobs in the finance sector; 28 percent wind up in consulting; and seven percent find jobs in the marketing arena.

Student Life and Environment

Life at Wharton offers "an amazing number of choices in terms of classes, activities, clubs, etc." It's an atmosphere students tell us is filled with a constant stream of unique opportunities they wouldn't otherwise have. One student cites these personal examples: "At Wharton I have done a four-week study trip to greater China; a consulting project to an Israeli company that wanted to enter the U.S. market; a marketing consulting project for AOL for the mobile location-based services product; a leadership venture to Ecuador next spring to learn about teamwork through a mountain climbing expedition; dozens of fantastic speakers; and finally, some great parties." MBAs appreciate that their "partners are involved in almost all campus-related activities here." One reports, "My wife and one-year-old daughter enjoy going to activities every Wednesday and Friday with the Wharton Kids Club. This has proved to be very helpful in providing an environment where my wife can make lots of friends in a new city, and my daughter can play with other kids her own age."

Hometown Philadelphia "is underrated but still needs work." One Bay Area native notes, "I was worried about Philadelphia after living in San Francisco, but I have been pleasantly surprised by the depth of culture, fun, and good food." Wharton's new facility, Huntsman Hall, is "top-of-the-line" but MBAs gripe that "sharing the building with undergraduates leads to scarce group study rooms. Most students do not use the library because it is overrun with undergrads." Still, Wharton does most things right. You realize this when you ask students what most needs improving here and all they can think to mention is "full-size lockers for each student."

Admissions

Wharton is among the most selective MBA programs in the country. On average, the school receives between seven and ten applications for each available slot. The school's website notes that "approximately 75 to 80 percent of all applicants are qualified for admission." Applicants are evaluated holistically by at least three members of the Admissions Committee. All prior academic experience, including graduate work and certifications, is considered. GMAT scores also figure into the decision. Quality of professional experiences, career choices, and stated goals for entering the program are all carefully reviewed. Committee members also look for evidence of leadership, interpersonal skills, entrepreneurial spirit, and good citizenship. International students must demonstrate competency in English through essays and interviews. Wharton offers three rounds of an admission each year; the first two rounds are equal with regard to a candidate's admissibility. The third round offers admission on a space-available basis and is generally more competitive.

FINANCIAL FACTS

Annual tuition (in-state/ out-of-state)	$57,026/$57,026
Fees	$5,008
Cost of books	$5,222
Room & board (on/off-campus)	$25,744/$25,744

ADMISSIONS

Admissions Selectivity Rating	**99**
# of applications received	6,408
Average GMAT	720
Range of GMAT	560–790
Accepts GRE scores	Yes
TOEFL required of international students	Yes
Application fee	$265
International application fee	$265
Application Deadline/Notification	
Round 1:	10/1 / 12/20
Round 2:	1/3 / 3/26
Round 3:	3/5 / 5/3
Deferment available	Yes
Maximum length of deferment	case by case for extenuating circumstances only
Transfer students accepted	No
Non-fall admissions	No
Need-blind admissions	Yes

EMPLOYMENT PROFILE

Career Rating	97	Grads Employed by Function	% Avg. Salary
Percent employed at graduation	80	Marketing	(9%) $106,468
Percent employed 3 months after graduation	92	Operations	(1%) $114,167
		Consulting	(31%) $127,811
Average base starting salary	$120,605	Management	(6%) $109,086
Primary Source of Full-time Job Acceptances		Finance	(40%) $121,087
School-facilitated activities	366 (62%)	Other	(13%) $116,683
Graduate-facilitated activities	221 (38%)	**Top 5 Employers Hiring Grads**	

McKinsey & Company (53), Boston Consulting Group (45), Bain & Company (25), Deloitte Consulting (16), Goldman Sachs (16)

UNIVERSITY OF PITTSBURGH
JOSEPH M. KATZ GRADUATE SCHOOL OF BUSINESS

GENERAL INFORMATION

Type of school	Public
Affiliation	No Affiliation
Academic calendar	August - April

SURVEY SAYS...

Classmates have diverse work experience, Friendly students, Happy students, Students love Pittsburgh, PA
Solid preparation in:
General management, Teamwork, Quantitative skills

STUDENTS

Enrollment of parent institution	34,934
Enrollment of MBA Program	535
% male/female	65/35
% out-of-state	59
% part-time	71
% underrepresented minority	19
% international	35
Average age at entry	28
Average years work experience at entry	5

ACADEMICS

Academic Experience Rating	95
Profs interesting rating	90
Profs accessible rating	93
Student/faculty ratio	6:1
% female faculty	25
% underrepresented minority faculty	5
% part-time faculty	34

Joint Degrees

MBA/MS-Engineering; MBA/Juris Doctorate; MBA/MS-Management Information Systems; MBA/Master of Public and International Affairs; MBA/Master of International Development; MBA/Master of International Business; MBA/Master of Public Health

Academics

The Joseph M. Katz Graduate School of Business at the University Pittsburgh attracts students that seek to find "academic rigor, stellar professors, a gifted peer group, an above-par post-MBA income, access to industry leaders, opportunities to prove one's mettle in case competitions, hackathons and start-up weekends, and above all . . . lifelong relationships with individuals." The school offers One-Year, Two-Year, Executive, and Part-time MBAs (as well as joint and dual degrees), focusing on giving students a core set of business skills and helping them customize their skill sets to their desired positions. Each program fosters "a cooperatively competitive attitude rather than an aggressively competitive attitude in the students." Katz also offers a specialized Masters in Accounting, Customer Insights, Supply Chain Management, Finance, and Management Information Systems.

The faculty makes the program "seamless"; they "manage class work, class discussions and assignments to maximize the value to the students." Accessibility of faculty members is high. Students say professors are "flexible with our work schedules," and they "easily relate real world problems into teachings." Most classes require team projects and exercises (in and out of class) to build interpersonal and communication skills, which is not a problem given the "driven, data-oriented, communicative" nature of the student body. Cross-cultural dimensions and global business themes run throughout the curriculum, and students in the Executive MBA program travel between the program's locations in Pittsburgh and Sao Paulo, Brazil for global executive forums in which they can "learn about global economies [and] cultural business differences and network with incredible business professionals." The other MBA programs include a Global Research Practicum, which is a short-term international immersion experience with a business project component.

Career and Placement

Katz is "tied into the entrepreneurship community in Pittsburgh and offers many experience-based fellowships and projects," and there is "no pressure to pursue top tier consulting and investment banking, but rather to give you the skills to get the position with your target company." The companies that recruit on campus "do have a manufacturing heavy tilt" as they are based on the surrounding area, but there "has been a shift toward medical, consulting, and IT industries as the economy of Pittsburgh has reinvented itself." The Career Services office "works tirelessly to connect students with corporate recruiters and the resources needed to fulfill our career goals," and the Executives in Residence (EIR) program (a mentorship setup that gives students access to top corporate executives with decades of experience) is "integral in interview preparation." EIRs are "deeply imbedded in many of the academic courses that require real-world, experienced-based learning such as our Consulting Field Project." Recent employers of Katz grads include Amazon, Crane Co, Deloitte, SDLC Partners, IBM, Nationwide Insurance, McKinsey, and PNC Financial Services.

ADMISSIONS CONTACT: THOMAS KELLER, DIRECTOR
ADDRESS: 301 MERVIS HALL, PITTSBURGH, PA 15260
PHONE: 412-648-1700 • FAX: 412-648-1659
E-MAIL: MBA@KATZ.PITT.EDU • WEBSITE: WWW.BUSINESS.PITT.EDU/INDEX.PHP

Student Life and Environment

Pittsburgh is "a hidden gem with low cost of living and great employment and social opportunities." People routinely study together, chat socially, and network at all levels (from students to faculty to alumni). "My fellow students are very intelligent, have great experiences to add to class discussions, and overall, offer nothing but encouragement in the program," says a student. A large portion of the student body is international—around a third—which contributes to the overall melting pot feel; the Katz student body truly feels as if it "is a family" and there are "lots of fun activities organized for students to network with folks from other programs," with one such session planned for every semester. Many activities involve other colleges at the university, including "theater tickets, Project Bundle Up, and happy hours (all on a regular basis)."

Admissions

Applicants to the Joseph M. Katz Graduate School of Business are evaluated on their demonstrated leadership skills, record of accomplishment, previous academic performance, and analytical skills as well as their future potential as leaders in business. The average GPA for the entering class of 2015 was 3.3 with an average GMAT of 608. Evaluative interviews are required for admission. Interviews for part-time candidates are arranged by invitation and take place after the admissions committee's initial review of a candidate's application.

Prominent Alumni

Frank Gaoning Ning, Chairman of Sinochem (China); Raymond William Smith, Chairman Verizon Ventures; Susan E. Arnold, Vice Chair/President, Procter & Gamble (retired)

FINANCIAL FACTS

Annual tuition (in-state/ out-of-state)	$24,998/$32,628
Fees	$3,800
Cost of books	$1,170
Room & board (on/off-campus)	$16,820/$16,820
% of students receiving grants	78
Average grant	$31,303

ADMISSIONS

Admissions Selectivity Rating	93
# of applications received	730
% applicants accepted	22
% acceptees attending	49
Average GMAT	608
Range of GMAT	553–658
Accepts GRE scores	Yes
Average Verbal GRE	154
Average Quantitative GRE	155
Average Writing GRE	3.9
Average GPA	3.3
TOEFL required of international students	Yes
Minimum TOEFL (paper/web)	600/100
Application fee	$50
International application fee	$50
Application Deadline/Notification	
Round 1:	10/15 / 12/15
Round 2:	12/1 / 2/15
Round 3:	2/1 / 4/15
Round 4:	4/1 / 5/15
Deferment available	Yes
Maximum length of deferment	One Year
Transfer students accepted	Yes
Transfer application policy	Matching coursework, accepting up to one-third total credits from an AACSB MBA program, provided that credits were not used to complete a previous MBA degree.
Non-fall admissions	Yes
Need-blind admissions	Yes

EMPLOYMENT PROFILE

Career Rating	94	Grads Employed by Function	% Avg. Salary
Percent employed at graduation	70	Marketing	(18%) $95,111
Percent employed 3 months after graduation	88	Operations	(10%) $95,120
		Consulting	(33%) $92,875
Average base starting salary	$88,027	Management	(2%)
Primary Source of Full-time Job Acceptances		Finance	(18%) $80,222
School-facilitated activities	36 (74%)	HR	(4%)
Graduate-facilitated activities	13 (27%)	MIS	(2%)
		Other	(12%) $76,787

Top 5 Employers Hiring Grads
Highmark (4), Nationwide Insurance (3), IBM (3), Model N (3), Deloitte (2)

UNIVERSITY OF PORTLAND
PAMPLIN SCHOOL OF BUSINESS ADMINISTRATION

GENERAL INFORMATION
Type of school   Private
Affiliation   Roman Catholic
Academic calendar   Semester

SURVEY SAYS...
Friendly students, Liberal students,
Happy students, Students love
Portland, OR
Solid preparation in:
Finance, General management,
Operations, Teamwork, Presentation
skills, Quantitative skills,
Environmental sustainability, Social
responsibility

STUDENTS
Enrollment of parent
  institution   4,337
Enrollment of MBA Program   142
% male/female   61/39
% out-of-state   49
% part-time   63
% underrepresented minority   47
% international   42
Average age at entry   30
Average years work
  experience at entry   7

ACADEMICS
Academic Experience Rating   89
Profs interesting rating   92
Profs accessible rating   95
Student/faculty ratio   13:1
% female faculty   26
% underrepresented
  minority faculty   23
% part-time faculty   0

Joint Degrees
Dual Degree MBA/MSF

Prominent Alumni
Dr. Robert B. Pamplin. Jr.,
Philanthropist / Entreprenuer;
Fedele Bauccio, Founder, Bon
Appetit Management Co.; Rich Baek,
Founder and Chairman, VTM Group;
John Heily, President and CEO,
Continental Mills, Inc.; Jim Murphy,
Senior Vice President, International,
Costco

Academics

The Pamplin School of Business Administration at the University of Portland features some of the Pacific Northwest's top-notch faculty and a curriculum "integrating professional experience into academic concepts." The program administrator has made this "wonderfully run" program "extremely easy to do while working," as many do, and the university even offers some tuition discounts to those who are seeking Nonprofit Management degrees (a notable program here), as well as scholarships for international students. The school is part of JEBNET, Jesuit Education in Business Network, which is a network of thirty AACSB-accredited universities nationwide that share similarly "strong mission statements" and provide students the ability to transfer credits and complete their MBA at another university.

The "good atmosphere within the classroom" is built on the foundation of "some of the most engaged professors I have had," according to one student. They "seem to really enjoy what they are teaching and a majority do a great job engaging students," and "are just as invested in your academic and career advancement" as the individual themselves. "Most of [the] professors treat me as their family or friends, and I've learned a lot of practical things from my school," says a student. Varied experiential backgrounds help instructors to provide a well-rounded curriculum.

The school's Catholic ties result in "an ideals driven environment," one that also happens to be "understanding of students working while attending classes." Most of the students are able to "work with professors one on one" outside of class. "The staff is amazing and the professors are intense, but it's an MBA program, so what'd you expect?!" says one happy student.

Career and Placement

Pamplin has an excellent "reputation against other schools locally," so those who are looking for jobs within the area have a leg up. Many people here are getting degrees for advancement in their current jobs, but the school does a good job of recruiting for the handful that are looking. "If you are young [and] under thirty...it's a good program because that is the age bracket that the recruiting companies pursue" at Pamplin. Since admission is rolling, students can begin immediately following their acceptance in the fall, spring, or summer, which is a huge advantage to working students.

Student Life and Environment

Pamplin has a "great facility, small class sizes," and a diverse student body that "is very professional and we are all in the same situation. We balance work, school, family, and friends." Students "tend to be younger than thirty," have "three to five years work experience at best," and are "career minded but not uptight." Many have careers in addition to school, which "makes relating easy," and the numerous nationalities of the student body beneficially "increases the world view of the program, as we are obviously moving towards a more world-based economy." Most of the students "like discussion and analysis," so one can learn "a lot of things not only from lecture, but [also from] my fellow students." Students work "in an incredibly tight cohort" and are "very, very supportive of one another's opinions and experiences."

The unique culture of the Pacific Northwest is reassuring to all who go here since many are regional locals, and the "gorgeous scenery" has more than a few fans. The UP campus itself "is breathtaking" and offers many "nice" transportation options.

Admissions

Applicants to the MBA program at the University of Portland must meet the following minimum requirements: an undergraduate GPA of at least 3.0; a GMAT score of at least 500; and an "admission index" of at least 1,100 under the formula [(undergraduate GPA x 200) + GMAT score]. Work experience, though strongly recommended, is not required; applicants with at least three years of post-baccalaureate professional experience are considered optimal candidates for the program. International students must score at least 570 on the TOEFL paper test or 230 on the computer-adaptive version of the TOEFL or a 7.0 on the IELTS exam. All applications to the University of Portland must include a completed application form, a resumé, a personal statement of goals, official transcripts for all postsecondary academic work, an official GMAT score report, and two letters of recommendation. International students must submit all of the above as well as an official TOEFL score report and a financial statement that indicates they will have adequate support throughout the duration of study. This is required before the I-20 form is issued to them.

FINANCIAL FACTS

Annual tuition	$31,590
Fees	$1,350
Cost of books	$1,200
Room & board	$12,000
% of students receiving aid	67
% of first-year students receiving aid	65
% of students receiving grants	22
Average award package	$13,538
Average grant	$4,591
Average loan	$21,164
Average student loan debt	$43,029

ADMISSIONS

Admissions Selectivity Rating	85
# of applications received	128
% applicants accepted	61
% acceptees attending	86
Average GMAT	536
Range of GMAT	490–590
Accepts GRE scores	Yes
Average Verbal GRE	153
Range of Verbal GRE scores	150–155
Average Quantitative GRE	152
Range of Quantitative GRE scores	149–154
Average Writing GRE	4.0
Range of Writing GRE scores	3.5–4.5
Average GPA	3.4
TOEFL required of international students	Yes
Minimum TOEFL (paper/web)	570/88
Application fee	$0
International application fee	$0
Application Deadline/Notification	
Deferment available	Yes
Maximum length of deferment	1 year
Transfer students accepted	Yes
Transfer application policy 9 semester hours of transfer credit from AACSB accredited program as long as the student received a B grade or higher in the course and the course has been taken within the last 5 years	
Non-fall admissions	Yes
Need-blind admissions	Yes

EMPLOYMENT PROFILE

Career Rating	72	Top 5 Employers Hiring Grads
Percent employed at graduation	80	Nike (3), M.J. Murdock Charitable Trust (2)
Percent employed 3 months after graduation	4	

UNIVERSITY OF RHODE ISLAND
COLLEGE OF BUSINESS ADMINISTRATION

GENERAL INFORMATION
Type of school	Public
Affiliation	No Affiliation
Academic calendar	Semesters

SURVEY SAYS...
Friendly students
Solid preparation in:
General management, Teamwork

STUDENTS
Enrollment of parent institution	16,700
Enrollment of MBA Program	237
% male/female	55/45
% out-of-state	45
% part-time	92
% underrepresented minority	10
% international	30
Average age at entry	30

ACADEMICS
Academic Experience Rating	**83**
Profs interesting rating	87
Profs accessible rating	91
% part-time faculty	0

Joint Degrees
MBA/Pharm.D - 7 years MBA/Engineering - 5 years MBA/Master of Oceanography - 2 years

Academics

The College of Business Administration at the University of Rhode Island has been providing MBAs to in-state and national students since 1961. With its emphasis on innovation and small class sizes, including the "flexibility of the program and the availability of the required classes," the school offers students a satisfying, affordable option for career advancement.

Students may complete a part-time MBA at the Providence campus—designed for individuals who want to pursue a degree while maintaining their personal and professional commitments—or the "unusual" One-Year MBA Program in Strategic Innovation at the Providence campus as well. The One-Year MBA was recently redesigned to promote critical thinking, analytical skills, hands-on projects, and organization among students requiring them to gather and analyze data before making critical decisions; it has many fans among the students, who sing its praises. The program's administration also receives high marks. It is "absolutely top shelf, [is] always helpful, [and] always encouraging." When students have questions, the staff, "responds via email/phone within minutes."

"I have been pleasantly surprised with how well the professors are able to adapt the 'book knowledge' to the real world," says a student. URI has many part-time students, and "all of the faculty, staff, and students are very aware and understanding of the strains put on the work-school-life balance." Professors "try to accommodate the students' needs without taking away from their curriculum." To this point, "the classes to this point have not wasted anyone's valuable time and provide pertinent course work and projects." Most professors are "good, with interesting and applicable professional backgrounds."

Career and Placement

Most here choose to go the part-time evening route, and so are not looking for any sort of help in the placement department. Though recruitment is not a huge concern here, some wish that URI would make efforts to "grow stronger partnerships with local companies in an effort to allow students a true-to-life work environment for projects and course work." Administration and faculty are very helpful "in assisting students in positioning the right pats to succeed in the MBA program and future careers." The timescale of the One-Year MBA, in particular, is "really convenient for students who are eager to get back in the workforce and do not wish to spend more than a year returning to or continuing school."

ADMISSIONS CONTACT: LISA LANCELLOTTA, COORDINATOR, MBA PROGRAMS
ADDRESS: 7 LIPPITT RD., BALLENTINE HALL, KINGSTON, RI 02881
PHONE: 401-874-4241 • FAX: 401-874-4312
E-MAIL: MBA@URI.EDU • WEBSITE: WWW.CBA.URI.EDU/MBA

Student Life and Environment

Students here are "bright, motivated individuals with a common goal towards career advancement." Most are just at the school to advance their careers, and appreciate the commonality of that goal. "I am a part-time student. I work full-time during the day and attend class at night. I am surrounded by individuals in the same situation," says one. There are plenty of "different ethnic backgrounds," and students are "very engaging in class, focused, cooperative, and willing to collaborate with others." Many who go here are from the sciences or engineering [fields], as the school offers a joint MBA/Master's of Oceanography program.

Aside from the program redesign, the school also features updated facilities and technology, including wireless classrooms, a trading room, and a computer lab. Though the Providence campus is located centrally downtown, the Kingston campus has "no real town and therefore no public transportation" and luckily, the "commute to school is easy." Almost all the MBA students live off campus and rely on their vehicles to get to and from campus. However, the area is "beautiful," and "great for people who like outdoors activities (hiking, biking, running, surfing, sailing, etc.)."

Admissions

URI offers many components of its application online and encourages applicants to submit materials online whenever possible. Students may provide all of the following materials via the Internet: a current resume, a personal statement of purpose, and two letters of recommendation (applicants e-mail referees, who then send their recommendations directly to the school). Students must also provide the admissions office with official transcripts for all postsecondary academic work and an official score report for the GMAT or GRE—scores must be no more than five years old. International applicants must provide all the above plus an official TOEFL or IELTS score report (scores must be no more than two years old); the minimum required score for admission is 575 on the paper-based TOEFL, 91 on the Internet-based TOEFL, or 6.5 on the IELTS. The school notes that most accepted applicants have an undergraduate GPA of at least 3.0 and GMAT/GRE scores ranked in at least the 50th percentile, but allows that grades and test scores are not the sole criteria for admission. The school seeks candidates with demonstrated strength in quantitative skills, work experience ("valued," but not required, according to university materials), leadership potential, motivation, and communication skills.

FINANCIAL FACTS

Annual tuition (in-state/ out-of-state)	$18,453/$36,434
Fees	$1,700
Cost of books	$4,000
Average grant	$0
Average loan	$0

ADMISSIONS

Admissions Selectivity Rating	**80**
# of applications received	106
% applicants accepted	92
% acceptees attending	82
Average GMAT	556
Accepts GRE scores	Yes
Average Verbal GRE	31
Average Quantitative GRE	35
Average Writing GRE	4.8
Average GPA	3.3
TOEFL required of international students	Yes
Minimum TOEFL (paper/web)	575/91
Application fee	$65
International application fee	$65
Early application deadline	4/15
Regular application deadline	6/30
Application Deadline/Notification	
Deferment available	Yes
Maximum length of deferment	1 year
Transfer students accepted	Yes
Transfer application policy Can take up to 20% of total credits from another AACSB accredited college/university.	
Non-fall admissions	Yes
Need-blind admissions	Yes

UNIVERSITY OF RICHMOND
ROBINS SCHOOL OF BUSINESS

GENERAL INFORMATION
Type of school   Private
Affiliation   No Affiliation
Academic calendar   Semester

SURVEY SAYS...
Classmates have diverse work experience, Friendly students, Conservative students, Abundant mentors available, Happy students, Students love University of Richmond, VA
Solid preparation in:
Teamwork, Communication/interpersonal skills, Presentation skills, Quantitative skills

STUDENTS
Enrollment of parent institution	4,180
Enrollment of MBA Program	83
% male/female	100/0
% out-of-state	0
% part-time	100
% underrepresented minority	0
% international	0
Average age at entry	29
Average years work experience at entry	5

ACADEMICS
Academic Experience Rating	90
Profs interesting rating	92
Profs accessible rating	95
Student/faculty ratio	3:1
% female faculty	22
% underrepresented minority faculty	8
% part-time faculty	19

Joint Degrees
Juris Doctor/Master of Business Administration (24 months)

Prominent Alumni
Michael Matthews, President & CEO, H&A Architects and Engineers; Margaret ("Lyn") McDermid, Chief Information Officer, Federal Reserve System; Anne Waleski, CFO, Markel Corporation; Kevin McQueen, CEO, CapTech Ventures

Academics

The MBA program at the University of Richmond is an engaging experience, which offers small classes and an interesting curriculum and boasts "top-tier faculty and staff." Students are challenged and rewarded here. The "amazing" professors "are quite accomplished" and "well-educated." Many students are pleased to discover that their professors are not just intellectually smart but are "great teachers" as well. "It is evident that the business school places teaching ability above research expertise when hiring faculty." "I feel fortunate to be in such a stimulating environment," a student explains. "I often leave class with a great sense of appreciation for the discussions I've had and the insight gained."

The administration as a whole won students' admiration for being "very responsive and engaged with the MBA program." "Whether I want to [meet] with the Dean, my professors, or the Program Director it is always easy to access those I need to speak with to resolve questions and concerns." Students are impressed that the administration and staff "know each student personally and really engage with us at every opportunity." "Part of that may be the small class size, which makes it a much more manageable experience and offers the opportunity to interact more on a personal level." One student feels "the personal attention that comes with [the small size] is the biggest strength of the program."

Equally appealing to students is the school's program of study. The convenience of having a program where adults do not "have to forego income and [can] attend in the evenings" gives many students the opportunities to apply their newfound skills to their jobs "on a daily basis," as it also makes the school a good option for those who may not otherwise be able to afford tuition. The program definitely requires a good amount of effort. One student suggests that the school might consider cutting down some of the required courses and offering more electives in their place, which would "allow students to more highly specialize in their chosen field of study."

Many students commented on the high caliber of fellow classmates that are "as motivated as I [am] to learn." "As a part-time program for working adults, the program does an exceptional job of promoting team work so that the students become a close-knit network of friends." There is also an added "international component" provided by several international students. This "real-world (vs. only theoretical cases in classroom) experience" is of great value to those wishing to expand their global knowledge.

Career and Placement

UR is situated in a "thriving business community that is strong in many realms, from finance (Harris Williams) to marketing (The Martin Agency)." The school's location draws many part-time MBA students who value the convenience of improving their education while working on the job. Sitting side-by-side with similar "top notch" students, "networking opportunities abound." In addition to fostering prospects with fellow students, the "administrative staff works hard to connect you with businesses and job opportunities." There are "many events with prominent speakers on campus," as well as "workshops, etc., outside of class to meet local business leaders." "The ability to network with alumni and the various panels and speakers that speak at the business school," create yet another layer of opportunities for graduate students. Still, some students feel that "the focus on job placement could stand to be improved . . . Career fairs on campus tend to be focused on undergraduates."

ADMISSIONS CONTACT: DR. RICHARD S. COUGHLAN
ADDRESS: MBA OFFICE, ROBINS SCHOOL OF BUSINESS, UNIVERSITY OF RICHMOND, VA 23173
PHONE: 804-289-8553 • FAX: 804-287-1228
E-MAIL: MBA@RICHMOND.EDU • WEBSITE: BUSINESS.RICHMOND.EDU/MBA

Student Life and Environment

Due to the nature of the program, student life as a graduate student is very different from that of an undergrad. "As a part-time program, most of the students commute to campus; some international students do live on campus. The students are friends with one another and will regularly meet off-campus, however, 'life at school' does not apply to most." "The program is taught entirely in the evening, almost exclusively to students who are working full-time. This makes networking and family involvement difficult, but there are some efforts made by the university to help on this front. Recently, UR opened an MBA lounge where MBA's can mingle before and after class. Also, spouses are invited to events like the annual holiday party."

Commitments of graduate students outside of school, however busy they may be, do not seem to affect this "energetic, intelligent" student body from their group work or their class bonding experience. The opening residency is "fantastic for creating relationships with students in your class" and the students are "exceptionally hard working leaders in the local business community," and are all quite capable of "maximizing the value of their time." "Richmond is a great city to live in as a business student. The graduate business school is a relatively small community on campus (with the undergraduate population being much larger, and the law school population being significantly larger as well), but MBA students often socialize together off-campus."

Admissions

The University of Richmond Robins School of Business accepts applications up to 05/18 on a rolling basis. GMAT scores, which average 606, as well as undergraduate GPAs, which average 3.3, are strongly taken into consideration as well as previous work experience and resume, all of which are required with your application. Interviews are also important.

FINANCIAL FACTS

Annual tuition (in-state/ out-of-state)	$1410/credit hr
Fees	$0
% of students receiving aid	44
% of first-year students receiving aid	35
% of students receiving grants	28
Average award package	$13,210
Average grant	$7,965
Average loan	$16,440
Average student loan debt	$48,015

ADMISSIONS

Admissions Selectivity Rating	**84**
# of applications received	46
% applicants accepted	76
% acceptees attending	100
Average Verbal GRE	150
Average Quantitative GRE	154
Average Writing GRE	4.0
Average GMAT	606
Range of GMAT	519–692
Accepts GRE scores	Yes
Average GPA	3.3
TOEFL required of international students	Yes
Minimum TOEFL (paper/web)	600/100
Application fee	$50
International application fee	$50
Regular application deadline	5/20
Regular application notification	5/25
Application Deadline/Notification	
Deferment available	Yes
Maximum length of deferment	1 Year
Transfer students accepted	Yes
Transfer application policy Maximum 9.0 hours of transfer credit accepted from an AACSB-accredited schools at the discretion of Program Director.	
Non-fall admissions	Yes
Need-blind admissions	Yes

UNIVERSITY OF ROCHESTER
WILLIAM E. SIMON GRADUATE SCHOOL OF BUSINESS ADMINISTRATION

GENERAL INFORMATION
Type of school	Private
Affiliation	No Affiliation
Academic calendar	Quarter

SURVEY SAYS...
Classmates have diverse work experience, Friendly students, Helpful alumni, Happy students, Abundant clubs and activities
Solid preparation in:
Finance, Accounting, General management, Teamwork, Quantitative skills

STUDENTS
Enrollment of parent institution	11,060
Enrollment of MBA Program	396
% male/female	62/38
% out-of-state	78
% part-time	47
% underrepresented minority	20
% international	54
Average age at entry	28
Average years work experience at entry	6

ACADEMICS
Academic Experience Rating	95
Profs interesting rating	93
Profs accessible rating	93
Student/faculty ratio	10:1
% female faculty	14
% underrepresented minority faculty	0
% part-time faculty	25

Joint Degrees
MBA/Master of Public Health; MD/MBA

Prominent Alumni
Douglas Petno, CEO, Commercial Banking, JP Morgan Chase; Mark Grier, Vice Chairman, Prudential Insurance Co.; Jay Benet, Vice Chairman/CFO- Travelers Companies; Mark Ain, Founder and Chairman/Kronos Incorporated

Academics

There's no denying that Rochester's William E. Simon Graduate School of Business Administration is an academic powerhouse. Trust us—you'll need a strong work ethic to get through the "rigorous" curriculum. After all, Simon places a "heavy emphasis on quantitative analysis and economics." On top of that, the school operates on a "ten-week quarter system" so classes "move very quickly."

Many MBAs are drawn to the program due to the school's high ranking finance and accounting departments. Fortunately, while it's definitely a "quant school," Simon still manages to foster a "very collaborative environment." As a very happy second-year adds, "I get the sense that I'm not only building a strong professional network once I graduate, but a whole new set of friends."

Additionally, Rochester MBAs are privy to "top-notch" professors who frequently demonstrate "progressive way[s] of approaching and solving problems." Simon instructors are also "incredibly knowledgeable in their fields and a source of invaluable information, mainly in the realms of finance and economics." And they tend to go "out of their way to ensure students are grasping the material." Indeed, they are "willing to meet outside of class to cover any material [with which] you are having difficulty." As a pleased first-year MBA explains, "All of them have responded to inquiries I've made outside of class rapidly and, due to the small class sizes, they quickly recognize you and get to know you as a student." MBAs here also happily report that the administration is equally "engaged" and "alert to [student] interest and concerns."

Career and Placement

The Career Management Center at Simon is designed to help turn students' professional dreams into a reality. MBA candidates can take advantage of individualized career counseling and reap the benefits of mock interviews and resume development sessions. Impressively, the center has dedicated experts on staff that cover specific industries like technology, healthcare, brand management, energy, consulting and operations and financial services. These specialists work aggressively to maintain relationships with employers and business leaders, connecting these individuals with Simon students and graduates.

Employers who frequently recruit and/or hire Simon MBAs include: Accenture, Expedia, Inc., American Express Company, PriceWaterhouseCoopers, LLP, Bank of America, Bureau of Labor Statistics, Citigroup, Comcast and Wells Fargo.

Student Life and Environment

Rochester MBAs take pride in describing their fellow students as "very ambitious," "hard working" and "intellectually capable." They are also "culturally diverse" and highly "welcoming." While everyone seems to be "proud of their backgrounds," they strive to "join together to form a common collective at Simon for the benefit of all." Indeed, they are truly "focused on ensuring the team does well [as opposed to] individual students."

During the week, most students are focused on the "academic grind," either attending classes or working on projects. And they can often be found hanging around local cafes "study[ing], mingl[ing] and coach[ing] each other." The campus itself is "beautiful" with "great facilities." And it's "always buzzing with activities."

Finally, we're told that "Rochester is a nice small city with enough things to do." However, "don't expect a NYC level of nightlife and entertainment." Thankfully, "there's enough to do, you just have to spend a little more time finding the options. A car/bike is a must, as public transit is really spotty. Overall, though, great place to spend two years."

Admissions

Admission to Simon is extremely competitive. Students with exceptional GPAs, applicable test scores, and relevant leadership experience (including post-baccalaureate work and extracurricular activities) rise to the top of the pool. Applicants to the school's MBA program must submit the following: an online application, one required essay, undergraduate transcripts, one letter of recommendation, a current résumé, an official GMAT report, and interview (if requested by the Admissions Committee). International students for whom English is not a primary language must submit an official score report for the TOEFL. This requirement is waived if students have studied for at least one full year in a college or university where English is the language of instruction.

FINANCIAL FACTS

Annual tuition (in-state/ out-of-state)	$53,223/$53,223
Fees	$1,053
Cost of books	$1,965
Room & board (on/off-campus)	$13,300/$13,300
% of students receiving aid	93
% of first-year students receiving aid	91
% of students receiving grants	90
Average award package	$43,319
Average grant	$31,122
Average loan	$29,974
Average student loan debt	$60,730

ADMISSIONS

Admissions Selectivity Rating	93
# of applications received	732
% applicants accepted	33
% acceptees attending	33
Average GMAT	667
Range of GMAT	640–710
Accepts GRE scores	Yes
Average Verbal GRE	158
Range of Verbal GRE scores	155–161
Average Quantitative GRE	157
Range of Quantitative GRE scores	156–161
Average Writing GRE	4.3
Range of Writing GRE scores	4.0–5.0
Average GPA	3.4
TOEFL required of international students	Yes
Application fee	$150
International application fee	$150
Early application deadline	10/15
Early notification date	12/15
Regular application deadline	1/5
Regular application notification	3/20
Application Deadline/Notification	
Round 1:	11/15 / 1/15
Round 2:	1/5 / 3/20
Round 3:	3/15 / 4/30
Round 4:	5/15 / 7/1
Deferment available	No
Transfer students accepted	Yes
Transfer application policy	
No more than 9 credit hours, may not be core courses; must complete full application for admission	
Non-fall admissions	No
Need-blind admissions	Yes

EMPLOYMENT PROFILE

Career Rating	95	Grads Employed by Function	% Avg. Salary
Percent employed at graduation	78	Marketing	(24%) $97,974
Percent employed 3 months after graduation	96	Operations	(3%) $79,000
		Consulting	(14%) $110,364
Average base starting salary	$98,206	Management	(10%) $110,000
Primary Source of Full-time Job Acceptances		Finance	(41%) $94,743
School-facilitated activities	66 (73%)	HR	(2%)
Graduate-facilitated activities	24 (27%)	MIS	(3%) $100,000
		Other	(1%)

Top 5 Employers Hiring Grads
bank of America (6), Citigroip (5), Constellation Brands, Inc. (5), Credit Suisse (3), Ernst & Young (3)

UNIVERSITY OF SAN DIEGO
SCHOOL OF BUSINESS

GENERAL INFORMATION

Type of school	Private
Affiliation	Roman Catholic
Academic calendar	August - May

SURVEY SAYS...

Classmates have diverse work experience, Friendly students, Good peer network, Good social scene, Cutting-edge classes, Abundant mentors available, Happy students
Solid preparation in:
Finance, Accounting, General management, Teamwork, Communication/interpersonal skills, Presentation skills, Quantitative skills, Doing business in a global economy

STUDENTS

Enrollment of parent institution	8,251
Enrollment of MBA Program	178
% male/female	55/45
% out-of-state	11
% part-time	50
% underrepresented minority	8
% international	57
Average age at entry	28

ACADEMICS

Academic Experience Rating	**88**
Profs interesting rating	93
Profs accessible rating	96
% female faculty	39
% underrepresented minority faculty	16
% part-time faculty	36

Joint Degrees

MBA/JD; MBA/MSRE

Prominent Alumni

Lowell McAdam, President and CEO, Verizon Communications; Garry Ridge, CEO, WD-40 Company; James Brennan, Chairman and Co-Founder, Suja Juice; Robert MacKay, Senior Vice President & Controller, PepsiCo Americas Beverages; Kenneth C.K. Koo, Chairman and CEO, TCC Group

Academics

A superb reputation for finance and international business precedes the School of Business at the University of San Diego, where a focus on the ideals of social responsibility, entrepreneurship, and diversity lead the way. The Full-Time MBA offers a General Management Track or International Business Track with optional short- and long-term study abroad options (Professional MBAs can participate in the short-term course), and course work is tailored to both the necessities of business and new business trends. Students can choose from "a great variety of electives" and are able "to work with real companies to consult on projects and learn from real world situations."

Professors all possess "extremely high accolades and work experience," and are always willing to go above and beyond for their students. They "prepare for class and work hard to help students succeed" and "are 100 percent committed to us getting good jobs and share their networks [to] support us in our efforts." No matter the course, everyone receives a "personal, intimate classroom experience" and the individual focus necessary for "learning, mentoring, and career coaching." The eye towards the future is even apparent in the building blocks of the program; the administration chooses the core classes and reevaluates every few years to ensure they are up-to-date on the best course work, and students find their flexibility to create a curriculum and staff it by the next semester to be impressive. "That shows they are paying attention to the economy and listening to the demands of the students," says one.

Career and Placement

"Career services are eager to help," and consulting projects, company site visits, guest speakers, and a mentorship program are just a few of the many assets that the "very hands-on and always available" office serves up. "The mentorship program is really special, in that it connects any willing student with prestigious San Diego business people," says a student. "Administrators have connected me with alumni and current students which allow me to expand my network, specifically in the industry I am aiming to work for," testifies one student. Some students do wish that there were more direct hiring relationships with larger companies, but "most students are equipped with soft skills like resume, conversational and interviewing skills to go on their own and find connections, follow up, interview, and land jobs," and fortunately business leaders in SoCal "know USD's reputation." Top employers for recent USD grads include Cymer, EDF Renewable Energy, Audacity, EHL, and Solar Turbines.

Student Life and Environment

The overwhelming majority of students here "are hard working go-getters that want to excel and get every bit of opportunity out of the MBA." This is a group of "charming, dedicated" people from a "vast number of countries around the world" who bring new experiences and cultures into the classroom. There is "a high level of support that students offer to each other inside and outside of the classroom," and "the course load is team-work-intensive and can, at times, be extensive." When school is out, there are several clubs, activities, networking events, and career events that students can attend or join every week, and USD has a "beautiful campus" that makes it "easy to know everyone and get what you want," and "the weather is amazing in San Diego so this is a great environment to relax in when class isn't in session." Many social opportunities arise via the school (and are open to Full-Time and Professional MBA students), such as "club activities, happy hours, baseball games, [and] boating trips."

Admissions

Prospective students must hold an undergraduate degree from an accredited college. GMAT scores, undergraduate academic performance, and work experience are all important factors in determining enrollment. Letters of recommendation, essays, and an interview are also required. Students may apply to more than one graduate program, but additional applications and associated fees apply. One set of transcripts can be used for both applications. The Full-Time MBA entering class of 2015 had a mean GMAT score of 621.

FINANCIAL FACTS

Annual tuition (in-state/out-of-state)	$37,498/$37,498
Fees	$632
Cost of books	$1,400
Room & board (on/off-campus)	$16,500/$16,500
% of students receiving aid	73
% of first-year students receiving aid	87
% of students receiving grants	65
Average award package	$21,443
Average grant	$12,391
Average loan	$28,729

ADMISSIONS

Admissions Selectivity Rating	85
# of applications received	169
% applicants accepted	55
% acceptees attending	47
Average GMAT	621
Range of GMAT	580–670
Accepts GRE scores	Yes
Average GPA	3.4
TOEFL required of international students	Yes
Minimum TOEFL (paper/web)	580/92
Application fee	$80
International application fee	$80
Application Deadline/Notification	
Round 1:	11/1
Round 2:	1/15
Round 3:	3/1
Round 4:	5/1
Deferment available	Yes
Maximum length of deferment	1 year
Transfer students accepted	Yes
Transfer application policy	
Only students in an affiliated "Jesuit MBA Network" program can be considered for transfer.	
Non-fall admissions	Yes
Need-blind admissions	Yes

EMPLOYMENT PROFILE

Career Rating	89	Grads Employed by Function	% Avg. Salary
Percent employed at graduation	49	Marketing	(6%) $70,000
Percent employed 3 months after graduation	64	Operations	(18%) $74,667
		Consulting	(35%) $80,000
Average base starting salary	$74,706	Management	(18%) $75,000
Primary Source of Full-time Job Acceptances		Finance	(12%) $58,000
School-facilitated activities	13 (62%)	MIS	(12%) $77,500
Graduate-facilitated activities	8 (38%)	**Top 5 Employers Hiring Grads**	

Cymer, EDF Renewable Energy, Audacity, DHL, Solar Turbines

UNIVERSITY OF SAN FRANCISCO
MASAGUNG GRADUATE SCHOOL OF MANAGEMENT

GENERAL INFORMATION
Type of school   Private
Affiliation   Roman Catholic-Jesuit
Academic calendar   Semester

SURVEY SAYS...
Classmates have diverse work experience, Friendly students, Liberal students, Students love San Francisco, CA
Solid preparation in:
Teamwork, Presentation skills

STUDENTS
Enrollment of parent institution	10,701
Enrollment of MBA Program	218
% male/female	61/39
% out-of-state	5
% part-time	44
% underrepresented minority	31
% international	43
Average age at entry	31
Average years work experience at entry	6

ACADEMICS
Academic Experience Rating	**88**
Profs interesting rating	90
Profs accessible rating	94
Student/faculty ratio	19:1
% female faculty	27
% underrepresented minority faculty	21
% part-time faculty	48

Joint Degrees
DDS/MBA (in conjunction with UCSF School of Dentistry); JD/MBA (Juris Doctor); MAPS/MBA (Asia Pacific Studies); MSEM/MBA (Environmental Management); MSFA/MBA (Financial Analysis)

Prominent Alumni
Mike Sangiacomo, President & CEO of Recology Inc.; Greg Suhr, San Francisco Police Chief; Paul Otellini, President and CEO of Intel Corporation; James Phelan, Former US Senator

Academics

"A great emphasis on entrepreneurship and finance" is among the program strengths that draw MBAs to the University of San Francisco's School of Management, which offers a variety of MBA program formats and optional concentrations to suit all needs. USF's MBA is available in three program formats: Full-Time MBA (two years), Part-Time MBA (three years), and an Executive MBA (twenty-one months).

In all programs, USF's "strong connections with venture capitalists in the area" as well as "the technology and innovation of the Silicon Valley" help make entrepreneurship "such a strength" of this MBA program. The MBA program's "international draw"—43 percent of students here are internationals—makes USF a great place for those interested in international business to learn and network. "I believe that anyone looking to get into international business would find USF a great fit," one student tells us. Each of USF's MBA programs maintains "small class sizes" that promote "personal relationships with professors," especially valuable since professors here "will get you business contacts." Each program embodies "the Jesuit approach toward a well-rounded education" and works at "ensuring ethics" throughout the curriculum.

The program places "an emphasis on group cooperation while nurturing individual growth."

Career and Placement

If you want to live and work in the Bay Area, USF will give you an edge in the local market. A staple in the community, USF has a strong alumni base and the school creates "good opportunities to network." Currently, USF graduates are employed at a range of prestigious companies, including Bank of the West, Gartner Consulting, Wells Fargo, Salesforce.com, Silicon Valley Bank, Pandora and Constellation Brands.

For those pursuing new positions after graduation, USF Graduate Career Services hosts a variety of workshops, events, and individual advising sessions to help students with career planning and professional development. The department typically collaborates with student clubs for speakers and strongly encourages student participation at various business community events. Despite these services, students feel the office can continue to improve. "The ability to bring in more big name companies or even jobs for the MBA students" is an area for improvement, one student writes, adding "I believe it is difficult because we have to compete with Stanford and Berkley, but USF MBA grads have a lot to offer and I believe being in San Francisco they should be marketing the MBA program much better to the job market."

Student Life and Environment

USF's "wired campus" in "one of the most beautiful cities in the world" offers "good resources" to students. "We have easy access to study rooms, computers, technology, and food (very important)," one student reports. Students' involvement on campus depends on their program. Part-timers, when balancing work, life, and school, can find it difficult to be "very involved [with the program] outside the classroom." The same holds true for the students in the "intense" Executive MBA program, who also happily report that the program "takes care of its students," a process that includes "catering all the food so you can concentrate on your classes."

Full timers, on the other hand, tell us that extracurricular life is "very active: a lot of clubs, good sport programs, a lot of speakers from Silicon Valley." There's also "Thirsty Thursday events, where students get together at local bars on Thursdays and have a drink." The event calendar is easy to track, as events "are summarized each week in an email from the VP of Marketing from the Graduate Business Association."

All here agree that San Francisco is an "excellent location" where there's "always something to do." There are "plenty of attractions nearby, including bars, parks, and museums. Students hang out with each other outside of school at these places." The MBA population is "a good mix of students in terms of background, gender, work experience" and include "many international students, students from across the U.S., married and single students, as well as students who come from all sorts of professional backgrounds."

Admissions

Application requirements vary among USF's MBA programs. All require that applicants submit the online application, a personal statement / essay(s), current résumé, transcripts, letters of recommendation, and an interview. All but the Executive MBA require a GMAT or GRE score. Two years of professional work experience is required for the Part-Time MBA and preferred for applicants to the Full-Time MBA; the Executive MBA requires a minimum of 8 years of experience. Depending on country of origin, international applicants may be required to demonstrate English proficiency through the TOEFL, IELTS or PTE Academic. A certification of finances is also required of all international applicants. It is important that all applicants demonstrate an interest in living USF's mission to change the world from here.

FINANCIAL FACTS

Annual tuition	$44,160
Fees	$250
Room & board	$18,000
% of students receiving aid	43
% of students receiving grants	35
Average grant	$12,582
Average student loan debt	$77,464

ADMISSIONS

Admissions Selectivity Rating	84
# of applications received	351
% applicants accepted	62
% acceptees attending	51
Average GMAT	554
Range of GMAT	500–610
Accepts GRE scores	Yes
Average Verbal GRE	154
Range of Verbal GRE scores	151–157
Average Quantitative GRE	151
Range of Quantitative GRE scores	147–155
Average Writing GRE	4.1
Range of Writing GRE scores	3.8–4.5
Average GPA	3.2
TOEFL required of international students	Yes
Minimum TOEFL (paper/web)	600/100
Application fee	$55
International application fee	$55
Application Deadline/Notification	
Round 1:	11/15 / 12/18
Round 2:	1/15 / 2/19
Round 3:	3/15 / 4/15
Round 4:	5/15 / 6/17
Deferment available	Yes
Maximum length of deferment	1 year
Transfer students accepted	Yes
Transfer application policy Students are eligible to transfer up to 6 credits when coming from another AACSB accredited program.	
Non-fall admissions	No
Need-blind admissions	Yes

EMPLOYMENT PROFILE

Career Rating		81
Percent employed at graduation		28
Percent employed 3 months after graduation		56
Average base starting salary		$70,357
Primary Source of Full-time Job Acceptances		
Graduate-facilitated activities	11 (61%)	
Unknown	7 (39%)	

Grads Employed by Function% Avg. Salary

Marketing	(21%)	$91,667
Other	(79%)	$64,545

Top 5 Employers Hiring Grads

UCSF, Johnson & Johnson, GuideSpark, First Data Corporation, Working Solutions

University of Scranton

Kania School of Management

GENERAL INFORMATION

Type of school	Private
Affiliation	Roman Catholic-Jesuit
Academic calendar	academic

SURVEY SAYS...

Friendly students, Happy students
Solid preparation in:
General management, Teamwork,
Presentation skills, Quantitative skills,
Environmental sustainability

STUDENTS

Enrollment of parent institution	5,422
Enrollment of MBA Program	474
% male/female	63/37
% out-of-state	47
% part-time	38
% underrepresented minority	14
% international	19
Average age at entry	25

ACADEMICS

Academic Experience Rating	90
Profs interesting rating	89
Profs accessible rating	93
Student/faculty ratio	13:1
% female faculty	7
% part-time faculty	26

Prominent Alumni

Christopher M. "KIP" Condron '70,
President, CEO & Director (retired),
AXA Financial, Inc. (New York, NY);
Paul M. Montrone , Ph. D. '62,
Chairman, Liberty Lane Partners;
Chairman Perspecta Trust, LLC,
Past Chair/CEO/President (Hampton,
New Hampshire); Susan M. Swain
'76, President and Co-COO, C-SPAN
(Washington, DC); John A. Walsh
'66, Executive Vice President &
Executive Editor, ESPN, Inc.
(Bristol, CT)

Academics

Most of the learning at the University of Scranton is informed by the principle of *Cura Personalis*, which translates from the Latin to mean "Care for the Entire Person." What this essentially describes is a respect for and appreciation of another's unique needs, circumstances, and gifts. These Jesuit values add an element of social responsibility to the work students do at the Kania School of Management (KSOM). Being a Jesuit institution does not, however, mean that the program is in any way light or insufficient. The MBA program at Scranton is accredited by the AASCB and "has a great reputation." It simply means that in the process of achieving their goals, students can rely on each other for a sense of camaraderie and support. The program places an emphasis on globalization and the intersection of technology and business. "At KSOM the diversity of the learning environment mirrors the global and diverse business setting of today's world. It offers an environment which is collaborative, values different ideas, encourages discussion, and lets the students think about phenomena in a very creative manner."

"The school offers many classes every term," and in addition to the general MBA, students are invited to specialize in the following disciplines: accounting, finance, international business management, information systems, marketing, and operations management. There are also programs that allows students to jointly pursue both a BS and an MBA. In addition to the University of Scranton's reputation and "forward thinking" attitude, are a multitude of amenities. The Irwin E. Alperin Financial Center has a simulated trading floor where students can learn via market simulations. It even has an electronic ticker and news and data feeds. Also, the wireless system at Kania ensures twenty-four-hour access to business applications and other online resources. The school prides itself on remaining "focused on what will be required of an MBA graduate in today's marketplace." Both a full-time and part-time track toward the MBA are offered at Kania, and those already in the workplace commend the "convenience" and "proximity" of the school. The Kania School of Management is described as an "excellent learning atmosphere," where "everyone is friendly and willing to help." "Professors are outstanding" and "provide critical insight." They are great at bringing real-world experience "into the four corners of a classroom." "They are all very well educated individuals, who take a lot of pride in teaching." Professors are also described as "accommodating to their students." As far as the administration is concerned, some say that "everything is smooth," while others complain of miscommunications with advisors and possible language barriers for international students.

Career and Placement

The Office of Career Services at the University of Scranton helps both graduate and undergraduate students find internships and full-time employment. They host workshops on various career-enhancing skills, as well as maintain an online job database. Still, students feel there are too "few job fairs," and that more of an effort needs to be made to assist students in finding "job opportunities after graduation." The Kania School of Management has "a very strong reputation" regionally. This means that students, who are up for jobs in Scranton usually get them. Of those students who responded to the poll, 95 percent had accepted employment three months after graduation. They were placed mainly in the Northeast and Middle Atlantic states. Some of the employers who hired graduates were Kraft Foods, Lowe's, PNC Bank, PricewaterhouseCoopers, and Sanofi Pasteur.

CAITLYN HOLLINGSHEAD, DIRECTOR, GRADUATE ADMISSIONS
ADDRESS: THE UNIVERSITY OF SCRANTON, OFFICE OF ADMISSIONS, THE ESTATE
800 LINDEN STREET, SCRANTON, PA 18510-4631 • PHONE: 570-941-7600 • FAX: 570-941-5995
E-MAIL:CGCE@SCRANTON.EDU WEBSITE: SCRANTON.EDU/MBA

Student Life and Environment

"The overall environment at the University of Scranton is very inviting. The University is open to its students and has created a very comfortable environment to learn and grow as a person." Students are "supportive, understanding, mature, and family-like." They also tend to help each other out and share "similar goals." They abide by "the founding moral principle of respect and care to all people." "There are limitless offerings of activities." It seems "everyone is involved in the University and the overall community." Students span a wide range. "Some are five-year MBA program majors with little real-world work experience, while others are working adults expanding their professional backgrounds and career opportunities." The MBA Student Association "works to get all MBA students involved outside of the classroom. They have socials and presentations a few times a semester in order to get MBA students socializing."

The campus is located in downtown Scranton, in the northeastern part of Pennsylvania. It is situated in the Lackawanna River Valley and has a population of roughly 76,000 people. The school itself encompasses fifty-eight acres and has been described by students as "scenic."

Admissions

The admissions committee requests the following from its applicants: Official GMAT scores, undergraduate GPA, personal essay, and letters of recommendation. Of those materials, GMAT score and GPA are of primary importance to the committee. Work experience will also be considered. Proficiency in English is an additional requirement. Admitted students had an average GPA of 3.2 and an average GMAT score of 515.

FINANCIAL FACTS

Annual tuition (in-state/ out-of-state)	$23,160/
Cost of books	$2,000
Room & board (on/off-campus)	$14,000/$14,000
% of students receiving grants	0

ADMISSIONS

Admissions Selectivity Rating	**89**
# of applications received	312
% applicants accepted	31
% acceptees attending	79
Average GMAT	515
Accepts GRE scores	No
Average GPA	3.3
TOEFL required of international students	Yes
Minimum TOEFL (web)	80
Application fee	$0
International application fee	$0
Application Deadline/Notification	
Deferment available	Yes
Maximum length of deferment	1 year
Transfer students accepted	Yes
Transfer application policy A transfer from an AACSB-accredited Jesuit school, otherwise 6 credits max	
Non-fall admissions	Yes
Need-blind admissions	Yes

EMPLOYMENT PROFILE

Career Rating	83	Top 5 Employers Hiring Grads
Percent employed 3 months after graduation	36	Price Waterhouse Coopers (6), Grant Thornton (3), Accenture (1), Lackawanna County (1),
Average base starting salary	$68,150	Princeton Review (1)

UNIVERSITY OF SOUTH CAROLINA
DARLA MOORE SCHOOL OF BUSINESS

Academics

Widely considered "one of the top institutions to study international business," the Darla Moore School of Business at University of South Carolina offers an "alternative program to traditional business school" through its flagship international MBA (IMBA) program (although it does offer a professional MBA and a one-year MBA as well). The IMBA program exposes Moore's students to a combination of "international work experience, education, and opportunity to learn a new language while completing [an] MBA." The program's required core classes make lead to "well-rounded" students. In the IMBA program, "the first seven months are spent doing a year's worth of core classes. Students are very tightly woven to provide each other academic, mental, and social support. The next three (or ten) months are spent overseas learning another language...then a five to seven-month internship, internationally or domestically, followed by a year of electives (in Columbia or abroad)."

Supporting the unique structure of the program are the school's "extremely talented" and "stellar" professors who "truly bring a wealth of international experience into the classroom." These professors "teach worldwide and use cases, simulations, and other situations to help us get a better understanding of how our decisions interact instead of just reading text." They make "the most abstract material understandable." As a result, students develop "a deep understanding of business fundamentals." Particularly noteworthy is the Global Supply Chain and Operations Management department which "prepares students to manage supply chains in a global environment, and provides students with operations management knowledge and practical training that puts them at the same level [as] engineers currently working at *Fortune* 500 companies."

While generally pleased with the quality of their professors, students are a bit more critical of the business school's administration which "is new and has some kinks to work out." On a more positive note, students feel that the administration is "open to working with the students to improve the school community, which makes up for a lack of organization and gives students a chance to gain valuable leadership skills." One recent development that is generating a lot of excitement among the students is the new "green" "multimillion dollar business school building" which was designed with "input from everyone," including "undergrads, master's [students], PhD [students], [and] staff" and which all hope will "bring unbelievable opportunities for future students."

Career and Placement

The majority of students surveyed expressed the need to improve the Office of Career Management (OCM) which they suggested should "spend less time 'coaching' students and more time focusing on building relationships with employers" as well as "reach out to a more diverse company base including ones from a wider geographic range." They also point out that "the highly-touted internship experience has suffered in recent years—the result of a failure to maintain relationships with companies (specifically in Latin America)." Students realize that not all of the blame falls on the OCM and acknowledge that "classes are small and our alumni network is small as a result. We attract some *Fortune* 500 companies who recruit on campus, but because there aren't as many of us out there in leadership, sometimes it is harder for us to get our foot in the door with these companies and during the recession we were one of the first schools cut from recruiting trips as a result." One of the more optimistic students has hopes for a brighter future and observes, "The Office of Career Management has partnered this year with a new external company and I believe they are doing a good job at providing students with placement services in a difficult hiring environment."

Student Life and Environment

The city of Columbia "is small but the student population makes going out fun" and "football is king." Despite its "good bar scene and nightlife," many of the students are "too busy during the core to enjoy the Columbia area. During your second year you have more of a chance, but it is a challenge to become involved in the community outside of the business school." The school campus provides "a lot of social and cultural activities" and has "everything from the normal Finance Club to Net Impact and even a Wine Society. We organize plenty of intramural teams and usually open them up to most people in the class."

The school attracts "a diverse set of students from Peace Corps volunteers to *Fortune* 500 company employees," to "Mormons with families" who all form a "very close-knit community." One student offers the more general observation that "half the students are more conservative and half are more liberal." While coming from a diverse set of backgrounds and experiences, "all are interested in new adventures and experiences particularly those having to do with learning aspects of other cultures and how their business practices differ from U.S. standards." "Overall, everyone is friendly and the atmosphere was one more of cooperation than competition."

Admissions

Applicants must submit an application, an application fee, official transcripts of post-secondary academic work, personal essays, letters of recommendation, and an official GMAT score report. International students must also submit TOEFL or IELTS scores unless they are graduates of an American college or university. Strong preference is shown for applicants with at least two years of work experience.

FINANCIAL FACTS

Annual tuition (in-state/ out-of-state)	$21,571/$35,790
Fees	$500
Cost of books	$1,016
Room & board (on/off-campus)	$12,957/$12,957
% of students receiving aid	69
% of first-year students receiving aid	89
% of students receiving grants	63
Average award package	$13,997
Average grant	$4,883
Average loan	$20,772
Average student loan debt	$41,740

ADMISSIONS

Admissions Selectivity Rating	85
# of applications received	379
% applicants accepted	72
% acceptees attending	69
Average GMAT	630
Range of GMAT	590–680
Accepts GRE scores	Yes
Average Verbal GRE	155
Range of Verbal GRE scores	152–159
Average Quantitative GRE	151
Range of Quantitative GRE scores	148–156
Average Writing GRE	4.0
Range of Writing GRE scores	3.6–4.5
Average GPA	3.3
TOEFL required of international students	Recommended
Minimum TOEFL (paper/web)	600/95
Application fee	$100
International application fee	$100
Application Deadline/Notification	
Round 1:	10/15 / 12/1
Round 2:	12/1 / 2/1
Round 3:	1/15 / 3/1
Round 4:	3/1 / 4/1
Deferment available	Yes
Maximum length of deferment	One year
Transfer students accepted	Yes
Transfer application policy	
Up to 12 hours can be considered for transfer from an AACSB accredited school.	
Non-fall admissions	Yes
Need-blind admissions	Yes

EMPLOYMENT PROFILE

Career Rating	88	Grads Employed by Function	% Avg. Salary
Percent employed at graduation	52	Marketing	(16%) $66,250
Percent employed 3 months after graduation	73	Operations	(31%) $76,777
		Consulting	(25%) $95,250
Average base starting salary	$85,100	Management	(13%) $95,750
Primary Source of Full-time Job Acceptances		Finance	(9%) $88,666
School-facilitated activities	20 (63%)	MIS	(6%)
Graduate-facilitated activities	5 (16%)	**Top 5 Employers Hiring Grads**	
Unknown	7 (22%)	Michelin (2), Accenture (1), The Coca-Cola Company (1), IBM (1), Bank of America (1)	

THE UNIVERSITY OF SOUTH DAKOTA
BEACOM SCHOOL OF BUSINESS

GENERAL INFORMATION

Type of school	Public
Affiliation	No Affiliation
Academic calendar	Semester

SURVEY SAYS...
Friendly students
Solid preparation in:
General management, Quantitative
skills

STUDENTS

Enrollment of parent institution	9,971
Enrollment of MBA Program	295
% male/female	74/26
% out-of-state	21
% part-time	94
% underrepresented minority	26
% international	21
Average age at entry	31
Average years work experience at entry	5

ACADEMICS

Academic Experience Rating	**86**
Profs interesting rating	89
Profs accessible rating	92
Student/faculty ratio	10:1
% female faculty	21
% underrepresented minority faculty	18
% part-time faculty	0

Joint Degrees
JD/MBA - approximately 3 years of
full time study

Prominent Alumni
John Thune, U.S. Senator from
South Dakota; Al Neuharth,
Founder of USA Today; Tom
Brokaw, American broadcaster; Tim
Johnson, U.S. Senator; Pat O'Brien,
Television presenter

Academics

The University of South Dakota Beacom School of Business is "quite the hidden gem." It has "a great reputation, reasonable tuition cost, and an MBA program that [can] be taken completely online." It is a non-profit, "affordable, high ranking," "established and accredited program,"—"a traditional brick and mortar school" that can be easily accessed "mainly via online courses." Students note that the MBA program "is very strong," "highly flexible" and "works well for working professionals." "The low student to teacher ratio" is "very attractive" as is "the low cost of tuition." And the "small community atmosphere allows openness among fellow students." In addition, The University of South Dakota offers health services and business analytics specializations. For many, it is "the best value" for an AACSB accredited school with a "healthcare specialization and online program."

The University of South Dakota Beacom School of Business—which offers an on-campus MBA, an online MBA, and a hybrid MBA—"has a good orientation program to help potential students familiarize themselves with the program," and makes it easy for undergraduates who were not business majors "to enter the program and complete prerequisites." "The MBA program managers are very knowledgeable and proactive in helping the students navigate the program," notes one student.

The program is known for "accessible," "quality professors" with "rigorous expectations." "The professors are well versed in the course subject matter and most have a vested interest in their students." They "strive to incorporate [the] newest practices," and have "excellent work-related experience." Students note that professors "do a great job of establishing communication with students" and ensuring "students understand that they will be accountable for the academic workload. There are no free handouts, but most professors are friendly and push students to achieve." One student notes that the "professors are a bit varied in their schedule availability, timeliness in grading and providing feedback, and effectiveness of their lectures." But also says that most of his "professors were very engaged in their courses, hosted live lessons, and gave meaningful homework and quizzes." For some, balancing course work and full-time jobs can be challenging, but the university provides weekly reviews for online MBAs to keep them on track. In addition, the administration makes it "very easy to enroll in classes and accommodate testing situations," and will go "the extra mile help get you through."

Overall, students call this program the "best bang for your buck," and say "the academic experience was outstanding." One student refers to the MBA program as "[t]he little engine that could." In other words, "a relatively small program [that] has a staff of professors and a group of students with tremendous work ethic." He goes on to say, "It was honestly a very difficult program but it shows in their national ranking." Another student says, "USD's MBA program is phenomenal. If you're looking for quality, flexibility, and affordability, then USD is the place to go."

Career and Placement

Professors and the administration alike are helpful in preparing resumes and helping students in their job search. Forty-one percent of students received job offers through school-facilitated activities. Over 50 percent of students who responded received a job offer by graduation, and an additional 44 percent received an offer within three months of graduating. Eighty-two percent of graduates accepted job offers in the Midwest. Notable alumni include John Thune, US Senator from South Dakota.

Student Life and Environment

The University of South Dakota Beacom School of Business boasts an "ethnically diverse" student body, "from a variety of backgrounds" and "different countries." "Many are from the financial sector, though there are some students from operations and human resource fields." Students are described as "very inviting and friendly" and as "having mid-western hospitality." One student says, "They are the types of people you want to grab a drink with after work and [they] will do anything to help you out." In the program, students often "work very well in groups" and though competition is present, it is not "really a focus."

The campus is considered "very well-run" and "feels safe and full of activities." Most students in the online and hybrid MBAs are employed full-time, and though many students in the online MBA program aren't regularly on campus, their program experience is not diminished. Online or off, they find their colleagues "business-minded, willing to share personal experiences, family-oriented, eager to help others, [and] flexible for group projects." "The school does well in accepting good students," notes one student. "Generally, classmates [are] engaged actively in class…. Some [are] busy with work life and family life, but they still manage time well to further their education at the school." This "creates a great collaborative learning environment."

Admissions

The Beacom School of Business offers the MBA program: on-campus, online, or hybrid (online and on-campus). All three require an undergraduate degree, GMAT scores, resume, statement of purpose, and three letters of recommendation. The average GMAT score for a recent class was 553. International students must submit a financial statement in addition to TOEFL or IELTS scores—a minimum TOEFL score of at least 550 (paper-based), 213 (computer-based), or 79 (Internet-based) is required. A 6.0 or higher is required for the IELTS.

FINANCIAL FACTS

Annual tuition (in-state/ out-of-state)	$7,239/$15,320
Fees	$6,233
Cost of books	$600
Room & board	$3,987
% of students receiving aid	30
% of students receiving grants	19
Average award package	$9,433
Average grant	$6,449
Average loan	$10,316
Average student loan debt	$6,088

ADMISSIONS

Admissions Selectivity Rating	80
# of applications received	69
% applicants accepted	90
% acceptees attending	87
Average GMAT	553
Range of GMAT	500–603
Accepts GRE scores	No
Average GPA	3.2
TOEFL required of international students	Yes
Minimum TOEFL (paper/web)	550/79
Application fee	$35
International application fee	$35
Application Deadline/Notification	
Deferment available	Yes
Maximum length of deferment	3 semesters
Transfer students accepted	Yes
Transfer application policy	
Maximum of 9 credit hours from an accredited institution may be transferred.	
Non-fall admissions	Yes
Need-blind admissions	Yes

EMPLOYMENT PROFILE

		Grads Employed by Function	% Avg. Salary
Career Rating	90		
Percent employed at graduation	56	Marketing	(16%) $53,760
Percent employed 3 months after graduation	80	Operations	(3%) $100,000
		Management	(26%) $48,485
Average base starting salary	$63,458	Finance	(36%) $71,850
Primary Source of Full-time Job Acceptances		HR	(6%) $48,573
School-facilitated activities	9 (29%)	MIS	(3%)
Graduate-facilitated activities	22 (71%)	Other	(10%) $84,333

Top 5 Employers Hiring Grads
Wells Fargo (2), Avera (2), KPMG (1), Goldman Sachs (1), Mutual of Omaha (1)

UNIVERSITY OF SOUTHERN CALIFORNIA
MARSHALL SCHOOL OF BUSINESS

GENERAL INFORMATION

Type of school	Private
Affiliation	No Affiliation
Academic calendar	Semester

SURVEY SAYS...

Good social scene, Good peer network, Helpful alumni
Solid preparation in:
Doing business in a global economy

STUDENTS

Enrollment of parent institution	43,401
Enrollment of MBA Program	951
% male/female	70/30
% part-time	54
% underrepresented minority	7
% international	27
Average age at entry	27
Average years work experience at entry	5

ACADEMICS

Academic Experience Rating	79
Profs interesting rating	71
Profs accessible rating	71
Student/faculty ratio	8:1
% female faculty	30
% underrepresented minority faculty	8
% part-time faculty	19

Joint Degrees

East Asian Area Studies (MBA/MA); Gerontology (MS/MBA); Industrial and Systems Engineering (MBA/MS); Jewish Non-profit Management (MBA/MA); Law (JD/MBA); Medicine (MD/MBA); Planning (MBA/MPL); Pharmacy (PharmD/MBA); Real Estate Development (MBA/MRED); Social Work (MBA/MSW); Education (MBA/EdD)

Academics

Offering "international business learning opportunities not available elsewhere" as well as solid programs in finance, consulting, entrepreneurship, real estate, marketing, and entertainment, the University of Southern California's Marshall School of Business excels in a broad range of areas. Best of all, perhaps, USC boasts "the most amazing alumni network in the nation," a huge asset when the time for job searches arrives. As one student explains, "I have never met another Trojan anywhere in the world who wasn't excited to meet another fellow Trojan!" "The Trojan Network is enormous and expansive, providing a lifetime equity of resources."

Marshall offers a two-year full-time MBA as well as a part-time evening MBA, an executive MBA, a one-year international MBA (called the IBEAR MBA), a global executive MBA, and an online MBA. The school "combines a rigorous curriculum" with "the personal attention of a private college." The MBA program here "has a strong emphasis on providing students an international perspective on business issues. It is more than just saying 'We think it is important that you consider other cultures.' At Marshall, it's mandatory that all students work on a consulting project for a company overseas and travel to that region through the PRIME program. As a result of PRIME and other programs, I've had meaningful work, educational, and fun experiences in Singapore, Thailand, Vietnam, and in Western Europe."

Marshall professors "are outstanding. They bring new research into the classroom and encourage students to actively participate in class." The faculty represents "a mixture of academics and recent career switchers from their fields in business...they do a very good job giving us a base to learn from." Course work is demanding; one student warns, "Marshall is much more difficult than I expected. I have nine years of work experience and consider myself a fairly bright individual. If I put in a decent amount of work and keep up with the reading, I can get a B-plus in our classes with relative ease, but it really is difficult to break the A barrier." Administrators "are committed to growth and innovation as an institution." According to one student, "chaos is inherent when new programs and classes are initiated. . . . This is a leading school's greatest challenge, and USC Marshall does everything in its power to attend to students' individual needs as well as meet their own goals and expectations."

Career and Placement

"Incredible changes" have been implemented at Marshall's Career Resources Center. "The resources and energy the career coaches bring to the students are head and shoulders above what students at [another prominent area business school] have. While I'm sure the CRC will continue to improve and bring in more high-profile companies, it is already a premier organization." Students praise the center's one-week winter inter-term program for first-years, through which "students learn how to fine tune their resume and interview skills. Additionally, they learn about networking, discover their inner interests, and come up with a value proposition. I believe this gives Marshall students a leg up in recruiting."

Companies most likely to employ Marshall MBAs include: Deloitte, PwC, EY, Google, AT&T, IBM, Amgen, GE, Autodesk, Johnson & Johnson, Mattel, Cognizant, Cisco, KPMG, Starbucks, SanDisk, Wells Fargo, Walt Disney Company, and Intel.

Student Life and Environment

Full-time students tell us that "there are numerous professional and social club opportunities in which to be involved at Marshall." Several point out that "being involved with the community is easy and fun due to the Challenge for Charity Club, which schedules regular volunteer days for junior achievement and hosts parties at popular LA night clubs where the entry fees are donated to the Special Olympics." And Marshall MBA students have won the Challenge for Charity Golden Briefcase for seven years in a row for a competition based on fundraising, volunteering, and athletics. One student adds, "With the numerous clubs and organizations, USC students are really only limited by the amount of time and energy they possess. Personally, I wanted to take a leadership role in the community, and have had the opportunity to do just that. That makes my schedule a little bit more hectic than normal, but that was a personal decision. Really, life at Marshall is as challenging as one has the ambition to make it." Throughout the program and the campus, students enjoy "a very communal atmosphere. Football season is amazing."

Los Angeles is a great hometown, "a fun and vibrant city" with "fabulous weather all year round." Students note that there are "nice apartments by the ocean for a decent price" within a twenty-minute commute of the campus. The city provides many opportunities "to spend time together outside of class." "There are parties or small get-togethers almost every weekend."

Admissions

The Marshall Admissions Office warns that its MBA programs are "highly selective," and that the Admissions Committee "carefully assesses each candidate on a number of dimensions, including prior academic, professional, and personal accomplishments." All applicants must provide the school with official transcripts for all postsecondary academic work, an official GMAT or GRE score report, an official TOEFL or IELTS score report (for international students who have not previously attended an English-language undergraduate or graduate program), an online application, a current resume, one required essay, and one letter of recommendation (a letter from a direct supervisor is preferred).

Prominent Alumni

Ronnie C. Chan, Chairman, Hang Lung Group Ltd.; Melissa Lora, President International, Taco Bell Corp, Yum! Brands, Inc.; Yang Ho Cho, Chairman & CEO, Korean Air

FINANCIAL FACTS

Annual tuition (in-state/ out-of-state)	$53,865/$53,865
Fees	$3,211
Cost of books	$1,350
Room & board (on/off-campus)	$18,111/$18,111

ADMISSIONS

Admissions Selectivity Rating	94
# of applications received	1,780
% applicants accepted	29
% acceptees attending	43
Average GMAT	679
Range of GMAT	650–710
Accepts GRE scores	Yes
Average GPA	3.3
TOEFL required of international students	Yes
Minimum TOEFL (paper/web)	600/100
Application fee	$150
International application fee	$150
Application Deadline/Notification	
Round 1:	10/19 / 12/18
Round 2:	1/8 / 4/1
Round 3:	4/8 / 5/20
Deferment available	No
Transfer students accepted	No
Non-fall admissions	No
Need-blind admissions	Yes

EMPLOYMENT PROFILE

Career Rating	92	Grads Employed by Function% Avg. Salary	
Percent employed at graduation	61	Marketing	(10%) $94,823
Percent employed 3 months after graduation	81	Operations	(4%) $85,333
		Consulting	(25%) $121,071
Average base starting salary	$105,171	Management	(8%) $103,215
Primary Source of Full-time Job Acceptances		Finance	(26%) $106,750
School-facilitated activities	52 (37%)	HR	(4%) $96,100
Graduate-facilitated activities	84 (60%)	Other	(14%) $97,667
Unknown	4 (3%)	**Top 5 Employers Hiring Grads**	
		Ernst & Young (8), Cognizant Technology Solutions (5), Deloitte (5), Wells Fargo (5), Johnson & Johnson (3)	

UNIVERSITY OF SOUTHERN MAINE
SCHOOL OF BUSINESS

GENERAL INFORMATION
Type of school   Public
Affiliation   No Affiliation
Academic calendar   Semester

SURVEY SAYS...
Students love Portland, ME
Solid preparation in:
Teamwork

STUDENTS
Enrollment of parent institution	9,382
Enrollment of MBA Program	135
% male/female	71/29
% out-of-state	0
% part-time	79
% underrepresented minority	0
% international	0
Average age at entry	30
Average years work experience at entry	5

ACADEMICS
Academic Experience Rating	86
Profs interesting rating	88
Profs accessible rating	91
Student/faculty ratio	17:1
% female faculty	24
% underrepresented minority faculty	0
% part-time faculty	0

Joint Degrees
3-2 Master of Business Administration, 5.5-6 years, B.S. and M.B.A. MS in Nursing and M.B.A., 3-4 years J.D./M.B.A., 4-5 years Master of Public Health and M.B.A., 3-4 years

Academics

University of Southern Maine's MBA program distinguishes itself through strong academics, "relatively low cost," and a decidedly local focus. This "internationally accredited" program is the best choice for Portland-area professionals, offering "convenient class times" and an easily accessible location on the school's main campus. Busy students appreciate that "most professors offer very organized courses with defined expectations and outcomes." Despite efficiency, USM is "not an online school or a 'three-week' MBA, but is a traditional business school with the rigors that come with it." The school augments the part-time program with a special 3-2 degree, through which business undergraduates can earn an MBA with just one additional year of full-time study.

With a strong background in the real world, "faculty is very professional, and topics covered are generally relevant and current." Students explain that "certain professors are more cutting edge and prepare you better for an innovative and sustainable professional culture than others, but the majority stay current and keep you up to date." Maine business plays a central role in the curriculum, and "the professors also do an excellent job using case studies from local companies." On that note, "USM has a lot of connections to the business community and works with them often, which helps create experience and visibility." While the program offers concentrations in accounting, finance, sustainability, or health management and policy, students would "absolutely love the school to offer targeted MBA courses (or someday concentrations) specific to some of Maine's fastest growing industries, such as biotechnology, medical devices, IT, etc." Students also note that "more interpersonal or organizational development classes could be offered as electives," along with a greater focus on entrepreneurship.

Drawing from the local business community, "the majority of USM MBA students study part time and are involved in diverse industry sectors, from food to music to finance to health care and to biotechnology." The varied experience among the student body "keeps business projects and case studies interesting, with diverse opinions and ideas to bring back to my own career." When it comes to staff and administrators, "some will do anything for students, while others will ignore their needs." In addition, students have noticed "political strife among the faculty and administration at the school." At the same time, "it's very easy to get into both required and popular classes" at University of Southern Maine, which distinguishes it from many other part-time business schools, and students are quick to point out that "the good side outweighs the bad by a large margin."

Career and Placement

Many of University of Southern Maine's graduate students are already working in the region, with plans to remain at their current companies after graduation. For those who'd like to make a career change, the School of Business Career Services and Internships Office operates an online job development website where current undergraduate and graduate students can search for open positions, take career assessments, and research companies and industries. The office offers resume and cover letter critiques, salary negotiation assistance, and individual career counseling. It also organizes a series of employer sessions, where students can meet with representatives from local companies. In addition to the services offered through the business school, there is a University-wide career fair every spring, which includes opportunities for MBA graduates.

ADMISSIONS CONTACT: ALICE B. CASH, ASSISTANT DEAN FOR STUDENT AFFAIRS
ADDRESS: 96 FALMOUTH STREET, P O BOX 9300, PORTLAND, ME 04104
PHONE: 207-780-4184 • FAX: 207-780-4662
E-MAIL: MBA@USM.MAINE.EDU • WEBSITE: WWW.USM.MAINE.EDU/SB

Within the business school, the administration is eager to present new professional opportunities to its students. In addition to online resources, "several times a week we get emails for job and intern openings." In fact, a current student shares, "I get more emails about job openings than anything else from USM. While I am employed, it's nice to see what other opportunities are available in the local market."

Student Life and Environment

On this Portland campus, students join the MBA program from a mix of industries, and encompass a "nice mix of ages, from twenty-two to fifty." In the part-time program, "most MBA students live off campus, work full time, and take classes part time," which means they are rarely able to participate in extracurricular or social activities. "There really isn't that much to do as far as clubs and student organizations are concerned," and, unfortunately, "due to budget issues, the childcare and spouse programs had to be cut last year." However, unlike many part-time programs, "commuter MBA students do have opportunities to join clubs, workshops, and more" at USM. A current student assures us "not many people stay on campus, but those who do have a great time" with their classmates. No matter what their involvement in campus life, "UMS MBA students are incredible friends, mentors, advisors, and team members."

Life at USM has recently made a big step up, as "new buildings were just added" to the business school campus, which "offer study areas and kitchen areas." On the greater campus, "the gym is excellent," and the range of "art and cultural events here are phenomenal." Off campus, "the city of Portland offers an amazing quality of life with affordable housing in the rural suburbs and a great, but safe, night life." With many wonderful restaurants and cafes near campus, "there is always a place to relax with your professors after class or meet with your teammates."

Admissions

Applications for University of Southern Maine's MBA program are accepted on a rolling basis, though prospective students who would like to be considered for a scholarship must apply early in the admissions cycle. Students are evaluated based on their undergraduate performance, potential for success in the program, and demonstrated leadership experience. For regular admission, prospective students must have a GMAT score of 500 or higher. The average GMAT for entering students is 556. Students may apply to the 3-2 program directly from high school or during their undergraduate studies at USM.

FINANCIAL FACTS

Annual tuition (in-state/ out-of-state)	$6,840/$18,468
Fees	$2,070
Cost of books	$1,500
Room & board (on/off-campus)	$11,230/

ADMISSIONS

Admissions Selectivity Rating	85
# of applications received	57
% applicants accepted	60
% acceptees attending	85
Average GMAT	556
Range of GMAT	500–610
Accepts GRE scores	Yes
Average GPA	3.3
TOEFL required of international students	Yes
Minimum TOEFL (paper/web)	550/79
Application fee	$65
International application fee	$65
Early application deadline	1/15
Regular application deadline	8/1
Application Deadline/Notification	
Deferment available	Yes
Maximum length of deferment	one year
Transfer students accepted	Yes
Transfer application policy A maximum of nine semester hours of transfer credit may be accepted. Please see catalog. http://usm.maine.edu/catalogs	
Non-fall admissions	Yes
Need-blind admissions	Yes

THE UNIVERSITY OF TAMPA
JOHN H. SYKES COLLEGE OF BUSINESS

GENERAL INFORMATION
Type of school	Private
Affiliation	No Affiliation
Academic calendar	Semester

SURVEY SAYS...
Classmates have diverse work experience, Friendly students, Good peer network, Cutting-edge classes, Abundant mentors available, Happy students, Students love Tampa, FL
Solid preparation in:
Marketing, Finance, Accounting, General management, Operations, Teamwork, Communication/interpersonal skills, Presentation skills, Quantitative skills, Doing business in a global economy

STUDENTS
Enrollment of parent institution	8,037
Enrollment of MBA Program	415
% male/female	66/34
% out-of-state	10
% part-time	32
% underrepresented minority	61
% international	49
Average age at entry	29
Average years work experience at entry	7

ACADEMICS
Academic Experience Rating	93
Profs interesting rating	94
Profs accessible rating	97
Student/faculty ratio	11:1
% female faculty	37
% underrepresented minority faculty	22
% part-time faculty	13

Joint Degrees
MS-ACC/MBA; MS-FIN/MBA; MS-MKT/MBA; MSN/MBA

Prominent Alumni
Dennis Zank, COO, Raymond James; John M. Barrett, President and CEO, First Citrus Bank; Robert Weisbord, CEO, Sinclair Digital

Academics

The MBA program at the University of Tampa's John H. Sykes College of Business provides "a great, friendly place to study," with "small class sizes" that "enhance class interaction and active participation" and a "cheap tuition" that students can't help but appreciate. The school offers students three curricular options: a full-time program that can be completed in sixteen months, a part-time program (with "a course schedule that is excellent for the working professional") that is typically completed in about three years, and a six-term Executive MBA program for business leaders ("the only true Saturday program in the area," one student tells us). Roughly one-third of the student body attends full time.

In all programs, students tout the curriculum, which "is outlined with a lower core, integrated core, and principal concentration that involves three electives. The program is flexible with the electives if you wanted to do a general MBA concentration." "Most of the classes require heavy interaction instead of just the instructor speaking," one MBA student writes, adding, "This leads to a lot of good insight and interesting conversations." Concentrations are available in entrepreneurship, finance, information systems management, international business, [innovation] management, marketing, and nonprofit management.

MBAs are just as sanguine about their instructors. UT Professors "are willing to give their personal cell phone numbers and adapt to office hours at the students availability." Their only complaint is that they feel some instructors aren't utilized "to their full potential. For example, for finance courses, it would be cool if students got a field trip to a trading floor somewhere in either Tampa, or anywhere in the U.S. Other more hands on activities like that for other majors too would be good." Still, students generally concur that, overall, "the academic experience is excellent. The school has built an environment that pushes the students to talk to each other, and ask each other for support." Administrators "focus on teamwork and building an environment that puts very little stress on the student." Students also appreciate how the administration "strives to remain cutting edge by preparing students as leaders in this new global marketplace." One student sums up, "The University of Tampa does an excellent job preparing you for the business world."

Career and Placement

UT's Office of Career Services provides Sykes MBAs with a battery of services, including assessment tests, workshops in business etiquette and business dress, one-on-one counseling, and job fairs. Students here praise "the professors' desire to help students obtain careers after graduation." Attendees of a recent on-campus career fair included ADP, Central Intelligence Agency, Chase Retirement Services, Deloitte, Franklin Templeton Investment, Geico, New York Life Insurance Company, Raymond James Financial, Syniverse Technologies Inc., Target Corporation, T. Rowe Price, The Nielsen Company, U.S. Department of State, and USAA.

Student Life and Environment

UT students reap the benefits of "a beautiful campus and of course, warm weather and beaches" as well as a "business building that is top notch, with up-to-date facilities." MBAs enjoy access to "outstanding educational, professional and social events for future business leaders," including "numerous seminars in which well-known CEOs and entrepreneurs make presentations throughout the semester. This provides excellent networking opportunities." The MBA program hosts "numerous clubs and local activities advertised weekly," and students with the time to spare also enjoy "sporting events on and around campus."

Not all can. About one-third of students here attend full-time, and they generally reap the benefits of the gorgeous, lively campus. The rest are part-timers, typically working full time in addition to their class work; they have little time for anything other than school assignments. The school draws a diverse student body "with people from different cultures and countries" as well as different professional backgrounds. The school works hard to build cohorts that exploit these differences "so that everyone brings something to the table. We get along great and have in-depth discussions."

Students' wish list for quality of life improvements include more parking facilities. One writes, "Parking has always been an issue for this school. The student population is constantly growing, thereby requiring an increase in faculty and staff. Most of the area on campus is developed with various types of buildings (administrative, classrooms, residence halls, etc.) and although there are two parking garages it is sometimes difficult to find convenient parking." Some full-timers also feel that "day care is needed as well as the introduction of family activities in order to get spouses and children more involved in students' lives. Many of us are so busy studying and doing assignments that our home life is highly affected."

Admissions

Admission to the full-time and part-time MBA programs at Sykes is based on undergraduate work; GMAT score (average score is 540); demonstration of proficiency in mathematics, computers, and written and oral communications skills; and professional experience. International students must demonstrate proficiency in English by scoring at least 577 on the written TOEFL, 230 on the computer-based TOEFL, 90 on the Internet-based TOEFL, or 7.0 on the IELTS. Admission to the Executive MBA program requires relevant work experience; applicants are required to have seven years of relevant work experience. Applicants to all programs must submit two letters of recommendation, a resume, and a personal statement.

FINANCIAL FACTS

Annual tuition (in-state/ out-of-state)	$9,168/$9,168
Fees	$80
Cost of books	$800
Room & board (on/off-campus)	$9,900/$6,500
% of students receiving aid	83
% of first-year students receiving aid	81
% of students receiving grants	42
Average award package	$15,324
Average grant	$11,137
Average loan	$15,814
Average student loan debt	$43,717

ADMISSIONS

Admissions Selectivity Rating	89
# of applications received	1,098
% applicants accepted	31
% acceptees attending	53
Average GMAT	540
Range of GMAT	480–600
Accepts GRE scores	Yes
Average GPA	3.5
TOEFL required of international students	Yes
Minimum TOEFL (paper/web)	577/90
Application fee	$40
International application fee	$40
Early application deadline	6/1
Regular application deadline	7/15
Application Deadline/Notification	
Deferment available	Yes
Maximum length of deferment	1 year
Transfer students accepted	Yes
Transfer application policy Up to 8 hrs. from an AACSB accredited school	
Non-fall admissions	Yes
Need-blind admissions	Yes

EMPLOYMENT PROFILE

Career Rating	88	Grads Employed by Function	% Avg. Salary
Percent employed at graduation	41	Marketing	(13%) $86,250
Percent employed 3 months after graduation	62	Consulting	(7%) $45,000
		Finance	(37%) $57,045
Average base starting salary	$71,563	MIS	(13%) $72,500
Primary Source of Full-time Job Acceptances		Other	(10%) $12,000
School-facilitated activities	10 (42%)	**Top 5 Employers Hiring Grads**	
Graduate-facilitated activities	11 (46%)	PriceWaterhouseCoopers (3), Ernst and	
Unknown	3 (13%)	Young (2), Bankers Financial Corporation (2),	
		Citibank (1), Ford Credit Company (1)	

THE UNIVERSITY OF TENNESSEE AT CHATTANOOGA
COLLEGE OF BUSINESS

Academics

The University of Tennessee-Chattanooga College of Business is offers a fast-paced, accelerated MBA program with an international component and a focus on group projects, not to mention being the only AACSB-accredited program in the area. With four required electives and two capstone courses (in Strategic Management and Entrepreneurship and New Ventures), and an optional accompanying graduate certificate in Data Analytics (through the Big Data Analytics and Research Center), the relatively young school is growing in name and offerings and is "excellent about staying up with current trends." "UTC is on the forefront of business advancement," says a student. The Online Professional MBA is taught by the same professors that teach on-campus, and these students say there is "always an opportunity to communicate with classmates and the professors."

The professors are "helpful" and "teach the classes to where it makes sense to those even without business backgrounds." They are "always reachable and eager to help and make sure you understand the material." Faculty "treat the students very much like peers . . . everyone is treated as an equal and we share a common goal of growth." Although some say that "it can be difficult at times to get into certain classes," the administration does a "good job of making sure that you have the correct classes, and they will do what they need to do to aid in your education." Administrators "are invested in the success of their students and have their institution's best interests at heart."

Career and Placement

Many students in the MBA program are already employed and so are mainly looking to "move their education to the next level," and these "very similar career goals . . . inspire a camaraderie." Still, the school's "connection to important local corporations" is one of its strongest assets, and the College of Business Center for Career Development hosts business expos, recruitment sessions, and luncheons to help further these connections. "Chattanooga is a great town!" says a student. "The area here is thriving with new businesses like Amazon, Volkswagen and other smaller start-up companies." Top employers of recent UTC grads include BlueCross BlueShield, Unum, TVA, Decosimo and Company, and Volkswagen.

Student Life and Environment

Classes are composed of small student bodies that are all centrally located in the College of Business building, and this proximity makes it easy to make acquaintances and "facilitates participation in extracurricular school activities." There is "a good mix between older students that have been working for years and younger students that graduated less than two years ago." Though most here have quite busy lives outside of the classroom, "students have always been friendly" and "it's extremely easy to create a group of friends who will work with you on every assignment you share." "Most of my fellow students are professionals in different industries and are extremely approachable," says one student. "I have more acquaintances from my classes than from my place of employment." Chattanooga is "a great city to live in. It is beautiful and has a good atmosphere."

Admissions

Gaining admittance to the UTC Graduate School is a prerequisite for applicants to the MBA program. Students must have a minimum 2.7 GPA and minimum 450 GMAT score for consideration. Applications are accepted on a rolling basis and due thirty days before the start of the semester. Official transcripts from one's universities are required as are GMAT scores, which average 498, and GPAs, which average 3.19. Work experience, although not mandatory, can prove to be advantageous in the admissions process. GRE scores may be submitted in lieu of GMAT scores. International students whose first language is not English must submit an official score report for the TOEFL (minimum grade required: 550, paper-based; 213, computer-based; 79 Internet-based) or the IELTS (minimum score 6.0).

FINANCIAL FACTS

% of students receiving aid	57
% of first-year students receiving aid	82
% of students receiving grants	6
Average award package	$16,489
Average grant	$5,836
Average loan	$19,664
Average student loan debt	$31,273

ADMISSIONS

Admissions Selectivity Rating	84
# of applications received	153
% applicants accepted	54
% acceptees attending	70
Average GMAT	498
Range of GMAT	450–538
Accepts GRE scores	Yes
Average Verbal GRE	153
Range of Verbal GRE scores	149–156
Average Quantitative GRE	149
Range of Quantitative GRE scores	146–153
Average Writing GRE	3.6
Range of Writing GRE scores	3.0–4.0
Average GPA	3.2
TOEFL required of international students	Yes
Minimum TOEFL (paper/web)	550/79
Application fee	$30
International application fee	$35
Application Deadline/Notification	
Deferment available	Yes
Maximum length of deferment	1 year
Transfer students accepted	Yes
Transfer application policy	
Students can transfer up to six hours from an AACSB accredited school. All transfer courses are subject to departmant approval.	
Non-fall admissions	Yes
Need-blind admissions	Yes

EMPLOYMENT PROFILE

Career Rating	72	Top 5 Employers Hiring Grads
		Blue Cross Blue Shield, Unum, TVA, Decosimo and Company, Volkswagen

THE UNIVERSITY OF TENNESSEE, KNOXVILLE
HASLAM COLLEGE OF BUSINESS

GENERAL INFORMATION

Type of school	Public
Affiliation	No Affiliation
Academic calendar	Semester

SURVEY SAYS...

Friendly students, Good social scene, Conservative students, Happy students
Solid preparation in:
Marketing, General management, Teamwork, Presentation skills, Computer skills

STUDENTS

Enrollment of parent institution	27,845
Enrollment of MBA Program	144
% male/female	80/20
% out-of-state	35
% part-time	0
% underrepresented minority	8
% international	22
Average age at entry	27
Average years work experience at entry	4

ACADEMICS

Academic Experience Rating	**91**
Profs interesting rating	90
Profs accessible rating	94
Student/faculty ratio	5:1
% female faculty	34
% underrepresented minority faculty	5
% part-time faculty	0

Joint Degrees

MBA/MS Business Analytics, 2 yrs; JD/MBA; MBA/MS Engineering, 2 yrs; MBA/ MS Agricultural Economics, 2 yrs; MBA/PharmD, 5 yrs

Prominent Alumni

Ralph Heath, VP & COO, Lockheed Martin Aeronautics; Kiran Patel, CFO, Solectron; Kevin Clayton, President & CEO, Clayton Homes; Bob Hall, CEO, Jewelry Television by ACN; James Gower, President & CEO, Rigel Pharmaceuticals

Academics

You'll be glad for the opportunity to join "an institution steeped in tradition and pride" and to "get an excellent education at an affordable price from professors who care, in an environment that promotes a full student life," but you'll have to work for it. Packing a full MBA program (including a required internship) into an intense three semesters is a challenge, but it is one students welcome thanks to educators who "are passionate about teaching their subject matter. There is not the overwhelming emphasis present in the classroom that they are 'too busy' to teach or help students that need it outside of class." The key is in making the subject matter engaging and interesting. "They have real world experience that they apply to the classroom, and they are very informed in all areas of business." These "very engaging" professors "have a great sense of humor, which makes the material 100 times more interesting."

Notably, "the professors all have lengthy experience working in industry prior to teaching, so the lessons are very well grounded in what actually takes place outside of academia." Even more important, these educators "continue to remain active in their previous fields, so they continue to infuse current lessons learned from industry into their classes." This means "they teach you skills that you can use in the real world." Those skills come through an education Knoxville students can tailor to suit their own needs, choosing to either focus on a single concentration or to pursue a dual degree with business analytics, engineering, or law. Supply chain management "is the program's flagship area of study," but concentrations in business analytics, entrepreneurship and innovation, finance, human resource management, operations management, and marketing are all on the agenda.

While "there have been a few communication issues between the professors and staff," by and large students praise the accessibility of their teachers and the work of the administration. "The administration works hard to make everything easy for potential and current students," while professors "are very easy to contact and very willing to help." Indeed, "faculty and staff are always available to talk about our career paths and advise us for the future." None of it comes easily—in the classroom, students "are challenged and expected to give maximum effort in order to succeed"—but students wouldn't have it any other way. One student sums it up: "Overall, this program has been a great academic experience and I learn something new about myself and my leadership skills every day."

Career and Placement

Connections and opportunities abound. "The program emphasizes career placement and devotes a lot of time to teaching business skills needed for effective job search and interviewing." The staff can be "instrumental in making professional connections." The program here provides "a lot of networking opportunities in the southeast." In addition, the faculty "are very active in helping find internships as well as providing interview prep and resume writing assistance. They provide a lot of networking lunches, dinners, and other opportunities as well as interesting speakers like the CEO of Walmart."

Most students find placement in the South (about 67 percent) and the Midwest (about 16 percent), with 51 percent of graduates taking jobs in logistics or operations. In recent years, graduating UTK students reported a mean base salary of about $79,000, with a salary range between $43,000 and $135,000.

ADMISSIONS CONTACT: DONNA POTTS, DIRECTOR OF ADMISSIONS, MBA PROGRAM
ADDRESS: 504 HASLAM BUSINESS BUILDING, KNOXVILLE, TN 37996-4150
PHONE: 865-974-5033 • FAX: 865-974-3826
E-MAIL: MBA@UTK.EDU • WEBSITE: MBA.UTK.EDU

Student Life and Environment

Expect a "positive, high energy atmosphere" here driven by a "very friendly and help-ful" student population. In part because "we take a lot of classes in a short period of time, which always keeps us on our toes," students here are quick to support one another. "Everyone is very friendly and willing to help in any way they can." The "fun college town" offers plenty to do, with football being one of the biggest draws, while the "very diverse academic and professional backgrounds (of your classmates) adds to the collec-tive learning." That diversity may be surprising to some. Between 25 and 30 percent of the class is from Europe and Asia, adding a broad mix of viewpoints to the "fast-paced and enjoyable" Knoxville culture.

"There is a very professional culture amongst my classmates that has proven to be quite contagious," but don't mistake that as meaning students don't know how to have fun. "It is not uncommon for a group of more than twenty MBA students to go out together on weekends or attend a cookout together. Overall, everyone gets along very well." Students find that their classmates are "fun to work with in class as well as great to be around outside of class. Everyone has very different backgrounds and stories, which makes our class diverse and interesting."

Admissions

A completed application form, undergraduate transcripts, a GMAT or GRE score report, two letters of recommendation, and four personal essays are required when applying for The University of Tennessee, Knoxville's MBA program. A personal interview is also recommended. Students from the United States are required to have a minimum GPA of 2.7 to be eligible for the program, while international candidates must have the equiv-alent GPA of 3.0 on a 4.0 scale. Incoming students tend to be high performers; in recent years, they had an average undergraduate GPA of 3.4, an average GMAT score of 616, and average work experience totaling over four years.

FINANCIAL FACTS

Annual tuition (in-state/ out-of-state)	$10,618/$28,806
Fees	$13,738
Cost of books	$3,500
Room & board (on/off-campus)	$10,000/$15,000
% of students receiving aid	66
% of first-year students receiving aid	67
% of students receiving grants	45
Average award package	$17,681
Average grant	$8,326
Average loan	$25,678
Average student loan debt	$28,627

ADMISSIONS

Admissions Selectivity Rating	87
# of applications received	205
% applicants accepted	51
% acceptees attending	68
Average GMAT	616
Range of GMAT	570–670
Accepts GRE scores	Yes
Average Verbal GRE	154
Range of Verbal GRE scores	149–160
Average Quantitative GRE	154
Range of Quantitative GRE scores	149–158
Average GPA	3.4
TOEFL required of international students	Yes
Minimum TOEFL (paper/web)	600/100
Application fee	$60
International application fee	$60
Early application deadline	2/1
Regular application deadline	2/1
Deferment available	No
Transfer students accepted	No
Non-fall admissions	No
Need-blind admissions	Yes

EMPLOYMENT PROFILE

Career Rating	92	**Grads Employed by Function% Avg. Salary**	
Percent employed at graduation	63	Marketing	(13%) $73,479
Percent employed 3 months after graduation	76	Operations	(51%) $88,140
		Consulting	(3%)
Average base starting salary	$79,407	Finance	(22%) $66,510
Primary Source of Full-time Job Acceptances		Other	(11%) $71,600
School-facilitated activities	38 (69%)	**Top 5 Employers Hiring Grads**	
Graduate-facilitated activities	17 (31%)	Deloitte (4), EY (3), Caterpillar Logistics (2), FedEx Express (2), PolyOne (2)	

THE UNIVERSITY OF TENNESSEE AT MARTIN

COLLEGE OF BUSINESS AND GLOBAL AFFAIRS

Academics

Offering part-time and full-time hybrid MBA options, as well as an online degree, University of Tennessee at Martin is a friendly, flexible, and low-key place to get a quality business education. The character of the MBA is largely defined by the fact that "UT Martin is a small campus and small school," which encourages relationships and networking within the College of Business. One of the many goals of the MBA curriculum includes developing strong communication and teamwork skills, and "the program requires regular engagement with faculty and fellow students" through both classes and group projects. A current student enthuses, "I love that my professors know my name and connect with me on a level deeper than just academics." The MBA curriculum is focused on the principles of general management, kicking off with a series of core courses in accounting, management, economics, and other key areas, followed by electives. Within the business school, "all professors are good, some are excellent," including strong faculty in finance, management, and other areas.

When students analyze the costs and benefits of pursuing an MBA, the numbers come out in favor of a UT Martin degree. At this state-run school, "the tuition cost is extremely low for an AACSB-accredited degree." Plus, many recent graduates are "offered a graduate assistant position," which helps cover the cost of their education in exchange for working with a UT professor. Convenience and flexibility are also key factors for local professionals. The school offers a hybrid program in Martin, which can be completed either full-time or part-time. MBA candidates attend classes 5 Saturdays per semester, while completing the remainder of the class online, while maintaining full-time employment during the day. While MBA students have a lot on their plate, "academically it is appropriately rigorous, but not too overwhelming for a working adult." Hybrid students can also opt for an MBA with Agricultural Option, which includes taking online Agricultural Economics courses in lieu of MBA elective courses.

In addition to its hybrid program, University of Tennessee—Martin operates a twenty-month fully online MBA for working professionals, whose schedules require the "flexibility of online classes." This program is principally directed at financial services professionals, though coursework covers all important business areas, from marketing to ethics. In the online program, students "usually watch recorded lectures and attend live meetings with the professor and the class once a week." In contrast to the hybrid program, the online curriculum is entirely "cohort-based," which means students complete the core "one class at a time" and in tandem with the same group of students throughout the program. While they do not benefit from face-to-face networking, online students "regularly work with students in workgroups from all around the US using video chat, email, and other collaboration tools." Students describe the experience as "relaxed but challenging," and say, "The professors are willing to go above and beyond to keep the students engaged." When it comes to running the online group, the "administration is absolutely excellent," and they help to "keep us on track" throughout the course of the year-and-a-half program.

Career and Placement

Outside of Memphis, UT Martin's College of Business offers the only AASCB-accredited MBA program in West Tennessee. Even though the campus is located in the small town of Martin, students benefit from the strong University of Tennessee brand name, as well as the extensive alumni network across the many UT campuses.

There is a university-wide Career Employment and Placement Services at the Student Success Center. This office typically assists undergraduate students in making career choices and applying for jobs. However, it does also have regional job opportunities for MBA graduates.

Student Life and Environment

UT Martin's traditional MBA programs attract ambitious professionals from the local region. Hybrid students represent "a good mix of twenty-somethings who are just out of undergraduate work, and career progressives in their thirties who are taking the next steps for success." Students visiting campus for hybrid courses have all the benefits of life in a small college town, which offers a relaxed and affordable environment for work and study. While they have access to the many clubs, organizations, and activities on the larger UT Martin campus, "as a graduate student, its pretty much just class and nothing else." A current student says, "My only extracurricular involvement is serving as a chapter adviser for my fraternity."

Though they may not meet face-to-face, online students still benefit from contact with their classmates—a group of "successful, intelligent, dependable, helpful, working professionals." Coming from Tennessee, as well as the greater United States, students in the online program have "very diverse work experience" and make great contributions to their cohort.

Admissions

University of Tennessee Martin determines a prospective student's admissions eligibility based on an index number, which is calculated using their GMAT or GRE score and GPA. To be accepted to the program unconditionally, students must achieve a score of at least 1050 when their cumulative undergraduate GPA is multiplied by 200 then added to their GMAT or GRE score. Students with a minimum of 7 years of progressive, relevant professional work experience may apply for a waiver of the GMAT or GRE, and those who do not meet published admissions standards may still be eligible for conditional acceptance to the program.

FINANCIAL FACTS

Annual tuition (in-state/ out-of-state)	$14,472/$35,388
Cost of books	$1,500
Room & board (on/off-campus)	$2,800/

ADMISSIONS

Admissions Selectivity Rating	82
# of applications received	22
% applicants accepted	68
% acceptees attending	80
Average GMAT	483
Range of GMAT	460–523
Accepts GRE scores	Yes
Average Verbal GRE	144
Range of Verbal GRE scores	143–145
Average Quantitative GRE	145
Range of Quantitative GRE scores	143–148
Average Writing GRE	3.3
Range of Writing GRE scores	3.0–3.5
Average GPA	3.0
TOEFL required of international students	Yes
Minimum TOEFL (paper/web)	525/
Application fee	$30
International application fee	$30
Application Deadline/Notification	
Deferment available	Yes
Transfer students accepted	Yes
Transfer application policy	
Transfer coursework must be from regionally accredited institution.	
See graduate section of the current catalog for further specifics.	
Non-fall admissions	Yes
Need-blind admissions	Yes

THE UNIVERSITY OF TEXAS AT ARLINGTON
COLLEGE OF BUSINESS

GENERAL INFORMATION

Type of school	Public
Affiliation	No Affiliation
Academic calendar	Semester

SURVEY SAYS...
Happy students
Solid preparation in:
General management, Teamwork,
Presentation skills

STUDENTS

Enrollment of parent institution	37,008
Enrollment of MBA Program	350
% part-time	100
Average age at entry	29
Average years work experience at entry	5

ACADEMICS

Academic Experience Rating	**90**
Profs interesting rating	89
Profs accessible rating	81
Student/faculty ratio	22:1
% female faculty	30
% underrepresented minority faculty	28
% part-time faculty	21

Joint Degrees
May combine two degrees (usually MBA and specialized program) or a business degree with others, such as Engineering, Architecture, and Science. Can obtain second degree with as few as 18 additional hours.

Prominent Alumni
Gen. Tommy Franks, U.S. Army (ret.); John Goolsby, President CEO (ret.) - Howard Hughes Corporation; Roy Williams, Chief Scot Exec. (ret.) - Boy Scouts America; Jerry Thomas, President & CEO - Decision Analyst, Inc.; Jackie Fouse, Sr. VP, CFO & Corp Strategy - Bunge, Ltd.

Academics

The University of Texas at Arlington is "a highly recognized" business program that is "a good value for the dollar" with "strong alumni," "a good reputation, and is fully AACSB accredited." Many students enjoy the "cohort format of the program," which allows students to grow and learn together. A real strength of the MBA program is how it "caters to people who have a full-time job. Almost all classes start about 7:00 P.M. so that commuters have time to get to class." Commuters can face some problems as "parking is horrendous, and it is extremely expensive." One student claims "I pay over $100 and still have to walk half a mile or more to class."

"The College of Business at UTA is at the cutting edge of the business world," one student says. "Our professors and administrators are always looking for the most innovative ideas or technologies, and the students get to research them and learn that not only the proven facts work, but also new ones." The campus is "very clean and very well organized" and "undergoing massive renovations to improve the quality of the campus. The overall appeal of the University should increase dramatically" once the renovations are done.

"The professors here are great," and the faculty is a real strength of the program. "Professors are tough, but they know well what they teach" and "have real-life work experience in what they are teaching." "The teaching styles have been diverse, but effective, and the professors are always interested in helping students succeed." One student says, "Ninety-five percent of the faculty is truly passionate about teaching students." Students who like to know where they stand academically may get slightly frustrated as "finding out grades is next to impossible," and you "very rarely know where you stand in class grade-wise until grades are posted."

"The administration must be the best in Texas," as they are "very helpful and there to answer any questions you have." "I liked the fact that it had two different programs to choose from: the cohort and the flexible," one student explains. Another student says the administration "even tailored a 'hybrid' program for me based on my situation." The career center "needs to bring in more companies" though, and "UTA should focus less on recruiting international students and more on recruiting U.S. students from other states."

Career and Placement

University of Texas at Arlington is "recognized by companies" around the country and has a good placement track record. UTA's brand is especially recognized in its region, and the "close proximity to Dallas" and Fort Worth gives students opportunities to establish connections with local businesses for when they graduate. "The school has established a very good rapport with businesses around the metroplex that easily absorb fresh graduates!" Some students did feel the school could do more to "partner with local, national, and international businesses." One caveat to note is that "members of the professional cohort MBA program" study on another campus, and "its students are not informed of the main campus job fairs or placement services."

Some prominent alumnae include John Goolsby, the retired CEO of Howard Hughes Corporation; Roy Williams, retired Chief Scout Exec. of Boy Scouts of America; and Jackie Fouse, President of Global Hematology and Oncology at Celgene.

ADMISSIONS CONTACT: REBECCA NEILSON, DIRECTOR OF GRADUATE BUSINESS SERVICES
ADDRESS: BOX 19376, ARLINGTON, TX 76019
PHONE: 817-272-3004 • FAX: 817-272-5799
E-MAIL: RNEILSON@UTA.EDU • WEBSITE: WWW.UTA.EDU/GRADBIZ

Student Life and Environment

"As the program is designed for working individuals, a large majority work," and most of the students are "less than thirty years old." Life on the UTA campus is "very casual and relaxed," although there is "practically no life at school other than to attend classes." "The campus is well designed to provide plenty of areas for students to gather and be respected." Graduate students "mostly all work full time" between jobs, classes, and studying. "We're very removed from the 'social' side of the University," one student explains.

UTA "has an extremely diverse makeup that includes students from all over the world," and "everyone of all races gets along very well." Although some students feel that despite the "very diverse" makeup, the student body is "segregated." In addition to racial and international diversity, the school sports "working professionals, working students, and non-working" students. Working students come "from the defense, pharmaceuticals, information technology, transportation, construction, and other service industries," and "we really teach each other, lending experience and hard-learned career knowledge to fellow classmates."

Admissions

UT Arlington carefully considers both quantitative and qualitative factors in every admissions decision. Although not required, professional experience after earning a bachelor's degree is factored heavily alongside GMAT scores, GPA, personal essay, and letters of recommendation. Average GMAT and GPA scores for last year's class were 550 and 3.4 respectively.

FINANCIAL FACTS

Annual tuition (in-state/ out-of-state)	$9,022/$17,775
Cost of books	$1,206
Room & board (on/off-campus)	$9,222/$9,222
% of students receiving aid	43
% of first-year students receiving aid	46
% of students receiving grants	24
Average award package	$14,781
Average grant	$4,343
Average loan	$15,047
Average student loan debt	$29,118

ADMISSIONS

Admissions Selectivity Rating	**88**
# of applications received	229
% applicants accepted	41
% acceptees attending	91
Average GMAT	518
Accepts GRE scores	Yes
Average Verbal GRE	156
Average Quantitative GRE	154
Average GPA	3.4
TOEFL required of international students	Yes
Minimum TOEFL (paper/web)	550/79
Application fee	$40
International application fee	$90
Regular application deadline	6/15
Application Deadline/Notification	
Deferment available	Yes
Maximum length of deferment	1 year
Transfer students accepted	Yes
Transfer application policy	
Maximum number of transferable credits is nine. Grades 'B' or better from an AACSB accredited university. Policy will vary based on the program.	
Non-fall admissions	Yes
Need-blind admissions	Yes

EMPLOYMENT PROFILE		
Career Rating	72	**Top 5 Employers Hiring Grads**
		Fidelity, TD Ameritrade, Lockheed Martin, BNSF, Bell Helicopter

THE UNIVERSITY OF TEXAS AT AUSTIN
McCOMBS SCHOOL OF BUSINESS

GENERAL INFORMATION

Type of school	Public
Affiliation	No Affiliation
Academic calendar	Semester

SURVEY SAYS...

Classmates have diverse work experience, Friendly students, Good peer network, Good social scene, Abundant mentors available
Solid preparation in:
Finance, Accounting, General management, Teamwork, Communication/interpersonal skills

STUDENTS

Enrollment of parent institution	50,950
Enrollment of MBA Program	979
% male/female	68/32
% out-of-state	36
% part-time	45
% underrepresented minority	11
% international	28
Average age at entry	28
Average years work experience at entry	5

ACADEMICS

Academic Experience Rating	96
Profs interesting rating	93
Profs accessible rating	97
Student/faculty ratio	4:1
% female faculty	22
% underrepresented minority faculty	5
% part-time faculty	21

Joint Degrees

MBA/Master of Arts in Asian Studies; MBA/Master of Arts in Advertising; MBA/Master of Arts in Communication Studies; MBA/Master of Arts in Journalism; MBA/Master of Arts in Radio-Television-Film; MBA/Master of Arts in Energy and Earth Resources; MBA/Master of Mechanical Engineering; MBA/Master of Global Policy Studies; MBA/Master of Arts in Latin American Studies; MBA/Doctor of Jurisprudence; MBA/Master of Arts

Academics

The University of Texas at Austin is "well-known for academic excellence in many aspects, such as accounting, entrepreneurial, IT management, marketing, and energy finance." The School's "good entrepreneurial track [record]" and "reasonable cost of living" in "one of the most fun cities in the United States" makes it attractive to students across the nation. "Austin provides a great environment for business school students" as it is "a hotbed of entrepreneurial activity." Some highlights of McCombs include the "Marketing Fellows organization in academics" and the "commitment to development of the top energy reputation among business schools." Students have "a great deal of freedom in which classes we take," and there is a "collaborative, yet competitive team-based atmosphere" where "students support each other." Academics are "very rigorous," and the "workload is pretty high, but people help each other." "It's intense but not insane," one student explains. "The course work is very intense for a semester and then frees up a bit." Overall, the Texas MBA "is a very rigorous program academically, yet students still find time to have fun." The School gives students the "ability to personalize your degree and supplement it with courses from other UT graduate programs."

The "administration does a good job of running things," "supporting the students," and improving "the overall academic experience." "Students have incredible freedom to start new programs with very few restrictions from administration," one student explains. The "administration is very involved with the MBA program," although it can be "a bit disorganized" and "disconnected from students." "The MBA program office is great and easy to work with; the only difficulties arise when we have to deal with the UT bureaucracy." "The UT campus in general is beautiful, but the business school buildings need some serious attention," and "the food available for the business school building is average at best." "I know you want to keep the revenues in house, but get us some real grub!" one student laments. The new Robert B. Rowling Hall, set to open in 2017, will house the MBA program and offer 504,000 sq ft of state-of-the-art classrooms, conference rooms, research centers, and a new cafe.

Students love their professors, who are "very accessible and knowledgeable" and "have had practical work experience that makes them that much better." "Ninety-five percent of the instructors are very engaging, accessible, intelligent, inspiring, and passionate about the material they teach." This "excellent" faculty is a "good mix of academics with a strong history of research and practitioners who have real-world knowledge," such as "leading researchers and ex-CEOs." "Class content is nicely divided up between theory, case, and simulation." One student says, "It has been more challenging than I could have ever imagined, but after going through this, I know I will be prepared for anything."

Career and Placement

McCombs has an "enthusiastic alumni base" and "strong employer connections," which help provide excellent career placement for its graduates. "Career services is one of the best in the nation," one student boasts. The "health of the Texas economy" in general offers "solid post-graduation job opportunities." "Texas is the place to be in terms of oil and gas and renewable," says one government and public policy student. McCombs' Investment Fund, Venture Fellows program, MBA+, and the Venture Labs Investment Competition are all excellent opportunities for hands-on learning" that the school provides to help students eventually find careers.

The school claims that 75 percent of students have job offers at graduation, and 91 percent find employment within three months of graduation. Some prominent alumni include Jim Mulva, President & CEO of Conoco Phillips; William Johnson, Chairman, President & CEO of Heinz; and Sara Martinez Tucker, President & CEO of the National Science & Math Initiative. Hewlett Packard, Dell, Advanced Micro Devices (AMD), Bank of America, and Deloitte Consulting are a handful of the many companies that recruit McCombs MBA graduates.

Student Life and Environment

The students at McCombs are "intelligent, clever, extremely hard working—the epitome of go-getters." Students "consistently beat top schools (including Ivy League) at National Case Competitions." "My classmates are from so many different backgrounds that it is impossible to characterize them," one student says. The student body is somewhat more "liberal" than your average business school, although it strikes "a good balance of conservative Texans and generally smart people who are open to social chemistry." "The culture really sets University of Texas at Austin apart," and students here are "very diverse and very competitive, but always willing to help." "Everyone is willing to help one another; it's not dog eat dog." "Everyone is very social, but this is NOT a party school," one student says. "I'm constantly in awe of the breadth and depth of the intelligence and experience that my peers have to offer." The school is also located in one of the most dynamic and interesting cities in the country. "I love Austin; it's a fantastic place to go to school," says one student. "While I'm very busy with school activities, our class always finds ways to socialize and enjoy Austin." Another student says, "Austin is the greatest city in the United States. I am going to miss it dearly."

Admissions

The McCombs School of Business only accepts online applications. A completed application must include a resume detailing work history (Two years of post-baccalaureate work experience is strongly recommended.), personal essays, official copies of transcripts for all post-secondary academic work, letters of recommendation, and an official score report for the GMAT. The average undergraduate GPA and GMAT scores for the most recent class were about 3.4 and 694 respectively.

in Middle Eastern Studies; MBA/ Master of Science in Nursing; MBA/ Master of Arts in Public Affairs; MBA/Master of Arts in Russian, East European, and Eurasian Studies

Prominent Alumni

Jim Mulva, Former President & CEO/Conoco Phillips; Robert B. Rowling, Founder, TRT Holdings (Omni Hotels, Golds Gym)

FINANCIAL FACTS

Annual tuition (in-state/ out-of-state)	$33,298/$48,832
Cost of books	$6,774
Room & board (on/off-campus)	$12,620/$12,620
% of students receiving aid	42
% of first-year students receiving aid	40
% of students receiving grants	29
Average award package	$38,634
Average grant	$10,197
Average loan	$40,041
Average student loan debt	$62,525

ADMISSIONS

Admissions Selectivity Rating	94
# of applications received	2,266
% applicants accepted	30
% acceptees attending	39
Average GMAT	694
Range of GMAT	680–720
Accepts GRE scores	Yes
Average Verbal GRE	160
Range of Verbal GRE scores	157–163
Average Quantitative GRE	158
Range of Quantitative GRE scores	156–161
Average GPA	3.4
TOEFL required of international students	Yes
Application fee	$200
International application fee	$200
Application Deadline/Notification	
Round 1:	10/13 / 12/17
Round 2:	1/12 / 3/29
Round 3:	3/31 / 5/12
Deferment available	Yes
Maximum length of deferment	1 year
Transfer students accepted	No
Non-fall admissions	No
Need-blind admissions	Yes

EMPLOYMENT PROFILE

Career Rating	97	Grads Employed by Function% Avg. Salary	
Percent employed at graduation	74	Marketing	(14%) $102,310
Percent employed 3 months after graduation	87	Operations	(6%) $92,814
		Consulting	(30%) $130,728
Average base starting salary	$113,787	Management	(11%) $101,679
Primary Source of Full-time Job Acceptances		Finance	(28%) $113,464
School-facilitated activities	149 (69%)	HR	(1%)
Graduate-facilitated activities	60 (28%)	Other	(10%) $105,450
Unknown	6 (3%)	**Top 5 Employers Hiring Grads**	
		Deloitte (19), Dell (13), PwC (12), Strategy& (5), Microsoft Corp (4)	

THE UNIVERSITY OF TEXAS AT DALLAS
NAVEEN JINDAL SCHOOL OF MANAGEMENT

Academics

UT Dallas's Naveen Jindal School of Management is a program on the rise. This "growing" program's "rankings are [...] skyrocketing and school is drawing more attention." Perhaps this is because it is "the only affordable school in Dallas," a city with "great economic opportunity." Students rave about UT Dallas's "great return on investment." The "fast track format" means "the length of the program is only sixteen months" and the school has a "high degree of flexibility." "Credits over fifteen are free" however restrictions on credits vary by program one student explains. "So, I can earn a discount on both time and money by working at my own pace." The school has a "hybrid on campus and online program" that is popular. "I wanted in-person classes, but the flexibility to attend some online classes as well," one student explains. The location in Dallas means "proximity to companies that hire MBAs." UT Dallas's "high educational standards" give it "a good reputation in the market and with area businesses."

"There are a few bad professors, but the majority" of them are "very committed and capable" and "some of the professors are absolute gems." "Most of the professors are experienced experts in their subjects, not just ivory tower academics." That said, most professors do have degrees from "top tier institutions" such as "The University of Chicago, UT Austin, Duke, and Harvard." Professors here apply the material "to real life situations." "I have NEVER had trouble contacting a professor by email when I have a question and they always respond within about 8 hours," one student says. "The program director and the administrative staff do an excellent job" and the staff is "smart, useful, and helpful." Some students do say that the "administration can be a little unorganized, particularly the career center." Overall, "the Jindal business school really does run like a well-oiled machine!"

Career and Placement

"The school is great for Dallas Area networking" and "well regarded by management professionals in the area." Some students think the Dallas focus can come at the expense of other areas. "The only companies that the career management center works with are local," one student explains. "This is a huge challenge for students who are not local." While one student says "career services is awful" another notes that "it did increase my earnings by 54 percent upon completion." "More companies are coming to the School of Management than before," and some companies that have hired recent grads include "AT&T, JP Morgan, Verizon, Ericsson, Southwest Airlines, [and] Dr. Pepper Snapple." The school says its placement rate is around 90 percent and that the average starting salary for graduates is around $81,000.

Student Life and Environment

The "awesome blossom" student body is "intelligent, global," "friendly," and, "diverse." Many students are "from India and Asia" and school is very "racially diverse." "They offer a unique view of business because of the many different backgrounds that are present at UT Dallas," one student explains. UT Dallas students are "hard working," "intelligent, and experienced." "I look forward to discussions because of their insight and ability to express thoughts carefully," one student says. Students interested in Greek life will be relieved to hear it is "improving" on campus, and there are thirty student organizations that business students can join. The experience of student life varies since students are divided between full-time, hybrid, evening, and online. "There was a strong sense of camaraderie amongst the Full-time class," but the evening program "attracts commuter students who want to get in, learn, and get out." Commuter students tend to not "make the effort to get involved with clubs and activities around the campus." Still, "even the busiest students with careers, families, night jobs, etc. give their best effort here. They participate as much as they can and have great work ethic, especially in teams."

Admissions

UT Dallas admissions are very completive and selective, especially for the full-time MBA program. The exact requirements for admission depend on which program you are applying to. The average student enters UT Dallas with five years of work experience and the average age is 28. Recent students have had an average GPA of 3.5 and GMAT scores ranging between 650 and 710 (25th to 75th percentiles).

FINANCIAL FACTS

Annual tuition (in-state/ out-of-state)	$15,242/$30,855
Fees	$3,800
Cost of books	$2,000
Room & board (on/off-campus)	$7,500/$7,500

ADMISSIONS

Admissions Selectivity Rating	96
# of applications received	484
% applicants accepted	22
% acceptees attending	53
Average GMAT	678
Range of GMAT	650–710
Accepts GRE scores	Yes
Average Verbal GRE	156
Range of Verbal GRE scores	152–161
Average Quantitative GRE	157
Range of Quantitative GRE scores	154–161
Average Writing GRE	4.0
Range of Writing GRE scores	3.5–4.0
Average GPA	3.5
TOEFL required of international students	Yes
Minimum TOEFL (paper/web)	550/90
Application fee	$100
International application fee	$150
Early application deadline	10/15
Early notification date	12/20
Regular application deadline	5/1
Regular application notification	6/15
Application Deadline/Notification	
Round 1:	10/15 / 12/20
Round 2:	1/15 / 2/20
Round 3:	3/1 / 4/15
Round 4:	5/1 / 6/15
Deferment available	Yes
Maximum length of deferment	one year
Transfer students accepted	Yes
Transfer application policy Full-Time (Cohort) MBA accepts 6 hours if they qualify. PMBA accepts 12 if they qualify.	
Non-fall admissions	Yes
Need-blind admissions	Yes

EMPLOYMENT PROFILE

Career Rating	85		
Percent employed at graduation	58	**Grads Employed by Function% Avg. Salary**	
Percent employed 3 months		Marketing	(19%) $83,000
after graduation	35	Operations	(13%) $78,250
Average base starting salary	$82,551	Consulting	(25%) $76,998
Primary Source of Full-time Job Acceptances		Management	(19%) $96,667
School-facilitated activities	13 (33%)	Finance	(9%) $87,000
Graduate-facilitated activities	27 (68%)	MIS	(16%) $74,728

Top 5 Employers Hiring Grads

Ericsson (4), Sabre (4), Tango Management Consulting (4), Deloitte (3), Hewlett Packard (3)

THE UNIVERSITY OF TEXAS AT SAN ANTONIO
COLLEGE OF BUSINESS

Academics

The University of Texas at San Antonio, or simply UTSA, is a school "developing rapidly in the UT system, and the College of Business is one of the top business schools in the South." With a "high reputation" for top-notch "finance and marketing courses," "generous scholarships," and "great professors," UTSA benefits greatly from the "UT name" and is a place where students are encouraged to "develop their own career paths." A good portion of students also mention that UTSA is a "conveniently located" and "relatively inexpensive" option for MBA students. One student with a concentration in supply chain/operations management tells us, "[my] coworkers graduated from UTSA and [gave it a] good recommendation."

Like a lot of large business schools, UTSA MBA candidates have both praise and criticism for their faculty. According to one student, of the 109 faculty members currently working in the business school, all are "excellent, with outstanding academic knowledge and contributions." But another student says, "Professors are quick to tell you they are only here for the research money and that they don't like teaching students . . . Professors are quick to judge and often make discouraging comments about the students who struggle." Given the feedback we have received, the consensus seems to be that "this school has really tried to attract great faculty and support them in teaching." In turn, while UTSA continues to grow in both size and reputation within the UT system, there is a balance of "great" professors, who infuse their courses with a "heavy research aspect," and others who "don't have any business teaching."

The College of Business at UTSA offers a flexible MBA (students can attend part time or full time). Students can choose a general MBA (no concentration) or an MBA in a variety of eleven concentrations. Additional degree options include an Executive MBA (designed for seasoned executives, professional, and entrepreneurs), a Ph.D. in business administration, and a Ph.D. in applied statistics. Discipline based Master's programs include a master of arts in economics; master of science degrees in applied statistics, finance, finance with real estate concentration, information technology, information technology with a cyber security concentration, and management of technology—all of which are thirty-three-credit hour programs. UTSA also offers a master of accountancy degree, which is thirty credit hours. In addition to the school's vast academic arsenal, the College of Business offers international immersion programs in Brazil, the Canary Islands, Chile, China, Finland, Italy, Morocco, Singapore, Spain and Vietnam. In short, UTSA MBA candidates have "attended programs all over the world."

Career and Placement

Based on recent feedback from students, it's apparent that UTSA has made improvements in recent years to its Career Services office, as well as to the school's recruitment events, where students are offered abundant "opportunities to meet with national and international companies." According to one student, "I find there to be many strong relationships between employers and the business school. Most of the professors and counseling staff seem well connected and ready to help students network. I would admit though, that many of the opportunities are either local or regional." "There are good companies that recruit and sponsor events." Regional companies, such as Valero, Ernst & Young, Deloitte, and KPMG, just to name a few, have actively recruited UTSA students in the past, but data also indicate many graduates end up finding work outside Texas and the Southwest region at large. One student, who works part time as a teaching assistant says, "There are so many opportunities for students to attend amazing workshops and certifications and hear interesting business speakers for free," all in addition to the College of Business's popular internship and faculty-led study abroad programs. "I think at other bigger-named schools," the same student continues, "it would be hard to be a name instead of a number and more challenging to get all the services and support that this program provides."

Student Life and Environment

The MBA program at UTSA is mostly geared toward the working professional, which would explain why "most of the MBA classes are at night." While this has obvious benefits for those with full-time jobs, "they could offer more classes during the day." "They are trying to change that," one student reminds us. "The staff and faculty really try to provide time for us to network and force us into groups so that we can connect." We are told there is "an excellent diversity of students" in the UTSA MBA program, many of whom describe their fellow students as "very kind and creative," "studious," "rich [with] work experience and a spirit of teamwork."

There is no shortage of activities on UTSA's campus. The library has been described to us as "one of the nicest in the country right now," although the "stacks are a bit dreary, but the aesthetics don't limit the selection." There is also a top-rated rec center, and the "food on campus is great, with recent additions, such as Chili's, Subway, Pita-Grill" and various other cuisine choices for all tastes.

Admissions

Applicants to the MBA program at The University of Texas at San Antonio are required to submit the following: GMAT scores, essay/personal statement, and an official undergraduate transcript. Letter of reference, resume, proof of state residency, and a list of extracurricular activities are all optional, but encouraged, if relevant to an applicant's planned course of study. Admissions will pay particularly close attention to GMAT scores and undergraduate GPA. Incoming students had an average of 588 and 3.2 respectively. International candidates are required to submit TOEFL scores (550 minimum for written test, 213 minimum for computer-based test).

FINANCIAL FACTS

Annual tuition (in-state/ out-of-state)	$4,671/$19,030
Fees	$3,025

ADMISSIONS

Admissions Selectivity Rating	**89**
# of applications received	146
% applicants accepted	39
% acceptees attending	81
Average GMAT	588
Range of GMAT	538–650
Accepts GRE scores	Yes
Average Verbal GRE	153
Range of Verbal GRE scores	149–156
Average Quantitative GRE	153
Range of Quantitative GRE scores	150–155
Average Writing GRE	4.0
Range of Writing GRE scores	3.6–4.0
Average GPA	3.2
TOEFL required of international students	Yes
Minimum TOEFL (paper/web)	550/79
Application fee	$50
International application fee	$90
Regular application deadline	7/1
Application Deadline/Notification	
Deferment available	Yes
Maximum length of deferment	2 terms
Transfer students accepted	Yes
Transfer application policy Please refer to Current Graduate Catalog.	
Non-fall admissions	Yes
Need-blind admissions	Yes

EMPLOYMENT PROFILE

Career Rating	87	Grads Employed by Function	% Avg. Salary
Percent employed at graduation	50	Other	(100%) $54,000
Percent employed 3 months after graduation	69		
Average base starting salary	$54,000		
Primary Source of Full-time Job Acceptances			
School-facilitated activities	4 (36%)		
Graduate-facilitated activities	7 (64%)		

THE UNIVERSITY OF TEXAS—PAN AMERICAN
COLLEGE OF BUSINESS ADMINISTRATION

GENERAL INFORMATION

Type of school	Public
Affiliation	No Affiliation
Academic calendar	Semester

SURVEY SAYS...
Friendly students, Happy students
Solid preparation in:
Finance, General management,
Operations

STUDENTS

Enrollment of parent institution	17,500
Enrollment of MBA Program	186
% male/female	68/32
% part-time	69
% underrepresented minority	75
% international	15
Average age at entry	31
Average years work experience at entry	2

ACADEMICS

Academic Experience Rating	**87**
Profs interesting rating	90
Profs accessible rating	93
Student/faculty ratio	27:1
% female faculty	30
% part-time faculty	0

Academics

The University of Texas—Pan American offers two tracks to an MBA, one through evening courses and another via online classes. Both are accredited by the American Assembly of Collegiate Schools of Business (AACSB). Students with an undergraduate degree in business can complete the evening program in just two years. Further specialization is offered upon completion of nine extra credit hours in one of the following disciplines: accounting, economics, finance, management, management information systems, and marketing.

Students agree that UTPA "offers quality education at an affordable cost." It's "close to the border" with a big focus on Latin American business. Class sizes are small. "You aren't only a number, but you have an identity." Students say professors know their names and are "dedicated" to their professions. They are also well versed in the material, and at the same time, "open to debate." The program's director "is always available and knows everyone in the program personally." She "demands the best of her instructors and makes changes if they are not providing the quality of work she expects." This results in classes that "are interesting and interactive. Everyone is given the chance to speak and have an opinion." "Each and every professor is knowledgeable in their field of study, and they are accessible." Professors respond "promptly to emails," "even late at night and on weekends." One student says, "I have enjoyed every class, and I utilize the knowledge gained on a daily basis." Students feel challenged, yet supported. "Every MBA class I have taken has required numerous case study reviews and numerous team projects. We have reviewed approximately fifty to sixty case studies of different subject matter in a year. These have been instrumental." Students "work well together, both in and out of the classroom environment." "Everyone is willing to contribute."

As far as the administration is concerned, "they do the best they can with what they have. Improvements can always be made." Students say, "The number of elective classes needs to be improved." They'd like to see more variety and perhaps different times for classes. Also, some feel frustrated when classes that are offered get cancelled. However, "for the most part, everything runs smoothly."

Career and Placement

The career office at UTPA serves both graduate and undergraduate students. CARIR, or the Center for Advisement, Recruitment, Internships, and Retention, offers career counseling and job-related assistance. However, most students feel that the "career center needs a lot of improvement." They would like to see "more efforts for career placement." One student believes that there are "no internships" readily available to students, and that it is "hard to be placed after graduation." However, both regional and national job databases do exist. Students can access them through their UTPA accounts. The office also hosts workshops on resume writing, networking, and other helpful career strategies. The following are just some organizations that hire UTPA graduates: Proctor and Gamble, Texas Instruments, Boeing Ernest and Young, and Northrop Grunman.

Student Life and Environment

Students describe fellow students as "the type of people who go the extra mile for anybody." They are "smart," "extremely friendly," and "always willing to lend a helping hand." The student body at UTPA is "honest," "mature," and "easy to talk to." UTPA "has a great cultural feel." "One of my classes has students from India, Mexico, Texas, China, Japan, Taiwan, Turkey, France, Romania, and I'm sure I've missed a couple others." Students are "very open to new cultures" and "create a learning environment that is conducive to expanding one's ideas." Another student says, "We are all like one big family." Students "keep in touch even when the final days of a course are over."

The University of Texas is located in Edinburg, Texas, where the cost of living is low and the "weather is good." UTPA is "far south of the northern snow." The gym "is brand new," and has "very good equipment." There are "movie nights when new releases come out for free" and other "events, from poker tournaments to trips to Europe." Some students "work full time" and have families, so their "time on campus is spent in the classroom during the week and in the library on the weekends." However, "a good portion of students don't have kids and often enjoy hanging out with each other on the weekends." There are also collaborative projects every semester, so even when students don't have time to socialize, they are still creating friendships through schoolwork.

Admissions

Applicants seeking admission to the College of Business are asked to submit the following materials to the Admissions Committee: sealed copies of official transcripts sent directly from all post-secondary institutions previously attended; official GMAT scores; three letters of recommendation; a current resume; a personal essay answering five specific questions; and the general application for the UPTA Graduate School. The most important criteria are the GMAT score and GPA. The committee will also consider extracurricular activities and work experience. Most applicants average two years work experience. The average GPA of accepted students is 3.0, and the average GMAT score is 450. Roughly one in two applicants is admitted.

FINANCIAL FACTS

Annual tuition (in-state/ out-of-state)	$2,797/$8,900
Fees	$314
Cost of books	$1,500
Average grant	$10,000
Average loan	$6,000

ADMISSIONS

Admissions Selectivity Rating	84
# of applications received	78
% applicants accepted	47
% acceptees attending	73
Average GMAT	450
Range of GMAT	380–555
Average GPA	3.0
TOEFL required of international students	Yes
Minimum TOEFL (paper/web)	500/
Application fee	$50
International application fee	$50
Early application deadline	12/1
Regular application deadline	8/1
Deferment available	Yes
Maximum length of deferment	One semester
Transfer students accepted	Yes
Transfer application policy Accept max. 3 courses	
Non-fall admissions	Yes
Need-blind admissions	Yes

THE UNIVERSITY OF TOLEDO
COLLEGE OF BUSINESS AND INNOVATION

GENERAL INFORMATION

Type of school	Public
Affiliation	No Affiliation
Academic calendar	Semester

SURVEY SAYS...
Friendly students
Solid preparation in:
General management, Teamwork, Presentation skills, Social responsibility

STUDENTS

Enrollment of parent institution	21,500
Enrollment of MBA Program	403
% male/female	61/39
% out-of-state	12
% part-time	74
% underrepresented minority	56
% international	30
Average age at entry	28
Average years work experience at entry	5

ACADEMICS

Academic Experience Rating	85
Profs interesting rating	89
Profs accessible rating	91
Student/faculty ratio	10:1
% female faculty	36
% underrepresented minority faculty	3
% part-time faculty	4

Joint Degrees
JD/MBA - 3-4 years, MD/MBA - 4-5 years, MPH/MBA- 20 months - 24 months

Prominent Alumni
Edward Kinsey, Co-Founder, Ariba, Inc.; Ora Alleman, VP, National City Bank; Michael Durik, Executive VP, The Limited Stores, Inc.; Marvin Herb, CEO Coca-Cola Bottling Company; Julie Higgins, Exective VP, The Trust Company of Toledo

Academics

Professionalism and value are just two of the reasons an MBA degree from The University of Toledo's College of Business and Innovation are an "immensely valuable" asset. Students can choose to begin the program in the Fall, Spring, or Summer semesters and proceed at their own pace without any formal declaration of full-time versus part-time; most people choose to work and attend classes at night, but "there is a growing group of younger MBA students who are attending full-time." The curriculum consists of Foundation Courses (which can be waived prior to enrollment for those who earned a C or better in equivalent undergraduate courses), Core Courses, and a minimum of three electives; these specialized classes are often "only offered at one time per semester" and students do report that they can be difficult to get into. The courses "are all around the same time so there is no leaving and coming back to campus," and for those with busy schedules or with geographic limitations, there are also opportunities to take classes online or in blended settings.

All professors are "extremely proficient and able to pass that knowledge along to their students," and "really interested in creating a learning environment for their students."

According to one student, "they made the decision on what aspect of business to get my degree in very hard. This is due to the fact they are all paragons of their field and make them all seem like a good career." These individuals take a progressive pedagogical approach and help change the course experience by "encouraging research and using modern technologies," and many of the MBA classes also "bring in external community leaders to give presentations and help prepare us to be future business leaders." The school administration similarly "does a great job of communicating with the students about beneficial events and speakers" and works hard "to put students' priorities first and operate as effectively and efficiently as possible."

Career and Placement

The Business Career Programs office "does an amazing job assisting MBAs with job placement if needed," and "treat you as a professional rather than a student." The office "works tirelessly to continually provide networking opportunities and career fairs." As the business school is known for being "extremely strict on GPA policies, and those who don't cut it get sent home," the UT reputation carries weight with the region's employers. The alumni base "creates a network that is global and more prominent than ever before," and activities such as the Advanced Leadership Academy provide opportunities for students "to listen and interact with UT alumni on discussion panels that encompass a broad range of business issues and provide invaluable information for students to take with them."

Recent employers of UT MBAs include Chrysler, University of Michigan Health System, First Solar, Ernst & Young, GM Powertrain, KeyBank, Heartland Information Systems, Hickory Farms, National City Corporation, Tenneco, Owens-Illinois, and Owens Corning.

Student Life and Environment

This slice of the UT population is "diverse in age, race, citizenship, and varying education backgrounds" and also happens to be "very nice and welcoming." This diversity "enriches class discussions and takes topics into a global level." As most students are working full-time, they commute in ("parking truly is a hassle on campus"), and the structure of the campus means that "unlike most schools, there are not spots students can go to" for long periods of downtime. This means there is not really much of a "scene of the university," though "there are lots arts-related activities on campus" for those who are looking. Downtown Toledo itself "has lots of clubs and restaurants, an awesome ballpark, the Huntington Arena, the Art Museum, [and] the Valentine Theatre," but it can be difficult to make time to take advantage. "People need to get down there and move around," says a student.

Admissions

Applicants to the MBA program at UT must submit the following materials: a completed application; official copies of transcripts from each undergraduate and graduate institution attended; three letters of recommendation; and an official score report for the GMAT. In addition to the above, all international applicants must submit a financial statement and supporting documents. International applicants from countries in which English is not the primary language must submit an official score report for the TOEFL. Students are encouraged to complete their applications online.

FINANCIAL FACTS

Annual tuition (in-state/ out-of-state)	$12,096/$21,984
Fees	$1,190
Cost of books	$1,200
Room & board (on/off-campus)	$0/$5,830
Average grant	$17,646
Average loan	$18,500

ADMISSIONS

Admissions Selectivity Rating	79
# of applications received	175
% applicants accepted	95
% acceptees attending	98
Average GMAT	525
Range of GMAT	450–680
Accepts GRE scores	No
Average GPA	3.2
TOEFL required of international students	Yes
Minimum TOEFL (paper/web)	550/80
Application fee	$45
International application fee	$75
Application Deadline/Notification	
Deferment available	Yes
Maximum length of deferment	1 semester
Transfer students accepted	Yes
Transfer application policy Maximum 9 credit hours with at least a B from an AACSB-accredited school.	
Non-fall admissions	Yes
Need-blind admissions	Yes

EMPLOYMENT PROFILE	
Career Rating	84
Percent employed at graduation	37
Percent employed 3 months after graduation	84

THE UNIVERSITY OF TULSA
COLLINS COLLEGE OF BUSINESS

GENERAL INFORMATION

Type of school	Private
Affiliation	No Affiliation
Academic calendar	Semester

SURVEY SAYS...
Friendly students
Solid preparation in:
Teamwork, General management,
Communication/interpersonal skills

STUDENTS

Enrollment of parent institution	4,671
Enrollment of MBA Program	86
% male/female	57/43
% out-of-state	12
% part-time	51
% underrepresented minority	10
% international	26
Average age at entry	27
Average years work experience at entry	2

ACADEMICS

Academic Experience Rating	69
Profs interesting rating	73
Profs accessible rating	68
Student/faculty ratio	11:1
% female faculty	19
% underrepresented minority faculty	9
% part-time faculty	19

Joint Degrees
MBA/MSF Dual Degree - 54 Hours
MSF/MSAM Dual Degree - 54 Hours
JD/MBA - 108 Hours/4 Years JD/
MSF - 108 Hours/4 Years

Prominent Alumni
Doug McMillon, President and CEO, Wal-Mart International; Al Walker, Chairman, President and CEO of Anadarko Petroleum Company; Chet Cadieux, Chairman and CEO Quiktrip Corporation; Paula Kuykendall, Retired Senior Vice President and Chief Accounting Officer, Hilton Hotels Worldwide; Stu Crum, President and CEO, Bridgestone Tires Retail Operations

Academics

The University of Tulsa operates a rigorous and contemporary MBA program within the context of a small, friendly, private school environment. With a "low student-to-professor ratio," class sizes are uniformly small, and "you really get a chance to develop relationships with the faculty and other students." In the classroom, the teaching staff gets top marks for experience: "Many of them are leaders in their fields and have remained very current and relevant to the vast changes we are seeing economically and globally." They are also excellent educators, and "although classes are difficult and grades are competitive, the professors are able to drive home the overall picture of what we are studying and why." Most importantly, TU is a thoroughly supportive environment, so it's easy to stay on the right track academically. If a student needs extra help (or just wants to chat), "Professors are all readily available outside of class and genuinely interested in the well-being of each student." In addition, staff and advisors "work with students to ensure that we follow the right path, are able to do what we want and need to do, and succeed in all areas of our academic lives." A current student adds, "I have had a great experience in regards to the administration, especially the graduate advisor. She has been instrumental in helping me navigate course loads."

Although TU is a small school, the MBA program is constantly working to remain on the cutting edge. With an eye towards industry trends, administrators "recently revamped the course work to reflect what companies stated that they were looking for in MBA grads, and they also are constantly injecting anything current into the courses, seminars, and lectures." A current student observes, administrators "are constantly seeking outside input from various companies and individuals so that their students are as best prepared upon graduation as they can be." To offer one example, business ethics has been introduced into the curriculum, which students say is "refreshing and relevant." In addition to course work, TU students have the opportunity to participate in co-curricular activities on and off campus. A particularly popular offering, "the Friends of Finance organization, brings in CEOs, presidents of *Fortune* 500 companies, etc., to speak to the business students, and also offers a special session afterwards for students to ask the speaker questions one-on-one."

Career and Placement

With a "strong reputation in the energy industry" and a "prestigious reputation" in the area, TU students are well-positioned to find a choice position after graduating from the MBA program. For assistance with the career planning and placement process, "TU has a Business Career Center that is entirely focused on job placement for business students." Through the Business Career Center, students have access to a myriad of services, including resume and cover letter revisions, mock interviews, salary information, career workshops, and various online resources and job boards. In addition, "the events and workshops...allow students to have one-on-one time with executives of *Fortune* 500 companies." Recently, TU graduates have taken jobs at organizations including Bank of Oklahoma, ConocoPhillips, Deloitte Consulting, DHL, GE, Grant Thornton, Honeywell International, IBM, Level 3 Communications, PriceWaterhouseCoopers, Toyota, Trammel Crow, and the U.S. Government.

Student Life and Environment

Drawing "a good mix of working professionals and recent graduates," TU students come from "a diverse background ethnically, academically, and professionally." Through group work and class discussions, "the diverse professional backgrounds of many of the students…lends itself to a very enriching atmosphere." Since the majority of students are "full-time working professionals or graduate student assistants that are taking classes full time," students admit that "there isn't much time to take part in social or community activities." Nonetheless, the school offers plenty of opportunities for TU students to get together socially. For example, "graduate student luncheons take place every month where all graduate students are invited to eat and mingle." In addition, "there are many opportunities to meet other graduate students and employers at company panel sessions, etiquette dinners, and meet-and-greet times off campus."

Located on the edge of downtown Tulsa, "the campus is not large, but it is very beautiful and has all of the amenities of a larger university, just on a smaller scale." Looking to the future, the school's administration is "continually improving the campus." For example, "over the past three to four years they have built suite-style dormitories for student housing," in an effort to promote "a more united student body, and a better overall… experience." In addition, "the fitness facility is first class" and many students make use of the well-stocked library. The surrounding area is home to many students, and they "feel very safe walking to class in the evening."

Admissions

The Graduate Business Programs office at University of Tulsa accepts applications on a rolling basis. A single scholarship application allows all students to be automatically considered for merit-based scholarships (more than 70 percent of current students receive some form of merit-based aid). Students may also apply to the graduate assistantship program, through which they receive a full-tuition scholarship in exchange for twenty hours of work each week on campus. In recent years, the entering class had an average undergraduate GPA of 3.5 and an average of two years professional work experience before entering the program.

FINANCIAL FACTS

Annual tuition (in-state/ out-of-state)	$30,875/$30,875
Fees	$150
Cost of books	$1,200
Room & board (on/off-campus)	$10,920/$10,920
% of students receiving aid	70
% of first-year students receiving aid	49
% of students receiving grants	67
Average award package	$19,130
Average grant	$16,644
Average loan	$16,582
Average student loan debt	$32,737

ADMISSIONS

Admissions Selectivity Rating	83
# of applications received	71
% applicants accepted	69
% acceptees attending	67
Average GMAT	575
Range of GMAT	530–607
Accepts GRE scores	Yes
Average Verbal GRE	151
Range of Verbal GRE scores	150–155
Average Quantitative GRE	153
Range of Quantitative GRE scores	148–158
Average GPA	3.3
TOEFL required of international students	Yes
Minimum TOEFL (paper/web)	575/90
Application fee	$55
International application fee	$55
Early application deadline	2/1
Regular application deadline	7/1
Application Deadline/Notification	
Deferment available	Yes
Maximum length of deferment	1 year
Transfer students accepted	Yes
Transfer application policy	
Maximum of 6 hours from an AACSB accredited institution.	
Non-fall admissions	Yes
Need-blind admissions	Yes

EMPLOYMENT PROFILE

Career Rating	73	Grads Employed by Function	% Avg. Salary
Percent employed at graduation	59	Marketing	(12%) $40,500
Percent employed 3 months after graduation	86	Operations	(18%) $51,667
		Consulting	(24%) $49,875
Average base starting salary	$55,682	Management	(12%) $85,000
		Finance	(24%) $62,250
		HR	(6%) $93,000
		Other	(71%) $53,333

Top 5 Employers Hiring Grads
ONEOK (4), NGL Energy Partners (2), Bank of Oklahoma Financial (1), JP Morgan Chase (1), ExxonMobil (1)

UNIVERSITY OF UTAH
DAVID ECCLES SCHOOL OF BUSINESS

GENERAL INFORMATION
Type of school	Public
Affiliation	No Affiliation
Academic calendar	Semester

SURVEY SAYS...
Classmates have diverse work experience, Friendly students, Conservative students, Happy students, Students love Salt Lake City, UT
Solid preparation in:
General management, Teamwork

STUDENTS
Enrollment of parent institution	41,751
Enrollment of MBA Program	447
% male/female	78/22
% out-of-state	34
% part-time	70
% underrepresented minority	15
% international	5
Average age at entry	27
Average years work experience at entry	3

ACADEMICS
Academic Experience Rating	89
Profs interesting rating	91
Profs accessible rating	93
Student/faculty ratio	11:1
% female faculty	31
% underrepresented minority faculty	7
% part-time faculty	36

Joint Degrees
MBA/MS (Bioengineering, Mechanical Eng., Chemical Eng., Electrical Eng., Comp. Sci.) 2.5 years MBA/JD 4 years MBA/Master of Health Administration, 3 years MBA/MEAE, 3 years MBA/MD, 5 years

Academics

The David Eccles School of Business is arguably the "best MBA [program] in the state of Utah." Indeed, it has a well-earned and well-deserved "reputation for excellence." Eccles tends to be a huge draw for "full-time, working professionals" as the school allows for a tremendous amount of "flexibility." In fact, the program "was designed [with] professionals [in mind.]" Some MBA hopefuls also set their sights on Utah for its innovative dual MBA/MHA (Master of Healthcare Administration) program. And there's plenty to pursue outside of healthcare as well. We're told that Utah really gives students "the ability to create the education [they] want to receive." We'd also be remiss if we neglected to mention that "small class sizes" are a hallmark of an Eccles education and frequently lead to "customized attention."

Utah MBAs speak quite highly of their professors whom they describe as "top-notch." Importantly, instructors here have "extensive academic and industry backgrounds which lead to more lively discussions of topics." And a happy second-year student shares, "They have pushed me very hard while at the same time they have been very understanding when I do not grasp a concept at first. I am so lucky to be a part of this program!" Finally, students also give high marks to the "very involved and helpful" administration. It's clearly evident that "they are very much interested in the well-being of the students."

Career and Placement

Utah's Career Center is certainly a boon to MBA students. Their dedicated staff work diligently to help MBAs maximize their investment. From networking seminars to interview workshops, Eccles students are certainly prepared for their job hunt. As an extremely satisfied second-year gushes, "The career advancement center was a huge help in improving my résumé, interviewing skills, and finding my worth. With graduation near, I have an offer that will increase my salary by 44 percent and my bonus by 300 percent. The program has definitely paid for itself in a short time." Additionally, students are privy to a "successful alumni" network that "continue[s] to give back" with their time, donations and connections.

Companies that frequently hire Eccles MBA include: American Airlines, Amazon, GE Healthcare, Capitol One, Hewlett Packard, General Mills, IBM, LDS Church, Oracle, TIAA-CREF and Pfizer.

Student Life and Environment

Given its location in Salt Lake City, it's not surprising that there's a "strong Church of Jesus Christ of Latter Day Saints influence" among those who attend Utah. Fortunately, the student body still manages to feel "diverse." And regardless of religious affiliation, MBA candidates here agree that their peers are "hardworking," "fun" and "very friendly." As one happy second-year shares, "My cohort is very active in supporting and assisting each other in and out of the classroom."

Students also report that the school is "very accommodating" for those balancing work and family life in addition to school. Eccles hosts "a lot of activities for [both] networking and for . . . families" and students and their partners can participate in everything from "museum days [to] BBQs." Moreover, the student leadership team is quite proactive when it comes to organizing events for "students to get to know each other in a relaxing and public atmosphere." However, though these future MBAs are "very committed to school" many are also "heavily committed to their...roles [outside of Eccles.]" Therefore, it's quite common for most students to simply head home after class.

Admissions

The Eccles admissions committee requires applicants to provide the following: an undergraduate transcript demonstrating a GPA of at least 3.0 (students failing to meet this requirement may gain entry based on evaluation of their performance during the final two years of undergraduate work); GMAT scores; two recommendations (submitted online); responses to essay questions; and a résumé. International students whose first language is not English must take the TOEFL. Two years of post-undergraduate professional experience are strongly encouraged but not required. The school reports that it administers "several privately-donated scholarships reserved for underrepresented groups and [designed] to help us build the gender, ethnic, and geographic diversity of our student body."

Prominent Alumni

J. Willard Marriott, II, Executive Chairman, Marriott International; Robert A. McDonald, Former Chair and CEO, Procter and Gamble; Norm Wesley, Former Chair and CEO, Fortune Brands; Geoffrey Wooley, Founding Partner, Dominion Ventures

FINANCIAL FACTS

Annual tuition (in-state/ out-of-state)	$26,083/$48,516
Fees	$850
Cost of books	$2,600
Room & board	$8,500
% of students receiving aid	84
% of first-year students receiving aid	86
% of students receiving grants	85
Average grant	$15,000
Average student loan debt	$19,846

ADMISSIONS

Admissions Selectivity Rating	85
# of applications received	170
% applicants accepted	64
% acceptees attending	60
Average GMAT	621
Range of GMAT	570–650
Accepts GRE scores	Yes
Average Verbal GRE	157
Range of Verbal GRE scores	150–165
Average GPA	3.4
TOEFL required of international students	Yes
Minimum TOEFL (paper/web)	600/100
Application fee	$55
International application fee	$65
Application Deadline/Notification	
Round 1:	11/1 / 12/13
Round 2:	1/1 / 2/12
Round 3:	3/1 / 4/12
Round 4:	5/1 / 6/12
Deferment available	No
Transfer students accepted	No
Non-fall admissions	No
Need-blind admissions	Yes

EMPLOYMENT PROFILE

Career Rating	85	Grads Employed by Function	% Avg. Salary
Percent employed at graduation	55	Marketing	(15%) $70,100
Percent employed 3 months after graduation	45	Operations	(36%) $76,111
		Consulting	(18%) $82,250
Average base starting salary	$76,728	Management	(6%)
Primary Source of Full-time Job Acceptances		Finance	(9%) $73,133
School-facilitated activities	23 (70%)	HR	(6%)
Graduate-facilitated activities	10 (30%)	MIS	(3%)
		Other	(6%)

Top 5 Employers Hiring Grads
InMoment (2), General Motors (1), T-Mobile (1), Adobe (1), eBay (1)

THE UNIVERSITY OF VERMONT
GROSSMAN SCHOOL OF BUSINESS

GENERAL INFORMATION
Type of school	Public
Affiliation	No Affiliation
Academic calendar	August to August

SURVEY SAYS...
Friendly students, Liberal students, Cutting-edge classes, Happy students, Students love Burlington, VT
Solid preparation in:
General management, Teamwork, Communication/interpersonal skills, Presentation skills, Environmental sustainability, Social responsibility

STUDENTS
Enrollment of parent institution	12,000
Enrollment of MBA Program	16
% male/female	44/56
% out-of-state	3
% part-time	0
% underrepresented minority	18
% international	0
Average age at entry	28
Average years work experience at entry	6

ACADEMICS
Academic Experience Rating	89
Profs interesting rating	90
Profs accessible rating	96
% female faculty	26
% underrepresented minority faculty	21
% part-time faculty	32

Joint Degrees
Dual-Degree between Vermont Law School and Sustainable Entrepreneurship Master of Business Administration.

Academics

The University of Vermont's Sustainable Entrepreneurship MBA (SEMBA) is one-year, full-time only program that focuses on social and environmental sustainability. SEMBA "is not just a traditional MBA with some sustainability courses attached." Instead, sustainability is woven through each course as a way to approach problems, instead of business as usual. UVM replaced its traditional MBA with SEMBA in 2014, and the past few years' of cultural change in students, administrators, faculty, and professors is "readily apparent." The small size of the program (target enrollment of 50) allows for it to be nimble, and "the directors ask for feedback regularly and respond quickly." "There is a genuine sense of pride and excitement at the Grossman School of Business," one student explains.

Through SEMBA's "rigorous and fast-paced" curriculum, students are exposed to both current and fundamental articles and encouraged to be forward-thinking. "SEMBA does not teach history, unless lessons can be learned from it. This is about the businesses of tomorrow," says one student. Everyone happily does the reading "because it's interesting, and because the best part about our classes are the discussions we have." The "deeply interested" professors "challenge [students] to do great work," even holding events for students in their homes, and will assist whenever needed, "even if not directly correlated to the coursework or if they are no longer teaching us." Similarly, the administration "does their absolute best to make things smooth for us students," including scheduling exams and projects so they don't all line up on the same day.

Career and Placement

All students are required to do a three-month summer Practicum Project with an existing company or new venture, and must successfully pitch their business plans to a panel in order to graduate. Experiential learning is a highlight for many students, who appreciate that UVM is "a place where you can take risks and be creative." The "great business clubs" at UVM also provide real-world experience. A sampling of the companies that participate in the summer Practicum Projects include Ben & Jerry's, CEMEX, DIVA, Facebook, Lancer, NativeEnergy, and Seventh Generation.

Student Life and Environment

SEMBA students are incredibly diverse in terms of backgrounds and work experience, from "a forty-seven-year-old mom with a background in forest conservation to a twenty-two-year-old recent grad interested in biomimicry to a thirty-year-old Iraq war veteran who is interested in community development." "The conversations we have are incredible and the support we give to one another is key," says a student of the "engaging discussions with well-articulated points of view." These students are "motivated people that still believe that they can have a positive impact on the world." Burlington and home university UVM are "all about eating well and being active." There are plenty of places to grab local food on campus, and many students walk to school or go for runs or bike rides during their lunch hour.

Admissions

Successful candidates will have scored higher than 500 on the GMAT, with a preference for those that scored higher than 550. Preference is also given to those with at least three years' of work experience under their belts. Applicants should also submit letters of reference. International applicants are required to submit TOEFL scores, with a minimum score of 90 on the web-based test. Above all else, those who are truly interested in the program should have a résumé and transcript that demonstrate a passion for sustainable entrepreneurship and the role of local and global communities in the marketplace.

FINANCIAL FACTS

Annual tuition (in-state/ out-of-state)	$28,331/$49,500
Fees	$2,016
Cost of books	$2,200
Room & board (on/off-campus)	$9,992/$9,992
% of students receiving aid	100
% of first-year students receiving aid	100
% of students receiving grants	100
Average award package	$30,025
Average grant	$6,096
Average loan	$34,804
Average student loan debt	$46,420

ADMISSIONS

Admissions Selectivity Rating	82
# of applications received	25
% applicants accepted	80
% acceptees attending	80
Average GMAT	558
Range of GMAT	450–600
Accepts GRE scores	Yes
Average Verbal GRE	158
Range of Verbal GRE scores	150–163
Average Quantitative GRE	151
Range of Quantitative GRE scores	145–159
Average Writing GRE	4.8
Range of Writing GRE scores	4.0–5.5
Average GPA	3.2
TOEFL required of international students	Yes
Minimum TOEFL (paper/web)	550/90
Application fee	$65
International application fee	$65
Regular application deadline	4/15
Application Deadline/Notification	
Deferment available	Yes
Maximum length of deferment	1 year
Transfer students accepted	No
Non-fall admissions	No
Need-blind admissions	Yes

EMPLOYMENT PROFILE

		Grads Employed by Function	% Avg. Salary
Career Rating	88		
Percent employed at graduation	0	Marketing	(25%) $48,500
Percent employed 3 months after graduation	80	Consulting	(42%) $38,000
		Management	(25%) $57,000
Average base starting salary	$51,319	Other	(8%) $36,000
Primary Source of Full-time Job Acceptances		**Top 5 Employers Hiring Grads**	
School-facilitated activities	3 (25%)	Pepsico (5), Ben & Jerry's (1), Burton	
Graduate-facilitated activities	7 (58%)	Snowboards (1), Rainforest Alliance (1), VEIC	
Unknown	2 (17%)	(1)	

UNIVERSITY OF VIRGINIA
DARDEN GRADUATE SCHOOL OF BUSINESS ADMINISTRATION

GENERAL INFORMATION
Type of school | Public
Academic calendar | Semester

SURVEY SAYS...
Classmates have diverse work experience, Friendly students, Good peer network, Good social scene
Solid preparation in:
Finance, Accounting, General Management, Teamwork, Quantitative skills

STUDENTS
Enrollment of parent
institution | 21,985
Enrollment of MBA Program | 656
% male/female | 67/34
% part-time | 0
% underrepresented minority | 11
% international | 32
Average age at entry | 27
Average years work
experience at entry | 5

ACADEMICS
Academic Experience Rating | 99
Profs interesting rating | 98
Profs accessible rating | 99
Student/faculty ratio | 6:1
% female faculty | 24
% underrepresented
minority faculty | 18
% part-time faculty | 30

Joint Degrees
MBA/JD; MBA/MA in East Asian Studies; MBA/MA in Government or Foreign Affairs; MBA/ME; MBA/MSN; MBA/PhD; MBA/MD; MBA/MPH; MBA/MPP; MBA/MEd

Academics

The University of Virginia's Darden Graduate School of Business Administration in Charlottesville, Virginia is a juggernaut among East Coast business programs, and is touted for its "rigorous core curriculum, excellent teaching faculty, [and] collaborative student body." While the workload is intense especially during the first-year "grind", the school's overwhelmingly "supportive spirit," fostered by learning teams, second-year coaches, and "very active" career-focused clubs, means that life here "is also a lot of fun." Academics are taught through the case study method and focus on collaborative learning, which students describe as "amazing."

First- and second-year Darden students have two distinct academic experiences. The first-year schedule is "pretty rigid as you have three classes every weekday except Friday, and you have to balance your workload in your learning teams." But there are plenty of opportunities "to spend time outside of the classroom developing personal relationships" through activities like "First Coffee, club events, and night time socials." The first year is "really demanding, but it is collaborative and engaging" as well, and "everyone works together to get through the material before entering the classroom." The second year "is focused on leadership in the school," as second-year students coach first years, helping them "navigate the job recruiting process," and lead clubs or "[help] faculty write cases." Second-year students pursue elective courses and build their own schedules—"a lot of students also use the time as an opportunity to travel."

Darden's "excellent" faculty are engaged in the program and "are genuinely invested in helping you be successful." "They want to know how your family is, how job searches are going, and who they can put you in touch with to help." Students appreciate that faculty "prioritize teaching and research equally," and often consult with companies and conduct research "to stay relevant" in their fields. Students are also "amazed at how well everything is run," especially by "how well different parts of the faculty (e.g. finance and ethics) coordinate their curriculum." One student reports, "I've never seen an organization run as smoothly as Darden. I'm sure there is tons of work and grinding going on in the background, but it almost seems automated."

Career and Placement

Darden's challenging curriculum and extensive alumni network pay dividends on the job market. "If I sent an email to ten different alums," one second year told us, "I'd be surprised if I didn't get at least nine responses." Darden has a great track record placing students in finance, but in recent years has been expanding its foothold in consulting and technology, counting Amazon and Microsoft among its top on-campus recruiters. The program also maintains "good relationships with top consulting firms." Darden has cultivated a reputation among "traditional MBA career firms (consulting, banking, general management) for creating professionals who are very smart and hardworking, but collaborative, team-focused, and friendly." For students plotting a different course, Darden has a "strong reputation with entrepreneurship," and the "Career Development Center is very helpful for students pursuing careers outside the 'traditional' paths," an investment advisory student reports.

Student Life and Environment

Darden "students are very, very social" and forge strong bonds with one another. "Because we are not in a large city," one technology student explains, "the majority of people that you meet and spend time with are your classmates which makes for an incredibly strong community with a strong affinity for the school and Charlottesville." Even though students are "graded on a significant curve," it has "never stopped students from helping one another." Students generally hang out together on Thursday nights and enjoy Charlottesville's "wonderful hiking, rafting, and biking trails" on weekends. While life as an MBA student can become hectic, at Darden "the degree of busyness depends on how much you want to get out of the program [. . .] students ultimately choose their balance in academics, activities, and recruiting."

Admissions

Darden evaluates a student's readiness for business school in three broad areas: academics, professional experience, and personal qualities and characteristics. These competencies are measured through the applicant's undergraduate record, GMAT or GRE scores, résumé and work experience, letters of recommendation, and admissions essays. In addition, interviews are required and are considered an important part of the application.

Prominent Alumni

Mr. Elie Maalouf, CEO, InterContinental Hotels Group, The Americas; Ms. Vanessa Wittman, CFO, Dropbox and Board Member for Ulta and Sirius; Mr. Michael E. O'Neil, Chairman, Citigroup, Inc.; Ms. Carolyn Miles, President and CEO, Save the Children; Mr. John R. Strangfeld, Chairman and CEO, Prudential Financial, Inc.

FINANCIAL FACTS

Annual tuition (in-state/ out-of-state)	$55,518/$57,836
Fees	$2,632
Cost of books	$2,000
Room & board (on/off-campus)	$16,690/$16,690
% of students receiving aid	75
% of first-year students receiving aid	76
% of students receiving grants	41
Average award package	$65,623
Average grant	$39,001
Average loan	$57,598
Average student loan debt	$100,083

ADMISSIONS

Admissions Selectivity Rating	95
# of applications received	2,578
% applicants accepted	28
% acceptees attending	46
Average GMAT	706
Accepts GRE scores	Yes
Average GPA	3.5
TOEFL required of international students	Yes
Minimum TOEFL (paper/web)	650/100
Application fee	$250
International application fee	$250
Application Deadline/Notification	
Round 1:	10/8 / 12/16
Round 2:	1/8 / 3/23
Round 3:	4/8 / 5/11
Deferment available	No
Transfer students accepted	No
Non-fall admissions	No
Need-blind admissions	Yes

EMPLOYMENT PROFILE

Career Rating	98		
Percent employed at graduation	89		
Percent employed 3 months after graduation	95		
Average base starting salary	$119,819		
Primary Source of Full-time Job Acceptances			
School-facilitated activities	240 (85%)		
Graduate-facilitated activities	42 (15%)		

Grads Employed by Function	% Avg. Salary
Marketing	(10%) $105,180
Consulting	(31%) $135,464
Management	(22%) $109,917
Finance	(31%) $118,177
Other	(6%) $108,636

Top 5 Employers Hiring Grads
McKinsey & Company (14), Boston Consulting Group, Inc. (13), Accenture (9), Amazon.com, Inc. (9), Microsoft Corp. (9)

UNIVERSITY OF WASHINGTON
MICHAEL G. FOSTER SCHOOL OF BUSINESS

GENERAL INFORMATION
Type of school	Public
Affiliation	No Affiliation
Academic calendar	Quarter

SURVEY SAYS...
Classmates have diverse work experience, Friendly students, Good peer network, Good social scene, Liberal students, Abundant mentors available, Helpful alumni, Happy students, Abundant clubs and activities, Students love Seattle, WA
Solid preparation in:
Marketing, Finance, General management, Teamwork, Communication/interpersonal skills, Presentation skills, Quantitative skills, Doing business in a global economy, Entreprenurial studies

STUDENTS
Enrollment of parent institution	54,223
Enrollment of MBA Program	887
% male/female	66/34
% out-of-state	41
% part-time	72
% underrepresented minority	7
% international	34
Average age at entry	29
Average years work experience at entry	6

ACADEMICS
Academic Experience Rating	97
Profs interesting rating	93
Profs accessible rating	96
Student/faculty ratio	5:1
% female faculty	31
% part-time faculty	32

Joint Degrees
JD/MBA; MBA/MAIS; MBA/MHA Health Administration; MBA/MPA

Prominent Alumni
William Ayer, Former CEO, Alaska Airlines; Dan Nordstrom, Former CEO, Nordstrom.com; Charles Lillis, Former CEO, Media One Group

Academics

MBA students at the University of Washington happily assert that the Foster School of Business has "the best reputation in the Pacific Northwest." Students here are privy to a relatively "small" program, which affords them the opportunity "to [get to] know [everyone] on a personal level, down to the professors and staff." The size also helps to ensure a "collaborative environment," one which students greatly value. And many are quick to highlight the "strong marketing, strategy and consulting [programs]." Foster also maintains "a big focus" on entrepreneurship, a fact that draws a number of students. As one second year brags, "The Buerk Center and Jones Foster Accelerator are awesome resources for anyone interested in starting their own company." Additionally, "the partnership with the university's engineering and science schools allows technical students to create startups with MBA students."

Both professors and the administration receive high marks. To begin with, the "energy and expertise that the professors at UW Foster bring to the classroom is unparalleled." Perhaps most impressive, "nearly all of [them] have great backgrounds that lend well to the subjects they teach. For instance, our global strategy classes are taught by a former McKinsey consultant. Finance courses are taught by former investment bankers. In addition to their experience, the institutions where they earned their PhD's are all top tier." And another pleased MBA candidate quickly adds, "[Professors] are accessible, patient, and incredibly intelligent...my interactions with them have only strengthened my resolve over time that I could not have chosen a better program to enroll in." Students also appreciate that "the administration operates by being extremely accessible...and keep[s] their ears and eyes open towards opportunities for improvement." Overall, it's abundantly clear that the Foster "deans and senior faculty go above and beyond [when it comes to both] teach[ing and] listen[ing]."

Career and Placement

MBA students here are a fortunate bunch. After all, the school is "a well-respected presence in Seattle" and "surrounded by Fortune 500 companies." Indeed, many proudly boast that "University of Washington [has] incredible connections to the numerous corporations and organizations in the community." As one grateful third-year shares, "[Foster has a] very good relationship with the local companies, especially with Amazon, Microsoft, Starbucks, Boeing, Expedia, etc. Seattle is the home for many big MNCs and my school is the first choice for their recruiting in many cases." Students are also privy to a "strong local and regional alumni network" as well. And they are quick to laud career services, which one happy student simply characterizes as "so good." He further gushes, "They are focused on getting everyone a job." Therefore, it's certainly no surprise that Foster maintains an "[excellent] job placement rate."

ADMISSIONS CONTACT: ERIN ERNST, DIRECTOR OF ADMISSIONS
ADDRESS: 110 MACKENZIE HALL, BOX 353200, SEATTLE, WA 98195-3200
PHONE: 206-543-4661 • FAX: 206-616-7351
E-MAIL: MBA@U.WASHINGTON.EDU • WEBSITE: WWW.FOSTER.WASHINGTON.EDU/MBA

Student Life and Environment

Foster MBAs speak very highly of their "diverse," "smart" and "friendly" peers. They tend to be "very supportive of one another" as well as "easy-going" and "fun." Students also tell us that "work-life balance is important" and that "there are plenty of social opportunities to get to know classmates." They also stress that it's "easy to spend the whole day on campus with class, activities, intramural sports, workshops, and event planning." As one thrilled student shares, "The amount of extracurricular activities and development opportunities available to us is exceptional. I was eager to be involved in club leadership, the student association, a student-to-student mentor program, and a number of other things, and because I was only competing against ninety other classmates, [I] was able to do these things and find many other ways to take on leadership roles." Lastly, students adore Seattle and see their location as "a huge strength." A satisfied student explains, "Seattle has an incredible wealth of employment opportunities right now, and the city is growing. The combination of access to the outdoors and urban nightlife means there is something for everyone."

Admissions

Admissions officers at Foster are on the lookout for individuals who have the potential to be leaders and innovators in management. Applicants need to demonstrate strong communication and computer skills. Solid quantitative skills are also a must. Post-undergraduate professional work is not required, though it is highly preferred. Finally, an academic background in business is not necessary.

FINANCIAL FACTS

Annual tuition (in-state/ out-of-state)	$30,129/$44,339
Fees	$1,071
Cost of books	$1,708
Room & board (on/off-campus)	$18,764/$18,764
% of students receiving aid	70
% of first-year students receiving aid	68
% of students receiving grants	62
Average award package	$33,144
Average grant	$18,341
Average loan	$28,111
Average student loan debt	$22,132

ADMISSIONS

Admissions Selectivity Rating	95
# of applications received	1,046
% applicants accepted	26
% acceptees attending	48
Average GMAT	688
Range of GMAT	640–710
Accepts GRE scores	No
Average GPA	3.4
TOEFL required of international students	Yes
Minimum TOEFL (paper/web)	600/100
Application fee	$85
International application fee	$85
Early application deadline	10/15
Early notification date	12/15
Regular application deadline	3/15
Regular application notification	5/15
Application Deadline/Notification	
Round 1:	10/15 / 12/15
Round 2:	11/15 / 1/15
Round 3:	1/15 / 3/30
Round 4:	3/15 / 5/15
Deferment available	Yes
Maximum length of deferment	1 year
Transfer students accepted	Yes
Transfer application policy	
Transfer applicants should apply as any other new student. The status of a transfer student is determined on a case by case basis, depending on the work completed at another school.	
Non-fall admissions	No
Need-blind admissions	Yes

EMPLOYMENT PROFILE

Career Rating		97	Grads Employed by Function	% Avg. Salary
Percent employed at graduation		83	Marketing	(37%) $100,452
Percent employed 3 months after graduation		96	Operations	(4%) $114,590
			Consulting	(26%) $116,360
Average base starting salary		$104,884	Management	(10%) $113,095
Primary Source of Full-time Job Acceptances			Finance	(16%) $96,140
School-facilitated activities		78 (60%)	HR	(2%) $80,573
Graduate-facilitated activities		47 (36%)	MIS	(1%)
Unknown		5 (4%)	Other	(4%) $93,500

Top 5 Employers Hiring Grads
Amazon.com, Microsoft, PricewaterhouseCoopers, Liberty Mutual, Intel

University of West Georgia
Richards College of Business

GENERAL INFORMATION

Type of school	Public
Affiliation	No Affiliation
Academic calendar	Semester

SURVEY SAYS...

Classmates have diverse work experience, Cutting-edge classes, Happy students
Solid preparation in:
General management, Teamwork, Presentation skills, Quantitative skills, Computer skills

STUDENTS

Enrollment of parent institution	12,834
Enrollment of MBA Program	95
% male/female	42/58
% out-of-state	0
% part-time	55
% underrepresented minority	42
% international	19
Average age at entry	27

ACADEMICS

Academic Experience Rating	**86**
Profs interesting rating	94
Profs accessible rating	95
Student/faculty ratio	2:1
% female faculty	33
% underrepresented minority faculty	33
% part-time faculty	0

Academics

The Richards College of Business at the University of West Georgia in Carrollton, GA offers an "affordable," highly accredited business program via evening or online classes that are "great for working students." Students can work out their own "flexible schedule" by enrolling in MBA courses at the main campus in Carrollton or in Newnan and Douglasville. Since many people are ambitious to get ahead in their current careers, the environment is often "very work intensive and challenging," but the "integrity" of the student body and the tremendous support provided by the school makes University of West Georgia (UWG) an excellent fit for the needs and goals of its students.

Professors here are what one student calls "the best I have ever had the pleasure to work with," and are "very knowledgeable, willing to help, and very understanding of needs that come up, be it work, family, etc." There is great diversity among instructors, and the various backgrounds—both educational and geographic—prove to be "a winning formula for our team and the MBA program." The terrific professor-to-student ratio feeds into the idea of a "big school with a cozy feeling of being small."

Richards College of Business also offers a 100 percent online MBA program, administered by The Georgia WebMBA®. "Not only do I get to interact with very intelligent, driven students from all over the world, but I am able to learn from top notch professors from various University of Georgia System [schools]," says one student. Professors at UWG are "great to work with," and students have "always been able to get help" when needed. "I have professors from several different schools in my program, and have seen an overall high quality in both the teaching and the support of the students," says one.

The school's "very fair" administration is "very competent and addresses issues timely and thoroughly," and "helps students to get the best out of their stay in the school." "My school understands that there is life beyond school hours and is flexible in both schedules and demands," says a student of the "around-the-clock assistance" provided. Together, the administration and professors have "created an excellent and dynamic learning environment." "My overall academic experience has been excellent, I wouldn't have picked any other school," says a student.

Career and Placement

"The diversity of both the student body and the professors" is one of the program's greatest preparatory measures for the real world, and the perspectives they bring to classes "are very practical and apply directly to career fields." The University of West Georgia is close to metropolitan Atlanta, so "many businesses are recruiting our graduates." "For a business school to be close to many major companies in the Atlanta area is great." Still, some students feel that "better career-oriented speakers or guests would be nice."

ADMISSIONS CONTACT: HOPE UDOMBON, ADMINISTRATIVE DIRECTOR OF GRADUATE PROGRAMS
ADDRESS: 1601 MAPLE STREET, CARROLLTON, GA 30118-3000
PHONE: 678-839-5355 • FAX: 678-839-5040
E-MAIL: HUDOMBON@WESTGA.EDU • WEBSITE: WWW.WESTGA.EDU/BUSINESS

Student Life and Environment

"My fellow students are diverse in demographics and background," according to one student, and "are very friendly and encouraging." People come to UWG of "all ages, ethnicities, income levels, married, singles, and many nationalities." Most students who go to UWG are local and commute, and since the MBA program is still relatively small, "life at UWG is very much like a community" where "you know everyone in your classes, semester after semester." "It's kind of like high school, without all the drama. We all meet up early/late in the library to study, etc.," says a student. The pleasant atmosphere is also helped by the fact that the location is great: there is "no heavy downtown traffic," and "campus is beautiful and well-kept."

There is definitely "a feeling of inclusion amongst the student body." Many MBA sutdents at UWG commute and work, so they "show up for class and leave afterward." Students have adopted an attitude of "let's get it done soon and right." Because of this, "there is a lot of teamwork." "Being an older student, I have had to rely heavily on the younger students, and they have been a saving grace for me!" says one student. "We are all in the program for the same reason, so everyone is willing to help!" A significant portion of the student body is international; many recently completed their undergraduate degrees (often at UWG), but some have long been out of school. Mostly, students "are getting an MBA to advance their career."

Admissions

Students are considered for regular admission to Richards College of Business based mainly on the student's undergraduate GPA and GMAT scores. An applicant must have a minimum of at least 950 points based on the formula: 200 x undergraduate GPA (4.0 system) + GMAT; or at least 1000 points based on the formula: 200 x upper division (last 60 hours) GPA (4.0 system) + GMAT. At the same time, students must also submit a current resume. Additionally to be considered for admission, the analytical writing section of the GMAT must be 3.0 or higher..

FINANCIAL FACTS

Annual tuition (in-state/ out-of-state)	$7,330/$25,264
Fees	$1,962
Cost of books	$1,500
Room & board (on/off-campus)	$9,798/$6,849

ADMISSIONS

Admissions Selectivity Rating	78
# of applications received	62
% applicants accepted	90
% acceptees attending	88
Average GMAT	476
Range of GMAT	445–525
Accepts GRE scores	Yes
Average Verbal GRE	144
Range of Verbal GRE scores	143–147
Average Quantitative GRE	141
Range of Quantitative GRE scores	139–143
Average Writing GRE	3.3
Range of Writing GRE scores	3.0–3.5
Average GPA	3.2
TOEFL required of international students	Yes
Minimum TOEFL (paper/web)	550/79
Application fee	$40
International application fee	$40
Regular application deadline	7/15
Application Deadline/Notification	
Deferment available	Yes
Maximum length of deferment	1 year without reapplying
Transfer students accepted	Yes
Transfer application policy A maximum of 6 semester hours of graduate credit may be transferred from another accredited institution. See catalog for more information.	
Non-fall admissions	Yes
Need-blind admissions	Yes

UNIVERSITY OF WISCONSIN—MADISON

SCHOOL OF BUSINESS

GENERAL INFORMATION

Type of school	Public
Affiliation	No Affiliation
Academic calendar	Semester

SURVEY SAYS...

Classmates have diverse work experience, Friendly students, Good peer network, Good social scene, Helpful alumni, Happy students, Abundant clubs and activities, Students love Madison, WI
Solid preparation in:
Marketing, Finance, Teamwork, Presentation skills, Quantitative skills

STUDENTS

Enrollment of parent institution	43,389
Enrollment of MBA Program	362
% male/female	64/36
% out-of-state	71
% part-time	45
% underrepresented minority	14
% international	23
Average age at entry	28
Average years work experience at entry	6

ACADEMICS

Academic Experience Rating	98
Profs interesting rating	91
Profs accessible rating	95
Student/faculty ratio	3:1
% female faculty	25
% underrepresented minority faculty	13
% part-time faculty	23

Joint Degrees

JD/MBA - 4 years

Prominent Alumni

Steve Bennett, CEO, Symantec; Thomas J. Falk, Chairman & CEO, Kimberly-Clark; John Morgridge, Chairman Emeritus, Cisco Systems; John Oros, Managing Director of J.C. Flowers & Co. LLC; Rob Pollock, Chairman & CEO of Assurant

Academics

The University of Wisconsin—Madison offers a unique and challenging MBA program, well suited to highly-focused students with clear career goals. Whereas most MBA programs require a wide array of course work in general management topics, the Wisconsin MBA curriculum is designed around career specializations, through which students focus their studies on a single business area such as real estate, brand management, or marketing research. Through their career specialization, students work within the business school's Centers for Expertise, which "ensure that students have lots of exposure to alumni, specific industry news, and professionals at various levels." A current student explains, "I chose the University of Wisconsin because they have a specialized program in marketing research that would give me the specialized skill set to continue in this field."

While career specializations are the hallmark of the Wisconsin MBA curriculum, "the program emphasizes strong learning within a specific discipline while allowing flexibility to learn cross-functional skills." Before beginning their studies within a specific center, students must complete the general management core curriculum, which provides a solid foundation in management essentials. Students comment that "the specified 'center' does make it difficult at times to expand into other departments." Throughout the curriculum, applied learning is an important component of the Wisconsin MBA, and students participate in live business projects for a wide range of companies. For example, students may conduct market research for leading companies, manage stock portfolios, or manage a portfolio of real estate securities.

The business school draws a team of top-notch faculty "committed to up-to-date teaching styles and topics." Student input here is valued. "Feedback is taken from the students at the end of every semester and the recommended changes are implemented for the next incoming class," says one MBA. "It's a constantly evolving and improving program that is viewed as a collaborative effort between the administration and students." On the whole, "Wisconsin represents a culture of collaboration and teamwork," and students reassure us that "when students compete, there is a general collegiate respect for one another." Another major perk of a Wisconsin MBA education is its public school price tag, made better by the fact that through assistantships: "The tuition is covered, benefits are covered, and you get a stipend." A student exclaims, "You might find it hard to catch your breath, but it's a great way to avoid loans."

Career and Placement

Starting at Orientation and through the first months of their MBA, students receive plenty of help to initiate their internship search, including instruction on resume writing, interviewing, researching companies and more. After that, students have access to the Career Center's Internet database as well as one-on-one career advising with professional counselors. However, the program's unique in-depth focus is what really makes the difference in career placement. A current student explains, "Access to corporate recruiters is unprecedented since we have a program which consists of specializations, rather than a generic MBA. You get put on a niche career track right away, so recruiters know exactly what they're getting during interviews."

With strong ties in the region, 60 percent of students take jobs in the Midwest. However, for those looking to expand their horizons, students reassure us that "last year and the current year, we have been utilizing our alumni and board member connections to send a significant number of finance students out to New York for positions with bulge bracket firms." Currently, the top five recruiters at UW are: Johnson & Johnson, Procter & Gamble, General Mills, State of Wisconsin Investment Board, and Cisco Systems, Inc.

Student Life and Environment

When they aren't hitting the books, Wisconsin MBA students say there are "plenty of activities to become involved in, such as fundraising events, guest lecturers and social get-togethers." Even if you aren't into extracurricular activities, it's easy to get to know your classmates, because "in addition to clubs, classes, and social events, most students are well connected with the other students in their centers." Most Wisconsin MBAs maintain a balanced perspective on life, work, and studies. A current student elaborates, "The students in the business school are very serious about their studies and put in long, dedicated hours to get things done. Then they go party. It takes a mature kind of mindset to be able to effectively balance the two." Another chimes in, "It's not uncommon to work on group projects until two or three in the morning."

At this famous university, the business school is located "in the middle of campus with the 42,000 other students, so there is a constant buzz of activity." The consummate college town, students love Madison, "a city with a thriving arts and cultural scene, and plenty of opportunities for recreation and entertainment." Since the business school is close to downtown, "you get the undergraduate as well as the professional demographic all within seven blocks." With so many entertainment options, it's no surprise that "most of the MBA students go out every Thursday night for a beverage—a great way to get to know everyone."

Admissions

The University of Wisconsin—Madison seeks students from diverse personal, professional, and cultural backgrounds, who have demonstrated success in business and management. Last year's class had an average GMAT score of 669 and average work experience of five years. In addition to their academic and professional achievements, Wisconsin looks for students who demonstrate intellectual curiosity, motivation, leadership, communication skills, and analytical ability. An applicant's fit with their chosen career specialization, academic record, standardized test scores, and work experience are among the most important factors in an admissions decision.

FINANCIAL FACTS

Annual tuition (in-state/ out-of-state)	$14,476/$29,293
Fees	$1,142
Cost of books	$1,200
Room & board	$9,990
% of students receiving aid	87
% of first-year students receiving aid	88
% of students receiving grants	87
Average award package	$28,175
Average grant	$28,175
Average loan	$19,567
Average student loan debt	$22,410

ADMISSIONS

Admissions Selectivity Rating	**98**
# of applications received	847
% applicants accepted	19
% acceptees attending	63
Average GMAT	669
Range of GMAT	640–710
Accepts GRE scores	Yes
Average Verbal GRE	162
Range of Verbal GRE scores	158–167
Average Quantitative GRE	159
Range of Quantitative GRE scores	158–161
Average Writing GRE	4.3
Range of Writing GRE scores	4.0–4.5
Average GPA	3.4
TOEFL required of international students	Yes
Minimum TOEFL (paper/web)	600/100
Application fee	$56
International application fee	$62
Application Deadline/Notification	
Round 1:	11/2 / 12/9
Round 2:	1/4 / 2/10
Round 3:	2/2 / 3/9
Round 4:	3/1 / 4/6
Deferment available	Yes
Maximum length of deferment	1 year
Transfer students accepted	No
Non-fall admissions	No
Need-blind admissions	Yes

EMPLOYMENT PROFILE

Career Rating	**95**	**Grads Employed by Function%**	**Avg. Salary**
Percent employed at graduation	77	Marketing	(31%) $98,059
Percent employed 3 months after graduation	90	Operations	(10%) $102,375
		Consulting	(14%) $117,700
Average base starting salary	$100,653	Management	(1%)
Primary Source of Full-time Job Acceptances		Finance	(22%) $103,000
School-facilitated activities	56 (66%)	HR	(5%) $90,667
Graduate-facilitated activities	22 (26%)	Other	(17%) $92,233
Unknown	7 (8%)	**Top 5 Employers Hiring Grads**	
		DISH Network (3), Target Corporation (3), General Mills (3), Kraft Foods Group (2), Kimberly-Clark Corporation (2)	

UNIVERSITY OF WISCONSIN—MILWAUKEE
SHELDON B. LUBAR SCHOOL OF BUSINESS

GENERAL INFORMATION
Type of school   Public
Affiliation   No Affiliation
Academic calendar   Semester

SURVEY SAYS...
Students love Milwaukee, WI

STUDENTS
Enrollment of parent
  institution   27,813
Enrollment of MBA Program   226
% male/female   71/29
% out-of-state   57
% part-time   71
% underrepresented minority   0
% international   57
Average age at entry   30
Average years work
  experience at entry   6

ACADEMICS
Academic Experience Rating   71
Profs interesting rating   66
Profs accessible rating   67
Student/faculty ratio   3:1
% female faculty   25
% underrepresented
  minority faculty   28
% part-time faculty   17

Joint Degrees
Master of Human Resources and
Labor Relations - 2-7 years Master
Of Public Administration, Non-Profit
Management - 2-7 years MBA/PhD
Nursing - 3-7 years MS-MIS.MBA
- 3-7 years

Prominent Alumni
Keith Nosbusch, CEO, Rockwell
Automation; Steve Davis, Chairman
& CEO, Bob Evans Farms Inc.;
Robert Probst, Exec VP, Tamarack
Petroleum; Mary Ellen Stanek,
Managing Director, Robert Baird &
Co; Jacquelyn Fredrick, President &
CEO, The BloodCenter of Wisconsin

Academics

The University of Wisconsin—Milwaukee Sheldon B. Lubar School of Business offers graduate students a "variety of classes" in a "convenient location." Students have "variety and flexibility" in choosing a part-time or full-time program. The MBA degree can be completed at the main campus in Milwaukee. The Lubar School's campus is located on Milwaukee's lovely east side, a few blocks from Lake Michigan. Classes generally take place in the evening, with the exception of a few courses scheduled on Saturdays or in a hybrid online format. Students in the Executive MBA program will meet over a seventeen-month period on alternating Fridays and Saturdays for a series of five ten-week sessions.

The graduate programs at Lubar do "an excellent job to prepare the business leaders and managers of tomorrow." Besides the core courses in management, students may also pursue an elective in cost management and ERP, e-business, entrepreneurship, financial strategy, global strategy, HR management, IT management, innovation management, investment management, leadership, manufacturing and service operations, managing change, health care management, supply chain management, marketing, or nonprofit management. The programs on the whole offer concrete "academic challenges." There is also a "good business community in Milwaukee" that students are able to take advantage of both during the program and after graduation.

Faculty at UWM consists of "strong professors with a business aptitude." They "do a great job in lecture explaining the material." One student comments about under-graduate teachers at a different university who "were intelligent about the subject matter, but could not teach at all." However, this same student avows, "The teachers at UW-Milwaukee really know how to teach." Having professors with direct experience of the business topics that they teach is deemed important to many students. "Most of the professors have been in the business world so they are able to provide practical examples during discussions." It was also noted that there are "some exceptional professors, dedicated to student learning and outcomes."

When asked about their school, UWM students "have nothing but good things to say about the administration, professors and [their] overall experience." Of course, there is always room for improvement. There were some suggestions regarding class offerings such as the addition of "online classes." Another student would like to see "more school spirit" on campus, especially at sporting events where it seems to be lacking.

Career and Placement

While most MBA students are employed full-time, UWM provides students at the Lubar School of Business with an array of programs and services to assist in job placement after graduation. There are career fairs, a resume referral service program that helps match students with the appropriate employers, a confidential alumni database placement service for employers to locate prospective candidates, on-campus recruiting services, and internships. Advisors are also available for mock interview sessions; job postings; help with resume design, cover letter writing, and interviewing; as well as scheduling on-campus interviews online via the e-Recruiting system. Recent top employers of Lubar graduates include US Bank, Kohler Company, Rockwell Automation, and Aurora Health Care. Other recent employers include Ernst & Young, Miller Brewing Company, Stark Investments, Cobalt Corp., and Wells Fargo. However, students did note the school's need of "getting more companies to recruit" on their list of improvements.

ADMISSIONS CONTACT: MATT JENSEN, MBA/MS PROGRAM MANAGER
ADDRESS: PO BOX 742, MILWAUKEE, WI 53201-0742
PHONE: 414-229-5403 • FAX: 414-229-2372
E-MAIL: MBA-MS@UWM.EDU • WEBSITE: WWW.UWM.EDU/BUSINESS

Student Life and Environment

Life at the University of Wisconsin—Milwaukee is "busy," though "great." For students looking for more ways to be involved, there is an abundance of professional business student organizations from which to choose. Although, many students are "not super involved" due to schedules that keep them away from campus, some manage to find the time for extracurricular activities. Although one student points out, there are "lots of activities for undergrads, not necessarily so for grads."

Students at UWM fall into a wide range of ages but the average student age is twenty-eight. The students are "professional, hard-working, [and] friendly," and most "look to be [in their] mid-thirties" and seem to "fall within a large range from 'Just graduated from College' to 'Mid-level managers.'" Students at UWM are "intelligent" and "down to earth." Working on team projects is a good way to get to know this "dynamic" group of students and is usually a rewarding experience since everyone is so "willing to learn." One student explains, "Everyone has been really great to work with. Whenever I've been in teams, everyone has pulled their weight and set a target of an A grade."

Admissions

Prospective candidates should send completed applications online to the UW-Milwaukee Graduate School website for review and recommendation. All applicants must submit a completed application form, an official GMAT score, one official copy of transcripts for all undergraduate work, and a personal statement. Letters of recommendation will also be considered. Students must achieve a minimum undergraduate GPA of 2.75 and have a GMAT score "that indicates a high probability of success in graduate school" to be considered for "admission in good standing." Applicants who fail to meet these minimum requirements may be granted "admission on probation" status. International students must meet all of the above requirements and must also submit an official TOEFL score report. Previous work experience is not necessary upon enrollment. Admissions are accepted on a rolling basis, and students in programs other than the EMBA or CO-20 MBA may start in any semester.

FINANCIAL FACTS

Cost of books	$900
Room & board	
(on/off-campus)	$9,000/$10,000
Average award package	$16,078
Average grant	$13,265
Average loan	$14,037
Average student loan debt	$21,056

ADMISSIONS

Admissions Selectivity Rating	**83**
# of applications received	161
% applicants accepted	63
% acceptees attending	48
Average GMAT	564
Range of GMAT	530–600
Accepts GRE scores	No
Average GPA	3.1
TOEFL required of	
international students	Yes
Minimum TOEFL	
(paper/web)	550/
Application fee	$56
International application fee	$960
Application Deadline	
Round 1:	8/1
Round 2:	1/1
Round 3:	5/1
Deferment available	Yes
Maximum length of	
deferment	One year
Transfer students accepted	Yes
Transfer application policy	
The application process is the	
same for all applicants.	
Non-fall admissions	Yes
Need-blind admissions	Yes

EMPLOYMENT PROFILE		
Career Rating	60*	**Top 5 Employers Hiring Grads**
		Kohler Company, Rockwell Automation, GE
		Healthcare, US Bank Corp, Aurora Health Care

UNIVERSITY OF WISCONSIN—WHITEWATER
COLLEGE OF BUSINESS AND ECONOMICS

GENERAL INFORMATION

Type of school — Public
Affiliation — No Affiliation
Academic calendar — Semester

SURVEY SAYS...
Happy students
Solid preparation in:
General management,
Communication/interpersonal skills,
Social responsibility

STUDENTS

Enrollment of parent institution	12,351
Enrollment of MBA Program	522
% male/female	56/44
% out-of-state	17
% part-time	83
% underrepresented minority	19
% international	17
Average age at entry	32
Average years work experience at entry	5

ACADEMICS

Academic Experience Rating	**86**
Profs interesting rating	90
Profs accessible rating	94
Student/faculty ratio	28:1
% female faculty	33
% underrepresented minority faculty	22
% part-time faculty	0

Joint Degrees
Students can simultaneously enroll in two graduate degree programs sharing 12 credits across programs. Available options: MBA-MPA for 54 credits, MBA-MS Applied Economics for 56 credits. Students must satisfy admission and graduation requirements for each program.

Academics

The University of Wisconsin-Whitewater offers "a great business school" for "anyone on a budget." One current student tells us, "I chose UW-Whitewater for my MBA because of the school's reputation, and they have the courses I want to be able to specialize in marketing." Adopting a two-pronged approach, UW-Whitewater offers students either a traditional in-class MBA or an online-only option, full- or part-time, both at "an affordable price compared to other AACSB-accredited programs." The online program in particular was recently ranked in U.S. News & World Report as one the country's top-twenty-five online MBA programs, and students can complete the program in one year with the proper prerequisites. Whatever one's time commitment or location, there are "two types of grad students" at UW-Whitewater: "The MBA students and MPA (master's of accountancy) students," both of whom can now take advantage of Hyland Hall, the school's new "state-of-the-art" business building, which has "changed the school 100 percent" for the better. What's more, MBA or MPA students getting their degree online—many of whom have "never stepped foot on campus"—enjoy the convenience of things "like chat groups [that] are not live meetings." According to one online student who lives in Japan, "When you are doing an online degree many students are in different time zones and have difficulty making meetings." Another online student, a self-proclaimed "full-time career woman and mother" shares with us that the online program "fits my lifestyle."

While UW-Whitewater "isn't as famous as UW-Madison," the school does boast "one of the best accounting master's programs in the nation," and according to many a student, "well-experienced" professors who are "accessible," "have high credentials," and "make themselves readily available outside of the classroom." As one pleasantly surprised student puts it, "I thought that a lot of my professors did not have real-world experience, but a majority of them have twenty plus years." "However," one full-time student offers, "a few should not be in the teaching career because of a lack of understanding."

There is no typical graduate student at UW-Whitewater; it's more of "a mix of students who are older and seeking greater academic qualifications, as well as those students . . . starting an MBA right after undergraduate" work. To add to this already diverse makeup, MBA students have a wide array of concentrations from which to choose, including finance, human resources management, international business, IT management, marketing, technology and training, and operations and supply chain management. Study-abroad programs are also available in France, Czech Republic, Mexico, Netherlands, Russia, Sweden, England, Switzerland, and Australia. The University also offers support services for international and minority students. "While I cannot say that UW-Whitewater is just as good as the expensive schools," one student tells us, "I would recommend this school over and over again to anyone considering an MBA."

Career and Placement

The University's Career Services Office offers "numerous programs and presentations" for students, including career counseling, career groups, a resource center and classes, resume and cover letter workshops, career fairs, interview prep, online job postings, on-campus interviews, and related resources. The career office is much more a resource for those students who attend classes on campus, while online-only students may feel left out for obvious reasons. However, one student reminds us, "There are so many ways to participate and always e-mails coming out for job openings and career fairs." But in terms of servicing this growing community of online students, the "Career Services Office seems lost as to how to help students search for jobs and how to help them connect with employers." For those students on campus, other improvement needs are cited, such as a "better mentoring program" and attracting a more diverse set of employers to the school's job fairs, besides Target and Walgreens. All the same, with a mean base salary of $54,000 for recently graduated full-time students, newly minted MBAs from UW-Whitewater aren't doing too badly these days.

Student Life and Environment

There's no two ways to cut it, "Whitewater is remote," but several students assure us that they've "enjoyed living in a small town," which can provide the quiet and seclusion many people need while earning their graduate degree. However, with few local employment opportunities, one student tells us, "No one really stays in Whitewater after graduation." Located "about an hour from the capital" of Madison, and not too far from Milwaukee either (from which several students hail), "the town itself is lacking in many ways," with "only one grocery store . . . and one or two clothing stores. Students must travel thirty minutes to a city that has a satisfactory place to shop." Several on-campus clubs and organizations allow students to get involved and apply their new skills and knowledge, but for the most part, UW-Whitewater is a school for commuters or those with full-time day jobs (85 percent of students attend part-time). "Convenience," above all else, is what UW-Whitewater students cite time and again about their school. Commuters have little trouble managing their class schedules, and online-only students praise the fact that they can "take classes from anywhere in the world." There is definitely "a lot of variety" in terms of classes and concentrations, although some students would like to see more "weekend classes for working professionals."

Admissions

With a mostly part-time student body of working professionals and online-only students, undergraduate GPAs and GMAT scores (both required for all applicants) tend to cover a wide range. The average undergrad GPA for MBA students is 3.3, and the average GMAT score is 482. However, those applicants with lower than average numbers in either category should not feel deterred, as optional materials like letters of reference, resume/work experience, and extracurricular activities can potentially shift the scales in one's favor. International applicants must submit TOEFL scores, with a minimum of 550 on the written test.

Prominent Alumni

Dean Amhaus, President & CEO at The Water Council; Barnali Goswami, Vice President, JP Morgan Chase; Jason Leigel, Vice President, Globus Medical; Sarah Lutz, Vice President - Corporate Banking, Associated Bank; Tobin Anderson, President, Tobin Anderson Consulting

FINANCIAL FACTS

Annual tuition (in-state/ out-of-state)	$9,126/$18,270
Fees	$0
Cost of books	$2,800
Room & board	$3,700
Average grant	$500
Average loan	$0

ADMISSIONS

Admissions Selectivity Rating	82
# of applications received	154
% applicants accepted	69
% acceptees attending	80
Average GMAT	482
Range of GMAT	418–540
Accepts GRE scores	Yes
Average GPA	3.3
TOEFL required of international students	Yes
Minimum TOEFL (paper/web)	550/79
Application fee	$56
Deferment available	Yes
Maximum length of deferment	1 year
Transfer students accepted	Yes
Transfer application policy	They must meet the same requirements as a non-transfer student. Nine credits may be transferred into the program.
Non-fall admissions	Yes
Need-blind admissions	Yes

EMPLOYMENT PROFILE

Career Rating	81
Percent employed at graduation	89
Average base starting salary	$80,211

VALPARAISO UNIVERSITY
COLLEGE OF BUSINESS—MBA PROGRAM

Academics

Valparaiso University College of Business offers "strong academic programs with an emphasis on values-based leadership and sustainability," thereby creating MBAs who are "well-equipped to be the leaders of the future green economy," students report. It's a big deal; Valpo's "commitment to moral and ethical standing" is frequently cited by students when asked to explain why they chose to attend this northwest Indiana university. Convenience, especially for the part-time students who make up about 36 percent of the MBA student body, is another factor. Valpo offers evening classes with the ability to attend remotely anf through which live on-campus classes are broadcast over the Internet (allowing those remote students to participate in class). Valpo's online software also allows students to collaborate on group projects remotely.

Valpo's MBA program is small and relatively new. It is also innovative, particularly in its scheduling. Valpo's eight-week bloc system creates six different entry dates during the academic year and allows a pick-and-choose approach that accommodates both fast-trackers and those who need take a little more time to complete the degree. The Valpo MBA entails eight core courses and four elective, or "enhancement" courses; the latter run the gamut from finance to management to e-commerce. Students who lack adequate undergraduate training in business can complete a series of foundational courses in addition to their core and enhancement work.

The small size of the MBA program and a "low student-to-professor ratio" mean plenty of "individual attention from professors," which students appreciate. "Access to mentors and extra projects is excellent" here, and students report that "it's easy to get into the classes you want" (although class selection, due to the size of the program, is limited). Professors bring "real-world experience" to the classroom to "provide real-world examples that we can immediately implement at work." Administrators are "constantly looking to improve the available programs. They seek student input [on] topics [ranging from]...new courses offered to the overall strategic plan of the university."

Career and Placement

Valpo's MBA program has been in existence since 2001. Students admit that "the word has not spread about Valpo," and the business community is just beginning to catch on to this new source of talented recruits. However, with the power of the Valparaiso name behind it and the strength of the MBA curriculum, students know it's just a matter of time before their program begins to draw its rightful share of attention from recruiters.

Many Valpo students are already employed when they begin their MBA and plan to continue at their current companies after graduation. However, those who are looking for new positions have access to the Valparaiso University Career Center. The Career Center serves the school's graduate and undergraduate community and offers a variety of professional development workshops and career counseling, campus career fairs, and a job search database.

ADMISSIONS CONTACT: CINDY A. SCANLAN, ASSISTANT DIRECTOR MBA
ADDRESS: 104 URSCHEL HALL, 1909 CHAPEL DRIVE, VALPARAISO, IN 46383
PHONE: 800-599-0840 • FAX: 219-464-5789
E-MAIL: MBA@VALPO.EDU • WEBSITE: WWW.VALPO.EDU/MBA

Student Life and Environment

Valpo MBAs are primarily part-time students. Part-timers range from twenty-two to fifty-five years old and have, on average, almost ten years of professional experience coming into the program. They typically "exhibit strong leadership skills with an emphasis on integrity, fairness, honesty and trust." Full-timers tend to be younger and less experienced. International students make up 1 percent of the part-time student body and 8 percent of the full-time population.

On campus, there are athletic events and multicultural events weekly for our enjoyment," and the program "encourages interaction with fellow students outside the classroom throughout the week." For those seeking big city entertainment, Chicago is only fifty miles to the northwest—you can't get much more "big city" than that! On the other hand, part-timers are typically too busy for any of that.

Admissions

Admissions decisions are made on a rolling basis with six different entry dates for part-time students and one start date for full-time students. Valparaiso makes admissions decisions holistically, assessing a combination of undergraduate and post-graduate academic performance, applicable professional experience, letters of recommendation, GMAT scores (working professionals can apply for a GMAT waiver), and a one-page personal statement describing the applicant's goals in order to determine the candidate's potential to benefit, and to benefit from, a Valpo MBA. In addition to the qualifications listed above, international students whose first language is not English must submit an official score report for the TOEFL or IELTS. All international students must submit an Affidavit of Financial Support. For students who have earned bachelor's outside the United States, a third-party transcript evaluation is required.

FINANCIAL FACTS

Annual tuition	$30,000
Fees	$553
Cost of books	$4,000
Room & board	$12,500
% of students receiving aid	33
% of first-year students receiving aid	10
% of students receiving grants	0
Average award package	$14,420
Average grant	$0
Average loan	$16,140
Average student loan debt	$35,000

ADMISSIONS

Admissions Selectivity Rating	79
# of applications received	58
% applicants accepted	88
% acceptees attending	76
Average GMAT	515
Range of GMAT	455–565
Accepts GRE scores	Yes
Average Verbal GRE	154
Range of Verbal GRE scores	152–155
Average Quantitative GRE	150
Range of Quantitative GRE scores	149–150
Average Writing GRE	4.0
Range of Writing GRE scores	4.0–4.0
Average GPA	3.2
TOEFL required of international students	Yes
Minimum TOEFL (paper/web)	577/90
Application fee	$30
International application fee	$50
Early application deadline	6/26
Early notification date	7/10
Regular application deadline	7/24
Regular application notification	8/7
Application Deadline/Notification Deferment available	Yes
Maximum length of deferment	1 Yr
Transfer students accepted	Yes
Transfer application policy Students must meet MBA admission requirements. Up to 6 credit hours from another AACSB-accredited program, subject to approval.	
Non-fall admissions	Yes
Need-blind admissions	Yes

EMPLOYMENT PROFILE

Career Rating	79	**Grads Employed by Function% Avg. Salary**	
Percent employed 3 months after graduation	20	Management	(50%) $40,000
		Other	(50%) $70,000
Average base starting salary	$53,000	**Top 5 Employers Hiring Grads**	
Primary Source of Full-time Job Acceptances		Aerotek (1), Georgia-Pacific (1), Medtronic Via	
Graduate-facilitated activities	2 (40%)	Groove Technical Resource (1), Blue Cross	
Unknown	3 (60%)	Blue Shield (1)	

VANDERBILT UNIVERSITY
OWEN GRADUATE SCHOOL OF MANAGEMENT

Academics

Students are drawn to Vanderbilt University's Owen Graduate School of Management for its "outstanding reputation, world-class professors, impressive network of alumni, prestigious program, [and] competitive employment rates upon graduation." However, above and beyond the prestige of attending a top university, students universally cite the "small school size" as the "number one" draw. The tight-knit community "gives Owen a big advantage when it comes to administration and classes." As one student attests, "There has never been a class that I was not able to take, with the professor I wanted to take it with. Furthermore, it is very easy to get access to the world-class faculty here. I have great experiences working for hours one-on-one with celebrity professors [that] it might be impossible to even get into class with at a different institution. I was particularly impressed by the school's ability to have classes taught by Senators, Congressmen, and *Fortune* 500 CEOs."

Owen has a great reputation for energizing "a sense of camaraderie between the students as well as between the students and faculty." Though course work is "a very challenging and demanding experience," "students are very driven to excel, but do so while supporting one another." The academic atmosphere is "competitive, while maintaining a sense of camaraderie." All students "have a strong sense of honor." In essence, Owen "gives back a multiple of your effort." Due to the small class sizes, students benefit from individual attention. "You really get to know everyone in your class which helps to develop a strong network for your professional career." This sense of camaraderie pays off down the line when it comes to seeking out a career; "Given the small size of the student body, alumni are very receptive when you reach out for networking and advice."

Owens's MBA program "is known for its strong performance in the finance sector," as well as "one of the best healthcare MBA programs in the country." The school "is efficiently run, and the professors are accessible, social, and are willing to help in any way they can." Overall, the academic experience here "is extremely pleasant." Garnering equal praise as that attributed to professors, the school administrators are "fantastic and accessible." "Both the Dean and other administrators are more than willing to meet with students to address concerns."

Career and Placement

From the top brass to those working in career management, "the school is extremely well-organized and unfailingly prepared." Owen's Career Management Center "has beefed up efforts significantly given the recession." That said, students are always hoping to "increase the volume of on-campus recruiting." Others add, it's "easy to navigate a wide range of social and cultural activities balanced by dozens of neighboring market leaders in diverse industries that allows insights into career tracks and opportunities. The alumni community, stretched all over the world, is very generous with [its] time and insight, too."

In a recent class, 87 percent of full-time MBA graduates seeking employment had received a job offer within three months of graduation. For those who accepted positions, the mean base salary was $91,653. Pharmaceutical/Biotechnology/Healthcare, Financial Services, and consumer products are the industries attracting the majority of recent Owen graduates with General Electric, Goldman Sachs, and Johnson and Johnson listed as the top five employers recently.

Student Life and Environment

By in large, students at Owen embrace the age-old, "work hard, play hard approach." Students "are competitive academically but not to the point [that] they are unwilling to help or that they don't have a social life." The Owen culture "embraces diversity but we are collaborative in our social, personal, and professional discourse. We work hard and intelligently and moreover, [we] take advantage of Nashville-based social outlets to reduce stress and activate an intense sense of camaraderie." A nostalgic second year adds, "I have developed friendships in business school at Owen that are just as strong as the friendships I had in college. It's important to have such a welcoming atmosphere like the one at Owen so that you can balance your life as well as possible while in business school."

Nashville "is a great city." As one resident confesses, "I'm from the north and was very reticent to move below the Mason Dixon line. I'm convinced Nashville is a diamond in the [rough]—a city that has yet to be discovered and appreciated for its great food, live music, and expanding economy." Every Thursday night, "students...and the faculty mingle at a social for several hours. The relationships we are building with each other and the teachers are a vital part of our education." In addition, "the city has plenty of options for outdoor activities, music, food, bars, and sports." However, students lament, "there is no on-campus housing for post-graduate students," and a "bigger library with more study rooms would be great!"

Admissions

With an incoming class size of approximately 175 students each year, the Vanderbilt MBA program is one of the world's most selective. Admission to the full-time MBA program is highly competitive. Admissions officers seek out an "exceptionally talented and diverse group of students who are willing and able to grow, prosper, and contribute in an environment that is academically rigorous, professionally rewarding, and personally enriching." In selecting candidates for admission, incoming students are evaluated for their academic aptitude and interest, experience and goals, and personal qualities and potential. A recent entering class had an average GPA of 3.4 and an average GMAT of 690.

Prominent Alumni

David Farr, CEO, Emerson; Martin Craighead, Chairman & CEO, Baker Hughes; Adena Friedman, President & COO, Nasdaq; Doug Parker, Chairman & CEO, American Airlines;

FINANCIAL FACTS

Annual tuition (in-state/ out-of-state)	$49,950/$49,950
Fees	$430
Cost of books	$1,842
Room & board	$14,376
% of students receiving aid	81
% of first-year students receiving aid	84
% of students receiving grants	71
Average award package	$48,522
Average grant	$28,066
Average loan	$46,922
Average student loan debt	$76,488

ADMISSIONS

Admissions Selectivity Rating	91
# of applications received	888
% applicants accepted	42
% acceptees attending	47
Average GMAT	690
Range of GMAT	660–710
Accepts GRE scores	Yes
Average Verbal GRE	158
Range of Verbal GRE scores	157–160
Average Quantitative GRE	156
Range of Quantitative GRE scores	153–160
Average Writing GRE	4.2
Range of Writing GRE scores	4.0–4.5
Average GPA	3.4
TOEFL required of international students	Yes
Minimum TOEFL (web)	100
Application fee	$175
International application fee	$175
Application Deadline/Notification	
Round 1:	10/27 / 12/11
Round 2:	1/12 / 3/15
Round 3:	3/1 / 4/21
Round 4:	5/3 / 6/1
Deferment available	Yes
Maximum length of deferment	1 year
Transfer students accepted	No
Non-fall admissions	No
Need-blind admissions	Yes

EMPLOYMENT PROFILE

Career Rating		97
Percent employed at graduation		81
Percent employed 3 months after graduation		92
Average base starting salary		$108,256
Primary Source of Full-time Job Acceptances		
School-facilitated activities		97 (78%)
Graduate-facilitated activities		28 (22%)

Grads Employed by Function	% Avg. Salary
Marketing	(15%) $94,057
Operations	(12%) $111,863
Consulting	(26%) $121,093
Management	(9%) $110,727
Finance	(24%) $106,889
HR	(7%) $95,125
Other	(6%) $99,500

Top 5 Employers Hiring Grads
Amazon (12), Deloitte (9), The North Highland Company (4), AT&T (4), Citi (4)

VILLANOVA UNIVERSITY
SCHOOL OF BUSINESS

Academics

For Philly professionals, the Villanova MBA is a smart choice, providing "solid academic rigor while allowing a degree of flexibility needed for working professionals." Widely known as the "best part-time program offered in the area," the MBA is offered on two urban campuses and in two distinct formats. Busy students with demanding jobs will appreciate the Flex MBA, which can be started any semester and allows students to complete coursework in three to five years of study. In the Flex MBA, "you can really move at your own pace based on work/life balance, financial readiness, and learning style." Those looking for maximum efficiency will likely prefer the cohort-based Fast Track program, which allows you to complete the MBA in two years while maintaining full-time employment. In addition to praising the speedy degree, Fast Track students say "the cohort environment is incredibly beneficial with regards to networking."

For students in either track, the MBA begins with core coursework, including accounting, economics, and management. After completing the core, students choose electives from a "large variety of course offerings," and have the option of tailoring their degree by pursuing a specialization in analytics, finance, health care management, international business, corporate management, or marketing, or by pursuing a real-estate concentration through the Daniel M. DiLella Center for Real Estate. "Elective courses are outstanding," and include special "opportunities for international travel and learning" through the overseas programs; recent trips have taken students to business capitals like Dubai and Milan. Villanova doesn't stop there: In addition to coursework, students must complete a consulting project with a local nonprofit company, and another with a global corporation. (Note that "the Fast Track curriculum includes a one-week international trip" as a part of the Strategic Management for Global Organizations class, though overseas programs are optional for Flex Track students.) Finally, "The Leadership Development classes that bookend the program are especially valuable in group work and networking for MBA students."

The faculty comprises both academics and career professionals, so "some core courses have more academic-oriented professors while some have professors with substantial work experience." While students might prefer one type of professor to the other, all agree that it's "a good balance" among the faculty. Just as important, most professors are accessible, friendly, and "really want to help students maximize their potential." A student adds, "So far, I have nothing but good things to say about the teaching quality at Villanova. I've never had a problem reaching a teacher outside of class, and I've never had a professor that I didn't understand." That said, the Villanova curriculum was recently revamped, and students mention that, "there have definitely been some serious kinks in the administrative side of the program." Fortunately, "the staff encourages and actually listens to student feedback," so problems rarely persist.

Career and Placement

As a part-time program, Villanova isn't focused on job placement as much as on preparing students to excel in their current field. Certainly, the Villanova MBA will help you "to improve your career options and ultimately to get a better job"; for most Villanova students, however, that better job is something they are pursuing at their current company, rather than through a career search. As such, the MBA program doesn't offer many recruitment or networking opportunities for graduate students.

Those looking to make a career change generally "have to create their own opportunities through networking sites such as LinkedIn, or postings on job sites." Fortunately, students note an improvement is already in process: "There is a new graduate career placement person who has been very diligent in working with students for positions after their MBA." In addition, the school offers a number of career-related resources, including corporate information sessions, career coaching, and online resources, and students can also reach out to Villanova's "strong alumni network."

Student Life and Environment

Given the inherent struggle of maintaining a full-time job while pursuing a graduate degree, it's no surprise that Villanova students are generally "engaged and hardworking," though they are a "friendly and collaborative" bunch, too. A huge benefit academically and socially, students at Villanova are "very diverse in terms of academic background, work experience, life experience, ethnicity, interests, and age." Here, you'll share a classroom (and chat over drinks) with "early- to mid-career professionals across a wide-range of industry sectors, ranging from healthcare to energy to financial services."

At Villanova, "most students work all day and then attend class at night," which makes for an incredibly busy schedule. Fortunately, that doesn't mean MBAs never socialize. While some students spend little time at school or with their MBA colleagues, others forge meaningful friendships in the program. "After class, a lot of the students go to the bar together," and the school schedules various events, including "regular casual happy hours, resume and LinkedIn profile counseling, lectures, [and] fundraisers," at both Villanova campuses. One student enthuses, "The networking opportunities that the program has provided me have far exceeded what I expected, especially in a part-time program. I have made a lot of friends who I expect will be lifelong contacts."

Admissions

For both the Flex Track and the Fast Track MBAs, students submit official academic transcripts, GMAT scores, two recommendations, a professional résumé, answers to two essay questions, and, for international students, the TOEFL. The current class has a GMAT range (for the middle 80 percent) of 563–640, an average undergraduate GPA of 3.3, and about six years of work experience before entering the program.

ADMISSIONS

Admissions Selectivity Rating	**76**
Average GMAT	600
Range of GMAT	563–640
Accepts GRE scores	Yes
Average GPA	3.3
TOEFL required of international students	Yes
Minimum TOEFL (paper/web)	550/90
Application fee	$50
International application fee	$50
Regular application deadline	6/30
Application Deadline/Notification	
Deferment available	Yes
Maximum length of deferment	up to one year
Transfer students accepted	Yes
Transfer application policy Up to nine credits from AACSB accredited MBA Programs	
Non-fall admissions	Yes
Need-blind admissions	Yes

VIRGINIA COMMONWEALTH UNIVERSITY
SCHOOL OF BUSINESS

Academics

Virginia Commonwealth University's School of Business is located in the heart of downtown Richmond, VA and is known for the "the quality of the faculty," "a good reputation," "low cost," and its "location." VCU's location places it squarely in the "backyard of many Fortune 500 companies" and "gives students direct access to executives of multinational companies" as well as "real-world knowledge." In addition to its full-time program, VCU offers a "part time program with night classes," which is a great "option for working professionals." The cost of tuition is also lower than the University of Richmond, making it a good fit for those who want a great education at an affordable price.

VCU's connection to a "thriving, growing city with a younger demographic" translates to its course offerings. They "realize that it's important to be innovative," and "update their curriculum with the times, and focus on business as it currently exists, not as it existed ten to fifteen years ago," notes a student from the Class of 2016. Students also praise the focus on "entrepreneurship" and the "great connections for learning and post-graduate opportunities."

Students cite "the real world experience the professors provide" as one of the "greatest strengths" of the VCU's MBA program. In fact, VCU's School of Business recently released its new strategic plan, EPIC (Experiential Learning, Problem-Solving Curricula, Impactful Research, Creative Culture) with an emphasis on problem-solving through innovation and creativity. The "professors are a good mixture of academics and experienced businesspeople." Many "professors have assignments pertaining to current business dealings," which students find especially informative. And "many of the professors make apparent efforts to incorporate very current topics and news into class discussion or assignments." In addition, at "the MBA level VCU uses tenured professors and does not rely exclusively on adjuncts." Students are "very impressed with professors" and say they are "very accommodating to working students." All are "accessible and willing to work with students outside of class time." Professors go out of their way to assist students "be it professional development, networking, classwork, etc." They are "involved in other activities in the business community and leverage that 'real world' experience in the classroom." As one student notes, "It's rare to find a group of people that, as a whole, are as dedicated to helping the population they support (the students) succeed as the faculty at VCU."

Career and Placement

Students say the "career development is great" and the administration of the "MBA program and other graduate business programs are stellar." While many "students do not have job placement needs, since the majority are full-time employees already," students say VCU is "great" when it comes to "development and job search resources." There is a" large job market in the Richmond area" and "Richmond contains a lot of VCU graduates, so often businesses in the community are willing to participate in campus activities." VCU's Business school "regularly has events" in "both professional and social environments"—from recruitment events "for various organizations," "networking and job search preparation events," and "leadership lunch-n-learns." Many departments have "set up connections with either public or private sector organizations so students can work on real projects, not simulations or artificial scenarios," which is "particularly important for an MBA degree so that you can build a portfolio from real experiences."

And as Richmond increases "its number of Fortune 500 companies," many "will most likely pay for their employees to attend," strengthening both the student body, and networking potential. The growing number of new start-up companies in Richmond provide other career opportunities for students as well as partnership opportunities with the School of Business and MBA faculty.

Student Life and Environment

VCU is a "modern, urban university" "centrally located to all of the Richmond events and destinations." Students say that "school/work life balance is very good" and that it is easy to make friends in the program that they "intend on networking with and keeping in touch with long after graduation." Students say their classmates are "outgoing," "smart," and "friendly." They are "driven," "collaborative," "competitive" and "engaged" students who are willing to do what it takes to complete the program." "Almost all of my classmates are part-time MBAs who bring many years of work experience," notes one student. While students say "the physical plant is quite good," "Snead Hall is a great environment to attend class" and "the gym is nice too," the "greatest strength is the accessibility of classes." For most VCU students the availability of classes and flexibility of the program have the most impact on their life and ability to succeed.

Admissions

Applicants must submit a completed application, an official GMAT score report, an official transcript for post-secondary academic work, a résumé, a personal statement, and three letters of recommendation. International applicants whose first language is not English must also provide proof of English proficiency.

FINANCIAL FACTS

Annual tuition (in-state/ out-of-state)	$10,258/$21,091
Fees	$2,911
Cost of books	$2,500
Room & board (on/off-campus)	$10,000/$12,000
% of students receiving aid	41
% of first-year students receiving aid	40
% of students receiving grants	20
Average award package	$12,803
Average grant	$7,484
Average loan	$14,899
Average student loan debt	$23,087

ADMISSIONS

Admissions Selectivity Rating	83
# of applications received	88
% applicants accepted	66
% acceptees attending	69
Average GMAT	545
Range of GMAT	493–600
Accepts GRE scores	Yes
Average Verbal GRE	150
Range of Verbal GRE scores	148–152
Average Quantitative GRE	153
Range of Quantitative GRE scores	150–155
Average Writing GRE	3.5
Range of Writing GRE scores	3.3–3.8
Average GPA	3.2
TOEFL required of international students	Yes
Minimum TOEFL (paper/web)	600/100
Application fee	$65
International application fee	$65
Regular application deadline	7/1
Regular application notification	7/15
Application Deadline/Notification	
Deferment available	Yes
Maximum length of deferment	1 year
Transfer students accepted	Yes
Non-fall admissions	Yes
Need-blind admissions	Yes

EMPLOYMENT PROFILE		
Career Rating	72	**Top 5 Employers Hiring Grads**
		Altria (1), Capital One (1), Alstom (1), DuPont (1), PepsiCo (1)

WAKE FOREST UNIVERSITY
SCHOOL OF BUSINESS

Academics

The Wake Forest University School of Business offers "a first-rate education delivered in a small school atmosphere that is conducive to high levels of interaction between students and the faculty." Students universally laud the "personal touch" the graduate business program employs with its "commitment to academic excellence, strong faculty, [and] small class size that enables plenty of interaction among students and faculty."

Academics at Wake Forest follow a holistic approach. The integrated curriculum helps students learn to analyze and solve problems by understanding the many components of a solution. Course content follows suit and is organized around a strong first-year core which includes essentials such as international business management, financial management, macroeconomics, operations management, and quantitative methods. In their second year students choose a career concentration within the broader areas of consulting/general management, finance, entrepreneurship, marketing, operations management, health, or an individually-designed concentration. As one student attests, "The workload...is generally much more intense than what most students expect coming into the school and in comparison to students at similar schools. However, this intense and well-rounded education has already proven beneficial in my summer internship and in job interviews."

The administration is "easily accessible and from faculty to staff, everyone is friendly. Student voices can be heard." When it comes to professors, at Wake Forest it's a first name, open-door policy. "All of my professors are engaged in my success. The level of dedication is a defining factor that sets Wake Forest apart," says one student. In addition, the "Dean has fantastic visions for the school."

Career and Placement

Wake Forest alumni "are very open to mentoring and helping with [students] job search." However, some current MBA students feel "Career Development needs to better prepare students for the internship and job search...clubs could have more activities that connect students with potential employers." In addition, current students would like to see more "diversity of companies that come to campus." Right now, "the focus is primarily on the Southeast, but they are taking strides to move to a more national scope." However, others note that the Career Management Center has already been making strides to improve: "For example, a dedicated mentoring program and alumni outreach program has been developed and is being implemented."

According the the School of Business, between all three MBA programs (evening programs offered in Winston-Salem and a Saturday program offered in Charlotte) there are 189 businesses represented, and 33 percent of current students have been promoted since starting the programs.

ADMISSIONS CONTACT: STACY POINDEXTER OWEN, DIRECTOR OF GRADUATE BUSINESS ADMISSIONS
ADDRESS: 1834 WAKE FOREST ROAD, FARRELL HALL, ROOM A54
WINSTON-SALEM, NC 27106 UNITED STATES • PHONE: 336-758-5422 • FAX: 336-758-5830
E-MAIL: BUSADMISSIONS@WFU.EDU@WFU.EDU • WEBSITE: WWW.BUSINESS.WFU.EDU

FINANCIAL FACTS

Cost of books	$1,000
% of students receiving aid	75
% of students receiving grants	47
Average grant	$29,818

ADMISSIONS

Admissions Selectivity Rating	75

Student Life and Environment

Wake Forest MBAs are "outgoing, dedicated, hard workers who are easy to get along with and fun to be around." There are countless student activities and the academic work is rigorous, but students love the atmosphere and enjoy getting together to debate key topics of the day or cheer on the Demon Deacons at a basketball game. "We are a tight-knit group. Everyone knows everyone for the most part. The week can get pretty busy, but a lot of us play intramurals or pickup games during the week." Fridays are the time "when we all go out and blow off some steam. Students, even ones on different teams, will help each other out."

Life on campus "is fast-paced and exciting." The workload is pretty demanding, but there is time for fun." The student government "puts on lots of social events that bring most people out to socialize." There are "tons of clubs, activities, both athletic, cultural, and community oriented," and "the town of Winston-Salem also has plenty of dining venues." The typical day at Wake "ranges from all-nighter's in the study room with your learning team to happy-hour events in the courtyard where students cut loose, to Alive at 5 concerts in downtown. It very much is a work hard play hard atmosphere," which "prepares you well for the future." "Quality of life is part of what makes Wake Forest such a great place to be." All of student organizations including SGA, honor council, finance club, entrepreneurship club, and charitable events are available to Working Professional students.

Admissions

The Wake Forest University School of Business "seeks individuals who have demonstrated achievement through academic course work, professional experience, and community involvement." Admissions Counselors "look for leadership ability, motivation, focus, enthusiasm, strong values, and teamwork skills in its prospective students." Postgraduate work is extremely important to the admissions process.

WASHBURN UNIVERSITY
SCHOOL OF BUSINESS

GENERAL INFORMATION
Type of school   Public
Affiliation   No Affiliation
Academic calendar Semesters: Fall;
                          Spring; Summer

SURVEY SAYS...
Classmates have diverse work experi-
ence, Happy students
Solid preparation in:
General management,
Communication/interpersonal skills,
Presentation skills

STUDENTS
Enrollment of parent
  institution   6,500
Enrollment of MBA Program   95
% male/female   67/33
% out-of-state   0
% part-time   70
% underrepresented minority   0
% international   25
Average age at entry   33
Average years work
  experience at entry   8

ACADEMICS
Academic Experience Rating   88
Profs interesting rating   90
Profs accessible rating   92
Student/faculty ratio   18:1
% female faculty   10
% underrepresented
  minority faculty   10
% part-time faculty   30

Joint Degrees
JD/MBA 108 Credit Hours approx-
iamtely eight semesters

Prominent Alumni
Greg Brenneman, Chairman of
CCMP Capital; Mayo Schmidt,
Former CEO/President of Viterra;
Dale C. Pond, Retired Former VP of
Marketing Lowe's

Academics

For Topeka professionals, the MBA at Washburn University's School of Business has a lot of selling points, among them its "location, reputation, cost, and appealing schedule for full-time workers." An "amazing value," this public school offers "lower tuition" than many business programs, yet maintains its standing as "one of the best business schools in [the] Midwest." No matter what your schedule and educational goals, Washburn makes it possible to complete a graduate degree without disrupting your career. "There are traditional day classes, as well as an abundance of night-class options," which gives busy professionals the opportunity to "work full-time and get a world-class MBA" simultaneously. Those who want to complete the program more quickly can enroll in more classes, taking up to a full course load. The school also offers a JD/MBA dual degree through which six hours of credit from the law school can be applied to the MBA.

As a true "teaching institution," Washburn's classroom experience is greatly enhanced by the fact that Washburn professors "love to teach and share what they know." They are also "skillful at encouraging students to lead the class," which makes coursework "interesting and engaging" across disciplines. The school boasts small class sizes and an excellent teacher-student ratio, so it's "easier to interact with professors and fellow students." "Accessible" professors keep regular office hours, and many "love collaborating with students on research or outside projects." In fact, "professors tend to form relationships with promising students, offering assistance whenever asked." The student-oriented faculty is complemented by a "very friendly and cooperative staff" and administration; however, students warn that, "outside of the School of Business, it can be difficult to get various tasks accomplished (i.e., financial aid, registrar issues, etc.)"

Washburn's curriculum is divided into nine foundation-level courses and eight upper-level business classes, followed by two advanced elective courses; students with an undergraduate degree in business can waive many or all of the foundational courses. Covering finance, quantitative methods, marketing, international business, strategy, and information systems, the Washburn curriculum is more academic than experiential. Through the school's professors come from "diverse backgrounds," contributing a great deal of "real world experience" to the academic environment, many students would like to see the school "provide opportunities for students to branch out, gain experience, and even earn credit through non-traditional routes." Students also note the general "lack of electives" makes it harder to specialize in a specific business discipline. Not to mention, most elective courses aren't offered every semester. A current MBA candidate notes, "I would love to have had the opportunity to engage in more specialized elective courses, aside from the general course requirements."

ADMISSIONS CONTACT: DR. ROBERT J. BONCELLA, MBA DIRECTOR
ADDRESS: SCHOOL OF BUSINESS, WASHBURN UNIVERSITY, TOPEKA, KS 66621
PHONE: 785-670-1308 • FAX: 785-670-1063
E-MAIL: MBA@WASHBURN.EDU • WEBSITE: WWW.WASHBURN.EDU/BUSINESS/MBA

Career and Placement

The Washburn MBA is an ideal program for "full-time workers that would like to grow in their company or look for upper-level positions." Classes are geared toward improving your business knowledge and skill set, and many students hope to leverage their education into a better job at their company or in their field. However, the school offers few on-campus recruitment programs, networking, or interviewing opportunities for students considering a career change. A student says, "I would expect more head-hunting from surrounding companies, but that just does not happen."

MBA candidates hoping to find a new gig after graduation can get assistance from the campus Career Services office. They offer career counseling services and host career fairs on campus that are open to undergraduates, graduate students, and alumni; recent career fairs were attended by local employers like Payless ShoeSource, CBW Bank, Cintas Corporation, and the City of Topeka. Prospective MBA candidates should note, however, that the majority of the opportunities offered through Career Services are geared toward undergraduates. As a result "most of the 'opportunities' that are presented to MBA students do not actually fit the ambitions of such individuals."

Student Life and Environment

Located in the heart of Topeka, "Washburn is a physically small institution, spanning just a few city blocks in each direction." The intimacy of the campus contributes to the close-knit feeling among the student body. With a limited enrollment of fewer than sixty students, it's an intimate atmosphere; a current student attests, "It feels like I know everyone in the MBA program." Students come to Washburn from "from diverse backgrounds and cultures," as well as from a range of professional backgrounds. In addition to locals, the school has "a great international student presence, as well, which adds a more worldly perspective to classroom discussions and reports."

Although the program was specifically designed to accommodate working professionals, there are also a handful of full-time students at Washburn. During the daylight hours, full-timers "study as a group in the library and participate in activities on campus," from sports to student clubs. Specifically aimed at graduate business students, the MBA Association is often involved in "inviting guest speakers and gathering MBA students in activities" around campus. Here, part-time students don't feel left out of campus life: "unlike some institutions, though, Washburn is 'alive' almost all hours of the day, due to its course flexibility."

Admissions

To be considered for admission at Washburn's MBA program, students must have an undergraduate GPA or 2.75 or better and a minimum GMAT score of 450, and those numbers must combine to meet a minimum "admissions index" number (which means that a higher GPA can offset a lower GMAT score and vice versa, though neither number can be excessively low). Students are also required to submit two letters of recommendation from former professors or employers. Applications are received and processed on a rolling basis.

FINANCIAL FACTS

Room & board	$12,000

ADMISSIONS

Admissions Selectivity Rating	83
# of applications received	61
% applicants accepted	66
% acceptees attending	78
Average GMAT	515
Range of GMAT	486–533
Accepts GRE scores	Yes
Average GPA	3.3
TOEFL required of international students	Yes
Minimum TOEFL (paper/web)	550/80
Application fee	$40
International application fee	$70
Application Deadline/Notification	
Deferment available	Yes
Maximum length of deferment	One Semester
Transfer students accepted	Yes
Transfer application policy Meet WU MBA Admission Requirements and we will accept up to nine hours from an AACSB Accredited Graduate Program.	
Non-fall admissions	Yes
Need-blind admissions	Yes

WASHINGTON UNIVERSITY IN ST. LOUIS
JOHN M. OLIN SCHOOL OF BUSINESS

Academics

Washington University's stellar MBA program "has a reputation for academic excellence without a hyper-competitive atmosphere." The small class sizes really allow for a "community based learning experience, [both] in and out of the classroom." Additionally, Olin affords students a "large degree of flexibility in course selection" and many "credits can be electives." Ultimately, this "provides students with a lot of freedom to design their own path." Further, most MBA candidates highlight both the finance and entrepreneurship programs as especially strong.

Just as essential, Olin manages to attract (and retain) "very friendly and smart" professors who are quite "approachable and...willing to spend time talking with you and discussing about current trends in business." Indeed, they "are generally very interested in individuals outside of their presence in the classroom, and they are even willing to share contacts with past students if a connection can be made."

For the most part, students have had positive interactions with the administration as well. A second-year shares, "The administration and staff [are] very engaging and willing to help out wherever possible...Every challenge I have faced was resolved within a week." A content peer chimes in, "The school's administration and faculty met and exceeded my expectations. They strive to make the program an individualized experience: one where you feel as though you, as an individual, have the potential to bring significant value to the program, the classroom, and the Olin community." Finally, a first-year student succinctly summarizes, "The overall academic experience has been phenomenal."

Career and Placement

When it comes to the job market, Olin MBAs are definitely competitive applicants (as evidenced by "very high post graduation employment rates"). Indeed, WashU "has a great reputation with a number of outstanding companies that hire for...general corporate management, finance, and operations." Additionally, as one marketing student proudly reveals, there's a "strong recruiting presence for brand management" as well. Many students are also "extremely impressed by [the] career services office." The counselors available provide fantastic, personalized advice tailored to each student's individual skill-sets and professional interests.

While you can definitely find a smattering of WashU MBAs scattered about the country, the majority of graduates finds jobs within the Midwest. Employers that frequently hire Wash. U. students include Citigroup, First National Bank of Omaha, IBM, Microsoft, Proctor & Gamble, Wells Fargo, Johnson & Johnson, Emerson, and Nestle Purina Pet Care.

Student Life and Environment

MBA candidates find Olin to be a "very inclusive" program, replete with "friendly" students who are definitely "open to building relationships." A first-year supports this notion stating, "As a small program, I can honestly say I knew everyone in my class by the end of the first semester and had the opportunity to work with a diverse team." And a second-year quickly follows up, "We know that our success requires teamwork and collaboration, so we are all sure to respect each other and help out where we can." Further, "We have insanely diverse backgrounds and experiences that lead to fun and engaging in-classroom and outside classroom discussion. We are passionate, but not cut-throat competitive."

Additionally, you can be assured that "there's never a dull moment" at Olin. To begin with, "you have so many ways to explore all of your interests and meet incredible thinkers and business leaders." Indeed, "there are events nearly every day of the week to attend. Workshops, fairs, club events, social events, etc can quickly fill up our schedules." Beyond the campus, students can readily take advantage of St. Louis, "a fantastic city [in which] to be a student. There are a ton of free museums and activities to take part in on the weekend, and the city as a whole is experiencing a renaissance right now. [And] because rents are cheap, it's possible to have a fantastic apartment or house on a student budget."

Admissions

Naturally, gaining admission to Olin is no cakewalk. The admissions committee truly wants to create a diverse class of students. Therefore, they do their utmost to select applicants from varying backgrounds. Moreover, they certainly take a holistic approach, considering experience, academic ability and leadership potential. The school offers six different application rounds (though from April 1st onward it operates on a rolling basis). If Olin is high on your list, we recommend applying as early as possible.

Prominent Alumni

Shelley Lavender, MBA 2003, President, Boeing Military Aircraft; Edward A. Mueller, MBA 1988, Chairman & CEO, Qwest Communications; Jim Weddle, MBA 1977, Managing Partner, Edward Jones; W. Patrick McGinnis MBA 1972, President & CEO, Nestle Purina Pet Care; Jerry Kent, BSBA 1978, MBA 1979, President & CEO, Cequel IIII

FINANCIAL FACTS

Annual tuition (in-state/ out-of-state)	$51,500/$51,500
Fees	$773
Cost of books	$5,564
Room & board	$17,696

ADMISSIONS

Admissions Selectivity Rating	95
# of applications received	1,685
% applicants accepted	27
% acceptees attending	31
Average GMAT	699
Range of GMAT	680–720
Accepts GRE scores	Yes
Average Verbal GRE	160
Average Quantitative GRE	159
Average Writing GRE	4.5
Average GPA	3.4
TOEFL required of international students	Recommended
Application fee	$0
International application fee	$0
Application Deadline/Notification	
Round 1:	10/1 / 12/15
Round 2:	11/15 / 1/25
Round 3:	1/5 / 3/31
Round 4:	4/1 / 6/1
Deferment available	Yes
Maximum length of deferment	If approved - 1 year
Transfer students accepted	Yes
Transfer application policy	
With approval, up to 9 credits from an AACSB-accredited graduate program.	
Non-fall admissions	No
Need-blind admissions	Yes

EMPLOYMENT PROFILE

Career Rating	96	Grads Employed by Function	% Avg. Salary
Percent employed at graduation	85	Marketing	(27%) $100,861
Percent employed 3 months after graduation	97	Operations	(12%) $90,686
		Consulting	(15%) $100,208
Average base starting salary	$98,297	Management	(11%) $99,000
Primary Source of Full-time Job Acceptances		Finance	(31%) $97,700
School-facilitated activities	69 (73%)	HR	(2%)
Graduate-facilitated activities	24 (26%)	MIS	(2%)
Unknown	1 (1%)	Other	(1%)

Top 5 Employers Hiring Grads
Citi (4), Emerson (4), ExxonMobil (4), Sigma-Aldrich (4), IBM (3)

WAYNE STATE UNIVERSITY
MIKE ILITCH SCHOOL OF BUSINESS

Academics

Asked why they chose the Mike Ilitch School of Business at Wayne State, most MBAs cite the affordability and convenience of the program. The school offers classes at its 203-acre main campus in Midtown Detroit, the Oakland Center in Farmington Hills and online; students extol these "convenient campus locations to choose from" and appreciate that "every MBA course can be taken at your choice of the two campuses or online." Evening classes and "a very flexible online class schedule" further help to facilitate the busy schedules of WSU MBAs, the great majority of whom work full-time while pursuing their degrees.

A "good finance" program and a strong local alumni network are among the other assets cited by students here. MBAs also point out that "WSU is an urban research-centered school," so "if you were interested in being a researcher, there are some great opportunities here." The downtown campus is "set in an urban environment" that "helps students get an education above and beyond classroom lectures," and because some adjunct "professors who teach the MBA classes work for local companies," participation in the program "is great for networking," not only with instructors but also with working classmates. Professors, students tell us, "have a nice mix of textbook-to-real world experience and knowledge… many published works and a few were either a CEO or high-ranking executive at a successful company. They challenge us to become better students but make themselves available to assist us in accomplishing our goals."

On the downside, some instructors have not yet figured out how to maximize the online course format even as it grows more popular with students. "Though some professors structure their in-class and online courses very, very well, this is not the norm at this school," one student explains. In many cases, "all we get are three to four-hour lectures, a talking head, and PowerPoint. The professors generally record their in-class lectures so we can't hear the students' questions," which students describe as "very annoying. It makes it hard to stay interested and focused." Some here also feel that the curriculum could use some revamping to place "more emphasis on core subjects and less on electives. Currently there is a 50/50 split."

Career and Placement

Dedicated solely to students in the Mike Ilitch School of Business, the Career Planning and Placement Office offers career counseling and professional development assistance to undergraduate and graduate students, as well as alumni of Wayne State. The center hosts a variety of on-campus interviews, career days, and meet-and-greet events. The center also offers career counseling services and comprehensive online resources. The school is well-integrated into the Detroit community; "In the Detroit area Wayne State business, medical, and law school alumni can be found in all industries and are happy to help fellow Wayne State alumni," one student reports.

A vast majority of Wayne State students are already working in a full-time, professional capacity when they begin their MBA. Therefore, many students are more focused on progressing in their current job, rather than making a career change or finding new positions.

Student Life and Environment

WSU has an "urban Detroit campus" and so must live with "the city's poor reputation" for poverty-related crime. Public safety "is better on campus than the surrounding areas, but many people need to park or walk to surrounding areas and have issues." While "the school is not responsible" for the city's crime rate, some here feel that "perhaps it could take measures to make the campus area very safe. This could include more police, security, and surveillance cameras." However, the university does have its own police department. Others are philosophical on the matter. "Until the auto industry rebounds, this urban Detroit campus will always have problems with the occasional stranger on campus. They don't pose any immediate threat, however it can be an unnerving experience for some people," one student observes. Students also note that "there are not a lot of healthy eating options around campus, and the rest of the restaurants are hit or miss."

"There aren't a lot of graduate-targeted activities or clubs" at either of the two WSU MBA locations, but most students are much too busy for such endeavors anyway. The student body, which "has got to be one of the most diverse student populations in the country," is a "mixed group of working adults and international students, mostly aged twenty-five to thirty-five." Students have "varying levels of work experience, although there are few who have management experience."

Admissions

The Wayne State University MBA program is predominately part-time, with nearly 600 students enrolled. Minimum qualifications for admission include a score of at least 390 on the GMAT and an undergraduate GPA of at least 2.75. The average entering student performs somewhat better: the median GMAT score among entering students is 485, while the median GPA is 3.2. The Wayne State University Mike Ilitch School of Business now accepts the GRE for admissions into our MBA program and a GMAT/GRE waiver option for highly qualified applicants. The admissions committee also evaluates a student's leadership potential and professional experience when making an admissions decision. Students may apply for admission in the fall, winter, or spring/summer semesters. International applicants must present an excellent academic record, demonstrate proficiency in English, and show sufficient means to cover tuition, supplies, and living expenses while enrolled in the program.

FINANCIAL FACTS

Annual tuition (in-state/ out-of-state)	$16,440/$32,904
Fees	$1,688
Cost of books	$1,196
Room & board (on/off-campus)	$9,430/$9,133
% of students receiving aid	40
% of first-year students receiving aid	49
% of students receiving grants	13
Average award package	$14,028
Average grant	$5,650
Average loan	$16,582
Average student loan debt	$41,267

ADMISSIONS

Admissions Selectivity Rating	89
# of applications received	807
# applicants accepted	454
# acceptees attending	292
Average GMAT	489
Range of GMAT	320–638
Accepts GRE scores	Yes
Average Verbal GRE	147
Range of Verbal GRE scores	140–157
Average Quantitative GRE	147
Range of Quantitative GRE scores	142–154
Average Writing GRE	4.0
Range of Writing GRE scores	4.0–4.0
Average GPA	3.2
TOEFL required of international students	Yes
Minimum TOEFL (paper/web)	550/79
Application fee	$0
International application fee	$0
Regular application deadline	7/1
Deferment available	Yes
Maximum length of deferment	One semester
Transfer students accepted	Yes
Transfer application policy	Must meet admission standards and a maximum of 6 credits are accepted. Students with a non-business undergraduate degree may only petition to transfer credit from an AACSB accredited M.B.A. program with a grade of B or better. Courses may not be over 6 years old.
Non-fall admissions	Yes
Need-blind admissions	No

EMPLOYMENT PROFILE

Career Rating		79
Average base starting salary		$74,551

Primary Source of Full-time Job Acceptances

School-facilitated activities	60	(53%)
Graduate-facilitated activities	5	(4%)
Unknown	48	(42%)

Grads Employed by Function% Avg. Salary

Marketing	(1%)	$61,800
Operations	(3%)	$60,000
Consulting	(5%)	$82,450
Management	(52%)	$87,200
Finance	(10%)	$58,500
HR	(2%)	$72,250
Other	(27%)	$62,400

Top 5 Employers Hiring Grads

General Motors (10), Ford Motor Company (9), Chrysler (5), Blue Cross Blue Shield (4), DTE Energy (4)

Weber State University

John B. Goddard School of Business & Economics

GENERAL INFORMATION

Type of school	Public
Affiliation	No Affiliation

SURVEY SAYS...

Classmates have diverse work experience, Friendly students, Conservative students, Happy students, Students love Layton, UT
Solid preparation in:
General management, Teamwork, Presentation skills, Social responsibility

STUDENTS

Enrollment of parent institution	26,000
Enrollment of MBA Program	186
% part-time	100
Average age at entry	35
Average years work experience at entry	4

ACADEMICS

Academic Experience Rating	88
Profs interesting rating	91
Profs accessible rating	91
Student/faculty ratio	8:1
% female faculty	5
% underrepresented minority faculty	0
% part-time faculty	25

Joint Degrees

MBA-Master of Health Administration combined degree program, length varies from 60 - 72 credit hours dependent upon undergraduate degree (business or non-business).

Academics

Designed specifically for working professionals, the MBA program at Weber State University in Utah offers one of the most flexible degree tracks around, allowing students to switch between full-time and part-time study at any time. With eight-week courses taught one night per week, the Goddard School MBA Program requires a "relatively low financial and time investment" and is "challenging enough to teach... something useful while recognizing that most students work full time," according to one student. "The experience is just what I wanted it to be: practical."

Registration is "simple," and "classes are scheduled to accommodate program progress without being in a cohort." There are six class blocks per year, and students can take a block off or take multiple classes in a block, and "can also take courses in any order as long as you have the prerequisites." The quality of instruction and the depth of professors' knowledge are "high," and teachers "bring a lot of outside experience to the table." The material they use is up to date and relevant, and if students "have questions or need additional help outside class, they are available." "They treat us like the working adults we are," says a student.

The administration is "very focused on the success of the students," are "very responsive," and "seem to have an honest desire to help students." The course schedules are released early, and individuals in the administration put in "consistent effort on their part to make clear where their offices are, what their respective roles are, and how best they can be contacted."

Career and Placement

Practically everyone who attends Goddard is working during the day, so recruitment and job placement is not a major concern for students, who are for the most part looking to further their existing careers. "The career personnel do more networking for the students than the students do on their own." Still, "the career counselor is the most connected job resource in the state" for those who are on the hunt, and the school "does an amazing job" of communicating "great and diverse" job opportunities to students. "We get weekly emails with links to [jobs]," says one.

ADMISSIONS CONTACT: DR. MARK A. STEVENSON, MBA ENROLLMENT DIRECTOR
ADDRESS: 2750 N. UNIVERSITY PARK BLVD. MC102, LAYTON, UT 84041-9099
PHONE: 801-395-3519 • FAX: 801-395-3525
E-MAIL: MBA@WEBER.EDU • WEBSITE: WEBER.EDU/MBA

Student Life and Environment

The program "caters to students who are working full-time and have families and who cannot take advantage of the student life offered," so "the majority are working and not involved in the many activities." The MBA program is at an extended campus, which lacks housing but does have its own clubs, programs, "bookstore, snacks, ample parking, nice library, and allows MBA students a dedicated, well-furnished classroom for study lab," as well as providing "an inviting environment for students to participate" should they so choose.

"The environment is great for a working professional and a terrific value for anyone wanting to further their career with an MBA," says a student of the "commuter" school. "I have been impressed with the professional nature of the students and their desire to do well in the program." Many interactions occur online, and students (who are accustomed to the working world) do their part. "I have yet to work in a group where I felt somebody did not pull their weight."

Admissions

To apply to the Goddard School MBA Program, students must possess a bachelor's degree from an accredited university. The primary criteria for selection are the student's undergraduate record and GMAT performance. Current students have a median GMAT score of 550 and an average GPA of 3.43 on a 4.0 scale. Other factors, such as work experience and professional progression, are also considered by the admissions committee. Each application is evaluated individually for the applicant's ability to succeed, potential for success, and possible strengths to contribute to the program. International applicants whose first language is not English must demonstrate English proficiency through testing; they must also have their undergraduate transcripts translated by a recognized service. Applications should be submitted online.

FINANCIAL FACTS

Annual tuition (in-state/ out-of-state)	$8,206/$16,884
Fees	$837
Cost of books	$1,000
Room & board (on/off-campus)	$6,700/$6,700
% of students receiving grants	5
Average grant	$5,000

ADMISSIONS

Admissions Selectivity Rating	82
# of applications received	112
% applicants accepted	86
% acceptees attending	98
Average GMAT	566
Range of GMAT	480–710
Accepts GRE scores	Yes
Average GPA	3.4
TOEFL required of international students	Yes
Minimum TOEFL (paper)	550
Application fee	$60
International application fee	$95
Application Deadline/Notification	
Round 1:	9/1 / 9/15
Round 2:	11/1 / 11/15
Round 3:	3/1 / 3/15
Round 4:	5/1 / 5/15
Deferment available	Yes
Maximum length of deferment	1 year
Transfer students accepted	Yes
Transfer application policy	
Full application required. Transfer credits from AACSB-accredited programs accepted, no more than one-third of degree total; from non-AACSB-accredited programs on a case-by-case basis.	
Non-fall admissions	Yes
Need-blind admissions	Yes

WEST VIRGINIA UNIVERSITY
COLLEGE OF BUSINESS AND ECONOMICS

Academics

The College of Business and Economics at West Virginia University "has a well-known business program with top professors," and this earns it "prestige within the state," students in this growing MBA program tell us. Full-time students love the one-year accelerated program that gets them in and out quickly, while those in the Executive MBA program love the convenience of being able to attend in one of nine satellite sites scattered about the Mountain State.

Students in both programs praise "the curriculum design," noting that "the sequence of courses is good, giving a good foundation in business: economics, accounting, marketing, finance, and operations." They appreciate that the WVU MBA program "teaches skills instead of memorization" and that administrators are always looking for ways to improve the curriculum. "There have been some significant improvements to make the program have a more global focus on business education," one impressed student reports.

WVU's full-time MBA is a forty-eight credit-hour program presented over a four-teen-month period. All domestic students are required to participate in an international trip to China, Poland, Italy, German, or the Czech Republic. The curriculum interweaves business themes and skills, building toward culminating coursework in planning and strategy. Students in the full-time program do not specialize in an area of concentration; however, WVU also offers an MBA in Finance, which can be completed in twelve months by students with substantial academic or professional experience in the field and in two years by students lacking such experience. Students in the EMBA program tell us that the program "provides students with one of the most diverse faculty groups in the country" and that "the diverse background of each faculty member provides students with a unique view of real life business experiences." (Students in the full-time program share this assessment of the faculty.)

All students here point out that "students not only focus on textbook examples, they get to participate in business experiences such as the Washington Campus and study-abroad programs to Italy, Czech Republic, Mexico, Germany, and China." These elements, they say, make for an "exceptional academic experience" and elevate the WVU MBA "a notch above the rest."

At the end of the day, the class sessions are very unique and productive based on multiple views from professionals working in various industries.

Career and Placement

The College of Business and Economics at WVU has its own dedicated Center for Career Development to serve business undergraduates and graduate students. The office provides counseling services, workshops, seminars, and on-campus recruiting events. Students tell us that the office seems geared mostly toward the needs of undergraduates. One writes that the office "is not geared well for MBA students. It is good for MSIR and MPA students. Even if they are for MBA students, the positions are only for entry level such as internships, leadership programs, etc." While students feel that "the career development center tries to give us information," they also feel that "it looks like they are working without any direction."

Student Life and Environment

WVU's full-time MBA program is attended by "a mix of professionals going back for MBAs and current college students." The program calls for a lot of group work; students tell us that "groups are very diverse, hardworking professionals that can appreciate the opinion of others…. The people in each group end up being the people you call for advice or to go out to dinner after class or on the weekend!" Some here, however, complain that the quality of students admitted to the full-time program needs to improve. One writes: "The class atmosphere is not that intellectually-motivating. Out of an entering class of sixty-five students, ten are very good and others are below average."

EMBA students may attend classes at the main campus in Morgantown or at any of nine satellite sites in Beckley, Charleston, Elkins, Keyser, Lewisburg, Martinsburg, Moorefield, Parkersburg, or Wheeling. One student calls these options "a blessing. The rural location where I live would not permit an economical pursuit of such a degree by traveling to the main campus for each class. The fact that classes are streamed to the distant location and the technology provides two-way communication and interaction is terrific!"

Admissions

Applicants to the MBA program must submit a completed application (paper or online), official transcripts for all postsecondary academic work, an official GMAT score report, and a resume. Letters of recommendation and a statement of purpose are optional. In addition, international students must submit an official TOEFL or IELTS score report (minimum score: 580, paper-and-pencil test; 237, computer-based test; 92, Internet-based test; or 6.5 IELTS). All students must have full use of a laptop PC that meets prescribed minimum software, memory, and processor-speed requirements; contact the school or visit the website for details. Applicants to the EMBA program must have at least two years of "significant work experience." For applicants with less than five years experience, GPA and GMAT figure most heavily in the admissions decision. Professional experience, especially managerial experience, is the greater factor for applicants with at least five years of experience.

FINANCIAL FACTS

Annual tuition (in-state/ out-of-state)	$11,776/$32,080
Cost of books	$1,800
Room & board (on/off-campus)	$9,080/$9,080
Average grant	$0
Average loan	$0

ADMISSIONS

Admissions Selectivity Rating	**87**
# of applications received	172
% applicants accepted	47
% acceptees attending	68
Average GMAT	536
Range of GMAT	450–630
Accepts GRE scores	No
Average GPA	3.4
TOEFL required of international students	Yes
Minimum TOEFL (paper)	580
Application fee	$60
International application fee	$60
Early application deadline	10/15
Early notification date	10/30
Regular application deadline	3/1
Regular application notification	3/15
Application Deadline/Notification	
Deferment available	Yes
Maximum length of deferment	1 year
Transfer students accepted	Yes
Transfer application policy Applicants request transfer credits and the admission committee reviews the request.	
Non-fall admissions	Yes
Need-blind admissions	Yes

WESTERN CAROLINA UNIVERSITY
COLLEGE OF BUSINESS

GENERAL INFORMATION

Type of school	Public
Affiliation	No Affiliation
Academic calendar	Semester

SURVEY SAYS...

Classmates have diverse work experience, Friendly students, Happy students, Students love Asheville, NC
Solid preparation in:
General management, Teamwork, Communication/interpersonal skills, Presentation skills, Quantitative skills

STUDENTS

Enrollment of parent institution	10,340
Enrollment of MBA Program	96
% male/female	67/33
% out-of-state	14
% part-time	78
% underrepresented minority	24
% international	10
Average age at entry	33

ACADEMICS

Academic Experience Rating	82
Profs interesting rating	90
Profs accessible rating	92
Student/faculty ratio	7:1
% female faculty	23
% underrepresented minority faculty	7
% part-time faculty	23

Prominent Alumni

Dr. David Ellis, Pardee Hospital; Carolyne Pelton, BB&T Corporate Banking - Senior Vice President; Wendy Cagle, Small Business Technology and Development Center; David Kemper, President - Kemper Strategies; Matthew Hutcherson, Regional Director for Mountain Bizworks

Academics

Located in a gorgeous, unique region of the Mid-Atlantic, the College of Business at Western Carolina University has worked hard to distinguish itself from other MBA programs, and has built a "reputation for not being an 'assembly-line' program." Students are encouraged to think for themselves and become effectively "better equipped to deal with future challenges." The small size of the school means that each student "has good learning opportunities" and "gets a lot of attention" from the "excellent, accessible professors with relevant professional experience." All in all, WCU offers a "quality MBA program with experienced, grounded faculty at a great price."

Although the school is based in Cullowhee—"an exceptional environment"—almost all of the MBA courses are held in Asheville. The school is very "oriented towards face-to-face classes" in Asheville and uses very little "new technology" (such as videoconferencing and electronic communications) for its courses. Professors and administrators "do a decent job of being available, considering that the main campus is over an hour away from our location." Both are "eager to tailoring course material to how students actually learn," and the professors "are very knowledgeable and have a lot of professional experience." The program heads and assistants are also "readily available and helpful with any questions that may arise."

The program's core courses are about mastering management in applied settings; students form small work groups and are trained to deal with real-world problems. Through the school's new MBA curriculum, developed in collaboration with faculty, recent graduates, and local employers, students learn and often perform the functions of chief officers in marketing, research and development, information technology, operations, legal affairs, finance, and the chief executive office.

Career and Placement

The fact that there are no online classes makes for "great networking opportunities." "Group projects help us network and the Graduate Business Students' Association is great," says a student. The "schedule flexibility for full-time employed students" is a great perk of the WCU program, as is the option for a 16-month "speedy graduation—in three semesters and a summer!" Although most students here are not looking for new jobs, students place great value on the real world applicability provided by the program design, which is "most beneficial to understanding the different aspects of business" and shows "how the different aspects work together to create a functioning business through real world examples."

Student Life and Environment

WCU really strives to create "a friendly, but competitive learning environment and the bonds you create with other students are very close." This "challenging and competitive" group is "very, very cooperative," "conscientious, mature, eager to learn, committed, and friendly." The student body tends to be a bit younger but still brings plenty of experience to bear. "As an older student, I am impressed and astonished by how astute the students are," says a student. "They are very helpful and supportive. I genuinely like them." Some "are Cherokee tribal members, some are from other local area businesses, and some are students continuing straight from school"; many are also "employees at the nearby casino. Though most students commute, there are enough distractions for those who want them, as Asheville is "a mid-sized city with plenty of activities in the area."

Admissions

Applicants to the MBA program at Western Carolina University must submit official copies of transcripts for all post-secondary academic work, an official score report for the GMAT or GRE, three letters of recommendation, a goal statement, and a resume. A minimum GMAT score of 450 and a minimum undergraduate GPA of 3.0 are generally required. Graduates of institutions in which the language of instruction is not English must also submit official score reports for the TOEFL and achieve a minimum score of 79–80 on the Internet-based test, 550 on the paper test, or 213 on the computer test. International applications are due by July 15 for the fall semester and by November 15 for the spring semester.

FINANCIAL FACTS

Annual tuition (in-state/ out-of-state)	$2,561/$8,214
Fees	$2,286
Cost of books	$744
Room & board (on/off-campus)	$9,290/$9,290
% of students receiving aid	53
% of first-year students receiving aid	65
% of students receiving grants	19
Average award package	$10,417
Average grant	$2,387
Average loan	$13,061

ADMISSIONS

Admissions Selectivity Rating	**74**
# of applications received	26
Average GMAT	489
Range of GMAT	410–530
Accepts GRE scores	Yes
Average GPA	3.2
TOEFL required of international students	Yes
Minimum TOEFL (paper/web)	550/79
Application fee	$65
International application fee	$65
Early application deadline	3/1
Application Deadline/Notification	
Deferment available	Yes
Maximum length of deferment	1 year
Transfer students accepted	Yes
Transfer application policy	
Up to 6 hours of graduate credit may be transferred from an AACSB institution	
Non-fall admissions	Yes
Need-blind admissions	Yes

WESTERN MICHIGAN UNIVERSITY
HAWORTH COLLEGE OF BUSINESS

GENERAL INFORMATION
Type of school   Public
Affiliation   No Affiliation
Academic calendar   Semester

SURVEY SAYS...
Friendly students, Happy students,
Students love Kalamazoo, MI
Solid preparation in:
General management, Teamwork,
Presentation skills, Doing business in
a global economy

STUDENTS
Enrollment of parent
institution   23,556
Enrollment of MBA Program   352
% male/female   63/37
% out-of-state   2
% part-time   44
% underrepresented minority   6
% international   22
Average age at entry   28

ACADEMICS
Academic Experience Rating   87
Profs interesting rating   90
Profs accessible rating   91
Student/faculty ratio   6:1
% female faculty   18
% underrepresented
minority faculty   9
% part-time faculty   0

Academics

Word of mouth plays a big part in many students' decision to attend the Graduate College at Western Michigan University with "great recommendations from family and friends." One student was even referred to the school by a CEO. Most students seem quite happy with their choice. They also like that the school "is nationally accredited," and ranked as a "top 100 school."

The graduate program at Western "is primarily a 'night school.' Most students work full-time jobs and take two classes a semester." "Classes are all from six to nine at night spread across three campuses. The MBA program is targeted at working people who want to pursue an MBA." Students find the program adaptable. One student agrees, saying, "I also like the ability to earn a specialization within my MBA program—I have some flexibility to change my curriculum if my interests change." The school also offers several online, weekend, and condensed-hybrid format courses.

While some classes are clearly more challenging than others, the workload is manageable for most students. "Academics are easy when you show up to class, pay attention, and do the work." The program also provides students with an "excellent emphasis on international business." This "global outlook" is "important in today's workforce."

Although not all the professors receive the same high praise, several do get excellent reviews. Considered "stellar" to "amazing people," these "teachers bring a great attitude and very effective teaching style[s]" to class. One student says, "Every semester I have entered into a new classroom and thought, 'Wow, this is my most favorite professor ever.' Now I'm struggling with which one is my favorite because there are so many and each one has helped me with situations that I will eventually face in my future." While one student claims to be "challenged to constantly find a way to incorporate what I am learning into my career," another student suggests, "WMU employs too many career educators, and I would like more real world applications of the materials we are learning." Class sizes are mostly adequate for sufficient student/teacher communication, usually "limited to thirty students so you get to interact quite a bit with the professors."

Career and Placement

The Career Services Center at WMU offers preparation services for graduate students at the Graduate College by way of resume, interviewing, and cover letter writing assistance. Students report satisfaction in their fellow peers' abilities of building "networking opportunities with fellow students." Simply going to class offers students "a great chance to meet people in my area." A student says, "It is amazing to me how much of an opportunity there is to network with international students from all around the globe here at Western Michigan University." Professors also do a good job in the classroom by teaching students "to grasp the knowledge of the subject and to incorporate that with their career fields." From one student's observations, professors "are willing to work with each student individually to help them make the right choices regarding career changes…. They also help with job placement and career fields."

The location of the school's main campus, "in a great city, Kalamazoo," also allows students a direct "community connection with local Fortune 500 companies." "The business school and WMU in general have a great relationship with what is a growing and vibrant city."

Student Life and Environment

Student life outside the classroom is "what you make it." "The school has many different social functions and sporting events to give student's the full college experience." Unfortunately, "family life for a lot of us limits the student involvement in clubs and activities." For the most part, though, students seem to get more out of [their] degree then just what they learn in class." At WMU, students come from many different cultures and backgrounds. "Western Michigan University is an international melting pot in the heart of west Michigan." One student attests, "Classmates are from as far away as China, India, and the Ukraine…. This opportunity to meet and collaborate with such a diverse student body is setting the stage for my ability to expand my professional network in the global economy."

Students in the graduate program as a whole are described as, "very team and school focused. "MBA students are largely uninvolved with campus as they are working full-time, commuting, and already established within their communities/workplaces." For example, one student recently "started an MBA social club to help build a greater sense of community." Overall, "people have a lot of school spirit and are very social. It is a fun school to go to."

Students make many positive remarks regarding WMU's Business School campus. "The campus is laid out well." The "landscaping is meticulous. The buildings are modern." However, another student says that as a commuter, "the parking is expensive and not that great." "WMU is in between a Big 10 school and a little private school; it has a great campus that is only becoming greater with reconstruction of more 'Green' space. The university is listening to the student population with regards to better housing, better food quality, and becoming green."

Admissions

Students with lower test scores and/or not so attractive grade point averages will take comfort in knowing that it is still possible to "get in with a lower GPA and GMAT score." These two scores are the only requirements along with the application; however, a personal statement and letters of recommendation can also be sent in for consideration.

FINANCIAL FACTS

Annual tuition (in-state/ out-of-state)	$12,727/$26,958
Fees	$923
Cost of books	$624
Room & board (on/off-campus)	$9,238/$9,238
% of students receiving aid	25
% of first-year students receiving aid	38
% of students receiving grants	4
Average award package	$13,896
Average grant	$9,497
Average loan	$14,947
Average student loan debt	$31,938

ADMISSIONS

Admissions Selectivity Rating	**82**
# of applications received	165
% applicants accepted	52
% acceptees attending	59
Average GMAT	532
Range of GMAT	485–580
Accepts GRE scores	Yes
TOEFL required of international students	Yes
Minimum TOEFL (paper/web)	550/80
Application fee	$50
International application fee	$100
Application Deadline/Notification	
Deferment available	Yes
Maximum length of deferment	One year
Transfer students accepted	Yes
Transfer application policy Students transferring from an AACSB accredited MBA program with the same admission requirements as WMU's MBA program may transfer six credit hours of work from their prior MBA program providing they have at least a 3.0 in the transfer course work and an overall gpa of 3.0 from the transfer institution.	
Non-fall admissions	Yes
Need-blind admissions	Yes

WICHITA STATE UNIVERSITY
BARTON SCHOOL OF BUSINESS

GENERAL INFORMATION

Type of school	Public
Affiliation	No Affiliation
Academic calendar	Semester

SURVEY SAYS...

Friendly students, Happy students,
Smart classrooms

STUDENTS

Enrollment of parent institution	14,495
Enrollment of MBA Program	168
% male/female	60/40
% part-time	45
% underrepresented minority	17
% international	13
Average age at entry	29
Average years work experience at entry	3

ACADEMICS

Academic Experience Rating	67
Profs interesting rating	62
Profs accessible rating	67
Student/faculty ratio	4:1
% female faculty	3
% underrepresented minority faculty	21

Academics

At the W. Frank Barton School of Business at Wichita State University, students benefit from a traditional, management-based MBA program that offers a broad range of course work in accounting, economics, finance, management, and marketing. Depending on a student's academic background (those who studied business as an undergraduate may be able to waive some requirements), the MBA is comprised of thirty-six to fifty-one credit hours, beginning with a core curriculum that covers business fundamentals. Throughout the core curriculum, particular attention is given to understanding the organization as an integrated system. Later, students may choose an area of concentration, taking up to nine credit hours of electives in finance, entrepreneurship, Business analytics and information management, or health care administration.

The school offers a fast-paced, 20 month executive MBA program for high-level professionals that meets on Saturday. There is also a traditional MBA program that holds its courses in the evening. Whether enrolled in the executive or traditional program, a majority of students work full-time while attending school. In fact, "most of them are professionals in the Wichita area," which means a double dose of work and responsibility. However, the school is aware of its students' special needs and "is very adept at offering programs that fit the schedules of its students." On top of that, students reassure us that the workload is manageable—"substantial at times, but for the most part, the average workload is within the expected output of a graduate program."

Reporting on the great classroom experience, WSU students generally describe their professors as "candid, well-spoken, knowledgeable, prepared, and fun." Unfortunately, students admit that a few staff members don't deserve such rave reviews. "There are some professors' classes I wish I could get a refund on, simply because the professors seem to be there only to earn a paycheck or a boosted ego," grumbles one student. In addition to their professors, classmates form an essential part of the learning experience at WSU. Drawing "a mix of mid-career business people and young business students," Wichita State students enjoy the fact that "everyone is very opinionated, which makes for great class discussions."

The "only AACSB-accredited school in the Wichita area," WSU is an excellent match for those who work or wish to start a career in the region, and WSU promotes a great deal of "community involvement with local businesses and entrepreneurs." Students appreciate the fact that "the school brings in wonderful special speakers and has a good reputation in the community." For example, "recently, the CEOs of Wal-Mart and PepsiCo visited the business school." Beyond Kansas, the school also runs an "international project with Berlin School of Economics and Law, where students taking the advanced strategic management course go to Berlin, Germany for one week and do the project there in conjunction with Berlin students."

Career and Placement

The Career Development Center (CDC) at Wichita State University serves the school's undergraduate and graduate community, including the business school. Through CDC, students have access to career counseling, an online job database, and an alumni database. The office also hosts several campus career fairs and on-campus interviews.

At Wichita State, "many students seem to be earning their MBAs in order to receive a raise or progress upward with their current employers," with a number of them also receiving tuition assistance. For those looking for a position with a new company after graduation, major employers in Wichita include Bank of America, Boeing, Bombardier Learjet, Cargill Meat Solutions, Textron Aviation, INTRUST Bank, Koch Industries, Spirit AeroSystems, Via Christi Health Systems, and York International.

Student Life and Environment

Those looking for a close-knit and community-oriented business school may be disappointed by "commuter-school" Wichita State. While they get a great business education, students admit that "the opportunities for networking are not particularly strong, as most students are too busy with work and families to attend mixers or be involved on campus." On the other hand, the atmosphere is pleasantly casual and friendly, and the community is "very diverse with local, national, and international students." A current student shares: "Even though we come from very different backgrounds and experiences, everyone seems to be incredibly open-minded and accepting to all students in the program."

The university provides plenty of extracurricular and recreational opportunities. In fact, students assure us that "if you want to do an activity and you look for one, you can find one." A case in point: One student who went from part-time to full-time status in his second year tells us, "I was surprised when I concentrated life to studies...I learned a lot that I missed when I was working in my first year." Off campus, Wichita is a pleasant, low-cost, medium-sized city with plenty of cultural, financial, shopping, performing arts, festivals, and entertainment options for graduate students.

Admissions

To be considered for admissions at Wichita State University, students must possess a four-year degree from an accredited college or university and be proficient in word processing, spreadsheet, and presentation software. Admissions decisions are made by evaluating the following: official GMAT scores (unless otherwise exempted), undergraduate transcript, an applicant's personal goals statement, two letters of recommendation, and a current resume. For the traditional MBA, career experience is a plus in an application package but is not required. Applicants to the executive MBA must have at least five years of relevant post-graduate work experience. Students may apply for entry in the spring and fall semesters.

FINANCIAL FACTS

Annual tuition (in-state/ out-of-state)	$4,927/$12,100
Fees	$1,336
Cost of books	$2,400
Room & board (on/off-campus)	$5,666/
% of students receiving aid	26
% of first-year students receiving aid	19
% of students receiving grants	11
Average award package	$5,318
Average grant	$1,306
Average loan	$7,123

ADMISSIONS

Admissions Selectivity Rating	86
# of applications received	139
% applicants accepted	49
% acceptees attending	72
Average GMAT	530
Accepts GRE scores	Yes
Average GPA	3.5
TOEFL required of international students	Yes
Minimum TOEFL (paper/web)	570/88
Application fee	$50
International application fee	$65
Regular application deadline	7/1
Application Deadline/Notification	
Deferment available	Yes
Maximum length of deferment	1 year
Transfer students accepted	Yes
Transfer application policy Only AACSB accredited classes may be transferred in. The maximum number of credit hours that can be transferred is 12.	
Non-fall admissions	Yes
Need-blind admissions	Yes

WILFRID LAURIER UNIVERSITY
SCHOOL OF BUSINESS & ECONOMICS

GENERAL INFORMATION
Type of school	Public
Affiliation	No Affiliation

SURVEY SAYS...
Good peer network

STUDENTS
Enrollment of parent institution	15,000
Enrollment of MBA Program	500
% male/female	60/40
% part-time	80
% international	10
Average age at entry	28
Average years work experience at entry	6

ACADEMICS
Academic Experience Rating	62
Profs interesting rating	60*
Profs accessible rating	63
% female faculty	36

Joint Degrees
MBA-CPA: approximately 4 years part time. MBA-MFin: approximately 3.3 years part time.

Academics

As Canada's largest full classroom-contact MBA program, there is something for everyone at the School of Business & Economics at Wilfrid Laurier University. Whether you want to take courses during the week, during the weekend, during the day, at night, on a part-time basis, on a full-time basis, at the Waterloo campus, or at the satellite campus in Toronto, chances are there is going to be an MBA format option at Laurier that suits your needs. In addition, the school's many MBA options cater to students from all professional and academic backgrounds. At Laurier, business executives have the opportunity to get a high-speed degree though the school's accelerated MBA program, while students with no previous work experience may apply to the "co-op" program, designed to help business newcomers develop their managerial and organizational skills. In addition, many students come to Laurier because it offers "the ability to get a professional designation (i.e., CMA, CFA) along with the MBA" through several joint-degree programs.

No matter how, when, or where they pursue an MBA, Laurier students appreciate the school's commitment to the case-based learning method, which "requires that you understand both the theory and then apply them in real-world situations." Emphasizing practical competence over strict academic theory, "the Laurier experience builds your thinking skills and allows you to attack complex problems from many angles." Discussion and debate are fundamental to the program, and "almost all courses include a group work component which promotes the teamwork abilities within each student." This interaction is an undeniable asset to the MBA education, since many "students are already at the manager/director level in their careers." A current student praises the professors, saying, "Not only do they contribute to the learning experience due to their vast work experiences, but they are very willing to help out both within the classroom and outside of it (networking)."

The core curriculum takes an "integrated" approach to business topics, which "allows you to cement concepts since you are dealing with them in multiple courses at the same time." After completing the core, students can tailor their education through a concentration in a number of fields (such as finance, accounting, brand communication management, supply chain management, or international business to name a few) by completing at least four courses in that subject area. They may also add breadth to their education through one of the school's international programs in Europe and Asia, or through the school's ample list of special seminars.

At the top of their field, Laurier professors are an excellent "mix of tenured professors and recognized, practicing professionals." Most "are PhDs and have recent/relevant consulting or real business experience." Friendly, down to earth, and well run, administrators at Laurier "communicate frequently with students and have always responded to questions very quickly."

Career and Placement

Career Services for the School of Business & Economics Graduate Programs provides assistance to MBA and MABE students and alumni. Their services include one-on-one career counseling and specialized workshops on topics such as resume writing, networking, interviewing, and cocktail and dining etiquette. Career Services also hosts special events, such as executive recruiter panels.

Maureen Ferraro or Aaron Miller, MBA Marketing Coordinators
Address: 75 University Avenue West, Waterloo, On N2L 3C5 Canada
Phone: 519-884-0710 • Fax: 519-886-6978
E-mail: mferraro@wlu.ca • Website: www.lauriermba.ca

Students agree that their school enjoys a great reputation in Canada, telling us that "employers love Laurier MBA students because they are much better educated and friendlier to work with." The following companies are among the extensive list of organizations recently recruiting Laurier MBAs: Accenture, American Express Canada, Bank of Canada, Canada Revenue Agency, CIBC World Markets, CPP Investment Board, Dell Canada, Deloitte Touche Tohmatsu, FedEx Canada, GE Canada, General Mills Canada, General Motors Canada, IBM Canada, The Loyalty Group, Managerial Design, Manulife Financial, National Bank Financial, Proctor & Gamble, Raytheon Canada, RLG International, Scotiabank Group, and TD Securities.

Student Life and Environment

With such a large and diverse student population, it's hard to summarize life at Laurier. Not surprisingly, there is something of a split between students who attend the program part-time and those who chose to pursue their studies full-time. There are two campuses in the Wilfrid Laurier University MBA program. One is on the Waterloo-based university campus and the other is a satellite campus right in downtown Toronto. Part-timers attending school at the Toronto MBA campus sometimes feel a little cut off from the main campus. However, Toronto students are required to participate in MBA events and competitions at the Waterloo campus.

In both locations, the majority of students are "mature with an established career and family life." For most, "life happens off campus," and students admit that there isn't much enthusiasm for campus activities or after-hours socializing. "Social activities with the satellite or main campus are limited due to work/family commitments in addition to academic demands," explains a current MBA candidate.

With many personal and professional commitments, most students at Laurier are talented multitaskers, who "are very good at balancing personal, work, and school life." However, they warn that the many group assignments, homework, and classes can make it difficult to juggle your educational, professional, and personal life. A student laments, "You have to be tough skinned to do an MBA on a part-time basis at WLU."

Admissions

To be considered for admission to Wilfrid Laurier University's MBA program, students must possess a four-year, undergraduate degree or equivalent (in any field of study) with at least a B average (73 percent) in the last ten half-credit courses taken. Except for the MBA with co-op option (for which no work experience is required), applicants must have at least two years of full-time work experience to apply for an MBA at Laurier. Students must also submit a GMAT score of at least 550. In addition to test scores and transcripts, students must send three letters of recommendation from professional and academic references to apply to the full-time or any of the part-time MBA Programs at Laurier. It is mandatory for students applying to the Co-op option to provide a 600+ GMAT score..

FINANCIAL FACTS

Annual tuition (in-state/ out-of-state)	$30,000/$30,000
Fees	$1,250
Cost of books	$3,000
Room & board (on/off-campus)	$8,000/$6,500

ADMISSIONS

Admissions Selectivity Rating	76
Average GMAT	620
Range of GMAT	550–750
Accepts GRE scores	Yes
Average GPA	3.2
TOEFL required of international students	Yes
Minimum TOEFL (paper/web)	573/100
Application fee	$125
International application fee	$125
Deferment available	No
Transfer students accepted	No
Non-fall admissions	Yes
Need-blind admissions	Yes

WILLAMETTE UNIVERSITY
ATKINSON GRADUATE SCHOOL OF MANAGEMENT

Academics

Willamette University's Atkinson Graduate School of Management certainly has a "reputation as a leader [throughout] the northwest." Indeed, the school is known for producing top-notch, innovative graduates. It also places a focus and priority on young professionals through its early career program, which prepares students for their first professional position, career change, and future career success. Additionally, Willamette emphasizes "experiential," "hands-on" and "cultural learning." And it provides "small classes" and a "comprehensive curriculum."

While MBA candidates can explore a wide variety of topics and interests, students rush to highlight Willamette's "exceptional entrepreneurship classes" and the school's "focus [on] sustainable development." Of course, Willamette's "greatest strength" might be its unique Angel Investor course. Open to second-year MBAs, the class pairs "each student . . . with an Angel Investor and [grants] access to a class fund of $1M. They invest alongside the Angels, evaluate opportunities and try to make money on the companies they decide to fund." As if that wasn't enticing enough, there's "also a new venture class where students create new products and then present their ideas to investors." We're told that "each year, the investors actually invest in the best ideas."

Willamette MBAs also have glowing remarks for their professors. They love that "the majority . . . have years of outside experience." Indeed, they're not "just academics who understand the concepts in theory but have never applied them in real life situations." Importantly, instructors are "also approachable and ready to help and offer advice." Praise extends to the administration as well. As one satisfied first-year sums up, "The school administration is amazing; every single person makes you feel at home and is always available to help you with any situation you encounter. I've only been here nine months but it's been a phenomenal experience in terms of learning and growing my skill set."

Career and Placement

Job prospects for Atkinson graduates are pretty rosy. This is certainly due in large part to the industrious administration which provides "amazing networking opportunities." Credit should also be given to Willamette's beloved Career Services office. After all, the office works diligently to "make sure all students have jobs over the summer break and by the time they graduate." More specifically, it runs a robust mentorship program, pairing students with business professionals whose expertise matches their development goals. The office also hosts numerous personalized, career-focused events like employer spotlights which give students the opportunity to interact with companies and corporate partners in small groups and/or one-on-one. And, of course, these MBAs are also privy to mock interviews, résumés workshops and programs of that ilk.

Companies that tend to recruit and hire Willamette MBAs include: Ford Motor Company, Ernst and Young, Sherpa Adventure Gear, Intel, Hitachi Consulting, Manzama, Rubicon International, Urban Science, Nike, Inc. and Vanguard.

Student Life and Environment

Willamette draws its MBAs from quite a diverse pool. In fact, "international students make up a large percentage of our class." Most students view this as an incredible asset. As one first-year explains, "It really brings a lot of interesting aspects into class discussions when students have such diverse experience and backgrounds!" No matter where they come from, most individuals prove to be "energetic," "creative," "bright" and "professional." Even better, they all seem to embrace the "prevailing notion is that if we help one another learn, we will all learn more down the road."

Outside of the classroom there is "always something to do." A first-year excitedly shares, "We have a weekly social get together at different local pubs where we get to relax, visit, and spend time not doing school work!" Additionally, "there are also several student associations that are very active so on nearly any given week at least one event is going on that is open to the students to enjoy." Best of all, these activities and social options help to foster a "close-knit community" at Atkinson.

Admissions

While the GMAT is the typical exam required for business school entry, Willamette also accepts the GRE. In recent years, the mean GMAT score and GPA for incoming Willamette students was 561 and 3.3, respectively. Previous work experience is not required for the Early Career/Career Change MBA. All students must have a personal interview with the admissions staff.

FINANCIAL FACTS

Annual tuition	$37,600
Fees	$80
Cost of books	$1,200
Room & board	$12,000
% of students receiving aid	80
% of first-year students receiving aid	80
% of students receiving grants	70
Average award package	$41,694
Average grant	$15,000
Average loan	$34,200
Average student loan debt	$68,590

ADMISSIONS

Admissions Selectivity Rating	86
# of applications received	406
% applicants accepted	45
% acceptees attending	45
Average GMAT	561
Range of GMAT	520–600
Accepts GRE scores	Yes
Average Verbal GRE	148
Range of Verbal GRE scores	141–153
Average Quantitative GRE	147
Range of Quantitative GRE scores	141–154
Average GPA	3.3
TOEFL required of international students	Yes
Minimum TOEFL (paper/web)	570/88
Application fee	$0
International application fee	$0
Early application deadline	3/15
Regular application deadline	5/1
Application Deadline/Notification	
Round 1:	12/15
Round 2:	2/1
Round 3:	3/15
Round 4:	5/1
Deferment available	Yes
Maximum length of deferment	1 year
Transfer students accepted	Yes
Transfer application policy	
May transfer up to six semester credits of MBA course work from an AACSB accredited MBA program to the Willamette Early Career and Career Change MBA program with the approval of the Dean.	
Non-fall admissions	No
Need-blind admissions	Yes

EMPLOYMENT PROFILE

		Grads Employed by Function	% Avg. Salary
Career Rating	89	Marketing	(20%) $48,507
Percent employed at graduation	35	Operations	(12%) $77,640
Percent employed 3 months after graduation	76	Consulting	(24%) $77,056
Average base starting salary	$63,917	Management	(10%)
Primary Source of Full-time Job Acceptances		Finance	(24%) $55,824
School-facilitated activities	19 (46%)	MIS	(2%)
Graduate-facilitated activities	22 (54%)	Other	(7%)

Top 5 Employers Hiring Grads
Avanade (2), Nike, Inc. (5), Intel Corporation (1), Ford Motor Company (1), HP (1), Ford Motor Company (1)

WILLIAM PATERSON UNIVERSITY
CHRISTOS M. COTSAKOS COLLEGE OF BUSINESS

GENERAL INFORMATION

Type of school	Public
Affiliation	No Affiliation
Academic calendar	Semester

SURVEY SAYS...
Happy students
Solid preparation in:
General management, Teamwork,
Presentation skills,
Social responsibility

STUDENTS

Enrollment of parent institution	11,414
Enrollment of MBA Program	107
% male/female	41/59
% part-time	70
% underrepresented minority	16
% international	25
Average age at entry	28

ACADEMICS

Academic Experience Rating	**81**
Profs interesting rating	88
Profs accessible rating	90
Student/faculty ratio	4:1
% female faculty	25
% underrepresented minority faculty	46

Academics

A state institution in New Jersey with an AACSB accredited MBA program, William Paterson University provides a "good academic atmosphere" for business professionals looking to enhance their skills. At this largely local school, the faculty comprises "very intelligent" business experts who have "valuable real-world experience to bring into the classroom." Eager to engage their students, William Paterson professors initiate "challenging discussions and clearly bring their experiences with them to the classroom." While the teaching staff boasts solid academic credentials, students say, "some are better teachers than others." For the best experience, a student says, "there are quite a few topnotch professors, and once you learn who they are, try to take as many classes with them as possible."

At William Paterson, MBA coursework is divided into three tiers: the lower core, the upper core, and concentration courses/electives. Students with advanced business experience or an undergraduate business degree may be able to place out of lower core courses, though they are required to complete at least thirty credits. Currently, the school offers MBA concentrations in accounting, marketing, entrepreneurship, finance, and general MBA study. They also operate a unique program in music management (one of two music management programs in the country), which capitalizes on the school's proximity to New York City. No matter what your field of interest, "professors promote teamwork" throughout the curriculum and soft skills are promoted alongside quantitative knowledge.

Principally catering to local professionals, William Paterson does its best to meet the needs and schedules of its busy student body. Of particular note, the majority of courses are taught in the evening (with additional offerings online and on weekends) so that students may continue with work and personal obligations during the day. In addition, there is a culture of support within the school community. A current MBA tells us "this is my first year back after ten years, and the school administration and professors have made coming back a smooth experience." With just over 130 students in the MBA program, "class sizes are typically small (fifteen or so students)," and the "intimate setting" is ideal for promoting camaraderie and fostering individual talents. For additional assistance, the majority of professors are also "willing and eager to answer questions outside the classroom."

While professors are well regarded, "the administration, on the other hand, has virtually no connection to its students." Additionally, there are administrative and scheduling glitches throughout the MBA. For example, it is "difficult to graduate on time as there is a limit to class offerings and restrictions on virtually every lower-core course offering." Even so, William Paterson is constantly improving its programs and appears to be on the up-and-up. If the positive changes continue, William Paterson's "MBA program may become one of the absolute best in the region."

Career and Placement

William Paterson's MBA program is specially designed for working professionals, and can also offer course rotations for full-time candidates. The business school maintains an online job board, where MBA candidates can browse career opportunities in the area. Registered employers can also use the site to view student resumes. Because William Paterson is located within commuting distance of New York, students can apply for jobs locally and throughout the metropolitan area, which is a definite advantage for those looking for big name employers or music industry contacts. Frequent alumni reunions on the William Paterson campus help graduates keep an ongoing network within the school community.

Beyond the business school, William Paterson graduate students and alumni can get additional job development assistance at the Career Development Center, the Gloria S. Williams Advisement Center, and the new William Pesce Family Mentoring Institute. Here MBA candidates may schedule an appointment for individual career counseling or a resume revision. However, the majority of the Center's services, including job fairs, are directed at the undergraduate community.

Student Life and Environment

William Paterson attracts professionals from across New Jersey, and there is a "diverse population of students." While the school community is "mostly young and ambitious," students "span a broad age range," from early professionals to seasoned managers. Across the board, students are "eager to learn" and bring enthusiasm to the classroom.

The Cotsakos College of Business is located in a newly constructed building at William Paterson's Valley Road campus, which is located just a few miles from the main University. Although there are campus housing options for graduate students, few students in the business program take advantage of them. With a class of working professionals, "the school is primarily a commuter school." In fact, for most MBA candidates, "life consists of the classroom experience" and little else. On the greater University campus, "activities are offered, but the MBA program isn't heavily involved." William Paterson has been making changes in this regard such as offering a host of guest speakers, over 150 enrichment seminars, and other added resources for MBA students.

Admissions

To be considered for admission to William Paterson's MBA program, students must submit official transcripts from undergraduate work, GMAT scores, and professional updated résumé. The average GMAT score is 500 or better, or a combination of a GMAT score of at least 450 and a GPA higher than 3.0. Students with a terminal degree in any field or an undergraduate GPA of 3.75 or better may be eligible to waive the GMAT.

FINANCIAL FACTS

Annual tuition (in-state/ out-of-state)	$9,213/$15,711
Fees	$2,594
Room & board	$10,600

ADMISSIONS

Admissions Selectivity Rating	**72**
# of applications received	102
% applicants accepted	64
% acceptees attending	68
Average GMAT	62
Accepts GRE scores	Yes
Average GPA	3.4
TOEFL required of international students	Yes
Minimum TOEFL (paper/web)	550/79
Application fee	$50
International application fee	$50
Application Deadline/Notification	
Deferment available	Yes
Maximum length of deferment	1 year
Transfer students accepted	Yes
Transfer application policy	
Maximum of 6 credits transferable; requires grade of B or better.	
Non-fall admissions	Yes
Need-blind admissions	Yes

WORCESTER POLYTECHNIC INSTITUTE
SCHOOL OF BUSINESS

Academics

Offering "more of a technical leadership program than a traditional MBA," the School of Business at Worcester Polytechnic Institute unites a broad-based degree in business essentials with highly specialized instruction in technology and technology management to fit the needs of graduate-level biz-savvy technophiles. Students appreciate the value of this approach; "The technology focus is great, considering where the business world is headed," one MBA observes. Another explains that the program "works very well in the intersection of business and technology, teaching us how to create and extract maximum value" from that nexus.

WPI's forty-eight-credit hour program features ten highly-integrated required courses; two major projects; and four electives. All coursework is taught from a technological perspective and practical applications to business theory are emphasized. Students tailor their education via electives in cutting-edge fields such as information security management, process design, or technological innovation. In addition to electives offered through the business school, WPI students can enroll in graduate-level electives in other departments, including computer science, biomedical engineering, and electrical engineering. Students may study on campus, online, or switch back and forth between the two formats, an arrangement they love. "You can take classes online or portions of it online in case you are away on business and can't make the class one night," creating a "high amount of schedule[ing] flexibility."

WPI is committed to keeping up with the Data Age, with "courses updated frequently" and online course delivery "allowing for larger numbers of students to take classes, so I have never been closed out of a class." It isn't just all-tech, all-the-time at WPI; professors "express strong concerns with teaching us the importance of ethics applied in business management." Course work, students warn, "is fairly extensive, averaging about three to six hours per week per credit for reading and homework," but "professors are fair in their grading and flexible to accommodate working student schedules," which helps. Administrators "operate the program seamlessly," another plus.

Career and Placement

A high percentage of WPI students work full time, many receiving tuition reimbursement from their current company while pursuing the MBA. Therefore, most will continue at the same company after completing the WPI program. However, those considering a career change can receive support and guidance through the university's Career Development Center, which serves the undergraduate, graduate, and alumni population. The CDC offers career counseling, workshops, and assessments, and maintains contact with regional employers and WPI alumni. The CDC also hosts several annual campus career fairs. Students appreciate "the way [WPI] fosters and enables networking opportunities and works with the students toward their career goals."

Employers who most frequently hire WPI MBAs include: BAE Systems, EMC, Fidelity, GE, Intel, Raytheon, Staples, Teradyne, and Textron.

Student Life and Environment

WPI occupies "a small urban campus with excellent access," making it easy for busy part-time students to zip in and zip out for classes, group meetings, etc. Students tell us that the library and student center are excellent resources; both "are well-staffed, clean, and contain useful equipment and products to support the learning environment." The program "offers a variety of activities and events throughout the year. These events range from academic to social to career-driven to special interests." To the extent that time permits, students "are not only actively engaged in school-related activities, but also go out of their way to actively participate in building a better world for the future. From holding forums on solar energy to fundraising for the community, WPI is always active in working to improve life for everyone [else]." Even the program's many distance-learning-only participants are surprised by their level of engagement. "It is not what I expected...it is very interactive. I love chat sessions most."

WPI MBAs tend to be "technical people in the stage of their careers [where they are ready] to transit[ion] from [a] professional role to [a] managerial position." There are "multiple nationalities represented" among the students, most of whom "have a good comprehension of English."

Admissions

The MBA program at Worcester Polytechnic Institute accepts students whose academic and professional record demonstrates the ability to excel in a challenging, technology-focused graduate program. Students are analyzed on the basis of their academic and professional performance, as well as their career goals and personal statement. In addition, all applicants must have demonstrated capacity to succeed in a technology-driven management program; therefore, a minimum of three semesters of college-level math or two semesters of college-level calculus are a prerequisite of the program. To apply, students must submit undergraduate transcripts, official GMAT or GRE scores, three letters of recommendation, and a completed application form. Applicants whose native language is not English and who have not earned degrees from English-language institutions must submit an official score report for the TOEFL or IELTS. WPI recruits underrepresented minorities through the Society of Hispanic Professional Engineers and the Society of Women Engineers, and maintains offices of diversity to increase recruitment among these groups.

FINANCIAL FACTS

Annual tuition (in-state/ out-of-state)	$32,784/$32,784
Fees	$60
Cost of books	$1,100
Room & board	$8,100
% of students receiving aid	25
% of first-year students receiving aid	25
% of students receiving grants	2
Average award package	$4,800
Average grant	$4,098
Average loan	$18,000

ADMISSIONS

Admissions Selectivity Rating	86
# of applications received	47
% applicants accepted	57
% acceptees attending	63
Average GMAT	603
Range of GMAT	560–630
Accepts GRE scores	Yes
Average Verbal GRE	151
Range of Verbal GRE scores	147–156
Average Quantitative GRE	159
Range of Quantitative GRE scores	156–163
Average Writing GRE	4.0
Range of Writing GRE scores	3.5–4.5
Average GPA	3.3
TOEFL required of international students	Yes
Minimum TOEFL (paper/web)	563/84
Application fee	$70
International application fee	$70
Regular application deadline	6/1
Regular application notification	7/1
Application Deadline/Notification	
Deferment available	Yes
Maximum length of deferment	1 year
Transfer students accepted	Yes
Transfer application policy	Accepted transfer applicants may transfer in up to 9 prior graduate-level credits toward the WPI MBA, provided those credits were not applied toward another earned degree.
Non-fall admissions	Yes
Need-blind admissions	Yes

EMPLOYMENT PROFILE		
Career Rating	85	**Top 5 Employers Hiring Grads**
		EMC (2), United Technologies Corp. (2)

WRIGHT STATE UNIVERSITY
RAJ SOIN COLLEGE OF BUSINESS

GENERAL INFORMATION
Type of school	Public
Affiliation	No Affiliation
Academic calendar	Semester

SURVEY SAYS...
Classmates have diverse work experience, Friendly students, Happy students
Solid preparation in:
General management, Teamwork, Presentation skills

STUDENTS
Enrollment of parent institution	17,789
Enrollment of MBA Program	449
% male/female	58/42
% out-of-state	7
% part-time	77
% underrepresented minority	11
% international	22
Average age at entry	30
Average years work experience at entry	6

ACADEMICS
Academic Experience Rating	**88**
Profs interesting rating	90
Profs accessible rating	91
Student/faculty ratio	10:1
% female faculty	24
% underrepresented minority faculty	20
% part-time faculty	15

Joint Degrees
MBA/MS Nursing (3 - 5 years)
MBA/MS Social & Applied Economics (2-3 years) MBA/MD (4 years)

Prominent Alumni
William Pohlman, Pohlman & Talmadge, Partner; Bradley Mayer, President Finance & IT, Speedway LLC; Gary McCullough, President & CEO, Career Education, Corp; Richard P. Davis, Founder Flagship Financial Service, (Retired); Thomas Duncan, CFO Premier Health Partners

Academics

Wright State University's Raj Soin College of Business offers a "great education for a low price." In addition to a traditional full-time MBA, Wright state offers cohort MBA programs that meet in the evenings or on the weekends to accommodate the needs of working students. The weekend program is held at three different campuses in the Dayton area to maximize convenience. The majority of students attend part time, and they appreciate that they can get a "great" education without "sacrificing too much of their work life," and that the school is "very commuter friendly." Students at other part-time MBA programs often complain about their ability to get into classes, but at Wright State, "picking and choosing classes online is very easy and convenient," and there are always "many seats available."

The academic program at Wright State provides an in-depth, multi-disciplinary understanding of business, while emphasizing ethics and sustainability and a global perspective. Some students are required to take foundation courses, though students who took similar classes as undergraduates and did well in them may be exempt. After that, students take eight core courses, such as Analysis of Global Economic Conditions, Leading Teams and Organizations, and Legal and Ethical Decision Making to gain a deeper understanding of business. Students can then choose a concentration in one of seven areas, including Economics, Finance, International Business, and Project Management to further specialize in their fields of interest. Wright University's study-abroad program is designed for working professionals and part-time students, which is rare. Trips to China and Paris are offered during Spring Break, and students have the opportunity to take classes and meet with international business leaders while learning more about global markets and economic issues.

Classes at Wright State "foster innovation and creativity." "Lectures and discussions revolve around real-world experiences," and professors create "safe spaces where students and their point of view is respected." The workload is "challenging," but "manageable," which is another bonus for working students. Most professors are "top-notch" and "passionate" and "provide students with the skills and knowledge needed to succeed in the real world," though there are some who "make students wish that tenure was eliminated." Overall, however, dedicated professors are one of the many aspects of life at Wright State that help students "become well-rounded business professionals." "This school is on the rise," one student says, "and is poised to be a leader not only in the country, but the world."

Career and Placement

Many Wright State students are already employed and are receiving tuition assistance from their current employers, so lots of students in the program aren't hoping to score a new job after graduation. Those who are, however, will benefit from Wright State's Career Services center, which actively works with local companies to determine their staffing needs. The Center hosts recruiting and networking events, as well as onsite interviews, and it provides personal career counseling. "Professors, administrative staff, and alumni are always willing to help any student in the job hunt" as well. Some students would like to see Wright State put more effort into its career services for business students and increase alumni networking opportunities.

Student Life and Environment

"Wright State University attracts students that are truly interested in their education." Students are "extremely hard-working and motivated, dedicated, and passionate about improving their breadth of knowledge and applying this to make a difference." The student body is a "mix of those just out of college undergraduate studies, students with a few years of experience, and students who have been in the workplace for a long time," and "many are pursuing a second or third master's degree." The student body at Wright State is also "very diverse." One student says, "You can meet hardworking students of all colors, nationalities, genders, ages, etc., in your classes." You're guaranteed to hear "different perspectives on issues," and students report that being exposed to "different viewpoints and life experiences enhances their learning experience."

Since the majority of students work full time and have demanding home lives, many of them don't have the opportunity to socialize with their peers. "I just drive to class after work and go to school and go home," one student explains. An upside of this is "the majority understand what each other are going through and are willing to help." Though many do disappear after class, one student says, "The lobby in the business school is always full with students socializing and working on school-related activities and projects." There are many business-oriented clubs, such as those dedicated to accounting and finance, as well as all kinds of organizations and intramural teams offered by Wright State University, should students find themselves with some free time.

Admissions

Students at Wright State University have an average of five years of work experience, but students are accepted with much less. Applicants must submit GMAT scores, a resume (required for the full-time MBA program), and three references; letters of recommendation are not required. Students who already have completed a master's degree in another discipline do not need to take the GMAT. The admission office ranks students according to an admissions index (College GPA X 200 + GMAT Score) and requires a minimum of 1,100 points for acceptance, though many students score much higher. The average undergraduate GPA for last year's incoming class was 3.2. The average GMAT score was 478. International students must submit a translated transcript where necessary, and if their primary language is not English, they must also take the TOEFL.

FINANCIAL FACTS

Annual tuition (in-state/ out-of-state)	$13,085/$22,224
Fees	$0
Cost of books	$3,200
Room & board (on/off-campus)	$10,000/$10,000
% of students receiving aid	15
% of first-year students receiving aid	20
% of students receiving grants	15
Average award package	$17,899
Average grant	$5,102
Average loan	$9,282
Average student loan debt	$36,006

ADMISSIONS

Admissions Selectivity Rating	84
# of applications received	356
% applicants accepted	55
% acceptees attending	70
Average GMAT	478
Range of GMAT	420–540
Accepts GRE scores	Yes
Average GPA	3.2
TOEFL required of international students	Yes
Minimum TOEFL (paper/web)	550/
Application fee	$40
International application fee	$40
Early application deadline	4/15
Early notification date	5/1
Regular application deadline	7/1
Regular application notification	8/1
Application Deadline/Notification	
Deferment available	Yes
Maximum length of deferment	1 year
Transfer students accepted	Yes
Transfer application policy	
They must meet WSU admissions requirements. Can transfer up to 15 credit hours with department approval.	
Non-fall admissions	Yes
Need-blind admissions	Yes

EMPLOYMENT PROFILE

Career Rating	81	Grads Employed by Function	% Avg. Salary
Percent employed 3 months		Consulting	(20%) $55,000
after graduation	30	Finance	(60%) $55,000
Average base starting salary	$51,272	Other	(20%) $49,000
Primary Source of Full-time Job Acceptances		**Top 5 Employers Hiring Grads**	
School-facilitated activities	8 (19%)	Wright Patterson Air Force Base (>10), Lexis-	
Graduate-facilitated activities	13 (32%)	Nexis (>10), Premier Health Partners (>5),	
Unknown	20 (49%)	CareSource (>5), Teradata (>5)	

XAVIER UNIVERSITY
WILLIAMS COLLEGE OF BUSINESS

GENERAL INFORMATION

Type of school	Private
Affiliation	Roman Catholic-Jesuit
Academic calendar	Semester

SURVEY SAYS...

Classmates have diverse work experience, Conservative students, Happy students
Solid preparation in:
Finance, General management, Teamwork, Quantitative skills, Doing business in a global economy

STUDENTS

Enrollment of parent institution	6,538
Enrollment of MBA Program	516
% male/female	67/33
% out-of-state	26
% part-time	77
% underrepresented minority	20
% international	24
Average age at entry	28
Average years work experience at entry	6

ACADEMICS

Academic Experience Rating	85
Profs interesting rating	91
Profs accessible rating	94
Student/faculty ratio	18:1
% female faculty	41
% underrepresented minority faculty	16
% part-time faculty	15

Joint Degrees

Master of Health Services Administration and Master of Business Administration Program Approximate Length; Master of Science in Nursing and Master of Business Adminstration Approximate Length; BS in Life Sciences and MBA; Approximate length; BSBA in Accounting and MBA

Academics

The Williams College of Business at Cincinnati's Xavier University offers multiple MBA programs across the main and satellite campuses, as well as five different study abroad locations as part of the school's International MBA program. The school "definitely caters to part time students": small classes take place at night and create an "atmosphere [that] is intimate," and the school works to provide great diversity in the MBA curriculum. Beyond the usual in concentrations like Health, Finance, and Management, they continue to add areas such as Business Intelligence and International Business in an effort to be "constantly improving." In addition, Xavier's roots in the Jesuit learning experience are "a remarkable approach to education."

"Excellent" professors and "efficient and understanding" administrators "put the student first." Most are working in the field or maintain contact with the business community, "therefore, the material is constantly evolving." Teaching is important here, but "Xavier still manages to keep on the cutting edge in terms of research." The faculty is "great, somewhat crazy, and always thoughtful," "highly analytical and intelligent, outgoing, and fun," and "very attentive to students' needs and business expectations." The students are as "strong contributors to the classroom as the professors."

Most professors have office hours outside of the standard nine-to-five, and the MBA office has later evening hours, "making it easy for part time students to reach someone after work." Administrative communication is "stellar." "Within the first week of class, the administration knew me by first name from our MBA orientation," says a student. "I feel I am valued."

Career and Placement

Though the school is completely "well respected in the Cincinnati area" and has "a strong alumni base," many admit that "Xavier needs a more national presence." "Right now it's mostly Cincy-based financial services companies that show up to the career fairs," says one student of the region, which has a high concentration of marketing and management companies. "Many *Fortune* companies located in the city don't directly recruit from my school, however they do send their current employees to get their MBA at my school," explains a student. Still, the school's star is on the rise, and "many of the big companies in the area recognize it as a leader."

Recent top employers of Xavier graduates are Procter & Gamble, Fidelity Investments, The Kroger Company, Fifth Third Bank, and General Electric.

Student Life and Environment

Most students in the MBA are part-time and working, though a recently added full-time program has changed the dynamics of the school somewhat (in a good way). Students are "a mix of quirky and straight-laced" ("ages range from early twenties to mid fifties") which "creates an eclectic atmosphere" in which everyone is "very friendly and willing to help others."

"Fine new facilities aid in the learning process" and are "beautiful, plus they are wired with technology," such as the Bloomberg trading center. Clubs and social gatherings take place in the "bustling" great lobby of the business college every night, and Xavier offers "a host of amenities" so commuting students can "easily pack up a bag and spend the day at the College of Business interacting with fellow classmates, studying on my own, and more." Students don't even have to stray far from the building, as "the library is across the street, there are restaurants within walking distance, [and] private study rooms and computer labs in the building." "It really is my home away from home," says a student.

Admissions

To be considered for admission to Xavier's graduate programs, students must have a GPA of at least 2.5 from their undergraduate studies—though, on average, entering students had a 3.2 GPA, on a 4.0 scale. Students must also have a minimum GMAT score of 470. Letters of recommendation are optional, but are recommended for students whose test scores or GPA fall below the average applicant. Previous career experience is not a requirement of the program; however, it is highly recommended.

Prominent Alumni

George Schaefer, President/CEO Fifth Third Bancorp; Robert J. Kohlhepp, Vice Chairman, Cintas Corporation

FINANCIAL FACTS

Annual tuition (in-state/ out-of-state)	$14,382/$14,382
Fees	$6
Cost of books	$1,500
Room & board	$11,000
% of students receiving aid	30
% of students receiving grants	41
Average award package	$15,038
Average grant	$530
Average loan	$17,667
Average student loan debt	$30,750

ADMISSIONS

Admissions Selectivity Rating	76
# of applications received	181
% applicants accepted	89
Average GMAT	512
Range of GMAT	480–590
Accepts GRE scores	Yes
Average Verbal GRE	147
Range of Verbal GRE scores	144–153
Average Quantitative GRE	146
Range of Quantitative GRE scores	143–152
Average Writing GRE	3.4
Range of Writing GRE scores	3.0–4.0
Average GPA	3.2
TOEFL required of international students	Yes
Minimum TOEFL (paper/web)	550/79
Application fee	$0
International application fee	$0
Application Deadline/Notification	
Deferment available	Yes
Maximum length of deferment	1 year
Transfer students accepted	Yes
Transfer application policy	
MBA admission required; XU MBA will accept 6 hours of core curriculum from AACSB accredited programs only and up to 18 hours of core curriculum from AACSB accredited Jesuit MBA Network Schools.	
Non-fall admissions	Yes
Need-blind admissions	Yes

EMPLOYMENT PROFILE

Career Rating	72	Grads Employed by Function	%	Avg. Salary
		Marketing	(21%)	$43,750
		Operations	(11%)	$35,000
		Consulting	(5%)	$81,000
		Management	(16%)	$86,333
		Finance	(11%)	$61,750
		HR	(5%)	$60,000
		MIS	(5%)	$105,000
		Other	(5%)	$17,000

YALE UNIVERSITY
SCHOOL OF MANAGEMENT

Academics

Established in 1976, the Yale School of Management is a "superbly run" institution that is "a model for the business school platform." Yale SOM provides resources and opportunities to non-traditional MBA candidates through avenues such as the Silver Scholars program, which admits and matriculates students directly from undergrad, and its numerous centers and initiatives (such as the Center for Customer Insights, the Program on Entrepreneurship, and the Initiative for Leadership and Organization) highlight the innovative thinking this "exceptionally well-positioned" program is known for. Professors are extraordinarily accessible, and students "can tell that they are here at SOM because they have a passion for teaching." The curriculum is "updated on a regular basis," and there are opportunities to take classes across the university. Yale SOM's Global Studies Requirement reinforces the school's worldly approach to business, and is often fulfilled by an International Experience course that caps off in a ten-day trip to foreign business capitals. The administration is incredibly open and always soliciting feedback: "You can meet with anybody at any level and have an intimate conversation about whatever is on one's mind." The "balance of business and society" is apparent in every artifice: "Most activities are rewarding and even casual conversation is thought-provoking."

Career and Placement

Students benefit from Yale SOM's close integration with its parent university. Business students are able to connect with Yale graduate, undergraduate and professional students through cross-campus clubs like Net Impact and the Yale Entrepreneurial Institute. "If a company does not recruit on campus, it is likely there is a Yale alumni connection that students can utilize to better access a firm," says a student. The Career Development Office has been improving steadily, and "recruiting results have been very impressive in recent years, with lots of success placing in both traditional business school jobs and a broader set of unique/more focused roles." The online job posting board has "thousands of opportunities" and "virtually every large company comes to campus." Top recruiters of Yale SOM grads include Accenture, PepsiCo, American Express, Citi, and Pfizer.

Student Life and Environment

New Haven is a small city that is "very accessible to New York," but most students stay busy on campus as life at SOM "encapsulates FOMO—fear of missing out." Yale SOM"s "collegial and open" community is a defining aspect of the school, and everyone—from students, their partners, faculty, staff, and alumni—is "extraordinarily welcoming, [and] will bend over backwards to help each other." This tight-knit bunch is "intellectually curious and socially conscious" and as many here are in dual degree programs, they can "provide unique and professional perspectives in class and teamwork." Students are very involved with daily events focused on topics such as "social impact, art, international relations, investment and technology." "Prioritization is a challenge here to an extreme I've never seen elsewhere," says a student.

Admissions

The Yale SOM program is competitive, and the school strives to create a student body with a diversity of backgrounds, experiences, and voices. The median undergraduate GPA for a recent class was 3.63 and the median GMAT was 720. In addition to traditional metrics, Yale admissions are decided by academic potential, personal values, professional accomplishment, and personal interviews.

Prominent Alumni

Timothy Collins, CEO & Senior Managing Director, Ripplewood Holdings; Indra Nooyi, Chairman and CEO, PepsiCo Inc.; Vivek Murthy, U.S. Surgeon General; Sandra Urie, Chairman & CEO, Cambridge Associates LLC

FINANCIAL FACTS

Annual tuition	$61,500
Fees	$1,880
Cost of books	$844
Room & board	
(on/off-campus)	$14,800/$14,800
% of students receiving aid	73
Average grant	$26,010
Average loan	$38,960

ADMISSIONS

Admissions Selectivity Rating	97
# of applications received	3,449
% applicants received	21
Average GMAT	721
Range of GMAT	710–740
Accepts GRE scores	Yes
Application fee	$225
Application Deadline/Notification	
Round 1:	9/14 / 12/6
Round 2:	1/10 / 3/23
Round 3:	4/15 / 5/18
Transfer student accepted	No

EMPLOYMENT PROFILE

Career Rating		97
Percent employed at graduation		77
Percent employed 3 months after graduation		92
Average base starting salary		$119,066
Primary Source of Full-time Job Acceptances		
School-facilitated activities		161 (72%)
Graduate-facilitated activities		63 (28%)
Unknown		1 (0%)

Grads Employed by Function % Avg. Salary

Marketing	(13%)	$109,229
Operations	(6%)	$114,542
Consulting	(37%)	$125,970
Management	(8%)	$119,493
Finance	(30%)	$116,687
Other	(5%)	$112,545

Top 5 Employers Hiring Grads

Amazon.com (8), McKinsey & Co. (8), Bain & Company, Inc. (8), Deloitte (7), Citi, The Boston Consulting Group, PricewaterhouseCoopers (6)

Part III-B
Business School Data Listings

ARKANSAS STATE UNIVERSITY
COLLEGE OF BUSINESS

ADMISSIONS CONTACT: DR. THOMAS WHEELER, DEAN, GRADUATE SCHOOL
ADDRESS: PO BOX 60, STATE UNIVERSITY, AR 72467 UNITED STATES
PHONE: 870-972-3029 • FAX: 870-972-3857
E-MAIL: GRADSCH@CHOCTAW.ASTATE.EDU • WEBSITE: BUSINESS.ASTATE.EDU

GENERAL INFORMATION

Type of school: Public Academic calendar: Semester

STUDENTS

Enrollment of MBA Program: 104 Average years work experience at entry: 0

ACADEMICS

Student/faculty ratio: 25:1 % female faculty: 24 % underrepresented minority faculty: 1

FINANCIAL FACTS

Annual tuition (in-state/out-of-state): $1,488/$3,744 Cost of books: $2,100 Room & board: $3,500 Average grant: $6,427 Average loan: $0

ADMISSIONS

Admissions Selectivity Rating: 65

# of applications received: 53 % applicants accepted: 85 % acceptees attending: 80 TOEFL required of international students: Yes

Deferment available: No Transfer students accepted: No Non-fall admissions: No Need-blind admissions: No

ASHRIDGE (UNITED KINGDOM)
ASHRIDGE BUSINESS SCHOOL

ADMISSIONS CONTACT: JULIET HARRY, ADMISSIONS OFFICER
ADDRESS: ASHRIDGE, BERKHAMSTED, HERTFORDSHIRE, HP41NS UNITED KINGDOM OF GREAT BRITAIN AND NORTHERN IRELAND
PHONE: +44 (0)1442 841120
E-MAIL: ADMISSIONS@ASHRIDGE.ORG.UK • WEBSITE: WWW.ASHRIDGE.ORG.UK

GENERAL INFORMATION

Type of school: Private

STUDENTS

Enrollment of MBA Program: 67 % male/female: 60/40 % part-time: 67 % international: 92 Average age at entry: 35 Average years work experience at entry: 11

ACADEMICS

% female faculty: 40

FINANCIAL FACTS

Annual tuition: $49,420 Cost of books: $800 Room & board (on/off-campus): $12,558/$16,100 % of students receiving aid: 30 % of first-year students receiving aid: 30 % of students receiving grants: 30 Average award package: $100,000 Average grant: $10,000

ADMISSIONS

Admissions Selectivity Rating: 81

# of applications received: 76 % applicants accepted: 67 % acceptees attending: 43 Average GMAT: 620 Range of GMAT: 550–750 Accepts GRE scores: No TOEFL required of international students: Yes Minimum TOEFL (paper/computer): 600/100 Application fee: $0 International application fee: $0

Deferment available: Yes Maximum length of deferment: 12 months Transfer students accepted: No Non-fall admissions: Yes Need-blind admissions: Yes

EMPLOYMENT PROFILE

Percent employed at graduation: 59 Percent employed 3 months after graduation: 59 Average base starting salary: $82,777

Primary Source of Full-time Job Acceptances

School-facilitated activities: ....7(32%)

Graduate-facilitated activities: ....6(27%)

Unknown: ....9(41%)

Grads Employed by Function ..... % Avg. Salary

Consulting:......................................(40%) $87,000

Management: ....(5%) $129,000

MIS: ....(5%)

Other: ....(23%) $67,000

Top 5 Employers Hiring Grads (number of hires in last class)
Coca Cola (1), Roland Berger Strategy Consulting (1), Aston Martin (1), British Telecom (1), Johnsons Controls (1)

ASIAN INSTITUTE OF MANAGEMENT (PHILIPPINES)
ASIAN INSTITUTE OF MANAGEMENT

ADMISSIONS CONTACT: MR. REY REYES, EXECUTIVE MANAGING DIRECTOR
ADDRESS: GROUND FLR. EUGENIO LOPEZ FOUNDATION BLDG., JOSEPH R. MCMICKING CAMPUS, ASIAN INSTITUTE OF MANAGEMENT, 123 PASEO DE ROXAS, MAKATI CITY, 1260 PHILIPPINES
PHONE: +63 2 8937631 • FAX: +63 2 8937631
E-MAIL: ADMISSIONS@AIM.EDU • WEBSITE: WWW.AIM.EDU

GENERAL INFORMATION

Type of school: Private Academic calendar: Sep. to Dec.

STUDENTS

Enrollment of parent institution: 393 Enrollment of MBA Program: 140 % male/female: 72/28 % out-of-state: 72 % part-time: 0 % international: 72 Average age at entry: 26 Average years work experience at entry: 4

ACADEMICS

Student/faculty ratio: 3:1 % female faculty: 28 % part-time faculty: 33

FINANCIAL FACTS

Annual tuition (in-state/out-of-state): /$16,130 Cost of books: $8,000 Room & board (on/off-campus): $4,100/ % of students receiving grants: 10

ADMISSIONS

Admissions Selectivity Rating: 83

# of applications received: 468 % applicants accepted: 45 Average GMAT: 656 Range of GMAT: 680–640 Accepts GRE scores: No Early notification date: 3/22 Regular application deadline: 8/5 Regular application notification: 10/1

Deferment available: Yes Maximum length of deferment: After one year Transfer students accepted: No Non-fall admissions: No Need-blind admissions: No

EMPLOYMENT PROFILE

Percent employed at graduation: 13 Percent employed 3 months after graduation: 32

Top 5 Employers Hiring Grads (number of hires in last class)

Cognizant India (9), Citibank (3), BPI (2), Renoir (2), JP Morgan (2)

ASTON UNIVERSITY
ASTON BUSINESS SCHOOL

ADDRESS: ASTON TRIANGLE, BIRMINGHAM B4 7ET, UK
PHONE: 011-44 (0) 121 204 3100
E-MAIL: ABSPG@ASTON.AC.UK • WEBSITE: WWW.ABS.ASTON.AC.UK

GENERAL INFORMATION

Type of school: Private

STUDENTS

Average years work experience at entry: 0

FINANCIAL FACTS

Annual tuition (in-state/out-of-state): $35,608/

ADMISSIONS

Admissions Selectivity Rating: 60*

Regular application deadline: 7/1

BARRY UNIVERSITY
ANDREAS SCHOOL OF BUSINESS

ADMISSIONS CONTACT: GUSTAVO CORDEIRO, MARKETING COORDINATOR
ADDRESS: GRADUATE ADMISSIONS, 11300 NE 2ND AVENUE, MIAMI SHORES, FL 33161-6695 UNITED STATES
PHONE: (305) 899-3100 • FAX: (305) 892-6412
E-MAIL: ADMISSIONS@MAIL.BARRY.EDU • WEBSITE: WWW.BARRY.EDU/BUSINESS

GENERAL INFORMATION

Type of school: Private Academic calendar: All year

STUDENTS

Enrollment of MBA Program: 119 % part-time: 100 Average age at entry: 29 Average years work experience at entry: 4

ACADEMICS

Student/faculty ratio: 7:1 % female faculty: 47 % underrepresented minority faculty: 47 % part-time faculty: 0

FINANCIAL FACTS

Annual tuition (in-state/out-of-state): $17,150/ Cost of books: $1,500 Room & board (on/off-campus): /$15,000 % of students receiving aid: 55 % of first-year students receiving aid: 52 % of students receiving grants: 29 Average award package: $25,308

Average grant: $7,719 Average loan: $28,219 Average student loan debt: $28,137

ADMISSIONS

Admissions Selectivity Rating: 86

# of applications received: 213 % applicants accepted: 31 % acceptees attending: 40 Average GMAT: 460 Range of GMAT: 400–450 Accepts GRE scores: Yes Average GPA: 3.6 TOEFL required of international students: Yes Minimum TOEFL (paper/computer): 550/79 Application fee: $30 International application fee: $30

Deferment available: Yes Maximum length of deferment: One year Transfer students accepted: Yes Transfer application policy: Up to six transfer credits (2 graduate classes) from an AACSB-accredited institution. Restrictions include (but not limited to): 1. All transfer credits must be a B (3.0) or better and courses must be directly parallel to required or elective courses in the MBA program. If the credits originate from a business program, that program must be accredited by AACSB International. 2. Graduate credits are not transferable if they were previously applied to a graduate degree that was awarded to the applicant. 3. No graduate credit will be allowed for correspondence or extension work. 4. Students may not transfer credits after they have entered the program. Non-fall admissions: Yes Need-blind admissions: Yes

EMPLOYMENT PROFILE

Percent employed at graduation: 20 Percent employed 3 months after graduation: 20 Average base starting salary: $75,700

Primary Source of Full-time Job Acceptances

Graduate-facilitated activities: ....6(33%)

Unknown: ....12(67%)

Top 5 Employers Hiring Grads (number of hires in last class)

Kony Solutions (1), South Florida Regional Extention Center (1), Telcome Argentina USA (1), Saudi Telecom Company (1), Lotificaciones Las Haciendes, SA (1)

BILKENT UNIVERSITY
FACULTY OF BUSINESS ADMINISTRATION

ADMISSIONS CONTACT: ZELIHA BEYDOGAN BARAN, EXECUTIVE MBA & MBA PROGRAMS COORDINATOR
ADDRESS: BILKENT UNIVERSITY, FACULTY OF BUSINESS ADMINISTRATION, BILKENT, 06800, ANKARA UNITED KINGDOM OF GREAT BRITAIN AND NORTHERN IRELAND
PHONE: +90 312 290 1611 • FAX: +90 312 266 49 58
E-MAIL: MBACOORDINATOR@BILKENT.EDU.TR
WEBSITE: WWW.MAN.BILKENT.EDU.TR

GENERAL INFORMATION

Type of school: Private

STUDENTS

Average age at entry: 25 Average years work experience at entry: 2

FINANCIAL FACTS

% of students receiving aid: 15 % of first-year students receiving aid: 15 % of students receiving grants: 30

ADMISSIONS

Admissions Selectivity Rating: 90

# of applications received: 66 **% applicants accepted:** 33 **% acceptees attending:** 77 **Average GMAT:** 601 **Range of GMAT:** 520–790 **TOEFL required of international students:** Yes **Minimum TOEFL (paper/computer):** /87

Deferment available: No **Transfer students accepted:** Yes **Transfer application policy:** The transfer applicant should contact the MBA Coordinator for the required materials and deadlines. **Non-fall admissions:** No **Need-blind admissions:** Yes

BIRMINGHAM-SOUTHERN COLLEGE

ADMISSIONS CONTACT: BRENDA D. DURHAM, DIRECTOR OF MPPM ADMISSION
ADDRESS: 900 ARKADELPHIA ROAD, BOX 549052, BIRMINGHAM, AL 35254 UNITED STATES
PHONE: 205-226-4803 • FAX: 205-226-4843
E-MAIL: GRADUATE@BSC.EDU • WEBSITE: WWW.BSC.EDU/MPPM

GENERAL INFORMATION

Type of school: Private **Academic calendar:** September - August

STUDENTS

Enrollment of parent institution: 1,400 **Enrollment of MBA Program:** 68 **% male/female:** 52/48 **Average age at entry:** 37 **Average years work experience at entry:** 15

ACADEMICS

Student/faculty ratio: 20:1 **% female faculty:** 29

FINANCIAL FACTS

Annual tuition (in-state/out-of-state): $13,825/$13,825 **Fees:** $300 **Cost of books:** $800

ADMISSIONS

Admissions Selectivity Rating: TK

# of applications received: 15 **% applicants accepted:** **TOEFL required of international students:** Yes **Minimum TOEFL (paper/computer):** 600/ **Application fee:** $25

Deferment available: Yes **Maximum length of deferment:** 1 year **Transfer students accepted:** Yes **Transfer application policy:** May transfer up to 6 graduate hours with a grade of B or better. Transfer coursework must be comparable to BSC-MPPM coursework and be approved by the Dean of Business Programs. **Non-fall admissions:** Yes **Need-blind admissions:** Yes

BOISE STATE UNIVERSITY
COLLEGE OF BUSINESS AND ECONOMICS

ADMISSIONS CONTACT: J. RENEE ANCHUSTEGUI, DIRECTOR, PROFESSIONAL MBA, MSA, MSAT
ADDRESS: BUSINESS GRADUATE STUDIES, 1910 UNIVERSITY DRIVE MS1600, BOISE, ID 83725-1600 UNITED STATES
PHONE: 208-426-3116
E-MAIL: GRADUATEBUSINESS@BOISESTATE.EDU
WEBSITE: COBE.BOISESTATE.EDU/GRADUATE

GENERAL INFORMATION

Type of school: Public **Academic calendar:** Semester

STUDENTS

Enrollment of parent institution: 18,447 **Enrollment of MBA Program:** 190 **% male/female:** 74/26 **% out-of-state:** 20 **% part-time:** 34 **% underrepresented minority:** 4 **% international:** 7 **Average age at entry:** 35 **Average years work experience at entry:** 12

ACADEMICS

Student/faculty ratio: 23:1 **% female faculty:** 20 **% underrepresented minority faculty:** 7 **% part-time faculty:** 2

FINANCIAL FACTS

Annual tuition (in-state/out-of-state): $0/$8,576 **Fees:** $6,898 **Cost of books:** $3,000 **Room & board (on/off-campus):** $6,800/$7,200 **% of students receiving aid:** 70 **% of first-year students receiving aid:** 23 **% of students receiving grants:** 22 **Average award package:** $16,700 **Average grant:** $19,492 **Average loan:** $14,599 **Average student loan debt:** $12,000

ADMISSIONS

Admissions Selectivity Rating: 86

# of applications received: 130 **% applicants accepted:** 55 **% acceptees attending:** 66 **Average GMAT:** 579 **Range of GMAT:** 510–665 **Accepts GRE scores:** **Average GPA:** 3.3 **TOEFL required of international students:** Yes **Minimum TOEFL (paper/computer):** 587/95 **Application fee:** $55 **International application fee:** $55 **Early notification date:** 3/15 **Regular application deadline:** 6/1 **Regular application notification:** 7/15

Deferment available: Yes **Maximum length of deferment:** 1 year **Transfer students accepted:** Yes **Transfer application policy:** Limit of up to 1/3 of total credits required to completed the degree at Boise State. Must receive grade of B or above from an AACSB accredited institution for transfer consideration. **Non-fall admissions:** Yes **Need-blind admissions:** Yes

EMPLOYMENT PROFILE

Percent employed at graduation: 78 **Percent employed 3 months after graduation:** 95 **Average base starting salary:** $73,077

Primary Source of Full-time Job Acceptances

School-facilitated activities: ....3(15%)

Graduate-facilitated activities: ....8(40%)

Unknown: ....9(45%)

Grads Employed by Function ..... % Avg. Salary

Marketing:......................................(5%) $70,000

Operations:...................................(10%) $61,667

Consulting:....................................(5%) $69,000

Management: ....(15%) $63,000

Finance:..(30%) $48,000

HR:...(5%) $53,000

MIS: ....(10%) $100,000

Other: ....(10%) $46,000

Top 5 Employers Hiring Grads (number of hires in last class)

Micron Technology (4), Northwest Mutual (2), Wells Fargo (2), Scentsy (2)

BRADLEY UNIVERSITY
FOSTER COLLEGE OF BUSINESS

ADMISSIONS CONTACT: ROB JOHANNSEN, DIRECTOR OF MBA PROGRAM
ADDRESS: 1501 WEST BRADLEY AVENUE, PEORIA, IL 61625 UNITED STATES
PHONE: 309-677-2256 • FAX: 309-677-3374
E-MAIL: MBA@BRADLEY.EDU • WEBSITE: WWW.BRADLEY.EDU/FCBA

GENERAL INFORMATION

Type of school: Private Academic calendar: Semester

STUDENTS

Enrollment of parent institution: 5,338 Enrollment of MBA Program: 49 % part-time: 57 Average age at entry: 27 Average years work experience at entry: 4

ACADEMICS

Student/faculty ratio: 2:1 % female faculty: 27 % underrepresented minority faculty: 9 % part-time faculty: 6

FINANCIAL FACTS

Fees: $400 Cost of books: $800

ADMISSIONS

Admissions Selectivity Rating: 81

# of applications received: 39 % applicants accepted: 85 % acceptees attending: 58 Average GMAT: 567 Range of GMAT: 520–620 Accepts GRE scores: No Average GPA: 3.5 TOEFL required of international students: Yes Minimum TOEFL (paper/computer): 550/79 Application fee: $40 International application fee: $50 Early notification date: 4/1 Regular application deadline: Deferment available: Yes Maximum length of deferment: 1 semester Transfer students accepted: Yes Transfer application policy: No more than 9 hours of credit from another AACSB-accredited school can transfer to Bradley MBA program. Non-fall admissions: Yes Need-blind admissions: Yes

CALIFORNIA STATE UNIVERSITY, SACRAMENTO
COLLEGE OF BUSINESS ADMINISTRATION

ADMISSIONS CONTACT: JEANIE WILLIAMS, GRADUATE PROGRAMS COORDINATOR
ADDRESS: 6000 J STREET, TAHOE HALL ROOM 1035, SACRAMENTO, CA 95819-6088 UNITED STATES
PHONE: 916-278-6772 • FAX: 916-278-4233
E-MAIL: CBAGRAD@CSUS.EDU • WEBSITE: WWW.CBA.CSUS.EDU

GENERAL INFORMATION

Type of school: Public Academic calendar: Semester

STUDENTS

Enrollment of parent institution: 23,280 Enrollment of MBA Program: 492 Average age at entry: 27 Average years work experience at entry: 4

ACADEMICS

% female faculty: 33

FINANCIAL FACTS

Annual tuition (in-state/out-of-state): $25,000/$37,276 Cost of books: $2,500 Room & board (on/off-campus): $8,435/$8,435

ADMISSIONS

Admissions Selectivity Rating: 86

# of applications received: 215 % applicants accepted: 52 % acceptees attending: 67 Average GMAT: 570 Range of GMAT: 440–740 Accepts GRE scores: Average GPA: 3.2 TOEFL required of international students: Yes Minimum TOEFL (paper/computer): 510/64 Application fee: $55 International application fee: $55 Regular application deadline: 4/1 Regular application notification: 5/30

Deferment available: No Transfer students accepted: Yes Transfer application policy: We accept up to 6 units of transfer coursework from other AACSB accredited institutions. Non-fall admissions: Yes Need-blind admissions: Yes

CALIFORNIA STATE UNIVERSITY, STANISLAUS
COLLEGE OF BUSINESS ADMINISTRATION

ADDRESS: , TURLOCK, CA 95382 UNITED STATES
PHONE: (209) 667-3070 OR 1-800-300-7420
E-MAIL: OUTREACH_HELP_DESK@CSUSTAN.EDU
WEBSITE: WWW.CSUSTAN.EDU/CBA

GENERAL INFORMATION

Type of school: Public

STUDENTS

Enrollment of parent institution: 9,246 Average age at entry: 28

ACADEMICS

% female faculty: 7 % underrepresented minority faculty: 42

FINANCIAL FACTS

Annual tuition (in-state/out-of-state): $7,930/$7,930 Fees: $254 Cost of books: $1,700 Room & board (on/off-campus): $9,000/$11,500

ADMISSIONS

Admissions Selectivity Rating: 74

# of applications received: 107 % applicants accepted: 78 Average GMAT: 500 Accepts GRE scores: Yes Average Verbal GRE: 149 TOEFL required of international students: Yes Minimum TOEFL (paper/computer): 550/ Application fee: $55 International application fee: $55 Regular application deadline: 6/14 Regular application notification: 8/14

Deferment available: No Transfer students accepted: Yes Transfer application policy: Proespective students may only transfer nine units of coursework into a graduate degree. Non-fall admissions: Yes

CANISIUS COLLEGE
RICHARD J. WEHLE SCHOOL OF BUSINESS

ADMISSIONS CONTACT: LAURA MCEWEN, DIRECTOR, GRADUATE BUSINESS PROGRAMS
ADDRESS: CANISIUS COLLEGE, 2001 MAIN ST, BAGEN HALL 201, BUFFALO, NY 14208-1098 UNITED STATES
PHONE: 716-888-2140 • FAX: 716-888-2145
E-MAIL: GRADBIZ@CANISIUS.EDU • WEBSITE: WWW.CANISIUS.EDU/MBA

GENERAL INFORMATION

Type of school: Private Academic calendar: Semester

STUDENTS

Enrollment of parent institution: 4,908 Enrollment of MBA Program: 311 % male/female: 97/3 % out-of-state: 10 % part-time: 93 % international: 0 Average age at entry: 26

ACADEMICS

% female faculty: 20 % underrepresented minority faculty: 10

FINANCIAL FACTS

Annual tuition (in-state/out-of-state): $25,992/ Cost of books: $500 Room & board (on/off-campus): $11,820/ Average grant: $0 Average loan: $0

ADMISSIONS

Admissions Selectivity Rating: 60*

Average GMAT: Accepts GRE scores: Yes TOEFL required of international students: Yes Minimum TOEFL (paper/computer): 500/ Application fee: $25

Deferment available: Yes Maximum length of deferment: 1 year Transfer students accepted: Yes Transfer application policy: Case-by-case basis. Non-fall admissions: Yes Need-blind admissions: No

CLARION UNIVERSITY OF PENNSYLVANIA
COLLEGE OF BUSINESS ADMINISTRATION

ADMISSIONS CONTACT: MS. DANA BEARER, ASSISTANT DIRECTOR
ADDRESS: CLARION UNIVERSITY OF PENNSYLVANIA, 840 WOOD STREET, CLARION, PA 16214 UNITED STATES
PHONE: 814-393-2605 • FAX: 814-393-1910
E-MAIL: MBA@CLARION.EDU • WEBSITE: WWW.CLARION.EDU/MBA

GENERAL INFORMATION

Type of school: Public Academic calendar: Semester

STUDENTS

Enrollment of parent institution: 5,712 Enrollment of MBA Program: 19 % male/female: 46/54 % out-of-state: 10 % part-time: 10 % underrepresented minority: 7 % international: 1 Average age at entry: 22 Average years work experience at entry: 1

ACADEMICS

Student/faculty ratio: 7:1 % female faculty: 13 % underrepresented minority faculty: 27 % part-time faculty: 0

FINANCIAL FACTS

Annual tuition (in-state/out-of-state): $5,448/$8,172 Fees: $2,367 Cost of books: $1,500 Room & board (on/off-campus): $4,500/ % of students receiving aid: % of first-year students receiving aid: 80 % of students receiving grants: Average award package: $22,203 Average grant: $14,424 Average loan: $18,117 Average student loan debt: $26,315

ADMISSIONS

Admissions Selectivity Rating: 76

# of applications received: 6 % applicants accepted: 100 % acceptees attending: 83 Average GMAT: 435 Accepts GRE scores: Yes Average GPA: 3.4 TOEFL required of international students: Yes Minimum TOEFL (paper/computer): 550/80 Application fee: $40 International application fee: $40

Deferment available: Yes Maximum length of deferment: 1 year Transfer students accepted: Yes Transfer application policy: May transfer up to nine approved credits. Non-fall admissions: Yes Need-blind admissions: Yes

CLARK ATLANTA UNIVERSITY
SCHOOL OF BUSINESS ADMINISTRATION

ADMISSIONS CONTACT: LORRI SADDLER RICE, DIRECTOR OF ADMISSIONS
ADDRESS: 223 JAMES P. BRAWLEY DRIVE, ATLANTA, GA 30314 UNITED STATES
PHONE: 404-880-8447 • FAX: 404-880-6159
E-MAIL: LRICE@CAU.EDU • WEBSITE: WWW.SBUS.CAU.EDU

GENERAL INFORMATION

Type of school: Private Academic calendar: Semester

STUDENTS

Enrollment of parent institution: 5,000 Enrollment of MBA Program: 120 % male/female: 38/62 % part-time: 10 % underrepresented minority: 90 % international: 10 Average age at entry: 28 Average years work experience at entry: 5

ACADEMICS

Student/faculty ratio: 11:1 % female faculty: 39 % underrepresented minority faculty: 92 % part-time faculty: 22

FINANCIAL FACTS

Annual tuition (in-state/out-of-state): $19,127/ Fees: $550 Cost of books: $800 Room & board (on/off-campus): /$4,875 % of students receiving aid: 95 % of first-year students receiving aid: 95 % of students receiving grants: 95 Average award package: $32,000 Average grant: $32,000 Average loan: $32,000 Average student loan debt: $65,000

ADMISSIONS

Admissions Selectivity Rating: 80

of applications received: 134 % applicants accepted: 67 % acceptees attending: 69 Average GMAT: 430 Range of GMAT: 340–520 Accepts GRE scores: Average GPA: 3.0 TOEFL required of international students: Yes Minimum TOEFL (paper): 175 Application fee: $40 International application fee: $55 Regular application deadline: 4/1 Deferment available: Yes Maximum length of deferment: one year Transfer students accepted: Yes Transfer application policy: We will accept up to 6 credit hours earned while enrolled in an accredited MBA program. Non-fall admissions: No Need-blind admissions: No

EMPLOYMENT PROFILE

Percent employed at graduation: 25 Percent employed 3 months after graduation: 2 Average base starting salary: $82,500

Primary Source of Full-time Job Acceptances

School-facilitated activities: ....7(25%)

Graduate-facilitated activities: ....15(50%)

Unknown: ....7(25%)

Grads Employed by Function ..... % Avg. Salary
Marketing:......................................(52%) $80,000
Operations:....................................(7%) $75,000
Finance:...(30%) $82,000
HR:...(7%) $75,000
Other: ....(4%) $50,000

Top 5 Employers Hiring Grads (number of hires in last class)
Chevron/Texaco, Coca Cola, American Express, Union Pacific, Delta Airlines

CLEVELAND STATE UNIVERSITY
MONTE AHUJA COLLEGE OF BUSINESS

ADMISSIONS CONTACT: RONALD MICKLER JR., ASSISTANT DIRECTOR GRADUATE BUSINESS
ADDRESS: 2121 EUCLID AVENUE, BU 327, CLEVELAND, OH 44115 UNITED STATES
PHONE: 216-687-3730 • FAX: 216-687-6888
E-MAIL: CBACSU@CSUOHIO.EDU • WEBSITE: WWW.CSUOHIO.EDU/BUSINESS/MBA/

GENERAL INFORMATION

Type of school: Public Academic calendar: Semester

STUDENTS

Enrollment of parent institution: 17,258 Enrollment of MBA Program: 602 % male/female: 57/43 % out-of-state: 3 % part-time: 71 % underrepresented minority: 25 % international: 17 Average age at entry: 26 Average years work experience at entry: 5

ACADEMICS

Student/faculty ratio: 26:1 % female faculty: 18 % underrepresented minority faculty: 13 % part-time faculty: 20

FINANCIAL FACTS

Annual tuition (in-state/out-of-state): $10,242/$19,334 Fees: $55 Cost of books: $1,500 Room & board (on/off-campus): $12,000/$12,000 % of students receiving aid: 43 % of first-year students receiving aid: 39 % of students receiving grants: 15 Average award package: $17,708 Average grant: $4,546 Average loan: $18,420 Average student loan debt: $36,648

ADMISSIONS

Admissions Selectivity Rating: 86

of applications received: 509 % applicants accepted: 42 % acceptees attending: 40 Average GMAT: 480 Range of GMAT: 440–670 Accepts GRE scores: Yes Average Verbal GRE: 147 Range of Verbal GRE scores: 144–158 Average Quantitative GRE: 142 Range of Quantitative GRE scores: 140–157 Average Writing GRE: 3.0 Range of Writing GRE scores: 2.0–5.0 Average GPA: 2.9 TOEFL required of international students: Yes Minimum TOEFL (paper/computer): 550/78 Application fee: $30 International application fee: $30 Regular application deadline: 7/1 Deferment available: Yes Maximum length of deferment: 12 months Transfer students accepted: Yes Transfer application policy: Must be in good academic standing, cumulative gpa of 3.00 or higher at Graduate Level. Non-fall admissions: Yes Need-blind admissions: Yes

EMPLOYMENT PROFILE

Percent employed at graduation: 50 Percent employed 3 months after graduation: 66 Average base starting salary: $55,000

Primary Source of Full-time Job Acceptances

School-facilitated activities: ....34(49%)

Graduate-facilitated activities: ....27(39%)

Unknown: ....8(12%)

Grads Employed by Function ..... % Avg. Salary
Marketing:......................................(10%) $55,000
Operations:....................................(10%) $55,000
Consulting:....................................(2%) $50,000
Management:..................................(18%) $55,000
Finance:...(15%) $55,000
HR:...(12%) $55,000
MIS:...(7%) $55,000
Other: ....(13%) $45,000

Top 5 Employers Hiring Grads (number of hires in last class)
Huntington National Bank (1), Cleveland Clinic (2), Key Bank (2), Lubrizol (1), Progressive Insurance (2)

COASTAL CAROLINA UNIVERSITY
WALL COLLEGE OF BUSINESS

ADMISSIONS CONTACT: DR. JAMES O. LUKEN, ASSOC. PROVOST/DIR. OF GRADUATE STUDIES
ADDRESS: P.O. BOX 261954, CONWAY, SC 29528-6054 UNITED STATES
PHONE: 843-349-2394 • FAX: 843-349-6444
E-MAIL: GRADUATE@COASTAL.EDU • WEBSITE: WWW.COASTAL.EDU/GRADUATE

GENERAL INFORMATION

Type of school: Public

STUDENTS

Enrollment of parent institution: 10,263 **Enrollment of MBA Program:** 69 % **male/female:** 68/32 % **out-of-state:** 32 % **part-time:** 41 % **underrepresented minority:** 22 % **international:** 12 **Average age at entry:** 25 **Average years work experience at entry:** 5

ACADEMICS

Student/faculty ratio: 5:1 % **female faculty:** 33 % **underrepresented minority faculty:** 13 % **part-time faculty:** 20

FINANCIAL FACTS

Annual tuition (in-state/out-of-state): $15,990/$29,100 **Fees:** $420 **Cost of books:** $3,218 **Room & board (on/off-campus):** /$7,850 % **of students receiving aid:** 70 % **of first-year students receiving aid:** 70 % **of students receiving grants:** 30 **Average award package:** $15,943 **Average grant:** $11,668 **Average loan:** $16,934 **Average student loan debt:** $43,989

ADMISSIONS

Admissions Selectivity Rating: 79

# of applications received: 59 % **applicants accepted:** 86 % **acceptees attending:** 78 **Average GMAT:** 482 **Range of GMAT:** 480–540 **Accepts GRE scores:** Yes **Average GPA:** 3.3 **TOEFL required of international students:** Yes **Minimum TOEFL (paper/computer):** 575/89 **Application fee:** $45 **International application fee:** $45 **Deferment available:** Yes **Maximum length of deferment:** 1 semester **Transfer students accepted:** Yes **Transfer application policy:** All course work must be 3.0 or higher. 6 hours - maximum transfer. **Non-fall admissions:** Yes **Need-blind admissions:** Yes

EMPLOYMENT PROFILE

Percent employed at graduation: 15 **Percent employed 3 months after graduation:** 85 **Average base starting salary:** $55,575

Primary Source of Full-time Job Acceptances

School-facilitated activities:	6(21%)
Unknown:	22(79%)

Grads Employed by Function ..... % Avg. Salary

Marketing:	(25%)
Operations:	(7%)
Consulting:	(7%)
Management:	(14%)
Finance:	(33%)
HR:	(4%)
MIS:	(4%)
Other:	(7%)

Top 5 Employers Hiring Grads (number of hires in last class)
Verizon, Lake Mary, FL (2)

COLORADO STATE UNIVERSITY— PUEBLO
MALIK AND SEEME HASAN SCHOOL OF BUSINESS

ADMISSIONS CONTACT: JOE MARSHALL, DIRECTOR OF ADMISSIONS
ADDRESS: 2200 BONFORTE BLVD, PUEBLO, CO 81001 UNITED STATES
PHONE: 719-549-2461 • FAX: 719-549-2419
E-MAIL: INFO@COLOSTATE-PUEBLO.EDU • WEBSITE: HSB.COLOSTATE-PUEBLO.EDU

GENERAL INFORMATION

Type of school: Public **Academic calendar:** Students may begin at any time

STUDENTS

Enrollment of parent institution: 5,100 **Enrollment of MBA Program:** 109 % **male/female:** 76/24 % **out-of-state:** 33 % **part-time:** 37 % **underrepresented minority:** 19 % **international:** 32 **Average age at entry:** 28

ACADEMICS

Student/faculty ratio: 11:1 % **female faculty:** 17 % **underrepresented minority faculty:** 50

FINANCIAL FACTS

ADMISSIONS

Admissions Selectivity Rating: 79

# of applications received: 56 % **applicants accepted:** 88 % **acceptees attending:** 100 **Average GMAT:** 440 **Range of GMAT:** 400–680 **Accepts GRE scores:** No **Average GPA:** 3.3 **TOEFL required of international students:** Yes **Minimum TOEFL (paper/computer):** 550/ **Application fee:** $35 **International application fee:** $35 **Deferment available:** No **Transfer students accepted:** Yes **Transfer application policy:** Students may transfer up to 9 credit hours of approved graduate courses. **Non-fall admissions:** Yes **Need-blind admissions:** Yes

COLUMBUS STATE UNIVERSITY
TURNER COLLEGE OF BUSINESS AND COMPUTER SCIENCE

ADMISSIONS CONTACT: BETHANY YANDELL, TURNER COLLEGE RECRUITER
ADDRESS: 4225 UNIVERSITY AVE., COLUMBUS, GA 31907 UNITED STATES
PHONE: 706-507-8800 OR 706-507-8186
E-MAIL: YANDELL_BETHANY@COLUMBUSSTATE.EDU
WEBSITE: COBCS.COLUMBUSSTATE.EDU/

GENERAL INFORMATION

Type of school: Public **Academic calendar:** Fall Spring Summer

STUDENTS

Enrollment of parent institution: 8,307 **Enrollment of MBA Program:** 100 % **male/female:** 65/35 % **out-of-state:** 59 % **part-time:** 83 % **underrepresented minority:** 35 % **international:** 41

Average age at entry: 33 Average years work experience at entry: 4

ACADEMICS

Student/faculty ratio: 30:1 % female faculty: 18 % underrepresented minority faculty: 0 % part-time faculty: 0

FINANCIAL FACTS

Annual tuition (in-state/out-of-state): $2,070/$8,271 Fees: $835 Cost of books: $600 Room & board (on/off-campus): / % of students receiving aid: 47 % of first-year students receiving aid: 47 % of students receiving grants: 11 Average award package: $499,653 Average grant: $16,074 Average loan: $477,829 Average student loan debt: $42,189

ADMISSIONS

Admissions Selectivity Rating: 83

# of applications received: 93 % applicants accepted: 56 % acceptees attending: 62 Average GMAT: 485 Range of GMAT: 430–550 Accepts GRE scores: Yes Average GPA: 3.1 TOEFL required of international students: Yes Minimum TOEFL (paper/computer): 550/79 Application fee: $40 International application fee: $40 Regular application deadline: 6/30 Deferment available: Yes Maximum length of deferment: 1 year Transfer students accepted: Yes Transfer application policy: No more than 6 semester hours may be transferred. Non-fall admissions: Yes Need-blind admissions: Yes

CONCORDIA UNIVERSITY
JOHN MOLSON SCHOOL OF BUSINESS

ADMISSIONS CONTACT: ANNA SOMMER, GRADUATE RECRUITMENT OFFICER
ADDRESS: 1450 RUE GUY, MB 6.201 (6TH FLOOR), MONTREAL, QC H3H 0A1
  CANADA
PHONE: 514-848-2424 EXT 2708 • FAX: 514-848-2816
E-MAIL: GRADPROGRAMS@JMSB.CONCORDIA.CA
WEBSITE: CONCORDIA.CA/JMSB.HTML

GENERAL INFORMATION

Type of school: Public Academic calendar: Trimester

STUDENTS

Enrollment of parent institution: 45,954 Enrollment of MBA Program: 322 % male/female: 67/33 % part-time: 69 Average age at entry: 29 Average years work experience at entry: 6

ACADEMICS

Student/faculty ratio: 12:1 % female faculty: 20 % underrepresented minority faculty: 0 % part-time faculty: 39

FINANCIAL FACTS

Annual tuition (in-state/out-of-state): $1,626/$14,801 Fees: $990 Cost of books: $4,000 Room & board (on/off-campus): $5,000/$10,750 % of students receiving grants: Average award package: $9,000 Average grant: $8,111 Average loan: $8,000

ADMISSIONS

Admissions Selectivity Rating: 89

# of applications received: 325 % applicants accepted: 42 % acceptees attending: 58 Average GMAT: 626 Accepts GRE scores:

No Average GPA: 3.3 TOEFL required of international students: Yes Minimum TOEFL (paper/computer): 577/90 Application fee: $100 International application fee: $100

Application Deadline/Notification:

Round 1: 6/1
Round 2: 10/1
Round 3: 2/15

Deferment available: Yes Maximum length of deferment: 1 year Transfer students accepted: Yes Transfer application policy: Applicants may be eligible for advanced standing Non-fall admissions: Yes Need-blind admissions: Yes

EMPLOYMENT PROFILE

Percent employed at graduation: Percent employed 3 months after graduation: 76 Average base starting salary: $79,071

Top 5 Employers Hiring Grads (number of hires in last class)

Bombardier, Deloitte Consulting, BMO, Ericsson Canada, Amazon. com

CRANFIELD UNIVERSITY
CRANFIELD SCHOOL OF MANAGEMENT

ADMISSIONS CONTACT: HELEN KNIGHT, ADMISSIONS EXECUTIVE
ADDRESS: CRANFIELD SCHOOL OF MANAGEMENT, CRANFIELD, BEDFORD,
  MK43 0AL
PHONE: 0044-1234-754432 • FAX: 0044-1234-752439
E-MAIL: MBAADMISSIONS@CRANFIELD.AC.UK
WEBSITE: WWW.CRANFIELDMBA.INFO

GENERAL INFORMATION

Type of school: Public Academic calendar: Year Long

STUDENTS

Enrollment of MBA Program: 284 % male/female: 78/22 % part-time: 48 % international: 90 Average age at entry: 31 Average years work experience at entry: 7

ACADEMICS

Student/faculty ratio: 3:1 % female faculty: 25

FINANCIAL FACTS

Annual tuition (in-state/out-of-state): $53,082/$53,082 Cost of books: $1,078 Room & board (on/off-campus): $9,973/$9,973 % of students receiving aid: 64 % of first-year students receiving aid: 64 % of students receiving grants: 64 Average award package: Average grant: $12,733

ADMISSIONS

Admissions Selectivity Rating: 86

# of applications received: 446 % applicants accepted: 50 % acceptees attending: 67 Average GMAT: 680 Range of GMAT: 640–710 Accepts GRE scores: No TOEFL required of international students: Yes Minimum TOEFL (paper/computer): 600/100 Application fee: $0 International application fee: $0

Deferment available: Yes Maximum length of deferment: 2 years Transfer students accepted: No Non-fall admissions: No Need-blind admissions: Yes

EMPLOYMENT PROFILE

Percent employed at graduation: 47 **Percent employed 3 months after graduation:** 49

Primary Source of Full-time Job Acceptances

School-facilitated activities: ....26(22%)

Graduate-facilitated activities: ....54(45%)

Unknown: ....39(33%)

Grads Employed by Function ..... % Avg. Salary

Marketing:.......................................(9%) $107,025

Operations:.....................................(6%) $94,448

Consulting:.....................................(16%) $99,919

Management: ....(18%) $92,172

Finance:...(8%) $72,330

MIS: ....(5%) $98,217

Other: ....(25%) $91,590

Top 5 Employers Hiring Grads (number of hires in last class)

Brambles Ltd., Newcastle Science City, CHEP, HCL Technologies, Rolls-Royce

CREIGHTON UNIVERSITY
HEIDER COLLEGE OF BUSINESS

ADMISSIONS CONTACT: GAIL S. HAFER, ASSISTANT DEAN, GRADUATE BUSINESS PROGRAMS
ADDRESS: HEIDER COLLEGE OF BUSINESS, 2500 CALIFORNIA PLAZA, OMAHA, NE 68178 UNITED STATES
PHONE: 402-280-2853 • FAX: 402-280-2172
E-MAIL: BUSGRADADMIT@CREIGHTON.EDU • WEBSITE: BUSINESS.CREIGHTON.EDU/

GENERAL INFORMATION

Type of school: Private

STUDENTS

Enrollment of parent institution: 8,236 **Enrollment of MBA Program:** 188 **% part-time:** 100 **Average age at entry:** 28

ACADEMICS

Student/faculty ratio: 2:1 **% female faculty:** 10 **% part-time faculty:** 35

FINANCIAL FACTS

Annual tuition (in-state/out-of-state): $10,206/ **Fees:** $764 **Cost of books:** $1,600 **Room & board (on/off-campus):** $7,000/$6,000 **% of students receiving aid:** 15 **% of first-year students receiving aid:** 8 **Average award package:** $19,653 **Average grant:** $0 **Average loan:** $0

ADMISSIONS

Admissions Selectivity Rating: 78

# of applications received: 50 **% applicants accepted:** 96 **Average GMAT:** 530 **Range of GMAT:** 518–580 **Accepts GRE scores:** Yes **Average Verbal GRE:** 161 **Average Quantitative GRE:** 156 **Range of Quantitative GRE scores:** – **Average Writing GRE:** 4.5 **Average GPA:** 3.3 **TOEFL required of international students:** Yes **Minimum TOEFL (paper/computer):** 550/80 **Application fee:** $50 **International application fee:** $50

Deferment available: Yes **Maximum length of deferment:** 1 year **Transfer students accepted:** Yes **Transfer application policy:** Maximum of 6 hours considered for transfer from AACSB accredited institution, unless student transferring from another AACSB accredited Jesuit institution in which case more than six hours may be considered for transfer. **Non-fall admissions:** Yes **Need-blind admissions:** No

Grads Employed by Function ..... % Avg. Salary

Other: ....(8%)

DePAUL UNIVERSITY
KELLSTADT GRADUATE SCHOOL OF BUSINESS

ADMISSIONS CONTACT: ROBERT RYAN, ASSISTANT DEAN AND DIRECTOR
ADDRESS: 1 EAST JACKSON BLVD, SUITE 7900, CHICAGO, IL 60604 UNITED STATES
PHONE: 312-362-8810 • FAX: 312-362-6677
E-MAIL: KGSB@DEPAUL.EDU • WEBSITE: KELLSTADT.DEPAUL.EDU

GENERAL INFORMATION

Type of school: Private **Academic calendar:** quarter

STUDENTS

Enrollment of parent institution: 25,398 **Enrollment of MBA Program:** 1,328 **% male/female:** 80/20 **% out-of-state:** 3 **% part-time:** 36 **% underrepresented minority:** 9 **% international:** 5 **Average age at entry:** 28 **Average years work experience at entry:** 4

ACADEMICS

Student/faculty ratio: 13:1 **% female faculty:** 25 **% underrepresented minority faculty:** 14 **% part-time faculty:** 41

FINANCIAL FACTS

Fees: $363 **Cost of books:** $1,134 **Room & board (on/off-campus):** $13,130/$13,130 **% of students receiving aid:** 61 **% of first-year students receiving aid:** 69 **% of students receiving grants:** 33 **Average award package:** $32,362 **Average grant:** $19,939 **Average loan:** $30,521 **Average student loan debt:** $51,891

ADMISSIONS

Admissions Selectivity Rating: 75

# of applications received: 660 **Average GMAT:** 573 **Range of GMAT:** 530–630 **Accepts GRE scores:** No **Average GPA:** 3.1 **TOEFL required of international students:** Yes **Minimum TOEFL (paper/computer):** 550/80 **Application fee:** $60 **International application fee:** $60 **Regular application deadline:** 7/1 **Application Deadline/Notification:**

Round 1: 2/1

Round 2: 4/1

Round 3: 7/1

Deferment available: Yes **Maximum length of deferment:** One year **Transfer students accepted:** Yes **Transfer application policy:** Must apply like any other applicant. **Non-fall admissions:** Yes **Need-blind admissions:** Yes

Percent employed at graduation: 67 **Percent employed 3 months after graduation:** 18 **Average base starting salary:** $70,488

Primary Source of Full-time Job Acceptances

School-facilitated activities: ....19(58%)

Graduate-facilitated activities: ....14(42%)

Grads Employed by Function ..... % Avg. Salary

Marketing:......................................(11%) $74,204

Operations:....................................(2%) $64,700

Consulting:.....................................(3%) $59,333

Finance:...(14%) $72,286

HR:...(2%) $57,250

Top 5 Employers Hiring Grads (number of hires in last class)

Sears (2), Kellogg's (2), Garret Popcorn (2), Nestle/Purina (1), Credit Suisse (1)

DRAKE UNIVERSITY
COLLEGE OF BUSINESS AND PUBLIC ADMINISTRATION

ADMISSIONS CONTACT: DANETTE KENNE, DIRECTOR OF GRADUATE PROGRAMS
ADDRESS: 2507 UNIVERSITY AVENUE, ALIBER HALL, SUITE 211, DES MOINES, IA 50311 UNITED STATES
PHONE: 515-271-2188 • FAX: 515-271-2187
E-MAIL: CBPA.GRADPROGRAMS@DRAKE.EDU
WEBSITE: WWW.CBPA.DRAKE.EDU/ASPX/PROGRAMS/PROGRAMDETAIL.ASPX?ID=6

GENERAL INFORMATION

Type of school: Private **Academic calendar:** Semester

STUDENTS

Enrollment of parent institution: 5,617 **Enrollment of MBA Program:** 167 **% male/female:** 20/80 **% part-time:** 97 **Average age at entry:** 28 **Average years work experience at entry:** 0

ACADEMICS

Student/faculty ratio: 19:1 **% female faculty:** 19 **% underrepresented minority faculty:** 5 **% part-time faculty:** 10

FINANCIAL FACTS

Annual tuition (in-state/out-of-state): $9,400/ **Fees:** $412 **Cost of books:** $800 **Room & board (on/off-campus):** $7,350/ **Average grant:** $0 **Average loan:** $0

ADMISSIONS

Admissions Selectivity Rating: 69

# of applications received: 98 **% applicants accepted:** 61 **% acceptees attending:** 65 **TOEFL required of international students:** Yes **Minimum TOEFL (paper/computer):** 550/ **Application fee:** $25 **International application fee:** $25 **Regular application deadline:** 7/6 **Deferment available:** Yes **Maximum length of deferment:** one term **Transfer students accepted:** Yes **Transfer application policy:** Case by case evaluation **Non-fall admissions:** Yes **Need-blind admissions:** Yes

EASTERN ILLINOIS UNIVERSITY
LUMPKIN COLLEGE OF BUSINESS AND APPLIED SCIENCES

ADMISSIONS CONTACT: DR. JOHN R. WILLEMS, COORDINATOR, GRADUATE BUSINESS STUDIES
ADDRESS: 600 LINCOLN AVENUE, 4025 LUMPKIN HALL, CHARLESTON, IL 61920-3099 UNITED STATES
PHONE: 217-581-3028 • FAX: 217-581-6642
E-MAIL: MBA@EIU.EDU • WEBSITE: WWW.EIU.EDU/~MBA

GENERAL INFORMATION

Type of school: Public **Academic calendar:** FA, SP, SU

STUDENTS

Enrollment of parent institution: 12,000 **Enrollment of MBA Program:** 128 **% male/female:** 61/39 **% out-of-state:** 3 **% part-time:** 47 **% underrepresented minority:** 7 **% international:** 8 **Average age at entry:** 28 **Average years work experience at entry:** 5

ACADEMICS

Student/faculty ratio: 23:1 **% female faculty:** 23 **% underrepresented minority faculty:** 31

FINANCIAL FACTS

Annual tuition (in-state/out-of-state): $7,887/$23,661 **Fees:** $2,330 **Cost of books:** $325 **Room & board (on/off-campus):** $7,626/$8,000 **% of students receiving aid:** 18 **% of first-year students receiving aid:** 30 **% of students receiving grants:** 18 **Average award package:** **Average grant:** $7,560

ADMISSIONS

Admissions Selectivity Rating: 84

# of applications received: 98 **% applicants accepted:** 63 **% acceptees attending:** 89 **Average GMAT:** 510 **Range of GMAT:** 450–545 **Accepts GRE scores:** No **Average GPA:** 3.3 **TOEFL required of international students:** Yes **Minimum TOEFL (paper/computer):** 550/79 **Application fee:** $30 **International application fee:** $30 **Early notification date:** 4/15 **Regular application deadline:** **Deferment available:** Yes **Maximum length of deferment:** 1 academic year **Transfer students accepted:** Yes **Transfer application policy:** Maximum of 9 semester hours at grade of "B" or better. **Non-fall admissions:** Yes **Need-blind admissions:** Yes

EMPORIA STATE UNIVERSITY

ADMISSIONS CONTACT: MARY SEWELL, ADMINISTRATIVE SPECIALIST
ADDRESS: 1200 COMMERCIAL STREET, CAMPUS BOX 4003, EMPORIA, KS 66801 UNITED STATES
PHONE: 620-341-5403 • FAX: 620-341-5909
E-MAIL: MSEWELL@EMPORIA.EDU • WEBSITE: WWW.EMPORIA.EDU

GENERAL INFORMATION

Type of school: Public **Academic calendar:** Semester and Summer

STUDENTS

Enrollment of parent institution: 6,404 **Enrollment of MBA Program:** 117 **% male/female:** 50/50 **% out-of-state:** 2 **% part-**

time: 28 % **underrepresented minority:** 2 % **international:** 57 **Average age at entry:** 26

ACADEMICS

Student/faculty ratio: 7:1 % **female faculty:** 13 % **underrepresented minority faculty:** 0 % **part-time faculty:** 0

FINANCIAL FACTS

Annual tuition (in-state/out-of-state): $3,976/$12,028 **Fees:** $842 **Cost of books:** $1,000 **Room & board (on/off-campus):** $7,090/$5,620

ADMISSIONS

Admissions Selectivity Rating: 77

# of applications received: 70 % **applicants accepted:** 96 % **acceptees attending:** 60 **Average GMAT:** 526 **Range of GMAT:** 490–540 **Accepts GRE scores:** **Average GPA:** 3.4 **TOEFL required of international students:** Recommended **Minimum TOEFL (paper/computer):** 550/80 **Application fee:** $40 **International application fee:** $75

Deferment available: Yes **Maximum length of deferment:** One Year **Transfer students accepted:** Yes **Non-fall admissions:** Yes **Need-blind admissions:** Yes

EMPLOYMENT PROFILE

Percent employed at graduation: 29 **Percent employed 3 months after graduation:** 54 **Average base starting salary:** $42,500

Primary Source of Full-time Job Acceptances

School-facilitated activities: ....3(23%)

Unknown: ....10(77%)

Grads Employed by Function ..... % Avg. Salary

Management: ....(4%)

Finance:..(38%) $40,000

MIS: ....(4%) $45,000

Top 5 Employers Hiring Grads (number of hires in last class)

Koch Industries (1), Grant Thornton (2), Emporia State University (2), BKD, LLP (1), CBIZ Accounting Tax & Advisory Services, LLC (1)

FAIRLEIGH DICKINSON UNIVERSITY
SILBERMAN COLLEGE OF BUSINESS

ADMISSIONS CONTACT: SUSAN BROOMAN, DIRECTOR OF GRADUATE RECRUITMENT & MARKETING
ADDRESS: FAIRLEIGH DICKINSON UNIVERSITY GRADUATE ADMISSIONS, FLORHAM CAMPUS 285 MADISON AVENUE (M-RIO-01), MADISON, NJ 7940 UNITED STATES
PHONE: 973-443-8905 • FAX: 973-443-8088
E-MAIL: GRAD@FDU.EDU • WEBSITE: WWW.FDU.EDU/BUSINESS

GENERAL INFORMATION

Type of school: Private **Academic calendar:** Academic Year

STUDENTS

Enrollment of parent institution: 12,247 **Enrollment of MBA Program:** 481 % **underrepresented minority:** 10 % **international:** 20

ACADEMICS

Student/faculty ratio: 20:1 % **female faculty:** 21 % **underrepresented minority faculty:** 41 % **part-time faculty:** 40

FINANCIAL FACTS

Annual tuition (in-state/out-of-state): $18,400/$18,400 **Fees:** $854 **Cost of books:** $1,200

ADMISSIONS

Admissions Selectivity Rating: 83

# of applications received: 184 % **applicants accepted:** 58 % **acceptees attending:** 72 **Average GMAT:** 480 **Accepts GRE scores:** Yes **Average GPA:** 3.4 **TOEFL required of international students:** Yes **Minimum TOEFL (paper/computer):** 550/79 **Application fee:** $40 **International application fee:** $40

Deferment available: Yes **Transfer students accepted:** Yes **Transfer application policy:** Foundation courses can be waived by meeting FDU waiver policy. 6 graduate level credits can be transferred from other AACSB schools if taken within the past five years with a grade of 3.0 or better. **Non-fall admissions:** Yes **Need-blind admissions:** Yes

Top 5 Employers Hiring Grads (number of hires in last class)

Johnson & Johnson, ADP, Verizon, Credit Suisse, Deloitte ()

FLORIDA ATLANTIC UNIVERSITY
COLLEGE OF BUSINESS

ADMISSIONS CONTACT: JANE HERBERT, ADMISSIONS COORDINATOR
ADDRESS: OFFICE DEPOT CENTER (BLDG 93) - ROOM 201, 777 GLADES ROAD, BOCA RATON, FL 33431 UNITED STATES
PHONE: 561-297-1086 • FAX: 561-297-2179
E-MAIL: FLEXMBA@FAU.EDU • WEBSITE: WWW.BUSINESS.FAU.EDU

GENERAL INFORMATION

Type of school: Public **Academic calendar:** Semesters

STUDENTS

Enrollment of parent institution: 30,803 **Enrollment of MBA Program:** 290 % **male/female:** 57/43 % **out-of-state:** 10 % **part-time:** 35 % **underrepresented minority:** 18 % **international:** 6 **Average age at entry:** 28

ACADEMICS

Student/faculty ratio: 15:1 % **female faculty:** 36 % **part-time faculty:** 13

FINANCIAL FACTS

Annual tuition (in-state/out-of-state): $5,467/$16,695 **Fees:** $1,190 **Cost of books:** $1,220 **Room & board (on/off-campus):** $11,556/$10,344

ADMISSIONS

Admissions Selectivity Rating: 90

# of applications received: 211 % **applicants accepted:** 34 % **acceptees attending:** 94 **Average GMAT:** 548 **Range of GMAT:** 505–605 **Accepts GRE scores:** Yes **Average Verbal GRE:** 151 **Range of Verbal GRE scores:** 148–154 **Average Quantitative GRE:** 150 **Range of Quantitative GRE scores:** 147–154 **Average Writing GRE:** 3.4 **Range of Writing GRE scores:** 3.0–3.5 **Average GPA:** 3.3 **TOEFL**

required of international students: Yes **Minimum TOEFL (paper/ computer): 600/ Application fee:** $30 **International application fee:** $30 **Regular application deadline:** 7/1 **Deferment available:** Yes **Maximum length of deferment:** Up to 1 year **Transfer students accepted:** Yes **Transfer application policy:** We allow the transfer of up to 6 semester credit hours from an AACSB accredited graduate program. Credits must be no more than 7 years old. **Non-fall admissions:** Yes **Need-blind admissions:** Yes

FU JEN CATHOLIC UNIVERSITY
COLLEGE OF MANAGEMENT, FU JEN CATHOLIC UNIVERSITY

ADMISSIONS CONTACT: MS. HSIU-HUA SHIH, SECRETARY OF THE COLLEGE
ADDRESS: 510, CHUNG-CHENG ROAD,, HSINCHUANG, TAIPEI COUNTY, 242 TAIWAN
PHONE: 886+2-2905-2651 • FAX: 886+2-2905-2186
E-MAIL: 003856@MAIL.FJU.EDU.TW
WEBSITE: WWW.MANAGEMENT.FJU.EDU.TW/

GENERAL INFORMATION
Type of school: Private

ADMISSIONS
Admissions Selectivity Rating: 60*

TOEFL required of international students: Recommended **Minimum TOEFL (paper/computer):** 550/ International **Early notification date:** 12/26 **Regular application deadline:** 3/1 **Regular application notification:** 5/2

Non-fall admissions: No **Need-blind admissions:** Yes

GEORGE MASON UNIVERSITY
SCHOOL OF MANAGEMENT

ADMISSIONS CONTACT: ANGEL BURGOS, MBA DIRECTOR
ADDRESS: 4400 UNIVERSITY DRIVE, MSN 5A2, ENTERPRISE HALL, ROOM 28, FAIRFAX, VA 22030 UNITED STATES
PHONE: (703) 993-2136 • FAX: 703-993-1778
E-MAIL: MBA@GMU.EDU • WEBSITE: WWW.SOM.GMU.EDU

GENERAL INFORMATION
Type of school: Public **Academic calendar:** Semester

STUDENTS
Enrollment of parent institution: 30,714 **Enrollment of MBA Program:** 342 **% male/female:** 54/46 **% part-time:** 88 **% international:** 28 **Average age at entry:** 29 **Average years work experience at entry:** 5

FINANCIAL FACTS
Annual tuition (in-state/out-of-state): $14,496/$26,112 **Fees:** $0 **Cost of books:** $1,000

ADMISSIONS
Admissions Selectivity Rating: 87

# of applications received: 296 **% applicants accepted:** 49 % **acceptees attending:** 68 **Average GMAT:** 580 **Accepts GRE scores:** **Average GPA:** 3.2 **TOEFL required of international students:** Yes

Minimum TOEFL (paper/computer): 650/93 **Application fee:** $60 **International application fee:** $60 **Early notification date:** 4/15 **Regular application deadline:** 4/15 **Regular application notification:** 5/15

Application Deadline/Notification:
Round 1:..3/15 / 4/15
Round 2:..4/15 / 5/15

Deferment available: No **Transfer students accepted:** No **Non-fall admissions:** Yes **Need-blind admissions:** Yes

GEORGIA COLLEGE & STATE UNIVERSITY
THE J. WHITNEY BUNTING COLLEGE OF BUSINESS

ADMISSIONS CONTACT: KATE MARSHALL, GRADUATE ADMISSIONS COORDINATOR
ADDRESS: GC&SU CAMPUS BOX 107, MILLEDGEVILLE, GA 31061 UNITED STATES
PHONE: 478-445-6289 • FAX: 478-445-1336
E-MAIL: GRAD-ADMIT@GCSU.EDU • WEBSITE: MBA.GCSU.EDU

GENERAL INFORMATION
Type of school: Public **Academic calendar:** Semester

STUDENTS
Enrollment of parent institution: 6,889 **Enrollment of MBA Program:** 54 **% male/female:** 33/67 **% out-of-state:** 67 **% part-time:** 95 **% underrepresented minority:** 67 **% international:** 67 **Average age at entry:** 34 **Average years work experience at entry:** 0

ACADEMICS
Student/faculty ratio: 18:1 **% female faculty:** 33 **% underrepresented minority faculty:** 19 **% part-time faculty:** 0

FINANCIAL FACTS
Cost of books: $1,350 **Room & board (on/off-campus):** $9,768/$10,872

ADMISSIONS
Admissions Selectivity Rating: 89

# of applications received: 37 **% applicants accepted:** 35 % **acceptees attending:** 69 **Average GMAT:** 550 **Range of GMAT:** 520–570 **Accepts GRE scores:** Yes **Average Verbal GRE:** 154 **Range of Verbal GRE scores:** 151–159 **Average Quantitative GRE:** 152 **Range of Quantitative GRE scores:** 150–154 **Average Writing GRE:** 4.0 **Range of Writing GRE scores:** 3.0–5.0 **Average GPA:** 3.1 **TOEFL required of international students:** Recommended **Minimum TOEFL (paper/computer):** 550/79 **Application fee:** $35 **International application fee:** $0

Deferment available: Yes **Maximum length of deferment:** One year **Transfer students accepted:** Yes **Transfer application policy:** Must meet regular admission requirements. Maximum of nine semester hours are transferable if equivalent to GC&SU curriculum and from an AACSB-accredited school. **Non-fall admissions:** Yes **Need-blind admissions:** Yes

Henderson State University
School of Business Administration

Admissions Contact: Missie Bell, Graduate School administrative assistant
Address: 1100 Henderson Street, Box 7802, Arkadelphia, AR 71999-0001 United States
Phone: (870) 230-5126 • Fax: (870) 230-5479
E-mail: grad@hsu.edu • Website: www.hsu.edu/SchoolofBusiness/

GENERAL INFORMATION

Type of school: Public

STUDENTS

Enrollment of parent institution: 3,754 **Enrollment of MBA Program:** 45 % **male/female:** 50/50 % **out-of-state:** 5 % **part-time:** 25 % **underrepresented minority:** 10 % **international:** 20 **Average years work experience at entry:** 0

ACADEMICS

Student/faculty ratio: 6:1 % **female faculty:** 38 % **underrepresented minority faculty:** 0 % **part-time faculty:** 0

FINANCIAL FACTS

Annual tuition (in-state/out-of-state): $2,916/$5,832 **Fees:** $411 **Room & board (on/off-campus):** $3,874/$3,874

ADMISSIONS

Admissions Selectivity Rating: 74

# of applications received: 19 % **applicants accepted:** 100 % **acceptees attending:** 32 **Average GMAT:** 450 **Range of GMAT:** 390–670 **Accepts GRE scores:** **Average GPA:** 3.0 **TOEFL required of international students:** Yes **Minimum TOEFL (paper/computer):** 550/ **Application fee:** $40 **International application fee:** $40

Deferment available: No **Transfer students accepted:** Yes **Transfer application policy:** 6 hours from an accredited university. **Non-fall admissions:** Yes **Need-blind admissions:** Yes

IE University
IE Business School

Admissions Contact: Julian Trigo, Admissions Director
Address: Maria de Molina, 11, 13, 15, Madrid, 28006 Spain
Phone: 34915689610
E-mail: adimisionss@ie.edu • Website: www.ie.edu

GENERAL INFORMATION

Type of school: Private **Academic calendar:** April - April & September - July

STUDENTS

Enrollment of MBA Program: 618 % **male/female:** 69/31 % **part-time:** 0 % **international:** 93 **Average age at entry:** 30 **Average years work experience at entry:** 6

ACADEMICS

% **female faculty:** 38

FINANCIAL FACTS

Annual tuition (in-state/out-of-state): $75,800/$75,800 **Fees:** $1,500 **Cost of books:** $2,500 **Room & board:** $25,000 % of stu-

dents receiving aid: 60 % of first-year students receiving aid: 60 % of students receiving grants: 35 **Average award package:** $19,000 **Average grant:** $18,000 **Average loan:** $20,000

ADMISSIONS

Admissions Selectivity Rating: 91

# of applications received: 3,389 % **applicants accepted:** 35 % **acceptees attending:** 52 **Range of GMAT:** 610–760 **Accepts GRE scores:** Yes **Average GPA:** 3.4 **TOEFL required of international students:** Yes **Minimum TOEFL (paper/computer):** 600/100

Deferment available: Yes **Maximum length of deferment:** 2 intakes **Transfer students accepted:** No **Transfer application policy:** Transfer applicants can apply to the IMBA pro-gram. They will be con-sidered as regular appli-cants and will lose all of their prior credits. Trans-fer credits are not **Non-fall admissions:** Yes **Need-blind admissions:** Yes

EMPLOYMENT PROFILE

Percent employed at graduation: **Percent employed 3 months after graduation:** 92

Primary Source of Full-time Job Acceptances

School-facilitated activities: ....(41%)
Graduate-facilitated activities: ....(59%)

Grads Employed by Function ..... % Avg. Salary

Marketing:.....................................(29%)
Operations:....................................(5%)
Consulting:....................................(20%)
Management: ....(14%)
Finance:...(17%)
HR:..(1%)
MIS:...(3%)
Other: ....(11%)

Top 5 Employers Hiring Grads (number of hires in last class)

Credit Suisse (7), McKinsey & Company (5), Accenture (4), Banco de Crédito del Peré (4), A T Kearny (3)

INCAE
INCAE Business School

Admissions Contact: Ryan Frazee, Director of Admissions and Recruitment
Address: 2 km Oeste Del Vivero Procesa N,Â°1, La Garita, Alajuela, Costa Rica
Phone:
E-mail: ryan.frazee@incae.edu • Website: www.incae.edu

GENERAL INFORMATION

Type of school: Private **Academic calendar:** modules

STUDENTS

Enrollment of parent institution: 172 **Enrollment of MBA Program:** 172 % **male/female:** 65/35 % **part-time:** 0 % **international:** 33 **Average age at entry:** 27 **Average years work experience at entry:** 4

ACADEMICS

Student/faculty ratio: 8:1 % female faculty: 75 % underrepresented minority faculty: 83 % part-time faculty: 0

FINANCIAL FACTS

Annual tuition (in-state/out-of-state): $37,150/ Fees: $1,655 Cost of books: $2,564 Room & board (on/off-campus): $11,556/ % of first-year students receiving aid: 85 Average award package: $5,900 Average grant: $4,700 Average loan: $2,200

ADMISSIONS

Admissions Selectivity Rating: 79

# of applications received: 345 % applicants accepted: 80 % acceptees attending: 62 Average GMAT: 602 Range of GMAT: 570–620 Accepts GRE scores: Yes TOEFL required of international students: Yes Minimum TOEFL (paper/computer): 600/100 Application fee: $110 International Regular application deadline: 7/15 Deferment available: Yes Transfer students accepted: No Non-fall admissions: No Need-blind admissions: No

EMPLOYMENT PROFILE

Average base starting salary: $53,000

INDIANA UNIVERSITY NORTHWEST
SCHOOL OF BUSINESS AND ECONOMICS

ADMISSIONS CONTACT: JOHN GIBSON, DIRECTOR, GRADUATE/UNDERGRADUATE PROGRAMS IN B
ADDRESS: 3400, BROADWAY, GARY, IN 46408-1197 UNITED STATES
PHONE: 219-980-6635 • FAX: 219-980-6916
E-MAIL: JAGIBSON@IUN.EDU • WEBSITE: WWW.IUN.EDU/BUSINESS/INDEX.HTM

GENERAL INFORMATION

Type of school: Public Academic calendar: Semester

STUDENTS

Enrollment of parent institution: 6,000 Enrollment of MBA Program: 115 % male/female: 100/0 % out-of-state: 0 % part-time: 99 % underrepresented minority: 0 % international: 0 Average age at entry: 35 Average years work experience at entry: 0

ACADEMICS

Student/faculty ratio: 10:1 % female faculty: 26 % underrepresented minority faculty: 37

FINANCIAL FACTS

Annual tuition (in-state/out-of-state): $6,750/$15,000 Fees: $500 Cost of books: $999 Room & board (on/off-campus): $0/$0 % of students receiving grants: 1 Average award package: Average grant: $999 Average loan: $999

ADMISSIONS

Admissions Selectivity Rating: 82

# of applications received: 50 % applicants accepted: 70 % acceptees attending: 100 Average GMAT: 475 Range of GMAT: 383–598 Accepts GRE scores: Yes Average Verbal GRE: 149 Range of Verbal GRE scores: 137–157 Range of Quantitative GRE scores: 146–156 Average Writing GRE: Range of Writing GRE scores: – Average GPA: 3.1 TOEFL required of international students: Yes

Minimum TOEFL (paper/computer): 550/80 Application fee: $35 International application fee: $60 Early notification date: 5/15 Regular application deadline: 8/1 Regular application notification: 8/15

Application Deadline/Notification:

Round 1: ....1/1 / 1/5
Round 2: ....5/1 / 5/5
Round 3: ....8/1 / 8/15

Deferment available: Yes Maximum length of deferment: One year Transfer students accepted: Yes Transfer application policy: Must be a student in Good Standing from an accredtied institution. Up to six credit hours may transfer in if the grade is 'B' or beter. Non-fall admissions: Yes Need-blind admissions: Yes

EMPLOYMENT PROFILE

Average base starting salary: $60,000

Primary Source of Full-time Job Acceptances

School-facilitated activities: ....(25%)
Graduate-facilitated activities: ....(65%)
Unknown: ....(10%)

INDIANA UNIVERSITY—PURDUE UNIVERSITY AT FORT WAYNE
SCHOOL OF BUSINESS AND MANAGEMENT

ADMISSIONS CONTACT: SANDY FRANKE, SECRETARY, MBA PROGRAM
ADDRESS: NEFF 366, 2101 COLISEUM BOULEVARD EAST, FORT WAYNE, IN 46805-1499 UNITED STATES
PHONE: 260-481-6498
E-MAIL: EMAIL@SCHOOL.EDU • WEBSITE: WWW.IPFW.EDU/BMS/MBA1.HTM

GENERAL INFORMATION

Type of school: Public Academic calendar: Semester

STUDENTS

Enrollment of parent institution: 10,749 Enrollment of MBA Program: 191 % male/female: 65/35 % part-time: 91 Average age at entry: 32 Average years work experience at entry: 0

ACADEMICS

Student/faculty ratio: 1:1

ADMISSIONS

Admissions Selectivity Rating: 65

# of applications received: 45 % applicants accepted: 91 % acceptees attending: 95 TOEFL required of international students: Application fee: $30 International Regular application deadline: 7/15 Regular application notification: 1/1

Deferment available: Yes Transfer students accepted: No Non-fall admissions: Yes Need-blind admissions: No

IOWA STATE UNIVERSITY
COLLEGE OF BUSINESS

ADMISSIONS CONTACT: AMY HUTTER, DIRECTOR, MBA RECRUITMENT & MARKETING
ADDRESS: 1360 GERDIN BUSINESS BUILDING, AMES, IA 50011 UNITED STATES
PHONE: 515-294-8118 • FAX: 515-294-2446
E-MAIL: BUSGRAD@IASTATE.EDU • WEBSITE: WWW.BUS.IASTATE.EDU/MBA

GENERAL INFORMATION

Type of school: Public **Academic calendar:** Semester

STUDENTS

Enrollment of parent institution: 26,380 **Enrollment of MBA Program:** 94 **% male/female:** 62/38 **% out-of-state:** 8 **% part-time:** 62 **% international:** 31 **Average age at entry:** 26 **Average years work experience at entry:** 3

ACADEMICS

Student/faculty ratio: 4:1 **% female faculty:** 9 **% underrepresented minority faculty:** 12 **% part-time faculty:** 9

FINANCIAL FACTS

Annual tuition (in-state/out-of-state): $7,718/$18,132 **Fees:** $930 **Cost of books:** $1,000 **Room & board (on/off-campus):** $10,200/$10,200 **% of students receiving aid:** 50 **% of first-year students receiving aid:** 50 **% of students receiving grants:** Average award package: $8,120

ADMISSIONS

Admissions Selectivity Rating: 84

# of applications received: 210 **% applicants accepted:** 69 **% acceptees attending:** 65 **Average GMAT:** 595 **Accepts GRE scores:** Average GPA: 3.4 **TOEFL required of international students:** Yes **Minimum TOEFL (paper/computer):** 600/ **Application fee:** $30 **International application fee:** $70

Deferment available: Yes **Maximum length of deferment:** One year **Transfer students accepted:** No **Non-fall admissions:** Yes **Need-blind admissions:** Yes

EMPLOYMENT PROFILE

Percent employed at graduation: 75 **Percent employed 3 months after graduation:** 94 **Average base starting salary:** $57,848

Primary Source of Full-time Job Acceptances

School-facilitated activities: ....23(69%)
Graduate-facilitated activities: ....12(31%)
Unknown: ....35(10%)

Grads Employed by Function ..... % Avg. Salary

Marketing:......................................(11%) $61,667
Operations:....................................(33%) $53,000
Consulting:.....................................(6%) $68,000
Management: ....(14%) $43,500
Finance:...(21%) $51,800
HR:..(3%)
MIS: ....(12%) $74,500

JACKSONVILLE STATE UNIVERSITY
COLLEGE OF COMMERCE AND BUSINESS ADMINISTRATION

ADMISSIONS CONTACT: DR. JEAN PUGLIESE, ASSOCIATE DEAN
ADDRESS: 700 PELHAM ROAD N, JACKSONVILLE, AL 36265 UNITED STATES
PHONE: 256-782-5329 • FAX: 256-782-5321
E-MAIL: PUGLIESE@JSU.EDU • WEBSITE: WWW.JSU.EDU

GENERAL INFORMATION

Type of school: Public

STUDENTS

Enrollment of parent institution: 9,100 **Enrollment of MBA Program:** 65 **% male/female:** 45/55 **% out-of-state:** 10 **% part-time:** 70 **% underrepresented minority:** 10 **% international:** 75 **Average age at entry:** 28 **Average years work experience at entry:** 3

ACADEMICS

Student/faculty ratio: 15:1 **% female faculty:** 33 **% underrepresented minority faculty:** 0 **% part-time faculty:** 0

FINANCIAL FACTS

Annual tuition (in-state/out-of-state): $6,048/$12,096 **Cost of books:** $2,000 **Room & board (on/off-campus):** $4,000/$10,000 **Average award package:** $18,000 **Average grant:** $1,000 **Average loan:** $10,000

ADMISSIONS

Admissions Selectivity Rating: 77

# of applications received: 37 **% applicants accepted:** 89 **% acceptees attending:** 61 **Average GMAT:** 477 **Range of GMAT:** 410–560 **Accepts GRE scores:** No **Average GPA:** 3.2 **TOEFL required of international students:** Yes **Minimum TOEFL (paper/computer):** 500/61 **Application fee:** $30 **International application fee:** $30 **Regular application deadline:** 7/1 **Deferment available:** No **Transfer students accepted:** Yes **Transfer application policy:** 6 hrs. of approved courses with grade of A or B. Must be from AACSB-International accredited institution. **Non-fall admissions:** Yes **Need-blind admissions:** Yes

JAMES MADISON UNIVERSITY

ADMISSIONS CONTACT: LYNETTE MICHAEL, DIRECTOR OF ADMISSIONS, THE GRADUATE SCHOOL
ADDRESS: GRACE STREET HOUSE, JAMES MADISON UNIVERSITY - MSC 6702, HARRISONBURG, VA 22807 UNITED STATES
PHONE: 540-568-6395 • FAX: 540-568-7860
E-MAIL: GRAD@JMU.EDU • WEBSITE: WWW.JMU.EDU/MBA

GENERAL INFORMATION

Type of school: Public **Academic calendar:** Aug-July

STUDENTS

Enrollment of parent institution: 21,227 **Enrollment of MBA Program:** 93 % male/female: 63/38 % out-of-state: 10 % part-time: 57 % underrepresented minority: 10 % international: 3 **Average age at entry:** 33 **Average years work experience at entry:** 10

ACADEMICS

Student/faculty ratio: 15:1 % female faculty: 19 % underrepresented minority faculty: 4 % part-time faculty: 8

FINANCIAL FACTS

Annual tuition (in-state/out-of-state): $12,000/$12,000 **Cost of books:** $5,676 % of students receiving aid: 79 % of first-year students receiving aid: 76 % of students receiving grants: 46 **Average award package:** $6,117 **Average grant:** $6,907 **Average loan:** $16,505 **Average student loan debt:** $13,623

ADMISSIONS

Admissions Selectivity Rating: 78

# of applications received: 70 % applicants accepted: 93 % acceptees attending: 71 **Average GMAT:** 530 **Range of GMAT:** 450–640 **Accepts GRE scores:** Yes **Average Verbal GRE:** 157 **Range of Verbal GRE scores:** 147–165 **Average Quantitative GRE:** 152 **Range of Quantitative GRE scores:** 144–158 **Average Writing GRE:** 4.5 **Range of Writing GRE scores:** 3.5–5.5 **Average GPA:** 3.2 **TOEFL required of international students:** Yes **Minimum TOEFL (paper/computer):** 570/88 **Application fee:** $55 **International application fee:** $55 **Regular application deadline:** 6/1 **Deferment available:** Yes **Maximum length of deferment:** 1 year **Transfer students accepted:** Yes **Transfer application policy:** Can transfer up to 9 credit hours from another AACSB accredited MBA program. **Non-fall admissions:** No **Need-blind admissions:** Yes

EMPLOYMENT PROFILE

Average base starting salary: $70,000

KANSAS STATE UNIVERSITY
COLLEGE OF BUSINESS ADMINISTRATION

ADMISSIONS CONTACT: LYNN WAUGH, GRADUATE STUDIES ASSISTANT
ADDRESS: 107 CALVIN HALL, MANHATTAN, KS 66506-0501 UNITED STATES
PHONE: 785-532-7190 • FAX: 785-532-7809
E-MAIL: GRADBUSINESS@KSU.EDU • WEBSITE: WWW.CBA.KSU.EDU

GENERAL INFORMATION

Type of school: Public **Academic calendar:** Semeters

STUDENTS

Enrollment of MBA Program: 91 % male/female: 70/30 % out-of-state: 4 % part-time: 18 % underrepresented minority: 9 % international: 22 **Average age at entry:** 24 **Average years work experience at entry:** 2

ACADEMICS

Student/faculty ratio: 5:1 % female faculty: 22 % underrepresented minority faculty: 4 % part-time faculty: 100

FINANCIAL FACTS

Annual tuition (in-state/out-of-state): $6,855/$19,340 **Fees:** $666 **Cost of books:** $1,000 **Room & board (on/off-campus):** $5,000/$6,000 % of students receiving aid: 18 % of first-year students receiving aid: 12 **Average grant:** $2,500 **Average loan:** $3,000

ADMISSIONS

Admissions Selectivity Rating: 90

# of applications received: 86 % applicants accepted: 40 % acceptees attending: 100 **Average GMAT:** 565 **Range of GMAT:** 500–660 **Accepts GRE scores:** No **Average GPA:** 3.4 **TOEFL required of international students:** Yes **Minimum TOEFL (paper/computer):** 550/ **Application fee:** $60 **International application fee:** $60 **Early notification date:** 4/15 **Regular application deadline:** 6/1 **Regular application notification:** 7/15

Deferment available: Yes **Maximum length of deferment:** 1 year **Transfer students accepted:** Yes **Transfer application policy:** Up to 9 graduate credit hours from an AACSB accredited institution for courses that are part of the K-State MBA program will be accepted **Non-fall admissions:** No **Need-blind admissions:** Yes

EMPLOYMENT PROFILE

Average base starting salary: $42,000

Grads Employed by Function	%	Avg. Salary
Marketing:	(8%)	$42,000
Consulting:	(22%)	$42,000
Finance:	(30%)	$46,000
HR:	(8%)	$52,000
MIS:	(8%)	$55,000

LEHIGH UNIVERSITY
COLLEGE OF BUSINESS AND ECONOMICS

ADMISSIONS CONTACT: JEN GIORDANO, DIRECTOR OF RECRUITMENT AND ADMISSIONS
ADDRESS: 621 TAYLOR STREET, BETHLEHEM, PA 18015 UNITED STATES
PHONE: 610-758-3418 • FAX: 610-758-5283
E-MAIL: MBA.ADMISSIONS@LEHIGH.EDU • WEBSITE: WWW.LEHIGH.EDU/MBA

GENERAL INFORMATION

Type of school: Private **Academic calendar:** Semester

FINANCIAL FACTS

Annual tuition (in-state/out-of-state): $17,100/$17,100 **Fees:** $0
Cost of books: $1,300 **Room & board (on/off-campus):** /$10,800
Average loan: $0

ADMISSIONS

Admissions Selectivity Rating: 60*

LOUISIANA STATE UNIVERSITY— SHREVEPORT
COLLEGE OF BUSINESS ADMINISTRATION

ADMISSIONS CONTACT: SUSAN WOOD, MBA DIRECTOR
ADDRESS: ONE UNIVERSITY PLACE, SHREVEPORT, LA 71115 UNITED STATES
PHONE: 318-797-5213 • FAX: 318-797-5017
E-MAIL: SWOOD@PILOT.LSUS.EDU • WEBSITE: WWW.LSUS.EDU/BA/MBA/

GENERAL INFORMATION

Type of school: Public **Academic calendar:** Semester

STUDENTS

Enrollment of parent institution: 4,237 **Enrollment of MBA Program:** 150 **% male/female:** 47/53 **% part-time:** 93 **% underrepresented minority:** 10 **% international:** 5 **Average years work experience at entry:** 0

ACADEMICS

Student/faculty ratio: 20:1 **% part-time faculty:** 0

FINANCIAL FACTS

Annual tuition (in-state/out-of-state): $3,245/$9,420 **% of students receiving aid:** 60

ADMISSIONS

Admissions Selectivity Rating: 67

# of applications received: 70 **% applicants accepted:** 71 **% acceptees attending:** 80 **TOEFL required of international students:** Yes **Minimum TOEFL (paper/computer):** 550/ **Application fee:** $10 International **Regular application deadline:** 6/30 **Deferment available:** No **Transfer students accepted:** No **Non-fall admissions:** Yes **Need-blind admissions:** No

EMPLOYMENT PROFILE

Average base starting salary: $40,000

LOUISIANA TECH UNIVERSITY
COLLEGE OF BUSINESS

ADMISSIONS CONTACT: DR. DOUG AMYX, ASSOCIATE DEAN OF GRADUATE STUDIES
ADDRESS: PO BOX 10318, RUSTON, LA 71272 UNITED STATES
PHONE: 318-257-4528 • FAX: 318-257-4253
E-MAIL: SSTRICK@LATECH.EDU • WEBSITE: WWW.BUSINESS.LATECH.EDU

GENERAL INFORMATION

Type of school: Public **Academic calendar:** quarter

STUDENTS

Enrollment of parent institution: 11,804 **Enrollment of MBA Program:** 57 **% male/female:** 68/32 **% underrepresented minority:** 5 **Average age at entry:** 0 **Average years work experience at entry:** 0

ACADEMICS

Student/faculty ratio: 25:1 **% female faculty:** 21

FINANCIAL FACTS

Annual tuition (in-state/out-of-state): $5,368/$9,700 **Fees:** $1,500 **Cost of books:** $1,100 **Room & board (on/off-campus):** $8,880/$8,880

ADMISSIONS

Admissions Selectivity Rating: 82

# of applications received: 48 **% applicants accepted:** 60 **% acceptees attending:** 72 **Average GMAT:** 460 **Range of GMAT:** 460–560 **Average GPA:** 3.2 **TOEFL required of international students:** Yes **Minimum TOEFL (paper/computer):** 550/80 **Application fee:** $40 **International application fee:** $40 **Regular application deadline:** 8/1 **Deferment available:** Yes **Maximum length of deferment:** 1 year **Transfer students accepted:** Yes **Transfer application policy:** Can only transfer 6 graduate hours from the university in which you are coming from. **Non-fall admissions:** Yes **Need-blind admissions:** No

MARIST COLLEGE
SCHOOL OF MANAGEMENT

ADMISSIONS CONTACT: KELLY HOLMES, DIRECTOR OF ADMISSION
ADDRESS: 3399 NORTH ROAD, POUGHKEEPSIE, NY 12601 UNITED STATES
PHONE: 845-575-3800 • FAX: 845-575-3166
E-MAIL: GRADUATE@MARIST.EDU
WEBSITE: WWW.MARIST.EDU/ADMISSION/GRADUATE/BUSINESSADMINISTRATION/

GENERAL INFORMATION

Type of school: Private **Academic calendar:** Semester

STUDENTS

Enrollment of parent institution: 6,474 **Enrollment of MBA Program:** 173 **% male/female:** 100/0 **% out-of-state:** 0 **% part-time:** 100 **% underrepresented minority:** 0 **% international:** 0 **Average age at entry:** 29

ACADEMICS

Student/faculty ratio: 8:1 **% female faculty:** 45 **% underrepresented minority faculty:** 18 **% part-time faculty:** 23

FINANCIAL FACTS

% of students receiving aid: 42 **% of first-year students receiving aid:** 71 **% of students receiving grants:** 40 **Average award package:** $6,622 **Average grant:** $2,080 **Average loan:** $12,459 **Average student loan debt:** $30,412

ADMISSIONS

Admissions Selectivity Rating: 88

# of applications received: 153 **% applicants accepted:** 40 **% acceptees attending:** 70 **Average GMAT:** 537 **Range of GMAT:** 530–580 **Accepts GRE scores:** Yes **Average Verbal GRE:** 153 **Range of Verbal GRE scores:** 150–154 **Average Quantitative GRE:** 150 **Range of Quantitative GRE scores:** 149–153 **Average Writing GRE:** 3.6 **Range of Writing GRE scores:** 3.0–4.0 **Average GPA:** 3.3 **TOEFL required of international students:** Yes **Minimum TOEFL (paper/computer):** 550/ **Application fee:** $50 **International application fee:** $50 **Regular application deadline:** 8/1 **Regular application notification:** 8/15

Deferment available: Yes **Maximum length of deferment:** 1 year **Transfer students accepted:** Yes **Transfer application policy:** No more than six credit hours of core courses. **Non-fall admissions:** Yes **Need-blind admissions:** Yes

Grads Employed by Function ..... % Avg. Salary

Marketing:.......................................(22%) $85,000
Operations:.....................................(6%)
Consulting:.....................................(28%)
Management: ....(13%) $85,000
Finance:...(3%) $68,333
HR:...(6%) $55,000
MIS:...(6%) $85,000
Other: ....(16%) $75,000

Top 5 Employers Hiring Grads (number of hires in last class)
U.S. Government (3), Pfizer (2), Central Hudson Gas & Electric (2), Westchester Medical Center Heath Network (1), NBC Universal, Inc (1)

MARSHALL UNIVERSITY
LEWIS COLLEGE OF BUSINESS

ADMISSIONS CONTACT: DR. MICHAEL A. NEWSOME, MBA DIRECTOR
ADDRESS: CORBY HALL 217, 400 HAL GREER BOULEVARD, HUNTINGTON, WV 25755-2305 UNITED STATES
PHONE: 304-696-2613 • FAX: 304-696-3661
E-MAIL: EMAIL@SCHOOL.EDU • WEBSITE: LCOB.MARSHALL.EDU/

GENERAL INFORMATION

Type of school: Public **Academic calendar:** Semesters

STUDENTS

Enrollment of MBA Program: 80 **% male/female:** 40/60 **% underrepresented minority:** 15 **% international:** 30 **Average years work experience at entry:** 2

ACADEMICS

Student/faculty ratio: 5:1 **% female faculty:** 10 **% underrepresented minority faculty:** 10 **% part-time faculty:** 25

FINANCIAL FACTS

Annual tuition (in-state/out-of-state): $2,020/$5,653 **Fees:** $1,100 **Cost of books:** $1,000 **Room & board (on/off-campus):** /$4,000 **% of students receiving aid:** 50 **% of first-year students receiving aid:** 50

ADMISSIONS

Admissions Selectivity Rating: 81

# of applications received: 100 **% applicants accepted:** 84 **% acceptees attending:** 95 **Average GMAT:** 530 **Accepts GRE scores:** Average **GPA:** 3.5 **TOEFL required of international students:** Yes **Minimum TOEFL (paper/computer):** 525/ **Application fee:** $40 **International application fee:** $25

Deferment available: No **Transfer students accepted:** Yes **Transfer application policy:** When a student's Plan of Study is approved, credit may be transferred with the approval of the Graduate Dean. The work must have been completed at another regionally accredited graduate institution and must be appropriate to the student's program. Grades earned must be at the grade level of B or better, and acceptable to the advisor and the Graduate Dean. A maximum of 12 hours will be accepted, provided that they meet time limitation requirements. Graduate credit transferred from other institutions will not become part of the Marshall University grade point average and will simply meet credit hour requirements toward graduation. **Non-fall admissions:** Yes **Need-blind admissions:** No

EMPLOYMENT PROFILE

Average base starting salary: $50,000

MCMASTER UNIVERSITY
DEGROOTE SCHOOL OF BUSINESS

ADMISSIONS CONTACT: STEVEN WALKER / DENISE ANDERSON / CAITLIN RIVERO, ADMINISTRATORS, RECRUITING & MBA ADMISSIONS
ADDRESS: 4350 SOUTH SERVICE RD, RJC 316, BURLINGTON, ON L7L 5R8 CANADA
PHONE: (905) 525-9140 EXT. 27024 • FAX: (905) 634-4985
E-MAIL: MBAINFO@MCMASTER.CA • WEBSITE: WWW.DEGROOTE.MCMASTER.CA

GENERAL INFORMATION

Type of school: Public **Academic calendar:** September to May

STUDENTS

Enrollment of MBA Program: 564 **% male/female:** 61/39 **% part-time:** 31 **% international:** 27 **Average age at entry:** 26 **Average years work experience at entry:** 2

ACADEMICS

% female faculty: 23

FINANCIAL FACTS

Annual tuition (in-state/out-of-state): $3,515/ **Fees:** $1,460 **Cost of books:** $1,000

ADMISSIONS

Admissions Selectivity Rating: 86

# of applications received: 574 **% applicants accepted:** 63 % **acceptees attending:** 64 **Average GMAT:** 625 **Accepts GRE scores:** No **Average Verbal GRE:** 159 **Average Quantitative GRE:** 160 **Average GPA:** 3.5 **TOEFL required of international students:** Yes **Minimum TOEFL (paper/computer):** 600/100 **Application fee:** $150 **International application fee:** $150 **Regular application deadline:** 6/1 **Deferment available:** No **Transfer students accepted:** Yes **Transfer application policy:** An application must be submitted and will be reviewed on a case-by-case basis **Non-fall admissions:** Yes **Need-blind admissions:** Yes

EMPLOYMENT PROFILE

Percent employed at graduation: 19 **Percent employed 3 months after graduation:** 81 **Average base starting salary:** $68,350

Primary Source of Full-time Job Acceptances

School-facilitated activities: 15 (19%)
Graduate-facilitated activities: 9 (11%)
Unknown: 55 (70%)

Grads Employed by Function ..... % Avg. Salary

Marketing:.....................................(13%) $65,400
Operations:....................................(8%) $51,000
Consulting:....................................(10%) $69,000
Management: ....(4%) $0
Finance:..(27%) $67,500
MIS:..(5%) $85,000
Other: ....(33%) $63,150

Top 5 Employers Hiring Grads (number of hires in last class)
CIBC (8), RBC (5), Deloitte (3), Maple Leaf Foods (3), Cancer Care Ontario (3)

McNeese State University
MBA Program

Admissions Contact: Tammy Pettis, University Admissions
Address: Box 92495, Lake Charles, LA 70609-2495 United States
Phone: 337-475-5145 • Fax: 337-475-5189
E-mail: info@mcneese.edu
Website: www.mcneese.edu/colleges/business/mba

GENERAL INFORMATION

Type of school: Public **Academic calendar:** Semester

STUDENTS

Enrollment of parent institution: 8,423 **Enrollment of MBA Program:** 98 **% male/female:** 68/32 **% out-of-state:** 3 **% part-time:** 64 **% underrepresented minority:** 1 **% international:** 36 **Average age at entry:** 30 **Average years work experience at entry:** 0

ACADEMICS

Student/faculty ratio: 16:1 **% female faculty:** 1 **% underrepresented minority faculty:** 45

FINANCIAL FACTS

Annual tuition (in-state/out-of-state): $3,097/$9,163 **Cost of books:** $1,200 **Room & board (on/off-campus):** $4,380/$3,600 **% of students receiving aid:** 0 **% of first-year students receiving aid:** 0 **% of students receiving grants:** 0 **Average award package:** **Average grant:** $0 **Average loan:** $0

ADMISSIONS

Admissions Selectivity Rating: 76

# of applications received: 36 **% applicants accepted:** 97 **% acceptees attending:** 51 **Average GMAT:** 480 **Range of GMAT:** 250–690 **Accepts GRE scores:** **Average GPA:** 3.6 **TOEFL required of international students:** Yes **Minimum TOEFL (paper/computer):** 550/79 **Application fee:** $20 **International application fee:** $30 **Deferment available:** Yes **Maximum length of deferment:** 1 year **Transfer students accepted:** Yes **Transfer application policy:** No more than 6 hours from AACSB Accredited School **Non-fall admissions:** Yes **Need-blind admissions:** Yes

Michigan State University
The Eli Broad Graduate School of Management

Admissions Contact: Paul North, Director, MBA Admissions and Marketing
Address: Full-Time MBA Program, 215 Eppley Center, East Lansing, MI 48824-1121 United States
Phone: 517-355-7604 • Fax: 517-353-1649
E-mail: mba@msu.edu • Website: mba.msu.edu

GENERAL INFORMATION

Type of school: Public **Academic calendar:** Semester

STUDENTS

Enrollment of parent institution: 47,131 **Enrollment of MBA Program:** 246 **% male/female:** 80/20 **% part-time:** 0 **% underrepresented minority:** 12 **% international:** 33 **Average age at entry:** 28 **Average years work experience at entry:** 4

FINANCIAL FACTS

Annual tuition (in-state/out-of-state): $24,900/$39,500 **Fees:** $35 **Cost of books:** $1,500 **Room & board (on/off-campus):** $10,737/$10,737 **% of students receiving grants:** **Average award package:** $27,575 **Average grant:** $7,840

ADMISSIONS

Admissions Selectivity Rating: 89

# of applications received: 508 **% applicants accepted:** 36 **% acceptees attending:** 50 **Average GMAT:** 638 **Accepts GRE scores:** Yes **Average GPA:** 3.3 **TOEFL required of international students:** Yes **Minimum TOEFL (paper/computer):** 600/100 **Application fee:** $85 **International application fee:** $85

Application Deadline/Notification:

Round 1: ....11/1 / 12/15

Round 2: ....1/9 / 3/29

Round 3: ....3/1 / 4/18

Round 4: ....4/16 / 5/23

Deferment available: No **Transfer students accepted:** No **Non-fall admissions:** No **Need-blind admissions:** Yes

EMPLOYMENT PROFILE

Percent employed at graduation: 67 **Percent employed 3 months after graduation:** 7 **Average base starting salary:** $88,672

Primary Source of Full-time Job Acceptances

School-facilitated activities: 53 (73%)

Graduate-facilitated activities: 20 (27%)

Grads Employed by Function ..... % Avg. Salary

Marketing:.....................................(15%) $86,800

Operations:....................................(40%) $87,500

Consulting:....................................(4%) $110,000

Finance:...(31%) $81,500

HR:..(10%) $80,100

Top 5 Employers Hiring Grads (number of hires in last class)

Cummins (4), Deloitte Consulting (3), General Motors (3), Intel (3), Sears (3)

MIDDLE TENNESSEE STATE UNIVERSITY
JENNINGS A. JONES COLLEGE OF BUSINESS

ADMISSIONS CONTACT: TROY A. FESTERVAND, DIRECTOR, GRADUATE BUSINESS STUDIES
ADDRESS: PO BOX 290 BAS N222, MURFREESBORO, TN 37132 UNITED STATES
PHONE: 615-898-2368 • FAX: 615-904-8491
E-MAIL: GBS@MTSU.EDU
WEBSITE: WWW.MTSU.EDU/~GRADUATE/PROGRAMS/BUAD.HTM

GENERAL INFORMATION

Type of school: Public

STUDENTS

Enrollment of MBA Program: 410 **% male/female:** 64/36 **% underrepresented minority:** 22 **Average age at entry:** 26 **Average years work experience at entry:** 0

ACADEMICS

Student/faculty ratio: 20:1 **% part-time faculty:** 0

FINANCIAL FACTS

Annual tuition (in-state/out-of-state): $3,250/$6,100 **Fees:** $300 **Cost of books:** $1,000 **Room & board (on/off-campus):** $2,500/$2,500 **Average grant:** $0 **Average loan:** $0

ADMISSIONS

Admissions Selectivity Rating: 75

# of applications received: 325 **% applicants accepted:** 93 **Average GMAT:** 490 **Accepts GRE scores:** **Average GPA:** 3.2 **TOEFL required of international students:** Yes **Minimum TOEFL (paper/computer):** 525/ **Application fee:** $25 **International application fee:** $30 **Regular application deadline:** 7/1 **Regular application notification:** 8/1

Deferment available: Yes **Maximum length of deferment:** varies **Transfer students accepted:** Yes **Transfer application policy:** Depends on courses and programs **Non-fall admissions:** Yes **Need-blind admissions:** No

MISSISSIPPI STATE UNIVERSITY
COLLEGE OF BUSINESS

ADMISSIONS CONTACT: DR. BARBARA SPENCER, DIRECTOR OF GRADUATE STUDIES IN BUSINESS
ADDRESS: P.O.DRAWER 5288, MISSISSIPPI STATE, MS 39762 UNITED STATES
PHONE: 662-325-1891 • FAX: 662-325-8161
E-MAIL: GSB@COBILAN.MSSTATE.EDU
WEBSITE: WWW.BUSINESS.MSSTATE.EDU/GSB/

GENERAL INFORMATION

Type of school: Public **Academic calendar:** Semester

STUDENTS

Enrollment of parent institution: 17,824 **Enrollment of MBA Program:** 75 **% male/female:** 71/29 **% out-of-state:** 26 **% part-time:** 44 **% underrepresented minority:** 10 **% international:** 10 **Average age at entry:** 27

ACADEMICS

Student/faculty ratio: 4:1 **% female faculty:** 28 **% underrepresented minority faculty:** 13 **% part-time faculty:** 19

FINANCIAL FACTS

Annual tuition (in-state/out-of-state): $7,726/$18,754 **Fees:** $0 **Cost of books:** $1,500 **Room & board (on/off-campus):** $14,073/$14,073 **% of students receiving aid:** 66 **% of first-year students receiving aid:** 75 **% of students receiving grants:** 47 **Average award package:** $15,793 **Average grant:** $3,880 **Average loan:** $10,887 **Average student loan debt:** $11,067

ADMISSIONS

Admissions Selectivity Rating: 82

# of applications received: 156 **% applicants accepted:** 71 **% acceptees attending:** 68 **Average GMAT:** 521 **Range of GMAT:** 460–560 **Average GPA:** 3.4 **TOEFL required of international students:** Yes **Minimum TOEFL (paper/computer):** 575/90 **Application fee:** $30 **International application fee:** $30 **Regular application deadline:** 7/1 **Deferment available:** Yes **Maximum length of deferment:** 1 year **Transfer students accepted:** Yes **Transfer application policy:** 6 hours of transfer credit from accredited institutions. **Non-fall admissions:** Yes **Need-blind admissions:** Yes

Morgan State University
Earl Graves School of Business and Management

Director of Graduate Admissions
Address: 1700 East Cold Spring Lane, Baltimore, MD 21251 United States
Website: www.morgan.edu/academics/sbm/academic/sbm.htm

GENERAL INFORMATION
Type of school: Public **Academic calendar:** Semester

STUDENTS
Enrollment of parent institution: 5,900 **Enrollment of MBA Program:** 103 % part-time: 100 **Average years work experience at entry:** 0

ACADEMICS
Student/faculty ratio: 12:1 % part-time faculty: 9

FINANCIAL FACTS
Room & board (on/off-campus): $2,990

ADMISSIONS
Admissions Selectivity Rating: 60*

# of applications received: 0 % applicants accepted: **TOEFL required of international students:** Yes **Minimum TOEFL (paper/computer):** 600/ **Application fee:** $20

Deferment available: Yes **Transfer students accepted:** No **Non-fall admissions:** No **Need-blind admissions:** No

Murray State University
College of Business and Public Affairs

Admissions Contact: Dr. Gerry Nkombo Muuka, Assistant Dean and MBA Director
Address: 109 Business Building, Graduate Admissions Office, Sparks Hall, Murray, KY 42071 United States
Phone: 270-762-6970 • Fax: 270-762-3482
E-mail: cbpa@murraystate.edu
Website: www.mursuky.edu/qacd/cbpa/mba/index.htm

GENERAL INFORMATION
Type of school: Public **Academic calendar:** Semester

STUDENTS
Enrollment of parent institution: 9,000 **Enrollment of MBA Program:** 160 % part-time: 53 **Average age at entry:** 31 **Average years work experience at entry:** 0

ACADEMICS
Student/faculty ratio: 20:1

FINANCIAL FACTS
Annual tuition (in-state/out-of-state): $4,185/$11,700 **Room & board (on/off-campus):** $3,800

ADMISSIONS
Admissions Selectivity Rating: 66

# of applications received: 121 % applicants accepted: 75 % acceptees attending: 52 **TOEFL required of international students:** Yes **Minimum TOEFL (paper/computer):** 525/ **Application fee:** $25

Deferment available: Yes **Transfer students accepted:** Yes **Transfer application policy:** none **Non-fall admissions:** Yes **Need-blind admissions:** No

Nanyang Technological University
Nanyang Business School

Admissions Contact: Associate Professor Ooi Lee Lee, Director (MBA)
Address: The Nanyang MBA, Nanyang Business School, Nanyang Avenue, Blk S3, B3a, Singapore, 639798 Singapore
Phone: 011-65-67906183 • Fax: 011-65-67913561
E-mail: nbsmba@ntu.edu.sg • Website: www.nanyangmba.ntu.edu.sg

GENERAL INFORMATION
Type of school: Public

STUDENTS
Enrollment of parent institution: 28,949 **Enrollment of MBA Program:** 282 % male/female: 72/28 % part-time: 34 % international: 81 **Average age at entry:** 31 **Average years work experience at entry:** 7

ACADEMICS
Student/faculty ratio: 2:1 % female faculty: 27 % part-time faculty: 7

FINANCIAL FACTS
Annual tuition (in-state/out-of-state): /$19,000 **Cost of books:** $5,000 **Room & board (on/off-campus):** $7,000/$10,000 **% of students receiving grants:** 9 **Average grant:** $17,300

ADMISSIONS
Admissions Selectivity Rating: 88

# of applications received: 904 % applicants accepted: 30 % acceptees attending: 62 **Average GMAT:** 652 **Range of GMAT:** 610–690 **TOEFL required of international students:** Yes **Minimum TOEFL (paper/computer):** 600/ **Application fee:** $35 **International application fee:** $35 **Early notification date:** 1/31 **Regular application deadline:** 3/31 **Regular application notification:** 4/30

Deferment available: Yes **Maximum length of deferment:** 1 year **Transfer students accepted:** Yes **Transfer application policy:** Reviewed on a case-by-case basis **Non-fall admissions:** Yes

EMPLOYMENT PROFILE
Percent employed at graduation: 51 **Percent employed 3 months after graduation:** 40 **Average base starting salary:** $57,797

Primary Source of Full-time Job Acceptances
School-facilitated activities: 45 (76%)
Graduate-facilitated activities: 14 (24%)

Grads Employed by Function ..... % Avg. Salary

Marketing:.....................................(15%)

Operations:...................................(12%)

Consulting:...................................(6%)

Management: ....(4%)

Finance:.......................................(57%)

MIS:..(2%)

Other: ....(4%)

Top 5 Employers Hiring Grads (number of hires in last class)

Cisco Systems (2), OCBC Bank (2), PricewaterhouseCoopers (2), ABN Amro Bank (1), Bain & Company (1)

NATIONAL CHENGCHI UNIVERSITY
COLLEGE OF COMMERCE, NATINOAL CHENGCHI UNIVERSITY

ADMISSIONS CONTACT: 29393091 EXT. 65406, PUBLICE RELATIONS SPECIALIST ADDRESS: RM. 406, YI-XIAN BUILDING,, 64, ZHI-NAN ROAD, SEC. 2, TAIPEI, 11605 TAIWAN PHONE: 886-2-29393091 EXT. 65406 • FAX: 886-2-29387882 E-MAIL: IMBA@NCCU.EDU.TW WEBSITE: HTTP://WWW.COMMERCE.NCCU.EDU.TW/INDEX.PHP?LANG=EN

GENERAL INFORMATION

Type of school: Public

STUDENTS

Average age at entry: 31 **Average years work experience at entry:** 6

FINANCIAL FACTS
ADMISSIONS

Admissions Selectivity Rating: 70

# of applications received: 152 **% applicants accepted:** 39 **Average GMAT: Accepts GRE scores:** Yes **TOEFL required of international students:** Recommended International **Regular application deadline:** 12/22 **Regular application notification:** 4/8

Deferment available: Yes **Maximum length of deferment:** 2 years **Transfer students accepted:** No **Non-fall admissions:** No **Need-blind admissions:** Yes

NICHOLLS STATE UNIVERSITY
COLLEGE OF BUSINESS ADMINISTRATION

ADMISSIONS CONTACT: BECKY LEBLANC-DUROCHER, DIRECTOR OF ADMISSIONS ADDRESS: PO BOX 2004, THIBODAUX, LA 70310 UNITED STATES PHONE: 985-448-4507 • FAX: 985-448-4929 E-MAIL: ESAI-BL@NICHOLLS.EDU • WEBSITE: WWW.NICHOLLS.EDU

GENERAL INFORMATION

Type of school: Public **Academic calendar:** Semester

STUDENTS

Enrollment of parent institution: 7,482 **Enrollment of MBA Program:** 90 **% male/female:** 80/20 **% part-time:** 54 **Average years work experience at entry:** 0

ACADEMICS

Student/faculty ratio: 15:1 **% female faculty:** 19 **% part-time faculty:** 0

FINANCIAL FACTS

Annual tuition (in-state/out-of-state): $7,129/$16,620 **Cost of books:** $2,000 **Room & board (on/off-campus):** $8,870/ **% of students receiving aid:** 20 **Average grant:** $4,000 **Average loan:** $0

ADMISSIONS

Admissions Selectivity Rating: 74

# of applications received: 26 **Average GMAT:** 494 **Accepts GRE scores: Average GPA:** 3.2 **TOEFL required of international students:** Yes **Minimum TOEFL (paper/computer):** 550/ **Application fee:** $20 **International application fee:** $30 **Regular application deadline:** 7/1 **Deferment available:** Yes **Maximum length of deferment:** 1 semester **Transfer students accepted:** Yes **Transfer application policy:** Maximum of 9 approved hours may be transferred from an accredited institution. **Non-fall admissions:** Yes **Need-blind admissions:** Yes

NORTHERN ILLINOIS UNIVERSITY, COLLEGE OF BUSINESS
MBA PROGRAMS

ADMISSIONS CONTACT: MONA SALMON, ASSISTANT DIRECTOR ADDRESS: BARSEMA 203, DEKALB, IL 60115 UNITED STATES PHONE: 866-648-6221 • FAX: 815-753-1668 E-MAIL: MBA@NIU.EDU • WEBSITE: WWW.COB.NIU.EDU/MBAPROGRAMS

GENERAL INFORMATION

Type of school: Public

STUDENTS

Enrollment of parent institution: 25,000 **Enrollment of MBA Program:** 528 **% male/female:** 100/0 **% part-time:** 99 **% underrepresented minority:** 0 **Average age at entry:** 32 **Average years work experience at entry:** 9

ACADEMICS

Student/faculty ratio: 24:1 **% female faculty:** 19 **% underrepresented minority faculty:** 4

FINANCIAL FACTS

Annual tuition (in-state/out-of-state): $8,154/$11,538 **Cost of books:** $750 **Average grant:** $0

ADMISSIONS

Admissions Selectivity Rating: 78

# of applications received: 262 **% applicants accepted:** 97 **% acceptees attending:** 70 **Average GMAT:** 550 **Average GPA:** 3.2 **TOEFL required of international students:** Yes **Minimum TOEFL (paper/computer):** 550/ **Application fee:** $30 **International Regular application deadline:** 6/1 **Deferment available:** Yes **Maximum length of deferment:** 24 months **Transfer students accepted:** Yes **Transfer application policy:** For the Evening MBA a limit of 9-semester-hours accepted for phase two credit from AACSB-accredited schools only. **Non-fall admissions:** Yes **Need-blind admissions:** Yes

Northern Michigan University
Walker L. Cisler College of Business

ADMISSIONS CONTACT: GERRI DANIELS, DIRECTOR
ADDRESS: 1401 PRESQUE ISLE AVENUE, MARQUETTE, MI 49855 UNITED
STATES
PHONE: 1-800-682-9797 • FAX: 906.227.1747
E-MAIL: ADMISSIONS@NMU.EDU • WEBSITE: WWW.NMU.EDU/BUSINESS

GENERAL INFORMATION
Type of school: Public

ACADEMICS
Student/faculty ratio: 15:1 **% female faculty:** 33 **% underrepresented minority faculty:** 0

FINANCIAL FACTS
Annual tuition (in-state/out-of-state): $8,640/$8,640 **Fees:** $308
Room & board (on/off-campus): $8,026

ADMISSIONS
Admissions Selectivity Rating: 60*

**# of applications received: % applicants accepted: TOEFL
required of international students:** Yes **Minimum TOEFL (paper/
computer):** 500/61 **Application fee:** $50 **International application
fee:** $50

Deferment available: Yes **Maximum length of deferment:** 1 year
Transfer students accepted: Yes **Transfer application policy:**
Transfer Credit More than 50 percent of the minimum credits for
graduate degrees must be Northern Michigan University credits. To
be accepted the following must occur: 1. The student must be in
good standing in the college or university from which credit is transferred. 2. Courses to be transferred must carry a grade of B or better. 3. Courses to be transferred must be appropriate to the graduate
program as determined by the program adviser. 4. Credit must have
been earned within the past seven years. 5. Official transcripts must
have been received by the College of Graduate Studies before transfer credit can be awarded. 6. All transfer credit must be reviewed by
the student, adviser and approved by the Dean of Graduate Studies.
The necessary documentation must be provided by the student.
7. Transfer grades will not be used in calculating the grade-point
average required for graduation. The transfer credit form, available
from the College of Graduate Studies Web site at www.nmu.edu/
graduate_studies, is to be completed by the adviser and submitted
to the College of Graduate Studies. This form will be used by the
adviser and department to signify approval of the appropriateness of
all courses. **Non-fall admissions:** Yes **Need-blind admissions:** Yes

North Dakota State University
College of Business Administration

ADMISSIONS CONTACT: PAUL BROWN, MBA DIRECTOR
ADDRESS: PO BOX 5137, FARGO, ND 58018 UNITED STATES
E-MAIL: PAUL.BROWN@NDSU.EDUX • WEBSITE: WWW.NDSU.EDU/CBA/

GENERAL INFORMATION
Type of school: Public

STUDENTS
Enrollment of MBA Program: 537 **% male/female:** 60/40 **% part-
time:** 89 **% international:** 8 **Average age at entry:** 29 **Average
years work experience at entry:** 0

ACADEMICS
Student/faculty ratio: 19:1 **% part-time faculty:** 28

FINANCIAL FACTS
Annual tuition (in-state/out-of-state): $4,600/$10,800 **Fees:** $340

ADMISSIONS
Admissions Selectivity Rating: 64

# of applications received: 162 **% applicants accepted:** 90 **%
acceptees attending:** 80 **TOEFL required of international students:**
Yes **Minimum TOEFL (paper/computer):** 550/ **Application fee:** $35
International **Regular application deadline:** 7/15 **Deferment avail-
able:** Yes **Transfer students accepted:** No **Non-fall admissions:** Yes
Need-blind admissions: No

Nyenrode Business Universiteit

ADMISSIONS CONTACT: VICTORIA BRESSERS, HEAD OF ADMISSIONS
ADDRESS: P.O. BOX 130, BREUKELEN, 3620 AC, NETHERLANDS
PHONE: 00 31 346 291 291 • FAX: 00 31 346 291 450
E-MAIL: INFO@NYENRODE.NL • WEBSITE: WWW.NYENRODE.NL

GENERAL INFORMATION
Type of school: Private

STUDENTS
Enrollment of MBA Program: 55 **% male/female:** 77/23 **% part-
time:** 45 **% international:** 90 **Average age at entry:** 31 **Average
years work experience at entry:** 7

ACADEMICS
Student/faculty ratio: 4:1 **% female faculty:** 16 **% part-time faculty:**
58

FINANCIAL FACTS
Annual tuition (in-state/out-of-state): $44,311/ **Cost of books:**
$1,597 **Room & board (on/off-campus):** $15,000/ **% of first-year
students receiving aid:** 20 **% of students receiving grants:**

ADMISSIONS

Admissions Selectivity Rating: 84

# of applications received: 103 **% applicants accepted:** 29 **Average GMAT:** 560 **TOEFL required of international students:** Yes **Minimum TOEFL (paper/computer):** 600/ **Application fee:** $80 International **Regular application deadline:** 8/31 **Deferment available:** Yes **Maximum length of deferment:** 2 years **Transfer students accepted:** No **Non-fall admissions:** No **Need-blind admissions:** No

EMPLOYMENT PROFILE

Average base starting salary: $50,000

Primary Source of Full-time Job Acceptances

School-facilitated activities: ....4 (%)

Unknown: ....18 (%)

Grads Employed by Function ..... % Avg. Salary

Marketing:.......................................(15%)

Consulting:....................................(31%)

Management: ....(8%)

Finance:...(31%)

HR:..(15%)

OHIO UNIVERSITY
COLLEGE OF BUSINESS

ADMISSIONS CONTACT: JAN ROSS, ASSISTANT DEAN, GRADUATE PROGRAM
ADDRESS: 514 COPELAND HALL, ATHENS, OH 45701 UNITED STATES
PHONE: 740-593-4320 • FAX: 740-593-1388
E-MAIL: ROSSJ@OHIO.EDU • WEBSITE: WWW.COB.OHIOU.EDU/GRAD/

GENERAL INFORMATION

Type of school: Public **Academic calendar:** quarters

STUDENTS

Enrollment of parent institution: 19,000 **Enrollment of MBA Program:** 119 **% male/female:** 68/32 **% out-of-state:** 67 **% part-time:** 64 **% underrepresented minority:** 12 **% international:** 16 **Average age at entry:** 25 **Average years work experience at entry:** 2

ACADEMICS

Student/faculty ratio: 4:1 **% female faculty:** 25 **% underrepresented minority faculty:** 10

FINANCIAL FACTS

Annual tuition (in-state/out-of-state): $12,675/$25,995 **Fees:** $5,000 **Cost of books:** $4,000 **Room & board (on/off-campus):** $10,000/$10,000 **% of students receiving aid:** 70 **% of first-year students receiving aid:** 70 **% of students receiving grants:** **Average award package:** $15,000 **Average grant:** $8,000 **Average loan:** $15,000

ADMISSIONS

Admissions Selectivity Rating: 90

# of applications received: 180 **% applicants accepted:** 32 **% acceptees attending:** 75 **Average GMAT:** 562 **Range of GMAT:** 480–670 **Accepts GRE scores:** **Average GPA:** 3.3 **TOEFL required of international students:** Yes **Minimum TOEFL (paper/computer):**

600/100 **Application fee:** $50 **International application fee:** $50 **Regular application deadline:** 2/1 **Regular application notification:** 4/1

Deferment available: Yes **Maximum length of deferment:** 1 year **Transfer students accepted:** No **Non-fall admissions:** Yes **Need-blind admissions:** Yes

EMPLOYMENT PROFILE

Percent employed at graduation: 58 **Percent employed 3 months after graduation:** **Average base starting salary:** $56,350

Primary Source of Full-time Job Acceptances

School-facilitated activities: 13 (25%)

Graduate-facilitated activities: 14 (25%)

Unknown: 27 (50%)

Grads Employed by Function ..... % Avg. Salary

Marketing:.....................................(53%) $56,350

Operations:....................................(14%) $56,350

Consulting:....................................(3%) $56,350

Management: ....(19%) $56,350

Finance:...(11%) $56,350

Top 5 Employers Hiring Grads (number of hires in last class)

Deloitte & Touche (2), Ernst & Young (1), KPMG (1)

OKLAHOMA STATE UNIVERSITY
SPEARS SCHOOL OF BUSINESS

ADMISSIONS CONTACT: JANICE ANALLA, ASSISTANT DIRECTOR, GRADUATE PROGRAMS
ADDRESS: OKLAHOMA STATE UNIVERSITY, 102 GUNDERSEN HALL, STILLWATER, OK 74078-4022 UNITED STATES
PHONE: 405-744-2951 • FAX: 405-744-7474
E-MAIL: SPEARSMASTERS@OKSTATE.EDU • WEBSITE: SPEARS.OKSTATE.EDU/MBA/

GENERAL INFORMATION

Type of school: Public **Academic calendar:** Semester

STUDENTS

Enrollment of MBA Program: 534 **% male/female:** 61/39 **% part-time:** 77 **% international:** 17 **Average age at entry:** 27

ACADEMICS

Student/faculty ratio: 25:1 **% female faculty:** 18 **% underrepresented minority faculty:** 2 **% part-time faculty:** 0

FINANCIAL FACTS

Annual tuition (in-state/out-of-state): $4,026/$15,652 **Fees:** $2,466 **Cost of books:** $730 **Room & board (on/off-campus):** $7,650

ADMISSIONS

Admissions Selectivity Rating: 81

# of applications received: 256 **% applicants accepted:** 82 **% acceptees attending:** 80 **Average GMAT:** 559 **Range of GMAT:** 510–603 **Accepts GRE scores:** No **Average GPA:** 3.3 **TOEFL required of international students:** Yes **Minimum TOEFL (paper/computer):** 575/89 **Application fee:** $40 **International application fee:** $75 **Regular application deadline:** 7/1 **Deferment available:** Yes **Maximum length of deferment:** 1 yr. **Transfer students accept-**

ed: Yes **Transfer application policy:** They must be a student in good standing at an AACSB accredited university. **Non-fall admissions:** Yes **Need-blind admissions:** Yes

EMPLOYMENT PROFILE

Percent employed at graduation: 67 **Percent employed 3 months after graduation:** 29 **Average base starting salary:** $52,855

Primary Source of Full-time Job Acceptances

School-facilitated activities: 17 (55%)

Graduate-facilitated activities: 10 (32%)

Unknown: 4 (13%)

Grads Employed by Function ..... % Avg. Salary

Marketing:.................................(20%) $48,250

Management: ....(35%) $62,429

Finance:....................................(45%) $47,456

THE OPEN UNIVERSITY
THE OPEN UNIVERSITY BUSINESS SCHOOL

ADMISSIONS CONTACT: STUDENT REGISTRATION & ENQUIRY SERVICE,
ADDRESS: THE OPEN UNIVERSITY BUSINESS SCHOOL, THE OPEN UNIVERSITY / PO BOX 197, MILTON KEYNES, MK7 6BJ UNITED KINGDOM OF GREAT BRITAIN AND NORTHERN IRELAND
PHONE: +44 8700100311 • FAX: +44 1908 654806
E-MAIL: OUBS-ILGEN@OPEN.AC.UK • WEBSITE: WWW.OPEN.AC.UK/OUBS/

GENERAL INFORMATION

Type of school: Public **Academic calendar:** Rolling May & November intakes

STUDENTS

Enrollment of parent institution: 5,500 **Enrollment of MBA Program:** 2,000 **% male/female:** 65/35 **% part-time:** 100 **Average age at entry:** 37 **Average years work experience at entry:** 14

ACADEMICS

Student/faculty ratio: 16:1 **% part-time faculty:** 413

FINANCIAL FACTS

Annual tuition (in-state/out-of-state): $19,880/ **% of students receiving aid:** 0 **% of first-year students receiving aid:** 0 **% of students receiving grants:** 0 **Average award package:** $0 **Average grant:** $0 **Average loan:** $0 **Average student loan debt:** $0

ADMISSIONS

Admissions Selectivity Rating: 64

# of applications received: 2,000 **% applicants accepted:** 100 **% acceptees attending:** 100 **TOEFL required of international students:** **Deferment available:** No **Transfer students accepted:** No **Non-fall admissions:** Yes **Need-blind admissions:** Yes

OREGON STATE UNIVERSITY
COLLEGE OF BUSINESS

ADMISSIONS CONTACT: ASHLEY MURPHY, MBA OPERATIONS DIRECTOR
ADDRESS: AUSTIN HALL 326, COLLEGE OF BUSINESS, CORVALLIS, OR 97331 UNITED STATES
PHONE: 541-737-5510 • FAX: 541-737-6033
E-MAIL: OSUMBA@BUS.OREGONSTATE.EDU
WEBSITE: BUSINESS.OREGONSTATE.EDU/MBA/

GENERAL INFORMATION

Type of school: Public **Academic calendar:** Quarter

STUDENTS

Enrollment of parent institution: 30,058 **Enrollment of MBA Program:** 219 **% male/female:** 56/44 **% out-of-state:** 86 **% part-time:** 43 **% underrepresented minority:** 4 **% international:** 83 **Average age at entry:** 26

ACADEMICS

Student/faculty ratio: 3:1 **% female faculty:** 26 **% underrepresented minority faculty:** 18 **% part-time faculty:** 1

FINANCIAL FACTS

Annual tuition (in-state/out-of-state): $18,873/$31,509 **Fees:** $524 **Cost of books:** $1,950 **Room & board (on/off-campus):** $11,874/$11,874 **% of students receiving aid:** 20 **% of first-year students receiving aid:** 22 **% of students receiving grants:** 7 **Average loan:** $0

ADMISSIONS

Admissions Selectivity Rating: 87

# of applications received: 196 **% applicants accepted:** 52 **% acceptees attending:** 83 **Average GMAT:** 571 **Range of GMAT:** 530–600 **Accepts GRE scores:** No **Average GPA:** 3.2 **TOEFL required of international students:** Yes **Minimum TOEFL (paper/computer):** 575/91 **Application fee:** $60 **International application fee:** $60 **Regular application deadline:** 8/1 **Deferment available:** Yes **Maximum length of deferment:** one year **Transfer students accepted:** Yes **Transfer application policy:** Up to 15 credits of approved coursework (AACSB-accredited) **Non-fall admissions:** Yes **Need-blind admissions:** Yes

EMPLOYMENT PROFILE

Percent employed at graduation: 51 **Average base starting salary:** $57,840

Grads Employed by Function ..... % Avg. Salary

Marketing:...................................(2%) $42,000

Operations:..................................(4%) $75,500

Management: ....(4%) $62,500

Finance:.......................................(7%) $46,350

MIS: ....(2%) $75,000

PACE UNIVERSITY
LUBIN SCHOOL OF BUSINESS

ADMISSIONS CONTACT: SUSAN FORD-GOLDSCHEIN, DIRECTOR OF GRADUATE ADMISSION
ADDRESS: ONE PACE PLAZA, NEW YORK, NY 10038 UNITED STATES
PHONE: 212-346-1531 • FAX: 212-346-1585
E-MAIL: GRADNYC@PACE.EDU • WEBSITE: WWW.PACE.EDU/LUBIN/

GENERAL INFORMATION

Type of school: Private **Academic calendar:** Semester

STUDENTS

Enrollment of parent institution: 12,857 **Enrollment of MBA Program:** 514 **% male/female:** 52/48 **% out-of-state:** 16 **% part-time:** 41 **% underrepresented minority:** 21 **% international:** 42 **Average age at entry:** 26 **Average years work experience at entry:** 2

ACADEMICS

Student/faculty ratio: 6:1 **% female faculty:** 20 **% underrepresented minority faculty:** 18 **% part-time faculty:** 25

FINANCIAL FACTS

Annual tuition (in-state/out-of-state): $20,790/$20,790 **Fees:** $632 **Cost of books:** $2,962 **Room & board (on/off-campus):** $16,400/$16,400 **% of students receiving aid:** 49 **% of first-year students receiving aid:** 48 **% of students receiving grants:** 33 **Average award package:** $18,055 **Average grant:** $8,916 **Average loan:** $20,381 **Average student loan debt:** $47,060

ADMISSIONS

Admissions Selectivity Rating: 83

# of applications received: 499 **% applicants accepted:** 64 **% acceptees attending:** 50 **Average GMAT:** 543 **Range of GMAT:** 510–570 **Accepts GRE scores:** Yes **Average GPA:** 3.3 **TOEFL required of international students:** Yes **Minimum TOEFL (paper/computer):** 600/100 **Application fee:** $70 **International application fee:** $70 **Regular application deadline:** 8/1 **Deferment available:** Yes **Maximum length of deferment:** one academic year **Transfer students accepted:** Yes **Transfer application policy:** maximum of 6 credits **Non-fall admissions:** Yes **Need-blind admissions:** Yes

EMPLOYMENT PROFILE

Percent employed at graduation: 85 **Percent employed 3 months after graduation:** 11 **Average base starting salary:** $67,615
Primary Source of Full-time Job Acceptances

School-facilitated activities:	49 (26%)
Graduate-facilitated activities:	13 (7%)
Unknown:	128 (67%)

Grads Employed by Function	% Avg. Salary
Marketing:	(11%) $66,200
Operations:	(15%) $80,000
Consulting:	(2%)
Management:	(9%) $80,000
Finance:	(43%) $64,054
HR:	(2%) $67,000
MIS:	(5%) $52,500
Other:	(13%) $77,800

Top 5 Employers Hiring Grads (number of hires in last class)
KPMG (9), PricewaterhouseCoopers (8), Ernst & Young (6), Deloitte (5), Pace University (2)

PENN STATE UNIVERSITY— GREAT VALLEY CAMPUS
SCHOOL OF GRADUATE PROFESSIONAL STUDIES

ADMISSIONS CONTACT: SUSAN HALDEMAN, GRADUATE ENROLLMENT COORDINATOR
ADDRESS: 30 EAST SWEDESFORD ROAD, MALVERN, PA 19355 UNITED STATES
PHONE: 610-648-3248 • FAX: 610-725-5296
E-MAIL: GVMBA@PSU.EDU • WEBSITE: WWW.GV.PSU.EDU

GENERAL INFORMATION

Type of school: Public **Academic calendar:** Semester

STUDENTS

Enrollment of parent institution: 2,000 **Enrollment of MBA Program:** 340 **% part-time:** 97 **Average age at entry:** 31 **Average years work experience at entry:** 8

ACADEMICS

Student/faculty ratio: 18:1 **% female faculty:** 40 **% underrepresented minority faculty:** 5 **% part-time faculty:** 20

FINANCIAL FACTS

Annual tuition (in-state/out-of-state): $16,752/$27,312 **Fees:** $600 **Cost of books:** $4,872 **Room & board (on/off-campus):** $0/$20,000 **% of students receiving aid:** 60 **% of first-year students receiving aid:** 50 **% of students receiving grants:** 1 **Average award package:** $4,500 **Average grant:** $15,000 **Average loan:** $4,500 **Average student loan debt:** $8,000

ADMISSIONS

Admissions Selectivity Rating: 82

# of applications received: 115 **% applicants accepted:** 72 **% acceptees attending:** 71 **Average GMAT:** 522 **Accepts GRE scores:** **Average GPA:** 3.2 **TOEFL required of international students:** Yes **Minimum TOEFL (paper/computer):** 550/ **Application fee:** $60 **International application fee:** $60

Deferment available: Yes **Maximum length of deferment:** one year **Transfer students accepted:** Yes **Transfer application policy:** Transfer applicants are encouraged and should submit all application materials, including official transcripts of courses already taken and course descriptions. **Non-fall admissions:** Yes **Need-blind admissions:** Yes

Grads Employed by Function ..... % Avg. Salary

Marketing:..(6%)

Operations:......................................(8%)

Consulting:......................................(5%)

Management: ....(10%)

Finance:..(10%)

HR:...(4%)

MIS: ....(7%)

Other: ....(11%)

THE PENNSYLVANIA STATE UNIVERSITY, CAPITAL COLLEGE
SCHOOL OF BUSINESS ADMINISTRATION

ADMISSIONS CONTACT: ROBERT COFFMAN, JR., DIRECTOR OF ENROLLMENT SERVICES
ADDRESS: 777 WEST HARRISBURG PIKE, UNIVERSITY PARK, PA 17057 UNITED STATES
PHONE: 717-948-6250 • FAX: 717-948-6325
E-MAIL: HBGADMIT@PSU.EDU
WEBSITE: WWW.HBG.PSU.EDU/PROGRAMS/GRADUATE/BUSINESSADMIN./PHP

GENERAL INFORMATION

Type of school: Public **Academic calendar:** Semester

STUDENTS

Enrollment of parent institution: 4,700 **Enrollment of MBA Program:** 196 **% male/female:** 98/2 **% out-of-state:** 18 **% part-time:** 91 **% international:** 2 **Average age at entry:** 29 **Average years work experience at entry:** 3

ACADEMICS

Student/faculty ratio: 7:1 **% part-time faculty:** 0

FINANCIAL FACTS

Average grant: $6,000

ADMISSIONS

Admissions Selectivity Rating: 75

Average GMAT: 558 **Accepts GRE scores:** No **Average GPA:** 3.3 **TOEFL required of international students:** Yes **Minimum TOEFL (paper/computer):** 550/80 **Application fee:** $65 **International application fee:** $65 **Regular application deadline:** 7/18 **Deferment available:** Yes **Maximum length of deferment:** 3 years **Transfer students accepted:** Yes **Transfer application policy:** 10 credits max will transfer **Non-fall admissions:** Yes **Need-blind admissions:** Yes

PURDUE UNIVERSITY CALUMET
SCHOOL OF MANAGEMENT

ADMISSIONS CONTACT: PAUL MCGRATH, COORDINATOR, GRADUATE MANAGEMENT PROGRAMS
ADDRESS: SCHOOL OF MANAGEMENT, PURDUE UNIVERSITY CALUMET, HAMMOND CITY, IN 46322-2094 UNITED STATES
PHONE: 219-989-2425 • FAX: 219-989-3158
E-MAIL: PMCGRAT@CALUMET.PURDUE.EDU
WEBSITE: WWW.CALUMET.PURDUE.EDU

GENERAL INFORMATION

Type of school: Public **Academic calendar:** Semester

STUDENTS

Enrollment of parent institution: 9,500 **Enrollment of MBA Program:** 213 **% male/female:** 100/0 **% out-of-state:** 0 **% part-time:** 96 **% underrepresented minority:** 0 **% international:** 0 **Average age at entry:** 28 **Average years work experience at entry:** 5

ACADEMICS

Student/faculty ratio: 10:1 **% female faculty:** 43 **% underrepresented minority faculty:** 24 **% part-time faculty:** 5

FINANCIAL FACTS

Annual tuition (in-state/out-of-state): $4,325/$9,322 **Cost of books:** $6,000 **Room & board (on/off-campus):** / **% of students receiving aid:** 0 **% of first-year students receiving aid:** 0 **% of students receiving grants:** 0 **Average grant:** $0 **Average loan:** $0

ADMISSIONS

Admissions Selectivity Rating: 79

# of applications received: 102 **% applicants accepted:** 93 **% acceptees attending:** 98 **Average GMAT:** 538 **Accepts GRE scores:** **Average GPA:** 3.2 **TOEFL required of international students:** Yes **Minimum TOEFL (paper/computer):** 550/ **Application fee:** $55 **International application fee:** $55 **Regular application deadline:** 8/1 **Regular application notification:** 8/1

Deferment available: Yes **Maximum length of deferment:** one year **Transfer students accepted:** Yes **Transfer application policy:** Six semester hours of B or better coursework, evaluated for equivalence by the Graduate Admissions Committee **Non-fall admissions:** Yes **Need-blind admissions:** Yes

EMPLOYMENT PROFILE

Average base starting salary: $37,000

QUEEN'S UNIVERSITY
QUEEN'S SCHOOL OF BUSINESS

ADMISSIONS CONTACT: 613-533-2302, PROGRAM MANAGER
ADDRESS: GOODES HALL, QUEEN'S UNIVERSITY, SUITE 338, KINGSTON, ON K7L 3N6 CANADA
PHONE: 613-533-2302/1-888-621-0060 • FAX: 613-533-6281
E-MAIL: MBA@QUEENSU.CA • WEBSITE: WWW.QUEENSMBA.COM

GENERAL INFORMATION

Type of school: Public **Academic calendar:** 12 months starting in January

STUDENTS

Enrollment of parent institution: 21,667 **Enrollment of MBA Program:** 67 **% male/female:** 69/31 **% international:** 42 **Average age at entry:** 28 **Average years work experience at entry:** 5

FINANCIAL FACTS

Annual tuition (in-state/out-of-state): $62,002/$70,054 **Room & board (on/off-campus):** $15,267/$15,267

ADMISSIONS

Admissions Selectivity Rating: 74

Average GMAT: 650 **Range of GMAT:** 580–770 **Accepts GRE scores:** No **TOEFL required of international students:** Yes **Minimum TOEFL (paper/computer):** 600/100 **Application fee:** $0 **International application fee:** $0

Application Deadline/Notification:

Round 1: 3/20
Round 2: 6/12
Round 3: 9/18
Round 4: 11/20

Deferment available: Yes **Maximum length of deferment:** 1 year **Transfer students accepted:** No **Non-fall admissions:** Yes **Need-blind admissions:** Yes

RIDER UNIVERSITY
COLLEGE OF BUSINESS ADMINSTRATION

ADMISSIONS CONTACT: JAMIE MITCHELL, DIRECTOR, GRADUATE ADMISSIONS
ADDRESS: PJ CIAMBELLI HALL, 2083 LAWRENCEVILLE ROAD, LAWRENCEVILLE, NJ 08648-3099
PHONE: 609-896-5036 • FAX: 609-895-5680
E-MAIL: GRADADM@RIDER.EDU
WEBSITE: HTTP://WWW.RIDER.EDU/ACADEMICS/COLLEGES-SCHOOLS/ COLLEGE-BUSINESS-ADMINISTRATION

GENERAL INFORMATION

Type of school: Private **Academic calendar:** Semester

STUDENTS

Enrollment of parent institution: 5,075 **Enrollment of MBA Program:** 136 **% male/female:** 37/63 **% out-of-state:** 5 **% part-time:** 86 **% underrepresented minority:** 53 **% international:** 47 **Average age at entry:** 29

ACADEMICS

Student/faculty ratio: 6:1 **% female faculty:** 32 **% underrepresented minority faculty:** 29 **% part-time faculty:** 23

FINANCIAL FACTS

Cost of books: $4,625

ADMISSIONS

Admissions Selectivity Rating: 82

# of applications received: 77 **% applicants accepted:** 66 **% acceptees attending:** 65 **Average GMAT:** 480 **Accepts GRE scores:** Yes **Average GPA:** 3.1 **TOEFL required of international students:** Yes **Minimum TOEFL (paper/computer):** 585/ **Application fee:** $50

International application fee: $50 **Regular application deadline:** 8/1 **Application Deadline/Notification:**

Round 1: 8/1
Round 2: 12/1
Round 3: 5/1

Deferment available: Yes **Maximum length of deferment:** 1 year **Transfer students accepted:** Yes **Transfer application policy:** Each case is evaluated individually. No more than 24 transferred credits against 52.5 required maximum. Maximum of 6 credits against 33 in the advance portion. **Non-fall admissions:** Yes **Need-blind admissions:** Yes

ROCKHURST UNIVERSITY
HELZBERG SCHOOL OF MANAGEMENT

ADMISSIONS CONTACT: ERIN STANDLEY, DIRECTOR GRADUATE BUSINESS ADMISSION
ADDRESS: MASSMAN HALL, 1100 ROCKHURST ROAD, KANSAS CITY, MO 64110 UNITED STATES
PHONE: 816-501-4632 • FAX: 816-501-4241
E-MAIL: MBA@ROCKHURST.EDU • WEBSITE: WWW.ROCKHURST.EDU/HELZBERG

GENERAL INFORMATION

Type of school: Private **Academic calendar:** Standard

STUDENTS

Enrollment of MBA Program: 235 **% male/female:** 85/15 **% out-of-state:** 19 **% part-time:** 61 **% underrepresented minority:** 6 **% international:** 0 **Average age at entry:** 29

ACADEMICS

% female faculty: 39 **% underrepresented minority faculty:** 10 **% part-time faculty:** 62

FINANCIAL FACTS

Annual tuition (in-state/out-of-state): $10,640/$10,640 **Fees:** $750 **Cost of books:** $2,000

ADMISSIONS

Admissions Selectivity Rating: 83

# of applications received: 200 **% applicants accepted:** 67 **% acceptees attending:** 74 **Average GMAT:** 516 **Range of GMAT:** 460–570 **Accepts GRE scores:** Yes **Average GPA:** 3.3 **TOEFL required of international students:** Yes **Minimum TOEFL (paper/computer):** 550/79 **Application fee:** $0 **International application fee:** $0

Deferment available: Yes **Maximum length of deferment:** two terms **Transfer students accepted:** Yes **Transfer application policy:** All credits transfer seamlessly for transfer students from universities that participate in the Jesuit Transfer Agreement (JTA). Transfer students from non-JTA universities may transfer up to 9 credit hours. **Non-fall admissions:** Yes **Need-blind admissions:** Yes

Saint Mary's University, Canada

Sobey School of Business

Admissions Contact: Leah Ray, Managing Director, MBA Program
Address: 923 Robie Street, Halifax, NS B3H 3C3 Canada
Phone: 902-420-5002 • Fax: 902-420-5119
E-mail: mba@smu.ca • Website: www.sobey.smu.ca

GENERAL INFORMATION

Type of school: Private **Academic calendar:** Semester

ACADEMICS

Student/faculty ratio: 25:1

FINANCIAL FACTS

Annual tuition (in-state/out-of-state): $9,235/ **Fees:** $480 **Cost of books:** $1,000 **Room & board (on/off-campus):** / **% of students receiving grants:** 50 **Average award package: Average grant:** $2,500

ADMISSIONS

Admissions Selectivity Rating: 60*

Saint Mary's University of Minnesota

Graduate School of Business and Technology

Admissions Contact: James Callinan, Director of Admissions
Address: 2500 Park Avenue, Minneapolis, MN 55404-4403 United States
Phone: 612-728-5100 • Fax: 612-728-5121
E-mail: tc-admission@smumn.edu
Website: www.smumn.edu/graduate-home/areas-of-study/ graduate-school-of-business-technology

GENERAL INFORMATION

Type of school: Private **Academic calendar:** Schools of Graduate & Professional

STUDENTS

Enrollment of parent institution: 5,688 **Enrollment of MBA Program:** 233 **% male/female:** 57/43 **% out-of-state:** 2 **% part-time:** 31 **% underrepresented minority:** 23 **% international:** 24 **Average age at entry:** 30

FINANCIAL FACTS

Annual tuition (in-state/out-of-state): $8,280/$8,280 **Fees:** $0

ADMISSIONS

Admissions Selectivity Rating: 63

# of applications received: 41 **% applicants accepted:** 100 **% acceptees attending:** 88 **TOEFL required of international students:** Yes **Minimum TOEFL (paper/computer):** 550/ **Application fee:** $25

Deferment available: Yes **Maximum length of deferment:** 1 year

Transfer students accepted: Yes **Transfer application policy:** May transfer up to six graduate credits from another regionally accredited institution. **Non-fall admissions:** Yes **Need-blind admissions:** Yes

Salisbury University

Franklin P. Perdue School of Business

MBA Director
Address: 1101 Camden Avenue, Salisbury, MD 21801-6837 United States
Phone: 410-548-5564 • Fax: 410-548-2908
E-mail: mba@salisbury.edu • Website: mba.salisbury.edu

GENERAL INFORMATION

Type of school: Public **Academic calendar:** Semester

STUDENTS

Enrollment of parent institution: 7,000 **Enrollment of MBA Program:** 73 **% male/female:** 58/42 **% part-time:** 56 **% underrepresented minority:** 1 **% international:** 12 **Average age at entry:** 26 **Average years work experience at entry:** 2

ACADEMICS

Student/faculty ratio: 25:1 **% female faculty:** 4 **% underrepresented minority faculty:** 0 **% part-time faculty:** 0

FINANCIAL FACTS

Annual tuition (in-state/out-of-state): $9,180/$19,244 **Fees:** $1,870 **Cost of books:** $1,100 **Room & board (on/off-campus):** /$8,500 **Average grant:** $9,680

ADMISSIONS

Admissions Selectivity Rating: 84

# of applications received: 50 **% applicants accepted:** 70 **% acceptees attending:** 100 **Average GMAT:** 550 **Range of GMAT:** 490–750 **Accepts GRE scores: Average GPA:** 3.4 **TOEFL required of international students:** Yes **Minimum TOEFL (paper/computer):** 550/79 **Application fee:** $45 **International application fee:** $45 **Early notification date:** 4/1 **Regular application deadline:** 3/1 **Regular application notification:** 4/1

Deferment available: No **Transfer students accepted:** No **Non-fall admissions:** No **Need-blind admissions:** Yes

EMPLOYMENT PROFILE

Percent employed at graduation: 61

SAMFORD UNIVERSITY
BROCK SCHOOL OF BUSINESS

ADMISSIONS CONTACT: ELIZABETH GAMBRELL, ASSISTANT DIRECTOR OF ACADEMIC PROGRAMS
ADDRESS: SAMFORD UNIVERSITY BROCK SCHOOL OF BUSINESS, 800 LAKESHORE DRIVE, BIRMINGHAM, AL 35229 UNITED STATES
PHONE: 205-726-2040
E-MAIL: GRADBUSI@SAMFORD.EDU • WEBSITE: WWW.SAMFORD.EDU/BUSINESS

GENERAL INFORMATION

Type of school: Private **Academic calendar:** Semester

STUDENTS

Enrollment of parent institution: 4,933 **Enrollment of MBA Program:** 77 % **part-time:** 100 **Average age at entry:** 27

ACADEMICS

Student/faculty ratio: 22:1 **% female faculty:** 26 **% underrepresented minority faculty:** 4 **% part-time faculty:** 11

FINANCIAL FACTS

Average award package: $28,500 **Average grant:** $3,000 **Average loan:** $28,500

ADMISSIONS

Admissions Selectivity Rating: 79

# of applications received: 44 **% applicants accepted:** 93 **% acceptees attending:** 78 **Average GMAT:** 538 **Accepts GRE scores:** Yes **Average Verbal GRE:** 149 **Average Quantitative GRE:** 144 **Average GPA:** 3.2 **TOEFL required of international students:** Yes **Application fee:** $35 **International application fee:** $35

Deferment available: Yes **Maximum length of deferment:** one year **Transfer students accepted:** Yes **Transfer application policy:** Applicants must apply as normal for the program by the appropriate deadline. A limited number of credits may transfer. **Non-fall admissions:** Yes **Need-blind admissions:** Yes

SAM HOUSTON STATE UNIVERSITY
COLLEGE OF BUSINESS ADMINISTRATION

ADMISSIONS CONTACT: DR. LEROY ASHORN, ASSOCIATE DEAN
ADDRESS: PO BOX 2056, HUNTSVILLE, TX 77341-2056 UNITED STATES
PHONE: 936-294-1239 • FAX: 936-294-3612
E-MAIL: BUSGRAD@SHSU.EDU • WEBSITE: COBA.SHSU.EDU/

GENERAL INFORMATION

Type of school: Public **Academic calendar:** September 1 to August 31

STUDENTS

Enrollment of parent institution: 17,580 **Enrollment of MBA Program:** 360 **% male/female:** 65/35 **% out-of-state:** 10 **% part-time:** 68 **% underrepresented minority:** 10 **% international:** 15 **Average years work experience at entry:** 0

ACADEMICS

Student/faculty ratio: 23:1 **% female faculty:** 33 **% underrepresented minority faculty:** 10

FINANCIAL FACTS

Annual tuition (in-state/out-of-state): $8,994/$18,471 **Cost of books:** $1,350

ADMISSIONS

Admissions Selectivity Rating: 81

# of applications received: 219 **% applicants accepted:** 73 **% acceptees attending:** 57 **Average GMAT:** 504 **Range of GMAT:** 460–540 **Accepts GRE scores:** Yes **Average GPA:** 3.4 **TOEFL required of international students:** Yes **Minimum TOEFL (paper/computer):** 550/79 **Application fee:** $40 **International application fee:** $75 **Regular application deadline:** 8/1 **Deferment available:** Yes **Maximum length of deferment:** One year **Transfer students accepted:** Yes **Transfer application policy:** Accept up to six semester hours from accredited universities **Non-fall admissions:** Yes **Need-blind admissions:** Yes

SOUTHEASTERN LOUISIANA UNIVERSITY
COLLEGE OF BUSINESS

ADMISSIONS CONTACT: MIKE RIVAULT, DIRECTOR OF ADMISSIONS
ADDRESS: SLU 10752, HAMMOND, LA 70402 UNITED STATES
PHONE: 800-222-7358 • FAX: 985-549-5882
E-MAIL: ADMISSIONS@SELU.EDU
WEBSITE: WWW.SELU.EDU/ACAD_RESEARCH/COLLEGES/BUS/INDEX.HTML

GENERAL INFORMATION

Type of school: Public **Academic calendar:** Semester

STUDENTS

Enrollment of parent institution: 14,594 **Enrollment of MBA Program:** 24 **% male/female:** 55/46 **% out-of-state:** 0 **% part-time:** 8 **% underrepresented minority:** 36 **% international:** 14 **Average age at entry:** 25

ACADEMICS

Student/faculty ratio: 3:1 **% female faculty:** 42 **% underrepresented minority faculty:** 16 **% part-time faculty:** 0

FINANCIAL FACTS

Annual tuition (in-state/out-of-state): $6,107/$18,584 **Fees:** $1,737 **Cost of books:** $3,220 **Room & board (on/off-campus):** $7,370/$7,370 **Average student loan debt:** $20,626

ADMISSIONS

Admissions Selectivity Rating: 76

# of applications received: 36 **% applicants accepted:** 100 **% acceptees attending:** 67 **Average GMAT:** 484 **Range of GMAT:** 440–500 **Accepts GRE scores:** No **Average GPA:** 3.3 **TOEFL required of international students:** Yes **Minimum TOEFL (paper/computer):** 525/75 **Application fee:** $20 **International application fee:** $30 **Regular application deadline:** 7/15 **Deferment available:** Yes **Maximum length of deferment:** 1 year **Transfer students accepted:** Yes **Transfer application policy:** Must earn 12 hours of graduate credit at Southeastern before applying for any transfer credit from another university. That university must be an accredited institution that regularly grants the master's degree or an equivalent foreign institution. The student must be eligible for readmission to the institution from which the credits are to be transferred and must have earned a minumun grade of "B" in each course to be transferred. No more than one-third of the hours required for graduation may be transferred. **Non-fall admissions:** Yes **Need-blind admissions:** Yes

SOUTHERN UTAH UNIVERSITY
SCHOOL OF BUSINESS

ADMISSIONS CONTACT: CHRISTINE PROCTOR, ASSOCIATE DIRECTOR OF ADMISSIONS
ADDRESS: SOUTHERN UTAH UNIVERSITY, 351 W. UNIVERSITY BLVD., CEDAR CITY, UT 84720 UNITED STATES
PHONE: 435-586-7742 • FAX: 435-865-8223
E-MAIL: PROCTOR@SUU.EDU • WEBSITE: SUU.EDU/BUSINESS/

GENERAL INFORMATION
Type of school: Public **Academic calendar:** Semester

STUDENTS
Enrollment of MBA Program: 63 **% male/female:** 86/14 **% part-time:** 33 **% underrepresented minority:** 14 **Average age at entry:** 27

ACADEMICS
Student/faculty ratio: 5:1 **% female faculty:** 8 **% underrepresented minority faculty:** 8 **% part-time faculty:** 8

FINANCIAL FACTS
Annual tuition (in-state/out-of-state): $9,048/$29,986 **Fees:** $540 **Cost of books:** $1,600 **Room & board (on/off-campus):** $6,189/$7,500 **% of students receiving aid:** 32 **% of first-year students receiving aid:** 36 **% of students receiving grants:** 17 **Average grant:** $7,750 **Average loan:** $11,099

ADMISSIONS
Admissions Selectivity Rating: 81

# of applications received: 42 **% applicants accepted:** 74 **% acceptees attending:** 71 **Average GMAT:** 420 **Range of GMAT:** 300–580 **Accepts GRE scores:** Yes **Average GPA:** 3.7 **TOEFL required of international students:** Yes **Minimum TOEFL (paper/computer):** 550/79 **Application fee:** $50 **International application fee:** $50 **Regular application deadline:** 3/1 **Deferment available:** Yes **Maximum length of deferment:** Two years **Transfer students accepted:** Yes **Non-fall admissions:** Yes **Need-blind admissions:** Yes

EMPLOYMENT PROFILE
Percent employed 3 months after graduation: 92 **Average base starting salary:** $42,293
Primary Source of Full-time Job Acceptances
Unknown: 50 (100%)

Grads Employed by Function ..... % Avg. Salary
Marketing:.....................................(2%) $47,500
Operations:....................................(2%) $47,500
Management: ....(24%) $47,272
Finance:..(39%) $44,111
HR:...(4%) $42,500
MIS: ....(2%) $37,500
Other: ....(26%) $34,500

Top 5 Employers Hiring Grads (number of hires in last class)
Southern Utah University (6), Boeing (3), First Equity Holdings (2), Hafen, Buckner, Everett & Graff (2), ()

ST. CLOUD STATE UNIVERSITY
HERBERGER COLLEGE OF BUSINESS

ADMISSIONS CONTACT: GRADUATE STUDIES OFFICE--ANNETTE DAY, GRADUATE ADMISSIONS MANAGER
ADDRESS: 720 4TH AVE. SOUTH, AS-121, ST. CLOUD, MN 56301-4498 UNITED STATES
PHONE: 320-308-2112 • FAX: 320-308-3986
E-MAIL: GRADUATESTUDIES@STCLOUDSTATE.EDU
WEBSITE: WWW.STCLOUDSTATE.EDU/MBA/

GENERAL INFORMATION
Type of school: Public **Academic calendar:** Semester

STUDENTS
Enrollment of parent institution: 16,334 **Enrollment of MBA Program:** 166 **% male/female:** 71/29 **% out-of-state:** 18 **% part-time:** 75 **% underrepresented minority:** 10 **% international:** 48 **Average age at entry:** 28 **Average years work experience at entry:** 5

ACADEMICS
Student/faculty ratio: 25:1 **% female faculty:** 27 **% underrepresented minority faculty:** 20 **% part-time faculty:** 8

FINANCIAL FACTS
Annual tuition (in-state/out-of-state): $14,292/$14,292 **Fees:** $165 **Cost of books:** $1,800 **Average grant:** $0 **Average loan:** $0

ADMISSIONS
Admissions Selectivity Rating: 76

% acceptees attending: 48 **Average GMAT:** 525 **Range of GMAT:** 470–700 **Accepts GRE scores:** **Average GPA:** 3.3 **TOEFL required of international students:** Yes **Minimum TOEFL (paper/computer):** 550/ **Application fee:** $35 **International application fee:** $35 **Early notification date:** 6/15 **Deferment available:** Yes **Maximum length of deferment:** 2 yr **Transfer students accepted:** No **Non-fall admissions:** Yes **Need-blind admissions:** No

EMPLOYMENT PROFILE
Average base starting salary: $38,000

Stephen F. Austin State University

Nelson Rusche College of Business

ADMISSIONS CONTACT: MICHAEL D. STROUP, MBA DIRECTOR
ADDRESS: PO BOX 13004, SFA STATION, STEPHEN F. AUSTIN STATE
UNIVERSITY, NACOGDOCHES, TX 75962-3004 UNITED STATES
PHONE: 936-468-3101 • FAX: 936-468-1560
E-MAIL: MBA@SFASU.EDU • WEBSITE: WWW.COB.SFASU.EDU

GENERAL INFORMATION

Type of school: Public

STUDENTS

Enrollment of parent institution: 10,000 **Enrollment of MBA Program:** 45 **% male/female:** 60/40 **% out-of-state:** 5 **% part-time:** 50 **% underrepresented minority:** 25 **% international:** 15 **Average age at entry:** 25 **Average years work experience at entry:** 3

ACADEMICS

Student/faculty ratio: 10:1 **% female faculty:** 30 **% underrepresented minority faculty:** 10 **% part-time faculty:** 0

FINANCIAL FACTS

Annual tuition (in-state/out-of-state): $1,134/$7,236 **Fees:** $126 **Cost of books:** $1,000 **Room & board (on/off-campus):** $5,000/$6,500 **% of students receiving aid:** 15 **% of first-year students receiving aid:** 5 **% of students receiving grants:** 0 **Average award package:** $3,500 **Average grant:** $3,500

ADMISSIONS

Admissions Selectivity Rating: 74

# of applications received: 60 **Average GMAT:** 510 **Range of GMAT:** 290–660 **Accepts GRE scores: Average GPA:** 3.0 **TOEFL required of international students:** Yes **Minimum TOEFL (paper/computer):** 550/ **Application fee:** $25 **International application fee:** $50 **Early notification date:** 8/1 **Regular application deadline:** 8/1 **Regular application notification:** 8/15

Deferment available: Yes **Maximum length of deferment:** one year **Transfer students accepted:** Yes **Transfer application policy:** Applicant may transfer in 6 hours graduate credit from an AACSB - International Accredited school. **Non-fall admissions:** Yes **Need-blind admissions:** Yes

EMPLOYMENT PROFILE

Average base starting salary: $52,000

Grads Employed by Function	% Avg. Salary
Marketing:................................(25%)	$45,000
Consulting:................................(20%)	$45,000
Management:...............................(15%)	$65,000

St. John Fisher College

School of Business

ADMISSIONS CONTACT: MS. REBECCA NORMAN, ASSOCIATE DIRECTOR OF
TRANSFER AND GRADUATE ADMISSIONS
ADDRESS: 3690 EAST AVENUE, SKALNY WELCOME CENTER, ROCHESTER, NY
14618 UNITED STATES
PHONE: 585.385.8064 • FAX: 585.385.8344
E-MAIL: GRAD@SJFC.EDU
WEBSITE: WWW.SJFC.EDU/ACADEMICS/BUSINESS/ABOUT/INDEX.DOT

GENERAL INFORMATION

Type of school: Private **Academic calendar:** Semester

STUDENTS

Enrollment of parent institution: 3,838 **Enrollment of MBA Program:** 156 **% male/female:** 56/44 **% out-of-state:** 1 **% part-time:** 58 **% underrepresented minority:** 14 **% international:** 2 **Average age at entry:** 25

ACADEMICS

Student/faculty ratio: 15:1 **% female faculty:** 24 **% underrepresented minority faculty:** 0 **% part-time faculty:** 24

FINANCIAL FACTS

Cost of books: $1,100 **% of students receiving aid:** 60 **% of first-year students receiving aid:** 93 **% of students receiving grants:** 30

ADMISSIONS

Admissions Selectivity Rating: 69

# of applications received: 108 **% applicants accepted:** 80 **% acceptees attending:** 64 **Average GMAT: Accepts GRE scores:** No **Average GPA:** 3.4 **TOEFL required of international students:** Yes **Minimum TOEFL (paper/computer):** 575/80 **Application fee:** $30 **International application fee:** $30

Deferment available: Yes **Maximum length of deferment:** One Semester **Transfer students accepted:** Yes **Transfer application policy:** Students can request transfer credit for graduate course work taken at accredited institutions. These credits must have been taken in an appropriate graduate program related to MBA graduate program of study. Only courses with a grade of "B" or better will be considered and the course must have been taken within 7 years prior to beginning graduate study at Fisher. A maximum of 9 credits may be permitted as transfer credit. **Non-fall admissions:** Yes **Need-blind admissions:** Yes

Tecnológico de Monterrey
Instituto de Emprendimiento Eugenio Garza Lagéra

Admissions Contact: Lic. Elsa Fernéndez, Director Admissions and Financial Aids
Address: Av. Eugenio Garza Sada 2501 Sur, Col. Tecnológico, Monterrey, NL 64849 Mexico
Phone: +52 (81) 8158 2269
E-mail: admisiones.mty@itesm.mx • Website: www.itesm.mx

GENERAL INFORMATION

Type of school: Private **Academic calendar:** quarter

STUDENTS

Enrollment of parent institution: 19,358 **Enrollment of MBA Program:** 597 **% male/female:** 79/21 **% part-time:** 90 **% underrepresented minority:** 0 **% international:** 66 **Average age at entry:** 28 **Average years work experience at entry:** 5

ACADEMICS

Student/faculty ratio: 14:1 **% female faculty:** 25 **% part-time faculty:** 39

FINANCIAL FACTS

Annual tuition (in-state/out-of-state): $17,500/ **Cost of books:** $780 **Room & board (on/off-campus):** $7,800/$6,400 **% of students receiving aid:** 26 **% of first-year students receiving aid:** 24 **% of students receiving grants:** 23 **Average grant:** $11,375 **Average loan:** $8,750

ADMISSIONS

Admissions Selectivity Rating: 84

# of applications received: 199 **% applicants accepted:** 73 **% acceptees attending:** 74 **Average GMAT:** 615 **Accepts GRE scores:** **Average GPA:** 3.5 **TOEFL required of international students:** **Application fee:** $115 **International application fee:** $115 **Regular application deadline:** 5/1 **Regular application notification:** 6/1

Deferment available: Yes **Maximum length of deferment:** 1 year **Transfer students accepted:** Yes **Transfer application policy:** The applicant has to fulfill all of the admission requisites **Non-fall admissions:** Yes **Need-blind admissions:** No

Grads Employed by Function ..... % Avg. Salary

Marketing:.......................................(12%)
Operations:.....................................(25%)
Finance:..(38%)
Other: ....(19%)

Tennessee State University

Admissions Contact: Sharon Thach, Coordinator, MBA
Address: 330 10th Avenue North, Suite K, Nashville, TN 37203 United States
Phone: 615-963-7133 • Fax: 615-963-7139
E-mail: mba@tnstate.edu • Website: www.cob.tnstate.edu

GENERAL INFORMATION

Type of school: Public **Academic calendar:** Semesters (3)

STUDENTS

Enrollment of MBA Program: 102 **% part-time:** 80 **% international:** 20

ACADEMICS

Student/faculty ratio: 12:1 **% female faculty:** 15 **% part-time faculty:** 0

FINANCIAL FACTS

Annual tuition (in-state/out-of-state): $15,000/$360,000 **Cost of books:** $2,000 **Room & board (on/off-campus):** / **% of students receiving aid:** 10 **% of first-year students receiving aid:** **% of students receiving grants:** 5

ADMISSIONS

Admissions Selectivity Rating: 74

Average GMAT: 510 **Accepts GRE scores:** Yes **Average GPA:** 3.2 **TOEFL required of international students:** Yes **Minimum TOEFL (paper/computer):** 500/ **Application fee:** $25

Application Deadline/Notification:

Round 1:.......................................7/1
Round 2:.......................................11/1
Round 3: 4/1

Deferment available: Yes **Maximum length of deferment:** 1 year **Transfer students accepted:** Yes **Transfer application policy:** Non AACSB on appeal 12 credits from AACSB college **Non-fall admissions:** No **Need-blind admissions:** Yes

Tennessee Tech University
College of Business

Address: Box 5023 TTU, 1105 N. Peachtree JH 112, Cookeville, TN 38505 United States
Phone: 931-372-3600 • Fax: 931-372-6544
E-mail: mbastudies@tntech.edu • Website: www.tntech.edu/mba/

GENERAL INFORMATION

Type of school: Public **Academic calendar:** Semester

STUDENTS

Enrollment of parent institution: 11,118 **Enrollment of MBA Program:** 45 **% male/female:** 55/45 **% out-of-state:** 0 **% part-time:** 40 **% underrepresented minority:** 12 **% international:** 7 **Average age at entry:** 27

ACADEMICS

Student/faculty ratio: 25:1 **% female faculty:** 25 **% underrepresented minority faculty:** 20 **% part-time faculty:** 0

FINANCIAL FACTS

Cost of books: $2,200 Room & board (on/off-campus): $8,400/$10,800 % of students receiving aid: 50 % of first-year students receiving aid: 45 % of students receiving grants: 25

ADMISSIONS

Admissions Selectivity Rating: 81

# of applications received: 91 % applicants accepted: 76 % acceptees attending: 65 Average GMAT: 536 Range of GMAT: 450–700 Accepts GRE scores: Yes Average Verbal GRE: 155 Range of Verbal GRE scores: 144–162 Average Quantitative GRE: 151 Range of Quantitative GRE scores: 147–157 Average GPA: 3.3 TOEFL required of international students: Yes Minimum TOEFL (paper/computer): 550/79 Application fee: $35 International application fee: $40

Deferment available: Yes Maximum length of deferment: 1 year Transfer students accepted: Yes Transfer application policy: As many as 9 semester hours may be transferred from other AACSB accredited schools. Each request for transfer credits will be evaluated by the MBA director on a case-by-case basis. Non-fall admissions: Yes Need-blind admissions: Yes

Top 5 Employers Hiring Grads (number of hires in last class)
Nissan, FedEx, Tennessee Valley Authority, HCA Corporation, Asurion

Texas A&M University— Commerce
College of Business and Technology

ADMISSIONS CONTACT: VICKY TURNER, GRADUATE ADMISSIONS
ADDRESS: P O BOX 3011, COMMERCE, TX 75429 UNITED STATES
PHONE: 903-886-5167 • FAX: 903-886-5165
E-MAIL: GRADUATE_SCHOOL@TAMU-COMMERCE.EDU • WEBSITE: WWW.
TAMU-COMMERCE.EDU/GRADUATEPROGRAMS

GENERAL INFORMATION

Type of school: Public Academic calendar: Semester

STUDENTS

Enrollment of parent institution: 8,875 Enrollment of MBA Program: 489 % male/female: 56/44 % part-time: 61 % underrepresented minority: 53 % international: 23 Average age at entry: 22 Average years work experience at entry: 0

ACADEMICS

Student/faculty ratio: 27:1 % female faculty: 10 % underrepresented minority faculty: 10 % part-time faculty: 20

FINANCIAL FACTS

Annual tuition (in-state/out-of-state): $7,000/$18,000 Cost of books: $1,000 Room & board (on/off-campus): $2,950/$2,200

ADMISSIONS

Admissions Selectivity Rating: 82

# of applications received: 1,215 % applicants accepted: 60 % acceptees attending: 65 Average GMAT: 460 Range of GMAT: 380–620 Accepts GRE scores: Average GPA: 3.0 TOEFL required

of international students: Yes Minimum TOEFL (paper/computer): 500/61 Application fee: $35 International application fee: $50 Regular application deadline: 6/1 Deferment available: Yes Maximum length of deferment: 2 Semesters Transfer students accepted: Yes Transfer application policy: Students can transfer up to 9 SH for the 30-33 HR. Non-fall admissions: Yes Need-blind admissions: No

Union Graduate College
School of Management

ADMISSIONS CONTACT: ERIN WHEELER, DIRECTOR OF STUDENT RECRUITMENT
ADDRESS: 80 NOTT TERRACE, SCHENECTADY, NY 12308 UNITED STATES
PHONE: 518-631-9850 • FAX: 518-631-9901
E-MAIL: INFO@UNIONGRADUATECOLLEGE.EDU
WEBSITE: WWW.UNIONGRADUATECOLLEGE.EDU

GENERAL INFORMATION

Type of school: Private Academic calendar: July-June

ACADEMICS

Student/faculty ratio: 15:1 % female faculty: 22 % underrepresented minority faculty: 11 % part-time faculty: 75

FINANCIAL FACTS

ADMISSIONS

Admissions Selectivity Rating: 60*

Accepts GRE scores: Yes TOEFL required of international students: Yes Minimum TOEFL (paper/computer): 550/80 Application fee: $75 International application fee: $75

Deferment available: Yes Maximum length of deferment: 1 year Transfer students accepted: Yes Transfer application policy: Will accepted up to 8 transfer courses. Non-fall admissions: Yes Need-blind admissions: Yes

EMPLOYMENT PROFILE

Percent employed at graduation: 70 Percent employed 3 months after graduation: 86

Grads Employed by Function ..... % Avg. Salary

Grads Employed by Function	% Avg. Salary
Marketing:	(13%)
Operations:	(13%)
Consulting:	(2%)
Management:	(11%)
Finance:	(29%)
HR:	(8%)
MIS:	(8%)
Other:	(16%)

Top 5 Employers Hiring Grads (number of hires in last class)

General Electric, Albany Medical Center

UNIVERSITE LAVAL
FACULTÉ DES SCIENCES DE L'ADMINISTRATION

ADDRESS: PAVILLON PALASIS PRINCE, 2325 RUE DE LA TERRASSE, QUÉBEC, QC G1V 0A6 CANADA
PHONE: 418-656-3080 • FAX: 418-656-5216
E-MAIL: REG@REG.ULAVAL.CA • WEBSITE: WWW.FSA.ULAVAL.CA

GENERAL INFORMATION

Type of school: Public **Academic calendar:** Semester

STUDENTS

Enrollment of parent institution: 40,690 **Enrollment of MBA Program:** 110 **% male/female:** 58/42 **% part-time:** 54 **% international:** 25 **Average age at entry:** 28 **Average years work experience at entry:** 4

ACADEMICS

Student/faculty ratio: 25:1 **% female faculty:** 36 **% part-time faculty:** 0

FINANCIAL FACTS

Annual tuition (in-state/out-of-state): $2,233/$12,157 **Room & board (on/off-campus):** $3,500/$9,200

ADMISSIONS

Admissions Selectivity Rating: 73

# of applications received: 1,305 **% applicants accepted:** 52 **% acceptees attending:** 45 **Average GMAT:** **Accepts GRE** scores: **Average GPA:** 3.2 **TOEFL required of international students:** Yes **Minimum TOEFL (paper/computer):** 550/ **Application fee:** $64 **International application fee:** $64 **Regular application deadline:** 3/1 **Deferment available:** Yes **Maximum length of deferment:** 1 year **Transfer students accepted:** No **Non-fall admissions:** Yes **Need-blind admissions:** No

EMPLOYMENT PROFILE

Percent employed at graduation: 46 **Percent employed 3 months after graduation:** 66

Top 5 Employers Hiring Grads (number of hires in last class)

Desjardins, Université Laval, Quebec government, Genivar, Arcelot Mittal

UNIVERSITY COLLEGE DUBLIN
MICHAEL SMURFIT GRADUATE SCHOOL OF BUSINESS

ADMISSIONS CONTACT: ELAINE MCAREE, ADMISSIONS MANAGER
ADDRESS: CARYSFORT AVENUE, BLACKROCK, DUBLIN, IRELAND
PHONE: 00353 1 7168862 • FAX: 00353 1 7168981
E-MAIL: MBA@UCD.IE • WEBSITE: WWW.SMURFITSCHOOL.IE

GENERAL INFORMATION

Type of school: Public **Academic calendar:** Sept-Aug

STUDENTS

Enrollment of MBA Program: 126 **% male/female:** 75/25 **% part-time:** 63 **% international:** 40

ACADEMICS

Student/faculty ratio: 2:1 **% female faculty:** 30

FINANCIAL FACTS

Annual tuition (in-state/out-of-state): /$29,500 **Fees:** $29,500 **Cost of books:** $1,000 **Room & board (on/off-campus):** $5,000/$5,500 **% of students receiving grants:** **Average award package:** $14,750

ADMISSIONS

Admissions Selectivity Rating: 85

# of applications received: 363 **% applicants accepted:** 48 **% acceptees attending:** 73 **Average GMAT:** 630 **Range of GMAT:** – **TOEFL required of international students:** Yes **Minimum TOEFL (paper/computer):** 600/100 International **Early notification date:** 1/15 **Regular application deadline:** 7/10 **Regular application notification:** 7/20

Application Deadline/Notification:

Round 1:	3/27
Round 2:	5/15
Round 3:	7/10

Deferment available: Yes **Maximum length of deferment:** 1 year **Transfer students accepted:** Yes **Transfer application policy:** Creditis may be awarded on the basis of ECTS (European Credit Transfer System) equivalency from accredited business schools only. **Non-fall admissions:** No **Need-blind admissions:** Yes

UNIVERSITY OF ALABAMA IN HUNTSVILLE
COLLEGE OF BUSINESS ADMINISTRATION

ADMISSIONS CONTACT: DR. DAVID BERKOWITZ, ASSOCIATE DEAN FOR GRADUATE PROGRAMS
ADDRESS: BAB 368, HUNTSVILLE, AL 35899 UNITED STATES
PHONE: 256-824-6681 • FAX: 256-824-7571
E-MAIL: GRADBIZ@UAH.EDU • WEBSITE: WWW.UAH.EDU

GENERAL INFORMATION

Type of school: Public **Academic calendar:** Semester

STUDENTS

Enrollment of MBA Program: 59 **% male/female:** 61/39 **% part-time:** 61 **% international:** 15 **Average age at entry:** 29 **Average years work experience at entry:** 5

ACADEMICS

Student/faculty ratio: 9:1 **% female faculty:** 22 **% underrepresented minority faculty:** 47 **% part-time faculty:** 39

FINANCIAL FACTS

Annual tuition (in-state/out-of-state): $10,671/$25,518 **Fees:** $17 **Cost of books:** $1,700 **Room & board (on/off-campus):** $9,410/ **% of students receiving aid:** 12 **% of first-year students receiving aid:** 1 **Average grant:** $0 **Average loan:** $0

ADMISSIONS

Admissions Selectivity Rating: 81

# of applications received: 70 % **applicants accepted:** 87 % **acceptees attending:** 97 **Average GMAT:** 556 **Range of GMAT:** 480–570 **Accepts GRE scores:** Yes **Average GPA:** 3.2 **TOEFL required of international students:** Yes **Minimum TOEFL (paper/computer):** /80 **Application fee:** $40 **International application fee:** $50 **Application Deadline/Notification:**

Round 1:.....................................7/18
Round 2:....................................11/30
Round 3: 4/30

Deferment available: No **Transfer students accepted:** Yes **Transfer application policy:** transfer credit evaluated by program advisor **Non-fall admissions:** Yes **Need-blind admissions:** Yes

Grads Employed by Function ..... % Avg. Salary

Marketing:.......................................(%) $60,000

Top 5 Employers Hiring Grads (number of hires in last class)

RedStone Arsenal, Boeing, ADTRAN, NASA, SAIC

UNIVERSITY OF ALASKA ANCHORAGE
COLLEGE OF BUSINESS AND PUBLIC POLICY

ADMISSIONS CONTACT: AL KASTAR, DIRECTOR OF ADMISSIONS
ADDRESS: PO BOX 141629, ANCHORAGE, AK 99514-1629 UNITED STATES
PHONE: 907-786-1480 • FAX: 907-786-4888
E-MAIL: AYADMIT@UAA.ALASKA.EDU
WEBSITE: HTTP://WWW.CBPP.UAA.ALASKA.EDU/BUSADMIN.ASP

GENERAL INFORMATION

Type of school: Public **Academic calendar:** Sep - May

STUDENTS

Enrollment of MBA Program: 143 % **male/female:** 43/57 % **out-of-state:** 28 % **part-time:** 66 % **underrepresented minority:** 33 % **international:** 9

ACADEMICS

Student/faculty ratio: 28:1 % **female faculty:** 6 % **underrepresented minority faculty:** 39

FINANCIAL FACTS

Annual tuition (in-state/out-of-state): $5,688/$11,628 **Fees:** $590 **Cost of books:** $900 **Room & board (on/off-campus):** $8,980

ADMISSIONS

Admissions Selectivity Rating: 70

# of applications received: 79 % **applicants accepted:** 76 % **acceptees attending:** 78 **Average GPA:** 3.1 **TOEFL required of international students:** Yes **Minimum TOEFL (paper/computer):** 550/ **Application fee:** $60

Deferment available: Yes **Maximum length of deferment:** One year **Transfer students accepted:** Yes **Transfer application policy:** Applicants must meet all UAA and MBA admissions requirements. Up to 9 semester credits not previously used to obtain any other

degree or certificate may be transferred to UAA from a regionally accredited institution and accepted toward a graduate degree or certificate. **Non-fall admissions:** Yes **Need-blind admissions:** Yes

UNIVERSITY OF ALASKA FAIRBANKS
SCHOOL OF MANAGEMENT

ADMISSIONS CONTACT: NANCY DIX, DIRECTOR
ADDRESS: P.O. BOX 757480, FAIRBANKS, AK 99775 UNITED STATES
PHONE: 907-474-7500 • FAX: 907-474-5379
E-MAIL: ADMISSIONS@UAF.EDU • WEBSITE: WWW.UAFSOM.COM/GPMBA.HTML

GENERAL INFORMATION

Type of school: Public

STUDENTS

Enrollment of parent institution: 5,025 **Enrollment of MBA Program:** 30 **Average age at entry:** 32 **Average years work experience at entry:** 10

ACADEMICS

Student/faculty ratio: 3:1 % **female faculty:** 30 % **underrepresented minority faculty:** 20

FINANCIAL FACTS

Annual tuition (in-state/out-of-state): $4,824/$9,846 **Fees:** $670 **Cost of books:** $1,076 **Room & board (on/off-campus):** $6,030/$10,413 **Average grant:** $16,928 **Average loan:** $6,083 **Average student loan debt:** $12,166

ADMISSIONS

Admissions Selectivity Rating: 79

% **acceptees attending:** 92 **Average GMAT:** 547 **Accepts GRE scores:** **Average GPA:** 3.5 **TOEFL required of international students:** Yes **Minimum TOEFL (paper/computer):** 550/ **Application fee:** $50 **International application fee:** $50 **Regular application deadline:** 8/1 **Regular application notification:** 8/1

Deferment available: Yes **Maximum length of deferment:** 1 year **Transfer students accepted:** Yes **Transfer application policy:** We take up to 3 courses. **Non-fall admissions:** Yes **Need-blind admissions:** Yes

University of Arkansas at Little Rock

College of Business

Admissions Contact: Dr. Sonya Premeaux, Associate Dean for Graduate Studies
Address: 2801 South University Avenue, Little Rock, AR 72204 United States
Phone: 501-569-3356 • Fax: 501-569-8898
Website: ualr.edu/cob

GENERAL INFORMATION

Type of school: Public **Academic calendar:** Semester

STUDENTS

Enrollment of parent institution: 9,925 **Enrollment of MBA Program:** 225 **% male/female:** 58/42 **% out-of-state:** 1 **% part-time:** 87 **% underrepresented minority:** 8 **% international:** 15 **Average age at entry:** 29 **Average years work experience at entry:** 0

ACADEMICS

% part-time faculty: 19

FINANCIAL FACTS

Annual tuition (in-state/out-of-state): $30,500/$30,500

ADMISSIONS

Admissions Selectivity Rating: 68

# of applications received: 87 **% applicants accepted:** 66 **% acceptees attending:** 74 **TOEFL required of international students:** Yes **Minimum TOEFL (paper/computer):** 550

Deferment available: Yes **Transfer students accepted:** No **Non-fall admissions:** No **Need-blind admissions:** No

EMPLOYMENT PROFILE

Average base starting salary: $40,000

University of Baltimore

Merrick School of Business

Admissions Contact: Dean Dreibelbis, Assistant Director of Admissions
Address: 1420 North Charles Street, Baltimore, MD 21201 United States
Phone: 888-664-0125 • Fax: 410-837-4774
E-mail: mba@towson.ubalt.edu • Website: www.ubtowsonmba.com

GENERAL INFORMATION

Type of school: Public **Academic calendar:** Semester

STUDENTS

Enrollment of parent institution: 5,240 **Enrollment of MBA Program:** 518 **% male/female:** 58/42 **% out-of-state:** 17 **% part-time:** 77 **% underrepresented minority:** 15 **% international:** 37 **Average age at entry:** 30 **Average years work experience at entry:** 4

ACADEMICS

Student/faculty ratio: 15:1 **% female faculty:** 30 **% underrepresented minority faculty:** 34

FINANCIAL FACTS

Cost of books: $900

ADMISSIONS

Admissions Selectivity Rating: 87

# of applications received: 434 **% applicants accepted:** 44 **% acceptees attending:** 81 **Average GMAT:** 525 **Range of GMAT:** 480–535 **Average GPA:** 3.2 **TOEFL required of international students:** Yes **Minimum TOEFL (paper/computer):** 550/ **Application fee:** $30 **International application fee:** $30

Deferment available: Yes **Maximum length of deferment:** 1 year **Transfer students accepted:** Yes **Transfer application policy:** Maximun 6 credits accepted in transfer. Must be from an AACSB accredited MBA program. **Non-fall admissions:** Yes **Need-blind admissions:** Yes

University of California, San Diego

Rady School of Management

Admissions Contact: Jay Bryant, Director, Graduate Recruiting & Admissions
Address: Otterson Hall, 2nd Floor, La Jolla, CA 92093 United States
Phone: 858-534-0864 • Fax: 858-822-5896
E-mail: RadyGradAdmissions@ucsd.edu • Website: rady.ucsd.edu

GENERAL INFORMATION

Type of school: Public **Academic calendar:** Quarters

STUDENTS

Enrollment of parent institution: 31,502 **Enrollment of MBA Program:** 126 **% male/female:** 78/22 **% out-of-state:** 78 **% part-time:** 46 **% underrepresented minority:** 7 **% international:** 69 **Average age at entry:** 31 **Average years work experience at entry:** 7

ACADEMICS

% female faculty: 18 **% underrepresented minority faculty:** 11 **% part-time faculty:** 53

FINANCIAL FACTS

Annual tuition (in-state/out-of-state): $11,220/$12,245 **Fees:** $43,938 **Cost of books:** $1,240 **Room & board (on/off-campus):** $20,502/$20,502

ADMISSIONS

Admissions Selectivity Rating: 89

# of applications received: 315 **% applicants accepted:** 44 **% acceptees attending:** 50 **Average GMAT:** 657 **Range of GMAT:** 610–710 **Accepts GRE scores:** Yes **Average GPA:** 3.3 **TOEFL required of international students:** Yes **Minimum TOEFL (paper/computer):** 60/80 **Application fee:** $200 **International application fee:** $200

Application Deadline/Notification:

Round 1: 12/1

Round 2: 2/1

Round 3: 4/1

Round 4: 6/1

Deferment available: Yes **Maximum length of deferment:** One academic year **Transfer students accepted:** No **Non-fall admissions:** No **Need-blind admissions:** Yes

EMPLOYMENT PROFILE

Percent employed at graduation: 48 **Percent employed 3 months after graduation:** 82 **Average base starting salary:** $80,265

Primary Source of Full-time Job Acceptances

School-facilitated activities: 9 (41%)

Graduate-facilitated activities: 9 (41%)

Unknown: 4 (18%)

Grads Employed by Function ..... % Avg. Salary

Marketing:......................................(39%) $94,223

Operations:....................................(11%)

Consulting:....................................(11%)

Management: ....(6%)

Finance:..(33%) $81,667

UNIVERSITY OF CENTRAL MISSOURI
HARMON COLLEGE OF BUSINESS ADMINISTRATION

ADMISSIONS CONTACT: LAURIE DELAP, ADMISSIONS EVALUATOR, GRADUATE SCHOOL
ADDRESS: WARD EDWARDS 1800, WARRENSBURG, MO 64093 UNITED STATES
PHONE: 660-543-4328 • FAX: 660-543-4778
E-MAIL: DELAP@UCMO.EDU • WEBSITE: WWW.UCMO.EDU/MBA

GENERAL INFORMATION

Type of school: Public **Academic calendar:** Semester

STUDENTS

Enrollment of parent institution: 10,980 **Enrollment of MBA Program:** 66 **% male/female:** 63/37 **% out-of-state:** 39 **% part-time:** 30 **% underrepresented minority:** 6 **% international:** 28 **Average age at entry:** 26 **Average years work experience at entry:** 2

ACADEMICS

Student/faculty ratio: 2:1 **% female faculty:** 30 **% underrepresented minority faculty:** 3 **% part-time faculty:** 0

FINANCIAL FACTS

Annual tuition (in-state/out-of-state): $5,904/$11,808 **Fees:** $604 **Cost of books:** $1,200 **Room & board (on/off-campus):** $6,000/$6,000 **% of students receiving aid:** 60 **% of students receiving grants:** 35 **Average grant:** $4,500

ADMISSIONS

Admissions Selectivity Rating: 85

# of applications received: 93 **% applicants accepted:** 55 **% acceptees attending:** 71 **Average GMAT:** 517 **Range of GMAT:** 450–560 **Accepts GRE scores:** No **Average GPA:** 3.4 **TOEFL required of international students:** Yes **Minimum TOEFL (paper/computer):** 550/79 **Application fee:** $30 **International application fee:** $50 **Deferment available:** Yes **Maximum length of deferment:** 2 semesters **Transfer students accepted:** Yes **Transfer application policy:** A maximum of 9 hours may be transferred and a "B" or higher is required for each transferred course. **Non-fall admissions:** Yes **Need-blind admissions:** Yes

UNIVERSITY OF COLORADO AT BOULDER
LEEDS SCHOOL OF BUSINESS

ADMISSIONS CONTACT: ANNE SANDOE, DIRECTOR OF PROFESSIONAL DEVELOPMENT
ADDRESS: 995 REGENT DRIVE, 419 UCB, BOULDER, CO 80309-0419 UNITED STATES
PHONE: 303-492-8397 • FAX: 303-492-1727
E-MAIL: LEEDSMBA@COLORADO.EDU • WEBSITE: WWW.COLORADO.EDU/BUSINESS

GENERAL INFORMATION

Type of school: Public **Academic calendar:** Semester

STUDENTS

Enrollment of parent institution: 30,000 **Enrollment of MBA Program:** 157 **% male/female:** 69/31 **% out-of-state:** 18 **% part-time:** 0 **% underrepresented minority:** 7 **% international:** 18 **Average age at entry:** 29 **Average years work experience at entry:** 5

ACADEMICS

Student/faculty ratio: 9:1 **% female faculty:** 20 **% part-time faculty:** 13

FINANCIAL FACTS

Annual tuition (in-state/out-of-state): $17,370/$32,328 **Fees:** $1,792 **Cost of books:** $1,800 **Room & board (on/off-campus):** $16,653/$16,653 **% of students receiving grants:** 36 **Average award package:** **Average grant:** $10,944 **Average loan:** $28,130 **Average student loan debt:** $56,255

ADMISSIONS

Admissions Selectivity Rating: 82

# of applications received: 259 **% applicants accepted:** 75 **% acceptees attending:** 44 **Average GMAT:** 616 **Range of GMAT:** 550–680 **Accepts GRE scores:** Yes **Average Verbal GRE:** 157 **Range of Verbal GRE scores:** 151–163 **Average Quantitative GRE:** 154 **Range of Quantitative GRE scores:** 151–163 **Average Writing GRE:** 4.3 **Range of Writing GRE scores:** 3.5–5.0 **Average GPA:** 3.3 **TOEFL required of international students:** Yes **Minimum TOEFL (paper/computer):** /100 **Application fee:** $70 **International application fee:** $70

Round 1: ....10/1 / 12/1

Round 2: ....12/1 / 2/1

Round 3: ....2/1 / 4/1

Round 4: ....4/1 / 6/1

Deferment available: Yes **Maximum length of deferment:** for one year **Transfer students accepted:** No **Non-fall admissions:** No **Need-blind admissions:** Yes

EMPLOYMENT PROFILE

Percent employed at graduation: 48 **Percent employed 3 months after graduation:** 36 **Average base starting salary:** $75,095

Primary Source of Full-time Job Acceptances

School-facilitated activities: 26 (59%)

Graduate-facilitated activities: 15 (34%)

Unknown: 3 (7%)

Grads Employed by Function ..... % Avg. Salary

Marketing:..................................(30%) $66,715

Operations:.................................(1136%) $64,200

Consulting:..................................(7%) $100,000

Management: ....(5%)

Finance:......................................(20%) $85,544

Other: ....(27%) $74,625

Top 5 Employers Hiring Grads (number of hires in last class)

Medtronic (3), Zayo Group (2), Tendril (2), Deloitte Consulting (1), FTI Consulting (1)

UNIVERSITY OF COLORADO COLORADO SPRINGS
GRADUATE SCHOOL OF BUSNIESS ADMINISTRATION

ADMISSIONS CONTACT: JOLENE SCHAULAND, GRADUATE PROGRAMS ADMISSIONS COORDINATOR
ADDRESS: GRADUATE SCHOOL OF BUSINESS ADMINISTRATION, 1420 AUSTIN BLUFFS PARKWAY, COLORADO SPRINGS, CO 80918 UNITED STATES
PHONE: 719-255-3122 • FAX: 719-255-3100
E-MAIL: MBACRED@UCCS.EDU • WEBSITE: WWW.UCCS.EDU/MBA

GENERAL INFORMATION

Type of school: Public **Academic calendar:** Semester

STUDENTS

Enrollment of MBA Program: 317 **% male/female:** 50/50 **% out-of-state:** 16 **% part-time:** 82 **% underrepresented minority:** 9 **% international:** 5 **Average age at entry:** 33 **Average years work experience at entry:** 4

ACADEMICS

Student/faculty ratio: 9:1 **% female faculty:** 26 **% part-time faculty:** 26

FINANCIAL FACTS

Annual tuition (in-state/out-of-state): $7,814/$13,610 **Fees:** $60 **Cost of books:** $800 **Room & board (on/off-campus):** $9,150/$10,400 **% of students receiving aid:** 35 **% of first-year**

students receiving aid: 35 **% of students receiving grants:** 11 **Average award package:** $12,385 **Average grant:** $5,545 **Average loan:** $12,799

ADMISSIONS

Admissions Selectivity Rating: 84

# of applications received: 155 **% applicants accepted:** 64 **% acceptees attending:** 67 **Average GMAT:** 532 **Range of GMAT:** 490–560 **Accepts GRE scores:** Yes **Average Verbal GRE:** 153 **Range of Verbal GRE scores:** 150–158 **Average Quantitative GRE:** 151 **Range of Quantitative GRE scores:** 148–155 **Average Writing GRE:** 3.8 **Range of Writing GRE scores:** 3.5–4.0 **Average GPA:** 3.3 **TOEFL required of international students:** Yes **Minimum TOEFL (paper/computer):** 550/80 **Application fee:** $60 **International application fee:** $100 **Regular application deadline:** 7/1 **Application Deadline/Notification:**

Round 1: 7/1

Round 2: 12/1

Round 3: 4/15

Deferment available: Yes **Maximum length of deferment:** 1 year **Transfer students accepted:** Yes **Transfer application policy:** Students may transfer up to a maximum of 6 credit hours from another AACSB-accredited school. All potential transfer courses must be approved by the program director and members of the graduate faculty. **Non-fall admissions:** Yes **Need-blind admissions:** Yes

UNIVERSITY OF COLORADO DENVER
BUSINESS SCHOOL

ADMISSIONS CONTACT: COURTNEY BURKETT, ADVISING & ADMISSIONS COORDINATOR
ADDRESS: CAMPUS BOX 165, PO BOX 173364, DENVER, CO 80217-3364 UNITED STATES
PHONE: 303-315-8100 • FAX: 303-315-8199
E-MAIL: BUSINESS@UCDENVER.EDU. • WEBSITE: WWW.BUSINESS.UCDENVER.EDU

GENERAL INFORMATION

Type of school: Public **Academic calendar:** Semester

STUDENTS

Enrollment of parent institution: 19,089 **Enrollment of MBA Program:** 790 **% male/female:** 63/37 **% out-of-state:** 48 **% part-time:** 67 **% underrepresented minority:** 7 **% international:** 7 **Average age at entry:** 28 **Average years work experience at entry:** 0

ACADEMICS

Student/faculty ratio: 35:1

FINANCIAL FACTS

Annual tuition (in-state/out-of-state): $7,844/$18,638 **Fees:** $594 **Cost of books:** $1,700 **Room & board (on/off-campus):** $9,950/$8,110 **% of students receiving aid:** 61 **% of first-year students receiving aid:** 24 **% of students receiving grants:** 22 **Average**

award package: $7,380 **Average grant:** $4,640 **Average loan:** $6,696 **Average student loan debt:** $33,815

ADMISSIONS

Admissions Selectivity Rating: 82

# of applications received: 265 **% applicants accepted:** 72 % **acceptees attending:** 77 **Average GMAT:** 547 **Range of GMAT:** 500–590 **Accepts GRE scores:** No **Average GPA:** 3.2 **TOEFL required of international students:** Yes **Minimum TOEFL (paper/computer):** 525/ **Application fee:** $50 **International application fee:** $75 **Regular application deadline:** 6/1 **Deferment available:** Yes **Maximum length of deferment:** 1 year **Transfer students accepted:** Yes **Transfer application policy:** Varies by student and program **Non-fall admissions:** Yes **Need-blind admissions:** Yes

EMPLOYMENT PROFILE

Average base starting salary: $57,903

Grads Employed by Function ..... % Avg. Salary
Marketing:.......................................(%) $61,250
Management: ....(%) $62,143
Finance:...(%) $50,625

UNIVERSITY OF DELAWARE
ALFRED LERNER COLLEGE OF BUSINESS & ECONOMICS

ADMISSIONS CONTACT: DENISE WATERS, DIRECTOR RECRUITMENT & ADMISSIONS
ADDRESS: 100, ONE SOUTH MAIN ST, NEWARK, DE 19716 UNITED STATES
PHONE: 302-831-2221 • FAX: 302-831-4835
E-MAIL: MBAPROGRAM@UDEL.EDU • WEBSITE: GRADUATE.LERNER.UDEL.EDU/

GENERAL INFORMATION

Type of school: Public **Academic calendar:** Semester

STUDENTS

Enrollment of parent institution: 22,166 **Enrollment of MBA Program:** 314 **% male/female:** 61/39 **% out-of-state:** 46 **% part-time:** 64 **% underrepresented minority:** 8 **% international:** 54 **Average age at entry:** 33 **Average years work experience at entry:** 6

ACADEMICS

Student/faculty ratio: 18:1 **% female faculty:** 35 **% underrepresented minority faculty:** 24 **% part-time faculty:** 2

FINANCIAL FACTS

Annual tuition (in-state/out-of-state): $18,000/$24,000 **Fees:** $850 **Cost of books:** $2,000 **Room & board (on/off-campus):** $9,500/$11,000 **% of students receiving aid:** 33 **% of first-year students receiving aid:** 25 **Average award package:** $17,324

ADMISSIONS

Admissions Selectivity Rating: 82

# of applications received: 154 **% applicants accepted:** 63 **Average GMAT:** 592 **Average GPA:** 3.3 **TOEFL required of international students:** Yes **Minimum TOEFL (paper/computer):** 600/100 **Application fee:** $75 **International application fee:** $75 **Regular application deadline:** 6/1 **Deferment available:** Yes **Maximum length of defer-**

ment: One academic year **Transfer students accepted:** Yes **Transfer application policy:** Up to nine semester hours of graduate credit earned at another AACSB accredited institution may be accepted toward the University of Delaware MBA degree. The courses must have completed with grades of "B" or better and within five years of the date of the requested transfer. Only those credits earned at an American Academy of Collegiate Schools of Business (AACSB) accredited institution are transferable and only after the candidate has completed at least nine credit hours as a matriculated MBA Program student at the University of Delaware. The student must submit a written request for credit evaluation and a waiver examination may be required. (Only the credits – not the grades – are transferable. **Non-fall admissions:** Yes **Need-blind admissions:** Yes

EMPLOYMENT PROFILE

Percent employed at graduation: 65 **Percent employed 3 months after graduation:** 25 **Average base starting salary:** $848,000

Grads Employed by Function ..... % Avg. Salary
Marketing:.....................................(16%) $105,200
Operations:....................................(13%) $96,400
Consulting:.....................................(3%) $117,500
Management: ....(6%) $78,000
Finance:...(12%) $80,000
MIS:...(6%) $85,300
Other: ....(13%) $73,500

Top 5 Employers Hiring Grads (number of hires in last class)
Astra Zeneca (4), J.P.Morgan (4), Bank of America (4), Barclay Card (4), CITI (6)

UNIVERSITY OF DETROIT MERCY
COLLEGE OF BUSINESS ADMINISTRATION

ADMISSIONS CONTACT: STEVEN CODDINGTON, ASSISTANT DIRECTOR OF ADMISSIONS
ADDRESS: 4001 W. MCNICHOLS ROAD, DETROIT, MI 48221-3038 UNITED STATES
PHONE: 313-993-1245 • FAX: 313-993-3326
E-MAIL: ADMISSIONS@UDMERCY.EDU • WEBSITE: WWW.BUSINESS.UDMERCY.EDU

GENERAL INFORMATION

Type of school: Private **Academic calendar:** Semester

STUDENTS

Enrollment of parent institution: 5,550 **Enrollment of MBA Program:** 200 **Average age at entry:** 29 **Average years work experience at entry:** 5

ACADEMICS

Student/faculty ratio: 30:1 **% female faculty:** 17 **% underrepresented minority faculty:** 13 **% part-time faculty:** 26

FINANCIAL FACTS

Annual tuition (in-state/out-of-state): $11,970/ **Fees:** $570 **Cost of books:** $1,200 **Room & board (on/off-campus):** $4,125/ **Average grant:** $40,000 **Average loan:** $18,500

ADMISSIONS

Admissions Selectivity Rating: 75

Average GMAT: 541 **Range of GMAT:** 410–720 **Accepts GRE scores:** Yes **Average GPA:** 3.4 **TOEFL required of international students:** Recommended

Application Deadline/Notification:

Round 1: 8/15
Round 2: 12/15
Round 3: 4/15
Round 4: 5/15

Deferment available: Yes **Maximum length of deferment:** 2 years **Transfer students accepted:** Yes **Transfer application policy:** Must submit transcripts and a GMAT for MBA program. GMAT can be waived. See website for conditions. **Non-fall admissions:** Yes **Need-blind admissions:** No

EMPLOYMENT PROFILE

Average base starting salary: $57,000

Top 5 Employers Hiring Grads (number of hires in last class)

Chrysler, Ford Motor, Bank One, Comerica, Henry Ford Health systems

UNIVERSITY OF HAWAII AT MANOA
SHIDLER COLLEGE OF BUSINESS

ADMISSIONS CONTACT: MICHELLE GARCIA, MBA ADMISSIONS DIRECTOR
ADDRESS: 2404 MAILE WAY, G202, HONOLULU, HI 96822 UNITED STATES
PHONE: 808-956-8266 • FAX: 808-956-9890
E-MAIL: MBA@HAWAII.EDU • WEBSITE: WWW.SHIDLER.HAWAII.EDU

GENERAL INFORMATION

Type of school: Public **Academic calendar:** Semester

STUDENTS

Enrollment of parent institution: 50,000 **Enrollment of MBA Program:** 75 % **male/female:** 69/31 % **out-of-state:** 56 % **part-time:** 40 % **underrepresented minority:** 58 % **international:** 18 **Average age at entry:** 28 **Average years work experience at entry:** 5

ACADEMICS

Student/faculty ratio: 25:1 % **female faculty:** 5 % **underrepresented minority faculty:** 10 % **part-time faculty:** 22

FINANCIAL FACTS

Annual tuition (in-state/out-of-state): $6,456/$9,912 **Fees:** $300 **Cost of books:** $1,200 **Room & board (on/off-campus):** $13,517/$13,517

ADMISSIONS

Admissions Selectivity Rating: 89

# of applications received: 224 % **applicants accepted:** 46 % **acceptees attending:** 73 **Average GMAT:** 628 **Range of GMAT:** 590–670 **Accepts GRE scores:** **Average GPA:** 3.3 **TOEFL required of international students:** Yes **Minimum TOEFL (paper/computer):** 600/100 **Application fee:** $60 **International application fee:** $60 **Early notification date:** 5/1 **Regular application deadline:** 5/1 **Regular application notification:** 7/1

Application Deadline/Notification:

Round 1: ....11/15 / 1/15
Round 2: ....1/15 / 3/15
Round 3: ....3/1 / 5/1
Round 4: ....5/1 / 7/1

Deferment available: No **Transfer students accepted:** Yes **Transfer application policy:** Credits may be transferred into the Part-time MBA program from other AACSB-accredited business schools, from other University of Hawaii graduate programs, or by petition as follows: Nine credits of coursework may be transferred into the PT MBA program. Transfer credit is appropriate for both Core classes(upon approval) and electives. Due to the cohort nature of the program, FT MBA's may not transfer in any credits. **Non-fall admissions:** No **Need-blind admissions:** Yes

UNIVERSITY OF HOUSTON—
CLEAR LAKE
SCHOOL OF BUSINESS

ADMISSIONS CONTACT: JANICE SAURWEIN, INTERIM REGISTRAR/DIRECTOR, ACADEMIC RECORDS
ADDRESS: 2700 BAY AREA BLVD, HOUSTON, TX 77058-1098 UNITED STATES
PHONE: 281-283-2500 • FAX: 281-283-2522
E-MAIL: ADMISSIONS@UHCL.EDU • WEBSITE: WWW.UHCL.EDU

GENERAL INFORMATION

Type of school: Public **Academic calendar:** Semester

STUDENTS

Enrollment of parent institution: 7,288 **Enrollment of MBA Program:** 368 % **male/female:** 55/45 % **out-of-state:** 10 % **part-time:** 62 % **underrepresented minority:** 23 % **international:** 15 **Average age at entry:** 30 **Average years work experience at entry:** 5

ACADEMICS

Student/faculty ratio: 18:1 % **female faculty:** 31 % **underrepresented minority faculty:** 19 % **part-time faculty:** 0

FINANCIAL FACTS

Annual tuition (in-state/out-of-state): $3,600/$13,608 **Fees:** $9,504 **Cost of books:** $1,800 **Room & board (on/off-campus):** $12,836/$12,836 % **of students receiving aid:** 20 **Average award package:** $8,300 **Average grant:** $1,000 **Average loan:** $8,000 **Average student loan debt:** $26,916

ADMISSIONS

Admissions Selectivity Rating: 78

# of applications received: 148 % **applicants accepted:** 80 % **acceptees attending:** 42 **Average GMAT:** 507 **Range of GMAT:** 460–570 **Average GPA:** 2.9 **TOEFL required of international students:** Yes **Minimum TOEFL (paper/computer):** 550/ **Application fee:** $35 **International application fee:** $75 **Regular application deadline:** 8/1 **Deferment available:** Yes **Maximum length of deferment:** 12 months **Transfer students accepted:** Yes **Transfer application policy:** Final 24 semester hours earned at UHCL-BUS **Non-fall admissions:** Yes **Need-blind admissions:** Yes

UNIVERSITY OF LONDON
LONDON BUSINESS SCHOOL

ADMISSIONS CONTACT: CAROLINE CHUKWUMA / NOEL CALISTE, CLIENT SERVICES
OFFICER
ADDRESS: REGENT'S PARK, LONDON NW1 4SA, UNITED KINGDOM OF GREAT
BRITAIN AND NORTHERN IRELAND
PHONE: +44 (0)20 7000 7500 • FAX: +44 (0)20 7000 7501
E-MAIL: MBAINFO@LONDON.EDU • WEBSITE: WWW.LONDON.EDU

GENERAL INFORMATION

Type of school: Public **Academic calendar:** August - July

STUDENTS

Average age at entry: 28

FINANCIAL FACTS

Cost of books: $345 **Room & board (on/off-campus):** /$22,500 %
of students receiving grants: 30 **Average award package:** $76,250
Average loan: $62,245 **Average student loan debt:** $65,500

ADMISSIONS

Admissions Selectivity Rating: 75

# of applications received: 2,765 **% applicants accepted:** Average
GMAT: 697 **Range of GMAT:** 600–790 **Accepts GRE scores:** No
TOEFL required of international students: Yes **Minimum TOEFL
(paper/computer):** /110

Application Deadline/Notification:

Round 1: ....10/7 / 12/17
Round 2: ....1/6 / 3/26
Round 3: ....3/3 / 5/21
Round 4: ....4/21 / 7/5

Deferment available: No **Transfer students accepted:** No **Non-fall
admissions:** No **Need-blind admissions:** Yes

EMPLOYMENT PROFILE

Percent employed 3 months after graduation: 81 **Average base
starting salary:** $108,212

Primary Source of Full-time Job Acceptances

School-facilitated activities: ....(77%)

Graduate-facilitated activities: ....(23%)

Top 5 Employers Hiring Grads (number of hires in last class)

McKinsey & Company (21), Credit Suisse (9), The Boston Consulting
Group (10), Barclays Group (11), Booz & Company (7)

THE UNIVERSITY OF MAINE
MAINE BUSINESS SCHOOL

ADMISSIONS CONTACT: CAROL L. MANDZIK, MANAGER OF MBA PROGRAMS
ADDRESS: 5723 DP CORBETT BUSINESS BUILDING, ORONO, ME 04469-5723
UNITED STATES
PHONE: 207-581-1971 • FAX: 207-581-1930
E-MAIL: CAROL.MANDZIK@MAINE.EDU • WEBSITE: WWW.UMAINE.EDU/BUSINESS

GENERAL INFORMATION

Type of school: Public **Academic calendar:** Semester

STUDENTS

Enrollment of parent institution: 10,901 **Enrollment of MBA
Program:** 54 **% male/female:** 87/13 **% out-of-state:** 18 **% part-time:**
30 **% underrepresented minority:** 1 **% international:** 1 **Average age
at entry:** 27 **Average years work experience at entry:** 7

ACADEMICS

Student/faculty ratio: 7:1 **% female faculty:** 31 **% underrepresented minority faculty:** 1 **% part-time faculty:** 5

FINANCIAL FACTS

Annual tuition (in-state/out-of-state): $7,524/$21,636 **Fees:**
$1,102 **Cost of books:** $800 **Room & board (on/off-campus):**
$10,466/$10,466 **% of students receiving aid:** 80 **% of students
receiving grants:** 55 **Average grant:** $5,000

ADMISSIONS

Admissions Selectivity Rating: 85

# of applications received: 38 **% applicants accepted:** 58 **% acceptees attending:** 50 **Average GMAT:** 572 **Range of GMAT:** 490–640
Accepts GRE scores: No **Average GPA:** 3.7 **TOEFL required of
international students:** Recommended **Minimum TOEFL (paper/
computer):** 550/79 **Application fee:** $65 **International application
fee:** $65 **Early notification date:** 1/20 **Regular application deadline:**
6/1 **Regular application notification:** 7/1

Deferment available: Yes **Maximum length of deferment:** 1 year
Transfer students accepted: Yes **Transfer application policy:** A
maximum of 6 hours accepted from accredited schools **Non-fall
admissions:** Yes **Need-blind admissions:** Yes

UNIVERSITY OF MANITOBA
I.H. ASPER SCHOOL OF BUSINESS

ADMISSIONS CONTACT: EWA MORPHY, GRADUATE PROGRAM MANAGER
ADDRESS: 324 DRAKE CENTER, WINNIPEG, MB R3T 5V4 CANADA
PHONE: 204-474-8448 • FAX: 204-474-7544
E-MAIL: ASPERMBA@UMANITOBA.CA • WEBSITE: WWW.UMANITOBA.CA/ASPER

GENERAL INFORMATION

Type of school: Public **Academic calendar:** Term based

STUDENTS

Enrollment of parent institution: 27,000 **Enrollment of MBA
Program:** 160 **% male/female:** 60/40 **% part-time:** 75 **% international:** 9 **Average age at entry:** 30 **Average years work experience
at entry:** 6

ACADEMICS

Student/faculty ratio: 30:1 % female faculty: 18 % underrepresented minority faculty: 32 % part-time faculty: 24

FINANCIAL FACTS

Annual tuition (in-state/out-of-state): $23,000/$32,000 Cost of books: $3,000 Room & board (on/off-campus): $6,000/$14,000 Average grant: $2,000

ADMISSIONS

Admissions Selectivity Rating: 75

# of applications received: 155 Average GMAT: 582 Range of GMAT: 500–720 Accepts GRE scores: Average GPA: 3.0 TOEFL required of international students: Yes Minimum TOEFL (paper/computer): 550/80 Application fee: $100 International application fee: $100 Regular application deadline: 5/1 Deferment available: No Transfer students accepted: Yes Transfer application policy: To earn an Asper MBA, at least half of the courses must be completed at Asper School of Business Non-fall admissions: Yes

EMPLOYMENT PROFILE

Percent employed at graduation: 75 Percent employed 3 months after graduation: 85 Average base starting salary: $80,000

Grads Employed by Function ..... % Avg. Salary
Marketing:.....................................(5%)

UNIVERSITY OF MINNESOTA DULUTH
LABOVITZ SCHOOL OF BUSINESS AND ECONOMICS

ADMISSIONS CONTACT: CARLEE WILLIAMS, DGS ASSISTANT
ADDRESS: 385 LSBE, 1318 KIRBY DRIVE, DULUTH, MN 55812 UNITED STATES
PHONE: 218-726-7757 • FAX: 218-726-7578
E-MAIL: UMDGRAD@UMN.EDU • WEBSITE: HTTP://Z.UMN.EDU/MBA/

GENERAL INFORMATION

Type of school: Public Academic calendar: Semester

STUDENTS

Enrollment of parent institution: 12,000 % part-time: 100 Average age at entry: 26 Average years work experience at entry: 6

ACADEMICS

Student/faculty ratio: 15:1 % female faculty: 27

FINANCIAL FACTS

Cost of books: $1,000 Room & board (on/off-campus): /$6,000

ADMISSIONS

Admissions Selectivity Rating: 83

# of applications received: 25 % applicants accepted: 52 Average GMAT: 505 Range of GMAT: 450–540 Accepts GRE scores: Yes Average GPA: 3.4 TOEFL required of international students: Yes Minimum TOEFL (paper/computer): 550/ Application fee: $75 International application fee: $95 Regular application deadline: 7/15 Regular application notification: 9/1

Application Deadline/Notification:
Round 1: ....7/15 / 8/31
Round 2: ....11/1 / 12/31
Round 3: ....5/1 / 5/30

Deferment available: Yes Maximum length of deferment: 1 year without reapp Transfer students accepted: Yes Transfer application policy: No more than 12 graduate credits can be transferred into program. Non-fall admissions: Yes Need-blind admissions: Yes

UNIVERSITY OF NEBRASKA AT OMAHA
COLLEGE OF BUSINESS ADMINISTRATION

ADMISSIONS CONTACT: LEX KACZMAREK, DIRECTOR, MBA PROGRAM
ADDRESS: 6708 PINE STREET, OMAHA, NE 68182-0048 UNITED STATES
PHONE: 402-554-2303 • FAX: 402-554-3747
E-MAIL: MBA@UNOMAHA.EDU • WEBSITE: CBA.UNOMAHA.EDU/MBA

GENERAL INFORMATION

Type of school: Public Academic calendar: Semester

STUDENTS

Enrollment of parent institution: 15,277 Enrollment of MBA Program: 247 % male/female: 69/31 % out-of-state: 19 % part-time: 83 % underrepresented minority: 6 % international: 21 Average age at entry: 27 Average years work experience at entry: 4

ACADEMICS

Student/faculty ratio: 9:1 % female faculty: 33 % underrepresented minority faculty: 6 % part-time faculty: 30

FINANCIAL FACTS

Annual tuition (in-state/out-of-state): $0/$0 Fees: $0 Room & board (on/off-campus): $8,500/$9,000 % of students receiving aid: 3 % of first-year students receiving aid: 4 % of students receiving grants: 8 Average award package: $10,490 Average grant: $9,738 Average loan: $10,905 Average student loan debt: $16,220

ADMISSIONS

Admissions Selectivity Rating: 83

# of applications received: 129 % applicants accepted: 73 % acceptees attending: 76 Average GMAT: 573 Range of GMAT: 530–610 Accepts GRE scores: Yes Average Verbal GRE: 152 Range of Verbal GRE scores: 147–157 Average Quantitative GRE: 152 Range of Quantitative GRE scores: 148–156 Average Writing GRE: 3.7 Range of Writing GRE scores: 3.0–4.5 Average GPA: 3.5 TOEFL required of international students: Yes Minimum TOEFL (paper/computer): 550/80 Application fee: $45 International application fee: $45 Regular application deadline: 7/1 Deferment available: Yes Maximum length of deferment: one year Transfer students accepted: Yes Transfer application policy: A maximum of nine hours of transfer credit may be accepted from another accredited (AACSB) institution. Non-fall admissions: Yes Need-blind admissions: Yes

UNIVERSITY OF NEBRASKA— LINCOLN
COLLEGE OF BUSINESS ADMINISTRATION

ADMISSIONS CONTACT: STEPHANIE OSTERTHUN, ON-CAMPUS MBA PROGRAM COORDINATOR/ADVISOR
ADDRESS: CBA 139, LINCOLN, NE 68588-0405 UNITED STATES
PHONE: 402-472-2338 • FAX: 402-472-5997
E-MAIL: CBAGRAD@UNL.EDU • WEBSITE: WWW.CBA.UNL.EDU

GENERAL INFORMATION

Type of school: Public **Academic calendar:** Semester

STUDENTS

Enrollment of parent institution: 24,207 **Enrollment of MBA Program:** 269 **% male/female:** 75/25 **% out-of-state:** 38 **% part-time:** 71 **% underrepresented minority:** 6 **% international:** 13 **Average age at entry:** 28 **Average years work experience at entry:** 3

ACADEMICS

Student/faculty ratio: 6:1 **% female faculty:** 25 **% underrepresented minority faculty:** 16 **% part-time faculty:** 16

FINANCIAL FACTS

Annual tuition (in-state/out-of-state): $6,345/$17,109 **Fees:** $1,280 **Cost of books:** $1,032 **Room & board (on/off-campus):** $9,722/$9,248 **% of students receiving aid:** 27 **% of first-year students receiving aid:** 38 **% of students receiving grants:** 12 **Average award package:** $12,821 **Average grant:** $5,861 **Average loan:** $12,294 **Average student loan debt:** $27,796

ADMISSIONS

Admissions Selectivity Rating: 85

# of applications received: 119 **% applicants accepted:** 61 **% acceptees attending:** 60 **Average GMAT:** 620 **Range of GMAT:** 600–650 **Accepts GRE scores:** Yes **Average GPA:** 3.4 **TOEFL required of international students:** Yes **Minimum TOEFL (paper/computer):** 550/80 **Application fee:** $50 **International application fee:** $50 **Regular application deadline:** 6/15 **Deferment available:** Yes **Maximum length of deferment:** one year **Transfer students accepted:** Yes **Transfer application policy:** 12 credit hours may be accepted from an AACSB accredited institution if approved by the MBA Committee **Non-fall admissions:** Yes **Need-blind admissions:** Yes

EMPLOYMENT PROFILE

Average base starting salary: $65,873

Grads Employed by Function	%	Avg. Salary
Marketing:	(14%)	$51,667
Operations:	(20%)	$66,600
Consulting:	(9%)	$42,500
Management:	(15%)	$72,760
Finance:	(8%)	$98,000
HR:	(1%)	
MIS:	(2%)	$59,500
Other:	(10%)	$45,000

Top 5 Employers Hiring Grads (number of hires in last class)
Cerner Corporation (2), IBM (2), Sandhills Publishing (2), Union Pacific Railroad (2)

UNIVERSITY OF NEW MEXICO
ROBERT O. ANDERSON GRADUATE SCHOOL OF MANAGEMENT

ADMISSIONS CONTACT: TRACY WILKEY, MANAGER, ACADEMIC ADVISEMENT
ADDRESS: THE UNIVERSITY OF NEW MEXICO, MSC05 3090, 1 UNIVERSITY OF NEW MEXICO, ALBUQUERQUE, NM 87131 UNITED STATES
PHONE: 505-277-3290 • FAX: 505-277-8436
E-MAIL: ANDERSONADVISING@UNM.EDU • WEBSITE: WWW.MGT.UNM.EDU/

GENERAL INFORMATION

Type of school: Public **Academic calendar:** Semester

STUDENTS

Enrollment of parent institution: 34,866 **Enrollment of MBA Program:** 307 **% male/female:** 56/44 **% out-of-state:** 18 **% part-time:** 48 **% underrepresented minority:** 63 **% international:** 15 **Average age at entry:** 26

ACADEMICS

Student/faculty ratio: 25:1 **% female faculty:** 33 **% underrepresented minority faculty:** 41 **% part-time faculty:** 16

FINANCIAL FACTS

Annual tuition (in-state/out-of-state): $7,883/$18,873 **Fees:** $1,036 **% of students receiving aid:** 71 **% of first-year students receiving aid:** 71 **% of students receiving grants:** 55 **Average award package:** $12,514 **Average grant:** $6,032 **Average loan:** $15,277

ADMISSIONS

Admissions Selectivity Rating: 87

# of applications received: 192 **% applicants accepted:** 50 **% acceptees attending:** 79 **Average GMAT:** 571 **Range of GMAT:** 510–620 **Accepts GRE scores:** Yes **Average Verbal GRE:** 155 **Range of Verbal GRE scores:** 152–158 **Average Quantitative GRE:** 155 **Range of Quantitative GRE scores:** 152–157 **Average Writing GRE:** 4.5 **Range of Writing GRE scores:** 4.0–5.0 **Average GPA:** 3.6 **TOEFL required of international students:** Yes **Minimum TOEFL (paper/computer):** 550/ **Application fee:** $50 **International application fee:** $50 **Regular application deadline:** 4/1 **Deferment available:** Yes **Maximum length of deferment:** 1 Year **Transfer students accepted:** Yes **Transfer application policy:** Up to 12 credit hours may transfer **Non-fall admissions:** Yes **Need-blind admissions:** Yes

Top 5 Employers Hiring Grads (number of hires in last class)
Sandia National Laboratories (10), University of New Mexico (4), Hewlett Packard, Los Alamos National Laboratories

University of New Orleans
College of Business Adminstration

Director of Admissions
Address: Admin Bldg Rm 103, 2000 Lakeshore Drive, New Orleans, LA 70148 United States
Phone: 504-280-6595 • Fax: 504-280-5522
E-mail: admissions@uno.edu • Website: www.uno.edu

GENERAL INFORMATION

Type of school: Public **Academic calendar:** Semester

STUDENTS

Enrollment of parent institution: 10,903 **Enrollment of MBA Program:** 384 **% male/female:** 70/30 **% out-of-state:** 19 **% part-time:** 40 **% underrepresented minority:** 15 **% international:** 13 **Average age at entry:** 29

ACADEMICS

Student/faculty ratio: 24:1 **% female faculty:** 25 **% underrepresented minority faculty:** 20 **% part-time faculty:** 3

FINANCIAL FACTS

Annual tuition (in-state/out-of-state): $4,644/$16,168 **Fees:** $4,467 **Cost of books:** $1,300 **Room & board (on/off-campus):** $11,793/$11,793 **% of students receiving aid:** 47 **% of first-year students receiving aid:** 54 **% of students receiving grants:** 8 **Average award package:** $13,504 **Average grant:** $2,643 **Average loan:** $14,663

ADMISSIONS

Admissions Selectivity Rating: 83

# of applications received: 274 **% applicants accepted:** 44 **% acceptees attending:** 85 **Average GMAT:** 481 **Range of GMAT:** 440–540 **Accepts GRE scores:** No **TOEFL required of international students:** Yes **Minimum TOEFL (paper/computer):** 550/80 **Application fee:** $50 **International application fee:** $50 **Regular application deadline:** 8/1 **Deferment available:** Yes **Maximum length of deferment:** 1 semester **Transfer students accepted:** Yes **Transfer application policy:** maximum number of credit hours transferrable = 12 **Non-fall admissions:** Yes **Need-blind admissions:** Yes

The University of New South Wales (UNSW)
AGSM MBA Programs

Admissions Contact: Recruitment & Admissions,
Address: AGSM Building, UNSW, Sydney NSW, 2052 Australia
Phone: 0061 2 99319490 • Fax: 0061 2 99319205
E-mail: admissions@agsm.edu.au
Website: www.agsm.edu.au/futureleaders

GENERAL INFORMATION

Type of school: Public **Academic calendar:** January

STUDENTS

% male/female: 81/19 **% part-time:** 0 **% international:** 56 **Average age at entry:** 29 **Average years work experience at entry:** 7

ACADEMICS

Student/faculty ratio: 4:1 **% female faculty:** 36 **% underrepresented minority faculty:** 0 **% part-time faculty:** 6

FINANCIAL FACTS

Annual tuition (in-state/out-of-state): $47,962/$47,962 **Cost of books:** $2,000 **Room & board (on/off-campus):** /$20,000

ADMISSIONS

Admissions Selectivity Rating: 77

Average GMAT: 664 **Range of GMAT:** 620–700 **Accepts GRE scores:** **Average GPA:** 3.0 **Minimum TOEFL (paper/computer):** 577/90 **Application fee:** $50 **International application fee:** $50 **Application Deadline/Notification:**

Round 1: ....5/1 / 5/30
Round 2: ....7/1 / 8/30
Round 3: ....9/3 / 9/30

Deferment available: Yes **Maximum length of deferment:** 1 year **Transfer students accepted:** Yes **Transfer application policy:** Transfer applicants must submit a completed application and meet all entry requirements; entry is January each year only; recognition of prior learning may be offered only for core courses correlations. **Non-fall admissions:** No **Need-blind admissions:** Yes

EMPLOYMENT PROFILE

Percent employed 3 months after graduation: 3 **Average base starting salary:** $116,411

Grads Employed by Function ..... % Avg. Salary

Marketing: ....(9%) $104,500
Consulting: ....(35%) $109,923
Management: ....(13%) $81,190
Finance: ....(17%) $92,821
Other: ....(4%) $78,413

Top 5 Employers Hiring Grads (number of hires in last class)

ABN AMRO, American Express (Brazil), Australian Stock Exchange, Australian Campus Network, Bain & Company

University of North Texas
College of Business

Admissions Contact: Stacy Buchanan or Brandi Everett, Graduate Academic Advisors
Address: P.O. Box 311160, Denton, TX 76203 United States
Phone: 940-369-8977 • Fax: 940-369-8978
E-mail: mbacob@unt.edu • Website: www.cob.unt.edu

GENERAL INFORMATION

Type of school: Public **Academic calendar:** Semester

STUDENTS

Enrollment of parent institution: 36,168 **Enrollment of MBA Program:** 776 **% male/female:** 55/45 **% part-time:** 46 **% underrep-**

resented minority: 24 % international: 33 **Average age at entry:** 28 **Average years work experience at entry:** 6

ACADEMICS

Student/faculty ratio: 8:1 **% female faculty:** 20 **% underrepresented minority faculty:** 8 **% part-time faculty:** 0

FINANCIAL FACTS

Annual tuition (in-state/out-of-state): $8,175/$17,949 **Fees:** $4,073 **Cost of books:** $1,000 **Room & board (on/off-campus):** $11,166/$17,100

ADMISSIONS

Admissions Selectivity Rating: 93

# of applications received: 705 **% applicants accepted:** 21 **% acceptees attending:** 72 **Average GMAT:** 532 **Accepts GRE scores:** No **Average GPA:** 3.3 **TOEFL required of international students:** Yes **Minimum TOEFL (paper/computer):** 550/79 **Application fee:** $60 **International application fee:** $95 **Regular application deadline:** 7/15 **Deferment available:** Yes **Maximum length of deferment:** Three semesters **Transfer students accepted:** Yes **Transfer application policy:** Transfer applicants must meet the same university application deadline. Only six to nine hours may transfer into our program. These hours will be determined by the departmental advisor. **Non-fall admissions:** Yes **Need-blind admissions:** Yes

EMPLOYMENT PROFILE

Percent employed 3 months after graduation:

Primary Source of Full-time Job Acceptances

School-facilitated activities: ....2(8%)

Unknown: ....24(92%)

Grads Employed by Function ..... % Avg. Salary

Marketing:......................................(8%) $33,500

Finance:...(77%) $42,000

HR:..(8%) $44,000

Other: ....(8%) $69,000

UNIVERSITY OF QUEENSLAND
UQ BUSINESS SCHOOL

ADMISSIONS CONTACT: THE MANAGER, STUDENT ADMIN,
ADDRESS: UQ BUSINESS SCHOOL, THE UNIVERSITY OF QUEENSLAND, ST LUCIA,
Q 4072 AUSTRALIA
PHONE: 011-617-3365 6475 • FAX: 011-617-3365 6988
E-MAIL: POSTGRAD_ENQUIRIES@BUSINESS.UQ.EDU.AU
WEBSITE: WWW.BUSINESS.UQ.EDU.AU

GENERAL INFORMATION

Type of school: Private

STUDENTS

Average years work experience at entry: 0

FINANCIAL FACTS

Annual tuition (in-state/out-of-state): $17,050/

Admissions Selectivity Rating: 60*

Regular application deadline: 1/30 **Regular application notification:** 1/30

UNIVERSITY OF SOUTHERN INDIANA
COLLEGE OF BUSINESS

ADMISSIONS CONTACT: DR. MAYOLA ROWSER, INTERIM DIRECTOR OF GRADUATE STUDIES
ADDRESS: 8600 UNIVERSITY BOULVARD, ROBERT D. ORR CENTER 1063, EVANSVILLE, IN 47712 UNITED STATES
PHONE: 812-465-7015 • FAX: 812-228-5018
E-MAIL: GSSR@USI.EDU • WEBSITE: BUSINESS.USI.EDU

GENERAL INFORMATION

Type of school: Public **Academic calendar:** Semester

STUDENTS

Enrollment of parent institution: 9,902 **Enrollment of MBA Program:** 80 **% male/female:** 67/33 **% out-of-state:** 13 **% part-time:** 81 **% underrepresented minority:** 27 **% international:** 20 **Average age at entry:** 26 **Average years work experience at entry:** 7

ACADEMICS

Student/faculty ratio: 22:1 **% female faculty:** 18 **% underrepresented minority faculty:** 23 **% part-time faculty:** 14

FINANCIAL FACTS

Annual tuition (in-state/out-of-state): $5,567/$10,917 **Fees:** $240 **Cost of books:** $1,200 **Room & board (on/off-campus):** $7,680/$9,640 **% of students receiving aid:** 40 **% of first-year students receiving aid:** 20 **% of students receiving grants:** 6 **Average award package:** $8,739 **Average grant:** $3,765 **Average loan:** $11,502

ADMISSIONS

Admissions Selectivity Rating: 79

# of applications received: 70 **% applicants accepted:** 90 **% acceptees attending:** 81 **Average GMAT:** 496 **Range of GMAT:** 440–528 **Accepts GRE scores:** Yes **Average Verbal GRE:** 153 **Range of Verbal GRE scores:** 149–153 **Average Quantitative GRE:** 154 **Range of Quantitative GRE scores:** 151–158 **Average Writing GRE:** 3.6 **Range of Writing GRE scores:** 3.0–4.0 **Average GPA:** 3.3 **TOEFL required of international students:** Yes **Minimum TOEFL (paper/computer):** 550/79 **Application fee:** $40 **International application fee:** $40

Deferment available: No **Transfer students accepted:** Yes **Transfer application policy:** Twelve accepted hours can be transferred into the program **Non-fall admissions:** Yes **Need-blind admissions:** Yes

EMPLOYMENT PROFILE

Average base starting salary: $52,400

Grads Employed by Function ..... % Avg. Salary

Marketing:.......................................(4%) $45,000

Management: ....(4%) $79,000

Finance:..(13%) $43,000

Other: ....(4%) $30,000

THE UNIVERSITY OF SOUTHERN MISSISSIPPI
COLLEGE OF BUSINESS

ADMISSIONS CONTACT: GABRIEL MCPHEARSON, ASSISTANT TO THE DIRECTOR
ADDRESS: 118 COLLEGE DRIVE #5096, HATTIESBURG, MS 39406-5096
UNITED STATES
PHONE: 601-266-4653 • FAX: 601-266-5814
E-MAIL: MBA@USM.EDU • WEBSITE: WWW.USM.EDU/MBA

GENERAL INFORMATION

Type of school: Public **Academic calendar:** Semester

STUDENTS

Enrollment of parent institution: 15,030 **Enrollment of MBA Program:** 93 % **male/female:** 58/42 % **out-of-state:** 24 % **part-time:** 59 % **underrepresented minority:** 8 % **international:** 8 **Average age at entry:** 27 **Average years work experience at entry:** 0

ACADEMICS

Student/faculty ratio: 30:1 % **female faculty:** 25 % **underrepresented minority faculty:** 15 % **part-time faculty:** 0

FINANCIAL FACTS

Annual tuition (in-state/out-of-state): $4,312/$4,312 **Fees:** $0 **Cost of books:** $1,600 **Room & board (on/off-campus):** $5,800/$7,600 % **of students receiving aid:** 75 % **of first-year students receiving aid:** % **of students receiving grants:** 25 **Average award package:** **Average grant:** $8,690 **Average loan:** $2,000

ADMISSIONS

Admissions Selectivity Rating: 85

# of applications received: 73 % **applicants accepted:** 56 % **acceptees attending:** 76 **Average GMAT:** 508 **Range of GMAT:** 450–560 **Accepts GRE scores:** **Average GPA:** 3.4 **TOEFL required of international students:** Yes **Minimum TOEFL (paper/computer):** 550/ **Application fee:** $25 **International application fee:** $25 **Regular application deadline:** 7/15 **Deferment available:** Yes **Maximum length of deferment:** 2 semesters **Transfer students accepted:** Yes **Transfer application policy:** They must fully apply to the program and can only transfer a total of 6 hours of graduate courses from other accredited institutions. The coursework must be graded (i.e., not pass/fail). **Non-fall admissions:** Yes **Need-blind admissions:** Yes

EMPLOYMENT PROFILE

Average base starting salary: $43,179

Primary Source of Full-time Job Acceptances

Unknown: 13 (100%)

Grads Employed by Function ..... % Avg. Salary

Marketing:.......................................(15%) $35,000

Operations:....................................(7%) $48,600

Management: ....(23%) $37,301

Finance:..(15%) $35,056

Other: ....(31%) $58,375

Top 5 Employers Hiring Grads (number of hires in last class)

Cintas, Frito Lay, Walgreen's, Sherman Williams Co., AmSouth Bank

UNIVERSITY OF SOUTH ALABAMA
MITCHELL COLLEGE OF BUSINESS

ADMISSIONS CONTACT: OFFICE OF ADMISSIONS,
ADDRESS: MEISLER HALL SUITE 2500, MOBILE, AL 36688-0002 UNITED STATES
PHONE: 251-460-6141 • FAX: 251-460-7876
E-MAIL: ADMISS@USOUTHAL.EDU • WEBSITE: MCOB.SOUTHALABAMA.EDU/

GENERAL INFORMATION

Type of school: Public

STUDENTS

Enrollment of parent institution: 13,500 **Enrollment of MBA Program:** 135 % **male/female:** 55/45 % **out-of-state:** 0 % **part-time:** 0 % **underrepresented minority:** 55 % **international:** 10 **Average age at entry:** 28 **Average years work experience at entry:** 0

ACADEMICS

Student/faculty ratio: 31:1 % **female faculty:** 21 % **underrepresented minority faculty:** 10 % **part-time faculty:** 0

FINANCIAL FACTS

Annual tuition (in-state/out-of-state): $4,008/$8,016 **Fees:** $2,460 **Cost of books:** $1,200 **Room & board (on/off-campus):** $4,750/$7,200 **Average grant:** $0 **Average loan:** $0

ADMISSIONS

Admissions Selectivity Rating: 82

# of applications received: 80 % **applicants accepted:** 78 % **acceptees attending:** 73 **Average GMAT:** 550 **Accepts GRE scores:** **Average GPA:** 3.4 **TOEFL required of international students:** Yes **Minimum TOEFL (paper/computer):** 525/ **Application fee:** $25 **International application fee:** $25 **Regular application deadline:** 7/15 **Regular application notification:** 7/25

Deferment available: No **Transfer students accepted:** Yes **Transfer application policy:** May transfer in up to 9 credits toward degeree. **Non-fall admissions:** No **Need-blind admissions:** Yes

UNIVERSITY OF SOUTH FLORIDA
MUMA COLLEGE OF BUSINESS

ADMISSIONS CONTACT: IRENE HURST, DIRECTOR OF MBA PROGRAMS
ADDRESS: 4202 E. FOWLER AVE.   BSN 3403, LOC BSN 103, TAMPA, FL
33620 UNITED STATES
PHONE: 813-974-3335 • FAX: 813-974-4518
E-MAIL: BSN-MBA@USF.EDU • WEBSITE: BUSINESS.USF.EDU

GENERAL INFORMATION

Type of school: Public **Academic calendar:** Semester

STUDENTS

Enrollment of parent institution: 48,330 **Enrollment of MBA Program:** 234 **% male/female:** 64/36 **% out-of-state:** 5 **% part-time:** 58 **% underrepresented minority:** 17 **% international:** 36 **Average age at entry:** 27 **Average years work experience at entry:** 7

ACADEMICS

Student/faculty ratio: 6:1 **% female faculty:** 25 **% underrepresented minority faculty:** 26 **% part-time faculty:** 0

FINANCIAL FACTS

Annual tuition (in-state/out-of-state): $11,216/$20,600 **Fees:** $37 **Cost of books:** $2,500 **Room & board (on/off-campus):** $15,500/$16,000 **% of students receiving aid:** 37 **% of students receiving grants:** 35 **Average award package:** $12,251 **Average grant:** $4,272 **Average loan:** $13,858 **Average student loan debt:** $32,239

ADMISSIONS

Admissions Selectivity Rating: 88

# of applications received: 288 **% applicants accepted:** 39 **% acceptees attending:** 61 **Average GMAT:** 572 **Range of GMAT:** 500–635 **Accepts GRE scores:** Yes **Average Verbal GRE:** 152 **Range of Verbal GRE scores:** 143–158 **Average Quantitative GRE:** 155 **Range of Quantitative GRE scores:** 152–159 **Average GPA:** 3.3 **TOEFL required of international students:** Yes **Minimum TOEFL (paper/computer):** 550/79 **Application fee:** $30 **International application fee:** $30

Deferment available: Yes **Maximum length of deferment:** 1 year **Transfer students accepted:** Yes **Transfer application policy:** 12 credits from an AACSB University with grades of B or better. **Non-fall admissions:** Yes **Need-blind admissions:** Yes

EMPLOYMENT PROFILE

Percent employed at graduation: 15 **Percent employed 3 months after graduation:** 3 **Average base starting salary:** $48,250
Primary Source of Full-time Job Acceptances
School-facilitated activities: 4 (14%)
Graduate-facilitated activities: 25 (86%)

Grads Employed by Function ..... % Avg. Salary
Marketing:......................................(9%) $0
Operations:....................................(9%) $61,000
Consulting:....................................(27%) $76,333
Management: ....(9%) $50,000
Finance:..(9%) $48,000
Other: ....(36%) $105,000

Top 5 Employers Hiring Grads (number of hires in last class)
Tribridge (2), USF (2), Raymond James (1), Lockheed Martin (1), Bloomin' Brands (1)

UNIVERSITY OF SOUTH FLORIDA
ST. PETERSBURG
COLLEGE OF BUSINESS

ADDRESS: 140 SEVENTH AVENUE SOUTH, BAY 104, ST. PETERSBURG, FL
33701 UNITED STATES
PHONE: 727-873-4142 • FAX: 727-873-4525
E-MAIL: ADMISSIONS@STPT.USF.EDU • WEBSITE: WWW.STPT.USF.EDU

GENERAL INFORMATION

Type of school: Public

STUDENTS

Enrollment of MBA Program: 162 **% male/female:** 100/0 **% out-of-state:** 0 **% part-time:** 100 **% underrepresented minority:** 0 **% international:** 0 **Average age at entry:** 29 **Average years work experience at entry:** 4

ACADEMICS

Student/faculty ratio: 9:1 **% female faculty:** 39 **% underrepresented minority faculty:** 6 **% part-time faculty:** 11

FINANCIAL FACTS
ADMISSIONS

Admissions Selectivity Rating: 86

# of applications received: 75 **% applicants accepted:** 59 **% acceptees attending:** 82 **Average GMAT:** 568 **Range of GMAT:** 530–590 **Accepts GRE scores:** Average GPA: 3.4 **TOEFL required of international students:** Recommended **Minimum TOEFL (paper/computer):** 550/ **Application fee:** $30 **International application fee:** $30 **Regular application deadline:** 7/1 **Regular application notification:** 7/8

Deferment available: Yes **Maximum length of deferment:** 1 year **Transfer students accepted:** Yes **Transfer application policy:** Students who meet our admission criteria may import up to two courses (6 credit hours) from any AACSB accredit business school. Courses require MBA Director approval **Non-fall admissions:** Yes **Need-blind admissions:** Yes

University of St. Gallen (Switzerland)

University of St. Gallen

Admissions Contact: Peggy van der Wallen, Admissions Manager
Address: Blumenbergplatz 9, St. Gallen, CH 9000 Switzerland
Phone: 41712247355 • Fax: 41712242473
E-mail: mba@unisg.ch • Website: www.mba.unisg.ch

GENERAL INFORMATION

Type of school: Public

FINANCIAL FACTS

Annual tuition (in-state/out-of-state): $56,000/$56,000 **Room & board (on/off-campus):** /$22,000

ADMISSIONS

Admissions Selectivity Rating: 60*

# of applications received: % applicants accepted: **TOEFL required of international students:** Recommended **Minimum TOEFL (paper/computer):** 600/100 **Application fee:** $0 **International application fee:** $0

Application Deadline/Notification:
Round 1: ....12/1 / 12/15
Round 2: ....2/1 / 2/15
Round 3: ....4/1 / 4/15
Round 4: ....6/1 / 6/15

Deferment available: Yes **Transfer students accepted:** No **Non-fall admissions:** No **Need-blind admissions:** No

University of Strathclyde, Glasgow

University of Strathclyde Graduate School of Business

Admissions Contact: 141-553- 6118, Lucy Reynolds
Address: 199 Cathedral Street, Glasgow, G4 0QU
Phone: 141-553-6118 • Fax: 141-553-6162
E-mail: admissions@gsb.strath.ac.uk • Website: www.gsb.strath.ac.uk

GENERAL INFORMATION

Type of school: Private

STUDENTS

Enrollment of MBA Program: 107 % male/female: 86/14 % part-time: 37 % underrepresented minority: 88 % international: 84
Average age at entry: 32 **Average years work experience at entry:** 9

ACADEMICS

Student/faculty ratio: 4:1 % female faculty: 11 % part-time faculty: 2

FINANCIAL FACTS

Annual tuition (in-state/out-of-state): $0/ **Fees:** $31,600 **Cost of books:** $150 **Room & board (on/off-campus):** $13,500/$15,300 **Average loan:** $0

ADMISSIONS

Admissions Selectivity Rating: 79

# of applications received: 280 % applicants accepted: 90 % acceptees attending: 42 **Average GMAT:** 560 **Accepts GRE scores: Average GPA:** 3.4 **TOEFL required of international students:** Yes **Minimum TOEFL (paper/computer):** 600/ **Application fee:** $0 **International application fee:** $0

Deferment available: Yes **Maximum length of deferment:** 2 years **Transfer students accepted:** No **Non-fall admissions:** Yes **Need-blind admissions:**

EMPLOYMENT PROFILE

Average base starting salary: $124,000

Grads Employed by Function	%	Avg. Salary
Marketing:	(5%)	$85,500
Consulting:	(10%)	$142,000
Finance:	(13%)	$130,000
Other:	(41%)	$95,000

Top 5 Employers Hiring Grads (number of hires in last class)
Mott McDonald (4), BT (3), RBoS (1), Standard Life (1), Prince and Princess of Wales Hospice (1)

The University of Texas at El Paso

College of Business Administration

Admissions Contact: Lorenie Orozco, Graduate Advisor
Address: College of Business Administration, Rm 102, 500 W University Avenue, El Paso, TX 79968 United States
Phone: 915-747-7726 • Fax: 915-532-8213
E-mail: mba@utep.edu • Website: www.mba.utep.edu

GENERAL INFORMATION

Type of school: Public **Academic calendar:** Semester

STUDENTS

Enrollment of parent institution: 22,309 **Enrollment of MBA Program:** 198 % male/female: 57/43 % out-of-state: 0 % part-time: 0 % underrepresented minority: 69 % international: 16
Average age at entry: 36 **Average years work experience at entry:** 12

ACADEMICS

Student/faculty ratio: 4:1 % female faculty: 27 % underrepresented minority faculty: 54 % part-time faculty: 8

FINANCIAL FACTS

Annual tuition (in-state/out-of-state): $11,017/$18,732 % of students receiving grants: 12 **Average student loan debt:** $35,898

ADMISSIONS

Admissions Selectivity Rating: 81

# of applications received: 125 % applicants accepted: 74 % acceptees attending: 71 **Average GMAT:** 476 **Accepts GRE scores:** No **Average GPA:** 3.2 **TOEFL required of international students:** Yes **Minimum TOEFL (paper/computer):** 600/100 **Application fee:** $45

International application fee: $80 **Regular application deadline:** 7/15 **Deferment available:** Yes **Maximum length of deferment:** 1 yr for US Applicants **Transfer students accepted:** Yes **Transfer application policy:** Limited transfer credits allowed. Must be from AACSB accredited institution and receive approval from Associate Dean for transfer courses to be considered. **Non-fall admissions:** Yes **Need-blind admissions:** Yes

EMPLOYMENT PROFILE

Percent employed at graduation: 21 **Percent employed 3 months after graduation:** 0 **Average base starting salary:** $82,750

Grads Employed by Function ..... % Avg. Salary

Operations:.....................................(1%) $89,000

Management: ....(1%) $79,000

Finance:..(3%) $79,000

MIS:...(1%) $109,000

Other: ....(3%) $75,667

Top 5 Employers Hiring Grads (number of hires in last class)

UTEP (2), El Paso Electric Company (1), VOTEC (1)

THE UNIVERSITY OF TEXAS AT TYLER
COLLEGE OF BUSINESS AND TECHNOLOGY

ADMISSIONS CONTACT: DR. MARY FISCHER, ASSOCIATE DEAN
ADDRESS: 3900 UNIVERSITY BOULEVARD, TYLER, TX 75799 UNITED STATES
PHONE: 903-566-7433 • FAX: 903-566-7372
E-MAIL: MFISCHER@UTTYLER.EDU • WEBSITE: WWW.UTTYLER.EDU/CBT

GENERAL INFORMATION

Type of school: Public **Academic calendar:** Semester

STUDENTS

Enrollment of parent institution: 6,150 **Enrollment of MBA Program:** 189 **% part-time:** 99 **Average age at entry:** 3 **Average years work experience at entry:** 0

ACADEMICS

Student/faculty ratio: 20:1 **% female faculty:** 45 **% underrepresented minority faculty:** 33 **% part-time faculty:** 12

FINANCIAL FACTS

Cost of books: $975

ADMISSIONS

Admissions Selectivity Rating: 82

# of applications received: 110 **% applicants accepted:** 76 **% acceptees attending:** 100 **Average GMAT:** 513 **Accepts GRE scores:** **Average GPA:** 3.1 **TOEFL required of international students:** Yes **Minimum TOEFL (paper/computer):** 550/ **Application fee:** $25 **International application fee:** $50

Deferment available: Yes **Maximum length of deferment:** 12 months **Transfer students accepted:** No **Non-fall admissions:** Yes **Need-blind admissions:** Yes

UNIVERSITY OF TORONTO
JOSEPH L. ROTMAN SCHOOL OF MANAGEMENT

ADMISSIONS CONTACT: CHERYL MILLINGTON, DIRECTOR OF MBA RECRUITING AND ADMISSIONS
ADDRESS: 105 ST. GEORGE STREET, TORONTO, ON M5S 3E6 CANADA
PHONE: 416-978-3499 • FAX: 416-978-5812
E-MAIL: MBA@ROTMAN.UTORONTO.CA • WEBSITE: WWW.ROTMAN.UTORONTO.CA

GENERAL INFORMATION

Type of school: Public **Academic calendar:** Sept-May

STUDENTS

Enrollment of parent institution: 70,000 **Enrollment of MBA Program:** 366 **% male/female:** 72/28 **% part-time:** 28 **% international:** 37 **Average age at entry:** 27 **Average years work experience at entry:** 5

ACADEMICS

Student/faculty ratio: 7:1 **% female faculty:** 24 **% part-time faculty:** 15

FINANCIAL FACTS

Annual tuition (in-state/out-of-state): $30,820/ **Fees:** $1,078 **Cost of books:** $5,000 **Room & board (on/off-campus):** $10,000/$10,000 **% of students receiving aid:** 70 **% of first-year students receiving aid:** 70 **% of students receiving grants:** 20 **Average award package:** **Average grant:** $8,000 **Average loan:** $20,000

ADMISSIONS

Admissions Selectivity Rating: 78

# of applications received: 1,100 **% applicants accepted:** **Average GMAT:** 660 **Range of GMAT:** 550–780 **Accepts GRE scores:** **Average GPA:** 3.4 **TOEFL required of international students:** Yes **Minimum TOEFL (paper/computer):** 600/100 **Application fee:** $150 **International application fee:** $150 **Regular application deadline:** 4/30 **Regular application notification:** 7/1

Application Deadline/Notification:

Round 1:..11/15 / 1/15

Round 2:..1/15 / 3/15

Round 3: ....4/30 / 7/1

Deferment available: Yes **Maximum length of deferment:** one year **Transfer students accepted:** No **Non-fall admissions:** No **Need-blind admissions:** Yes

EMPLOYMENT PROFILE

Percent employed 3 months after graduation: 93 **Average base starting salary:** $83,067

Primary Source of Full-time Job Acceptances

School-facilitated activities: ....(60%)

Graduate-facilitated activities: ....(40%)

Grads Employed by Function ..... % Avg. Salary

Marketing:......................................(8%) $78,000

Operations:....................................(2%) $68,300

Consulting:....................................(23%) $103,000

Management: ....(10%) $80,000

Finance:...(23%) $77,600

Other: ....(34%)

Top 5 Employers Hiring Grads (number of hires in last class)

CIBC (19), RBC Financial Group (12), Deloitte (11), BMO Financial Group (9), Scotiabank (7)

UNIVERSITY OF WARWICK
WARWICK BUSINESS SCHOOL

ADMISSIONS CONTACT: EMMA SHAW, MBA ADMISSIONS OFFICE
ADDRESS: WARWICK BUSINESS SCHOOL, COVENTRY, CV4 7AL
PHONE: 011-44 (0)24 7652 4100
E-MAIL: WARWICKMBA@WBS.AC.UK • WEBSITE: WWW.WBS.AC.UK

GENERAL INFORMATION

Type of school: Public **Academic calendar:** trimester

STUDENTS

Enrollment of parent institution: 16,000 **Enrollment of MBA Program:** 575 **% male/female:** 73/27 **% part-time:** 90 **% international:** 91 **Average age at entry:** 30 **Average years work experience at entry:** 6

ACADEMICS

Student/faculty ratio: 4:1 **% female faculty:** 39

FINANCIAL FACTS

Annual tuition (in-state/out-of-state): $47,931/$47,931 **Cost of books:** $1,000 **Room & board (on/off-campus):** $13,000/$13,000 **% of students receiving aid:** 25 **% of first-year students receiving aid:** **% of students receiving grants:** 25 **Average award package:** $24,000 **Average grant:** $24,000 **Average loan:** $0

ADMISSIONS

Admissions Selectivity Rating: 86

# of applications received: 249 **% applicants accepted:** 39 **% acceptees attending:** 57 **Average GMAT:** 647 **Range of GMAT:** 560–720 **Accepts GRE scores:** No **TOEFL required of international students:** Yes **Minimum TOEFL (paper/computer):** /105 **International Regular application deadline:** 7/31 **Deferment available:** Yes **Maximum length of deferment:** 12 months **Transfer students accepted:** No **Non-fall admissions:** No **Need-blind admissions:** Yes

EMPLOYMENT PROFILE

Percent employed 3 months after graduation: 96

Primary Source of Full-time Job Acceptances

School-facilitated activities: ....(36%)

Graduate-facilitated activities: ....(44%)

Unknown: ....(20%)

Grads Employed by Function ..... % Avg. Salary

Marketing:......................................(20%)

Operations:....................................(8%)

Consulting:....................................(12%)

Management: ....(22%)

Finance:...(10%)

HR:..(6%)

MIS:...(4%)

Other: ....(2%)

Top 5 Employers Hiring Grads (number of hires in last class)

Deloitte, Accenture, Johnson & Johnson, Pepsico, Proctor & Gamble

UNIVERSITY OF WEST FLORIDA
COLLEGE OF BUSINESS

ADMISSIONS CONTACT: GRADUATE ADMISSIONS OFFICE, GRADUATE ADMISSIONS OFFICERS
ADDRESS: 11000 UNIVERSITY PKWY, BLDG 18, PENSACOLA, FL 32514 UNITED STATES
PHONE: 850-474-2230 • FAX: 850-474-3360
E-MAIL: ADMISSIONS@UWF.EDU • WEBSITE: UWF.EDU/MBA

GENERAL INFORMATION

Type of school: Public

STUDENTS

Enrollment of MBA Program: 178 **% male/female:** 60/40 **% out-of-state:** 80 **% part-time:** 90 **% international:** 80 **Average age at entry:** 29 **Average years work experience at entry:** 0

ACADEMICS

Student/faculty ratio: 25:1 **% female faculty:** 13 **% underrepresented minority faculty:** 13 **% part-time faculty:** 28

FINANCIAL FACTS

Annual tuition (in-state/out-of-state): $8,325/$30,093 **Cost of books:** $1,000 **Average grant:** $1,400

ADMISSIONS

Admissions Selectivity Rating: 87

# of applications received: 71 **% applicants accepted:** 49 **% acceptees attending:** 80 **Average GMAT:** 537 **Range of GMAT:** 460–600 **Accepts GRE scores:** **Average GPA:** 3.4 **TOEFL required of international students:** Yes **Minimum TOEFL (paper/computer):** 550/ **Application fee:** $30 **International application fee:** $30 **Regular application deadline:** 6/1 **Deferment available:** Yes **Maximum length of deferment:** One year **Transfer students accepted:** Yes **Transfer application policy:** Student can transfer in no more than 6 credit hours from an AACSB Accredited School. Student must meet the minimum GMAT score of 450. **Non-fall admissions:** Yes

University of Wisconsin— Eau Claire

College of Business

Admissions Contact: Ms. Jan Stewart, MBA Program Associate
Address: 105 Garfield Avenue, Eau Claire, WI 54702-4004 United
States
Phone: 715-836-4733 • *Fax:* 715-836-2409
E-mail: admissions@uwec.edu
Website: http://www.uwec.edu/COB/graduate/index.htm

GENERAL INFORMATION

Type of school: Public **Academic calendar:** Semester

STUDENTS

Enrollment of parent institution: 10,500 **Enrollment of MBA Program:** 130 **% male/female:** 55/45 **% out-of-state:** 80 **% part-time:** 90 **% underrepresented minority:** 5 **% international:** 80 **Average age at entry:** 28 **Average years work experience at entry:** 7

ACADEMICS

Student/faculty ratio: 5:1 **% female faculty:** 30 **% part-time faculty:** 0

FINANCIAL FACTS

Annual tuition (in-state/out-of-state): $8,186/$18,276 **Cost of books:** $1,000 **Room & board (on/off-campus):** $5,630/ **Average grant:** $0 **Average loan:** $0

ADMISSIONS

Admissions Selectivity Rating: 75

# of applications received: 0 **% applicants accepted:** Average **GMAT:** 540 **Accepts GRE scores:** Yes **Average GPA:** 3.3 **TOEFL required of international students:** Yes **Minimum TOEFL (paper/computer):** 550/79 **Application fee:** $56 **International application fee:** $56

Deferment available: Yes **Maximum length of deferment:** 1 year **Transfer students accepted:** Yes **Transfer application policy:** Transfer credits are accepted from other AACSB accredited schools. **Non-fall admissions:** Yes **Need-blind admissions:** Yes

Grads Employed by Function ..... % Avg. Salary

Marketing:	(20%)
Operations:	(10%)
Management:	(30%)
MIS:	(10%)

University of Wisconsin— La Crosse

College of Business Administration

Admissions Contact: Cory Sjoquist, Director
Address: 1725 State Street, La Crosse, WI 54601 United States
Phone: 608-785-8939 • *Fax:* 608-785-6695
E-mail: admissions@uwlax.edu • *Website:* www.uwlax.edu

GENERAL INFORMATION

Type of school: Public **Academic calendar:** Semester

STUDENTS

Enrollment of parent institution: 10,408 **Enrollment of MBA Program:** 40 **% part-time:** 65 **Average age at entry:** 27

ACADEMICS

% female faculty: 35 **% part-time faculty:** 0

FINANCIAL FACTS

Annual tuition (in-state/out-of-state): $9,235/$18,822

ADMISSIONS

Admissions Selectivity Rating: 81

# of applications received: 36 **% applicants accepted:** 81 **% acceptees attending:** 79 **Average GMAT:** 524 **Accepts GRE scores:** Average GPA: 3.3 **TOEFL required of international students:** Yes **Minimum TOEFL (paper/computer):** 550/79 **Application fee:** $56

Deferment available: Yes **Maximum length of deferment:** rolling **Transfer students accepted:** Yes **Transfer application policy:** Maximum of nine credits may be transferrable. **Non-fall admissions:** Yes **Need-blind admissions:** Yes

University of Wisconsin— Oshkosh

College of Business Adminstration

Admissions Contact: Lynn Grancorbitz, MBA Program Assistant
Director and Advisor
Address: 800 Algoma Blvd., Oshkosh, WI 54901 United States
Phone: 800-633-1430 • *Fax:* 920-424-7413
E-mail: mba@uwosh.edu
Website: www.uwosh.edu/colleges/coba/assets/grad/index.php

GENERAL INFORMATION

Type of school: Public **Academic calendar:** Semester

STUDENTS

Enrollment of parent institution: 10,528 **Enrollment of MBA Program:** 525 **% male/female:** 55/45 **% out-of-state:** 2 **% part-time:** 95 **% underrepresented minority:** 2 **% international:** 3 **Average age at entry:** 32 **Average years work experience at entry:** 5

ACADEMICS

Student/faculty ratio: 11:1 **% female faculty:** 15 **% underrepresented minority faculty:** 5

FINANCIAL FACTS

Annual tuition (in-state/out-of-state): $4,664/$13,622 % of students receiving aid: 5 % of first-year students receiving aid: 5 % of students receiving grants: 0

ADMISSIONS

Admissions Selectivity Rating: 80

# of applications received: 115 % applicants accepted: 90 % acceptees attending: 93 Average GMAT: 540 Range of GMAT: 470–610 Accepts GRE scores: Average GPA: 3.1 TOEFL required of international students: Yes Minimum TOEFL (paper/computer): 550/ Application fee: $45 International application fee: $45 Regular application deadline: 7/1 Deferment available: Yes Maximum length of deferment: 3 years Transfer students accepted: Yes Transfer application policy: Accept up to 9 credits from an AACSB accredited MBA program. Non-fall admissions: Yes Need-blind admissions: No

EMPLOYMENT PROFILE

Percent employed at graduation: 30 Percent employed 3 months after graduation: 50

Primary Source of Full-time Job Acceptances

Graduate-facilitated activities: 100 (100%)

UNIVERSITY OF WISCONSIN— PARKSIDE
COLLEGE OF BUSINESS, ECONOMICS, AND COMPUTING

ADMISSIONS CONTACT: MICHELE GEE, ASSOCIATE DEAN
ADDRESS: 900 WOOD ROAD, BOX 2000, KENOSHA, WI 53141-2000 UNITED STATES
PHONE: 262-595-2243 • FAX: 262-595-2680
E-MAIL: ADMISSIONS@UWP.EDU
WEBSITE: WWW.UWP.EDU/LEARN/COLLEGES/BUSINESSECONOMICSCOMPUTING/

GENERAL INFORMATION

Type of school: Public Academic calendar: Semester

STUDENTS

Enrollment of parent institution: 5,000 Enrollment of MBA Program: 85 % male/female: 58/42 % out-of-state: 7 % part-time: 81 % underrepresented minority: 25 % international: 13 Average age at entry: 33 Average years work experience at entry: 5

ACADEMICS

Student/faculty ratio: 5:1 % female faculty: 37 % underrepresented minority faculty: 45

FINANCIAL FACTS

Annual tuition (in-state/out-of-state): $8,658/$17,789 Fees: $277 Cost of books: $700

ADMISSIONS

Admissions Selectivity Rating: 77

# of applications received: 44 % applicants accepted: 100 % acceptees attending: 84 Average GMAT: 472 Range of GMAT:

440–530 Accepts GRE scores: Yes Average GPA: 3.3 TOEFL required of international students: Yes Minimum TOEFL (paper/computer): 550/79 Application fee: $56 International application fee: $56 Regular application deadline: 8/1 Deferment available: Yes Maximum length of deferment: 12 months Transfer students accepted: Yes Transfer application policy: Must be accepted and max of 12 credits in transfer Non-fall admissions: Yes Need-blind admissions: Yes

UNIVERSITY OF WYOMING
COLLEGE OF BUSINESS

ADMISSIONS CONTACT: TERRI L. RITTENBURG, DIRECTOR OF MBA PROGRAM
ADDRESS: P.O. BOX 3275, LARAMIE, WY 82071 UNITED STATES
PHONE: 307-766-2449 • FAX: 307-766-4028
E-MAIL: MBA@UWYO.EDU • WEBSITE: BUSINESS.UWYO.EDU/MBA

GENERAL INFORMATION

Type of school: Public Academic calendar: Semester

STUDENTS

Enrollment of parent institution: 11,904 Enrollment of MBA Program: 63 % male/female: 64/36 % part-time: 48 % underrepresented minority: 0 % international: 18 Average age at entry: 28 Average years work experience at entry: 0

ACADEMICS

Student/faculty ratio: 3:1

FINANCIAL FACTS

Annual tuition (in-state/out-of-state): $2,988/$8,676 Fees: $246 Cost of books: $300 Room & board (on/off-campus): $6,212/ % of students receiving aid: 0 % of first-year students receiving aid: 0 Average grant: $0 Average loan: $0

ADMISSIONS

Admissions Selectivity Rating: 75

# of applications received: 0 % applicants accepted: % acceptees attending: 0 Average GMAT: 558 Accepts GRE scores: Average GPA: 3.2 TOEFL required of international students: Yes Minimum TOEFL (paper/computer): 525/ Application fee: $40 International application fee: $0 Regular application deadline: 2/1 Deferment available: Yes Maximum length of deferment: 1 year Transfer students accepted: Yes Transfer application policy: Maximum number of transferable credits is nine with a minimum grade of B from an AACSB-accredited school. Non-fall admissions: No Need-blind admissions: Yes

EMPLOYMENT PROFILE

Average base starting salary: $38,878

UTAH STATE UNIVERSITY
JON M. HUNTSMAN SCHOOL OF BUSINESS

ADMISSIONS CONTACT: SCHOOL OF GRADUATE STUDIES, ADMISSIONS OFFICER
ADDRESS: 0900 OLD MAIN HILL, LOGAN, UT 84322-0900 UNITED STATES
PHONE: (435) 797-1190 • FAX: (435) 797-1192
E-MAIL: APRIL.FAWSON@USU.EDU • WEBSITE: WWW.HUNTSMAN.USU.EDU

GENERAL INFORMATION

Type of school: Public **Academic calendar:** Semester

STUDENTS

Enrollment of parent institution: 28,994 **Enrollment of MBA Program:** 234 **% male/female:** 71/29 **% out-of-state:** 15 **% part-time:** 69 **% underrepresented minority:** 5 **% international:** 18 **Average age at entry:** 28 **Average years work experience at entry:** 8

ACADEMICS

Student/faculty ratio: 3:1 **% female faculty:** 19 **% underrepresented minority faculty:** 6 **% part-time faculty:** 0

FINANCIAL FACTS

Annual tuition (in-state/out-of-state): $21,686/$35,179 **Cost of books:** $1,800 **Room & board (on/off-campus):** $5,000/$5,000 **% of students receiving aid:** 20 **% of first-year students receiving aid:** 20 **% of students receiving grants:** 20 **Average award package:** $6,000 **Average grant:** $2,800 **Average loan:** $4,000 **Average student loan debt:** $13,000

ADMISSIONS

Admissions Selectivity Rating: 84

# of applications received: 211 **% applicants accepted:** 67 **% acceptees attending:** 86 **Average GMAT:** 532 **Range of GMAT:** 488–574 **Accepts GRE scores:** Yes **Average GPA:** 3.4 **TOEFL required of international students:** Yes **Minimum TOEFL (paper/computer):** 550/79 **Application fee:** $55 **International application fee:** $55

Application Deadline/Notification:

Round 1: ....12/1 / 1/15
Round 2: ....2/1 / 3/1
Round 3: ....3/1 / 4/1
Round 4: ....4/1 / 5/1

Deferment available: Yes **Maximum length of deferment:** 1 year **Transfer students accepted:** Yes **Transfer application policy:** Classes to be transferred are reviewed and approved on an individual basis to ensure that equivalent course content is covered. **Non-fall admissions:** No **Need-blind admissions:** Yes

EMPLOYMENT PROFILE

Percent employed 3 months after graduation: 81 **Average base starting salary:** $55,889

Grads Employed by Function ..... % Avg. Salary	
Marketing:	(27%) $50,012
Operations:	(9%) $54,025
Management:	(15%) $54,383
Finance:	(29%) $57,000
HR:	(10%) $57,500
MIS:	(5%) $63,250
Other:	(5%) $95,000

Top 5 Employers Hiring Grads (number of hires in last class)
Harris Research Inc. (2), Goldman Sachs (1), Honeywell Inc. (1), Monsanto Corp. (1), Hewlett Packard (1)

VALDOSTA STATE UNIVERSITY
LANGDALE COLLEGE OF BUSINESS ADMINISTRATION

ADMISSIONS CONTACT: JUDY TOMBERLIN, GRADUATE SCHOOL
ADDRESS: 903 N. PATTERSON STREET, VALDOSTA, GA 31698-0005 UNITED STATES
PHONE: (229) 333-5696 • FAX: (229) 245-3853
E-MAIL: MBA@VALDOSTA.EDU • WEBSITE: WWW.VALDOSTA.EDU/LCOBA/GRAD/

GENERAL INFORMATION

Type of school: Public **Academic calendar:** Semester

STUDENTS

Enrollment of parent institution: 10,500 **Enrollment of MBA Program:** 31 **% male/female:** 50/50 **% part-time:** 100 **% underrepresented minority:** 0 **% international:** 8 **Average age at entry:** 30 **Average years work experience at entry:** 8

ACADEMICS

Student/faculty ratio: 3:1 **% female faculty:** 20 **% underrepresented minority faculty:** 0 **% part-time faculty:** 0

FINANCIAL FACTS

Annual tuition (in-state/out-of-state): $3,766/$12,544 **Fees:** $708 **Cost of books:** $800 **Room & board (on/off-campus):** $2,684/$2,684 **Average grant:** $1,000 **Average loan:** $8,966

ADMISSIONS

Admissions Selectivity Rating: 87

# of applications received: 21 **% applicants accepted:** 48 **% acceptees attending:** 80 **Average GMAT:** 534 **Range of GMAT:** 500–640 **Accepts GRE scores:** **Average GPA:** 3.3 **TOEFL required of international students:** Yes **Minimum TOEFL (paper/computer):** 550/ **Application fee:** $25

Deferment available: Yes **Maximum length of deferment:** One semester **Transfer students accepted:** Yes **Transfer application policy:** Maximum of 6 hours transfered from AACSB institution. **Non-fall admissions:** Yes **Need-blind admissions:** Yes

Virginia Tech
Pamplin College of Business

Admissions Contact: Robin Camputaro, Associate Director
Address: 1044 Pamplin Hall, Virginia Tech, Blacksburg, VA 24061
United States
Phone: 540-231-6152 • Fax: 540-231-4487
E-mail: mba@vt.edu • Website: www.mba.vt.edu

GENERAL INFORMATION

Type of school: Public **Academic calendar:** Fall 2010

STUDENTS

Enrollment of parent institution: 31,087 **Enrollment of MBA Program:** 316 **% male/female:** 68/32 **% out-of-state:** 66 **% part-time:** 47 **% underrepresented minority:** 2 **% international:** 48 **Average age at entry:** 26 **Average years work experience at entry:** 2

ACADEMICS

Student/faculty ratio: 27:1 **% female faculty:** 25 **% underrepresented minority faculty:** 18 **% part-time faculty:** 11

FINANCIAL FACTS

Annual tuition (in-state/out-of-state): $10,677/$20,926 **Fees:** $5,636 **Cost of books:** $8,340 **Room & board (on/off-campus):** $8,820/$8,820 **% of students receiving aid:** 94 **% of first-year students receiving aid:** 78 **% of students receiving grants:** 81 **Average award package:** $22,975 **Average grant:** $13,857 **Average loan:** $17,310 **Average student loan debt:** $34,375

ADMISSIONS

Admissions Selectivity Rating: 87

# of applications received: 173 **% applicants accepted:** 52 **% acceptees attending:** 54 **Average GMAT:** 627 **Range of GMAT:** 610–650 **Accepts GRE scores:** Yes **Average GPA:** 3.5 **TOEFL required of international students:** Yes **Minimum TOEFL (paper/computer):** 550/80 **Application fee:** $65 **International application fee:** $65 **Early notification date:** 12/15 **Deferment available:** Yes **Maximum length of deferment:** 1 year **Transfer students accepted:** No **Non-fall admissions:** No **Need-blind admissions:** Yes

EMPLOYMENT PROFILE

Percent employed at graduation: 53 **Percent employed 3 months after graduation:** 66 **Average base starting salary:** $67,392

Primary Source of Full-time Job Acceptances

School-facilitated activities: ....17(68%)
Graduate-facilitated activities: ....8(32%)

Grads Employed by Function ..... % Avg. Salary

Marketing: ....(12%) $65,333
Operations: ....(12%) $64,000
Consulting: ....(20%) $81,200
Management: ....(8%) $60,000 Finance: (20%) $65,000
MIS: ....(12%) $70,667
Other: ....(16%) $55,405

Top 5 Employers Hiring Grads (number of hires in last class)
PWC (3), Ernst & Young (1), Deloitte (1), KPMG (1), Capitol One (1)

Vlerick Leuven Gent
Management School

Admissions Contact: Yolanda Habets, Programme Manager
Address: Vlamingenstraat 83, 3000 Leuven, BELGIUM., Reep 1, 9000
Gent, BELGIUM, Leuven, VB 3000 Belgium
Phone: + 32 16 24 88 86 • Fax: + 32 16 24 88 11
E-mail: MBA@vlerick.be • Website: www.vlerick.com

GENERAL INFORMATION

Type of school: Public

STUDENTS

Enrollment of parent institution: 30,000 **Enrollment of MBA Program:** 320 **% male/female:** 75/25 **% out-of-state:** 90 **% part-time:** 55 **% international:** 90 **Average age at entry:** 30 **Average years work experience at entry:** 6

ACADEMICS

Student/faculty ratio: 4:1 **% female faculty:** 25 **% underrepresented minority faculty:** 100 **% part-time faculty:** 0

FINANCIAL FACTS

Annual tuition (in-state/out-of-state): $42/$42 **Cost of books:** $0 **Room & board (on/off-campus):** $12,000/$12,000 **% of students receiving aid:** 10 **% of first-year students receiving aid:** 10 **% of students receiving grants:** 10 **Average award package:** $630,000 **Average grant:** $15,000 **Average loan:** $22,000 **Average student loan debt:** $12,500

ADMISSIONS

Admissions Selectivity Rating: 91

# of applications received: 600 **% applicants accepted:** 34 **% acceptees attending:** 43 **Average GMAT:** 660 **Range of GMAT:** 600–700 **Accepts GRE scores:** No **Average GPA:** 3.5 **TOEFL required of international students:** Yes **Minimum TOEFL (paper/computer):** /95 **Application fee:** $50 **International application fee:** $50 **Early notification date:** 4/14 **Regular application deadline:** 6/30 **Regular application notification:** 7/14

Application Deadline/Notification:

Round 1: ....1/22 / 2/1
Round 2: ....3/24 / 4/1
Round 3: ....6/30 / 7/14

Deferment available: Yes **Maximum length of deferment:** 1 year **Transfer students accepted:** No **Non-fall admissions:** No **Need-blind admissions:** Yes

EMPLOYMENT PROFILE

Percent employed at graduation: 50 **Percent employed 3 months after graduation:** 90 **Average base starting salary:** $120,000

Primary Source of Full-time Job Acceptances

School-facilitated activities: ....25(45%)

Graduate-facilitated activities: ....15(30%)

Unknown: ....14(25%)

Grads Employed by Function ..... % Avg. Salary

Marketing:.....................................(10%) $120,000

Consulting:....................................(15%) $120,000

Management: ....(10%) $120,000

Finance:..(15%) $120,000

Top 5 Employers Hiring Grads (number of hires in last class)

Bechtel (1), Inbev (1), Belgacom (1), ING Bank (1), US Foreign Service (1)

WASHINGTON STATE UNIVERSITY
CARSON COLLEGE OF BUSINESS

ADMISSIONS CONTACT: MITCH SWANGER, DIRECTOR OF ADMISSIONS
ADDRESS: , PO BOX 644750, PULLMAN, WA 99164 UNITED STATES
PHONE: 509-335-7617 • FAX: 509-335-3851
E-MAIL: MBA@WSU.EDU • WEBSITE: BUSINESS.WSU.EDU/GRADUATE-PROGRAMS

GENERAL INFORMATION

Type of school: Public **Academic calendar:** Semester

STUDENTS

Enrollment of parent institution: 30,069 **Enrollment of MBA Program:** 85 % **male/female:** 71/29 % **out-of-state:** 19 % **part-time:** 51 % **underrepresented minority:** 2 % **international:** 5 **Average age at entry:** 26 **Average years work experience at entry:** 6

ACADEMICS

Student/faculty ratio: 25:1 % **female faculty:** 17 % **part-time faculty:** 17

FINANCIAL FACTS

Annual tuition (in-state/out-of-state): $21,000/$40,000 **Fees:** $960 **Cost of books:** $4,676 **Room & board (on/off-campus):** $11,356/$11,356 % **of students receiving aid:** % **of first-year students receiving aid:** 57 % **of students receiving grants:** **Average award package:** $12,074 **Average grant:** $4,994 **Average loan:** $11,154

ADMISSIONS

Admissions Selectivity Rating: 88

# of applications received: 148 % **applicants accepted:** 45 % **acceptees attending:** 71 **Average GMAT:** 500 **Range of GMAT:** 530–595 **Accepts GRE scores:** No **Average GPA:** 3.4 **TOEFL required of international students:** Yes **Minimum TOEFL (paper/computer):** 580/93 **Application fee:** $75 **International application fee:** $75 **Early notification date:** 1/17 **Regular application deadline:** 3/1 **Regular application notification:** 3/8

Deferment available: Yes **Maximum length of deferment:** One year **Transfer students accepted:** Yes **Transfer application policy:** Transfer students will only be able to apply 6 credits of elective coursework to the WSU MBA on a case-by-case basis. **Non-fall admissions:** Yes **Need-blind admissions:** Yes

WESTERN ILLINOIS UNIVERSITY
COLLEGE OF BUSINESS AND TECHNOLOGY

DIRECTOR OF MBA PROGRAM
ADDRESS: 1 UNIVERSITY CIRCLE, 115 SHERMAN HALL, MACOMB, IL 61455 UNITED STATES
PHONE: 309-298-3157 • FAX: 309-298-3111
E-MAIL: ADMISSIONS@WIU.EDU • WEBSITE: WWW.WIU.EDU/USERS/MICOBTD/

GENERAL INFORMATION

Type of school: Public **Academic calendar:** Semester

STUDENTS

Enrollment of parent institution: 13,000 **Enrollment of MBA Program:** 111 % **male/female:** 52/48 % **part-time:** 55 % **underrepresented minority:** 2 % **international:** 26

ACADEMICS

Student/faculty ratio: 24:1 % **female faculty:** 29 % **underrepresented minority faculty:** 15 % **part-time faculty:** 7

FINANCIAL FACTS

Annual tuition (in-state/out-of-state): $5,696/$11,392 **Fees:** $1,453 **Cost of books:** $1,150 **Room & board (on/off-campus):** $7,210/$9,000 % **of students receiving aid:** 17 % **of first-year students receiving aid:** 37 % **of students receiving grants:** 20 **Average award package:** **Average grant:** $4,696

ADMISSIONS

Admissions Selectivity Rating: 79

# of applications received: 47 % **applicants accepted:** 89 % **acceptees attending:** 64 **Average GMAT:** 549 **Range of GMAT:** 500–600 **Accepts GRE scores:** **Average GPA:** 3.3 **TOEFL required of international students:** Yes **Minimum TOEFL (paper/computer):** 550/ **Application fee:** $30

Deferment available: Yes **Transfer students accepted:** No **Non-fall admissions:** Yes **Need-blind admissions:** No

WESTERN NEW ENGLAND UNIVERSITY
COLLEGE OF BUSINESS

ADMISSIONS CONTACT: MATTHEW FOX, DIRECTOR OF RECRUITING AND MARKETING
ADDRESS: 1215 WILBRAHAM RD, SPRINGFIELD, MA 1119 UNITED STATES
PHONE: 413 782 1517 • FAX: 413-702-1777
E-MAIL: STUDY@WNE.EDU • WEBSITE: WWW.WNE.EDU

GENERAL INFORMATION

Type of school: Private **Academic calendar:** Four 11-week terms

FINANCIAL FACTS

Annual tuition (In-state/out-of-state): $25,560/$25,560 **Fees:** $0 **Cost of books:** $3,100 **Room & board:** $8,000

ADMISSIONS

Admissions Selectivity Rating: 60*

Accepts GRE scores: Yes **TOEFL required of international students:** Yes **Minimum TOEFL (paper/computer):** 550/79 **Application fee:** $30 **International application fee:** $30

Deferment available: Yes **Maximum length of deferment:** One year **Transfer students accepted:** Yes **Transfer application policy:** The College will consider up to 12 credits from an AACSB accredited program. **Non-fall admissions:** Yes **Need-blind admissions:** Yes

WESTERN WASHINGTON UNIVERSITY
COLLEGE OF BUSINESS AND ECONOMICS

ADMISSIONS CONTACT: DANIEL PURDY, MBA PROGRAM ASSOCIATE DIRECTOR ADDRESS: 516 HIGH ST., PARKS HALL 419, BELLINGHAM, WA 98225-9072 UNITED STATES
PHONE: 360-650-3825 • FAX: 360-650-4844
E-MAIL: DANIEL.PURDY@WWU.EDU • WEBSITE: WWW.CBE.WWU.EDU/MBA

GENERAL INFORMATION

Type of school: Public **Academic calendar:** Fall thru Spring - Quarter System

STUDENTS

Enrollment of parent institution: 14,979 **Enrollment of MBA Program:** 97 **% male/female:** 53/47 **% out-of-state:** 16 **% part-time:** 40 **% underrepresented minority:** 22 **% international:** 7 **Average age at entry:** 29 **Average years work experience at entry:** 6

ACADEMICS

Student/faculty ratio: 2:1 **% female faculty:** 21 **% underrepresented minority faculty:** 20 **% part-time faculty:** 9

FINANCIAL FACTS

Annual tuition (in-state/out-of-state): $7,344/$17,190 **Fees:** $846 **Cost of books:** $1,000 **Room & board (on/off-campus):** $11,000/ **% of students receiving aid:** 18 **% of first-year students receiving aid:** 11

ADMISSIONS

Admissions Selectivity Rating: 82

# of applications received: 116 **% applicants accepted:** 77 **% acceptees attending:** 70 **Average GMAT:** 575 **Range of GMAT:** 458–690 **Accepts GRE scores:** Yes **Average GPA:** 3.3 **TOEFL required of international students:** Yes **Minimum TOEFL (paper/computer):** 567/86 **Application fee:** $50 **International application fee:** $50 **Regular application deadline:** 5/1 **Deferment available:** Yes **Maximum length of deferment:** 1 year, fee required **Transfer students accepted:** Yes **Transfer application policy:** Transfer maximum of 9 quarter (six semester) credits; graded with a b, 3.0, or better; taken no more than three years prior to a student's quarter of admission; be acceptable to the granting institution for its master's degree; and meet the requirements and conditions of approved courses offered by WWU. **Non-fall admissions:** Yes **Need-blind admissions:** Yes

WIDENER UNIVERSITY
SCHOOL OF BUSINESS ADMINISTRATION

ADMISSIONS CONTACT: ANN SELTZER, GRADUATE ENROLLMENT PROCESS ADMINISTRATOR
ADDRESS: 1 UNIVERSITY PLACE, CHESTER, PA 19013 UNITED STATES
PHONE: 610-499-4305 • FAX: 610-499-4615
E-MAIL: SBAGRADV@MAIL.WIDENER.EDU • WEBSITE: WWW.WIDENER.EDU

GENERAL INFORMATION

Type of school: Private **Academic calendar:** Semester

STUDENTS

Enrollment of MBA Program: 105 **% male/female:** 40/60 **% part-time:** 90 **% international:** 10 **Average age at entry:** 29 **Average years work experience at entry:** 7

ACADEMICS

Student/faculty ratio: 6:1 **% female faculty:** 39 **% underrepresented minority faculty:** 5 **% part-time faculty:** 27

FINANCIAL FACTS

Annual tuition (in-state/out-of-state): $21,600/ **Fees:** $200 **Cost of books:** $850 **Room & board (on/off-campus):** /$7,650 **% of students receiving aid:** 9 **% of first-year students receiving aid:** 3 **% of students receiving grants:** 5 **Average award package:** $19,174 **Average grant:** $9,660 **Average loan:** $15,283

ADMISSIONS

Admissions Selectivity Rating: 87

# of applications received: 130 **% applicants accepted:** 45 **% acceptees attending:** 85 **Average GMAT:** 533 **Range of GMAT:** 450–540 **Accepts GRE scores:** Average **GPA:** 3.2 **TOEFL required of international students:** Yes **Minimum TOEFL (paper/computer):** 550/ **Application fee:** $25 **International Regular application deadline:** 5/1 **Deferment available:** Yes **Maximum length of deferment:** 1 year **Transfer students accepted:** Yes **Transfer application policy:** Students may transfer all foundation level courses from other institutions. Up to 6 credits of core or elective courses may be transferred from AACSB accredited programs. **Non-fall admissions:** Yes **Need-blind admissions:** Yes

WINTHROP UNIVERSITY
COLLEGE OF BUSINESS ADMINISTRATION

ADMISSIONS CONTACT: PEGGY HAGER, DIRECTOR OF GRADUATE PROGRAMS
ADDRESS: 213 THURMOND BUILDING, ROCK HILL, SC 29733 UNITED STATES
PHONE: 803-323-2409 • FAX: 803-323-2539
E-MAIL: MBAOFFICE@WINTHROP.EDU • WEBSITE: WWW.WINTHROP.EDU/CBA/MBA

GENERAL INFORMATION

Type of school: Public **Academic calendar:** Semester

STUDENTS

Enrollment of parent institution: 6,249 **Enrollment of MBA Program:** 168 **% male/female:** 64/36 **% out-of-state:** 41 **% part-time:** 57 **% underrepresented minority:** 38 **% international:** 26 **Average age at entry:** 29 **Average years work experience at entry:** 5

ACADEMICS

Student/faculty ratio: 4:1 **% female faculty:** 40 **% underrepresented minority faculty:** 12 **% part-time faculty:** 8

FINANCIAL FACTS

Cost of books: $1,400

ADMISSIONS

Admissions Selectivity Rating: 78

# of applications received: 102 **% applicants accepted:** 90 **% acceptees attending:** 70 **Average GMAT:** 470 **Range of GMAT:** 400–550 **Accepts GRE scores:** Average GPA: 3.2 **TOEFL required of international students:** Yes **Minimum TOEFL (paper/computer):** 550/ **Application fee:** $50 **International application fee:** $50 **Regular application deadline:** 7/15 **Deferment available:** Yes **Maximum length of deferment:** 1 year **Transfer students accepted:** Yes **Transfer application policy:** 9 graduate semester hours of approved coursework may be transferred **Non-fall admissions:** Yes **Need-blind admissions:** Yes

YOUNGSTOWN STATE UNIVERSITY
WILLIAMSON COLLEGE OF BUSINESS ADMINISTRATION

ADMISSIONS CONTACT: SUE DAVIS, INTERIM DIRECTOR
ADDRESS: ONE UNIVERSITY PLAZA, YOUNGSTOWN, OH 44555 UNITED STATES
PHONE: 330-742-2000 • FAX: 330-742-1658
E-MAIL: ENROLL@YSU.EDU • WEBSITE: WWW.WCBA.YSU.EDU

GENERAL INFORMATION

Type of school: Public

STUDENTS

Average years work experience at entry: 0

FINANCIAL FACTS

Annual tuition (in-state/out-of-state): $5,670/$8,520

ADMISSIONS

Admissions Selectivity Rating: 60*

SCHOOL SAYS . . .

In this section you'll find schools with extended listings describing Admissions, curriculum, internships, and much more. This is your chance to get in-depth information on programs that interest you. The Princeton Review charges each school a small fee to be listed, and the editorial responsibility is solely that of the university.

AMERICAN UNIVERSITY
Kogod School of Business

AT A GLANCE

The Kogod School of Business, established in Washington, D.C. more than fifty years ago, has a diverse population that is driven to make a difference in the world. American University is known as a place where students learn from leaders in their fields, are engaged in active citizenship, and where Washington, D.C., serves as a laboratory for learning through work, internships, and other forms of experiential education. The Kogod School of Business embodies this character. We know that doing business in the capital, where all industries and sectors meet, is unlike doing business anywhere else. We are committed to preparing our graduates to excel in this elite environment. Kogod is the oldest accredited business school in Washington, D.C. The school is accredited by The Association to Advance Collegiate Schools of Business (AACSB International), which represents the highest standard of achievement for business schools worldwide.

ADMISSIONS

Complete your application for Kogod School of Business online at http://kogod.american.edu/apply.

DEGREES OFFERED

Full-Time MBA; Professional MBA; MS Accounting; MS Analytics; MS Finance; MS Marketing; MS Real Estate; MS Sustainability Management; MS Taxation; LLM/MBA; JD/MBA; MBA/MA in International Studies; Graduate Business Certification

ACADEMIC PROGRAMS

Kogod offers two distinct MBA programs to meet students' unique personal and professional needs. Students may choose the immersive full-time MBA, or select the part-time Professional MBA, designed for professionals who wish to continue working while pursuing their degree. The Kogod full-time MBA is designed to be a career catalyst for ambitious professionals. In 21 months, graduates acquire the knowledge, skills, and experience required to achieve professional success. Students complete the core in the first year, leaving the second year open to electives. Students gain knowledge and skills in both domestic and global business through experience and interaction with clients, professors, business leaders, and fellow students, both inside and outside of the classroom. Students may pursue a specialized consulting focus, developed with leading federal and commercial consulting firms, to prepare for consulting in human capital, finance, IT or strategy. Alternatively, students may choose electives with an emphasis on accounting, entrepreneurship, sustainability management, or other business disciplines. Internships, career development, and volunteer opportunities ensure students graduate with an extensive network of contacts from the American University community and beyond.

Kogod's Professional MBA (PMBA) is designed for working professionals seeking to advance their careers. The PMBA's comprehensive, cohort-based design allows students to continue working and complete their degree in 27 consecutive months by attending class one night a week. The program's concierge-style services and hybrid teaching approach helps students achieve a positive work-life balance. Course materials, an iPad, meals during class time, course registration, and an international travel-study experience are all included in the tuition. The program is structured so students can take courses one at a time, with classes sequenced to build upon one another. This allows students to absorb and retain material better, and provides the opportunity s to work with peers in a collaborative environment. Kogod also offers specialized masters programs in Accounting, Analytics, Finance, Marketing, Real Estate, Sustainability Management, and Taxation that provide advanced training from real-world professionals and thought leaders. Students gain expertise in their chosen field through a combination of classroom, practical, and career management experience. Kogod leverages its connections within each industry to help students broaden their knowledge about career options, current industry trends, and the general industry landscape.

SAMPLE FULL-TIME CURRICULUM

First Year: Accounting (3) Finance (3) Strategic Decision-Making in a Global Environment I-II (6) Marketing (1.5) Managerial Economics (1.5) Quantitative Methods I-II (3) Organizational Behavior (1.5) Legal, Ethical & Social Issues (1.5) Global Issues (1.5) Management Information Systems (1.5) Productions & Supply Chain Management (1.5)

Second Year: Career Track Course (3) Career Track Course (3) Career Track Course (3) Consulting Project/Elective (3) Consulting Project/Elective (3) Consulting Project/Elective (3) Consulting Project/Elective (3)

AREAS OF INTEREST

Accounting; Asset and Money Management; Consulting; Banking, Investment and Finance; Global Emerging Market; Entrepreneurship; International Trade and Global Supply Chain Management; Leadership; Marketing Management and Research; Real Estate; and Taxation.

SPECIAL ACADEMIC PROGRAMS

Kogod offers an extensive set of interdisciplinary programs that include three dual-degree programs: LLM/MBA, JD/MBA, and the MA/MBA.

FACULTY

Our faculty are experts in their fields and regularly conduct research in the industries distinctive to the Washington, D.C. region. In addition to their research and classroom responsibilities, our faculty curate Kogod's Business in the Capital Event Series, which focuses on multiple industry tracks and regularly brings experts to campus to expand our community's knowledge base.

CAREERS

The Kogod Center for Career Development (KCCD) is committed to helping both students and employer partners meet their unique business goals, including transitioning to a new career or finding talented candidates for an organization. KCCD's team of experienced career development professionals proactively partner with students to assess current strengths and employ creative strategies to reach future career goals. Kogod's career development curriculum is led by KCCD and teaches students how to leverage their individual educational and professional backgrounds. Students learn how to apply a project-management approach to the career management process with plans, metrics, and benchmarks. The career management team works with students individually and in the classroom on developing strategies for effective networking, interview and negotiation skills,, and how to cultivate offers.

TUITION & FINANCIAL AID

Full-Time MBA and Master of Science Programs (2016-2017 Academic Year)
Per Credit Hour Rate: $1,579 per credit hour
Graduate Student Fees:
Graduate Student Fee: $30
Technology Fee: $120
Sport Center Fee: $65
Professional MBA program Tuition
•Flat Rate for Total Program: $ 84,632*. This includes tuition, program fees, global learning experience, textbooks, software, and light meals on class days.
*For cohort entering Fall 2016 only

STUDENT BODY

At Kogod, we believe education should extend beyond the classroom. Hands-on experiences enhance leadership ability, communication skills, and self-confidence. Kogod Leadership and Applied Business (K-LAB), Kogod Global Learning, and the Kogod Center for Business Communications allow students to learn valuable professional skills in real-world settings, including the annual case competition, student clubs, international travel, and community volunteer programs.

BABSON COLLEGE
F.W. Olin Graduate School of Business

AT A GLANCE

At Babson's F.W. Olin Graduate School of Business, we believe that entrepreneurship is applicable-and-crucial-in organizations of all types and sizes, in established businesses as well as new ventures. Babson is the only business school that has developed and advanced an innovative teaching method, Entrepreneurial Thought and Action®. Unlike most business schools that teach entrepreneurship as a discrete, siloed subject, Babson incorporates Entrepreneurial Thought and Action across all disciplines. In fact, Babson's MBA program has been ranked number one in the country for entrepreneurship for 22 consecutive years by U.S. News & World Report, as well as by the Princeton Review. Building off the classroom curriculum are the Signature Learning Experiences (SLEs). These experiences reinforce and expand classroom learning through hands-on activities that require graduate students to put theories into practice. To supplement, there is a wide array of elective courses for deeper experiential and field-based learning. Students can customize their portfolio of electives to meet their career aspirations and may decide to further focus their studies through a concentration.

ADMISSIONS

Students are admitted to the program based on a careful evaluation of academic records, professional qualifications, GMAT or GRE scores, and personal attributes. Interviews are required for admission to all programs. International students must submit TOEFL or IELTS results and official English translations of all academic documents.

Application deadlines and decision dates for all programs may be found at: http://www.babson.edu/admission/graduate/apply/Pages/deadlines.aspx

For more information, contact: Telephone: 781-239-4317; 800-488-4512 (toll-free within the U.S.)

E-mail: gradadmissions@babson.edu Website: www.babson.edu/graduate

ACADEMIC PROGRAMS

The Babson MBA: With four programs, the Babson MBA allows you to choose the program that best suits your lifestyle and objectives. With the unified curriculum across all programs, students will take the same core courses with the same faculty and can choose from a common set of electives.

One-Year Program: Suited for those with a strong academic foundation in business and a career-track that demands an accelerated, full-time MBA experience.

Two-Year Program: Ideal for individuals who need a comprehensive business focus to redirect their careers and want a full-time campus experience.

Evening Program: Ideal for working professionals who seek a part time MBA program that allows flexibility to accommodate professional or personal demands.

Blended Learning Program: Favorable to working professionals seeking a part-time MBA that allows for increased flexibility through a blend of web-based and face to face sessions.

MS Programs: Master of Science in Management in Entrepreneurial Leadership: A 9-month Master's program that prepares leaders to make an impact in their career by providing a combination of foundation business knowledge, entrepreneurial leadership skills, and hands-on experience.

Master of Science in Accounting: The program prepares graduates for public accounting careers and the CPA exam. Graduates gain technical accounting knowledge and an entrepreneurial mindset that gives Babson graduates a competitive advantage.

Master of Science in Finance: A 9-month program that provides in-depth financial and quantitative knowledge combined with sophisticated problem-solving, practical application, ethical judgment, and professional development, and communication skills.

SPECIAL ACADEMIC PROGRAMS

Babson provides many on and off campus opportunities for you to connect and learn from other students, faculty, and the global alumni network, as well as collaborate and get involved. Here are just a few of the graduate clubs and organizations: Babson Entrepreneurship Forum, Asian Business Forum, Babson Association of Women MBAs, Babson Consulting Group, Babson Marketing Club, Babson Energy and Environmental Club and Net Impact. In addition to clubs and organization, Babson offers a variety of opportunities to analyze a real-time organizational opportunity and create value-added solutions. Through experiential learning, students enhance their classroom learning through real world experience, team dynamic skill building, and career insight. Learn more about experiential learning: http://www.babson.edu/Academics/graduate/mba/experiential-learning/Pages/default.aspx

FACULTY

Babson's faculty is an internationally and professionally diverse group. The faculty includes seasoned corporate executives, visionary entrepreneurs, and academic thought leaders. Learn more about Babson's faculty: www.babson.edu/Faculty

CAREERS

The Graduate Center for Career Development provides students comprehensive support in three interrelated areas: personal skill development, exploring industries and career paths, and targeting and securing opportunities. Each advisor aligns with a specific industry to better enhance relationships in the marketplace and establish expertise. Babson graduates are constantly making a difference as entrepreneurial leaders in organizations of all types and sizes. Learn more about our graduates at: http://www.babson.edu/student-life/career-development/graduate/Pages/default.asp

STUDENT BODY

The graduate student population reflects the global landscape as it is today-diverse, fast paced, and forward thinking. Students are pursuing their graduate degrees with varying focuses: switching careers, starting businesses, advancing careers, refining organizational impact in the near term, and poising themselves for continued growth with their employer in the long term. Babson students represent a variety of geographic and professional backgrounds, but their desire to become entrepreneurial leaders is the common thread.

Learn more about our students: http://www.babson.edu/admission/graduate/class-profile/Pages/default.aspx

CAMPUS AND LOCATION

Babson College has three campus locations—Wellesley, MA, Boston, MA and San Francisco CA. Main campus: Wellesley, MA; Boston campus; Blended Learning program offered at San Francisco campus

FACILITIES

Babson students have access to extensive business resources. For more information, go to: http://www.babson.edu/Academics/centers/Pages/home.aspx

BELMONT UNIVERSITY
The Jack C. Massey Graduate School of Business

AT A GLANCE

The Jack C. Massey Graduate School of Business provides graduate business programs (MBA and MACC) to working and aspiring professionals in the Nashville area. All classes are offered in a weeknight, evening format.

The Jack C. Massey Graduate School of Business was founded in 1986 through a gift from one of the country's most successful entrepreneurs. Mr. Massey remains as the only U.S. businessperson to ever take three different private companies (i.e., Kentucky Fried Chicken, HCA, and Winners Corp.) public to the New York Stock Exchange. The School was created to offer graduate business programs to Nashville area working professionals and offers a part-time and full-time MBA, as well as the Masters of Accountancy and a specialized part-time healthcare MBA--each in a weeknight, evening format on the Belmont University campus. Belmont is the only private university in Tennessee to maintain AACSB International accreditation in business and accounting. Massey's part-time MBA program was 28th in BusinessWeek's most recent national ranking of part-time MBA programs, and Fortune Magazine identified Belmont as one of the top five universities in the U.S. at which to study entrepreneurship.

DEGREES OFFERED

The Massey Graduate School offers two degree programs:

The Master of Business Administration (MBA) degree requires 34 credits, with 9 specialty tracks across accounting, business intelligence, entrepreneurship, finance, healthcare management, international business, marketing, music business and business negotiation. The MBA is offered in three formats: (1) a part-time "Professional MBA" version designed for working professionals with prior business experience and (2) a full-time "Accelerated MBA" version for individuals with little to no business work experience and (3) a part-time "Health Care MBA" version for industrials already in the health care industry. Classes for all programs are offered Monday–Thursday evenings throughout the year.

The Master of Accountancy (MACC) degree requires 30 credits and is designed to prepare students to meet the 150 hour CPA requirement, and a Becker CPA Review program is also available. MACC classes are offered year-round, Monday-Thursday evenings.

ACADEMIC PROGRAMS

The Jack C. Massey College of Business also includes the Center for Entrepreneurship, the Center for Business Ethics, Center for International Business, and the Center for Executive Education, each of which houses additional learning opportunities for students. A Summer Accounting Institute option for aspiring MACC students offers non-accounting undergraduates a fast-track opportunity to begin their graduate accounting course work and a Summer Business Institute offers aspiring MBA students who did not major in business as undergraduates a similar opportunity to complete all MBA prerequisites in a single summer .

All graduate students complete a brief study-abroad experience course as part of their degree requirements. Trips are scheduled between terms and typically last 8-10 days. Destination options for 2016-17 include Great Britain, Ireland, Peru, South Africa, South Korea, and Taiwan.

The curriculum is designed with 2-credit hour courses instead of the traditional 3-credit format. This gives Massey students a greater breadth of curriculum in the core business/accounting offerings, while also assuring a greater number of electives for matching to a particular student career plan. All students also complete a required entrepreneurship course, as well as preparation in business ethics.

Massey alumni appreciate the existence of the "Massey Passport" program that provides a lifetime opportunity for graduates to return to campus and attend graduate business classes for free on a space-available basis.

SPECIAL ACADEMIC PROGRAMS

Massey graduate students who complete elective coursework (2 courses) in business negotiation and mediation are eligible for listing as an "Approved Rule 31 Mediator; by the Supreme Court of the State of Tennessee. MBA and MACC students alike are also eligible to earn industry certifications in lean management and six sigma (both green and black belts).

FACULTY

Over 90% of graduate faculty are doctorally-qualified and full-time professors, while the remaining minority are full-time business executives. Continuing faculty are hired on the basis of their academic and professional preparation, as well as a demonstrated commitment to high-quality instruction.

CAREERS

The Massey School has a dedicated Career Development Center that provides comprehensive career services to graduate business students and alumni. Career Services are a lifetime benefit for alumni of The Massey School.

TUITION & AID

Tuition charges per course for 2016-17 are calculated at $3,170 for all MBA students and $2,460 for all MACC students. There are a limited number of scholarship opportunities (e.g., merit, financial need, minority status), as well as graduate assistant opportunities.

STUDENT BODY:

The typical Massey Professional MBA student has 6 years of business experience, is 29 years old, and works full-time, while completing the degree program in 2 years. The typical Accelerated MBA student has less than 2 years of business experience, is 23 years old, and is focused full-time on completing the degree program in 1 year. MACC students also tend to be somewhat younger as a group, with less business experience and are preparing to sit for the CPA exam. Many MACCs are full-time graduate students. Healthcare MBA students are similar to Professional MBAs but are already working within the health care industry prior to admission.

CAMPUS AND LOCATION

As an academic unit within Belmont University, The Massey Graduate School is located in the heart of Nashville, Tennessee, a rare place combining big-city charisma and small-town charm. Known internationally as "music city," Nashville is also a hotbed for entrepreneurship, healthcare, and international trade. Belmont University, a host campus for the 2008 U.S. Presidential Debates, is located on a 62-acre campus and maintains a total enrollment of—~7,500 students.

FACILITIES

All classes are held in the Jack C. Massey Business Center, which includes a variety of high-tech classrooms, computer labs, a finance trading center, and student support offices. Graduate students also have a separate computer lab workspace, as well as well-equipped study areas and high-tech collaboration spaces.

BENTLEY UNIVERSITY

AT A GLANCE

Bentley is a national leader in business education, blending the breadth and technological strength of a large university with the values and student focus of a small college. A Bentley education is designed to help our students thrive, with the ability to identify, create, and adapt to the changes inevitable in work and life. Located on a classic New England campus minutes from Boston, Bentley is a dynamic community of leaders, scholars and creative thinkers. The university enrolls approximately 1,430 graduate students and 43 doctoral students. Bentley is accredited by the New England Association of Schools and Colleges; AACSB International — The Association to Advance Collegiate Schools of Business; and the European Quality Improvement System, which benchmarks quality in management and business education.

Graduate study at Bentley University delivers expert preparation for what's next. Bentley's dynamic graduate courses are developed by faculty with industry-tested expertise, and informed by input from corporate leaders, giving our students exposure to current concepts and skills. The collection of centers and labs on campus features the latest tools for gathering and analyzing information in finance, marketing, information design, accountancy, and emerging technologies. And Bentley graduate students routinely tackle real business challenges for companies and other organizations, in team-driven consulting projects in the U.S. and abroad, giving them the opportunity to fine-tune their abilities in project management, presentation and collaboration.

At Bentley, students can pursue their degree on a schedule that fits their life. Our Professional MBA and eight MS programs offer options to study full time or part time; and many classes meet both on campus and online. And Bentley graduate programs draw professionals at every career stage, from a cross-section of industries. So they forge connections with accomplished individuals of different backgrounds, but with similar drive and focus. In this way, Bentley graduates become members of a lifelong global network of peers and alumni.

ADMISSIONS

Required documents include: completed online application and supplements, official transcripts from all prior course work, two written recommendations, résumé, GMAT/GRE scores and TOEFL scores for international applicants. Refer to the Graduate Admissions website for more information: bentley.edu/graduate/admission-financial-aid

DEGREES OFFERED

As a business university, Bentley offers academic programs targeted at the intersection of business and technology. An emphasis on continuous innovation underlies everything we do, from curriculum development to teaching methods to program delivery options.

ACADEMIC PROGRAMS

Three MBA Programs

No matter where students are right now in their careers and lives, Bentley has an MBA program to take them further. The three MBA programs, two full time and one part time, are tailored to students' academic backgrounds and professional experiences.

The Bentley MBA

The groundbreaking Bentley MBA takes a dramatically different approach to business education. This 11-month program replaces the traditional classroom setting with a powerful studio model that emphasizes collaboration. A select group of highly motivated students pursue four 10-week themes: Innovation, Value, Environments and Leadership. During three field-based trips — two of them international — students examine the role of business in different cultures and how organizations address urgent issues.

The Emerging Leaders MBA

The Emerging Leaders MBA is designed for recent college graduates who want to launch their career quickly with an added credential. Students gain technical knowledge of the key business disciplines, as well as a solid grounding in leadership, values, creativity and innovation. And our Emerging Leaders MBA program delivers real-world experience through a Business Process Management field project, Corporate Immersion class and a 10-day international Global Business Experience — so you'll be 100 percent prepared to make immediate contributions upon being hired.

The Professional MBA Program

The Professional MBA program is designed for those who need to balance the demands of work and family, offering flexibility, choice and the possibility of credit for prior academic work. In addition to foundation courses that expose students to all areas of business, the core of the program focuses on business process, strategic thinking, the application of technology, effective communication and ethical management. Students have opportunities to customize their MBAs with concentrations by choosing electives from eight specialty business disciplines. The program is available online in hybrid format.

Eight MS Programs

Bentley also offers eight Master of Science programs, giving our students the chance to develop expertise in a specific business discipline. They are grouped into two areas of focus: accounting and finance, and technology and analytics.

CAREERS

Our dedicated graduate team helps student learn how to leverage a graduate degree in the job market, fine tune personal and professional goals and connect with leading employers in a range of industries. Resources include the Career Management Series, recruitment and internship programs, career fairs, online databases, and more. One-on-one advising with an experienced career counselor helps sharpen career development goals. An active campus recruiting program links graduate students with top U.S. companies such as Liberty Mutual, Deloitte, EMC Corporation, and Raytheon.

TUITION & AID:

Tuition figures are program-dependent. Tuition for 2015-2016:

$77,930 Emerging Leaders MBA (foundation waivers are possible and will reduce the overall tuition cost)

$72,730 Bentley MBA (scholarships available)

$4,225 Cost per course for Professional MBA and MS Programs

CAMPUS AND LOCATION

Bentley is located in Waltham, Massachusetts, just 10 miles from Boston. Getting to Boston from Bentley is easy. The college runs a free shuttle bus to Harvard Square in Cambridge, where public transportation connects to the heart of the city.

CALIFORNIA STATE UNIVERSITY—LOS ANGELES
College of Business & Economics

AT A GLANCE
Accredited by the AACSB since 1960, the Cal State L.A. College of Business & Economics has consistently been a facet of the Los Angeles community that creates individuals who thrive in the ever-changing business world.

The college offers a range of graduate business programs that include MBA (with options in various fields of business), MS Accountancy, MA Economics, MS Health Care Management, and MS Information Systems.

With an emphasis on hands-on learning, students can expect to gain the type of knowledge that will not only prepare them for their future careers, but also act as the catalyst for innovative thinking.

PROGRAMS OFFERED
- MBA (Full-Time, Part-Time, Executive MBA)

With options in:
- Accounting
- Business Analytics
- Entertainment Business Management
- Entrepreneurship
- Finance
- Health Care Management
- Human Resource Management
- Information Systems
- International Business
- Management
- Marketing
- MS Accountancy
- MA Economics
- MS Health Care Management
- MS Information Systems

ACADEMIC PROGRAMS
As many of our students have full-time work responsibilities, our graduate business programs are designed to enable them to realize their career ambitions while successfully balancing their professional schedules. Typically, new students can expect to obtain their degrees within 18-24 months.

The College of Business & Economics is designed to offer a range of business disciplines to concentrate in while also providing a strong foundation giving students an enterprise-wide view. Our MBA provides our students with knowledge that widens their perspective and helps them to think strategically. For instance, an MBA candidate in marketing can expect to finish our program more experienced in quantitative areas of business, which becomes an asset to the student as they begin to work with the data that defines their marketing goals.

FACULTY
Cal State L.A.'s business faculty are award-winning teachers, scholars and mentors. With over 150 full-time and part-time professors coming from all walks of life, our faculty is proud to make an impact at the College of Business & Economics and provide their students with the knowledge they have obtained from their careers and life in general.

CAREERS
Cal State L.A. has many services available to all of its graduate students. Within the College of Business & Economics, the Student Services Center is available to offer services exclusive to our graduate students. Our Placement Coordinator is available to help our graduate students connect with Cal State L.A. partners for career and internship opportunities and hosts multiple workshops and events throughout the year. In addition, a full-time faculty advisor and international office are available to serve all our graduate students. Currently, the College of Business & Economics is partnered with local employers such as NBCUniversal, Boeing, NASA JPL, UPS, and many others.

TUITION & AID
Tuition for the program is approximately $25,000 ($36,000 for international students) and typically takes 18-24 months to complete. Scholarships and financial aid are available to qualified students.

STUDENT BODY
Residing in Southern California, our student body is extremely diverse and provides the backdrop for an educational experience that cannot be obtained anywhere but here. While many of our students are Los Angeles natives, a growing number of them are international and continue to bring a new sense of diversity as cultures from around the world converge in our programs.

The average age of our graduate students is 28 years old and typically they have several years of work experience (domestic or international). Typically, our students are in our program as a means for career development or career advancement.

CAMPUS AND LOCATION
Located only minutes away from Los Angeles' business hub, the College of Business & Economics offers the ideal situation for students pursuing their graduate business degree while gaining exposure to a huge urban laboratory where many kinds of business can thrive.

The College has the added luxury of being in the middle of a diverse set of neighboring communities and it gives our students a better understanding of the expanding landscape of business that they will soon be venturing into. Furthermore, on-campus events like the annual Business Pitch and other competitions bring our students together to collaborate and share new perspectives and experiences from within the Cal State L.A. community.

Our campus is spacious and gives its student body the perfect Southern California experience. We are extremely proud to offer modern campus amenities that continue to push the boundaries of education, but also showcase everything that has helped sculpt who we are today.

FACILITIES
The Cal State L.A. campus offers a variety of facilities that are open to graduate students from the College of Business & Economics. A 2-winged library sits adjacent to the newly renovated student union that is populated by numerous restaurants and outdoor dining areas. A few yards in either direction finds you next to the Luckman Fine Arts Complex or the University Athletics Center. Exclusive to the College of Business & Economics are the Nongshim Innovation Lab and 2 computer labs where graduate students can utilize state of the art technology to develop their ideas and collaborate with peers

CLARK UNIVERSITY
Graduate School of Management

The AACSB-accredited Clark Graduate School of Management offers quality programs in management, accounting, and finance. We offer the benefits of a large business school, in a smaller, more intimate setting.

AT A GLANCE
We Rank Among the Best Business Schools
Clark GSOM is a small, academically rigorous, AACSB-accredited business school that offers a personalized, collaborative learning experience. Since its launch in 1982, GSOM has embodied its mission to develop a diverse community of learners, researchers, and business professionals who think critically, manage collaboratively and contribute to their organizations and society.

Professors Who Don't Just Teach Best Practices; They've Helped Define Them.
Our faculty members are highly regarded experts in their fields. They lead all of your classes—not teaching assistants—and they are scholar-practitioners with significant experience and research in the fields of leadership, finance and corporate social responsibility. GSOM faculty are eager to provide students personal attention and professional insights. They truly love to teach, mentor and help students advance their careers.

LOCATION AND ENVIRONMENT
An Affordable East Coast Location that Keeps You Connected.
Clark's beautiful, tree-lined campus is located in Worcester, Massachusetts—the second largest city in New England. Living and studying in Worcester offers several distinct advantages, including affordable living options. The city is a center for biotechnology research, healthcare, financial services, higher education and green energy—an ideal setting for landing the right internship or job, and launching an enduring career.

Worcester's location in central Massachusetts is one of its greatest assets, with the cities of Boston, Providence, Hartford and Springfield—and the terrific prospects they offer in the media, financial, healthcare and insurance fields—only a short drive away. The campus is also only three hours from New York City.

OFF-CAMPUS OPPORTUNITIES:
Worcester is a diverse community with distinctive cultures that shape and flavor the city. Clark faculty and students engage with the city as partners through class projects and other collaborations. The city offers numerous cultural and recreational opportunities. Broadway-quality shows hit town at the Hanover Theatre for the Performing Arts, and the hiking trails in the Broad Meadow Brook Wildlife Sanctuary carve out a natural oasis within the city limits. From small local diners, to fine-dining on Shrewsbury Street, to cultural and ethnic eateries, the restaurant opportunities are endless. If you want more, you can be skiing in New Hampshire, swimming at Narragansett Beach in Rhode Island, or make a dinner run to Boston's North End within an hour.

ACADEMIC PROGRAMS
Degree Formats
Clark GSOM offers numerous options for completing your degree. Full or part-time options are available for the MBA, the Master of Science in Accounting, and the Master of Science in Management. A select number of courses are offered online each semester, and accelerated courses are offered during summer and certain school breaks. Day and evening options are available at both the Southborough, MA campus and the main campus in Worcester. In addition, MBA applicants with three or more years of managerial experience in a professional position are considered for the Professional Track, which offers up to two course waivers. Students can begin in January or September.

The Master of Science in Finance (MSF) and the various dual-degrees are offered only as full-time programs.

Beta Gamma Sigma Honor Society
GSOM is pleased to offer the prestigious Beta Gamma Sigma (BGS) honor society to its top students in each graduate program. BGS is an international honor society of students and scholars from business programs accredited by AACSB International. Every year, GSOM celebrates the academic achievement of its top performing students with a Beta Gamma Sigma induction ceremony and reception.

STUDY ABROAD
GSOM students can travel outside the U.S. to gain hands-on experience addressing global business issues through Clark's Global Programs. The Global Business Seminar is a capstone course that includes a week-long trip to an international business hub. The course focuses on a different country each year examining its business and economic environment and culminating with a visit to a variety of companies within the country. Past trips have included the Netherlands, Greece, Argentina, France, and China. The Doing Business in Northern Europe Program is an accelerated four-week business course that takes place at a major university in Sweden. Students may also apply to study for one semester at the Sorbonne in France.

CAMPUS FACILITIES AND EQUIPMENT
Libraries
GSOM students have access to numerous libraries and research spaces on campus, including the following:

Academic Commons at Goddard Library—The University's main library consists of a cutting-edge facility for research, teaching and learning by centralizing academic and research support services for students and faculty. It provides hundreds of thousands of traditional and electronic resources.

Jeanne X. Kasperson Research Library—The Kasperson Research Library offers one of the most extensive research collections in North America on environmental risk and hazards, and human dimensions of global environmental change.

Computer Labs
GSOM students have access to a dedicated computer lab, with necessary course software including Bloomberg and MATLAB. There are a number of general computing lab spaces throughout campus.

Athletic Facilities
All students have access to the athletic facilities on campus. The Kneller Athletic Center is the center of athletic life, featuring the primary basketball court, a recreational court, and space for indoor badminton, baseball, field hockey, lacrosse, running, soccer, softball, tennis, four racquetball courts and two squash courts. Also housed in the building is a six-lane, 25-yard competition-sized pool. Attached to the Kneller is the James and Ada B. Bickman Fitness Center, encompassing two floors of cardio and free weight equipment, as well as multipurpose space for our wellness-related classes and group fitness activities.

TUITION, ROOM, BOARD, AND FEES
Tuition varies by master's degree program. Applicants are encouraged to visit program web pages for accurate degree costs.

DUQUESNE UNIVERSITY
Donahue Graduate School of Business

AT A GLANCE

The Donahue Graduate School of Business at Duquesne University in Pittsburgh, Pennsylvania, prepares responsible leaders who are capable of transforming organizations, communities and the world. We challenge our students to reach their full potential, reflecting our university's century-long commitment to ethics and service, excellence and innovation. Among the graduate business schools accredited by AACSB-International, Duquesne was among the first 100 endorsers of the Principles for Responsible Management Education (PRME). The Donahue School was cited among the top three graduate business schools for ethics by the Academy of Management Learning and Education.

Duquesne's Donahue School offers contemporary and managerially relevant graduate programs to meet the needs of full-time students and working professionals:

JOINT DEGREE PROGRAMS:

The Donahue School offers MBA degrees in conjunction with advanced degrees in corporate communication, environmental science and management, health-management systems, industrial pharmacy, liberal studies, law, nursing, and pharmacy. To pursue a joint or dual degree program, candidates must apply to and be accepted by both schools.

COST OF STUDY

The MBA Sustainability program is billed in three equal installments. Tuition for 2016-17 is $18,277 per semester, totaling $54,831 for the three semester program. Tuition and fees do not include airfare, incidentals or some meals for the mandatory international study trip or any required pre-MBA coursework.

The Professional MBA, MAcc and MS-ISM programs are billed on a per credit basis. Tuition for the 2016-17 academic year is $1,234 per credit. Students may also qualify for a 25% tuition discount subject to availability.

The Master of Science in Management and Master of Science in Sports Business are billed on a per credit hour basis. Tuition for the 2016-17 academic year is $900 per credit.

LIVING AND HOUSING COSTS

Graduate housing is available on campus. Furnished and unfurnished studio, one and two bedroom apartments on campus can be rented at annual rates ranging from $15,370 to $26,830. Most graduate students prefer off-campus housing, which is abundant and affordable. The University's Office of Residence Life assists students in finding off-campus housing in Pittsburgh's many residential communities.

FINANCIAL AID

Full-time MBA Sustainability: All applicants are considered for merit scholarships, research fellowships and graduate assistantships based on the strength of application materials. A competitive GMAT or GRE score is required to be considered for a graduate assistantship or fellowship.

Professional MBA, MAcc, MS-ISM programs: A limited number of graduate assistantships, which provide up to 9 credits of tuition remission each semester, are available on a merit basis to high potential students who take the equivalent of a full-time course load (8 or more credits). A competitive GMAT or GRE score is required to be considered for a graduate assistantship.

STUDENT BODY

The Donahue Graduate School student body of approximately 350 students is diverse. Duquesne actively recruits and enrolls students from Africa, Asia, India, Europe, and Latin America, bringing an international dimension to every classroom. Professional MBA students make up about 85% of the study body. Many work at Pittsburgh's multinational and regional firms and bring real-world issues to the classroom experience. The MBA Sustainability students, over half of whom hail from outside the region, take their core courses as a cohort during the daytime. They bring a broad range of geographic, ethnic, educational and professional backgrounds to their studies and fieldwork. MAcc students take day and evening classes as a cohort of approximately 20 students. All graduate students interface regularly for idea cafes with corporate partners, symposia, case competitions, speaker events, intramural sports, and student organizations such as Net Impact and the Donahue Business Society.

CAMPUS AND LOCATION

Long noted as one of the world's great business centers, Pittsburgh combines the features of big-city living with many of the charms and personal characteristics of a much smaller town. Consistently ranked among the most livable cities for its safe neighborhoods and living standards, Pittsburgh has a large concentration of corporate headquarters, a strong civic identity and a sense of pride in its rebirth as a modern urban community. Duquesne and neighboring universities participate in a wide variety of cultural, social, recreational and sporting activities in Western Pennsylvania.

FACILITIES

Rockwell Hall, is a 10-story building which houses the John F. Donahue Graduate School of Business. Graduate students have access to sixteen classrooms, labs, and an investment center. Rockwell Hall also houses a student lounge, Carfang Commons, team suites, the School of Business Technology Center, Computing and Technology Services, Small Business Development Center, Career Services Center, and the Mills Complex.

The Investment Center offers access to syndicated databases and sophisticated analytical tools in a classroom setting that mimics worldwide trading operations with real-time data feeds for stocks, bonds, international markets, futures, options and other securities. Students have regular access to historical and current data from Bloomberg, Reuters, Morningstar, Ibbotson, Compustat, CSI and KLD and Trucost. Adjacent technology labs offer state-of-the-art software for enterprise resource planning (ERP), networking, modeling and computing.

Gumberg Library brings over 200 world-class e-research databases to students' fingertips. The university library itself houses over 710,500 volumes, more than 19,000 journal titles, and an extensive microprint and audiovisual center. Other library facilities include an online card catalog and interlibrary loan capabilities that gives students access to hundreds of additional periodicals not physically housed in the library.

INDIANA UNIVERSITY OF PENNSYLVANIA
Eberly College of Buisness and Information Technology

AT A GLANCE

The Eberly College of Business and Information Technology MBA program (accredited by AACSB International), with its global strategy focus and highly international student and faculty composition, is designed to sharpen students' managerial, analytical, and decision-making skills so that they can compete in today's global environment. The Eberly MBA program has a long tradition of providing cost-effective preparation for a successful career in business. IUP is consistently ranked among the best institutions in the region for cost and academic quality by a wide variety of sources such as: The Princeton Review's Best Business Schools; Kiplinger's Personal Finance Magazine; Barron's Best Buys in College Education; Forbes Magazine's America's Best Colleges, The New York Times; Money magazine; Entrepreneur Magazine and U.S. News and World Report.

ADMISSIONS

Requirements for admission include a completed undergraduate degree in any field with a superior academic track record from an accredited college/university, GMAT scores, academic/professional letters of recommendation, and the applicant's career goal statement and resume. The GMAT score of admitted candidates range from 450-710 with an average GMAT of 510; the average undergraduate grade point average is 3.1/4.0. GRE scores are accepted as a substitute for GMAT. International applicants must also submit an official TOEFL score report with a minimum score of 76 (iBT Score) or IELTS minimum score of 6.0 and an affidavit of financial support indicating availability of sufficient funds to study in the U.S. For information and a complete application packet, visit www.iup.edu/mba ; contact Dr. Krish Krishnan, Eberly College MBA Program, 421 Eberly College of Business and Information Technology, IUP, 664 Pratt Drive, Indiana, PA 15705; or e-mail iup-mba@iup.eduor Krishnan@iup.edu; Telephone: 1-724-357-2522, Fax: 1-724-357-6232

DEGREES OFFERED

Eberly College offers a full-time, on-campus MBA program for young professionals and recent college graduates that can be completed in 12 months. In addition, an executive MBA program for experienced working professionals is available at IUP's off-campus sites in the Monroeville, Northpointe (Pittsburgh) and Johnstown area. In collaboration with our international partner universities we offer the IUP MBA program in Bangalore, India and executive MBA program in Palestine. The college also offers bachelor's degrees in accounting, entrepreneurship and small business management, finance, general management, human resource management, supply chain management, international business, management information systems, and marketing.

ACADEMIC PROGRANS

The Eberly MBA is a 36-credit, integrated, general management program with an option to complete concentrations/specializations (nine/twelve additional credits) in Finance, Human Resource Management, International Business, Management Information Systems, Marketing, Professional Accountancy or Supply Chain Management. The MBA courses focus on business applications and current analytical tools and techniques, and strongly emphasize information technology utilization in managerial problem solving. A variety of elective courses are available in each of the concentration areas. Opportunities are available for internships with local, national, and international organizations.

FACULTY

Eberly MBA courses are taught by faculty members who have doctoral degrees in their fields of specialization and extensive research and publication track records. Their international backgrounds and/or exposure, experience in industry, and current research projects bring an ideal blend of theory and practice to the MBA courses. Eberly faculty members serve as editors on nine national/international journals.

CAREERS

IUP assists MBA students with job placement through its recruiting programs, computerized job-search database, resume referrals, individual counseling, workshops, and job fairs. Many major corporations recruit on the IUP campus, and recent MBA graduates have accepted positions with companies such as Accenture, Amazon.com, BNY Mellon, BearingPoint, Citizens Bank, PNC Bank, Coca-Cola, Deloitte & Touche, Deutsche Bank, Dow Chemical, Ernst & Young, GE, IBM, Merrill Lynch, MetLife,, PPG, Renault, Rockwell International, Siemens, Symantec, Walt Disney, and World Bank. During 2016, the Eberly College held a "Business Day" that attracted more than 48 businesses and governmental agencies. Eberly College of Business also assists international students with career workshops and placement support for summer internships as well as practical training positions after graduation.

STUDENT BODY

Eberly provides students with an opportunity to learn with a diverse group of individuals. More than half the students are from 24 countries other than the U.S., 22 percent have previous business work experience, and 8 percent are currently working full-time in professional careers. Eberly College takes great pride in the activities and initiatives of its College of Business Student Advisory Council and the members of its 14 student organizations. Eberly College of Business Graduate Business Students Association provides MBA students professional development opportunities including participation in regional and national case competitions, company visits, career-fair visits and group visits to professional and business organizations in New York, Chicago and Washington DC.

CAMPUS AND LOCATION

Indiana University of Pennsylvania enrolls 14,369 students from across the nation and around the globe. Located in the heart of Indiana, Pa. (70 miles Northeast of Pittsburgh, PA), IUP's main campus has grown from twelve acres and one building in 1875, to 374 acres, 59 major buildings and 11 athletic fields. There are 892 international students at IUP representing 44 states and 61 countries. In recent years, IUP has replaced more than a dozen residential and academic buildings to enhance the campus's living-learning environment. The small town atmosphere of Indiana PA brings the double advantage of low cost of living as well as safe and friendly living environments to the students. Proximity to the city of Pittsburgh brings the connections with major businesses and corporations of the area to enhance internship and career building opportunities.

FACILITIES

A state-of-the-art, $12-million facility houses the MBA classrooms. The Eberly complex is a beautiful, four-story facility that offer a spacious atrium for student interaction and studying, complete wireless access, a cafe, a 450-seat auditorium, and a public computing lab operation. Students of the Eberly College study in one of the most technologically advanced business schools in the country. The Eberly complex houses more than 600 computer workstations, more than 20 file servers, nine computing labs (including a financial trading room and advanced financial trading room), digital production studio; wireless technology throughout the campus, and online access to comprehensive business periodicals and journals databases. The college also houses a Small Business Institute, Small Business Development Center, and a Small Business Incubator where MBA students can gain business consulting and entrepreneurship experience. The Financial Trading Room in Eberly offers students databases and related software to conduct financial analysis and learn valuation techniques, arbitrage techniques, and portfolio risk-management strategies. Eberly also offers the Bloomberg Professional service software system, an industry-grade comprehensive data-monitoring and analytical tool used to train students to study real-time movements in global markets. The marketing department of the college houses the Consumer Neuroscience lab for research in the field of buyer behavior in which MBA students can participate as research assistants.

RICE UNIVERSITY
Jesse H. Jones Graduate School of Business

AT A GLANCE

Rice University aspires to path-breaking research, excellence in teaching and contributions to the enhancement of our world. As the university's business school, The Jesse H. Jones Graduate School of Business adheres to those same values to cultivate a diverse community of learning and discovery. More specifically, the Jones School develops principled, innovative thought leaders in global communities. Through a combination of rigorous curriculum, elite faculty and impressive facilities, students receive an outstanding business school experience. The result is innovative leadership that engages the entrepreneurial spirit and impacts business on a global level. The Jones School is one of the world's best teaching and research universities, offering Full-Time MBA, MBA for Executives, and MBA for Professionals programs. A Ph.D. program debuted in 2009 and business concentrations highlight the school's strengths while allowing full-time MBA students to focus on areas of interest.

ADMISSIONS

The Jones School considers each aspect of the application when making admissions decisions. The application requirements include: GMAT or GRE (GRE or MCAT for joint degree candidates); TOEFL or PTE for some international applicants; transcripts from educational institutions; resume; confidential evaluations; essays; interview (invitation only); completed application form and application fee. Academic Background: A four-year undergraduate degree from an accredited college or university is required for U.S. applicants. International applicants must have an undergraduate degree equivalent to a four-year U.S. degree. Undergraduate and graduate GPAs, GMAT or GRE scores (GRE or MCAT for joint degree candidates), choice of major, electives, course load, and grade patterns are all considered. Leadership Potential: Demonstrated leadership and management experiences, both on the job and through extracurricular activities, will help us assess leadership potential. We look for individuals with at least two years of professional work experience although there is always room for superstars. Confidential Evaluations: Evaluations from employers provide perspective on potential student capabilities, enabling us to assess your qualifications more accurately. Essays: Essays articulating career goals, work experience, and reasons for choosing the Rice MBA program are a crucial component of the application process. These essays are designed to convey intangibles such as reasons for pursuing an MBA; benefits of academic, professional and personal opportunities; and personal expectations of the Jones School experience.

DEGREES OFFERED

The Jones School focuses all of its energy on graduate business education. A Rice MBA is available three distinct programs (Full-Time, MBA for Professionals and MBA for Executives) designed to accommodate students at every stage of their career. Also available are an MBA/Masters in Engineering (MBA/ME) in conjunction with the George R. Brown College of Engineering at Rice, and MBA/Professional Science Masters (MBA/PSM) in conjunction with the Wiess School of Natural Sciences at Rice, and an MBA/MD in conjunction with Baylor College of Medicine. Also available is the Master of Accounting (MAcc) degree which is a one-year degree program. The Jones School also offers a Ph.D. in Management to develop business school faculty.

ACADEMIC PROGRAMS

Every course offers unparalleled opportunity to work one-on-one with an accessible, involved, and energetic faculty. The Jones School faculty maintains an important balance between teaching and research, believing that current industry knowledge is as critical as textbooks to your education.

A comprehensive core curriculum focuses on managerial and leadership skills, ethics, information technology, and communication skills in addition to the functional areas. Students take elective credit hours, which allow them to custom design their curriculum to suit career goals.

FACULTY

The Jones School's faculty is consistently recognized for their knowledge, research, teaching ability, and student focus. Each member of the Jones faculty maintains a balance between teaching and research, ensuring that students receive the most current, leading-edge education. Recognized for their exceptional academic achievements as evidenced by peer-reviewed journal publications and other scholarly activity, the business school faculty at Rice University have distinguished themselves nationally and internationally. To find clear, quick translations of their bold ideas, try reading ricebusinesswisdom.com. It will change the way you think.

CAREERS

The Career Management Center (CMC) is housed within the Jones School building and works only with Rice MBA students and alumni. The CMC serves to support each student's development of a career plan throughout their two years at the Jones School. From day one of immersion to graduation, the CMC works individually with students and alumni to ensure they develop the strategy, job search skills, and networking opportunities that will help them succeed in the MBA job market.

TUITION & AID

Tuition: $53,000 for the 2016-2017 academic year for the Full-Time program. The total two-year tuition for the MBA for Professionals program for students beginning in fall 2016 is $98,500 (evenings) or $102,000 (weekends). The total two-year tuition for the MBA for Executives program for students beginning in fall 2016 is $115,000.

FINANCIAL AID

Over 82 percent of students attending the Full-Time MBA program receive merit-based scholarships. Rice University's Office of Student Financial Services also administers a variety of federally and privately funded loan programs. The Jones Graduate School has over 40 distinct, named, merit-based scholarships. Our top three flagship scholarships are: James W. Crownover Scholarship, The Military Scholars Program, The McNair Scholars Program sponsored by the Robert and Janice McNair Foundation. We are thrilled to support military veterans who are making a transition to civilian life after serving our country. In addition, we have been designated to be a 2016 Military Friendly school by Victory Media. The Jones Graduate School is focusing a portion of its recruiting efforts on U.S. veterans. This military student support encompasses scholarships, extensive funding of the Post 911 Yellow Ribbon Program, access to our renowned Veterans in Business Association (VIBA), along with a network of alumni and community members who support our military veterans.

STUDENT BODY

The Jones School attracts students both nationally and internationally. In fact, 36 percent of the first year students hail from outside the United States and an additional 18 percent are from outside of Texas. A variety of student organizations are available and many sponsor guest speakers, visit area businesses, and take on special projects. In addition, weekly corporate-sponsored "partios"—parties on the Jones School patio—provide relaxation and opportunities to network and bond with fellow students.

CAMPUS AND LOCATION

Rice University is located on a beautiful wooded 300-acre campus in central Houston, minutes from the downtown business district and the city's world-class theater district. The campus is located across the street from the renowned Texas Medical Center and within walking distance to the museum district, Houston Zoological Gardens, and Hermann Park.

RENSSELAER POLYTECHNIC INSTITUTE
Lally School of Management

AT A GLANCE

The Lally School of Management was founded in 1963 as an integral part of Rensselaer Polytechnic Institute.

Building on Rensselaer's heritage of more than 190 years of leadership in science and engineering, the Lally School develops technologically-savvy, entrepreneurial business leaders who can initiate and guide innovation for commercial success. All programs enable the next generation of business leaders to combine their passion for technology with the management ability to succeed in today's challenging global marketplace.

ADMISSIONS

The Lally School of Management attracts candidates who clearly articulate and act on their personal and professional goals. Accepted candidates share a strong entrepreneurial spirit and are confident about their analytical and quantitative skills. Required items include completion of the online Rensselaer graduate application, essay, resume, transcripts, letters of recommendation, and a GMAT or GRE score. The TOEFL is required for international applicants.

DEGREES OFFERED

- MBA
- MS Business Analytics
- MS Management
- MS Quantitative Finance & Risk Analytics
- MS Supply Chain Management
- MS Technology Commercialization and Entrepreneurship
- PhD research program
- Part-time study is available for most programs

ACADEMIC PROGRAMS

The Lally MBA program prepares business leaders with the skills and thinking that are essential for meeting the day-to-day, real-world challenges of running a business within the evolving dynamics of the global economy. Through experiential hands-on instruction, students acquire an overall understanding of the new sources of value creation brought about by the convergence of globalization and the information technology (IT) revolution.

The curriculum enables students to gain critical expertise in launching, running, and growing a successful business: creating and managing an enterprise; value creation, managing networks, and driving innovation; developing innovative products and services; formulating and executing competitive business strategies; and managing the business implications of emerging technologies. Courses focus on critical business issues in today's global marketplace and integrate all discrete business functions, from finance and operations to global marketing and supply chain management. Key modules include global business, decision models, social responsibility and business ethics, and succeeding in knowledge intensive organizations. Additional programs: See http://lallyschool.rpi.edu

FACULTY

Lally's faculty are scholars of significant standing and deep experience in a wide range of business contexts. They are research-oriented and focus on advancing business through using the basic disciplines of economics, behavioral science, and analytical methods.

Our clinical faculty strive to exploit their experience and professional expertise to turn theory into practice. They bring real world business experiences into the Lally learning environment.

CAREERS

The Lally School Career Resource Center provides extensive career resources including workshops, mock interview sessions, and career counseling. Lally's industry partners work with us to influence curriculum to meet the most current demands in an ever-changing workplace; provide meaningful internship and co-op experiences for students; and create industry programs that become the platform for cutting-edge faculty research.

TUITION & AID

Full-time graduate tuition for the 2016–17 academic year is $49,520. Other costs (estimated living expenses, insurance, etc.) are projected to be about $19,250. Therefore, the cost of attendance for full-time graduate study is approximately $68,770 per year. Part-time study and cohort programs are priced separately.

Upon application to the Lally School for the full-time graduate programs, students are automatically considered for financial aid. Financial aid is competitive and granted based on merit.

Financing options include:
Federal Stafford Loans—contact the Rensselaer Financial Aid Office at 518-276-6813.

Merit-based:
- Tuition scholarship– MBA and MS students automatically considered
- Tuition scholarship and teaching or research assistantships—PhD students

Named fellowships:
- Herman Family Foundation Fellowship for Women in Entrepreneurship
- Bozzone Fellowship (Production and Operations concentration).
- Reinert Raider Fellowship (Finance concentration).
- Raymond A. and Ina C. Best Fellowship—Tau Beta Pi Fellowship

Third-party loans:
- GMAC MBA (1-888-440-4622).
- Sallie Mae.
- Access Group.org

Internship opportunities may also be available via the Rensselaer Entrepreneur Internship Program and the Office of Career Services.

CAMPUS AND LOCATION

Rensselaer's 275 acre campus is a blend of modern style and classic design. Built into a hillside, it overlooks the Hudson River and the city of Troy, which is experiencing a rebirth as an emerging hotbed of startups, restaurants and artist galleries. The area offers a relaxed lifestyle with many cultural and recreational opportunities, with easy access to both the high-energy metropolitan centers of the Northeast—Boston, New York City, and Montreal, Canada—and the quiet beauty of the neighboring Adirondack Mountains. Rensselaer is committed to a campus culture and engaging student experience where students can learn and grow in an environment that encourages discovery, creativity, innovation, and diversity.

FACILITIES

The Lally School of Management is located in one of Rensselaer's most historic buildings, now a technology-intensive center for teaching and research.

The facility features four large classrooms with facilities that are computer-interactive, and set up for videoconferencing. The building also includes fully networked faculty and staff offices, wireless access, a computer study hall, student and faculty lounges, a centrally located student services suite, and a food service concession.

UNIVERSITY OF HOUSTON—VICTORIA
School of Business Administration

AT A GLANCE

Quality—The University of Houston-Victoria School of Business Administration is accredited by AACSB International, the hallmark of excellence in management education. The business school has been ranked number one for the Greatest Opportunity for Minority Students, serving students from nearly 25 countries by award winning faculty from more than 12 countries. Value—The school has been named nationally as one of the "Top 25 Ranked Best Buys" in distance learning by GetEducated.com for the past five years, and UHV consistently ranks in the top four best value Texas Universities for affordability. Convenience—Face-to-face evening courses are offered in Katy, Texas, as well as online. Students outside the Houston area may complete all their Master of Business Administration coursework online. The Global MBA students have an online capstone assignment and the Strategic MBA students are required to participate in person in a one-day MBA conference prior to completing their degree. Houston-area students may combine face-to-face and online courses and create a schedule to fit around their professional life. UHV is considered a national leader in distance education and online course delivery and the MBA has been offered completely online since 1999. The convenient program formats allow students to continue their education part time in conjunction with a full-time career or accelerate degree completion as a full-time student.

LOCATION AND ENVIRONMENT

Victoria is located 30 miles inland from the Gulf of Mexico in the Coastal Bend of Texas, within two hours of Corpus Christi, Austin, San Antonio and Houston. The city is a safe, small city that serves as the regional hub for a seven-county area known as the Crossroads because of its location. The population is about 65,000 people. Business programs also are offered at an off-campus location in Katy close to the energy corridor.

GRADUATE DEGREES OFFERED

The University of Houston-Victoria's School of Business Administration has one of the largest AACSB accredited MBA programs in Houston for a reason. We make it our mission to transform your life's aspirations into reality through our unique and specialized MBA degrees. Here are some reasons that UHV stands out:

- Affordable tuition that is lower than most private online schools
- Faculty who are full-time researchers with Ph.Ds
- Classes taught by full time faculty, not adjuncts

Our degrees are designed to boost our graduates' careers and elevate their knowledge base in a targeted specialty. We offer three unique degrees and two special programs that allow students who received their undergraduate degrees with 90 hours to obtain an MBA degree in the U.S.

- Global MBA
- Strategic MBA
- MS in Economic Development & Entrepreneurship
- Fourth-year Bridge Global MBA
- Fourth-year Bridge Strategic MBA

The MBA concentration comprises one fourth of the curriculum and allows student to customize their program to best fit their interests and career goals. The concentration choices are: Accounting, Economic Development; Entrepreneurship, Finance, General Business, Human Resources Management, International Business (except Global MBA), Management and Marketing.

Fourth-year Bridge MBA and Global MBA programs are designed for students holding a three-year bachelor's degree from outside the U.S. to earn an MBA.

The Master of Science in Economic Development and Entrepreneurship program is a 36-credit-hour, entirely online curriculum ideal for entrepreneurs and those working in the economic development field of attracting and growing businesses.

EXPENSES AND FINANCIAL AID

For 2016-2017, tuition and fees for Texas residents are $477.40 per graduate credit hour. Non-residents pay $835.39 per credit hour. The UHV School of Business Administration has been named one of the "Top 25 Ranked Best Buys" in distance learning by GetEducated.com for the past five years. UHV offers scholarships, grants and loan options as well as payment plans to assist students with funding their education. A limited number of graduate assistantships and fellowships also are available.

FACULTY

Business programs are taught by faculty from more than 12 countries, with Ph.Ds from schools such as University of Texas in Austin, Arizona State, Indiana University, Michigan State, University of Illinois, Georgia State and Syracuse. Most importantly, faculty members are dedicated teachers who are responsive and accessible to students, and are active researchers with publications in leading journals in their fields.

STUDENT ORGANIZATIONS AND ACTIVITIES

The Business Student Association, Beta Gamma Sigma Honor Society, the Houston chapter of the National Society of Hispanic MBAs and the UHV chapter of the National Association of Women MBAs are amongst the organizations available to join.

The Dean's Distinguished Speaker series is held in the fall and spring semesters and brings business leaders to campus where they candidly share their experiences for the benefit of students. During the spring semester, alumni speak to classes, connecting the MBA program to a wide range of careers in finance, information technology, engineering management, healthcare administration, accounting and real estate.

ADMISSIONS PROCESS

Applications are processed on a rolling admission basis. Application deadlines only apply to international students. The individual attention for which UHV School of Business Administration is known begins with the admission process. Admission requirements for the MBA program include the following:

- An overall GPA of 2.5, or a GPA of 2.5 based on your last 60 hours of coursework.
- A GMAT score of 450 or a GRE score of 292. Students may enroll in ONE semester (maximum nine hours of gradu¬ate coursework) without official GMAT scores on file. Students who have earned an undergraduate GPA of 3.0 or higher and have relevant professional work experience are eligible to apply for a GMAT waiver.
- International student admission is listed at www.uhv.edu/international.
- Online application with no application fee.
- Admissions decisions are made promptly and early application is encouraged but not required.
- Temporary graduate admission allows one semester of enrollment before GMAT/GRE scores are filed.

To apply, complete the Apply Texas application form and send official, sealed transcripts to:

Admissions Office
University of Houston-Victoria
3007 N. Ben Wilson St.
Victoria, TX 77901

UNIVERSITY OF ROCHESTER
Simon Business School

AT A GLANCE

Simon Business School at the University of Rochester in Rochester, New York offers a highly personalized, global business education experience. Our world-class faculty and diverse student body create a truly international experience and help make Simon one of the nation's top-ranked business schools. At Simon, you'll be part of a results-oriented but highly intimate community that values teamwork in addition to academic excellence. Programs offered are Full-Time MBA and MS programs, Executive MBA, Professional MBA, and Part-Time MS programs. The school is accredited by the AACSB-The Association to Advance Collegiate Schools of Business since 1966.

ADMISSIONS

The Simon Business School Admissions Committee reads each application individually and evaluates recommendations, teamwork, and communication skills, the nature and scope of prior work experience, the undergraduate academic record, and GMAT or GRE scores. All undergraduate majors are represented in the program.

DEGREES OFFERED
Full-Time Study

Simon Business School offers several exciting and challenging MBA program options. Whether you are a young professional just starting your career, or a seasoned veteran looking to sharpen and update your skills, these programs offer full immersion into the business school experience. It's a deep dive that delivers results and helps prepare you for today's business challenges.

Simon's traditional Two-Year MBA program is truly the hallmark option for full-time students who are looking to propel their careers with a fully immersive experience. This program includes the opportunity for a summer internship and offers competitive concentrations that provide the practical experience and business skills every professional needs.

- Competitive and Organizational Strategy, including tracks in Strategy and Organizations and Pricing
- Corporate Accounting
- Entrepreneurship
- Finance
- Marketing, including tracks in Marketing Strategy, Pricing, and Brand Management
- Business Systems Consulting
- Computers and Information Systems
- Health Sciences Management
- International Management
- Operations Management
- Public Accounting

Professional MBA (PMBA)

The PMBA program utilizes a partial lockstep, class cohort system in which teams of students take their nine core courses together in a structured program. Then 11 electives are required to complete the desired concentrations. Continuing at two classes per quarter, cohort members typically complete their degrees in 2.5 years. There are two entrance dates, March or September.

Executive MBA Program (EMBA)

The EMBA program offers candidates the same curriculum, resources, and faculty as the full-time program without career interruption. Classes meet every other Saturday, and one Friday per month. Blackboard Collaborate technology allows students to attend the second Saturday online, as needed. As a result, students have the option to attend on campus one weekend per month. Simon Business School also offers an EMBA program in Bern, Switzerland. (The program is completed in 22 months).

MS Programs

Full-Time MS program options include: Accountancy, Finance, Marketing Analytics and Business Analytics. Simon Business School also offers Part-Time MS programs in Finance, Marketing Analytics, Business Analytics, Management, and Medical Management.

MS Programs in NYC

The School also offers two 13-month Master of Science programs in New York City: Finance starts each year in March and Health Care Management starts each year in July. These programs are designed for working professionals who seek an advanced degree on an accelerated part-time basis.

ACADEMIC PROGRAMS

Simon Business School's analytic, economics-based curriculum provides students with powerful and enduring frameworks to explain and predict the behavior of markets, organizations, and individual decision makers. As a result, our graduates are thoroughly prepared to take on the ever-changing marketplace throughout their careers. Our faculty helps them get there not only through a challenging, rigorous education, but also with support, coaching, and personalized instruction. Simon emphasizes teamwork, allowing each student to benefit from the diverse makeup of the student body that has hailed from over 130 different countries over the years and a variety of personal and professional backgrounds. Over 15,000 graduates form an influential network extending around the globe, and contribute in varied and significant ways to the worlds of business, academia, and public policymaking.

CAREERS

The Career Management Center team works diligently to develop new and enhance existing corporate partnerships to provide a wide range of career opportunities for both summer internships and full-time career positions. The Career Management Center's staff offers a targeted, personalized approach to assist students in identifying, initiating, and implementing highly effective career search plans. 2015 Full-Time MBA Career Placement Results 96 percent of students secured job placement three months post graduation Simon ranks No. 8 among US business schools for job placement three months post graduation among ranked business schools (Bloomberg Businessweek, October 2015).

TUITION & AID

In addition to the $150 application fee, estimated tuition is $46,000/year for 2015-2016. Books, fees, room and board, personal, and health insurance expenses are estimated at approximately $21,352 for the 2015-2016 academic year. Both US and international applicants are eligible for merit awards. In fact, Simon Business School offers merit-based scholarship support to over 80% of our incoming Full-Time MBA students each year.

STUDENT BODY

Approximately 400 full-time MBA and MS students join the Simon community every year. August entrants complete the first-year core courses during the fall and winter quarters. The majority of January entrants complete core courses during the winter, spring, and summer quarters. In the MBA Class of 2017, 18 countries are represented; prior full-time work experience averages 5.5 years, and the average age is 28. Women comprise 44 percent of the class.

CAMPUS AND LOCATION

Simon Business School is situated on the River Campus of the University of Rochester, near the banks of the Genesee River, and three miles from downtown Rochester, New York. It is one of seven schools and colleges within the University of Rochester. Simon also has a presence in New York City, where it offers part-time MS programs in Finance and Health Care Management.

WILLAMETTE UNIVERSITY

AT A GLANCE

Willamette's Early Career MBA prepares students for their first professional position or career change. In 21 months, students build the knowledge and experience they need to fast-track their career. As a national leader in experiential learning, the Willamette MBA builds knowledge, experience and professional career management skills needed for successful careers in business, government and not-for-profit organizations. Programs include the Early Career and Career Change MBA for students preparing for their first professional position, career change or advancement; and the MBA for Professionals for experienced students seeking career enhancement or advancement. All of Willamette MBA programs emphasize hands-on learning and are accredited by AACSB International—the global hallmark of excellence in business education.

ADMISSIONS

Applicants for the Early Career and Career Change MBA program should visit http://willamette.edu/mba/programs/eccc/index.html for information.

Applicants for the MBA for Professionals program should visit http://willamette.edu/mba/programs/professionals/index.html for information.

ACADEMIC PROGRAMS

The Early Career and Career Change MBA is designed for students seeking career entry, change or advancement. The program emphasizes learning-by-doing, and does not require previous work experience. From the first day of class, students apply what they learn to real organizations and develop the tools they need to manage, lead and succeed. In 21 months, Early Career and Career Change MBA students learn the core principles of management and strategic decision-making; refine their career interests; build a resume of respected professional experience; and develop in-depth expertise in one or more career areas of interest:

Accounting
Entrepreneurship
Finance
Global Management
Human Resources
Marketing
Operations, Analysis & Systems
Organizational Analysis
Public & Not-for-Profit Management
Sustainability Management

The MBA for Professionals allows individuals with three or more years of professional work experience to complete their MBA while employed. The program is 24 months long, and features experiential learning and convenient evening classes. Students immediately apply what they learn to their job and accelerate their careers.

SPECIAL ACADEMIC PROGRAMS

The Willamette Early Career MBA builds professional experience through internships; consulting projects with client organizations; and innovative elective courses. Students have the opportunity to learn SAP and other analytical tools; manage the student investment fund; participate as a member of an angel investing group; launch an entrepreneurial venture; and apply management skills to real organizations through class projects and internships.

FACULTY

Willamette MBA faculty are award-winning teachers, scholars and mentors. They believe that great MBA teaching emphasizes the importance of an integrated understanding of management decision-making and the application of what you learn to real organizations. Our faculty are also easily accessible and dedicated to the success of their students and alumni.

CAREERS

An outstanding career services team supports the goals of Willamette MBA students. Services include the best practices of career management, workshops, internships, networking, employment connections and interviews, individual counseling, mentoring, coaching, career and networking events and professional student organizations.

Nearly all of Early Career and Career Change students participate in an internship. Sample internship employers includes Adidas, Deloitte, Hewlett Packard, Morgan Stanley Smith Barney, Intel, Microsoft, Nike, Tektronix, Willamette Humane Society, Mercy Corps Northwest, and State of Oregon.

More than 85% of Early Career and Career Change students receive a job offer within three months of graduation. Typical employers include Avanade, Bank of America, Ford Motor Company, Nike Inc., Hewlett Packard Company, Intel Corporation, Overstock.com, State of Oregon and Tektronix.

TUITION & AID

2016-17 tuition for the Early Career and Career Change MBA is $39,100 for the two semester academic year. Merit-based scholarships, Federal Unsubsidized Loans and Federal Graduate Plus Loans are available to eligible students.

2016-17 tuition for the MBA for Professionals is $69,200 (total cost) for the six semester program. MBA for Professionals tuition includes the cost of books and fees. Merit-based scholarships, Federal Unsubsidized Loans and Federal Graduate Plus Loans are available to eligible students.

STUDENT BODY

Our students are energetic, creative, ethical, exceptional, friendly, mature, hardworking, insightful, professional, reliable, team-players and leaders. Early Career and Career Change students come from around the world and across the U.S. The average age of student is 24, has zero to five years of work experience, and is utilizing the MBA to prepare for career entry or career change.

MBA for Professionals students have three or more years of work experience and are preparing for career advancement and enhancement. The average age is 33 years old and employed while completing their MBA. Students represent a wide variety of businesses and organizations from the Portland/Salem metropolitan areas.

CAMPUS AND LOCATION

The Salem and Portland metro areas offer an excellent quality of life, friendly people, mild climate and the recreational resources of the beautiful Pacific Northwest. Professionally, the Portland-Salem corridor provides convenient access to a multitude of businesses (including Northwest legends Nike and Intel) and a number of government and not-for-profit organizations.

Willamette MBA students are an active community who benefit from a vibrant recreational and social life. Students can ski the Cascade Mountains; enjoy Oregon's Pacific Coast; windsurf in the Columbia River Gorge; hike forested areas; participate in student activities and professional organizations; and enjoy the big city opportunities of Portland. Willamette's campus is spacious and beautiful, and located across the street from the state capitol in downtown Salem.

FACILITIES

The Salem campus includes two libraries, recreational and fitness facilities, dining centers, student center, concert hall, art museum, and more. The Portland Center is conveniently located in the Pearl District with easy access to public transportation and public parking. All facilities offer WiFi, email, network software and printing services.

DECODING DEGREES

Many business programs offer a number of degrees, including joint- or combined-degree programs with other departments (or with other schools) that you can earn along with your MBA. You'll find the abbreviations for these degrees in the individual school profiles, but we thought we'd give you a little help in figuring out exactly what they are.

AGSIM	American Graduate School of International Management Social Service Administration		MA	Master of Arts
			MAB	Master of Agribusiness
APC	Advanced Professional Certificate		MAcc	Master of Accountancy (or Accounting)
BA	Bachelor of Arts		MAAE	Master of Arts in Applied Economics
BASC	Bachelor in Engineering		MAEcon	Master of Arts in Economics
BBA	Bachelor of Business Administration		MAg	Master of Agriculture
BPA	Bachelor of Public Affairs		MAIB	Master of Arts in International Business
BS	Bachelor of Science		MAIS	Master of Accounting and Information Systems
BSB	Bachelor of Science in Business			
BSBA	Bachelor of Science in Business Administration		MALL	Master of Arts in Language Learning
			MAPS	Master of Asian Pacific Studies
CIS	Computer Information Systems (or Sciences)		MAR	Master of Arts in Religion
			MArch	Master of Architecture
DBA	Doctor of Business Administration		MAS	Master of Actuarial Science
DDS	Doctor of Dental Surgery		MBA	Master of Business Administration
DMD	Doctor of Dental Medicine		MBE	Master of Business Education
DO	Doctor of Osteopathic Medicine		MBI	Master of Business Informatics
DPS	Doctor of Professional Studies		MBS	Master of Business Studies
EdD	Doctor of Education		MD	Doctor of Medicine
EDM	Executive Doctor of Management		MDIV	Master of Divinity
EMBA	Executive MBA		ME	Master of Engineering
EMIB	Executive Master of International Business		MECOM	Master of Electronic Commerce
EMPA	Executive Master of Public Administration		MEd	Master of Educational Leadership/ Master of Education
EMS	Executive Master of Science			
EMSM	Executive Master of Science in Management		MEM	Master of Engineering and Management
			MEng	Master of Engineering
EMSMOT	Executive Master of Science in Management of Technology		MF	Master of Forestry
			MFA	Master of Fine Arts
EMST	Executive Master of Science in Taxation		MHA	Master of Health Administration
GDPA	Graduate Diploma in Accounting		MHR	Master of Human Resources
GEMBA	Global Executive Master of Business Administration		MHRM	Master of Human Resources Management
HRIM	Hotel, Restaurants and Institutional Management		MIA	Master of International Affairs
			MIAS	Master of International and Area Studies
IAMBA	Information Age Master of Business Administration		MIB	Master of International Business
			MIE	Master of Industrial Engineering
IMBA	International MBA		MILR	Master of Industrial and Labor Relations
IPD	Interdisciplinary Product Development		MIM	Master of International Management
JD	Juris Doctorate		MIS	Management Information Systems
LLB	Bachelor of Law			

MISM	Master of Information Systems Management	MSIM	Master of Science in Industrial Management
MLAS	Master of Liberal Arts and Science	MSIMC	Master of Science in Integrated Marketing Communications
MMIS	Master of Management Information Systems	MSIR	Master of Science in Industrial Relations
MMR	Master of Marketing Research	MSIS	Master of Science in Information Systems
MMS	Master of Management Science	MSISE	Master of Science in Industrial and Systems Engineering
MNO	Master of Nonprofit Organizations	MSISM	Master of Science in Information Systems Management
MOD	Master of Science in Organizational Development	MSIT	Master of Science in Information Technology
MPA	Master of Public Administration	MSITM	Master of Science in Information Technology Management
MPAcc	Master of Professional Accounting	MSM	Master of Science in Management
MPH	Master of Public Health	MSMIS	Master of Science in Management Information Systems
MPIA	Master of Public and International Affairs	MSMOT	Master of Science in Management of Technology
MPL	Master of Planning	MSN	Master of Science in Nursing
MPP	Master of Public Policy	MSOD	Master of Science in Organization Development
MRED	Master of Real Estate Development	MSpAd	Master of Sports Administration
MS	Master of Science	MSRE	Master of Science in Real Estate
MSA	Master of Science in Accountancy (or Accounting)	MSS	Master of Social Science
MSAIS	Master of Science in Accounting Information Systems	MSSA	Master of Science in Social Administration
MSAT	Master of Science in Accountancy, Taxation	MST	Master of Science in Taxation
MSB	Master of Science in Business	MSTM	Master of Science in Telecommunications Management
MSBA	Master of Science in Business Administration	MSW	Master of Social Work
MSE	Master of Science in Engineering	MTAX	Master of Taxation
MSEC	Master of Science in Electronic Commerce	MTLM	Master of Transportation and Logistics Management
MSF	Master of Science in Finance	NEMBA	National Executive Master of Business Administration
MSFA	Master of Science in Financial Analysis	PharmD	Doctor of Pharmacy
MSFS	Master of Science in Foreign Services	PhD	Doctor of Philosophy
MSG	Master of Science in Gerontology	SM	Master of Science
MSGFA	Master of Science in Global Financial Analysis	TSM	Telecommunications Systems Management
MSHA	Master of Science in Health Administration	VMD	Doctor of Veterinary Medicine
MSHFID	Master of Science in Human Factors in Information Design		
MSIAM	Master of Science in Information Age Marketing		
MSIB Business	Master of Science in International		
MSIE	Master of Science in Industrial Engineering		

INDEX

ALPHABETICAL INDEX

INDEX BY LOCATION

INTERNATIONAL

INDEX BY COST

$15,000–$25,000

OVER $55,000

INDEX BY MBA CONCENTRATION

ENTREPRENEURSHIP

FINANCE

HEALTHCARE ADMINISTRATION

HUMAN RESOURCES

MARKETING